CANADIAN EDITION

Excellence in Business Communication

John V. Thill
Chief Executive Officer
Communication Specialists of America

Courtland L. Bovée
Professor of Business Communication
C. Allen Paul Distinguished Chair
Grossmont College

Ava Cross
Department of Business and Technical Communication
Ryerson University

Toronto

National Library of Canada Cataloguing in Publication Data

Thill, John V.
Excellence in business communication

Canadian ed.
Includes bibliographical references and index.
ISBN 0-13-019355-0

1.Business communication–Case studies. I. Bovée, Courtland L. II. Cross, Ava, date III. Title.

HF5718.2.C3T45 2002 658.4'5 C2001-900879-1

0-13-019355-0

Vice President, Editorial Director: Michael Young
Editor-in-Chief: David Stover
Senior Editor: Sophia Fortier
Marketing Manager: Sharon Loeb
Executive Developmental Editor: Marta Tomins
Senior Production Editor: Sherry Torchinsky
Copy Editor: Jim MacLachlan
Production Coordinator: Peggy Brown
Page Layout: Joan M. Wilson
Photo Research: Susan Wallace-Cox
Art Director: Mary Opper
Interior & Cover Design: Monica Kompter
Cover Image: Anthony Marsland/Tony Stone

Original edition published by Prentice Hall, Inc., a division of Pearson Education, Upper Saddle River, NJ.

3 4 5 05 04 03

Printed and bound in the United States of America.

To my husband and

my children.

Contents in Brief

Contents

HANDBOOK Fundamentals of Grammar and Usage 567

✔ Checklists

Preface

The classic text *Excellence in Business Communication* by John V. Thill and Courtland L. Bovée is an engaging business communication textbook, valued for bringing the real world of work into the classroom. This first Canadian edition retains the dynamic features of the original but adds a further dimension by involving students in communication tasks and problems faced by many Canadian companies.

What attributes of the original text carried it through five successful editions? Why is it an effective tool for helping Canadian students hone their skills for the world of work? Two of the many features that distinguish this book immediately spring to mind.

First, students will benefit from the real-world simulations using actual companies. These simulations provide unique opportunities for applying business communication concepts to real events and for sharpening students' problem-solving skills. *Excellence in Business Communication* deals in a comprehensive way with the fundamentals of theory and practice and presents them in a logical sequence that builds upon each step as students progress through the book. But, in addition, real-life simulations, compelling case studies, a friendly writing style, and clear graphics bring to life the nuances of workplace communication in a realistic and meaningful way. The text will instill in students respect for the subject and confidence that the skills can be mastered.

Second, students will enjoy meeting a cross-section of employees from all levels of companies of varying sizes and complexities, as well as small business owners who, on a typical day, face their own variety of communication problems. In each chapter, students are asked to work with business people to solve their problems. Through this process, students gain not only essential knowledge of the workplace, but also the satisfaction of applying their communication skills successfully. Students often find it easy to relate to highly visible companies when applying the communication skills taught in the classroom and, in this edition, they will consider the communication issues of such well-regarded Canadian organizations as Indigo, Suncor, and the Confederation Centre of the Arts. Each day we also read of smaller Canadian companies drawing national and international attention for their innovative products and services. Students will enjoy interacting with people from lesser-known firms such as Zero-Knowledge Systems and *Business$ense* magazine, two companies making their mark on both the Canadian and global business scene.

Features Link Concepts to the Real World

Excellence in Business Communication paints a vivid picture of the world of business communication, offering an overview of the wide range of communication skills used by business people to present ideas clearly and persuasively. It also gives specific examples of the communication techniques that have led to sound decision making and effective teamwork. In addition, the book's insights into the way organizations operate help clarify student career interests by identifying the skills needed for a lifetime of career success.

"On-the-Job" Simulations

The opportunity to learn by doing informs this textbook. Students not only learn from other people's successes and failures but also make "on the job" decisions about communication problems. As the table of contents shows, this Canadian edition was written with the cooperation of both well-known and growing businesses, Canadian and multinational, including Dofasco, Telus, Suncor, Malkam Cross-Cultural Training, and Hewlett-Packard.

Each chapter opens with an exclusive feature, "On the Job: Facing a Communication Dilemma." This slice-of-life vignette summarizes a communication problem being faced by an actual company. The solution to the dilemma is found in the concepts presented in the chapter, and the dilemma reappears from time to time throughout the chapter to dramatize the connection between the principles discussed and life on the job.

Furthermore, each chapter ends by expanding on the introductory communication problem with the feature, "On the Job: Solving a Communication Dilemma," a simulation based on a real company. Students are asked to solve the dilemma by applying the principles discussed in the text, by making decisions about the communication process, and by selecting the best alternatives from the choices offered. Not only do these simulations give students the opportunity to practise real-world decision making, but they also tie the textual information to real-life examples, providing a concrete basis for analyzing chapter principles. This chapter-spanning feature adds an important dimension of reality to the learning process.

"Behind the Scenes" Special Features

Strategically placed within each chapter, "Behind the Scenes" boxes extend the chapter material by focussing on real people, real products, and real companies. This Canadian edition incorporates firsthand interviews with accomplished business communicators at actual companies and research into their activities in eighteen "Behind the Scenes" special features that bring more of the business world into the classroom. Examples include

- Behind the Scenes at Dofasco: Planning Environmental Performance Reports
- Behind the Scenes at the Aboriginal Banking Newsletter: Partnership: The Key to Success
- Behind the Scenes at the Confederation Centre of the Arts: Celebrating Canadian Culture and Heritage

The discussion questions at the end of each of these special features give students numerous opportunities to analyze business communication principles and practices.

Up-to-Date Internet Resources

The World Wide Web, a component of the Internet, contains a wealth of valuable resources. To acquaint students with Web sites that relate to the content of *Excellence in Business Communication*, a "Going Online" feature describing an especially useful site is included in each chapter.

Examples of the "Going Online" feature include

- Create Your Own Web site
- Connect Now with a Virtual Library
- Search Thousands of Full-Text Articles Instantly
- Link Your Way to a Better Résumé

To give students practice in exploring the rich resources of the Web, "Developing Your Internet Skills" exercises are included at the end of each chapter. These exercises are directly tied to the "Going Online" sites showcased within the chapters.

Gallery of Business Communication Professionals

Another special feature of this text is a photo gallery of numerous highly successful professionals from business, industry, and the media who give an expert's view about a particular aspect of business communication. Among the individuals featured are Heather Reisman (Indigo Books); Firoz Rasul (Ballard Power Systems); Peter Mansbridge (CBC's *The National*); and Rick Hansen (former paralympic athlete and fundraiser for research into spinal injuries). Each profile relates specifically to the text and adds another dimension to student learning.

Example After Example of Letters, Memos, and Reports

This first Canadian edition of *Excellence in Business Communication* contains numerous up-to-date sample documents. These examples show students how businesses apply the principles taught in the book to get desired results.

The chapters on letters and memos contain examples from many types of organizations and from people working in a variety of functional areas. Many of these documents are fully formatted, and some are presented on the letterheads of well-known organizations, both profit and not-for-profit, such as the Royal Ontario Museum and Mott's Canada. The accompanying analyses help students see precisely how to apply the principles discussed in the text. Poor examples, followed by improved versions, illustrate common errors and effective techniques for correcting them.

The report-writing chapters give numerous examples as well. And the last chapter of the report unit illustrates the step-by-step development of a long report, which appears in its entirety to show how all the parts fit together.

Real-World Issues

The boundaries of business communication are always expanding. In addition to covering all the traditional subjects, this Canadian edition of *Excellence in Business Communication* provides material to help students manage a variety of the current issues in business communication which they are likely to face.

The process approach. Because both the communication product and the process to achieve it are equally important, this edition accentuates the process approach while maintaining a strong product orientation.

Ethics. Every message, whether verbal or non-verbal, communicates something about our values and ethics. Students must be given the means to anticipate and analyze the ethical dilemmas they will face on the job. Ethical questions addressed in this book include how much to emphasize the positive in business messages (Chapter 6), how to handle negative information in recommendations (Chapter 9), where to draw the line between persuasion and manipulation in sales letters (Chapter 11), and how to use photographs in reports without misleading the audience (Chapter 14). "Promoting Workplace Ethics" boxes showcase areas of special interest throughout the text.

Crisis communication. Discussion of mismanagement by the Canadian Red Cross (taken over by Canadian

Blood Services) when reporting the risk of AIDS through blood transfusions emphasizes the connection of ethics and crisis communication (Chapter 1).

Communication barriers. The shift toward a customer-service orientation means that more and more careers will depend on interpersonal skills. Whether working on an assembly line or at the front desk of a hotel, people interacting with people make it vital to overcome communication barriers (Chapter 2).

Cultural diversity and intercultural communication. The changing nature of the domestic workforce requires strong communication skills. Regardless of the organization you join, you are likely to be dealing with colleagues from various national, religious, and ethnic backgrounds, both within and across national borders. Moreover, with such international agreements as Europe 1992, the North American Free Trade Agreement (NAFTA), the General Agreement on Tariffs and Trade (GATT), and the World Trade Organization (WTO), the continuing globalization of business necessitates strong skills to communicate effectively with people from other cultures. This important element of global business practice is looked at in-depth in Chapter 3 and further examined in "Achieving Intercultural Communication" boxes throughout the text.

Business technology. Constant advances in technology alter the ways of communication in organizations. To excel in the business world of today and tomorrow, students need to quickly become comfortable with changing communication channels (Chapter 4). "Using the Power of Technology" and "Effective E-Business Communication" boxes throughout the book showcase areas of communication technology and highlight communication methods related to e-business. An icon marks technology-related end-of-chapter activities. Students will also

- learn how to judge Web sites for reliability and credibility when using the Internet for research.
- read about cutting-edge software, created by a Canadian company and used by Canadian firms, that facilitates the job search process.
- discover how to format résumés for online submission.

Law. The possibility of litigation makes it important to understand the legal implications of written and oral communication, such as the pitfalls of writing letters of recommendation (Chapter 9).

Employment search. Radical mid-career job changes are becoming more common, whether by choice or because of downsizing and flattening hierarchies. The ability to master new skills as well as information pertaining to new jobs is essential (Chapter 12).

Communication versatility. Small businesses create most of the new jobs and employ more people than large corporations do. Since small businesses are unable to support communication specialists for specific tasks, staff need to be versatile in their communication skills–writing letters and reports, interacting on the phone, giving speeches, making sales presentations, creating presentation slides, and producing professional documents.

Collaborative writing. Collaboration brings multiple perspectives and various skills to a project. It combines the strengths of all the team members to increase productivity, enrich knowledge and enhance interpersonal relationships. Making sure everyone works together effectively can be part of the challenge. An icon marks those end-of-chapter assignments that involve teamwork.

Tools That Help Develop Skills and Enhance Comprehension

This edition emphasizes the skills and real-world competencies necessary for students to make the transition from academia to the workplace. It is essential that students develop the academic and occupational skills that business requires. Interactive pedagogy, much of which is grounded in real-world situations, helps them accomplish this goal.

Lively, Conversational Writing Style

The lucid writing style in *Excellence in Business Communication* makes the material easy to read and comprehend, helps stimulate interest, and promotes learning. The writing style also exemplifies the principles presented in this book.

Learning Outcomes and Summary

Each chapter begins with a concise list of numbered goals that students can expect to achieve by reading the chapter and completing the simulations, exercises, and cases. The outcomes appear again in the margins throughout the chapter and are summarized at the end to guide the learning process, to motivate students to master the material, and to aid them in measuring their success.

Documents for Analysis

Students evaluate and revise a broad selection of documents, including letters, memos, e-mail messages, a letter of application, and a résumé. The hands-on experience of analyzing and improving sample documents will help students revise their own writing.

Margin Notes

Short summary statements in the margins highlight key points and reinforce learning. While they are no substitute for reading the chapters, they are useful for quickly getting the gist of a section, rapidly reviewing a chapter, and locating areas of greatest concern.

Checklists

To help students organize their thinking when they begin a communication project, make decisions as they write, and check their own work, this edition contains 28 checklists. Appearing as close as possible to the related discussion, the checklists are reminders, not hard-cast formulas. They provide useful guidelines for writing, without limiting creativity. Students will find them handy references when they're on the job and need to refresh their memory about effective communication techniques.

End-of-Chapter Pedagogy

The acronym TAP (Test, Apply, Practise) reminds students that they can "tap" their knowledge.

TEST YOUR KNOWLEDGE

The Summary of Learning Outcomes and more than 100 **Review Questions** will refresh memory and start students thinking about the concepts introduced in each chapter.

APPLY YOUR KNOWLEDGE

More than 100 **Critical Thinking Questions** prompt students to stretch their learning beyond the chapter content. Not only will students find them useful in studying for examinations, but the instructor may also draw on them to promote classroom discussion of issues that have no easy answers.

PRACTISE YOUR KNOWLEDGE

A wealth of **Exercises** and **Cases** provides assignments such as those students will face at work. The exercises and cases deal with all types and sizes of organizations, domestic and international. Each chapter also includes an exercise or a case that requires access to the World Wide Web. These activities are suitable for a range of fields of study: management, marketing, accounting, finance, information systems, office administration, and many others. With such variety to choose from, students will have ample opportunity to test their problem-solving skills. Most cases feature real companies including Ballard Power Systems, Campbell Soup Canada, and Blockbuster Video.

Appendixes

The Canadian edition of *Excellence in Business Communication* contains two appendixes. Appendix A, "Format and Layout of Business Documents," discusses formatting for all types of documents in one convenient place. Appendix B, "Documentation of Report Sources," presents information on conducting secondary research and gives basic guidelines for handling reference citations, bibliographies, and source notes (and includes Web sites, e-mail, and newsgroups).

Grammar Handbook

A useful handbook, "Fundamentals of Grammar and Usage," is a primer-in-brief, presenting the basic tools of language. Engaging exercises test understanding of each section.

Correction Symbols

Convenient charts of correction symbols on the inside covers clarify the use of correction symbols and abbreviations so students can easily understand teacher evaluations.

Colour Art and Strong Visual Program

The dramatic use of colour not only provides exceptional visual appeal but also guides the reader to important features. In each chapter, students learn from a rich selection of carefully chosen and crafted illustrations–graphs, charts, tables, and photographs–that demonstrate important concepts.

Book Design

The state-of-the-art design is based on extensive research and invites students to delve into the content. It also makes reading easier, reinforces learning, and increases comprehension. The design of this book, like much communication, has the simple but essential objective of gaining interest and making a point.

Chapter Content Overview

The Canadian edition incorporates the extensive revisions John V. Thill and Courtland L. Bovée made to the fourth and fifth editions of *Excellence in Business Communication.* Members of the academic and business communities, both in the US and Canada, carefully reviewed it, and Thill and Bovée tested the book in the classroom. Instructors, business people, and students have all praised its superior coverage of subject matter, up-to-date examples, flexible organization, and authentic portrayal of business. The addition of Canadian context brings currency and relevance. For example:

- **Business communication and Canada's two official languages.** Students will learn how organizations handle messages that are sent in both English and French.
- **Aboriginal concerns.** Students will read about the *Aboriginal Business Newsletter*, an important communication medium between the Business Development Bank of Canada and the Aboriginal population.
- **Communicating environmental concerns.** Students will read about the communication processes two Canadian natural resource companies use to covey their environmental programs.

Here is an overview of the key content of *Effective Business Communication, Canadian edition.* Explorations of communications issues with Canadian companies are highlighted in *italic.*

Chapter 1: Communicating Successfully in an Organization includes two "In-Depth Critique" sample documents to expose students as early as possible to business letters and memos and maintains emphasis on the six vital themes that recur throughout the book: open communication climate, ethics, intercultural messages, technological tools, audience-centred thinking, and efficient message flow. Students learn about electronic tools that both protect privacy and may compromise it during the communication process between customers and companies.

- *Behind the Scenes at Zero-Knowledge, Montreal: The Freedom to Communicate*

Chapter 2: Understanding Business Communication presents a new transactional model of the communication process to help students clearly envision this basic tenet of business communication and emphasizes the overcoming of communication barriers.

- *Behind the Scenes at Enterprise Mediation Inc., Ottawa: Resolving Communication Problems Without Going to Court*

Chapter 3: Communicating Interculturally clarifies the relationship between growing technology and increasing global opportunities and demonstrates how intercultural differences can block successful communication, both in the Canadian workforce and across national boundaries.

- *On the Job with Malkam Cross-Cultural Training, Ottawa: Working with Cultural Diversity*
- *Behind the Scenes at Terra Cognita: Should You Say It with Flowers? And with What Kind?*

Chapter 4: Communicating Through Technology discusses how technology affects communication, guides students toward choosing the right medium for the message, and shows how the Internet is changing business communication.

- *Behind the Scenes at Telus: Using Technology to Communicate Change*

Chapter 5: Planning Business Messages covers collaborative writing while emphasizing the composition process: planning (defining your purpose, analyzing your audience, establishing your main idea, and selecting the appropriate channel and medium), composing (organizing and outlining your message, and formulating the message), revising (editing, rewriting, producing, and proofing your message), and compares electronic channels to oral and written channels.

- *Behind the Scenes at The Aboriginal Banking Newsletter: Partnership – The Key to Success*

Chapter 6: Composing Business Messages offers guidelines on e-mail etiquette and shaping an e-mail message, and clarifies the three levels of style–informal, conversational, and formal–explaining why most business writing is conversational.

- *Behind the Scenes at* Business $ense *Magazine: Helping Graduates into the World of Business*

Chapter 7: Revising Business Messages includes coverage of evaluating the writing of others so that students can collaborate more smoothly, and discusses active and passive voice and parallelism, giving numerous examples.

- *Behind the Scenes at the Confederation Centre of the Arts: Celebrating Canadian Heritage and Culture*

Chapter 8: Writing Direct Requests discusses internal and external direct messages, includes many fully formatted sample documents showing such requests as orders, claims, and adjustments, and reviews requesting information via the Internet and e-mail.

- *On the Job with Indigo: May the Best Seller Win!*

  Chapter 9: Writing Routine, Good-News, and Goodwill Messages stresses the process of writing neutral and positive messages such as claim and adjustment grants and inquiry replies.

- *Behind the Scenes with CRM Software: Big Brother is Watching You*

  Chapter 10: Writing Bad-News Messages discusses strategy and techniques of both the direct and indirect approaches to negative messages such as denying requests for assistance, favours, claims, and adjustments, and stresses the importance of maintaining goodwill when dealing with negative situations.

- *Behind the Scenes at Your Bank's Ombudsman: Is the Customer Always Right?*

  Chapter 11: Writing Persuasive Messages considers the issues of ethics, audience, and emotion in persuasive writing, shows how to avoid faulty logic, and provides guidance on writing a variety of persuasive messages such as fund-raising letters, sales letters (presented in hard copy and on the World Wide Web), and messages that sell an idea on the job.

- *On the Job with The Young Entrepreneurs' Association: Promoting a Good Thing*
- *Behind the Scenes at the Canadian Soccer Association: Scoring Goals and Sponsors*

  Chapter 12: Writing Short Reports incorporates material on electronic reports, discusses business plans, clearly defines and differentiates the types of reports used in business applications, links to concepts presented in earlier chapters (such as style, tone, "you" attitude, positive language, and concise wording), discusses structural clues that help readers understand and navigate a document, and considers formatting features.

- *Behind the Scenes at AchieveGlobal: Consulting, Clarifying, Communicating*

  Chapter 13: Planning Long Reports covers the relative merit and hypothesis methods of problem-solving and explains report planning steps, including problem definition, factoring, structuring, research, and data analysis.

- *Behind the Scenes at Dofasco: Planning Environmental Performance Reports*

  Chapter 14: Writing Long Reports covers a variety of formal reports and proposals. This chapter discusses how to introduce sources, guides students on computerized report design, and discusses report features–the prefatory parts, including the executive summary; the report body, including the introduction, conclusions, and recommendations; and supplementary elements, such as the bibliography and index. This chapter also discusses visual support and documentation and citation procedures, and provides an entire sample report, including citation references.

- *Behind the Scenes of Annual Reports: Telling a Company's Story, Once a Year, Every Year*

  Chapter 15: Writing Résumés and Application Letters discusses computer-generated documents, the Internet and job searching, scannable résumés, employment portfolios, and building job experience through internships and temporary job assignments.

- *Behind the Scenes at Recruitsoft: The Wired World of E-cruiting*

  Chapter 16: Interviewing for Employment and Following Up discusses different interview formats, including video interviews, demonstrates the advantages of videotaping mock interviews for evaluation and the importance of thank-you messages, and offers guidance on writing letters of resignation.

- *Behind the Scenes at IBM: Secrets to Winning an Interview*

  Chapter 17: Listening, Interviewing, and Conducting Meetings reviews components of oral communication at work, including types of listening and improving listening skills; discusses the different kinds of interviews students may participate in at work; covers the mechanics and dynamics of meetings; and incorporates issues relating to intercultural barriers mentioned in Chapters 2 and 3.

- *Behind the Scenes at 3M: The Keys to Masterful Meetings*

  Chapter 18: Giving Speeches and Oral Presentations discusses planning and preparation, understanding the audience, and developing the speech, including preview and review statements. It also considers the benefits of using an outliner from software packages (such as PowerPoint) and the question-and-answer period following a speech or presentation.

- *On the Job at Lucent Technologies Canada with CEO Carol Stephenson: Speaking Her Mind, Persuading Her Listeners*

A Teaching and Learning Package that Meets Real Needs

The instructional package for this textbook is specially designed to simplify the tasks of teaching and learning.

Instructor's Resource Manual

This comprehensive manual is an instructor's tool kit that provides suggested solutions to exercises, and suggested solutions and fully formatted letters for *every* case in the letter-writing chapters. A grammar pre-test and a post-test are accompanied by additional exercises.

Study Guide

An accompanying study guide provides chapter-by-chapter exercises designed to reinforce comprehension of key concepts presented in the text and to promote good language and writing skills.

Test Item File

This manual is organized by text chapters and includes a mix of multiple-choice, true-false, and fill-in-the-blank questions for each chapter, approximately 1500 objective items in all, carefully written and reviewed to provide a fair, structured program of evaluation.

Test Manager, Windows Version

Based on a state-of-the-art test-generation software program, *Test Manager* is suitable for your course and can be customized to your class needs. This user-friendly software allows you to generate error-free tests quickly and easily. You can edit our questions and answers and even add some of your own. You can then create an exam, administer it traditionally or online, evaluate and track student results, and analyze the success of the examination–all with a simple click of the mouse.

Companion Website

Visit our Companion Website at **www.pearsoned.ca/thill**. This text-specific site offers a wealth of materials for students and instructors, including multiple-choice, true-or-false, and essay questions so students can quiz themselves chapter-by-chapter.

Acetate Transparency Program

A set of transparency acetates is available to instructors upon request. These visuals help bring concepts alive in the classroom and provide a starting point for discussing communication techniques.

PowerPoint Presentation Software

Enhance your classroom presentations with this well-developed PowerPoint presentation set. Hundreds of colourful, text-specific electronic slides are available to highlight and reinforce the important concepts of the text.

Business Communication Update Newsletter for Faculty

Delivered exclusively by e-mail every month, this newsletter provides interesting materials that can be used in class and offers a wealth of practical ideas about teaching methods. To receive a complimentary subscription, send an e-mail to **bovee-thill@uia.net**. In the subject line, put '"BCU" Subscription Request.' In the message area, please list your name and institutional affiliation.

Perils of Pauline CD-ROM

This interactive, multimedia product uses exercises, activities, and a bit of humour to draw students into the material and help them deal with real-world communication challenges while in a simulated working environment.

Online Learning Solutions

Pearson Education Canada supports instructors interested in using online course management systems. We provide text-related content in WebCT, Blackboard, and our own private label version of Blackboard called CourseCompass. To find out more about creating an online course using Pearson content in one of these platforms, contact your local Pearson Education Canada sales representative.

Acknowledgments

This Canadian edition was created with the help of many people. I would like to thank the professional communicators who generously answered my questions for many of the Behind the Scenes features: Wendy MacNair, Editor, *Aboriginal Banking Newsletter*; Anne Hoekstra, Editor-in-Chief, *Business $ense*; Laurie Murphy, Publicist (on leave), Confederation Centre of the Arts; David Bedford, Managing Director, Soccer Canada Properties; Bill Stevens, Senior Consulting Partner, Achieve Global; and Ian Hamilton, Manager, Corporate Communications, Dofasco.

Many educators in Canada read my manuscript and made thoughtful suggestions. I would like to thank Les Hanson, Red River Community College; Kay McFadyen, University of Alberta; Kendra Carmichael, Acadia University; Isobel Findlay, University of Saskatchewan; Deborah Meredith, University of British Columbia; Alberta Smith, Algonquin College; Martha Finnigan, Durham College; Heather Thompson, St. Mary's University; Helen Cook, St. Mary's University; Ritva Seppanen, Concordia University; and David Patient, Simon Fraser University. And a special thanks to Diane Harris who prepared the exercises for the grammar handbook.

At Pearson Education Canada, David Stover offered me the opportunity to work on this textbook. I am grateful to him, and to Marta Tomins and Sherry Torchinsky, who guided the book through the editorial and production process. Thank you also to Jim MacLachlan for copyediting the text.

Finally, my love and affection to John, Miriam, and David, whose unfailing love, support, and good humour kept me going through the duration of this project. Bill Cross was interested, as always; and this was another project Eleanor Cross would have enjoyed seeing to fruition. David Cross and Michal Calder Cross supplied some material. My family in the US, Sharon Barbanel Geier and Leslie Gordon Politzer, always took the time to listen. My mother, as ever, was there for me.

The Pearson Education Canada companion Website...

Your Internet companion to the most exciting, state-of-the-art educational tools on the Web!

The Pearson Education Canada Companion Website is easy to navigate and is organized to correspond to the chapters in this textbook. The Companion Website comprises these distinct, functional features:

Customized Online Resources

Online Interactive Study Guide

Communication

Table of Contents

Explore these areas in this Companion Website. Students and distance learners will discover resources for indepth study, research, and communication, empowering them in their quest for greater knowledge and maximizing their potential for success in the course.

A NEW WAY TO DELIVER EDUCATIONAL CONTENT

Course Management

Our Companion Websites provide instructors and students with the ability to access, exchange, and interact with material specially created for our individual textbooks.

- **Syllabus Manager** provides instructors with the option of creating online classes and constructing an online syllabus linked to specific modules in the Companion Website.
- **Grader** allows the student to take a test that is automatically marked by the program. The results of the test can be e-mailed to the instructor and then added to the student's record.
- **Help** includes an evaluation of the user's system and a tune-up area that makes updating browsers and plug-ins easier. This new feature will facilitate the use of our Companion Websites.

Instructor Resources

This section features modules with additional teaching material organized by chapter for instructors. Downloadable PowerPoint Presentations, Electronic Transparencies, and an Instructor's Manual are just some of the materials that may be available in this section. Where appropriate, this section will be password protected. To get a password, simply contact your Pearson Education Canada representative or call Faculty Sales and Services at 1-800-850-5813.

General Resources

This section contains information that is related to the entire book and that will be of interest to all users of the site. A Table of Contents and a Glossary are just two examples of the kind of information you may find in this section.

The General Resources section may also feature *Communication facilities* that provide a key element for distributed learning environments:

- **Message Board** – This module takes advantage of browser technology to provide the users of each Companion Website with a national newsgroup to post and reply to relevant course topics.
- **Chat Room** – This module enables instructors to lead group activities in real time. Using our chat client, instructors can display website content while students participate in the discussion.

Visit www.pearsoned.ca/thill for great student resources

Want some practice before an exam?

The Student Resources section contains the modules that form the core of the student learning experience in the Companion Website. The modules presented in this section may include the following:

- Learning Outcomes
- Multiple-Choice Questions
- True/False Questions
- Essay Questions
- Short Answer Questions
- Destinations

The question modules provide students with the ability to send answers to our grader and receive instant feedback on their progress through our Results Reporter. Coaching comments and references to the textbook may be available to ensure that students take advantage of all available resources to enhance their learning experience.

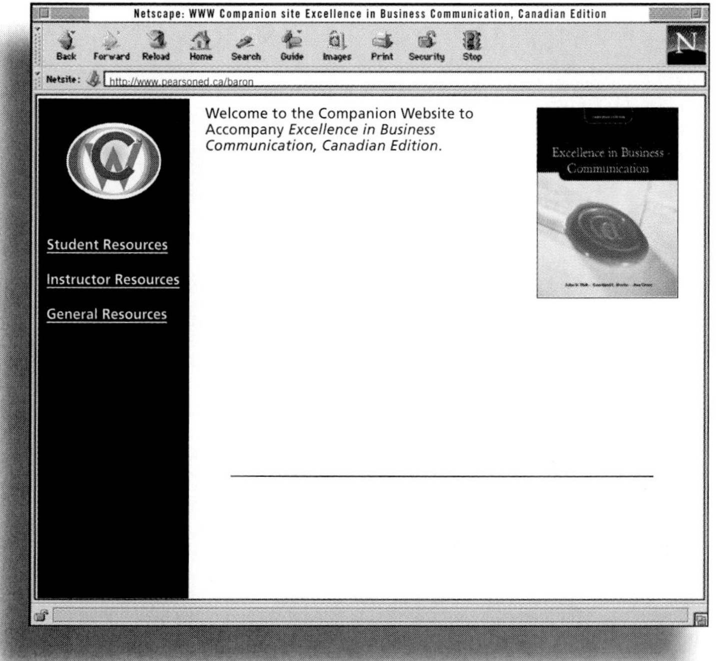

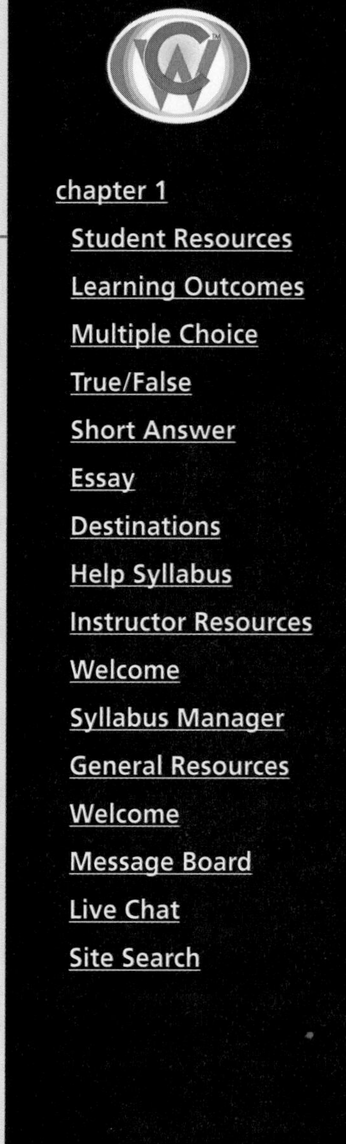

PEARSON EDUCATION CANADA

26 Prince Andrew Place
Toronto, Ontario M3C 2T8

To order:
Call: 1-800-567-3800
Fax: 1-800-263-7733

For samples:
Call: 1-800-850-5813
Fax: (416) 299-2539
E-mail:
phabinfo_pubcanada@pearsoned.com

The Companion Website for this text can be found at:

www.pearsoned.ca/thill

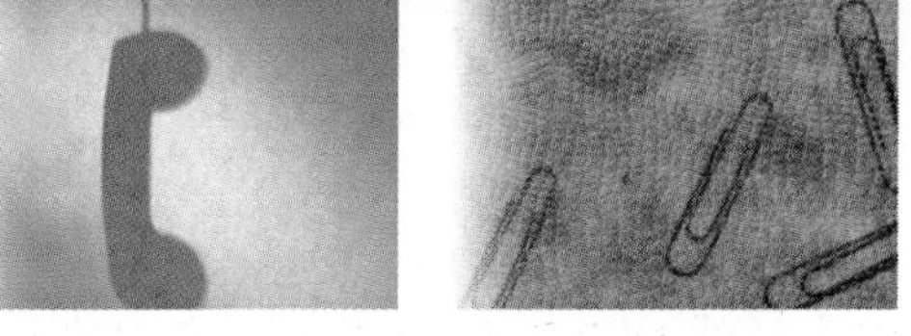
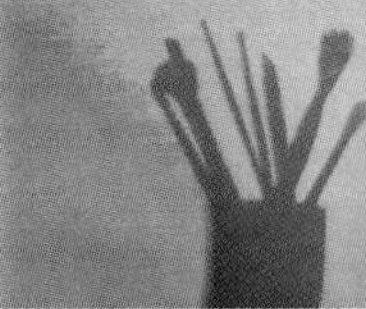

CHAPTER 1

Communicating Successfully in an Organization

AFTER STUDYING THIS CHAPTER, YOU WILL BE ABLE TO

1. Describe how managers use communication
2. Contrast formal and informal communication channels within an organization
3. Explain how companies communicate with outside audiences
4. Analyze how companies communicate successfully in a crisis
5. Discuss the six factors that contribute to effective business communication
6. Develop goals for acquiring the communication skills you will need in your career

ON THE JOB
Facing a Communication Dilemma at Hallmark

When You Care Enough to Send the Very Best—Inside or Outside the Company

Have you ever needed to discuss a sensitive topic with someone and been unsure of how to start the conversation? Chances are you can find a Hallmark card to help you. Hallmark is in the communication business, helping people share their thoughts and feelings. The company introduces thousands of new paper cards each year and has recently introduced online electronic greeting cards and software for customers to design their own greeting cards. Because Hallmark has more than 12 000 employees and such a diverse range of products, communicating within the company is at least as important as communicating with customers.

When people browse through Hallmark greeting cards, they are looking for the best way to express a sentiment—whether with joy, sympathy, or humour. In fact, strong communication is the key to success at Hallmark, whether helping people share their thoughts and feelings or conducting operations within the organization.

As Hallmark's internal communications and publications manager, Andy McMillen is responsible for ensuring that employees receive all the information they need to be both productive and satisfied and to help the company achieve its goals for growth. Most Hallmark employees are organized into teams, and Hallmark's success depends heavily on strong communication within and between all its teams, as well as between these teams and upper management. McMillen is responsible for maintaining the flow of information. For example, information about changes in employee benefits must be distributed to all employees, whereas information about a specific project might be important only for that project team.

McMillen also knows that each team has its own responsibilities and special communication needs, so he must determine the right medium and format for each kind of information. For example, creative teams of writers and artists must come up with new ideas for cards. Their responsibilities require a unique combination of individual creativity and team cooperation, and McMillen needs to keep that fact in mind when communicating with them. On the other hand, cross-functional teams include people from marketing, sales, customer service, and operations. Because both creative and cross-functional teams make decisions by reaching a consensus rather than by relying on decisions passed down from upper management, McMillen pays particular attention to tone when he communicates with them.

Hallmark works hard to attract and keep high-quality employees, viewing them as the company's most important resource. It's up to McMillen to make sure that internal communication not only keeps employees motivated and informed about company strategies, progress, and business, but also enables them to understand how they can help move the company forward.

If you were in McMillen's position, what would you do to keep communication flowing smoothly and efficiently throughout the organization? What sort of communication climate could you instill to help guarantee that everyone receives necessary information? How would you decide which communication method is best for each of the many messages you need to share with all the people inside Hallmark?[1]

Communication, Business, and You

Communication enables organizations to function.

Organizations such as Hallmark believe that communication both inside and outside the company should be open, honest, and clear. Your ability to communicate increases productivity, both yours and your organization's. It shapes the impressions you make on your colleagues, employees, supervisors, investors, and customers. It allows you to perceive the needs of these **stakeholders** (the various groups you interact with), and it helps you respond to those needs. Whether you run your own business, work for an employer, invest in a company, buy or sell products, design computer chips, run for public office, or raise money for charities, your communication skills determine your success.[2]

Good communication skills are vital because every member of an organization is a link in the information chain. The flow of information along that chain is a steady stream of messages, whether from inside the organization (staff meetings, progress reports, project proposals, research results, employee surveys, and persuasive interviews) or from outside the organization (loan applications, purchasing agreements, help-wanted ads, distribution contracts, product advertisements, and sales calls). Your ability to receive, evaluate, use, and pass on information affects your company's effectiveness, as well as your own.

Ask yourself what information your co-workers and supervisors need from you, and then figure out how you can supply it. Also ask yourself what information you need to do your job, and then find ways to get it.

Within the company, you and your co-workers use the information you obtain from one another and from outsiders to guide your activities. The work of the organization is divided into tasks and assigned to various organizational units, each reporting to a manager who directs and coordinates the effort. This division of labour and delegation of responsibility depends on the constant flow of information up, down, and across the organization. So by feeding information to your boss and peers, you help them do their jobs, and they help you to do yours.

You are a contact point in the external and internal communication networks.

LEARNING OUTCOME 1
Describe how managers use communication.

If you are a manager, your day consists of a never-ending series of meetings, casual conversations, speaking engagements, and phone calls, interspersed with occasional periods set aside for reading or writing. From these sources, you cull important points and pass them on to the people who need them. In turn, you rely on your employees to provide you with useful data and to interpret, transmit, and act on the messages you send them.

The manager's role is to make and carry out decisions by collecting facts, analyzing them, and transmitting directions to lower-level employees.

If you are a relatively junior employee, you are likely to find yourself on the perimeter of the communication network. Oddly enough, this situation puts you in an important position in the information chain. Although your span of influence may be limited, you are in a position to observe firsthand things that your supervisors and co-workers cannot see: a customer's immediate reaction to a product display, a supplier's momentary hesitation before agreeing to a delivery date, an odd whirring noise in a piece of equipment, or a slowdown in the flow of customers. These are the little gems of information that managers and co-workers need to do their jobs. If you don't pass that information along, nobody will–because nobody else knows. Such an exchange of information within an organization is called **internal communication.**

Employees serve as the eyes and ears of an organization, providing direct impressions from the front line.

The Internal Communication Network

LEARNING OUTCOME 2
Contrast formal and informal communication channels within an organization.

Communication among the members of an organization is essential for effective functioning, so each organization approaches internal communication in a particular way, depending on its requirements. In a small business with only five or six employees, much information can be exchanged casually and directly. In a large organization such as Hallmark, transmitting the right information to the right people at the right time can be a real challenge, whether communicating by phone, e-mail, fax, or inter-office memo (see Figure 1.1).

Formal Communication Channels

The **formal communication network** is the official structure of an organization, which is typically shown as an organization chart like the one in Figure 1.2. Such charts summarize the lines of authority; each box represents a link in the chain of command, and each line represents a formal channel for the transmission of official messages. Information may travel down, up, and across an organization's formal hierarchy.

The formal flow of information follows the official chain of command.

INTERNAL MEMORANDUM

TO: Jacqueline Rogeine
FROM: Tom Beatty
DATE: April 10, 2001
SUBJECT: First-Quarter Sales to Disney

The first paragraph gives the reader specific information related to the subject.

Our first-quarter sales to Disney theme parks show a continuing trend toward growth, although margins remain thin. We supplied 38 retail outlets with 52 licensed or personalized items. Gross profits rose 18% from the first quarter last year, so the severe winter evidently had less impact than we originally expected.

The second paragraph presents an easy-to-read chart of data selected from the overall report.

Although you can look over the attached raw data, the items below enjoyed continued popularity:

Product & Number	2000 First Quarter	2001 First Quarter	Percent Increase
Minnie's Tea Set (M30)	$ 102 477	$ 122 460	16.3%
Mickey's Mighty Ball (B44)	204 112	249 425	18.2
"My-Name" Note Cards (P26)	98 934	121 689	18.7
"Needs-a-Name" Doll (D88)	407 332	534 827	23.8
Character T-shirt (P102)	804 231	1,147 638	29.9
TOTAL	$ 1 617 086	$ 2 176 039	25.7%

The third and fourth paragraphs provide pertinent information related to other areas in the company.

I'm recommending to Ted in marketing that we supply our field reps with character T-shirts (P102) to present to buyers. We can break two million with this product if we keep promoting it.

Our Asian suppliers assure us that they can keep the products moving our way; however, we need to carefully monitor the spelling of all names. I recommend that we request a fax to proof before signing off on imprinting any item produced overseas.

The final paragraph summarizes the information, asks for follow-up by a certain time, and ends on a positive note.

In general, the figures suggest continued strong growth with no appreciable change in our investment ratio other than adjusting for inflation. After you look over the numbers, let me know whether you have any questions or concerns before the board meets next month. If the trend continues, 2001 may prove to be a record-setting year for PPI.

FIGURE 1.1

In-Depth Critique: Internal Communication by Memo

As a supplier to vacation spots such as Disney theme parks, Personalized Products, Inc. (PPI) produces souvenirs and toys printed with a wide variety of common names. In this memo, sales manager Tom Beatty reports first-quarter sales to Jacqueline Rogeine, vice-president of finance.

The communication climate suffers when management distorts or ignores information from below, or when management limits the flow of information to employees.

When managers depend on formal channels for communicating they risk encountering **distortion** or misunderstanding. Every link in the communication chain opens up a chance for error. So, by the time a message has made its way all the way up or down the chain, it may bear little resemblance to the original idea. People at lower levels may have only a vague idea of what top management expects of them, and executives may get an imperfect picture of what's happening lower down the chain.

One way to reduce distortion is to reduce the number of levels in the organizational structure. The fewer the links in the communication chain, the less likely it is

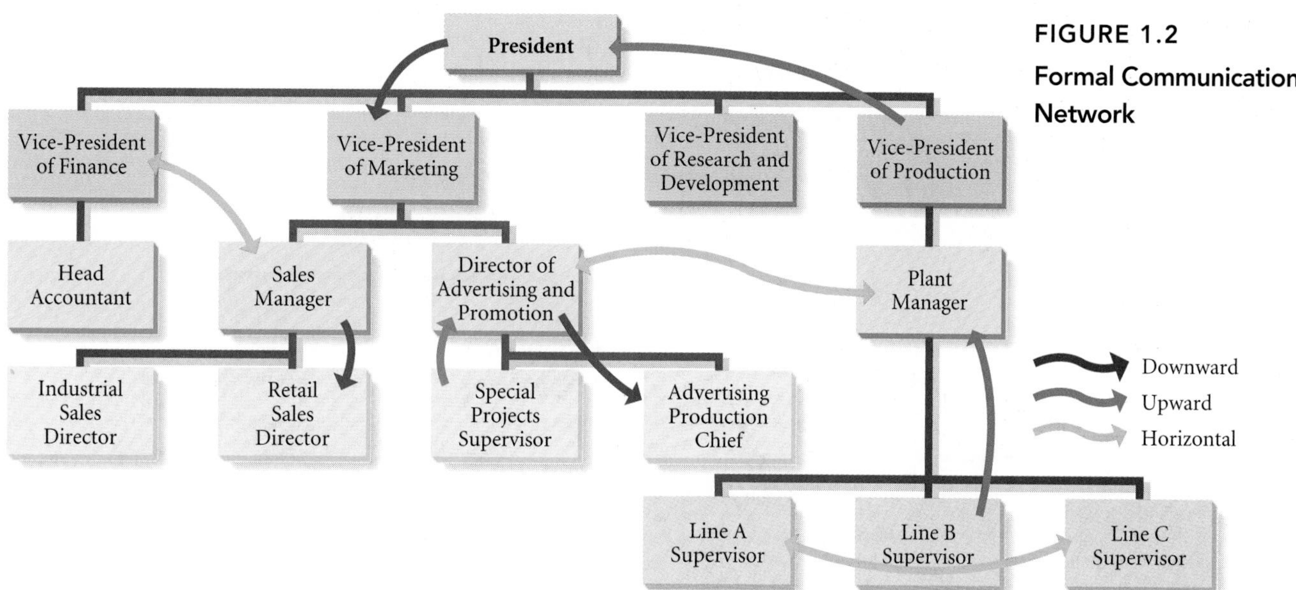

FIGURE 1.2
Formal Communication Network

that misunderstandings will occur.[3] In general, big corporations have more levels than small corporations. But, as Figure 1.3 illustrates, size doesn't necessarily force a company to have a hierarchy with many levels. By increasing the number of people who report to each supervisor, the company can reduce the number of levels in the organization and simplify the communication chain. In other words, a **flat structure** (having fewer levels) and a wide span of control (having more people reporting to each supervisor) are less likely to introduce distortion than are a **tall structure** and a narrow span of control. The best way to fight distortion is to make sure communication flows freely down, up, and across the organization chart.

DOWNWARD INFORMATION FLOW

Managers direct and control the activities of lower-level employees by sending messages down through formal channels.

In most organizations, decisions are made at the top and then flow down to the people who will carry them out.[4] Downward messages might take the form of a casual conversation or a formal interview between a supervisor and an individual employee, or they might be communicated orally in a meeting, in a workshop, on videotape, or on voice mail. Messages might also be written for e-mail or for a memo, training manual, newsletter, bulletin board announcement, or policy directive. At Hallmark, Andy McMillen oversees the publication of employee newsletters that help get the word out. From top to bottom, each person in the organization must be careful to understand the message, apply it, and pass it along.

Most of what filters downward is geared toward helping employees do their jobs. Typical messages include briefings on the organization's mission and strategies, instructions on how to perform various jobs, explanations of policies and procedures, feedback on the employees' performance, and motivational pep talks. Downward communication is especially important in hard times; it lets employees know how the organization is doing, what problems it faces, and what is expected to happen in the future.

UPWARD INFORMATION FLOW

Messages directed upward provide managers with the information they need to make intelligent decisions.

Upward communication is just as vital as downward communication. To solve problems and make intelligent decisions, managers must learn what's going on in the organization. Because they can't be everywhere at once, executives depend on lower-level employees to furnish them with accurate, timely reports on problems, emerging trends, opportunities for improvement, grievances, and performance.

FIGURE 1.3

Organizational Structure and Span of Control

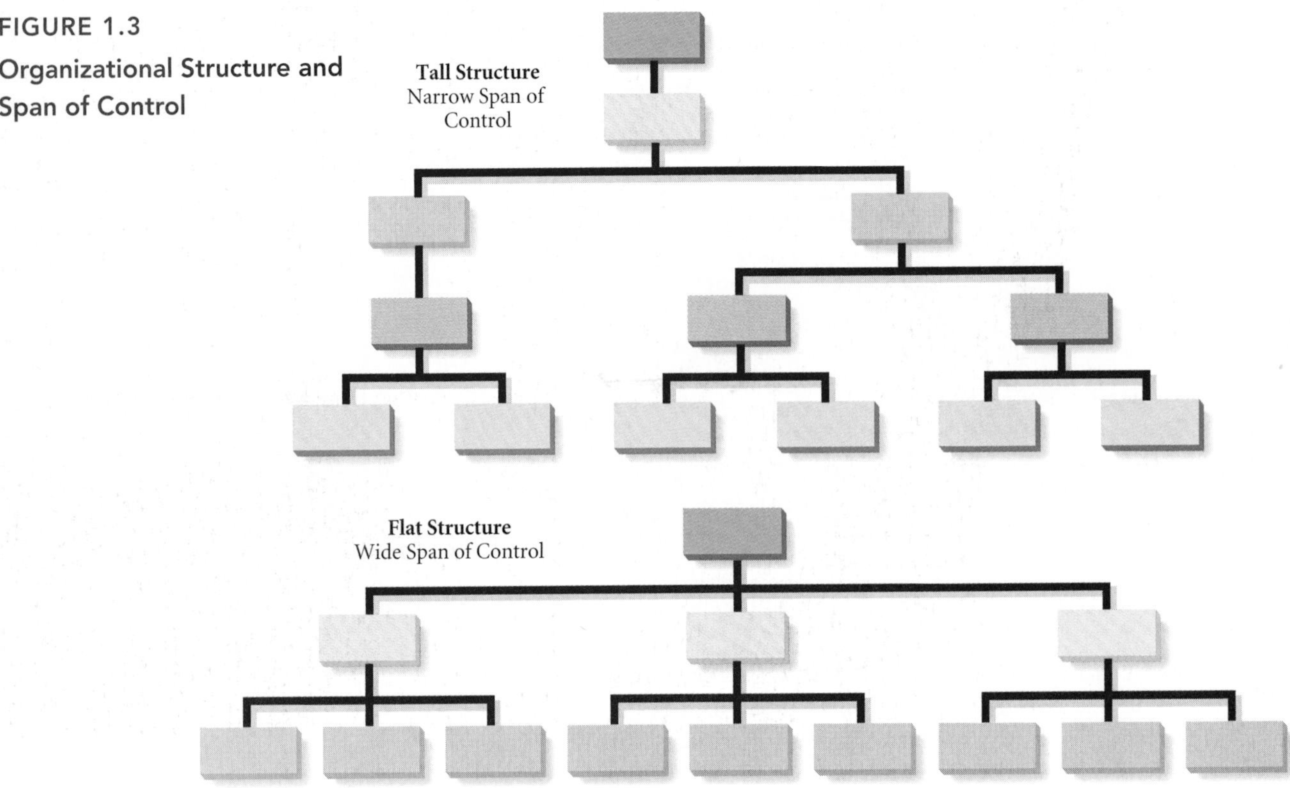

The danger, of course, is that employees will report only the good news. People are often afraid to admit their own mistakes or to report data that suggest their boss was wrong. Companies try to guard against the "rose-coloured glasses" syndrome by creating reporting systems that require employees to furnish vital information on a routine basis. Many of these reports have a *red-flag* feature that calls attention to deviations from planned results. Other formal methods for channelling information upward include e-mail, group meetings, interviews with employees who are leaving the company, and formal procedures for resolving grievances. Hallmark's McMillen often helps to arrange meetings between various levels of management and their employees.

In recent years, many companies have also set up suggestion systems, partnership councils, and open forums. These mechanisms encourage employees to question policies and to submit ideas for improving the work environment. The management-employee council at Aetna Canada, for example, successfully created a new overtime policy.[5]

HORIZONTAL INFORMATION FLOW

Official channels also permit messages to flow from department to department.

In addition to the upward and downward flow of communication in the formal communication network, horizontal communication flows from one department to another, either laterally or diagonally. It helps employees to coordinate tasks, and is especially useful for solving complex and difficult problems.[6] For example, in Figure 1.2, the sales manager might send a memo or an e-mail message to the vice-president of finance, outlining sales forecasts for the coming period, or the plant manager might phone the director of advertising and promotion to discuss changes in the production schedule.

In many companies, advanced technology provides the physical foundation for interdepartmental communication. Nortel Networks uses a worldwide computer network to link its 60 000 employees in Canada, Australia, Singapore, Malaysia, Japan, Ireland, France, and the United States. Whether implemented through technology or not, horizontal communication is crucial. Without it, coworkers aren't able to share information, resulting in missed deadlines, duplicated efforts, increased costs (due to rework), decreased product quality, and deteriorating employee relationships.[7]

Informal Communication Channels

The grapevine is an important source of information in most organizations.

Formal organization charts illustrate how information is supposed to flow. In actual practice, however, lines and boxes on a piece of paper cannot prevent people from talking with one another. Every organization has an **informal communication network**–a grapevine-that supplements official channels. As people go about their work, they have casual conversations with their friends in the office. They joke and kid around and discuss many things: their apartments, their families, restaurants, movies, sports, and other people in the company.

The informal communication network carries information along the organization's unofficial lines of activity and power.

Although some of these conversations deal with personal matters, business is often discussed. In fact, about 80 percent of the information that travels along the grapevine pertains to business, and 75 to 95 percent of it is accurate.[8] Figure 1.4 illustrates a typical informal communication network, which often provides the company's real power structure.

Some top executives are wary of the informal communication network, possibly because it threatens their power to control the flow of information. However, attempts to quash the grapevine generally have the opposite effect. Informal communication increases when official channels are closed or when the organization faces periods of change, excitement, or anxiety. Instead of trying to eliminate the grapevine, sophisticated companies minimize its importance by making certain that the official word gets out.

Some companies try to tap into the grapevine.[9] One service, called In Touch, helps executives keep up with grapevine news by providing an 800 number that employees can call anonymously with any problems or worries. The recorded mes-

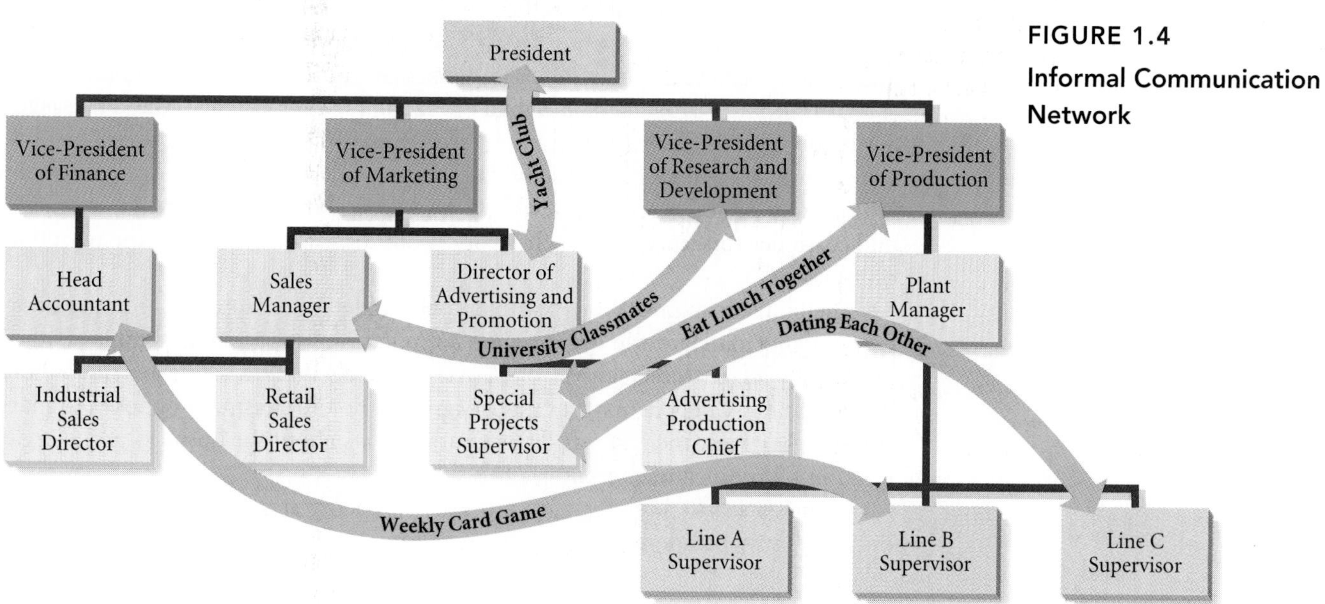

FIGURE 1.4
Informal Communication Network

sages are either summarized or transcribed verbatim for top management.[10] Better yet, successful managers tap into the grapevine themselves to avoid being isolated from what's really happening. Hewlett-Packard trains its managers in **management by walking around (MBWA),** encouraging them to be interested in employees' personal lives as well as their work lives. Brian McLean, the CEO of Mediacom, a leading Canadian outdoor advertising firm, practices MBWA by keeping in touch with the operations specialists in Mediacom's client companies. He says, "We had consultants consulting consultants, and I and my people seemed to be spending all of our time in meetings inventing some new complexity. We got rid of all that … and now my job is very simply keeping my ear to the ground."[11]

LEARNING OUTCOME 3
Explain how companies communicate with outside audiences.

The External Communication Network

The external communication network links the organization with the outside world of customers, suppliers, competitors, and investors.

Just as internal communication carries information up, down, and across the organization, **external communication** carries it into and out of the organization. Companies constantly exchange messages with customers, vendors, distributors, competitors, investors, journalists, and government and community representatives. Whether by phone, fax, e-mail, videotape, or letter (see Figure 1.5), much of this communication is carefully orchestrated, and some occurs informally.

Formal Contacts with Outsiders

The marketing and public relations departments are responsible for managing much of the organization's formal communication with outsiders.

Even though much of the communication with outsiders is casual and relatively unplanned, most organizations attempt to control the information they convey to customers, investors, and the general public. Two functional units are particularly important in managing the flow of external messages: the marketing department and the public relations department.

Marketing focuses on selling goods and services, whereas public relations is more concerned with developing the organization's overall reputation.

THE ROLE OF MARKETING AND PUBLIC RELATIONS

As a consumer, you are often on the receiving end of marketing messages: face-to-face or telephone conversations with salespeople, direct-mail solicitations, TV and radio commercials, newspaper and magazine ads, advertising banners on the Internet, product brochures, and mail-order catalogues. Although these messages are highly visible, they represent only a small part of marketing communication. In addition to advertising and selling products, the typical marketing department is also responsible for product development, physical distribution, market research, and customer service, all of which involve both the transmission and the reception of information.

The public relations (PR) department (also called the corporate communication department) manages the organization's reputation with various groups, including employees, customers, investors, government agencies, and the general public. Professional PR people may have a background in journalism, as opposed to marketing. They view their role as disseminating news about the business to the organization's various audiences.

Whereas marketing messages are usually openly sponsored and paid for by the company, public relations messages are carried by the media if they are

August 16, 2001

Dear Ms. McCallum,

Thank you for your interest in our products. Swift Canoe & Kayak is a canoe and kayak manufacturing and retailing business, located just outside Algonquin Park. Many of our products have been developed in conjunction with our neighbouring business, Algonquin Outfitters.

To purchase a Swift canoe and/or kayak, you can visit one of our two factory-direct outlets or attend one of the many factory sales we hold throughout the province each spring and fall. Both our Swift stores and all our special events offer on-site test paddling and a tremendous selection. Our annual newsletter on our stores and sales events is available upon request.

Many people choose to order their boat ahead of time or consult with one of our staff members before test paddling and purchasing our canoes and kayaks. In this case, we recommend that you first read through the catalogue, then call us and talk to one of our factory sales representatives. They are all expert paddlers, non-commissioned, and available from 9 AM to 6 PM, 7 days a week. You can also visit our Web site and use our interactive canoe selector!

When we receive your order, we will send confirmation and give you a date that your boat will be finished. Most orders can be picked up immediately, while custom orders may take two to four weeks. We can ship your boat to any of the sales events we hold. Factory-direct shipping is also available through most parts of Ontario.

Next is the hard part–waiting for your custom-made Swift craft! When it is ready, it will come with a Swift Owner's Manual and lots of information on how to take care of your boat. For your added assurance, all of our boats are backed with a lifetime warranty and Swift's personal guarantee to provide years of paddling enjoyment.

Please take the time to review our information. We're looking forward to serving your needs.

Happy Paddling,

Karen McDonald
Swift Canoe & Kayak–Algonquin
www.swiftcanoe.com

R.R. #1, Oxtongue Lake, Dwight, ON P0A 1H0
Phone: 705-635-1167 Fax: 705-635-9456 e-mail: swift@bconnex.net

The first paragraph establishes the company's credibility by describing its products and affiliation with a nearby outdoor equipment retailer.

The second and third paragraphs provide helpful information about how products can be selected and ordered. The detail provided is meant to reassure readers that their questions will be answered by qualified salespeople.

The fourth and fifth paragraphs continue to reassure readers with detail about shipping and the warranty. The light tone created in the beginning of paragraph five enhances the letter's personal tone.

The final paragraph reinforces key ideas in the message by inviting readers to examine the enclosed catalogue and repeating the company's interest in helping them.

FIGURE 1.5

In-Depth Critique: External Communication by Letter

When canoeing enthusiasts request a catalogue from Swift Canoe & Kayak, they also receive a letter summarizing how to select and order a product. External messages such as these not only provide useful information, but also establish goodwill between the company and its potential customers, cultivating a relationship that may lead to a purchase.

considered newsworthy. The communication tools used by PR departments include news releases, lobbying programs, special events, booklets and brochures about the organization, letters, annual reports, audiovisual materials, speeches and position papers, tours, and internal publications for employees.

LEARNING OUTCOME 4
Analyze how companies communicate successfully in a crisis.

CRISIS COMMUNICATION

One of the most visible functions of the PR department is to help management plan for and respond to crises. A good PR professional looks for potential problems, constantly scans the business environment, then alerts management to the implications of such problems and suggests the best course of action.

The way a company handles a crisis can have a profound impact on the organization's subsequent performance.

Sudden, violent accidents form one type of public-relations nightmare. Plane crashes, oil spills, chemical leaks, and product defects all belong to this group. The other type of crisis is the sort that builds slowly and occurs because of a company's conscious, but ill-founded, decisions. One example is the role of the Canadian Red Cross in concealing the risk of AIDS through blood transfusion. The Krever inquiry, led by Justice Horace Krever, found that top Red Cross executives publicly claimed that the danger of AIDS was overrated while privately recognizing the risk. The inquiry also found that the Red Cross wasted time establishing preventive measures. The actions of the Canadian Red Cross resulted in public loss of faith in the organization and its replacement by the Canadian Blood Services.[12]

Most experts recommend handling a crisis with candour and honesty.

According to public relations professionals, when disaster strikes, a defensive posture is generally counterproductive. The best course is to be proactive, admit your mistakes, and apologize (see Table 1.1). That's the course Johnson & Johnson followed in its now classic handling of the Tylenol poisoning scare in 1982.

When a crisis hits, most firms respond, to some degree, through their public relations department, but they sometimes ignore the audience that is likely to be affected most–their own employees. When Alberta energy company Suncor developed its cost-cutting measures in 1992, the organization was "in a state of fear.

TABLE 1.1 Dos and Don'ts of Crisis Communication

When a Crisis Hits:	
Dos	***Don'ts***
Do be prepared for trouble. Identify potential problems. Appoint and train a response team. Prepare and test a crisis management plan.	Don't blame anyone for anything.
Do get top management involved as soon as the crisis hits.	Don't speculate in public.
Do set up a news centre for company representatives and the media, equipped with phones, computers, and other electronic tools for preparing news releases. • Issue at least two news updates a day, and have trained personnel on call to respond to questions around the clock. • Provide complete information packets to the media as soon as possible. • To prevent conflicting statements and provide continuity, appoint a single person, trained in advance, to speak for the company. • Tell receptionists to direct all calls to the news centre.	Don't refuse to answer questions.
Do tell the whole story—openly, completely, and honestly. If you are at fault, apologize.	Don't release information that will violate anyone's right to privacy.
Do demonstrate the company's concern by your statements and your actions.	Don't use the crisis to pitch products or services.
	Don't play favourites with media representatives.

People didn't know what was going to happen next," says Mike O'Brien, executive vice-president of the Sunoco Group, Suncor's petroleum products division. To explain and to minimize the impact of the changes on employees, management "communicated our vision over and over again–through every channel we had–bulletins, voice mail messages, face-to-face meetings ... all kinds of forums ... brainstorming sessions and focus groups." In the end, management achieved its goals because the process for reaching them was made clear to employees.[13]

Don't ignore the impact of a crisis on employees.

Informal Contacts with Outsiders

Every employee informally accumulates facts and impressions that contribute to the organization's collective understanding of the outside world.

As a member of an organization, you are inherently an informal conduit for communicating with the outside world. In the course of your daily activities, you unconsciously absorb bits of information that add to the collective knowledge pool of your company. During a trip to the shopping mall, you notice how a competitor's products are selling; as you read the paper, you pick up economic and business news related to your work; when you have a problem at the office, you ask your family or friends for advice.

What's more, every time you speak for or about your company, you send a message. In fact, if you have a public contact job, you don't even have to say anything. All you have to do is smile. Many outsiders may form their impression of your organization on the basis of the subtle, unconscious clues you transmit through your tone of voice, facial expression, and general appearance.

Top managers rely heavily on informal contacts with outsiders to exchange information that might be useful to their companies. Although much of the networking involves interaction with fellow executives, plenty of high-level managers recognize the value of keeping in touch with the real world. For example, when Stanley Gault was chairman of Rubbermaid, he cornered travellers in airports to ask for ideas on new products. Xerox executives spend one day each month handling customer complaints, and senior executives at Hyatt Hotels serve as bellhops. As Wal-Mart founder Sam Walton used to say when someone asked why he visited Kmart stores: "It's all part of the educational process. I'm just learning."[14]

Characteristics of Effective Organizational Communication

LEARNING OUTCOME 5
Discuss the six factors that contribute to effective business communication.

If good management depends on effective communication, it follows that the best-managed companies are those that have built the best internal and external communication networks. What makes their networks the best? What characteristics contribute to effective communication? Six factors are involved:

1. fostering an open communication climate
2. committing to ethical communication
3. understanding the difficulties involved in intercultural communication
4. becoming proficient in communication technology
5. using an audience-centred approach to communication
6. creating and processing messages efficiently

An Open Communication Climate

The organization's communication climate affects the quantity and quality of the information that passes through the pipeline.

An organization's communication climate is a reflection of its **corporate culture:** the mixture of values, traditions, and habits that give a place its atmosphere or personality. Some companies tend to choke off the upward flow of communication, believing that it tends to result in time-consuming and unproductive debate. Other companies, such as Hallmark, foster candour and honesty: employees feel free to confess their mistakes, to disagree with the boss, and to express their opinions.

The management style of the top executives influences the organization's communication climate.

Many factors influence an organization's communication climate, including the nature of the industry, the company's physical setup, the history of the company, and passing events. However, as Hallmark's Andy McMillen confirms, one of the most important factors is the style of the top management group.[15]

Of all the many ways to categorize management styles, one of the most widely used is Douglas McGregor's Theory X and Theory Y.[16] Theory X managers consider workers to be lazy and irresponsible, motivated to work only by fear of losing their jobs. These managers adopt a directive style. Theory Y managers, on the other hand, assume that people like to work and to take responsibility when they believe in what they are doing. These managers adopt a more supportive management style.

Today more and more companies are recognizing the value of an open communication climate.

Yet another management approach, called Theory Z, was developed by William Ouchi.[17] Like athletic coaches, Theory Z managers encourage employees to work together as a team. Although the company still looks after employees, it also gives them the opportunity to take responsibility and to participate in decision making. The trend today is toward any style that encourages open communication climates. In such a climate, managers spend more time listening than issuing orders, and workers not only offer suggestions but also help set goals and collaborate on solving problems.[18]

A Commitment to Ethical Communication

Ethics are the principles of conduct that govern a person or group.

The second factor contributing to effective communication is the organization's commitment to **ethics,** the principles of conduct that govern a person or a group. Unethical people are essentially selfish and unscrupulous, saying or doing whatever it takes to achieve an end. Ethical people are generally trustworthy, fair, and impartial, respecting the rights of others and concerned about the impact of their actions on society. Ethics has been defined as "knowing the difference between what you have a right to do and what is the right thing to do."[19]

A McGill University graduate, Darren Entwistle is CEO of TELUS, Canada's second largest telecommunications company. He believes that "honest and honourable business dealings are the cornerstone of quality customer service" and of a company's success. TELUS's code of business ethics is clearly communicated in its Corporate Social Responsibility Report. You can read it at **about.telus.com.**

Ethics plays a crucial role in communication. Language itself is made up of words that carry values. So merely by saying things a certain way, you influence how others perceive your message, and you shape expectations and behaviours.[20] Likewise, when an organization expresses itself internally, it influences the values of its employees; when it communicates externally, it shapes the way outsiders perceive it. **Ethical communication** includes all relevant information, is true in every sense, and is not deceptive in any way.

When sending an ethical message, you are accurate and sincere. You avoid language that manipulates, discriminates, or exaggerates. You do not hide negative information behind an optimistic attitude, you don't state opinions as facts, and you portray graphic data fairly. You are honest with employers, co-workers, and clients and never seek personal gain by making others look better or worse than they are. You don't allow personal preferences to influence your perception or the perception of others, and you act in good faith. On the surface, such ethical practices appear fairly easy to recognize. But deciding what is ethical can be quite complex.

RECOGNIZING ETHICAL CHOICES

An **ethical dilemma** involves choosing among alternatives that aren't clear-cut (perhaps two conflicting alternatives are both ethical and valid, or perhaps your alternatives lie somewhere in the vast grey area between right and wrong). Suppose you're president of a company that's losing money. You have a duty to your shareholders to try to cut your losses and a duty to your employees to be fair and honest. After looking at various options, you conclude that you'll have to lay off 500 people immediately. You suspect that you may have to lay off another 100 people later on, but right now you need those 100 workers to finish a project. What do you tell them? If you confess to them that their jobs are shaky, many may quit just when you need them most. However, if you tell them that the future is rosy, you'll be stretching the truth.

Conflicting priorities and the vast grey areas between right and wrong pose ethical problems for an organization's communicators.

Unlike a dilemma, an **ethical lapse** is making a clearly unethical or illegal choice. Suppose you have decided to change jobs and have discreetly landed an interview with your boss's largest competitor. You get along great with the interviewer, who is impressed enough with you to offer you a position on the spot. Not only is the new position a step up from your current job, but the pay is double what you're getting now. You accept the job and agree to start next month. Then as you're shaking hands with the interviewer, she asks that when you begin your new job, you bring along profiles of your present company's ten largest customers. Do you comply with her request? How do you decide between what's ethical and what is not?

Laws provide ethical guidelines for certain types of messages.

Ask yourself how you would feel if you were on the receiving end of the message.

MAKING ETHICAL CHOICES

One place to look for guidance is the law. If saying or writing something is clearly illegal, you have no dilemma: You obey the law. However, even though legal considerations will resolve some ethical questions, you'll often have to rely on your own judgment and principles. You might apply the rule of "Do unto others as you would have them do unto you." You might examine your motives: If your intent is honest, the statement is ethical, even though it may be factually incorrect; if your intent is to mislead or manipulate the audience, the message is unethical, regardless of whether it is true. You might look at the consequences of your decision and opt for the solution that provides the greatest good to the greatest number of people. You might also ask yourself a set of questions:[21]

- Is this decision legal? (Does it violate civil law or company policy?)
- Is it balanced? (Does it do the most good and the least harm? Is it fair to all concerned in the short term as well as in the long term? Does it promote positive win-win relationships?)
- Is it a decision you can live with? (Does it make you feel good about yourself? Does it make you proud? Would you feel good about your decision if a newspaper published it? If your family knew about it?)
- Is it feasible? (Can it work in the real world? Have you considered your position in the company, your company's competition, its financial and political strength, the likely costs or risks of your decision, and the time available?)

MOTIVATING ETHICAL CHOICES

Ethical communication promotes long-term business success and profit. However, improving profits isn't reason enough to be ethical. So how can an organization motivate employees to be ethical? First and foremost, the personal influence of chief executives and managers plays an important role. Top managers can begin encouraging ethical behaviour and decision making by being receptive communicators themselves (which requires mastering many of the skills presented in this text). They can also send the right message to employees by rewarding ethical behaviour. Managers can lay out an explicit ethical policy, and, in fact, more and more companies are using

Going Online

Use the Power of the Internet to Help You Learn About Business Communication

One of the best ways to find information on the Internet about business communication or any other topic is by metasearch tools. They are like master search engines, enabling you to access individual engines, such as Yahoo! and Looksmart simultaneously. Bookmark the following metasearch engines on your list:

www.savvysearch.com

www.metacrawler.com

allinone.com

Note: To reach the Web sites you find throughout this book, you don't have to type every single URL (universal resources locator) into your browser. Type just one–**www.pearsoned.ca/thill**–the Web site for this book. There, you'll find live links that take you straight to the site of your choice.

PROMOTING WORKPLACE ETHICS

Ethical Boundaries: Where Would You Draw the Line?

At the very least, you owe your employer an honest day's work for an honest day's pay: your best efforts, obedience to the rules, a good attitude, respect for your employer's property, and a professional appearance. Such duties and considerations seem clear-cut, but where does your obligation to your employer end? For instance, where would you draw the line in communication situations such as the following?

- ✧ Writing your résumé so that an embarrassing two-year lapse won't be obvious
- ✧ Telling your best friend about your company's upcoming merger right after mailing the formal announcement to your shareholders
- ✧ Hinting to a co-worker (who's a close friend) that it's time to look around for something new, when you've already been told confidentially that she's scheduled to be fired at the end of the month
- ✧ Saying nothing when you witness one employee taking credit for another's successful idea
- ✧ Preserving your position by presenting yourself to supervisors as the only person capable of achieving an objective
- ✧ Buying one software package for use by three computer operators
- ✧ Making up an excuse when (for the fourth time this month) you have to pick up your child from school early and miss an important business meeting
- ✧ Calling in sick because you're taking a few days off and you want to use up some of the sick leave you've accumulated.

The ethics involved in these situations may seem perfectly unambiguous ... until you think about them. But, wherever you are, whatever the circumstances, you owe your employer your best efforts. And time and again, it will be up to you to decide whether those efforts are ethical.

CAREER APPLICATIONS

1. List ethical behaviours you would expect from your employees, and compare your list to those of your classmates.
2. As the supervisor of the office typing pool, you must deal with several typists who have a tendency to gossip about their co-workers. List five things you might do to resolve the situation.

Sources: Adapted from Ben Stein, "An Employer's Bill of Rights," *Business Month*, April 1990, 55; Thomas A. Young, "Ethics in Business: Business of Ethics," *Vital Speeches*, 15 September 1992, 725–730; "Business Ethics: What Are Your Personal Standards?" *Working Woman*, February 1990, 61–62; Kyle Herger, "One Communicator's Gold Star Is Another's Scarlet Letter," *IABC Communication World*, September 1989, 34–36; Barbara D. Langham, "Ethics: Where Do You Stand?" *IABC Communication World*, May 1989, 21–22, 24–25; Frank Yanacek, "A Question of Ethics," *Transportation and Distribution*, December 1988, 48–50.

BEHIND THE SCENES AT ZERO-KNOWLEDGE SYSTEMS

The Freedom to Communicate

Subsidized massages and laundry service are two of the employee perks at Zero-Knowledge Systems, a Montreal software company located in the city's lively Latin quarter, noted for its sidewalk cafés, jazz bars, and summer festival. Their product is Freedom, a technology that allows people to maintain their privacy while surfing or communicating via the Internet. Zero-Knowledge believes that freedom of expression on the Internet is threatened when information such as e-mail addresses or online messages can be accessed by third parties. The company's mission is to empower Internet users to control their personal data completely, disclosing it only when they want to. With Freedom software, messages can be posted anonymously to newsgroups and identities concealed when sending e-mail or chatting online. Zero-Knowledge is "committed to building the tools to ensure that the Internet develops as a borderless platform for economic, democratic and social advancement."

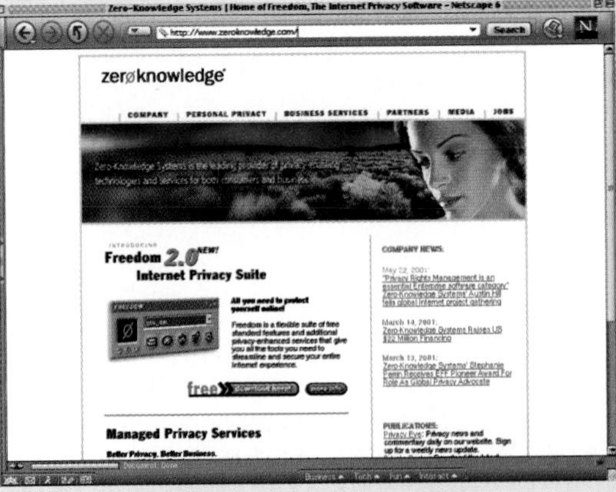

Founded by brothers Austin and Hamnett Hill and their father, Hammie Hill, in 1997, Zero-Knowledge grew dramatically within a year, from a staff of 15 to 200, as they have been developing and marketing their product.

One way Zero-Knowledge encourages employee commitment is by nurturing individuals and emphasizing rewards over rules. Material benefits include a gym, a meditation room,

a written **code of ethics** to help employees determine what is acceptable. In addition, managers can use ethics audits to monitor ethical progress and to point up any weaknesses that need to be addressed.[22]

Organizations can foster ethical behaviour
- ✧ By helping top managers become more sensitive communicators
- ✧ By rewarding ethical actions
- ✧ By using ethics audits

An Understanding of Intercultural Communication

The third factor contributing to a positive communication climate is understanding intercultural communication. Not only are more and more businesses crossing national boundaries to compete on a global scale, but the makeup of the global and domestic workforce is changing rapidly. European, Asian, and North American firms are establishing offices around the world and are creating international ties through global partnerships, cooperatives, and affiliations.[23] These companies must understand the laws, customs, and business practices of their host countries, and they must deal with business associates and employees who are native to those countries (who perhaps speak another language and who are certainly more familiar with the culture). Multiculturalism is a defining feature of the Canadian workplace. Of the one million people who immigrated to Canada between 1991 and 1996, almost 80 percent speak a native language other than English or French. It is estimated that about one-third of Torontonians speak that native language at home.[24] So, whether you work abroad or at home, you will encounter more and more cultural diversity in the workplace. To compete successfully in today's multicultural environment, businesspeople must overcome the communication barriers not only of language but of culture as well (see Chapter 3).

Intercultural communication plays an important role both abroad and at home.

Intercultural communication is discussed in detail in Chapter 3.

A Proficiency in Communication Technology

The fourth factor contributing to effective organizational communication is the ability to use and adapt to technology. The increasing speed of communication

Technology's effects on communication are discussed in detail in Chapter 4.

magazine subscriptions, a cafeteria with an espresso machine, and a games room.

As a high-tech company, Zero-Knowledge focuses on creating a stimulating environment that can be called a community, rather than a workplace. The public relations officer, Dov Smith, notes that the corporate culture at Zero-Knowledge is "a shift from people in sheep pens." Smith says that at his previous job, "They would stick you in a pen and you would be stuck there all cooped up to work, work, work ... there was no quality to the work life."

The Hills supply more than a lively environment. They also nurture their employees by giving them the freedom to communicate. For example, job titles aren't assigned—workers choose their own. Cryptographers call themselves "evil geniuses"; customer service people are "support gurus." Such self-expression helps to foster open communication, a keynote of the Zero-Knowledge culture.

So does the flat organizational structure. New employees work alongside world-class scientists, and the company founders may be seen playing ping-pong with staff in the games room. Teams are diverse, filled with people of different cultures, ages, lifestyles, and opinions. Such teams are seen as "smarter, faster and more flexible than homogeneous teams." Decisions, whether from upper management or staff, are subject to open and intense scrutiny. Emplyees say that the Hills encourage them to speak their minds, and to raise issues. The Hills believe that "the more varied the perspectives on the problem, the more likely you're going to get fresh, original solutions." [25]

APPLY YOUR KNOWLEDGE

1. Today's organizations try to open communication channels by managing through teams. Briefly discuss the advantages of team decision making. Are there any disadvantages? Explain.
2. Can the interior design of a workplace inhibit or encourage communication among employees? Discuss the benefits and limitations of both "open-concept" work environments, where employees share large common areas, and cubicle environments, where employees are physically separated from their colleagues.

and the growing amount of information to be communicated are only two results of the ever-changing technology you will encounter on the job. To succeed, business people today must be able to understand, use, and adapt to the technological tools of communication (see Chapter 4).

An Audience-Centred Approach to Communication

Using an audience-centred approach means keeping your audience in mind at all times when communicating.

The fifth factor contributing to effective organizational communication is an **audience-centred approach:** Keep your audience in mind at all times during the process of communication. Empathizing with, being sensitive to, and generally considering your audience's feelings is the best approach for effective communication. The audience-centred approach is more than an approach to business communication; it's actually the modern approach to business in general, behind such concepts as total quality management and total customer satisfaction.

Communicate from your audience's point of view.

Because you care about your audience, you use every possible way to make your message meaningful to them. You might actually create lively individual portraits of readers and listeners to predict how they will react. You might simply try to put yourself in your audience's position. You might try adhering strictly to guidelines about courtesy, or you might be able to gather information about the needs and wants of your audience. Whatever your tactic, the point is to write and speak from your audience's point of view.

Paul Tellier, CEO of Canadian National Railways, sees informal communication as a powerful way to communicate with CN's employees at all levels. After taking the helm in 1992, Tellier used face-to-face meetings with managers and line workers to transmit the changes needed for greater productivity and competitiveness in order to ensure the pre-eminent position of Canada's railways.

An Efficient Flow of Communication Messages

The sixth factor contributing to effective organizational communication is an efficient flow of communication messages. Think for a minute about the number of messages we send and receive, both within the organization and throughout the world.

- Despite computer manufacturers' promises of the paperless office, paper consumption in Canada grows 10 to 15 per cent each year.[26]
- Canadians now use almost 8 million wireless devices almost daily. There are 5.3 million wireless phones, over 1.5 million pagers, and 10 000 mobile satellite phones in use today.[27]
- In one year, 11.9 billion messages were left on voice mailboxes.[28]
- A 1999 survey found that 56 per cent of respondents use the Internet every day or several times a week, up 48 per cent from 1998.[29]

All companies can hold down costs and maximize the benefits of their communication activities if they just follow three simple guidelines:

Organizations save time and money by sending only necessary messages.

- *Reduce the number of messages.* Think twice before sending a message. The average cost of dictating, transcribing, and mailing a business letter is between $19.02 and $27.28.[30] So if a message must be put in writing, a letter or memo is a good investment. But if the message merely adds to the information overload, it's probably better left unsent or handled in some other way–say, by a quick telephone call or a face-to-face chat.
- *Speed up the preparation of messages.* First, save time by making sure that written messages are prepared correctly the first time around. Second, save time with standardization. Most organizations use form letters to handle repetitive correspondence, and most employ a standard format for memos, reports, and e-mail messages prepared on a recurring basis. In addition, standardization saves your audience's time because the familiar format enables people to absorb the information quickly.

By streamlining the preparation of messages, companies make sure that information is transmitted in a timely manner.

- *Train the writers and speakers.* When the American Society for Training and Development surveyed major employers, it found that 41 percent provide writing-skills programs for their employees.[31] Many others, including Hallmark, offer seminars and workshops on handling common oral communication situations (such as dealing with customers, managing subordinates, and getting along with co-workers) as well as training in computers and other electronic means of communication.

In-house training benefits even experienced communicators.

LEARNING OUTCOME 6
Develop goals for acquiring the communication skills you will need in your career.

Even though you may ultimately receive training on the job, you can start mastering business communication skills right now, in this course. Begin with an honest assessment of where you stand. In the next few days, watch how you handle the communication situations that arise. Then in the months ahead, try to focus on building your competence in areas where you need the most work.

Focus on building skills in the areas where you've been weak.

This book has been designed to provide the kind of communication practice that will prepare you for whatever comes along later in your career. The next chapter introduces some concepts of communication in general so that you will be better able to analyze and predict the outcome of various situations. Chapters 3 and 4 discuss the importance of intercultural and technological communication. Chapters 5, 6, and 7 explain how to plan and organize business messages and how to perfect their style and tone. Chapters 8 through 18 deal with specific forms of communication: letters and memos; reports, résumés and application letters; interviews and meetings; and speeches and presentations. As you progress through this book, you will also meet many business communicators like Andy McMillen of Hallmark. Their experiences will give you an insight into what it takes to communicate effectively on the job.

Is Telecommuting Right for You?

USING THE POWER OF TECHNOLOGY

Telecommuting sounds like the perfect life. No commute. No morning rush to get ready for. No expensive wardrobe. No daycare for kids. But for many people, telecommuting also means no social life.

Many home-based workers soon find that they miss interacting with colleagues. Some worry that if they're not in the office—if they're not seen—they'll be forgotten. Others find that they actually put in longer hours or they encounter too many distractions, such as young children requiring attention. Still others discover that it takes a lot of willpower and self-discipline to be productive when the refrigerator and a nice warm bed are just a few feet away.

Is telecommuting right for you? Here's a checklist to help you determine whether you'd be a good candidate. If you answer "yes" to all the questions, go for it. But if you answer "no" to any of them, you need to think the issue through carefully before taking the leap.

- ✧ Have you worked at your company long enough to thoroughly understand its culture and expectations?
- ✧ Does your home have a separate room in which to work, with a door that shuts?
- ✧ Can others perform their jobs without you being physically available?
- ✧ Does your home workspace have a separate phone line for a fax/modem, computer, and other equipment?
- ✧ Are you content to work in isolation?
- ✧ If you have a child, will you have daycare available while you work?
- ✧ Can you perform your job, complete projects, and meet your deadlines without supervision?
- ✧ If you live with someone else who works at home, will this pose any problems?
- ✧ Can you physically take your work home with you in a briefcase?
- ✧ Are you disciplined enough to stop working at the end of the day?
- ✧ Can you communicate everything you need for your daily workload via phone or e-mail?
- ✧ If you were your boss, would you let you telecommute?

CAREER APPLICATIONS

1. Based on your answers to the telecommuting questions, do you think telecommuting is right for you? Why or why not?
2. What sort of person do you think would be happy as a telecommuter?

Sources: Adapted from Bronwyn Fryer, "WorkShop," *Working Woman*, April 1997, 59–60; Lisa Chadderdon, "Merrill Lynch Works—at Home," *Fast Company*, April:May 1998, 70–72; Peg Verone, "House Rules," *Success*, July 1998, 22–23.

Applying What You've Learned

At the beginning of this chapter, you read about the challenge faced by Hallmark as it tried to keep internal communication flowing smoothly and efficiently. Each chapter begins with a similar slice-of-life vignette titled "On the Job: Facing a Communication Dilemma." As you read through the chapter, think about the communication problems faced by the company highlighted in the vignette, and become familiar with the various concepts presented there.

At the end of each chapter you'll find an innovative simulation called "On the Job: Solving a Communication Dilemma." Each simulation starts by explaining how the organization actually solved its communication dilemma. Then you'll play the role of a person at the organization introduced in the vignette, and you'll face a situation you'd encounter on the job in that organization. You will be presented with several communication scenarios, each with several possible courses of action. It's up to you to recommend one course of action from the available choices, even though some of the questions have more than one acceptable answer and some have no truly satisfactory answers. Your instructor may assign the simulations as homework, as teamwork, as material for in-class discussion, or in several other ways. These scenarios let you explore various communication ideas and apply the concepts and techniques from the chapter.

Now you're ready for the first simulation. As you tackle each question, think about the material you covered in this chapter and consider your own experience as a communicator. You'll probably be surprised to discover how much you already know about business communication.

ON THE JOB
Solving a Communication Dilemma at Hallmark

When You Care Enough to Send the Very Best—Inside or Outside the Company

Hallmark relies on effective communication to supply employees with important information such as new products, the company's financial status, and changes in employee benefits. To keep Hallmark's communication climate open and to ensure that all employees receive the information they need, McMillen uses many communication channels.

He oversees several company publications. *Noon News* is a daily newsletter for all company employees. Like a small-town newspaper, it fosters a sense of community by including bits of personal information (such as birthdays and anniversaries), want ads, reminders of such things as health-plan enrolment deadlines, and information on company products and finances. Another internal publication, *Directions*, is published to distribute information to managers. It has no established publication schedule, because its purpose is to give managers important company information before it becomes public. In addition, computer-monitor signboards in various locations throughout the headquarters building display information that was too late for print deadlines.

Face-to-face communication is also common at Hallmark. Several times a year McMillen schedules CEO Forums, at which company president and CEO Irvine Hockaday meets with about 50 employees selected at random from all company divisions. For 90 minutes employees can discuss their concerns directly with the head of the company. With no predetermined agenda, the participants are free to bring up anything they want to discuss. Says McMillen, "The forums are purely for midmanagement and below, so there's no intimidation factor. You can talk to Irv about anything, and you don't have to worry about your VP sitting there taking notes. It's a terrific opportunity for dialogue." Four times a year, McMillen arranges a Corporate Town Hall, at which Hockaday holds sessions for 400 employees. Unlike the CEO Forums, these meetings have an agenda and a specific topic. For the first 30 minutes, Hockaday talks about a specific company issue, and then opens the meeting for an hour of discussion.

Of course, communication also occurs informally when people talk face to face and by telephone, or write memos and electronic mail. Whatever the channel used, Hallmark cares enough to strive for the very best internal communication, and it's McMillen's job to make sure that all necessary information is delivered effectively and efficiently.[32]

Your Mission: You are manager of communications at Hallmark's corporate headquarters. In this position, you're responsible for both internal and external communication. Use your knowledge of communication to choose the best response for each of the following situations. Be prepared to explain why your choice is best.

1. The company's medical insurance plan for the next year contains substantial changes from this year's plan. How should information about these changes first be distributed to employees?
   a. Have the company president present the information at Corporate Town Hall meetings so that employees can give him feedback on their reactions to the changes.
   b. Detail the changes in *Noon News.*
   c. Publish details in *Directions,* the document distributed to managers, and then outline the changes in *Noon News.*
   d. Describe the changes in the annual benefits statement sent to each employee.

2. Suppose the team that handles the shipping of party products is falling behind schedule. The management adviser says that many team members are just going through the motions and are not giving their best to the job. As one way of improving performance, she wants to send a memo to everyone in the department. Which of the following approaches would you recommend that she use?
   a. Tell employees that the team's performance is not as good as it could be, and ask for their ideas on how to improve the situation.
   b. Explain that you'll have to fire the next person you see giving less than 100 percent (even though you know that company policy prevents you from actually doing so).
   c. Ask employees to monitor one another and to report problems to the department manager.
   d. Tell all employees that if team performance does not improve, wages will be reduced and evaluations will not be positive.

3. A rumour begins circulating that a major product line will be dropped and the workers in that area will be laid off. The rumour is false. What is the first action you should take?
   a. Put a notice on the computer-monitor signboards denying the rumour.
   b. Publish a denial in *Directions* asking all managers to tell their employees that the rumour is false.
   c. Schedule a meeting with all employees on the affected product line. At the meeting, have the company president explain the facts and publicly state that the rumour is false.
   d. Ignore the rumour. Like all false rumours it will eventually die out.

4. In collaboration with a software company, Hallmark has developed PC software for users to design their own greeting cards. At this time, only the team working on the new cards and upper management know about the product. How will you spread the information to all employees?
   a. Announce the product in *Noon News.*
   b. Publish an edition of *Directions* explaining the new product.
   c. Have the president announce the introduction at a Corporate Town Hall session.
   d. Send e-mail to all employees.

TAP Your Knowledge

Summary of Learning Outcomes

1. Describe how managers use communication. A manager's day is filled with meetings, casual conversations, speaking engagements, and phone calls. Interspersed with these oral activities are periods set aside for reading and writing. From these sources, managers glean important information to keep staff informed, from executives and other managers to lower-level employees.

2. Contrast formal and informal communication channels within an organization. The formal communication channels form the official structure of an organization. These channels are characterized by downward flow, where decisions are made at the top and transmitted to the people who will implement them; upward flow, where lower-level employees will send messages to managers and executives; and horizontal flow, which may be lateral or diagonal, from one department to another. Informal communication channels are also called the grapevine, characterized by casual conversations in the workplace. Top executives are sometimes wary of the grapevine because it may threaten their power to control information. Effective managers try to keep in touch with employees by tapping into the grapevine.

3. Explain how companies communicate with outside audiences. Companies communicate both informally and formally with outside audiences. The marketing department is used to advertise and develop products, which involves contact with the general public. The public relations department manages the corporation's reputation with various groups, including employees, customers, investors, and government agencies. Marketing messages are usually openly sponsored by the company; public relations messages are carried by the media if they are considered newsworthy.

4. Analyze how companies communicate successfully in a crisis. A good public relations department looks for potential problems, alerts management to them, and suggests the best course of action. When communicating in a crisis, a company must tell the whole story–openly, completely, and honestly.

5. Discuss the six factors that contribute to effective business communication. Effective business communication is based on (1) an open communication climate, where employees feel comfortable about expressing their honest opinions; (2) a commitment to ethical communication, where employees communicate relevant, honest, and complete information; (3) an understanding of intercultural communication and overcoming the barriers of both language and culture; (4) proficiency in communication technology, so that today's employees can adapt to technological changes; (5) an audience-centred approach to communication, which is sensitive to the audience's feelings and situation; and (6) creating and processing messages efficiently, by reducing their number, preparing them more quickly, and training employees to communicate effectively.

6. Develop goals for acquiring the communication skills you will need in your career. In your communication course, develop goals that will help you communicate effectively in the workplace. This will enhance your reputation in the eyes of fellow staff and employers, and give you opportunities you might not otherwise have.

Test Your Knowledge

Review Questions

1. What are stakeholders?
2. What are the strengths of formal communication channels? Their weaknesses?
3. What are the strengths of informal communication channels? Their weaknesses?
4. In what ways are individual members of an organization an informal communication medium with the outside world? Why is it important to be aware of this dimension of the company?
5. What are the different management styles?
6. What is meant by ethical communication? How does an employee make ethical choices?

Apply Your Knowledge

Critical Thinking Questions

1. Why do you think good communication in an organization improves employees' attitudes and performance? Explain briefly.
2. Whenever you report negative information to your boss, she never passes it along to her colleagues or supervisors. You believe that the information is important, but who do you talk to? Your boss? Your boss's supervisor? A co-worker who also reports to your boss? A co-worker who reports to a different boss? Briefly explain your answer.
3. You've just been promoted to manager and you've developed a good rapport with most of your employees, but Richardson and Blake keep going to your supervisor with matters that should go through you. Both employees have been at the company for at least 10 years longer than you have, and both know your supervisor very well. Should you speak with them about this problem? Should you speak with your supervisor? Explain briefly.
4. Because of your excellent communication skills, your boss always asks you to write his reports for him. When you overhear the CEO complimenting him on his logical organization and clear writing style, he responds

as if he'd written all those reports himself. You're angry, but he's your boss. What can you do? Briefly explain your answer.

5. To save time and money, your company is considering limiting all memos to one page or less. The CEO asks your opinion. Is it a good idea? Explain briefly.

6. As long as you make sure that everyone involved receives some benefit and that no one gets hurt, is it okay to make a decision that's just a little unethical? Briefly explain your answer.

Practise Your Knowledge

Exercises

1. For the following tasks, identify the necessary direction of communication (downward, upward, horizontal), suggest an appropriate type of communication (casual conversation, formal interview, meeting, workshop, videotape, newsletter, memo, bulletin board notice, and so on), and briefly explain your suggestion.
   a. As personnel manager, you want to announce details about this year's company picnic.
   b. As director of internal communication, you want to convince top management of the need for a company newsletter.
   c. As production manager, you want to make sure that both the sales manager and the finance manager receive your scheduling estimates.
   d. As marketing manager, you want to help employees understand the company's goals and its attitudes toward workers.
2. Name three ways you might encourage your employees to give you feedback on daily operations. Explain briefly.
3. In your small publishing firm, you have three top-notch editors, and, as the firm grows, you need them to work more often as a team. One of the editors, Wilson, is rigid and unforgiving, constantly reminding others of his 20 years' experience, and is unwilling to compromise. Pick an option and briefly explain why it's the best course of action. Should your first step be to
   a. Fire Wilson and look for a replacement?
   b. Talk privately with Wilson about your need for his cooperation?
   c. Meet with all three of your editors to forge team spirit?
4. An old university chum phoned you out of the blue to say: "I had to call you. You'd better keep this under your hat, but when I heard that my company was buying you guys out, I was dumbfounded. I had no idea that a company as large as yours could sink so fast. Your group must be in pretty bad shape over there!" Your stomach turned suddenly queasy, and you felt a chill go up your spine. You'd heard nothing about any buyout, and before you could even get your friend off the phone, you were wondering what you should do. Of the following, choose one course of action and briefly explain it.
   a. Contact your CEO directly and relate what you've heard.
   b. Ask co-workers whether they've heard anything about a buyout.
   c. Discuss the phone call confidentially with your immediate supervisor.
   d. Keep quiet about the whole thing (there's nothing you can do about the situation anyway).
5. When Solid State Circuits accidentally released chlorine and endangered the surrounding district, local neighbours were up in arms. Two years later, thanks to a company-wide community relations campaign, the neighbourhood is filled with goodwill and friendship for the company. Solid State's open-door policy ranges from quarterly meetings with the local Environmental Concerns Committee to tours of the plant to regular softball games between company employees and neighbourhood residents–with picnics afterward. Solid State even lends facilities for neighbours to use for holiday socials and rummage sales. One local resident has said, "As the years go by, Solid State will be associated with community interests and involvement." In less than a page, explain why becoming involved in the surrounding community and openly sharing information with local residents should result in such support and goodwill for the company.[33]
6. Briefly explain why you think each of the following is or is not ethical.
   a. De-emphasizing negative test results in a report on your product idea.
   b. Taking a computer home to finish a work-related assignment.
   c. Telling an associate and close friend that she'd better pay more attention to her work responsibilities or risk being fired.

   d. Recommending the purchase of excess equipment to use up your allocated funds before the end of the fiscal year so that your budget won't be cut next year.

7. Your boss wants to send a message welcoming employees recently transferred to your department from your Hong Kong branch. They all speak English, but your boss asks you to review his message for clarity. What would you suggest your boss change in the following paragraph? (Briefly explain your decisions.)

   I wanted to welcome you ASAP to our little family here in Canada. It's high time we shook hands in person and not just across the sea. I'm pleased as punch about getting to know you all, and I for one will do my level best to sell you on Canada.

8. Technological devices such as fax machines, cellular phones, e-mail, and voice mail are making business people more accessible at any time of day or night both at work and at home. What kind of impact might frequent intrusions have on a business person's professional and personal life? Explain your answer in less than a page.

9. As a manufacturer of telecommunications hardware, Nortel Networks has developed a code of ethics that it expects employees to follow. Visit Nortel's Web site at **www.nortelnetworks.com/ethics/living7.html** and review its seven major provisions (such as Gathering Competitive Information). In a brief paragraph, describe three specific things you could do that would violate any of these provisions. In another brief paragraph, describe how you would use these Web pages to avoid ethical problems as you write business letters, memos, and reports. Submit both paragraphs to your instructor.

10. Top management has asked you to speak at an upcoming executive meeting to present your arguments for a more open communication climate. Which of the following would be most important for you to know about your audience before giving your presentation? (Briefly explain your choice.)
    a. How many top managers will be attending.
    b. What management style members of your audience prefer.
    c. How firmly these managers are set in their ways.

11. What would be the most efficient way (phone call, interview, memo, or newsletter) to handle each of the following communication situations? (Briefly explain your answer.)
    a. Informing everyone in the company of your department's new procedure for purchasing equipment.
    b. Leaving final instructions for your secretary to follow while you're out of town.
    c. Disciplining an employee for chronic tardiness.
    d. Announcing the installation of ramps for employees who use wheelchairs.

12. Write a memo introducing yourself to your instructor. Keep it under one page, and use Figure 1.1 as a model for format.

13. Your boss often uses you as a sounding board for her ideas. Now she seems to want you to act as an unofficial messenger, passing her ideas along to the staff without mentioning her involvement and informing her of what staff members say without telling them you're going to repeat their responses. What questions should you ask yourself as you consider the ethical implications of this situation? Write a short paragraph explaining the ethical choice you will make in this situation.[36]

Developing Your Internet Skills

Going Online: Use the Power of the Internet to Help You Learn About Business Communication, p. 13

What role do you think the Internet might play in your business future? For instance, will you use it as a research tool? As a communications tool? As a marketing tool? Use this mental exercise to train yourself to take advantage of all the Internet has to offer by thinking ahead now, so that in a business crunch, you'll automatically know where to turn. The metasearch engines should help spur your thinking.

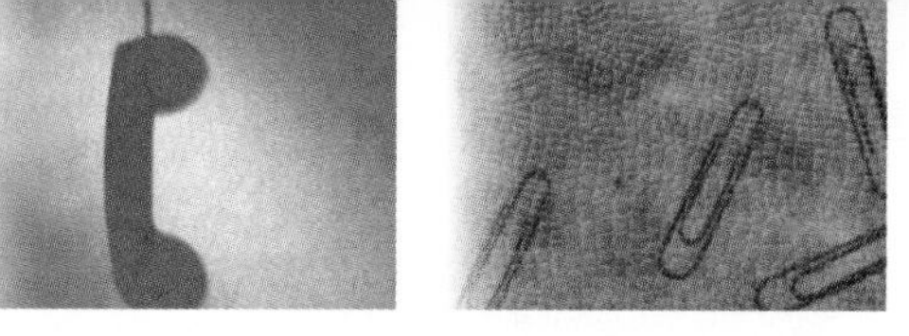

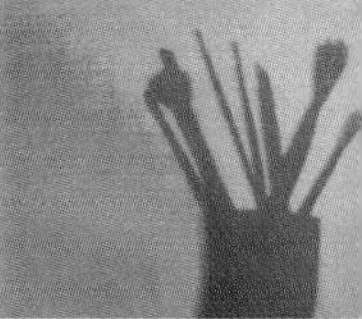

CHAPTER 2

Understanding Business Communication

AFTER STUDYING THIS CHAPTER, YOU WILL BE ABLE TO

1. List the general categories of non-verbal communication
2. Explain the four channels of verbal communication
3. Identify the steps in the communication process
4. Describe what can go wrong when you're formulating messages
5. Discuss communication barriers and how to overcome them
6. Summarize what you can do to improve communication

ON THE JOB
Facing a Communication Dilemma at Suncor Energy Inc.

Communicating a Green Message

Every company communicates with its customers, employees, and a variety of other groups. Although most are seldom challenged to defend their practices and policies, there are certain industries where communicating can make unusual demands. Suncor Energy Inc. of Calgary, Alberta, operates in the environmentally sensitive oil industry. Like all companies, Suncor produces many routine communications, such as responses to inquiries or progress reports on current projects, that keep the company functioning day to day. But Suncor also works hard to maintain the trust of the public as an environmentally responsible energy producer. Involved in oil exploration and fuel development, Suncor mines the Alberta oil sands and other regions of Western Canada and refines oil in Ontario. Its operations, supplying an essential resource, are seen by many as harmful to the land and contributing to the deterioration of the atmosphere. But Suncor has developed programs to minimize the impact of its operations on the environment. The company has committed millions of dollars to alternative and renewable energy projects, such as funding research into the generation of wind power in Alberta. They support education and training programs, teaching their customers and partners how to be good environmental citizens. Suncor views sustainable development—the focus on renewable energy sources that are profitable for the company and its shareholders—as a critical element in the company's balance sheet. So how does a Canadian resource company communicate its activities as an environmental citizen to the public at large and to activist groups critical of its practices?

Images are influential communication tools. Suncor Energy uses pictures of alternative power generators in their brochures and on their Web site to communicate their environmental mission.

This difficult situation presents Suncor with major communication challenges. As a publicly owned company, it has a commitment to its investors to improve shareholder value—to make sure their investment in the company grows. As an employer, Suncor has a responsibility to its workers to ensure their livelihood. And as an energy producer, Suncor has a responsibility to society to operate in an environmentally sound way. The challenge for Suncor's corporate communications staff is to make known to both supporters and critics the company's progress in minimizing the environmental impact of its operations. What tools do the communication professionals at Suncor use to get their messages out to activist groups, consumers, and employees? How do they select their communication media to transmit their environmental vision in the most effective manner to their audiences? Answers to such questions help the company to build goodwill with its stakeholders, improve its profits, and maintain its reputation as a principled energy producer.[1]

The Basic Forms of Communication

Actions speak louder than words.

As Suncor's managers are well aware, effective communicators have many tools at their disposal. They know how to put together the words that will convey their meaning. They reinforce their words with gestures and actions. They look you in the eye, listen to what you have to say, and think about your feelings and needs. At the same time, they study your reactions, picking up the nuances of your response by watching your face and body, listening to your tone of voice, and evaluating your words. They absorb information just as efficiently as they transmit it, relying on both non-verbal and verbal cues.

LEARNING OUTCOME 1
List the general categories of non-verbal communication.

Perhaps a certain amount of inconsistency between words and actions is unavoidable. We don't always say what we really mean; in fact, we don't always *know* what we really mean. Unravelling the mysteries of communication requires perception, concentration, and an appreciation of the communication process.

Non-verbal Communication

Non-verbal communication is the process of communicating without words.

The most basic form of communication is **non-verbal communication:** all the cues, gestures, vocal qualities, spatial relationships, and attitudes toward time we use to communicate without words. Anthropologists theorize that long before human beings used words to talk things over, our ancestors communicated by using their bodies. They gritted their teeth to show anger; smiled and touched one another to indicate affection. Although we have come a long way since those primitive times, we still use such non-verbal cues to express superiority, dependence, dislike, respect, love, and many other feelings.[2]

Non-verbal communication has few rules and often occurs unconsciously.

Non-verbal communication differs from verbal communication in fundamental ways. For one thing, it's less structured, so it's more difficult to study. It also differs in intent and spontaneity. We generally plan our words. When we say, "Please get back to me on that order by Friday," we have a conscious purpose. We think about the message, if only for a moment. However, when we communicate nonverbally, we often do it unconsciously. We don't mean to raise an eyebrow or blush. Those actions come naturally, without our consent.

THE IMPORTANCE OF NON-VERBAL COMMUNICATION

Although non-verbal communication is often unplanned, it can have more impact than verbal communication alone. Non-verbal cues are especially important in conveying feelings; some researchers maintain that they account for 93 percent of the emotional meaning that is exchanged in any interaction.[3] The total impact of any message is probably most affected by the blending of non-verbal and verbal communication.[4]

Non-verbal communication is more reliable and more efficient than verbal communication.

One reason for the power of non-verbal communication is its reliability. Most people can deceive us much more easily with words than with their bodies. Words are relatively easy to control; body language, facial expressions, and vocal characteristics are not. By paying attention to these non-verbal cues, we can detect deception or affirm a speaker's honesty. Not surprisingly, we have more faith in non-verbal cues than we do in verbal messages. If a person says one thing but transmits a conflicting message non-verbally, we almost invariably believe the non-verbal signal.[5] To a great degree, then, an individual's credibility as a communicator depends on non-verbal messages.

People use non-verbal signals to support and clarify verbal communication.

Non-verbal communication is important for another reason: It can be efficient from both the sender's and the receiver's standpoints. You can transmit a non-verbal message without even thinking about it, and your audience can register the meaning unconsciously. At the same time, when you have a conscious purpose, you can often achieve it more economically with a gesture than you can with words. A wave of the hand, a pat on the back, a wink–all are streamlined expressions of thought.

THE TYPES OF NON-VERBAL COMMUNICATION

The meaning of non-verbal communication lies with the observer, who both reads and interprets specific signals in the context of a particular situation and a particular culture. Although there are more than 700 000 specific forms of non-verbal communication,[6] they can be grouped into six general categories:

The face and eyes command particular attention as a source of non-verbal messages.

- *Facial expressions and eye behaviour.* Your face is the primary site for expressing your emotions; it reveals both the type and the intensity of your feelings.[7] Your eyes are especially effective for indicating attention and interest, influencing others, regulating interaction, and establishing dominance.
- *Gestures and postures.* By moving your body, you can express both specific and general messages, some voluntary and some involuntary. Many gestures–a wave of the hand, for example–have a specific and intentional meaning, such as "hello" or "good-bye." Other types of body movement are unintentional and express a more general message. Slouching, leaning forward, fidgeting, and walking briskly are all unconscious signals that reveal whether you feel confident or nervous, friendly or hostile, assertive or passive, powerful or powerless.

Body language and tone of voice reveal a lot about a person's emotions and attitudes.

- *Vocal characteristics.* Like body language, your voice carries both intentional and unintentional messages. On a conscious level, you can use your voice to create various impressions. Consider the sentence "What have you been up to?" If you repeat that question four or five times, changing your tone of voice and stressing various words, you can convey quite different messages. However, your vocal characteristics also reveal many things that you are unaware of. The tone and volume of your voice, your accent and speaking pace, and all the little *um*'s and *ah*'s that creep into your speech say a lot about who you are, your relationship with the audience, and the emotions underlying your words.

Physical appearance and personal style contribute to your identity.

- *Personal appearance.* Your appearance helps establish your social identity. People respond to us on the basis of our physical attractiveness. Although an individual's body type and facial features impose limitations, most of us are able to control our attractiveness to some degree. Our grooming, our clothing, our accessories, our style–all modify our appearance. If your goal is to make a good impression, adopt the style of the people you want to impress. In most businesses, a professional image is appropriate, but many new high-tech companies, such as Zero-Knowledge, profiled in Chapter 1, encourage their employees to dress casually.

Your use of touch, your attitude toward time, and your use of space (all of which are affected by culture) help establish your social relationships.

- *Touching behaviour.* Touch is an important vehicle for conveying warmth, comfort, and reassurance. Even the most casual contact can create positive feelings. The accepted norms of touching vary, depending on the gender, age, relative status, and cultural background of the persons involved. In business situations, touching suggests dominance, so a higher-status person is more likely to touch a lower-status person than the other way around. Touching has become controversial, however, because it can sometimes be interpreted as sexual harassment.
- *Use of time and space.* Like touch, time and space can be used to assert authority. In many cultures, people demonstrate their importance by making other people wait, or they show respect by being on time. People can also assert their status by occupying the best space. In Canadian companies, the chief executive usually has the corner office and the most attractive view. Apart from serving as a symbol of status, space can determine how comfortable people feel talking with each other. When people stand too close or too far away, we feel ill at ease.

Non-verbal communication can be different for men and women.

Attitudes toward punctuality and comfort zones and all other non-verbal communication vary from culture to culture. In addition, gender has an impact on non-verbal communication. For example, some studies show that women are generally better than men at decoding non-verbal cues. And in the company boardroom, ideas put forth by women may be ignored by their male counterparts. One Canadian female executive has said that, in her career, she has "learned what it is like to be invisible, having a suggestion dismissed by male peers, only to have the same proposal raised by one of them at a meeting, and subsequently endorsed."[8]

Improve non-verbal skills by paying more attention to cues, both yours and those of others.

To improve your non-verbal skills, pay more attention to non-verbal cues (especially facial expressions), engage in more eye contact, and probe for more information when verbal and non-verbal cues conflict. Most employees are frustrated and distrustful when their supervisors give them conflicting signals. So try to be as honest as possible in communicating your emotions.[9]

Verbal Communication

LEARNING OUTCOME 2
Explain the four channels of verbal communication.

Although you can express many things non-verbally, there are limits to what you can communicate without the help of language. If you want to discuss past events, ideas, or abstractions, you need symbols that stand for your thoughts. **Verbal communication** consists of words arranged in meaningful patterns. In the English language, the pool of words is growing; English currently contains about 750 000 words, although many of us recognize fewer than about 3 percent of them.[10] To create a thought with these words, we arrange them according to the rules of grammar, putting the various parts of speech in their proper sequence. We then transmit the message in spoken or written form, anticipating that someone will hear or read what we have to say.

Verbal communication is the process of communicating with words.

Language is composed of words and grammar.

SPEAKING AND WRITING

As Figure 2.1 illustrates, business people tend to prefer oral communication channels to written ones. The trade-offs between speaking and writing are discussed in more depth in Chapter 5, but basically, it's generally quicker and more convenient to talk to somebody than to write a memo or letter. Furthermore, when you're speaking or listening, you can pick up added meaning from non-verbal cues and benefit from immediate feedback.

Business people rely more heavily on oral than on written communication channels for sharing information on a day-to-day basis, but they often put important messages in writing.

On the other hand, relying too heavily on oral communication can cause problems in a company. At Ben & Jerry's Homemade, a US ice cream manufacturer that has entered the Canadian market, this reliance has been one of the main sources of the company's growing pains. The founders, Ben Cohen and Jerry Greenfield, are by nature face-to-face communicators. They want their organization to function like a big, happy family in which people share ideas openly and informally, and, for a while, it did. However, as Ben & Jerry's grew and the number of employees increased, keeping everyone adequately informed by word of mouth became difficult. As one employee pointed out, "It's hard to feel you're part of a big family if you don't know the brothers and sisters."[11] For maximum impact, be sure to use both written and spoken channels.

Effective business communication depends on skill in receiving messages as well as skill in sending them.

LISTENING AND READING

Take another look at Figure 2.1. Apart from underscoring the importance of oral communication, it illustrates that people spend more time receiving information than transmitting it. Listening and reading are every bit as important as speaking and writing.

Unfortunately, most of us aren't very good listeners. Immediately after hearing a ten-minute speech, we typically remember only half of what was said. A few days later, we've forgotten three-quarters of the message.[12] Worse, we often miss the subtle, underlying meaning entirely. To some extent, our listening problems stem from our education, or lack of it. We spend years learning to express our ideas, but few of us ever take a course in listening. Nevertheless, developing better listening abilities is crucial if we want to foster the understanding and cooperation so necessary for an increasingly diverse workforce.[13]

If you're listening, as opposed to reading, you have the advantage of being able to ask questions and interact with the speaker. Instead of just gathering information, you can cooperate in solving problems. This interactive process requires additional listening skills, discussed in Chapter 17.

Rick George, CEO of Suncor Energy, Inc., credits the company's success to a policy of listening to employees and to the community—local, provincial, and federal governments, regulators, First Nation groups, and environmentalists. By soliciting their input and advice, George and his leadership team are able to improve Suncor's performance and maintain good relationships with their stakeholders.

FIGURE 2.1

The Percentage of Communication Time Business People Spend on Various Communication Channels

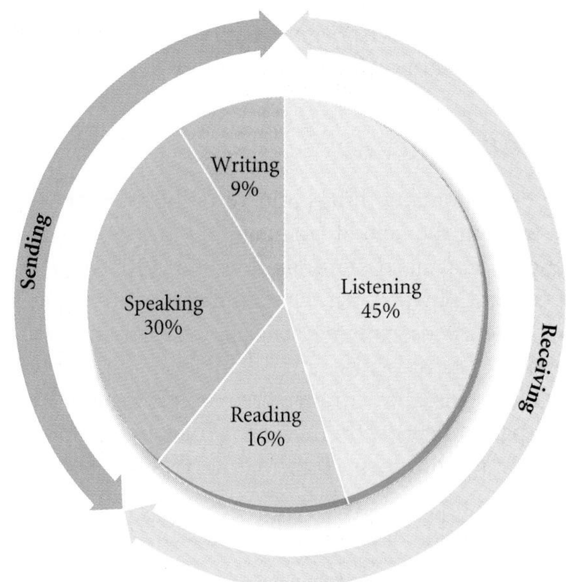

Likewise, our reading skills often leave a good deal to be desired. According to Statistics Canada, 22 per cent of adult Canadians have "serious problems dealing with printed material" and a further 24 to 26 per cent can manage only simple reading tasks.[14] Even those who read adequately often don't know how to read effectively. They have trouble extracting the important points from a document, so they can't make the most of the information contained in it.

LEARNING OUTCOME 3
Identify the steps in the communication process.

The Process of Communication

Whether you are speaking or writing, listening or reading, communication is more than a single act. Instead, it is a transactional (two-way) process that can be broken into six phases, as Figure 2.2 illustrates:[15]

The communication process consists of six phases linking sender and receiver.

1. *The sender has an idea.* You conceive an idea and want to share it.
2. *The sender transforms the idea into a message.* When you put your idea into a message that your receiver will understand, you are **encoding**, deciding on the message's form (word, facial expression, gesture), length, organization, tone, and style–all of which depend on your idea, your audience, and your personal style or mood.
3. *The sender transmits the message.* To physically transmit your message to your receiver, you select a **communication channel** (verbal, non-verbal, spoken, or written) and a **medium** (telephone, computer, letter, memo, report, face-to-face exchange, and so on). The channel and medium you choose depend on your message, the location of your audience, your need for speed, and the formality of the situation.
4. *The receiver gets the message.* For communication to occur, your receiver must first get the message. If you send a letter, your receiver has to read it before understanding it. If you're giving a speech, the people in your audience have to be able to hear you, and they have to be paying attention.
5. *The receiver interprets the message.* Your receiver must cooperate by **decoding** your message, absorbing and understanding it. Then the decoded message has to be stored in the receiver's mind. If all goes well, the message is interpreted correctly; that is, the receiver assigns the same basic meaning to the words as the sender intended and responds in the desired way.

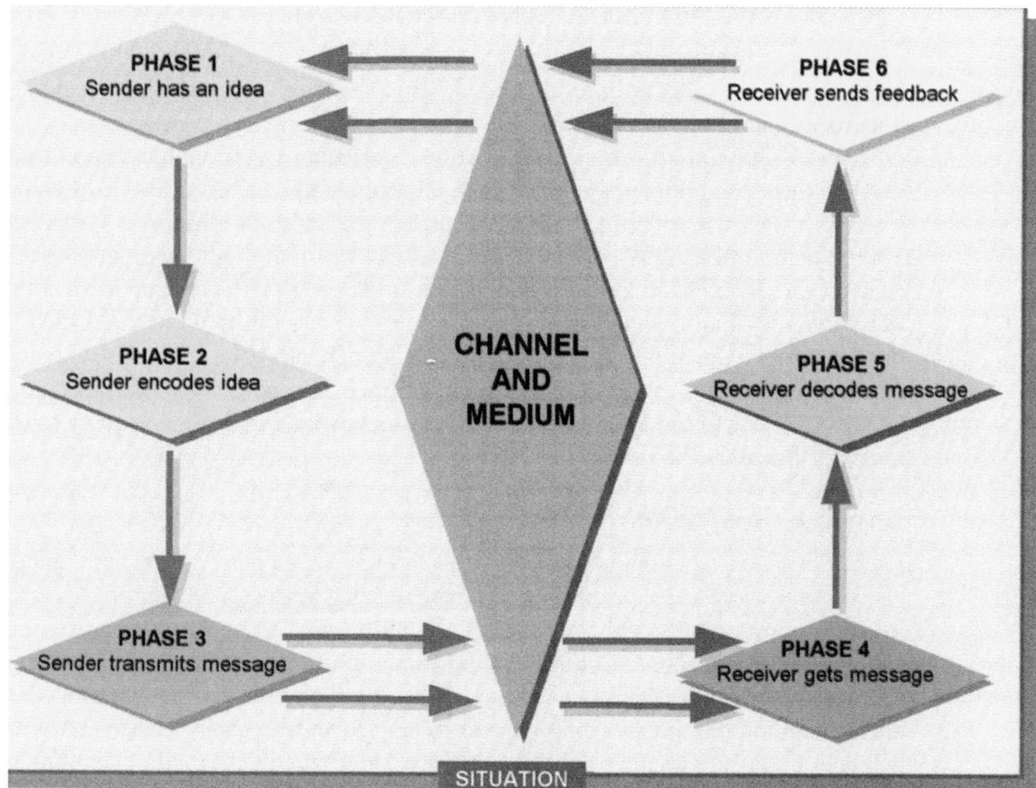

FIGURE 2.2
The Communication Process

6. *The receiver reacts and sends feedback to the sender.* **Feedback** is your receiver's response, the final link in the communication chain. After getting the message, your receiver responds in some way and signals that response to you. Feedback is a key element in the communication process because it enables you to evaluate the effectiveness of your message. If your audience doesn't understand what you mean, you can tell by the response and refine your message.

Feedback is your audience's response; it permits you to evaluate your message's effectiveness.

The process is repeated until both parties have finished expressing themselves, but communication is effective only when each step is successful.

Formulating a Message

LEARNING OUTCOME 4
Describe what can go wrong when you're formulating messages.

Communication is a dynamic process. Your idea cannot be communicated if you fail to perform any step in that process. Unfortunately, the process can be interrupted before it really begins–while you're trying to put your idea into words. Several things can go wrong when you're formulating a message, including indecision about the content of your message, lack of familiarity with the situation or the receiver, and difficulty in expressing ideas.

INDECISION ABOUT CONTENT

Include only the information that is useful to your audience, and organize it in a way that encourages its acceptance.

Deciding what to say is the first hurdle in the communication process. Many people make the mistake of trying to convey everything they know about a subject. Unfortunately, when a message contains too much information, it's difficult to absorb. If you want to get your point across, decide what to include and what to leave out, how much detail to provide, and what order to follow. If you try to explain something without first giving the receiver adequate background, you'll create confusion. Likewise, if you recommend actions without first explaining why they are justified, your message may provoke an emotional response that inhibits understanding.

LACK OF FAMILIARITY WITH THE SITUATION OR THE RECEIVER

Ask why you are preparing the message and for whom you are preparing it.

Creating an effective message is difficult if you don't know how it will be used. Unless you know why a report is needed, you are forced to create a very general document, one that covers a little bit of everything.

Lack of familiarity with your audience is an equally serious handicap. You need to know something about the biases, education, age, status, and style of your receiver in order to create an effective message. If you're writing for a specialist in your field, for example, you can use technical terms that might be unfamiliar to a lay person. If you're addressing a lower-level employee, you might approach a subject differently than if you were talking to your boss. Decisions about the content, organization, style, and tone of your message all depend, at least to some extent, on the relationship between you and your audience. If you don't know your audience, you will be forced to make these decisions in the dark, and at least part of your message may miss the mark.

DIFFICULTY EXPRESSING IDEAS

An inability to put thoughts into words can be overcome through study and practice.

Lack of experience in writing or speaking can also prevent a person from developing effective messages. Some people lack expertise in using language. Such problems can be overcome, but only with some effort. The important thing is to recognize the problem and take action. Taking courses in communication is a good first step. Many companies offer their own in-house training programs in communication; others have tuition reimbursement programs to help cover the cost of outside courses. Self-help books are another good, inexpensive alternative. You might even join a professional organization or other group (such as Toastmasters) to practise your communication skills in an informal setting.

The fact is that innumerable barriers to communication can block any phase of the communication process. Effective communicators do all they can to remove such barriers. By thinking about some of these barriers, you increase your chances of overcoming them.

LEARNING OUTCOME 5
Discuss communication barriers and how to overcome them.

Overcoming Communication Barriers

Noise is any interference in the communication process that distorts or obscures the sender's meaning. Such communication barriers can exist between people and within organizations.[16]

COMMUNICATION BARRIERS BETWEEN PEOPLE

Communication barriers exist between people and within organizations.

When you send a message, you intend to communicate meaning, but the message itself doesn't contain meaning. The meaning exists in your mind and in the mind of your receiver. To understand one another, you and your receiver must share similar meanings for words, gestures, tone of voice, and other symbols.

Perception is our individual interpretation of the world around us.

Differences in Perception The world constantly bombards us with information: sights, sounds, scents, and so on. Our minds organize this stream of sensation into a mental map that represents our **perception** of reality. In no case is the map in a person's mind the same as the world itself, and no two maps are exactly alike. As you view the world, your mind absorbs your experiences in a unique and personal way. For example, if you go out for pizza with a friend, each of you will notice different things. As you enter the restaurant, one of you may notice the coolness of the air-conditioning; the other may notice the aroma of pizza.

Because your perceptions are unique, the ideas you want to express differ from other people's. Even when two people have experienced the same event, their mental images of that event will not be identical. As senders, we choose the details that seem important and focus our attention on the most relevant and general. As receivers, we try to fit new details into our existing pattern. If a detail doesn't quite fit, we are inclined to distort the information rather than rearrange the pattern.

Overcoming perceptual barriers can be difficult. Try to predict how your message will be received, anticipate your receiver's reactions, and shape the message accordingly–constantly adjusting to correct any misunderstanding. Try not to apply the same solution to every problem, but look for solutions that fit the specific problems. Frame your messages in terms that have meaning for your audience, and try to find something useful in every message you receive.[17]

Incorrect Filtering **Filtering** is screening out or abbreviating information before a message is passed on to someone else. In business, the filters between you and your receiver are many: secretaries, assistants, receptionists, and answering machines, to name a few. Just getting through by telephone can take a week if you're calling someone who's protected by layers of gatekeepers (operators, secretaries, assistants). Worse yet, your message may be digested, distilled, and probably distorted before it's passed on to your intended receiver. Those same gatekeepers may also translate, embellish, and augment your receiver's ideas and responses before passing them on to you. To overcome filtering barriers, try to establish more than one communication channel (so that information can be verified through multiple sources), eliminate as many intermediaries as possible, and decrease distortion by condensing message information to the bare essentials.

Filtering is screening out or abbreviating information before passing the message on to someone else.

Language Problems When you choose the words for your message, you signal that you are a member of a particular culture or subculture and that you know the code. The nature of your code–your language and vocabulary–imposes its own barriers on your message. For example, the language of a lawyer differs from that of an accountant or a doctor, and the differences in their vocabularies affect their ability to recognize and express ideas.

Your denotative (literal) and connotative (subjective) definitions of words may differ dramatically from those of other people.

Barriers also exist because words can be interpreted in more than one way. Language uses words as symbols to represent reality; nothing in the word *cookie* automatically ties it to the physical thing that is a cookie. We might just as well call a "cookie" a "zebra." Language is an arbitrary code that depends on shared definitions, but there's a limit to how completely any of us can share the same meaning for a given word.

Even on the literal (denotative) level, words are imprecise. People in Canada generally agree on what a cookie is. However, your idea of a cookie is a composite of all the cookies you have ever tasted or seen: oatmeal cookies, chocolate chip cookies, sugar cookies, and vanilla wafers. Someone from another culture may have a different range of cookie experiences: meringues, florentines, and spritz. You both agree on the general concept of cookie, but the precise image in your minds differs.

On the subjective (connotative) level, the differences are even greater. Your interpretation of the word *cookie* depends partly on how you feel about cookies. You may have very pleasant feelings about them: You may remember baking them with your mother or coming home from school on winter afternoons to cookies and milk. Or you may be on a diet, in which case cookies will be an unpleasant reminder that you think you're too fat and must say no to all your favorite foods.

To overcome language barriers, use the most specific and accurate words possible. Always try to use words your audience will understand. Increase the accuracy of your messages by using language that describes rather than evaluates and by presenting observable facts, events, and circumstances.

As anchor of CBC's news program, *The National*, Peter Mansbridge addresses a Canada-wide audience daily. He must be careful to use words that mean the same thing to everyone, regardless of background or region of the country. Your chances of being easily understood increase if you are as accurate and as specific as you can be.

Listening ability decreases when information is difficult to understand and when it has little meaning for your audience.

Poor Listening Perhaps the most common barrier to reception is simply a lack of attention on the receiver's part. We all let our minds wander now and then, regardless of how hard we try to concentrate. People are especially likely to drift off when they are forced to listen to information that is difficult to understand or that has little direct bearing on their own lives. If they are tired or concerned about other matters, they are even more likely to lose interest. As already mentioned, too few of us listen well.

To overcome listening barriers, verify your interpretation of what's been said (by paraphrasing what you've understood). Empathize with speakers (by trying to view the situation through their eyes), and resist jumping to conclusions. Clarify meaning by asking non-threatening questions, and listen without interrupting.

Your audience may react either to the content of a message or to the relationship between sender and receiver that it implies.

In business communication, try to maintain your objectivity.

Differing Emotional States Every message contains both a *content meaning*, which deals with the subject of the message, and a *relationship meaning*, which suggests the nature of the interaction between sender and receiver. Communication can break down when the receiver reacts negatively to either of these meanings. You may have to deal with people when they are upset–or when you are. You may also have conflicting emotions about the subject of your message or the audience for it.

To overcome emotional barriers, be aware of the feelings that arise in yourself and in others as you communicate, and attempt to control them. For example, choose neutral words to avoid arousing strong feelings unduly. Avoid attitudes, blame, and other subjective concepts. Most important, be alert to the greater potential for misunderstanding that accompanies emotional messages.

Try to understand the other person's point of view, and respect the inevitable differences in background and culture.

Differing Backgrounds Differences in background can be one of the hardest communication barriers to overcome. When your receiver's life experience differs substantially from yours, communication becomes difficult. Age, education, gender, social status, economic position, cultural background, temperament, health, appearance, popularity, religion, political belief, even a passing mood can all separate one person from another and make understanding difficult. Communicating with someone from another country is probably the most extreme example of how background may impede communication; culture clashes can also arise in the workplace (see Chapter 3). But you don't have to seek out a person from an exotic locale to run into cultural gaps. You can misunderstand even your best friends and closest relatives, as you no doubt know from personal experience.

To overcome the barriers associated with differing backgrounds, avoid projecting your own background or culture onto others. Clarify your own and understand others' backgrounds, spheres of knowledge, personalities, and perceptions. And don't assume that certain behaviours mean the same thing to everyone.

Going Online

Beef Up Your Internet Language Skills

Your success in Internet communication depends on how well you understand the language. That's where Netlingo can help. Keep the site's pocket-dictionary floating toolbar on your desktop while you surf, and you'll have instant access to definitions of common Net terms, which don't always mean what you'd expect. For instance, you know from this chapter that *cookie* means different things in different cultures–but do you know what *cookie* means to a Netizen? Better look it up.

www.netlingo.com

COMMUNICATION BARRIERS WITHIN ORGANIZATIONS

Although all communication is subject to misunderstandings, business communication is particularly difficult. The material is often complex and controversial. Moreover, both the sender and the receiver may face distractions that divert their attention. Further, because the opportunities for feedback are often limited, it is difficult to correct misunderstandings.

Information Overload Too much information is as bad as too little because it reduces the audience's ability to concentrate effectively on the most important messages. People who face information overload sometimes try to cope by ignoring some of the messages they receive or by delaying responses to messages they deem unimportant. They may also answer only parts of some messages or respond inaccurately to certain messages. People also try to manage information overload by responding hastily to each message, or by reacting only superficially to all messages.

Some information isn't necessary.

To overcome information overload, realize that some information is not necessary, and make necessary information easily available. Give information meaning, rather than just passing it on, and set priorities for dealing with the information flow.

Message Complexity When formulating business messages, you communicate both as an individual and as a representative of an organization. Thus you must adjust your own ideas and style so that they are acceptable to your employer. In fact, you may occasionally be asked to write or say something that you disagree with personally.

The complexity of messages is related to
- ✧ Your conflicts about the content
- ✧ The dry or difficult nature of the subject

Business messages may also deal with subject matter that can be technical or difficult to express. Imagine trying to write an interesting insurance policy, a set of instructions on how to operate a scraped-surface heat exchanger, the guidelines for checking credit references, an explanation of why profits have dropped by 12 percent in the last six months, or a description of your solid-waste-management program. These topics are dry, and making them clear and interesting is a real challenge.

To overcome the barriers of complex messages, keep them clear and easy to understand. Use strong organization, guide readers by telling them what to expect, use concrete and specific language, and stick to the point. Be sure to ask for feedback so that you can clarify and improve your message.

Message Competition Communicators are often faced with messages that compete for attention. If you're talking on the phone while scanning a report, both messages are apt to get short shrift. Even your own messages may have to compete with a variety of interruptions–the phone rings every five minutes, people intrude, meetings are called, crises arise. In short, your messages rarely have the benefit of the receiver's undivided attention.

Business messages rarely have the benefit of the audience's full and undivided attention.

To overcome competition barriers, avoid making demands on a receiver who doesn't have the time to pay careful attention to your message. Make written messages visually appealing and easy to understand, and try to deliver them when your receiver has time to read them. Oral messages are most effective when you can speak directly to your receiver (rather than to intermediaries or answering machines). Also, be sure to set aside enough time for important messages that you receive.

Differing Status Employees of low status may be overly cautious when sending messages to a manager and may talk only about subjects they think the manager is interested in. Similarly, higher-status people may distort messages by refusing to discuss anything that would tend to undermine their authority in the organization. Moreover, belonging to a particular department or being responsible for a particular task can narrow your point of view so that it differs from the attitudes, values, and expectations of people who belong to other departments or who are responsible for other tasks.

To overcome status barriers, keep managers and colleagues well informed. Encourage lower-status employees to keep you informed by being fair-minded and respectful of their opinions. When you have information that you're afraid your boss might not like, be brave and convey it anyway.

Status barriers can be overcome by a willingness to give and receive bad news.

Lack of Trust Building trust is difficult. Other organization members don't know whether you'll respond in a supportive or responsible way, so trusting can be risky. Without trust, free and open communication is effectively blocked, threatening the organization's stability. However, just being clear in your communication isn't enough.

For communication to be successful, organizations must create an atmosphere of fairness and trust.

Structural barriers block upward, downward, and horizontal communication.

To overcome trust barriers, be visible and accessible. Don't insulate yourself behind assistants or secretaries. Share key information with colleagues and employees, communicate honestly, and include employees in decision making.

Inadequate Communication Structures Organizational communication is impaired by formal restrictions on who may communicate with whom and who is authorized to make decisions. Having too few formal channels blocks effective communication. Strongly centralized organizations, especially those with a high degree of formalization, reduce communication capacity and decrease the tendency to communicate horizontally–thereby limiting effective coordination of activities and decisions. Tall organizations tend to provide too many vertical communication links, so messages become distorted as they move through the organization's levels. To overcome structural barriers, forward-thinking companies offer opportunities for communicating upward, downward, and horizontally (using such techniques as employee surveys, open-door policies, newsletters, memos, e-mail, and task groups). They try to reduce hierarchical levels, increase coordination between departments, and encourage two-way communication.

Your choice of a communication channel and medium depends on the

- ✧ Message
- ✧ Audience
- ✧ Need for speed
- ✧ Situation

Incorrect Choice of Medium If you choose an inappropriate communication medium, your message can be distorted so that the intended meaning is blocked. You can select the most appropriate medium by matching your choice with the nature of the message and the group or the individual who will receive it. **Media richness** is the value of a medium in a given communication situation. It is determined by a medium's ability (1) to convey a message using more than one informational cue (visual, verbal, vocal), (2) to facilitate feedback, and (3) to establish personal focus (Figure 2.3).

BEHIND THE SCENES AT ENTERPRISE MEDIATION INC.

Resolving Communication Problems Without Going to Court

Barbara Benoliel, an industrial psychologist and long-time workplace mediator, notes that today "Old ways of getting rid of a problem, such as transferring a worker elsewhere, aren't feasible. Pared-down companies rarely have room to move someone." To solve employee-management disputes, many Canadian firms are resorting to neutral and impartial third-party professional mediators invited by the company to resolve conflicts in their workplace. Christine Hart, director of the Toronto Alternative Dispute Resolution Centre, established in 1994, says that 40 percent of civil court cases are referred there, and that half these cases come to a resolution.

To help people settle their differences, mediators focus on helping them communicate more effectively.

Enterprise Mediation Inc., an Ottawa-based mediation firm, has a variety of approaches to resolve employment, contract, interpersonal, and other workplace conflicts. They use face-to-face communication in their Ottawa offices or at their clients' locations, teleconferencing, videoconferencing, the Internet, or a combination of these. Whatever the medium, the ten-member staff of lawyers and certified mediators bring opposing parties together to solve the problem. Enterprise Mediation's Peter Bishop, a lawyer and registered practitioner in dispute resolution, says, "Resolving interpersonal or group conflicts doesn't mean that former adversaries will come to like each other or that conflict emotions or interests will be completely eliminated. Generally it means that, having recognized and discussed their adverse personal feelings and conflicting interests, people have found ways to work productively in spite of them."

The professional mediator fulfills a number of functions, all requiring strong communication skills. The staff at Enterprise Mediation establish the ground rules for the mediation sessions. They outline and explain the meeting structure to the participants and get agreement from the opposing parties about the process to be followed. The mediators then manage the session, ensuring that participants use the agreed approach, guiding them through it, and dealing with obstacles that can obstruct the path to a resolution. The mediators also ensure that the principle of objectivity is applied in the mediation session. Participants are taught to

Face-to-face communication is the richest medium because it is personal, provides immediate feedback, transmits information from both verbal and non-verbal cues, and conveys the emotion behind the message. Telephones and some other interactive electronic media aren't as rich; although they allow immediate feedback, they don't provide visual non-verbal cues such as facial expressions, eye contact, and body movements.[18] Written media can be personalized through addressed memos, letters, and reports, but they lack the immediate feedback and the visual and vocal non-verbal cues that contribute to the meaning of the message. The leanest media are generally impersonal written messages such as bulletins, fliers, and standard reports. Not only do they lack the ability to transmit non-verbal cues and to give feedback, they also eliminate any personal focus.

To overcome media barriers, choose the richest media for non-routine, complex messages. Use rich media to extend and humanize your presence throughout the organization, to communicate caring and personal interest to employees, and to gain employee commitment to organizational goals. Use leaner media to communicate simple, routine messages. You can send information such as statistics, facts, figures, and conclusions through a note, memo, or written report.[19]

FIGURE 2.3

A Continuum of Media Richness

To ensure effective communication, use richer media for messages that are complex, ambiguous, and non-routine.

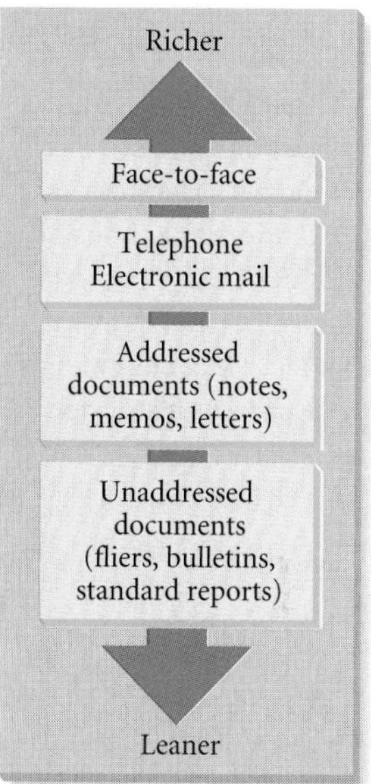

Closed Communication Climate As discussed in Chapter 1, communication climate is influenced by management style, and a directive, authoritarian style blocks the free and open exchange of information that characterizes good communication. At Suncor, management works hard to maintain an open communication climate. To overcome communication barriers, spend more time listening than issuing orders. Make sure you respond constructively to employees; and, of course, encourage employees and colleagues to offer suggestions, participate in solving problems, and help to set goals and make decisions.

acknowledge and understand the viewpoint of the opposing disputant without attacking it, and to express themselves as impartially as possible. Says Bishop, "The mediator can help parties discuss past events at the level of their actual experience, perceptions and feelings ... Issues and conflicts can be explored honestly and assertively in a way that is non-aggressive and relatively non-threatening." It is the mediator's job to clarify the issues on all sides and to steer all parties toward settlement by acting as facilitators. They interpret and reframe the issues, brainstorm possible solutions, identify the pros and cons of each suggestion, and provide an opportunity for the parties involved to listen to each other.

A key mediation skill is listening. Dwight Golann, a senior mediator and trainer in mediation techniques, believes that "people don't listen well." Most conflicts don't get resolved until both parties feel they have been heard and reach a point at which they can listen to each other. So Golann teaches his students a mixture of techniques to show they are listening effectively: taking notes, maintaining direct eye contact, nodding, rephrasing what they hear, and listening for the feelings behind the words.

Golann also recognizes the importance of training mediators to analyze body language—a silent form of communication. He shows his students how to look for emotional *hot spots* by observing the body language of the parties involved—including gestures, nervousness, and avoiding direct eye contact. Once emotional hot spots have been identified, mediators can "discuss the issue, trace it back to its source, and help people distinguish the past problem from the present situation—so they can move on and focus on resolving it."

According to the professionals at Enterprise Mediation, mediation can improve workplace relationships. By resolving conflicts and having opposing parties deal with issues in a collaborative manner, mediation can preserve relationships and create productive business environments.[20]

APPLY YOUR KNOWLEDGE

1. As a junior mediator for Enterprise Mediation, you have been asked to speak to the owners of a company that has experienced an unusually high rate of employee turnover in the past year. The owners are concerned that their communication practices are ineffective. What general advice can you offer regarding employer-employee communication?
2. You have been invited to observe the intial mediation session of two partners in a software venture who have been embroiled in a conflict for two years. During the initial session, the mediator allows both parties to explain their side of the story. One of them is plainly very angry and at one point seems near tears. Can this approach be productive? Please give your reasons.

The CEO of Habitat for Humanity, Bobbye Goldenberg must effectively communicate Habitat's mission: to build affordable housing with families in need. Her organization works in partnership with their clients and local communities, supported by donations of goods and services from suppliers and volunteers.

Unethical Communication An organization cannot be credible or successful in the long run if it creates illegal or unethical messages. Relationships within and outside the organization depend on trust and fairness. Make sure your messages contain all the information that ought to be there. Make sure that information applies to the situation. And make sure your message is completely truthful.

Inefficient Communication Producing worthless messages wastes time and resources, and contributes to the information overload already mentioned. Reduce the number of messages by thinking twice before sending one. Then speed up the process: first, by preparing messages correctly the first time and, second, by standardizing format and material when appropriate. Be clear about the writing assignments you accept as well as the ones you assign.

Physical Distractions Communication barriers are often physical: bad connections, poor acoustics, illegible copy. Although noise of this sort seems trivial, it can completely block an otherwise effective message. Your receiver might also be distracted by an uncomfortable chair, poor lighting, or some other irritating condition. In some cases, the barrier may be related to the receiver's health. Hearing or visual impairment or even a headache can interfere with reception of a message. These annoyances don't generally block communication entirely, but they may reduce the receiver's concentration.

To overcome physical barriers, exercise as much control as possible over the physical transmission link–if you're preparing a written document, make sure its appearance doesn't detract from your message. If you're delivering an oral presentation, choose a setting that permits the audience to see and hear you without straining. When you are the audience, learn to concentrate on the message rather than the distractions.

LEARNING OUTCOME 6
Summarize what you can do to improve communication.

How to Improve Communication

As you learn how to overcome more and more communication barriers, you become more and more successful as a business communicator. Think about the people you know. Which of them would you call successful communicators? What do these people have in common? Chances are, they share five traits:

Effective communication requires perception, precision, credibility, control, and congeniality.

- *Perception.* They are able to predict how you will receive their message. They anticipate your reaction and shape the message accordingly. They read your response correctly and constantly adjust to correct any misunderstanding.
- *Precision.* They create a meeting of the minds. When they finish expressing themselves, you share the same mental picture.
- *Credibility.* They are believable. You have faith in the substance of their message. You trust their information and their intentions.
- *Control.* They shape your response. Depending on their purpose, they can make you laugh or cry, calm down, change your mind, or take action.
- *Congeniality.* They maintain friendly, pleasant relations with you. Regardless of whether you agree with them, good communicators command your respect and goodwill. You are willing to work with them again, despite your differences.

Effective communicators overcome the main barriers to communication by creating their messages carefully, minimizing noise in the transmission process, and facilitating feedback.

Create the Message Carefully

The best way to create messages carefully is to focus on your audience so you can help them understand and accept your message. You want to create a bridge of words that leads audience members from their current position to your point, so you have to know something about your audience's attitudes and opinions. If you're addressing strangers, try to find out more about them; if that's impossible, try to project yourself into their position by using your common sense and imagination. Then you'll be ready to create your message:

In general terms, your purpose is to bring your audience closer to your views.

- Tell your audience at the outset what to expect from your message. Let them know the purpose of your message, and tell them what main points they will encounter. Even if you don't want to reveal controversial ideas at the beginning of a message, you can still give your audience a preview of the topics you plan to cover.

Give your audience a framework for understanding the ideas you communicate.

- Balance general concepts with specific illustrations. Once you've stated your overall idea at the beginning of your message, develop that idea by using vivid, concrete examples. The most memorable words are the ones that create a picture in your audience's mind by describing colours, objects, scents, sounds, and tastes. Specific details such as numbers, figures, and percentages can also be vivid.

To make your message memorable
- ✧ Use words that evoke a physical, sensory impression
- ✧ Use telling statistics

- Keep your messages as brief and as clear as possible. With few exceptions, one page is easier to absorb than two, especially in a business environment, where so many messages compete for attention. However, you have to be careful to develop each main idea adequately. You're better off covering three points thoroughly than eight points superficially.

The key to brevity is to limit the number of ideas, not to restrict their development.

- Show how new ideas are related to ideas that already exist in the minds of your audience. The meaning of the new concept is clarified by its relationship to the old. Such connections also help make the new concepts acceptable.

Tie the message to your audience's frame of reference.

- When you come to an important idea, say so. By explicitly stating that an idea is especially significant, you wake people up; you also make it easier for them to file the thought in the proper place. You can call attention to an idea visually, using headlines, bold type, and indented lists and by using charts, graphs, maps, diagrams, and illustrations. If you're delivering your message orally, use your body and voice to highlight the important concepts.

By highlighting and summarizing key points, you help your audience understand and remember the message.

- Before concluding your message or even a major section of a long message, take a moment or two to review the points you've just covered. Restate the purpose, and show how the main ideas relate to it. This simple step will help your audience remember your message and will help simplify the overall meaning of complex material.

Minimize Noise

Even the most carefully constructed message will fail to achieve results if it does not reach your audience. As far as possible, try to eliminate potential sources of interference. Then make sure your choice of communication channel and medium doesn't interfere with your message. Choose the method that will be most likely to attract your audience's attention and enable them to concentrate on the message. If a written document seems the best choice, try to make it physically appealing and easy to comprehend. Use an attractive, convenient format, and pay attention to such details as the choice of paper and the quality of type. If possible, deliver the document when you know the reader will have time to study it.

The careful choice of channel and medium helps focus your audience's attention on your message.

USING THE POWER OF TECHNOLOGY

Using the Internet to Explore International Business Communication

Skillful communication is critical to the success of your business or organizational relationships. To help you communicate more effectively, the International Association of Business Communicators (IABC) offers analyses of issues, case studies, models of communication practices, and advice. All of these can help you develop strategies for managing communication in international business. IABC is a source for real-world examples, as well as manuals and handbooks on a variety of topics. IABC's Web site (**www.iabc.com**) provides a career and job posting area for students, communicators seeking jobs, and employers. You'll also find a regularly updated list of topics on the home page, including news items and announcements of conferences and workshops. Explore IABC's resources including its links to a global network of communicators.

CAREER APPLICATIONS

1. Describe several of IABC's resources. What are some of IABC's goals that can benefit business professionals? What is the purpose of the IABC Research Foundation? How could the manual *Business Management for Communicators* be useful to you in public relations or organizational communication? If you do not think the manual would be useful, explain why (give details).
2. What professional benefits does IABC offer to business communicators? Why should a businessperson affiliate with an organization such as IABC? What is the advantage to a business communicator?
3. What is the IABC Code of Ethics? Why is a code of ethics important for business communicators?

If the message calls for an oral delivery channel, try to eliminate physical barriers. The location should be comfortable and quiet, with adequate lighting, good acoustics, and few visual distractions. In addition, think about how your own appearance will affect the audience. An outfit that screams for attention creates as much noise as a squeaky air-conditioning system. Another way to reduce interference, particularly in oral communication, is to deliver your message directly to the intended audience. The more people who filter your message, the greater the potential for message distortion.

Facilitate Feedback

In addition to minimizing noise, giving your audience a chance to provide feedback is crucial. But one thing that makes business communication difficult is the complexity of the feedback loop. If you're talking face to face with another person, feedback is immediate and clear. However, if you're writing a letter, memo, or report that will be read by several people, feedback will be delayed and mixed. Some of the readers will be enthusiastic or will respond promptly; others will be critical or reluctant to respond, and revising your message to take their feedback into account will be difficult.

Make feedback more useful by
- ✧ Planning how and when to accept it
- ✧ Being receptive to your audience's responses
- ✧ Encouraging frankness
- ✧ Using it to improve communication

When you plan a message, think about the amount of feedback you want to encourage. Although feedback is generally useful, it reduces your control over the communication situation. You need to know whether your message is being understood and accepted, but you may not want to respond to comments until you have completed your argument. If you are communicating with a group, you may not have the time to react to every impression or question.

So think about how you want to obtain feedback, and choose a form of communication that suits your needs. Some channels and media are more compatible with feedback than others. If you want to adjust your message quickly, talk to the receiver face to face or by phone. If feedback is less important to you, use a written document or give a prepared speech.

Feedback isn't always easy to get, even when you encourage it. In some cases, you may have to draw out the other person by asking questions. If you want to know specific things, ask specific questions, but also encourage your audience to express general reactions; you can often learn something very interesting that way.

Regardless of whether the response to your message is written or oral, encourage people to be open and to tell you what they really think and feel. Of course, you have to listen to their comments, and you must do so objectively. You can't say "Please tell me what you think" and then get mad at the first critical comment. So try not to react defensively. Your goal is to find out whether the people in your audience have understood and accepted your message. If you find they haven't, don't lose your temper. After all, the fault is at least partially yours. Instead of saying the same thing all over again, only louder this time, try to find the source of the misunderstanding. Then revise your message. Sooner or later, if you keep trying, you'll succeed. You may not win the audience to your point of view, but at least you'll make your meaning clear, and you'll part with a feeling of mutual respect.

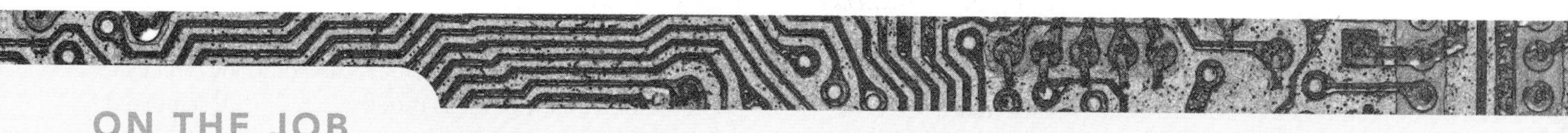

ON THE JOB
Solving a Communication Dilemma at Suncor Energy

Communication plays a key role in Suncor's work as an energy producer. The company uses a variety of means to get its environmental message across to its stakeholders—employees, activist groups, consumers, the general public, and local, provincial, and federal governments—the people with a special interest in the company's operations. For example, Suncor's media relations division produces various kinds of documents to explain and promote the company's business. This material includes brochures that discuss Suncor's research on alternative and renewable energy and their Alberta oil sands operations; newsletters that inform local communities about the company's current projects and their impact on the environment; reports on the company's health and safety policies; news releases announcing such events as new appointments and projects; and speeches for Suncor executives to deliver to community, professional, and social groups.

Annual reports are documents for communicating with shareholders. At Suncor, they not only disclose financial information but also discuss the company's environmental concerns. They explain the company's alternative energy research program and its progress in controlling greenhouse gases that damage the atmosphere.

Corporate Web sites are major promotional and informational tools for business. For Suncor, a Web site is another means for communicating their environmental message. Along with the information usually found on corporate Web pages—company background, biographies of company officers, a description of the company's operations, media information, such as news releases, and investor news—Suncor's Web site includes the ARE (Alternative and Renewable Energy) pages. Here Suncor details their environmental vision and action plan, and provides environmental reports for readers to download. The "Know Us" page broadcasts Suncor's formal environmental mission statement:

> Our Mission: We will met the needs of a changing world by establishing Suncor as a renewable-energy provider. We will build a successful portfolio of alternative business opportunities to ensure our continued growth as a unique and sustainable energy company.

Communicating what the company is about and what it wants to accomplish is a vital purpose of Suncor's corporate communications team.[21]

Your Mission: You've recently been hired as a communications specialist in Suncor's corporate communications division. You have three responsibilities: (1) giving input on guidelines and practices to help the company communicate more effectively; (2) helping managers in various divisions—marketing, research and development, human resources—with communication problems; and (3) acting as one of the company's official voices by talking to reporters and tour groups, and so on.

1. A reporter from *The Globe and Mail* is writing an article on alternative energy resources in Canada. She wants to know how Suncor can claim to be environmentally friendly when the company is expanding its Alberta oil-sands operations and will increase significantly the number of barrels of oil produced each day. The article is running in tomorrow's edition, so the reporter doesn't have time to let you think about her question and call back with an answer. Which is the best response?

a. You know anything you say might provoke a negative reaction, so you simply say, "I'm sorry. I can't comment on that issue."

b. You know that you have to establish some credibility, and pretending that the expansion has little or no impact on the environment is foolish. You say, "Yes, it is true that we are expanding our oil-sands operations and that output of oil will increase significantly. However, the technology we will use is more environmentally friendly than existing methods. Furthermore, Suncor will spend $100 million over the next five years on alternative and renewable energy projects."

c. You want to take control of the conversation, so you tell her that she should speak to other oil producing companies and ask them about their environmental programs.

d. Simply say, "We are satisfying the needs of consumers and cannot be held entirely responsible for impacting

Canada's environment. People need gas to drive their cars and heat their homes."

2. The manager of one of the production plants realizes that his communication skills are important for several reasons: he holds primary responsibility for successful communication inside the plant; he needs to communicate with the managers who report to him; and his style sets an example for other managers. He asks you to sit in on face-to-face meetings for several days to observe his non-verbal messages. You witness the following four habits; which do you think is the most negative?
   a. He rarely comes out from behind his massive desk when meeting people; at one point he gave an employee a congratulatory handshake, and the employee had to lean way over his desk just to reach him.
   b. When an employee hands him a report and then sits down to discuss it, he alternates between making eye contact and making notes on the report.
   c. He is consistently pleasant, even if the person he is meeting is delivering bad news.
   d. He interrupts meetings to answer the phone, rather than letting an assistant get the phone; then he apologizes to visitors for the interruption.
3. In any company, employees have questions about workplace safety, company goals, benefits and pensions, and other issues. As a company that promotes open communication, Suncor wants to encourage employees to communicate with management on matters of concern to them. You have been asked to advise on the best ways for the company to answer employee questions. Be prepared to discuss the pros and cons of each of the following choices, and select the best one. Keep in mind that Suncor's employees work in various locations—the company's headquarters in Calgary, Alberta; the oil sands in Fort McMurray, Alberta; and the Sunoco refinery in Sarnia, Ontario.
   a. Institute a question-and-answer section in the company newsletter.
   b. Ask employees to submit questions by e-mail to designated staff who will respond to them.
   c. Ask employees to submit questions by internal snail mail to designated staff who will respond to them.
   d. Have a monthly forum at company headquarters where management will answer questions from the audience. This forum will be simultaneously broadcast by satellite to remote locations where employees will use telephones to ask questions.
4. As a major Canadian corporation, Suncor is the subject of many school reports and case studies. Many of the people working on these projects contact the company directly for information. Many of these requests ask for the same information, such as quarterly financial reports. How should the company respond to this huge task?
   a. Use the Internet and World Wide Web to make standardized information available to all researchers. Most students now have Internet access at home or at school, so this option will meet their needs while saving the company time and money.
   b. Write and publish a book that answers the most frequently asked questions. When people phone or e-mail for help, suggest that they visit the library or purchase the book.
   c. The people asking for help are likely to be customers or potential customers, so it's vital to give them all the help they need. Hire sufficient staff to address every inquiry.
   d. The buying potential of an individual student is not likely to compensate for all the work of helping him or her find information for a school report. Set up a phone line with a recorded message thanking people for calling but explaining that you just don't have the staff time available to help researchers.

TAP Your Knowledge

Summary of Learning Outcomes

1. List the general categories of non-verbal communication. Non-verbal communication contains six categories: (1) facial expressions and eye behaviour, your primary site for expressing emotions; (2) gestures and postures, which communicate nervousness, confidence, and other attitudes; (3) vocal characteristics, which carry both intentional and unintentional messages about your emotions; (4) personal appearance, which is an indicator of your social identity through your grooming and clothing; (5) touching behaviour, which can convey warmth and reassurance; and (6) time and space, which can be used to assert authority and status.

2. Explain the four channels of verbal communication. The four channels of communication are speaking, writing, listening, and reading. People tend to prefer oral communications to written ones, because it is quicker to convey information through speaking than through writing. However, written communication is a better means for keeping a large number of people within an organization fully informed. People spend about 45 percent of their communication time listening, but often forget the message or miss underlying meaning. Unfortunately, the level of functional illiteracy in Canada is high. Even people who know how to read effectively have trouble extracting key points from a document.

3. Identify the steps in the communication process. Six steps form the communication process. In the first step, the sender of the message conceives an idea. When the sender puts the idea into a message the receiver will understand, the message is encoded. Then the sender transmits the message through a communication channel, verbal or non-verbal. For communication to occur, the receiver must get the message. The receiver decodes, or interprets, the message. At the end of the communication process, the receiver sends feedback to the sender.

4. Describe what can go wrong when you're formulating messages. The communication process can be interrupted before it really begins. The process can be thwarted by indecision about the content of the message, when the sender can't decide what to say. The process can be obstructed by a lack of familiarity with members of the audience and their needs. It is important to know something about their biases, education, age, and status if the sender is to create an effective message. Furthermore, the sender can have difficulty expressing ideas. Many people have trouble putting their thoughts into words, but this obstacle can be overcome by taking courses and even participating in professional organizations such as Toastmasters.

5. Discuss communication barriers and how to overcome them. Communication barriers exist between people and within organizations. Communication barriers between people may be caused by differences in perception, since no two people perceive an environment or language in the same way. Communication barriers may also be caused by incorrect filtering (screening out information), language problems, poor listening, differing emotional states, and differing backgrounds. Within organizations, communication barriers may be caused by information overload, which reduces an audience's ability to concentrate effectively on the most important messages. Other barriers can be found in the complexity of the message, the fact that receivers may be faced with more than one message competing for their attention, differing status within an organization, lack of trust, inadequate communication structures, and a closed communication climate. It is important to choose the right approach to overcoming a specific communication barrier. To deal with incorrect filtering, the sender of the message should try to establish more than one communication channel, so that the message can be verified by more than one source. To overcome language barriers, the sender must choose the most specific and accurate words. To overcome information overload, the sender must give the information meaning and set priorities for dealing with information flow.

6. Summarize what you can do to improve communication. To improve communication, you must create your messages carefully, minimize noise or potential sources of interference with your message, and facilitate feedback by deciding the form of communication you want your audience to use for response.

Test Your Knowledge

Review Questions

1. Why is non-verbal communication important?
2. What are the drawbacks of relying only on written communication?
3. What are the benefits of oral communication?
4. Choose three communication barriers within organizations and discuss ways to overcome them.
5. Define "media richness."
6. Choose three kinds of inappropriate communication media and discuss how they can distort messages.
7. What are effective ways to create messages?
8. How can noise be minimized?

Apply Your Knowledge

Critical Thinking Questions

1. How can non-verbal communication help you run a meeting? How can it help you call the meeting to order, emphasize important topics, show approval, express reservations, regulate the flow of conversation, and invite a colleague to continue with a comment?
2. Which communication channels are more susceptible to noise, written or spoken? Why?
3. How can you as the receiver help a sender successfully communicate a message? Briefly explain.
4. Do you think it is easier to communicate with members of your own sex? Why or why not?
5. How can you impress on your employees the importance of including negative information in messages?
6. Under what circumstances might you want to limit the feedback you receive from an audience of readers or listeners? Briefly explain.

Practise Your Knowledge

Document for Analysis

Read the following document; then (1) analyze the strengths and weaknesses of each sentence and (2) revise the document so that it follows this chapter's guidelines.

> It has come to my attention that many of you are lying on your time cards. If you come in late, you should not put 8:00 on your card. If you take a long lunch, you should not put 1:00 on your time card. I will not stand for this type of cheating. I simply have no choice but to institute a time-clock system. Beginning next Monday, all employees will have to punch in and punch out whenever they come and go from the work area.
>
> The time clock will be right by the entrance to each work area, so you have no excuse for not punching in. Anyone who is late for work or late coming back from lunch more than three times will have to answer to me. I don't care if you had to take a nap or if you girls had to shop. This is a place of business, and we do not want to be taken advantage of by slackers who are cheaters to boot.
>
> It is too bad that a few bad apples always have to spoil things for everyone.

Exercises

1. Write a short description of your classroom's communication potential. What furniture is in the room? How is the room arranged? Are students seated in rows? In a circle? Where is the instructor's space? At the front of the room? In the middle? What are the acoustics like? Are there any windows in the room? Do they offer pleasing views? Could they be distracting? Are there any chalkboards or other visual aids that might affect communication? Is the temperature comfortable? Are heaters or air conditioners noisy? Explain how these and other factors influence the communication that goes on in your classroom. Conclude your description with a statement about the kind of communication your classroom encourages. (An inflexible atmosphere for one-way lectures? An open forum of give and take? An intimate setting for private conversations between members of small groups?)
2. On the World Wide Web, visit the home pages for Air Canada at **www.aircanada.ca** and for Singapore Airlines at **www.singaporeair.com**. Identify the verbal and non-verbal cues that help you understand each company as well as the products and services that each company offers. Examine the presentation of both text and visual elements, including photographs and graphics. Consider the layout of the page, background "noise," and repetition. Think about the needs of the audience. Is each page informative and easy to use? Do the links take the user to appropriate and clearly presented data? In 500 words, explain which site is more effective and why.
3. Your boss has asked you to research and report on corporate child-care facilities. Of course, you'll want to know who (besides your boss) will be reading your report. Working with two team members, list four or five other things you'll want to know about the situation and about your audience before starting your research. Briefly explain why the items on your list are important.

4. Use the six phases of the communication process to analyze a miscommunication you've recently had with a co-worker, supervisor, classmate, teacher, friend, or family member. What idea were you trying to share? How did you encode and transmit it? Did the receiver get the message? Did the receiver correctly decode the message? How do you know? Based on your analysis, identify and explain the barriers that prevented your successful communication in this instance.
5. Basing your decisions on the relative richness of communication media, such as face-to-face interviews, telephone conversations, written messages (such as memos, letters, and reports), and bulletins or newsletters, advise your employees how best to send the following messages, and explain your rationale.
   a. A technical report on the durability of your production equipment
   b. A reminder to employees about safety rules
   c. A performance evaluation of an employee who has been consistently missing deadlines
   d. A confirmation of tomorrow's luncheon meeting with an important client
   e. The quarterly statistics on inventory control
   f. Your resignation before joining another company
6. You've accepted an invitation from the chamber of commerce to speak about controlled growth in the community. You know that your audience will consist mostly of local business people, but how can you find out more? Is it possible to determine where they stand on the issue of growth, how much they know about the topic, and what information they need to have before they'll accept your message? You have one month before the speech. List any methods you can think of that will help you learn as much as you can about the audience you'll be addressing.
7. You've agreed to help a colleague by reviewing his report. His language needs to be more specific and more memorable, so you've compiled a list of words and phrases that should be replaced. Please suggest one or two appropriate alternatives for the underlined sections in the following:
   a. A <u>pale, grayish yellow</u> cover
   b. <u>Soft</u> leather
   c. The <u>people buying this product</u>
   d. During this <u>period of business prosperity</u>
   e. Concern for <u>seriously declining profits</u>
8. You are writing a report on the Canadian sales of your newest product. Of the following topics, identify those that should and should not be included in your report (please explain your choices):
   a. Regional breakdowns of sales across the country
   b. Sales figures of competitors who are selling similar products worldwide
   c. Predictions of how the improving Canadian economy will affect sales over the next six months
   d. The impact of Japanese competitors' selling similar products in Canada
   e. An evaluation of your company's selling this product internationally
9. Describe the kinds of vocal signals and body movements you can use to highlight the key points of your speech.
10. You're stuck. Your boss has asked you to make your presentation to the board at lunch. You dread the prospect. It's bad enough that you have to convince such a stuffy group to spend more money on employee training and education, but to have to do it over lunch at a formally set table for nine in the middle of a busy restaurant is too much. What can you do to get the board members' attention, keep it, and overcome the interruptions and noise of the restaurant's waiters and lunch crowd?
11. In order to obtain just the right amount of feedback, choose the appropriate form of communication for the following (briefly explain your choices).
    a. Disclosing your idea for a new product to your five-member team
    b. Obtaining comments from your boss on your approach to completing the annual shareholders' report
    c. Convincing top management and co-workers that your plan for improving companywide communication is the best plan
    d. Getting opinions from your co-workers about remodelling the local office
12. Whenever your boss asks for feedback on an idea, she blasts anyone offering criticism no matter how gently the news is broken to her. This defensive reaction has caused people to start agreeing with everything she says. You think that the situation is unhealthy for the company and for your boss. So, despite the likelihood of her reacting defensively, you want to talk to her about it. List some of the things you'll say when you meet with her tomorrow.

Developing Your Internet Skills

Going Online: Beef Up Your Internet Language Skills, p. 32

Do you think the Internet is creating a new language recognized and understood worldwide? How might this benefit the business world? Can you think of any terms coined by Net users that have spilled over into everyday usage? Does this kind of lingo exclude certain groups, or does it broaden everyone's knowledge?

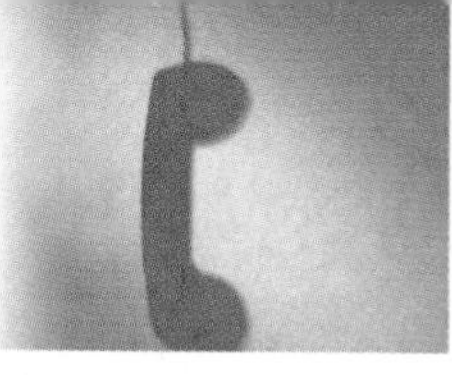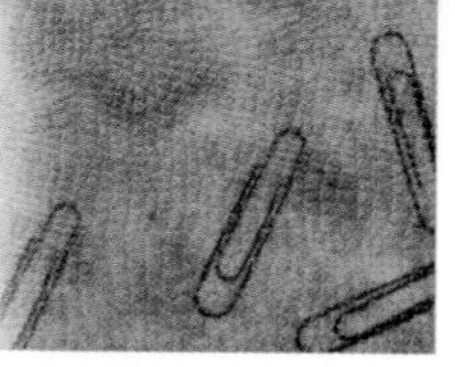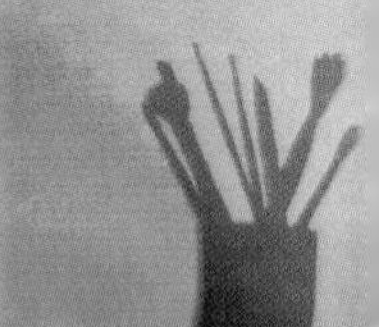

CHAPTER 3

Communicating Interculturally

AFTER STUDYING THIS CHAPTER, YOU WILL BE ABLE TO

1. Outline the two trends that have made intercultural business communication so important
2. Define culture and intercultural communication
3. Discuss at least four of the nine ways people can differ culturally
4. Summarize how to learn about a particular culture
5. Discuss some general skills to help communicate in any culture
6. Identify some of the common sources of misunderstanding that occur when negotiating across cultures
7. Explain the importance of speaking and listening effectively when communicating face to face with people from other cultures

ON THE JOB

Facing a Communication Dilemma at Malkam Cross-Cultural Training

Working with Cultural Diversity

Let's imagine that the Chinese manager of your unit, a recent immigrant to Canada, has dramatically increased your firm's sales in the Far East. Your company's vice-president of marketing wants to recognize his achievement, and assigned you the task of buying your manager a small gift. Do you choose (a) a radio; (b) a watch; or (c) a silver coin?

Laraine Kaminsky, President of Ottawa-based Malkam Cross-Cultural Training, helps her clients overcome obstacles that might interfere with their adaptation to the Canadian workplace as well as the world of international business. Her firm of eight full-time staff and 50 consultants creates cross-cultural, language, and diversity training programs and delivers them to Canadian companies, individual business people, and immigrants to Canada. The rapidly growing global marketplace and Canada's position as a magnet for immigrants from all over the world have provided Malkam with many opportunities to help people communicate across cultures.

South African–born Laraine Kaminsky founded her company in 1989 after an unexpected job transfer to Canada. Her firm helps new immigrants become accustomed to Canadian ways as well as helping employees at all levels to work with people from different cultures within and outside Canada. She says, "These days it's not the transfer of technology that's confusing. It's the transfer of culture. In today's world, what people need to learn is how to be effective in the new culture to which they are exposed."

The unique combination of influences present in one culture can condition people to think, feel, and behave quite differently from people in another culture. Some differences are dramatic, as in the importance of social status. Other differences, such as personal values and decision-making approaches, can be more subtle and more difficult to perceive. Basic language barriers often prevent employees from understanding each other, but the potential for misunderstanding goes beyond language differences. As one example, Kaminsky cites the employer-employee relationship. In Canada, it is often on a first-name basis. In Korea, she says, the workplace is very formal. Coming from a culture where employees and employers keep their distance, Korean immigrants will find this casual interaction startling.

Cultural differences—and the misconceptions that might result from them—can affect teamwork, productivity, and job satisfaction. If you worked for Malkam, how would you approach teaching clients about the Canadian workplace? How would you help immigrants adapt to Canadian culture? What advice would you give to Canadians to improve their communication with immigrant colleagues?

By the way, if you answered radio or silver coin to the question, you would be right. Kaminsky says that in Chinese culture anything that connotes the passage of time represents death. Such a gift would be certain to create some awkwardness.[1]

The Importance of Intercultural Business Communication

Figure 3.1 lists some of the programs played on CHIN radio in Toronto on a typical broadcasting day. The station transmits in more than 30 languages to more than 30 cultural communities throughout southern Ontario. While the organization you join may not be that diverse, you will very likely be dealing with people from various national, religious, and ethnic backgrounds. You may find yourself trying to bridge differences in both language and culture as you exchange business messages with co-workers, customers, suppliers, investors, and competitors from other cultures.

AM 1540 FM 100.7
CHIN
RADIO/TV INTERNATIONAL
TORONTO • CANADA

Time		Sunday	
12:00 AM	Spanish	T.O. Latino Show	Magda De La Torre
2:00 AM	English	Dr. Love Show	Fitzroy Gordon
6:00 AM	English	Arts Show "café express"	Rene Jerez
6:30 AM	Caribbean	Shabnam	Richard Aziz
7:30 AM	Dobro J. Hrvatska	Croatian Religion	
8:00 AM	Italian Religion	La Voce Della Speranza	Pastor G. DeMeo
8:30 AM	Jewish	Shalom	Zelda Young
10:00 AM	Irish/Scottish	Songs From Home	Hugh Straney
11:00 AM	Eng/Religion	Timothy Eaton Church	Live Service
NOON	Croatian Program	John Loncaric	
1:00 PM	Italian	Weekend Italiano	Various Hosts
6:00 PM	Filipino	Pearl Of The Orient	Joel Recla & Agatha Luna
7:00 PM	Bengali	Sringar Radio	Sujoy Kanungo
8:00 PM	Romanian	Miorita	Maria Cojocaru
8:30 PM	Japanese	Sunday Night Japan	Shin Kawai
9:00 PM	Iranian Gospel Voice	Iranian Religion	
9:30 PM	Somali Voice	Mohammed Hassan	
10:30 PM	Lithuanian Show	Violet Laurin	
11:00 PM	Urdu/Arabic	Voice of Pakistan	

FIGURE 3.1

Cultural Diversity in Central Canada

During a week, radio station CHIN-AM in Toronto broadcasts in their native languages to 30 cultural groups located in southern Ontario. This Sunday program schedule reflects some of the diversity of Canadian society.

Of course, communicating across language and cultural barriers at home is only one way your communication skills will be challenged. Communicating across national borders will also challenge your skills. More and more companies around the world are hopping national borders to conduct business.

Communicating with Cultures Abroad

LEARNING OUTCOME 1
Outline the two trends that have made intercultural business communication so important.

Thanks to technological advances in communication and transportation, companies can quickly and easily span the globe in search of new customers and new sources of materials and money. Even firms that once thought they were too tiny to expand into a neighbouring city have discovered that they can tap the sales potential of overseas markets with the help of fax machines, the Internet, overnight delivery services, and e-mail. This rise of international business has expanded international business communication by increasing exports, relaxing trade barriers, and increasing foreign competition in domestic markets.

Technology has made global communication both quick and easy.

The globalization of business is accelerating as more companies cross national borders to find customers, materials, and capital.

More and more businesses report that a large part of their overall sales now come from **exports** (products sold to customers in other countries). Nestlé, which is based in Switzerland, sells over 95 percent of its products in other countries. Likewise, with some Canadian companies, exports are strong. Bombardier, the Montreal-based aerospace and transportation world leader, saw 90 percent of its revenues generated in markets outside Canada in its 1999 fiscal year.[2]

Relaxing trade barriers has also quickened the pace of international trade. Mexico, Canada, and the United States have agreed to lower trade barriers throughout the continent, creating a single market of 400 million people. Moreover, discussions are under way to extend that agreement throughout the Americas.[3] The goal is to increase **imports** (products purchased from businesses in other countries) by reducing the obstacles to moving goods across borders. Similarly, the nations of the European Union have been eliminating trade barriers. Since 1993, capital, products, and employees have been flowing freely across European borders, creating a unified market of 380 million people.[4]

As companies move into the global marketplace, they increase the competition in domestic markets for employees, customers, and materials. Within Canada, many Canadian manufacturers compete domestically with non-Canadian firms. In this fast-paced global marketplace, companies are finding that good communication skills are essential for meeting customers, making sales, and working effectively with colleagues in other countries.

Communicating with a Culturally Diverse Workforce

In addition to communicating with people in other countries, you'll be communicating with people in Canada whose culture and language differ from yours. First, if you work in the local branch of a foreign firm or if your company does business with local branches of foreign firms, you may find that differences in language and culture interfere with communication.

Cultural diversity is the degree to which the population is made up of people from varied national, ethnic, racial, and religious backgrounds.

Second, no matter where you work, you'll face language and cultural barriers as you communicate with members of an increasingly diverse domestic workforce. A country's workforce reflects its **cultural diversity,** the degree to which the population is made up of people from various national, ethnic, racial, and religious backgrounds.

In Canada, for example, the high degree of cultural diversity in the domestic workforce has been partially shaped by immigration trends. Eighty percent of the immigrants who arrived here between 1991 and 1996 speak a native language other than English or French.[5] The 1996 Census showed that almost half of these immigrants were from Eastern, Southeast, and Southern Asia, 7 percent from Central and South America, 6 percent from the Caribbean and Bermuda, 14 percent from Eastern and Southern Europe, and 7 percent from Africa.[6] As immigrants have joined the Canadian workforce, they bring their own language and culture.

Of course, people also differ in their gender, age, physical abilities, family status, and educational background. Like language and culture, these elements contribute to the diversity of the workforce. They shape how people view the world. And they also affect how business messages are conceived, planned, sent, received, and interpreted.

The Basics of Intercultural Business Communication

As discussed in Chapter 2, differences in background can be a difficult communication barrier to overcome. When you plan to communicate with people of another culture–whether in another country or in your own country–it's important to be aware of cultural differences. Consider the communication challenge that Mazda's managers faced when the Japanese auto manufacturer opened a plant in the United

States. Mazda officials passed out company baseball caps and told their US employees they could wear the caps at work, along with their mandatory company uniform (blue pants and khaki shirts). The employees assumed that the caps were a *voluntary* accessory, and many decided not to wear them. The Japanese managers, who regarded failure to wear the caps as a sign of disrespect, were upset. Managers acknowledged that the caps were voluntary but believed that employees who really cared about the company would *want* to wear the caps. However, the US employees had a different view: They resented being told what they should want to do, and they began cynically referring to all Mazda's directives as "mandatory-voluntary."[7] How do you think Canadian auto workers would react to Mazda's policies? Would Canadians demonstrate an attitude like that of their US counterparts?

Test Your Intercultural Knowledge

ACHIEVING INTERCULTURAL COMMUNICATION

Never take anything for granted when you're doing business in a foreign country. All sorts of assumptions that are valid in one place can trip you up elsewhere if you fail to consider that customs may vary. Here are several true stories about business people who blundered by overlooking some simple but important cultural differences. Can you spot the erroneous assumptions that led these people astray?

1. You're tired of the discussion and you want to move on to a new topic. You ask your Australian business associate, "Can we table this for a while?" To your dismay, your colleague keeps right on discussing just what you want to put aside. Are Australians that inconsiderate?
2. You finally made the long trip overseas to meet the new German director of your division. Despite slow traffic, you arrive only four minutes late. His door is shut, so you knock on it and walk in. The chair is too far away from the desk, so you pick it up and move it closer. Then you lean over the desk, stick out your hand and say, "Good morning, Hans, it's nice to meet you." Of course, you're baffled by his chilly reaction. Why did he react that way?
3. Your meeting went better than you'd ever expected. In fact, you found the Japanese representative for your new advertising agency to be very agreeable; she said yes to just about everything. When you share your enthusiasm with your boss, he doesn't appear very excited. Why not?
4. You've finally closed the deal, after exhausting both your patience and your company's travel budget. Now, two weeks later, your Chinese customers are asking for special considerations that change the terms of the agreement. How could they do this? Why are they doing it? And, most important, what should you do?

In each case the problems have resulted from inaccurate assumptions. Here are the explanations of what went wrong:

1. To "table" something in Australia means to bring it forward for discussion. This is the opposite of what North Americans usually mean. The English that's spoken in Australia is closer to British than to North American English. If you are doing business in Australia, become familiar with the local vocabulary. Note the tendency to shorten just about any word whenever possible, and add "ie" to it is a form of familiar slang: for example, *brolly* (umbrella) and *lollie* (candy). And yes, it's true: "G'day" is the standard greeting. Use it.
2. You've just broken four rules of German polite behaviour: punctuality, privacy, personal space, and proper greetings. In time-conscious Germany, you should never arrive even a few minutes late. Also, Germans like their privacy and space, and they adhere to formal greetings of "Frau" and "Herr," even if the business association has lasted for years.
3. The word *yes* may not always mean *yes* in the Western sense. Japanese people may say *yes* to confirm they have heard or understood something but not necessarily to indicate that they agree with it. You'll seldom get a direct no. Some of the ways that Japanese people say no indirectly include "It will be difficult," "I will ask my supervisor," "I'm not sure," "We will think about it," and "I see."
4. For most North American business people, the contract represents the end of the negotiation. For Chinese business people, however, it's just the beginning. Once a deal is made, Chinese negotiators view their counterparts as trustworthy partners who can be relied on for special favours—such as new terms in the contract.

Sources: Adapted from David A. Ricks, "International Business Blunders: An Update," *Business & Economic Review,* January–March 1988, 25; Valerie Frazee, "Keeping Up on Chinese Culture," *Global Workforce,* October 1996, 16–17; Valerie Frazee, "Establishing Relations in Germany," *Global Workforce,* April 1997, 16–17; James Wilfong and Toni Seger, *Taking Your Business Global* (Franklin Lakes, N.J.: Career Press, 1997), 282.

Understanding Culture

LEARNING OUTCOME 2
Define culture and intercultural communication.

You belong to several cultures. The most obvious is the culture you share with all the people who live in your own country. You also belong to other cultural groups, including an ethnic group, a religious group, and perhaps a profession that has its own special language and customs. **Culture** is a shared system of symbols, beliefs, attitudes, values, expectations, and norms for behaviour. All members of a culture have similar assumptions about how people should think, behave, and communicate, and they all tend to act on those assumptions in much the same way.

Culture is a shared system of symbols, beliefs, attitudes, values, expectations, and norms for behaviour.

Distinct groups that exist within a major culture are referred to as **subcultures.** Groups that might be considered subcultures in Canada are Indo-Canadians, wrestling fans, Russian immigrants, and Memorial University graduates.

Subcultures are distinct groups that exist within a major culture.

By bridging cultural differences, you can successfully achieve **intercultural communication,** the process of sending and receiving messages between people of different cultures. When communicating with a person from another culture, you will be most effective if you can identify the differences between your cultures and accommodate those differences without expecting either the other party or yourself to give up your identity.[8]

Intercultural communication is the process of sending and receiving messages between people of different cultures.

Recognizing Cultural Differences

LEARNING OUTCOME 3
Discuss at least four of the nine ways people can differ culturally.

Laraine Kaminsky says, "While conducting business internationally, you are faced with different sets of cultural rules. While cultural awareness is not always considered a key success factor, ... failure to recognize cultural differences could lead to serious misunderstandings, thus jeopardizing business relationships."[9] When you write to or speak with someone in another culture, you encode your message using the assumptions of your own culture. However, the receiver decodes it according to the assumptions of the other culture, so your meaning may be misunderstood. The greater the difference between the two cultures, the greater the chance for misunderstanding.[10]

Cultural misunderstandings often arise when companies with entirely different ways of doing business join forces. Look at Daimler-Benz and Chrysler. When these two companies announced their engagement, employees and investors alike were stunned.[11] Except for the fact that both companies make cars, they couldn't be more different in culture and product. Pegged as a middle-class company that is willing to take chances, Chrysler sells over 2.3 million cars, Jeeps, vans, and rugged pickup trucks annually–mostly to North American customers. Daimler-Benz, by contrast, is slow-moving and intensely conservative. Each year it sells about 726 000 cars that ooze quality and luxury and appeal to an elite group of mostly European buyers.[12]

Deepak Chopra, M.D., is one of the most prolific (and profitable) authors on the planet, with bestsellers, clinics, audiotapes, and other communication products featuring his name and smiling face. What brought him fame and fortune? A sincere objective of helping people—and a keen talent for translating Eastern concepts to a Western audience. His speaking and writing skills are exceptional, and his intercultural communication talents are unsurpassed.

Operational differences such as these are just the tip of the problem iceberg. Cultural differences will also show up in employees' social values, ideas of status, decision-making habits, attitudes toward time, use of space, cultural context, body language, manners, and legal and ethical behaviour. Acknowledging and exploring these differences is an important step toward understanding how meshed cultures affect the way we do business and communicate. Without an understanding of these differences, business people can unknowingly act improperly and unacceptably, hurting their own reputations and those of their organizations.[13]

SOCIAL VALUES

In 1994, the Department of Citizenship and Immigration asked thousands of Canadians to define the Canadian character. People felt that Canadians "value honesty and fairness," "respect hard work and people with integrity," and expect fellow citizens and residents "to respect the system that is in place, and not to take advantage of [its] generosity." Many people said that two great Canadian strengths are a diverse population and an atmosphere "where individuals are not merely tolerant, but seek and encourage cultural exchange." Other values seen as Canadian are an appreciation of the country's bilingual culture, respect for Aboriginal peoples, and conservation of the environment and the Canadian landscape. Immigrants are seen as contributing to the vibrancy of Canada and helping to define Canada as a country.[14]

Canadians value a diverse population, honesty and fairness, the country's bilingual culture, Aboriginal peoples, and conservation of the environment.

A 1996 poll conducted by Environics, a social research firm, found that Canadians "like trying to take advantage of the unforeseen opportunities that present themselves." Canadians are placing less faith in hierarchical institutions, such as government, and are taking more control of their own lives.[15] In business, this attitude can be seen in the many new high-tech companies, such as Zero-Knowledge, profiled in Chapter 1, that encourage individualism and independence in their employees. However, according to Paul Tellier, CEO of Canadian National Railways, "Canadians are becoming more entrepreneurial; but risk-taking, individualism, and the ambition to create wealth have not been part of our national psyche for as long as they have in the United States."[16]

ROLES AND STATUS

Culture dictates the roles people play, including who communicates with whom, what they communicate, and in what way. For example, in many countries women still don't play a prominent role in business, so female executives who visit these countries may find some resistance when first introduced to foreign clients and colleagues. However, experience has shown that female international managers benefit from a halo effect: the host-nation clients realize that women executives sent abroad are rare, so they assume these managers are of a high calibre.[17]

People from other cultures demonstrate their status differently than Canadians do.

Concepts of status also differ. Many Canadian executives send status signals that reflect materialistic values. The CEO often has a large corner office, deep carpets, an expensive desk, and handsome accessories. In other cultures, status is communicated in other ways. The highest-ranking executives in France sit in the middle of an open area, surrounded by lower-level employees. In the Middle East, fine possessions are reserved for the home, and business is conducted in modest quarters. An executive from another culture who assumes that such office arrangements indicate a lack of status would be incorrect.

DECISION-MAKING CUSTOMS

In Canada and the United States, business people try to reach decisions as quickly and efficiently as possible. The top people are concerned with reaching an agreement on the main points, and then leave the details to be worked out later by others. In Greece, that approach would backfire. A Greek executive assumes that anyone who ignores the details is being evasive and untrustworthy. Spending time on each little point is considered a mark of good faith. Similarly, Latin Americans prefer to make their deals slowly, after much discussion.

Many cultural groups take longer than Canadian and US business people to reach decisions, and many rely more heavily on group consensus.

Cultures also differ in terms of who makes the decisions. In Canada, many organizations are dominated by a single figure who says yes or no to the major deals. It is the same in Pakistan, where you can get a decision quickly if you reach the highest-ranking executive.[18] In other cultures, decision making is shared. In Japan, the negotiating team arrives at a consensus through an elaborate, time-consuming process. Agreement must be complete–there is no majority rule. And, as do businesses everywhere, Japanese firms expect their managers to follow the same decision-making process whether they're in Tokyo or in Toronto.

CONCEPTS OF TIME

Although business people in Canada, the United States, Germany, and some other nations see time as a way to organize the business day efficiently, people in other cultures see time as more flexible.

Differing perceptions of time are another factor that can lead to misunderstandings. German, Canadian, and US executives see time as a way to plan the business day efficiently, focusing on only one task during each scheduled period. Because time is so limited, German and North American executives try to get to the point quickly when communicating.

However, executives from Latin America and Asia see time as more flexible. In those cultures, building a foundation for the business relationship is more important than meeting a deadline for completing a task. Seen in this light, it's not surprising that people in such cultures do not observe strict schedules. Instead, they take whatever time is needed to get to know each other and to explore the background issues.[19]

A salesperson from Calgary calling on a client in Mexico City and kept waiting 30 minutes might infer that the client attaches a low priority to the visit and might feel angry and insulted. In fact, the Mexican client doesn't mean to imply anything at all by the delay. In Mexico, a wait of 30 minutes is a matter of course; the workday isn't expected to follow a rigid, preset schedule.[20]

CONCEPTS OF PERSONAL SPACE

People from various cultures have different comfort zones.

Like time, space means different things in different cultures. The classic anecdote of a conversation between a US executive and a Latin American executive can also apply to Canadians. As the story goes, the interaction may begin at one end of a hallway and end up at the other, with neither party aware of having moved. During the conversation the Latin American executive instinctively moves closer to the US executive, who unconsciously steps back, resulting in an intercultural dance across the floor.

People in Canada and the United States usually stand about five feet apart during a business conversation. Five feet is uncomfortably close for people from Germany or Japan, but for Arabs or Latin Americans it is uncomfortably far. Because of these differing concepts of personal space, a Canadian manager may react negatively (without knowing exactly why) when a Latin American colleague moves closer during their conversation. And the Latin American colleague may react negatively (again, without knowing why) when the Canadian manager backs away.

CULTURAL CONTEXT

Whereas Canadian and US business people rely mostly on words to convey meaning, people in other cultures rely heavily on situational cues and implicit understanding.

One of the ways we assign meaning to a message is according to its **cultural context:** the pattern of physical cues and implicit understanding that convey meaning between two members of the same culture. However, people convey contextual meaning differently from culture to culture. In the **high-context culture** of South Korea or Taiwan, people rely less on verbal communication and more on the context of nonverbal actions and environmental setting to convey meaning. The rules of everyday life are rarely explicit in high-context cultures; as they grow up, people learn how to recognize situational cues (such as gestures and tone of voice) and how to respond as expected.[21]

In the **low-context cultures** of Canada, the United States, or Germany, people rely more on verbal communication and less on circumstances and implied meaning. Expectations are usually spelled out in a low-context culture through explicit statements, such as "Please wait until I'm finished," or "You're welcome to browse." In this way, business people in a low-context culture not only explains their own actions but also cue the other person about what to do or what to expect next.[22]

Imagine the confusion and frustration of someone from a low-context culture trying to sell products to a client from a high-context culture. If the client says nothing after the salesperson names a price, the salesperson may assume that the silence means rejection and may try to save the sale by naming a lower figure. However, in the high-context culture, silence means only that the client is considering the first offer. By misinterpreting the silence and lowering the price, the salesperson loses needed income.

BODY LANGUAGE

Gestures help members of a culture clarify confusing messages, but differences in body language provide a major source of misunderstanding during intercultural communication. Furthermore, don't make the mistake of assuming that someone from another country who speaks your language has mastered the body language of your culture. Instead, learn some of the basic differences in the way people supplement their words with body movement. Take the signal for *No*. People in Canada and the United States shake their heads back and forth; people in Bulgaria nod up and down; people in Japan move their right hands; people in Sicily raise their chins. Or take eye contact. Many business people in Canada and the US assume that a person who won't meet their gaze is evasive and dishonest. However, in many parts of Latin America and Asia, keeping your eyes lowered is a sign of respect, and among many Aboriginal groups, a child's maintaining eye contact with an adult is a sign of disrespect.[23]

Variations in the meaning of body language can cause problems because people are unaware of the messages they are transmitting.

Sometimes people from different cultures misreads an intentional signal sent by body language; sometimes they overlook the signal entirely or assume that a meaningless gesture is significant. For example, an Egyptian might mistakenly assume that a Westerner who exposes the sole of his or her shoe is offering a grave insult. The more you understand nonverbal messages, the better you will communicate in your own and other cultures.[24]

SOCIAL BEHAVIOUR AND MANNERS

The rules of polite behaviour vary from country to country.

What is polite in one culture may be considered rude in another. In Arab countries, it's impolite to take gifts to a man's wife but acceptable to take gifts to his children. In Germany, giving a woman a red rose is considered a romantic invitation, inappropriate if you are trying to establish a business relationship with her. In India you might be invited to visit someone's home "Any time." If you're not familiar with the culture, you may be reluctant to make an unexpected visit, and you might therefore wait for a definite invitation. But your failure to take the invitation literally is an insult, a sign that you do not care to develop the friendship.

In any culture, rules of etiquette may be formal or informal. Formal rules are the specifically taught rights and wrongs of how to behave in common social situations, such as table manners at meals. When formal rules are violated, members of a culture can explain why they feel upset. In contrast, informal social rules are more difficult to identify and are usually learned by watching how people behave and then imitating that behaviour. Informal rules govern how males and females are supposed to behave, when it is appropriate to use a person's first name, and so on. When informal rules are violated, members of a culture are likely to feel uncomfortable, although they may not be able to say exactly why.[25]

Going Online

Mastering the Art of Intercultural Communication

Check out the International Business & Technology Web site for links to dozens of practical and fascinating sites that will help you learn about different nations and peoples and communicate more effectively with intercultural audiences.

www.brint.com/International.htm

LEGAL AND ETHICAL BEHAVIOUR

From culture to culture, what is considered legal and ethical behaviour varies widely. In some countries, companies, whether domestic or foreign, are expected to pay government officials extra fees for approving government contracts. These payments aren't always seen as bribes, but as recompense for easing the process of negotiating a contract abroad. However, depending on the size of the payment and the circumstances under which it is made, Canada, the United States, Sweden,

People often encounter differing standards of legal and ethical behaviour in the course of doing business in other countries.

and many other countries may consider it a bribe, which is both illegal and unethical. In fact, in 1999, Canada signed an international bribery convention negotiated by nations belonging to the Organization for Economic Cooperation and Development (OECD). In the same year, federal legislation was instituted that would make bribing a foreign official a criminal offence in Canada.[26]

When you conduct business around the world, you may also find that other legal systems differ from what you're accustomed to. In the United Kingdom and the United States, someone is innocent until proven guilty, a principle that is rooted in English common law. In Mexico and Turkey, often someone is presumed guilty until proven innocent, a principle that is rooted in the Napoleonic code.[27] These distinctions can be particularly important if your firm must communicate about a legal dispute in another country.

Dealing with Language Barriers

Language shapes our world view, dictating our perception of the universe, so the potential for misunderstanding cross-cultural interaction is great.[28] Even the way information is approached and processed can differ greatly among cultures. For example, an English speaker feels responsible for transmitting the meaning of a message, but a Chinese speaker is more likely to expect the receiver to discover the meaning in a message that uses indirectness and metaphor. Further, an English speaker often places sentences in a chronological sequence to establish a cause-and-effect pattern. However, a Chinese speaker often begins by creating a context with generalizations that form a web (or frame) to receive and support a given topic.[29]

BEHIND THE SCENES AT TERRA COGNITA

Should You Say it with Flowers? And with What Kind?

In France, do you give an even number or odd number of flowers? Are dahlias and chrysanthemums suitable flowers as gifts in Spain? And, should you shake hands with your foreign host with one hand in your pocket?[30]

Terra Cognita, an intercultural training company, can help you understand other cultures and communicate effectively in the international world of business. The creator of audio and videotapes, interactive multimedia cross-cultural learning tools, the Internet training site **www.culturesavvy.com**, and seminars designed for individuals or groups, Terra Cognita helps people living or working abroad to understand the host society and the business practices of different cultures. A client using Terra Cognita's services, for example, will learn about the influence of culture on employer-employee relationships, teamwork, training, and negotiating—all essential elements of business. Terra Cognita recommends the following basic rules to help you navigate the cultural seas of international business.

When trying to communicate with people in a culture different from your own, eating unfamiliar foods may be a challenge. Even so, experts advise you to eat at least a little, even if you choice is between mealworms and crickets.

1. *What gift should I bring to a host?* Mary Bosrock of Terra Cognita notes that gift-giving varies among countries and observing local customs fosters business. Generally speaking, the gift should be appropriate to the relationship and to the culture, and should be suitably priced–neither cheap nor extravagant. In Europe, business gifts are rarely given at the initial meeting, and may even be considered poor taste. If you decide to bring flowers should your host invite you to his or her home, keep in mind that in France an odd number is considered unlucky, and that in Spain dahlias and chrysanthemums are traditional for funerals.
2. *How do I greet someone?* A positive first impression goes a long way. As the experts at Terra Cognita say, it can create a fruitful relationship (conversely, a negative first impression takes a lot of work to erase). Be prepared to shake hands with everyone present upon arrival and departure, as most Europeans do. In many countries, people give and receive a lighter handshake than we are accustomed to in North America. And never shake hands with one hand in your pocket. Doing so might be considered unprofessional and may suggest that you are not focusing completely on your hosts. It is also necessary to understand the customs regarding titles. In Europe, they are very important

Language differences can be confusing even if you are a Canadian executive doing business in an English-speaking country. For example, a Canadian paper products manufacturer wishing to sell a brand of paper serviettes in the US would have to use the word "napkins" instead, as the Canadian word is not used south of the border. Furthermore, it is entertaining to note how miscommunication tripped up a US paper products manufacturer trying to penetrate the English market for paper napkins by using its usual advertising slogan: "There is no finer paper napkin for the dinner table." Unfortunately for the US company, *napkin* is the British term for *diaper*.[31]

English is the most prevalent language in international business, but you cannot assume that all words mean the same to everyone.

Also likely are misunderstandings involving vocabulary, pronunciation, or usage when Canadian business people deal with people who use English as a second language–some 650 million people fall into this category. Some of these millions are extremely fluent; others have only an elementary command of English. Although you may miss a few subtleties when dealing with those less fluent in your own language, you'll still be able to communicate. However, don't assume that the other person understands everything you say. Your message can be mangled by slang, idioms, and local accents.

Watch for clues to be sure that your message is getting through to people who don't speak your language.

When you deal with people who don't speak your language at all, you have three options: You can learn their language, use an intermediary or a translator, or teach them your language. Becoming fluent in a new language requires a major commitment. Canadian foreign service officers take months of language training and then continue their studies at their foreign posts. Even the Berlitz method, famous for the speed of its results, requires a month of intensive effort. Language courses can be quite expensive as well. So unless you're planning to spend several years abroad or to make frequent trips over an extended period, learning another language may take more time and more money than you can afford.

If you have a long-term business relationship with people of another culture, it is helpful to learn their language.

because they imply a great deal of information about family background, education, profession, and personal achievement. If possible, learn beforehand the titles of the people you will be meeting. Furthermore, don't use first names unless your host clearly invites you to do so. Violating this rule demonstrates disrespect, and consequently can damage business negotiations.

3. *Cheers!* If you don't know the language of the host country, learning a few phrases goes a long way, because you show that you care about the people and their culture. Bosrock suggests learning how to greet and thank your hosts and deliver a brief toast. For example, the common toast "to your health" is "prosit" (PRO-sit) in German and "op uw gezondheid" (op uv ge-ZOND-hite) in Dutch. Even if your pronunciation isn't perfect, your effort will be recognized.
4. *What time is the meeting?* In Mexico, the concept of time is often different from that in Canada, the United States, and Western European countries. According to Terra Cognita, Mexicans sometimes refer to time as *la hora americana*, indicating the regard for punctuality customary in Canada and the US, or as *la hora mexicana*, denoting their preference for a flexible timetable. Because people in Canada and the US consider time a limited resource, they will have to adjust to business schedules in Mexico, where appointment calendars are used for planning meetings, but are not closely followed. Interpersonal relationships are prized more than punctuality, and social encounters are not abruptly ended so that the person can go to his or her next appointment. When setting deadlines with Mexican counterparts, according to Terra Cognita, Canadian and US business people should discuss their objectives, and explain any need for a tight deadline, allowing flexibility if it cannot be met.

APPLY YOUR KNOWLEDGE

1. Select a non-English-speaking nation that trades with Canada. With the help of either a foreign language instructor or a translation dictionary, type or print the accepted translation for the following business terms: (a) contract, (b) sale, (c) delivery date, (d) duplicate copies, and (e) negligence. Separately, show three friends the list of translated terms only. Ask each to pronounce the terms. In your notebook, spell phonetically the pronunciations you hear. When finished, compare the pronunciations. How different are they? Which terms produced the greatest variety?
2. Should colleges and universities that offer a business major require a separate degree or certification program for international business? What courses from the curriculum at your school would you require for such a degree or certificate? What new courses can you suggest?

A more practical approach is to use an intermediary or a translator. An experienced translator can analyze a message, understand its meaning in the cultural context, consider how to convey the meaning in another language, and then use verbal and nonverbal signals to encode or decode the message for someone from another culture. If your company has an overseas subsidiary, you may want to seek help from local employees who are bilingual. You can also hire bilingual professionals such as advertising consultants and lawyers.

The option of teaching other people to speak your language doesn't appear to be very practical at first glance. However, many companies do, in fact, offer language-training programs for employees, be they in English, French, or the languages of their customers. For example, Canadian Airlines (now part of Air Canada) developed language-training programs for employees serving its Asian routes so that reservation agents and flight attendants could speak to passengers in their own language.[32] But sometimes, requiring employees to use a specific language when they're on the job can create communication problems. In general, the magnitude of the language barrier depends on whether you are writing or speaking. Written communication is generally easier to handle.

BARRIERS TO WRITTEN COMMUNICATION

Because so many international business letters are written in English, Canadian firms don't always worry about translating their correspondence. Moreover, regardless of where they're located, some multinational companies ask all their employees to use English when writing to employees in other lands. For example, Nissan employees use English for internal memos to colleagues in other countries, even though the corporation is based in Japan. Similarly, English is the official business language of Philips, the global electronics giant based in the Netherlands.[33]

Most routine business correspondence is written in English, but marketing messages are generally translated into the language of the country where the product is to be sold.

However, many other forms of written communication must be translated. Advertisements are almost always translated into the language of the culture in which the products are being sold. Warranties, repair and maintenance manuals, and product labels also require translation. In addition, many multinational companies translate policy and procedure manuals for use in overseas offices. Reports from foreign branches to the home office may be written in one language and then translated into another. One multinational company, E. I. Du Pont de Nemours & Company, translates roughly 70 000 pages of documents a year.[34]

When documents are translated literally, communication can break down. For example, the advertising slogan "Come alive with Pepsi" was once mistranslated for German audiences as "Come out of the grave" and for Thai audiences as "Bring your ancestors back from the dead."[35] To overcome barriers to written communication, follow these recommendations:[36]

- Use the skills of bilingual employees or professional translators.
- Write short messages.
- Keep your wording clear and simple.
- Avoid slang.
- Use your fax machine to transmit the information (with speed and clarity).

BARRIERS TO ORAL COMMUNICATION

Differences in pronunciation, vocal inflections, and vocabulary can pose problems when you're speaking to people from other cultures.

Oral communication usually presents more problems than written communication. If you've ever studied another language, you know it's easier to write in that language than to conduct a conversation. Even if the other person speaks your language, you may have a hard time understanding the pronunciation if the person isn't proficient. For example, many non-native English speakers can't distinguish between the English sounds *v* and *w,* so they say "wery" for "very." At the same time, many people from the United States cannot pronounce the French *r* or the German *ch.*

Also, because people use their voices in different ways, listeners might misunderstand their intentions. Russian speakers, for instance, tend to speak in flat, level tones in their native tongue. When they speak English, they maintain this pattern, and non-Russian listeners may assume that the speakers are bored or rude. Middle Easterners tend to speak more loudly than Westerners and may therefore mistakenly be considered more emotional. On the other hand, the Japanese are soft-spoken, a characteristic that implies politeness or humility to Western listeners.

Idiomatic expressions are another source of confusion. If a Canadian executive tells an Egyptian executive that a certain product "doesn't cut the mustard," chances are communication will fail. Even when the words make sense, their meanings may differ according to the situation. For example, suppose you are dining with a German woman who speaks English quite well. You inquire, "More bread?" She says, "Thank you," so you pass the breadbasket. She looks confused; then she takes the breadbasket and sets it down without taking any bread. In German, *thank you (danke)* can be used as a polite refusal as well as a signal of acceptance. If the woman had wanted more bread, she would have used the word *please* (*bitte* in German).

President of Latin Access, a PEI-based intercultural training company, Patricia Diaz has taught English as a second language both to executives in Mexico, her home country, and Canadians. She also delivers courses in intercultural communication, human relations, social etiquette and business protocol to Canadians working globally, and wrote *A Guide to Mexican Customs and Manners.*

When speaking in English to people who speak English as a second language, you may find these guidelines helpful:

- *Try to eliminate noise.* Pronounce words clearly, stop at distinct punctuation points, and make one point at a time.
- *Look for feedback.* Be alert to signs of confusion in your listener. Realize that nods and smiles don't necessarily mean understanding.
- *Rephrase your sentence when necessary.* If someone doesn't seem to understand you, choose simpler words; don't just repeat the sentence in a louder voice.
- *Don't talk down to the other person.* Try not to over-enunciate, and don't blame the listener for not understanding. Use phrases such as "Am I going too fast?" rather than "Is this too difficult for you?"
- *Use objective, accurate language.* Avoid overusing adjectives such as *fantastic* and *fabulous,* which people from other cultures might consider unreal and overly dramatic.
- *Let other people finish what they have to say.* If you interrupt, you may miss something important. You'll also show a lack of respect.

Dealing with Ethnocentric Reactions

Although language and cultural differences are significant barriers to communication, they can be overcome by maintaining an open mind. Unfortunately, many of us lapse into **ethnocentrism,** the tendency to judge all other groups according to our own group's standards, behaviours, and customs. When we make such comparisons, we too often decide that our group is superior.[37]

Ethnocentrism is the tendency to judge all other groups according to your own group's standards, behaviours, and customs and to see other groups as inferior by comparison.

By reacting ethnocentrically, you ignore the distinctions between your own culture and another person's culture. You assume that others will act the same way you do, that they will operate from the same assumptions, and that they will use language and symbols in the same way you do. If they do not, you may mistakenly believe that they are in error or that their way is invalid or inferior to your own. An ethnocentric reaction makes you lose sight of the possibility that your words and actions will be misunderstood. It also makes you likely to misinterpret or belittle the behaviour of others.

Ethnocentric people are often prone to **stereotyping,** attempting to predict individuals' behaviour or character on the basis of their membership in a particular group or class. When people first start to investigate the culture of another group, they may stereotype characteristics as a way of understanding common tendencies of that group's members. However, the next step is to move beyond the stereotypes to relationships with real people. Unfortunately, when ethnocentric

Stereotyping is the attempt to categorize individuals by trying to predict their behaviour or character on the basis of their membership in a particular group.

people stereotype an entire group of people, they do so on the basis of limited, general, or inaccurate evidence, and they frequently develop biased attitudes toward the group.[38] They fail to communicate with individuals as they really are. Instead of talking to someone of another culture as a unique human being, ethnocentric people tend to see that person as embodying the stereotypes of that culture. The individual's personal qualities become insignificant in the face of preconceptions. That person's actions, attitudes, and behaviour are forced to fit a preconceived image.

Often, both parties in an intercultural exchange are guilty of ethnocentrism, stereotyping, and prejudice. It is little wonder, then, that misunderstandings arise. Fortunately, a healthy dose of open-mindedness can prevent a lot of problems. Laraine Kaminsky and her staff at Malkam Cross-Cultural Training clearly help their clients move beyond stereotypes.

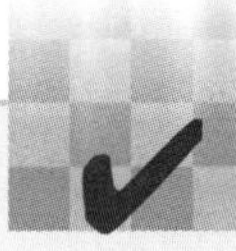

Checklist for Doing Business Abroad

A. Social Customs

1. How do people react to strangers? Are they friendly? Hostile? Reserved?
2. What words and gestures do people use to greet each other?
3. What are the appropriate manners when you enter and leave a room? Should you bow? Nod? Shake hands?
4. How are names used for introductions? How are introductions handled (by age, gender, authority)?
5. What are the attitudes toward touching people?
6. How do you express appreciation for an invitation to lunch or dinner or to someone's home? Should you bring a gift? Send flowers? Write a thank-you note?
7. Does custom dictate how, when, or where people are expected to sit in social or business situations?
8. Are any phrases, facial expressions, or hand gestures considered rude?
9. How close do people stand when talking?
10. How do you attract the attention of a waiter in a restaurant? Do you tip the waiter?
11. When is it rude to refuse an invitation? How do you politely refuse?
12. What are the acceptable eye contact patterns?
13. What gestures indicate agreement? Disagreement? Respect?
14. What topics may be discussed in a social setting? In a business setting? What topics are unacceptable?

B. Concepts of Time

1. How is time expressed?
2. What are the generally accepted working hours?
3. How do business people view scheduled appointments?
4. How do people react to time in social situations?

C. Clothing and Food

1. What occasions require special clothing? What colours are associated with mourning? With love? With joy?
2. Are some types of clothing considered taboo for one sex or the other?
   a. What is appropriate business attire for men?
   b. What is appropriate business attire for women?
3. What are the attitudes toward human body odours? Are deodorants/perfumes used?
4. How many times a day do people eat? How are hands or utensils used when eating?
5. What types of places, food, and drink are appropriate for business entertainment? Where is the seat of honour at a table?

D. Political Patterns

1. How stable is the political situation? How does its stability (or instability) affect business inside and outside the country?
2. How is political power manifested? Military power? Economic strength?
3. What are the traditional institutions of government?
4. What channels are used for expressing political opinion?
   a. What channels are used to express official government positions?
   b. What channels are used to express unofficial government positions?

Tips for Communicating with People from Other Cultures

You may never completely overcome linguistic and cultural barriers or ethnocentric tendencies, but you can communicate more effectively with people from other cultures if you work at it. Once you've acknowledged that cultural differences exist, the next step is to learn as much as possible about the cultures in which you plan to do business. You can also develop general skills for dealing with cultural diversity in your own and in other countries. If you'll be negotiating across cultures, it's important to learn how to conduct yourself and what to expect. Finally, you'll want to consider how to handle both written and oral communication with people from other cultures.

5. What media of information are important? Who controls them?
6. In social or business situations, is it appropriate to talk politics?

E. Workforce Diversity

1. Is the society homogeneous?
2. What ethnic groups are represented?
3. What languages are spoken?
4. How diverse is the workforce?
5. What are the current and projected immigration patterns? How do these trends influence the composition of the workforce?

F. Religion and Folk Beliefs

1. To which religious groups do people belong? Is one predominant?
2. How do religious beliefs influence daily activities?
3. Which places have sacred value? Which objects? Which events?
4. Is there a tolerance for minority religions?
5. How do religious holidays affect business and government activities?
6. Does religion affect attitudes toward smoking? Drinking? Gambling?
7. Does religion require or prohibit eating specific foods? At specific times?
8. What objects or actions portend good luck? Bad luck?

G. Economic and Business Institutions

1. What are the primary resources and principal products?
2. What kinds of vocational and technological training are offered?
3. What are the attitudes toward education?
   a. Do most business persons have a university degree?
   b. Are women educated as well as men?
4. Are businesses generally of one type?
   a. Are they large public corporations?
   b. Are they government owned or controlled?
   c. Are they family businesses?
5. Is it appropriate to do business by telephone? By e-mail?
6. Do managers make business decisions unilaterally, or do they involve employees?
7. Are there any customs related to exchanging business cards?
8. How are status and seniority shown in an organization? In a business meeting?
9. Are business people expected to socialize before conducting business?

H. Ethics, Values, and Laws

1. Is money or a gift expected in exchange for arranging business transactions? What are the legal, ethical, and business consequences of giving what's expected? Of not giving?
2. What ethical issues might affect business transactions?
3. What legal issues might affect business transactions?
4. Is competitiveness or cooperation of greater importance?
5. What are the attitudes toward work? Toward money?
6. Is politeness more important than factual honesty?
7. How is a *friend* defined? What are the responsibilities of a friend?
8. What virtues are admired in a business associate? In a friend?

Learning About a Culture

LEARNING OUTCOME 4
Summarize how to learn about a particular culture.

When you're preparing to do business with people from a particular culture, you'll find that you can communicate more effectively if you study that culture in advance. Before Procter & Gamble advertises a new product outside Canada and the US, company researchers thoroughly investigate what people want and need. That way, P&G marketers can shape the advertising message to the language and customs of the particular culture.

Learning as much as possible about another culture will enhance your ability to communicate with its members.

If you're planning to live in another country or to do business there repeatedly, you might want to learn the language. The same holds true if you'll be working closely with a subculture that has its own language, such as Vietnamese Canadians. Even if you're doing business in your own language, you show respect by making the effort to learn the subculture's language. In addition, you'll learn something about the culture and the customs of its people. If you don't have the time or the opportunity to learn a new language, at least learn a few words.

Learning general intercultural communication skills will help you adapt in any culture, which is important if you interact with people from a variety of cultures or subcultures.

Read books and articles about the culture and talk to people who have done business with that culture's members. Concentrate on learning something about the culture's history, religion, politics, values, and customs. Find out about a country's subcultures, especially its business subculture, and any special rules or protocol. Here is a brief sampling of intercultural communication tips from seasoned business travellers:

- In Spain let a handshake last five to seven strokes; pulling away too soon may be interpreted as rejection. In France, however, the preferred handshake is a single stroke.
- Don't give a gift of liquor in Arab countries.
- In Pakistan don't be surprised when business people excuse themselves in the middle of a meeting to conduct prayers. Muslims pray five times a day.
- Allow plenty of time to get to know the people you're dealing with in Africa; they're suspicious of people who are in a hurry.
- You'll insult your hosts if you turn down food, drink, or hospitality of any kind in Arab countries. But don't accept too quickly, either. A polite refusal (such as "I don't want to put you to any trouble") is expected before you finally accept.
- Stress the longevity of your company when dealing with German, Dutch, and Swiss firms.

These are just a few examples of the variations in customs that make intercultural business so interesting. This chapter's Checklist for Doing Business Abroad can help you start your investigation of another culture by examining its social customs, concepts of time, clothing and food, political patterns, workforce diversity, religion and folk beliefs, economic and business institutions, and its ethics, values, and laws.

Developing Intercultural Communication Skills

LEARNING OUTCOME 5
Discuss some general skills to help communicate in any culture.

Learning all you can about a particular culture is a good way to figure out how to send and receive intercultural messages effectively, but remember two important points: first, don't expect ever to understand another culture completely. No matter how much you study Italian culture, for example, you'll never be an Italian or share the experiences of having grown up in Italy. Second, don't fall into the overgeneralization trap; don't look at people stereotypically and then never move beyond that view. The trick is to learn useful general information and, at the same time, to be aware of and open to variations and individual differences.

This cultural sensitivity is especially important when you interact with people from a variety of cultures or subcultures. You may not have the time or interest to learn a lot about every culture, but you can communicate more effectively if you develop general skills that help you adapt in any culture:[39]

- *Take responsibility for communication.* Don't assume that it's the other person's job to make the communication succeed.
- *Withhold judgment.* Learn to listen to the whole story and accept differences in others without judging them.
- *Show respect.* Learn how respect is communicated–through gestures, eye contact, and so on–in various cultures.
- *Empathize.* Imagine the other person's feelings and point of view; consider what he or she is trying to communicate and why.
- *Tolerate ambiguity.* Learn to control your frustration when placed in an unfamiliar or confusing situation.
- *Look beyond the superficial.* Don't be distracted by such things as dress, appearance, or environmental discomforts.
- *Be patient and persistent.* If you want to communicate with someone from another culture, don't give up easily.
- *Recognize your own cultural biases.* Learn to identify when your assumptions are different from the other person's.
- *Be flexible.* Be prepared to change your habits and attitudes when communicating with someone from another culture.
- *Emphasize common ground.* Look for similarities from which to work.
- *Send clear messages.* Make both your verbal and nonverbal signals clear and consistent.
- *Increase your cultural sensitivity.* Learn about variations in customs and practices so that you'll be more aware of potential areas for miscommunication.
- *Deal with the individual.* Communicate with each person as an individual, not as a stereotypical representative of another group.
- *Learn when to be direct.* Investigate each culture so that you know when to send your message in a straightforward manner and when to be indirect.

Seema Narula is President and CEO of The Associates Group of Companies, a human resource and information-technology recruiting and consulting firm. The company's founder, she built the Ottawa-based business from a staff of two in 1988 to 22 in-house employees and over 225 outside consultants, with locations in Calgary, North Carolina, and India. Awarded the Businesswoman of the Year Award in 1998 by the Indo-Canadian Chamber of Commerce, she has been recognized for her business success and service to the Indo-Canadian community.

These skills will help you communicate with anybody, regardless of culture. For more ideas on how to improve communication in the workplace, see this chapter's Checklist for Communicating with a Culturally Diverse Workforce.

Negotiating Across Cultures

LEARNING OUTCOME 6
Identify some of the common sources of misunderstanding that occur when negotiating across cultures.

Whether you're trying to make a sale, buy a business, or rent an office, negotiating with people from other cultures can test your communication skills. More Canadian companies than ever are trying to form alliances with foreign companies. First, you may find that your approach to negotiation differs from the approach of the people with whom you're negotiating. For example, negotiators from Canada tend to take a relatively impersonal view of negotiations. They see their goals in economic terms and usually presume, at least at the outset, that the other party is trustworthy. In contrast, Chinese and Japanese negotiators prefer a more sociable negotiating atmosphere. They try to forge personal ties as the basis for building trust throughout the negotiating process. In their view, any immediate economic gains are less important than establishing and maintaining a long-term relationship. French negotiators are likely to be even less personal than Canadian, US, Chinese, and Japanese negotiators. They may favour an atmosphere of formal hospitality and start by distrusting the other party.[40]

Second, cultures differ in their tolerance for open disagreement. Although Canadian and US negotiators typically enjoy confrontational, debate-oriented negotiation, Japanese negotiators shun such tactics. To avoid the unpleasant feelings that might result from open conflict, Japanese companies use a go-between, or a third

People from other cultures often have different approaches to negotiation and may vary in their tolerance for open disagreement.

person, to assist in the negotiation. Chinese negotiators also try to prevent public conflict. They make concessions slowly and stay away from the technique of proposal-counterproposal. If you try to get a Chinese negotiating team to back down from a position they have taken, you will cause them to lose face—and you will very likely lose the deal.

In addition, negotiators from other cultures may use different problem-solving techniques, protocols, schedules, and decision-making methods. If you learn about your counterparts' culture before you start to negotiate, you'll be better equipped to understand their viewpoints. Moreover, showing flexibility, courtesy, patience, and a friendly attitude will go a long way toward finding a solution that works for both sides.

Handling Written Communication

Unless you are fluent in the language of your intended audience, you will ordinarily write in your own language and, if needed, have your letters or other written materials translated by a professional translator. Be especially concerned with clarity:

- Use short, precise words that say exactly what you mean.
- Rely on specific terms and concrete examples to explain your points.
- Stay away from slang, idioms, jargon, and buzz words. Abbreviations, acronyms (such as CAD/CAM), and unfamiliar product names may also lead to confusion.
- Construct sentences that are shorter and simpler than those you might use when writing to someone fluent in your own language.
- Use short paragraphs. Each paragraph should stick to one topic and should be no more than eight to ten lines.
- Help readers follow your train of thought by using transitional phrases. Precede related points with expressions such as *in addition* and *first, second, third.*

Checklist for Communicating with a Culturally Diverse Workforce

A. Accepting Cultural Differences

1. Adjust the level of communication to the education level of your employees.
2. Encourage employees to openly discuss their culture's customs so that differences won't seem strange or inexplicable.
3. Create a formal forum in which all employees can become familiar with the specific beliefs and practices of the cultures represented in the company workforce.
4. Provide training to help employees recognize and overcome ethnocentric reactions and stereotyping.
5. Make available books, articles, and videotapes about various cultures so interested employees can learn more.
6. Help stamp out negative or stereotyped labels by paying attention to how people identify their own groups.

B. Handling Oral and Written Communications

1. Define and explain key terms people will need to know on the job.
2. Repeat and summarize information frequently to emphasize important points.
3. Use familiar words whenever possible.
4. Don't cover too much information at one time.
5. Be specific and explicit, using descriptive words, exact measurements, and examples when possible.
6. Give the reason for asking employees to follow a certain procedure and explain what will happen if the procedure is not followed.
7. Use written summaries and visual aids (when appropriate) to clarify your points.
   a. Give employees written information they can take away to go over later.
   b. Use pictures that show actions (especially when explaining safety procedures).
   c. Use international symbols (such as ∅), which are understood cross-culturally.

Your word choice should also reflect the relationship between you and your audience. In general, Canadian business people will want to be somewhat more formal than they would be when writing to people in their own country. In many cultures, people use a more elaborate style, so your audience will expect more formal language in your letter. Consider the letter in Figure 3.2. It might sound stilted to a Canadian reader, but it is typical of business letters in many other countries. In Germany, business letters usually open with a reference to the business relationship and close with a compliment to the recipient. Of course, be careful not to carry formality to extremes, or you'll sound unnatural.

International business letters generally have a formal tone and a relatively elaborate style.

Letter writers in other countries also use various techniques to organize their thoughts. If you are aware of some of their practices, you'll be able to concentrate on the message without passing judgment on the writers. Letters from Japanese business people, for example, are slow to come to the point. They typically begin with a remark about the season or weather. This is followed by an inquiry about your health or congratulations on your success. A note of thanks for your patronage might come next. After these preliminaries, the main idea is introduced.

Handling Oral Communication

LEARNING OUTCOME 7
Explain the importance of speaking and listening effectively when communicating face to face with people from other cultures.

Some transactions simply cannot be handled without face-to-face contact. In many countries, business relationships are based on personal relationships–until you establish rapport nothing happens. In addition, personal contact gives you the benefit of immediate feedback so you can clarify your own message as well as the other person's. As a consequence, executives in charge of international operations often have a hectic travel schedule. When a Procter & Gamble CEO was head of the international division, he spent nearly 70 percent of his time meeting with managers and high-level contacts in other countries.[41]

Face-to-face communication lets you establish a personal relationship with people from other cultures and gives you the benefit of immediate feedback.

d. Augment written material with video presentations to make the material come alive.

8. Demonstrate and encourage the right way to complete a task, use a tool, and so on.
9. Reduce barriers caused by language differences.
   a. Offer managers training in the language of the employees they supervise.
   b. Offer employees training in the language that most people in the company (and customers) use.
   c. Ask bilingual employees and managers to serve as translators when needed, but rotate this assignment to avoid resentment.
   d. Recruit bilingual employees and managers or have trained translators available to give the organization greater flexibility in dealing with linguistic differences.
   e. Print important health and safety instructions in as many languages as needed to enable all employees to understand them.

C. Assessing How Well You've Been Understood

1. Be alert to facial expressions and other nonverbal signs that indicate confusion or embarrassment.
2. Encourage employees to ask questions in private and in writing.
3. Observe how employees use the information you've provided to do their jobs, and review any points that may have been misunderstood.
4. Research the nonverbal reactions of other cultures so you're prepared to spot subtle signs of misunderstanding.

D. Offering Feedback to Improve Communication

1. Focus on the positive by explaining what *should* be done rather than on the negative by discussing what *shouldn't* be done.
2. Offer feedback in terms of the person's behaviours and the situation, rather than a judgment about the person.
3. Be supportive as you offer feedback, and reassure individuals that their skills and contributions are important.

Herrn
Karl Wieland
Geschäftsführer
Schwarzwald-Geschenke
Friedrichstraße 98

70174 Stuttgart
GERMANY

15. Mai 2001

Sehr geehrter Herr Wieland,

Da die Touristensaison bald beginnt, möchten wir die Gelegenheit ergreifen, Ihnen unsere neue Reihe handgeschnitzter Kuckucksuhren vorzustellen. Im letzten Jahr waren Sie so freundlich, zwei Dutzend unserer Uhren zu kaufen. In Anerkennung unserer guten Geschäftsbeziehugen bieten wir Ihnen nunmehr die Möglichkeit, die neuen Modelle auszuwählen, bevor wir diese Reihe anderen Geschäften zum Kauf anbieten.

Wie Sie wissen, verwenden unsere Kunsthandwerker nur das beste Holz. Nach altbewährten Mustern, die von Generation zu Generation weitergereicht werden, schnitzen sie sorgfältig jedes Detail von Hand. Unsere Uhrwerke sind von hervorragender Qualität, und wir testen jede Uhr, bevor sie bemalt und versandt wird. Auf alle Furtwangener Kunsthandwerk-Uhren geben wir eine Garantie von 5 Jahren.

Beiliegend erhalten Sie eine Ausgabe unserer neuesten Broschüre und ein Bestellformular. Um unserer Wertschätzung Ausdruck zu verleihen, übernehmen wir die Versandkosten, wenn Sie vor dem 15, Juni bestellen.

Wir wünschen Ihnen weiterhin viel Erfolg in Ihrer neuen Stuttgarter Niederlassung. Wir sind davon überzeugt, daß Sie mit Ihrer größeren Ausstellungsfläche und erweitertem Angebot Ihre Stammkunden zufriedenstellen werden und viele neue Besucher gewinnen werden.

Mit freundlichen Grüßen

Frederick Semper

Frederick Semper

FIGURE 3.2

In-Depth Critique: German Business Letter, with Translation

This letter was written by a supplier in Germany to a nearby retailer. The tone is more formal than would be used in Canada, but the writer clearly focuses on his audience.

When using oral communication, be alert to the possibilities for misunderstanding. Recognize that you may inadvertently be sending conflicting signals or that you may be misreading the other person's cues. To help overcome language and cultural barriers, follow these suggestions:

- Try to be aware of unintentional meanings that may be read into your message. Clarify your true intent with repetition and examples.
- Listen carefully and patiently. If you do not understand a comment, ask the person to repeat it.

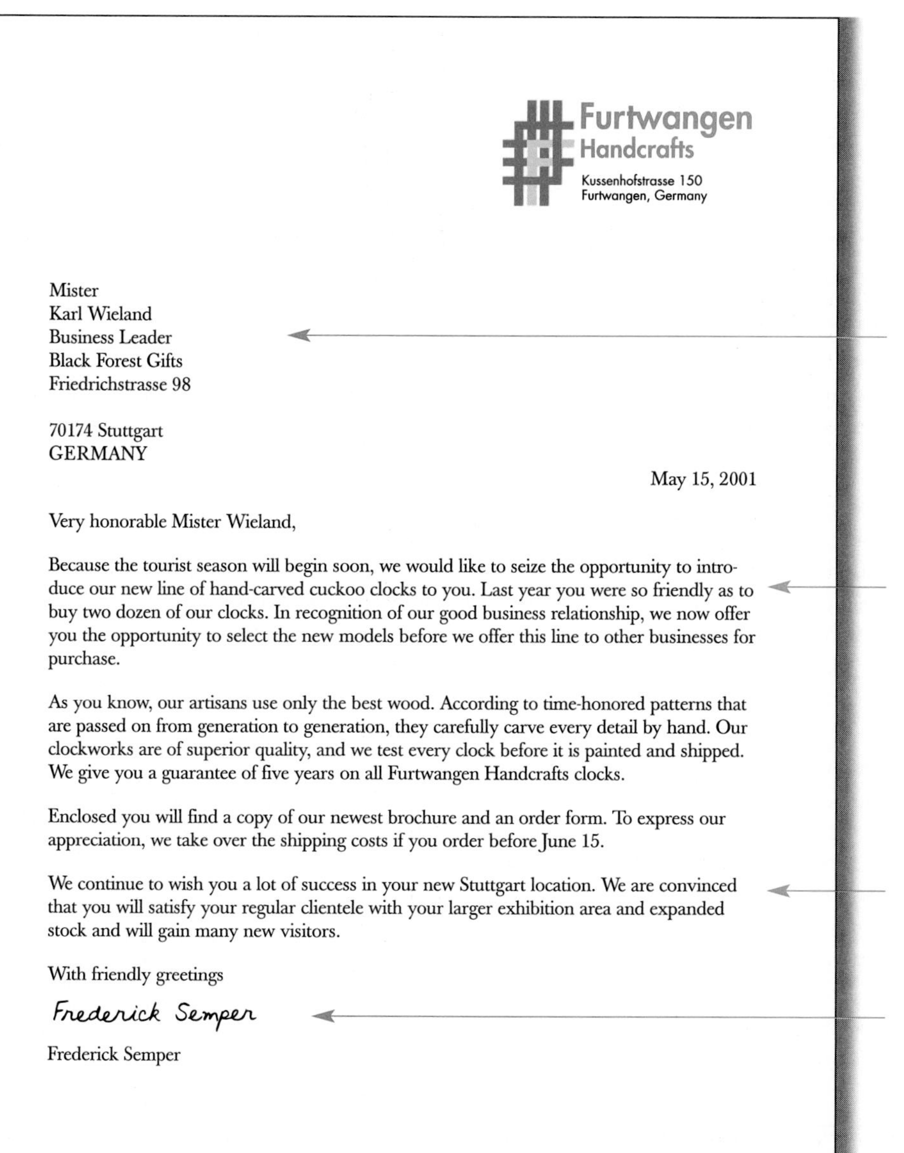

Mister
Karl Wieland
Business Leader
Black Forest Gifts
Friedrichstrasse 98

70174 Stuttgart
GERMANY

May 15, 2001

Very honorable Mister Wieland,

Because the tourist season will begin soon, we would like to seize the opportunity to introduce our new line of hand-carved cuckoo clocks to you. Last year you were so friendly as to buy two dozen of our clocks. In recognition of our good business relationship, we now offer you the opportunity to select the new models before we offer this line to other businesses for purchase.

As you know, our artisans use only the best wood. According to time-honored patterns that are passed on from generation to generation, they carefully carve every detail by hand. Our clockworks are of superior quality, and we test every clock before it is painted and shipped. We give you a guarantee of five years on all Furtwangen Handcrafts clocks.

Enclosed you will find a copy of our newest brochure and an order form. To express our appreciation, we take over the shipping costs if you order before June 15.

We continue to wish you a lot of success in your new Stuttgart location. We are convinced that you will satisfy your regular clientele with your larger exhibition area and expanded stock and will gain many new visitors.

With friendly greetings

Frederick Semper

Frederick Semper

The addressee's title, Geschäftsführer, literally means "business leader": A common English translation would be "managing director."

By offering the retailer an early selection of products, a five-year guarantee, and free shipping costs for an early order, Herr Semper shows his concern for his audience.

The closing compliment is typical of German business letters.

Also note that, in German business letters, the sender's title is not included under the typed name on the closing block.

FIGURE 3.2
continued

- ➤ Recognize that gestures and expressions mean different things in different cultures. If the other person's body language seems at odds with the message, take time to clarify the meaning.
- ➤ Adapt your conversation style to the other person's. Whether the other person appears to be direct and straightforward or indirect and oblique, adjust your style to match.
- ➤ At the end of a conversation, be sure that you and the other person agree on what has been said and decided. Clarify what will happen next.
- ➤ If appropriate, follow up by writing a letter or memo summarizing the conversation and thanking the person for meeting with you.

In short, take advantage of the other person's presence to make sure that your message is getting across and that you understand his or her message too.

USING THE POWER OF TECHNOLOGY

Communicating with a Global Audience on the Web

As access to the World Wide Web grows, Canadian companies can promote their products and services globally. But, reaching an international audience on the Web involves more than simply offering translations of English and French. Successful global sites address the needs of international customers in five ways:

1. ***Consider the reader's viewpoint.*** Assume your audience is unfamiliar with common Canadian phrases and references. To avoid confusion, use universal terms for times, dates, and geographical names. For example, consider expressing time in military format ("16:00" for 4 p.m.). Since Europeans read "10/04/2001" as April 10, 2001, be sure you spell out the month and year. And offer complete locations, such as "Halifax, Nova Scotia, Canada."
2. ***Be sensitive to cultural differences.*** Since humour is rooted in cultural norms, a touch of Canadian humour may not be funny to Asian or European readers. Don't risk offending or slighting your audience with cultural stereotypes or expressions. Avoid idioms and references that aren't universally recognized, such as "putting all your eggs in one basket" or "jumping out of the frying pan into the fire."
3. ***Keep the message clear.*** Use simple words and write in the active voice. Avoid complicated sentence structure to achieve a simple, straightforward tone. And don't forget to define abbreviations and acronyms.
4. ***Break through language barriers with graphics.*** Clarify written concepts with graphics. However, even though most graphical icons are internationally recognized, some images are more widely accepted than others. In some countries, for example, a mailbox doesn't necessarily convey the idea of sending mail. So an envelope might be a more appropriate symbol to reinforce the message, "Contact us."
5. ***Consult local experts.*** Work with local experts and webmasters to develop native-language keywords that will direct international customers to your site. Also seek the advice of local experts about customary phrases and references. Even simple terms like "home page" differ from country to country. Spanish readers refer to the "first page," or "pagina inicial."

CAREER APPLICATIONS

1. Visit the World of Sony Music Entertainment on the Web at **www.sonymusic.com/world** and examine Sony's sites for Argentina, France, and Germany. How does Sony "localize" each country's site?
2. Compare Sony Music's international sites to IBM's global Web pages at **www.ibm.com**. How does Sony's approach differ from IBM's? Do both corporations successfully address the needs of a global audience? Write a two-paragraph summary that compares the international sites of both companies.

Sources: Laura Morelli, "Writing for a Global Audience on the Web," *Marketing News*, 17 August 1998, 16; Yuri and Anna Radzievsky, "Successful Global Web Sites Look Through Eyes of the Audience," *Advertising Age's Business Marketing*, January 1998, 17; Sari Kalin, "The Importance of Being Multiculturally Correct," *Computerworld*, 6 October 1997, G16–G17; and B.G. Yovovich, "Making Sense of All the Web's Numbers," *Editor & Publisher*, November 1998, 30–31.

ON THE JOB
Solving a Communication Dilemma at Malkam Cross-Cultural Training

Malkam Cross-Cultural Training provides diversity, cultural awareness, and language training services to individual and corporate clients. Their diversity training program, for example, teaches how culture may affect decisions and communication in the workplace. Their communication seminars help employees at all levels to improve their written, oral, and behavioural skills when dealing with people from other cultures.

Malkam's cultural awareness program educates organizations about etiquette and protocols when dealing with business people from different cultures, abroad or at home, and provides insight into different communication styles. Malkam also trains managers and executives to negotiate effectively with different cultures, teaching them about a host country's specific negotiating style and providing strategies that can help a Canadian firm conclude a contract successfully with their foreign counterpart. Furthermore, Malkam assists companies in developing strategies to settle intercultural conflicts by teaching employees about gender and psychological factors of other cultures.

Malkam's language training programs for non-native speakers of English help them develop their written and oral skills. The staff offers group and individual programs in effective business writing style, mastering the mechanics of English, and speaking idiomatically and confidently.

Malkam works with government, industry, banking and finance, small businesses and major corporations, so they can take advantage of growing opportunities in the global marketplace. Their facilities include up-to-date language laboratories, several classrooms, as well as a supervised on-site daycare and an employment opportunity program to assist newcomers to Canada while they study with Malkam's specialists.[42]

Your Mission: Imagine you are a trainer at Malkam Consultants working with a variety of classes: one is composed of newcomers who are learning English and about Canadian ways, another is made up of managers who will be travelling abroad for business. You want to foster cooperation among your students and encourage them to interact effectively with each other. Use your skill in intercultural communication to choose the best response in each of the following situations. Be prepared to explain why your choice is best.

1. It's important that students in your class for English as a second language develop their ability in speaking conversational English. How do you accomplish this?
   a. You have each student prepare at least two presentations in English on aspects of their culture that they will deliver to the class.
   b. From time to time you take the class to a coffee shop and have them order food in English and speak English while they are there.
   c. You pair off students and have them prepare scenarios in English, such as job interviews, to present in front of the class.
   d. From time to time you invite the class to your home where you lead conversations in English.

2. One of your students is having trouble following the instructions for using the audiotape machine in the language laboratory. It is obvious to you that she does not understand the instructions, even though she insists she does. How do you help her?
   a. You have her memorize the instructions and have her recite them to you.
   b. You ask a student who speaks her language to help her through the instructions.
   c. You repeat the instructions several times in front to the entire class.
   d. You demonstrate how the machine is used and have her repeat the process until she is able to operate it easily.

3. Several of your students in your class for English as a second language do not make eye contact when delivering speeches because in their cultures it is considered rude to make eye contact when speaking to other people. How do you persuade them to look at the audience?
   a. You gently encourage the students to make eye contact. You explain that in Canada it is common for business people to make eye contact when giving a presentation, and that people who don't are not considered effective speakers.
   b. You don't discuss the issue with the students at all and let them avoid making eye contact. You believe they will understand the importance of eye contact when they give presentations in their jobs in Canada.
   c. You show videos about making effective presentations, hoping the students will be encouraged to make eye contact after watching them.
   d. You set up team presentations, creating teams with students who are comfortable making eye contact with the audience and those who are not. You expect that while these teams rehearse their presentations, students who avoid looking at the audience will be persuaded to make eye contact after working with peers who do.

4. Your students are breaking into ethnically based cliques. Members of ethnic groups eat together, socialize together, and chat in their native language while they are together. Some other students feel left out and alienated. How do you encourage a unified class attitude?
   a. Ban the use of languages other than English in class.
   b. Do nothing. This is normal behaviour.
   c. Encourage people to mingle and get to know each other better.
   d. Send all of your students to diversity training classes.

TAP Your Knowledge

Summary of Learning Outcomes

1. Outline the two trends that have made intercultural business communication so important. Advances in communication and transportation, such as the Internet, e-mail, and overnight delivery services, have helped businesses to find new customers and establish new partnerships with companies worldwide. Because of these advances, many businesses report that a large part of their sales come from exports. The growth of a culturally diverse workforce is another trend that has made intercultural business communication vital. In all workplaces in Canada today, staff deal with language and cultural barriers that may interfere with the exchange of messages.

2. Define culture and intercultural communication. Culture is a shared system of symbols, beliefs, attitudes, values, expectations, and norms for behaviour. All members of a culture have similar assumptions about how people should think, behave, and communicate, and they all tend to act on those assumptions. Intercultural communication is the process of sending and receiving messages between people of different cultures.

3. Discuss at least four of the nine ways people can differ culturally. (1) By holding different social values, people can differ culturally. For example, Canadians value a diverse population, honesty and fairness, the country's bilingual culture, Aboriginal peoples, and conservation of the environment. (2) The roles people play and concepts of status also create cultural differences. For example, in Canada and the United States women play a prominent role in business; in other countries, women may not play a significant part in an organization. Concepts of status also differ culturally. In Canada, materialistic values, such as well-appointed private offices for executives, may signal their rank in an organization. In France, however, high-ranking managers may have their desks in the middle of an open area, surrounded by lower-level employees. (3) Decision-making customs also differ between cultures. In Canada and the United States, business people prefer to reach decisions quickly. In Latin America, people prefer to make their deals slowly, after much discussion. (4) Body language is another mark of different cultural behaviour, and mannerisms common to one culture may be misinterpreted by another. Canadian business people tend to believe that a lack of eye contact signals evasiveness and dishonesty. In many Latin American and Asian cultures, keeping one's eyes lowered is a sign of respect.

4. Summarize how to learn about a particular culture. You can learn about another culture by learning the language, reading books and articles and talking to people who have done business with that culture's members.

5. Discuss some general skills to help communicate in any culture. One skill to help you communicate across cultures is to take responsibility for communication–don't rely on the other person to make the communication succeed. Also show respect, and learn how it is communicated. Look beyond the superficial–avoid being distracted by dress and appearance. Recognize your own cultural biases, and be flexible by identifying when your assumptions are different from the other person's.

6. Identify some of the common sources of misunderstanding that occur when negotiating across cultures. One source of misunderstanding is the different approaches taken to negotiating. Canadian business people tend to take an impersonal view of negotiations, whereas Chinese and Japanese negotiators prefer a more sociable atmosphere. Cultures also differ in their tolerance for open disagreement when negotiating. Although Canadians may enjoy debate-oriented negotiation, the Japanese shun such tactics.

7. Explain the importance of speaking and listening effectively when communicating face to face with people from other cultures. Some transactions cannot take place without face-to-face communication. Speaking and listening effectively encourages clear feedback and demonstrate your respect of the other person.

Test Your Knowledge

Review Questions

1. Distinguish between high-context and low-context cultures and give examples of each.
2. Give three examples of language barriers and discuss why it is important to recognize them.
3. What are four barriers to written communication across cultures?
4. Discuss methods of improving oral communication across cultures.
5. Define stereotyping. How can it impact on cross-cultural communication?
6. How can you improve your written communications to people of other cultures?

Apply Your Knowledge

Critical Thinking Questions

1. Your office in another country desperately needs the supplies that have been sitting in Turkish customs for a month. Should you bribe a customs official to speed up delivery? Explain.
2. What actions might you take to minimize the potential problems of differing concepts of time between your office in Calgary and your office in Venezuela?
3. A Canadian retail chain is opening a new store in Tijuana, Mexico (a border city south of San Diego, California). What cultural differences might this retailer's managers encounter when they start to hire and train local employees?
4. Your company has relocated to a US city where a Vietnamese subculture is strongly established. Many of your employees will be from this subculture. What can you do to ensure effective communication between your management and the Vietnamese Americans you are currently hiring?
5. What are some of the intercultural communication issues to consider when deciding whether to accept an overseas job with a firm that's based in your own country? A job in your own country with a local branch of a foreign-owned firm? Explain.
6. How do you think company managers from a country that has a relatively homogeneous culture might react when they have to do business with the culturally diverse staff of a company in a less homogeneous country? Explain your answer.

Practise Your Knowledge

Exercises

1. A Canadian manager wants to export T-shirts to another country, but an official expects a special payment before allowing the shipment into his country. How can the two sides resolve their different approaches without violating Canadian rules against bribing foreign officials? Team up with a classmate to role-play a meeting in which the Canadian manager tries to convince the official to authorize the shipment without being paid. Then discuss how the two parties handled their cultural differences.
2. You've been assigned to host a group of Swedish university students who are visiting your university for the next two weeks. They've all studied English and speak the language well. What can you tell them that will help them fit into the culture on your campus? Make a brief list of the important formal and informal behavioural rules they should understand to communicate effectively with students on your campus. Next to each item, note one problem that might occur if the Swedish visitors don't consider that rule when communicating.
3. Choose a specific country, such as India, Portugal, Bolivia, Thailand, or Nigeria–the less familiar you are with it, the better. Research the culture and write a brief summary of what a Canadian manager would need to know about concepts of personal space and rules of social behaviour to conduct business successfully in that country.
4. As the director of marketing for a telecommunications firm based in Germany, you're negotiating with an official in Guangzhou, China, who's in charge of selecting a new telephone system for the city. You insist that the specifications be spelled out in detail in the contract. However, your Chinese counterpart argues that in developing a long-term business relationship, such minor details are unimportant. What can you do or say to break this intercultural deadlock and obtain the contract without causing the official to lose face?

5. Although English is the international language of business, the English spoken in Canada differs from that spoken in Australia. By going to the library or interviewing someone who has lived in Australia, research five specific phrases that have different meanings in these two cultures. What problems would you have if you were unaware of the different meanings and misinterpreted these phrases during a business conversation?
6. Germany is a low-context culture; by comparison, France and England are more high-context. These three translations of the same message were posted on a lawn in Switzerland: the German sign read, "Walking on the grass is forbidden"; the English sign read, "Please do not walk on the grass"; and the French sign read, "Those who respect their environment will avoid walking on the grass."[43] How does the language of each sign reflect the way information is conveyed in the cultural context of each nation? Write a brief (two- to three-paragraph) explanation.
7. Team up with two other students and list ten examples of slang or idiom (in your own language) that would probably be misinterpreted or misunderstood during a business conversation with someone from another culture. Next to each example, suggest other words you might use to convey the same message. Do the alternatives mean *exactly* the same as the original slang or idiom?
8. Differences in gender, age, and physical abilities contribute to the diversity of today's workforce. Working with a classmate, role-play a conversation in which:
   a. A woman is being interviewed for a job by a male human resources manager
   b. An older person is being interviewed for a job by a younger human resources manager
   c. A person who uses a wheelchair is being interviewed for a job by a person who can walk.

   How did differences between the applicant and the interviewer shape the communication? What can you do to improve communication in such situations?
9. Imagine that you're the lead negotiator for a company that's trying to buy a factory in Prague. Your parents grew up near Prague and speak Czech at home, so you understand and speak the language fairly well. However, you wonder about the advantages and disadvantages of using a translator anyway. For example, you may have more time to think if you wait for an intermediary to translate the other side's position. Decide whether to hire a translator, and then write a brief (two- to three-paragraph) explanation of your decision.
10. What communication problems would you face if you had to defend yourself in court in another country but didn't understand the language or the legal traditions? If you were assigned a translator, how might this additional person affect the communication process? Explain.
11. Suppose you transferred to a university in another country. How would you learn appropriate classroom behaviour? Make a list of what you would need to know. For example, you might want to find out how to approach your professors when you have questions. To get the answers to these questions, draft a letter to a university student in another nation.
12. Choose two countries from the following list: Argentina, Belgium, Cuba, Egypt, Japan, Korea, Indonesia, Malaysia, Vietnam, Zimbabwe. On the World Wide Web, read about three cultural or business aspects of each country, and then (in not more than 500 words) explain (a) why it's important to understand those aspects when communicating in your chosen country, (b) how computers and other electronic technology can help such intercultural communication, and (c) how computers and other electronic technology can hinder such intercultural communication. To locate information on the World Wide Web, start your search at **globaldirekt.com**. The site provides direct access to various search engines, and is arranged geographically.
13. When a company knows that a scheduled delivery time given by an overseas firm is likely to be flexible, managers may buy in larger quantities or may order more often to avoid running out of product before the next delivery. Identify three other management decisions that may be influenced by differing cultural concepts of time, and make notes for a short (two-minute) presentation to your class.

Developing Your Internet Skills

Going Online: Mastering the Art of Intercultural Communication, p. 53

Your manager has asked you to write up an information sheet for an executive who is going abroad to conduct business. Using a country of your choice, go to **www.brint.com/International.htm** and employ the various links to find information that would be useful to the executive.

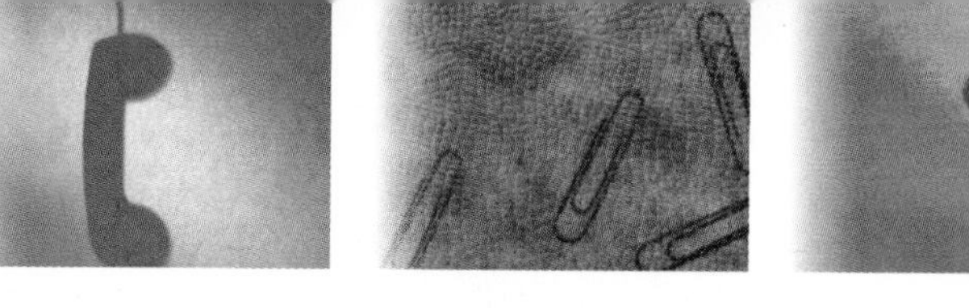

CHAPTER 4

Communicating Through Technology

AFTER STUDYING THIS CHAPTER, YOU WILL BE ABLE TO

1. Describe the technological tools now available for creating printed documents
2. Discuss the internal and external databases used in business research
3. Judge the benefits and limitations of spell checkers and grammar checkers
4. Explore the communication role of electronic mail and Internet technologies in today's business organizations
5. Describe the technologies available for group communication
6. Assess the ways technology is changing business communication

ON THE JOB
Facing a Communication Dilemma at Hewlett-Packard

From Trauma to Triumph, One Step at a Time

Hewlett-Packard (HP) relies on communication to keep the company operating smoothly. With more than 85 400 employees in dozens of divisions and hundreds of sales and support centres worldwide, including 1300 workers in 21 locations across Canada, Hewlett-Packard needs to keep in touch. New communication technologies make it possible for people on opposite sides of the globe to work together almost as easily as people sitting in adjoining cubicles. Technology like this is changing the workplace, requiring a new way of thinking about work.

Technology helps Hewlett-Packard employees communicate with speed and convenience. HP employees understand that besides adapting to evolving electronics, they need good writing and speaking skills now more than ever.

Systems technology specialists at HP spend a lot of their time looking at business processes to decide how they can be redesigned (or re-engineered) for greater efficiency. That often means helping the company "reinvent the way it does business," says Mike Stevens, who has spent part of his HP career as a systems technology expert. It also means using good communication skills to coordinate interaction with co-workers.

Even though it's relatively easy for specialists like Stevens to use technology in their own jobs, they must also help others to adapt to changes in the communication processes and the technology they must use. It's a delicate situation: Some people enjoy change (particularly at a fast-moving company like HP); others are reluctant to give up methods that have been successful in the past. In order to communicate clearly and effectively with co-workers outside of their team, Stevens and his fellow specialists must first communicate well with each other.

If you were Mike Stevens, what steps would you take to help other employees understand and adapt to changing processes? How would you use technology to improve communication with your team members and other HP employees who rely on you for help?[1]

Technology in Contemporary Business Communication

As Hewlett-Packard and other companies try to compete in the global economy, they are always looking for better ways to communicate. Business people such as HP's Mike Stevens must choose from an ever-expanding list of communication tools to remain competitive. You'll probably use most of the technologies discussed in this chapter, as well as future innovations we can only dream about right now. The better you understand the technological issues involved, the more effective you'll be as a communicator.

In business communication today, you not only have to think about what you're going to say and how you're going to say it; you also have to decide which technological tools you'll use to do so. No hard rules dictate which tool to use in each case (partly because the technology keeps changing), but here are some factors to consider:

- *Audience expectations.* How would you like your university to deliver your degree by fax machine? It would seem a little strange, wouldn't it? You expect your school to use a certain set of technologies (such as mail delivery or a phone-in system). Business audiences have similar expectations for various kinds of messages. Knowing what people expect is part of getting to know your audience.

- *Time and cost.* Time is often the biggest factor in your technology choice. You'd probably choose the phone to send an urgent message, for instance. Many of the technologies discussed in this chapter were designed specifically to help people communicate faster, but cost can be an issue as well, both how much you have to spend and how much is appropriate for the situation. Spending $500 to create a presentation for customers might be appropriate, but spending that much to tell your colleagues when you'll be on vacation would be wasteful.
- *Nature of the message.* What you need to say in a document also affects your choice of technologies. For instance, business messages often require some sort of visual support (diagrams, photographs, or tables). A telephone call wouldn't be a good choice in such cases, but a printed report would be. If you need to convey emotion and excitement, delivering your message in person might be best. However, if you can't visit every member of your audience, sending your message on videotape might be a good substitute.
- *Presentation needs.* Sometimes the way you need to present your document will dictate which tools you use. If you're sending a report to an important client, you might want to stretch your budget to use a commercial printer, colour graphics, and professional binding. For short internal messages, however, you probably would not want to spend that amount of time or money.
- *Work environment.* One of the most significant communication advances in recent years is the dramatically improved quality and availability of portable tools for creating, sending, and receiving messages. Millions of business people spend some or all of their time outside traditional office settings, working from their cars, homes, hotel rooms, or other locations. Well-equipped "road warriors" can now communicate with as much convenience and impact as their deskbound colleagues.

General guidelines for choosing communication technology include considering
- ✧ Audience expectations
- ✧ Time and cost
- ✧ Nature of the message
- ✧ Presentation needs
- ✧ Work environment

Some tools can create more than one type of message or document. Likewise, you may have two or three technological options when it comes to one particular message or document. The trick is to pick the tool that does the best overall job in each situation.

Technology in Written Communication

LEARNING OUTCOME 1
Describe the technological tools now available for creating printed documents.

When preparing written documents, you can take advantage of technological developments at every step. You're probably familiar with some of them, but others are just now starting to appear. In business communication, a variety of tools can help you create both printed and electronic documents.

Creating Printed Documents

The most common means for creating printed documents is word-processing software.

Whether you're writing a one-paragraph memo or a 500-page report, technology can help you create an effective document quickly and efficiently. Some of these tools apply only to printed documents, but others can help you with electronic documents as well. **Word-processing software** is the dominant tool for creating printed documents, and it can do far more than you could ever attempt on a typewriter. If two or more people are developing a single document, they can use a category of software known as **groupware**. These systems keep track of revisions, let people attach electronic notes to one another's sections, enforce a common format for all sections, and take care of other issues that come up in any collaborative writing project. Groupware can include a variety of computing and communication tools to help people work together.[2]

The tool most appropriate for assembling finished pages with graphics elements is desktop publishing (DTP) software.

In the same way that word-processing software was created to computerize typewriters, **desktop publishing (DTP)** software was created to computerize the process of assembling finished pages. If you wanted a first-class report with photos and drawings, the old way of doing things involved cutting strips of printed text and pasting them onto a blank page along with the photos and drawings. Desktop publishing software does the same thing, only it all happens on your computer screen. Word processing and DTP are the core technologies for creating printed documents, and you can take advantage of a growing selection of specialized tools as well. The following sections present a brief overview of document creation to give you a better idea of how the various pieces of hardware and software can help you with planning, composing, revising, producing, printing, and distributing documents.

PLANNING DOCUMENTS

Some of the writing you'll do on the job requires very little planning. For a memo to your staff regarding the company picnic or a letter requesting information from a supplier, you can often collect a few facts and get right down to writing. In other cases, however, you won't be able to start writing until you've done extensive research. This research often covers both the audience you'll be writing to and the subject matter you'll be writing about. Technology can help you with planning tasks, with research tasks, and with outlining your thoughts once you've done your research.

Technology helps you manage communication with

- ✧ Contact managers
- ✧ Personal information managers
- ✧ Project management software

Managing Communication Projects Some computer software can actually help you plan and manage communication projects. These tools fall into three general (sometimes overlapping) categories. First, **contact managers** help you maintain communication with a large number of people. They store information about the people you need to contact (names, addresses, product preferences, and so on) and help to automate many tasks, such as generating follow-up letters after you've spoken with someone on the phone. Second, **personal information managers (PIMs)** help you manage all kinds of information, from to-do lists to document outlines to e-mail messages. Personal information managers are similar in some ways to contact managers, but they are generally much more powerful when it comes to managing, sorting, and storing information. Third, **project management software** helps you plan and coordinate the activities needed to complete projects, and it helps you communicate with others regarding project status.

LEARNING OUTCOME 2
Discuss the internal and external databases used in business research.

Researching Audience and Content Sometimes the information you need for a document can be found inside your company, in its sales records, existing research reports, and other *internal sources*. At other times, the information you need will be found outside the company, in books, magazines, and other *external sources*. Technology can help in both cases.

Much of your company's internal information may be stored in one or more **databases,** which are collections of facts ranging from financial figures to the text of reports. For information on sales trends, you might use a computer to search through your company's sales records. You can use **spreadsheets** or **statistical analysis software** to sort through numerical data and **text retrieval software** to sort through reports and other textual material.

Research is often one of the most important steps in business communication, and technology provides several helpful tools, including

- ✧ Online databases, both private and public
- ✧ Statistical analysis software
- ✧ Text retrieval software
- ✧ Web sites
- ✧ CD-ROM information sources

The list of external sources of business information is long and is getting longer all the time. If you need some data on the Canadian economy, you can tap into Statistics Canada's Web site. If you need to see whether Parliament passed any tax laws in the last week that might affect your company, you can try accessing *The Tax Page*, which explains many recent government taxation actions.[3] These and thousands of other databases, on topics ranging from accounting to zoology, are available to anyone with a properly equipped computer–although usually for a fee. By using commercial online services or the Internet, you can access a huge number of databases and even the catalogues in many academic libraries around the world.

Another useful research tool is the **CD-ROM** (compact disc–read only memory), a type of compact disc that can be read by a computer's CD drive. An individual CD-ROM can contain either a single volume of information or collections of documents ranging from back files of newspapers to sets of books on a particular subject. For example, Microsoft *Encarta* is a multimedia encyclopedia that contains not only textual information but also animated drawings, short video clips, and audio tracks.[4]

From his purchase of Canada's first FM station CHFI-FM in 1962, Ted Rogers built Rogers Communications into a telecommunications and media powerhouse. A true pioneer in the communications industry, Ted Rogers focused on developing technologies to make his company a leader in wireless communication, mass media, high-speed Internet service, and retail video stores. Designated a "Caring Company" by the Canadian Centre for Philanthropy, Rogers Communications supports numerous Canadian charities.

Outlining Content Once you've collected the necessary information for your report, the next step is to create an outline, which will help you give order to your ideas. You've probably created outlines for reports, possibly using note cards to arrange and sort the various sections. The outlining feature found in word-processing software performs the same functions you did manually, but much more efficiently. You can quickly move sections around and easily experiment with order and organization. Electronic outlining further boosts your productivity because you can copy and paste section titles from the outline into the text of a presentation or report. If you want to look at outlining tools that are more specialized than the one found in your word-processing software, try a product called Inspiration. This tool lets you outline and organize ideas visually by moving and connecting blocks and arrows that represent a flow of ideas.[5]

COMPOSING DOCUMENTS

When you're ready to start writing, the computer once again demonstrates how it can enhance the communication process. Composing a document on your computer involves keyboarding, of course, but that's just the beginning. Technology offers a number of ways to get text into your document, and you're no longer limited to just text, either. The right software makes it relatively easy to add a wide variety of graphic elements to your document, and even audio notes if you have the right equipment.

Technology provides several options for entering text into a document:
- ✧ Keyboarding (typing)
- ✧ Digital notepads
- ✧ Voice recognition systems
- ✧ Scanning and OCR

Entering Text Composing means sitting at the keyboard and typing. Word processors help make this task as painless as possible, by enabling you to erase and move text easily. The fact that you're on a computer, however, opens up some interesting possibilities for text entry.

To start with, if you don't know how to keyboard or don't like to, you can try **digital notepads**. Using a digital pen, you write on regular paper. The pen saves your handwritten notes and transfers them into the computer. Once in the computer, your notes can be handled like any computerized text: they can be organized, searched, attached to e-mail messages or inserted into presentations. Digital notepads are most commonly used by business people who travel and need an easy way to record and save information.

With some computers, you don't have to write or type at all. **Voice recognition systems**, which convert your voice to text, free you from keyboard or pen input. Such breakthroughs are particularly important for people with physical impairments, giving them the means to become more active communicators.

A boilerplate is any standard block of text used in various documents without being changed.

Some of the text that business communicators use in their documents is prewritten; it already appears in other documents. Say that you want to announce to the media that you've developed a new product or hired an executive. Such announcements are called press releases, and they usually end with a standard paragraph about the company and its line of business. Any standard block of text used in various documents without being changed is called a **boilerplate**. With a good word processor, you don't have to retype the boilerplate each time you write a press release. You simply store the paragraph the first time you write it and then copy it into a document whenever you need it. Not only does this save time, it also reduces mistakes, because you're not retyping the paragraph every time you use it. A related concept applies to manipulating existing text. If you're a national sales manager compiling a report that includes summaries from your four regional managers, you can use your word processor's **file merge** capability to combine the four documents into one, saving yourself the trouble of retyping all four.

Scanning provides a digital image of a page; OCR converts text images into strings of electronic characters.

Using a boilerplate or file-merge capability assumes that the text you want to include is in electronic format, saved on a computer disk. But sometimes you have only printed versions of the document. In such cases you can use a **scanner,** a device that essentially takes a picture of a printed document and converts it to an electronic format that your computer can handle. Scanners produce just a visual image of the document, though, and the process requires an additional step if you want to use the words from the document as normal input to your word processor. A technology called **optical character recognition (OCR)** lets your computer "read" the scanned image, picking out the letters and words that make up the text.

Scanning and OCR technologies raise the legal and ethical issues of plagiarism and image manipulation. Of course, people have had the ability to copy words and images for quite some time, but computer tools make copying even easier. Now you can scan a photo you have on file, retouch it as you see fit, and then include it in your own document. It's also possible to make products and people look better than they really are and to depict situations or events that never actually happened. As technology continues to expand these options, business communicators will continue to face new and challenging ethical issues.

Graphics software can add a visual element to your message.

Adding Graphics and Sound to Documents Computers can do some amazing things with text entry, but that's only part of their capabilities. With the right equipment, you can add full-colour pictures and even sound recordings to your documents. The software for creating business visuals falls into two basic groups: presentation software and graphics software. **Presentation software** helps you create overhead transparencies and computer slide shows for meetings, discussed later in the chapter. **Graphics software** ranges from products that can create simple diagrams and flowcharts to comprehensive tools designed for artists and graphic designers. You can create your pictures from scratch, use **clip art** (collections of uncopyrighted images), or scan in drawings or photos. Much of the graphic design and artwork that you see in business publications was created with software packages such as CorelDRAW! and Freehand.

Inserting your visuals into a document used to be a chore, but increasing standardization of computer file formats has made the task easier. Say you want to distribute some ideas you have for a new corporate logo, and you want to include your sketches in a memo. You've already created several logos in CorelDRAW!, but your memo is in Microsoft Word. No problem–you simply save the CorelDRAW! file in a special transfer format, then switch to your memo in Microsoft Word and activate a command to insert the picture. The logos pop into your memo, and you can shrink or enlarge them to fit.

Adding sound bites to your documents is an exciting way to get your message across. Several systems allow you to record a brief message or other sound and attach it to particular places in a document. Of course, to actually hear the sound, the person receiving the memo has to load the memo into his or her multimedia computer.

REVISING DOCUMENTS

When it's time to revise and polish your message, your word processor can help in a variety of ways, starting with the basics of adding, deleting, and moving text.

Cut and paste is a term used in both word processing and desktop publishing to indicate cutting a block of text out of one section of a document and pasting it in somewhere else. The *find and replace function* helps you track down words or phrases and change them if you need to. This can be a great time saver in long documents if you need to change a word or phrase that appears in several places.

Beyond the basic revision tools, three advanced software functions can help bring out the best in your documents. A **spell checker** compares your document with an electronic dictionary stored on your disk drive, highlights words that it doesn't recognize, and suggests correct spelling. Spell checkers are a wonderful way to weed major typos out of your documents, but it's best not to use them as replacements for good spelling skills. If you use *their* when you mean to use *there,* your spell checker will fly right past the error, because *their* is in fact spelled correctly. If you're in a hurry and accidentally omit the *p* at the end of *top,* your spell checker will read *to* as correct. Or if you mistakenly type the semicolon instead of the *p,* your spell checker will read *to;* as a correctly spelled word.

LEARNING OUTCOME 3
Judge the benefits and limitations of spell checkers and grammar checkers.

Spell checkers, grammar checkers, and computerized thesauruses can all help with the revision process, but they can't take the place of good writing and editing skills.

A computer **thesaurus** gives you alternative words, just as your printed thesaurus does, but you can get them faster and more easily. Another advantage is that, like the printed thesaurus, you can seek relations among words as well rather than a mere listing of synonyms. At **www.thesaurus.com**, you will find several routes to the word you're looking for. You can type a word and see its synonyms and (sometimes) antonyms too. You can also browse the thesaurus by broader categories for classifying words. And if you're looking for a word by sound, there is a rhyming dictionary at **www.writeexpress.com/online.html**. This will allow you to rhyme either the end or the beginning of a word, or a double rhyme.

The third major revision tool is the **grammar checker**, which tries to do for your grammar what a spell checker does for your spelling. The catch here is that checking your spelling is much easier than checking your grammar. A spell checker simply compares each word in your document with a list of correctly spelled words. A grammar checker has to determine whether you're using words correctly and constructing sentences according to the complex rules of composition. The computer doesn't have a clue about what you're trying to say, so determining whether you've said it correctly is monstrously difficult. Moreover, even if you've used all the rules correctly, a grammar checker still can't tell whether your document communicates clearly. However, grammar checkers can perform some helpful review tasks and point out things you should consider changing, such as passive voice, long sentences, and words that tend to be misused or overused.[6]

PRODUCING FINISHED DOCUMENTS

Consider the letter shown in Figure 4.1. Many simple hardware and software packages are capable of producing documents like this one, formatting text so that the appearance is both professional and inviting. The way you package your ideas has a lot to do with how successful your communication will be. A document that looks out of date will make even your innovative ideas seem dull. Today's computer software makes it easy for anyone to produce great-looking documents. Word processors and desktop publishing software can help you by:

Computer software can help you add a first-class look to your most important business documents.

- *Adding a first-class finish.* From selecting attractive typefaces to adding colour graphics, you can use your computer tools to turn a plain piece of text into a dazzling and persuasive document. Used improperly, however, these same tools can turn your text into garish, high-tech rubbish. Knowing how to use the tools of technology is a key issue for today's business communicators.
- *Managing document style.* With so many design and formatting choices at your fingertips, it's often difficult to maintain consistency throughout your

A neatly formatted letterhead and logo can add to a professional appearance.

A contemporary typeface, such as Times New Roman, can make your document inviting to read.

The use of bullets and boldface can make information easily accessible by highlighting it.

Royal Ontario Museum

100 Queen's Park
Toronto, Ontario
Canada
M5S 2C6

Membership

Telephone (416) 586-5700
Facsimile (416) 586-5703
Web Site http://www.rom.on.ca
E-Mail membership@rom.on.ca

ROM

January 22, 1999

Ms. Nancy Nau & Mr. Andrew Cheston
1707 Altona Road
Pickering, ON L1V 1M5

Dear Ms. Nau & Mr. Cheston,

One of my greatest pleasures as Head of Membership Services is welcoming new Members to the Royal Ontario Museum. You're now part of a group of over 35 000 individuals who, as Members, contribute so significantly to the Museum's vitality. Most of our Members stay with us for many years. In the hope that you will too, please consider this the first of many welcomes.

You've picked a terrific year to join the ROM, and here are a few reasons why:

- Opening in February is our new expanded **Discovery Centre**. The gallery will be organized in diverse environmental 'zones' such as a glittering starlight or an enchanted forest. Older children can dress up in costume, examine minerals under an ultraviolet light, and much more. Families with toddlers and babies have their own special area complete with stroller parking.
- In May the spectacular **Inco Gallery of Earth Sciences** opens. This gallery which promises to be visually exciting, interactive and educational will be divided into four major sections: **Dynamic Earth, Restless Earth, Earth: The Alien Planet** and **Treasures of the Earth**.

Of course, I hope you'll take advantage of all your membership benefits–visit the Members' Lounge, use your discount in all the ROM shops and the ROM restaurant, enjoy the *Rotunda* magazine and *Atria* newsletter. Also, the next time you visit, inquire at the membership desk about our discounted parking.

But most of all, come to the ROM as often as possible. We truly treasure your attendance and hope you'll be part of the Royal Ontario Museum's great future.

Yours sincerely,

Ania Kordiuk

Ania Kordiuk
Director, Membership and Annual Giving

FIGURE 4.1
In-Depth Critique: The Importance of Appearance

document. **Style sheets** are collections of formatting rules available in full-featured word processors and DTP packages that can save a lot of formatting effort. Every time you need to add a section to your report, for instance, your style sheet can ensure that all the sections are formatted consistently (with the same typeface, margins, word spacing, etc.). You can also use style sheets to make sure that all the documents created by everyone in a department or even an entire company have a consistent look.

➤ *Generating supporting elements.* If you've ever written a report with footnotes or endnotes, an index, and a table of contents, you know how much work these supporting elements can be. Fortunately, a computer can help keep track of your footnotes; it will renumber them all every time you add or delete a reference. For indexes and tables of contents, you simply flag the terms you want to include, and the software assembles the lists for you.

High-end word-processing software can handle most aspects of final document production, but some communicators prefer to finish off their documents with desktop publishing instead. In addition to giving you more control over spacing, graphics, colour, and other elements, DTP makes many layout and design tasks easier than word processing can. When moving a column of text, for instance, with DTP you can grab it, move it wherever you want, and resize it along the way if you like.

PRINTING AND DISTRIBUTING DOCUMENTS

Laser and inkjet printers are popular ways of producing documents in business today.

With a thoroughly revised document, you're ready to print and distribute copies to your audience. **Printers** come in a variety of shapes, sizes, and capabilities, from low-cost portables that fit in your briefcase to inkjet and high-resolution colour units that can print photographs. Most offices today are equipped with laser printers, which produce a printed image by drawing with a low-power laser beam. For results that look the very best, pages can be printed using a **typesetter** or an **imagesetter**, both of which are similar in concept to laser printers but which produce sharper images.

Technology also simplifies the distribution of your documents. For multiple copies of your document, you can print as many as you like on your office printer or print a single copy and reproduce it with a **photocopier**. For high-volume and complex reproduction (involving colours or photographs, for instance), you'll want to take your document to a **print shop**, a company that has the special equipment needed for such jobs.

When you need to send the same document (sales letter, invoice, or other customer communication) to a large number of people, *mail merge* automatically combines a standard version of the document with your list of names and addresses. It will produce one copy for each person on your mailing list, saving you the trouble of inserting the name and address each time. The names and addresses can come from your own customer databases or from mailing lists you can rent from firms that specialize in collecting names and addresses.

Fax machines (and computers equipped with fax modems) are an integral part of the business communication process, providing fast transmission of printed documents all over the world.

Fax machines have had a major impact on the distribution of printed documents. Using regular telephone lines, you can transmit (*fax*) an exact reproduction (a *facsimile*) of a document from one machine to another. Fax machines are indispensable for international business, particularly since they overcome the delay problems of regular mail and the time-zone problems of trying to contact someone by telephone.[7] Personal computers (PCs) can be equipped with **fax modems**, which combine data transmission with fax capabilities.

Many companies now distribute information on CD-ROM rather than on paper. For instance, several of HP's product catalogues are available either on CD-ROM or in printed form. The cost of producing CD-ROMs is very low, and most personal computers include CD-ROM drives. CD-ROMs hold a large amount of information, and their small size saves money in postage and shipping.

Creating Electronic Documents

A growing number of business documents are never put on paper; they're written on a computer and sent to other computers on the same network. A **network** is a group of computers that are connected so that they can share information. Networks vary greatly in size and nature. Small, private-office setups, sometimes called **local area networks (LANs)**, connect computers in a single building or local area. **Wide area networks (WANs)**, a group of LANs, connect computers in separate locations. Some internal networks also include software such as e-mail programs and search tools. Many LANs, WANs, or intranets (discussed later in this chapter) are also connected to larger outside networks. A **gateway** controls the passage of information between internal and external networks.

The Internet is actually a network of networks.

The world's largest network is the **Internet,** which is actually a network of networks.[8] It is the fastest-growing means of communication in the business world today. Microsoft CEO Bill Gates says, "The Internet is the most important single development to come along since the IBM PC was introduced in 1981."[9]

Some of the software available on the Internet includes

- ✧ Electronic mail
- ✧ Telnet
- ✧ File transfer protocol
- ✧ Search engines
- ✧ World Wide Web

You can access the Internet through a commercial online service, such as CompuServe Canada or America Online Canada, or directly through a service provider. Once you are connected, you need additional software to actually do anything:

- ➢ Electronic mail lets you send and receive mail via the Internet. There is more information on e-mail later in this chapter.
- ➢ **Telnet** lets you connect to a remote computer and run programs on that computer. (You must be authorized and have an account on the remote computer.)
- ➢ **File transfer protocol (FTP)** lets you copy files from a remote computer to your computer.
- ➢ Search engines (Yahoo!, Lycos, and Excite are among the most popular) help you locate information on other computers. Because the Internet is growing so fast, new search tools appear and existing ones become obsolete very quickly. You can find an annotated list of most of the currently available Internet search tools at **www.search.com** on the Web.
- ➢ The **World Wide Web,** or the **Web,** is a graphical approach to storing and accessing information on the Internet. There is more information on the Web later in this chapter.

E-MAIL

LEARNING OUTCOME 4
Explore the communication role of electronic mail and Internet technologies in today's business organizations.

Electronic mail, generally called e-mail, is one of the most useful Internet features for business. **E-mail** refers to documents created, transmitted, and read entirely on computer (Figure 4.2). If you can save a file on your computer, you can probably send it via e-mail. For the people who use it, e-mail has changed the style of business communication in dramatic ways. The advantages of e-mail include the following:[10]

Electronic mail (e-mail) helps businesses communicate quickly and informally.

- ➢ *Speed.* An e-mail message often arrives at its destination anywhere in the world in a matter of seconds. With e-mail, you can correspond back and forth repeatedly in the time it used to take for one message to be delivered.
- ➢ *Cost.* The cost of sending an e-mail message is usually less than the cost of a first-class stamp. It is definitely less than the cost of overnight delivery services ($6 to $20 or more).
- ➢ *Portability.* You can receive and send e-mail anywhere you can connect your computer to the Internet.
- ➢ *Convenience.* The person you want to contact need not be sitting at the computer or even have the computer turned on when your message arrives. This feature solves the problems of *phone tag* (two people calling back and forth leaving messages without ever connecting) and of coordinating phone calls across time zones. For instance, HP has employees in almost every time zone around the world, and many of them need to communicate with far-flung colleagues. With e-mail, a sales representative in Germany can easily communicate with a technical specialist in Saskatchewan, even though the two are separated by nine time zones.

Date: Tue, 15 Aug 2001 10:05:00-0700
From: Pixelar List Control<ListControl@mail1.pixelar.com>
To:jkhan@idirect.com
Subject: Re: Subscribe

Please save a copy of this message for future reference.

You (jkhan@idirect.com) have been added to the Yukon Brewing Co. announcements mailing list. Periodically you will receive announcements about new products or just plain old exciting news. We won't send out messages often, just every few months or so to help keep you up to date with what's brewing in the Yukon. :-)

Does this sound like it might get annoying? To be removed from the list, send the following message to ListControl@mail1.pixelar.com:

unsubscribe YukonBeer

Otherwise, if you begin to miss us terribly, you can visit our web site at:

http://www.yukonbeer.com

Thanks for your interest in the Yukon Brewing Company!

The addressing information shows that a company may employ an outside firm to manage electronic functions, such as e-mail subscriptions, related to the business's Web site.

The first paragraph confirms the subscription request and gives some detail about the content and frequency of outgoing messages.

The message uses humour to establish a light tone and to project a particular image of the company. The layout of the message makes it easy for the reader to follow instructions regarding list removal or accessing the firm's Web site. The recipient can usually go directly to the Web site by clicking on the Web address.

The e-mail ends courteously.

FIGURE 4.2

In-Depth Critique: Electronic Mail

Like many companies that promote themselves on the World Wide Web, the Whitehorse-based Yukon Brewing Company offers a free e-mail subscription to update interested parties on company events.. This message is one example of an electronic confirmation to a subscription request.

- *Record keeping.* You can save and organize messages you send and receive, so e-mail can provide a good record of the communication on a specific project.
- *News services.* Several electronic news services are available. You specify the topic or the key words of interest to you, and the service gathers articles on those topics from newspapers, magazines, and wire services, and sends you the results via e-mail. Some of the services are free; others cost up to $400 a year or more.[11]
- *Egalitarianism.* With most e-mail systems, anybody can send messages to just about anybody else. Lower-level employees (who may otherwise have no contact with upper management) can send e-mail messages to top managers as easily as to their colleagues–the electronic equivalent of an open-door policy.[12]
- *Open communication.* People sometimes write things in e-mail they wouldn't dream of saying in person or typing in a printed document.[13] This new openness can help companies communicate better and circulate useful opinions from more people. As you can imagine, however, such openness can also create tension and interpersonal conflict.
- *Distribution lists.* Within an e-mail program, you can create distribution lists–groups of people to whom you routinely send information. Then when you want to send a message, you specify the name of the list rather than typing all the names again.

Grace Clark is AOL Canada's Vice President of Technology. Her group is responsible for all technology-related components of AOL Canada and CompuServe Canada, including network design implementation and client and systems development.

Going Online

Create Your Own Web Site

You'll learn how to create your own Web site using valuable Web development links, utilities, and online tutorials. Through this massive, user-friendly resource library, you'll learn about document and Web-page design, navigation, structure, and more. You'll even learn how to have your Web site translated into a foreign language.

www.stars.com

- *Automated mail.* Some companies use software that automatically retrieves or distributes information. For example, say you want to get information about the services and prices of ATT Canada Communication Services, an Internet service provider. You simply send e-mail (without an actual message) to **info@attcanada.ca**, and the computer automatically responds.

Some of the main benefits of e-mail also create its worst problems. Because it's so easy and cheap to send e-mail, people tend to overuse it, distributing messages more widely than necessary. Also, some company executives receive hundreds of messages a day, many of which are the electronic equivalent of junk mail. Besides wasting time, overuse can overload e-mail systems, resulting in lost messages or even system crashes.

Privacy is another problem with e-mail. E-mail messages may seem more private than phone calls, but it is surprisingly easy for e-mail to end up in places you did not intend it to go. People do not always screen the distribution list carefully and send information to people who should not have it or do not need it. Even if your message originally goes only where you intended it to go, a recipient can easily forward it on to someone else. Like paper mail, e-mail can be used as evidence in court cases.[14] Moreover, employers can monitor your e-mail on the job.[15] A good rule of thumb is not to put anything in e-mail that you would not write in any other business correspondence.[16]

INTERNET DISCUSSION GROUPS

Two forms of discussion groups are common on the Internet: discussion mailing lists and Usenet newsgroups. A **discussion mailing list** (of which there are more than 100 000) consists of people with a common interest. You can subscribe by sending a message to the list's e-mail address. From then on, you will automatically receive via e-mail a copy of any message posted to that list by any other subscriber to that list. It's like subscribing to an electronic newsletter to which everyone can contribute.[17]

Usenet newsgroups are similar to mailing lists, but they are accessed differently. Mailing lists are accessed by e-mail. Newsgroups are accessed by a newsgroup reader program in Netscape, Internet Explorer, or some other browser. Once you subscribe, you can read messages posted by other subscribers and leave messages for the other subscribers to read. You can get and submit information on more than 10 000 subjects. For example, the newsgroup **alt.business.misc** is a forum for small-business owners.[18]

WORLD WIDE WEB

The World Wide Web is the part of the Internet that can accommodate graphics.

The **World Wide Web, WWW,** or **Web,** is a very powerful system of interconnections on the Internet. Being familiar with terms helps you use the Web:

- *Multimedia.* When using the Web, you can access not only text files but also graphic, photographic, audio, and video files. Figure 4.3 shows a Web page with text and graphics.
- *Browser.* To find your way around the Web, you need a piece of software called a **browser.** Two popular browsers are Netscape Navigator and Microsoft's Internet Explorer.
- *Home page.* Every site on the Web has its own **home page,** or starting place. This site might be a very complex document containing graphics and hyperlinks (as in Figure 4.3), or it might be quite simple.

- *URL.* Each resource or site on the Web has a unique address called a **uniform resource locator (URL)**. The URL for Hewlett-Packard's Web site is **www.hp.com**.
- *Hyperlinks.* Hyperlinks, or **links,** are interactive connections among sites on the Web.
- *Hypertext.* Hypertext is a method of cross-referencing between files by using links. When you click on a link, hypertext uses the URL to find the file or site. This is a convenient way of finding related information. For example, look at HP's site in Figure 4.3. If you want more information on HP products, click on the button labeled *Products & Services.*
- *Web site.* Thousands of companies and individuals now have their own Web sites. At HP's site, for instance, clicking on buttons or links provides information about new products, the company's annual report, a current press release, any job openings, or a variety of other topics. A Web site provides an interactive means of advertising.

Intranets

An intranet is an Internet-type network whose information and access are restricted to a single organization.

Not all Web sites are available to anyone cruising the Net. Some are reserved for the private use of a single company's employees and stakeholders. An **intranet** uses the same technologies as the Internet and the World Wide Web, but the information provided and the access allowed are restricted to the boundaries of a companywide LAN or WAN. In some cases, suppliers, distribution partners, and key customers may also have access, but intranets are protected from unauthorized access through the Internet by a **firewall**, a special type of gateway that controls

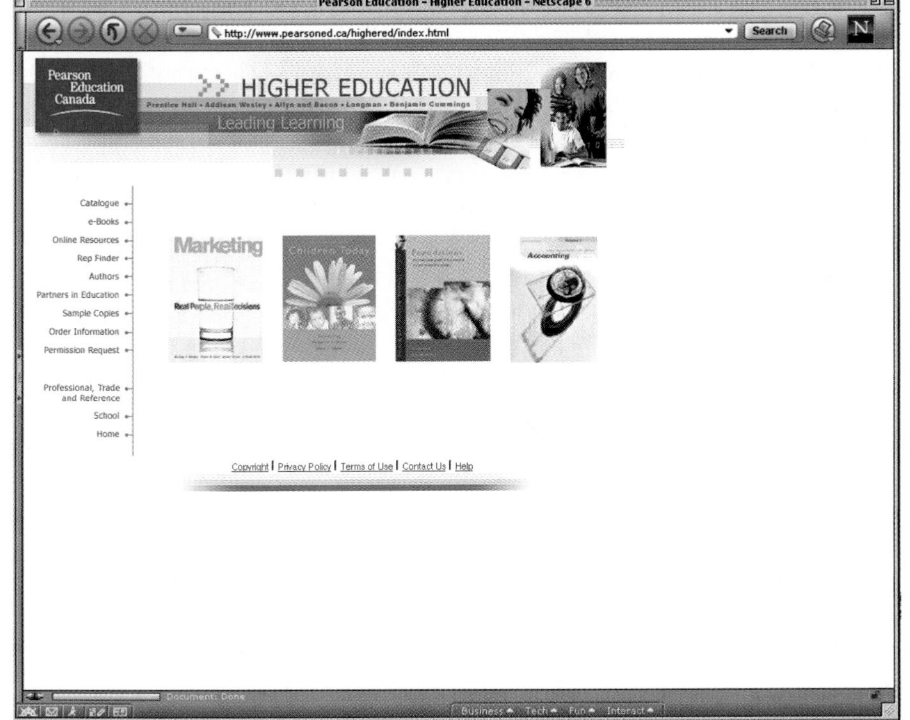

FIGURE 4.3

Web Pages Help Businesses Communicate Internally and Externally

This site on the World Wide Web shows a typical home page with graphics and hyperlinks.

USING THE POWER OF TECHNOLOGY

Elements of Cyberstyle

In cyberspace, "you are what you write," says Charles Rubin, author of 30 books about technology. People's opinion of you online is determined to a large extent by your command of the written word. And writing for the Web is indeed different.

People go to the Web because they want to get information efficiently. Ninety percent of the people reading Web pages don't scroll down. Which is why you need to grab the reader's attention and make your main points on the first screen. Furthermore, Web readers have short attention spans, so you must hook them quickly.

To hook readers and keep them, experts suggest that you use a more conversational tone and that you keep words, sentences and paragraphs short. Many readers will just scan a Web page, so use meaningful—not clever—subheads to break up text. Use lists whenever possible, and cut excess verbiage. Accuracy is also important. People have a zillion other sites to choose from. If the first thing a reader sees has an error in it, you may lose the reader forever.

Along with conciseness and accuracy comes comprehensiveness. While Web surfers may be in a hurry, if they like what they see, they'll want as much of it as they can get. The Web allows you to be concise and comprehensive at the same time. You do this by using your first Web page to present the big picture. Then you unfold the rest of your story through links to other pages. But be sure to make it clear how many links are involved. Readers like to know what they are getting into. They don't like to be forced into following one path, but at the same time, subdividing pages too much and forcing readers to tunnel through too many links will only frustrate them. Moreover, readers like to be in control. If you don't let them take control, they will anyway. But they'll do it by clicking to another site.

CAREER APPLICATIONS

1. Do you notice any elements of cyberstyle that also apply to business messages? Make a list, and discuss why each element is important in business.
2. Visit any two Web sites, and compare their cyberstyles. Do both Web sites contain all the elements recommended here? If not, briefly outline how the sites might be improved by applying good cyberstyle.

Sources: Jennifer L. Rewick, "Elements of Cyberstyle," *Wall Street Journal*, 22 November 1999, R64; Reid Goldsborough, "Words for the Wise: Writing for the Web" *Office Systems*, November 1999, 52+; Carol Holstead, "Three Steps to Web-Smart Editing," *Folio Supplement*, 2000, 195–196.

Vice-Chairman and Chief Information Officer of Royal Bank, Marty Lippert directs the bank's e-business strategies and initiatives. He says that it is crucial for today's small businesses to become "Internet-enabled" and to provide their customers electronic convenience in order to survive.

access to the local network. People on an intranet can get out to the Internet, but unauthorized people on the Internet cannot get in.[19] As a leading computer company, Hewlett-Packard, not surprisingly, owns one of the largest intranets in the world.[20]

Possibly the biggest advantage of an intranet is that it eliminates the problem of employees using different types of computers within a company. On an intranet, all information is available in a format compatible with Macintosh, PC, or UNIX-based computers. The need to publish internal documents on paper is virtually eliminated because everyone can access the information electronically.

Besides saving paper, an intranet can save a company money in the form of employee hours. Employees can find information much faster and more easily by using a well-designed database on an intranet than by digging through a filing cabinet or card catalogue. Companies use intranets for updating policy manuals, posting job openings and submitting job applications, accessing marketing and sales presentations from anywhere in the world, updating and managing employee benefits, accessing company records and databases, collaborating from anywhere in the world to develop new products, scheduling meetings, setting up company phone directories, and publishing company newsletters.[21] In fact, just about any information that can help employees communicate is a good candidate for an intranet. As video and audio technologies progress, you can expect to see more multimedia applications on intranets as well.

Apply Your Knowledge

Critical Thinking Questions

1. Is it important for everyone in a company to know how to use the latest technological tools for document preparation? Why or why not?
2. Would you choose word-processing or desktop publishing software as a tool for writing memos to your staff? Why?
3. Considering how fast and easy it is, should e-mail replace meetings and other face-to-face communication in your company? Why or why not?
4. Why are companies interested in group technologies such as teleconferencing, groupware, and intranets?
5. How could a global corporation such as Coca-Cola take advantage of Internet technology to keep its people around the world in touch with each other?
6. What are the implications for companies that are slow to adopt new communication technologies and for employment candidates who have limited experience with such technologies?

Practise Your Knowledge

Exercises

1. You are responsible for recommending word-processing software to the headquarters staff at Federal Express Canada. Using computer magazines available in the library, read reviews of leading word-processing products. On the basis of your research, select the one product you think is best, and write a brief recommendation.
2. You're a consultant hired by Chrysler Canada to investigate how the company and its dealers can use technology to communicate with potential customers. Interview several people who've bought a car, and ask them what types of communication technology the manufacturers and car dealers used. Ask them what types of technology they expected manufacturers and dealers to use. Did one technology seem to work better than another? Write a couple of paragraphs explaining to Chrysler what you've learned.
3. For each of the following tasks, decide which communication technology, if any, would be the best to use, and be prepared to explain your choices in class.
   a. The CEO of a major corporation wants to explain the company's performance to 27 000 employees, who are located in 14 sites across North America and Europe.
   b. A small-business owner wants to convince her bank that the normal loan qualification shouldn't apply in her case and that the bank should approve her request for a $2 million business-expansion loan.
   c. A manager needs to warn three employees that their job performance is below company standards.
4. Computer viruses are software programs designed to wreak havoc in computer systems. They can cause millions of dollars of damage in lost time and destroyed data, so they are understandably an important concern for businesses. By interviewing a computer expert or researching library articles, learn the extent of the virus problem. Then draft a brief (less than one page) explanation, listing the things that companies can do to protect themselves.
5. List the technological skills you already have and could discuss in a job interview. Can you type? Have you used e-mail or online services? Have you surfed the Web? Have you used photocopiers, calculators, answering machines, voice-mail systems? What experience do you have with video cameras, video players, videoconferencing equipment? Which brands, models, or systems are you familiar with? Which software packages do you have experience using?
6. Interview several local business people or university administrators to find out the following (write a one-page summary of your findings):
   a. What communication technology they use
   b. What tasks they use the technology for
   c. The advantages of using the technology
   d. The disadvantages of using the technology
   e. How technology has affected their ability to communicate on the job.

7. You will be out of town for the next week, attending an important meeting that was called at the last minute. While you're away, you want your clients to be able to get the personal attention they deserve, so you've made arrangements with an associate to cover for you. Of course, not every client will need help before your return on May 16; most of them should be able to leave a message on your voice mail so that you can get back to them when you return. Compose a message to record on your voice-mail system letting your clients know that you haven't abandoned them and that they can either leave a message or contact your associate (Bill Comden at 578-3737). Make sure the message is brief while still containing all the necessary information.
8. Many magazines have established Web pages in addition to using print. For example, the *Canadian Geographic* Web site at **www.Canadiangeographic.ca** aims to give the magazine a wider audience through the Web. Consider whether the information provided on the home page and linked pages effectively addresses the needs of the intended audience. Send an e-mail message to *Canadian Geographic*, or to one of the linked information pages (including the companies that designed and maintain the home page) asking for additional information. Print both your query and your response for submission.

Developing Your Internet Skills

Going Online: Create Your Own Web Site, p. 82

Think of a Web site you might like to create, either now or in some imaginary future. Picture the kind of graphics and text you'd use, the overall style and tone (irreverent? funny? serious? all business?) that would be appropriate to your purpose (which you will need to define). After looking over the Web Developer's Virtual Library–or WDVL (stars.com)–how do you think these tools might help you accomplish your imaginary Web site?

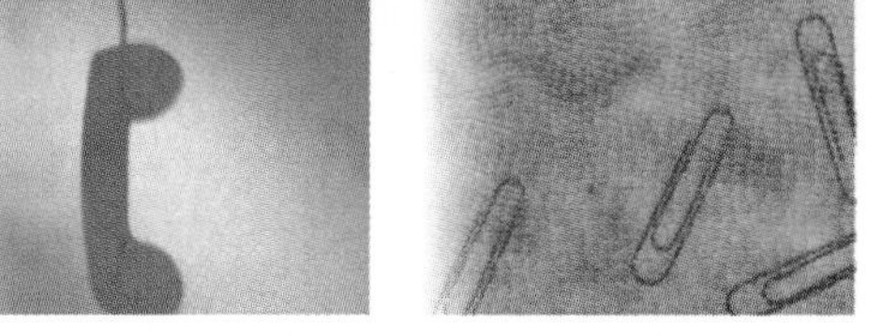

CHAPTER 5

Planning Business Messages

AFTER STUDYING THIS CHAPTER, YOU WILL BE ABLE TO

1. Describe the basic tasks in the composition process
2. Define both the general and the specific purposes of your business messages
3. Test the purpose of your business messages
4. Develop an audience profile
5. Analyze the needs of your audience
6. Establish the main idea of your messages
7. Select an appropriate channel and medium for transmitting a particular message to a particular audience

ON THE JOB
Facing a Communication Dilemma at Mattel

The Best-Selling Doll in the World

She has been called timeless, ageless, and perfect. She has been styled an inspiration to children, encouraging them to realize their hopes and dreams. Children and adults have been collecting her for the past 40 years, and enjoying endless hours of pleasure in her company. Her name? Barbie.

Since Barbie's debut, the Mattel toy company has sold more than a billion copies of the 11-inch-tall dolls and family members. In fact, if placed head to toe, Barbie and her clan would circle the earth more than seven times. Many Barbie fans also own her boyfriend Ken and a group of her girlfriends, not to mention her $200 dream house, her red Ferrari, her vacation hideaway, her horse, her cats, and her ever-expanding wardrobe. Mattel has even extended into Barbie software. Barbie's appeal is practically universal. She appears in 67 countries around the world, modified in facial characteristics and clothing to suit local tastes: Asian Barbie, Greek Barbie, Icelandic Barbie, Peruvian Barbie ...

Careful planning helps Mattel's employees compose effective messages that are meaningful to the consumers, business contacts, and other employees who receive them. When people at Mattel plan business messages, they clarify their purpose for communicating, try to understand their audience, focus on the main idea of the message, and decide on the best way to send it.

Still, not everybody loves her. Feminists complain that Barbie is a materialistic airhead concerned only with possessions, popularity, and appearances. Susan Reverby, director of the women's studies program at a US college, won't allow her own little girl to play with Barbie. "I don't want my daughter to think that being a woman means she has to look like Barbie and date someone like Ken," Reverby says.

The people at Mattel are sensitive to the criticism. Jill Barad, a former president and chief executive officer, set out to redeem Barbie's reputation by giving her a career. She added a new dimension to Barbie's appeal by giving her not just one job, but many. After plunging into the workforce in 1983 as an employee of McDonald's, Barbie has gone on to bigger and better things. She's been an astronaut, a surgeon, a veterinarian, an Olympic athlete, and the leader of a rock band—and she has the clothes to prove it.

Barbie's managers face the communication challenge of sending a message that will satisfy both Barbie's critics and her faithful fans. The critics want Barbie to be a strong, serious woman with a social conscience—the type of person who volunteers at a settlement house for homeless people after putting in a ten-hour day on Wall Street. The fans want Barbie to be what she has always been—a popular, pretty girl who wears glamorous clothes and has fun all the time.

How can Mattel plan messages that will appease one group without upsetting the other? What consideration should be given to purpose? Audience? What is the best communication channel for these messages? What is the best medium?[1]

Understanding the Composition Process

LEARNING OUTCOME 1
Describe the basic tasks in the composition process.

Mattel's dilemma is not unique. In your own career, some of your tasks will be routine, needing little more than jotting down a few sentences on paper or in an e-mail message; others will be more complex, requiring reflection, research, and careful document preparation. Regardless of the job you hold, the amount of time you actually spend composing messages, or the complexity of your task, effective communication will be the key.[2] Even if you have trouble thinking of what you'll say, you can gain control over your messages by separating the various composition activities into a process.

A Three-Step Process

Although some communicators reject any structured composition process as artificial, the fact is that your final message (the product) and the way you achieve it (the process) are irrevocably linked. So, successful communicators like Jill Barad concentrate on both.[3] The process presented here will be most valuable if you view it not as a recipe, not as a list of how-to directives, not as a fixed sequence of steps, but as a way to understand the various tasks involved in composition.[4] The composition process varies with the situation, the communicator, and the organization. So the stages do not necessarily occur in 1-2-3 order. Communicators often jump back and forth from one stage to another.

The composition process helps you gain control over your messages.

The composition process is flexible; it's not a fixed prescription of sequenced steps.

The **composition process** includes three steps–planning, composing, and revising–which can be divided into 10 stages (see Figure 5.1):

- *Planning.* During the planning phase, you think about the fundamentals of your message: your reason for communicating, your audience, the main idea of your message, and the channel and medium that will best convey your thoughts. The stages of planning include (1) defining your purpose, (2) analyzing your audience, (3) establishing your main idea, and (4) selecting the appropriate channel and medium.
- *Composing.* Having collected all the information you'll need, you decide on the organization of ideas and the tone you'll adopt. Then you formulate the message, committing your thoughts to words, creating sentences and paragraphs, and selecting illustrations and details to support your main idea. The stages of composing include (5) organizing your message and (6) formulating your message.
- *Revising.* Having formulated your thoughts, you step back to see whether you have expressed them adequately. You review the content and organization of your message, its overall style and readability, and your word choice. You revise and rewrite until your message comes across as clearly and effectively as possible. Then, once you have produced the message, you proofread it for details such as grammar, punctuation, and format. The stages of revision include (7) editing your message, (8) rewriting your message, (9) producing your message, and (10) proofing your message.

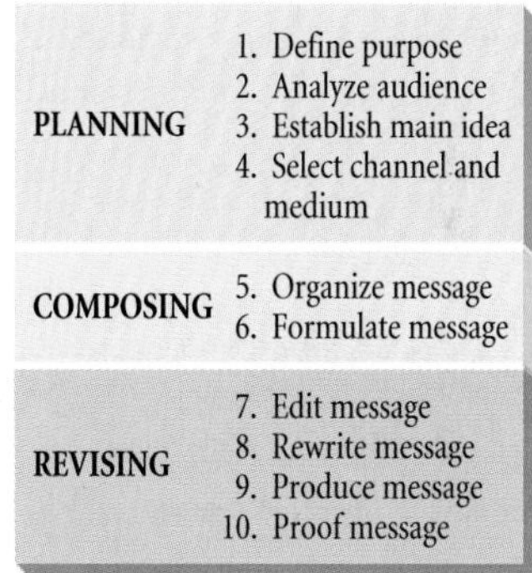

FIGURE 5.1

The Composition Process

Good communicators realize that the composition process often occurs out of order as they jump back and forth from one stage to another.

Good composition includes such important considerations as spelling and usage, but the central part of any composition process is thinking.[5] This three-step process helps you assess the possibilities for achieving a specific objective. It gives you control over your composition by helping you focus on the specific tasks that make up successful composition.

Collaboration

In many organizations, the process of preparing a message is a team effort. **Collaborative writing,** in which more than one writer works on a document, can result in a better product than one person could produce alone. Collaboration brings multiple perspectives and various skills to a project. It combines the strengths of all the team members to increase productivity, enrich knowledge, and enhance interpersonal relationships.[6]

Collaboration affects the composition process.

Today's computers make collaborative writing more feasible than it once was. They allow you the freedom to experiment and explore various approaches to the writing process and the subject matter. Electronic tools such as groupware, e-mail, and computer conferencing help you communicate quickly and effectively as you maintain an ongoing dialogue with other team members.[7]

Firoz Rasul, CEO of Ballard Power Systems, Inc., is leading his company to develop fuel-cell technology as a viable energy alternative. His efforts include informing, persuading, and collaborating with the transportation industry so that his company's research can be transformed into reality.

Collaborative writing isn't without problems. As a member of a collaborative team, you need writing skills such as researching, drafting, editing, and proofreading. However, team members coming from different backgrounds will have different concerns–a technical expert may focus on accuracy and meeting scientific standards; an editor may focus on organization and coherence; a manager may focus on schedules, cost, and corporate goals. So, in addition to being able to write, you must also be able to attend meetings regularly, plan and organize efficiently, accept responsibility, volunteer willingly, contribute ideas freely, elicit and listen to ideas, cooperate, and resolve conflicts.[8] You must be able and willing to overcome differences in writing styles, working styles, and personality traits. You must be open to the opinions of others and focus on your team's objectives instead of your own.

Collaborative writing is used in any number of business situations, ranging from one writer asking a co-worker's opinion to many writers cooperating in an all-out team effort. You might sit down with your boss to plan a memo, work independently during the writing phase, and then ask your boss to review the message and suggest revisions. Or your message may be particularly long and important so that the process involves more people: a project manager, researchers, writers, typists, graphic artists, and editors.[9] For efforts of this type, the review and revision stages might be repeated several times to respond to input not only from various team members but also from various departments.

To get organized, your team will select a leader, clarify goals, and resolve conflicts.[10] To be effective, your team will agree on purpose, audience awareness, and writing style.

Schedules

Scheduling affects the composition process.

When composing a message, whether alone or in collaboration with co-workers, you should allot your time properly. Any realistic schedule will give you the time you need for thoroughly planning, composing, and revising your message. But business messages are often composed under pressure and on a schedule that is anything but realistic. Especially when time is short, carefully schedule yourself, and stick to your schedule. Of the time you're given, try using roughly half for planning, gathering material, and immersing yourself in the subject matter. Try using less than a quarter of your time for composing, and use more than a quarter of the time for revising–so that you don't shortchange important final steps such as polishing and proofing.[11]

Examining the Composition Process

This textbook breaks the composition process into three chapters. Chapter 5 focuses on planning business messages (Stages 1–4). Chapter 6 discusses composing business messages (Stages 5, 6), and Chapter 7 covers revising business messages (Stages 7–10). The result of planning can be as simple as a handwritten checklist of topics to cover in a phone conversation, or it can be a detailed strategy that spells out scheduling and collaborative responsibilities, objectives, audience needs, and media choices. By defining your purpose, you set clear objectives for measuring your efforts. By analyzing your audience, you focus on their needs and point of view. By establishing your main idea, you shape and control your message. By selecting a channel and medium, you present your message in the best light possible.[12]

Stage 1: Defining Your Purpose

When planning a business message, think about your purpose. Of course you want to maintain the goodwill of the audience and create a favourable impression for your organization, but you also have a particular goal you want to achieve. That purpose may be straightforward and obvious (placing an order), or it may be more difficult to define (Barad's purpose of satisfying both critics and fans of Barbie). When the purpose is unclear, it pays to spend a few minutes thinking about what you hope to accomplish.

The purpose of the message helps you decide whether to proceed, how to respond to your audience, which information to focus on, and which channel and medium to use.

Common Purposes of Business Messages

LEARNING OUTCOME 2
Define both the general and the specific purposes of your business messages.

All business messages have a **general purpose:** to inform, to persuade, or to collaborate with your audience. The purpose determines both the amount of audience participation you need and the amount of control you have over your message. If your message is intended strictly to inform, you require little interaction with your audience. Your readers or listeners absorb information, accept it, or reject it, but they don't contribute to message content–you control the message. If your message is persuasive, you require a moderate amount of audience participation, and you'll retain a moderate amount of message control. Finally, if you seek collaboration from your audience, you require maximum audience participation, so your control of the message is low; you can't adhere to a rigid plan because you will need to adjust to new input and unexpected reactions.

Your general purpose may be to inform, to persuade, or to collaborate.

In addition to having a general purpose, your messages also have a **specific purpose.** Ask yourself, "What should my audience do or think after reviewing this message?" Then state your purpose as precisely as possible, identifying the members of the audience who should respond.

To determine the specific purpose, think of how the audience's ideas or behaviour should be affected by the message.

How to Test Your Purpose

LEARNING OUTCOME 3
Test the purpose of your business messages.

Once you've established your purpose, pause for a moment to consider whether it's worth pursuing at this time. There's no point in creating a message that is unlikely to accomplish its purpose. Before you decide to send the message, ask yourself these questions:

- *Is the purpose realistic?* Most people resist change. So if your purpose involves a radical shift in action or attitude, you'll do better to go slowly. Instead of suggesting your whole program at once, consider proposing the first step and viewing your message as the beginning of a learning process.
- *Is this the right time?* An idea that is unacceptable when profits are down, for example, may easily win approval when business improves. If an organization is undergoing changes of some sort, you may want to defer your message until things stabilize and people can concentrate on your ideas.
- *Am I the right person to deliver the message?* Even though you may have done all the work yourself, your boss may have a better chance of accomplishing results because of her or his higher status. Achieving your objective is more important than taking the credit. In the long run, people will recognize the quality of your work. Also bear in mind that some people are simply better writers or speakers than others. If the stakes are high and you lack experience or confidence, you might want to play a supporting role rather than take the lead.
- *Is the purpose acceptable to the organization?* As the representative of your company, you are obligated to work toward the organization's goals. Say you're a customer service representative who answers letters from customers. If you receive an

Defer a message or do not send it at all if
- ✧ The purpose is not realistic
- ✧ The timing is not right
- ✧ You are not the right person to deliver the message
- ✧ The purpose is not acceptable to the organization

abusive letter that unfairly attacks your company, your initial reaction might be to fire back an angry reply. Would top managers want you to counterattack, or would they want you to regain the customer's goodwill? Your response should reflect the organization's priorities.

Stage 2: Analyzing Your Audience

Ask yourself some key questions about your audience:
- ✧ Who are they?
- ✧ What is their probable reaction to your message?
- ✧ How much do they already know about the subject?
- ✧ What is their relationship to you?

Once you are satisfied that you have a legitimate purpose in communicating, take a good look at your intended audience. Who are its members, what are their attitudes, and what do they need to know? The answers to these questions will indicate something about the material you'll cover and the way you'll cover it.

Develop Your Audience's Profile

LEARNING OUTCOME 4
Develop an audience profile.

If you're communicating with someone you know well, perhaps your boss or a co-worker, audience analysis is relatively easy. You can predict their reactions pretty well without a lot of research. On the other hand, if your audience is made up of strangers, you have to do some investigating to learn about them before you can use common sense to anticipate their reactions.

Focus on the common interests of the audience, but be alert to their individual concerns.

- ➤ *Determine audience size and composition.* Audience size affects the amount of audience participation in oral presentations and the degree of formality in written documents. Audience size also affects the diversity of backgrounds and interests you'll encounter, so you need to look for the common denominators that tie the members of an audience together. At the same time, you want your message to deal with the concerns of particular individuals. Because a marketing manager and a production or finance manager need different information, be sure to include a variety of evidence that touches on everyone's area of interest.
- ➤ *Identify the primary audience.* When several people will be receiving your message, try to identify those who are most important to your purpose. If you can reach the decision makers or opinion moulders, other members of the audience will follow their lead. Although higher-status people usually make the decisions, occasionally a person in a relatively low position will have influence in one or two particular areas.
- ➤ *Estimate the audience's probable reaction.* Your approach to organizing your message depends on your audience's probable reaction. If you expect a favourable response with very little criticism or debate, you can be straightforward about stating your conclusions and recommendations. You can also use a minimal amount of evidence to support your points. On the other hand, when you face a skeptical audience, you may have to introduce your conclusions and recommendations more gradually and provide more proof.

A gradual approach and plenty of evidence are required to win over a skeptical audience.

- ➤ *Gauge the audience's level of understanding.* If you and your audience share the same general background, you can assume they will understand your material without any difficulty. Otherwise, you'll have to decide how much you need to educate them. The trick is to provide the information they need without being stodgy or obvious.
- ➤ *Define your relationship with the audience.* If you're unknown to your audience, you'll have to earn their confidence before you can win them to your point of view. If you're communicating with a familiar group, your credibility has already been established, so you can get down to business immediately. You can build credibility or overcome people's preconceptions of you by providing ample evidence for any material outside your usual area of expertise. Your status relative to your audience also affects the style and tone of your presentation, depending on whether you're addressing your boss, your peers, employees of lower status, customers, or suppliers.

Vary the tone and structure of the message to reflect your relationship with the audience.

Satisfy Your Audience's Informational Needs

LEARNING OUTCOME 5
Analyze the needs of your audience

The key to effective communication is determining your reader's needs and then responding to them. You do that by telling people what they need to know in terms that are meaningful to them. A good message answers all the audience's questions.

- *Find out what the audience wants to know.* In many cases, the audience's information needs are readily apparent. When consumer affairs specialists answer letters requesting information about Barbie, all they normally have to do is respond to the consumers' questions. In other cases, an audience may not be particularly good at telling you what is needed. Your boss might say, "Find out everything you can about the Tim Horton's, and write a memo on it." That's a pretty big assignment. Ten days later, you submit your 25-page report, and, instead of heaping you with praise, your boss says: "I don't need all this. All I want is Tim Horton's five-year financial record." So when you get a vague request, pin it down. One good approach is to restate the request in more specific terms. Another approach is to get a fix on its priority. You might ask, "Should I drop everything else and devote myself to this for the next week?"
- *Anticipate unstated questions.* Try to think of information needs that your audience may not even be aware of. Suppose your company has just hired a new employee from out of town, and you've been assigned to coordinate this person's relocation. At a minimum, you would write a welcoming letter describing your company's procedures for relocating employees. With a little extra thought, however, you might decide to include some information about the city: perhaps a guide to residential areas, a map or two, brochures about cultural activities, or information on schools and transportation.
- *Provide all the required information.* Once you've defined your audience's needs, be certain to satisfy those needs completely. One good way to test the thoroughness of your message is to use the journalistic approach: Check to see whether your messages answer *who, what, when, where, why,* and *how* questions. Whenever you request any action, take particular care to explain exactly what you are expecting. Until readers get a clear picture of what they're supposed to do, they can't possibly do it. If you want them to send you a cheque for $5, tell them; if you want them to turn in their time cards on Friday by 3:00 P.M., say so.
- *Be sure the information is accurate.* There's no point in answering all your audience's questions if the answers are wrong. In business, you have a special duty to check things before making a written commitment, especially if you're writing to someone who is outside the company. Your organization is obligated to fulfill any promises you make, so make sure that your company will be able to follow through. You may sincerely believe that you have answered someone's questions correctly and then later realize that your information was incorrect. If that happens, the most ethical thing for you to do is to contact the person immediately and correct the error. Most people will respect you for your honesty.
- *Emphasize ideas of greatest interest to the audience.* When deciding how to respond to your audience's information needs, remember that some points will be of greater interest and importance than others. The head of engineering and someone from the shipping department might be interested in different things. If you don't know the audience, or if you're communicating with a large group of people, you'll have to use your common sense to identify points of particular interest. Such factors as age, job, location, income, or education can give you a clue. Remember that your main goal as a business communicator is to tell your audience what they need to know.

Five questions to ask yourself that will help you satisfy the audience's information needs:

- What does the audience want to know?
- What does the audience need to know?
- Have I provided all desired and necessary information?
- Is the information accurate?
- Have I emphasized the information of greatest interest to the audience?

Going Online

Learn More About Analyzing an Audience

Find out more about audience analysis with a table that's based on developing information for the Web. A carefully constructed audience cluster diagram graphically illustrates the discussion and reinforces the points made in this textbook.

www.december.com/web/develop/wdaudience.html

In the race against Nike for market share, Reebok International's founder and chairman, Paul Fireman, plans his advertising messages for specific audiences rather than trying to appeal to the entire shoe market at one time.

Satisfy Your Audience's Motivational Needs

Some types of messages, particularly persuasive and bad news messages, are intended to motivate audience members to change their beliefs or behaviour. The problem is that people resist ideas that conflict with their existing beliefs and practices. They may selectively screen out threatening ideas or distort your message to fit their preconceived map of reality. To overcome resistance, arrange your message so that the information will be as acceptable as possible (see Chapter 1).

Satisfy Your Audience's Practical Needs

Many business messages are directed toward people who are themselves in business: your customers, suppliers, co-workers. So, regardless of where these people work or precisely what they do, their days are filled with distractions:

- First-level supervisors are involved in at least 200 separate activities or incidents in an eight-hour day.
- Most activities are very brief. One study of supervisors shows one activity every 48 seconds.
- A study of chief executives reports that periods of desk work average 10 to 15 minutes each.
- Responding to mail takes less than 5 percent of a manager's time, and most executives react to only about 30 percent of the mail they receive.[13]

In other words, many in your audience will review your message under difficult circumstances with many interruptions, and they are likely to give it a low priority. So make your message as convenient as possible for your audience. Try to be brief. In general, a 5-minute talk is easier to follow than a 30-minute presentation; a two-paragraph letter is more manageable than one that's two pages long, and a two-page memo is more likely to be read than a ten-page report.

If your written message has to be long, make it easy for readers to follow so they can pick it up and put it down several times without losing the thread of what

Playing the Dating Game

EFFECTIVE E-BUSINESS COMMUNICATION

Dating your online messages is one of the best ways to reassure readers that the information is still accurate and pertinent. Although many printed messages are undated, a Web page should show when it was posted or most recently updated—including the time, if it helps readers better assess the accuracy of the information. Details such as product prices, inventory availability, and even management appointments can change at any hour, so dates and times help readers keep track. For example, CBC.ca includes both the date and the time to allow online readers to see exactly when news stories were posted.

APPLY YOUR KNOWLEDGE

1. What kinds of online messages might need dates but not times of posting?
2. CBC.ca shows the date and time at the top of an online story. Is this an appropriate position for the date and time of every online message? Explain your answer.

you're saying. Begin with a summary of key points, use plenty of headings, and put important points in list format so they'll stand out. Put less important information in separate enclosures or appendices, and use charts and graphs to dramatize important ideas.

Remember that your audience
- ✧ May have little time
- ✧ May be distracted
- ✧ May give your message low priority

If you're delivering a long message orally, be sure to give listeners an overview of the message's structure, and then express your thoughts clearly and logically. You might also use flip charts, slides, or handouts to help listeners understand and remember key points. You're the guide; lead audience members through your message by telling them where they've been and where they're going.

Stage 3: Establishing the Main Idea

LEARNING OUTCOME 6
Establish the main idea of your messages.

Every business message can be boiled down to one main idea. Regardless of the issue's complexity, one central point sums up everything. This point is your theme. Everything else in the message either supports this point or demonstrates its implications.

A topic and a main idea are different. The **topic** is the broad subject of the message. The **main idea** makes a statement–one of many possible statements–about the topic. It provides a rationale, explaining your purpose in terms that the audience can accept. A Mattel executive might give a presentation on the topic of Barbie's image, with the aim of persuading critics that Barbie has become an acceptable role model for young girls. Her main idea might be that Barbie's careers have made the character a more rounded person.

The main idea is the hook that sums up why a particular audience should do or think as you suggest.

The main idea has to strike a response in the intended audience. It has to motivate people to do what you want by linking your purpose with their own. When you're preparing a brief letter, memo, or meeting agenda, the main idea may be pretty obvious, especially if you're dealing with simple facts that have little or no emotional content for the audience. In such cases, the main idea may be nothing more than "Here is what you wanted." If you're responding to a request for information about the price and availability of your company's products, your main idea would be something like "We have these items at competitive prices."

Wendy MacNair is the editor of the Aboriginal Banking newsletter, published by the Aboriginal Banking Unit of the Business Development Bank of Canada. She helps contributors to the newsletter bring out the best in their writing by reading their drafts and commenting on matters of style and expression. What sort of advice do you think MacNair gives to her authors to help them become effective communicators?

Finding the angle or hook is more complicated when you're trying to persuade someone or when you have disappointing information to convey. In those situations, look for a main idea that will establish a good relationship between you and your audience. Focus on some point of agreement or common interest.

In longer documents and presentations, in which a mass of material needs to be unified, the problem of establishing a main idea becomes still more challenging. You need to identify a generalization that encompasses all the individual points you want to make. For these tough assignments, you may need to take special measures to pinpoint your main idea.

Use Pre-writing Techniques

Identifying the main idea often requires creativity and experimentation. The best approach is to **brainstorm,** letting your mind wander over the possibilities, testing various alternatives against your purpose, your audience, and the facts at your disposal. How do you generate those possibilities? Successful communicators use various approaches. You have to experiment until you find a pre-writing method that fits your mental style. Here are a few approaches that might work for you:

- *Storyteller's tour.* Turn on your tape recorder and pretend that you've just run into an old friend on the street. She says, "So, what are you working on these days?" Give her an overview of your message, focusing on your reasons for com-

Some techniques for establishing the main idea:
✧ Storyteller's tour
✧ Random list
✧ FCR worksheet
✧ Journalistic approach
✧ Question-and-answer chain

municating, your major points, your rationale, and the implications for your intended audience. Listen critically to the tape; then repeat the exercise until you are able to give a smooth, two-minute summary that conveys the gist of your message. The summary should reveal your main idea.

- *Random list.* On a computer screen or a clean sheet of paper, list everything that pops into your head pertaining to your message. When you've exhausted the possibilities, study the list for relationships. Sort the items into groups, as you would sort a deck of cards into suits. Look for common denominators; the connection might be geographical, sequential, spatial, chronological, or topical. Part of the list might break down into problems, causes, and solutions; another part, into pros and cons. Regardless of what categories finally emerge, the sorting process will help you sift through your thoughts and decide what's important and what isn't.
- *FCR worksheet.* If your subject involves the solution to a problem, you might try using an **FCR worksheet** to help you visualize the relationships among your findings (F), your conclusions (C), and your recommendations (R). For example, you might find that you're losing sales to a competitor who offers lower prices than you do (F). From that finding, you might conclude that your

BEHIND THE SCENES AT THE ABORIGINAL BANKING NEWSLETTER

Partnership—The Key to Success

"The focus of the Aboriginal Banking newsletter," explains editor Wendy MacNair, "is on our motto, Partnership—The Key to Success." Published quarterly by the Aboriginal Banking Unit of the Business Development Bank of Canada (BDC), this colourful, high-quality newsletter directs both Aboriginal and non-Aboriginal entrepreneurs to the bank's programs and products for starting and maintaining a small business. It is distributed widely among Canada's Aboriginal community—to all First Nations across Canada, Friendship Centres, Aboriginal Capital Corporations—as well as to business leaders, entrepreneurs, and other interested parties. Based in Winnipeg, the Aboriginal Banking newsletter helps the BDC fulfill its mandate to be more visible and accessible to Canada's small business owners.

Today, more than 20 000 First Nations, Métis, and Inuit in Canada run their own business, operating in the so-called traditional areas of trapping, fishing, and farming as well as in knowledge-based business and in exporting. But there are obstacles to growing an Aboriginal-owned firm. According to a 1997 Industry Canada study, about half of Aboriginal entrepreneurs perceive that they have inadequate access to capital. They indicate that they lack the personal resources lenders require for collateral and that there are few financial institutions in their communities.

Mirroring the significance of images and spirituality to Aboriginal peoples, Aboriginal art is included in each issue of the Aboriginal Banking newsletter.

A mandate of the BDC, a Crown financial institution, is to provide financial support to small business by complementing commercial lenders. Through the Aboriginal Banking Unit, established in 1996, the BDC commits funds to supporting Aboriginal business—by the end of fiscal 2000, they had lent a total of $42 million. With the Aboriginal Banking newsletter, the BDC builds awareness of its financial products and business know-how available to its varied client base.

Launched in the summer of 1997, the Aboriginal Banking newsletter, produced in-house by the BDC, saw its circulation quickly grow to its current 3500 copies. Its objective, states Wendy MacNair, "is to profile success stories and other items of interest as they relate to access to capital and Aboriginal entrepreneurism." The staff consists of editor MacNair and Jim Richardson, the Unit's National Director. Yet, as MacNair comments, "Although I am editor, the newsletter is a collaborative effort by many individuals—BDC staff and clients, loss of sales is due to your pricing policy (C). This conclusion would lead you to recommend a price cut (R). To make an FCR worksheet, divide a computer screen or a sheet of paper into three columns. List the major findings in the first column, then extrapolate conclusions and write them in the second column. These conclusions form the basis for the recommendations, which are listed in the third column. An analysis of the three columns should help you focus on the main idea.

- *Journalistic approach.* For informational messages, the journalistic approach may provide a good point of departure. The answers to six questions–who? what? when? where? why? and how?–should clarify the main idea.
- *Question-and-answer chain.* Perhaps the best approach is to look at the subject from your audience's perspective. Ask yourself: "What is the audience's main question? What do they need to know?" Examine your answers to those questions. What additional questions emerge? Follow the chain of questions and answers until you have replied to every conceivable question that might occur to the audience. By thinking about your material from their point of view, you are more likely to pinpoint the main idea.

Aboriginal leaders and entrepreneurs as well as public affairs staff at our head office in Montreal, and many, many others."

MacNair states that "a quality product has always been very important." Produced on semi-glossy, letter-size paper, the 16-page newsletter is published in both English and French, with each version beginning on opposing covers. Format tends to be consistent with each issue, with MacNair and Richardson determining how to arrange the articles and artwork within the standard framework. Aboriginal art and prayers provided by spiritual leaders and elders are interspersed throughout each newsletter, reflecting the importance of images and spirituality to Aboriginal peoples.

Each issue features a cover story written by an Aboriginal leader or entrepreneur discussing the importance of Aboriginal economic development and entrepreneurship. The sensitive issue of balancing BDC's policy on editorial content with the message contained in the guest editorial is sometimes challenging. The challenge is to make required changes without offending the guest writer and keep their message intact by sometimes adjusting the tone of the article.

At least two pages are devoted to profiling Aboriginal clients. Readers learn about the success of specific businesses that have benefited from the BDC's financial support and advice, such as Stu McKay Outfitters, Ltd., a cat-fishing guide service. Short articles about special events also fill each issue, such as stories relating the achievements of Aboriginal college and university students.

The planning process starts four months before the publication date. At their first meeting, the staff select story ideas. Three weeks later, staff members read draft articles and offer their comments. Stories written by BDC clients are edited for spelling, grammar, and punctuation, but the writer's voice, or writing style, is retained. About midway between the first meeting and the publication date, MacNair prepares stories for placement into a PageMaker desktop publishing file and meets with Jim Richardson to review the newsletter. Then, MacNair e-mails the PageMaker file to a Winnipeg design firm, which arranges the text and visuals. She also sends the text to BDC's Public Affairs department, where the material is translated.Upon receiving the formatted file from the designer, MacNair and her staff check it for accuracy, placement of text and images, and overall visual appeal. When the designer receives MacNair's approval, the French text is inserted, and, after more checking, the issue is sent to the printer about one week before hard copies are distributed.

The result of all this careful planning and attention to detail? MacNair reports that feedback about the newsletter has been universally positive. You can find a sample of the Aboriginal Banking newsletter on the BDC site at **www.bdc.ca/bdc/home/Default.asp**. Choose Aboriginal Business from the site map.[14]

APPLY YOUR KNOWLEDGE

1. As editor of the Aboriginal Banking newsletter, how would you plan to communicate the following changes in the newsletter as being in the best interest of the readers: (a) having the newsletter written by staff rather than including guest columnists; (b) cutting out illustrations entirely.
2. Collaboration is necessary to producing the Aboriginal Banking newsletter. What are the benefits of collaboration? The problems?

Limit the Scope

Limit the message to three or four major points, regardless of its length.

There's a limit to how much you can communicate in a given number of words. What can be accomplished depends on the nature of the subject, the audience members' familiarity with the topic, their receptivity to your conclusions, and your credibility. In general, presenting routine information to a knowledgeable audience that already knows and respects you can be done quickly. Building consensus about a complex and controversial subject takes longer, especially if the audience is composed of skeptical or hostile strangers.

Although you should adjust your message to fit the time or space available, don't change the number of major points. Regardless of how long the message will be, stick with three or four major points–five at the very most. According to communication researchers, that's all your audience will remember.[15] If you're delivering a long message, say, a 60-minute presentation or a 20-page report, the major points can be developed in considerable detail. You can spend about ten minutes or ten paragraphs (or over three pages of double-spaced, printed text) on each of your key points and still have room for the introduction and conclusion. If your message is brief, four minutes or one page, you'll have only a minute or a paragraph each for the introduction, conclusion, and major points.

Stage 4: Selecting the Appropriate Channel and Medium

LEARNING OUTCOME 7
Select an appropriate channel and medium for transmitting a particular message to a particular audience.

The communication media available to business people have mushroomed in the past two decades: audiotapes, videotapes, faxes, e-mail, Web sites, voice mail, teleconferences–to name a few. You can now select not only from the traditional oral and written channels but also from the newer electronic channels, which include some features of the other two. Your selection of channel and medium can make the difference between effective and ineffective communication.[16] So, when choosing a channel (oral, written, or electronic) and a medium (face-to-face conversation, telephone conversation, e-mail, voice mail, videotape, written report, and so on), do your best to match your selections to your message and your intentions.[17]

A variety of messages requires a variety of communication channels.

Every medium has limitations that filter out parts of the message. For example, flyers or bulletin boards are undynamic and ineffective for communicating extremely complex messages, but they're perfect for simple ones. Moreover, every medium influences your audience's perception of your intentions. If you want to emphasize the formality of your message, use a formal medium, such as a written memo or letter. If you want to emphasize the confidentiality of your message, use voice mail rather than a fax, send a letter rather than a memo, or address the matter in an interview rather than during a meeting. If you want to instill an emotional commitment to corporate values, consider a visual medium, such as a videotape or videoconference.[18]

Various cultures tend to favour one channel over another. For example, Canada, the US, and Germany emphasize written media, whereas Japan emphasizes oral media–perhaps because its high-context culture carries so much of the message in nonverbal cues and between-the-lines interpretation.[19] Within Canada, the basic choice of oral, written, or electronic channels depends on the purpose, the audience, and the characteristics of the three communication channels (see Table 5.1).

TABLE 5.1 When to Talk It Over, Write It Out, or Apply Technology

An Oral Message Is Best When	A Written Message Is Best When	An Electronic Message Is Best When
You want immediate feedback from the audience	You don't need immediate feedback	You don't need immediate feedback, but you do need speed
Your message is relatively simple and easy to accept	Your message is detailed, complex, and requires careful planning	Your message is emotional; you may or may not need immediate feedback, but you're physically separated (videotape, teleconference)
You don't need a permanent record	You need a permanent, verifiable record	You don't need a permanent record, but you want to overcome time-zone barriers (voice mail, fax)
You can assemble the audience conveniently and economically	You are trying to reach an audience that is large and geographically dispersed	You want to minimize oral distortion, but you're in a hurry and in a distant location (e-mail)
You want to encourage interaction to solve a problem or to reach a decision	You want to minimize the chances for distortion that occur when a message is passed orally from person to person	You are trying to reach an audience that is large and geographically dispersed, and you want to reach them personally (teleconference, videotape)

Oral Communication

The chief advantage of oral communication is the opportunity it provides for immediate feedback. This is the channel to use when you want the audience to ask questions and make comments or when you're trying to reach a group decision. Face-to-face communication is useful when you're presenting controversial information, because you can read the audience's body language and adjust your message accordingly.[20]

In general, use oral communication if your purpose is to collaborate with the audience.

Your choice between a face-to-face conversation and a telephone or conference call depends on the location of your audience, importance of your message, and your need for the sort of non-verbal feedback that only body language can reveal. In fact, oral communication takes many forms, including conversations, telephone calls, interviews, small group meetings, seminars, workshops, training programs, formal speeches, and major presentations. Chapters 17 and 18 explore these channels in more detail.

In general, the smaller the audience, the more the interaction among its members. If your purpose involves reaching a decision or solving a problem, select an oral medium geared toward a small audience. Be sure the program is relatively informal and unstructured so that ideas can flow freely. Gatherings of this sort can be arranged quickly and economically.

At the opposite extreme are formal presentations to large audiences, which are common at events such as sales conventions, shareholder meetings, and ceremonial functions. Often these major presentations take place in a big facility, where the audience can be seated auditorium-style. The formality of such occasions makes them unsuitable for collaborative purposes requiring audience interaction.

Written Communication

Written messages also take many forms. At one extreme are the scribbled notes people use to jog their own memories; at the other are elaborate, formal reports that rival magazines in graphic quality. Regardless of the form, written messages have

Written communication increases the sender's control but eliminates the possibility of immediate feedback.

one big advantage–they let you plan and control the message. A written format is appropriate when the information is complex, when a permanent record is needed for future reference, when the audience is large and geographically dispersed, and when immediate interaction with the audience is either unimportant or undesirable.

For extensive coverage of letters and memos, see Chapters 8 through 11. Reports are thoroughly discussed in Chapters 12 through 14. In addition, Appendix A presents a detailed discussion of the accepted formats for business documents. Although many types of written communication are specialized, the most common are letters, memos, and reports.

LETTERS AND MEMOS

Letters and memos are organized according to their purpose; the relationship between writer and reader dictates their style and tone.

With a few exceptions, most letters and memos are relatively brief documents, generally one or two pages. Memos are the workhorses of business communication; they are used for the routine, day-to-day exchange of information within an organization. Letters go to outsiders, and they perform an important public-relations function in addition to conveying a particular message. Memos are usually brief, lacking a salutation and emphasizing the needs of readers who have time only to skim messages. They can also be sent to any number of receivers, whereas letters are sent to only one. Because of their open construction and method of delivery, memos are less private than letters. You often use memos to designate responsibility, communicate the same material to many people, communicate policy and procedure, confirm oral agreements or decisions, and place specific information on record.

Letters (see Figure 5.2), memos, and e-mail messages (see Figure 5.3) can be classified by function into four categories: direct requests; routine good-news and goodwill messages; bad-news messages; and persuasive messages. Their function determines their organization, but style and tone are governed by your relationship with your audience.

Many organizations rely on form letters (and sometimes form memos) to save time and money on routine communication. Form letters are particularly handy for such one-time mass mailings as sales messages about products, explanations of policies and procedures, information about organizational activities, goodwill messages such as seasonal greetings, and acknowledgements of job applications. A variation of the form letter is the **boilerplate**, or standard paragraph, that can be selected to suit an occasion or an audience. Letters containing boilerplates are used for messages that need to be slightly more individualized than a form letter, such as the replies from a consumer affairs specialist to inquiries about Mattel's products and activities.

REPORTS AND PROPOSALS

Reports are generally longer and more formal than letters and memos, and they have more components.

Factual, objective documents such as reports and proposals may be distributed either to insiders or outsiders, depending on their purpose and subject. They come in many formats–including preprinted forms, letters, memos, and manuscripts. They range in length from a few pages to several hundred. In general, reports and proposals are longer than letters and memos and have a larger number of distinct elements.

Reports and proposals also tend to be more formal than letters and memos. As in all forms of business communication, the organization, style, and tone of reports and proposals depend on the message's purpose, on the relationship between writer and reader, and on the traditions of the organization. Thus the basic composition process is much the same for all.

MOTT'S

MOTT'S CANADA

2700 Matheson Boulevard East
East Tower, Suite 500
Mississauga, Ontario L4W 4X1
Phone (905) 629-1899
Fax (905) 629-3534

September 19, 2000

Ms. Mita Nemani
84 Plum Road
Willowdale, ON M2R 3J2

Dear Ms. Nemani:

Thank you very much for your interest in our Mott's Bake Lite program.

We have enclosed our free recipe pamphlet which contains a selection of tested and proven recipes which replace the butter and oil in baking with Mott's Apple Sauce.

Many consumers have asked us if they can use Mott's Apple Sauce as a substitute in all their baking recipes. We can only recommend the recipes we have developed in our test kitchens, because they are proven to succeed very well and to produce excellent, healthy results.

We can, however, provide a rule of thumb for those wanting to experiment with their own favourite recipes; butter and oil can normally be substituted with equal amounts of apple sauce. However, you must consider that apple sauce is sweeter, and thinner, which may call for less sugar, and more flour.

Again, we would like to thank you for your interest in Mott's and wish you the best of luck and enjoyment in your baking.

Sincerely,

Holly Prentice

Holly Prentice
Consumer Affairs Specialist

encl.

A MEMBER OF THE CADBURY SCHWEPPES PLC GROUP

The formal salutation indicates Prentice's respect for a customer she doesn't know.

The body of the letter includes advice for using the product. Additional information in a response to a request for a pamphlet or other company publication is included to maintain goodwill.

The close is cordial and alludes to the main idea of the message.

FIGURE 5.2

In-Depth Critique: A Typical Letter

When Mott's consumer affairs specialists respond to requests for information, they are careful to make their messages personal and detailed.

Electronic Communication

Although oral messages can be in person and face to face, they can also be transmitted electronically using voice mail, teleconferencing, audiotape, videotape, closed-circuit television, and so on. Similarly, although written messages can be handwritten, typed, or printed, they can also be transmitted electronically using

In general, use electronic communication for speed, to overcome time-zone barriers, and to reach a widely dispersed audience personally.

Because Goshal has all managers' e-mail addresses in one file, she needs to key in only the name of that file to reach each manager.

Goshal states the essential information and gives an overview of the workshop.

Goshal also tries to anticipate other questions managers might have.

Date: Thursday, 12 October 2000. 10:04:58
From: Neema Goshal, HR
To: IS Managers
Subject: Presentations course

On Wednesday, November 15, Jack Stoller of Tech Training, Inc. is offering a four-hour workshop from 10 to 2, covering presentation skills. He will discuss planning, organizing, and delivering a technical presentation and incorporating visual support.

If you wish to take advantage of this opportunity, please call me by Tuesday, November 8 to reserve a spot. The workshop will be held in the fourth floor board room, and lunch will be served.

Contact me with any questions at x1209.

Neema Goshal

FIGURE 5.3

In-Depth Critique: A Typical E-Mail Message

Many Canadian corporations use internal e-mail lists to contact an entire functional level or a division. Here, the Vice President of Human Resources, Neema Goshal, is notifying Information Systems managers of a training opportunity. By choosing to e-mail these employees, rather than calling each one individually or posting a notice on a central bulletin board, Goshal saves time and minimizes her efforts.

e-mail, faxes, computer conferencing, and so on. Electronic media are useful when you need speed, when you're physically separated from your audience, when you need to overcome time-zone barriers, and when you need to reach a dispersed audience personally. Chapter 4 introduced the technological features of electronic

Checklist for Planning Business Messages

A. Purpose

1. Determine whether the purpose of your message is to inform, to persuade, or to collaborate.
2. Identify the specific behaviour you hope to induce in the audience.
3. Make sure that your purpose is worthwhile and realistic.

B. Audience

1. Identify the primary audience.
2. Determine the size and composition of the group.
3. Analyze the audience's probable reaction to your message.
4. Determine the audience's level of understanding.
5. Evaluate your relationship with the audience.
6. Analyze the audience's informational, motivational, and practical needs.

C. Main Idea

1. Stimulate your creativity with brainstorming techniques.
2. Identify a hook that will motivate the audience to respond to your message in the way you intend.
3. Evaluate whether the main idea is realistic given the length limitations imposed on the message.
4. Collect any necessary information.

media; following are a few pointers on when to select electronic media over traditional oral or written media:[21]

- *Voice mail* is usually used to replace short memos and phone calls that need no response. It is most effective for short, unambiguous messages.
- *Teleconferencing* is best for informational meetings, but it's ineffective for negotiation. It's an efficient alternative to a face-to-face meeting, but it can't totally simulate it. For example, because it discourages the secondary conversations that usually occur during a meeting of more than four or five people, it could prevent participants from sharing valuable information. On the other hand, discouraging secondary conversations might help participants focus on the topic.
- *Videotape* is often effective for sending a motivational message to a large number of people. By communicating nonverbal cues, it can strengthen your image of sincerity and trustworthiness; however, it offers no opportunity for immediate feedback.
- *Fax* messages are usually used to overcome time-zone barriers when a hard copy is required. A fax has all the characteristics of a written message, except that it may lack the privacy of a letter, and depending on the quality of your audience's machine (thermal versus plain-paper, for example), your message may appear less crisp, perhaps even less professional, than other written messages.
- *E-mail* offers advantages of speed, lower cost, and increased access to other employees. This medium is best at communicating brief, noncomplex information that's time sensitive, but its effectiveness depends on the skills of the people using it.
- *Computer conferencing* offers the advantage of democracy; that is, more attention is focused on an idea than on who communicates it. However, too much emphasis on the message (to the neglect of the person communicating it) can threaten corporate culture, which needs a more dynamic medium of communication.

Message planning encompasses valuable tasks that help you gain more control over the composition process. Use this chapter's Checklist for Planning Business Messages not as a recipe for well-planned messages but as a reminder of what tasks and choices to address as you develop your business messages. Also remember that the planning stages discussed here may be useful at any time during the composition process, depending on your purpose, your audience, and your message.

D. Channel and Medium

1. If your purpose is to collaborate, give an informal, relatively unstructured oral presentation to a small group.
2. If you are celebrating an important public occasion, give a prepared speech to a large audience.
3. If you need a permanent record, if the message is complex, or if immediate feedback is unimportant, prepare a written message.
   a. Send a letter if your message is relatively simple and the audience is outside the company.
   b. Send a memo if your message is relatively simple and the audience is inside the company.
   c. Write a report if your message is objective and complex.
4. If you need to communicate quickly, overcome time-zone differences, or personally reach a widely dispersed audience, choose electronic communication.
   a. Use voice mail if your message is short and clear.
   b. Use teleconferencing for informational meetings.
   c. Use videotape for sending motivational messages to a large number of people.
   d. Use fax machines to overcome time-zone barriers.
   e. Use e-mail for speed, lower cost, and increased access to other employees.
   f. Use computer conferencing to focus attention on ideas instead of status.

ON THE JOB
SOLVING a Communication Dilemma at Mattel

Convincing the world that Barbie is more than a fashion doll is not an easy task, but Mattel's brand managers are doing their best with careful planning and a thorough understanding of their audience. Part of the problem is that Mattel's purposes are mixed. On the one hand, the company wants Barbie to be a worthy role model for little girls. On the other hand, Mattel wants to sell dolls and accessories—and that means that Barbie must retain her traditional appeal. After all, hundreds of millions of people have voted with their pocketbooks for the Barbie doll whose number one priority is what to wear. Nearly $2 billion in yearly sales—40 percent of Mattel's total revenue—is at stake. Completely changing Barbie's image could jeopardize the doll's mystique and hurt sales.

To a great extent, that mystique depends on Barbie's lack of a strong identity. Mattel intentionally says very little about Barbie's character because they want little girls to decide what Barbie is like. Her bland personality and her wide assortment of clothes and accessories allow for endless possibilities. Barbie can be whatever a child wants her to be.

Still, an image of Barbie emerges from a variety of messages—advertising, public relations events, the official Barbie Web site, and *Barbie* magazine, a glossy publication sent to 650 000 members of Barbie's fan club. The magazine describes Barbie's clothes and activities. In a recent issue, for example, Ken took Barbie out to dinner at a "sumptuous restaurant." For the occasion, Barbie chose her "ravishing new pink ruffled evening dress." Perhaps the strongest statement about Barbie's personality was a two-hour cartoon special, featuring her experiences with her all-girl rock band. But even there, Barbie's character remained a mystery. All she did on the show was sing and play music.

Although in many ways Mattel has reinforced the popular image of Barbie, the company has also raised her consciousness. In the mid-1970s, the company surveyed mothers and asked their opinion of Barbie. Many responded that she lacked ambition and should get a job. According to Jill Barad (the former president of the Barbie brand), the public was delighted when Mattel reacted by launching Barbie's career. Now Barbie is a better person, says Barad, who comments that Barbie "does have talent and skills, and goes to work and makes money, and that's how she affords her car!" She has also embraced cultural diversity. Barbie's pals are African, Asian, and Hispanic versions of Barbie herself.

As a symbol of popular culture, Barbie has also gained a measure of respectability. Scholars write learned articles analyzing her significance. The Toy Manufacturers of America have acknowledged her unique place in the history of toys. International conventions are held annually to celebrate Barbie. In 1999, Calgary, Alberta was the first Canadian city to host one, and it attracted visitors from across Canada, the US, and Europe. Barbie has impressed not only young girls but adult collectors, artists, and fashion designers with her varied wardrobes and accessories.[22]

Your Mission: You have recently joined Mattel's marketing department. One of your responsibilities is to respond to letters about Barbie. Your goals are to emphasize Barbie's positive qualities, to reinforce her popularity with youngsters, and to handle her critics as diplomatically as possible. Choose the best alternatives for handling the following correspondence, and be prepared to explain why your choice is best:

1. You have received a letter from Alice Brown, a reporter for a feminist oriented magazine, who is writing an article tentatively entitled "Barbie: Reflection or Moulder of Contemporary Values?" Brown has asked you for information about the marketing campaign that Mattel has employed to mould Barbie's image over the years. When responding to Brown's request, what should your purpose be?
   a. The general purpose is to inform. The specific purpose is to provide Brown with a brief summary of the evolution of Mattel's marketing campaign for Barbie over the past 30 years.
   b. The general purpose is to persuade. The specific purpose is to convince Brown that Barbie is a worthy role model for young girls and that the marketing campaign portrays Barbie as a socially aware, successful career woman.
   c. The general purpose is to collaborate. The specific purpose is to work with Brown to develop an article that examines the evolution of Mattel's marketing campaign for Barbie.
   d. The general purpose is to respond. The specific purpose is to convey details requested by a journalist.
2. Assume that your purpose is to convince Brown of Barbie's worthiness as a role model who is a socially aware, successful career woman. Does this purpose meet the tests suggested in the chapter?
   a. Yes. The purpose is realistic. The timing is right. You are the right person to send the message. And the purpose is acceptable to the organization.
   b. Not completely. Realistically, Brown may not accept Barbie as an admirable role model for young girls. Even though Barbie now has a career and some friends from other cultural backgrounds, her basic image has not changed a great deal.
   c. The purpose is fine, but you are not the right person to send the message. Mattel's president should respond.

d. The timing is right for this message. Stress Barbie's involvement in social causes and in career activities. Show how unimportant fashion is to Barbie's new lifestyle.

3. When planning your reply, what assumptions can you safely make about your audience?

a. The audience includes not only Alice Brown but also the readers of her magazine. Given their feminist bias, the readers will probably be hostile to business in general and to Barbie in particular. They probably know virtually nothing about the toy business. Furthermore, they probably mistrust you because you are a Mattel employee.

b. Alice Brown will probably be the only person who reads the letter directly. She is the primary audience; the readers of her article are the secondary audience. Brown will be happy to hear from Mattel and will read the information with an open mind. As a journalist, Brown is probably intelligent and objective. However, she may not know a great deal about Mattel or about marketing. Although she is a stranger to you, she trusts your credibility as a Mattel spokesperson.

c. Alice Brown is probably the sole and primary audience for the letter. The fact that she is writing an article about Barbie suggests that she enjoyed playing with the doll as a child and that she knows a great deal about Barbie already. In all likelihood, she will respond positively to your reply and will trust your credibility as a Mattel representative.

d. Alice Brown may be an industrial spy working for a rival toy company. She will show your reply to people who work for your competitor; they will analyze the information and use it to improve their own marketing program at your expense.

4. Which channel and medium of communication should you use in replying to Alice Brown?

a. Call her on the phone to ask for clarification of her needs; then follow up with a letter report (4 to 20 pages, written in letter format).

b. Call her on the phone, ask for clarification of her needs, and answer her while you have her on the line.

c. Write a letter asking for clarification of her needs, and follow up with a letter report.

d. Send a form letter used for replying to all inquiries about Barbie.

TAP Your Knowledge

Summary of Learning Outcomes

1. Describe the basic tasks in the composition process. The composition process essentially involves planning, composing, and revising. During the planning phase, define your purpose, analyze your audience, establish your main idea, and select the appropriate channel and medium for communicating. During the composing phase, organize and formulate your message. During the revising phase, edit, rewrite, produce, and proofread your message.

2. Define both the general and the specific purposes of your business messages. The general purpose of your message is to inform, persuade, or collaborate with your audience. The specific purpose requires stating your purpose as precisely as possible and identifying the members of the audience who should respond.

3. Test the purpose of your business messages. When testing the purpose of your message, you need to ask yourself several questions: (1) Is the purpose realistic? (2) Is this the right time to send the message? (3) Am I the right person to deliver the message? (4) Is the purpose acceptable to the organization?

4. Develop an audience profile. Understanding your audience is essential to creating an effective message. To develop an audience profile, (1) determine the size of your audience and its composition; (2) identify the primary audience; (3) judge your audience's probable reaction; (4) gauge your audience's level of understanding; (5) define your relationship with your audience.

5. Analyze the needs of your audience. The needs of your audience are informational, motivational, and practical. To analyze the informational needs, you must learn what the audience needs to know, anticipate unstated questions, provide all the required information, certify the information is accurate, and emphasize the ideas of greatest interest to the audience. To analyze your audience's motivational needs, determine what their existing beliefs and practices are, so that you can arrange your message in the manner that is most acceptable to them. To analyze your audience's practical needs, determine their position and activities to understand how much time they may have to read your message.

6. Establish the main idea of your messages. Every message has a topic and a main idea. The topic is the broad subject of the message. The main idea makes a statement about the topic.

7. **Select an appropriate channel and medium for transmitting a particular message to a particular audience.** Selecting the channel and medium of your message can make the difference between effective and ineffective communication. When choosing a channel (oral, written, or electronic) and a medium (face-to-face conversation, telephone conversation, e-mail, voice mail, videotape, or written report), try to match your selections to your message and your intentions.

Test Your Knowledge

Review Questions

1. Describe the benefits and drawbacks of collaboration.
2. Discuss the three components of audience analysis.
3. Describe the five techniques of pre-writing.
4. Why is it important to limit the scope of your message?
5. Compare the uses of letters and memos, and reports and proposals.
6. Discuss the advantages and disadvantages of voice mail, teleconferencing, and fax messages.

Apply Your Knowledge

Critical Thinking Questions

1. Some writers argue that it's a waste of time for them to plan messages because they inevitably change their plans as they go along. How would you respond to this argument? Briefly explain.
2. Your supervisor has asked you to prepare a message that, in your opinion, serves no worthwhile purpose. What will you do? Explain.
3. As editor of your company's newsletter, how would you go about discovering the needs of your fellow employees? Write a one-page explanation.
4. List several main ideas you might use if you were trying to persuade top management to invest in word-processing equipment and software.
5. What would be the best medium for a personnel manager to use for explaining employee benefits to new employees? Explain your answer.
6. If you were a member of the public relations department, what medium would you recommend using to inform the local community that your toxic-waste cleanup program has been successful? Why?

Practise Your Knowledge

Exercises

1. For each of the following communication tasks, state a specific purpose (if you have trouble, try beginning with "I want to …").
   a. A report to your boss, the store manager, about the outdated items in the warehouse
   b. A memo to clients about your booth at the upcoming trade show
   c. A letter to a customer who hasn't made a payment for three months
   d. A memo to employees about the office's high water bills
   e. A phone call to a supplier checking on an overdue parts shipment
   f. A report to future users of the computer program you have chosen to handle the company's mailing list.

2. Make a list of communication tasks you'll need to accomplish in the next week or so (a job application, a letter of complaint, a speech to a class, an order for some merchandise, etc.). For each, determine a general and a specific purpose.

3. List five messages you have received lately, such as direct-mail promotions, letters, e-mail messages, phone solicitations, and lectures. For each, determine the general and the specific purpose; then answer the following questions: Was the message well timed? Did the sender choose an appropriate channel and medium for the message? Did the appropriate person deliver the message? Was the sender's purpose realistic?

4. Barbara Marquardt is in charge of public relations for a cruise line that operates out of Vancouver, B.C. She is shocked to read a letter in a local newspaper from a disgruntled passenger, complaining about the service and entertainment on a recent cruise. Marquardt will have to respond to these publicized criticisms in some way. What audiences will she need to consider in her response? What channels and media should she choose? If the letter had been published in a travel publication widely read by travel agents and cruise travellers, how might her course of action differ?

5. For each of the following communication tasks, write brief answers to three questions: Who is my audience? What is my audience's general attitude toward my subject? What does my audience need to know?

   a. A final-notice collection letter from an appliance manufacturer to an appliance dealer, sent ten days before legal collection procedures will be initiated

   b. An unsolicited sales letter asking readers to purchase computer disks at near-wholesale prices

   c. An advertisement for peanut butter

   d. Fliers, to be attached to doorknobs in the neighbourhood, announcing reduced rates for chimney lining or repairs

   e. A cover letter sent along with your résumé to a potential employer

   f. A request (to the seller) for a price adjustment on a piano that incurred $150 in damage during delivery to a banquet room in the hotel you manage

6. Rewrite the following message so that it includes all the information the reader needs. (Make up any necessary details.)

   I am pleased to offer you the position of assistant buyer at Fontaine and Sons at an annual salary of $29 500. I hope to receive notice of your acceptance soon.

7. Your team has been studying a new method for testing the durability of your company's electric hand tools. Now the team needs to prepare three separate reports on the findings: first, a report for the administrator who will decide whether to purchase the equipment needed for this new testing method; second, a report for the company's engineers who design and develop the hand tools; and third, a report for the trainers who will be showing workers how to use the new equipment. To determine the audience's needs for each of these reports, the team has listed the following questions: (1) Who are the readers? (2) Why will they read my report? (3) Do they need introductory or background material? (4) Do they need definitions of terms? (5) What level or type of language is needed? (6) What level of detail is needed? (7) What result does my report aim for? Working with two other students, answer the questions for each of these audiences:

   a. The administrator

   b. The engineers

   c. The trainers.

8. Choose an electronic device that you know how to operate well (videocassette recorder, personal computer, telephone answering machine, etc.). Write two sets of instructions for operating the device: one set for a reader who has never used that type of machine and one set for someone familiar with that type of machine in general but who has never operated the specific model.

9. Work with a classmate to complete this task. Each partner must independently visit the site at **www.bell.ca.** Working together only by e-mail (not in person and not using any other electronic technology), plan, compose, and revise your joint explanation of the Web site. Summarize *what* is on the Web page and linked pages, and then evaluate the site. Explain why it does or does not communicate efficiently and effectively, and whether it provides complete and accessible information for the intended audience. When you and your collaborator are satisfied with your explanation, print it out for submission to your instructor.

10. You're looking for a job as a salesperson, so you'd better be able to sell yourself first. What special qualities do you have that make you a desirable sales employee? Use the techniques described in the chapter to come up with a main idea you can use in your efforts to market yourself. In no more than a paragraph, draft a statement of your main idea that tells your audience (potential employers) what to do or think about you and why.

11. Suggest short, simple words to replace each of the following.

a. inaugurate
b. terminate
c. utilize
d. anticipate
e. assistance
f. endeavour
g. ascertain
h. procure
i. consummate
j. advise
k. alteration
l. forwarded
m. fabricate
n. nevertheless
o. substantial

Developing Your Internet Skills

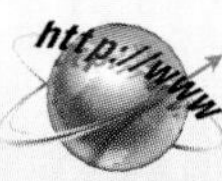

Going Online: Learn More About Analyzing an Audience, p. 99

Recalling the imaginary Web site you developed for the Going Online exercise in Chapter 4, draw a cluster diagram for your primary and secondary audiences. If time permits, go ahead and use the categories in the audience-analysis table to compile more information about your own imagined audience. What new ideas does this give you about content?

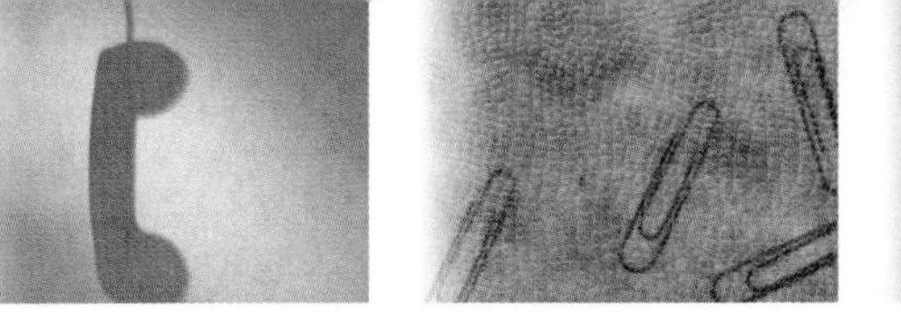
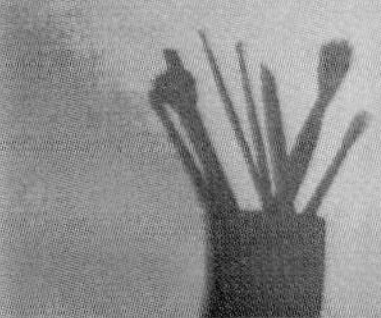

C H A P T E R 6

Composing Business Messages

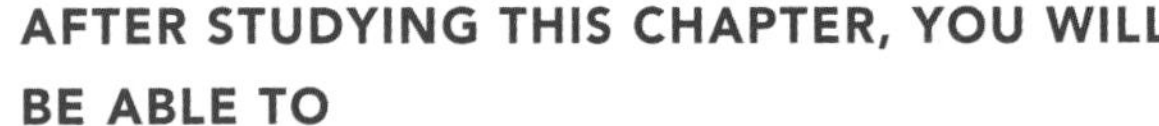

AFTER STUDYING THIS CHAPTER, YOU WILL BE ABLE TO

1. Identify the characteristics of a well-organized message
2. Explain why organization is important to both the audience and the communicator
3. Break a main idea into subdivisions grouped under logical categories
4. Arrange ideas in direct or indirect order, depending on the audience's probable reaction
5. Compose a message using a style and tone that are appropriate to your subject, purpose, and audience.
6. Use the "you" attitude to interest the audience in your message
7. Compose an appropriate e-mail message

ON THE JOB
Facing a Communication Dilemma at Club Med

Fun in the Sun—For Everyone This Time

When you think about Club Med, what comes to mind? You probably envision sunny skies, blue water, and carefree single adults relaxing and mingling on the beach in some tropical paradise. That was the image the French company cultivated for many years, from its humble camping-club beginnings in the 1950s to its emergence as a worldwide resort operator in the 1970s and 1980s. In fact, one business reference even uses the phrase "sun, sea, and sex" to describe the company's philosophy during those decades of growth.

Employees at Club Med use their strong communication skills not only to communicate with travel agents but also to attract guests of all ages, including families with children, singles, and retired people. Serge Trigano motivates his marketing staff to work hard to support Club Med's new image.

That philosophy was certainly profitable—until the 1990s, when people began to shift away from freewheeling lifestyles. Then a series of unfortunate events put an end to society's enchantment with travelling to exotic locations. These events were not like anything that business executives normally have to face: French tourists were kidnapped in Turkey; political tension and sporadic violence broke out in Israel; civil war erupted in the former Yugoslavia—just a few of the locations where Club Med has resorts. Also, Japanese and Australian tourists boycotted Club Med resorts to protest French nuclear tests in the South Pacific, and a hurricane destroyed a Club Med village in the Caribbean. The result of all this upheaval was a dramatic decline in business, leading to losses that bottomed out at $50 million in 1993.

So in 1993, when Serge Trigano took the company's reins from his father, one of the fundamental appeals of Club Med—its exotic locations—was no longer all that appealing; many of its resorts seemed to be in hot spots whose very names had become more frightening than enchanting. Trigano knew he couldn't control the world, but he could control Club Med's strategy and, to a large extent, its reputation. Recognizing society's shifting concerns, he set about expanding the company's market by adding vacation programs that were aimed not only at singles but also at married couples, families with children, and senior citizens.

Once these new programs were in place, Trigano needed to inform travel agents of the new programs and encourage the agents to recommend Club Med vacations for everyone, not just young singles. Travel agents account for 85 percent of Club Med business, so their support is crucial if the new programs are to succeed.

If you were Serge Trigano, what sort of letter could you write to stimulate a travel agent's interest in your resorts and new vacation programs? How important will organization be to your letter? Will an outline help? What style will work best?[1]

Stage 5: Organizing Your Message

Like Serge Trigano, all business communicators face the problem of conveying a complicated web of ideas in an understandable fashion. Since people simply don't remember dissociated facts and figures, successful communicators rely on organization to make their messages meaningful.[2] Before thinking about how to achieve good organization, however, think about what it means and why it's important.

What Good Organization Means

LEARNING OUTCOME 1
Identify the characteristics of a well-organized message.

The definition of a well-organized message varies from country to country, but in Canada and the United States, it generally refers to a linear message that proceeds point by point. If you've ever received an unorganized message, you're familiar with the frustration of trying to sort through a muddle of ideas. Consider this letter from Jane Creston, the office manager at Johnson & Associates Appraisers:

> Johnson and Associates Antiques Appraisers has been doing business with Microplus since I was hired six years ago. Our building was smaller then, and it was located at the corner of Sloane and Rockland.
>
> Mr. Johnson bought our first laser printer there, and I still remember the day. It was the biggest purchase order I'd ever written. Of course, over the years, I've gotten used to larger orders.
>
> We have five employees. Although not all of them are directly involved in appraising antiques and collectibles, they all use the scanner to do their jobs. The flatbed scanner we bought for the office has been a problem. We have taken it for repairs twice to the authorized service centre, and Suzanne has been very careful with the machine and hasn't abused it. She likes scanning photographs of her pet dog on her lunch breaks. The scanner still doesn't work right, and she's tired of hauling it back and forth. We're all putting in longer hours to make up for Mr. Johnson's not being here, and none of us has a lot of spare time.
>
> This is the first time we've returned anything to your store, and I hope you agree that we deserve a better deal.

This letter displays the sort of disorganization that Canadian and US readers find frustrating. By taking a closer look at the letter, you can identify the four most common faults responsible for organization problems:

Most unorganized communication suffers from problems with content, grouping, or sequence.

- Taking too long to get to the point. Creston wrote two paragraphs before introducing the topic: the faulty scanner. Then she waited until the final paragraph to state her purpose: requesting an adjustment.
- Including irrelevant material. Creston introduced information that has no bearing on her purpose or her topic. Does it matter that their shop used to be smaller or that it was in a different location? What difference does it make whether an employee likes scanning personal photos during lunch?
- Getting ideas mixed up. Creston seems to be making five points: (1) her company is an old customer; (2) she writes purchase orders; (3) all of the company's employees use the scanner; (4) the scanner doesn't work; and (5) Creston wants an adjustment. However, the ideas are in the wrong places. It would be more logical to begin with the request for a refund. Some of the other points should be combined under the general idea that the company is a valuable customer.
- Leaving out necessary information. The customer service representative may want to know the make, model, and price of the scanner; the date on which it was purchased; the specific problems it has had; and whether the repairs were covered by the warranty. Creston also failed to specify what she wants the store to do. Does she want a new scanner of the same type? A different model? Or simply her money back?

A message is well organized when all the pieces fit together in a coherent pattern.

Marie Delorme is President of ImagiNATION Cards, Inc., a small business that sells Aboriginal art cards to the corporate and retail markets. She contributes her time and expertise to the Boards of the Canadian Youth Business Foundation, the Canadian Council for Aboriginal Business, and the University of Calgary Cultural Diversity Institute. Why do professionals like Delorme appreciate messages that are well organized and clearly written?

Achieving good organization can be a challenge. Nevertheless, by reorganizing these four common faults, you can establish what good organization means. Four guidelines can help you to create a well-organized message:

- Make the subject and purpose clear.
- Include only information that is related to the subject and purpose.
- Group the ideas and present them in a logical way.
- Include all the necessary information.

Each guideline not only helps you communicate clearly and logically but also helps you communicate ethically–by making sure you state all information as truthfully, honestly, and fairly as possible. Observing these four rules changes the original letter so that the message can be effectively communicated (see Figure 6.1).

Johnson and Associates Appraisers
Appraiser of Fine Antiques
257 Laurier E., Montreal, Quebec H2T 1G3
Phone: 514-555-9735 Fax: 514-555-9750 Email: jaa7@sympatico.ca

March 22, 2000

Microplus
4535 Du Park
Montreal, QC H2V 4E4

Attention: Customer Service

We would like to return the Vision 1200E scanner we purchased in January because its performance is below standard.

We bought the scanner on January 14 for $349.99 (marked down from $399.99) during your millennium sale. The scanner has produced incomplete images on three occasions since we have owned it. It is an essential tool for our business, because we scan photographs of items we appraise for storage in our computer.

On January 17, we took the scanner to the authorized service centre, Electronic Systems Repair, after it first produced poor images. The technician told us the problem was a faulty connection. On February 4, we returned to the repair shop with the scanner after the second breakdown. We were again told there was a faulty connection. Yesterday, the scanner once more produced images with very poor resolution.

We purchased the Vision scanner because its output was rated excellent; reviews cited its crisp and vivid images. Although the scanner is still covered by the one-year warranty, we are not happy with the unit's performance. We would like to return it and receive a refund.

Johnson and Associates bought our computer systems and printers from Microplus two years ago. We have always been pleased with your prompt and reliable service. Please let me know when your courier will pick up the Vision 1200E scanner from our shop.

Sincerely,

Jane Creston

Jane Creston

The first paragraph clearly states the purpose of this letter.

The second and third paragraphs explain the situation so that the reader will understand the problem. The writer includes no irrelevant information, and the ideas are presented logically.

The fourth paragraph states precisely what adjustment is being requested.

The last paragraph motivates a response by reminding the reader of previous business (which implies future business) and seeking a specific action.

FIGURE 6.1

In-Depth Critique: Letter with Improved Organization

This letter from Johnson and Associates Appraisers asking for a refund is organized to give all needed information in a sequence that helps the reader understand the message.

Why Good Organization Is Important

LEARNING OUTCOME 2
Explain why organization is important to both the audience and the communicator.

You might be asking yourself whether it matters that the message is well organized, as long as the point is eventually made. Why not just let the ideas flow naturally and trust that the audience will grasp the meaning? But when you consider the cost of misinterpreted messages–such as wasted time reading and rereading unclear messages, poor decision making, and shattered business relationships–you begin to realize the value of clear writing and good organization.[3] By arranging your ideas logically and diplomatically, you increase the chances of satisfying your audience's needs for information, motivation, and practicality. You also simplify your communication task.

- *Helping your audience understand your message.* The less work required of your audience to figure out your message, the better they will understand what you're trying to say. As Club Med's Serge Trigano points out, you want your information to be "user-friendly and understandable." If you're interested in getting your message across, good organization is one of the handiest tools because it makes your message easier to understand. A well-organized message satisfies the audience's need for information.

The main reason for being well organized is to improve the chances that people will understand exactly what you mean.

- *Helping your audience accept your message.* Good organization helps motivate your audience to accept your message. As the letter in Figure 6.2 shows, you can soften refusals, leave a good impression, and be more convincing by organizing messages diplomatically. You can also use good organization to enhance your credibility and add authority to your messages.

Good organization also helps you get your ideas across without upsetting the audience.

- *Saving your audience's time.* Well-organized messages are efficient. They contain only relevant ideas, so your audience doesn't waste time on superfluous information. Moreover, all the information in a well-organized message is in a logical place. The audience can follow the thought pattern without a struggle, and they can save even more time by looking for just the information they need instead of reading everything.

Well-organized messages are efficient because they contain only relevant information.

- *Simplifying your communication task.* Finally, being well organized helps you compose your message more quickly and efficiently. By thinking about what you're going to say and how you're going to say it before you begin to write, you can proceed more confidently. You can use your organization plan to get some input from your boss to be sure you're on the right track before you spend hours working on a draft. If you're working on a large and complex project, you can use the plan to divide the writing job among co-workers to finish the assignment as quickly as possible.

Organizing what you're going to say before you start to write makes the job much easier.

How Good Organization Is Achieved

Understanding the need for good organization is half the battle. Knowing how to organize your messages well is the other half. Serge Trigano of Club Med achieves good organization by following this two-step process: first define and group the ideas; then establish their sequence with a carefully selected organizational pattern.

To organize a message, first group the ideas, then put them in sequence.

DEFINE AND GROUP IDEAS

LEARNING OUTCOME 3
Break a main idea into subdivisions grouped under logical categories.

The pre-writing techniques described in Chapter 5 will help you generate your main idea, but they won't necessarily tell you how to develop it or how to group the supporting details in the most logical and effective way. To decide on the final structure of your message, you need to visualize how all the points fit together. One way to do this is to construct an outline. Whether you use the outlining features provided with word-processing software or simply jot down three or four points on the back of an envelope, making a plan and sticking to it will help you cover the important details.

In business, deciding what to say is more important than deciding how to say it.

When you're preparing a long and complex message, an outline is indispensable because it helps you visualize the relationship among the various parts. Without an outline, you may be inclined to ramble. As you're describing one point, another point may occur to you–so you describe it. One detour leads to another, and, before you know it, you've forgotten the original point. With an outline to guide you, however, you can communicate in a more systematic way, covering all the necessary ideas in an effective order and with proper emphasis. Following an outline

An outline or a schematic diagram will help you visualize the relationship among parts of a message.

Microplus

4535 Du Park, Montreal, QC H2V 4E4
Tel: 514-444-2480 Fax: 514-444-2486 Email: plus@micronet.com

March 26, 2000

Ms. Jane Creston
Johnson and Associates Appraisers
257 Laurier E.
Montreal, Quebec H2T 1G3

Dear Ms. Creston:

The letter begins with a neutral statement that the reader should not find objectionable. →

Thank you for your letter of March 22 describing your situation with the Vision 1200E scanner that you bought at our store on January 14, 2000. We always appreciate knowing of any problems our customers have with equipment purchased from Microplus.

The refusal is stated indirectly and is linked with a solution to the reader's problem. →

Our refund policy (printed on the back of your receipt) states that Microplus will refund the price of any new equipment within 30 days of purchase. The manufacturer's warranty still covers your Vision 1200E scanner. You will receive immediate attention if you call Mr. Jean LaVigne, a Vision technician, at 514-555-1212. If you wish to write to the manufacturer, the address is Vision Industries, 123 Main Street, Montreal Quebec, H2T 2L4. I have dealt with Mr. LaVigne, and I can assure you that he will provide satisfactory service.

The letter closes on an appreciative note and confidently assumes normal dealings in the future. →

Ms. Creston, your firm has been a long-standing customer of our store. Please take advantage of our spring sale, held during the first two weeks of April, when we feature special discounts on computer accessories and other equipment. We look forward to seeing you.

Sincerely,

Anna Wong

Anna Wong
Customer Service

FIGURE 6.2

In-Depth Critique: Letter Demonstrating a Diplomatic Organizational Plan
This letter from Microplus responds to the inquiry from Johnson & Associates about the unsatisfactory scanner. Although the information is effectively negative, the letter diplomatically achieves a positive feeling.

also helps you express the transitions between points so that your message is coherent and the audience will understand the relationship among your ideas.

You're no doubt familiar with the basic alphanumeric outline, which uses numbers and letters to identify each point and indents them to show which ideas are of equal status. (Chapter 13 tells more about formats for outlining.) A more schematic approach illustrates the structure of your message in an organization chart like one that depicts a company's management structure (Figure 6.3). The main idea is shown in the highest-level box, and, like a top executive, it establishes the big

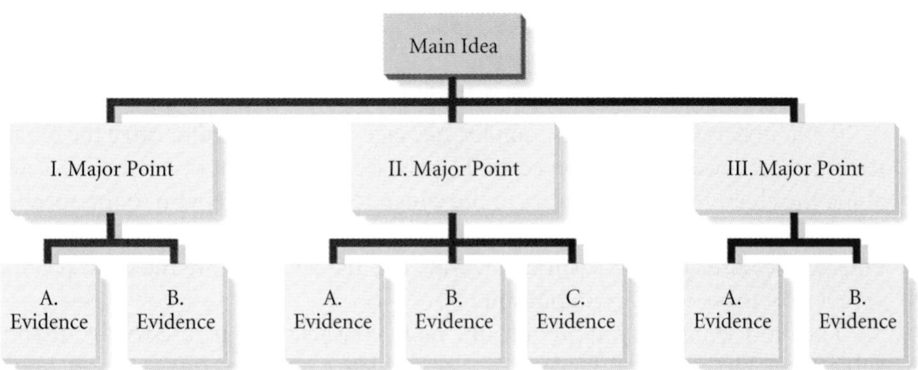

FIGURE 6.3
Organization Chart for Organizing a Message

picture. The lower-level ideas, like lower-level employees, provide the details. All the ideas are logically organized into divisions of thought, just as a company is organized into divisions and departments.[4]

Start with the Main Idea The main idea, placed at the top of an organization chart, helps you establish the goals and general strategy of the message. This main idea summarizes two things: (1) what you want your audience to do or think, and (2) why they should do so. Everything in the message should either support this idea or explain its implications.

The main idea is the starting point for constructing an outline.

State the Major Points In an organization chart, the boxes directly below the top box represent the major supporting points, corresponding to the main headings in a conventional outline. These are the "vice-presidential" ideas that clarify the message by expressing it in more concrete terms. To fill in these boxes, break the main idea into smaller units. In general, try to identify three to five major points. If you come up with more than seven main divisions of thought, go back and look for opportunities to combine some of the ideas. The big question then is deciding what to put in each box. Sometimes the choices are fairly obvious. At other times you may have hundreds of ideas to sort through and group together. In either case, be sure to consider both your purpose and the nature of the material.

The main idea should be supported by three to five major points, regardless of the message's length.

If your purpose is to inform and the material is factual, the groupings are generally suggested by the subject itself. They are usually based on something physical that you can visualize or measure: activities to be performed, functional units, spatial or chronological relationships, parts of a whole. When you're describing a process, the major support points are almost inevitably steps in the process. When you're describing a physical object, the vice-presidential boxes correspond to the components of the object. When you're giving a historical account, each box represents an event in the chronological chain.

When your purpose is to persuade or collaborate, the major support points may be more difficult to identify. Instead of relying on a natural order imposed by the subject, develop a line of reasoning that proves your central message and motivates your audience to act. The boxes on the organization chart then correspond to the major elements in a logical argument. Basically, the supporting points are the main reasons your audience should accept your message.

Director of Communications and Public Affairs for Dofasco, Gordon Forstner is responsible for promoting the steel manufacturer's reputation and vision. What must Forstner know about his audience so that he can choose the right strategy and language for his message?

Illustrate with Evidence The third level on the organization chart shows the specific evidence you'll use to illustrate your major points. This evidence is the flesh and blood that helps your audience understand and remember the more abstract concepts. Say you're advocating that the company increase its advertising budget. To support this point, you could provide statistical evidence that your most successful competitors spend more on advertising than you do. You could also describe a specific case in which a particular competitor increased its ad budget and achieved an impressive sales gain. As a final bit of evidence, you could show that, over the past five years, your firm's sales have gone up and down in unison with the amount spent on advertising.

If you're developing a long, complex message, you may need to carry the organization chart (or outline) down several levels. Remember that every level is a step along the chain from the abstract to the concrete, from the general to the specific. The lowest level contains the individual facts and figures that tie the generalizations to the observable, measurable world. The higher levels are the concepts that reveal why those facts are significant.

Each major point should be supported with enough specific evidence to be convincing, but not so much that it's boring.

The more evidence you provide, the more conclusive your case will be. If your subject is complex and unfamiliar to your audience or if they are skeptical, you'll need a lot of facts and figures to demonstrate your points. On the other hand, if your subject is routine and the audience is positively inclined, you can be more sparing with the evidence. You want to provide enough support to be convincing, but not so much that your message becomes boring or inefficient. Of course you'll need to document your sources of information, and you may sometimes need to obtain permission to use copyrighted material.

Another way to keep the audience interested is to vary the type of detail. As you plan your message, try to incorporate the methods described in Table 6.1. Switch from facts and figures to narration; add description for vividness; include examples or references to authority to enhance your credibility. Reinforce your message with visual support. A judicious use of these elements will add to the richness of your communications.

ESTABLISH SEQUENCE WITH ORGANIZATIONAL PATTERNS

LEARNING OUTCOME 4
Arrange ideas in direct or indirect order, depending on the audience's probable reaction.

Once you've defined and grouped your ideas, you're ready to decide on their sequence. When you're addressing a Canadian or US audience with minimal cultural differences, you have two basic options:

- Direct approach (deductive): putting the main idea first, followed by the evidence
- Indirect approach (inductive): putting the evidence first and the main idea later.

These two basic approaches may be applied either to short messages (memos and letters) or to long ones (reports, proposals, presentations). To choose between the two alternatives, you must first analyze your audience's likely reaction to your purpose and message. As Club Med's Serge Trigano knows, the direct approach is generally fine when your audience will be receptive: eager, interested, pleased, or even neutral. If they'll be resistant to your message–displeased, uninterested, or unwilling–you'll usually have better results with the indirect approach.

Use direct order if the audience's reaction is likely to be positive and indirect order if it is likely to be negative.

Bear in mind, however, that each message is unique. You can't solve all your communication problems with a simple formula. If you're sending bad news to outsiders, for example, an indirect approach is probably best. On the other hand, you might want to get directly to the point in a memo to an associate, even if your message is unpleasant. The direct approach might also be the best choice for long messages, regardless of the audience's attitude, because delaying the main point could cause confusion and frustration. Just remember that the first priority is to make the message clear.

Short messages follow one of four organizational plans, depending on the audience's probable reaction.

Patterns for Short Messages Once you've analyzed your audience's probable reaction and chosen a general approach, you can choose the most appropriate organizational pattern: direct request; routine, good news, or goodwill message; bad news message; or persuasive message. Table 6.2 summarizes how each type of message is structured.

TABLE 6.1 Six Types of Details

Type of Detail	Example	Comment
Facts and figures	Sales are strong this month. We have received two new contracts worth $5 million and have a good chance of winning another with an annual value of $2.5 million.	Most common form of detail in business messages. Adds more credibility than any other form of development. May become boring if used in excess.
Example or illustration	We've spent the past four months trying to hire recent accounting graduates for our internal audit staff, and, so far, only one person has agreed to join our firm. One woman told me that she would love to work for us, but she can get $5000 more a year elsewhere.	Adds life to a message, but one example does not prove a point. Idea must be supported by other evidence as well.
Description	Upscale hamburger restaurants are designed for McDonald's graduates who still love the taste of a Big Mac but who want more than convenience and low prices. The adult hamburger establishments feature attractive waitresses, wine and beer, half-pound burgers, and substantial side dishes, such as nachos and potato skins. Atmosphere is a key ingredient in the formula for success.	Useful when you need to explain how something looks or functions. Helps audience visualize the subject by creating a sensory impression. Does not prove a point, but clarifies points and makes them memorable. Begins with overview of object's function; defines its purpose, lists major parts, and explains how it operates; relies on words that appeal to senses.
Narration	Under former management, the company operated in a casual style. Executives came to work in blue jeans, meetings rarely started on time, and lunch rarely ended on time. When Mr. Wilson took over as CEO, however, the company got religion—financial religion. A University of Western Ontario MBA who favours conservative suits, Mr. Wilson has embarked on a complete overhaul of the operation. He has cut the product line from 6000 items to 1200 and has chopped $12 million of expenses.	Good for attracting attention and explaining ideas, but lacks statistical validity.
Reference to authority	I talked with Jackie Lohman in the Quebec plant about this idea, and she was very supportive. As you know, Jackie has been in charge of that plant for the past six years. She is confident that we can speed up the number 2 line by 150 units per hour if we add another worker.	Bolsters a case and adds variety and credibility. Works only if authority is recognized and respected by audience, although he or she may be an ordinary person.
Visual aids	Graphs, charts, tables	Essential when presenting specific information. Used more often in memos and reports than in letters.

TABLE 6.2 Four Organizational Plans for Short Messages

Audience Reaction	Organizational Plan	Opening	Body	Close
Eager or interested	Direct requests	Begin with the request or main idea.	Provide necessary details.	Close cordially and state the specific action desired.
Pleased or neutral	Routine, good news, or goodwill messages	Begin with the main idea or the good news.	Provide necessary details.	Close with a cordial comment, a reference to the good news, or a look toward the future.
Displeased	Bad news messages	Begin with a neutral statement that acts as a transition to the reasons for the bad news.	Give reasons to justify a negative answer. State or imply the bad news, and make a positive suggestion.	Close cordially.
Uninterested or unwilling	Persuasive messages	Begin with a statement or question that captures attention.	Arouse the audience's interest in the subject. Build the audience's desire to comply.	Request action.

In each organizational plan, the opening, the body, and the close all play an important part in getting your message across. When used with good judgment, these basic types of business messages can be powerful tools of communication.[5]

Direct requests get straight to the point because the audience usually wants to respond.

- *Direct requests.* The most straightforward business message is the direct request. This type of message lets you get to the point in the first paragraph or, if you're talking with someone face to face or on the phone, allows you to get right down to business. Use this organizational pattern when your audience will be interested in complying or eager to respond. The direct approach is the most natural approach, perhaps the most useful and businesslike. This type of message is discussed in greater detail in Chapter 8.

The direct approach is effective for messages that will please the reader or will cause no particular reaction.

- *Routine, good news, and goodwill messages.* Other messages that call for the direct approach are also easy to organize. Use this organizational pattern when the audience will feel neutral about your message or will be pleased to hear from you. If you're providing routine information as part of your regular business, the audience will probably be neutral, neither pleased nor displeased. If you're announcing a price cut, granting an adjustment, accepting an invitation, or congratulating a colleague, the audience will be pleased to hear from you. Using the direct approach for routine, good news, and goodwill messages has many advantages. You put your audience in a good frame of mind, encourage readers to be receptive to whatever else you have to say, and emphasize the pleasing aspect of your message by putting it right up front. This type of message is discussed in more detail in Chapter 9.
- *Bad news messages.* This organizational pattern uses the indirect approach and is appropriate when the audience will be displeased about what you have to say.

If you're turning down a job applicant, refusing credit, or denying a request for an adjustment, the audience will be disappointed. Astute business people know that every person encountered has the potential to be a customer, a supplier, or a contributor or to influence someone who is a customer, a supplier, or a contributor. So they take a little extra care with their bad news messages (Figure 6.4). The first and last sections of any letter make the biggest impression.

If you have bad news, try to put it somewhere in the middle, cushioned by other, more positive ideas.

Johnson and Associates Appraisers

Appraiser of Fine Antiques

257 Laurier E., Montreal, Quebec H2T 1G3

Phone: 514-555-9735 Fax: 514-555-9750 Email: jaa7@sympatico.ca

April 3, 2000

Ms. Frances Witherspoon
President
Canadian Association of Antiques Appraisers
6132 Bay Street
Halifax, NS B3L 1Z3

Dear Frances,

I am indeed honoured by your invitation to be the keynote speaker at this year's convention of the Association of Antiques Appraisers. As a member of the association, I have enjoyed meeting my colleagues from across Canada at our annual event and have learned a great deal from them over the years.

> The letter begins with a neutral statement that provides a transition to the refusal.

This year, I have agreed to speak at our local Young Entrepreneurs of Canada convention on the day of the gala dinner, when the keynote speech is delivered. My involvement with the Young Entrepreneurs is long-standing, and I see my speech as an opportunity to introduce them to the business of antique appraising and the fascination it holds for us.

> The body explains the reason for the refusal and then implies the bad news.

May I suggest an alternative speaker? I have consulted Karl Van den Broek of Victoria, B.C. over the years on a number of projects. Karl told me he is coming to this year's convention. As you know, he is well known in the field, and has written several articles on clock and watch appraisals. I'm sure he would be able to both inform and entertain our colleagues with his knowledge and experience.

> The writer takes care to introduce a positive thought.

Thank you again for the invitation to deliver the keynote speech. I look forward to speaking with you and members of the planning committee after the convention to hear about the seminars that were held.

> The letter closes on a cordial note.

Best wishes,

James Johnson

James Johnson
President

FIGURE 6.4

In-Depth Critique: Letter Delivering Bad News

This letter shows how James Johnson responded when asked to speak at a dinner sponsored by the Association of Antiques Appraisers. Note how he cushions the bad news.

In Figure 6.4, if Johnson had refused in the first sentence, the reader might never have bothered to go on to the reasons or might have been in the wrong frame of mind to consider them. By putting the explanation before the refusal, Johnson focused attention on the reasons. Of course, you have to be sincere about your reasons. A reader can spot a phony excuse right away. The indirect approach is neither manipulative nor unethical. As long as you can be honest and reasonably brief, you're better off opening a bad news message with a neutral point and putting the negative information after the explanation. This type of message is discussed further in Chapter 10.

Using the indirect approach gives you an opportunity to get your message across to a skeptical or hostile audience.

- *Persuasive messages.* The indirect approach is also useful when you know that your audience will resist your message–will be uninterested in your request or unwilling to comply without extra coaxing. Resistance might be the likely reaction to a sales or collection letter, an unsolicited job application, or a request for a favour of some kind. Although you might argue that people are likely to feel manipulated by the indirect approach, the fact remains that you have to capture people's attention before you can persuade them to do something. If you don't, you really have no way to get the message across. You also have to get your audience to consider with an open mind what you have to say; to do that, you have to make an interesting point and provide supporting facts that encourage the audience to continue paying attention. Once you have them thinking, you can introduce your real purpose. This type of message is discussed at greater length in Chapter 11.

The organization of a longer message should reflect both the purpose of the message and the audience's probable reaction.

Patterns for Longer Messages Most short messages can use one of the four basic organizational patterns. Longer messages (namely, reports and presentations) require a more complex pattern to handle the greater mass of information. These patterns can be broken into two general categories: informational and analytical.

When your purpose is to inform, the major points are organized in a natural order implied by the subject's characteristics.

In general, the direct approach is used to organize informational reports and presentations. Operating instructions, status reports, technical descriptions, and descriptions of company procedures all fall into this category. Long informational messages have an obvious main idea, often with a descriptive or "how to" overtone. The development of subordinate ideas follows the natural breakdown of the material to be explained; subtopics can be arranged in order of importance, sequentially, chronologically, spatially, geographically, or categorically.

When your purpose is to persuade or collaborate, the approach is analytical, with major points corresponding to logical arguments or to conclusions and recommendations.

Analytical reports and presentations are designed to lead the audience to a specific conclusion. When your purpose is to collaborate with your audience to solve a problem or to persuade them to take a definite action, your organizational pattern must highlight logical arguments or focus the audience's attention on what needs to be done. Your audience may respond in one of two ways to your material, and your choice of organizational plan should depend on the reaction you anticipate:

- If you expect your audience to agree with you, use a structure that focuses attention on conclusions and recommendations.
- If you expect your audience to be skeptical about your conclusions and recommendations or hostile toward them, use a structure that focuses attention on the rationale that supports your point of view.

You'll learn more about organizing longer messages in Chapter 12. For now, the important thing is to master the basic steps in structuring a message.

SHARPENING YOUR CAREER SKILLS

Beating Writer's Block: Nine Workable Ideas to Get Words Flowing

Putting words on a page or on screen can be a real struggle. Some people get stuck so often that they develop a mental block. If you get writer's block, here are some ways to get words flowing:

- *Use positive self-talk.* Stop worrying about how well or easily you write, and stop thinking of writing as difficult, time consuming, or complicated. Tell yourself that you're capable and that you can do the job. Also, recall past examples of your writing that were successful.
- *Know your purpose.* Be specific about what you want to accomplish with this particular piece of writing. Without a clear purpose, writing can indeed be impossible.
- *Visualize your audience.* Picture audience backgrounds, interests, subject knowledge, and vocabulary (including the technical jargon they use). Such visualization can help you choose an appropriate style and tone for your writing.
- *Create a productive environment.* Write in a place that's for writing only, and make that place pleasant. Set up "writing appointments." Scheduling a session from 9:30 to noon is less intimidating than an indefinite session. Also, keep your mind fresh with scheduled breaks.
- *Make an outline or a list.* Even if you don't create a formal outline, at least jot down a few notes about how your ideas fit together. As you go along, you can revise your notes. Eventually you will end up with a plan that gives direction and coherence.
- *Just start.* Put aside all worries, fears, distractions—anything that gives you an excuse to postpone writing. Then start putting down any thoughts you have about your topic. Don't worry about whether these ideas can actually be used; just let your mind range freely.
- *Write the middle first.* Start wherever your interest is greatest and your ideas are most developed. You can follow new directions, but note ideas to revisit later. When you finish one section, choose another without worrying about sequence. Just get your thoughts down.
- *Push obstacles aside.* If you get stuck at some point, don't worry. Move past the thought, sentence, or paragraph, and come back to it later. Prime the pump simply by writing or talking about why you're stuck: "I'm stuck because ..." Also try brainstorming. Before you know it, you'll be writing about your topic.
- *Read a newspaper or magazine.* Try reading an article that uses a style similar to yours. Choose one you'll enjoy so that you'll read it more closely.

When deadlines loom, don't freeze in panic. Concentrate on the major ideas first, and save the details for later, after you have something on the page. If you keep things in perspective, you'll succeed.

CAREER APPLICATIONS

1. List the ways you procrastinate, and discuss what you can do to break these habits.
2. Analyze your own writing experiences. What negative self-talk do you use? What might you do to overcome this tendency?

Stage 6: Formulating Your Message

Once you've completed the planning process, you're ready to begin composing the message. If your schedule permits, put your outline or organization chart aside for a day or two; then review it with a fresh eye, looking for opportunities to improve the flow of ideas. When you feel confident that your structure will achieve your purpose with the intended audience, you can begin to write.

Composing Your First Draft

Composition is the process of drafting your message; polishing it is a later step.

As you compose the first draft, don't worry about getting everything perfect. Just put down your ideas as quickly as you can. You'll have time to revise and refine the material later. Composition is easier if you've already figured out what to say and in what order, although you may need to pause now and then to find the right word. You may also discover as you go along that you can improve on your outline. Feel free to rearrange, delete, and add ideas, as long as you don't lose sight of your purpose.

If you're writing the draft in longhand, leave space between lines so that you'll have plenty of room for making revisions. The best tool for drafting the message is word-processing software, which allows you to make changes easily. You might try dictating the message into a tape recorder, particularly if you're practising for an oral delivery or if you're trying to create a conversational tone.

Controlling Your Style and Tone

LEARNING OUTCOME 5
Compose a message using a style and tone that are appropriate to your subject, purpose, audience, and format.

Style is the way you use words to achieve a certain tone, or overall impression. You can vary your style—your sentence structure and vocabulary—to sound forceful or passive, personal or impersonal, colourful or colourless. The right choice depends on the nature of your message and your relationship with the reader.

When composing the message, vary the style to create a tone that suits the occasion.

Your use of language is one of your credentials, a badge that identifies you as being a member of a particular group. Try to make your style clear, concise, and grammatically correct, and try also to make it conform to the norms of your group. Every organization has its own stylistic conventions, and many occupational groups share a particular vocabulary.

Although style can be refined during the revision phase (see Chapter 7), you'll save time and a lot of rewriting if you compose your message in an appropriate style.

BEHIND THE SCENES AT *BUSINESS $ENSE*

Helping Graduates into the World of Business

From an award-winning student project to a nationwide magazine in two short years, *Business $ense* has been helping Canadian students move from the world of school into the world of business. Its tips on résumés and interviews, perspectives on careers, and profiles of Canada's top business people, make *Business $ense* a key source for the information students seek as they decide on their futures. Billed as "The first and only national magazine for Canadian business students," its stated mission is "To unite, inspire and educate business students across Canada by engaging their minds, informing them of issues related to their interests, and supporting their activities."

As editor of Business $ense, Anne Hoekstra's goal is to help Canadian students move from the world of school to the world of business.

Back in 1996, David Sher was a business student at Toronto's Ryerson University. For a course assignment, he wrote a business plan with some classmates that developed his idea for a national magazine aimed at college and university students. The project earned a "Best Business Plan" award from Ryerson's business school, as well as national awards when he submitted the plan to two Canada-wide competitions. Encouraged by these achievements, Sher put his plan into action after graduation in 1997 with magazine co-founder Anne Hoekstra. Today, *Business $ense* is distributed free to all business students in college and university programs across Canada four times a year, in September, November, January, and March, reaching a circulation of 120 000. As another sign of its growing popularity, the magazine has been available at newsstands since January 2000. Sher and Hoekstra's dream of uniting, inspiring, and educating students has become a reality.

Sher is the magazine's publisher and Hoekstra editor-in-chief, but *Business $ense* is a collaborative venture, the product of a shared vision. The pair's audience is their priority. Hoekstra explains that the magazine's content and style "is guided by the needs and desires of the average *Business $ense* reader—the Canadian business student. A great deal of time was spent in the formation stages of the publication and is continuously being spent on liaison with the audience on finding out what is important to them." Focus groups, letters to the magazine, regular readership surveys conducted on the Web site, **www.businesssense.com**, after every issue, all help Sher and Hoekstra target the magazine to their readers' needs.

Each issue has four main sections: features, general interest, business perspectives, and FYI. The first includes the cover story and a "guest of honour" piece, focusing on a prominent

Your tone is affected by planning-stage elements such as your purpose and your audience's probable reaction to your message. Other elements affecting the tone of your message include thinking about the relationship you want to establish with your audience, using the "you" attitude, emphasizing the positive, establishing credibility, being polite, and projecting your company's image.

THINK ABOUT THE RELATIONSHIP YOU WANT TO ESTABLISH

The first step toward getting the right tone is to think about your relationship with the audience. Who are you and who are they? Are you friends of long standing with common interests or are you total strangers? Are you equal in status, experience, and education, or are you clearly unequal? Your answers to these questions will help you define your relationship with the audience so that you can give the right impression in your message.

The tone of your business messages may span a continuum from informal to conversational to formal. Club Med's Trigano writes in a somewhat informal style, appropriate for his company's size and atmosphere. Most business messages fall around the conversational level of formality, using plain language that is neither stiff nor full of slang. Your conversational tone may become less or more formal, depending on the situation.

If you're addressing an old friend, your conversational tone might tend toward an informal level. Of course, in business messages, your tone would never be as

Going Online

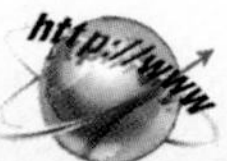

Connect Now with a Virtual Library

You can have more than 200 essential sources of information right at your fingertips with the Virtual Reference Desk. The site includes an almanac, encyclopedia, dictionary, thesaurus, atlas, virtual newspaper, weather site, e-mail address locater, 260 search engines in 19 categories, and more.

www.refdesk.com

Canadian business figure. "General interest" contains articles on a wide range of topics of concern to all business students regardless of specialization; here, readers can learn about career opportunities or courses at a particular school. "Business perspectives" is directed more toward specific disciplines, such as finance or marketing, but written so that non-specialists can learn something new. And FYI—for your information—advises students on résumés, scholarships, health, and other matters. Like the content, the writing style is also student-centred. *Business $ense*, says Hoekstra, is "written in a language that business students can understand, relate to, and process with ease and comfort. The objective of the writing style is to adjust to the mindset and perception of the business student reader. It is informative, educational, and inspirational in nature." A conversational tone, humour, and the "you" attitude make the magazine a relaxing yet informative read.

The process of creating each issue is a "laborious one." After choosing story ideas, Hoekstra recruits a writer—an industry expert, a distinguished professor, a business leader, business student or a freelancer. Stories undergo three or four rounds of editing. Working with her art director and designers from the staff of ten, Hoekstra selects artwork to accompany each article and the magazine goes to the design and production department for layout. Distribution soon follows.

Other *Business $ense* features include the "La Page Française" section, which Sher and Hoekstra aim to enlarge with the help of Québecois business leaders, professors, and students. And there is the *Business $ense* Web site, a critical tool that allows Hoekstra and Sher to add timely information and conduct their online surveys between issues. In January 2000, for example, starting salary data was published in cooperation with the Hay Group, a leading consulting firm, gaining an extra 50 000 page views that month.

Hoekstra remarks that "being the editor-in-chief has been a wonderful and enriching experience, both personally and professionally. Publishing is one of the most challenging industries, and has taught me a lot. My writing skills have been enhanced as I was fortunate enough to be exposed to a great variety of talented writers and editors who have helped us shape *Business $ense* into the highly appreciated publication it is today."[6]

APPLY YOUR KNOWLEDGE

1. As an assistant editor at *Business $ense* magazine you are responsible for keeping track of authors' submissions. Some authors submit their articles past the assigned deadlines, thus jeopardizing the production schedule. Anne Hoekstra has asked you to draft a polite letter to authors expressing the importance of deadlines and asking them to notify you when they cannot meet them. How would you begin this letter? How would you organize the key points in the body of the letter? Would you use the direct or indirect approach? Why?
2. Your company wants to publish a quarterly company newsletter for its employees. What are some of the main issues that should be resolved before a company newsletter is published? Please explain.

informal as it would with family members or school chums. On the other hand, if you're in the lower echelon of a large organization, your conversational tone would tend to be more formal and respectful when communicating with the people above you. Some people in high positions are extremely proud of their status and resent any gesture from a lower-level employee that is remotely presumptuous. They may not like you to offer your own opinions, and they may resent any implied criticism of their actions or decisions. If you're writing to someone of this type, your message may be ineffective unless you show a deep appreciation of rank. Also remember that businesspeople in North America are generally less formal than their counterparts in most other cultures.[7] So, to avoid embarrassment or misunderstanding when communicating across cultures, increase your level of formality.

Although various situations require various tones, most business communication sounds businesslike without being stuffy. The tone suggests that you and your audience are sensible, logical, unemotional people–objective, interested in the facts, rational, competent, and efficient. You are civilized people who share a mutual respect for each other.

To achieve a warm but businesslike tone

- ✧ Don't be too familiar
- ✧ Use humour only with great care
- ✧ Don't flatter the other person
- ✧ Don't preach
- ✧ Don't brag
- ✧ Be yourself

To achieve this tone, avoid being too familiar. Don't mention things about anyone's personal life unless you know the individual very well. Such references are indiscreet and presumptuous. Avoid phrases that imply intimacy, such as "just between you and me," "as you and I are well aware," and "I'm sure we both agree." Also, be careful about sounding too folksy or chatty; the audience may interpret this tone as an attempt on your part to seem like an old friend when, in fact, you're not.

Humour is another type of intimacy that may backfire. It's fine to be witty in person with old friends. It's difficult, however, to hit just the right note of humour in business messages, particularly if you don't know the readers very well, because what seems humorous to you may be deadly serious to others. When you are communicating across cultures, the chances are slim that your audience will appreciate your humour or even realize that you're trying to be funny.[8]

Also avoid obvious flattery. Although most of us respond well to honest praise and proper respect, we're suspicious of anyone who seems too impressed. When someone says, "Only a person of your outstanding intellect and refined tastes can fully appreciate this point," little warning lights flash in our minds. We suspect that we're about to be conned.

Avoid preaching to your audience. Few things are more irritating than people who assume that they know it all and that we know nothing. People who feel compelled to give lessons in business are particularly offensive. If, for some reason, you have to tell your audience something obvious, try to make the information unobtrusive. Place it in the middle of a paragraph, where it will sound like a casual comment as opposed to a major revelation. Alternatively, you might preface an obvious remark with "as you know" or some similar phrase.

Bragging is closely related to preaching and is equally offensive. When you praise your own accomplishments or those of your organization, you imply that you're better than your audience. References to the size, profitability, or eminence of your organization may be especially annoying (unless, of course, those in your audience work for the same organization). You're likely to evoke a negative reaction with comments such as "We at McMann's, which is the oldest and most respected firm in the city, have a reputation for integrity that is beyond question."

Perhaps the most important thing you can do to establish a good relationship with your audience is to be yourself. People can spot falseness very quickly, and they generally don't like it. If you don't try to be someone you're not, you'll sound sincere.

LEARNING OUTCOME 6
Use the "you" attitude to interest the audience in your message.

USE THE "YOU" ATTITUDE

By using an audience-centred approach, you try to see the subject through your audience's eyes. Then you can project this approach in your messages by adopting a "you" attitude; that is, by speaking and writing in terms of your audience's wishes, interests, hopes, and preferences. Talk about the other person, and you're talking about the thing that most interests him or her. Too many business messages have an "I" or "we" attitude, which causes the sender to sound selfish and uninterested in the receiver. The message tells what the sender wants; the recipient is expected to go along with it.

The "you" attitude is best implemented by expressing your message in terms of the audience's interests and needs.

On the simplest level, you can adopt the "you" attitude by replacing terms that refer to yourself and your company with terms that refer to your audience. In other words, use *you* and *yours* instead of *I*, *me*, and *mine* or *we*, *us*, and *ours*:

INSTEAD OF THIS	USE THIS
To help us process this order, we must ask for another copy of the requisition.	So that your order can be filled promptly, please send another copy of the requisition.
We are pleased to announce our new flight schedule from Montreal to St. John's, which is any hour on the hour.	Now you can take a plane from Montreal to St. John's any hour on the hour.
We offer the printer cartridges in three colours: black, blue, and green.	Select your printer cartridge from three colours: black, blue, and green.

Using *you* and *yours* requires finesse.[9] If you overdo it, you're likely to create some rather awkward sentences. You also run the risk of sounding like a high-pressure carnival barker at the county fair.[10] The "you" attitude is not intended to be manipulative or insincere. It is an extension of the audience-centred approach. In fact, the best way to implement the "you" attitude is to be sincere in thinking about your audience. It isn't just a matter of using one pronoun as opposed to another; it's a matter of genuine empathy. You can use *you* 25 times in a single page and still ignore your audience's true concerns. Look back at the letter in Figure 6.4. The first paragraph uses the pronoun *your* quite correctly and effectively. The third paragraph also displays effective use of the "you" attitude, and communicates a warm, personal approach. In the final analysis, it's the thought that counts, not the pronoun. If you're talking to a retailer, try to think like a retailer; if you're dealing with a production supervisor, put yourself in his or her position; if you're writing to a dissatisfied customer, imagine how you would feel at the other end of the transaction. The important thing is your attitude toward the members of your audience and your appreciation of their position.

Avoid using *you* and *yours*
- ✧ To excess
- ✧ When assigning blame
- ✧ If your organization prefers a more formal style

The word *you* does not always indicate a "you" attitude, and the "you" attitude can be displayed without using the word *you*.

On some occasions, you'll do better to avoid using *you*. For instance, when someone makes a mistake and you want to point it out impersonally to minimize the possibility of ill will, you might say, "We have a problem," instead of "You caused a problem." Using *you* in a way that might sound dictatorial is also impolite:

INSTEAD OF THIS	USE THIS
You should never use that kind of paper in the copy machine.	That type of paper doesn't work very well in the copy machine.
You must correct all five copies before noon.	All five copies must be corrected by noon.
You need to make sure the staff follows instructions.	The staff may need guidance in following instructions.

In addition, remember that the use of personal pronouns may not be acceptable in other cultures. In Japan, for example, people are uncomfortable with the personal touch of the "you" attitude. Japanese writers refer to their audience's company rather than to their receiver: "Your company [not you] will be pleased with the survey results."[11] You're always better off using the style and tone preferred by the culture you're dealing with.

Keep in mind the attitudes and policies of your organization as well. Some companies have a tradition of avoiding references to you and I in their memos and formal reports. If you work for a company that expects a formal, impersonal style, confine your use of personal pronouns to informal letters and memos.

EMPHASIZE THE POSITIVE

Explain what you have done, what you can do, and what you will do—not what you haven't done, can't do, or won't do.

Another way of showing sensitivity to your audience is to emphasize the positive side of your message.[12] Focus on the silver lining, not on the cloud. Stress what is or will be instead of what isn't or won't be. Most information, even bad news, has at least some redeeming feature. If you can make your audience aware of that feature, you will make your message more acceptable.

INSTEAD OF THIS	USE THIS
It is impossible to repair this vacuum cleaner today.	Your vacuum cleaner will be ready by Tuesday.
We apologize for inconveniencing you during our remodelling.	The renovations now under way will help us serve you better.
We never exchange damaged goods.	We are happy to exchange merchandise that is returned to us in good condition.

When you are offering criticism or advice, focus on what the person can do to improve.

In addition, when you're criticizing or correcting, don't hammer on the other person's mistakes. Avoid referring to failures, problems, or shortcomings. Focus instead on what the person can do to improve:

INSTEAD OF THIS	USE THIS
The problem with this department is a failure to control costs.	The performance of this department can be improved by tightening up controls.
You filled out the order form wrong. We can't send you the paint until you tell us what colour you want.	So that your order can be processed properly, please check your colour preferences on the enclosed card.
You broke the dish by running cold water on it right after you took it from the oven.	These dishes are sensitive to temperature shock and should be allowed to cool gradually after they are removed from the oven.

Show your audience how they will benefit from complying with your message.

If you're trying to persuade the audience to buy a product, pay a bill, or perform a service for you, emphasize what's in it for them. Don't focus on why you want them to do something. Instead of saying, "Please buy this book so that I can make my sales quota," say, "The plot of this novel will keep you in suspense to the last page." Instead of saying, "We need your contribution to the Boys and Girls Club," say, "You can help a child make friends and build self-confidence through your donation to the Boys and Girls Club." An individual who sees the possibility for personal benefit is more likely to respond positively to your appeal.

Avoid words with negative connotations; use meaningful euphemisms instead.

In general, try to state your message without using words that might hurt or offend your audience. Substitute mild terms (euphemisms) for those that have unpleasant connotations. Instead of advertising "cheap" merchandise, announce your bargain prices. Don't talk about "pimples and zits"; refer more delicately to complexion problems. You can be honest without being harsh. Gentle terms won't change the facts, but they will make those facts more acceptable:

INSTEAD OF THIS	USE THIS
toilet paper	bathroom tissue
used cars	resale cars
high-calorie food	high-energy food

On the other hand, don't carry euphemisms to extremes. If you're too subtle, people won't know what you're talking about. "Derecruiting" workers to the "mobility pool" instead of telling them they have six weeks to find another job isn't really very helpful. When using euphemisms, you walk a fine line between softening the blow and hiding the facts. It would not be ethical to speak to your community about relocating refuse when you're really talking about your plans for disposing of toxic waste. Such an attempt to hide the facts would very likely backfire, damaging your business image and reputation. In the final analysis, people respond better to an honest message delivered with integrity than they do to sugar-coated double-talk.

PROMOTING WORKPLACE ETHICS

Spin Cycle: Deciphering Corporate Doublespeak

If there's one product businesses can produce in large amounts, it's doublespeak. Doublespeak is language that only pretends to say something but that in reality hides, evades, or misleads. Like most products, doublespeak comes in many forms, from the popular buzzwords that everyone uses but no one really understands—such as "competitive dynamics" and "empowerment"—to words that try to hide meaning, such as "re-engineering," "synergy," and "restructure."

With doublespeak, bribes and kickbacks are called *rebates* or *fees for product testing*, junk and used-car-parts dealers have become *auto dismantlers and recyclers*, and travel agents are called *vacation specialists, destination counselors*, or *reservation specialists*. Plus, just about everyone's job title has the word *chief* in it: Chief Learning Officer, Chief Cultural Officer, Chief Ethics Officer, and Chief Creative Officer. After all the "operations improvement" that corporations have undergone, you have to wonder who all those "chiefs" are leading. Never before have so many led so few.

With doublespeak, banks don't have *bad loans* or *bad debts*; they have *nonperforming credits* that are *rolled over* or *rescheduled*. And corporations never lose money; they just experience *negative cash flow, deficit enhancement*, or *negative contributions to profits*.

Of course, no one gets fired these days. If you're high enough in the corporate pecking order, you *resign for personal reasons*. But for those below the lofty heights of corporate power, you're *involuntarily terminated* as the result of *downsizing, workforce adjustments*, and *headcount reductions*. Some companies even *assign candidates to a mobility pool, implement a skills mix adjustment*, or *eliminate redundancies in the human resources area*. One automobile company (which closed an entire assembly plant and eliminated over 8000 jobs) calls it *a volume-related production schedule adjustment*.

But don't worry, if you're *dehired, deselected, surplused*, or *uninstalled*, corporations will offer you a *career change opportunity*, or *vocational relocation*. In fact, hardly anyone is laid off these days. "We don't characterize it as a layoff," said one corporate doublespeaker (sometimes called a spin-doctor). "We're managing our staff resources. Sometimes you manage them up, and sometimes you manage them down."

CAREER APPLICATIONS

1. The president of one company just learned that some of his employees have been playing a popular game called "buzzword bingo," in which participants ridicule doublespeak by tracking the jargon their bosses use during staff meetings on bingo-like cards. Some managers are complaining that it's getting out of control. In fact, as one meeting dragged on, employees tried to steer the conversation to use all the buzzwords on their cards. What can managers do to avoid these silly games?
2. Visit the following buzzword-bingo Web sites and print out a card or two. Read the current business section of your favourite newspaper. How many buzzwords did you find?
   Sites: **fooz.com/bingo**
   www.ksquared.net/~key/ietf-bingo.cgi
   www.buzzkiller.net

Source: Adapted from William Lutz, "Life under the Chief Doublespeak Officer," *USA Today*, 17 October 1996, 15A.

ESTABLISH CREDIBILITY

Don't make false promises.

Because the success of your message may depend on the audience's perception of you, their belief in your competence and integrity is important. You want people to believe that you know what you're doing and that your word is dependable. Club Med's Trigano believes in building credibility over time by carefully building one's reputation. The first step is to promise only what you can do and then to do what you promise. After that, you can enhance credibility through your writing and speaking style.

If you're communicating with someone you know well, your previous interactions influence your credibility. The other person knows from experience whether you're trustworthy and capable. If the person is familiar with your company, the firm's reputation may be ample proof of your credibility.

To enhance your credibility
- ✧ Show that you understand the other person's situation
- ✧ Establish your own credentials or ally yourself with a credible source
- ✧ Back up your claims with evidence, not exaggerations
- ✧ Use words that express confidence
- ✧ Believe in yourself and your message

But what if you are complete strangers? Even worse, what if the other person starts off with doubts about you? First and foremost, show an understanding of the other person's situation by calling attention to the things you have in common. If you're communicating with someone who shares your professional background, you might say, "As a fellow engineer (lawyer, doctor, teacher, or whatever), I'm sure you can appreciate this situation." Another approach is to use technical or professional terms that identify you as a peer.

You can also gain the audience's confidence by explaining your credentials, but you need to be careful that you don't sound pompous. Generally, one or two aspects of your background are all you need to mention. Possibly your title or the name of your organization will be enough to impress the audience with your abilities. If not, perhaps you can mention the name of someone who carries some weight with your audience. You might begin a letter with "Professor Goldberg suggested that I contact you," or you could quote a recognized authority on a subject, even if you don't know the authority personally. The fact that your ideas are shared by a credible source adds prestige to your message.

Your credibility is also enhanced by the quality of the information you provide. If you support your points with evidence that can be confirmed through observation, research, experimentation, or measurement, your audience will recognize that you have the facts, and they will respect you. Exaggerated claims, on the other hand, are unethical and do more harm than good.

You also risk losing credibility if you seem to be currying favour with insincere compliments. So support compliments with specific points:

When Body Shop founder Anita Roddick decided to use her business as a vehicle for social and environmental change, she focused worldwide attention on her credibility with customers. Indeed, as Roddick and her business have become symbols of social responsibility, they have drawn criticism and investigation. Any mistakes and errors will be magnified, says Roddick, "but by emphasizing social issues in addition to profits, we are trying to change the focus of business."

INSTEAD OF THIS	USE THIS
My deepest heartfelt thanks for the excellent job you did. It's hard these days to find workers like you. You are just fantastic! I can't stress enough how happy you have made us with your outstanding performance.	Thanks for the fantastic job you did filling in for Gladys at the convention with just an hour's notice. Despite the difficult circumstances, you managed to attract several new orders with your demonstration of the new line of coffeemakers. Your dedication and sales ability are truly appreciated.

The other side of the credibility coin is too much modesty and not enough confidence. Many writing authorities suggest that you avoid such words as *if*, *hope*, and *trust*, which express a lack of confidence on your part:

INSTEAD OF THIS	USE THIS
We hope this recommendation will be helpful.	We're glad to make this recommendation.

If you'd like to order, mail us the reply card.	To order, mail the reply card.
We trust that you'll extend your service contract.	By extending your service contract, you can continue to enjoy top-notch performance from your equipment.

The ultimate key to being believable is to believe in yourself. If you are convinced that your message is sound, you can state your case with authority so that the audience has no doubts. When you have confidence in your own success, you automatically suggest that your audience will respond in the desired way. If you lack faith in yourself, however, you're likely to communicate an unsteady attitude that undermines your credibility.

BE POLITE

The best tone for business messages is almost always a polite one. By being courteous to your audience, you show consideration for their needs and feelings. You express yourself with kindness and tact.

Although you may be tempted now and then to be brutally frank, try to express the facts in a kind and thoughtful manner.

Undoubtedly, you'll be frustrated and exasperated by other people many times in your career. When that happens, you'll be tempted to say what you think in blunt terms. To be sure, it's your job to convey the facts, precisely and accurately. Nevertheless, venting your emotions will rarely improve the situation and may jeopardize the goodwill of your audience. Instead, be gentle when expressing yourself:

INSTEAD OF THIS	USE THIS
You really fouled things up with that last computer run.	Let me tell you what went wrong with that last computer run so that we can make sure things run smoothly next time.
You've been sitting on my order for two weeks now. When can I expect delivery?	As I mentioned in my letter of October 12, we are eager to receive our order as soon as possible. Could you please let us know when to expect delivery.

Use extra tact when writing and when communicating with higher-ups and outsiders.

Of course, some situations require more diplomacy than others. If you know your audience well, you can get away with being less formal. However, when corresponding with people who outrank you or with those outside your organization, you usually include an added measure of courtesy. In general, written communication requires more tact than oral communication. When you're speaking, your words are softened by your tone of voice and facial expression. You can adjust your approach depending on the feedback you get. Written communication, on the other hand, is stark and self-contained. If you hurt a person's feelings in writing, you can't soothe them right away. In fact, you may not even know that you have hurt the other person, because the lack of feedback prevents you from seeing his or her reaction.

In addition to avoiding things that give offence, try to find things that might bring pleasure. Remember a co-worker's birthday, send a special note of thanks to a supplier who has done a good job, acknowledge someone's help, send a clipping to a customer who has expressed interest in a subject. People remember the extra little things that indicate you care about them as individuals. In this impersonal age, the human touch is particularly effective.

Another simple but effective courtesy is to be prompt in your correspondence. If possible, answer your mail within two or three days. If you need more time to pre-

CEO William Gates wants Microsoft to maintain its image of competitiveness well into the future, when he predicts that his company's software "will be used in business, in the home, in the pocket, and in the car." But a company's image is also projected through its employees, so when you're speaking for your company, it's important to align your personal values with those of your organization.

pare a reply, write a brief note or call to say that you're working on an answer. Most people are willing to wait if they know how long the wait will be. What annoys them is the suspense.

PROJECT THE COMPANY'S IMAGE

Even though establishing the right tone for your audience is your main goal, give some thought to projecting the right image for your company. When you communicate with outsiders, on even the most routine matter, you serve as the spokesperson for your organization. The impression that you make can enhance or damage the reputation of the entire company. Thus your own views and personality must be subordinated, at least to some extent, to the interests and style of the company.

You can save yourself a great deal of time and frustration if you master the company style early in your career. In a typical corporation, 85 percent of the letters, memos, and reports are written by someone other than the higher-level managers who sign them. Most of the time, managers reject first drafts of these documents for stylistic reasons. In fact, the average draft goes through five revisions before it is finally approved.[13]

You might wonder whether all this effort to fine-tune the style of a message is worthwhile. The fact is, people in business care very much about saying precisely the right thing in precisely the right way. Their willingness to go over the same document five times demonstrates just how important style really is. For a reminder of the tasks involved in composition, see this chapter's Checklist for Composing Business Messages.

Shaping Your E-Mail Message

LEARNING OUTCOME 7
Compose an appropriate e-mail message.

An e-mail message is more than an electronic memo or a one-way telephone call.[14] You can send e-mail to co-workers, supervisors, and staff, but you can also send e-mail outside the company to customers, suppliers, and competitors. Moreover, you can send it across the globe as easily as across the hall.

Organization and style are just as important for e-mail messages as for any other type of message. So communicate your points quickly and efficiently by making your e-mail message audience centred, easy to follow, and interesting.

Make your e-mail messages
✧ Audience centred
✧ Easy to follow
✧ Interesting

MAKE YOUR E-MAIL AUDIENCE CENTRED

Even though e-mail may have an image of speed and informality, take enough time to compose your e-mail messages carefully. Think about your audience. Consider your reader's interests, needs, and feelings.

Checklist for Composing Business Messages

A. Organization

1. Recognize good organization.
   a. Subject and purpose are clear.
   b. Information is directly related to subject and purpose.
   c. Ideas are grouped and presented logically.
   d. All necessary information is included.
2. Achieve good organization through outlining.
   a. Decide what to say.
      i. Main idea
      ii. Major points
      iii. Evidence
   b. Organize the message to respond to the audience's probable reaction.
      i. Use the direct approach when your audience will be neutral, pleased, interested, or eager.
      ii. Use the indirect approach when your audience will be displeased, uninterested, or unwilling.
3. Choose the appropriate organizational plan.
   a. Short messages

How formal you make your message depends on your audience, as well as on your purpose. Although e-mail may at times seem transitory, it can emulate snail mail by having conventional business language, a respectful style, and a more formal format (including a traditional greeting, formalized headings, and a formal closing and signature).[15] Of course e-mail can be as informal and casual as a conversation between old friends–just be sure that such a style is appropriate for the situation. Regardless of the level of formality required, do your best to use correct spelling and proper grammar. Some e-mail users insist that spelling and grammar take a back seat to your readiness to communicate.[16] But in business communication, e-mail needs to be as clear and as easy to understand as possible.

The formality of your e-mail depends on your audience.

Because e-mail is so effortlessly sent abroad, focusing on your audience also means being culturally aware. When communicating with someone in another culture, take into account cultural differences. For example, be sure to give metric measurements (followed by English-system equivalents); spell out what format or system you're using for dates, times, numbers, and money; and use more formal greetings for people in those parts of the world that expect them.[17]

You need to be culturally aware when writing e-mail.

Because e-mail is read on-screen, keep your audience's terminal in mind (Figure 6.5). Computers and e-mail systems vary, so you want to ensure that your readers won't be confused by message lines that run off the screen or that wrap incorrectly. Make sure that your line length is fewer than 80 characters (or fewer than 60 characters if your message is likely to be forwarded, because forwarding often indents messages a tab length). And, of course, don't use font features such as boldface and italics unless you're certain your reader's computer and e-mail software can reproduce such features.[18]

Consider how your message will appear on your audience's screen.

Remember to make responding easy. State clearly the type of response you need. Give enough information in your e-mail message for your audience to be able to respond. Word your message so that your audience can reply as briefly as possible, perhaps with a yes or a no. Also, ask for your audience's response early in your message, perhaps even in your subject line.[19]

Make responding easy.

MAKE YOUR E-MAIL EASY TO FOLLOW

Some readers receive more e-mail than they can read, so your best chance of getting your message across is to make your e-mail easy to follow. Use short, focused paragraphs that are organized in a logical fashion. Consider using the method newspaper reporters use–writing from the top down. That way you'll be sure to get your point across as early as possible, in case your reader doesn't have the time or interest to finish reading your message.[20]

Consider writing e-mail from the top down.

---

i. Direct request
ii. Routine, good news, or goodwill message
iii. Bad news message
iv. Persuasive message

b. Long messages
  i. Informational pattern
  ii. Analytical pattern

B. Formulation

1. Compose your first draft.
  a. Get ideas down as quickly as you can.
  b. Rearrange, delete, and add ideas without losing sight of your purpose.

2. Vary the style to create a tone that suits the occasion.
  a. Establish your relationship with your audience.
    i. Use the appropriate level of formality.
    ii. Avoid being overly familiar, using inappropriate humour, including obvious flattery, sounding preachy, bragging, or trying to be something you're not.
  b. Extend your audience-centred approach by using the "you" attitude.
  c. Emphasize the positive aspects of your message.
  d. Establish your credibility to gain the audience's confidence.
  e. Use a polite tone.
  f. Use the style that your company prefers.

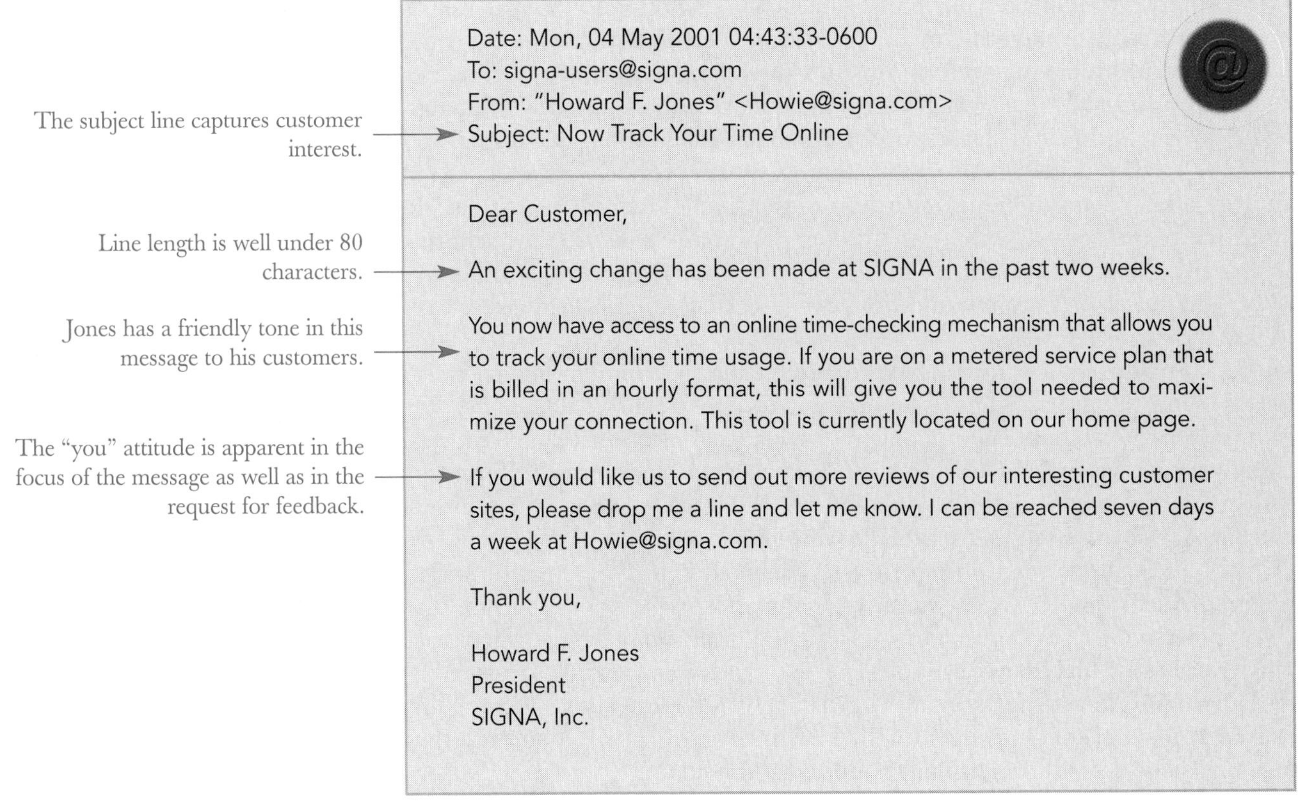

The subject line captures customer interest.

Line length is well under 80 characters.

Jones has a friendly tone in this message to his customers.

The "you" attitude is apparent in the focus of the message as well as in the request for feedback.

Date: Mon, 04 May 2001 04:43:33-0600
To: signa-users@signa.com
From: "Howard F. Jones" <Howie@signa.com>
Subject: Now Track Your Time Online

Dear Customer,

An exciting change has been made at SIGNA in the past two weeks.

You now have access to an online time-checking mechanism that allows you to track your online time usage. If you are on a metered service plan that is billed in an hourly format, this will give you the tool needed to maximize your connection. This tool is currently located on our home page.

If you would like us to send out more reviews of our interesting customer sites, please drop me a line and let me know. I can be reached seven days a week at Howie@signa.com.

Thank you,

Howard F. Jones
President
SIGNA, Inc.

FIGURE 6.5
In-Depth Critique: On-Screen E-Mail Message
This e-mail message is formatted in an accessible manner.

In fact, try to keep your message short and concise. Many e-mail messages are less than three paragraphs long and fit into one screen. Whenever possible, try to limit your message to one screen or window. Of course, some e-mail messages will be longer than one screen; a few may even be longer than several screens. When it's necessary to send a long e-mail message, consider including a brief table of contents in the first screen, perhaps with a short paragraph that summarizes and highlights the key points. Also, use headings to break up long passages of text. Not only do they help your reader understand you, but they can serve as shortcuts, highlighting the material your reader may want to read or skip. And remember that lists are an efficient way to present information. You can use bullets (asterisks) to emphasize key points and numbered lists for sequential points. Embedding a list within text can also save you some space.[21]

MAKE YOUR E-MAIL INTERESTING

When your readers are deciding which messages to spend time on, they look at whom each is from, they check the subject line, and they may scan the first screen. If your message can't attract your reader's attention by that time, your e-mail will probably go unread and will probably be deleted.[22] You can make your e-mail more interesting–from start to finish.

An e-mail's subject line offers you an opportunity to gain your reader's interest.

An interesting subject line does more than just describe or classify the content of your message. By applying key words, humour, quotations, or questions, you can grab your reader's attention. You have 25 to 30 characters to build interest for you message (longer lines are often truncated). Try wording your subject line so that it tells your reader what to do. For example: "Send figures for July sales" is much more informative than "July sales figures." Of course, you don't want to use wild statements just to attract your reader's attention. Using "Urgent" in your subject lines too often will soon have an effect quite different from the one you intend.

Use a greeting to make your e-mail more personal.

Your e-mail header displays who your message is to and from. Even so, adding a greeting makes your e-mail message more personal.[23] Naturally, whether you use a formal greeting (Dear Professor Van Nest) or a more casual one (Hi Marty!) depends on your audience and your purpose.

Create interesting typographical effects with keyboard characters.

Even though you can't usually use underlining, fonts, or graphics to emphasize various parts of your message, you can use keyboard characters such as asterisks, dashes, carets, hyphens, colons, slashes, pipes, and capital letters. For example, you can surround a word with asterisks to *make* it stand out. Or you can indicate underlining like _this_. You can open up your message by using white space

```
-----------------------------------------------------------------------
|                                                                     |
|and by inserting lines or boxes made of asterisks or hyphens and pipes.|
|_____________________________________________________________________|
```

You can make a headline with all capital letters, but don't overdo it. TOO MANY CAPITAL LETTERS LOOKS LIKE SHOUTING! You can even use extra character spaces to emphasize your most i m p o r t a n t points.[24] Of course, you must guard against overusing any of these techniques, or else your message will look jumbled and confusing.

To emphasize or clarify the meaning of a comment in a less formal message, you can also use your keyboard to create **emoticons** (little sideways pictures). For example, you can make a sideways happy face with a colon, a hyphen, and a closing parenthesis as :-). Variations might look like :-> or <:-) or <(:-> and so on. Other emotions can also be expressed, such as boo hoo :-< and uh oh :-o and my lips are sealed :-x. As with other enhancement techniques, emoticons can be overdone. When used sparingly, they can add interest, but when overused, they can make your message look too much like graffiti.[25]

Be careful not to overdo emoticons.

Your closing and signature also personalize your e-mail message. In most cases, use simple closings, such as *Thanks* or *Regards*, rather than more traditional business closings such as *Sincerely yours*. Of course, you may want to use a more formal closing for international e-mail, such as *Respectfully yours*.

For your signature, you can simply type your name or initials on a separate line. You might put one or two hyphens before your name to set it off from the body of your e-mail. Or you may want to use a signature file, a short identifier that may include your name, company name, postal address, fax number, other e-mail addresses, and sometimes even a short quotation or thought. Some users think you should include only the information needed to contact you. Once you create a signature file, you can save it in your mail program and add it to e-mail messages without retyping. You can also use a digital copy of your handwritten signature, which is becoming acceptable as legal proof of business transactions in the United States, especially when accompanied by a date stamp that is automatically inserted by your mail program.[26]

ON THE JOB
Solving a Communication Dilemma at Club Med

For many years Club Med targeted single adults, promising them a relaxing yet socially active vacation. To combat disasters in and around many of its locations in the early 1990s and to respond to the shifts in society's view of freewheeling lifestyles, the company began targeting senior citizens and families with children. Families spend billions of dollars on vacations every year, and the 50-plus age group is growing at a rate triple that of the general population, making both groups attractive to the Club Med marketing staff.

Many Club Med resorts added facilities and entertainment aimed at children and older people. The company introduced the "Forever Young" program tailored for older customers, sending them to resorts featuring accessibility, interesting day trips, and sports such as tennis and golf. The headline for the ad campaign was: "With age comes wisdom and patience, not to mention a great deal at Club Med." The company significantly increased its advertising budget to promote the new programs.

But advertising alone was not enough to make the programs successful. Up to 85 percent of Club Med's business comes through travel agents, so success depended heavily on agents' recommendations. Club Med reorganized its marketing staff to optimize relationships with travel agents. And in the fall of 1996, Club Med published a sales manual describing its vacation programs and including demographic profiles of guests (to help travel agents match potential clients with appropriate resorts).

The new programs have been very successful, and travel agents have responded well to Club Med's efforts. According to a recent study, half of the company's clients were married couples and another 15 percent were children. And 15 percent of the company's revenues came from clients over the age of 50. The changes also improved Club Med's financial picture. After substantial losses in 1993, company profits increased significantly for three years, including an 87 percent increase from 1995 to 1996.

Your Mission: You are on the sales staff at Club Med. The company recently introduced new vacation programs geared toward senior citizens, a market quite different from the typical Club Med visitor. You know that travel agents are your best source of business, and you want the agents you work with to support the new programs. You plan to send them brochures describing the program, and you have also written a draft of a letter to introduce yourself and encourage the agents to recommend Club Med vacations for a wider range of customers.

Here is a copy of your draft. Read it and then select the best responses to the questions that follow. Be prepared to explain why your choice is best.[27]

Dear travel partner:

Do you think of Club Med as a vacation destination for swinging singles? Our resorts are popular with young adults, but that is not all that Club Med has to offer.

I'm sure it isn't news to you that the 55-and-older age group is the fastest growing vacation market today. People in this older group are looking for new and different places to vacation, and we think they would enjoy Club Med resorts. Our new "Forever Young" program is geared to people 55 and older. The enclosed brochure describes the program, and I'm sure you will find the program to be a great way to satisfy your clients.

I am excited about working with you to help a wider range of customers enjoy Club Med vacations. Please feel free to call me if I can be of any assistance to you.

1. Does the letter conform to the guidelines for good organization?
   a. No. The opening sentence is unprofessional, and it might be offensive to some people. The letter does not get to the point until the end of the second paragraph, and even then it is vague. There is not enough information to support the main purpose, and the information is poorly organized. The first paragraph should introduce the new program, then subsequent paragraphs should contain supporting information, describing how the For-ever Young program meets the needs of senior citizen vacationers.
   b. The letter includes unnecessary information. You are including a brochure, so you just need to refer the reader to the brochure.
   c. The letter is basically well organized, but there is not enough information to support the main point. It says that senior citizens would enjoy Club Med, but it does not have enough detail to convince a travel agent to risk sending customers there.
   d. The letter is well organized. The subject and purpose are clear. All necessary information is included, and the information is directly related to subject and purpose. Information is grouped and presented logically.
2. You decide to rewrite the draft. Your first step is to develop an outline. What should you use as your main idea?
   a. The 55-and-older age group is a rapidly growing source of vacation business.
   b. Club Med is not just for singles anymore.
   c. Club Med's sales staff has been reorganized to better support travel agents.

d. New programs at Club Med can help agents arrange successful vacations for a broader range of clients.

3. What basic points will you use to develop and support the main idea?

a. People go on vacation to have fun. Senior citizens will be attracted to Club Med because of its reputation for providing fun vacations.

b. Senior citizens have more money and time for vacations than ever before. They like to feel younger, so they would enjoy being around the younger clients at Club Med resorts. Because business has been declining, Club Med is putting a lot of effort into attracting the older crowd. The program's success depends on the travel agents' support.

c. As baby boomers mature, the senior citizen vacation market will grow quickly. Today's senior citizens are more active than the seniors of previous generations, so they are looking for a different kind of vacation. Club Med provides a good balance of activities and relaxation. Senior citizens will like the all-inclusive price because they know up front how much their vacation will cost. Return business is important at Club Med as well as for travel agents, and 40 percent of Club Med clients return within two years for another vacation.

d. Senior citizens as a group are fussy about how they spend their money; they want top value for their dollar. They will be attracted to Club Med because of its reputation for quality and service.

4. Which organizational plan should the letter follow?

a. Indirect. You are targeting a totally different customer than the agents are used to sending to your resorts, so agents may be skeptical. By reminding the agents of your past success and describing how the new program was developed, you will pique interest in the program. Include information on how the senior citizen vacation market is changing, and describe how Club Med is responding to those changes. Close by asking the agents to send you a broader range of clients, and offer your assistance.

b. Indirect. Open by saying Club Med wants to expand its customer base and explain why. Refer the agents to the brochure for information on the program. Close by asking the agents to recommend your resorts to their senior citizen clients.

c. Indirect. Start by mentioning the rapid growth in the senior citizen vacation market. Describe what kind of vacation typical senior citizens are looking for. Refer the agents to the brochure for information on Club Med's program for senior citizens. Close by asking the agents to recommend your resorts to their senior citizen clients.

d. Direct. The new programs will benefit the agents as well as Club Med, so they will be eager to recommend the resorts for their senior clients. State in the first paragraph that you want the agents to recommend Club Med vacations to a broader range of clients, then explain why doing so is a good idea. Finish by providing your phone number so that they can contact you for assistance or more information.

TAP Your Knowledge

Summary of Learning Outcomes

1. Identify the characteristics of a well-organized message. In Canada and the US, a well-organized message proceeds point by point, in a linear fashion. You can follow four guidelines to effectively organize your message: (1) make the subject and purpose clear; (2) include only information that is related to the subject and the purpose; (3) group the ideas and present them in a logical way; (4) include all the necessary information.

2. Explain why organization is important to both the audience and the communicator. Audiences benefit from good organization in several ways. When audience members receive a message that is well organized, they don't have to read and reread a message to make sense of it, so they save time. They are also better able to understand the content, so they can accept the message more easily, and they can make better decisions based on its information. Communicators also benefit from good organization. When a message is well organized, communicators save time because preparing the message is quicker. Communicators can also use their organizational plan to get advance input from their audience members, making sure they're on the right track. Finally, good organization allows communicators to divide portions of the writing assignment among co-workers.

3. Break a main idea into subdivisions grouped under logical categories. To create a message efficiently, create an organizational chart that groups your major points and evidence under the appropriate main idea. The main idea summarizes (1) what you want your audience to do or think; and (2) why they should do so. The major points support your main idea. They are usually suggested by your subject, and may be based on activities that can be performed, functional units, spatial or chronological relationships, or parts of a whole. For example, if you're describing a process, the major points are the steps in the process.

4. Arrange ideas in direct or indirect order, depending on the audience's probable reaction. You are ready to decide on the sequence of your ideas after you have arranged and grouped them. The direct approach is deductive: the main idea is first, followed by the evidence. The indirect approach is inductive: the evidence first, and then the main idea. If you believe your audience will be receptive to your idea, or neutral, you'll usually have better results with the direct approach. If you believe they'll be resistant, you may decide to use the indirect approach.

5. Compose a message using a style and tone that are appropriate to your subject, purpose, audience. Style is the way you use words to achieve a certain tone, or overall impression. When composing a message, think about your purpose, the relationship you want to establish with your audience, and how your audience might react to your message. When you communicate with an audience whose education, experience, and status are similar to yours, your tone may be somewhat informal. When you communicate with an audience whose experience is greater than yours and whose status is higher, your tone will likely be more formal.

6. Use the "you" attitude to interest the audience in your message. The "you" approach means that you try to see the subject through your audience's eyes. You speak and write in terms of the audience's wishes, interests, hopes, and preferences, and use the pronouns "you" and "yours" instead of "I," "me," "we," or "us" in your oral and written communications. Overdoing the "you" attitude, however, can project insincerity, so it is necessary to use it judiciously.

7. Compose an appropriate e-mail message. Organization and style are as important for e-mail messages as they are for any other. Make your message audience centred, take into account cultural differences between you and your audience, make your message easy to follow by using short, focused paragraphs, create an effective subject line, and ensure that your greeting suits your audience and your purpose.

Test Your Knowledge

Review Questions

1. Describe the pitfalls of poor organization.
2. Give examples of the types of detail suitable for example or illustration, description, and narration.
3. When is the indirect approach chosen for bad news messages?
4. When is the indirect approach chosen for persuasive messages?
5. Give two examples of how the "you" attitude can be used to accentuate the positive.
6. Give two examples of how the "you" attitude can be used to establish credibility.
7. What are some techniques for making your e-mail messages interesting?

Apply Your Knowledge

Critical Thinking Questions

1. When organizing the ideas for your business message, how can you be sure that what seems logical to you will also seem logical to your audience?
2. Do you think that cushioning bad news is manipulative?
3. Which organizational plan would you use to ask employees to work overtime to meet an important deadline: a direct request or a persuasive message? Why?
4. Which organizational plan would you use to let your boss know that you'll be out a full day next week to attend your uncle's funeral: a routine message or a bad news message? Why?
5. When composing business messages, how can you be yourself and project your company's image at the same time?
6. Is it ever acceptable to use an indirect approach when writing e-mail? How can you use a buffer when you have to state your purpose in the subject line? Explain.

Practise Your Knowledge

Exercises

1. Suppose you are preparing to recommend to top management the installation of a new heating system (called cogeneration). The following information is in your files. Eliminate from the list topics that aren't essential; then arrange the other topics so that your report will give management a clear understanding of the heating system and a balanced, concise justification for installing it.

   History of the development of the cogeneration heating process

   Scientific credentials of the developers of the process

   Risks assumed in using this process

   Your plan for installing the equipment in your building

   Stories about its successful use in comparable facilities

   Specifications of the equipment that would be installed

   Plans for disposing of the old heating equipment

   Costs of installing and running the new equipment

   Advantages and disadvantages of using the new process

   Detailed ten-year cost projections

   Estimates of the time needed to phase in the new system

   Alternative systems that management might wish to consider

2. Indicate whether the direct or indirect approach would be best in each of the following situations, then briefly explain why. Would any of these messages be inappropriate for e-mail? Explain.
   a. A letter from a consumer asking when next year's automobiles will be put on sale locally
   b. A letter from a recent college graduate requesting a letter of recommendation from a former instructor
   c. A letter turning down a job applicant
   d. An announcement that because of high air-conditioning costs, the plant temperature will be held at 25 degrees during the summer months
   e. A final request to settle a delinquent debt

3. If you were trying to persuade people to take the following actions, how would you organize your argument?
   a. You want your boss to approve your plan for hiring two new people.
   b. You want to be hired for a job.
   c. You want to be granted a business loan.
   d. You want to collect a small amount from a regular customer whose account is slightly past due.
   e. You want to collect a large amount from a customer whose account is seriously past due.

4. Suppose that end-of-term frustrations have produced this e-mail message to Professor Anne Koyama from a student who feels that he should have received a B in his accounting class. If this message were recast into three or four clear sentences, the teacher might be more receptive to the student's argument. Rewrite the message to show how you would improve it.

   I think that I was unfairly awarded a C in your accounting class this term, and I am asking you to change the grade to a B. It was a difficult term. I don't get any money from home, and I have to work mornings at the Pancake House (as a cook), so I had to rush to make your class, and those two times that I missed class were because they wouldn't let me off work because of special events at the Pancake House (unlike some other students who just take off when they choose). On the midterm examination, I originally got a 75 percent, but you said in class that there were two different ways to answer the third question and that you would change the grades of students who used the "optimal cost" method and had been counted off 6 points for doing this. I don't think that you took this into account, because I got 80 percent on the final, which is clearly a B. Anyway, whatever you decide, I just want to tell you that I really enjoyed this class, and I thank you for making accounting so interesting.

5. Substitute inoffensive phrases for the following:
   a. you claim that
   b. it is not our policy to
   c. you neglected to
   d. in which you assert
   e. we are sorry you are dissatisfied
   f. you failed to enclose
   g. we request that you send us
   h. apparently you overlooked our terms
   i. we have been very patient
   j. we are at a loss to understand

6. Rewrite the following letter to Ms. Joanne Aglukark (597 Corydon Avenue, Winnipeg, Manitoba R3L 0N9)

so that it conveys a helpful, personal, and interested tone:

> We have your letter of recent date to our Ms. Dobson. Owing to the fact that you neglected to include the size of the dress you ordered, please be advised that no shipment of your order was made, but the aforementioned shipment will occur at such time as we are in receipt of the aforementioned information.

7. Rewrite these sentences to reflect your audience's viewpoint.
   a. We request that you use the order form supplied in the back of our catalogue.
   b. We insist that you always bring your credit card to the store.
   c. We want to get rid of all our 14-inch monitors in order to make room in our warehouse for the new 20-inch models. Thus we are offering a 25 percent discount on all sales this week.
   d. I am applying for the position of bookkeeper in your office. I feel that my grades prove that I am bright and capable, and I think I can do a good job for you.
   e. As requested, we are sending the refund for $25.
8. Revise these sentences to be positive rather than negative.
   a. To avoid the loss of your credit rating, please remit payment within ten days.
   b. We don't make refunds on returned merchandise that is soiled.
   c. Because we are temporarily out of Baby Cry dolls, we won't be able to ship your order for ten days.
   d. You failed to specify the colour of the blouse that you ordered.
   e. You should have realized that waterbeds will freeze in unheated houses during winter months. Therefore, our guarantee does not cover the valve damage, and you must pay the $9.50 valve-replacement fee (plus postage).
9. Provide euphemisms for the following words and phrases.
   a. stubborn
   b. wrong
   c. stupid
   d. incompetent
   e. loudmouth
10. Nortel Networks is a world leader in telecommunications hardware and services. This Canadian company also believes "that a company doesn't operate in a vacuum. It is part of the society and the communities where it's located," in the words of CEO John Roth. Visit their Web site at **www.nortel.ca/corporate/community/citizenship/index2.html**, and consult their e-citizenship index. Click on various topics and consider how Nortel's image is projected and the causes they support. Write an e-mail message to a fellow student explaining how the Web site enables Nortel to advocate their causes and advertise their business. Print your e-mail message for submission to your instructor, or send it electronically.

Documents for Analysis

Document 6.A: Defining and Grouping Ideas

The writer of the following list is having trouble grouping the ideas logically for an insurance information brochure. Revise the list and develop a logical outline, paying attention to appropriate subordination of ideas. Rewrite where necessary to give phrases a more consistent sound.

Accident Protection Insurance Plan

- Coverage is only pennies a day
- Benefit is $100 000 for accidental death on common carrier
- Benefit is $100 a day for hospitalization as result of motor vehicle or common carrier accident
- Benefit is $20 000 for accidental death in motor vehicle accident
- Individual coverage is only $17.85 per quarter; family coverage is just $26.85 per quarter
- No physical exam or health questions
- Convenient payment–billed quarterly
- Guaranteed acceptance for all applicants
- No individual rate increases
- Free, no-obligation examination period
- Cash paid in addition to any other insurance carried
- Covers accidental death when riding as fare-paying passenger on public transportation, including buses, trains, jets, ships, trolleys, subways, or any other common carrier
- Covers accidental death in motor vehicle accidents occurring while driving or riding in or on automobile, truck, camper, motor home, or non-motorized bicycle

Document 6.B: Controlling Your Style and Tone

Read the following document; then (1) analyze the strengths and weaknesses of each sentence and (2) revise the document so that it follows this chapter's guidelines.

I am a new publisher with some really great books to sell. I saw your announcement in *Quill & Quire* about the bookseller's show you're having this summer, and I think it's a great idea. Count me in, folks! I would like to get some space to show my books. I thought it would be a neat thing if I could do some airbrushing on T-shirts live to help promote my hot new title, *T-Shirt Art*. Before I got into publishing, I was an airbrush artist, and I could demonstrate my techniques. I've done hundreds of advertising illustrations and have been a sign painter all my life, so I'll also be promoting my other book, hot off the presses, *How to Make Money in the Sign Painting Business.*

I will be starting my PR campaign about May 2001 with ads in *Q&Q* and some art trade papers, so my books should be well known by the time the show comes around in August. In case you would like to use my appearance there as part of your publicity, I have enclosed a biography and photo of myself.

P.S. Please let me know what it costs for booth space as soon as possible so that I can figure out whether I can afford to attend. Being a new publisher is mighty expensive!

Developing Your Internet Skills

Going Online: Connect Now with a Virtual Library, p. 129

After exploring the virtual reference desk at this site, list as many ways as you can think of to use this extensive site effectively in a business setting.

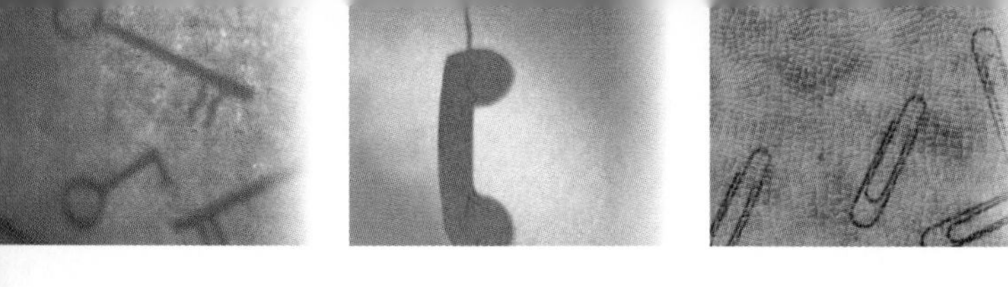

CHAPTER 7

Revising Business Messages

AFTER STUDYING THIS CHAPTER, YOU WILL BE ABLE TO

1. Edit your messages for content and organization, style and readability, and word choice
2. Choose the most correct and most effective words to make your point
3. Rewrite sentences to clarify the relationships among ideas and to make your writing interesting
4. Identify elements of paragraphs
5. Rewrite paragraphs using the appropriate development technique
6. Choose the best design for written documents
7. Proofread your messages for mechanics and format

ON THE JOB
Facing a Communication Dilemma at McDonald's

A Little More Polish on the Golden Arches, Please

If you yearn for a Big Mac, a Coke, and fries, you might enjoy working as a McDonald's quality control representative. David Giarla has been one for 10 years during his career at McDonald's and still likes the smell of Egg McMuffins in the morning. If you filled Giarla's shoes, you would visit seven or eight McDonald's each day, sample the food, inspect the kitchen, survey the storeroom, and chat with the manager and employees. If you like what you eat and see, everyone breathes a sigh of relief and goes back to flipping burgers and wiping tables. But if the food, service, or facilities are not up to standard, employees begin to worry that you will file a negative report with headquarters. If enough bad reports pile up, McDonald's might cancel the franchisee's licence.

Professionals such as David Giarla at McDonald's understand the importance of careful revision. The most successful communicators make sure their messages are the best they can be.

Your aim, however, is not to get people into trouble. On the contrary, you want the store managers to succeed. Quality control reps like Giarla believe that by holding local managers to McDonald's high standards they can help them build their businesses. When Giarla spots a problem, he always points it out and gives the manager a chance to fix it before filing a negative report. Giarla's aim is to offer criticism in a diplomatic and constructive manner, and he is usually successful.

Next time you're in a McDonald's, put yourself in Giarla's position. What would you tell the manager and employees to help them improve their operation? How would you phrase your suggestions? What words would you choose, and how would you arrange them in sentences and paragraphs?[1]

Stage 7: Editing Your Message

Whether offering criticism or praise, David Giarla understands that once you've completed the first draft of your message, you owe it to yourself and to your audience to review and refine it. Plan to go over a document at least three times: once for content and organization, once for style and readability, and once for mechanics and format. The letter in Figure 7.1 has been edited using the proofreading marks shown on page 616. The letter in Figure 7.2 shows how the thoroughly revised letter looked when completed.

LEARNING OUTCOME 1
Edit your messages for content and organization, style and readability, and word choice.

The tendency is to separate revision from composition, but editing is an ongoing activity that occurs throughout the composition process. You edit and revise as you go along; then you edit and revise again after you've completed the first draft. Although the basic editing principles discussed here apply to both written and oral communication, the steps involved in revising a speech or an oral presentation are slightly different, as Chapter 18 explains.

Evaluating Your Content and Organization

After a day or two, review your message for content and organization.

Let your draft sit a day or two before you begin the editing process so that you can approach the material with a fresh eye. Then read through the document quickly to evaluate its overall effectiveness. You're mainly concerned with content, organization, and flow. Compare the draft with your original plan. Have you covered all points in the most logical order? Is there a good balance between the

Content and organization: In the first paragraph, stick to the point (the main idea). In the middle highlight the key advantage of the frequent-guest program, and discuss details in a subsequent paragraph. Eliminate redundancies.

Style and readability: Reword to stress the "you" viewpoint. Clarify the relationships among ideas through placement and combination of phrases. Moderate the excessive enthusiasm, and eliminate words (such as *amenities*) that might be unfamiliar to your reader.

Mechanics and format: To prevent confusion, spell out the abbreviated phrase FG.

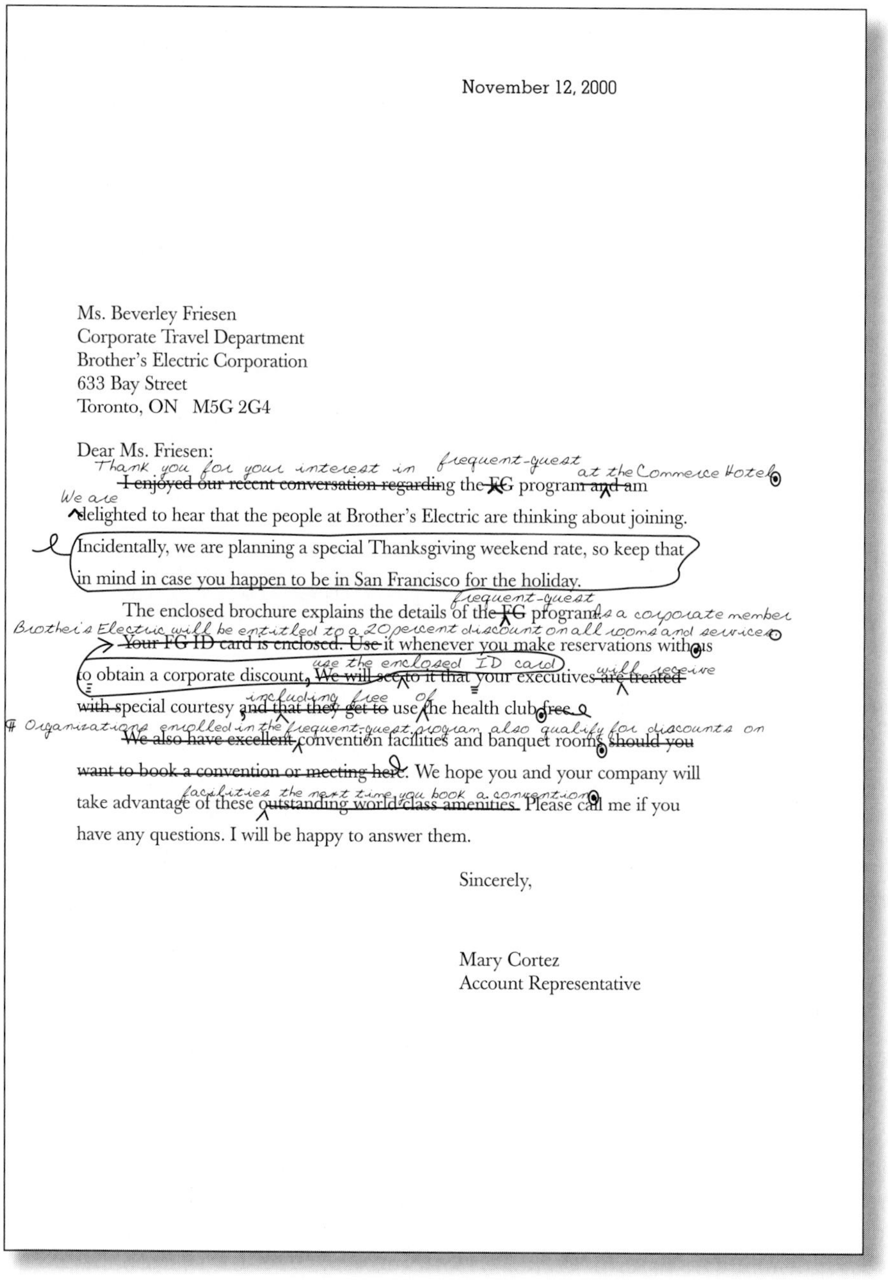

November 12, 2000

Ms. Beverley Friesen
Corporate Travel Department
Brother's Electric Corporation
633 Bay Street
Toronto, ON M5G 2G4

Dear Ms. Friesen:

Thank you for your interest in ~~I enjoyed our recent conversation regarding~~ the frequent-guest ~~FG~~ program at the Commerce Hotel. ~~and am~~ We are delighted to hear that the people at Brother's Electric are thinking about joining. ~~Incidentally, we are planning a special Thanksgiving weekend rate, so keep that in mind in case you happen to be in San Francisco for the holiday.~~

The enclosed brochure explains the details of the frequent-guest ~~FG~~ program. As a corporate member Brother's Electric will be entitled to a 20 percent discount on all rooms and services. ~~Your FG ID card is enclosed. Use~~ it whenever you make reservations with us to obtain a corporate discount. Use the enclosed ID card ~~We will see to it that~~ your executives will receive ~~are treated with~~ special courtesy including free ~~and that they get to~~ use of the health club ~~free~~.

Organizations enrolled in the frequent-guest program also qualify for discounts on ~~We also have excellent~~ convention facilities and banquet rooms. ~~should you want to book a convention or meeting here~~. We hope you and your company will take advantage of these ~~outstanding world-class amenities~~ facilities the next time you book a convention. Please call me if you have any questions. I will be happy to answer them.

Sincerely,

Mary Cortez
Account Representative

FIGURE 7.1

In-Depth Critique: Sample Edited Letter

This letter responds to Beverley Friesen's request for information about the Commerce Hotel's frequent-guest program.

general and the specific? Do the most important ideas receive the most space, and are they placed in the most prominent positions? Have you provided enough support and double-checked the facts? Would the message be more convincing if it were arranged in another sequence? Do you need to add anything? On the other hand, what can you eliminate? In business, it's particularly important to weed out unnecessary material.

In the first phase of editing, spend extra time on the beginning and ending of the message. As Dave Giarla knows, these are the sections that have the greatest impact on the audience. Be sure that the opening of a letter or memo is

333 Sansome Street ➢ San Francisco, CA 94104
(800) 323-7347 ➢ (415) 854-2447 ➢ Fax (415) 854-7669
www.CommerceHotel.com

November 12, 2000

Ms. Beverley Friesen
Corporate Travel Department
Brother's Electric Corporation
633 Bay Street
Toronto, ON M5G 2G4

Dear Ms. Friesen:

Thank you for your interest in the frequent-guest program at the Commerce Hotel. We are delighted to hear that the people at Brother's Electric are thinking about joining.

The enclosed brochure explains the details of the frequent-guest program. As a corporate member, Brother's Electric will be entitled to a 20 percent discount on all rooms and services. To obtain your corporate discount, use the enclosed ID card whenever you make reservations with us. Your executives will receive special courtesy, including free use of the health club.

Organizations enrolled in the frequent-guest program also qualify for discounts on convention facilities and banquet rooms. We hope you and your company will take advantage of these facilities the next time you book a convention. Please call me if you have any questions. I will be happy to answer them.

Sincerely,

Mary Cortez

Mary Cortez
Account Representative

The first paragraph now provides a "you" attitude, spells out what was previously abbreviated, and contains only relevant material.

The second paragraph now clarifies the benefits of the frequent-guest program and personalizes those benefits with the "you" style.

The last paragraph now combines a final benefit with more information about services available. It also concludes with a friendly tone.

FIGURE 7.2

In-Depth Critique: Final Revised Letter

The revised letter gives the information of Figure 7.1 in a more organized fashion and has a friendlier style and clearer mechanics.

Michael D. Eisner, chairman and CEO of the Walt Disney Company, has kept Walt Disney's legacy alive and fiscally healthy through recent years of dramatic change and growth. His detail-oriented business sense is apparent in every branch of Disney's operations, including the renewed stature of Disney's animation studios as the best in the industry. For Eisner, careful review and revision of budgets, reports, and strategic-growth proposals are critical to running a company.

relevant, interesting, and geared to the reader's probable reaction. In longer messages, check to see that the first few paragraphs establish the subject, purpose, and organization of the material. Review the conclusion to be sure that it summarizes the main idea and leaves the audience with a positive impression.

Reviewing Your Style and Readability

When editing a message's style and readability, ask yourself whether you've achieved the right tone for your audience. Look for opportunities to make the material more interesting through the use of lively words and phrases. At the same time, be particularly conscious of whether your message is clear and readable. Check your vocabulary and sentence structure to be sure you're relying mainly on familiar terms and simple, direct statements. You might even apply a readability formula to gauge the difficulty of your writing.

Readability depends on word choice, sentence length, sentence structure, organization, and the message's physical appearance.

The most common readability formulas measure the length of words and sentences to give you a rough idea of how well educated your audience must be to understand your message. Figure 7.3 shows how one readability formula, the Fog Index, has been applied to an excerpt from a memo. (The "long" words in the passage have been underlined.) As the calculation shows, anyone who reads at a grade nine level should be able to read this passage with ease.

FIGURE 7.3
The Fog Index

1. Select writing Sample.
   Keep the sample between 100 and 125 words long.

   I called Global Corporation to ask when we will receive copies of its <u>insurance policies</u> and <u>engineering</u> reports. Cindy Turner of Global said that they are putting the <u>documents together</u> and will send them by Express Mail next week. She told me that they are late because most of the <u>information</u> is in the hands of Global's <u>attorneys</u> in Montreal. I asked why it was in Montreal; we had <u>understood</u> that the account is serviced by the client's Halifax branch. Turner explained that the account <u>originally</u> was sold to Global's Montreal <u>division</u>, so all paperwork stays there. She promised to <u>telephone</u> us when the package is ready to ship.

2. Determine average sentence length.
   Count the number of words in each sentence. Treat independent clauses (stand-alone word groups containing subject and predicate) as separate sentences. For example, "In school we studied; we learned; we improved" counts as three sentences. Then add the word counts for all the sentences to get the total word count, and divide that by the number of sentences. This excerpt has an average sentence length of 14 words:

   $$18 + 21 + 21 + 7 + 13 + 12 + 5 + 12 = 109$$
   $$109 \text{ words} \div 8 \text{ sentences} = 14$$

3. Determine percentage of long words.
   Count the number of long words–that is, all words that have three or more syllables (underlined in excerpt). Do not count proper nouns, combinations of short words (such as paperwork and anyway), and verbs that gain a third syllable by adding -es or -ed (as in trespasses and created). Divide the number of long words by the total number of words in the sample and multiply the answer by 100. The percentage of long words in this excerpt is 10 percent:

   $$11 \text{ long words} \div 109 \text{ total words} = 10 \text{ percent}$$

4. Determine the grade level required to read the passage.
   Add the numbers of average sentence length and percentage of long words. Multiply the sum by 0.4, and drop the number following the decimal point (if there is one). The grade level required to easily read this excerpt is 9:

   $$14 \text{ words per sentence} + 10 \text{ percent long words} = 24$$
   $$24 \times 0.4 = 9.6 - 0.6 = 9 \text{ (Fog Index)}$$

Of course, readability indexes can't be applied to languages other than English. Counting syllables makes no sense in other languages. For example, compare the English *forklift driver* with the German *Gabelstaplerfahrer*. Chinese and Japanese characters don't lend themselves to syllable counting at all.[2]

Although readability formulas can easily be applied, they ignore some important variables that contribute to reading ease, such as sentence structure, the organization of ideas, and the appearance of the message on the page.[3] To fully evaluate the readability of your message, ask yourself whether you have effectively emphasized the important information. Are your sentences easy to decipher? Do your paragraphs have clear topic sentences? Are the transitions between ideas obvious?

Assessing Your Word Choice

LEARNING OUTCOME 2
Choose the most correct and most effective words to make your point.

When choosing and revising words,[4] business communicator Dave Giarla pays attention to two things: correctness and effectiveness. Even though the rules of grammar are constantly changing to reflect changes in the way people speak, grammatical errors decrease your credibility with your audience. So if you have doubts about what is correct, don't be lazy. Look up the answer, and use the proper form of expression. Check the grammar and usage guide in this book (Appendix C), or consult any number of special reference books available in libraries and bookstores. You can find such references on the Internet, including **www.dictionary.com/writing** and **www.bartleby.com**. Most authorities agree on the basic conventions.

The two key aspects of word choice are
✧ Correctness
✧ Effectiveness

Just as important as using the correct words is choosing the best words for the job at hand. Word effectiveness is generally more difficult to achieve than correctness, particularly in written communication. Following are some of the techniques professional writers use to improve the effectiveness of their style.

If in doubt, check it out.

PLAIN ENGLISH

Plain English is close to spoken English and can be easily understood.

Plain English is a way of writing and arranging language so that your audience can understand your meaning. If you've ever tried to make sense of an obtusely worded legal document or credit agreement, you can understand the movement toward requiring contracts and other such documents to be written in plain English. Because it's close to the way we speak, plain English is easily understood by anyone with a grade eight or grade nine education.[5]

The growing focus on plain English has already led to plain-English loan and credit-card application forms, insurance policies, and real estate contracts. Even so, plain English has some limitations. It lacks the precision necessary for scientific research, intense feeling, and personal insight. Moreover, it fails to embrace every culture and dialect equally.[6] Needless to say, it's intended for areas where English is the primary language; however, the lessons of plain English can also help you simplify messages intended for audiences who may speak English only as a second or even third language.

FUNCTIONAL WORDS AND CONTENT WORDS

Functional words (conjunctions, prepositions, articles, and pronouns) express relationships among content words (nouns, verbs, adjectives, and adverbs).

Words can be divided into two categories. Functional words express relationships and have only one unchanging meaning regardless of the context. They include conjunctions, prepositions, articles, and pronouns. Your main concern with functional words is to use them correctly. Content words–nouns, verbs, adjectives, and adverbs–are multidimensional and therefore are subject to various interpretations. These words carry the meaning of a sentence. Content words are the building blocks; functional words are the mortar. In the following sentence, all the content words are in italics:

> *Some objective observers* of the *cookie market give Mr. Christie* the *edge* in *quality*, but *President's Choice is lauded* for *superior distribution*.

Both functional words and content words are necessary, but your effectiveness as a communicator depends largely on your ability to choose the right content words for your message. So take a closer look at two important dimensions for classifying content words.

Content words have both a denotative (dictionary) meaning and a connotative (associative) meaning.

Connotation and Denotation As you know from reading Chapter 2, content words have both a denotative and a connotative meaning. The **denotative meaning** is the literal, or dictionary, meaning; the **connotative meaning** includes all the associations and feelings evoked by the word. Some words have more connotations than others. If you say "Malcolm bought a used car," you may be suggesting that its condition is poor and that the car will need repairs. On the other hand, if you say "Malcolm bought a 'pre-owned' car" (a term used in the automobile industry), you replace the negative connotations of "used" with the more positive connotation that the car was carefully maintained.

In business communication, generally use terms that are low in connotative meaning. Words that have relatively few possible interpretations are less likely to be misunderstood. Furthermore, because you are usually trying to write about projects, policies, and other business concerns in an objective, rational manner, you want to avoid emotion-laden comments.

The more abstract a word, the more it is removed from the tangible, objective world of things that can be perceived with the senses.

In business communication, use concrete, specific terms whenever possible; use abstractions only when necessary.

Abstraction and Concreteness Content words also vary in their level of abstraction. An abstract word expresses a concept, quality, or characteristic instead of standing for something you can touch or see. Abstractions are usually broad concepts that encompass a category of ideas. They are often intellectual, academic, or philosophical. *Love, honour, progress, tradition,* and *beauty* are abstractions. Concrete terms are anchored in the tangible, material world. They stand for something particular: *chair, table, horse, rose, kick, kiss, red, green, two.* These words are direct and vivid, clear and exact.

You might suppose that concrete words are better than abstract words, because they are more precise. However, imagine trying to talk about business without referring to such concepts as *morale, productivity, profits, quality, motivation,* and *guarantees.* Nevertheless, abstractions can be troublesome. They tend to be fuzzy and subject to many interpretations. They also tend to be boring. It isn't always easy to get excited about ideas, especially if they're unrelated to concrete experience. The best way to minimize such problems is to blend abstract terms with concrete ones, the general with the specific. State the concept, and then pin it down with details expressed in more concrete terms. Save the abstractions for ideas that cannot be expressed any other way. For example, instead of referring to McDonald's "principles of operation," Dave Giarla talks about specifics such as "fast service, good food, and clean facilities."

Going Online

Improve Your Writing Style with Proven Techniques

You can improve your work quickly and easily with the *Elements of Style,* by William Strunk Jr., a classic in its field. The contents include rules of usage, principles of composition, commonly misused words and expressions, words commonly misspelled, and dozens of before-and-after examples.

www.bartleby.com/141

WORDS THAT COMMUNICATE

Wordsmiths are journalists, public relations specialists, editors, letter and report writers–anyone who earns a living by crafting words. Unlike poets, novelists, or dramatists, wordsmiths don't try for dramatic effects. They are mainly concerned with being clear, concise, and accurate in their use of language. To reach this goal, they emphasize words that are strong, familiar, and short, and they avoid hiding them under unnecessary syllables. When you edit your message, do your best to think like a wordsmith.

Strong Words Nouns and verbs are the most concrete words in any message, so use them as much as you can. Although adjectives and adverbs obviously have parts to play, use them sparingly. They often call for subjective judgments, and business communication strives to be objective. Verbs are especially powerful because they carry the action; they tell what's happening in the sentence. The more dynamic and specific the verb, the better. Instead of settling for *rise* or *fall,* look for something more meaningful and descriptive, like *soar* or *plummet*. However, be sure that your choice of verb precisely communicates your meaning. You wouldn't want to say that a corporation's share price "soared" if it rose only 3 percent over the previous day's price.

Verbs and nouns are more concrete than adverbs and adjectives.

Familiar Words You'll communicate best with words that are familiar to your readers. At the same time, bear in mind that words familiar to one reader might be unfamiliar to another:

Familiar words are preferable to unfamiliar ones, but try to avoid overworked terms (clichés).

AVOID UNFAMILIAR WORDS	USE FAMILIAR WORDS
ascertain	find out, learn
consummate	close, bring about
peruse	read, study

Although familiar words are generally the best choice, beware of terms so common that they have become trite. Consider the following clichés and their plain language equivalents:

CLICHÉ	PLAIN LANGUAGE
He calls the shots.	He is in charge.
It cost an arm and a leg.	It was expensive.
It was a new ball game.	It was a fresh start.

Also handle technical or professional terms with care. Used in moderation, they add precision and authority to a message. However, many people don't understand them, and even a technically sophisticated audience will be lulled to sleep by too many. Let your audience's vocabulary be your guide. When addressing a group of telecommunication engineers, you might use the term "ADSL line"; but when speaking to consumers planning to access the Internet, you should probably say "high-speed phone line."

Short Words Although certainly not true in every case, short words are generally more vivid and easier to read than are long words. Thus they often communicate better than long words:

Short words are generally more vivid than long ones and improve the readability of a document.

AVOID LONG WORDS	USE SHORT WORDS
During the preceding year, the company accelerated productive operations.	Last year the company sped up operations.
The action was predicated on the assumption that the company was operating at a financial deficit.	The action was based on the belief that the company was losing money.

Camouflaged Verbs In the words you use, watch for endings such as *-ion, -tion, -ing, -ment, -ant, -ent, -ence, -ance,* and *-ency*. Most of them change verbs into nouns and adjectives–the words that result are camouflaged verbs. Removing the camouflage to restore the verbs will strengthen your writing:

Turning verbs into nouns or adjectives weakens your writing style.

AVOID CAMOUFLAGED VERBS	USE VERBS
The manager undertook implementation of the rules.	The manager implemented the rules.
Verification of the shipments occurs weekly.	Shipments are verified weekly.

BIAS-FREE LANGUAGE

Avoid biased language that might offend the audience.

Respect is a basic principle of communication. **Bias-free language** is language that demonstrates your consideration of your audience's gender, race, ethnicity, age, and physical ability. Thoughtful communicators are alert to avoid language that may offend their audiences.

Don't use slang, idioms, or restrictive viewpoints when communicating interculturally, and don't judge associates by their grammar or language structure.

Cultural Bias Whether working with employees from diverse cultures or dealing with businesses and customers in other countries, be careful to avoid cultural bias in your business messages. Avoid using slang ("white elephant," "going down the tubes"), abbreviations and acronyms ("FYI, the MIS is back on line"), and idioms ("You need to go with what you have").[7] If you're having your message translated into another language, one effective way to check for undetected cultural bias is to have it back-translated.

Replace words that inaccurately exclude women or men.

Gender Bias For many years, the word *man* was used to denote humanity, describing people of either gender and any age. Today, however, man is associated more with adult males. Some of the most commonly used words contain the word *man,* but some gender-free alternatives exist:

UNACCEPTABLE	PREFERABLE
mankind	humanity, human beings, human race, people
if a man drove 100 km at 90 km/h	if a person (or someone or a driver) drove 100 km at 90 km/h
man-made	artificial, synthetic, manufactured, constructed, of human origin
manpower	human power, human energy, workers, workforce, personnel

Here are some simple ways to replace occupational terms that contain the word *man* with words that can represent people of either gender:

UNACCEPTABLE	PREFERABLE
businessman	business executive, business manager, business person
salesman	sales representative, salesperson, sales clerk
insurance man	insurance agent
foreman	supervisor

As publisher of *Business $ense* magazine, David Sher sees his work as "an endless quest for adding value to the life of a business student." He reviews each issue from concept to completion, making sure that the result will be a unified product where visuals and text mesh and where readers can get the information they need to succeed in their careers.

Avoid using female-gender words such as *authoress* and *actress; author* and *actor* denote both women and men. Similarly, avoid special designations, such as *woman doctor* or *male nurse*. Use the same label for everyone in a particular group. Don't refer to a woman as a *chairperson* and then call the man a *chairman.*

The pronoun *he* has also traditionally been used to refer to both males and females. Here are some simple ways to avoid this outdated usage:

UNACCEPTABLE	PREFERABLE
The average worker... he	The average worker... he or she *or* Average workers... they
The typical business executive spends four hours of his day in meetings.	Most business executives spend four hours a day in meetings.

Avoid identifying certain roles with a specific gender:

UNACCEPTABLE	PREFERABLE
the engineer ... he	engineers ... they
the nurse/teacher ... she	nurses/teachers ... they

Another way to avoid bias is to make sure you don't always mention men first. Vary the traditional pattern with *women and men, gentlemen and ladies, she and he, her and his*. Finally, identify women by their own names, not by their role or marital status—unless it is appropriate to the context:

UNACCEPTABLE	PREFERABLE
Don Harron and Catherine	Don Harron and Catherine McKinnon
Don Harron and Ms McKinnon	Mr. Harron and Ms. McKinnon

The preferred title for women in business is Ms., unless the individual asks to be addressed as Miss or Mrs. or has some other title, such as Dr.

Racial and Ethnic Bias The guidelines for avoiding racial and ethnic bias are much the same as those for avoiding gender bias. The central principle is to avoid language suggesting that members of a racial or ethnic group have the same stereotypical characteristics:

Eliminate references that reinforce racial or ethnic stereotypes.

UNACCEPTABLE	PREFERABLE
our new black CEO	our new CEO
Jim Wong is an unusually tall Asian.	Jim Wong is tall.

The best solution is to avoid identifying people by race or ethnic origin unless such a label is relevant:

UNACCEPTABLE	PREFERABLE
Frank Clementi, Italian-Canadian CEO	Frank Clementi, CEO

Be correct when you refer to Canada's Aboriginal peoples. The Canadian constitution recognizes three groups of Aboriginal peoples: Indians, Métis, and Inuit. They each have their own heritage, language, cultural practices, and spiritual beliefs. The term "Indian" describes all the Aboriginal people in Canada who are not Inuit or Métis. Many Aboriginal people today are offended by the term "Indian" and prefer "First Nation." Many First Nations peoples have adapted the term "First Nation" to replace the term "band" to designate their community. As an accurate and ethical communicator, be sure to use the terms Canada's Aboriginal peoples prefer when you refer to them.

Age Bias As with gender, race, and ethnic background, mention the age of a person only when it is relevant:

Avoid references to an individual's age or physical limitations.

UNACCEPTABLE	PREFERABLE
Mary Kirazy, 58, has just joined our trust department.	Mary Kirazy has just joined our trust department.

When referring to older people, avoid such stereotyped adjectives as *spry* and *frail*. For example, do not say, "Frank, a spry old man, ran in the Masters' marathon." Instead, simply say "Frank ran in the Masters' marathon."

Always refer to people first and their disabilities second.

Disability Bias Thoughtful communicators also avoid discriminatory language when referring to people with disabilities. When you must refer to people's limitations, avoid using terms such as *handicapped, crippled,* or *retarded,* and be sure to put the person first and the disability second.[8]

UNACCEPTABLE	PREFERABLE
Crippled workers face many barriers on the job.	Workers with physical disabilities face many barriers on the job.

Most of all, avoid mentioning a disability unless it is pertinent. When it is pertinent, present the whole person, not just the disability, by showing the limitation in an unobtrusive manner:

UNACCEPTABLE	PREFERABLE
An epileptic, Tracy has no trouble doing her job.	Tracy's epilepsy has no effect on her job performance.

The Canadian Human Rights Commission guarantees equal opportunities for people who have or have had a condition that might handicap them. The goal of bias-free communication is to abandon stereotyped assumptions about what a person can do or will do and to focus on an individual's unique characteristics.

Evaluating the Writing of Another

When critiquing someone else's writing, focus on
✧ Purpose
✧ Accuracy
✧ Clear language

In business, many documents are written for someone else's signature.[9] When you need to critique the work of another, you want to help that person communicate effectively, and to do that you must provide specific, constructive comments. To help the writer make meaningful changes, concentrate on three elements:[10]

- *Does the document accomplish the intended purpose?* Is the purpose clearly stated? Does the body support the stated purpose? You might outline the key points to see whether they support the main idea. Is the conclusion supported by the data? Are the arguments presented logically? Be sure to determine whether the directions given with the initial assignment were clear and complete. If the document fails to accomplish its purpose, it must be rewritten.
- *Is the factual material correct?* A proposal to provide nationwide computer-training services for $15 million would be disastrous if your intention was to provide those services for $150 million. Be sure you pay strict attention to detail. All factual errors must be corrected.
- *Does the document use ambiguous language?* Readers must not be allowed to interpret the meaning in any way other than intended. If you interpret a message differently from what an author intended, the author is at fault, and the document must be revised to clarify problem areas.

Requesting other changes depends on whether they are
✧ Cosmetic
✧ Time consuming
✧ Bad for morale

If any one of these elements needs attention, the document must be rewritten, revised, or corrected. However, once these elements are deemed satisfactory, the question is whether to request other changes. If the three elements are in fact acceptable, consider three points before requesting a major revision.[11]

- *Can the document truly be improved?* If the changes you want are purely subjective and cosmetic, they will not actually improve the document.
- *Can you justify the time needed for a rewrite?* If time is short, you may need to use what you have–as long as the elements of purpose, accuracy, and specificity are fulfilled.
- *Will your request have a negative impact on morale?* If unexplained or inconsistent changes are regularly made to a person's writing she can become demoralized.

Stage 8: Rewriting Your Message

LEARNING OUTCOME 3
Rewrite sentences to clarify the relationships among ideas and to make your writing interesting.

As you edit your business message, you'll find yourself rewriting passages, sentences, and even whole sections to improve its effectiveness. David Giarla would caution you to remember that in your search for perfection, you're probably also facing a deadline, so try to stick to the schedule you set during the planning stage. Do your best to revise and rewrite thoroughly but economically. Also, you'll probably want to keep copies of your revised versions. As you rewrite, concentrate on how each word contributes to an effective sentence and how that sentence develops a coherent paragraph.

Create Effective Sentences

Every sentence contains a subject (noun or noun equivalent) and a predicate (verb and related word).

In English, words don't make much sense until they're combined in a sentence to express a complete thought. Thus, *Jill, receptionist, the, smiles,* and *at* can be organized into "Jill smiles at the receptionist." Now you can begin exploring the possibilities for improvement, looking at how well each word performs its particular function. Nouns and noun equivalents are the topics (or subjects) you're communicating about, and verbs and related words (or predicates) make statements about those sub-

Warding Off Digital Disaster

USING THE POWER OF TECHNOLOGY

Today's data is being threatened. Computer viruses such as the Lovebug and Anna Kournikova wreaked havoc on computers around the world. Not only can computer viruses turn detailed records into electronic confetti, but the very media carrying our precious bits of information aren't lasting as long as we had expected. Moreover, chances are good that the software (or even the hardware) needed to get at today's data might not be readily available in 10 years. Anyone who has tried wresting information from a $5\frac{1}{4}$-inch floppy disk knows that.

You can help prevent your digits from turning to dust by taking these precautions:

- *Keep your PC clean.* Keep food and drink away from your equipment.
- *Maintain your hard drive.* Scan your drive for errors often, and correct them. Defragment your hard drive once a year (but only after performing a complete system backup).
- *Install surge protectors.* Make sure your protectors have a UL1449 rating of 330 volts or less, and install a backup power supply.
- *Exit your system correctly.* Shut down all applications before you turn off your computer; then shut down your computer in proper sequence.
- *Register your hardware and software.* Send in registration cards so that you are eligible for customer support and are notified about major problems or upgrades.
- *Install antivirus programs.* Use a good virus-scanning program, and update it at least quarterly. Run a virus scan on everything that comes into your computer: new software, new floppy disks, and Internet downloads. Don't open e-mail attachments from strangers.
- *Back up your system regularly.* Make sure you flag all important files and keep a regular backup schedule. Back up your entire system before installing any new software.
- *Store your backups properly.* Store your backup media offsite in a cool, dry cabinet away from heat, humidity, light, dust, and smoke. Keep them away from electric motors, speakers, phone handsets, monitors, TV screens, and transformers (which can cause electromagnetic radiation and erasure). Serious PC users may want to consider online backup services, a safe and inexpensive option.
- *Keep your copies clean and organized.* Label your backup media clearly. Twice a year buy and use new backup media, and clean the magnetic heads on your backup hardware. Do a test restore monthly to make sure your backups are usable.

By taking these steps, you can substantially reduce your risk should a data disaster strike.

CAREER APPLICATIONS

1. Your office has just decided to electronically store all written communications, reports, policies, and so on. Express your concerns about this policy in a brief memo to the president of the company.
2. Trade memos with a classmate. Review and edit each other's writing. Then answer the bulleted questions appearing in the section "Evaluating the Writing of Another."

jects. In a more complicated sentence, adjectives and adverbs modify the subject and the statement, and various connectors hold the words together.

To give your writing variety, use the three types of sentences:
- ✧ Simple
- ✧ Compound
- ✧ Complex

THE THREE TYPES OF SENTENCES

Sentences come in three basic varieties: simple, compound, and complex. A **simple sentence** has a single subject and a single predicate, although it may be expanded by nouns and pronouns serving as objects of the action and by modifying phrases. In the following examples, the subject is underlined once, and the predicate verb is underlined twice:

> Profits have increased in the past year.

A **compound sentence** expresses two or more independent but related thoughts of equal importance, joined by *and, but,* or *or.* In effect, a compound sentence is a merger of two or more simple sentences (independent clauses) that deal with the same basic idea:

> Wage rates have declined by 5 percent, and employee turnover has been high.

The independent clauses in a compound sentence are always separated by a comma (followed by a conjunction), or by a semicolon (in which case the conjunction–*and, but, or*–is dropped).

A **complex sentence** expresses one main thought (the independent clause) and one or more subordinate thoughts (dependent clauses) related to it, often separated by a comma. The subordinate thought, which comes first in the following sentence, could not stand alone:

> Although you may question Gerald's conclusions, you must admit that his research is thorough.

When constructing a sentence, use the form that best fits the thought you want to express. The structure of the sentence should match the relationship of the ideas. If you have two ideas of equal importance, express them as two simple sentences or as one compound sentence. However, if one idea is less important than the other, place it in a dependent clause to form a complex sentence. This compound sentence uses a conjunction to join two ideas that aren't truly equal:

> The chemical products division is the strongest in the company, and its management techniques should be adopted by the other divisions.

In the following complex sentence, the first thought has been made subordinate to the second. Note how much more effective the second idea is when the cause-and-effect relationship has been established:

> Because the chemical products division is the strongest in the company, its management techniques should be adopted by the other divisions.

As a publicist for the Confederation Centre of the Arts, Laurie Murphy must adapt her messages to a variety of audiences. Her work requires thorough revision to make the language and writing style is well suited for her intended readers.

In complex sentences, the placement of the dependent clause should be geared to the relationships of the ideas expressed. If you want to emphasize the idea in the dependent clause, put it at the end of the sentence (the most emphatic position) or at the beginning (the second most emphatic position). If you want to downplay the idea, bury the dependent clause within the sentence.

> MOST EMPHATIC: The handbags are manufactured in Mexico, *which has lower wage rates than Canada.*

EMPHATIC: *Because wage rates are lower there,* the handbags are manufactured in Mexico.

LEAST EMPHATIC: Mexico, *which has lower wage rates,* was selected as the production point for the handbags.

To make your writing as effective as possible, use all three sentence types. If you use too many simple sentences, you can't properly express the relationship among ideas. If you use too many long, compound sentences, your writing will sound monotonous. On the other hand, an uninterrupted series of complex sentences is hard to follow.

SENTENCE STYLE

Of course, sentence style varies from culture to culture. German sentences are extremely complex with a lot of modifiers and appositives; Japanese and Chinese languages don't have sentences in the same sense that Western languages do.[12] Basically, whether a sentence in English is simple, compound, or complex, it should be grammatically correct, readable, and appropriate for your audience. In general, strive for simplicity.

Break long sentences into shorter ones to improve readability.

Keep Sentences Short Long sentences are usually harder to understand than short sentences because they are packed with information that must all be absorbed at once. Most good business writing therefore has an average sentence length of 20 words or fewer. That figure is the average, not a ceiling. To be interesting, your writing should contain both longer and shorter sentences.

Long sentences are especially well suited for grouping or combining ideas, listing points, and summarizing or previewing information. Medium-length sentences (those with about 20 words) are useful for showing the relationships among ideas. Short sentences are tailor-made for emphasizing important information.

Active sentences are stronger than passive ones.

Rely on the Active Voice Active sentences are generally preferable to passive sentences because they are easier to understand.[13] You're using **active voice** when you put the subject (the "actor") before the verb, and the object of the sentence (the "acted upon") after the verb: "John rented the office." You're using **passive voice** when you put the subject after the verb and the object before it: "The office was rented by John." As you can see, the passive verb combines the helping verb *to be* with a form of the verb that is usually similar to the past tense. Using passive verbs makes sentences longer and de-emphasizes the subject. Active verbs produce shorter, stronger sentences:

AVOID PASSIVE SENTENCES	USE ACTIVE SENTENCES
Sales were increased by 32 percent last month.	Sales increased by 32 percent last month.
The new procedure is thought by the president to be superior.	The president thinks the new procedure is superior.

Use passive sentences to soften bad news, to put yourself in the background, or to create an impersonal tone.

Of course, in some situations, using the passive voice makes sense. You may want to be diplomatic when pointing out a problem or error of some kind, so you might say, "The shipment was lost" rather than "You lost the shipment." The passive version seems less like an accusation because the emphasis is on the lost shipment rather than on the person responsible. Similarly, you may want to point out what's being done without taking or attributing either the credit or the blame, so you might say something like "The production line is being analyzed to determine the source of problems." You may want to avoid personal pronouns in order to create an objective tone, so in a formal report, you might say, "Criteria have been established for evaluating capital expenditures."

Be on the lookout for
- ✧ Inefficient phrases
- ✧ Redundancies
- ✧ Unneeded relative pronouns and articles

Eliminate Unnecessary Words and Phrases Some words and combinations of words have more efficient, one-word equivalents. So you can avoid "This is to inform you that we have begun production" by saying "We have begun production."

COMBINATIONS TO AVOID	EFFICIENT EQUIVALENTS
for the sum of	for
in the event that	if
on the occasion of	on
prior to the start of	before

Relative pronouns such as *who, that,* and *which* frequently cause clutter, and sometimes even articles are excessive (mostly too many *thes*). However, well-placed relative pronouns and articles serve an important function by preventing confusion. For example, without *that,* the following sentence is ambiguous:

CONFUSING: The project manager told the engineers last week the specifications were changed.

CLEAR: The project manager told the engineers last week *that* the specifications were changed.

CLEAR: The project manager told the engineers *that* last week the specifications were changed.

Here are some other ways to prune your prose:

POOR	IMPROVED
consensus of opinion	consensus
at this point in time	at this time, now
irregardless	(no such word; use regardless)
each and every	(either word, but not both)
due to the fact that	because
at an early date	soon (or a specific date)
at the present time	now
in view of the fact that	because
until such time as	when
we are of the opinion	we believe, we think
as a result of	because
for the month of December	for December

Avoid needless repetition.

In general, be on the lookout for the needless repetition of words or ideas. Try not to string together a series of sentences that all start with the same word or words, and avoid repeating the same word too often within a given sentence.

Another way to write economically is to use infinitives in place of some phrases. This technique not only shortens your sentences but makes them clearer as well:

Use infinitives to replace some phrases.

POOR	IMPROVED
In order to be a successful writer, you must work hard.	To be a successful writer, you must work hard.
He went to the library for the purpose of studying.	He went to the library to study.
The employer increased salaries so that she could improve morale.	The employer increased salaries to improve morale.

Avoid Obsolete and Pompous Language The language of business used to be much more formal than it is today. A few out-of-date phrases remain from the earlier style of writing. Perhaps the best way to eliminate them is to ask yourself, "Would I say this if I were talking with someone face to face?"

Obsolete formal phrases can obscure meaning.

OBSOLETE	UP-TO-DATE
as per your letter	as in your letter (do not mix Latin and English)
hoping to hear from you soon, I remain	(omit)
yours of the 15th	your letter of June 15
awaiting your reply, we are	(omit)
in due course	today, tomorrow (or a specific time)
permit me to say that	(permission is not necessary; just say what you wish)
we are in receipt of	we have received
pursuant to	(omit)
in closing, I'd like to say	(omit)
attached herewith is	here is
the undersigned	I, me
kindly advise	please let us know
under separate cover	in another envelope, by parcel post
we wish to inform you	(just say it)
attached please find invoice	invoice is enclosed
it has come to my attention	I have just learned; Ms. Garza has just told me
our Mr. Lydell	Mr. Lydell, our credit manager
please be advised that	(omit)

Being a good communicator, McDonald's Dave Giarla understands that pompous language is similar to out-of-date phrases. It also sounds stiff and roundabout. Do not use pretentious language, trite expressions, or overly complicated sentences, because they will block communication and lower your esteem in the eyes of your audiences.

The use of pompous language suggests you are a pompous person.

POOR	IMPROVED
Upon procurement of additional supplies, I will initiate fulfillment of your order.	I will fill your order when I receive more supplies.

Business writing shouldn't be gushy.

Moderate Your Enthusiasm An occasional adjective or adverb intensifies and emphasizes your meaning, but too many ruin your writing:

POOR	IMPROVED
We are extremely pleased to offer you a position on our staff of exceptionally skilled and highly educated employees. The work offers extraordinary challenges and a very large salary.	We are pleased to offer you a position on our staff of skilled and well-educated employees. The work offers challenges and an attractive salary.

In many cases, the parts of a compound sentence should be separated into two sentences.

Break Up Strung-Out Sentences A strung-out sentence is a series of two or more sentences unwisely connected by *and*–in other words, a compound sentence taken too far. You can often improve your writing style by separating the string into individual sentences:

POOR	IMPROVED
The magazine will be published January 1, and I'd better meet the deadline if I want my article included.	The magazine will be published January 1. I'd better meet the deadline if I want my article included.

Don't be afraid to present your opinions without qualification.

Avoid Hedging Sentences Sometimes you have to write *may* or *seems* to avoid stating a judgment as a fact. Nevertheless, when you have too many such hedges, you aren't really saying anything:

POOR	IMPROVED
I believe that Mr. Johnson's employment record seems to show that he may be capable of handling the position.	Mr. Johnson's employment record shows that he is capable of handling the position.

Avoid starting sentences with *it* and *there.*

Watch for Indefinite Pronoun Starters If you start a sentence with an indefinite pronoun (an expletive) such as *it* or *there,* odds are that the sentence could be shorter:

POOR	IMPROVED
It would be appreciated if you would sign the lease today.	Please sign the lease today.
There are five employees in this division who were late to work today.	Five employees in this division were late to work today.

Express Parallel Ideas in Parallel Form When you have two or more similar (parallel) ideas to express, try to use a **parallel construction**; that is, use the same grammatical pattern. The repetition of the pattern tells readers that the ideas are comparable and adds a nice rhythm to your message. In the following examples, parallel construction makes the sentences more readable:

POOR	IMPROVED
Miss Simms had been drenched with rain, bombarded with telephone calls, and her boss shouted at her.	Miss Simms had been drenched with rain, bombarded with telephone calls, and shouted at by her boss.

Parallelism can be achieved through a repetition of words, phrases, clauses, or entire sentences:

PARALLEL WORDS: The letter was approved by Clausen, Makryk, Merlin, and Carlucci.

PARALLEL PHRASES: We have beaten the competition in supermarkets, in department stores, and in specialty stores.

PARALLEL CLAUSES: I'd like to discuss the issue after Vicki gives her presentation but before Marvin shows his slides.

PARALLEL SENTENCES: In 1997 we exported 30 percent of our production. In 1998 we exported 50 percent.

Eliminate Awkward Pointers To save words, business writers sometimes direct their readers' attention elsewhere with such expressions as *the above-mentioned, as mentioned above, the aforementioned, the former, the latter, respectively.* These words cause the reader to jump from one point in the message to another, a process that hinders effective communication. A better approach is to be specific in your references, even if you must add a few more words:

POOR	IMPROVED
Computer supplies for legal secretaries and beginning clerks are distributed by the Law Office and Stenographic Office, respectively.	Computer supplies for legal secretaries are distributed by the Law Office; those for beginning clerks are distributed by the Stenographic Office.

Avoid Dangling Modifiers Sometimes a modifier is not just an adjective or adverb but an entire phrase defining a noun or verb. Be careful to construct your sentences so that this type of modifier refers to something in the main part of the sentence in a way that makes sense. Consider this sentence:

Make sure that modifier phrases are really related to the subject of the sentence.

Walking to the office, a red sports car passed her.

The construction implies that the red sports car has the office and the legs to walk there. The modifier is said to be **dangling** because it has no real connection to the subject of the sentence–in this case, the sports car. This is what the writer is trying to say:

Dangling modifiers make sentences confusing and sometimes ridiculous.

A red sports car passed her while she was walking to the office.

Flipping the clauses produces another correct sentence:

While she was walking to the office, a red sports car passed her.

POOR	IMPROVED
Working as fast as possible, the budget was soon ready.	Working as fast as possible, the committee soon had the budget ready.
After a three-week slump, we increased sales.	After a three-week slump, sales increased.

The first example shows one frequent cause of dangling modifiers: passive construction in the independent clause. When you make the clause active instead of passive, you can see the connection with the dangling modifier more clearly.

Stringing together a series of nouns may save a little space, but it causes confusion.

Avoid Long Sequences of Nouns When nouns are strung together as modifiers, the resulting sentence is hard to read. You can clarify the sentence by putting some of the nouns in a modifying phrase. Although you add a few more words, your audience won't have to work as hard to understand the sentence.

POOR	IMPROVED
The window sash installation company will give us an estimate on Friday.	The company that installs window sashes will give us an estimate on Friday.

Subject and predicate should be placed as close together as possible, as should modifiers and the words they modify.

Keep Together Words That Work Together To avoid confusing readers, keep the subject and predicate of a sentence as close together as possible. Otherwise, readers will have to read your sentence twice to figure out who did what.

The same rule applies to other parts of speech. Adjectives, adverbs, and prepositional phrases usually make the most sense when they're placed as close as possible to the words they modify:

POOR	IMPROVED
A 10 percent decline in market share, which resulted from quality problems and an aggressive sales campaign by Armitage, the market leader in the Northwest Territories, was the major problem in 1999.	The major problem in 1999 was a 10 percent loss of market share, which resulted from both quality problems and an aggressive sales campaign by Armitage, the market leader in the Northwest Territories.

POOR	IMPROVED
We will deliver the pipe that you ordered last Tuesday soon.	We will soon deliver the pipe that you ordered last Tuesday.

Emphasize parts of a sentence by
- ✧ Giving them more space
- ✧ Putting them at the beginning or the end of the sentence
- ✧ Making them the subject of the sentence

Emphasize Key Thoughts In every message, some ideas are more important than others. You can emphasize these key ideas through your sentence style. One obvious technique is to give important points the most space. When you want to call attention to a thought, use extra words to describe it. Consider this sentence:

> The chairperson of the board called for a vote of the shareholders.

To emphasize the importance of the chairperson, you might describe her more fully:

> The chairperson of the board, who has considerable experience in corporate takeover battles, called for a vote of the shareholders.

You can increase the emphasis even more by adding a separate, short sentence to augment the first:

> The chairperson of the board called for a vote of the shareholders. She has considerable experience in corporate takeover battles.

Another way to emphasize an idea is to place it at either the beginning or the end of a sentence:

LESS EMPHATIC	MORE EMPHATIC
We are cutting the price to stimulate demand.	To stimulate demand, we are cutting the price.

You can also call attention to a thought by making it the subject of the sentence. In the following example, the emphasis is on the person:

I can write letters much more quickly using a computer.

In this version, the computer takes centre stage:

The *computer* enables me to write letters much more quickly.

Techniques like this give you a great deal of control over the way your audience interprets what you have to say.

Develop Coherent Paragraphs

A paragraph is a cluster of sentences that are all related to the same general topic. It is a unit of thought. A series of paragraphs makes up an entire composition. Each paragraph is an important part of the whole, a key link in the train of thought. As you edit a message, think about the paragraphs and their relationship to one another.

Paragraphs are functional units that revolve around a single thought.

LEARNING OUTCOME 4
Identify elements of paragraphs.

ELEMENTS OF THE PARAGRAPH

Paragraphs vary widely in length and form. You can communicate effectively in one short paragraph of two or three sentences or in pages of long paragraphs of eight to ten sentences, depending on your purpose, your audience, and your message. The typical paragraph contains three basic elements: a topic sentence, related sentences that develop the topic, and transitional words and phrases.

Most paragraphs consist of a topic sentence, related sentences, and transitional elements.

Topic Sentence Every properly constructed paragraph is **unified**; it deals with a single topic. The sentence that introduces that topic is called the **topic sentence.** In informal and creative writing, the topic sentence may be implied rather than stated. In business writing, the topic sentence is generally explicit and often is the first sentence in the paragraph. The topic sentence gives readers a summary of the general idea that will be covered in the rest of the paragraph. The following examples show how a topic sentence can both introduce the subject and suggest the way that subject will be developed:

The topic sentence
- ✧ Reveals the subject of the paragraph
- ✧ Indicates how it will be developed

The medical products division has been troubled for many years by public relations problems. [In the rest of the paragraph, readers will learn the details of the problems.]

To get a refund, you must supply us with some additional information. [The details will be described.]

Related Sentences The sentences that explain the topic sentence complete the unified thought of the paragraph. These related sentences must all have a bearing on the general subject, and they must provide enough specific details to make the topic clear:

Paragraphs are developed through a series of related sentences that provide details about the topic sentence.

The medical products division has been troubled for many years by public relations problems. Since 1991 the local newspaper has published 15 articles that portray the division in a negative light. We have been accused of everything from mistreating laboratory animals to polluting the local groundwater. Our facility has been described as a health hazard. Our scientists are referred to as "Frankensteins," and our profits are considered "obscene."

The developmental sentences are all more specific than the topic sentence. Each one provides another piece of evidence to demonstrate the general truth of the main thought. Also, the clear relation of each sentence to the general idea being developed gives the paragraph its unity. A paragraph is well developed when it contains enough information to make the topic sentence convincing and interesting.

Transitional words and phrases show readers how paragraphs and the ideas within them are related.

Transitional Elements Some ideas are simply too big to be handled conveniently in one paragraph. Unless you break up the thoughts somehow, you'll end up with a three-page paragraph that will intimidate even the most dedicated reader. What do you do when you want to package a big idea in short paragraphs? Break the idea into subtopics, treat each subtopic in a separate paragraph, and be careful to provide plenty of transitional elements.

It's a fact that short paragraphs (of 100 words or fewer) are easier to read than long ones. So, in addition to being unified and well developed, effective paragraphs are **coherent;** that is, they are arranged in a logical order so that the audience can understand the train of thought. In Figure 7.4, coherence is achieved through the use of transitions that show how one thought is related to another. You can establish transitions in various ways:

Some transitional devices:
✧ Connecting words (conjunctions)
✧ Repeated words or phrases
✧ Pronouns
✧ Words that are frequently paired

- Use connecting words: *and, but, or, nevertheless, however, in addition,* and so on.
- Echo a word or phrase from a previous paragraph or sentence: "A *system* should be established for monitoring inventory levels. This *system* will provide … "
- Use a pronoun: "Ms. Arthur is the leading candidate for the president's position. *She* has excellent qualifications."
- Use words that are frequently paired: "The machine has a *minimum* output of … Its *maximum* output is … "

LEARNING OUTCOME 5
Rewrite paragraphs using the appropriate development technique.

FIVE WAYS TO DEVELOP A PARAGRAPH

Paragraphs can be developed in many ways. Your choice of technique depends on your subject, your intended audience, and your purpose. Remember also that in actual practice you'll often combine two or more methods of development in a single paragraph.

Five ways to develop paragraphs:
✧ Illustration
✧ Comparison or contrast
✧ Cause and effect
✧ Classification
✧ Problem and solution

Before settling for the first approach that comes to mind, think about the alternatives. Think through various methods before committing yourself. If you fall into the easy habit of repeating the same old paragraph pattern time after time, your writing will be boring.

Illustration When you develop a paragraph by illustration, you give examples that demonstrate the general idea:

> Some of our most popular products are available through local distributors. For example, Everett & Lemmings carries our frozen soups and entrees. The J. B. Green Company carries our complete line of seasonings, as well as the frozen soups. Wilmont Foods, also a major distributor, now carries our new line of frozen desserts.

Comparison or Contrast Similarities or differences among thoughts often provide a strong basis for paragraph development:

> In previous years, when the company was small, the recruiting function could be handled informally. The need for new employees was limited, and each manager could comfortably screen and hire her or his own staff. Today, however, Gambit Products must undertake a major recruiting effort. Our successful bid on the Owens contract means that we will be doubling our labor force over the next six months. To hire that many people without disrupting our ongoing activities, we will create a separate recruiting group within the human resources department.

Marty Grieve
Director, Consumer Printer Division
Lexmark Canada Inc.
160 Royal Crest Court
Markham, Ontario CANADA
L3R 0A2
e-mail:martyg@lexmark.com

Dear Friend,

We know that there are many printer choices in the market. So it is with sincere appreciation that I thank you, on behalf of all the employees of Lexmark Canada, for choosing Lexmark for your printing needs.

I assure you that your investment is a good one. Aside from now owning renowned printing technology, you have access to customer service that's second-to-none in the industry. We call our service Total Lexmark Care (TLC), and it's our commitment to you.

From hereon, we're by your side. Whether you require technical support or product information, we're just a phone call or a click of the mouse away.

Here's how you can reach us:

1. For technical support or product information, simply call toll-free: **1-800-539-6275**.
2. Visit our web site at: www.lexmark.ca for on-line technical support or to download the latest in driver updates.

There will be times when we will want to inform you about updates to your printer and exciting promotions. To ensure you receive this important information, please complete and return the postage-paid registration card today.

Again, thank you for entrusting Lexmark with your printer investment. We're determined to build on that trust to ensure your complete satisfaction.

Sincerely,

Marty Grieve

Marty Grieve
Director, Consumer Printer Division

Short paragraphs increase clarity and effectiveness.

Each paragraph is organized around a topic sentence. The writer employs the "you" attitude and varies short and long sentences for a conversational tone.

Access information is itemized for easy reference.

Separate paragraphs are linked by transitional elements such as repeating the word "you".

FIGURE 7.4

In-Depth Critique: Letter with Short, Focused Paragraphs

This letter accompanied a Lexmark-brand printer.

Cause and Effect When you develop a paragraph using the cause-and-effect technique, you focus on the reasons for something:

> The heavy-duty fabric of your Wanderer tent probably broke down for one of two reasons: (1) a sharp object punctured the fabric, and, without reinforcement, the hole was enlarged by the stress of erecting the tent daily for a week, or (2) folding and storing the tent while it was still wet gradually rotted the fibres.

Classification Paragraphs developed by classification show how a general idea is broken into specific categories:

> Successful candidates for our supervisor-trainee program generally come from one of several groups. The largest group, by far, consists of recent graduates of

> accredited data-processing programs. The next largest group comes from within our own company, as we try to promote promising clerical workers to positions of greater responsibility. Finally, we do occasionally accept candidates with outstanding supervisory experience in related industries.

Problem and Solution Another way to develop a paragraph is to present a problem and then discuss the solution:

> Selling handmade toys by mail is a challenge because consumers are accustomed to buying heavily advertised toys from major chains. However, if we develop an appealing catalogue, we can compete on the basis of product novelty and quality. In addition, we can provide craftsmanship at a competitive price: a rocking horse made from birch wood, with a hand-knit tail and mane; a music box with the child's name painted on the top; Inuit sculptures made by Inuit artisans.

Stage 9: Producing Your Message

LEARNING OUTCOME 6
Choose the best design for written documents

Once you've planned, composed, edited, and rewritten your message, give some thought to its presentation. Oral presentations are discussed in Chapter 18, and visual aids are discussed in Chapter 14. In the following sections, you'll get an

BEHIND THE SCENES AT THE CONFEDERATION CENTRE FOR THE ARTS

Celebrating Canadian Heritage and Culture

"Communicating the creative work of Canada's best writers, visual artists, playwrights, designers, performers, musicians, and technicians is fun, rewarding, and full of variety," says Laurie Murphy, publicist at Charlottetown's Confederation Centre of the Arts in Prince Edward Island. On a typical day, while actors, dancers, and musicians rehearse, the art-going public strolls through the museum and art gallery, and kids enjoy hands-on activities, Murphy is at her computer crafting the media releases, brochures, fact sheets, biographies and Web site copy that promote the centre's events. The only cultural institution in Canada designated as the National Memorial to the Fathers of Confederation, the centre is most famous for *Anne of Green Gables, The Musical,* its longest-running production. Officially opened in 1964 by Her Majesty Queen Elizabeth II, the centre is the focal point for the annual Charlottetown Festival. It is also a place where the public can experience theatre, music, dance, and art year-round. Without the material Murphy and her marketing colleagues write, the Confederation Centre could easily slip from public view.

Laurie Murphy's job includes publicizing such plays as the perennial favourite, *Anne of Green Gables*, the Musical.

Murphy's challenge is to attract local, national, and international media attention to reach audiences, critics, and theatre artists, directors, and technicians.

On a typical day Murphy has to balance writing and networking, as she produces promotional and informational documents and maintains her contacts with the media. Ideas "are generated based on the programming offered to the public," she says. "There are obvious story ideas, such as the appointment of a new director, a new actor in a lead role, or a new set or new costumes." Another source for interesting story ideas are "informal discussions I have within the marketing department as well as with a show's director, cast members, stage managers, or other theatre professionals backstage. For example, a supporting cast member who gets an opportunity to fill in for a lead actor unable to perform because of illness is an interesting story that the public always seems to enjoy hearing."

The centre offers an eclectic mix of art forms—plays, such as the musical *Anne of Green Gables* or Young Company and community theatre productions; visual art in its museum and idea of basic decisions about the design of written documents. To help people comprehend long, uninterrupted pages of text, you can use design elements such as white space, headings, and boldface type (just as this textbook does) to provide visual clues to the importance of various ideas and their relationships.[14]

Written documents require decisions about design elements.

- *White space.* The blank space free of text or artwork is known as **white space.** It provides contrast, and, perhaps even more important, it gives readers a resting point. White space includes the open area surrounding headings, the margin space, the vertical space between columns, the space created by ragged line endings, the paragraph indents or extra space between unindented paragraphs, and the horizontal space between lines of type. You'll decide how much white space to allow for each of these areas.
- *Margins and line justification.* Margins define the space around your text and between text columns. They're influenced by the way you have your word processor format the lines. Your choices are (1) full-justified (text is aligned on both the left and right margins), (2) left-justified (with a ragged-right margin), (3) right-justified (with a ragged-left margin), or (4) centred. Full-justified text will "darken" your message's appearance and will make it look like a form letter. Full-justified text is often considered more difficult to read because large gaps can appear between words and because more words are hyphenated; excessive hyphenation is distracting and hard to read. Even so, many magazines and newspapers use justified type because it yields greater word

White space is free of text and artwork.

gallery, such as exhibits of traditional crafts or the work of nineteenth and twentieth century Canadian artists; and choral and instrumental recitals. It also conducts educational programs targeted at elementary, middle, and high school students. So, Murphy is challenged to capture the mood of each project and write for its specific audience. Media releases follow standard formats and include both an "in brief" section of no more than 160 words and an "in full" section of 500 words maximum. She explains that these formats "provide the media with the option to print or broadcast as a public-service-announcement item, or in a news release format." Seasonal brochures, such as those describing the Charlottetown Festival, held from May to October, are directed toward a general audience. They are written in a "promotional style," with appealing, pithy phrases readers will easily remember. Copy written for generic brochures feature an "educative" style that explains the Centre's projects and activities more fully. When successful, her copy has a direct effect on ticket sales, sponsorship, and future productions.

Since her office services the programming directors and management of the Confederation Centre of the Arts, collaboration is a key element in her work. Her role is to provide assistance in presenting and disseminating information to the public, media, and staff. "Regardless of the document and its intended audience," explains Murphy, "I will ask others in the marketing department to proofread before sending it to the program director for fact-checking. Upon return, changes are made before final edit and approval by the director of Marketing and Development." Documents involving the CEO, executive director, or board members must have their stamp of approval before release. Upon authorization, the document is sent to the centre's French translator.

Murphy's work on the centre's Web site, originally created in 1997, also involves collaboration and editing. While a graphic designer oversees the project and works with the Webmaster, she writes the site's text. In 1999 the site was "completely rebuilt," making it easier for online visitors to get information "with more streamlined and reorganized text and images. The photographs and graphics were made as small as possible without detracting from the look and feel of the site to ensure a quick download time for the end user." No doubt, the changes did their magic, as visits have skyrocketed since the Web site's creation. As Laurie Murphy says, "Handling publicity at a national arts centre is always exciting, given that the programming is usually new and creative."[15]

APPLY YOUR KNOWLEDGE

1. To demonstrate that writing can almost always be improved, select an article on any subject from a newspaper or magazine. (1) Make a list of the words you would exchange for more colourful, more precise, or less biased words. (2) List your revisions on a separate sheet. (3) Rewrite any sentences that could be enlivened by the active voice. (4) Look for paragraphs that could be shortened or simplified without losing meaning.
2. One of the most frustrating problems business writers face is having their words and work misunderstood. List the steps you can take to avoid uttering, "But that's not what I meant!"

Flush-left–ragged-right type gives your message an open feeling.

density. Flush-left text "lightens" your message's appearance, giving it an informal, contemporary feeling of openness. Centred text lends a formal tone to your message but slows reading because readers have to search for the beginning of each line. The same problem is also true of flush-right–ragged-left type.

Headings help your readers quickly identify the content and organization of your message.

➤ *Headings and captions.* Headings and subheadings are usually set larger than the type used for text and are often set in a different typeface. They invite readers to become involved in your message. Heads are often centred, but you should avoid centring heads that contain more than two lines because, like centred text, they slow your readers as they search for the beginning of each line. You can link headings as closely as possible with the text they introduce by providing more space above the heading than below it. Next to headings, captions are the most widely read part of a message, tying photographs and illustrations into the rest of your message. Although usually placed below the figures they describe, captions can also be placed beside or above their figures.

Serif typefaces are commonly used for text.

Sans serif typefaces are commonly used for headings.

➤ *Typefaces.* **Typeface** refers to the physical design of letters, numbers, and other characters, which can make your message look authoritative, friendly, classy, or casual. **Serif typefaces** have small crosslines (called serifs) at the ends of each letter stroke.[16] (See Figure 7.5.) Serif faces such as Times New Roman (which is built into most laser printers) are commonly used for text. Typefaces with rounded serifs can look friendly; those with squared serifs can look official. **Sans serif typefaces** have no serifs. Faces such as Helvetica are ideal for display treatments that use larger type. Many great-looking documents are based on a single sans serif typeface for heads and subheads with a serif typeface for text and captions. Using too many typefaces clutters the document.

Checklist for Revising Business Messages

A. Editing Your Message

1. Content and organization
   a. Review your draft against the message plan.
   b. Cover all necessary points in logical order.
   c. Organize the message to respond to the audience's probable reaction.
   d. Provide enough support to make the main idea convincing and interesting.
   e. Eliminate unnecessary material; add useful material.
   f. Be sure the beginning and ending are effective.
2. Style and readability
   a. Be sure you've achieved the right tone.
   b. Increase interest with lively words and phrases.
   c. Make sure your message is readable.
      i. Check vocabulary.
      ii. Check sentence structure.
      iii. Consider using a readability index.
3. Word choice
   a. Use plain English.
   b. Use concrete words that avoid negative connotations.
   c. Rely on nouns, verbs, and specific adjectives and adverbs.
   d. Select words that are strong, familiar, and short; avoid clichés, camouflaged verbs, and hedging words.
   e. Use bias-free language.

B. Rewriting Your Message

1. Sentence style
   a. Fit the sentence structure to the thought.
   b. Tailor the sentence style to the audience.
   c. Aim for an average sentence length of 20 words.
   d. Write mainly in the active voice, but use the passive voice to achieve specific effects.
   e. Eliminate unnecessary words and phrases
   f. Avoid obsolete and pompous language.
   g. Moderate your enthusiasm.
   h. Break up strung-out sentences.
   i. Avoid hedging sentences.
   j. Watch for indefinite pronoun starters.
   k. Express parallel ideas in parallel form.
   l. Eliminate awkward pointers.
   m. Avoid dangling modifiers.

Serif Typeface	Sans Serif Typeface
Times Roman is often used for text. TIMES ROMAN IS HARDER TO READ IN ALL CAPS.	Helvetica is often used for headings. HELVETICA IS A CLEANER FACE EVEN IN ALL CAPS.

FIGURE 7.5

Common Typefaces
Although serif typefaces are considered easier to read than sans serif, both have their place in document design.

- *Type styles.* **Type style** is any modification that lends contrast or emphasis to type. Using **boldfaced** type for subheads breaks up long expanses of text, but too much will darken your document's appearance. Use *italic* type for emphasis, or in captions. Be careful to avoid any style that slows your audience's reading. Underlining can interfere with your reader's ability to recognize the shapes of words, and using all capitals slows reading.[17] Shadowed or outlined type can seriously hinder legibility, so use these styles carefully.

Avoid using type styles that slow your readers down.

You decide on each design element according to its function. Effective design guides your readers through your message, so be sure to be consistent, balanced, restrained, and detail oriented:

For effective design, pay attention to
✧ Consistency
✧ Balance
✧ Restraint
✧ Detail

- *Consistency.* Be consistent in your use of design elements within a message (and sometimes even from message to message). Margins, typeface, type size, and spacing (in paragraph indents, between columns, and around photographs)

n. Avoid long sequences of nouns.

o. Keep subject and verb close together, and keep adverbs, adjectives, and prepositional phrases close to the words they modify.

p. Emphasize key points through sentence style.

2. Effective paragraphs

a. Be sure each paragraph contains a topic sentence, related sentences, and transitional elements.

b. Edit for unity, effective development, and coherence.

c. Choose a method of development that suits the subject: illustration, comparison or contrast, cause and effect, classification, problem and solution.

d. Vary the length and structure of sentences within paragraphs.

e. Mix paragraphs of different lengths, but aim for an average of 100 words.

C. Producing Your Message

1. Design elements

a. Use appropriate white space around headings, in margins, between columns, at line endings, in paragraph indents or between unindented paragraphs, and between lines of type.

b. Choose margins and line justification that won't darken your document.

c. Use headings to break up long passages of text and to guide your readers through your message.

d. Select typefaces that complement the tone of your message.

e. Use only as many type styles as you actually need, avoiding any style that slows the reader's progress.

2. Design decisions

a. Be consistent, balanced, restrained, and detail oriented.

b. Avoid last-minute compromises.

D. Proofing Your Message

1. Mechanics and format

a. Review sentences to be sure they are grammatically correct.

b. Correct punctuation and capitalization errors.

c. Look for spelling and typographical errors.

d. Review the format to be sure it follows accepted conventions.

e. Use the format consistently throughout the message.

2. Electronic grammar and spell checkers

a. Use electronic checkers to point out errors you might overlook.

b. Be aware of program limitations so that you don't rely too heavily on electronic checkers.

should be consistent throughout a message. Also be sure that all recurring elements, such as vertical lines, columns, and borders, are handled consistently.

- *Balance.* To create a pleasing design, balance the space devoted to text, artwork, and white space.
- *Restraint.* Strive for simplicity in design. Don't clutter your message with too many design elements, too much highlighting, or too many decorative touches.
- *Detail.* Track all details that affect your design and thus your message. Headings and subheads that appear at the bottom of a column or a page (orphans) can offend readers when the promised information doesn't appear until the next column or page. A layout that appears off balance can be very distracting, and any typographical errors can sabotage an otherwise good-looking design.

Avoid last-minute compromises. Don't reduce type size or white space to squeeze in text. On the other hand, avoid increasing type size or white space to fill space. If you've planned your message so that your purpose, your audience, and your message are clear, you can design your document to be effective.[18]

SHARPENING YOUR CAREER SKILLS

How to Proofread Like a Pro: Tips for Creating the Perfect Document

You've carefully revised and polished your document, and it's been sent off to the word-processing department to be put into final form. You can breathe a sigh of relief, but only for the moment. You'll still be proofreading what comes out of the printer. To ensure that any document is error-free, always proofread the final version. Following are some hints to help make your proofreading more effective.

- ✧ ***Multiple passes.*** Go through the document several times, focusing on a different aspect each time. The first pass might be to look for omissions and errors in content; the second pass could be for layout, spacing, and other aesthetic features; a final pass might be to check for typographical, grammatical, and spelling errors.
- ✧ ***Perceptual tricks.*** Your brain has been trained to ignore transposed letters, improper capitalization, and misplaced punctuation. Try (1) reading each page from the bottom to the top (starting at the last word in each line), (2) placing your finger under each word and reading it silently, (3) making a slit in a sheet of paper that reveals only one line of type at a time, and (4) reading the document aloud and pronouncing each word carefully.
- ✧ ***Impartial reviews.*** Have a friend or colleague proofread the document for you. Others are likely to catch mistakes that you continually fail to notice. (All of us have blind spots when it comes to reviewing our own work.)
- ✧ ***Typos.*** Look for the most common typographical errors (typos): transposition (such as *teh*), substitution (such as *ecomonic*), and omission (such as *productvity*).
- ✧ ***Mechanics.*** When looking for errors in spelling, grammar, punctuation, and capitalization, if you're unsure about something, look it up in a dictionary, a usage book, or another reference work.
- ✧ ***Accuracy.*** Double-check the spelling of names and the accuracy of dates, addresses, and all numbers (quantities ordered, prices, and so on). It would not do to order 500 staplers when you want only 50.
- ✧ ***Distance.*** If you have time, set the document aside and proofread it the next day.
- ✧ ***Vigilance.*** Avoid reading large amounts of material in one sitting, and try not to proofread when you're tired.
- ✧ ***Focus.*** Concentrate on what you're doing. Try to block out distractions, and focus as completely as possible on your proofreading task.
- ✧ ***Caution.*** Take your time. Quick proofreading is not careful proofreading.

Proofreading may require patience, but it adds credibility to your document.

CAREER APPLICATIONS

1. What qualities does a person need to be a good proofreader? Are such qualities inborn, or can they be learned?
2. Proofread the following sentence:

   aplication of thse methods in stores in Regina and Trois Rivières have resultted in a 30 drop in roberies an a 50 precent decling in violnce there, acording ot thedevelpers if the securty sytem, Hanover brothrs, Inc.

Stage 10: Proofreading Your Message

LEARNING OUTCOME 7
Proofread your messages for mechanics and format.

When you proofread your message, you ensure that it's letter perfect. Although grammar, spelling, punctuation, and typographical errors may seem trivial to some people, most readers will view your attention to detail as a sign of your professionalism. If a writer lets mechanical errors slip through, the reader automatically wonders whether the writer is unreliable in more important ways.

Credibility is affected by your attention to the details of mechanics and format.

Also, give some attention to the finer points of format. Have you followed accepted conventions and company guidelines for laying out the document on the page? Have you included all the traditional elements that belong in documents of the type you are creating? Have you been consistent in handling margins, page numbers, headings, exhibits, source notes, and other details? To resolve questions about format and layout, see Appendix A.

Finally, if you compose your business messages on a computer, many of the mechanical and grammatical problems discussed in this chapter can be checked electronically. Spell checkers and grammar checkers were discussed in Chapter 4. They're available either as part of word-processing programs such as Microsoft Word, Corel WordPerfect, Word Pro, and Claris Works, or as special stand-alone programs for medical, technical, and foreign-language applications. Although both types of programs can flag problem areas, they can't actually fix any of those errors for you. For a reminder of the tasks involved in revision, see this chapter's Checklist for Revising Business Messages.

Electronic grammar and spell checkers can be helpful if you don't rely too heavily on them.

ON THE JOB
Solving a Communication Dilemma at McDonald's

What do quality control representatives look for when they inspect a McDonald's restaurant? If you were one, you might visit seven or eight outlets a day. The staff in one of your restaurants would know you were coming, but not when. Would they be serving you breakfast, lunch, or dinner?

As you drive into the parking lot, you check for rubbish; the ideal McDonald's is blindingly clean from the street to the storeroom. As you enter the restaurant, you check if the lines are moving quickly. Are order takers smiling? Are tables spotless?

You taste the food, and note if it is fresh and if the portion size is right. In the kitchen, you check the dates stamped on the hamburger wrappers and other items, and note if the cooks are working as a team. If you see a problem—be it a messy storeroom or a soft-serve cone piled six inches high instead of the regulation three inches—you notify the restaurant manager and suggest improvements. You keep your tone positive, avoiding words like "bad" or "unacceptable," offering constructive advice instead. You might expect the restaurant manager and employees to resent your suggestions, but by and large they welcome them, because you know how to communicate in a friendly manner.[19]

Your Mission: You have recently joined McDonald's as a quality control representative. Most of the managers are cooperative, and most of the restaurants maintain high standards. But there is one exception. Over the past few months, you have pointed out a variety of problems to a particular McDonald's manager. You have been friendly, polite, and constructive in your suggestions, but nothing has been done to correct most of the problems. On your last visit, you warned the manager that you would have to file a negative report with headquarters if you didn't see some improvement immediately. You have decided to put your suggestions in writing and to give the manager one week to take action. Here is the first draft of your letter. Using the questions that follow, analyze it according to the material in this chapter. Be prepared to explain your analysis.

> Please correct the problems listed below. I will visit your facility within the next few days to monitor your progress. If nothing has been done toward rectifying these infractions of McDonald's principles of operation, you will be reported to headquarters for noncooperation and unsatisfactory levels of performance. As you know, I have mentioned these deviations from acceptable practice on

previous visits. You have been given ample opportunity to comply with my suggestions. Your failure to comply suggests that you lack the necessary commitment to quality that has long been the hallmark of McDonald's restaurants.

On two occasions, I have ascertained that you are using expired ingredients in preparing hamburgers. On February 14, a package of buns with a freshness date of January 31 was used in your facility. Also, on March 2, you were using cheese that had expired by at least ten days. McDonald's is committed to freshness. All our ingredients are freshness dated. Expired ingredients should be disposed of, not used in the preparation of products for sale to the public. For example, you might contact local charities and offer the expired items to them free of charge, provided, of course, that the ingredients do not pose a health hazard (e.g., sour milk should be thrown out). The Community Resource Centre in your area can be reached by calling 555-0909. Although I have warned you before about using old ingredients, the last time I visited your facility I found expired ingredients in the storeroom.

Your bathrooms should be refurbished and cleaned more frequently. The paper towel dispenser in the men's room was out of towels the last time I was there, and the faucet on the sink dripped. This not only runs up your water bill but also creates a bad impression for the customer. Additionally, your windows need washing. On all my visits, I have noticed fingerprints on the front door. I have never, in fact, seen your door anything but dirty. This, too, creates a negative impression. Similarly, the windows are not as clean as they might be. Also, please mop the floors more often. Nobody wants to eat in a dirty restaurant.

The most serious infraction pertains to the appearance of store personnel. Dirty uniforms are unforgivable. Also, employees, particularly those serving the public, must have clean fingernails and hands. Hair should be neatly combed, and uniforms should be carefully pressed. I realize that your restaurant is located in an economically depressed area, and I am aware that many of your employees are ethnic minorities from impoverished backgrounds and single-parent families. Perhaps you should hold a class in basic cleanliness for these people. It is likely that they have not been taught proper hygiene in their homes.

In addition, please instruct store personnel to empty the trash more frequently. The bins are constantly overflowing, making it difficult for customers to dispose of leftover food and rubbish. This is a problem both indoors and outdoors.

Also bear in mind that all patrons should be served within a few minutes of their arrival at your place of business. Waiting in line is annoying, particularly during the busy lunch hour when people are on tight schedules. Open new lines when you must in order to accommodate the flow of traffic. In addition, instruct the order takers and order fillers to work more rapidly during busy times. Employees should not be standing around chatting with each other while customers wait in line.

As I mentioned above, I will visit your facility within a few days to check on your progress toward meeting McDonald's criteria of operation. If no visible progress has been made, I will have no alternative other than to report you to top management at headquarters. If you have any questions or require clarification on any of these items, please feel free to contact me. I can be reached by calling 506-555-3549.

1. How would you rate this draft in terms of its content and organization?

a. Although the style of the letter needs work, the content and organization are basically okay.
b. The draft is seriously flawed in both content and organization. Extensive editing is required.
c. The content is fine, but the organization is poor.
d. The organization is fine, but the content is poor.

2. What should be done to eliminate the biased tone of the fourth paragraph?

a. Omit the last three sentences of the paragraph.
b. Omit the last three sentences and add something like the following: "Please have your employees review the videotape that deals with McDonald's standards of personal appearance."
c. Revise the last three sentences along the following lines: "Given the composition of your labour force, you may need to stress the basics of personal hygiene."

3. Which of the following is the best alternative to this sentence: "If nothing has been done toward rectifying these infractions of McDonald's principles of operation, you will be reported to headquarters for noncooperation and unsatisfactory levels of performance."

a. "If nothing has been done to correct these infractions, you will be reported to headquarters for noncompliance."
b. "If you don't shape up immediately, headquarters will hear about it."
c. "By correcting these problems promptly, you can avoid being reported to headquarters."
d. "You can preserve your unblemished reputation by acting immediately to bring your facility into compliance with McDonald's principles of operation."

4. Take a look at the third paragraph of the letter. What is its chief flaw?

a. There is no topic sentence.
b. The topic sentence is too narrow for the ideas encompassed in the paragraph.
c. The transition from the previous paragraph is poor.
d. The paragraph deals with more than one subject.
e. The topic sentence is not adequately developed with specific details in subsequent sentences.

TAP Your Knowledge

Summary of Learning Outcomes

1. Edit your messages for content and organization, style and readability, and word choice. Start the editing process after you have distanced yourself from your draft for a couple of days. With a fresh eye, you can determine if you have covered all your points and presented them in the most effective manner when you compare your draft with your original plan. In the first phase of editing, try to spend time on the beginning and ending of your messages, as they have the most impact on your audience. When editing your message's style and readability, ask yourself whether you've achieved the right tone for your audience, and look for opportunities to make the material more interesting through the use of lively words and phrases, familiar terms, and simple, direct statements

2. Choose the most correct and most effective words to make your point. The most correct and effective words that make your point are those that are understandable, familiar, and free of bias. Use both functional and content words in your messages; be sensitive to both the connotation and denotation of the words you use; and try to write as concretely as possible. Use strong words, the words that are the most concrete in any message, familiar words, and short words. Change camouflaged verbs into real verbs. Be sure that your language is free of cultural, gender, racial, ethnic, and disability bias.

3. Rewrite sentences to clarify the relationships among ideas and to make your writing interesting. Create effective sentences to send clear and easy-to-read messages. Follow some common-sense guidelines to help you accomplish this task efficiently: keep your sentences short; rely on the active voice; eliminate unnecessary words and phrases; avoid obsolete and pompous language; moderate your enthusiasm; and break up strung-out sentences (a series of two or more sentences connected by "and"). Also keep words together that work together and emphasize key thoughts.

4. Identify elements of paragraphs. Paragraphs vary widely in length and form, but all properly constructed paragraphs are unified. The typical paragraph consists of a topic sentence, related sentences, and transitional words and phrases. The topic sentence introduces the topic of the paragraph, and related sentences develop and explain the topic sentences. Transitional words and phrases give coherence through connective words, echoing a word or phrase from a previous paragraph, and using pronouns or words that are frequently paired.

5. Rewrite paragraphs using the appropriate development technique. Rewriting a paragraph requires familiarity with different ways of developing ideas. First, you can illustrate the main idea through examples. Second, you can use comparison or contrast to highlight similarities or differences among thoughts. Third, use the cause-and-effect method, which demonstrates the reasons for something. Fourth, use classification to show how a general idea is broken down into specific categories. Finally, use the problem-and-solution approach, in which you present a problem and then discuss the solution.

6. Choose the best design for written documents. Good design invites your audience to read your message and aids their comprehension. Good document design includes sufficient white space, proper margin and line justification, use of headings and captions, and correct choice of typeface and type styles, such as boldface and italics.

7. Proofread your messages for mechanics and format. Proofreading leads to a letter-perfect message. Checking for correct grammar, punctuation, spelling, and typographical errors–the mechanics–will show your attention to detail. Pay attention to format too. Following company guidelines for formatting, consistent handling of margins, page numbers, headings, exhibits, source notes, and other details will also demonstrate your professionalism. Remember that spell checkers and grammar checkers flag problem areas, but that they are no substitute for eagle-eyed proofreading, which will fix mistakes that electronic aids will miss.

*T*est Your Knowledge

Review Questions

1. What is a Fog Index, and how can it help you become a better writer?
2. Define the terms "denotation" and "connotation."
3. Define the terms "abstract" and "concrete."
4. Give three examples of weak phrases and their corresponding strong terms that are not listed in this chapter.

5. Give examples of three unfamiliar words and their corresponding familiar terms that are not listed in this chapter.
6. What are camouflaged verbs? Give three examples.
7. What is cultural bias? Define other types of bias.
8. What questions should you ask when you evaluated the writing of a friend or colleague?
9. Distinguish between the active voice and the passive voice.

Apply Your Knowledge

Critical Thinking Questions

1. You have so little time for your current project that you have to skip a few of the tasks in the composition process. You've already cut down everything you can in the planning and composing categories. Which tasks in the revision category would be best to cut: editing, rewriting, producing, or proofreading? Explain.
2. In what business situations might you want to use words of high connotative value?
3. How could cultural bias differ from racial and ethnic bias? What examples can you think of?
4. What specific techniques of style could you use to create a formal, objective tone? An informal, personal tone?
5. Which design elements are necessary to consider when designing your formal business letter? Which are not necessary?
6. Given the choice of only one, would you prefer to use a grammar checker or a spell checker? Why?

Practise Your Knowledge

Exercises

1. Write a concrete phrase for each of these vague phrases.
   a. sometime this spring
   b. a substantial saving
   c. a large number attended
   d. increased efficiency
   e. expanded the work area
2. List words that are stronger than the following:
   a. ran after
   b. seasonal ups and downs
   c. bright
   d. suddenly rises
   e. moves forward
3. As you rewrite these sentences, replace the clichés with fresh, personal expressions.
   a. Being a jack-of-all-trades, Dave worked well in his new selling job.
   b. Moving Leslie into the accounting department, where she was literally a fish out of water, was like putting a square peg into a round hole, if you get my drift.
   c. I knew she was at death's door, but I thought the doctor would pull her through.
   d. Movies aren't really my cup of tea; as far as I am concerned, they can't hold a candle to a good book.
   e. It's a dog-eat-dog world out there in the rat race of the asphalt jungle.
4. Revise the following sentences, using shorter, simpler words.
   a. The antiquated calculator is ineffectual for solving sophisticated problems.
   b. It is imperative that the pay increments be terminated before an inordinate deficit is accumulated.
   c. There was unanimity among the executives that Ms. Jackson's idiosyncrasies were cause for a mandatory meeting with the company's personnel director.
   d. The impending liquidation of the company's assets was cause for jubilation among the company's competitors.
   e. The expectations of the president for a stock dividend were accentuated by the preponderance of evidence that the company was in good financial condition.

5. Rewrite each of the following to eliminate bias.

a. For a recent immigrant, Ranesh is outgoing.

b. He needs a wheelchair, but he doesn't let his handicap affect his job performance.

c. A pilot must have the ability to stay calm under pressure, and then he must be trained to cope with any problem that arises.

d. Candidate Renata Parsons, married and the mother of a teenager, will attend the debate.

e. Senior citizen Sam Vitelli is still an active salesman.

6. Rewrite each sentence so that it is active rather than passive.

a. The raw data are submitted to the data-processing division by the sales representative each Friday.

b. High profits are publicized by management.

c. The policies announced in the directive were implemented by the staff.

d. Our computers are serviced by the Milton Company.

e. The employees were represented by Janet Sanchez.

7. Condense these sentences to as few words as possible.

a. We are of the conviction that writing is important.

b. In all probability, we're likely to have a price increase.

c. Our goals include making a determination about that in the near future.

d. When all is said and done at the conclusion of this experiment, I'd like to summarize the final windup.

e. After a trial period of 3 weeks, during which time she worked for a total of 15 full working days, we found her work was sufficiently satisfactory so that we offered her full-time work.

8. Write up-to-date versions of these phrases; write *none* if you believe there is no appropriate substitute.

a. as per your instructions

b. attached herewith

c. in lieu of

d. in reply I wish to state

e. please be advised that

9. Remove all the unnecessary modifiers from these sentences.

a. Tremendously high pay increases were given to the extraordinarily skilled and extremely conscientious employees.

b. The union's proposals were highly inflationary, extremely demanding, and exceptionally bold.

10. Rewrite these sentences so that they no longer contain any hedging.

a. It would appear that someone apparently entered illegally.

b. It may be possible that sometime in the near future the situation is likely to improve.

c. Your report seems to suggest that we might be losing money.

d. I believe Nancy apparently has somewhat greater influence over employees in the typing pool.

e. It seems as if this letter of resignation means you might be leaving us.

11. Rewrite these sentences to eliminate the indefinite starters.

a. There are several examples here to show that Elaine can't hold a position very long.

b. It would be greatly appreciated if every employee would make a generous contribution to Mildred Radic's retirement party.

c. It has been learned in Ottawa today from generally reliable sources that an important announcement will be made shortly by the Prime Minister's office.

d. There is a rule that states that we cannot work overtime without permission.

e. It would be great if you could work late for the next three Saturdays.

12. Present the ideas in these sentences in parallel form.

a. Mr. Hakim is expected to lecture three days a week, to counsel two days a week, and must write for publication in his spare time.

b. She knows not only accounting, but she also reads Latin.

c. Both applicants had families, college degrees, and were in their thirties, with considerable accounting experience but few social connections.

d. This book was exciting, well written, and held my interest.

e. Dragan is both a hard worker and he knows bookkeeping.

13. Rewrite these sentences to clarify the dangling modifiers.

a. Running down the railroad tracks in a cloud of smoke, we watched the countryside glide by.

b. Lying on the shelf, Anita saw the seashell.

c. Based on the information, I think we should buy the property.

d. Being cluttered and filthy, Sandy took the whole afternoon to clean up her desk.

e. After proofreading every word, the memo was ready to be signed.

14. Rewrite the following sentences to eliminate the long strings of nouns.

a. The focus of the meeting was a discussion of the bank interest rate deregulation issue.

b. Following the government task force report recommendations, we are revising our job applicant evaluation procedures.

c. The production department quality assurance program components include employee training, supplier cooperation, and computerized detection equipment.

d. The supermarket warehouse inventory reduction plan will be implemented next month.

e. The university business school graduate placement program is one of the best in the country.

15. Rearrange the following sentences to bring the subjects closer to their verbs.

a. Trudy, when she first saw the bull pawing the ground, ran.

b. It was Terri who, according to Ted, who is probably the worst gossip in the office (Tom excepted), mailed the wrong order.

c. William Oberstreet, in his book *Investment Capital Reconsidered,* writes of the mistakes that bankers through the decades have made.

d. Judy Schimmel, after passing up several sensible investment opportunities, despite the warnings of her friends and family, invested her inheritance in a jojoba plantation.

e. The president of U-Stor-It, which was on the brink of bankruptcy after the warehouse fire, the worst tragedy in the history of the company, prepared an announcement for the press.

16. Explore the Web site at **owl.english.purdue.edu/lab/owl/index.html**, and briefly explain (a) the services of each presentation listed at this site and (b) the benefits each offers to writers.

17. Working with four other students, divide up the following five topics and write one paragraph on your selected topic. Be sure one student writes a paragraph using the illustration technique, one using the comparison or contrast technique, one using a discussion of cause and effect, one using the classification technique, and one using a discussion of problem and solution. Then exchange paragraphs within the team and pick out the main idea and general purpose of the paragraph one of your teammates wrote. Was everyone able to correctly identify the main idea and purpose? If not, suggest how the paragraph might be rewritten to clarify.

a. Types of cameras (or dogs or automobiles) available for sale

b. Advantages and disadvantages of eating at fast-food restaurants

c. Finding that first full-time job

d. Good qualities of my car (or house, or apartment, or neighbourhood)

e. How to make a dessert recipe (or barbecue a steak or make coffee)

Documents for Analysis

Read the following documents; then (1) analyze the strengths and weaknesses of each sentence and (2) revise each document so that it follows this chapter's guidelines.

DOCUMENT 7.A: Creating Effective Sentences

The move to our new offices will take place over this coming weekend. For everything to run smooth, everyone will have to clean out their own desk and pack up the contents in boxes that will be provided. You will need to take everything off the walls too, and please pack it along with the boxes.

If you have a lot of personal belongings, you should bring them home with you. Likewise with anything valuable. I do not mean to infer that items will be stolen, irregardless it is better to be safe than sorry.

On Monday, we will be unpacking, putting things away, and then get back to work. The least amount of disruption is anticipated by us, if everyone does their part. Hopefully, there will be no negative affects on production schedules, and current deadlines will be met.

DOCUMENT 7.B: Assessing Your Word Choice

Dear Ms. Giraud:

Enclosed herewith please find the manuscript for your book, *Careers in Woolgathering.* After perusing the first two chapters of your 1500-page manuscript, I was forced to conclude that the subject matter, handicrafts and artwork using wool fibres, is not coincident with the publishing program of Caribou Press, which to this date has issued only works on environmental endeavours, avoiding all other topics completely.

Although our firm is unable to consider your impressive work at the present time, I have taken the liberty of recording some comments on some of the pages. I am of the opinion that any feedback that a writer can obtain from those well versed in the publishing realm can only serve to improve the writer's authorial skills.

In view of the fact that your residence is in the Winnipeg area, might I suggest that you secure an appointment with someone of high editorial stature at the Red River Press, which I believe might have something of an interest in works of the nature you have produced.

Wishing you the best of luck in your literary endeavours, I remain

Arthur J. Cogswell
Editor

DOCUMENT 7.C: Developing Coherent Paragraphs

For delicious, air-popped popcorn, please read the following instructions: The popper is designed to pop 1/2 cup of popcorn kernels at one time. Never add more than 1/2 cup. A half cup of corn will produce three to four litres of popcorn. More batches may be made separately after completion of the first batch. Popcorn is popped by hot air. Oil or shortening is not needed for popping corn. Add only popcorn kernels to the popping chamber. Standard grades of popcorn are recommended for use. Premium or gourmet type popping corns may be used. Ingredients such as oil, shortening, butter, margarine, or salt should never be added to the popping chamber. The popper, with popping chute in position, may be preheated for two minutes before adding the corn. Turn the popper off before adding the corn. Use electricity safely and wisely. Observe safety precautions when using the popper. Do not touch the popper when it is hot. The popper should not be left unattended when it is plugged into an outlet. Do not use the popper if it or its cord has been damaged. Do not use the popper if it is not working properly. Before using the first time, wash the chute and butter/measuring cup in hot soapy water. Use a dishcloth or sponge. Wipe the outside of the popper base. Use a damp cloth. Dry the base. Do not immerse the popper base in water or other liquid. Replace the chute and butter/measuring cup. The popper is ready to use.

Developing Your Internet Skills

Going Online: Improve Your Writing Style with Proven Techniques, p. 152

While you're doing one of the exercises in this chapter–revising your writing–make it a point to log on and check *Elements of Style* to see what tips you can glean for improving your prose. When you're working on a document, which do you think you're more likely to use–a print version of a writing stylebook that might be on a bookshelf across the room (or in a library) or an online version just a few moments and clicks away? Why? Will your answer be different when you're working in a business office?

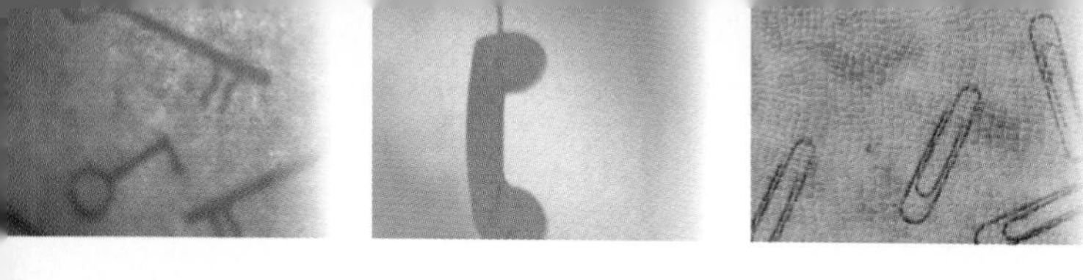

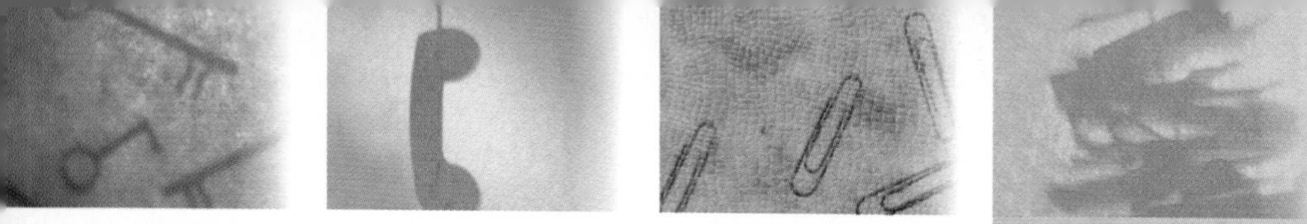

CHAPTER 8

Writing Direct Requests

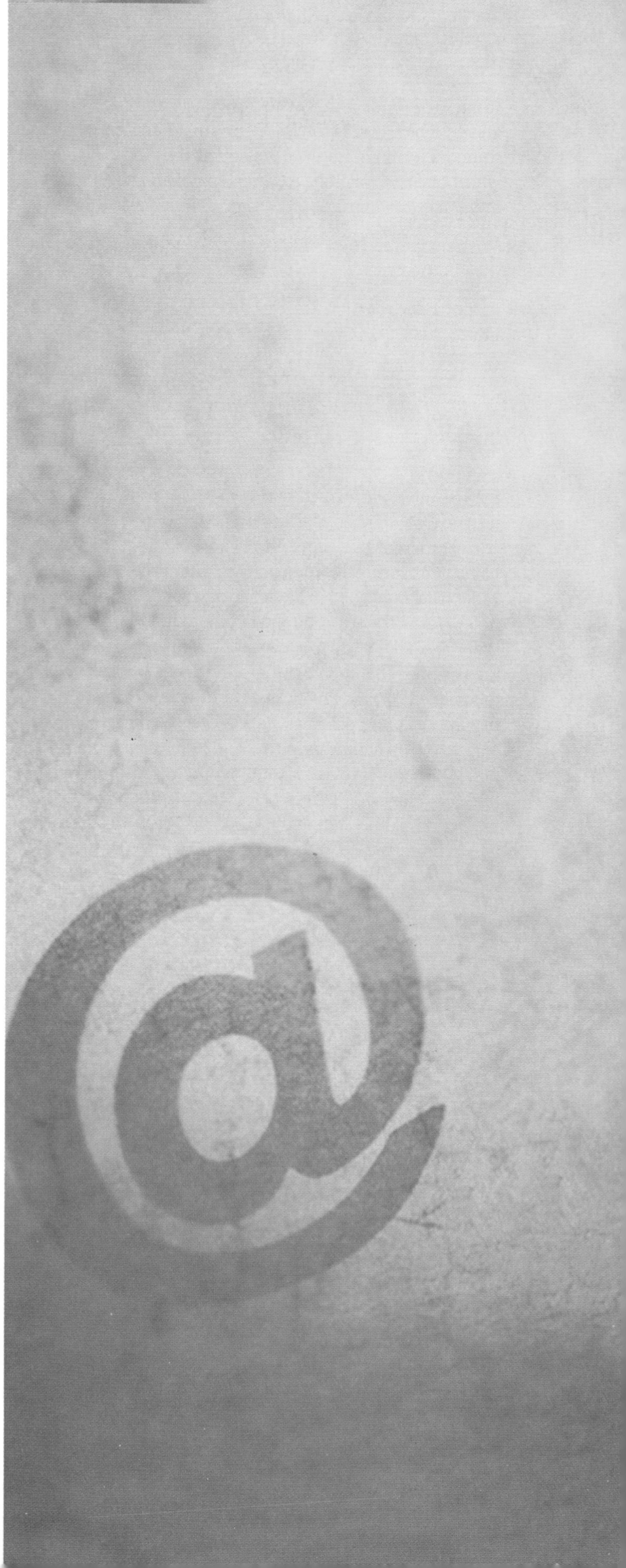

AFTER STUDYING THIS CHAPTER, YOU WILL BE ABLE TO

1. Clearly state the main idea of each direct request you write
2. Provide sufficient explanation for the reader to be able to comply with your request
3. Close with a courteous request for specific action
4. Apply the direct strategy to claim and adjustment messages
5. Apply the direct strategy to routine inquiries about people

ON THE JOB
Facing a Communication Dilemma at Indigo Books and Music

May the Best Seller Win!

With films, videos, video games, television, and surfing the Internet as highly popular forms of visual entertainment, it's easy to become gloomy about the state of reading in Canada, but the book business has been booming in recent years. Canadian consumers bought in the neighbourhood of $50 million worth of books in 1998, including $10 million in online sales. In just the last decade, Canadians have seen book superstores built from coast to coast, a phenomenon that both generates and feeds their interest in reading.

As Indigo's founder and CEO, Heather Reisman is the primary decision-maker when it comes to her firm's image and activities. Her goal is to create an environment where book lovers can enjoy "the best of a proprietor-run shop combined with the selection of a true emporium." Indigo's success in the Canadian book market is testimony to her ability to communicate her vision clearly to both Indigo executives and front-line staff.

One leader in this reading rebirth is Heather Reisman, CEO of Indigo Books and Music. Reisman is a book lover herself. She holds literacy fundraisers in her home and includes her "personal picks" in Indigo's holiday gift catalogue. She was formerly the president of soft-drink manufacturer Cott Corporation and before that headed a change-management consulting firm for 15 years. In 1996, she created Indigo as the "world's first cultural department store," where consumers can not only buy books, but also music, gift items, and fine stationery. There are now 15 Indigo stores across Canada and an Indigo.ca Web site for Internet sales. Of course, Reisman is hardly alone in the Canadian book market, online or off.

Bookstores fall into three categories: (1) independent bookstores, which are individually owned outlets ranging from tiny specialty shops to warehouse-sized giants, such as Winnipeg's McNally Robinson, the largest independent bookseller in Canada; (2) chains such as the Chapters book superstores, which Reisman has recently acquired; and (3) online booksellers, such as Amazon.com, which let customers search for and order books by visiting a Web site on the Internet. Reisman's chief competitors now are online stores.

As you read this chapter, put yourself in Heather Reisman's position. To maintain your market share, you must send messages to customers and store managers, requesting both information and action. How can you obtain the information you need to make your decisions? How will you phrase your requests so that store managers will respond with positive action in the race against competitors, both the bookstores that occupy physical building space and those that occupy the new virtual space of the Internet?[1]

Organizing Direct Requests

For direct requests
- ✧ State the request or main idea
- ✧ Give necessary details
- ✧ Close with a cordial request for specific action

When you believe your audience will have a favourable (or, at least, neutral) reaction to your message, use the direct, or deductive, plan to organize your message. Present the request or the main idea first, follow up with relevant details, and close with a cordial statement of the action you want. This approach works well when your request requires no special tact or persuasion.

People making direct requests may be tempted to begin with a personal introduction: "I am a book buyer for Indigo, and I'm interested in expanding our selection of reference books." However, this type of beginning is usually a mistake. The essence of the message, the specific request, is obscured. A better way to organize a direct request is to state what you want in the first sentence or two and let the explanation follow.

Assume that your reader will comply once she or he understands your purpose.

Even though you expect a favourable response, the tone of your opening is important. Don't demand immediate action ("Send me your catalogue no. 33A"). Instead, show courtesy with such words as *please* and *I would appreciate*. Through politeness you will get your reader's respect as well as the response you want.

The middle part of a direct request usually amplifies the opening ("I would like to order a sample of several of your reference works to determine whether they would appeal to our customers"). The details you provide will help your audience to fulfill your request correctly.

Word the request itself carefully so that it says exactly what you want.

In the last section, clearly state the action you're requesting. You may wish to tell the audience where to send the information or product, indicate any time limits, or list details of the request that were too complex or numerous to cover in the opening. Then close with a brief, cordial note reminding the audience of the importance of the request ("If the sample books sell well, you can expect to receive additional orders from Indigo").

Now let's take a closer look at the three main sections of a direct request. Although this discussion focuses on letters and memos, remember that this organizational plan may be appropriate for brief oral and electronic messages as well.

LEARNING OUTCOME 1
Clearly state the main idea of each direct request you write.

Direct Statement of the Request or Main Idea

The general rule for the first part of a direct request is to write not only to be understood but also to avoid being misunderstood. If you request "2000 sales figures" from your company's sales department, the person who handles your request won't know if you want regional or national figures, a one-page summary or a 10-page detailed report. So be as specific as possible in the sentence or two that begins your message.

Edward Lewis, publisher and CEO, and Clarence O. Smith, president of Essence Communications Inc. (ECI), together launched *Essence* magazine in 1970. It quickly became a leading source of information for African-American and African-Canadian women. During ECI's growth to its present status as a large and diverse media company, the pair's success has depended on a unique relationship with readers and strong alliances with leading corporations and financial institutions. Building these relationships meant writing thousands of direct requests, skillfully presented to ensure positive replies.

Also, be aware of the difference between a polite request in question form (which requires no question mark) and a question that is part of a request:

POLITE REQUEST IN QUESTION FORM	QUESTION THAT IS PART OF A REQUEST
Would you please help us determine whether Kate Kingsley is a suitable applicant for a position as landscape designer.	Did Kate Kingsley demonstrate an ability to work smoothly with clients?

Many direct requests include both types of statements, so be sure to distinguish between the polite request that is your overall reason for writing and the specific questions that belong in the middle section of your letter or memo.

Finally, if you have more than one request, consider the following ways of writing them:

- When you have several requests, use headings to express categories of requests, with each category containing several requests. Categorizing your needs makes the reader's job easier.
- When you have an unusual or complex request, state the request and then provide supporting details right underneath it. In other words, make each request a short paragraph.
- When you have a list of requests, include space beneath each request so that the reader can write on your letter or memo. This method saves everyone's time and effort. It also controls the length of the reader's response.

Justification, Explanation, and Details

LEARNING OUTCOME 2
Provide sufficient explanation for the reader to be able to comply with your request.

The body, or middle section, of your message should continue logically from your opening. One way to continue your message is to show how the reader might benefit from responding to it. For example, the owner of a gift shop that sells picture frames, crafts, stationery, and other small items might write the following to a potential supplier: "By keeping me informed about your products, I will be able to determine which ones are suitable for my store. If my customers like the samples you send me, I will contact your sales representative."

In the middle section
- ✧ Call attention to how the reader will benefit from granting your request
- ✧ Give details of your request

Another possible approach for the middle section is to ask a series of questions, particularly if your inquiry concerns machinery or complex equipment. You might ask about technical specifications, exact dimensions, and the precise use of the product. The most important question is asked first. If cost is your main concern, you might begin with a question such as "What is the price of your least expensive laser printer?" Then you may want to ask more specific but related questions about, say, the cost of toner cartridges and maintenance service.

Ask the most important question first; then ask related, more specific questions.

If you're requesting several items or answers, number the items and list them in logical order or in descending order of importance. Furthermore, so that your request can be handled quickly, ask only the questions that are central to your main request. Also, avoid asking for information that you can easily find on your own, even if your effort takes considerable time.

Use numbered lists when you're requesting several items or answers.

If you're asking many people to reply to the same questions, consider wording them so that they can be answered yes or no, or with some other easily counted response. You may even want to provide respondents with a form or with boxes they can check to indicate their answers. If you need more than a simple yes-or-no answer, pose an open-ended question. For example, a question such as "How fast can you repair computer monitors?" is more likely to elicit the information you want than "Can you repair computer monitors?" Keep in mind also that phrasing questions in a way that hints at the response you want is not likely to get you accurate information. So try to phrase your questions objectively. Finally, deal with only one topic in each question. If the questions need amplification, keep each question in a separate paragraph.

When you prepare questions
- ✧ Ask only questions that relate to your main request
- ✧ Don't ask for information you can find yourself
- ✧ Make your questions open-ended and objective
- ✧ Deal with only one topic in each question

Other types of information that belong in this section include data about a product (model number, date and place of purchase, condition), your reason for being concerned about a particular matter, and other details about your request. Upon finishing this middle section, your audience should understand why the request is important and should be willing to satisfy it.

Courteous Close with Request for Specific Action

LEARNING OUTCOME 3
Close with a courteous request for specific action.

Close your letter with two important elements: (1) a request for some specific response (complete with any time limits that apply), and (2) an expression of appreciation or goodwill. Help your reader respond easily by including your phone number, office hours, and other helpful information.

However, don't thank the reader "in advance" for cooperating. If the reader's reply warrants a word of thanks, send it after you've received the reply. If you're requesting information for a research project, you might offer to forward a copy of your report in gratitude for the reader's assistance. If you plan to reprint or publish materials that you ask for, indicate that you'll get any necessary permission. When asking for information about an individual, be sure to indicate that you'll keep all responses confidential.

Close with
- ✧ A request for some specific response
- ✧ An expression of appreciation
- ✧ Information about how you can be reached

How Direct Is Too Direct?

ACHIEVING INTERCULTURAL COMMUNICATION

Being direct is civil, considerate, and honest—or so say people in Canada and the United States. Other folks view that same directness as being abrupt, rude and intrusive—even dishonest and offensive. Countries such as France, Mexico, Japan, Saudi Arabia, Italy, and the Philippines all tend to be high-context cultures (see discussion in Chapter 3). That is, the people in these countries depend on shared knowledge and inferred messages to communicate; they gather meaning more from context and less from direct statement.

Offering a little constructive criticism may actually hurt your Japanese assistant's dignity. In fact, in high-context cultures, avoid saying outright, "You are wrong." You could cause the other person to lose face. When making requests, determine whether to use a direct or an implied message by considering audience attitudes toward destiny, time, authority, and logic:

- *Destiny.* Do audience members believe they can control events themselves or do they see events as predetermined and uncontrollable? If you're supervising employees who believe that fate controls a construction deadline, your crisp e-mail message requesting them to stay on schedule may be hard for them to understand. It may even be insulting.
- *Time.* Do audience members view time as exact, precise, and not to be wasted or do they see time as relative, relaxed, and necessary for developing interpersonal relationships? If you see time as money and you get straight to business in your memo to your Mexican manager, your message may be overlooked in the confusion over your disregard for social propriety.
- *Authority.* Do audience members conduct business more autocratically or more democratically? In Japan, rank and status are highly valued, so when communicating downward, you may need to be even more direct than you're used to being in Canada. And when communicating upward, you may need to be much less direct than usual.
- *Logic.* Do audience members pursue logic in a straight line, from point A to point B, or do they communicate in circular or spiral patterns of logic? If you organize a speech or letter in a straightforward and direct manner, your message may be considered illogical, unclear, and disorganized.

You may want to decide not only how direct to be in written messages but also whether to write at all. Perhaps a phone call or a visit would be more appropriate. By finding out how much or how little a culture tends toward high-context communication, you'll know whether to be direct or to rely on nuance when communicating with the people there.

CAREER APPLICATIONS

1. Research a high-context culture such as Japan, Korea, or China, and write a one- or two-paragraph summary of how someone in that culture would go about requesting information.
2. When you are writing to someone in a high-context culture, would it be better to (a) make the request directly in the interest of clarity or (b) try to match your audience's unfamiliar logic and make your request indirectly? Explain your answer.

Online bookseller Jeffrey Bezos, founder and CEO of Amazon.com, uses the Internet not only to sell books but also to make constant direct requests of his customers. He asks them to add Amazon.com links to their own Web sites, write book reviews, explore new Web pages, and read features. Once they're interacting, they're hooked.

Placing Orders

Orders are considered one of the simplest types of direct request. Suppliers view them favourably because they are profitable, so as a writer you do not need to spend time trying to get the attention of your readers: the simple fact that you are placing an order provokes their interest. All you need do is state your needs clearly and directly.

To see what to include in a good order letter, examine any mail or online order form supplied by a large firm or an Internet retailer such as Lee Valley Tools (**www.leevalley.com**). An effective form offers complete and concise directions for providing all the information needed to fill an order. After the date, the order form probably starts with "Please send the following" or "Please ship."

Order blanks are arranged to document precisely the goods you want, describing them by catalogue number, quantity, name or trade name, colour, size, unit price, and total amount due. This complete identification helps prevent errors in filling the order. When drafting an order letter, follow the same format, presenting information about the items you want in column form, double-spacing between the items, and totalling the price at the end.

Order blanks provide space for delivery information, such as how and where to send the shipment. In your letter be sure to specify the delivery address, especially if the billing and delivery addresses are different. Also indicate how the merchandise is to be shipped: by truck, air freight, parcel post, air express, or courier. Unless you specify the mode of transportation, the supplier chooses.

If any letter is sent with payment, mention the amount, explain how it was calculated, and if necessary, the account the vendor should charge. Again, the order form provides an excellent format. Here's an example:

Please send the following items to the above address by air freight. I am ordering from your current spring-summer catalogue:

The general request is stated first.

Quantity	Stock I.D.	Description	Price Per Item	Price Totals
5	342	Dreamcatchers (blue w/white feathers)	$7.98	$39.90
5	343	Dreamcatchers (red and blue with white feathers)	7.98	39.90
10	671	Inuit art calendar	12.98	129.80
10	771	Inuit baskets (medium size)	22.98	229.80
3	848	Soapstone sculptures (seal)	34.98	104.94
		Total Sales		543.34
		Shipping		46.00
		GST		41.25
		Amount Due		630.59

All necessary details are provided (in a format similar to an order form).

Information about tax and shipping was provided in the catalogue, so the writer calculated the amount due.

Not every item ordered through the mail, via e-mail, or by fax is neatly displayed in a catalogue, Web site, or newspaper advertisement. If the goods are somewhat unusual, the problem of identifying them becomes more complex. For instance, a general contractor ordering supplies for several ongoing jobs at different sites mailed this order to Jefferson's Windows:

When ordering nonstandard items, include a complete description.

Our customers have selected the following windows to replace existing construction:

- 3647 John Street
  - 2 Bowen CW2836-4 (Casement bow window, wood, true divided lite)
  - 1 Bowen CW2836-5 (Casement bow window, wood, true divided lite)
- 3647 815 Silverton Avenue
  - 4 Falbo FN 236 (French casement, wood, true divided lite)
  - 2 Bowen D2830 (Double-hung, wood, true divided lite)
- 3647 7700 Main Street
  - 3 Fibretec G436 (Gliding window, Perma-Shield, mullion fillers)

Once you have confirmed the item numbers and availability with each manufacturer, please call me at 905-555-6040 to verify the pricing. We need these delivered by September 17, so please inform me of any possible delay.

Note the specific details included in the letter and the clarity about what is needed at each location. In any order for nonstandard items, the additional description helps the reader identify your needs accurately. In special cases, such as ordering machine parts, you may even make drawings of the parts you need and add an explanation of their particular use.

A final suggestion about placing orders: be thorough and clear. If you supply unclear or insufficient information, your reader must make an extra effort to obtain the missing details. The delays and cross-communications that result will hold up delivery of your order and may lead to mistakes in filling it.

To make sure your order is filled correctly, retain a copy of your letter, fax, or e-mail message. If you haven't received a response in a reasonable time (two weeks, in most cases), write or call to see whether your order has arrived and is being processed. (To remind yourself of the tasks involved in placing orders, see this chapter's Checklist for Orders.)

Requesting Routine Information and Action

When making a routine request, say
- ✧ What you want to know
- ✧ Why you want to know
- ✧ Why it is in the reader's interest to help you

When you need to know about something, elicit an opinion from someone, or suggest a simple action, you usually need only ask. In essence, simple requests say, "This is what I want to know (or what I want you to do), why I want to know it, and how you might benefit from helping me." If your reader is able and willing to do what you want, such a straightforward request will get the job done with a minimum of fuss.

Exactly what do you want the reader to understand or do as a result of reading your request for action?

Despite their simple organization, routine requests deserve a tactful touch. In many organizations, e-mail, memos, and letters like these are sent to hundreds or even thousands of employees, customers, clients, and shareholders. So the potential for creating a positive impression is second only to the risk of causing ill will through ambiguous wording or a discourteous tone. When writing even a routine request, keep the purpose of your message in mind. That is, ask yourself what you want recipients to understand or do as a result of reading the message. As you prepare the request, remember that even the briefest note can create confusion and hard feelings.

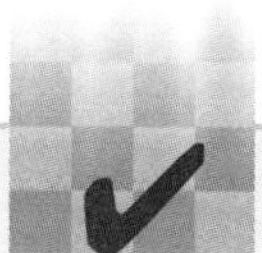

Checklist for Orders

A. Direct Statement of the Request

1. Use wording that indicates an order rather than a request: "Please send me" or "please ship" instead of "I want" or "I need," which are neither polite nor appropriate for an order.
2. Open with a general description of your order that foreshadows all the details.

B. Justification, Explanation, and Details

1. For complex orders, provide a general explanation of how the requested materials will be used.
2. Provide all specifications: quantity, price (including discounts), size, catalogue number, product description, shipping instructions (date and place), arrangements for payment (method, time, deposits), and cost totals.
3. Use a format that presents information clearly and makes it easy to total amounts.
4. Double-check the completeness of your order and the cost totals.

C. Courteous Close with Request for Specific Action

1. Include a clear summary of the desired action.
2. Whenever possible, suggest a future reader benefit from complying with the order.
3. Close on a cordial note.
4. Clearly state any time limits that apply to your order, and explain why they are important.

Requests to Company Insiders

Although requests to fellow employees are often oral and casual, some messages are better sent by e-mail or put in permanent, written form. A clear, thoughtfully written memo or e-mail message can save time and questions by helping readers understand precisely what is required.

A request in memo form
✧ Provides a permanent record
✧ Saves time and questions
✧ Tells precisely what is needed

Hydel Interior Alternatives

INTERNAL MEMORANDUM

To: All Employees
From: Mike Ortega, Human Resources
Date: October 10, 2000
Subj: New Wellness Program Opportunity

The benefits package committee wants you to consider participating in a wellness program. As you know, we've been meeting to decide on changes in our benefits package. We need your response on this matter, so please read the following information carefully and complete the bottom half of this memo.

The readers are busy, so the purpose of the communication is stated in the first paragraph.

Last week, we sent you a memo detailing the Synergy Wellness Program. In addition to the package as described in the memo (life, major medical, dental, hospitalization), Synergy offered HIA a 10 percent discount. To meet the requirements for the discount, we have to show proof that at least 25 percent of our employees participate in aerobic exercise at least three times a week for at least 20 minutes. (Their actuarial tables show a resulting 10 percent reduction in claims.)

During warm weather, many of us walk the nature trail on our lunch break. Those walks will satisfy Synergy's requirements, but we have those nasty winters when no one can venture outside. After looking around, we discovered a gymnasium with an indoor track just a few blocks south on Grant Street. The Keep Fit Sports Centre will give our employees unlimited daytime access to their indoor track, gym, and pool for a group fee that comes to approximately $4.50 per month per employee if at least half of us sign up. Payroll says you can have the amount automatically deducted, if you wish.

The second and third paragraphs present the situation that makes the inquiry necessary.

In addition to walking, we can swim, play volleyball, jazzercise, form our own intramural basketball teams, and much more. Our spouses and children can also participate at a deeply discounted monthly fee. If you have questions, please e-mail or call me or any member of the committee. Let us know your wishes on the following form.

The final paragraph lists reader benefits, requests action, and provides an easy-to-use response form.

Sign and return the following no later than Friday, October 27.

==

_____ Yes, I will participate in the Synergy Wellness program and pay $4.50 a month.
_____ Yes, I am interested in a discounted family membership.
_____ No, I prefer not to participate.

Signature ______________________________

Employee ID Number ______________________________

FIGURE 8.1

In-Depth Critique: Memo Requesting Routine Action from Employees

Hydel Interior Alternatives (HIA) provides interior office designs for businesses. HIA recently decided to upgrade its wellness and benefits program, but it will have to charge employees a nominal fee to pay for use of a sports complex. This memo seeks employee response about the new program and the possible fee.

A routine request follows the standard direct plan. Start with a clear statement of your reason for writing; then provide whatever explanation is needed to justify the request. Close with a specific account of what you expect, and include a deadline if appropriate. The memo in Figure 8.1 was sent to all employees of an interior design company.

In the following memo, the writer refers to a previous memo on the same topic and then requests a response from employees:

The memo begins with the central question.

Are you interested in having a day-care centre on site?

A little background information orients the reader.

Several suggestions in the cafeteria suggestion box indicate that parents at Timken want convenient, affordable child care. Therefore, your answers to the following questions will help us determine your needs.

The numbered questions focus responses so that they will be easier to tally.

1. How many children would you enrol in the new centre?
2. How much do you currently pay each week for each child in day care?
3. Do you think the cost is too high? In your opinion, what would be a reasonable weekly charge for each child?
4. What qualities do you look for in a day-care centre?
5. What qualifications do you expect of the caregivers?

Specific instructions for replying close the memo. The courteous tone helps ensure a prompt response.

You may respond on this form and return it to Human Resources by Friday. We appreciate your prompt response so that we may begin analyzing the possibilities.

BEHIND THE SCENES AT NUMA FINANCIAL SYSTEMS

Promoting a Business on the Internet

Stephen Eckett is founder and managing director of Numa Financial Systems, a virtual consulting company—that is, his company's only existence is a Web site on the Internet. Although Eckett's company is registered in the United Kingdom, he works mainly from France, and his clients live all over the world.

Like many consultants, Eckett is a one-man operation. He markets his knowledge through Numa's Web site and offers advice on how to connect to the Internet to research financial markets and manage investment portfolios. Eckett knows that responding to direct requests is one way to promote his business. Of course, Eckett doesn't charge you for his online advice; rather, he hopes that if you interact with Numa's Web site you will eventually hire him as a consultant or purchase his book *Investing Online* (a practical guide to using the Internet for investing in the global stock market and trading currencies). In fact, Eckett sells his book directly through his Web site to customers all over the world. He also plans to offer investment software, conference registrations, and journal subscriptions in the near future.

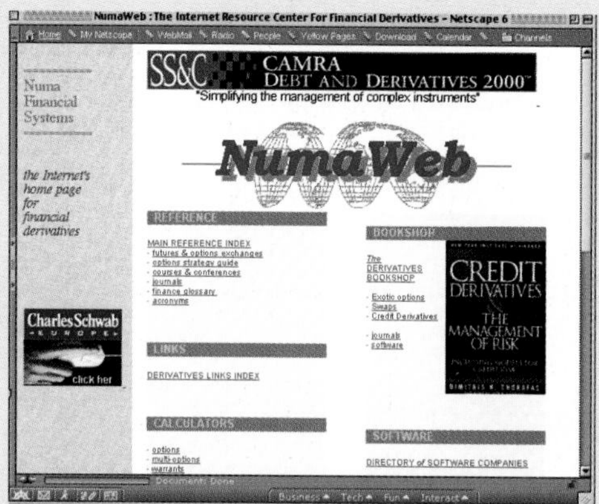

Through his Web site, Stephen Eckett of Numa Financial Systems receives more than 50 requests a day for information.

Eckett believes that the key to building his consulting business is effective customer interaction. That's why he takes online information requests very seriously. He gets more than 50 requests for information each day, including requests for investment advice, job applications, book orders, and information on advertising services via the Numa Web site. Because he's received so many of these online requests, Eckett has some practical advice on how to compose direct requests for e-mail so that people will respond by taking positive action.

"Be concise," says Eckett. "Get straight to the point. Include the reason for the request in the first few lines, and don't write

This matter-of-fact memo assumes some shared background. Such a style is appropriate when you're communicating about a routine matter to someone in the same company.

Adjust the writing style to take shared reference points into account.

When used well, memos and e-mail messages can communicate efficiently, concisely, and powerfully. When misused, they can waste time and effort, swell the ocean of information that offices must deal with, and even tarnish your business reputation. So avoid writing frequent, long, unneeded messages. And don't put anything in a memo or e-mail message that you wouldn't want to share with absolutely everyone.

Requests to Other Businesses

Many letters and e-mail messages to other businesses are requests for information about products, such as an Indigo letter requesting a catalogue from a reference book distributor. They are among the simplest of all letters to write because businesses welcome the opportunity to tell you about their goods and services. In fact, you can often fill out a coupon, a response card, or an online form and then mail or e-mail it to the correct address. In other cases, you might write a brief note requesting further information about something you saw or heard about in an advertisement. One or two sentences will most likely do the job. Companies commonly check on the effectiveness of their advertisements, so mention where you saw the advertisement or heard about the product.

When writing a letter in response to an advertisement

- ✧ Say where you saw the ad
- ✧ Specify what you want
- ✧ Provide a clear and complete return address on the letter

long paragraphs of text; it's awkward and tiring to read on a computer screen. Break your messages up into smaller units, and make each paragraph only a few lines long. Don't try to get too clever with the layout of the message because the recipient may be using a different e-mail program that alters the text presentation entirely."

Be sure to keep the subject heading as precise and detailed as space allows. If the editor of a newsletter on gold investment receives 50 e-mail information requests a day, the subject heading "Gold" will not be very useful.

Eckett notes that informality is a big advantage of e-mail. He adds, however, that it is fine to be informal if you are writing to your brother, an old school friend, or an established work colleague—but not when making contact with someone for the first time or when it is still early in a business relationship. He emphasizes the importance of perfect grammar and spelling—especially if you want to get positive action. For example, if he receives a message littered with spelling errors, or even just phrased inelegantly, chances are strong that he will respond with a pre-written auto-reply message.

According to Eckett, e-mail information requests have a tremendous advantage over the fax and phone. Not only is e-mail faster and cheaper, but the recipient can immediately file the requests by topic and wait until later to perform an automatic search by date, sender, subject heading, or key words. So, if you need to find or follow up on an information request, it's a matter of five seconds to filter, search, or sort though 5000 messages. Eckett personally sorts his e-mail into some 60 categories. "It's far better than wading though a filing cabinet of curled fax paper."

Eckett does note a situation in which e-mail might not be a good choice. He believes that, even though e-mail is a great tool for simple information requests, it may not be effective for initiating contact with a more senior person (such as a corporate manager). Eckett says that it is best to contact that person by phone. He adds that e-mail requests from unknown parties will seldom reach the senior person, even if they are sent to that person's direct e-mail address.

APPLY YOUR KNOWLEDGE

1. Eckett has hired you to help him respond to his Web site inquiries. Knowing that he is a stickler for good grammar and spelling, you are concerned because your e-mail software does not have a grammar or spelling checker. You are not the best typist. What easy steps can you take to prevent errors in your e-mail communications?
2. Aside from good grammar, spelling, and short paragraphs, please list some (perhaps creative) ways that you can make sure that your e-mail request will evoke a positive response.

If the reader is not expecting your letter, supply more detail.

Of course, many inquiries are prompted by something other than an advertisement, and they demand a more detailed letter or e-mail message. If the message will be welcome, or if the reader won't mind answering it, the direct approach is still appropriate. The following is such a letter:

The overall request is stated at the beginning. Phrased politely in question form, it requires no question mark.

> Would you please supply me with information about the lawn services you provide.

The explanation for the request keeps the reader's attention by hinting at the possibility of future business.

> Pralle Realty owns approximately 27 pieces of rental property in Kingston, and we're looking for a lawn service to handle all of them. We are making a commitment to provide quality housing in this university town, and we are looking for an outstanding firm to work with us.

To avoid burdening the reader with an impossibly broad request, the writer asks a series of specific questions, itemized in a logical sequence.

> 1. **Lawn care:** What is your annual charge for each location for lawn maintenance, including mowing, fertilizing, and weed control?
>
> 2. **Shrubbery:** What is your annual charge for each location for the care of deciduous and evergreen bushes, including pruning, fertilizing, and replacing as necessary?

To avoid receiving useless yes-or-no answers, the writer asks some open-ended questions.

> 3. **Contract:** How does Agri-Lawn Service structure large contracts? What kind of additional information do you need from us?

The courteous close specifies a time limit.

> We hope to hear from you by February 15. We want to have a lawn-care firm in place by March 15.

This letter should bring a prompt and enthusiastic reply because the situation is clearly described, the possibility of current and future business is suggested, and the questions are specific and easy to answer. Also, the letter implies confidence in the opinion and assistance of the reader. Because the letter will be sent to a business and pertains to a possible sale, the writer did not enclose a stamped, preaddressed envelope.

If you aren't using letterhead stationery, be sure to type your address on the letter clearly and completely. Many inquiries are not answered because the address was written only on the return envelope, which the recipient discarded.

Requests to Customers and Other Outsiders

Requests to customers often spell out in detail
- ✧ What exactly is needed
- ✧ How filling the request will benefit them

Businesses often ask individuals outside the organization to provide information or to take some simple action: attend a meeting, return an information card, sign a document, confirm an address, supplement information on an order. These messages are often short and simple, but some situations require a more detailed explanation. Readers might be unwilling to respond unless they understand how the request benefits them. So more complex letters, with several paragraphs of explanation, are sometimes necessary.

Routine requests to customers can be used to re-establish communication.

Businesses sometimes need to re-establish a relationship with former customers. In many cases, customers who are unhappy about some purchase or about the way they were treated make no complaint–they simply stay away from the offending business. A letter of inquiry encouraging customers to use idle credit accounts offers them an opportunity to register their displeasure and then move on to a good relationship. In addition, a customer's response to an inquiry may provide the company with insights into ways to improve its products and customer service. Even if they have no complaint, customers still welcome the personal attention. Such an inquiry to the customer might begin this way:

> When a good credit-card customer like you has not bought anything from us in six months, we wonder why. Is there something we can do to serve you better?

Letters of inquiry sent to someone's home frequently include a stamped, pre-addressed envelope to make it easy for the customer to reply.

When sending routine requests to individuals rather than to other businesses, consider enclosing a stamped, pre-addressed envelope.

Inquiry letters similar to the one above are also sent from one business to another. For example, a sales representative of a housewares distributor might send this type of letter to a retailer. To review material discussed here, see this chapter's Checklist for Routine Requests.

Writing Direct Requests for Claims and Adjustments

LEARNING OUTCOME 4
Apply the direct strategy to claim and adjustment messages.

Satisfied customers bring additional business to the firm; dissatisfied customers do not. In addition, dissatisfied customers complain to anyone who will listen, creating poor public relations. So, even though **claims** (or formal complaints) and **adjustments** (or claim settlements) may seem like unpleasant concepts, progressive organizations such as Indigo want to know when their clients or customers are dissatisfied with their services or merchandise. So if you have a complaint, it's in your best interests, and the company's, to bring your claim or request for an adjustment to the organization's attention. Communicate at once with someone in the company who can make the correction. A phone call or visit may solve the problem, but a written claim letter is better because it documents your dissatisfaction.

You are entitled to request an adjustment whenever you receive a product or service that doesn't live up to the supplier's standards.

Your first reaction to a clumsy mistake or a defective product is likely to be anger or frustration, but the person reading your letter probably had nothing to do with the problem. Making a courteous, clear, concise explanation will impress the reader much more favourably than an abusive, angry letter. Asking for a fair and reasonable solution will increase your chances of receiving a satisfactory adjustment.

Tone is of primary importance; keep your claim businesslike and unemotional.

Checklist for for Routine Requests

A. Direct Statement of the Request

1. Phrase the opening to reflect the assumption that the reader will respond favourably to your request.
2. Phrase the opening so clearly and simply that the main idea cannot be misunderstood.
3. Write in a polite, undemanding, personal tone.
4. Preface complex requests with a sentence or two of explanation, possibly a statement of the problem that the response will solve.

B. Justification, Explanation, and Details

1. Justify the request, or explain its importance.
2. Explain to the reader the benefit of responding.
3. State desired actions in a positive and supportive, not negative or dictatorial, manner.
4. Itemize parts of a complex request in a numbered series.
5. List specific questions.
   a. Avoid asking questions that you could answer by yourself.
   b. Arrange questions logically.
   c. Number questions.
   d. Word questions carefully to get the types of answers you need: numbers, or *yeses* and *noes* if you need to tally many replies; lengthier, more-detailed answers if you want to elicit more information.
   e. Word questions to avoid clues about the answer you prefer so as not to bias the reader's answers.
   f. Limit each question to one topic.

C. Courteous Close with Request for Specific Action

1. Courteously request a specific action and make it easy to comply, perhaps by enclosing a return, postage-paid envelope or by explaining how you can be reached.
2. Indicate gratitude, possibly by promising to follow up in a way that will benefit the reader.
3. Clearly state any important deadline or time frame for the request.

In your claim letter
- ✧ Explain the problem and give details
- ✧ Provide backup information
- ✧ Request specific action

In most cases, and especially in your first letter, assume that a fair adjustment will be made, and follow the plan for direct requests. Begin with a straightforward statement of the problem, and give a complete, specific explanation of the details. In the middle section of your claim letter, provide any information the adjuster will need to verify your complaint about faulty merchandise or unsatisfactory service. Politely request specific action in your closing, and suggest that the business relationship will continue if the problem is solved satisfactorily.

Be prepared to document your claim. Send copies and keep the original documents.

Since companies usually accept the customer's explanation of what's wrong, you must be entirely honest when filing claims for adjustment or refund. Also, be prepared to back up your claim with invoices, sales receipts, cancelled cheques, dated correspondence, catalogue descriptions, and any other relevant documents. Send copies and keep the originals for your files.

If the remedy is obvious, tell your reader exactly what will return the company to your good graces–for example, an exchange of merchandise for the right item or a refund if the item is out of stock. If you're uncertain about the precise nature of the trouble, you could ask the company to make an assessment. When you're dissatisfied with an expensive item, you might request that an unbiased third person either estimate the cost of repair or suggest another solution. Be sure to supply your telephone number and the best time to call (as well as your address) so that the company can discuss the situation with you if necessary.

The following letter was written to an office cleaning company. As you read it, compare the tone with the one in Figure 8.2. If you were the person receiving the complaint, which version would you respond to more favourably?

> We have used your service since March 1998, and we are disgusted by the condition the shop has been left in this week. I found full wastebaskets, smudge marks on the countertops, and coffee cups on the desks. Furthermore, the floor was full of scuff marks and dirt; remember that we contracted with your firm to polish the floors on Wednesday and Friday nights. This carelessness is very disappointing. I expect you to hire good workers, and to check up on them.

In general, it's a good idea to suggest specific and fair compensation when asking for an adjustment. However, in some cases you wouldn't request a specific adjustment but ask the reader to resolve the problem. In a letter like this, define the problem and express your dissatisfaction in as much detail as possible, while conveying a sincere desire to find a fair solution. A courteous tone will allow the reader to save face and still make up for the mistake. (This chapter's Checklist for Claims and Requests for Adjustment will remind you of the tasks involved in such messages.)

Going Online

Expand Your Knowledge About Credit

Visit "The Credit Book" on the Canadian Credit Union System Web site to understand what consumer credit is all about. You will learn about types of credit, security for loans, sources of credit, and the loan application process. Educate yourself as well about your responsibilities and rights when you are granted a loan.

www.westfortcu.on.ca/finance/creditbk.htm

Making Routine Credit Requests

If your credit rating is sound, your application for business credit may be as direct as any other type of simple request. Whether the application is directed to a local bank; to a supply company, wholesaler, or manufacturer; or to a national credit-card company, the information needed is the same. You might phone the company for a credit application, write a letter, or send an e-mail as simple as this:

> We would like to open a credit account with your company. Please send an application blank, and let us know what references you will need.

Before you get a credit account, you'll have to supply such information as the name of your company, the length of time you've been in business, the name of your bank, and the addresses of businesses where you have existing accounts.

Baltic Instaprint
620 Broadway Ave • Saskatoon, SK S7N 1A8
306-555-6543
pol@baltprint.com

June 8, 2000

Stepan Mikolovic, Manager
Brightspot Cleaning and Maintenance
1515 Arlington Ave
Saskatoon, SK S7Y 2Y3

Dear Mr. Mikolovic:

For the last two weeks, my store has not been properly cleaned. I am asking you to replace the current staff with new cleaners.

I have contracted with you since March 1998, and had been very satisfied with your service. However, when I opened the store on Tuesday, Wednesday, and Thursday morning this week, I found full wastebaskets, smudge marks on the countertops, and coffee cups on the desks. Furthermore, the floor wasn't polished, a job that we have contracted with your firm to do on Tuesday and Friday nights. This lack of care is very unusual. Until this past week your cleaners have been meticulous in looking after our shop.

Assigning new cleaners to our store may solve the problem. We are a very busy photocopy and print shop and see a steady stream of customers from the time we open until we close. Our customers expect us to do clean and neat work; accordingly, the appearance of our shop must reflect our high standards.

Thank you for looking into this matter. I hope to hear from you by the end of next week; you can reach me at 555-6543 between 8 a.m. and 7 p.m.

Yours truly,
Vassily Polikoff
Owner

The problem is stated clearly and calmly in the first paragraph.

The second paragraph explains the particulars of the situation so that the person reading the letter will understand why the writer thinks a problem exists.

The last paragraph requests specific action and makes responding easy by providing a phone number.

FIGURE 8.2

In-Depth Critique: The Importance of a Polite Tone

Most people would react much more favourably to this version of the complaint letter about inadequate cleaning. As this rational and clear message demonstrates, a courteous approach is best for any routine request. If you must write a letter that gives vent to your anger, go ahead; but then tear that one up and write a letter that will actually help solve the problem.

Businesses trying to establish credit are also expected to furnish a financial statement and possibly a balance sheet. In general, the lender wants proof that your income is stable and that you can repay the loan. You might put this information in your original letter, but it will probably be requested again on the standard credit application form.

The second step is to supply the necessary information.

Order letters are often combined with a request for credit.

A request to buy on credit is sometimes included with a company's first-time order for goods. In such cases, the customer often sends copies of the latest financial statement along with the order letter. If the order is made by e-mail or on the Internet, indicate that financial statements are available. A company whose credit standing is good can confidently ask that the order be accepted on a credit basis. Because the main idea in this situation is to get permission to buy on credit, the letter should open with that request. Figure 8.3 is an example of the way an order may be combined with a request for credit. Note how the request for credit is supported by documentation of financial stability. In addition, the writer has encouraged a favourable response by adopting a confident tone and mentioning the probability of future business.

A request for credit
- ✧ Is supported by documentation
- ✧ Adopts a confident tone
- ✧ Hints at future business

Inquiring About People

LEARNING OUTCOME 5
Apply the direct strategy to routine inquiries about people.

The need to inquire about people arises often in business. For example, some companies ask applicants to supply references before awarding credit, contracts, jobs, promotions, scholarships, and so on. If you're applying for a job and your potential employer asks for references, you may want to ask a close personal or professional associate to write a letter of recommendation. Or, if you're an employer considering whether to hire an applicant, you may want to write directly to the person the applicant named as a reference. Whatever the situation, just remember that the approach to writing letters of inquiry about people is similar to the approach for requests already discussed; that is, such inquiries include a direct statement of the request (or main idea), a justification of the request (explanation of the situation with details), and a courteous close that includes a request for specific action.

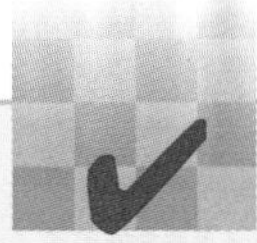

Checklist for Claims and Requests for Adjustment

A. Direct Statement of the Request

1. Write a claim letter as soon as possible after the problem has been identified.
2. State the need for reimbursement or correction of the problem.
3. Maintain a confident, factual, fair, unemotional tone.

B. Justification, Explanation, and Details

1. To gain the reader's understanding, praise some aspect of the product or service, or at least explain why it was originally purchased.
2. Present facts honestly, clearly, and politely.
3. Eliminate threats, sarcasm, exaggeration, and hostility.
4. Specify the problem: product failed to live up to advertised standards; product failed to live up to sales representative's claims; product fell short of company policy; product was defective; customer service was deficient.
5. Make no accusation against any person or company, unless you can back it up with facts.
6. Use a nonargumentative tone to show your confidence in the reader's fairness.
7. If necessary, refer to documentation (invoices, cancelled cheques, confirmation letters, and the like), but mail only photocopies.
8. Ask the reader to propose fair adjustment, if appropriate.
9. If appropriate, clearly state what you expect as a fair settlement, such as credit against the next order you place, full or partial refund of the purchase price of the product, replacement or repair of the defective merchandise, or performance of services as originally contracted.
10. Do not return the defective merchandise until you have been asked to do so.
11. Avoid uncertainty or vagueness that might permit the adjusters to prolong the issue by additional correspondence or to propose a less-than-fair settlement.

C. Courteous Close with Request for Specific Action

1. Summarize desired action briefly.
2. Simplify compliance with your request by including your name, address, phone number, and hours of availability.
3. Indicate how complying with your request will benefit the reader.

04/12/01 THU FAX [403-555-7999] 002

VIA

FAX

Climbers' Cabin
4011 7 St SE
Calgary AB T2G 2Y9
403-555-7966/fax 403-555-7999
www.up-n-up.com/kirsten@up-n-up.com

April 12, 2001

VIA FAX SUBMISSION: 514-555-6747

Mr. Jack Silva
Silva Outerwear
214 Sherbrooke E
Montreal QC H2X 1E6

Dear Mr. Silva,

We are getting ready for the fall and winter season, and would like to order some of your polyester fibre outerwear. If you can send the shipment by August 10, we will be able to feature some of your items in our display window. We need the following:

Quantity	Item #	Description	Color	Size	Price	Extension
20	H21	Andes hat, multicolour	multi	S	$6.00	$120.00
20	H23	Andes hat, multicolour	"	M	6.00	120.00
20	H25	Andes hat, multicolour	"	L	6.00	120.00
12	V36	Vest	blue	M	24.00	288.00
12	V38	Vest	black	M	24.00	288.00
12	V40	Vest	leaf pattern	M	24.00.	288.00
12	V36	Vest	blue	L	24.00	288.00
12	V38	Vest	black	L	24.00	288.00
12	V40	Vest	leaf pattern	L	24.00.	288.00
8	V36	Vest	blue	XL	24.00	192.00
8	V38	Vest	black	XL	24.00	192.00

I am sending our financial statement and references by courier. We seek terms of 2/10, net 30, FOB your warehouse. I'll provide more information upon request.

We know how popular your outerwear is, and we look forward to selling it to our customers.

Sincerely yours,

Kirsten Magnusson
Buyer

The message starts strong with a positive statement and a possible reader benefit.

The order is clearly stated in an easy-to-read table.

Financial information necessary for granting credit is being provided. The message also states the terms of credit that are being requested.

Terms of 2/10 refers to a request for a 2 percent discount if the bill is paid within 10 days of receipt rather than the standard 30 days. "Net 30" means that the bill is due in full within 30 days of receipt. "FOB (freight on board) your dock" means that shipping will be paid by the purchaser from the point of loading indicated, in this case, Silva Outerwear's warehouse.

The message ends on a positive note with a compliment to the receiver and an additional reader benefit.

FIGURE 8.3

In-Depth Critique: Combining an Order with a Routine Credit Request
A sports clothing store combines an order with a request for credit.

ON THE JOB
Solving a Communication Dilemma at Indigo Books and Music

Since 1997, Heather Reisman has been building an impressive presence on the Canadian book scene with Indigo Books and Music, most recently acquiring Larry Stevenson's Chapters chain. Reisman has achieved her prominence as a Canadian bookseller through a mix of the right locations, books and gift items that differentiate Indigo from her competitors, and the ability to communicate her business vision effectively to employees and customers. As Indigo's chief manager, she must also request information from her executive team, store managers, and other employees. Reisman uses the feedback to help her company evolve and gain market share.

In Canada the battle for the book-reading public has moved from independent booksellers to big-box bookstores. Although the growth of the big stores has forced many independents out of business, some, such as Nicholas Hoare Booksellers with locations in Montreal, Ottawa, and Toronto, and McNally Robinson in Winnipeg, have withstood the onslaught. Reisman's Indigo tries to be a megastore with the personal appeal of the smaller booksellers. Indigo is targeted toward an upscale market, with an emphasis on travel, home decor, gardening, and art books, as well as trade fiction, rather than mass-market paperbacks. The atmosphere of each Indigo outlet speaks refinement in the large, portico windows, uncluttered floor space, and winding staircases. Book-industry observers note that these qualities were a marked difference from rival Chapters stores, which seemed more densely filled with products.

Reisman is also building Indigo's presence in shopping malls with smaller, so-called "Indigo Lite" stores, about 8000 square feet as compared to 20 000 to 40 000 square feet of a typical Indigo Books and Music store. One "Lite" Indigo exists in Montreal's Jean Talon retail complex. In the competitive arena of the Internet, the Indigo.ca Web site, which Reisman started in 1999, is designed not only as a convenient location to browse for and order books, music, and gifts, but also as a cultural experience. Here booklovers can watch one of the three Indigo "channels" which list current and past store events and transmit author readings and Reisman's interviews with writers through streamed audio. Web site visitors can also become an "Indigo Insider" by subscribing to their mailing list to be the "first to know" about special offers, read various best-seller lists, and join on-line discussions about books.

Reisman wants to offer Canada's booklovers "the best of a small proprietor-run shop combined with the selection of a true emporium." The impact she has made in only a few years demonstrates her ability to communicate with customers and employees.[2]

Your Mission: You have recently taken a job at Indigo's head office as an administrative assistant on the management team. One of your jobs entails drafting letters to Indigo store managers and outside contacts. Using the principles outlined in this chapter for writing direct requests, handle each of the following letters to the best of your ability. Be prepared to explain your choices.

1. You are asked to contact the store managers to find out whether the company's new Web site is affecting sales in retail stores. Which of the following is the best opening for this letter?

a. I have recently joined Heather Reisman's staff as an administrative assistant. She has asked me to write to you to obtain your input on the impact of the company's new Web site on store sales. Please reply to the following questions within five working days. [List of questions follows.]

b. Please tell us what you think of Indigo.ca. Ms. Reisman is trying to evaluate its impact on our business. Within the next few days, can you take a few moments to jot down your thoughts on its impact. Specifically, Ms. Reisman would like to know ... [List of questions follows.]

c. By April 15, please submit written answers to the following questions on the new Indigo Web site. [List of questions follows.]

d. Is the new Web site affecting sales in your store? We're polling all store managers for their reaction to online retailing. Is it thumbs up or thumbs down on the Web?

2. Which of the following is the best choice for the middle section of the letter?

a. Specifically, has store business decreased since the Web site went online? If so, what is the percentage decrease in sales over the previous six months? Over the comparable period last year? Have customers mentioned the Web site? If so, have their comments been positive or negative? Has employee morale been affected by the site? How?

b. By replying to the following questions, you will help us decide whether to continue with the Web site as is, revise it, or drop it entirely:

1. Has business decreased in your store since the Web site went live? If it has, what is the percentage decrease in sales over the previous six months? Over the comparable period last year?
2. Have customers mentioned the site? If so, have their comments been positive or negative? Give some typical examples.
3. Has employee morale been affected by the Web site initiative? How?

c. By circling the response that most accurately reflects your store's experience, please answer the following questions regarding the company's new Web site:

1. Since the Web site went live, sales have
   a. increased
   b. decreased
   c. remained about the same
2. Customers (have/have not) mentioned the Web site. Their comments have been primarily (positive/negative).
3. Employee morale (has/has not) been affected by the Web site.

d. Ms. Reisman needs to know the following: (1) How have overall store sales changed since the company's new Web site went live? (2) What do customers think of the site? Attach complimentary customer comments. (3) What do employees think of the site? Attach complimentary employee comments.

3. For a courteous close with a request for specific action, which of the following paragraphs is the best?

a. Thank you for your cooperation. Please submit your reply in writing by April 15.

b. Ms. Reisman is meeting with her senior staff on April 17 to discuss the Web site. She would like to have your reaction in writing by April 15 so that she can present your views during that meeting. If you have any questions, please contact me at 697-2886.

c. You may contact me at 697-2886 if you have any questions or need additional information about this survey. Ms. Reisman requires your written response by April 15 so she can discuss your views with her senior staff on April 17.

d. Thank you for your input. As the frontline troops in the battle for sales, you are in a good position to evaluate the impact of the new Web site. We here at corporate headquarters want to increase overall company sales, but we need your feedback. Please submit your written evaluation by April 15 so that Ms. Reisman can use the results as ammunition in her meeting with senior staff on April 17.

4. To promote the new Harry Potter children's book, Ms. Reisman has ordered 30 large cutout cardboard displays of the new cover. The Indigo warehouse has received the shipment; however, seven of the displays are bent and cannot be used in promoting the book. You have been asked to prepare a letter requesting an adjustment. Select the best version.

a. On March 25, we ordered 30 cardboard cutouts (item #90067-C in your April catalogue). When the shipment arrived last week, we discovered that 7 of the cutouts were bent. Whether the damage occurred during shipping or at your place of business, I do not know. However, I do know that we cannot use the cutouts in their present form. If you can replace them before April 25, please do so. We are withholding payment until the matter is straightened out.

b. Please call me immediately at (416) 697-2886 to discuss a problem with the Harry Potter cutouts that we ordered from you. Seven of them are bent and cannot be used in our nationwide book promotion scheduled for May 1.

Time is running short, I know, but we would really like you to replace the 7 damaged cutouts if you can do so in time for our promotion. If that is not possible, we will adjust our payment to reflect a sale of 23 cutouts as opposed to 30. Thanks for your cooperation. The good cutouts are really cute, and we expect they will boost our book sales.

c. Of the 30 Harry Potter cardboard cutouts received last week, 7 are not in good condition. I inspected them myself, and several of us tried to fix the cutouts, but they don't look very good. Therefore, please replace these 7 before April 25.

d. Seven of the Harry Potter cardboard cutouts that we ordered from your firm on March 25 arrived in poor condition. Can you replace them before April 25? If so, we would still like to use them in our May 1 book promotion. I am enclosing a copy of the invoice for your convenience. As you can see, our original order was for 30 cutouts (catalogue item #90067-C), priced at $35.00 each. Our bill for the total order is $1050.00. We will send payment in full when we receive the 7 undamaged cutouts. If replacements are not available by April 25, we will send you a cheque for the 23 good cutouts, which we plan to use in any case. Including tax and handling costs, the adjusted total would be $955.75. Would you like us to return the damaged items? Perhaps they can be salvaged for another purpose.

Please call me at (416) 697-2886 any time this week to discuss the situation. We are eager to receive the replacement cutouts so that our bookstores can benefit from the Harry Potter display during our nationwide book promotion scheduled for May 1.

TAP Your Knowledge

Summary of Learning Outcomes

1. Clearly state the main idea of each direct request you write. To be clearly understood by your audience, be specific in the opening part of your message and be sure to express your request politely. When you have several requests, use headings to express categories of requests. When you have a complex request, state the request and provide supporting details immediately underneath it. When you have a list of requests, include space beneath each request so that the reader has room to make notes.

2. Provide sufficient explanation for the reader to be able to comply with your request. The middle section of your direct messages should be a logical outgrowth of your opening remarks. If your inquiry concerns complex equipment or the cost of something, your middle section may include a series of questions about technical specifications, or the cost breakdown. Data about a product and your reasons for being concerned about a particular matter are other details that clarify your message for your audience.

3. Close with a courteous request for specific action. In your close, be sure you request a specific response, including time limits, and show appreciation or goodwill. Courtesy and helpfulness will motivate your reader to answer promptly.

4. Apply the direct strategy to claim and adjustment messages. Claim and adjustment messages seek a solution to a problem with a product or service. To motivate a helpful response, make sure your tone is polite and include a clear and concise explanation of the problem in your message. Begin with a straightforward statement of the problem and follow with the details. Ask for corrective action, politely, in your conclusion. You can suggest that the business relationship will continue if the problem is solved satisfactorily.

5. **Apply the direct strategy to routine inquiries about people.** In business, companies frequently need to inquire about job applicants, contracts, or promotions. In inquiry letters like these, also open with a direct statement of the request, justify the request in the letter body with details, and close courteously with a request for specific action.

Test Your Knowledge

Review Questions

1. What is the basic strategy of direct requests?
2. What is an effective format for order letters that do not use order forms?
3. What are three kinds of routine requests?
4. What are some types of requests to customers and other outsiders?
5. What kinds of information do you need to provide when seeking a credit account?

Apply Your Knowledge

Critical Thinking Questions

1. Why is it important to know about any cultural differences between you and your audience when you're organizing a request?
2. Why is it inappropriate to begin your request with a brief personal introduction?
3. What precautions should be taken when writing secondary questions in a direct request? Explain what harm could be done by overlooking such precautions.
4. Which is the most important element of an order letter: the legality of the offer, the clarity of the order, or the explanation of how items will be used? Briefly explain.
5. Every time you send a direct-request memo to Ted Jackson, he's slow to answer or refuses to comply. You're beginning to get impatient. Should you send Jackson a memo to ask what's wrong? Complain to your supervisor about Jackson's uncooperative attitude? Arrange a face-to-face meeting with Jackson? Bring up the problem at the next staff meeting? Explain.
6. You have a complaint against one of your suppliers, but you have no documentation to back it up. Should you request an adjustment anyway? Why or why not?

Practise Your Knowledge

Documents for Analysis

Read the following documents; then (1) analyze the strengths and weaknesses of each sentence and (2) revise each document so that it follows this chapter's guidelines.

Document 8.A: Requesting Routine Information from a Business

Our university is closing its dining hall for financial reasons, so we want to do something to help the students prepare their own food in their residence rooms if they so choose. Your colourful ad in *University Management Magazine* caught our eye. We need the following information before we make our decision.

1. Would you be able to ship the microwaves by August 15? I realize this is short notice, but our board of trustees just made the decision to close the dining hall last week and we're scrambling around trying to figure out what to do.
2. Do they have any kind of a warranty? Students can be pretty hard on things, as you know, so we will need a good warranty.
3. How much does it cost? Do you give a discount for a big order?
4. Do we have to provide a special outlet?
5. Will students know how to use them, or will we need to provide instructions?

As I said before, we're on a tight time frame and need good information from you as soon as possible to help us make our decision about ordering. You never know what the board might come up with next. I'm looking at several other companies also, so please let us know ASAP.

Document 8.B: Requesting Routine Information from a Customer

I'm writing to inquire about your recent order for a High Country backpack. You didn't tell us which backpack you wanted, and you know they make a lot of different ones. They have the canvas models with the plastic frames and vinyl trim and they have the canvas models with leather trim and they have the ones that have more pockets than the other ones. Plus they come in lots of different colours.

Also they make the ones that are large for a big-boned person and the smaller versions for little women or kids. So you can see why I didn't know which one to send you. Also, we have to have payment when you place your order and you didn't include a cheque or credit card number (we need your signature if you order by credit card).

Actually, if you could drive to our store in Medicine Hat it would help a lot because then you could see all of them and try them on. Plus we have a lot of other neat equipment you could look at. I realize you live kind of far from here, but it would be worth the trip. If you really can't come, then you just need to do the things I mentioned and we'll get it right out to you.

Cases

Placing Orders

1. Paper shortage: Order faxed to Leslie Office Supplies Your environmental consulting company, Environmental Services, is a microbusiness–a small business with only one or two employees. Because most of your business is conducted by phone, fax, or modem, last year you moved out of Calgary and into the countryside nearby.

Serene as the woods may be, your company still demands a lot of your time. You are everything from CEO to janitor and cafeteria chef. That's why Leslie's Office Supplies, a mail-order distributor, attracted your attention.

Leslie's catalogue offered you credit, free same-day shipping, 24-hour operators, and a gift of a mouse pad and 20 Bic pens with your first order. How many times had you wasted half a day trekking into the city for a ream of paper? You gave Leslie's a chance. You called the 800 number on Saturday, and by Tuesday the paper was on your doorstep. Then, a few weeks later, you received a special sale catalogue:

> SALE!! All Cascade and PlusBright copier and printer paper 20% off regular price during the month of February. Call or fax us today!

How could you resist? Moreover, the time you've been losing shopping for "bargains" at the discount store is costing you hundreds of dollars, whereas Leslie's pricing is sometimes only a few dimes higher.

Your Task: You plan to fax an order to Leslie's. You need six reams of the Plus Bright Laser Paper; one carton of CF brand standard one-ply, 6-cm calculator rolls (stock no. 2PF8677; $46.00); one C0 brand QS200 high-yield laser printer toner cartridge (stock no. 02QS0200; $125.99); and one dozen $8\frac{1}{2}$ by 11-inch Acme brand perforated legal pads in buff (stock no. Q2TP31, colour code 4; $18.29).

You want to save the catalogue's order blank, so type the information in memo form and fax it to Leslie's at 1-800-626-3111. Your account number is BB5554432-999, and your address is PO Box 777, Cremona AB T0M 0R0. You don't have information on shipping charges, so request that the amount be included on your bill.

2. Wakeboard mania: Letter from Performance Ski & Surf ordering more equipment Your boss is amazed. Bill Porter, owner of Performance Ski & Surf, hasn't seen sporting equipment sell this rapidly in Mahone Bay, Nova Scotia, since in-line skating became popular. Since May, you haven't been able to keep wakeboards in stock. It doesn't seem to matter much which brand–Wake Tech, Neptune, or Full Tilt–your customers are snapping them up and heading out to the water, locals and tourists alike. Wakeboards are outselling traditional trick water skis by 20 to 1.

"Maybe it's because they don't require big, fast boats," you suggest. "I heard they're using fishing trawlers in Halifax, and they're still catching wind because the slower boats make bigger wakes to launch from."

Porter nods thoughtfully as he gazes at a photograph of professional wakeboarder Dean Lavelle. He's holding the same kind of rope any water skier holds, but he's 15 feet in the air. His short, stubby, fiberglass wakeboard (which is strapped to his feet) is higher than his head and from the grimace on his face, it looks as if he's mid-flip.

"I just hope none of these kids get hurt trying to imitate the pros," Butler says.

"Nah," you say. "Extreme sports–it's the way of the millennium. Look at what happened to snowboarding. You'll see wakeboarders at the Olympics soon."

Your Task: Butler has asked you to order another 12 Wake Techs, 8 Neptunes, and 10 Full Tilts. "Don't worry about colours or models; we'll be lucky to get this order filled at all from what I hear." He suggests that you draft a form letter for the three orders, and he'll supply the addresses and account numbers when you're finished.[3]

3. Vacation dreams: E-mail message ordering tourist information from Trinidad and Tobago For two years, you've been working hard at your first management job as an assistant branch manager for the Royal Bank. The promotion has kept you more than busy (you never realized how much overtime salaried managers are expected to put in). You're really looking forward to that two-week paid vacation you've worked so hard to earn.

"So what's it going to be?" the branch manager asked you this morning. "Hawaii or Disneyworld?"

"Huh?" you mumbled–after all, it was only 7 A.M. You caught yourself, cleared your throat, and politely answered that you hadn't decided yet. (Your vacation isn't until December, and this is a cold day in February.)

"I know your vacation is 10 months away," your manager said, "but I need to know your plans today for a report I'm filing with the head office. Just drop your first and second choices for vacation dates on my desk by 3 P.M. I'll let you know by next week how that fits into everyone else's schedule." Then she turned on her heel and strode off toward the vault.

By 3 P.M.? First and second choices? You don't even know where you're going! In the heat of desperation, an idea strikes. You hurry over to the customer waiting area, pick up a glossy copy of *Saveur* magazine, and begin flipping through the ads. You already know you don't want any ordinary vacation; you want to go somewhere exotic, somewhere tropical, like the spot where those two people are lounging in front of that plummeting waterfall. (How they got that beach umbrella to balance on the rocks, you'll never understand.) "In Tobago, Nature is in balance, as well as in abundance," reads the caption. Yes, that's it!

Your Task: Striding confidently back to your computer, you spread the ad out on your desk, call up your e-mail program, and tap in the address for ordering the *Trinidad & Tobago: Come to Life* tourist information booklet: **tourism.info@tidco.co.tt**. You can almost feel those tropical breezes warming your snow-weary bones as you type the order. Create this e-mail message and print it out for your instructor.[4]

4. Canary Cam: E-mail order across the border When you bought your first canary, you had no inkling the little guy might lead you to a new job. You put Sam in your bedroom, feeding him the seed you gave your parakeet when you were a kid. Almost immediately, Sam stopped singing and flumped down on his perch, looking miserable. You were worried, so you turned to the Internet to find help.

First you found the Canary List users group. Mostly breeders with large flocks to tend, they nevertheless directed you to Canadian "Robirda" McDonald, owner of www.robirda.com, Web home of the Canary Cam, *Flock Talk* e-zine, and the Birds Board. At **robirda.com**, no question is too trivial for Robirda's personal attention. You quickly discovered why some call her the "Canary Godmother."

With her special combination of TLC and straight-shooting education, Robirda had Sam perked up in no time and you out in the kitchen chopping greens, grating carrots, and baking "birdie muffins." Sam has now taken over your bedroom, where you've installed a larger cage, a full-spectrum light that keeps pace with sunrise and sunset, and a radio to keep Sam company when you're gone. But he's rewarding you. He warbles opera with Andrea Bocelli and chirps along with Garth Brooks, changing keys and matching rhythms as if he were reading a score. Truly amazing.

Feeling grateful, you wrote to ask Robirda how you could help her campaign to save canaries from ignorant owners and thoughtless breeders. She put you to work answering e-mail–mostly directing worried new owners to information on her site and responding to the schoolchildren who enjoy visiting the live Canary Cam to watch canary moms and dads hatching chicks in Robirda's bird room.

Today, the good news is that Robirda's applied for status as a nonprofit educational society, and you might be her first employee! The bad news is that her local supplier went out of business, and she urgently needs 50 pounds each of canary 80/20 seed mix and soak seed. She sent you e-mail, "Can you help me find a new source?" with a reminder, "One that will ship grains to Canada?"

Your Task: You've located Herman Brothers Pet Products in Detroit, and their Web address is **www.hermanbros-seed.com/**. The company has assured you it can legally ship across the border, and president Richard Herman (**rcherman@ hermanbros-seed.com**) asks you to e-mail him the complete order so that he can calculate shipping charges. His site lists the 80/20 canary seed mix at $15.45 for 50 lbs. The soak seed is $20.25. Seeds need to be shipped to Roberta C. McDonald, 1725 E. 3rd Avenue, Vancouver, BC, V5M-5R6.[5]

Requesting Routine Information and Action

5. Please tell me: Request for information about a product You're a consumer, and you've probably seen hundreds of products that you'd like to buy (if not, look at the advertisements in your favourite magazine for ideas). Choose a big-ticket item that is rather complicated, such as a stereo system or a vacation in the Caribbean.

Your Task: You surely have some questions about the features of your chosen product or about its price, guarantees, local availability, and so on. Write to the company or organization offering it, and ask four questions that are important to you. Be sure to include enough background information so that the reader can answer your questions satisfactorily.

If requested to do so by your instructor, mail a copy of your letter (after your instructor has had an opportunity to review it) to the company or organization. After a few weeks, you and your classmates may wish to compare responses and to answer this question: How well do companies or organizations respond to unsolicited inquiries?

6. Web site: E-mail message from Knitsmart Yarn and Needles requesting additional information An enjoyable hobby that whiled away cold winter evenings in Corner Brook, Newfoundland has given cousins Lee O'Reilly and Siobhan Gavin a local following and fame throughout the hand-knitting community in the Maritimes as well as in fashionable shops in Canada's large cities. First teaching their young relatives and neighbours the art of knitting, they soon branched into selling yarn out of Lee's basement and then running small classes for different skill levels. After opening a small yarn shop in Corner Brook's shopping district, they began creating their own knitwear designs and selling them as kits, supplied with yarn and knitting needles, through their shop and catalogue. After their designs caught the eye of a Holt Renfrew buyer, their business took off beyond what the cousins ever imagined. Their colourful sweater and hat designs are worn not only by socialites but also film and stage performers attracted to their uniqueness. Little did the cousins think that their hobby would become a cottage industry and then a major business.

You've been working at Knitsmart Yarn and Needles during your summer break from university, and you think it's time that Lee and Siobhan branch into new territory: the World Wide Web. You think that the cousins should build a Web site where they can gain new customers, interest other people in their craft, and inspire knitters around the world with their patterns. You find an advertisement in the local newspaper for a company that creates Web sites (Webtech), but the classified ad gives little information beyond a phone number and an e-mail address.

Your Task: You will be setting aside time next week to discuss the opportunities a Knitsmart Web site offers to the Lee and Siobhan. Write an e-mail message requesting more information from Webtech about what the company can do for Knitsmart Yarn and Needles.

7. Shrinking vacation: E-mail to a *Chatelaine* advice columnist "Hey," you exclaim to no one in particular after ripping open your paycheque and glancing at the stub. "They cheated me!"

Reza sticks her head up from the next cubicle. "What are you screaming about?"

"They ripped me off for vacation time!" you fume, waving the slip under Reza's nose. "Look right there, in the little square. It says I've only got 45.36 accrued hours for vacation and sick time. What happened to the 71 hours I had two weeks ago?"

Your colleague just smiles sweetly at you. "You didn't read the memo they sent around, did you?"

"What memo?" You're really not interested in memos right now. You're just wondering how soon you can get in to see the boss–or maybe you should go straight to personnel.

"The memo that explained a new company policy wherein every time we're late"–she looks at you pointedly–"and that includes late coming back from lunch, they're going to deduct the time from our sick leave and vacation time. Looks like you've been busted," she adds with a less than sympathetic grin.

"They can't do this to me! It's not fair!" you sputter. "I'll take it to a lawyer!"

"Hey, if you really think it's not fair, why don't you write to the job expert at the *Chatelaine* Web site," your colleague suggests. Reza always did enjoy office controversies.

"What expert," you mumble morosely, resigning yourself to your fate. You've been counting in your head, and they're probably accurate with their figures. You never could get anywhere on time and you estimate you've been late about 10 times in the last 14 working days–that is, if you count the extra 15 minutes you took for lunch a few times. And you thought no one noticed!

"Why not look at the Web site right now?"

You look over the Ask an Expert Web pages and see they cover many job-related topics. What harm could it do to get an opinion? You just might have a point of contention, because no one discussed lateness with you before deducting the vacation time and you received no detailed listing of the dates and exact amounts of time you were late. Is this a legal action for an employer to take?

Your Task: Write an e-mail message addressed to a suitable job expert at the *Chatelaine* Ask an Expert page (**www.chatelaine.com/experts/askanexpert.html**). Keep in mind that only questions selected for publication in the magazine will be answered. If the response suggests you have a legitimate case, you might want to consult an employment lawyer.[6]

8. Helping out: E-mail request about donations to the Computers for Schools Initiative As a computer-literacy volunteer at a local high school, you have heard of the Computers for Schools Initiative, an Industry Canada program that works with private business, industry, and volunteer organizations to collect, refurbish, and distribute "retired" computers to Canada's schools and public libraries free of charge. Since its creation in 1993 by Industry Canada and the Telephone Pioneers, the largest industry-related volunteer organization globally, more than 230 000 computers have been placed across Canada. There are so many benefits: older technology is recycled, saving it from the dump; kids develop skills they can use for education and the job market; and the donors do something beneficial for society.

You are intrigued and inspired by this national initiative, and you get thinking. At your part-time job as a customer service representative at a local bank you've already seen the desktop computers replaced twice in the last three years. You've also seen the laptops used by managers replaced with newer, faster ones with more bells and whistles. Where does this old equipment go, you wonder. Is it used as landfill, or just taking up space in a warehouse? You want to find out.

Your Task: Visit the Computers for Schools Web site at **www.schoolnet.ca** to learn about this worthy project. Then go to the Web site of a bank of your choice, and compose an e-mail message to their contact address. Asking suitable questions, find out about the bank's computer recycling program, if any, and tell them about the Computers for Schools project.[7]

9. Blockbuster Video shake-up: Memo from top brass requesting info from retail managers Everyone knew there was trouble at Blockbuster's new headquarters in Dallas when CEO Bill Fields, a former Wal-Mart whiz, suddenly resigned. Then Sumner Redstone and Tom Dooley (chairman and deputy chairman of Blockbuster's parent company, Viacom) flew in to assess the damage wrought by Fields's departure. They started by giving orders, particularly to you, Fields's former executive assistant.

Before he resigned to take a position with Hudson's Bay Company in Canada, Fields's strategy had been to boost Blockbuster's revenues and profits by establishing a new niche as a "neighbourhood entertainment centre." Using tricks he'd learned at Wal-Mart, he ordered the reconfiguration of more than 1000 Blockbuster outlets, surrounding the cash registers with flashy displays of candy, potato chips, new and used videotapes for sale, magazines, and tie-in toys. His stated goal was to add $1 in retail purchases to every video rental transaction. Meanwhile, he also moved Blockbuster's headquarters from Florida to Dallas, losing some of the company's top staff when they declined to make the move. Then Fields started construction on an 818 000-square-foot warehouse 40 km outside Dallas to centralize a new, sophisticated distribution operation for Blockbuster's North American outlets. But revenues were still falling.

Redstone and Dooley's new plan is to get Blockbuster back into its core business–video rentals–ignoring gloomy analysts who say satellite dishes and cheap tape sales are slowly sinking the rental industry. "This is still a healthy, growing business," Dooley insists. He believes that consumers coming in to rent videos were confused by the array of retail products they saw. "We want people to think of Blockbuster as the place to go to rent tapes," he says.

Dooley and Redstone have brought in new management and are making changes in everything from store format to marketing and advertising to inventory control and overhead reduction. Now they've turned to you. "We've got a job you'll love," Dooley smiles. "We know you can handle it."

Your Task: "Draft a memo that will pick the brains of retail managers in the stores that Fields reconfigured," Dooley orders. "I want to know whether customers walk out when current hits aren't available, whether the emphasis on retail products affected cash flow, and whether sales and rental figures have changed now that we've ordered all that clutter out of the limelight. Ask them where the cash is coming from: tape rentals, tape sales, or candy bars? More importantly, what about profit margins? I want a full report from every manager by the end of next week!" To get that kind of cooperation, you'd better organize your questions effectively.[8]

10. Follow that lead: E-mail message requesting information on Patagonia Your editor has asked you to gather information for a business profile about a unique company that would interest the local businesses. One such company, Patagonia, has created quite a stir in the business community, and you want to find out more about it.

Your Task: Explore Patagonia's Web site, **www.patagonia.com**. While you're online, get any information you can for the profile: Where is the company headquarters located? What is the company best known for? What types of stores carry Patagonia's products? What products does Patagonia offer? Where are Patagonia dealers? Finally, request product information by linking to the online guide service, sign the guest registry, order a Patagonia catalogue, and send an e-mail message requesting further information.

Requesting Claims and Adjustments

11. Bolga mix-up: E-mail to Getrade (Ghana) Ltd. from Pier 1 Imports The way you heard it, in 1993 your employer, Pier 1 Imports, sent a buyer to Accra, Ghana, to find local handicrafts to slake your customers' insatiable thirst for African art. Free-market reforms in Ghana during the 1980s helped ease export procedures, but so far the Ghanaian entrepreneurs who sprang forward to take advantage of the change are having trouble meeting demand from large-quantity buyers like Pier 1. The shipment that just arrived from Getrade (Ghana) Ltd., one of your best Ghanaian suppliers, is a good example of what's been going wrong.

Your customers love the bowl-shaped Bolga baskets woven by the Fra-fra people of northern Ghana. You can't keep them in stock. So this was to be a huge shipment—3000 Bolga baskets. You requested baskets in the traditional Bolga shape but woven in solid colours, since your customers prefer solid to mixed colours. Getrade was to ship 1000 green, 1000 yellow, and 1000 magenta. Your overseas buyer heard that the Body Shop ordered similar baskets with traditional mixed-colour patterns and a flatter shape. You sympathize with Ladi Nylander, chairman and managing director of Getrade, who is trying hard to adapt to the specific tastes of his North American buyers. He's hiring local artisans to carve, shape, and weave all sorts of items—often from designs provided by Pier 1. Personally, you can understand how Getrade got confused. But you know Pier 1 can't sell the 3,000 mixed-colour, flat Bolga baskets that you've been shipped.

Your Task: As assistant buyer, it's your job to compose the e-mail message alerting Getrade to the mix-up. You decide that if you want the mistake corrected, you'd better direct your message to Nylander at **Nylander@Getrade.co.za**. If you're lucky, it may be simply that the Body Shop's order got mixed up with yours.[9]

12. Unmannered manor: Letter requesting reimbursement from Property Vision in London As executive assistant to Barry Lansdon, CEO of Lansdon Holdings, you often handle routine letter-writing tasks. But this situation is stretching your abilities.

Last May, Lansdon decided to invest in some property in Great Britain. He'd heard that some of the most historically significant manor houses were on the market, and the notion of joining the landed British gentry—even part-time—fired his imagination. He contacted the people at Property Vision of London (with your help), and they replied with a dozen suggestions, including Testcombe Manor in Chilbolton, Hampshire ($5.6 million Cdn), where Edward VII once halted his private train to go fishing. You liked the seventeenth-century farmhouse in Kent ($625 000 Cdn), but it was Hunsdon House that caught your employer's fancy. This 87-acre estate ($5.6 million Cdn) had supposedly been Henry VIII's hunting lodge.

When Lansdon and his wife flew over to inspect this genuine Tudor mansion, they suffered quite a shock. The kingly aura conferred by wall-mounted rhinoceros trophies and wallpaper flecked with real gold was impressive. But only a quarter of the building could ever have heard Henry VIII's footsteps. It turned out that Hunsdon House had been demolished, then rebuilt in the 1700s—nearly two centuries after Henry's death. Moreover, the Lansdons discovered that "medieval" also applied to the plumbing system. They learned that insurers would require them to hire a full-time caretaker (at $80 000 a year), and the sheer size of the estate demanded a butler ($110 000 Cdn), a housekeeper ($70 000 Cdn), and a gardener ($70 000 Cdn) to keep the spectacular gardens in bloom. And, if the Lansdons stayed for more than 90 days a year, they'd have to pay British taxes.

"We never would have made the trip if they'd told us even half of this," Mr. Lansdon sighed as he handed you a folder. "I think we have every right to ask for a reimbursement. You'll find an itemized expense list inside."

Your Task: Write the claim letter to Mr. William Gething of Property Vision, 36 Brock Street, London, England W1Y 1AD, UK (Voice: 0171-493-4944, Fax: 0171-491-2548).[10]

Making Routine Credit Requests

13. Beanie Babies: Letter requesting credit from Ty, Inc. Bubbles (the fish), Inch (the worm), Ziggy (the zebra)—if you hear another parent ask for them, you're going to walk out the door of Sandy's Gifts and never return. No, not really. You love the brightly coloured, fuzzy little bean-bag toys as much as anyone, but you hate seeing adults look as disappointed as their kids when you tell them you don't carry them.

"You mean you don't even have Bongo the monkey or Pinky the flamingo?"

"Sorry, not yet," you apologize. "But we've had so many requests, we're hoping to have them in stock soon. If you leave your name and phone number ..."

Sandy Applegate, the store's owner, is sympathetic when you tell her what's been happening, but she doesn't know what to do. Her cash flow situation just doesn't allow for any new stock purchases until after Christmas. Who would have thought the $12 bean-bag animals (called Beanie Babies by manufacturer Ty, Inc.) would be so popular?

"But think of the sales we're missing," you interject. "Won't they give you credit?"

"Well, we've never done business with them before," Sandy says thoughtfully, "but you might have a point. After all, Sandy's Gifts has been in business for almost ten years, at the same location. How many retail shops can

say that today? And our credit with other vendors is excellent. Why don't you give it a try? You've been wanting to learn more about managing the store, haven't you?"

She's right. This is a great opportunity!

Your Task: Write a letter for Sandy's signature to New Account Sales, Ty, Inc., P.O. Box 5377, Oakbrook, Illinois 60522, requesting credit to purchase two dozen Beanie Babies. Introduce the store, its reputation, and the reasons Ty might like to comply.[11]

14. Please, Mr. Spear: Fax requesting credit for movie-scene banquet ingredients A few months ago you landed the most exciting job you could imagine, as a production assistant for Meg McComb, one of the best known movie food stylists in Canada and the US. But some days it's just a little too exciting. Like today, your boss has been hired to concoct a twelfth-century feast for a period costume drama directed by Kenneth Branagh. You have to get authentic-looking food for 150 actors ready by shooting time—tomorrow at 1 P.M.

McComb is a pro, and you have full confidence in her as she races about the office, handing out assignments to a cluster of nervous assistants. You know that she knows what to do with a banquet for 150 if the shooting is cancelled at the last moment (feed it to friends), and how to handle temperamental ingredients (avoid them) and star-quality special requests (indulge them if the budget's right). She previously created a circa-1948 wedding banquet for Branagh's *Dead Again*. After four days of shooting, her fancy tower of cheeses melted into what McComb called a *quesadilla muerte*. Then Branagh cut the scene from the movie anyway. For *Apollo 13,* McComb spent a full week recreating a 1969 picnic complete with hams and Jell-O molds, and for *Star Trek: The Next Generation,* she found puffy green cakes at an Oriental market that earned her fame as the inventor of "algae puff hors d'oevres."

Zipping by your desk, McComb tosses you a catalogue of food retailers, blurting only one word, "Asparagus." Thank goodness the set is in Vancouver, not London. She means asparagus for 150, and luckily most of your produce suppliers are in California. Flipping through the pages, you come across Mr. Spear, a grower/shipper in the San Joaquin Valley who specializes in overnight retail shipments of jumbo spears, picked in the morning, shipped in the afternoon, on your table the next day–three pounds for $16.95, plus shipping. Quick work with your calculator tells you that you need about 75 pounds, or $424 worth, if you have to pay retail. It's already noon.

You've never worked with Mr. Spear before, but you need the grower to ship the asparagus without prepayment in order to get it to McComb's kitchens by 10 A.M. tomorrow. Standard office practice is to ask for a wholesale price and free shipping when ordering such large amounts. But if those terms aren't available, you'll pay full retail price as long as Mr. Spear can meet the deadline. You'll have to pass on the extra cost to Branagh's ever-growing production budget.

Your Task: Mr. Spear's people will want to review Meg McComb's credentials before they'll ship on credit, so write your request and fax it immediately. Be sure to include a copy of McComb's highly impressive client list. Call the number they list in the catalogue, 1-800-677-7327, to get the fax number.[12]

Developing Your Internet Skills

Going Online: Expand Your Knowledge About Credit, p. 192

Explore the links on this site to learn about credit. What are the different types of credit? What are your responsibilities and rights as a debtor? Review "The Credit Book" and consider how this information might help you in future evaluations of the risk involved in offering credit to a potential client or customer. How will you incorporate this knowledge in any credit refusal letters you might need to write?

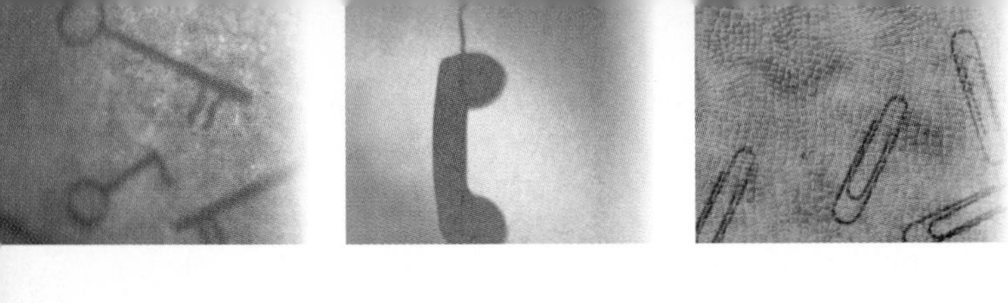

CHAPTER 9

Writing Routine, Good-News, and Goodwill Messages

AFTER STUDYING THIS CHAPTER, YOU WILL BE ABLE TO

1. Adjust the basic organizational pattern to fit the type of message you are writing
2. Add resale and sales promotion material when appropriate
3. Explain the main differences in messages granting a claim when the company, the customer, or a third party is at fault.
4. Write credit approvals and recommendation letters
5. Use the correct form for such specialized messages as instructions
6. Establish the proper tone when writing goodwill letters

ON THE JOB
Facing a Communication Dilemma at Campbell Soup Company

Keeping Millions of People Happy, One Spoonful at a Time

If you worked in consumer response at Campbell's Soup, you'd be in the problem business. You might be like Karen Donohue, who has been a supervisor in the department during her career with the prepared-food giant. You would answer consumer questions and respond to consumer complaints, both of which require strong communication skills and a special talent for working with people.

Working with customers can be a challenge in any business, but consider the size of Campbell's customer base. Every second of every hour, consumers around the world buy 100 packages of Campbell's soups and other products—that's more than 8.6 million purchases every single day. In addition to the well-known soup brands, Campbell's markets Pace Picante sauce, Pepperidge Farm cookies, Prego pasta sauces, V8 vegetable juice, and Spaghetti-Os, among others. Walk into just about any kitchen in North America, and you'll find a Campbell's brand on the shelf.

Campbell's has a history of high-quality products stretching back to the latter 19th century. Soup sales took off after 1897, when an executive in the company, who was also a chemist, figured out how to remove most of the water from soup, making it easier and cheaper to ship long distances. This distribution advantage helped Campbell's become one of the first North American companies to market products nationwide.

In an effort to promote company products as wholesome food that tastes good, the people at Campbell Soup Company do their very best to communicate positive messages to consumers. They also strive to maintain good relationships with fellow employees and outside contacts. All these messages focus on clearly stating the main idea while showing a genuine understanding of the audience.

Campbell's stumbled a bit during the 1980s, thanks in part to changing consumer tastes and some diversification efforts away from the core business lines. However, with new management, new products tailored to local markets, and a narrower focus on key products, Campbell's has been back on track through the late 1990s.

Now the challenge is to maintain that healthy growth as the company continues to hold its own in Canada and the United States and to grow overseas. A consumer response supervisor at Campbell's is an in-house customer advocate, an important link between the public and the research kitchens. In this job, you would be Campbell's eyes and ears, relaying information back to the company while at the same time making sure consumers are satisfied with Campbell's products. If you were Karen Donohue, how would you communicate with the public to answer inquiries and complaints? How would you plan and write positive business messages?[1]

Organizing Positive Messages

LEARNING OUTCOME 1
Adjust the basic organizational pattern to fit the type of message you are writing.

As Campbell Soup's Karen Donohue understands, much business communication consists of messages that present neutral information, answer requests positively, and establish positive relationships, so you'll probably write many **routine, good-news,** and **goodwill messages** on the job. Whether you use letters, memos, e-mail, or phone, understanding how positive messages are organized will allow you to compose them quickly. Of course, as Campbell's Karen Donohue knows, cultural context does influence how business messages are organized (see the box "How Direct Is Too Direct?" in Chapter 8). However, when sending positive messages to audiences in Canada and the US, you will most likely use the direct plan. Begin with a clear statement of the main idea, follow with the relevant details, and end with a courteous close.

Clear Statement of the Main Idea

Organizational plan for routine, good-news, and goodwill messages:
✧ Main point
✧ Details
✧ Close

Almost all business communication has two basic purposes: (1) to convey information and (2) to produce in the audience a favourable (or at least accepting) attitude or response. When you begin a message with a statement of your purpose, you're preparing your audience for the explanation that follows. Make your opening clear and concise. The following introductory statements make the same point; however, one is cluttered with unnecessary information that buries the purpose, whereas the other is brief and to the point:

INSTEAD OF THIS	WRITE THIS
I am pleased to inform you that after deliberating the matter carefully, our human resources committee has recommended you for appointment as a staff accountant.	You've been selected to join our firm as a staff accountant, beginning March 20.

Before you begin, have a clear idea of what you want to say.

The best way to write a clear opening is to have a clear idea of what you want to say. Before you put one word on paper, ask yourself this: What is the single most important message I have for this audience?

Relevant Details

The body of a routine, good-news, or goodwill message develops the main idea. Your reason for communicating can usually be expressed in a sentence or two,

BEHIND THE SCENES WITH CRM SOFTWARE

Big Brother Is Watching You

Your car dealer sends you birthday greetings. Your bank sends a letter announcing a credit card targeted toward your student status. A catalogue company you used last year sends an e-mail asking about your current needs. Your mail box and in-box fill with messages you never asked for, which sometimes seem to pry into your personal life. You are experiencing the results of CRM (Customer Relationship Management) software, one of the most influential electronic communication tools businesses use to maintain and cultivate links with their all-important customers.

CRM software is a powerful tool for cultivating relationships with consumers. But does its ability to record and store information enable unethical business people to invade their customers' privacy?

Norm Francis, president and CEO of Vancouver's Pivotal Software Inc., a major player in the field, says, "CRM is about companies wanting to do a better job interacting with and understanding their customers." Simply put, customer relationship software permits businesses to create databases of information about their customers and clients, current as well as prospective. The database stores essential contact information—addresses, phone numbers—as well as order histories, preferences about when they'd like to be contacted, personal facts such as birth date, anniversary, children's names, kinds of pets, hobbies, and interests. In other words, whatever information a firm can obtain will be stored electronically and accessed whenever that customer has contact with the company, in person, by phone, or over the Internet.

Banks, investment houses, catalogue companies, car dealers and car rental agencies, hotels, and countless other businesses use CRM software. So do non-profit organizations—hospitals and volunteer and social agencies. The reason CRM software has become so popular is obvious: it simplifies the creation of customer profiles and helps a company to target events and occasions in consumers' business and personal lives that might stimulate further sales. For example, hotels may use the product to determine their guests' preferences. You may find your favourite bottled water and chocolate waiting if you ordered these brands on a previous visit. Retailers will send goodwill messages based on personal information: a birthday letter with a discount or upgrade for your next vehicle is common with car rental agencies. Announcements are another favourite: after you've made a but you'll need more space to explain your point completely so that your audience will not be confused. The task of providing information is easiest when you're responding to a series of questions. You can simply answer them in order, possibly in a numbered sequence.

Answer questions in the order they were asked.

In addition to providing details in the body of your positive messages, maintain the supportive tone established at the beginning. This tone is easy to continue when your message is purely good news, as in this example:

> Your educational background and internship have impressed us, and we believe you would be a valuable addition to Green Valley Properties. As discussed during your interview, your salary will be $3 300 per month, plus benefits. In that regard, you will meet with our benefits manager, Paula Sanchez, at 8:00 A.M. on Monday, March 20. She will assist you with all the paperwork necessary to tailor our benefit package to your family situation. She will also arrange for various orientation activities to help you become familiar with our company.

Sometimes a routine or positive message must convey information that will disappoint your audience. When the message includes negative information, put the bad news into as favourable a context as possible. Look at the following example:

INSTEAD OF THIS	WRITE THIS
No, we no longer carry the Sportsgirl line of sweaters.	The new Olympic line has replaced the Sportsgirl sweaters that you asked about. Olympic features a wider range of colours and sizes and more contemporary styling.

large deposit—perhaps a graduation gift or first paycheque—your bank may send a message describing their investment products. CRM software enables business to anticipate their customers' purchasing patterns based on past transactions or life events. A business can manipulate the software so that it is alerted when an occasion makes contact ripe—and potentially fruitful for the sender.

In fact, CRM software is ideal for gathering information from "invisible customers": people whose interactions with companies are through "lower-touch" channels, such as the Internet or debit cards, or through banking machines. Here too CRM software can capture customer data and create a profile to generate messages suited to the purchase patterns these impersonal channels reveal. According to Bob Angel, a senior business consultant with NCR Canada and an expert on CRM products, "Powerful databases ... can store ... detailed information for analysis of complex relationships, account by account. The key is to understand the individual customer's behaviour and to be able to identify when a change occurs."

For generating routine, good-news, and goodwill messages—such as product announcements, special deals, business events of interest to customers—CRM software is hard to beat. It also enables firms to deal with their suppliers more easily: a business place can not only place online orders more efficiently, but it can also review its order history and account information.

But managing a customer relationship with this electronic marvel also has its dangers. How does a company know that the data they're collecting is true? A survey revealed that of the millions of people who interact with firms online, 42% falsify the information they transmit. And how can consumers trust a company to treat their personal and business information ethically? The Canadian Marketing Association has established standards to protect the public from unethical use of personal data: for example, firms must provide a warning before collecting personal information and get permission to pass on names and addresses to other businesses. Without a doubt, the power of CRM software is double-edged: while it can help businesses to retain customers and raise profits, it can violate one of our most prized possessions, our privacy.[2]

APPLY YOUR KNOWLEDGE

1. You work for a company that is considering the purchase of CRM software. Write a brief memo addressed to the Vice-President, Operations, outlining the software's strengths and weaknesses as a tool for sending good-news and goodwill messages.
2. Your e-mail inbox has been filling with spam, or junk e-mail, from an online catalogue company with whom you recently dealt. You are fed up with all the offers of special deals you don't want. Compose an e-mail to the company outlining their obligation to respect your privacy and the action you will take if they continue violating it.

Ann Cavoukian is Ontario's Information and Privacy Commissioner. Her office investigates privacy complaints, ensures compliance with the privacy acts, and educates the public about privacy laws. Cavoukian believes that electronic commerce can succeed only if companies invest in technologies that safeguard their customers' privacy.

A bluntly negative explanation was replaced with a more complete description that emphasized how the audience could benefit from the change. Be careful, though: you can use negative information in this type of message only if you're reasonably sure the audience will respond positively to your message. (Otherwise, use the indirect approach, which is described more thoroughly in Chapter 10.)

Courteous Close

Your message is most likely to succeed if your audience is left with the feeling that you have their personal welfare in mind. In addition, if follow-up action is required, clearly state what your reader should do. By highlighting a benefit to the reader, this closing statement clearly summarizes the desired procedure: "Mail us your order this week so that you can be wearing your Shetland coat by the first of October."

Replying to Requests for Information and Action

Whether sent by snail mail, fax, or e-mail, many memos and letters are written in response to an inquiry or a request. If the answer is yes or is straightforward information, then the direct plan is appropriate. Any request is important to the person making it, whether inside or outside the organization. That person's opinion of your company and its products, your department, and you yourself will be influenced by how promptly, graciously, and thoroughly you handle the request. Readers' perceptions are the reason Campbell's consumer response specialists like Karen Donohue are so sensitive to the tone of their memos, letters, and other messages.

Admittedly, complying with a request isn't always easy. The information may not be immediately at hand, and decisions to take some action must often be made at a higher level. Fortunately, however, many requests are similar. For example, a human resources department gets a lot of inquiries about job openings. Companies usually develop form responses to handle repetitive queries like these. Although form responses are often criticized as being cold and impersonal, you can put a great deal of thought into wording them, and you can use computers to tailor your messages to suit individual needs. Thus a computerized form letter prepared with care may actually be more personal and sincere than a quickly typed, hastily prepared personal reply.

When a Potential Sale Is Involved

LEARNING OUTCOME 2
Add resale and sales promotion material when appropriate.

Prospective customers often request a catalogue, a brochure, a swatch of material, or some other type of sample or information to help them decide whether to buy a product seen in an advertisement. A polite and helpful response may prompt them to buy. However, when the customer has not requested information and is not looking forward to a response, you must use persuasive techniques like those described in Chapter 11. But in a solicited letter that the customer is anticipating, you may use the direct plan.

Three main goals when a potential sale is involved:
- ✧ Respond to the immediate request
- ✧ Encourage a sale
- ✧ Convey a good impression of you and your firm

When you're answering requests and a potential sale is involved, you have three main goals: (1) to respond to the inquiry and answer all questions, (2) to encourage the future sale, and (3) to leave your reader with a good impression of you and your firm. The following letter succeeds in meeting those three objectives:

Thank you for requesting a copy of Radio World's short-wave radio catalogue. You will find in it complete descriptions of our portable and tabletop lines.

A clear statement of the main point is all that's required to start.

You were especially interested in radios under $250.00. Please look at pages 6 to 8, where you will find our compact digital line. The Airtone 200 covers all of the major short-wave bands as well as AM, FM, and long-wave. With the Airtone 200 you can enjoy BBC World Service, Deutsche Welle, Radio Italia Internazionale, Radio Japan, and numerous other stations. The large LCD display shows frequency, station name, city, and time for easy reference.

The Airtone 200 stores up to 40 stations in its memory and features a 12/24 hour clock, dual antennae, earphones, pouch, and handbook. It operates on four AA batteries or the included AC adaptor.

Key information is presented immediately, along with sales promotion.

Radio City sells the Airtone 200 for $199.00, a 20 percent discount off the suggested retail price. We back up all our products with a 30-day satisfaction guarantee and a one-year warranty on parts and labour. We service what we sell in our on-site repair shop, both in and out of warranty.

Describing this product's warranty encourages readers to take one more step toward purchase.

Please call toll-free 1-800-293-0098 to speak with a customer service representative or to order one of our short-wave radios. Imagine the excitement of listening to news and music from almost any country in the comfort of your home.

The personal close confidently points toward the sale.

USING THE POWER OF TECHNOLOGY

Spam: Putting a Lid on It

From exasperated consumers to giant online services, everyone is trying to stamp out irritating electronic junk mail called spam. The Canadian Association of Internet Providers is one organization that is involved in educating the ISP industry on how to control this scourge of cyberspace. If spam is jamming your mailbox, don't wait for governments to step in. You can wage your own counterassault.

Keep a Low Profile

The best way to avoid junk e-mail is to stay off the spammers' lists—which can be difficult. Some marketers use automated robot programs. But savvy surfers can use a few tricks of their own to fool the robots:

- *When possible, use an online alias.* Many Internet service providers (ISPs) allow users to create multiple screen names. Create one to use only in chat rooms and forums, thus hiding your original e-mail address from spammers.
- *Keep your e-mail address unlisted.* Don't list yourself in your ISP's member directory.
- *Alter your e-mail address on bulletin boards.* Use an e-mail address that is recognizable to humans but imperceptible to stupid robot programs. For example, instead of using your real address (Jason@msn.com) disguise it (JasonNOSPAM @NOSPAM.msn.com).

Don't Reply to Spam

No matter how careful you are, you will end up on some spammers' lists. Some junk mail even offers you a civil choice: "If you don't wish to receive any more e-mail, click on the reply button and ask to be removed." But experts warn that replying to spammers is the worst possible reaction. Doing so can actually promote your address to a "premium" spam list—because it's clear that someone is actually reading the e-mail at that account.

Drown Out the Noise

When the barrage of junk e-mail gets to be too much, you can use technology to trash some of it. Most e-mail packages and online services offer filtering programs that try to get rid of stuff you don't want. You can set up a filter (1) by instructing it to accept e-mail from a list of specified users or services, or (2) by instructing it to weed out specific people or services. Of course, no filter is perfect; some desirable e-mail may get tossed out in the process.

Fight Back

You can even take more extreme steps. You might send a complaint to the spammer's ISP. When service providers get a lot of complaints about a mass marketer on their system, they can shut down the account and put the spammer out of business—at least temporarily. So far, Canada has no laws regulating the Internet. In 2000, the CRTC decided not to consider applying the Broadcasting Act to the Internet.

CAREER APPLICATIONS

1. Do you think the Canadian government should create a law to curb unsolicited e-mail? Would such a law violate free speech? Why or why not?
2. Do you think legislation should be created to force senders of unsolicited commercial e-mail to include their name, phone, and address? Would such legislation actually legitimize spamming—making it okay to spam as long as you include your contact information. Why or why not?

Two goals when no sale is involved:
- ✧ Respond to the request
- ✧ Leave a favourable impression of your company or foster good working relationships

When No Potential Sale Is Involved

Some requests from outsiders and most requests from fellow employees are not opportunities to sell a product. In replies to those requests, you have two goals: (1) to answer all the questions honestly and completely and (2) to leave a favourable impression that prepares the way for future business or smoothes working relationships. Figure 9.1 is an e-mail message responding to requests from fellow employees. See the Checklist for Positive Replies to review the primary tasks involved in this type of business message.

FIGURE 9.1

In-Depth Critique: E-Mail Replying to a Routine Request

This message is a reply that the advertising director wrote to a housewares manager whose merchandise wasn't being featured correctly in regional newspaper ads. The tone of the memo, although respectful, is less formal than the tone would be in a message in which a potential sale is involved.

Date: Tuesday, 5 January 2001, 10:15:32
To: "Avery Mendoza, Housewares Manager" <amendoza@lvn.woolworth.com>
From: "Wilimina Simmons" <wsimmons@west.woolworth.com>
Subject: Sale ads for 30 cL glass tumblers

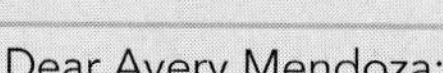

Dear Avery Mendoza:

At last we've traced the problem and have corrected the newspaper ads you alerted us to in your last message:

1. Incorrect stock numbers have been corrected and cross-checked on all paperwork, both at the main warehouse and in advertising.
2. The ads that mistakenly featured 50 cL glass tumblers have been revised to feature the 30 cL glass tumblers you intended.
3. Ad layout people have been alerted to prevent future discrepancies by getting department managers' approval before printing.

The good news is announced without any fanfare. The specific actions are enumerated for easy reference.

Apparently, the housewares vendor transposed the item numbers for these glasses on the packing slips, and the error made its way all the way through inventory at our main warehouse and onto our stock-number sheets here in the advertising department. So every time you sent us your weekly features for 30 cL glass tumblers (stock number HW779-898), our layout people traced the number on our stock sheets and mistakenly came up with 50 cL tumblers.

The problem's cause and eventual solution are explained to demonstrate awareness and goodwill.

I know you had to sell the more expensive 50 cL tumblers for the 30 cL sale price until we could get the ads corrected. I'm sending a message to your store manager, explaining the mix-up and taking full responsibility for it. If there is any way I can help you with ad features in the future, please contact me.

An appreciative, personal, cooperative close confirms the desire to foster good working relationships.

Thanks,

Wilimina Simmons
Regional Advertising Director

Responding Favourably to Claims and Adjustment Requests

LEARNING OUTCOME 3
Explain the main differences in messages granting a claim when the company, the customer, or a third party is at fault.

As anyone in business knows, customers sometimes return merchandise to a company, complain about its services, and ask to be compensated. Such complaints are golden opportunities for companies to build customer loyalty.[3] The most sensible reaction is to assume that the customer's account of the transaction is an honest statement of what happened–unless the same customer repeatedly submits dubious claims, a customer is patently dishonest (returning a dress that has obviously been worn, claiming it's the wrong size), or the dollar amount in dispute is very large. Few people go to the trouble of requesting an adjustment unless they actually have a problem. Once the complaint is made, however, customers may come to view the original transaction as less important than the events that come after the complaint.[4]

In general, it pays to give customers the benefit of the doubt.

The usual human response to a bad situation is to say, "It wasn't my fault!" However, business people like Karen Donohue who receive requests for claims or adjustments can't take that stance. Even when the company's terms of adjustment are generous, a grudging tone can actually increase the customer's dissatisfaction.

An ungracious adjustment may increase customer dissatisfaction.

To protect your company's image and to regain the customer's goodwill, refer carefully to your company's errors. Don't blame an individual or a specific department, and avoid such lame excuses as "Nobody's perfect" or "Mistakes will happen." Don't promise that problems will never happen again; such guarantees are unrealistic and often beyond your control. Instead, explain your company's efforts to do a good job; in so doing, you imply that the error was an unusual incident.

Imagine that a large mail-order clothing company has decided to create a form letter to respond to the hundreds of claims it receives each year. The most common customer complaint is not receiving exactly what was ordered. The form letter can be customized through word processing and individually signed:

> Your letter concerning your recent Kitimat order has been forwarded to our director of order fulfillment. Your complete satisfaction is our goal. Our customer service representative will contact you soon to assist with the issues raised in your letter.
>
> Whether you are skiing or driving a snowmobile, Kitimat Gear offers you the best protection from wind, snow, and cold–and Kitimat has been taking care of your outdoor needs for over 27 years! Because you're a loyal customer, enclosed is a $5 gift certificate. You may wish to consider our new line of quality snow goggles.
>
> Thank you for taking the time to write to us. Your input helps us better serve you and all our customers.

This letter exemplifies the following points:

- Because a form letter like this is sent to people with various types of requests or complaints, it cannot start with a clear good-news statement.
- The letter starts instead with what might be called a "good-attitude" statement; it is *you*-oriented to put the customer at ease.
- At no time does this letter suggest that the customer was mistaken in writing to Kitimat about the order in question.
- The letter includes some resale and sales promotion, made more personal by the use of *you*.
- The letter closes with a statement of the company's concern for all its customers.

You may send form letters in response to claims, but word them carefully so that they are appropriate in a variety of circumstances.

A claim letter written as a personal answer to a unique situation would start with a clear statement of the good news: the settling of the claim according to the customer's request. Here is a more personal response from Kitimat Gear:

> Here is your heather-blue wool-and-mohair sweater (size large) to replace the one returned to us with a defect in the knitting on the left sleeve. Thanks for giving us the opportunity to correct this situation. Customers' needs have come first at Kitimat Gear for 27 years. Our sweaters are handmade by the finest knitters in this area, and Kitimat inspects all our sweaters before sending them on to our customers.
>
> Our newest catalogue is enclosed. Browse through it, and see what wonderful new colours and patterns we have for you. Whether you are skiing or driving a snowmobile, Kitimat Gear offers you the best protection available from wind, snow, and cold. Let us know how we may continue to serve you and your sporting needs.

Suppose that a customer is technically wrong (he washed a permanent-press shirt in hot water) but feels he's right ("The washing instructions were impossible to find!"). Remember that refusing to make an adjustment may mean losing that customer as well as many of the customer's friends, who will hear only one side of the dispute. It makes sense, therefore, to weigh the cost of making the adjustment against the cost of losing future business from one or more customers.

When complying with an unjustified claim, let the customer know that the merchandise was mistreated, but maintain a respectful and positive tone.

If you choose not to contest the claim, start off with a statement of the good news: You're replacing the merchandise or refunding the purchase price. The explanatory section needs more attention, however. Your job is to make the customer realize that the merchandise was mistreated without falling into a condescending tone ("Perhaps you failed to read the instructions carefully") or preachy ("Next time, please allow the machine to warm up before using it at full power"). Keep in mind that a courteous tone is especially important to the success of your message, regardless of the solution you propose. For example, an explanation of correct handling might be phrased in the following way:

> Our washing instructions, included on the tag attached to the sweater as well as the label sewn into the seam, indicate that the sweater should be washed by hand in cold water using a detergent specially formulated for wool garments, or dry cleaned. Following these methods ensures that the sweater will retain its original shape.

Note that the explanation is straightforward and objective; it doesn't cast blame on the customer.

At times a customer will submit a legitimate claim for a defect or damage that was not caused by either of you. If the merchandise was damaged while in transit,

Checklist for Positive Replies

A. Initial Statement of the Good News or Main Idea

1. Respond promptly to the request.
2. Indicate in your first sentence that you are shipping the customer's order or fulfilling the reader's request.
3. Avoid such trite and obvious statements as "I am pleased to," "We have received," "This is in response to," or "Enclosed please find."
4. If you are acknowledging an order, summarize the transaction.
   a. Describe the merchandise in general terms.
   b. Express appreciation for the order and the payment, if they have arrived.
   c. Welcome a new customer aboard.
5. Convey an upbeat, courteous, *you*-oriented tone.

B. Middle, Informational Section

1. Imply or express interest in the request.
2. If possible, answer all questions and requests, preferably in the order posed.
   a. Adapt replies to the reader's needs.
   b. Indicate what you have done and will do.
   c. Include any details or interpretations that the reader may need in order to understand your answers.
3. Provide all the important details about orders.
   a. Provide any necessary educational information about the product.
   b. Provide details of the shipment, including the approximate arrival time.

the carrier is responsible. If the defect was caused by the manufacturer, you have a claim for replacement from that firm.

When a third party is at fault, you have three options: (1) Honour the customer's claim with the standard good-news letter and no additional explanation; (2) honour the claim but explain that you were not really at fault; or (3) take no action on the claim and suggest that your customer file against the firm that caused the defect or damage. Common business sense tells you, however, that the third option is almost always a bad choice. The exception is when you're trying to dissociate yourself from any legal responsibility for the damaged merchandise, especially if it has caused a personal injury, in which case you would send a bad-news message.

Three options when a third party is at fault:
- ✧ Honour the claim
- ✧ Honour the claim with an explanation of what went wrong
- ✧ Refer the customer to the third party for satisfaction of the claim

Of the other two options, the first is more attractive. By honouring the claim without explanation, you are maintaining your reputation for fair dealing at no cost to yourself; the carrier or manufacturer that caused the damage in the first place will reimburse you. To review the tasks involved in this type of message, see this chapter's Checklist for Favourable Responses to Claims and Adjustment Requests.

Approving Routine Credit Requests

LEARNING OUTCOME 4
Write credit approvals and recommendation letters.

These days, much of our economy runs on credit. Consumers often carry a wallet full of credit cards, and businesses of all sizes operate more smoothly because they can pay for their purchases over time. Because credit is so common, most credit requests are routine.

Letters approving credit are good-news messages and the first step in what may be a decades-long business relationship. So open your letter with the main idea.

In the middle section, include a reasonably full statement of the credit arrangements: the upper limit of the account, dates that bills are sent, possible arrangements for partial monthly payments, discounts for prompt payments, interest charges for unpaid balances, and due dates. State the terms positively and objectively, not negatively or in an authoritarian manner:

State credit terms factually and in terms of the benefits of having credit.

INSTEAD OF THIS	WRITE THIS
Your credit balance cannot exceed $5000.	With our standard credit account, you can order up to $5000 worth of fine merchandise.
We expect your payment within 30 days of receipt of our statement.	Payment is due 30 days after you receive our statement.

c. Clear up any questions of charges (shipping costs, insurance, credit charges, or discounts for quick payment).

4. Use sales opportunities when appropriate.
   a. Enclose a brochure that provides routine information and specifications, if possible, pointing out its main value and the specific pages of potential interest to the reader.
   b. Call the customer's attention to related products with sales promotion material.
   c. Introduce price only after mentioning benefits, but make price and the method of payment clear.
   d. Send a credit application to new customers and cash customers, if desirable.

5. If you cannot comply with part of the request, perhaps because the information is unavailable or confidential, tell the reader why and offer other assistance.

6. Embed negative statements in positive contexts, or balance them with positive alternatives.

C. Warm, Courteous Close

1. Direct a request to the reader (such as "Please let us know if this procedure does not have the effect you're seeking") or specify the action you want the reader to take, if appropriate.
   a. Make the reader's action easy to perform.
   b. Refer to the reader benefit of fulfilling your request.
   c. Encourage the reader to act promptly.

2. Use resale material when acknowledging orders to remind the reader of benefits to be derived from this order.

3. Offer additional service, but avoid suggestions of your answer's being inadequate, such as "I trust that," "I hope," or other statements that imply doubt.

4. Express goodwill or take an optimistic look into the future, if appropriate.

Include resale and sales promotion information in a credit letter.

Because a letter approving credit can have significant implications for a business's financial health, it is essential to check the wording for accuracy, completeness, and clarity.

The final section of the letter provides resale information and sales promotion highlighting the benefits of buying from you. The following letter was written both to approve credit and to bring in customers:

The good-news opening gets right to the point.

> Congratulations! Your credit application to Jake's Building Centre has been approved, with $3000 in credit available to you. Just use the enclosed card when you shop at any of our three Jake's Building Centres. With this card, you can purchase tools, appliances, paint, plumbing and electrical supplies, lawn products, and much more.

An objective statement of the terms constitutes a legal contract. Positive, you-oriented wording avoids an authoritarian tone.

> Our statements are sent out on the twentieth of each month and will list each credit purchase, the total amount due, and the monthly payment due. If you pay the total amount by the fifteenth of the following month, no interest is charged. If you elect to pay the smaller monthly amount, interest will be calculated at the rate of 1.5 percent a month on the amount still owed and added to your next statement.

The courteous close provides resale for the store and sales promotion noting a range of customer benefits.

> Jake's Building Centres are located in Edmonton, Dawson Creek, and Jasper, with free delivery within 50 km of each store. Come to us for everything you need to build, repair, or remodel your home or business. Count on our high quality and low prices whenever you purchase one of our top-of-the-line products. Come see us for your next building project!

See this chapter's Checklist for Credit Approvals to quickly review the tasks involved in this type of message.

Checklist for Favourable Responses to Claims and Adjustment Requests

A. Initial Statement of the Good News or Main Idea

1. State immediately your willingness to honor the reader's claim.
2. Accept your reader's account as entirely accurate unless good business reasons demand a different interpretation of some points.
3. Adopt a tone of consideration and courtesy; avoid being defensive, recriminatory, or condescending.
4. Thank the reader for taking the time to write.

B. Middle, Informational Section

1. Minimize or, if possible, omit any disagreements with your reader's interpretation of events.
2. Maintain a supportive tone through such phrases as "Thank you for," "May we ask," "Please let us know," and "We are glad to work with you."
3. Apologize only under extreme circumstances; then do so crisply and without an overly apologetic tone.
4. Admit your firm's faults carefully.
   a. Avoid blaming any particular person or office.
   b. Avoid implying general company inefficiency.
   c. Avoid blaming probability ("Mistakes will happen").
   d. Avoid making unrealistic promises about the future.
   e. Remind the reader of your firm's quality controls.
5. Be careful when handling the customer's role in producing the problem.
   a. If appropriate, honour the claim in full but without negative comment.
   b. If appropriate, provide an objective, non-vindictive, impersonal explanation.

C. Warm, Courteous Close

1. Clarify any necessary actions that your reader must take.
2. Remind the reader of how you have honoured the claim.
3. Avoid negative information.
4. Encourage the customer to look favourably on your company and/or the product in question (resale information).
5. Encourage the customer to continue buying other goods from you (sales promotion), but avoid seeming greedy.

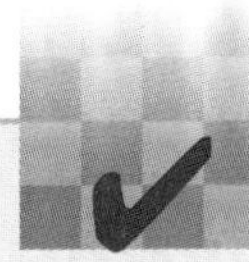

Checklist for Credit Approvals

A. Initial Statement of the Good News or Main Idea

1. Cheerfully tell the reader that he or she now has approved credit with your firm.
2. Tell the reader, with brief resale, that he or she will soon be enjoying the use of any goods that were ordered with the request; specify the date and method of shipment and other purchase details.
3. Establish a tone of mutual warmth and trust.

B. Middle, Informational Section

1. Explain the conditions under which credit was granted.
2. Include or attach a full explanation of your firm's credit policies and expectations of payment.
3. Stress the advantages of prompt payment in a way that assumes your reader will take advantage of them ("When you pay your account in full within ten days ...").
4. Include disclosure statements.
5. Inform or remind the reader of the general benefits of doing business with your firm (resale).
   a. Tell the consumer about free parking, mail and phone shopping, personalized shopping services, your home-decorating bureau, bridal consultants, restaurants, child care, gift wrapping, free deliveries, special discounts or purchase privileges, and other benefits, if your firm offers them.
   b. If the customer is a retailer or wholesaler, tell about nearby warehouses, factory representatives, quantity discounts, free window or counter displays, national advertising support, ads for local newspapers and other media, repair services, manuals, factory guarantees, prompt and speedy deliveries, toll-free phone number, research department, and other benefits, if your firm offers them.
6. Inform or remind the reader of a special sale, discount, or promotion (sales promotion).
7. Avoid exaggerations or flamboyant language that might make this section of your letter read like an advertisement.

C. Warm, Courteous Close

1. Summarize the reasons the reader will enjoy doing business with your firm.
2. Use the "you" attitude, and avoid clichés.
3. Invite the reader to a special sale or the like or provide resale information to motivate him or her to use the new account.

Conveying Positive Information About People

Many circumstances call for writing a letter of recommendation. Professors write letters of reference for students seeking jobs. A manager can be asked for a letter recommending an employee for an award. You may write a letter for a neighbour seeking to join a club. Such letters may take the direct approach when the recommendation is generally positive. Employers use the same type of organizational plan when telling job applicants the good news—that they got the job.

Recommendation Letters

Letters of recommendation have an important goal: to convince readers that the person being recommended has the characteristics required for the job or other benefit. It is important, therefore, that they contain all the relevant details:

- The full name of the candidate
- The job or benefit that the candidate is seeking
- Whether the writer is answering a request or taking the initiative
- The nature of the relationship between the writer and the candidate
- Facts relevant to the position or benefit sought
- The writer's overall evaluation of the candidate's suitability for the job or benefit sought

Use concrete, specific examples to convince the reader when the candidate is outstanding.

Recommendation letters are usually confidential; that is, they're sent directly to the person or committee who requested them and are not shown to the candidate. However, some colleges and universities use an application-for-reference form that includes a confidentiality option. Students can check a box indicating that they want to read the recommendation after their referee has completed it.

Oddly enough, the most difficult recommendation letters to write are those for truly outstanding candidates. Your audience will have trouble believing uninterrupted praise for someone's talents and accomplishments. So illustrate your general points with specific examples that point out the candidate's abilities.

A recommendation letter presenting negatives may be carefully worded to satisfy both the candidate and the person or company requesting the information.

Most candidates aren't perfect, however. Omitting reference to a candidate's shortcomings may be tempting, especially if the shortcomings are irrelevant to the demands of the job in question. Even so, you have an obligation to your audience, to your own conscience, and even to the better-qualified candidate who's relying on honest references, to refer to any shortcoming that is serious and related to job performance.

A serious shortcoming cannot be ignored, but beware of being libellous:

- ✧ Include only relevant, factual information
- ✧ Avoid value judgments
- ✧ Balance criticisms with favourable points

The danger in writing a critical letter is that you might **libel** the person–that is, make a false and malicious written statement that injures the candidate's reputation. On the other hand, if the negative information is truthful and relevant, it may be unethical and illegal to omit it from a recommendation. So if you must refer to a possible shortcoming, you can best protect yourself by providing the specific facts that support your statements and by consulting with the legal department in your organization on the issues relating to the reference.[5]

You can also avoid trouble by asking yourself the following questions before sending a recommendation letter:

- ➢ Does the person receiving this frank, personal information have a legitimate right to the information?
- ➢ Is all the information I have presented related directly to the job or other benefit being sought?
- ➢ Have I put the candidate's case as strongly and as honestly as I can?
- ➢ Have I avoided overstating the candidate's abilities or otherwise misleading the reader?
- ➢ Have I based all my statements on first-hand knowledge and provable facts?

Suncor Energy's Human Resources Management System is a valuable tool for helping management communicate effectively with employees, notes Sue Lee, Suncor's senior Vice-President of Human Resources and Communications. "The wealth of information tracked and stored in this database helps communicators develop better communication strategies and plans by better understanding their employee audience," she says. Routine communication is one way Suncor keeps employees informed.

Good News About Employment

Finding suitable job applicants and then selecting the right person is a task fraught with hard choices and considerable anxiety. In contrast, writing a letter to the successful applicant is a pleasure. Most of the time, such a letter is eagerly awaited, so the direct approach is appropriate:

> Welcome to Lake Valley Rehabilitation Centre. A number of excellent candidates were interviewed, but your educational background and recent experience at Memorial Hospital make you the best person for the position of medical records coordinator.
>
> As we discussed, your salary is $39 400 a year. We would like you to begin on Monday, February 1. Please come to my office at 8:00 A.M. I will give you an in-depth orientation to Lake Valley and discuss the various company benefits available to you. You can also sign all the necessary employment documents.
>
> After lunch, Vanessa Jackson will take you to the Medical Records department and help you settle in to your new responsibilities at Lake Valley Home. I look forward to seeing you on February 1.

This letter takes a friendly, welcoming tone, and it explains the necessary details: job title, starting date, salary, and benefits. The explanation of the first day's routine helps allay the bewilderment and uncertainty that might bother the new employee.

Although letters like these are pleasant to write, it is usual to have a supervisor or human resources specialist read them for accuracy.

A letter telling someone that she or he got the job is a legal document, so make sure all statements are accurate.

Writing Directives and Instructions

LEARNING OUTCOME 5
Use the correct form for such specialized messages as instructions

Directives are memos that tell employees *what* to do. Instructions tell people inside and outside the company *how* to do something and may take the form of e-mail messages, memos, letters, or even booklets. Directives and instructions are both considered routine messages because readers are assumed to be willing to comply.

The goal in writing directives and instructions is to make the point so obvious and the steps so self-explanatory that readers won't have to ask for additional help. Directives and instructions are especially important within companies: Faulty internal directives and bungled instructions are expensive and inefficient. The following directive does a good job of explaining what employees are expected to do:

Directives tell employees what to do; instructions tell readers how to do something.

> New security badges will be issued to all employees between January 20 and January 24. Each employee must report in person to the Human Resources Office (Building B, Room 106) to exchange the old (red) security badges for the new (yellow) security badges. The electronic security system will not recognize the old badges on February 1 and thereafter.
>
> If you are unable to make this exchange between January 20 and January 24, contact Theresa Gomez before January 15 either by phone at 4-6721 or by e-mail at <tgomez@biotech.com>.

In our highly technological world, instructions must accompany the computers that make our work and daily lives easier. Users must read the manuals that accompany popular electronic devices like the *personal digital assistant*, or PDA, in order to enjoy their full benefits for managing time, maintaining contact lists, jotting memos, and many other applications.

This directive is brief and to the point. Drawn-out explanations are unnecessary because readers are expected simply to follow through on a well-established procedure. Yet it also covers all the bases, answering these questions: Who? What? When? Where? Why? How?

Instructions answer the same questions, but they differ from directives in the amount of explanation they provide. You might write a simple three-sentence directive to employees to tell them of a change in the policies regarding employee scholarships; however, a detailed set of instructions would be more appropriate to explain the procedure for applying for a scholarship.

When writing instructions, take nothing for granted. Assuming that readers know nothing about the process you're describing is better than risking confusion and possible damage or harm by overlooking some basic information. Figure 9.2 is a set of instructions for writing instructions.

Writing Business Summaries

Business people are bombarded with masses of information, and at one time or another, everyone in business relies on someone else's summary of a situation, publication, or document. To write a summary, gather the information (whether by reading, talking with others, or observing circumstances), organize that information, and then present it in your own words. Although many people assume that summarizing is a simple skill, it's actually more complex than it appears. A well-written summary has at least three characteristics.

Writing summaries involves
- ✧ Gathering information
- ✧ Organizing information
- ✧ Presenting information in your own words

How to Write Useful Instructions

When you need to explain in writing how to do something, a set of step-by-step instructions is your best choice. By enumerating the steps, you make it easy for readers to perform the process in the correct sequence. Your goal is to provide a clear, self-sufficient explanation so that readers can perform the task independently.

Gather Equipment
1. Writing materials (pen and paper, computer, typewriter)
2. Background materials (previous memos, policy manuals, manufacturer's booklets, etc.)
3. When necessary, the apparatus being explained (machine, software package, or other equipment)

Prepare
1. Perform the task yourself, or ask experts to demonstrate it or describe it to you in detail.
2. Analyze prospective readers' familiarity with the process so that you can write instructions at their level of understanding.

Make Your Instructions Clear
1. Include four elements: an introduction, a list of equipment and materials, a description of the steps involved in the process, and a conclusion.
2. Explain in the opening why the process is important and how it is related to a larger purpose.
3. Divide the process into short, simple steps presented in order of occurrence.
4. Present the steps in a numbered list, or if presenting them in paragraph format, use words indicating time or sequence, such as first and then.
5. If the process involves more than ten steps, divide them into groups or stages identified with headings.
6. Phrase each step as a command ("Do this" instead of "You should do this"); use active verbs ("Look for these signs" instead of "Be alert for these signs"); use precise, specific terms ("three weeks" instead of "several weeks").
7. When appropriate, describe how to tell whether a step has been performed correctly and how one step may influence another. Warn readers of possible damage or injury from a mistake in a step, but limit the number of warnings so that readers do not underestimate their importance.
8. Include diagrams of complicated devices, and refer to them in appropriate steps.
9. Summarize the importance of the process and the expected results.

Test Your Instructions
1. Review the instructions to be sure they are clear and complete. Also judge whether you have provided too much detail.
2. Ask someone else to read the instructions and tell you whether they make sense and are easy to follow.

FIGURE 9.2
Instructions for Writing Instructions

Three characteristics of a well-written summary:
- ✧ Accuracy
- ✧ Comprehensiveness and balance
- ✧ Clear sentence structure and good transitions

First, as in writing any business document, be sure the content is accurate. If you're summarizing a report or a group of reports, make sure you present the information without error. Check your references, and then check for typos.

Second, make your summary comprehensive and balanced. The purpose of writing your summary is usually to help colleagues or supervisors make a decision, so include all the information necessary for your readers to understand the situation, problem, or proposal. If the issue you're summarizing has more than one side, present all sides fairly and equitably. Make sure you include all the information necessary. Even though summaries are intended to be as brief as possible, your readers need a minimum amount of information to grasp the issue being presented.

Third, make your sentence structure clear, and include good transitions.[6] The only way your summary will save anyone's time is if your sentences are uncluttered, use well-chosen words, and proceed logically. Then, to help your readers move from one point to the next, your transitions must be just as clear and logical. When writing your summary, be sure to cut through the clutter. Identify those ideas that belong together, and organize them in a way that's easy to understand.[7]

Writing Goodwill Messages

LEARNING OUTCOME 6
Establish the proper tone when writing goodwill letters.

Business isn't all business. To a great extent, it's an opportunity to forge personal relationships. You can enhance your relationships with customers and with other business people by sending friendly, unexpected notes with no direct business purpose. Goodwill messages like these have a positive effect on business because people prefer to deal with organizations that are warm and human and interested in more than just money.

Goodwill is the positive feeling that encourages people to maintain a business relationship.

Such goodwill messages might be considered manipulative and thus unethical unless you make every attempt to be sincere, honest, and truthful. Without sincerity, skillful writing is nothing more than clever, revealing the writer as interested only in personal gain and not in benefiting customers or fellow workers. One way to come across as sincere is to avoid exaggeration. What do you think a reader's reaction would be to these two sentences?

Make sure your messages are grounded in reality.

> We were overjoyed to learn of your promotion.
>
> Congratulations on your promotion.

Most likely, your audience wouldn't quite believe that anyone (except perhaps a relative or very close friend) would be "overjoyed." On the other hand, readers will accept your simple congratulations–a human, understandable intention.

To demonstrate your sincerity, back up any compliments with specific points:

INSTEAD OF THIS	WRITE THIS
Words cannot express my appreciation for the great job you did. Thanks. No one could have done it better. You're terrific! You've made the whole firm sit up and take notice, and we are ecstatic to have you working here.	Thanks for taking charge of the meeting in my absence. You did an excellent job. With just an hour's notice, you managed to pull the legal and public relations departments together so that we could present a united front in the negotiations. Your dedication and communication abilities have been noted and are truly appreciated.

Note also the difference in the words used in these two examples. Your reader would probably believe the more restrained praise to be more sincere. Offering help in a goodwill message is fine, but promise only what you can and will provide. Avoid giving even the impression of an offer of help when none is intended.

Offer help only when you are able and willing to provide it.

Although goodwill messages have little to do with business transactions, they might include some sales information if you have the opportunity to be of particular service or want to remind the reader of your company's product. However, any sales message should be subdued and secondary to the helpful, thoughtful message. In the following example, the owner of a children's clothing shop succeeds in establishing a relationship with the new mother at a very special time in her life:

If a sales pitch ever appears in a goodwill message, make it only the slightest hint.

> Congratulations on the birth of your son at Valleyfield Memorial Hospital. Nothing matches the joy of a new mother welcoming her tiny baby into the

> world. To commemorate this joyful occasion, Bundles from Heaven is sending you this special gift–a beautifully illustrated book for you to keep track of all the important events in your son's life.
>
> Our shop serves Valleyfield, meeting the clothing and equipment needs of babies like yours. That's our only business. Stop in sometime and introduce us to your little son!

The mothers receiving this letter won't feel a great deal of pressure to buy but will feel that the owner took notice of this very special event in their lives. If you include a sales pitch in this type of letter, make sure that it takes a back seat to your goodwill message. Honesty and sincerity must come across above all else.

Going Online

Send an Electronic Goodwill Message

Send a free electronic greeting card from the My Sentiments Fine Art Greeting Cards collection. You can choose from a variety of backgrounds and even add music. Many languages are available. Recipients will receive an e-mail notice that a greeting is waiting for them. Consider using these cards for holidays, birthdays, or announcing a new product or service.

www.bluemountain.com

Congratulations

One prime opportunity for sending congratulations is news of a significant business achievement: for example, being promoted or attaining an important civic position. Highlights in people's personal lives–weddings and births, graduations, success in non-business competitions–are another reason for sending congratulations. You may congratulate business acquaintances on their achievements or on their spouse's or children's achievements. You may also take note of personal events, even if you don't know the reader well. Of course, if you're already friendly with the reader, you may use a personal tone.

Taking note of significant events in someone's personal life helps cement the business relationship.

Some alert companies develop a mailing list of potential customers by assigning an employee to clip newspaper announcements of births, engagements, weddings, and graduations or by obtaining information on real estate transactions in the local community. Then they introduce themselves by sending out a form letter that might read like this:

> Congratulations on your new home! Our wish is that it brings you much happiness.
>
> To help you commemorate the occasion, we've enclosed a key chain with your new address engraved on the leather tab. Please accept this with our best wishes.

In this case, the company's letterhead is enough of a sales pitch. This simple message has a natural, friendly tone, even though the sender has never met the recipient.

Messages of Appreciation

A message of appreciation documents a person's contributions.

An important managerial quality is the ability to see employees (and other business associates) as individuals and to recognize their contributions (Figure 9.3). People often value praise more highly than monetary rewards. A message of appreciation may also become an important part of an employee's personnel file.

With its references to specific qualities and deeds, this note may provide support for future pay increases and promotions.

Anyone who does you or your organization a special favour should receive written thanks.

Suppliers also like to know that you value some exceptional product or the service you received. Long-term support deserves recognition too. Your praise doesn't just make the supplier feel good; it also encourages further excellence. The brief message that follows expresses gratitude and reveals the happy result:

> Thank you for sending the air-conditioning components via overnight delivery. You allowed us to satisfy the needs of two customers who were getting very impatient with the heat.
>
> Special thanks to Susan Brown who took our initial call and never said "it can't be done." We greatly appreciate her initiative on our behalf.

From: Amir Rizvi, Vice-President, Sales and Marketing
To: Miriam David, Finance
Cc: Eric Jaegar, Human Resources
Date: September 16, 2000
Subject: Thank you

Thank you for creating the computerized spreadsheets to track our marketing efforts and sales by both region and product. Your understanding of the scope of this division's responsibilities is evident in the spreadsheets' detail and thoroughness.

I particularly appreciate the historical data you included and the fine documentation and training you provided. Because of your efforts, the marketing staff will be able to manipulate and update the data easily.

Your talents in judging the scope of the project, executing it on time, and following through with the final details are a great asset to our division.

The reason for congratulating the reader is expressed early and concisely.

The compliment is most effective when coupled with statements that show your knowledge of the recipient's work.

The message ends with remarks on the recipient's general management skills.

FIGURE 9.3

In-depth Critique: E-mail message of appreciation to employee

This sample note of appreciation immediately gets to the point and cites the details that justify the message. With its references to specific qualities and deeds, this note may provide support for future pay increases and promotions.

When you write a message of appreciation to a supplier, try to mention specifically the person or people you want to praise. Your expression of goodwill might net the employee some future benefit. In any case, your message honours the company the individual represents.

Be sure to thank guest speakers at meetings, even if they've been paid an honorarium or their travel expenses–and surely if they have not. They may have spent hours gathering and organizing material for an informative and interesting presentation, so reward their hard work. Messages of appreciation are also appropriate for acknowledging donations to campaigns or causes. They usually include a few details about the success of the campaign or how the funds are being used so that the donors will feel good about having contributed.

Steinway & Sons manufactures pianos and wants them to be played by such special artists as Elton John and Vladimir Ashkenazy. As vice-president of the worldwide concert and artist department, Peter Goodrich uses goodwill messages to let these artists know that "we are thinking about them and that we appreciate the fact that they play our pianos."

Condolences

In times of serious trouble and deep sadness, people appreciate receiving written condolences and expressions of sympathy. Granted, such messages are hard to write, but don't let the difficulty of the task keep you from responding promptly. Those who have experienced a health problem, the death of a loved one, or a business misfortune like to know they're not alone.

Begin condolences with a brief statement of sympathy, such as "I was deeply sorry to hear of your loss." In the middle, mention the good qualities or the positive contributions made by the deceased. State what the person or business meant to you. In closing, you can offer your condolences and your best wishes. One considerate way to end this type of message is to say something that will give the reader a little lift, such as a reference to a brighter future.

You're not obligated to offer help to the reader; a good condolence message is often help enough. However, if you want to and can offer assistance, do so. Remember, the bereaved and grieving often suffer financially as well as emotionally, and re-establishing a business or a life often takes a great deal of time and effort. A simple gesture on your part may mean much to the reader.

Here are a few general suggestions for writing condolence messages:

- *Keep reminiscences brief.* Recount a memory or an anecdote (even a humorous one), but don't dwell on the details of the loss, lest you add to the reader's anguish.
- *Write in your own words.* Write as if you were speaking privately to the person. Don't quote "poetic" passages or use stilted or formal phrases. If the loss is a death, refer to it as such rather than as "passing away" or "departing."
- *Be tactful.* Mention your shock and dismay, but keep in mind that the bereaved and distressed loved ones take little comfort in such lines as, "Richard was too young to die" or "Starting all over again will be so difficult." Try to strike a balance between superficial expressions of sympathy and heartrending references to a happier past and a possibly bleak future.
- *Take special care.* Be sure to spell names correctly and to be accurate in your review of facts.
- *Write about special qualities of the deceased.* You may have to rely on reputation to do this, but let the grieving person know the value of her or his loved one.
- *Write about special qualities of the bereaved person.* A few simple words of encouragement may help a bereaved family member feel more confident about handling things during such a traumatic time.[8]

In condolence messages, try to find a middle path between being superficial and causing additional distress.

Checklist for Goodwill Messages

A. Planning Goodwill Messages

1. Choose the appropriate type of goodwill message for your purpose.
   a. Offer congratulations to make the reader feel noticed.
   b. Express praise or thanks to show your appreciation for good performance.
   c. Offer condolences to show appreciation for the deceased or the person suffering a loss.
2. Be prompt when sending out goodwill messages so that they lose none of their impact.
3. Send a written goodwill message rather than a verbal one by telephone, because a written message can be enjoyed more than once; but realize that a telephone message is better than none at all.

B. Format

1. Use the format most appropriate to the occasion.
   a. Use letter format for condolences and for any other goodwill message sent to outsiders or mailed to an employee's home.
   b. Use memo format for any goodwill messages sent through interoffice mail, except for condolences.
2. Hand-write condolences (and replies to handwritten invitations); otherwise, type the goodwill message.
3. Use personalized stationery, if available.
4. For added impact, present congratulations in a folder with a clipping or photo commemorating the special event.

C. Opening

1. State the most important idea first to focus the reader's attention.
2. Incorporate a friendly statement that builds goodwill right at the beginning.
3. Focus on the good qualities of the person or situation.

D. Middle

1. Provide sufficient details, even in a short message, to justify the opening statement.
2. Express personalized details in sincere, not gushy, language.
3. Be warm but concise.
4. Make the reader, not the writer, the focus of all comments.

E. Close

1. Use a positive or forward-looking statement.
2. Restate the important idea, when appropriate.

Above all, don't let the fear of saying something wrong keep you from saying anything at all. A supervisor, George Bigalow, sent the following condolence letter to his administrative assistant, Janice Case, after learning of the death of Janice's husband:

> My sympathy to you and your children. All your friends at Carter Electric were so very sorry to learn of John's death. Although I never had the opportunity to meet him, I do know how very special he was to you. Your tales of your family's camping trips and his rafting expeditions were always memorable.

A few kind words can go a very long way.

ON THE JOB
Solving a Communication Dilemma at Campbell Soup Company

Campbell Soup has been steadily climbing away from its past business troubles with solid performance throughout the 1990s. Products matched to local and regional tastes and carefully chosen acquisitions continue to help the company grow. For example, Germany and France are two of the largest soup-consuming markets in the world (the French consume four times as much soup per capita as people in the United States do), and Campbell has lately made major acquisitions in both countries. The company barely turned a profit in 1990, but it earned more than $714 million in 2000 (on sales of $6.27 billion).

With growth come more customers, of course, and more customers mean more questions for Campbell's consumer-response supervisors, like Karen Donohue. Whenever people write, phone, or send e-mail, these specialists are in charge of making sure questions and complaints are answered satisfactorily. Many of the questions are routine and repetitive ("What are the most popular flavours of Campbell's Soup?"), but many others require special, personalized communication skills.

Like many companies these days, Campbell uses the World Wide Web as a two-way communication vehicle between the company and its customers. The company's home page provides links to recipes, financial and investment news, educational support programs, and an online store, as well as the consumer response centre. Here, specialists like Donohue answers some of the most frequently asked questions (for example: How many Os are in a 15-ounce can of Spaghetti-Os? Answer: 1750), and she invites consumers to e-mail other questions and comments. Consumers who wish to speak with a Campbell's representative instead of sending e-mail can call a toll-free number listed on-screen.

Not surprisingly, workers like Karen Donohue play a major role in Campbell's efforts to better meet the needs of its millions of customers worldwide. The job of consumer-response staff is to assist dissatisfied customers and answer simple questions. But, while helping to satisfy customers, they can also gain important insights into consumers' needs and purchasing behaviours. As Campbell continues in this millennium, the consumer marketing staff will be communicating with customers and employees to make sure the giant food producer keeps sales and profits cooking.[9]

Your Mission: You have joined Campbell's consumer marketing staff. You are responsible for handling correspondence with both consumers and Campbell employees. Your objective is to improve the flow of communication between the public and the company so that Campbell can respond quickly and knowledgeably to changing consumer needs. Choose the best alternatives for responding to the situations described below, and be prepared to explain why your choice is best.

1. Donohue has received a letter from a Mrs. Felton who is pleased that Campbell offers a line of Healthy Request reduced-sodium soups but would like to see more flavours added. Which of the following is the best opening paragraph for your reply?

   a. The Campbell Soup Company was founded in 1869 in Camden, New Jersey. The Dorrance family took control from the founders in 1894. At the turn of the century, John Dorrance invented the soup condensation process, which enabled the company to sell a 10-ounce can for a dime. He was a conservative man and a stickler for quality. His only son, the late Jack Dorrance, followed his father into the business and had a similar management philosophy. As chairperson of the company, he used to pinch the tomatoes and taste the carrots occasionally to be sure that the folks in the factory were maintaining high standards. Mr. Dorrance took personal interest in the development of the low-salt line and would be pleased to know that it appeals to you.
   b. Thank you for your enthusiastic letter about Campbell's Healthy Request soups. We are delighted that you enjoy the flavours currently available, and we are working hard to add new varieties to the line.
   c. Good news! Our world-renowned staff of food technologists is busy in the test kitchen at this very moment, experimenting with additional low-sodium recipes for Healthy Request soups. Hang on to your bowl, Mrs. Felton, more flavours are on the way!

2. Which of the following versions is preferable for the middle section of the letter to Mrs. Felton?

   a. You can expect to see several exciting new Healthy Request soups on your supermarket shelf within the next year. Before the new flavours make their debut, however, they must undergo further testing in our kitchens and in selected markets across the country. We want to be sure our soups satisfy consumer expectations.

      While you're waiting for the new flavours of Healthy Request, you might like to try some of Campbell's other products designed especially for people like you who are concerned about health and nutrition. I'm enclosing coupons that entitle you to sample both Pepperidge Farm Five-Star Fibre bread and Pace Picante sauce "on the house." We hope you enjoy them.

   b. We are sorry that the number of Healthy Request flavours is limited at this time. Because of the complexities of testing flavours both in the Campbell kitchens and in test markets around the country, we are a bit behind schedule in releasing new varieties. But several new flavours should be available by the end of the year, if all goes according to plan. In the meantime, please accept these coupons; they can be redeemed for two other fine Campbell products designed for the health-conscious consumer.

   c. Additional flavours of Healthy Request reduced-sodium soups are currently in formulation. They will arrive on supermarket shelves soon. In the meantime, why not enjoy some of Campbell's other fine products designed for the health-conscious consumer? The enclosed coupons will allow you to sample Pace Picante sauce and Pepperidge Farm Five-Star Fibre bread at our expense.

3. Campbell has received a letter from the Heart and Stroke Foundation asking for information on the fat and sodium content of Campbell's products. Your department has developed a brochure that provides the necessary data, and you plan to send it to the association. Which of the following cover letters should you send along with the brochure?

   a. Please consult the enclosed brochure for the answers to your questions regarding the composition of Campbell's products. The brochure provides detailed information on the sodium and fat content of all Campbell's products, which include such well-known brands as V8, Pepperidge Farm, and Franco-American, as well as Campbell's Soups.

   b. Thanks for your interest in Campbell's products. We are concerned about nutrition and health issues and are trying to reduce the salts and fats in our products. At the same time, we are striving to retain the taste that consumers have come to expect from Campbell. In general, we feel very good about the nutritional value of our products and think that after you read the enclosed brochure you will too.

   c. Thank you for your interest in Campbell's Soup. The enclosed brochure provides the information you requested about the fat and sodium content of our products. Over the past ten years, we have introduced a number of reduced-sodium and low-fat products designed specifically for consumers on restricted diets. In addition, we have reformulated many of our regular products to reduce the salt and fat content. We have also revised our product labels so that information on sodium and fat content is readily apparent to health-conscious consumers. If you have any questions about any of our products, please contact our consumer information specialists at 1-800-227-9876.

4. Campbell has received a letter from a disgruntled consumer, Mr. Max Edwards, who was disappointed with his last can of Golden Classic beef soup with potatoes and mushrooms. It appears that the can contained an abundance of potatoes, little beef, and few mushrooms. You have been asked to reply to Mr. Edwards. Which of the following drafts is best?

   a. We are extremely sorry that you did not like your last can of Golden Classic beef soup with potatoes and mushrooms. Although we do our very best to ensure that all our products are of the highest quality, occasionally our quality-control department slips up and a can of soup comes out a bit short on one ingredient or another. Apparently you happened to buy just such a can–one with relatively few mushrooms, not much beef, and too many potatoes. The odds against that ever happening to you again are probably a million to one. And to prove it, here's a coupon that entitles you to a free can of Golden Classic soup. You may pick any flavour you like, but why not give the beef with potatoes and mushrooms another try? We bet it will meet your standards this time around.

   b. You are right, Mr. Edwards, to expect the highest quality from Campbell's Golden Classic soups. And you are right to complain when your expectations are not met. Our goal is to provide the best, and when we fall short of that goal, we want to know about it so that we can correct the problem. And that is exactly what we have done. In response to your complaint, our quality-control department is re-examining its testing procedures to ensure that all future cans of Golden Classic soup have an even blend of ingredients. Why not see for yourself by taking the enclosed coupon to your supermarket and redeeming it for a free can of Golden Classic soup? If you choose beef with potatoes and mushrooms, you can count on getting plenty of beef and mushrooms this time.

   c. Campbell's Golden Classic soups are a premium product at a premium price. Our quality-control procedures for this line have been carefully devised to ensure that every can of soup has a uniform distribution of ingredients. As you can imagine, your complaint came as quite a surprise to us, given the care that we take with our products. We suspect that the uneven distribution of ingredients was just a fluke, but our quality-control department is looking into the matter to ensure that the alleged problem does not recur. We would like you to give our Golden Classic soup another try. We are confident that you will be satisfied, so we are enclosing a coupon that entitles you to a free can. If you are not completely happy with it, please call me at 1-800-227-9876.

TAP Your Knowledge

Summary of Learning Outcomes

1. Adjust the basic organizational pattern to fit the type of message you are writing. Routine messages present neutral information, answer requests positively, and establish relationships. These messages begin with the main idea, followed by the necessary details, and end with a courteous close. The opening should be concise, to the point, and use the you-attitude whenever possible. The middle part should sufficiently develop the main idea and maintain the supportive attitude established in your opening. The close should include reader benefits and summarize the action you want your reader to take. Sometimes routine messages convey mildly disappointing information; in cases such as these, put the negative information into as positive a context as possible, but use negative information only if you're reasonably sure your audience will respond favourably to your message.

2. Add resale and sales promotion material when appropriate. Prospective customers often request annual reports, catalogues, and brochures. Respond to the inquiry, answer all questions, and leave your reader with a good impression of you and your firm. Include information that highlights the key features and benefits of the product or service; doing so will motivate readers to consider purchase.

3. Explain the main differences in messages granting a claim when the company, the customer, or a third party is at fault. When granting a claim, the explanatory section of your reply differs, depending on who is at fault. If your company is at fault, avoid reacting defensively, and be careful when referring to company errors. Rather than placing blame, explain your company's efforts to do a good job. Remember not to make any unrealistic promises or guarantees. If the customer is at fault, you must help your reader realize what went wrong so it won't happen again. However, you don't want to sound condescending, preachy, or insulting. If a third party is at fault, you can honour the claim with no explanation, or you can honour the claim and explain that the problem was not your fault.

4. Write credit approvals and recommendation letters. Credit approvals may be the first stage in a long-term business relationship, so be sure to accentuate the positive in your message. Employ a friendly, rather than authoritarian, tone in your message. Be sure to end with resale information and sales promotion that highlights the benefits of buying from your firm. Recommendation letters must contain all the relevant details about the candidate, including your relationship to the person and your overall evaluation of the candidate's suitability for the job. Remember that you have an obligation to your audience to include the candidate's shortcomings that are related to job performance, as well as strengths. You must base your recommendation on first-hand knowledge and provable facts.

5. Use the correct form for such specialized messages as instructions. Instructions tell people inside and outside the company how to do something. Your goal is to make the point obvious and the steps self-explanatory; otherwise, your readers will have to ask for additional help. Directives tell employees what they have to do, and should be fairly brief and to the point, as the reader is expected to follow through on a well-established procedure. Business summaries, another type of specialized message, should be accurate, comprehensive, and balanced. Make your sentence structure clear, and use correct transitions when writing summaries.

6. Establish the proper tone when writing goodwill letters. Goodwill messages include congratulations, messages of appreciation, and condolences. To project sincerity, avoid exaggeration. When congratulating someone or demonstrating appreciation, try to refer to specific qualities and actions. When writing condolences, keep reminiscences brief, write in your own words, be tactful, and cite the special qualities of the deceased and the bereaved person.

Test Your Knowledge

Review Questions

1. What question should you ask yourself when planning a routine or positive message?
2. What are your goals when responding to requests that are not opportunities to sell a product?
3. What strategy should you take when writing a response to a claim letter that does not contest the claim?

4. What questions should you ask yourself before mailing a recommendation letter?
5. Why are business summaries written? What are the characteristics of effective business summaries?
6. What are the differences between messages of congratulation and messages of appreciation?
7. Why is it important to use your own words when writing a condolence letter?

Apply Your Knowledge

Critical Thinking Questions

1. As a local retailer, would you take the time to reply to requests for information and action when no potential sale is involved? Why or why not?
2. An error by your company cost an important business customer a new client–you know it and your customer knows it. Do you apologize, or do you refer to the incident in a positive light without admitting any responsibility? Briefly explain.
3. Your customer is clearly at fault and lying. Will you disallow her claim? Why or why not?
4. You've been asked to write a letter of recommendation for an employee who is disabled and uses a wheelchair. The disability has no effect on the employee's ability to do the job, and you feel confident about writing the best recommendation possible. Nevertheless, you know the prospective company, and its facilities aren't well suited to wheelchair access. Do you mention the employee's disability in your letter? Explain.
5. Should resale and sales promotion be subdued (if included at all) in goodwill messages? Explain.

Practise Your Knowledge

Documents for Analysis

Read the following documents; then (1) analyze the strengths and weaknesses of each sentence and (2) revise each document so that it follows this chapter's guidelines.

Document 9.A: Responding to Claims and Adjustment Requests When the Buyer Is at Fault

We read your letter requesting your rental deposit refund. We couldn't figure out why you hadn't received it, so we talked to our maintenance engineer as you suggested. He said you had left one of the doors off the hinges in your apartment in order to get a large sofa through the door. He also confirmed that you had paid him $26.00 to replace the door since you had to turn in the U-Haul trailer and were in a big hurry.

This entire situation really was caused by a lack of communication between our housekeeping inspector and the maintenance engineer. All we knew was that the door was off the hinges when it was inspected by Sally Tarnley. You know that our policy states that if anything is wrong with the apartment, we keep the deposit. We had no way of knowing that George just hadn't gotten around to replacing the door. But we have good news. We approved the deposit refund, which will be mailed to you from our home office in Halifax, NS. I'm not sure how long that will take, however. If you don't receive the cheque by the end of next month, give me a call.

Next time, it's really a good idea to stay at your apartment until it's inspected as stipulated in your lease agreement. That way, you'll be sure to receive your refund when you expect it. Hope you have a good summer.

Document 9.B: Responding to Claims and Adjustment Requests When the Company Is at Fault

Thank you for contacting us about your purchase of the "Knights of Balthazar" game for your Macintosh. We apologize for the problem and want you to know how it happened.

We outsource our packaging to a firm called TriTech, which does the design work and prints the boxes. Unfortunately, the box that contained your CD for Balthazar was mistakenly labelled. It will work only on an IBM (or compatible) platform.

We are taking care of our customers even though this problem was caused by TriTech. If you will send the entire CD, the box, the warranty card, and your receipt, we will gladly replace it with a CD that will work in your computer. We also need to know how much memory you have and the system you are running. (Balthazar won't work on anything less than a System 7.)

Thanks for your patience. Again, we apologize for this even though it was beyond our control. We always want to do the right thing for our customers. Incidentally, I am enclosing our latest catalogue of interactive CD games. We hope to do business with you in the future.

Document 9.C: Letter of Recommendation

Your letter to Tanaka Asata, President of Sony, was forwarded to me because I am the human resources director. In my job as head of HR, I have access to performance reviews for all of the Sony employees in Canada. This means, of course, that I would be the person best qualified to answer your request for information on Nick Oshinski.

In your letter of the 15th, you asked about Nick Oshinski's employment record with us because he has applied to work for your company. Mr. Oshinski was employed with us from January 5, 1992, until March 1, 1997. During that time, Mr. Oshinski received ratings ranging from 2.5 up to 9.6 with 10 being the top score. As you can see, he must have done better reporting to some managers than to others. In addition, he took all vacation days, which is a bit unusual. Although I did not know Mr. Oshinski personally, I know that our best workers seldom use all the vacation time they earn. I do not know if that applies in this case.

In summary, Nick Oshinski performed his tasks well depending on who managed him.

Cases

Replying to Requests for Information and Action

1. Window shopping at Wal-Mart: Writing a positive reply via e-mail The Wal-Mart chain of discount stores is one of the most successful in the world, designing, importing, and marketing across national borders. In particular, Wal-Mart rarely fails to capitalize on a marketing scheme, and its online shopping page is no exception. To make sure the Web site remains effective and relevant, the webmaster asks various people to review the site and give their feedback. As administrative assistant to Wal-Mart's director of marketing, you have just received a request from the Web master to visit Wal-Mart's Web site and give feedback on the shopping page.

Your Task: Visit Wal-Mart at **www.walmart.com** and do some online window shopping. As you browse through the shopping page, consider the language, layout, graphics, ease of use, and background noise. Then compose a positive reply to the Web master, and send your feedback to **cserve@walmart.com**. Print a copy of your e-mail message for submission to your instructor.

Responding Favourably to Claims and Adjustment Requests

2. Mercedes merchandise: Form letter announcing a new, upscale catalogue Mercedes-Benz owners take their accessories seriously, so many of them are upset when they purchase "rip-off" Mercedes baseball caps that fall apart. Such merchandise is produced by sweatshop entrepreneurs, your boss's polite term for merchandisers who pirate the Mercedes logo, paste it onto cheap baseball caps, and then sell their wares at swap meets and flea markets. When the logo falls off, you get the irate letters.

You're working for the vice-president of accessories marketing for Mercedes-Benz. This is big business; today nearly every brand of automobile has its accompanying goods for proud owners: ties, T-shirts, watches, shoes, hats, jackets, sweaters. Most are sold right in the showrooms, and they're extremely popular. Some of the upscale manufacturers have been striving to provide logo-bearing clothing and gadgets that meet their customers' high-class budgets as well as their tastes. But simply raising prices has backfired. The second most common customer complaint you've been receiving is, "Why should I pay twice the price for an ordinary shirt just because it carries the Mercedes logo?"

The V-P agrees with these customers, so he went to work with other company executives to produce a brand new, 55-page, glossy, full-colour *Mercedes-Benz Personal & Automotive Accessories* catalogue loaded with expensive stuff. Mercedes-Benz has recruited world-class, top-of-the-line manufacturers and designers to produce merchandise worthy of the company's highly refined clientele. The new catalogue presents Wittnauer watches, Caran D'Ache ballpoints and Bally bomber jackets–all emblazoned with the triangle logo or images of Mercedes-Benz models, past and present. The catalogue even features a $3300 collapsible aluminum mountain bike for slipping into the trunk of your 500SL.

Your Task: The vice-president of accessories marketing wants you to develop a form letter–a very classy one, of course–to send with a copy of the new catalogue to all the customers who have sent complaints about shoddy or overpriced merchandise during the last year or so. He thinks they'll be quite happy with this reply.[10]

3. Cable hiccups: e-mail reply to an unhappy cable Internet customer. As a customer service agent working for your local cable company, you've received the occasional complaint like the one you're looking at on your computer monitor. The writer says,

> I'm fed up with the your cable Internet service. I've had my new computer for about a year and used the slow dial-up ISP service only because the manufacturer included it for free. I got your high-speed cable Internet service because your advertising promised it was 30 times faster than dial-up. I've used it since March, and I'm very disappointed. I'm paying $39.95 a month, plus taxes, but twice in the last month I've been unable to connect and service is a lot slower than advertised. What a rip-off!
>
> I'm a student and I work part-time. I do a lot of my research for essays and reports over the Internet. Not to mention e-mail. I have deadlines to meet. I want you to cancel my service and refund me my last two months' payments.

You know that many people complain that the cable line is shared with neighbours, which might slow down service. But slowdowns are rare with cable and happen with high-speed phone lines too. Cable Internet service has a lot of capacity and can provide rapid access to the Internet, even though lines are shared with neighbours. You think the writer is exaggerating and just wants to get his money back because the message is dated April 6, near the end of the school term.

Your Task: You'll be sending a positive e-mail to the writer indicating that your company will refund the amount he requests. Write to **TopGuy@ihome.com** You've been trained to educate consumers about cable Internet service in these messages and to provide a month's free service if they decide to use your company again. Look at the Web site for your local cable Internet provider for background information about the speed of cable Internet service.

4. Try us again: Letter and coupons from M&M/Mars You took a lot of teasing from friends when you went to work for M&M/Mars candy manufacturers. If they only knew: after a few weeks, you finally got tired of sampling the wares, and now the only desserts you want to see are the kind Mom bakes from scratch. Still, working in consumer relations is fun. Especially when you answer letters like this one:

> I bought a box of frozen Dove Bars at the local Ralph's supermarket and when I got them home and opened them, the chocolate coating was crushed on every single bar! I live 20 km from the market. Returning them was just too inconvenient. And at $6 for only 4 bars, one expects perfection! Imagine my disappointment!

The letter didn't include the proof-of-purchase panel from the end of the box, but company policy is to respond favourably to anyone who takes the time to write a letter.

Your Task: You're going to send the consumer, Tom Doppler 88 George St., St. Catharines, ON L2R 5N6, two coupons: one for a free box of Dove Bars and one for $1 off any M&M/Mars frozen dessert product.

Approving Routine Credit Requests

5. Satellite farming: Letter granting credit from Deere & Company The best part of your job with Deere & Co., a heavy machinery manufacturer, is saying yes to a farmer. In this case, it's Arlen Ruestman in Broadview, Saskatchewan.

Ruestman wants to take advantage of new farming technology. Your company's new GreenStar system uses satellite technology: the Global Positioning System (GPS). By using a series of satellites orbiting Earth, the system can pinpoint (to the metre) exactly where a farmer is positioned at any given moment as he drives his GreenStar-equipped combine over a field. For farmers like Ruestman, that means a new ability to micromanage even 10 000 acres of corn or soybeans.

For instance, using the GreenStar system, farmers can map crop yields from a given area and then examine potential causes of yield variations. After careful analysis, they can determine exactly how much herbicide or fertilizer to spread over precisely which spot–eliminating waste and achieving better results. With cross-referencing and accumulated data, farmers can analyze why crops are performing well in some areas and not so well in others.

Then they can program farm equipment to treat only the problem area–for example, spraying an insect infestation two metres wide, 300 m down the row.

Some farms have already saved as much as $10 an acre on fertilizers alone. For 10 000 acres, that's $100 000 a year. Once Ruestman retrofits your GreenStar precision package on his combine and learns all its applications, he should have no problem saving enough to pay off the $7350 credit account you're about to grant him.

Your Task: Write a letter to Mr. Ruestman, P.O. Box 992, Broadview, SK S0G 0K0 informing him of the good news.[11]

Conveying Positive Information About People

6. On course for the Ivey School of Business: Reply to a request for a recommendation letter After working for several years for Karen Donohue in Campbell Soup Company's consumer response department, one of your co-workers, Angela Cavanaugh, has decided to apply for admission to the Richard Ivey School of Business at the University of Western Ontario. She has asked Donohue to write a letter of recommendation for her. Here are the facts about Angela Cavanaugh:

1. She has an undergraduate degree in journalism from Carleton University, where she was an honours student.
2. She joined Campbell's directly after graduating and has worked for the firm for the past five years.
3. Her primary responsibility has been to answer letters from consumers; she has done an outstanding job.
4. Her most noteworthy achievement has been to analyze a year's worth of incoming mail, categorize the letters by type and frequency, and create a series of standardized replies. The department now uses Cavanaugh's form letters to handle approximately 75 percent of its mail.
5. Although Cavanaugh has outstanding work habits and is an excellent writer, she lacks confidence as a speaker. Her reluctance to present her ideas orally has prevented her from advancing more rapidly at Campbell's. This could be a problem for her at the Ivey School of Business, where skill in classroom discussion influences a student's chances of success.

Your Task: Because you have worked closely with Cavanaugh, Karen Donohue has asked you to draft the letter, which Donohue will sign.[12]

7. Cold comfort: Letter offering a regional sales position with Golight Winter in Saskatchewan ranch country is something to sneeze at–and to shiver over. That's why rancher Jerry Gohl invented the Golight, a portable spotlight that can be mounted on a car or truck roof and rotated 360 degrees horizontally and 70 degrees vertically by remote control. No more getting out of the truck in freezing, pre-dawn temperatures to adjust a manual spotlight in order to check on his livestock in the dark. In fact, Gohl hardly has any time left to check the livestock at all these days: His invention has become so popular that three-year-old Golight, Inc., expects to sell more than $2 million worth of the remote-controlled lights next year.

The company expanded fast, with Golights becoming popular all over the world among hunters, boaters, commuters who fear dark-of-night roadside tire changes, and early morning fishing enthusiasts who can scope out the best shoreline sites by controlling the spotlight from inside their warm and cozy vehicles. Sales reps have been hired for every part of the country and overseas, but Gohl has been holding out for just the right person to replace him in Saskatchewan. After all, the company president knows better than anyone what the local ranchers need and how they think–that's why his invention was such a success there. He didn't want to jinx his good fortune by choosing the wrong replacement.

Finally, last week he met a young man named Robert Victor who seems to fit the bill. Robert grew up on a Saskatchewan ranch, helping his dad with those 4 A.M. chores. He's young, but he's felt the bite of the Prairie's cold, he knows the rancher mind, and best of all, he's been bringing in top dollar selling agricultural equipment in Alberta for the past few years. Now he wants to return to his home province. Jerry liked him from the first moment they shook hands. "He's got the job if he wants it," the boss tells you. "Better send him some e-mail before someone else grabs him. He can start as soon as he's settled."

Your Task: Compose the message communicating Gohl's offer to Robert Victor: salary plus commission as discussed, full benefits (paid vacation, health and dental insurance) if he's still around in six months. His address is **robv7@sympatico. ca**. Sign with your name, as Gohl's personnel manager.[13]

Writing Directives and Instructions

8. Help for the hopeless: Instructions for working a VCR. As the only receptionist in a hectic pediatrician's office, you are busy from 9 to 5 taking appointments, calling patients with lab results, making sure the coffee pot is full, filing records–the list goes on. Dr. Makryk, your boss, hired his nephew, a high school student, to help you after school, and Frank has been great with the filing and playing with the kids while they wait to see Dr. M. But Frank seems to have a phobia with the two office VCRs. He is always asking you to help him load the machine his uncle uses to study medical videos as well as the waiting room VCR that shows cartoons. You weren't counting on Frank being techno-phobic!

Your Task: You decide the best way to help Frank is to write a clear set of instructions for using the VCRs. Be sure to frame the instructions with some goodwill comments so that Frank won't feel demeaned by his lack of techno-skills.

Writing Business Summaries

9. Gardening by computer: Summary of CD-ROM releases for Rodale executives Rodale Press has been publishing gardening magazines and books sold throughout Canada and the US since 1942. First came J. I. Rodale's demonstration farm in Emmaus, Pennsylvania, and his resulting *Organic Gardening* magazine–which is still the most widely read gardening publication in the world, according to the company history you read when you came on board. Now the company has its own Web site, selling its popular books and magazines about gardening, health, fitness, backpacking, running, bicycling, and woodworking to a new generation of computer literates. That's why Rodale executives are thinking hard about releasing the company's first CD-ROM, and gardening is the subject of choice. After all, it's the foundation on which the entire company was built.

"Microsoft is doing well with its *Complete Gardening* CD-ROM," says your boss, who is vice-president of sales and marketing for Rodale. "And I've heard about one called *3-D Landscape* from a company named Books That Work. But has anyone duplicated what Rodale does so well?"

You know she means a CD-ROM that matches the company's mission statement (a framed version of which

hangs over your desk): "Our mission is to show people how they can use the power of their bodies and minds to make their lives better. 'You can do it,' we say on every page of our magazines and books.'" Any CD-ROM would also have to emphasize organic gardening techniques to be approved by Rodale family members, who still own the company.

Your Task: You've volunteered to research other gardening CD-ROMs currently in the marketplace, writing a brief summary for Rodale's top management that will indicate what's out there for consumers already, who's published them, and how Rodale's special expertise might fit into the mix.[14]

10. How did Nike do it? Summary of a PR disaster Jill Montaine has been the proud owner of Jill's Jackets in Toronto for seven years, ever since her designs started showing up on celebrities. Word of mouth spread so fast that it wasn't long before she moved out of her converted garage studio and into her own showcase shop on Bloor Street.

Now she's worried.

"I don't know what I'm going to do. This could ruin me," she confesses to you (her store manager). She showed up worrying this morning before you opened the shop. She had originally sewn all her own designs and sold them on consignment at local boutiques. When her popularity grew, she hired subcontractors outside Canada, most recently in Southeast Asia, to keep up with the orders. Yesterday she learned that one of her overseas subcontractors has imposed new, harsh rules on his workers. Long hours, no breaks, unsanitary and hazardous working conditions–in other words, he's turned the operation into the worst kind of overseas sweatshop. And Jill's Jackets is his only client.

Montaine is worried about how much of her money has gone into his pockets instead of workers' paycheques, and she has already taken steps to replace him with another subcontractor. Now she's worried over how quickly this news might spread and destroy her reputation in

Canada. Word of mouth is everything in the upscale fashion business, and similar stories have nearly ruined others–including some more famous than Jill's Jackets.

"Why don't you find out how other companies have handled this kind of situation?" you suggest gently.

"Oh, you're right! That's a great idea." Relief spreads quickly over Montaine's face. "What did Nike do? Can you find out? How did they handle this kind of PR disaster?"

Your Task: Grateful for your suggestion, Montaine has left the shop in haste, heading off to a luncheon fashion show that she hopes will take the sting out of the bad publicity. Meanwhile, she's asked you to leave the clerks in charge of the store and zip over to the library. She wants you to read up on Nike's response to the accusations of overseas labour abuse that arose during the spring of 1997. Then you are to type up a summary of your findings and fax it to her home machine.[15]

Conveying Good News About Products and Operationss

11. A rising star: Letter congratulating award recipient You read in your university alumni magazine, *McGill News*, that Melissa Thanh won this year's Student Entrepreneur of the Year Award from ACE, the Association of Canadian Entrepreneurs. Melissa worked in your desktop publishing firm part-time during her high school years to help with family expenses. She was a very diligent employee and caught on very fast to the technology. You check out the ACE Canada Web site and learn that the CIBC Student Entrepreneur of the Year Award is "presented annually to a full-time Canadian university or college student running a business." Finalists are chosen based on "operating success, job creation, involvement in new economy activities, innovation, community involvement, and school performance." Melissa wins a package of products and services that will be useful for her business, and $1000 cash.

You've heard through a friend in the industry that Melissa started her own desktop-publishing firm out of her family's basement and created a Web site to advertise her business–putting together newsletters, brochures, letterheads, and other documents. As long as a client provides the text, she is able create an attractive package. Obviously her skills are known, for, your friend tells you, she has gained clients across Canada. She's also been a straight-A student at McGill University, captain of the women's soccer team, and a volunteer in soup kitchens.

Your Task: Write a letter of congratulation to Melissa. Address it to 2505 35th Ave. W, Vancouver BC V6N 2L9.[16]

12. ABCs: Form letter thanking volunteers Working together with government, educators, labour, and business, ABC Canada, a national literacy organization, promotes awareness of literacy and works to involve the private sector in supporting literacy. Its aim is "to promote a fully literate Canadian population." People in your firm, Fine Paper Company, participated in the annual PGI Golf Tournament for Literacy, which was founded by Peter Gzowski, one of Canada's great broadcasters and writers, and best known for his morning show on the CBC. The PGI is a very successful fundraising event, having generated $5 million over more than a decade. PGI tournaments are held in every province and territory.

Statistics Canada's report, *Literary Skills for the Knowledge Society*, notes that "22 percent of adult Canadians have serious problems with printed materials" and that "24 to 26 percent of Canadians can only deal with simple reading tasks."

Not only does your firm support the PGI Golf Tournament with monetary donations–and golf lovers–but the CEO, Laurent DesLauriers, established a volunteer program for employees to donate their time at local community centres to help adults learn to read. This program has become a success at Fine Paper Company.

Your Task: As a human resources specialist at Fine Paper Company, you are sometimes asked to write goodwill letters to employees, a job you enjoy doing. Mr. DesLauriers has directed the office to send a thank-you letter to all the volunteers, those who participated in the golf tournament and those who volunteer their time at the community centres. You will compose a form letter, which will be merged with individual employee's names and addresses.[17]

Developing Your Internet Skills

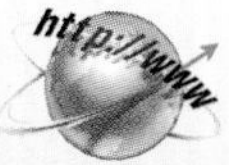

Going Online: Send an Electronic Goodwill Message, p. 222

Send a message to someone you think needs some encouragement. Now send another of your own choice. Was the digital postcard as easy to complete as you expected? Did you run into any snags? How could you make this process simpler, and how might this service improve business relations?

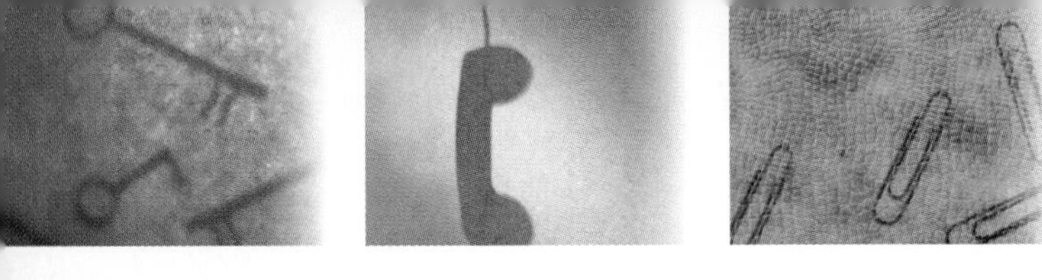

CHAPTER 10

Writing Bad-News Messages

AFTER STUDYING THIS CHAPTER, YOU WILL BE ABLE TO

1. Choose correctly between indirect and direct approaches to a bad-news message
2. Establish the proper tone from the beginning of your message
3. Present bad news in a reasonable and understandable way
4. Write messages that motivate your audience to take constructive action
5. Close messages so that your audience is willing to continue a business relationship with your firm

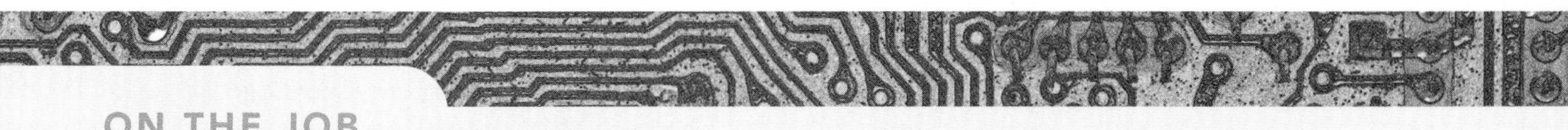

ON THE JOB
Facing a Communication Dilemma at Wal-Mart

When Saying No Is Part of Your Job

With 1722 stores, 472 Sam's Clubs, and 868 Supercenters in the US, 173 outlets in Canada, and 889 other locations around the world, all filled with housewares, hardware, electronics, music, movies, toys, tools, car supplies, and clothing for the entire family, Wal-Mart is a shopper's paradise and a supplier's dream. With total company sales of $165 billion for 1999, Sam Walton's company has grown from its first store in Rogers, Arkansas, in 1962, to an international powerhouse. Wal-Mart's relationship with its suppliers accounts in large part for the chain's success. To deliver its "everyday low price," or EDLP in Wal-Mart jargon, the store works with manufacturers and service providers to lower costs–and still be profitable–through reduced packaging and streamlined distribution systems.

Although Wal-Mart will reject some potential suppliers, the firm still wants to maintain good relationships with them. By clearly explaining the reasons for the rejection in a clear and helpful way, Wal-Mart communicates their understanding and good will–essential elements for maintaining a positive link in a difficult situation.

Suppliers are eager to work with Wal-Mart, but they must meet Wal-Mart's stringent criteria in order to get their wares onto Wal-Mart's shelves and their services to Wal-Mart's customers. To start the process of becoming a Wal-Mart supplier, manufacturers and service providers must complete a comprehensive proposal. They must answer key questions about their customers' demographics—age, family size, income, geographical location. Potential suppliers must discuss how their product will help Wal-Mart gain market share while controlling costs. They must analyze product benefits, direct and indirect competition, and their product's impact on other related products sold at Wal-Mart. Along with their answers, potential suppliers must provide financial statements, product literature and price lists, and samples. To become a Wal-Mart supplier is a demanding process, with no guarantee of success.

Final approval for Wal-Mart suppliers rests with the purchasing agent at the Wal-Mart home office in Bentonville, Arkansas. If you were a Wal-Mart purchasing agent, how would you respond to requests from companies that want to become partners with Wal-Mart but can't meet all of the chain's requirements? How would you respond to a supplier who has gone through this rigorous process but does not meet Wal-Mart's standards? How would you plan and compose messages that deliver bad news in a professional manner, in a way that doesn't affront or demean your audience, while still getting your point across?[1]

Organizing Bad-News Messages

As Wal-Mart's purchasing agents realize, some people interpret being rejected for a job or for credit as a personal failure; even rejections in less sensitive areas usually complicate people's lives. Admittedly, business decisions should not be made solely to avoid hurting someone's feelings. Mixing bad news with consideration for your readers' needs helps them understand that the unfavourable decision is based on a business judgment, not on any personal judgment.

Like direct requests and routine, good-news, and goodwill messages, bad-news messages are best communicated across cultures by using the tone, organization, and other cultural conventions that your audience expects. Only then can you avoid inappropriate or even offensive approaches that could jeopardize your business relationship.[2] For example, people in Germany tend to be more direct with bad news, but in Japan, bad news can be presented so positively that a Canadian business person might not detect it at all.[3]

When you need to communicate bad news to a Canadian or US audience that has minimal cultural differences, consider tone and organization. Your tone contributes to your message's effectiveness by supporting three specific goals:

- Helping your audience understand that your bad-news message represents a firm decision
- Helping your audience understand that, under the circumstances, your decision was fair and reasonable
- Helping your audience remain well disposed toward your business and possibly toward you

With the right tone, you can make an unwelcome point while preserving your audience's self-esteem.

In a bad-news message, the "you" attitude translates into
- ✧ Emphasizing the audience's goals instead of your own
- ✧ Looking for the best in your audience
- ✧ Using positive rather than negative phrasing

To accomplish the right tone, make liberal use of the "you" attitude–for example, by pointing out how your decision might actually further your audience's goals. In addition, convey concern by looking for the best in your audience; assume that your audience is interested in being fair, even when they are at fault. Finally, you can ease disappointment by using positive words rather than negative ones. Just be sure that your positive tone doesn't hide the bad news behind ambiguous language.[4] You want to convey the bad news, not cover it up.

How you arrange the main idea and supporting data can also ease your audience's disappointment. The two basic strategies described in Chapter 6 are (1) the indirect plan, which presents supporting data before the main idea, and (2) the direct plan, which presents the main idea before the supporting data.

LEARNING OUTCOME 1
Choose correctly between indirect and direct approaches to a bad-news message

Indirect Plan

The indirect plan is actually a familiar approach. You've probably used it many times to say something that might upset another person. Instead of beginning a business message with a blunt no, which could keep your audience from reading or listening to your reasons, use the indirect plan to ease your audience into the part of your message that demonstrates that you're fair-minded and eager to do business on some other terms.

The indirect plan consists of four parts: (1) a buffer; (2) reasons supporting the negative decision; (3) a clear, diplomatic statement of the negative decision; and (4) a helpful, friendly, and positive close. By presenting the reasons for your decision before the bad news itself, you gradually prepare the audience for disappointment. In many cases, this approach is more appropriate than an abrupt statement of the bad news.

LEARNING OUTCOME 2
Establish the proper tone from the beginning of your message

BUFFER

A buffer is a neutral lead-in to bad news.

The first step in using the indirect plan is to put the audience in a receptive mood by making a neutral, non-controversial statement closely related to the point of the message. This statement is called a **buffer.** In a letter telling a client that you cannot run a training session until a date later than desired, you might begin with a statement like this: "Thank you for the opportunity to hold a software seminar at your firm. I do understand that you would like to have your staff develop proficiency in the software as soon as possible."

If possible, base the buffer on statements made by the person you're responding to. If you use an unrelated buffer, you seem to be avoiding the issue; that is, you appear unethical and you lose your audience's respect. Another goal when composing your buffer is to avoid giving the impression that good news will follow. Building up the audience at the beginning only makes the subsequent letdown even more painful. Imagine your reaction to the following openings:

> Your résumé indicates that you would be well suited for a management trainee position with our company.
>
> Your résumé shows very clearly why you are interested in becoming a management trainee with our company.

The second opening emphasizes the applicant's favourable interpretation of her qualifications rather than the company's evaluation, so it's less misleading but still positive. Here are some other things to avoid when writing a buffer:

Use a buffer that is
- ✧ Neutral
- ✧ Relevant
- ✧ Not misleading
- ✧ Assertive
- ✧ Succinct

- ➤ *Avoid saying no.* An audience encountering the unpleasant news right at the beginning usually reacts negatively to the rest of the message, no matter how reasonable and well phrased it is.
- ➤ *Avoid using a know-it-all tone.* When you use phrases such as "You should be aware that," the audience expects your lecture to lead to a negative response and therefore resists the rest of your message.
- ➤ *Avoid wordy and irrelevant phrases and sentences.* Sentences such as "We have received your letter," "This letter is in reply to your request," and "We are writing in response to your request" state the obvious. You make better use of the space by referring directly to the subject of the letter.
- ➤ *Avoid apologizing.* An apology weakens your explanation of the unfavourable decision.
- ➤ *Avoid writing a buffer that is too long.* The point is to identify briefly something that both you and your audience are interested in and agree on before proceeding in a businesslike way.

Should you use the indirect or direct strategy when communicating all bad news? Many people in finance believe that, when communicating the falling fortunes of one's investments, the direct strategy is best. Why?

Table 10.1 shows types of buffers you could use to open a bad-news message tactfully.

Some critics believe that using a buffer is manipulative, dishonest, and thus unethical. In fact, buffers are unethical only if they're insincere. Breaking bad news with kindness and courtesy is the human way. Consideration for the feelings of others is never dishonest, and that consideration helps your audience accept your message.

After you've composed a buffer, evaluate it by asking yourself four questions: Is it pleasant? Is it relevant? Is it neutral, saying neither yes nor no? Does it provide for a smooth transition to the reasons that follow? If you can answer yes to every question, you may proceed confidently to the next section of your message.

REASONS

LEARNING OUTCOME 3
Present bad news in a reasonable and understandable way.

If you've done a good job of composing the buffer, the reasons will follow naturally. Cover the positive points first; then move to the less positive ones. Provide enough detail for the audience to understand your reasons, but be concise; a long, roundabout explanation may make the audience impatient.

Present reasons to show that your decision is reasonable and fair.

The goal is to explain *why* you have reached your decision before you explain *what* that decision is. If you present your reasons effectively, they will help convince the audience that your decision is justified, fair, and logical. However, someone who realizes you're saying no before he or she understands why may either quit paying attention altogether or be set to refute the reasons when they're finally given.

Focus on how the audience might benefit from your negative message.

When giving your reasons, be tactful by highlighting just how the decision benefits your audience instead of focusing on why the decision is good for you or your company. For example, when saying no to a credit request, show how your decision will keep the person from becoming overextended financially. Facts and figures are often helpful in convincing members of your audience that you're acting in their best interests.

As you explain your reasons, avoid hiding behind company policy to cushion the bad news. If you say, "Company policy forbids our hiring anyone who does not have two years' management experience," you seem to imply that you haven't considered the person on her or his own merits. Although skilled and sympathetic communicators may sometimes quote company policy, they also briefly explain it so that the audience can try to meet the requirements at a later time.

Avoid apologizing when giving your reasons. Apologies are appropriate only when someone in your company has made a severe mistake or has done something terribly wrong. If no one in the company is at fault, an apology gives the wrong impression.

The tone of the language you use to explain your reasons greatly influences your audience's reception of the bad news that follows. So avoid negative, counterproductive words like these:

TABLE 10.1 Types of Buffers

When a Crisis Hits:		
Buffer	**Strategy**	**Example**
Agreement	Find a point on which you and the reader share similar views.	We both know how hard it is to make a profit in this industry.
Appreciation	Express sincere thanks for receiving something.	Your cheque for $127.17 arrived yesterday. Thank you.
Cooperation	Convey your willingness to help in any way you realistically can.	Employee Services is here to smooth the way for all of you who work to achieve company goals.
Fairness	Assure the reader that you've closely examined and carefully considered the problem, or mention an appropriate action that has already been taken.	For the past week, we have carefully monitored those using the photocopying machine to see whether we can detect any pattern of use that might explain its frequent breakdowns.
Good news	Start with the part of your message that is favourable.	A replacement knob for your range is on its way, shipped February 10 via UPS.
Praise	Find an attribute or an achievement to compliment.	Your résumé shows an admirable breadth of experience, which should serve you well as you progress in your career.
Resale	Favourably discuss the product or company related to the subject of the letter.	With their heavy-duty, full-suspension hardware and fine veneers, the desks and file cabinets in our Montclair line have become a hit with value-conscious professionals.
Understanding	Demonstrate that you understand the reader's goals and needs.	So that you can more easily find the printer with the features you need, we are enclosing a brochure that describes all the Panasonic printers currently available.

INSTEAD OF THIS	SAY THIS
We have received your *broken* clock.	We have received the clock you sent us.
I *cannot understand* what you mean.	Please clarify your request.
The *damage* won't be fixed for a week.	The item will be repaired next week.
There will be a *delay* in your order.	We will ship your order as soon as possible.
You are clearly *dissatisfied.*	We are doing what we can to make things right.
Your account is in *error.*	Corrections have been made to your account.
The breakage was not our *fault.*	The merchandise was broken during shipping.
Sorry for your *inconvenience.*	The enclosed coupon will save you $5 next time.
We *regret* the misunderstanding.	I'll try my best to be clearer from now on.
I was *shocked* to hear the news.	The news reached me yesterday.
Unfortunately, we haven't received it.	It hasn't arrived yet.
The enclosed statement is *wrong.*	Please recheck the enclosed statement.

Furthermore, protect the audience's pride by using language that conveys respect: avoid an accusing tone. Use third-person, impersonal, passive language to explain your audience's mistakes in an inoffensive way. Say, "The appliance won't work after being immersed in water" instead of "You shouldn't have immersed the appliance in water." In this case, the "you" attitude is better observed by avoiding the word *you.*

Sometimes the "you" attitude is best observed by avoiding the word *you.*

When refusing the application of a management trainee, a tactfully worded letter might give these reasons for the decision not to hire:

> Because these management trainee positions are quite challenging, our human resources department has researched the qualifications needed to succeed in them. The findings show that the two most important qualifications are a bachelor's degree in business administration and two years' supervisory experience.

This paragraph does a good job of stating the reasons for the refusal:

Well-written reasons are
✧ Detailed
✧ Tactful
✧ Individualized
✧ Unapologetic
✧ Positive

- ➢ It provides enough detail to make the reason for the refusal logically acceptable.
- ➢ It implies that the applicant is better off avoiding a program in which she would probably fail, given the background of others who would be working alongside her.
- ➢ It doesn't rest solely on company policy. A relevant policy exists but is presented as logical rather than rigid.
- ➢ It offers no apology for the decision.
- ➢ It avoids negative personal expressions ("You do not meet our requirements").

Although specific reasons help the audience accept bad news, reasons cannot always be given. When reasons involve confidential, excessively complicated, or

Sometimes detailed reasons should not be provided.

purely negative information, or when the reasons benefit only you or your firm (such as enhancing the company's profits), don't include them. Move directly to the next section.

THE BAD NEWS

To make bad news less painful

- ✧ De-emphasize the bad news visually and by sentence structure
- ✧ Use a conditional statement
- ✧ Tell what you did do, not what you didn't do
- ✧ Minimize the space or time devoted to it.

When the bad news is a logical outcome of the reasons that come before it, the audience is psychologically prepared to receive it. However, the audience may still react emotionally if the bad news is handled carelessly. Three techniques are especially useful for saying no as clearly and as painlessly as possible.

First, de-emphasize the bad news:

- ➤ Subordinate it in a complex or compound sentence ("My department is already shorthanded, so I'll need all my staff for at least the next two months").
- ➤ Embed it in the middle of a paragraph.

LEARNING OUTCOME 4
Write messages that motivate your audience to take constructive action.

Second, use a conditional (*if* or *when*) statement to imply that the audience could possibly have received, or might someday receive, a favourable answer: "When you have more managerial experience, you are welcome to reapply." Such a statement could motivate applicants to improve their qualifications.

Third, tell the audience what you did, can do, or will do rather than what you did not do, cannot do, or won't do. Say "We sell exclusively through retailers, and the one nearest you that carries our merchandise is ..." rather than "We are unable to serve you, so please call your nearest dealer." Helpful comments reinforce a

BEHIND THE SCENES AT YOUR BANK'S OMBUDSMAN

Is the Customer Always Right?

Your bank refuses to grant you a loan. You feel service charges are high. You are liable for withdrawals on your ATM card that you didn't make. Your bank refuses to honour a life insurance claim. What do you do?

You can, of course, switch banks, as 2 percent of Canadians did in 1997, the most recent year available. Or, you can complain. But will your complaint be treated in a fair and impartial manner?

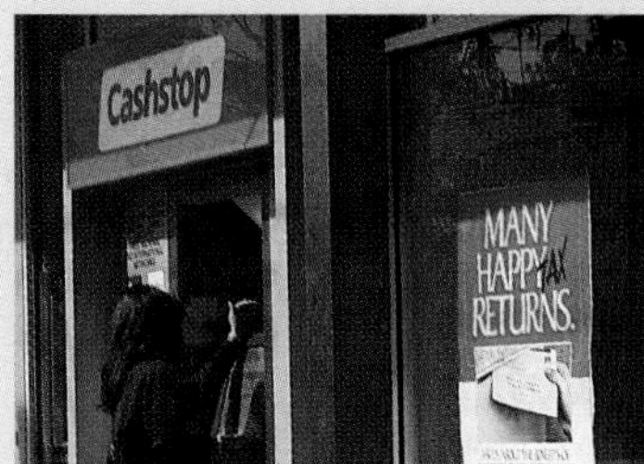

The ombudsman of Canada's banks face the same challenges confronting many business people who must communicate bad news—how to retain the customer's business and goodwill while justifying the negative decision.

If you cannot get satisfaction from your branch, call centre, or head office executive responsible for customer complaints, appeal to your bank's ombudsman. Each of Canada's chartered banks has an ombudsman's office as part of the bank structure, acting independently from the bank itself. According to Bill Bailey, ombudsman for Scotiabank, his staff cannot "jump in" to solve a customer's problem. Instead, they can only listen to customers after they have sought help at the local level, the procedure Canada's other banks also follow. Says Bailey, with Scotiabank's 40 000 employees there will be "foul-ups along the way." The 2000 Annual Report produced by his office indicates that Bailey and his staff received 229 complaints, from both personal banking and small business customers. Of these, 225 were handled. Agreement between customers and the bank was reached in 76 cases, or 34 percent; partial agreement in 31 cases, or 14 percent; and no agreement in 118 cases, or 52 percent.

The process all Canada's chartered banks follow in resolving customer complaints embraces communication and education. As with all bad-news situations, communication must be timely, open, clear, and specific. Dennice Leahey, ombudsman for Royal Bank Financial Group, comments, "The best solutions are found when conflicts are handled quickly and by the people directly involved." She urges Royal Bank customers to "plan for a quality conversation and take action when they have a complaint." And she urges both the customer and the Bank to "listen to each other and find the common ground."

Leahey, like other bank ombudsmen, uses a variety of methods to resolve disputes. One method is to bring customers and bank employees together to talk out the disagreement. Bank customers are urged to arrive with all relevant documentation, the names of staff involved, and a clear idea of both the basis of their complaint and the solution they want. Often, she notes, a lack of understanding or unclear information may be grounds for a customer's dissatisfaction. In instances such as these, listening and clarifying the facts can positive impression of your firm in your readers' minds and encourage them to remain your customers.

When writing a bad-news message, avoid negative wording and personal language.

Of course, when implying bad news, be sure your audience understands the entire message–including the bad news. It would not be ethical or practical to overemphasize the positive. So if an implied message might leave doubt, state your decision in direct terms. Just be sure to avoid blunt statements that are likely to cause pain and anger. Replace the following phrases, which are particularly likely to offend:

INSTEAD OF THIS	USE THIS
I must refuse your request to meet with your staff.	I will be seeing an out-of-town client on the day of the meeting.
We must deny your application.	The position has been filled.
I am unable to grant your request.	Contact us again when you have established ...
We cannot afford to continue the program.	The program will conclude on May 1.
We must reject your proposal.	We've accepted the proposal from another vendor.
We must turn down your extension request.	Please send in your payment by June 14.

settle problems arising from miscommunication. When the parties find it difficult to talk, however, because their relationship has broken down, mediators are brought in to facilitate the discussion, attempting to draw out information and opinions and identifying the options that can settle the dispute. Leahey makes it clear that her office cannot reverse a branch's decision; one example is when a client is refused a loan. But if her investigation reveals a customer has been treated unfairly, or that the bank violated procedure, she can make a recommendation to resolve the problem.

When a bank's ombudsman finds that the bank is at fault, typically the bank makes some sort of restitution. The outcome works to the benefit of both parties: customers receive a degree of satisfaction, and the bank learns where they must improve their service or products, or their communication with customers. However, what happens when the ombudsman cannot give the customer the result he or she seeks?

If customers wish to pursue a matter beyond their bank's ombudsman, they can contact the Canadian Banking Ombudsman for a final, independent review. But this ultimate arbitrator makes clear that his office can refuse complaints considered "frivolous or vexatious, or if there is clearly no reasonable prospect of success." One example is the customer who demands compensation "that is measurably beyond any amount the ombudsman considers fair in the circumstances and where the customer's position was so inflexible as to make resolution impossible."

In the words of Scotiabank's Bill Bailey, "The customer isn't always right." Yet like most businesses, banks want to educate their customers so that they become more knowledgable and thus better consumers. Canada's banks believe that teaching their customers about rules and policies is essential to keeping their business when disputes cannot be resolved to the customer's satisfaction. One educational tool is a bank's Web site. For example, Bank of Montreal specifies that their ombudsman, Don Willis, cannot resolve complaints about operating hours and services. Another category is unauthorized use of an ATM (automatic teller machine) card or allowing another person to use a confidential PIN (personal identification number). To communicate bank policy, the language used is specific and direct. For more information on the ombudsman's role, look at the Web site for any of the chartered Canadian banks, or go to www.bankingombudsman.com.[5]

APPLY YOUR KNOWLEDGE

1. Frequently, Canada's chartered banks receive complaints about service fees for low account balances. Investigate your bank or a competitor to determine the fee structure. Now, imagine you work at a local branch as a customer service representative who must deal with complaints from customers who do not maintain the minimum balance in their account. How would you respond to these complaints? Should you use the direct or the indirect approach? Explain your choice of strategy.
2. When you are explaining the reasons for bad news, is it beneficial to discuss the process involved in reaching the decision? Why?

LEARNING OUTCOME 5
Close messages so that your audience is willing to continue a business relationship with your firm.

POSITIVE CLOSE

After giving your audience the bad news, your job is to end your message on an upbeat note whenever possible. In a message to a customer or potential customer, an off-the-subject ending that includes resale information or sales promotion is appropriate. If you've asked someone to decide between alternatives or to take some action, make sure she or he knows what to do, when to do it, and how to do it with ease. Whatever type of close you choose, follow these guidelines:

An upbeat, positive close
✧ Builds goodwill
✧ Offers a suggestion for action
✧ Provides a look toward the future

- Keep your close as positive as possible. Don't refer to, repeat, or apologize for the bad news, and refrain from expressing any doubt that your reasons will be accepted. Avoid statements such as "I trust our decision is satisfactory."
- Encourage additional communication *only* if you're willing to discuss your decision further. Avoid phrases such as "If you have further questions, please write."
- Keep a positive outlook on the future. Do not anticipate problems. Avoid statements such as "Should you have further problems, please let us know."
- Be sincere. Steer clear of clichés that are insincere in view of the bad news. Avoid saying, "If we can be of any help, please contact us."
- Be confident about keeping the person as a customer. Avoid phrases such as "We hope you will continue to do business with us."

Keep in mind that the close is the last thing the audience has to remember you by. Try to make the memory a positive one.

Direct Plan

A bad-news message organized on the direct plan starts with a clear statement of the bad news, proceeds to the reasons for the decision, and ends with a courteous close. Stating the bad news at the beginning can have two advantages: (1) It makes a shorter message possible, and (2) the audience needs less time to reach the main idea of the message, the bad news itself.

Use the direct plan when
✧ Your boss prefers that internal messages come right to the point
✧ The message has little personal impact
✧ You want to make your point emphatically

Although the indirect approach is preferable for most bad-news messages, you may sometimes want to move right to the point. Memos are often organized so that the bad news comes before the reasons. In fact, some managers expect all internal correspondence to be brief and direct, regardless of whether the message is positive or negative. Routine bad-news messages to other companies often follow the direct plan, especially if they relay decisions that have little or no personal impact. Using a buffer can actually cause ill will in people who see them frequently–such as people searching for employment.[6] In addition, you'll sometimes know from experience that your audience simply prefers reading the bad news first in any message. Of course, the direct plan is also appropriate when you want to present an image of firmness and strength; for example, the last message in a collection series, just before the matter is turned over to an attorney, usually gets right to the point.

So, in any number of circumstances, you may want to use the direct plan and save your positive comments for the close. Whichever approach you choose, remember that a tactful tone and a focus on reasons will help make any bad-news message easier to accept.

Conveying Bad News About Orders

The basic goal of a bad-news letter about orders is to protect or make a sale.

Businesses must sometimes convey bad news concerning orders. When you must relate bad news to suppliers, focus your audience's attention on what can be done rather than on what cannot. When writing to a would-be customer, you have three basic goals:

EFFECTIVE E-BUSINESS COMMUNICATION

Transforming Wrongs Into Rights

"Problems are opportunities in disguise"—an apt description of how savvy e-businesses approach customer service. Every complaint gives you a chance to strengthen your customer's loyalty, if you make full use of Internet technology to show that you're really interested in making things right. Web-based businesses can offer customers a wider choice of contact methods: phone, mail, fax, e-mail, or instant online customer-service chat, just the way Lands' End does. Online customers expect speed, so respond quickly, ideally within 24 hours. If you need more time to resolve sticky problems, send prompt e-mail updates to let customers know you're working on their behalf.

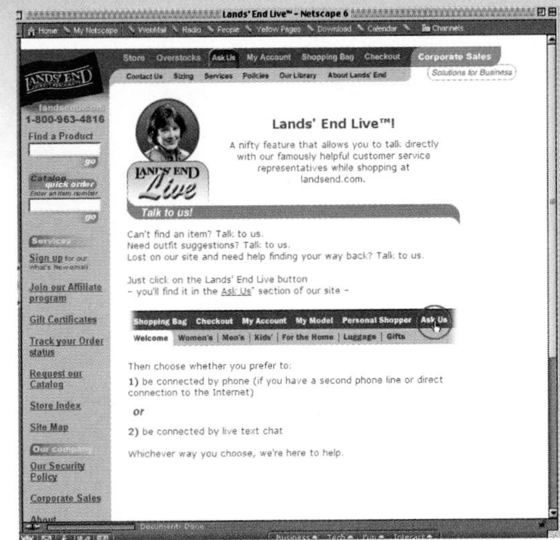

1. When you send an e-mail message to update a customer whose problem will take several days to resolve, what can you say to maintain her or his goodwill?
2. When you send an e-mail message to update customers whose problems are taking more time to resolve, would the direct or the indirect approach be more appropriate? Why?

- To work toward an eventual sale along the lines of the original order
- To keep instructions or additional information as clear as possible
- To maintain an optimistic, confident tone so that your reader won't lose interest

Use the indirect plan when telling a customer that you cannot immediately ship the entire order.

For example, when you must back order for a customer, you have one of two types of bad news to convey: (1) you're able to send only part of the order, or (2) you're able to send none of the order. When sending only part of the order, you actually have both good news and bad news. In such situations, the indirect plan works very well. The buffer contains the good news (that part of the order is en route) along with a resale reminder of the product's attractiveness. After the buffer come the reasons for the delay of the remainder of the shipment. A strong close encourages a favourable attitude toward the entire transaction (Figure 10.1).

Even when you're unable to send the customer any portion of an order, you can still use the indirect approach. However, because you have no good news to give, your buffer only confirms the sale, and the explanation section states your reason for not filling the order promptly. For a brief outline of back-order tasks, see this chapter's Checklist for Bad News About Orders.

Communicating Negative Answers and Information

The business person who tries to say yes to everyone probably won't win many promotions or stay in business for long. Occasionally, your response to inquiries must simply be no. It's a mark of your skill as a communicator to be able to say no clearly yet not cut yourself off from future dealings with the other person.

Depending on your relationship with the reader, you could use either the direct plan or the indirect plan when writing negative messages. If the reader is unlikely to

In the indirect plan, the buffer conveys the good news and confirms the wisdom of the customer's choice.

The reasons for the shipping delay are stated in a way that indicates that the ottoman is a popular choice. The bad news is cushioned by the pledge to take care of the problem by a definite time.

The bad news itself is implied by telling the reader what is being done, not what cannot be done.

The positive close also opens the door to future business.

Chair ◆ House

5405 Doyle St., Halifax, NS B3J 1H9 902-555-6789/fax 902-555-6775

October 9, 2000

Dr. Elizabeth Fawnworth
45 O'Leary Ave
St. John's, NF A1B 2C9

Dear Dr. Fawnworth:

Thank you for your order of the special edition recliner and matching ottoman. The recliner with custom features will be shipped today. The leather trim you designated turned out beautifully, and we're sure the recliner will make a handsome addition to your study.

The roll-around ottoman has proved to be one of our most popular items. Our plant manager reports that, even though he has almost doubled production this year, we are still experiencing some delays. We estimate that your ottoman will be shipped no later than November 15 to arrive by December 1.

Remember that all Chair House products carry a lifetime guarantee. We know you will enjoy your recliner and ottoman for many years. I've enclosed a catalogue that includes our latest designs. Please call me at (902) 555-6785 if you'd like to talk about any of our special fabrics or custom designs. We look forward to serving you again in the future.

Cordially,

Suzanne Godfrey

Suzanne Godfrey
Manager, Custom Designs

Enclosure

FIGURE 10.1

In-Depth Critique: Letter Advising of a Back Order

For a customer whose order for a recliner and ottoman will be partly filled, your letter might read like this one.

Use the direct plan when your negative answer or information will have little personal impact; use the indirect plan in more sensitive situations.

be deeply disappointed, use the direct plan. Otherwise, use a buffer that expresses your appreciation for being thought of, assures the reader of your attention to the request, compliments the reader, or indicates your understanding of the reader's needs. Continue with the reasons for the bad news and the bad news itself, couched in terms that show how the reader's problem can be solved and what you can do to help. Then close with a statement of interest, encouragement, or goodwill. You can demonstrate your sincerity (and minimize the reader's hostility or disappointment) by promptly fulfilling any promises you make.

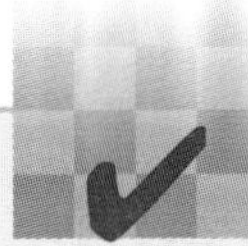

Checklist for Bad News About Orders

A. Overall Strategy

1. Use the indirect plan in most cases.
2. Use the direct plan when the situation is routine (as between employees of the same company), when the reader is not emotionally involved in the message, or when you know that the reader would prefer the bad news first.

B. Buffer

1. Express appreciation for the specific order.
2. Extend a welcome to a new customer.
3. Avoid negative words *(won't, can't, unable to)*.
4. Use resale information on the ordered merchandise to build the customer's confidence in the original choice (except for unfillable orders).

C. Reasons

1. Emphasize what the firm is doing rather than what it isn't doing, what it does have rather than what it lacks.
2. Avoid apologies and expressions of sorrow or regret.
3. Handle back orders carefully.
   a. Specify shipping dates.
   b. Give reasons why the item is out of stock, such as high popularity or exceptional demand, that may stimulate the customer's desire for the item.
   c. Reinforce the customer's confidence with resale. For consumers, emphasize personal attention, credit, repair services, free delivery, special discounts, telephone shopping, and other services; for dealers, emphasize free counter and window displays, advertising materials, sales manuals, factory guarantees, and nearby warehousing.
   d. Refer to sales promotion material, if desirable.

D. The Bad News

1. State the bad news as positively as possible.
2. State the bad news clearly.
3. Stress the benefit to the reader of their decision to buy your product.

E. Positive, Friendly, Helpful Close

1. Remind the reader of how her or his needs are being met, if appropriate.
2. Use resale information to secure the sale, especially for back orders.
3. Adopt a tone that shows you remain in control of the situation and will continue to give customers' orders personal attention.

Providing Bad News About Products

When you must provide bad news about a product, the situation and the reader will dictate whether to use the direct or the indirect plan. If you are writing to tell your company's bookkeeping department about increasing product prices, use the direct plan. The reader will have to make some arithmetical adjustments to put the increases into effect but presumably won't be emotionally involved in the matter. However, you should probably use the indirect plan to convey the same information to customers because they will be disappointed or angry.

Consider the direct or indirect plan for telling the reader bad news about a product.

The e-mail message in Figure 10.2 was written to tell one company's sales managers that their request for a licensing agreement had been rejected. The middle section of the memo presents an honest statement of the bad news. The effect of the bad news is diminished by the problem-solving tone, by the avoidance of any overt statement that such a setback may affect commissions, and by the upbeat close.

Denying Cooperation with Routine Requests

When people ask you for information or want you to do something and you can't honour the request, you may answer with either the direct plan or the indirect plan. Say that you have asked a company to participate in your research project concerning sales promotion. However, that company has a policy against disseminating any information about projected sales figures. How would you react to the following letter?

Consider the direct or indirect plan to tell someone you cannot do what has been requested.

> Our company policy prohibits us from participating in research projects in which disclosure of discretionary information might be necessary. Therefore, we decline your invitation to our sales staff to fill out questionnaires for your study.
>
> Thank you for trying to include Quallcom Corporation in your research. If we can be of further assistance, please let us know.

This letter would offend most readers, for several reasons:

Date: Thu, 27 Aug 2000 08:09:19
From: Frank Leslie <leslie@Sybervant.com.>
To: All Sales Managers
Subject: August 29 Meeting

The memo begins on a complimentary note to buffer the bad news. →

Thank you for your continuing efforts to make Sybervantage a leader in video-game development. Recent reports indicate that we captured a 10% increase in market share over the second quarter of last year. That increase is directly attributable to your energy and enthusiasm. Now we're facing a situation that will put us to the test.

The bad news is presented along with possible explanations. →

As you know, many of us in R&D have been working to develop computer games based on Looney Tunes characters. Currently, we have eight games in various stages of development. However, Warner has turned down our requests for licensing agreements. It wasn't a matter of money; we offered them top dollar. I believe that Warner saw the tremendous potential and simply decided to develop its own character-based computer games.

The third paragraph indicates the action that will be taken to lessen the impact of the bad news and actively involves the readers in the possibility of a solution. →

On August 29, we will hold day-long meetings here in Orlando to discuss our options. We'd like all of you to be present. Our purpose will be to decide whether we want to pursue another licensing agreement, or continue as we started, by developing our own character-based games. Meetings will take place at the Ramada Renaissance by the airport. Lunch will be provided. Call or e-mail Shirley in my office for reservations.

We have an opportunity to reshape Sybervantage in the 21st century. Our company has a great future, and I'm looking forward to the energy we can create.

See you there,

Frank Leslie

President

FIGURE 10.2

In-Depth Critique: E-Mail Message Providing Bad News About Products
When Sybervantage pursued licensing agreements with Warner, the company expected to be entering into a lucrative arrangement in which both companies would profit. Now that Warner has rejected the request, Sybervantage must adjust its strategic planning and must keep its sales force both motivated and involved.

- The direct plan is used, even though the reader is outside the company and may be emotionally involved in the response.
- The tone of the first paragraph is unnecessarily negative and abrupt.
- The writer hides behind company policy, a policy that the reader may find questionable.
- The offer to help is an unpleasant irony, given the writer's unwillingness to help in this instance.

Wording, tone, and format conspire to make a letter either offensive or acceptable. The letter in Figure 10.3 conveys the same negative message as the preceding letter without sounding offensive.

Quallcom Corporation

687 Portage Ave, Suite 1700, Winnipeg, MB R3G 0M5
204-555-2354/fax 204-555-2349
contact@quallcom.net

February 12, 2000

Phillippe DiCastro
Analyst
Morrissey Financial Advisors
30 Cumberland St N
Thunder Bay, ON P7A 4K9

Dear Mr. DiCastro:

We at Quallcom Corporation appreciate and benefit from the research conducted by companies such as yours. Your present study sounds interesting, and we are certainly willing to help within the constraints of our firm's policies governing outside researchers.

The buffer is supportive and appreciative.

Our board requires strict confidentiality of all sales information until quarterly reports are mailed to stockholders. As you know, we release news reports at the same time quarterly reports go out. We will include you in all our future mailings.

Instead of hiding behind "company policy," the writer explains the reason for the policy. The bad news is implied, not stated explicitly in the second paragraph.

Although we cannot release projected figures, we are, of course, able to share data that are part of the public record. I've enclosed several of our past earnings reports for your inspection.

We look forward to the results of your study. Please let us know if there is any additional way we can help.

The close is friendly, positive, and helpful.

Yours truly,

Lisa McKinnon
Customer Service
Investor Relations

Enclosure

FIGURE 10.3
In-Depth Critique: Letter Refusing a Routine Request for Information

As you think about the different impacts these two versions might have on you, you can see why effective business writers take the time and the trouble to give negative messages the attention they deserve.

Declining Invitations and Requests for Favours

Consider the direct or indirect plan to turn down an invitation or a request for a favour.

When you must say no to an invitation or a requested favour, your use of the direct or the indirect plan depends on your relationship with the reader. For example, suppose your former business-management professor wants to take her students on a tour of your company's facilities, and she contacts you to arrange it. However, the company-wide sales meeting will take place at the same time. If you didn't know the teacher, you would probably use the indirect plan. But if you are friendly with her, and keep in touch, you might use the direct approach.

> Thank you, Professor Wong, for asking Plastics Injection Inc. to host a plant tour for your students. We know that in past years the students have learned a great deal about how a business like ours operates. This year, however, I will have to book a date other than the one you suggested.
>
> We are having our company-wide sales meeting from March 12 to 14. During this time, our auditorium is fully booked for presentations and the staff who conduct the tours will be updating the sales reps on current projects.
>
> As an alternative, can your class come here the following week, on March 21? As usual, a tour guide will meet your group at 10:00 A.M. at the main entrance.
>
> Let me know if this date is good for you and how many students to expect. As in the past, the tour lasts two hours, and the students can enjoy lunch in the staff cafeteria. Please call me at 555-2232 (my direct line) to discuss the new date.
>
> Professor Wong, I appreciate your understanding and look forward to speaking with you.
>
> Sincerely,
>
> Mohammed Mansour

The letter gets to the point in the first paragraph, but presents both the reason for the refusal and an alternative, thus softening the rejection and maintaining goodwill.

Refusing Adjustment of Claims and Complaints

Use the indirect plan in most cases of refusing to make an adjustment.

Almost every customer who requests an adjustment is emotionally involved; therefore the indirect plan is generally used for a refusal. Your job as a writer is to avoid accepting responsibility for the unfortunate situation and yet avoid blaming or accusing the customer. To steer clear of these pitfalls, pay special attention to the tone of your letter. Keep in mind that a tactful and courteous letter can build goodwill while denying the claim (Figure 10.4).

When refusing to make an adjustment

- ✧ Demonstrate understanding of the complaint
- ✧ Explain your refusal
- ✧ Suggest alternative action

When refusing to adjust a claim, avoid language that might have a negative impact on the reader. Instead, demonstrate that you understand and have considered the complaint. Then, even if the claim is unreasonable, rationally explain why you are refusing the request, but don't apologize or rely on company policy. End the letter on a respectful and action-oriented note. This chapter's Checklist for Refusals to Make Adjustments reminds you of the tasks involved in such messages.

extend credit to a business, explain your reasons as factually and as impersonally as possible–perhaps the firm's latest financial statements don't meet your criteria, or its credit rating has fallen below an acceptable minimum. Also, explain the steps that must be taken to restore credit. Emphasize the benefits of continued dealings on a cash basis until the firm's creditworthiness has been established or restored. You might offer discounts for cash purchases or assistance in cooperative merchandising to reduce the firm's inventory and increase its cash flow. Third-party loans are another possibility you might suggest.

In a letter denying credit to a business

- ✧ Be more factual and less personal than in a letter to an individual
- ✧ Suggest ways to continue doing business

Whether dealing with business customers or consumers, companies that deny credit exercise good judgment in order to avoid legal action. A faulty decision may unfairly do damage to a person's reputation, which in turn may provoke a lawsuit and other bad publicity for the company. Handling credit denials over the phone instead of in writing is no guarantee of avoiding trouble; companies that orally refuse credit still proceed with caution. For a reminder of the tasks involved in this type of message, see this chapter's Checklist for Credit Refusals.

Be aware that credit is a legally sensitive subject.

Conveying Unfavourable News About People

From time to time, most managers must convey bad news about people. Letters to prospective employers may be written in direct order. On the other hand, letters to job applicants and employees are often written in indirect order, because the reader will most certainly be emotionally involved.

Use the indirect plan when giving someone bad news about his or her own job; use the direct plan when giving bad news about someone else's job.

Refusing to Write Recommendation Letters

If your position at work requires you to write recommendation letters, it is important to seek the advice of someone who understands the legal pitfalls to be avoided when terminating employment. You can consult human resources personnel or a lawyer who specializes in employment matters.[7] Many former employers refuse to write recommendation letters, especially for people whose job performance has been unsatisfactory. Generally speaking, letters written to a prospective employer that refuse to provide a recommendation are typically brief and direct:

In letters informing prospective employers that you will not provide a recommendation, be direct, brief, and factual.

> We received your request for a recommendation for Yolanda Johnson. According to the guidelines from our human resources department, we are authorized to confirm only that Ms. Johnson worked for Freemont Inc. for three years, from June 1996 to July 1999.

For letters to applicants themselves, also seek professional advice. Any refusal to cooperate may seem a personal slight and a threat to the applicant's future. To avoid potential ill feeling, it is important to handle the situation with diplomacy. The following example is brief but polite:

In letters telling job applicants that you will not write a recommendation, use the utmost tact.

> Although I am unable to write a formal recommendation for your position, I can send Freemont Inc. a confirmation of your employment dates. You may want to consult with your professors at university for detailed references. Best of luck in your career.

This message attempts to maintain good will while refusing the recipient's request for a job reference by suggesting an alternative avenue for assistance.

Giving Negative Performance Reviews

In performance reviews, say what's right as well as what's wrong, and explain how the employee can improve performance.

A performance review is a manager's formal or informal evaluation of an employee. Few other communication tasks require such a broad range of skill and strategy as what's needed for performance reviews, whether positive or negative. The main purpose of these reviews is to improve employee performance by (1) emphasizing and clarifying job requirements, (2) giving employees feedback on their efforts at fulfilling those requirements, and (3) guiding their continued efforts by developing a plan of action, along with rewards and opportunities. In addition to improving employee performance, performance reviews help companies set organizational standards and communicate organizational values.[8]

Positive and negative performance reviews share several characteristics: The tone is objective and unbiased, the language is nonjudgmental, and the focus is on resolving the problem.[9] Also, to increase objectivity, more organizations are giving their employees feedback from multiple sources.[10]

Checklist for Credit Refusals

A. Buffer

1. Introduce a topic that is relevant and that both you and the reader can agree on.
2. Eliminate apologies and negative-sounding words.
3. Phrase the buffer to avoid misleading the reader.
4. Limit the length of the buffer.
5. Express appreciation for the credit request.
6. Introduce resale information.

B. Reasons

1. Check the lead-in from the buffer for smoothness.
2. Make a transition from the favourable to the unfavourable message.
3. Make a transition from the general to the specific.
4. Avoid a condescending lecture about how credit is earned.
5. Avoid relying on unexplained company policy.
6. Stress the benefits of not being overextended.
7. Encourage a later credit application, if future approval is realistic.
8. Phrase reasons in terms of experience with others.
9. Carefully present reasons for the refusal.
   a. Clearly state the reasons if the reader will accept them.
   b. Explain your general credit criteria.
   c. Refer to a credit-reporting agency you have used.
   d. Use *insufficient information* as a reason only if this is the case.
   e. To avoid the risk of legal action, omit reasons entirely for extraordinarily sensitive or combative readers or when evidence is unusually negative or involves behavioural flaws. Consider seeking legal advice in situations such as these.
10. Remind the reader of the benefits of cash purchases.

C. The Bad News

1. Make the refusal clear to the reader.
2. Offer only honest encouragement about considering the credit application at a later date.
3. Avoid negative words, such as "must decline."
4. Suggest positive alternatives, such as cash and layaway purchases.
5. Handle refusals of business credit differently.
   a. Recommend cash purchases for small, frequent orders.
   b. Describe cash discounts (include figures).
   c. Suggest reducing inventory so that the business can strengthen its credit rating.
   d. Offer promotional and marketing aid.
   e. Suggest a later review of the credit application, if future approval is realistic.

D. Positive, Friendly, Helpful Close

1. Avoid business clichés, apologies, and words of regret.
2. Suggest actions the reader might take.
3. Encourage the reader to look to the future, when the application may be approved.
4. Include sales promotion material only if the customer would not be offended.

Be aware that employee performance reviews can play an important role in lawsuits. It's difficult to criticize employees face to face, and it's just as hard to include criticism in written performance evaluations. Nevertheless, if you fire an employee for incompetence and the performance evaluations are all positive, the employee can sue your company, maintaining you had no cause to terminate employment.[11] So, as difficult as it may be, make sure your performance evaluations are well balanced and honest.

When you need to give a negative performance review, remember the following guidelines:[12]

- *Confront the problem right away.* Avoiding performance problems only makes them worse. The one acceptable reason to wait is if you need time to calm down and regain your objectivity.
- *Plan your message.* Be clear about your concerns, and include examples of the employee's specific actions. Think about any possible biases you may have, and get feedback from others. Collect all relevant facts (both strengths and weaknesses).
- *Deliver the message in private.* Whether in writing or in person, make sure you address the performance problem privately. Don't send performance reviews by e-mail or fax. If you're reviewing an employee's performance face to face, conduct the review in a meeting arranged expressly for that purpose, and consider holding the meeting in a conference room, the employee's office, or some other neutral area.
- *Focus on the problem.* Discuss the problems caused by the employee's behaviour (without attacking the employee). Compare the employee's performance with what's expected, with company goals, or with job requirements (not with other employees' performance). Identify the consequences of continuing poor performance, and show you're committed to helping solve the problem.
- *Ask for a commitment from the employee.* Help the employee understand that planning for and making improvements are the employee's responsibility. However, finalize decisions jointly so that you can be sure any action to be taken is achievable. In fact, set a schedule for improvement and for following up with evaluations of that improvement.

Even if your employee's performance has been disappointing, you would do well to mention some good points in your performance review. Then you must clearly and tactfully state how the employee can better meet the responsibilities of the job. If the performance review is to be effective, be sure to suggest ways that the employee can improve.[13]

Going Online

Protect Yourself When You Write—and Receive—a Job Reference

Learn about exit interviews and guidelines for terminating employment by examining Employers Online, a Government of Canada sponsored Web site that informs small business owners and entrepreneurs about hiring and firing employees. Find out about employment standards legislation, just cause, constructive dismissal, and other topics related to employment termination. At the government of Canada site for employers, start with Human Resource Management and then look at the Layoffs and Terminations page. You can also see regulations for particular provinces on this site:

employers.gc.ca

SHARPENING YOUR CAREER SKILLS

Mastering the Art of Constructive Criticism

To improve, people need to be evaluated, but criticism from others is often hard to take. The way you tell someone "You did it wrong" can destroy goodwill and cooperation, or it can build the relationship and help the person retain self-esteem, learn from the mistake, and improve performance. To criticize constructively, follow these suggestions:

- ✧ **Get all the facts first.** Don't accept hearsay or rumours. Find out who did or said what, when, where, why, and how—and be specific.
- ✧ **Don't act in haste.** Never act while you're angry. Think things out before you write or speak, and then explain your criticism calmly, rationally, and objectively.
- ✧ **Phrase your remarks impersonally.** Criticize the mistake, not the person. Focus your remarks on the action only, and analyze it thoughtfully.
- ✧ **Never criticize in an offhand manner.** Treat the situation seriously. Take the time to state the problem in detail, explaining what was wrong and why.
- ✧ **Don't ridicule, talk down, or use sarcasm.** An abusive tone prevents people from accepting what you have to say. Respect readers and listeners, giving them the benefit of the doubt.

- **Make the offence clear.** Don't talk in generalities. Be specific about exactly what was done wrong.
- **Preface the criticism with a kind word or a compliment.** Start with a few words of praise or admiration, saying how much you value the person. First the good news; then the bad.
- **Supply the answer.** Explain how to do things right. Don't dwell on the mistake; emphasize how to correct it and avoid repeating it.
- **Ask for cooperation.** Don't demand cooperation. Asking makes the person feel like a team member and provides an incentive to improve.
- **Limit yourself to one criticism for each offence.** Don't dredge up or rehash past mistakes. Focus on the current problem.
- **End on a friendly note.** Don't leave things up in the air, to be discussed again later. Settle them now, and make the close friendly. Let the last memory of the matter be a good one.
- **Forgive and forget.** Once the criticism has been made, let the person start with a clean slate. Avoid looking for more mistakes, and give the person a chance to improve.
- **Take steps to prevent a recurrence.** Follow up to make sure the person is acting on your suggestions and doing things right.

If you follow these guidelines, constructive criticism can benefit you, your company, and—most important—the person you're criticizing.

CAREER APPLICATIONS

1. Think back over the lessons you've learned in life. How did you benefit from someone telling you the truth about something you were doing wrong?
2. With a partner, role-play a situation in which one of you is a manager and the other a lower-level employee. The manager is angry because the employee repeatedly arrives late for work, takes long lunches, and leaves five to ten minutes early. However, the employee's work is always excellent. After the role-play, analyze what the manager did right and what could be improved.

ON THE JOB
Solving a Communication Dilemma at Wal-Mart

Manufacturers who want to sell their products through Wal-Mart undergo a gruelling process to receive the approval that will put their goods on the shelves of a major multinational retailer. The Wal-Mart *Supplier Proposal Guide*, which all potential suppliers must read before submitting their products, gives them the facts about Wal-Mart's philosophy, standards, and practices—the policies and rules suppliers must observe if they are chosen to sell their products through Wal-Mart stores.

When Wal-Mart receives a proposal, the supplier-development staff direct the products to the appropriate buyers for review and evaluation. Potential suppliers are guaranteed a reply by phone or letter from Wal-Mart within 90 days of receipt of the completed proposal package, but are not guaranteed a supplier number. Final judgment lies in the office of the purchasing agent at head office, with no certainty of success.

The proposal process benefits Wal-Mart by giving them suppliers whose products and services can enhance the giant retailer's bottom line. But the process also benefits companies, even if Wal-Mart rejects them, because it helps the firms to analyze their own businesses practices and improve them. Undoubtedly, effective communication is one of the key skills Wal-Mart's purchasing agents must have to refuse potential suppliers after they have worked hard to become a Wal-Mart partner and still maintain their good will.[14]

Your Mission: You're on the purchasing staff at Wal-Mart at the home office. Your job includes responding to requests and proposals from companies that would like to become Wal-Mart suppliers. These requests cover a variety of topics, from meetings to making sales presentations.

1. You have received a proposal from a company whose product, you believe, would be attractive to current Wal-Mart customers. But the applicant has not effectively discussed future demand for the product, one of the key questions in the proposal package. You'd like the applicant to resubmit the proposal, but he will have to wait an additional 90 days for a response. Which of the following paragraphs does the best job of presenting the bad news?
   a. It's too bad you neglected to answer fully the key question about future demand for your product. If you want us to consider your product for display at Wal-Mart, you'd better fill out the questionnaire completely.
   b. We know completing the supplier proposal is a demanding and time-consuming process. As the instructions indicate, all key questions must be fully answered if the proposal is to receive consideration. We are returning your proposal package so that you can review your answer to Question #2, dealing with future competition for your product.

c. We appreciate the work you put into completing your supplier proposal. You did a thorough job. But please expand on Question #2.

2. Continuing with the case of the incomplete proposal, which of the closing paragraphs would you choose and why?

a. We do appreciate that you took a lot of time to work on the proposal, but we can't read it until you complete it. And you won't be hearing from us for another 90 days.

b. If you need further assistance in completing your proposal, please consult the Internet bookmarks listed in the guidebook. We look forward to receiving your revised supplier proposal.

c. Thank you for your attention to this matter.

3. Personal contacts are an important source of new business opportunities in many industries. In some cases, business people develop these contacts through active participation in industry or professional groups, visits to trade shows, alumni societies, and other groups. You've recently received a request from a former classmate (Marcia DeLancey) who is now a sales manager for a plastics manufacturer. She wants to visit your office to present her company's plastic containers. However, you are already familiar with the company and know that it is too small to meet your needs for on-time global deliveries. You didn't know DeLancey all that well; in fact, you had to think for a minute to remember who she was (this is the first contact you've had with her since you both graduated five years ago). Which of the following openings would be most appropriate, keeping in mind that you know her company can't make the grade?

a. Congratulations on reaching such an impressive position at your new company. I hope you enjoy your work as much as I enjoy mine. Thank you for your recent inquiry–evaluating such requests is one of my key responsibilities.

b. Great to hear from you; I'd love to catch up on old times with you and find out how you're doing in your new job. I bounced around a bit after university, but I really feel that I've found my niche here at Wal-Mart.

c. I'm sorry to say that Wal-Mart has already evaluated your company and found its resources were not a good match for our international delivery needs. However, I do appreciate your getting in touch, and I hope all is well with you.

4. Wal-Mart, like many corporate buyers, wants to establish stable, dependable relationships with suppliers. Having a supplier falter on the job or even go out of business without warning would be a huge disruption for Wal-Mart. As a result, your department is concerned about every supplier's financial health. The company that provides Wal-Mart with linens has done a good job for years, but recent events have left the company in precarious financial shape. Your office has already told the company that Wal-Mart would be forced to find another linen source if the company's finances didn't improve. Unfortunately, they've gotten even worse, and it's time to act. You've already written the buffer, reasons, and bad news, and now you need a positive close. Which of these would you choose?

a. Thank you very much for the products you've provided in the past. All of us here at Wal-Mart wish you the best in resolving your current situation. If you are able to meet our financial criteria in the future, by all means please get back in touch with us.

b. I understand that you're bound to be disappointed by our decisions. If you don't think our decision was valid or if there is more information that you believe we need to evaluate, please feel free to call me or my immediate supervisor to discuss the situation. We have to deal with quite a few suppliers, as you know, and I suppose there is a chance that we missed something in our initial evaluation.

c. I'm very sorry that we have to terminate our purchasing agreement with you. We relied on your company's products for many years, and it's a shame that we won't be able to in the future. I hope this decision doesn't affect your workforce too negatively. If there's anything we can do to help, please don't hesitate to call.

TAP Your Knowledge

Summary of Learning Outcomes

1. Choose correctly between indirect and direct approaches to a bad-news message. The direct approach to bad-news messages puts the bad news up front, then states the reasons (and perhaps offers an alternative), and closes with a positive statement. On the other hand, the indirect approach begins with a buffer (a neutral or positive statement), explains the reasons, clearly states the bad news (de-emphasizing it as much as possible), and closes with a positive statement. It's best to use the direct approach when you know your audience prefers receiving bad news first or if the bad news will cause readers little pain or disappointment. Otherwise, the indirect approach is best.

2. Establish the proper tone from the beginning of your message. To create an audience-centred tone, be aware of and use the cultural conventions that your audience expects. For audiences with few cultural differences, use the "you" attitude, choose positive words, and use language that is respectful. Adopting this tone helps your readers accept that your decision is firm, understand that your decision is fair and reasonable, remain well-disposed toward your company, and preserve their pride.

3. **Present bad news in a reasonable and understandable way.** To help your audience accept your message, place the positive points first, then the negative ones, when presenting your explanation. Explain why you have reached your decision before telling what the decision is. Try to highlight why the decision benefits the audience instead of your company, and provide enough detail in a concise manner.

4. **Write messages that motivate your audience to take constructive action.** To say no and still be diplomatic, use three techniques. First, de-emphasize the bad news by minimizing the space devoted to it, subordinating it in a complex or compound sentence, or embedding it mid-paragraph. Second, relate the bad news in a conditional (*if* or *when*) statement to imply that readers could have received or might someday receive a favourable answer. Third, imply the bad news by saying what you will do, not what you won't do.

5. **Close messages so that your audience is willing to continue a business relationship with your firm.** To maintain a business connection with your audience, use five techniques. First, keep your close as positive as possible. Second, encourage additional communication *only* if you are willing to discuss your decision further. Third, keep a positive outlook on the future. Fourth, be sincere. Fifth, be confident about keeping the person as a customer.

Test Your Knowledge

Review Questions

1. Define the term "buffer."
2. Describe four kinds of buffer statements, and give examples for each.
3. Why shouldn't you apologize when giving your reasons for your decision in a bad-news message?
4. When should you state your decision in direct terms in bad-news messages?
5. What are the dangers of using negative language in bad-news messages?
6. What circumstances warrant the direct approach in bad-news messages?
7. Define "defamation" and explain why it must be avoided in claim refusals.
8. What guidelines should you follow when refusing to write recommendation letters?

Apply Your Knowledge

Critical Thinking Questions

1. You have to tell a local restaurant owner that your plans have changed and you have to cancel the 90-person banquet scheduled for next month. Do you need to use a buffer? Why or why not?
2. Why is it important to end your bad-news message on a positive note?
3. If company policy changes, should you explain those changes to employees and customers at about the same time, or should you explain to employees first? Why?
4. If the purpose of your letter is to convey bad news, should you take the time to suggest alternatives to your reader? Why or why not?
5. The policy at your company is to refuse refunds on merchandise after 30 days. An important customer has written to request a refund on a purchase made 31 days ago, or he'll take his business elsewhere. How do you respond? Explain your answer.
6. When giving a negative performance review, should the impact be softened by addressing the problem a little at a time? Why or why not?

Practise Your Knowledge

Documents for Analysis

Read the following documents; then (1) analyze the strengths and weaknesses of each sentence and (2) revise each document so that it follows this chapter's guidelines.

Document 10.A: Conveying Bad News About Orders

We want to take this opportunity to thank you for your past orders. We have included our new catalogue of books, videos, films, and slides to let you know about our great new products. We included our price list also. Please use this list rather than the old one as we've had a slight increase in prices.

Per your request, we are sorry we can't send you the free examination copies of the textbooks you requested. The books, *Communication for Business* and *Winning the Presentation Game,* are two of our new titles that are enjoying brisk sales. It seems everyone is interested in communication skills these days.

We do apologize for not sending the exam copies for free. Our prices continue to rise along with everyone else's, and it's just not feasible to send everyone free copies. If you'd still like to have a look, please notice the prices in the list I've included and don't forget shipping and handling. You can also fax your order to the number shown on the sheet or e-mail your order over the Internet.

I'm sure these books would make a great addition to your collection. Again, we are sorry we couldn't grant your request, but we hope you order anyway.

Document 10.B: Communicating Negative Answers and Information

Your spring fraternity party sounds like fun. We're glad you've again chosen us as your caterer. Unfortunately, we have changed a few of our policies, and I wanted you to know about these changes in advance so that we won't have any misunderstandings on the day of the party.

We will arrange the delivery of tables and chairs as usual the evening before the party. However, if you want us to set up, there is now a $100.00 charge for that service. Of course, you might want to get some of the brothers and pledges to do it, which would save you money. We've also added a small charge for cleanup. This is only $3.00 per person (you can estimate because I know a lot of people come and go later in the evening).

Other than that, all the arrangements will be the same. We'll provide the skirt for the band stage, tablecloths, bar setup, and of course, the barbecue. Will you have the tubs of ice with soft drinks again? We can do that for you as well, but there will be a fee.

Please let me know if you have any problems with these changes and we'll try to work them out. I know it's going to be a great party.

Document 10.C: Refusing Adjustment of Claims and Complaints

I am responding to your letter of about six weeks ago asking for an adjustment on your fax/modem, model FM39Z. We test all our products before they leave the factory; therefore, it could not have been our fault that your fax/modem didn't work.

If you or someone in your office dropped the unit, it might have caused the damage. Or the damage could have been caused by the shipper if he dropped it. If so, you should file a claim with the shipper. At any rate, it wasn't our fault. The parts are already covered by warranty. However, we will provide labour for the repairs for $50.00, which is less than our cost since you are a valued customer.

We will have a booth at the upcoming trade fair there and hope to see you or someone from your office. We have many new models of office machines that we're sure you'll want to see. I've enclosed our latest catalogue. Hope to see you there.

Cases

Conveying Bad News About Orders

1. More to come: Letter explaining delay of Anne of Green Gables T-shirts Each year thousands of people attend the Charlottetown Festival to see plays featuring Lucy Maud Montgomery's fictional characters. Montgomery's stories have been loved by Canadians and by millions around the world, since the publication of her first novel, *Anne of Green Gables*, in 1908. Prince Edward Island has benefited immensely from tourists who travel there during the Festival season to enjoy not only the theatre but the sea, beaches, and Montgomery's birthplace. Souvenirs are popular among both Canadian and foreign visitors, who buy them for friends and relatives back home.

This summer's Festival was so successful that your local store, Little Things, has sold out its stock of child and youth size T-shirts featuring Anne's image. You've received a letter from a German tourist explaining that when his nieces and nephews saw his daughter's T-shirt, they each wanted one too. He's included his credit card number and expiry date, and wants two green T-shirts in size 6X, three white shirts in size 10-12, and two in size 14-16. His letter is dated October 6, 2001, and he is hoping to get the shirts in time for Christmas. Your problem is that you only have two blue shirts, size 6X–no green–in stock, and one white shirt, size 10-12. You do have lots of white shirts in size 14-16. More T-shirts won't be available until March 2001 as the product is seasonal. You also have some other items in stock, such as stickers, always popular with kids, and buttons.

Your Task: Write to Josef Mandelheim, Sonnenstrasse 4, 86669 Erlingshofen, Germany. Explain what you can do. Child-size shirts are $8.95 each, youth size $10.95, duty is 12% of the total, there is no GST, and shipping is $32.00.

2. BC blend: Letter explaining delays for Cedar Grove compost Ever since word got out about your company's "gourmet compost" (with a little help from your marketing department), Pacific Northwest gardeners can't seem to get enough of Cedar Grove Composting's $20 a cubic yard blend of rotting plant materials, vegetables, and of course, coffee grounds. The fact that your company picks up its composting materials as part of a mandatory recycling program in Vancouver is probably part of the appeal.

"It has a good, rich smell," Mary Heide, manager of Sky Nursery in Nanaimo, BC, told the press, while one of her employees raved about its "rich, brown coffee colour–kind of a mocha colour from a BC point of view." That was it. The orders from gardening retailers started pouring in as their customers heard of the stuff and demanded it for their gardens, despite the fact that your prices are 30 percent higher than everyone else's. It didn't help matters that your general manager, Jan Allen, publicized your $3 million, high-speed fans, cooling chambers, and other devices that "air out" the compost as it cures by telling the media that competing brands just "sit around in static piles. Ours has a higher degree of intelligence."

Your Task: As manager of Cedar Grove's wholesale division, you have a backlog of requests from retailers who are eager to fill their customers' orders, and you have to let them know that it's going to be about four weeks before you can fill them. Better write this bad-news form letter with as much care and concern as Cedar Grove puts into its compost.[15]

Communicating Negative Answers and Information

3. No time for talking: Memo from Trident Aquaculture Farming the ocean? You thought it was a crazy idea when you first heard of Trident Aquaculture, but you went for an interview anyway, offering your skills as an office manager. You changed your mind after winding up as administrative assistant for Michael D. Willinsky, president of the company and a skilled biologist and fish farmer who helped create the most innovative and promising sea-farming cage ever tested in the open ocean.

After trials in the blustery, icy seas off Nova Scotia and in the frozen St. Lawrence River, Willinsky's research team proved that their unique cage design–measuring about 12 m in diameter and based on Buckminster Fuller's geodesic dome–could survive 130–180 km/h winds, 2 to 4 m waves, strong currents, and fast-moving ice floes. Thanks to regular hand-feeding and protection from predators, the Arctic char salmon raised inside the Nova Scotia dome matured in a record 18 months (wild Arctic char mature in 6 to 8 years).

Seaside communities are desperate for economic alternatives to the traditional fishing industry, now that overfishing, pollution, and coastal development have depleted the world's natural fish supply. About 70 000 US and Canadian fishers lost their livelihood in 1993, when several major Atlantic fishing areas were closed to commercial fishing because of severe depletion. Yet the demand for fish products has increased. Willinsky's prototype sea dome promises to provide a sustainable supply of fresh- or salt-water fish, renew economic activity in coastal areas, and provide new jobs in the fishing industry.

One result is that Willinsky has become a popular speaker among government and industry leaders. But your boss has to divide his time between pursuing research and development, promoting aquaculture, and managing his company. Next month he travels to Hawaii to speak at an international conference on ocean farming, sponsored by the United Nations Food and Agriculture Organization. Willinsky's US research partner, Michael A. Champ, wants Willinsky to appear at a joint speaking engagement for the Halifax, NS, chamber of commerce. Unfortunately, the date falls during Willinsky's week in Hawaii.

Your Task: Willinsky has asked you to fax Champ. Write the informal memo to Michael A. Champ, President, Environmental Systems Development Company (at 1-703-899-7326 in Falls Church, Virginia) and suggest an alternative date.[16]

4. Feeling at home in Denmark: Letter to Web House critiquing its homepage Web House is an award-winning Danish company that designs Web sites and other Internet materials for international clients. Christian Broberg has hired you as an independent consultant to evaluate the company's home page from a Canadian point of view. You'll need to visit the Web House site, **www.webhouse.dk**, and study it from the perspective of a Canadian business manager. Consider all aspects of clear intercultural communication.

Your Task: Write a letter to Christian Broberg, Assistant Director (Web House, Hasserisgade 30, 9000 Aalborg, Denmark), and explain why the design of the Web House site may cause problems for English-speaking clients. Your message is not entirely good news, so take extra care in the way you explain your viewpoints to someone from another country.

5. Music Mania: Letter rejecting Web site proposal Your amateur band, Four Guys, plays at parties and in clubs. You have a lot of fun entertaining your audience with popular rock and original compositions, and your group usually has a gig. All the members have thought that getting a Web site would be great for business–you can advertise your band, the music you play, who you are–as well as provide references from previous customers and give contact numbers. You also thought links to other musical sites would draw interest to your band's Web site. A Web site would be a great opportunity for more exposure. Who knows? Maybe you'd get the attention of a music producer, and get a recording contract! One of the guys, Jim McKay, has a buddy who wants to start his own Web site company and is happy to create a site for the band on spec.

The result isn't exactly what you and your band expected. Colours are black, purple, and green. The text is very small and hard to read. The site is difficult to navigate. Jim's friend neglected to include a contact e-mail address and links to other sites. The guys are really disappointed. At least they didn't have to put down a deposit for the work.

Your Task: Since you are the band's manager, you've been designated as the bearer of bad news. Write a letter to Jim's buddy, Grant Roberts, telling him you won't be needing his services.

6. The cheque's in the mail–almost: Letter from Sun Microsystems explaining late payments You'd think that a computer company could install a new management information system without a hitch, wouldn't you? The people at Sun Microsystems thought so too, but they were wrong. When they installed their own new computerized system for getting information to management, a few things, such as payments to vendors, fell through the cracks.

It was embarrassing, to say the least, when Sun's suppliers started clamouring for payment. Terence Lenaghan, the corporate controller, found himself in the unfortunate position of having to tell 6000 vendors why Sun Microsystems had failed to pay its bills on time–and why it might be late with payments again. "Until we get these bugs ironed out," Lenaghan confessed, "we're going to have to finish some of the accounting work by hand. That means that some of our payments to vendors will probably be late next month too. We'd better write to our suppliers and let them know that there's nothing wrong with the company's financial performance. The last thing we want is for our vendors to think our business is going down the tubes."

Your Task: Write a form letter to Sun Microsystems' 6000 vendors explaining that bugs in their new management information system are responsible for the delays in payment.[17]

7. Everything old is new again: E-mail message reporting polyester findings Polyester got a bad rap in the 1980s. Now it's making a comeback in both fashion and food. What? Eat and drink from polyester containers? It's an idea whose time has come, according to chemical companies ranging from Dow to Amoco. An ice-cold Coke sipped from a polyester container may be tough for some people to swallow, but experts predict that a new generation of plastic may solve many of the problems, such as carbonation loss and heat sensitivity, caused by the containers now being used.

Today's drink bottles use a plastic called PET (polyethylene terephthalate). When stressed by heat, PET is too porous to contain the "fizz." But PET can now be mixed with a recently developed polyester called PEN (polyethylene naphthalate) to create a new generation of tougher plastic. Shell Chemical's director of polyester research and development, David Richardson, believes in the product. "In a few years, I'll be able to fix you a nice meal, and everything in it will come out of a polyester container."

Why make the switch from aluminum or glass to plastic? "Plastic is less deadly than glass when you throw it at a soccer match," says Richard Marion, an executive at Amoco Corporation's Amoco Chemical Company. Airlines like it because it's lightweight. Their little jelly containers used in First Class will weigh less. Consumers like it because it's clear, resealable, lightweight, and easily recycled. Polyester is definitely making a comeback. But one segment of the population is proving resistant to the trend: young adults. In a market research study, students preferred aluminum cans: Of all the container materials, aluminum ranked highest, achieving an 84 percent acceptance rate.

According to the study, students like the feel of the aluminum cans (plastic feels slippery and is harder to hold) and believe that aluminum keeps drinks colder. They also believe that aluminum keeps the carbonation longer, creating a "mouth buzz," whereas plastic lets the fizz out. And finally, they think that aluminum cans look "cool" and that plastic containers look "dorky."

Your market research team has come up with a couple of ways to deal with these perceptions. One approach would be an ad campaign showing "cool" young adults drinking from plastic bottles. Another would be ads showing that new technology is helping the plastic containers to hold in the "fizz."

Your Task: As assistant director of marketing for Coca-Cola, write an e-mail message to your boss, Tom Ruffenbach, <TomRuf@marketing.coca-cola.com>, in which you report your findings and suggest ways to overcome this consumer bias.[17]

Refusing Adjustment of Claims and Complaints

8. Your monkey, your choice: Letter from Choquette's Exotic Pets refusing a damage claim As a well-known exotic animal dealer in the Montreal area, your boss, Roger Choquette, has dealt with his share of customers experiencing buyer's regret. Despite his warnings, many of them still buy their exotic pets for the wrong reasons. When Melissa Carpenter bought Binky, a red-tailed guenon monkey, she begged Mr. Choquette to reduce his price to $10 000 because she had "fallen in love with Binky's soulful eyes and adorable button nose." Now she wants to return poor Binky, and you have never seen your boss so angry.

"Listen to this!" fumes Mr. Choquette as he reads Carpenter's letter:

> While I was at work, I locked your monkey in his own room–which I equipped with his own colour TV (with cable) and which I spent days wallpapering with animal pictures. Then last night your monkey somehow unlocked the door, ripped out my telephone, opened the refrigerator, smashed eggs all over my kitchen and my new Persian carpet, broke 14 of the china dishes my mother gave me when I got married, and squeezed toothpaste all over the Louis XIV settee I inherited from my grandmother!

"Not only does she demand that I take poor Binky back after she's abused him through her ignorance and neglect," snapped Mr. Choquette, "but she wants me to pay $150 000 in damages for her car, her apartment, and her state of mind."

Your boss is so upset that you decide to write Ms. Carpenter yourself.

Your Task: Write to Lisa Carpenter (22 Oakland Ave, Westmount, QC H3Y 1N9) and include a copy of her contract. It clearly states Roger Choquette's policy: refunds only if animals are returned in good health, and absolutely no warranty against damages. Each pet comes with specific care instructions, including warnings about certain idiosyncrasies that could cause problems in the wrong environment.

Despite the fact that Binky is probably traumatized by his experiences, Mr. Choquette has generously agreed to accept his return, refunding Ms. Carpenter's $10 000. However, he will not accept liability for any loss of property or for any claims of mental duress on the part of Ms. Carpenter.[19]

9. Not so good: Bill 180 says no way As a Campbell's Soup Canada corporate affairs employee, you've been working on the Labels for Education program since its start here in the fall of 1998. You've enjoyed watching schools across the country receive free audio-visual, computer, sports, and electronic equipment as well as books, videocassettes, and CD-ROMs in exchange for the labels the kids save from Campbell's Soup tins and packages. The program has been in place in US schools since 1973, and now cash-strapped Canadian schools can obtain much-needed equipment to enhance their students' education. Although it takes thousands of labels to exchange for products, kids, parents, teachers, and administrators think the program is very worthwhile, especially with limited funding for education.

But Campbell's has to discontinue the program in Quebec. The company didn't know that Bill 180, passed by the provincial legislature in 1998, the same year Campbell's Labels for Education began in Canada, prohibits commercial solicitation in public schools. Said Alain Leclerc, press attaché to Quebec's Minister of Education, Bill 180 makes it unacceptable for companies to "incite or put pressure on children to consume products." You saw Kellogg's end its Education is Tops program in Quebec, for which kids brought Kellogg's box tops to their schools, giving educators the pleasure of seeing 10 cents from each top going to educational materials. Now, Campbell's has received notice from Ministry of Education officials on February 22 to end the program in two weeks. "If you don't do anything, we will," Campbell's was told. In Canada, 3600 schools have registered for Labels for Education, and only 70 are in Quebec. Yet, although Campbell's must pull the plug on their educational program, companies like Scholastic Books of Markham, Ontario continue to sell their products through catalogues distributed in the classroom, and chocolate manufacturers have kids sell their candies door-to-door for fundraising programs, with the companies reaping the profits. You don't see the fairness.

Your Task: As a public affairs specialist with Campbell's, compose a form letter, to be mailed to Quebec parents, who want to know what's happening with Campbell's Labels for Education program.[20]

10. It's our right: Memo to office staff introducing e-mail surveillance When you were hired as Alicia DelFranco's personal assistant at DelFranco Advertising, you signed a contract agreeing to use e-mail, the Internet, and other electronic tools only for work-related activities. But everyone e-mails jokes around the office and sends messages to friends and family during the day. This happens in every wired business–and no one (as far as you know) gets fired. So it came as a shock to you and everyone else when Jack Kwan and Marci Stone, two of the firm's best account managers, emptied their desks and were escorted out of the building by a security guard. Sure, you used to get lots of jokes on your computer from Jack and Marci–maybe they did online shopping, too, and even looked at offensive sites. But they earned a lot of money for the firm, and clients liked working with them.

Calling you into her office after Jack and Marci have left, Alicia DelFranco discusses these developments. As an employer, she explains, she has a right to monitor how her employees use electronic communications in her firm. Sure, she expects her people to do some personal e-mailing in the office and some Web surfing during the day–she knows it goes on. But Jack and Marci were too free with the privilege. They may have revealed some company secrets to friends in other advertising firms. The new ads for Woofgang dog biscuits, created by rival Smith Advertising, was just too full of ideas Jack and Marci discussed with Alicia for a cat-food producer on DelFranco's books. Alicia has to protect her company and her employees who rely on her for their paycheques. So, Alicia tells you, she has hired a company called stalker.com to set up an electronic surveillance system that will monitor how employees use the Internet and e-mail. They'll analyze computer logs to see if staff have been doing anything improper online and submit weekly reports to her.

Your Task: Alicia wants you to draft a memo to all staff about these new developments. The trick is to communicate this news but to maintain their goodwill. She'll review the memo with you after you've completed it.[21]

Refusing to Extend Credit

11. Photo finish: No credit to Tod Rooker, photographer You've dealt with Tod Rooker, a photographer of weddings and family events, for the last 13 years with no problem. He's sent numerous jobs to you for developing and has always paid on time. But for the last two jobs he has asked your company, Best Photo Labs, to extend credit. He says the wedding and special events market is drying up in his neighbourhood, and he's getting few referrals from old customers. He has to work as an industrial photographer during the day for a friend's firm, and can only work evenings at his own business. He isn't making the money he used to, but he hopes to get enough cash flowing from his day job to pay Best Labs for developing his photos. He sure can't ask for money from his customers until they see the finished pictures.

But Best Photo Labs has a business to run, and they can't rely on goodwill to pay their technicians, developing chemicals, photographic paper, as well as their rent and utilities.

Your Task: As the office manager for Best Photo Labs, you've dealt with Tod Rooker's account for several years. You know he's a nice guy, and a good photographer. Write Tod a tactful letter refusing credit. Tod's address is Tod Rooker, Professional Photographer, 195 Argyle St., Fredericton, NB E3B 1T6

12. Pay or sell: Last chance to settle condo management fees You don't like writing such letters, but during your five years as a property manager for Provide Corporation you've had to tell condo owners that if they don't pay their monthly maintenance fees, Provide will attach a lien to their bank accounts, as they are permitted to do by provincial law. The problem you're having now is with Mrs. Edith Bookman, a recent widow who has fallen behind two months in her maintenance fees. The money she–and all the other apartment owners pay each month–goes towards maintaining the building and grounds in order to keep the property healthy and attractive. Without the monthly maintenance fee from each owner, the condo would fall into disrepair, and everyone would have to pay a special assessment to bring it back to standard. No one wants that to happen.

You know that things are difficult for Mrs. Bookman right now. You've consulted with the condo's board of directors, made up of owners who give direction to the property manager when needed. They've told you not to attach Mrs. Bookman's account now, although provincial law says you could. Instead, they want to give her another month to pay the arrears.

Your Task: Write a letter to Mrs. Bookman following the Board's direction. Explain that she must pay her two months arrears with her third payment, and why doing so is important. If she doesn't, Provide will attach her bank account for the balance owed as well as a $500 administrative lien fee, which they are legally allowed to do. Mrs. Bookman lives at 1335 St. Albert Trail NW, Suite 3E, Edmonton, AB T5L 4R3.

Developing Your Internet Skills

Going Online: Protect Yourself When You Write a Job Reference, p. 253

As you explore the Layoffs and Terminations section at employers.gc.ca you'll see how complicated the ins and outs of reference writing have become. Do you think these constraints are good for employees? For employers? Why or why not?

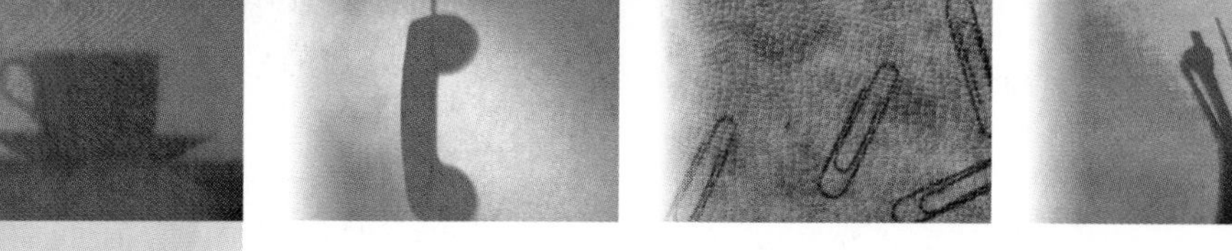

CHAPTER 11

Writing Persuasive Messages

AFTER STUDYING THIS CHAPTER, YOU WILL BE ABLE TO

1. Discuss the planning tasks that need extra attention when preparing persuasive messages
2. Distinguish between emotional and logical appeals, and discuss how to balance them
3. Describe the AIDA plan for persuasive messages
4. Compare sales messages with fund-raising messages
5. List at least four attention-getting devices for sales messages
6. List the ten guidelines that will help you strengthen your fund-raising messages

ON THE JOB
Facing a Communication Dilemma at the Young Entrepreneurs' Association

Promoting a Good Thing

It started as a thought, and grew into a nation-wide support group for young business people with original ideas and the need for advice and encouragement. Picking up on the energy from meeting and talking with fellow winners of the 1991 Young Entrepreneur of the Year Awards, sponsored by the Federal Business Development Bank, Robert French established the Young Entrepreneurs' Association. Since the group's founding in 1992, members can find peer support and business contacts, as well as develop lifelong friendships, by taking advantage of the YEA's many educational and social programs. Currently, the YEA has local chapters in British Columbia, Alberta, Manitoba, Ontario, Nova Scotia, New Brunswick, and Newfoundland, with more being established.

To persuade students and young entrepreneurs to join the YEA, staff must craft messages that get attention, create interest, encourage desire, and motivate action. Strong communication skills are essential for members of the non-profit organization's board of directors.

With 500 members in the year 2000, the YEA certainly has room to grow and to provide numerous benefits to young Canadian business people. The non-profit organization offers a pitch-free environment where members can discuss their achievements and challenges and share knowledge and information that can help other entrepreneurs, seasoned or new, to attain success. In addition to peer-mentoring groups, YEA members also receive referrals to the media that will give them publicity and recognition, a subscription to *The YEA Spirit*, the organization's newsletter filled with useful resources, and invitations to many social occasions where they can both relax and make important contacts for growing their businesses.

The YEA itself, however, is still in its infancy. Open to anyone under 35 who owns a business, the YEA also offers associate and student memberships. Creating a grassroots network of young business people is a challenge, because YEA staff, like co-presidents Roger Van Maris and Jason Thistle, must persuade busy students and entrepreneurs to join in order to gain both the personal and professional benefits that participation offers. And, because the YEA has limited resources, Van Maris and Thistle must also persuade established companies, such as Royal Bank, IBM, and InternetDirect, the YEA's Internet service provider, to provide financial support, guest speakers, and in-kind services. The entire seven-member board of directors is acutely aware of the need for members and sponsors to keep the organization alive. If you worked as YEA director, how would you persuade students and business people of the group's value? How would you convince companies to support the YEA? How would you organize such messages? What would you do to get your audience's attention?[1]

Planning Persuasive Messages

LEARNING OUTCOME 1
Discuss the planning tasks that need extra attention when preparing persuasive messages.

Much more than simply asking somebody to do something, **persuasion** is the attempt to change an audience's attitudes, beliefs, or actions.[2] Persuasive messages aim to influence audiences who are inclined to resist, so they depend heavily on strategic planning. Before you begin to write a persuasive message, consider some important questions: What legal and ethical issues apply here? Who is my audience? How will my credibility affect my message? What tools can help me persuade my audience? Would emotional or logical appeals be best?

Ethical Persuasion

The word *persuasion* is used negatively when associated with dishonest and unethical practices, such as coaxing, urging, and sometimes even tricking people into accepting an idea, buying a product, or taking an action they neither want nor need. However, the positive meaning of *persuasion* is influencing your audience members by informing them and by aiding their understanding, thereby allowing them the freedom to choose.[3] Ethical business people inform customers of the benefits of an idea, an organization, a product, a donation, or an action so that customers can recognize how well it will fill a need they truly have.

When you are trying to influence people's actions, knowledge of the law is crucial. However, merely avoiding what is illegal may not always be enough. To maintain the highest standards of business ethics, make every attempt to persuade without manipulating. Choose words that won't be misinterpreted when de-emphasizing negatives, and be sure you don't distort the truth. Show consideration for your audience by adopting the "you" attitude with honest concern for their needs and interests. Your consideration of audience needs is more than ethical; it's the proper use of persuasion. Moreover, it's more likely to achieve the response you intended and to satisfy your audience's needs.

Questions to ask before you begin to write a persuasive message:

- ✧ What legal and ethical issues apply here?
- ✧ Who is my audience?
- ✧ How will my credibility affect my message?
- ✧ What tools can help me persuade my audience?
- ✧ Would emotional or logical appeals be best?

Audience Needs

The best persuasive messages are closely connected to your audience's existing desires and interests.[4] One of the most effective ways to motivate members of your audience is to offer to satisfy their needs. Of course, people have many needs, but some researchers believe that certain needs have priority and that the most basic needs (such as security and safety) must be met before a person will seek to fulfill higher-level needs (such as esteem and status).[5] For example, say that you supervise someone who consistently arrives late for work. Once you've analyzed the need that motivates him to arrive late, you can craft an appeal that will interest him in your message about changing his behaviour.

To motivate members of your audience, offer to satisfy their needs.

Because people's needs differ, people respond differently to any given message. Not everyone is interested in economy, for instance, or fair play. As a matter of fact, some people have innermost needs that make appeals to status and greed much more effective. To accommodate these individual differences, analyze your audience and then construct a message that appeals to their needs. A letter requesting an adjustment for defective merchandise could focus on issues of fairness or on legal issues, depending on the reader. A sales letter for sheepskin seat covers might emphasize prestige to Porsche drivers and comfort to Chevrolet drivers.

To assess various individual needs, you can refer to specific information such as **demographics** (the age, gender, occupation, income, education, and other quantifiable characteristics of the people you're trying to persuade) and **psychographics** (the psychological characteristics of a person, such as personality, attitudes, and lifestyle). In addition, both types of information are strongly influenced by culture.

Demographics include characteristics such as age, gender, occupation, income, and education.

Psychographics include characteristics such as personality, attitudes, and lifestyle.

When analyzing your audience, take into account their cultural expectations and practices so that you don't undermine your persuasive message by using an inappropriate appeal or by organizing your message in a way that seems unfamiliar or uncomfortable. Persuasion is different in different cultures. For example, in France using an aggressive, hard-sell technique is no way to win respect from your audience. In fact, such an approach would probably antagonize your audience. In Germany, where people tend to focus on technical matters, plan on verifying any figures you use for support, and make sure they are exact. In Sweden, audiences tend to focus on theoretical questions and strategic implications, whereas in Canada and the United States audiences are usually concerned with more practical matters.[6] Your understanding and respect for cultural differences will not only help you satisfy the needs of audience members but also help them respect you.

Writer Credibility

For you to persuade a skeptical or hostile audience, you must make them believe you know what you're talking about and that you're not trying to mislead them. Your **credibility** is your ability to be believed because you're reliable and worthy of confidence. Without credibility, your efforts to persuade will seem manipulative.

One of the best ways to gain credibility is to support your message with facts. Testimonials, documents, guarantees, statistics, research results, and the like all provide seemingly objective evidence for what you have to say, so they can add to your credibility. The more specific and relevant your proof, the better. Another good way to improve your credibility is to name your sources, especially if they're respected by your audience. Still other ways of gaining credibility include:

Gain credibility by supporting your argument with facts such as testimonials, documents, guarantees, statistics, and research results.

Your credibility is improved if you are enthusiastic, objective, sincere, expert, and trustworthy and if your intentions are good and you establish common ground.

- *Being enthusiastic.* Your excitement about the subject of your message can infect your audience.
- *Being objective.* Your understanding of and willingness to acknowledge all sides of an issue help you present fair and logical arguments in your persuasive message.
- *Being sincere.* Your honesty, genuineness, good faith, and truthfulness help you focus on your audience's needs.
- *Being an expert.* Your knowledge of your message's subject area (or even of some other area) helps you give your audience the quality information they need to make a decision.
- *Having good intentions.* Your willingness to keep your audience's best interests at heart helps you create persuasive messages that are ethical.
- *Being trustworthy.* Your honesty and dependability help you earn your audience's respect.
- *Establishing common ground.* Any beliefs, attitudes, and background experiences you have in common with members of your audience will help them identify with you.

Once you are committed to ethical persuasion, to satisfying the needs of your audience, and to building your credibility, you can concentrate on strengthening your message with some important persuasive tools.

Language and Other Persuasive Tools

Semantics is the meaning of words and other symbols.

Two ways of using semantics are choosing your words carefully and using abstractions to enhance emotional content.

When you're trying to build your credibility, how do you let your audience know that you're enthusiastic and trustworthy? Simply claiming outright that you have these traits will not convince them. But a careful use of language can communicate your sincerity and interest. Pay close attention to the subtle meanings of words—their **semantics**. The words you choose say much more than their dictionary definition. For instance, *useful, beneficial,* and *advantageous* may be considered synonyms, yet they are not interchangeable:

> She suggested a useful compromise. (The compromise allowed the parties to get to work.)
>
> She suggested a beneficial compromise. (The compromise not only resolved the conflict but also had a positive effect, perhaps for both parties.)
>
> She suggested an advantageous compromise. (The compromise benefited her or her company more than it benefited the other party.)

Building Credibility Online

EFFECTIVE E-BUSINESS COMMUNICATION

When you use printed messages to build credibility, you generally have limited space for testimonials and other persuasive evidence. On the Internet, however, space is never a problem—you can easily add pages of evidence to convince your audience of your expertise and reliability. Business people and consumers often browse Web sites to find out more before contacting potential suppliers. You can build credibility by conspicuously posting detailed problem–solution case studies and satisfied-customer testimonials. When IBM uses this technique, it also includes special links for readers to offer feedback, ask questions, and request additional information.

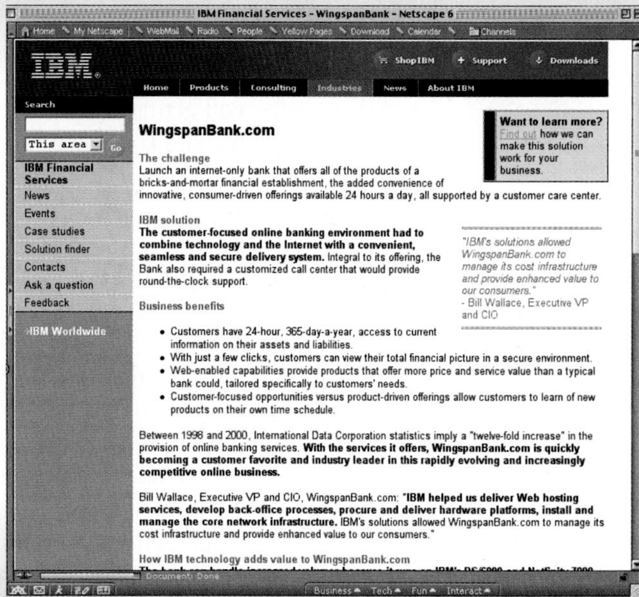

CAREER APPLICATIONS

1. You can use case studies and testimonials to build credibility. Would this technique be best for persuasive messages that use logical appeals or those that use emotional appeals?
2. How do case studies and testimonials help reinforce your position in a persuasive message?

Another way language can affect persuasive messages lies in the variety of meanings that people attribute to certain words. Abstractions are subject to interpretation because they refer to things that people cannot experience with their senses. So use abstractions to enhance the emotional content of a persuasive message. For example, you may be able to sell more flags by appealing to your audience's patriotism (which may be interpreted in many ways) than by describing the colour and size of the flags. You may have better luck collecting an overdue bill by mentioning honesty and fair play than by repeating the sum owed and the due date. However, be sure to include the details along with the abstractions; the very fact that you're using abstract words leaves room for misinterpretation.

Of course, even if you do use language skillfully, you may be able to accomplish your purpose only with the use of other methods. Persuading audience members to change their attitudes or to take action can be difficult. Here are some other tools to use in persuasive messages:[7]

Other persuasive tools include focusing on your goals, using simple language, anticipating opposition, being specific, being moderate, providing sufficient support, and creating a win-win situation.

- *Focus on your goal.* Your message will be clearest if you shift your focus away from changing minds and emphasize the action you want your audience to take.
- *Use simple language.* In most persuasive situations, your audience will be cautious, watching for fantastic claims, unsupportable descriptions, and emotional manipulation. So speak plainly and simply.
- *Anticipate opposition.* Think of every possible objection in advance. In your message, you might raise and answer some of these counter-arguments, to prove you're fair-minded.
- *Be specific.* Back up your claims with evidence, and when necessary cite facts and figures. Let your audience know that you've done your homework.
- *Be moderate.* Asking your audience to make major changes in attitude or beliefs will most likely evoke a negative response. Asking audience members to take one step toward that change may be a more reasonable goal.

- *Provide sufficient support.* It is up to you to prove that the change you seek is necessary.
- *Create a win-win situation.* Make it possible for both you and your audience to gain something. Audience members will find it easier to deal with change if they stand to benefit.

All of these tools will help your persuasive message be accepted, but none of them will actually convince your audience to take the action you want. To persuade people, you'll need a strong argument, whether based on emotion or on logic.

Emotion and Logic

You can defuse negative emotions in ways that help people accept your message.

You can defuse negative emotions by planning carefully. For example, when people's needs are not being met, they're likely to respond emotionally. A person who lacks a feeling of self-worth is likely to be sensitive to the tone of respect in a message. So in a collection letter to such a person, you can carefully avoid any hint that the person might be considered dishonourable. Otherwise, the person might become upset and ignore your message. Not even the best-crafted, most reasonable message will persuade someone who is emotionally unable to accept it.

Both emotional and logical appeals are needed to write successful persuasive messages.

But aside from simply avoiding negative emotions, how do you actually convince an audience that your position is the right one, that your plan will work best, that your company will do the most with a reader's donations? Is it better to appeal to your readers' emotions? Perhaps you're better off appealing strictly to their logic? For the best results when writing persuasive messages, appeal to both.

To persuade your audience, you can call on human emotion by basing your argument on the needs or sympathies of audience members, as long as your

BEHIND THE SCENES AT THE CANADIAN SOCCER ASSOCIATION

Scoring Goals and Sponsors

David Bedford's job requires getting the sponsors that keep kids and adults playing the sport they love—soccer. In 2000 total Canadian soccer registration reached 729 142, surpassing 1999 figures by 26 533, and more than 50 percent above 10 years earlier. 2000 soccer registration beat hockey by over 200 000 enthusiasts and figure skating by 570 000. Demographically, more than a third of 2000 soccer players were female, and 87 percent were under the age of 19. In this land of ice and snow, soccer has become a true Canadian pastime.

The goal of the Canadian Soccer Association is to sustain and promote the game in Canada. To deliver their programs, the organization must seek private support.

Yet the Canadian Soccer Association receives only 8 percent of its funding from Sport Canada, threatening the health of an organization whose mission is to promote "the growth and development of soccer for all Canadians at all levels." The remaining support must be obtained through the private sector, and it is the job of professionals such as David Bedford to help keep the sport going. As managing director of Soccer Canada Properties, a unit created by the CSA in partnership with IMG Canada, a sports management firm, Bedford and his team solicit and administer sponsorship for the CSA's amateur activities. Bedford explains that the sponsorship funds he raises, or products or services that he persuades companies to donate, are earmarked for such activities as the 13 different national team programs, national championships involving domestic clubs, mini-soccer festivals, and coaching development.

Persuading companies to sponsor CSA activities is rarely easy. Some companies want to be associated with the sport, so they contact the CSA seeking sponsorship opportunities. For example, notes Bedford, "Some leads come from a company's natural association with soccer, either via equipment sponsorship—Adidas, for instance—or by virtue of the company's involvement in other

emotional appeal is subtle.[8] You can make use of the emotion surrounding certain words. *Freedom,* for instance, brings forth strong feelings, as do words such as *success, prestige, credit record, savings, free, value,* and *comfort.* Using words like these puts the audience in a certain frame of mind and helps them accept your message. Also, emotion works with logic in a unique way: People need to find rational support for an attitude they've already embraced emotionally.

LEARNING OUTCOME 2
Distinguish between emotional and logical appeals, and discuss how to balance them.

A **logical appeal** calls on human reason. In any argument you might use to persuade an audience, you make a claim and then support your claim with reasons or evidence. When appealing to your audience's logic, you might use several types of reasoning:

Emotional appeals are best if they're subtle.

- **Analogy** is reasoning from specific evidence to a *specific* conclusion. To persuade employees to attend a planning session, you might use a town meeting analogy, comparing your company to a small community and your employees to valued members of that community.
- **Induction** is reasoning from specific evidence to a *general* conclusion. To convince potential customers that your product is best, you might report the results of test marketing in which individuals preferred your product over others.
- **Deduction** is reasoning from a generalization to a specific conclusion. To persuade your boss to hire additional employees, you might point out industrywide projections that industry activity (and thus your company's business) will be increasing rapidly over the next three months.

Logical appeals use more than one type of reasoning:
✧ Analogy
✧ Induction
✧ Deduction

Of course, regardless of the reasoning used, an argument or statement can easily appear to be true when it's actually false. Whenever you appeal to your audience's reason, do everything you can to ensure that your arguments are logically sound.

jurisdictions." One example here is JVC, an electronics leader, which provides sponsorship to both FIFA (Federation of International Football Associations) and the CSA.

Bedford contacts other companies because of their obvious demographic link with some of the CSA's programs. He cites fast-food giant McDonald's as a "natural fit" with the mini-soccer programs because of its appeal to kids and families. Another way the CSA approaches sponsors "is by target categories." Says Bedford. "We pick the targets that we think have the most affinity to soccer and its demographics, or we target services or products for which the CSA has a need—Air Canada, for instance."

Research and planning play a critical part in finding a sponsor. Bedford and his team investigate the market of a potential company, analyzing such areas as a firm's target audience, competitors, sales-distribution channels, and pricing. They will also meet with potential sponsors to understand their objectives, budgets, and timing. Doing this background work helps Bedford to prepare a persuasive presentation that shows "how an integrated soccer sponsorship package will work for them." Presentations are often delivered by a team, typically formed by Bedford with corporate sales and marketing representatives from IMG Canada. Their multimedia presentations incorporate video, pictures, and logos—each one is different—tailored to different audiences.

Establishing the credibility of the CSA is another key element in persuading companies to sponsor Soccer Canada programs. One approach Bedford often takes is to demonstrate the overwhelming popularity of the sport in Canada, by providing telling statistics. His audiences learn how many more kids play soccer than hockey, with 38 percent young women as compared to 7 percent in hockey. Another way Bedford establishes the CSA's credibility is to show that "soccer is the most popular game in the world, and the CSA is the keeper of that trust in Canada."

The CSA seeks new funding constantly; as Bedford remarks, "the more we bring in, the more programs we can run for our constituents." Sponsors benefit by getting more exposure for their brands, leading, of course, to more customers. The CSA benefits by delivering programs that provide "goals and excitement" for thousands of Canadians through training, competitions, and fun.[9]

APPLY YOUR KNOWLEDGE

1. Imagine you work for Soccer Canada Properties, the unit that solicits and administers sponsorship for the Canadian Soccer Association. How would you formulate a message that explains the needs of the CSA to potential sponsors and the benefits of sponsorship to them?
2. List some reasons why it is important to know your audience when writing persuasive messages.

AVOIDING FAULTY LOGIC

In any rational appeal, your high ethical standards dictate that you provide information, facts, and knowledge that can be used in decision making. To make this information persuasive, you must make your arguments relevant, well-grounded, and systematic. You make your points lucid and your arguments sound by steering clear of faulty logic:[10]

Avoid faulty logic such as hasty generalizations, begging the question, attacking your opponent, oversimplifying, assuming a false cause, using faulty analogies, and using illogical support.

- *Avoid hasty generalizations.* Make sure you have plenty of evidence before drawing conclusions.
- *Avoid begging the question.* Make sure you can support your claim without simply saying the same thing in different words.
- *Avoid attacking your opponent.* Be careful to address the real question. Attack the argument your opponent is making, not your opponent's character.
- *Avoid oversimplifying a complex issue.* Make sure you present all the facts rather than relying on an "either/or" statement that makes it appear as though only two choices are possible.
- *Avoid assuming a false cause.* Make sure to use cause-and-effect reasoning correctly so that you do not assume one event caused another just because it happened first.
- *Avoid faulty analogies.* Be careful that the two objects or situations being compared are similar enough for the analogy to hold. Even if *A* resembles *B* in one respect, it may not in other respects.
- *Avoid illogical support.* Make sure the connection between your claim and your support is truly logical and not based on a leap of faith, a missing premise, or irrelevant evidence.

The Toulmin model of logic helps you uncover hidden assumptions that your audience may not accept.

When organizing and shaping your persuasive message, always think carefully about the argument you're using. You can test your argument to see whether it's logical. For example, you can use the Toulmin model of logic developed by philosopher Stephen Toulmin. It can help you discover whether you've made hidden assumptions that your audience may not accept.

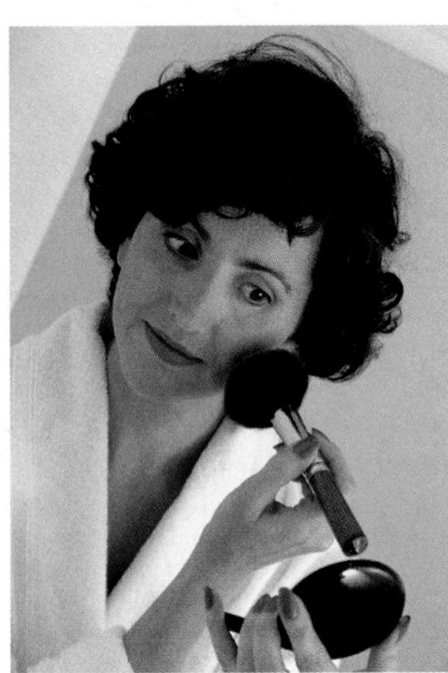

Companies work hard to persuade consumers to buy their products. What appeals do manufacturers of cosmetics make? Are these appeals successful? Are they ethical?

USING THE TOULMIN MODEL

As you shape your argument, you'll make it stronger (1) by finding common ground (basing your major argument on points that your audience already accepts) and (2) by stating the points in your case clearly.[11]

1. State your claim clearly.
2. Support your claim with a clear reason.
3. If your audience already accepts your reason (already holds the same belief, value, or principle presented in your reason), you may proceed to your conclusion.
4. If your audience does not already accept your reason, you must support it with another clearly stated claim, and support that claim with another clear reason, and so forth until you achieve common ground (find a reason based on beliefs, values, or principles that your audience already agrees with). Only then may you return to step 3.

As you can see, you are basically supporting your claim with evidence that is itself backed by a chain of reasons (all of which your audience must accept before you can move forward). This approach may remind you of the question-and-answer chain discussed briefly in Chapter 5 and at more length in Chapter 12.

Organizing Persuasive Messages

LEARNING OUTCOME 3
Describe the AIDA plan for persuasive messages.

Once you have carefully and thoroughly planned your persuasive message, you're ready to organize it. One way to organize persuasive messages is the **AIDA** plan, which has four phases: (1) attention, (2) interest, (3) desire, and (4) action.

Organize persuasive messages using the AIDA plan:
- ✧ Attention
- ✧ Interest
- ✧ Desire
- ✧ Action

In the **attention** phase, you convince your audience right at the beginning that you have something useful or interesting to say. The audience wants to know "What's in this message for me?" So try to tell them in the attention phase, without making extravagant claims or threats and without bringing up irrelevant points (Figure 11.1).

Begin every persuasive message with an attention-getting statement that is
- ✧ Personalized
- ✧ You-oriented
- ✧ Straightforward
- ✧ Relevant

In the **interest** phase, you explain how your message is related to the audience. Continuing the theme that you started with, you paint a more detailed picture with words. Your goal is to get the audience thinking, "This is an interesting idea; could it possibly solve my problem?" In Figure 11.1, the interest section ties together a factual description and the benefits of instituting the new recycling plan. Also, the benefits relate specifically to the attention phase that precedes this section.

In the interest section
- ✧ Continue the opening theme in greater detail
- ✧ Relate benefits specifically to the attention-getter

In the **desire** phase of a persuasive message, you back up claims and thereby increase your audience's willingness to take the action that you'll suggest in the next section. Whatever evidence you use to prove your claim, make sure it's directly relevant to your point.

In the desire section
- ✧ Provide relevant evidence to prove your claim
- ✧ Draw attention to any enclosures

In the **action** phase, you suggest the action you want your audience to take. All persuasive messages end with a section that urges specific action, but the ending is more than a statement such as "Institute this program as soon as possible" or "Send me a refund." In fact, this section offers a good opportunity for one last reminder of the main benefit the audience will achieve by taking the action you want. The secret of the action phase is to make the action easy. In sales letters, you might ask readers to call a toll-free number for more information or fill out an enclosed order form.

Close a persuasive message with an action ending that suggests a specific step the audience may take.

The Indirect Approach

The AIDA plan is tailor-made for using the indirect approach, allowing you to save your main idea for the action phase. Be sure to use the indirect approach when:

- ➤ Your audience is negative (has strong resistance to your message)
- ➤ Your message is relatively short and clear (so that readers don't have to wait long for your main idea)
- ➤ You know your readers won't object to the indirect plan

Using AIDA with the indirect approach allows you to save your idea for the action phase.

When you use the indirect approach in persuasive messages, your goal is to explain your reasons and build interest before revealing your purpose. So the attention phase takes on increased importance. Getting your readers' attention is thoroughly covered in the discussion of sales letters later in this chapter.

The Direct Approach

The AIDA plan can also be adapted for the direct approach, allowing you to use your main idea as the attention-getter. You build interest with your argument, build desire with your evidence, and emphasize your main idea in the action phase with the specific action you want your audience to take. The direct approach is often shorter than the indirect approach, so it is appreciated by readers who are busy and pressed for time. Use the direct approach when:

Using AIDA with the direct approach allows you to use your main idea as your attention-getter.

INTERNAL MEMORANDUM

To: Eleanor Tran, Comptroller
From: Randy Thumwolt, Purchasing Director
Date: August 22, 2001
Subject: Cost Cutting in Plastics

In the attention phase, background information and specific numbers grab the reader's attention.

As you know, we purchase five tons of plastic product containers each year. The price of the polyethylene terephthalate (PET) tends to rise and fall as petroleum costs fluctuate.

You asked me earlier to find some ways to cut our annual costs for plastics. In my memo of January 5, I suggested that we bulk-purchase plastics during winter months, when petroleum prices tend to be lower. Thanks for approving that suggestion. So far, I estimate that we will realize a 10 percent savings this year.

In the interest phase, the writer clearly describes the problems the company is still facing.

Even so, our costs for plastic containers are exorbitant ($2 million annually). In addition, we have received an increasing number of consumer letters complaining about our lack of a recycling program for the PET plastic containers both on the airplanes and in the airport restaurants. I've done some preliminary research and have come up with the following ideas:

The desire phase makes suggestions in an easy-to-read list and provides detailed support in an attachment.

1. Provide recycling containers at all Host Marriott airport restaurants.
2. Offer financial incentives for the airlines to collect and separate PET containers.
3. Set up a specially designated dumpster at each airport for recycling plastics.
4. Contract with A-Batt Waste Management for collection.

I've attached a detailed report of the costs involved. As you can see, our net savings the first year should run about $500,000. I've spoken to Ted Macy in marketing. If we adopt the recycling plan, he wants to build a PR campaign around it.

In the action phase, the writer provides another reader benefit and urges action within a specific time frame.

The PET recycling plan will help build our public image while improving our bottom line. If you agree, let's meet with Ted next week to get things started.

FIGURE 11.1

In-Depth Critique: Persuasive Letter Using the AIDA Plan

Randy Thumwolt uses the AIDA plan in this persuasive memo about a program that could solve two problems at once: (1) the high annual cost of plastics and (2) the rising number of consumer complaints about the company's failure to recycle plastics.

- Your audience is objective (and has no real resistance to your message)
- Your message is long and complex (so that you satisfy your reader's curiosity)
- You know that your reader prefers the direct plan (for example, most supervisors appreciate messages that save them time and communicate the subject matter quickly)

However, even though you're presenting your main idea first, make sure you include a brief justification or explanation so that your reader doesn't have to accept your idea on blind faith.

POOR	IMPROVED
I recommend building our new retail outlet on the West Main Street site.	After comparing the four possible sites for our new retail outlet, I recommend West Main Street as the only site that fulfills our criteria for visibility, proximity to mass transportation, and square footage.

Remember that your persuasive messages take careful planning and organization. Your success depends on your commitment to being ethical, analyzing your audience's needs, maintaining your own credibility, using language carefully, balancing emotion and logic, and choosing the most appropriate organizational plan. Following these guidelines will help you craft strong persuasive messages, no matter what the situation.

Preparing Persuasive Messages on the Job

When writing persuasive messages within an organization consider three influences:
- ✧ Corporate culture
- ✧ Subcultures
- ✧ Position

Within an organization, you may write persuasive messages for any number of reasons. You may want to implement top management's decisions, sell a supervisor on your idea for cutting costs, suggest more efficient operating procedures, elicit cooperation from competing departments, or win employee support for a new benefits package. When writing a persuasive message to someone within your organization, consider three special aspects affecting your approach: corporate culture, corporate subcultures, and position or power.[12]

Every message written for a corporation adds to the corporate tradition.

An organization's culture heavily influences the types of message considered effective. All the previous messages in the organization establish a tradition and practice that define persuasive writing within that culture. If you accept and use that tradition, you are thereby establishing a certain common ground with your audience, and you will be rewarded by being accepted into the corporate culture. If you never learn the tradition or reject it, you'll have difficulty achieving common ground, and your attempts at persuasion will suffer.

Each functional area within a corporation develops its own subculture.

Organizations are made up of various functional areas such as accounting, finance, manufacturing, marketing, research, and human resources. Each of these areas (or subcultures) tends to have its own approaches to helping the corporation succeed, and its own traditions in valuing other functional areas, communicating, using language, and persuading. So, each subculture tends to mistrust the language and customs of other subcultures. When writing a persuasive message within your subculture, you can use its accepted communication and language traditions with confidence. When writing a persuasive message outside your subculture, however, anticipate problems from readers whose general mind-set and specific business traditions may differ from yours.

Your position relative to your audience's position within an organization influences how you approach your persuasive message.

Your position in an organization affords you a commensurate amount of authority, expertise, and power. Therefore, the position you hold will affect how you organize and write persuasive messages. Say you are a first-line manager. When writing a persuasive message to top management, you may try to be diplomatic and to persuade by using an indirect approach. But some managers may perceive your indirect persuasion as manipulative and time wasting. On the other hand, you may consciously try to save your supervisors time by using a direct approach. But some supervisors might perceive your direct persuasion as brash and presumptuous.

Similarly, when writing a persuasive message to employees, you may try to ease into a major change by persuading with an indirect approach, but your employees might perceive your indirect approach as weak. Or you may decide to persuade them with a direct approach to reinforce your image of authority, in which case your employees might perceive your direct approach as rude and unfeeling.

The way you word and organize persuasive messages that will be read within the organization depends on organizational culture, your position, and your audience's position, not to mention the particular situation. So be sure to analyze your company's traditions, your department's practices, and your audience before deciding on an approach. In Figure 11.2, Bette McGiboney has chosen the direct plan to persuade her boss to accept her idea.

Three problems with external requests for action:

- ✧ They reach people who are already busy and reluctant to comply.
- ✧ They frequently offer nothing tangible in return.
- ✧ They must compete with so many other requests.

Writing Persuasive Requests for Action

Many persuasive messages are written to solicit funds, favours, information, or cooperation. Within an organization, persuasive techniques are often required to get someone to change policies or procedures, to spend money on new equipment and services, to promote a person, or to protect turf.[13] Persuasive letters to outsiders might solicit donations, request an adjustment, or ask for some other type of help.

As the YEA's young board of directors know well, creating an external persuasive message is one of the most difficult persuasive tasks you could undertake. First, people are busy, so they're reluctant to do something new. Second, the request offers no guarantee of any tangible reward in return. Third, competing requests are plentiful. Royal Bank, for example, receives hundreds of sponsorship proposals each week, and applies a strict set of criteria when evaluating them.[14]

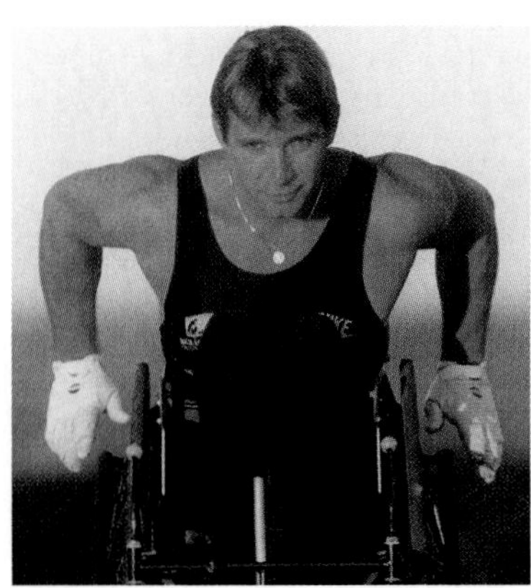

Paralyzed in a motor vehicle crash in 1973 at the age of 15, Rick Hansen has worked tirelessly to raise awareness of the impact of spinal cord injury. He came to international prominence with his 1985-87 round-the-world tour which raised $24 million for rehabilitation research. Wheeling 40 000 kilometers through 34 countries on four continents, Hansen showed what perseverance and determination can achieve. Today, Rick is President and CEO of the Rick Hansen Institute, an organization determined to accelerate the discovery of a cure for spinal cord injury.

Why do people respond to requests for action on an issue that is more important to you than to them? If you're lucky, they may believe in the project or cause that you're writing about. Even so, you must convince them that your request will give them some benefit, perhaps an intangible benefit down the road or a chance to make a meaningful contribution. Also, especially in the case of requests for professional favours or information, people may think that they are obliged to "pay their dues" by helping others.

Highlight the direct and indirect benefits of complying with your request.

When making a persuasive request, therefore, take special care to highlight both direct and indirect benefits. Direct benefits might include a reduced work load for the supervisor who institutes flex-time or a premium for someone who responds to a survey. Indirect benefits might include better employee morale or the prestige of giving free workshops to small businesses.

The attention-getting device at the beginning of a persuasive request for action usually serves to show readers that you know something about their concerns and that you have some reason for making such request. In this type of persuasive message, more than in most others, a flattering comment about your reader is acceptable, especially if it's sincere. The body of the letter or memo covers what you know about the problem you're trying to solve with the reader's help: the facts and figures, the benefits of helping, your experience in attacking the problem. The goal is to give you and your request credibility, to make the reader believe that helping you will indeed help solve a significant problem. Once you've demonstrated that your message is relevant to your reader, you can request some specific action. Be aware, however, that a persuasive memo is somewhat more subdued than a letter to an outsider might be.

Date: Wednesday, 22 July 2001, 3:44:05
To: housel@ath.cait.ab.ca
From: "Bette McGiboney" <mcgibon@ath.cait.ab.ca>
Subject: Savings on toll-free number

Dear David:

As you know, our billing for the toll-free number coming into the ticket office usually runs at least $1500 for the month of August, compared with an average of $293 for the other eleven months. Fans who call in August usually have at least a five-minute wait on hold. Here's an idea that will not only save us money but also help us manage our time and better serve our fans.

Under this plan, callers will hear the same messages and be offered the same options as before. However, if an operator isn't available when a caller presses "0" for ticket information, a new message will request a name and phone number so that we can return the call within the next two business days.

I estimate that reducing the on-hold time could eliminate at least $900 from our August bill (based on a conversation with our phone representative). The good news is that the idea costs nothing and can be implemented immediately. We can use quiet times of the day to return phone calls, thus spreading our work more evenly.

I've discussed the idea informally with our operators, and they would like to try it. After hockey season, we can use our spring interns to call a random selection of customers to see how they liked the new message system. The plan will help us in the following ways:

- Provide better customer service
- Help us manage our time and stress levels
- Save us money on our toll-free line

I've attached a sheet with possible wording for the new message. Please let me know by the end of the month whether you'd like to give this a try.

Thank you,

Bette

This message follows the AIDA plan. The attention paragraph convinces the reader that Bette has something useful to say by opening with a statement of the problem.

The interest paragraph explains how the new plan will work, creating more interest in the idea.

The third and fourth paragraphs create desire by presenting supporting evidence such as cost savings, and the bulleted benefits draw the reader to the essence of the message.

The action paragraph is simple and direct with a specific time frame. It also takes care of a chore that might have caused the reader to delay.

FIGURE 11.2

In-Depth Critique: E-Mail Selling an Idea to a Boss

Bette McGiboney is administrative assistant to the athletic director of Central Alberta Institute of Technology. Each year, after season tickets have been mailed out, the cost of the athletic department's toll-free number skyrockets as fans call to complain about their seats, or about receiving the wrong number of tickets, or to order last-minute tickets. The August phone bill is usually over $1500, in part because each customer is put on hold while operators serve others. McGiboney has an idea that may solve the problem.

Make only reasonable requests.

The most important thing to remember when preparing a persuasive request for action is to keep your request within bounds. Nothing is so distressing as a request so general, all-encompassing, or inconsiderate that it seems impossible to grant, no matter how worthy the cause. Also be careful not to doom your request to failure by asking your reader to do all your work for you: to provide information that you were too lazy to seek, to spend time saving you from embarrassment or inconvenience, or to provide total financial support for a cause that nobody else is supporting. To review the tasks involved in such messages, see this chapter's Checklist for Persuasive Requests for Action on page 280.

Writing Sales and Fund-Raising Messages

LEARNING OUTCOME 4
Compare sales messages with fundraising messages.

Two distinctive types of persuasive messages are sales letters and fund-raising letters. These messages often come in special direct-mail packages that can include brochures, reply forms, or other special inserts. Both types of messages are often written by specialized and highly skilled professionals.

How do sales messages differ from fund-raising messages? Sales messages are usually sent by for-profit organizations seeking to solve readers' problems by persuading them to spend money on products. On the other hand, fund-raising messages are usually sent by non-profit organizations seeking to solve other people's problems by persuading readers to donate their money or time. Nevertheless, the fact is that sales and fund-raising messages are competing for business and public attention, time, and dollars.[15] Both types of messages attempt to persuade readers to spend their time or money on the value being offered–whether that value is the convenience of a more efficient vacuum cleaner or the satisfaction of helping save children's lives. Sales and fund-raising messages require a few more steps than other types of persuasive messages.

Going Online

Lobby Your Leaders

A Canadian Government site offers information about the structure of the Canadian government. It identifies ministers and their portfolios, and how to contact them. Persons wishing to persuade a minister or other official about an issue of importance can have direct access through this site. It provides easy access in several ways: by the ministers' names, by their areas of responsibility, and by government departments. This site also leads to members of parliament.

canada.gc.ca/howgoc/glance_e.html

Sales Letters

Whether you're selling a product, service, or company image, remember that the focus of your message is your audience. As with any message, persuasive or not, knowing the standard of practice can help you avoid serious legal problems. Keep in mind the following issues:

- Making a false statement in a sales letter is fraud if the recipient can prove that (1) you intended to deceive, (2) you made the statement regarding a fact rather than an opinion or a speculation, (3) the recipient was justified in relying on the statement, and (4) the recipient was damaged by it (in a legal sense). Misrepresenting the price, quality, or performance of a product in a sales letter is fraud. So is a testimonial by a person misrepresented to be an expert.
- Using a person's name, photograph, or other identity in a sales letter without permission constitutes invasion of privacy. Protect yourself from potential legal action by seeking permission. Doing so is not only prudent but also courteous, and will establish a good relationship between you and the subject.
- Publicizing a person's private life in a sales letter can also result in legal problems. Stating that the manager of a local bank (mentioned by name) served six months in prison for income-tax evasion is a potentially damaging fact that may be considered an invasion of privacy. You would also risk a lawsuit by

publicizing another person's past-due debts or by publishing without consent another person's medical records, x-rays, or photograph.

Knowing standards of practice will help you send messages that are ethical and abide by legal guidelines.

As with other persuasive messages, following the letter of the law isn't always enough. To write sales letters of the highest ethical character, focus on solving your readers' problem rather than on selling your product. If you're genuinely concerned about your audience's needs and interests, you'll find it easier to avoid legal or ethical pitfalls. Once you're firmly committed to focusing on your audience, you can begin planning your sales letter by figuring out what features would most interest your readers.

DETERMINING SELLING POINTS AND BENEFITS

Know your products' selling points, but talk about their benefits to consumers.

Selling points are the most attractive features of an idea or product; benefits are the particular advantages that readers will realize from those features. One selling point of a security system for students' residence rooms is its portability. The benefit to students is the ability to protect their possessions from theft without investing in a full-blown permanently installed alarm system (Figure 11.3).

Start with a thorough knowledge of the product.

Obviously, you can't write about selling points or benefits without a thorough understanding of your subject as well as of your audience. So take a good look at your product. Ask yourself (or someone else, if necessary) everything that you think a potential buyer might want to know about it. If you were writing the sales letter in Figure 11.3, you would need to have a full description of what the portable security system looks like, what it does, and how it works. Some selling points of the SecureAbel Alarms are that they can be installed with a screwdriver, have an activator that hooks to your key chain or belt loop, and have a blinking red light to warn intruders to stay away. You should also investigate prices and discounts, delivery schedules, and packaging.

Form a mental picture of the product's typical buyer; then relate selling points and benefits to that picture.

Once you have a complete file on your product, collect data about your audience and try to form a mental image of the typical buyer for the product. This mental image will help you focus on the central concerns of potential buyers in your audience. Then you can check the selling points you've already come up with against your audience's actual needs.

Think about how the product's features can help potential buyers; then concentrate on how your product's selling points can actually satisfy your audience's needs.

Now think about how your product can benefit your audience. Some benefits of the SecureAbel Alarms are their ease of installation, their ease of activation, and their giving you a feeling of safety and security. Be sure to focus on relatively few product benefits, and determine which benefits are most appealing to your audience. Ultimately, you'll single out one benefit that will become the hallmark of your campaign. Safety seems to be the key benefit emphasized by SecureAbel Alarms.

CHOOSING THE FORMAT AND APPROACH

Once you know what you need to say and who you want to say it to, decide how you're going to say it. Will you send just a letter, or will you include brochures, samples, response cards, and the like? Will the letter be printed with an additional colour or special symbols or logos? How many pages will it run? You'll also need to decide whether to conduct a multi-stage campaign, with several mailings and some sort of telephone or in-person follow-up, or rely on one hard-hitting mailing.

All these decisions depend on the audience you're trying to reach–their characteristics, their likely acceptance of or resistance to your message–and what you're trying to get them to do. In general, expensive items and hard-to-accept propositions call for a more elaborate campaign than low-cost products and simple actions.

SecureAbel Alarms, Inc.

584 Crawford Ave • Windsor ON N9A 5C4 • 519-555-4424 • Fax 519-555-4422 • www.secure.com

October 14, 2000

Mr. Samuel Zolezzi
Elgin Hall, West Wing
University of Western Ontario
London, ON N6A 5B9

Dear Mr. Zolezzi:

Beginning with a provocative question draws the reader into the letter and raises the awareness of a need. Benefits have both a logical appeal (protecting possessions) and an emotional appeal (personal safety).

Did you know that one out of four university students becomes a victim of theft? How would you feel if you returned to your residence room and discovered that your hard-earned stereo, computer, or microwave had been stolen? Remember, locked doors won't stop a determined thief.

In the second paragraph, the writer seeks to establish a common bond with the reader and explains how the product works by comparing it with something the reader is familiar with, a car alarm.

It happened to me when I was in university. That's why I've developed a portable security system for your residence room. It works like an auto alarm and can be installed with an ordinary screwdriver. The small activator hooks to your key chain or belt loop. Just press the "lock" key. A "beep" tells you your room is secure, and a blinking red light warns intruders to stay away.

The third paragraph mentions an additional threat to safety and hence another benefit of the security system.

If a thief tries to break in, a loud alarm sounds. Your possessions will be safe. And, even more important, you can activate the system from your bedside, so you're safe while you sleep.

You'd expect this peace of mind to cost a fortune–something most college students don't have. But we're offering the SecureAbel Dorm Alarm System for only $75. Here's what you'll receive by return mail:

The bulleted list creates the sense of added value to the offer.

- The patented alarm unit
- Two battery-operated programmable remote units
- A one-year warranty on all parts
- Complete and easy-to-follow installation instructions

The final paragraph urges quick action.

Order additional alarm boxes to install on your window or bathroom door for only $50. Act now. Fill out the response card, and mail it along with your choice of payment method in the enclosed envelope. Don't give thieves and criminals a chance. Protect yourself and your belongings. Send in your card today.

Sincerely,

Dan Abel

Dan Abel, President

Enclosures

FIGURE 11.3

In-Depth Critique: Letter Selling a Product

This sales letter for SecureAbel Alarms uses the AIDA plan to persuade students to buy its residence-room alarm systems.

LEARNING OUTCOME 5
List at least four attention-getting devices for sales messages.

Several tried-and-true attention- getting devices are used in sales letters for a wide variety of products.

GETTING ATTENTION

Sales letters are prepared according to the AIDA plan used for any persuasive message, so they start with an attention-getting device. Professionals use some common techniques to attract audience attention. When you're preparing a sales letter, consider emphasizing:

➢ *A piece of genuine news.* "In the past 60 days, auto manufacturers' inventories have shrunk by 12 percent."

- *A personal appeal to the reader's emotions and values.* "The only thing worse than paying taxes is paying taxes when you don't have to."
- *The most attractive feature plus the associated benefit.* "New control device ends problems with employee pilferage!"
- *An intriguing number.* "Here are three great secrets of the world's most loved entertainers."
- *A sample of the product.* "Here's your free sample of the new Romalite packing sheet."
- *A concrete illustration with story appeal.* "In 1985 Earl Colbert set out to find a better way to process credit applications. After ten years of trial and error, he finally developed a procedure so simple but thorough that he was cited for service to the industry by his industry association."
- *A specific trait shared by the audience.* "Busy executives need another complicated 'time-saving' device like they need a hole in the head!"
- *A provocative question.* "Are you tired of watching inflation eat away at your hard-earned profits?"
- *A challenge.* "Don't waste another day wondering how you're going to become the success you've always wanted to be!"
- *A solution to a problem.* "Tired of arctic air rushing through the cracks around your windows? Stay warm and save energy with StormSeal Weather-stripping."

Each year more than a million people throughout North America receive Easter Seal services, which requires both money and volunteers. What sorts of appeals would you include in an Easter Seal letter?

A look at your own mail will show you the prevalence of these few techniques in sales letters. Using these proven attention-getting devices will give your sales letters added impact. Look again at Figure 11.3 and see how many of them it uses.

Choose an attention-getter that encourages the reader to read more.

Of course, not all attention-getting devices are equally effective. The best is the one that makes your audience read the rest of the letter. Look closely at the following three examples. Which seems most interesting to you?

> How would you like straight A's this semester?
>
> Get straight A's this semester!
>
> Now you can get straight A's this semester, with …

If you're like most people, you'll find the first option the most enticing. The question invites your response–a positive response designed to encourage you to read on. The second option is fairly interesting too, but its commanding tone may make you wary of the claim. The third option is acceptable, but it certainly conveys no sense of excitement, and its quick introduction of the product may lead you to a snap decision against reading further.

Sales letters prepared by professionals also use a variety of formatting devices to get your attention, including personalized salutations, special sizes or styles of type, underlining, colour, indentions, and so on. Whatever special techniques are used, the best attention-getter for a sales letter is a hook that gets the reader thinking about the needs your product might be able to help fill.

EMPHASIZING THE CENTRAL SELLING POINT

Suppose that your company's alarm device is relatively inexpensive, durable, and tamper-proof. Although these are all attractive features, you want to focus on only one. Ask yourself what the competition has to offer, what most distinguishes your product, and what most concerns potential buyers. The answers to these questions will help you select the **central selling point,** the single point around which to build your sales message. Highlight this point in your heading or first paragraph, and make it stand out through typography, design, or high-impact writing.[16]

To determine your product's central selling point, ask

- ✧ What does the competition offer?
- ✧ What is special about my product?
- ✧ What are potential buyers really looking for?

HIGHLIGHTING BENEFITS

Determining the central selling point will help you define the benefits to potential buyers. Perhaps your company's alarm device has been built mainly to overcome the inability of your competitors' products to resist tampering by would-be burglars. Tamper resistance is your central selling point; its benefits are that burglars won't be able to break in easily and therefore the likelihood of a burglary will be reduced. You'll want to mention this benefit repeatedly, in words and pictures (if possible), near the beginning and the end of your letter. You might get attention by using a news item to stress this benefit: "Burglaries of businesses in our county have increased 7.7 percent over the past year; police department officials cite burglars' increasing sophistication and familiarity with conventional alarm devices." You might pose a provocative question: "Worried about the reliability of your current alarm system in repelling today's sophisticated burglars?"

Selling points + "you" attitude = benefits.

In the rest of the letter, continue to stress the central selling point but weave in references to other benefits: "You can get this worry-free protection for much less than you might think." Also, "The same technology that makes it difficult for burglars to crack your alarm system makes it durable, even when it must be exposed to the elements." Remember, sales letters reflect the "you" attitude through references to benefits, so always phrase the selling points in terms of what such features will do for potential customers.

USING ACTION TERMS

To give force to a message
✧ Use action terms
✧ Use colourful verbs and adjectives

Active words give force to any business message, but they are especially important in sales letters. Compare the following:

INSTEAD OF THIS	WRITE THIS
The NuForm desk chair is designed to support your lower back and relieve pressure on your legs.	The NuForm desk chair supports your lower back and relieves pressure on your legs.

The second version says the same thing in fewer words and puts more emphasis on what the chair does for the user ("supports") than on the intentions of the design team ("is designed to support").

Checklist for Persuasive Requests for Action

A. Attention

1. Demonstrate that you understand the audience's concerns.
2. Introduce a direct or indirect benefit that can be developed as a central selling point.
3. Construct statements so that they don't sound like high-pressure sales tactics or bribes.
4. Use an effective opening: a comment or assertion the audience will agree with, a compliment (if sincere), a frank admission that you need the audience's help, a problem that is the basis of your request, one or two rhetorical questions, a statement of what is being done or has been done to solve a problem.

B. Interest and Desire

1. Early in the body of the message, introduce the reason you are writing.
   a. Mention the main audience benefit before the actual request.
   b. Thoroughly explain your reason for asking the favour.
2. Include all necessary description: physical characteristics and value of the product or project.
3. Include all facts and figures necessary to convince members of your audience that their contribution will be enjoyable, easy, important, and of personal benefit (as much as is true and possible).
   a. In a request for cooperation, explain the problem, facts, suggestions, other participants' roles, and the audience's part.
   b. In a request for a donation, explain the problem, past and current attempts to remedy it, future plans, your organization's involvement, and projected costs, along with suggestions about how the audience can help.

In general, use colourful verbs and adjectives that convey a dynamic image. Be careful, however, not to overdo it: "Your factory floors will sparkle like diamonds" is hard to believe and may prevent your audience from believing the rest of your message.

TALKING ABOUT PRICE

The price people will pay for a product depends on the prices of similar products, the general state of the economy, and the psychology of the buyer. Price is therefore a complicated issue and often a sensitive one.

Whether the price of your product is highlighted or downplayed, prepare your readers for it. Such words as *luxurious* and *economical* provide unmistakable clues about how your price compares with competitors' prices, and they help your readers accept the price when you finally state it. If your price is relatively high, definitely stress features and benefits that justify it. If the price is low, you may wish to compare the features of your product with those of the competition's products, either directly or indirectly. In either case, if the price you eventually mention is a surprise to the reader, you've made a mistake that will be hard to overcome.

You can prepare readers for your product's price by subtle choice and arrangement of words.

Here's an example from a sales letter offering a product at a bargain price:

> All the Features of Name-Brand Sunglasses at Half the Price!
>
> Why pay for a designer name when you can enjoy wearing stylish sunglasses with polarized lenses for half the price?

If the price is an attractive feature, emphasize it by displaying it prominently.

In this excerpt, the price falls right at the end of the paragraph, where it stands out. In addition, the price issue is featured in a bold headline. This technique may even be used as the opening of a letter if the price is the most important feature and the audience for the letter is value conscious.

If price is not a major selling point, you can handle it in several ways. You could leave out the price altogether or mention it only in an accompanying brochure. You could de-emphasize the price by putting the actual figures in the middle of a paragraph close to the end of your sales letter, well after you've presented the benefits and selling points. The same paragraph might include a discussion of related

To de-emphasize price
- ✧ Bury actual figures in the middle of a paragraph near the end
- ✧ Mention benefits and favourable money matters before the actual price
- ✧ Break a quantity price into units
- ✧ Compare the price with the cost of some other product or activity

---

c. Describe the possible direct benefits.

d. Describe the possible indirect benefits.

4. Anticipate and answer possible objections.
   a. Ignore objections if they are unimportant or might not occur to the audience or if you can focus on positive facts instead.
   b. Discuss objections (usually) about half or two-thirds of the way through the body of the letter or memo.
   c. Acknowledge objections calmly; then overcome them by focusing on more important and more positive factors.
   d. Turn objections into an advantage by looking at them from another viewpoint or by explaining the facts of the situation more clearly.
   e. Overcome objections to providing restricted material by giving assurance that you will handle it in whatever limited way is specified.
5. Introduce any enclosures after you have finished the key message, with an emphasis on what to do with them or what information they offer.

C. Action

1. Confidently ask for the audience's cooperation.
2. Make the desired action clear and easy.
3. Stress the positive results of action.
4. Include the due date for a response (if necessary), and tie it in with audience benefits (if possible): adequate time for ordering supplies, prominent billing on the program, and so forth.
5. Replace negative or tentative statements, such as "If you can donate anything," with positive, confident statements, such as "To make your contribution, just return …"
6. Tie in the last sentence with an appeal or a statement featured in the opening paragraph (if appropriate), as a last audience-benefit plug.

topics, such as credit terms, special offers, and volume discounts. Mentioning favourable money matters before the actual price also reduces its impact.

Emphasis on the rarity of the edition signals value and thus prepares the reader for the big-ticket price that follows. The actual price, buried in the middle of a sentence, is tied in with another reminder of the exclusivity of the offer.

> Only 100 prints of this exclusive, limited-edition lithograph will be created. On June 1, they will be made available to the general public, but you can reserve one now for only $350, the special advance reservation price. Simply rush the enclosed reservation card back today so that your order is in before the June 1 publication date.

Professional writers use two other techniques in sales letters to minimize price. One is to break a quantity price into units. Instead of saying that a case of wine costs $144, you might say that each bottle costs $12. The other is to compare your product's price with the cost of some other product or activity: "The cost of owning your own spa is less than you'd pay for a health-club membership." Your aim is to make the cost seem as small and affordable as possible, thereby eliminating price as a possible objection.

SUPPORTING YOUR CLAIMS

Types of support for product claims:
- Samples
- Brochures
- Examples
- Testimonials
- Statistics
- Guarantees

You can't assume that people will believe what you say about your product just because you said it in writing. You'll have to prove your claims, especially if your product is complicated, expensive, or representative of some unusual approach.

Support for your claims may take several forms. Samples and brochures, often with photographs, are enclosed in the sales package and are referred to in the letter. The letter also uses boldfacing or bulleted lists for highlighting claims. Examples of how the product has benefited others, includes testimonials (actual quotations) from satisfied customers, or cites statistics from scientific studies of the product's performance. Guarantees of exchange or return privileges, which may also be woven into the letter or set off in a special way, indicate that you have faith in the product and are willing to back it up.

It's almost impossible to provide too much support. Try to anticipate every question your audience may ask. Put yourself in your audience's place so that you can ask, and answer, all the what-ifs.[17]

MOTIVATING ACTION

The overriding purpose of a sales letter is to get your reader to do something. Many consumer products sold through the mail simply ask for a cheque–in other words, an immediate decision to buy. On the other hand, non-profit organizations such as the Young Entrepreneurs' Association and companies selling big-ticket and more complex items frequently ask for just a small step toward the final decision to buy or to donate, such as sending for more information or authorizing a call by a fund-raiser sales representative.

Aim to get the reader to act as soon as possible.

Try to persuade readers to take action, whatever it is, right away. Convince them that they must act now, perhaps to guarantee a specific delivery date. If there's no particular reason to act quickly, many sales letters offer discounts for orders placed by a certain date or prizes or special offers to, say, the first 500 people who respond. Others suggest that you charge purchases to a credit card or pay them off over time. Still others offer a free trial, an unconditional guarantee, or a no-strings request card for information, all in an effort to overcome readers' natural inertia. Motivating action can be a challenge in sales letters and even more of a challenge when you're trying to raise funds.

Fund-Raising Letters

Fund-raising letters use many of the same techniques used in sales letters.

Most of the techniques used to write sales letters can be used to write fund-raising letters, as long as your techniques match your audience, your goals, and the cause or organization you're representing (Figure 11.4). Be careful to establish value in the minds of your donors. Above all, don't forget to include the "What's in it for me?" information–for example, telling your readers how good they'll feel after making a donation.[18]

PLANNING FUND-RAISING MESSAGES

To make sure that your fund-raising letters outshine the competition's letters, take some time to get ready before you actually begin writing.[19] You can begin by reading the mail you receive from donors. Learn as much as you can about your audience by noting the tone of their letters, the language they use, and the concerns they raise. This exercise will help you write letters that donors will both understand and relate to.

By reading your mail from donors, you can learn about the tone, language, and concerns your donors prefer.

You might also keep a file of competing fund-raising letters. Study these samples to find out what other fund-raisers are doing and what new approaches they're taking. Most important, find out what works and what doesn't. Then you can continue with your other research efforts such as performing interviews, holding focus groups, and reading trade journals to find out what people are concerned about, what they're interested in, and what gets their attention.

By keeping a file of competing fund-raising letters, you can find out what works and what doesn't.

Finally, before you start writing, know whose benefits to emphasize. Make a two-column list, and, on one side, list what your organization does; on the other side, list what your donors want. You'll discover that the two columns are quite different. Make sure that the benefits you emphasize relate to what your donors want (not to what your organization does). Then you can work on stating those donor benefits in specific detail. For example: "Your donation of $100 will provide 15 people with a Christmas dinner."

Be sure to focus on the concerns of your readers, not the concerns of your organization.

PERSONALIZING FUND-RAISING MESSAGES

Because fund-raising letters depend so heavily on emotional appeals, keep your message personal. A natural, real-life lead-in is usually the best. People seem to respond best to slice-of-life stories. In fact, storytelling is perfect when your narrative is unforced and goes straight to the heart of the matter.[20] Professional fund raiser Conrad Squires advises you to "find and use relevant human-interest stories," to "show donors the faces of the people they are helping," and to "make the act of sending a contribution as real and memorable and personal" as you can.[21] Those devices make people feel the warmth of other lives.[22]

Human-interest stories are the best way to interest your readers in fund-raising letters.

So that your letters remain personal, immediate, and effective, steer clear of three common mistakes:[23]

- Avoid letting your letter sound like a business communication of any kind.
- Avoid wasting space on warm-up (the things you write while you're working up to your real argument).
- Avoid assuming that the goals of your organization are more important than your readers' concerns (a deadly mistake).

To personalize fund-raising letters
- ✧ Avoid sounding businesslike
- ✧ Avoid warming up to your real argument
- ✧ Avoid assuming that your organization's goals are more important than your reader's concerns

The last item is crucial when writing fund-raising letters. Squires says: "The more space you spend writing about the reader, the better response you're likely to get."[24]

> "You've proven you are somebody who really cares what happens to children, Mr. Jones."

> "Ms. Smith, your company's kindness can change the world for Meta Singh and his family."

Also, it's up to you to help your donors identify with recipients. A busy company executive may not be able to identify with the homeless person she passes on the street every day. But every human being understands pain. So do your best to portray that homeless person's situation in words the busy executive can understand.[25]

The "you"-oriented opening focuses on the reader's generosity and grabs attention.

The next three paragraphs create interest by emphasizing benefits to the reader and by providing details of the trip and costs.

The easy-to-read list of benefits creates desire to participate in a worthwhile project.

The last paragraph urges action by naming additional reader benefits and enclosing a response card.

Brandon High School Band

27 Linden Blvd. • Brandon, MB R7B 1C1
(204) 555-7768

Dear Corporate Friend:

You have been a loyal supporter of our award-winning Brandon High School Band, and we appreciate what you've helped us accomplish. Because of you, we were able to participate in three festival competitions this year, and we brought home three "Grand Champion" trophies.

Now we have the unprecedented opportunity to represent Brandon in the Osaka International Band Festival in 2003. Only 25 top bands from Canada have been invited, and, thanks to your sponsorship, Brandon High School Band is one of them.

Your continued support will help the Brandon High School Band accept Osaka's exciting invitation. The Brandon City Council, the Brandon School Board, and our own Parents Association Board believe that the trip will be an opportunity for our 130 band members to learn about another culture. Even more important, our Brandon ambassadors will bring their experiences back to our community and their classmates in speeches, photographs, and interviews with the local media.

Let us paint your logo on our band trailer as one of our Golden Sponsors. We'll also include your name in all our programs and mailings between now and the time of the trip. You'll be helping band members

1. Learn about other cultures
2. Share information abroad about our way of life in Canada
3. Teach others in Brandon what they learn
4. Help Brandon become recognized as a good home for international businesses

We estimate total costs at $500 000. The city of Osaka has pledged $25 000 toward financing the trip, and we have already received pledges from Akworth Nissan and the city for $25 000 each. Our band members will be holding fund-raising events such as car washes, bake sales, a spring fair, and many others over the next two years. But your support will make our dream a reality.

Please help our young ambassadors make this trip. Mark your pledge card and return it today. You'll receive personal letters from the kids expressing their appreciation. And you'll be proof of our city's motto, "Dreams come true in Brandon."

Cordially,

Monty Nichols

Monty Nichols
President
Brandon High School Band Parents Association

Enclosure

FIGURE 11.4

In-Depth Critique: Letter Raising Funds

As president of the non-profit Brandon High School Band Parents Association, Monty Nichols is faced with the daunting task of raising half a million dollars to help send the band to Osaka, Japan, for an international band festival. Nichols and his board have decided to contact local businesses for help. This letter makes a compelling case for donations.

LEARNING OUTCOME 6
List the ten guidelines that will help you strengthen your fundraising messages.

STRENGTHENING FUND-RAISING MESSAGES

The best fund-raising letters do four things: (1) thoroughly explain a specific need, (2) show how important it is for readers to help, (3) spell out exactly what amount of help is being requested, and (4) describe in detail the benefits of helping.[26] Here are some fund-raising guidelines that will help you accomplish these four major tasks:[27]

Strong fund-raising letters
✧ Explain a specific need thoroughly
✧ Show how important it is for readers to help
✧ Spell out exactly what amount of help is being requested
✧ Describe in detail the benefits of helping

- Do whatever you can to interest your readers at the absolute beginning of your letter. If you can't catch your readers' interest then, you never will.
- Tell your story with simple, warm, and personal language.
- Be sure to give readers an opportunity to accomplish something important.
- Make the need so urgent and strong that your readers find it hard to say no. "Won't you send a gift now, knowing children's lives are on the line?" Donors want to feel needed. They want the excitement of coming to your rescue.
- Make it extremely easy to respond by asking for a small gift.
- Make the amount of money you want absolutely clear and appropriate to your audience.
- Explain why the money is needed as soon as possible.
- Write no longer than you have to. For example, people expect telegram-type messages to be short. For fund-raising letters, however, longer messages are usually the most effective, as long as you keep your sentences and paragraphs short, maximize content, and minimize wordiness. If you're writing a long message, just make sure it's interesting and no longer than necessary.
- Include all the basics in your reply form–your name, address, telephone number; a restatement of your request and the gift amount; your donor's name, address, and code number (or space enough for a label); information on how to make out the cheque; and information on tax deductibility.
- Use interesting enclosures. Enclosures that simply give more information about a project or the purpose of your organization don't inspire readers to respond. To increase returns, use enclosures that are fun or that give the donor something to do, sign, send, or keep. Examples include bumper stickers and short surveys.

These guidelines should help you engage the humanity and compassion of your readers by focusing on specific reader benefits, detailing the unique need, emphasizing the urgency of the situation, and spelling out the exact help needed.

Like sales letters, fund-raising letters are simply particular types of persuasive messages. Each category has its unique requirements, some of which only professional writers can master. (See this chapter's Checklist for Sales and Fund-Raising Letters as a reminder of the tasks involved in these messages.)

Writing Collection Messages

The purpose of the collection process is to maintain goodwill while collecting what is owed. Collection is a sensitive issue. The following practices must be *avoided* to ensure that your messages meet legal and ethical standards:

- Falsely implying that a lawsuit has been filed
- Contacting the debtor's employer or relatives about the debt
- Communicating to other persons that the person in debt
- Using abusive or obscene language
- Using defamatory language (such as calling the person a *deadbeat* or a *crook*)
- Intentionally causing mental distress
- Threatening violence
- Communicating by postcard (not sufficiently confidential)
- Sending anonymous COD communications
- Misrepresenting the legal status of the debt
- Communicating in such a way as to make the receiver physically ill
- Giving false impressions, such as labelling the envelope "Tax Information"
- Misrepresenting the message as a government or court document

To protect people from unreasonable persecution and harassment by debt collectors, the law also delineates when you may contact a debtor, how many times you may call, and what information you must provide to the debtor (timely responses, accurate records, and understandable documents). However, that doesn't mean you can't be firm in a collection letter. As long as what you state is true and lawful, it can't be construed as harassment or misrepresentation.

A debtor's response is likely to be emotional, especially when the debtor is conscientious, so use tact.

Conscientious customers are embarrassed about past-due accounts. In such an emotional state, they may consciously or unconsciously blame you for the problem, procrastinate, avoid the situation altogether, or react aggressively. Your job is to neutralize those feelings by using **positive appeals,** by accentuating the benefits of complying with your request for payment. If positive appeals fail, you may have to consider a **negative appeal,** which stresses the unpleasant consequences of not acting rather than the benefits of acting. Of course, using abusive or threatening language and harassing your customer are ineffective and illegal–continue to use a polite and businesslike tone as you point out some of the actions legally available to you.

Positive appeals are usually more effective than negative ones.

If positive appeals fail, you may need to point out the actions legally available to you.

Don't forget that your real aim is to persuade the customer to make the payment. So your best approach is to try to maintain the customer's goodwill. One key to success in collecting is remembering that collection is a process, not just a single demand.[28] As the past-due period lengthens, a series of collection letters reflecting the increasing seriousness of the problem is sent to the customer at predetermined intervals: notification, reminder, inquiry, urgent notice, and ultimatum. At the later stages, the customer's credit and buying history, the amount of money owed, and the customer's overall credit rating determine the content and style of collection messages.

Steps in the collection series:
- ✧ Notification
- ✧ Reminder
- ✧ Inquiry
- ✧ Urgent notice
- ✧ Ultimatum

Checklist for Sales and Fund-Raising Letters

A. Attention

1. Design a positive opening that awakens in the reader a favourable association with the product, need, or cause.
2. Write the opening so that it's appropriate, fresh, honest, interesting, specific, and relevant.
3. Promise a benefit to the reader.
4. Keep the first paragraph short, preferably two to five lines, sometimes only one.
5. Design an attention-getter that uses a human-interest story for fund-raising letters or any of the following techniques for sales letters: significant facts about the product, solution to a problem, special offer or gift, testimonial, stimulation of the senses or emotions, reference to current events, action picture, startling fact, agreeable assertion, comparison, event or fact in the reader's life, problem the reader may face, quotation.

B. Interest

1. State information clearly, vividly, and persuasively, and relate it to the reader's concerns.
2. Develop the central selling point, or explain the urgency of the fund-raising need.
3. Feature the product or need in two ways: physical description and reader benefits.
   a. Interweave benefits with a physical description; or place benefits first.
   b. Describe the objective details of the need or of the product (size, shape, colour, scent, sound, texture, and so on).
   c. Through psychological appeals, present the sensation, satisfaction, or pleasure your reader will gain translating the product, service, or donation into the fulfillment of needs and desires.
   d. Blend cold facts with warm feelings.

C. Desire

1. Enlist one or more appeals to support the central idea (selling point or fund-raising goal).
   a. Provide one paragraph of desire-creating material in a one-page letter with a descriptive brochure; provide several paragraphs if the letter itself is two or more pages long, with or without an enclosed brochure.
   b. Emphasize reader benefits.
   c. If the product is valued mainly because of its appearance, describe its physical details.

Notification

Most creditors send bills to customers on a regular schedule, depending on the terms of the credit agreement. Typically, this standard notification is a form letter or statement, often computerized, stating clearly the amount due, the date due, the penalties for late payment, and the total amount remaining to be paid. The standardized form, far from being an insult to the recipient, indicates the creditor's trust that all will go according to plan.

The standardized notification is a sign of trust.

Reminder

If the payment has not been received within a few days after the due date, most creditors send out a gentle reminder. Again, the tone of the standardized letter is reassuring, conveying the company's assumption that some minor problem has delayed payment. In other words, the firm still believes that the customer has every intention of paying what is due and needs only to be reminded. Thus the tone is not too serious:

The reminder notice, which still assumes only a minor problem, may be a standardized form or an informal message.

> Our records show that your September payment is more than a week overdue. If you have recently mailed your cheque for $154.87, we thank you. If not, please send it in quickly.

Using a different strategy, some companies send out a copy of the unpaid bill at this stage, with a handwritten note or preprinted stamp or sticker indicating that payment has not yet been received.

- d. If the product is machinery or technical equipment, describe its sturdiness of construction, fine crafting, and other technical details in terms that help readers visualize themselves using it.
- e. Include technical sketches and meaningful pictures, charts, and graphs, if necessary.
- f. If the main point is to elicit a donation, use strong visual details, good narrative, active verbs, and limited adjectives to strengthen the desire to help.

2. Anticipate and answer the reader's questions.
3. Use an appropriate form of proof.
   - a. Include facts about users' experience with the charitable organization or product, including verifiable reports and statistics from donation recipients or product users.
   - b. Provide names (with permission only) of other satisfied buyers, users, or donors.
   - c. Present unexaggerated testimonials from persons or firms who have used the product or donated funds and whose judgment the reader respects.
   - d. For sales letters, provide the results of performance tests by recognized experts, testing laboratories, or authoritative agencies.
   - e. For fund-raising letters, provide the details of how donations are spent, using recognized accounting or auditing firms.
   - f. In sales letters, offer a free trial or a guarantee, and refer to samples if they are included.
4. Note any enclosures in conjunction with a selling point or reader benefit.

D. Action

1. Clearly state the action you desire.
2. Provide specific details on how to order the product, donate money, or reach your organization.
3. Make action easy through the use of a mail-back reply card, preaddressed envelope, phone number, or promise of a follow-up call or visit.
4. Offer a special inducement to act: time limit or situation urgency, special price for a limited time, premium for acting before a certain date, free gift for buying or donating, free trial, no obligation to buy but more information or a suggested demonstration, easy payments with no money down, credit-card payments.
5. Supply a final reader benefit.
6. Include a postscript conveying important donation information or an important sales point (if desired for emphasis).

Inquiry

The inquiry
- ✧ Assumes that something unusual is preventing payment
- ✧ Is personalized
- ✧ Avoids any suggestion of customer dissatisfaction

As frustrating as it may be to send out a reminder and still get no response, don't assume that your customer plans to ignore the debt, especially if the customer has paid bills promptly in the past. So avoid accusations in your inquiry message. However, the time has passed for assuming that the delay is merely an oversight, so you may assume that some unusual circumstance is preventing payment:

> According to our records, we have not received your September payment of $154.87. Because this payment is four weeks overdue, we are quite concerned. You have a history of paying your bills on time, so we must conclude that there is a problem. Please contact us at (800) 536-4995 to discuss this payment, or send us your cheque for $154.87 right away. We want to help you correct this situation as quickly as possible.

Personalization at this stage is appropriate because you're asking your customer to work out an individualized solution. The letter also avoids any suggestion that the customer might be dissatisfied with the purchase. Instead, it emphasizes the reader's obligation to communicate about the problem and the creditor's willingness to discuss it. Including the writer's name and a phone number helps motivate a response at this stage.

Urgent Notice

An urgent notice
- ✧ Might be signed by a top company official
- ✧ Might indicate the negative consequences of noncompliance
- ✧ Should leave an opening for payment without loss of face

The urgent notice stage represents a significant escalation. Convey your desire to collect the overdue payment immediately and your willingness to get serious, but avoid any overt threats. To communicate a sense of urgency, you might have a top official in the company sign the letter or resort to a negative appeal. Whatever the strategy, an urgent notice still leaves an opening for the debtor to make a payment without losing face:

An attention-getter focuses on the unusual circumstances leading to this letter.

> I was very surprised this morning when your file reached my desk with a big tag marked OVERDUE. Usually, I receive customer files only when a serious problem has cropped up.

The recipient is reminded of the order. Personalization and an attempt to emphasize common ground may motivate the reader to respond.

> Opening your file, I found the following facts: Your order for five cases of Panza serving trays was shipped six months ago. Yet we still haven't received the $232.70 due. You're in business too, Ms. Demisov, so you must realize that this debt needs to be paid at once. If you had a customer this far behind, you'd be equally concerned.

The preferred action is spelled out; an option is also suggested in case of serious trouble.

> Please see that a cheque for $232.70 is mailed to us at once. If you need to work out an alternate plan for payment, call me now at (712) 693-7300.

> Sincerely,

The name of a ranking official lends weight to the message.

> Artis Knight
> Vice-President

Ultimatum

An ultimatum
- ✧ Should state the exact consequences of nonpayment
- ✧ Must avoid any hint of defamation or harassment
- ✧ Need not take a personal, helpful tone

Some people's finances are in such disorder that you won't get their attention until the ultimatum stage. But don't send an ultimatum unless you intend to back it up and are well supported by company policy. Even then, maintain a polite, businesslike manner and avoid defaming or harassing the debtor.

By itemizing the precise consequences of not paying the bill, you can encourage debtors to re-evaluate their priorities. You're no longer interested in hearing why it has taken them so long to respond; you're interested in putting your claim at the top of their list. The tone of the ultimatum need not be as personal or individualized as the inquiry or urgent notice. At this stage, you're in a position of justified authority and should no longer be willing to return to an earlier stage of communication and negotiation:

> On December 12, 2000, you placed a catalogue order with Karting Klothes for our extra-large wheeled duffle bag, and you applied for a credit account with us. We approved your application, and on December 17 mailed the duffle bag to you with an invoice for $92.87. According to our credit application, which you signed, payment is due within 20 days of the date of the invoice. As of February 7, your payment was significantly overdue.
>
> Karting Klothes sent you reminders on January 7 and again on February 7. In both these letters, we asked you to contact us to discuss your payment. We also asked you to make a partial payment as a show of your good faith. You did neither.
>
> Karting Klothes has already cancelled your credit privileges and will turn your account over to a collection agency if we do not receive your payment for $92.87 by March 10. To reinstate your account and to avoid the problems associated with a bad credit rating, mail your cheque immediately.

This letter outlines the steps that have already been taken, implying that the drastic action to come is the logical next step. Although earlier collection messages were based on persuasion, this one is essentially a bad-news letter.

If a letter like this doesn't yield results, the only remaining remedy is to begin legal collection procedures. As a final courtesy, you might want to send the debtor a notice of the action you're about to take. By maintaining your respect for the customer until the bitter end, you may still salvage some goodwill.

ON THE JOB
Solving a Communication Dilemma at the Young Entrepreneurs' Association

Since its founding in 1992, the Young Entrepreneurs' Association has helped hundreds of young Canadians to start and develop their businesses and students to make contacts and discuss their plans with peers and mentors. Meetings are conducted in an environment where members can "comfortably share their triumphs and challenges, ideas, experiences and knowledge." Members receive the group's newsletter, *The YEA Spirit*, which presents "news, information, and inspiration for entrepreneurs," and may attend programs such as the "Successful Entrepreneurs' Series," "Presidents' Roundtables," the "Business Expert Series," and "Breakfast Brainstorming." Growing quickly in Ontario, the YEA began to expand nationally in 1997 and now has chapters established in Victoria, Vancouver, Halifax, and St. John's and under development in Kelowna, Calgary, Regina, Winnipeg, Moncton, and Fredericton. A non-profit organization, the YEA is assisted by such established companies as Royal Bank, IBM, and Hewlett-Packard, and is eager to receive any kind of help that will enable them to further their goals.

Your Mission: As a member of the YEA's Board of Directors, one of your duties is to contact the chairpersons of business programs at Canadian universities and colleges seeking their support for YEA activities and programs . Use your knowledge of persuasive messages to choose the *best* alternative in each of the following situations. Be prepared to explain why your choice is the most effective one.[29]

1. You have been allocated the job of drafting a form letter to be sent to the chairpersons of business programs in Canada where new chapters of the Young Entrepreneurs' Association are established, but the members don't yet have a designated office. The chairpersons are already familiar with the work of the YEA. Which of the following versions is the best attention-getter for this letter?

a. No, this isn't a letter asking for a financial contribution. We know are looking for a valuable resource you may be able to share with us: a few hundred square feet of unused office space.
b. Don't let that unused office space go to waste! Let the YEA take that space off your hands. We're looking for a vacant room in your department. If you let us have any office space you're not using, you'll be giving your students a chance to meet with their fellow YEA members.
c. If you could put your empty office space to productive use by helping your students, wouldn't you be interested? Donate some of your department's unused space to the Young Entrepreneurs' Association chapter at your school. You'll gain the satisfaction of helping your students by giving them a central place to meet and to learn from the success of other young business people.

2. Which of the following versions is the most effective interest and desire section for your letter?

a. You may have one medium-sized office, or even a portion of an open work space, that you no longer use. Just 400 square feet would allow the chapter president and secretary to have enough space to maintain a place where they can perform administrative work and hold meetings with members. We would be able to adapt any empty office to our needs, regardless of its location. We would supply our own computers, printer, fax machine, and furniture.

   By donating space to your school's chapter of the Young Entrepreneurs' Association, you will be able to enhance your students' studies by providing a location where they can share ideas and information in a relaxed atmosphere. You will see them take into the classroom the enthusiasm they've developed from seeing how entrepreneurs started their own businesses and became successful.
b. The officers of your school's YEA branch can work productively in as little as 400 square feet of office space. So please look around. Check every nook and cranny in your facility. See whether you have a large office, or a portion of an open work area you no longer use that may be suitable.

   You will be proud of your department's donation, which will help the YEA serve your students. Help us educate the next generation of entrepreneurs by donating your unused office space today!
c. The Young Entrepreneurs' Association needs your help. Any office space–as little as 400 square feet–will help us put local representatives near the students they serve. Please take a moment to see whether you have one large office, or a portion of an open work area, that you no longer use.

   If you donate this empty space, we'll take care of the details. We'll both benefit. You'll unload space you don't need, and we'll be able to have a place to operate. But the people who will benefit most will be your students.

3. Which of the following versions would be the best action section for your letter?

a. Your donation of unused office space will make a real difference to the YEA and to the students we serve. If you have any questions about donating office space, please call me at 905-555-6541. I'd be happy to discuss the details with you.
b. Your donation of free office space for our local chapter of the YEA would be much appreciated. If you have any space that you are able to donate, call me immediately at 905-555-6541 and I will be ready to answer any questions about donating space that you have.
c. If you can donate unused office space, you will help your student members of the YEA immeasurably. If you are willing to donate space, please take a moment to call me at 905-555-6541. I will try to answer any questions you have about donating space.

4. University and college newspapers managed and written by students are common on many campuses. Imagine that the YEA has put together an advertisement they would like to place in as many of these newspapers as possible, but because of limited funds, they would like the advertising space to be donated. Which of the following appeals to your audience would be most effective in a letter seeking free advertising space?

a. An entirely emotional appeal stressing the needs of the YEA and the satisfaction of helping a worthy cause.
b. An entirely logical appeal stressing that the advertisements can be inserted whenever the newspapers have unused space, thus saving editors the trouble of rearranging articles and other advertisements to make the page look good, or using meaningless filler.
c. A combination of emotional and logical appeals, stressing both the satisfaction of helping a worthy cause and the rationale behind printing the advertisement whenever the editors have available space.

TAP Your Knowledge

Summary of Learning Outcomes

1. Discuss the planning tasks that need extra attention when preparing persuasive messages. Because persuasive messages can be complicated and sensitive, several planning tasks need extra attention. You'll be persuading people to take action that they probably wouldn't have taken without your message, so analyzing your purpose is crucial. In addition, audience analysis may need to be more detailed for persuasive messages, gauging psychological and social needs in addition to cultural differences. Also, when persuading a skeptical audience, your credibility must be unquestionable, so you may need to spend some extra effort to establish it. And since your attempts to persuade could be viewed by some as manipulative, you need to strive for the highest ethical standards.

2. Distinguish between emotional and logical appeals, and discuss how to balance them. Emotional appeals call on human feelings, using arguments that are based on audience needs or sympathies. However, these appeals aren't effective by themselves. Logical appeals call on human reason (whether using analogy, induction, or deduction). If you are careful to avoid faulty logic, you can use logic together with emotion, thereby supplying rational support for an idea that readers have already embraced emotionally. In general, logic will be your strongest appeal, with only subtle emotion. However, when persuading someone to purchase a product, join a cause, or make a donation, you can heighten emotional appeals.

3. Describe the AIDA plan for persuasive messages. When using the AIDA plan, you open your message by getting *attention* with a reader benefit, a problem, a stimulating question, a piece of news, or an unexpected statement. You build *interest* with facts, details, and additional reader benefits. You increase *desire* by providing more evidence and reader benefits and by anticipating and answering possible objections. You conclude by motivating a specific *action,* emphasizing the positive results of that action, and making it easy for the reader to respond.

4. Compare sales messages with fundraising messages. Sales messages are used by for-profit companies to persuade readers to make a purchase for themselves. In contrast, fund-raising messages are used by non-profit organizations to persuade readers to donate their time or their money to help others. However, these two types of persuasive message have a lot in common. Primarily, they both try to persuade readers to "buy" (with time or money) the value that is being offered (the product or the cause). In addition, both types of persuasive message generally use the AIDA plan.

5. List at least four attention-getting devices for sales messages. Professionals use common techniques to attract audience attention in sales messages. In the openings of your sales messages, you can make a personal appeal to the reader's emotions and values, highlight the product's most attractive features and benefits, offer a sample of the product, present a short, intriguing anecdote, or ask a provocative question.

6. List the ten guidelines that will help you strengthen your fundraising messages. To strengthen your fundraising messages, follow these guidelines: (1) interest your readers immediately, (2) use simple language, (3) give your readers the chance to do something important, (4) make it hard to say no, (5) ask for a *small* gift, (6) make your needs clear, (7) explain the urgency, (8) write no longer than you have to, (9) make your reply form complete and thorough, (10) use interesting enclosures.

Test Your Knowledge

Review Questions

1. How do emotional appeals differ from logical appeals?
2. What is the AIDA plan, and how does it apply to persuasive messages?
3. What are five kinds of faulty logic?
4. What are the similarities and differences between sales messages and fund-raising messages?
5. What role do demographics and psychographics play in audience analysis during the planning of a persuasive message?
6. What are four of the ways you can build credibility with an audience when planning a persuasive message?
7. What three types of reasoning can you use in logical appeals?
8. How can semantics affect a persuasive message?
9. How do benefits differ from features?

Apply Your Knowledge

Critical Thinking Questions

1. If you must persuade your audience to take some action, aren't you being manipulative and unethical? Explain.
2. How many of a manager's daily tasks require persuasion? List as many as you can think of.
3. Are emotional appeals ethical? Why or why not?
4. Is it honest to use a hook before presenting your request? Explain.
5. Why is it important to maintain goodwill in your collection letter? Briefly explain.
6. For over a year, you've tried repeatedly to collect $6000 from a client who is able to pay but simply refuses. You're writing one last letter before turning the matter over to your attorney. What sort of things can you say in your letter? What things should you avoid saying? Explain your answers.

Practise Your Knowledge

Documents for Analysis

Read the following documents; then (1) analyze the strengths and weaknesses of each sentence and (2) revise each document so that it follows this chapter's guidelines.

Document 11.A: Writing Persuasive Requests for Action

At Tolson Auto Repair, we have been in business for over 25 years. We stay in business by always taking into account what the customer wants. That's why we are writing. We want to know your opinions to be able to better conduct our business.

Take a moment right now and fill out the enclosed questionnaire. We know everyone is busy, but this is just one way we have of making sure our people do their job correctly. Use the enclosed envelope to return the questionnaire. And again, we're happy you chose Tolson Auto Repair. We want to take care of all your auto needs.

Document 11.B: Writing Sales and Fund-Raising Letters

We know how awful dining hall food can be, and that's why we've developed the Mealaweek Club. Once a week, we'll deliver food to your residence room or apartment. Our meals taste great. We have pizza, buffalo wings, hamburgers and curly fries, veggie roll-ups, and more!

When you sign up for just six months, we will ask what day you want your delivery. We'll ask you to fill out your selection of meals. And the rest is up to us. At Mealaweek we deliver! And payment is easy. We accept MasterCard and VISA or a personal cheque. It will save money especially when compared with eating out.

Just fill out the enclosed card and indicate your method of payment. As soon as we approve your credit or cheque, we'll begin delivery. Tell all your friends about Mealaweek. We're the best idea since sliced bread!

Cases

Writing Persuasive Requests for Action

1. Selling sales letters: E-mail message promoting a new idea at Sears Canada As marketing manager for Sears Canada, you know that sales messages can make or break a business. One of your company's most difficult tasks is getting customers to read a sales letter. During a recent seminar, you heard a reference made to the "PSALM" method, and you decide to learn more about it. Explore the Web site at **www.so-cal.com/writingbiz/page1.htm** and find out what is meant by the PSALM approach. What does the author of this approach identify as the most common mistakes in sales letters? You are enthusiastic about how this new approach has changed your thinking about sales letters, and you would like everyone in your department to seriously consider it.

Your Task: Write an e-mail message to everyone in your department, selling the idea of the PSALM method to your colleagues.

2. Selling an idea: E-mail message to your instructor You went browsing the Web to find out about the Toulmin model for reasoning. You were intrigued by what you found at **www.unl.edu/speech/comm109/Toulmin/ index.htm**. Spend a few minutes exploring the site. Do you think that this Web site is well designed?

Your Task: Write an e-mail message to your instructor to persuade her or him of your opinion.

3. Avoiding depression: Letter requesting severance package at Intermed You've heard the old saying that when your next door neighbour loses her job, it's a recession; when you lose yours, it's a depression. After 15 years as a loyal manager at Intermed, a surgical equipment manufacturer, you might be about to experience your own "depression." In a companywide meeting this morning, your CEO informed everyone that Intermed has just been bought by Urohealth Systems and that a substantial number of layoffs are anticipated.

As manager of Intermed's technical support department, you're glad to know that Urohealth is unlikely to let most of your hourly staff go. But you've also heard that after Urohealth's last acquisition, middle managers like you were, to put it politely, "downsized" in large numbers. You're fairly certain your job will disappear within weeks.

Not one to go down without a fight–and preferring to keep a positive perspective–you decide to take a proactive approach. Before they have a chance to fire you, you're going to negotiate a reasonable, friendly, and equitable parting of company. And better to negotiate the terms of your voluntary termination now, with your Intermed superiors, before Urohealth brings in new upper management staff.

So you buckle down to study the inevitable. First, you look at your current compensation and decide to ask for four weeks' severance pay for each of your 15 years of service. (You want to start high, but you're prepared to settle for three weeks' severance pay, or even two, if you have to.) Second, you consider your stock purchases over the years (part of your benefits program). You've heard that some managers lost their recent stock purchases when they were terminated, and since the company's stock is likely to increase in value after Urohealth's acquisition, you'd like to keep all of yours. You're willing to trade some of your severance pay to keep all of your stock, you decide.

Also, your RSP may be in jeopardy. The company's agreement has been to match your savings to the plan each year, so long as you are still employed by them. Since you won't be on the payroll through December 31, they're likely to balk at this year's matching amount. Better make this part of your severance request, for the company to make its matching contribution despite your early departure.

Finally, conventional wisdom says it can take up to a year for someone with your skills and experience to find another job. You'd like Intermed to provide outplacement counselling and the use of an office, telephone, and office equipment, plus payment of your job-hunting expenses, for at least 90 days. Considering all you've done for them over the years–and your current managers are quite happy with your work–your requests aren't going to be extravagant.

Your Task: Write a persuasive letter to Shirley Barnett, Intermed's Director of Human Resources, Room 1735, 649 Bay St., Toronto, ON M5G 2L4, outlining your proposed voluntary termination and suggested severance package.[30]

4. Helping out: Persuasive memo to Good Eats store managers Good Eats is a chain of organic food stores with locations in Ottawa. The stores are big and well lit, like their more traditional grocery store counterparts. They are also teeming with a wide variety of attractively displayed foods and related products.

However, Good Eats is different from the average supermarket. Its products include everything from granola sold in bulk to environmentally sensitive household products. The meats sold come from animals that were never fed antibiotics, and the cheese is from cows said to be raised on small farms and treated humanely.

Along with selling these products to upscale shoppers, the company has been giving food to homeless shelters. Every third weekend, Good Eats donates non-perishable food to three soup kitchens downtown. Company executives believe they are in a unique position to help others.

You work for the Chief Operating Officer (COO) of Good Eats. You've been asked to find ways to expand the donation program by involving the company's eight branches, most of which are in the suburbs. Ideally, the

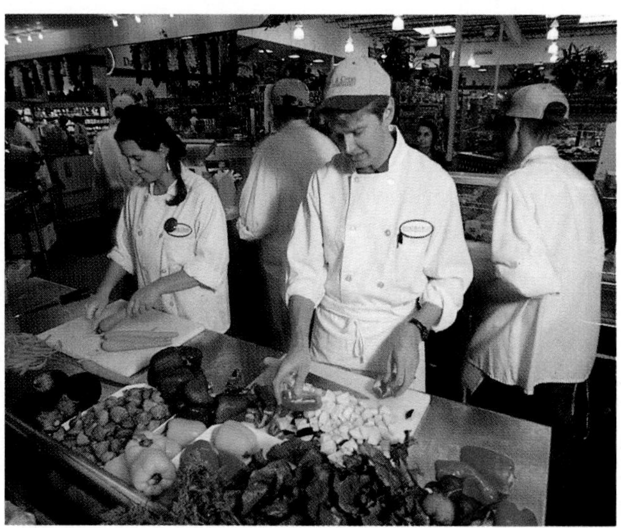

company would be able to increase the number of people it helps and to get more of its employees involved.

You don't have a great deal of extra money for the program, so the emphasis has to be on using resources already available to the stores. One idea is to use trucks from suburban branches to make the program mobile. Another idea is to join forces with a retailing chain to give food and clothing to individuals. The key is to be original and not exclude any idea, no matter how absurd it might seem. The only stipulation is to keep ideas politically neutral. Good Eats executives do not want to be seen as supporting any party or candidate. They just want to be good corporate citizens.

Your Task: Send persuasive memos to all managers at Good Eats, requesting ideas to expand the program. Invite employees to contribute ideas, for this or any other charitable project for the company.[31]

5. The glass bicycle: Persuasive letter from Owens-Corning requesting bids for manufacturing rights A student design group from Brazil's University of São Paulo has come up with the winning bicycle design in the Global Design Challenge. Sponsored by Owens-Corning, the competition called on teams from eight top design and engineering schools in the United States, Canada, Europe, Asia, and South America to design a bicycle that would cost less than $100 and would incorporate mainly glass-fibre composites in the construction. The winning entry is called the Kangaroo. Its framework is made of polyester reinforced with glass fibre, and its estimated manufacturing cost is $82. Moreover, some unique features make it a product of truly worldwide potential. An adjustable wheelbase can be shortened to allow easy manoeuvring in city traffic, and the seat and handlebars can be adjusted within a range to suit 95 percent of the world's population. Since more than half of the people on the globe depend on bicycles as their primary means of transportation, and since bicycles require no fossil fuel for operation, this product has tremendous potential in countries from Abu Dhabi to Zimbabwe.

As Owens-Corning's North American licensing manager, your job is to sign up companies to produce and market the Kangaroo bicycle for the Canadian, Mexican, and US markets. A manufacturing deal has been arranged with a Chinese producer who can deliver the bicycles to any West Coast NAFTA port for $86, including shipping, taxes, and tariffs. Your problem is that you have no distribution system to handle bicycles, so you must find a marketing partner who will license the rights to distribute and market the Kangaroo in North America. Your preference is to find a single marketer to serve the entire region, and priority will be given to companies such as Schwinn, Nishiki, and Cannondale Bicycles who are currently using Owens-Corning materials in their products. You are planning to license the marketing rights for a five-year term for an initial payment of $350 000 plus 8 percent of the gross sales.

Your Task: Write a persuasive letter to Mr. Gregg Bagni, Marketing Director, Schwinn Bicycle & Fitness (1690 38th Street, Boulder, CO 80301-2602), requesting a bid on the North American marketing rights and offering him first refusal. Point out the features you think will make the Kangaroo a widespread success, and be sure to spell out the financial terms. He can then determine whether the deal makes sense from his perspective. But don't give him too much time–ask for a response within ten days.[32]

6. Nap Time: Memo requesting space for "day sleepers" at Bild & Associates It's been one of those days … you were dragging by 10 A.M., ready to slump over onto your drafting table at Bild & Associates architectural firm in Halifax. Even that incredibly bright harbour view outside the office windows hasn't helped perk you up, and the coffee is just giving you stomach pains. Now how are you supposed to be creatively inspired when you can barely get your eyes to focus and your head feels like it's full of cotton? No, you weren't out partying last night–you've just been working long, late hours on a rush job for one of the firm's biggest clients. If only you could stretch out for a little catnap, you'd be good as new in 15 minutes …

Groggily, your mind brings up the memory of an item you spotted in *The Herald* a year ago and tore out. You seem to remember stuffing it into a desk drawer with the vague notion of presenting it during one of those officewide, corporate-spirit pep rallies your employers are so fond of. You rummage around in the drawer–ah, there it is, a short article about a minitrend toward "nap rooms" in the workplace. At first, your work ethic was shocked at the concept, but then your creative self started to glow at the thought. After all, didn't they teach you in school that Thomas Edison kept a cot in his office and got his best ideas when he was napping? And the article quotes an expert, William A. Anthony, author of *The Art of Napping*. He says that most people aren't sleep deprived, they're "nap ready."

It's not as if there haven't been precedents or pioneers out there in the business world. Shelly Ginenthal, the human resources director of *Macworld Magazine,* says their two-person nap room was installed in 1986 and usually has a waiting line. Must not be interfering with productivity if they're still using it more than ten years later, you muse. And here's another firm, Yarde Metals in Bristol, Connecticut, whose president, Bruce Yarde, says, "A quick little nap can rejuvenate you." So he's fighting employee stress with a 25-person nap room. Wow! That's almost like your old kindergarten. And yet another–you like this one best–an architectural firm in Montreal, Smith, Gold Associates, has plans on its drawing boards to add a nap space to its offices. If they can do it in Montreal, why not here?

Your Task: After you've had a good night's sleep, write a memo to Gerhardt M. Bild, the senior partner, persuading him that the distinguished offices of Bild & Associates could benefit from the addition of a corporate nap room. Be sure you've used your best persuasive skills, though, or you might send the wrong message to your employer.[32]

7. Caribbean Recognition: E-mail to city council The request seems simple enough: members of the Caribbean Business Association of your city have asked the city council to erect two signs designating the neighborhood where many Caribbean businesses are located as the Caribbean Business District. The area has been home to your family's restaurant, the Island Tastes, for many years.

But some members of the community complained when the issue was brought up during a city council session. "We should be focusing on unifying the community as a whole and its general diversity," they argued, "not dividing the city up into small ethnic districts." Some of the council members had been intrigued, however, by the prospect of creating a new tourist destination by marking the Caribbean Business District officially–that's what it actually is and has been for as long as you can remember. However, the issue was tabled for later consideration.

As the manager of your family's restaurant, you agree with those council members who think the designation would attract visitors. Moreover, the Caribbean Business Association has returned to the city council with an offer to pay for the cement structures which will designate the neighbourhood as the Caribbean Business District. The Association is willing to spend up to $30 000 for the design and installation of the signs.

Your Task: As a member of the Caribbean Business Association, you've been asked to support the request with an e-mail message to Cathy Stanford, your city's deputy mayor, at cstanford@council.yc.[34]

8. Too good to be true: E-mail to Page North requesting adjustment Page North offered its pager services for a mere $5 a month. Two weeks ago, you bought an inexpensive pager and signed a two-year contract. You had expected your pager to be up and running as soon as you bought it, but your co-workers and clients have been getting a busy signal when they dial your pager number. You've called Page North to get the problem resolved, but it's going to take them a week to fix it. Obviously, you don't want to be charged for any time the pager isn't in service, so you discuss the situation with the local manager. She tells you to contact Judy Hinkley at the company's regional business office.

Your Task: Send an e-mail message to Hinkley at Judy@pgnorth.com and request an adjustment to your account. Request credit or partial credit for one month of service. Remember to write a summary of events in chronological order, supplying exact dates for maximum effectiveness.

9. Phone frustration: Persuasive letter to Western Tel requesting resolution of telephone service overcharges You are a freelance business researcher, and your time is valuable, especially when you're using online research facilities. These valuable resources are becoming more and more important in your work, so you can't afford to sit around waiting for your Internet searches to download files at 56 000 bits per second (56 kbps). You often deal with massive files that can take forever to transfer at these rates. You determined that an ISDN (Integrated Services Digital Network) connection would be a faster alternative for your online work. You contacted Western Tel in November and requested residential ISDN service (you work from home).

When the confirming work order arrived, you discovered that Western Tel had your account set up as business service, so you called the service representative to change it to the lower residential rate. As a result, your business service was disconnected, and it took Western Tel two weeks to reconnect you. On top of that, when the initial bill arrived, there was a $125 charge for disconnecting the business service, and another $75 charge for reinstallation, but no credit for the two weeks of downtime. You have made at least 13 calls to the customer service department, both locally and at Western Tel headquarters in Edmonton. You even left a message on the customer feedback section of Western Tel's Internet Web site. But none of these actions have resolved the situation.

Your Task: Compose a persuasive letter to Ms. Claire Abell (Western Tel's director of consumer affairs at Western Tel, Edmonton, AB T5A 1B0), explaining your frustration with this billing problem and asking for immediate adjustment.[35]

10. Where Teens Gather: Memo Urging Partnership with Goosehead.com Your company is Blue Nitro, and you sell sports shoes–at least you hope to, as soon as your fledgling company makes enough commotion in the ever-fickle teen marketplace. As marketing director, it's your job to find out where to position the company's advertising resources to best advantage. Sure, MTV–but television chews up your budget faster than you can say "blue-soled shoes."

Early on, you hired a teen-market consultant, with disappointing results. Today you think you've hit the jackpot. You've discovered Goosehead.com, a Web site started by an 11-year-old girl. And this young entrepreneur has been basking in the kind of media attention you'd love to have: a feature story in *People* magazine.

Ashley Power is now 15 and president of Goosehead.com Inc. Her site now flies the banner "Goosehead Teen Entertainment Network" and has spawned its own clothing line, in addition to the live video chats, games, advice columns, and other entertainment featured online. Ashley's newest partner? Academy Award-winning actor Richard Dreyfuss, father of teens himself. He's helping Ashley improve her teenage cyber-sitcom, "Whatever," which she originated on the site. The actor will also help her develop new shows. Meanwhile, she's fielding offers to take "Whatever" to television.

Admittedly, Ashley's stepdad helped her get started. He's a TV-commercial director, he co-authors the sitcom, and he introduced Ashley to the William Morris agent who first encouraged "Whatever." Ashley's mom is a commercial artist, and she helped Ashley learn Photoshop to develop the site's alluring graphics.

But it was Ashley's original vision that won attention. She wanted "a Web site that won't talk down to teens as if they're little kids." After she listed the new site with search engines, she started getting 45 000 hits a day. Now Goosehead.com averages 100 000 visitors a day, and Ashley personally supervises the work of 30 adult staffers to make sure the content satisfies her own tastes and measures up to the feedback from her audience.

That's *your* audience she's got there. You could easily sign up to trade links with Goosehead. But you're thinking that Blue Nitro needs to become an investment partner to buy more visibility on the site–probably as a sponsor for "Whatever" episodes. Or you might be able to get in on the bottom rung of future Dreyfuss-inspired shows. You've already seen impressive partners on the site, including some in your industry, such as Quiksilver, Oakley, Kipling. You need to act fast.

Your Task: Write a persuasive memo to your Blue Nitro president Kevin Hawkins, convincing him that Ashley Power's site is hot and that your company should make this move. The first step will be to begin partnership discussions with Power and company.

11. Ouch, that hurts! Persuasive memo at Technology One requesting equipment retrofit Mike Andrews leaves your office, shutting the door behind him. The pain in his arm is reflected on his face. He's about to file a worker's compensation claim–your third this month. As human resources director for Technology One, a major software-development firm, you're worried not only about costs but also about the well-being of your employees.

Mike's complaints are much the same as those already reported by two other computer technicians: sharp pains in the wrist, numbness, and decreased range of motion. You know that the average technician spends at least six hours a day working on the computer, yet you've never had this many complaints in a short time, and the severity of the symptoms seems to be increasing.

You decide to seek the advice of experts. A local sports and orthopedic medicine clinic gives you a detailed description of repetitive strain injuries (RSIs). The symptoms described are virtually identical to those exhibited by your technicians. You're distressed to learn that, if the cause of these injuries is not found and corrected, your technicians could require surgery or could even become permanently disabled.

The physical therapist at the clinic feels that exercises and wrist splints may help relieve symptoms and could even prevent new injuries. However, she also recommends that you consult an ergonomic analyst who can evaluate the furniture and equipment your technicians are using.

On her advice, you bring in an analyst who spends an entire day at your facility. After measuring desk and chair height, watching technicians at work, and conducting a detailed analysis of all your equipment, he makes two recommendations: (1) Throw out all your computer keyboards and replace them with ergonomic keyboards, and (2) replace every mouse with a trackball. Suddenly you realize that the RSI complaints began shortly after your controller and purchasing manager bought a truckload of new computer equipment at a local merchant's going-out-of-business sale. You begin to wonder about the quality and design of that equipment, and you ask the analyst what benefits the changes will provide.

The ergonomic keyboard actually splits the traditional rows of keys in half and places the rows of keys at different angles, allowing the wrists to stay straight and relieving pressure on the forearm. The repetitive motions involved in using a mouse further aggravate the symptoms created by use of the traditional keyboard. Using a trackball does not require the repetitive clicking motion of the forefinger.

Your task: You know that replacing peripheral equipment on more than 50 computers will be costly, especially when the existing equipment is nearly new. However, increasing RSIs and disability claims could be even more costly. Write a persuasive memo to Katherine Wilson, your controller, and convince her of the immediate need to retrofit the technicians' computer equipment.

Writing Sales and Fund-Raising Messages

12. All natural: Letter promoting crystal Deodorant Stones of America When Larry Morris first walked into your advertising office and placed what looked like a large piece of rock salt in your hand, proclaiming that this product could make Arid, Dial, Ban, and all the others obsolete, all you could do was stare at the thing. You couldn't imagine how this clear, hard rock could keep anyone's underarms sweet smelling. In the first place, what were you supposed to do with it? Wear it around your neck? You looked at Morris with a skeptical squint–was this some new crystal-healing device?

But Morris, owner of Deodorant Stones of America (DSA), smiled patiently and sat down to explain his new product. The only ingredients are mineral salts, used for centuries in Thailand to get rid of body odours by destroying the skin bacteria that cause the unpleasant smells. The stones contain no perfumes, preservatives, oils, emulsifiers, alcohol, propellants, or harsh chemicals. The naturally occurring minerals (potassium alum, ammonium, barium, calcium, iron, magnesium, manganese, phosphorus, silicon, sodium, strontium, and titanium) are crystallized over a period of several months, then hand-shaped and smoothed for rubbing over the skin. When either the skin or the stone is wet, an invisible layer of the mineral salts sticks to the skin, but it won't stain clothing or clog pores. Morris says the minerals kill odour-causing bacteria so thoroughly that the stones are 200 percent more effective than conventional chemical deodorants.

Deodorant Stones of America now sells about 7 million stones annually, throughout North America and in seven countries overseas, under several brand names: Fresh Foot (Foot Deodorant Stone), The Jock's Rock (World Class Deodorant), Nature's Crystal (Body Deodorant), Thai Deodorant Stone, and Pure & Natural (push-up sticks and spray). Morris wants to expand, and he's hired you to write an all-purpose sales letter directed to both consumers and retailers.

Your Task: You've tried the stone and signed the contract. You especially liked the fact that it gave off absolutely no odour at all and worked for a full 24 hours. Write the sales letter for one or all of the product names listed above.[37]

13. Power pioneers: Sales letter touting Ballard Power Systems fuel cells If you can turn water (H_2O) into hydrogen and oxygen by running an electrical current through it (electrolysis), can you produce an electrical current by combining hydrogen and oxygen? A British lawyer, Sir William Robert Grove, proved in 1839 that you could. He produced the world's first electricity-generating fuel cell. But until recently, no one could produce a commercially viable version of Grove's invention.

The simple device is somewhat like a battery; it produces an electrical current by means of an electrochemical reaction. It's also like a combustion or turbine engine; it continues to operate as long as it's supplied with fuel (some form of hydrogen and oxygen). Best of all, the fuel cell's only by-products are water, heat, and, if certain fuels are used, carbon dioxide.

Analysts predict that two decades from now fuel cells will account for 15 percent of growth in the global power-producing industry. Burnaby, BC's Ballard Power Systems develops and manufactures fuel cells to power buses, cars, and trucks. They also produce stationary fuel-cell power generators which could supply enough power to meet the electricity needs of homes and businesses. In 1999 Ballard introduced the Xcellsis Fuel Cell Engine, manufactured by their associated company Xcellsis. These engines were used on three buses operated with TransLink in Vancouver and three buses operated by the Chicago Transit Authority during two-year field trials, which concluded successfully in 2000. These trials showed that fuel cells make engines for mass transportation cleaner and environmentally more friendly than conventionally powered ones.

Your task: If the trials were so successful in Vancouver, why not hold a trial in your city or town? Write a letter selling the idea of a fuel-cell trial to the head of your local transit service. Plan to enclose Ballard Power Systems's most recent annual report, which will give your reader more information about fuel cell technology.[38]

14. The bride wore hiking boots: Persuasive letter to "We Do" bridal superstore When Shari and Randy Almsburg of Burnaby, BC, decided to tie the knot, they knew just what they wanted. "We always enjoyed hiking. In fact, we met each other on a hike. That's why we wanted to wrap our wedding plans around our favourite hobby." Enter Tie the Knot, a one-owner company specializing in bizarre wedding plans.

"Actually, the bride wearing a white dress and a pair of hiking boots was *not* our most unusual wedding," says owner and wedding consultant, Todd Dansing (whose own wedding took place a mile high just before the happy couple plunged to Earth by parachute). "We recently helped plan an underwater wedding in a shark tank at the aquarium for two marine biologists whose work involved feeding the fish. Our main problem there was this huge turtle that kept bumping into the preacher." Dansing tells you of other unusual weddings that took place in airplanes, on boats, under water, and in exotic locations such as Alberta's Badlands. Whatever your wedding plans, Todd believes he can find the necessary resources and save you time and money in the process.

Todd's marketing efforts to date have involved mostly word of mouth and free press coverage of his unusual weddings (although reporters kept their distance when two snake handlers from the zoo tied the knot). But his brother-in-law has invested capital in the business, so Todd hires you to help him tell the world about his services. You suggest that he consider affiliating with an established wedding service or store.

You and Todd visit We Do, a bridal superstore located in Winnipeg, Manitoba, and you help Todd see the potential for marketing his unusual, offbeat wedding service to this large company. We Do is a 26 000-square-foot matrimonial Mecca that sells 600 styles of bridal gowns and everything else traditional couples need for a wedding. The franchise hopes to open 40 stores eventually, so if Todd can strike a deal with We Do, his future profit potential will be high.

Your Task: Write a letter for Todd's signature to Carol Feinberg, CEO of We Do. Suggest that Tie the Knot would make a great consultant for couples with offbeat wedding tastes. Emphasize Todd's experience, and point out the ways this venture will provide additional market share for We Do. Think of possible objections, such as Todd's lack of capital and small company size, and try to assure Feinberg that Tie the Knot is the right business to help capitalize on a unique opportunity.[39]

15. Finding money creatively: Fund-raising letter from Bel Canto Opera Bel Canto Opera is a small, creative opera company, renowned for its daring, sometimes offbeat, performances. Located in a major metropolitan area, it has been hampered by having to compete with larger, more affluent opera companies that have large followings and budgets to match.

Despite the competition, Bel Canto Opera has benefited from critical acclaim, and it has built a small but loyal following since its premier performance more than 18 years ago. Now the company is at a crossroads. Most recently it mounted a production of *Elegy for Young Lovers*. However, the show had to close after only a week because of poor attendance. Bills continue to come in, and the bank account is bare. The creative director won't even discuss continuing the season unless a solution can be found.

Out of the darkness comes an angel. A local university with a brand-new performing arts centre would like to form an alliance with Bel Canto Opera. Although the university isn't offering large sums of cash, its board members are willing to let the company use the performing arts centre and other campus facilities at no cost. They would also consider some joint ventures in money-making educational events such as lectures and exhibitions. These events would be fairly easy and inexpensive to produce, and they could generate some immediate cash flow.

But the *coup de théâtre* for Bel Canto Opera would be access to the university's key donors, alumni, and supporters of the arts. The company's management team believes that, properly cultivated, this group could provide the sound financial base the company needs for future operations. Everyone on the team is excited.

The chairperson of the opera's board, the creative director, the development director, and the head of the university's fine arts department recently held a strategy session. After agreeing in principle to finalize the alliance between Bel Canto Opera and the university, all agreed that the first order of business is to raise funds. It was generally agreed that business and community leaders should be informed and invited to lend their financial support to the new venture.

A symposium is planned, at which the new venture will be introduced. The symposium will include musical previews of Bel Canto's upcoming season, a presentation by the creative director, and messages from key university staff. The goal of the symposium is to raise $500 000 in pledges.

Your Task: As development director of Bel Canto Opera, you have been asked to draft a letter to community and business leaders. Your goals are to convince them of the opera's viability, get them to attend the symposium, and convince them to pledge their financial support.[40]

16. Buses for seniors: Fundraising letter from King County Senior Centre The King County Senior Centre is one of Nova Scotia's oldest non-profit institutions for the elderly. Over the past 50 years, it has relied on financial support from government, businesses, and individuals.

Unfortunately, recent provincial cutbacks have dug into the organization's budget. In addition, in the last five years two of the county's largest companies, Hardwick Industries and McCarthy Electrical Motors, have moved offshore and shut down local operations. Both businesses were supporters of the center, as were many of the workers who lost jobs.

However, the needs of the center keep growing. For many of the county's roughly 1000 seniors who live alone, it's the only place where they can meet their peers, use a special library, avoid extreme weather, or get a well-balanced meal. The centre is not a nursing home and has no overnight facilities. Most individuals get to the facility on one of the three shuttle-type vans belonging to the centre. The buses are also used for various day trips to museums, plays, and similar functions. Occasionally, they are used to help the temporarily disabled get to doctors' offices or pharmacists.

Each van is more than eight years old. Although not unsafe, the vans are showing their age. The constant repairs are stopgap measures at best, and most weeks at least one of the vehicles is inoperable. Monthly repairs are averaging a total of $600 for the three vehicles. In addition, when the vans aren't working, the clients, staff, and budget all suffer. Seniors can't get to the centre, trips are cancelled, and drivers are sometimes paid for coming to work even though they weren't able to drive.

Conservatively, it would cost about $42 000 to replace each van with a new one: $126 000 total. This includes estimates on how much the centre could gain from selling the old vans. It's a fair amount of money, but in the opinion of your board of directors, buying new vans would be better than continuously repairing the old ones or risking the purchase of used ones.

Your Task: As director of the centre, draft a fund-raising letter to send to all of the businesses in the county. Stress the good work the centre does and the fact that this is a special fund-raising effort. Mention that all the money collected will go directly toward the purchase of the vans.

Writing Collection Messages

17. A firm but gentle nudge: Urgent notice collection letter at People's Trust You are the director of marketing at People's Trust, a consumer-oriented bank with branches mainly in southern Ontario. Because your bank is surrounded by some of the top educational institutions in the country, you have long considered student loans to be an important product.

You've just finished reviewing this month's collection reports and you realize that, for the sixth straight month, your bad-debt ratio (loans over 90 days past due) has increased. In addition, your average collection time has increased more than 20 days in the same period. This trend disturbs you, and you know your loan committee will be even more disturbed.

When People's Trust began an aggressive marketing campaign for student loans a little over ten years ago, tuition costs at local universities were less than half what they are today. As the cost of education has skyrocketed (creating a growing demand for financing), your interest rates on these loans have remained virtually unchanged. And with your collection ratio going downhill, you can see profits eroding rapidly.

You're also concerned because many of your student loans were made to parents of university and college students as part of the PLUS (Parent Loans to Undergraduate Students) program. These parents are some of the bank's best customers, local executives and community leaders with whom you have other important business dealings. You want to maintain your good image and relationship with these customers, so you're hesitant to implement a get-tough collection policy.

You're beginning to develop a strategy to improve collection of student loans. You plan to stress loyalty to your customers, commitment to supporting local educational institutions, and your desire to work with people who will demonstrate good-faith efforts. You think that refinancing and extended payment options might encourage some people to improve their payment records.

Your loan committee will meet in three days. You're aware that the more conservative committee members may recommend selling the entire delinquent student-loan business to a collection firm. You feel this action would be extremely detrimental to your bank's reputation and long-term growth.

Your Task: Develop a customer-relations collection letter designed to encourage these borrowers to improve their payment records. Assume that your bank's computer program will personalize each letter with the customer's name and address. Make your communication personal and directed to the individual customer.[41]

18. One last try: Ultimatum collection letter from Arciero Brothers Tony Arciero was ecstatic when his concrete company, Arciero Brothers, was selected as one of the construction subcontractors for a huge entertainment complex being built by Moorfield Construction. Located near one of the country's leading vacation destinations, the complex was designed to include restaurants, theatres, a video arcade, and a kiddyland play park.

With a venture of this magnitude it wasn't surprising that more than 200 subcontractors were needed to handle the building and infrastructure work. Arciero Brothers specializes in building foundations, sidewalks, and parking lots. Although Arciero has been in business for more than 20 years, the entertainment complex is the largest contract he's ever been awarded.

The project took nearly 24 months to complete. Arciero Brothers was on site throughout the first 21 months of the job. Phil Arciero hired new employees, including labourers and skilled tradespeople, and bought extra equipment to handle the new work and continue to meet the needs of his existing customers.

Moorfield Construction paid Arciero 10 percent of his estimate at the beginning of the job. Interim payments were made monthly, until the total payments reached 85 percent of the contract bid. Moorfield was to withhold the final 15 percent until the entire project was approved by the city building inspectors, a common practice in the construction industry. It has been nearly five months since the entertainment complex passed final inspection and opened for business.

Your Task: As the comptroller at Arciero Brothers, you've already paid your workers, drawing against your credit line at the bank to do it. You've called Moorfield Construction once a week, requesting payment of the more than $100 000 that is still outstanding on your contract. Moorfield officials say paperwork foul-ups are the reason for the slow payment. You're aware that none of the other subcontractors have received their final payments and that some of them are hiring attorneys to file mechanic's liens (legal collection proceedings) directly against the owner of the complex. You've talked to Tony Arciero about the dilemma. Neither of you wants to jeopardize potential future business from Moorfield Construction or from the entertainment complex owners. But to preserve your rights, and to increase your chances of being paid (liens are paid in the order filed), you and Arciero decide to have your attorney file a mechanic's lien. You recommend to Arciero that you write a polite but firm letter to Moorfield, with a copy to the owners of the entertainment centre, demanding immediate payment of the full amount owed you and informing Moorfield of the lien. Address your letter to Moorfield Construction (380 Gage Ave N, Hamilton, ON L8L 7B2), and address the copy to James Penny, Vice-President of Finance, Edwards Theatres Inc. (517 Adelaide St W, M5V 1T6).[42]

Developing Your Internet Skills

Lobby Your Leaders, p. 276

Follow the links to the home page of one of your MPs from the "how Canada is governed" Web site. Draft and send a persuasive but short e-mail message about an issue that concerns you. Be sure to apply the best persuasive strategy you've learned in this chapter for writing your message.

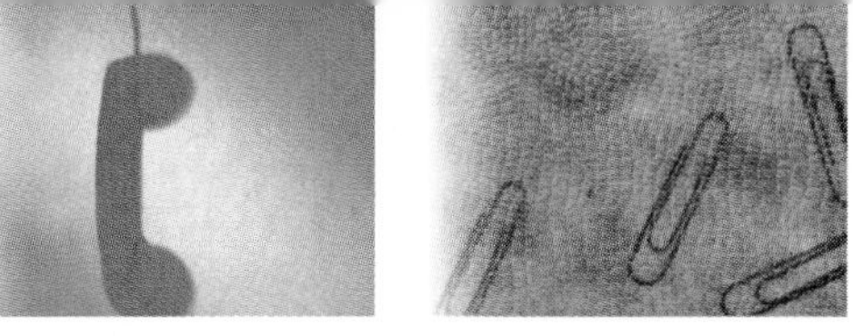
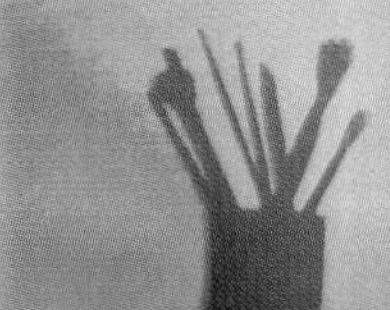

CHAPTER 12

Writing Short Reports

AFTER STUDYING THIS CHAPTER, YOU WILL BE ABLE TO

1. Define what is meant by a business report
2. Discuss six general purposes of reports
3. Make decisions about report format, style, and organization based on six factors: who, what, when, where, why, and how
4. Weigh the advantages and disadvantages of electronic reports
5. Explain how short reports are developed
6. Make reports readable

ON THE JOB

Facing a Communication Dilemma at Federal Express

Delivering On Time, Every Time

Imagine collecting, transporting, and delivering more than 3 million letters and packages every day. Now imagine that every one of these parcels absolutely, positively has to arrive at its destination when expected. That's the standard against which Federal Express managers—and customers—measure performance. Living up to this exacting standard day in and day out presents founder and CEO Frederick W. Smith and his entire management team with a variety of communication challenges.

At Federal Express, reports of all kinds are used to track both system and employee performance, as well as to assemble information needed for making managerial decisions. Not only does Frederick Smith read innumerable reports, he wrote a very famous one, which detailed the idea of his air express delivery service and persuaded investors to fund his idea.

When Federal Express began operation in 1973, its services covered 22 US cities. Today it delivers throughout the United States and Canada, and to 210 countries overseas. To make these deliveries on time, every time, in Canada, Federal Express employs 3500 people in 66 facilities. Worldwide, Federal Express counts 145 000 employees and a fleet of 643 airplanes and 41 500 vehicles.

But keeping packages in motion is only part of the challenge. Federal Express must also battle a host of rivals, including United Parcel Service (UPS), Airborne Express, DHL, and other delivery companies. Competition is fierce, so Federal Express is constantly on the lookout for innovative ways to serve customers better. One important way Federal Express helps commercial and industrial customers is by taking over their warehouse and inventory chores. Instead of just acting as a shipping service, Federal Express operates like part of the customer's organization.

Smith's newest service innovations involve electronic commerce in general and the Internet in particular. To get around the tedious work of filling out shipping forms and telephoning a pickup request, Federal Express now lets customers place orders online with a new service called FedEx interNetShip. Also, to help customers capitalize on the selling power of the World Wide Web, the FedEx VirtualOrder service can handle everything from setting up a product catalogue on a Web site to the more traditional service of delivering the goods.

With competitors offering more and customers expecting more, Smith and his management team have their work cut out for them. Monitoring and controlling the Federal Express operation, training new employees, making a host of decisions—all these activities require the communication of timely, accurate information. To keep the business running smoothly, maintain satisfied customers, and hold competitors at bay, Federal Express managers receive and prepare reports of all kinds. How can Smith and his managers use reports for internal communication? How can writers make their reports readable? What makes one report better than another?[1]

What Makes a Good Business Report

LEARNING OUTCOME 1
Define what is meant by a business report.

Business reports are like bridges spanning time and space. Organizations such as Federal Express use them to provide a formal, verifiable link among people, places, and times. Some reports are needed for internal communication; others are vehicles for corresponding with outsiders. Some are required as a permanent record; others are needed to solve an immediate problem or to answer a passing question. Many move upward through the chain of command to help managers monitor the various units in the organization; some move downward to explain management decisions to lower-level employees responsible for day-to-day operations.

A business report is any factual, objective document that serves a business purpose.

You may be surprised at the variety of messages that qualify as reports. The term covers everything from a fleeting image on a computer screen to preprinted forms to informal letters and memos to formal three-volume manuscripts. Many reports are delivered orally, as discussed in Chapter 18. In general, however, most business people think of **reports** as written, factual accounts that objectively communicate information about some aspect of the business. Reports can be printed on paper or distributed electronically. Although business reports serve hundreds of purposes, six basic uses are common (Table 12.1).

LEARNING OUTCOME 2
Discuss six general purposes of reports.

TABLE 12.1 The Six Most Common Uses of Reports

Purpose of Report	Common Examples	Preparation and Distribution	Features
To monitor and control operations	Plans, operating reports, personal activity reports	Internal reports move upward on a recurring basis; external reports go to selected audiences	**Format:** Standard memo or preprinted form **Style:** Telegraphic **Organization:** Topical **Order:** Direct
To implement policies and procedures	Lasting guidelines, position papers	Internal reports move downward on a non-recurring basis	**Format:** Matches policies and procedures manual **Style:** Fully developed text **Organization:** Topical **Order:** Direct
To comply with regulatory requirements	Reports for Canada Customs and Revenue Agency, Canadian Human Rights Commission, and other industry regulators	External reports are sent on a recurring basis	**Format:** Standardized; perhaps preprinted or electronic form **Style:** Skeletal **Organization:** To follow reader's instructions **Order:** Direct
To obtain new business or funding	Sales proposals	External reports are sent on a non-recurring basis	**Format:** Letter or manuscript **Style:** Fully developed text **Organization:** Problem-solution **Order:** Commonly direct
To document client work	Interim progress reports, final reports	External reports are sent on a non-recurring basis	**Format:** Letter or manuscript **Style:** Fully developed text **Organization:** Around sequential steps or key findings **Order:** Usually direct
To guide decisions	Research reports, justification reports, troubleshooting reports	Internal reports move upward on a non-recurring basis	**Format:** Memo or manuscript **Style:** Fully developed text **Organization:** Around conclusions or logical arguments **Order:** Direct or indirect

In large part, a report is a managerial tool. Even the most capable managers must rely on other people to observe events or collect information for them. Like Frederick Smith, managers are often too far away to oversee everything themselves, and they don't have enough time. In addition, they often lack the specialized background required to research and evaluate certain subjects. Thus reports are usually prepared for managers or on their behalf.

The goal in developing a report is to make the information as clear and convenient as possible. If Frederick Smith received information that was inaccurate, incomplete, or difficult to decipher, any decisions he based on it would be bad ones, so Federal Express would suffer along with Smith's reputation. Because time is precious, you tell your readers what they need to know–no more, no less–and you present the information in a way that is geared to their needs. Some managers like to use a computer to compare information from the reports they receive. Some managers like to get their reports orally, face to face. However, many managers prefer the convenience and permanence of paper reports and, increasingly, of electronic reports distributed over the Internet or corporate intranets.

LEARNING OUTCOME 3
Make decisions about report format, style, and organization based on six factors: who, what, when, where, why, and how.

Regardless of the medium you use for your message, try to keep the likes and dislikes of your readers in mind. As you make decisions about the content, format, style, and organization of the report, your readers' needs are your main concern. Before you write, decide whether to use letter, memo, or manuscript format (see Appendix A for details), whether to employ a formal or an informal style; and how to group your ideas.

When thinking about these issues, ask yourself the following questions and tailor the report accordingly:

- *Who initiated the report?* **Voluntary reports,** which are prepared on your own initiative, usually require more detail and support than **authorized reports,** which are prepared at the request of someone else. When writing a voluntary report, you give more background on the subject, and you explain your purpose more carefully. An authorized report is organized to respond to the reader's request.
- *What subject does the report cover?* A report's vocabulary and format are dictated by its subject matter. For example, audit reports (that verify an accountant's inspection of a firm's financial records) contain a lot of numbers, often in the form of tables. Reports from the legal department (perhaps on the company's patents) contain many legal terms. When you and your reader are familiar with the subject and share the same background, you don't need to define terms or explain basic concepts. The presentation format, style, and organization are dictated by the characteristics of the subject.

When making decisions about the format, style, and organization of a report, consider its
✧ Origin ✧ Distribution
✧ Subject ✧ Purpose
✧ Timing ✧ Probable reception

- *When is the report prepared?* **Routine reports** are submitted on a recurring basis (daily, weekly, monthly, quarterly, annually) and require less introductory and transitional material than needed for **special reports** (non-recurring reports that deal with unique situations). Routine reports are often prepared on preprinted or computerized forms (either of which the writer simply fills in), or they're simply organized in a standard way.
- *Where is the report being sent?* **Internal reports** (used within the organization) are generally less formal than **external reports** (sent to people outside the organization). Many internal reports, especially those under ten pages, are written in memo format. On the other hand, external reports may be in letter format (if they are no longer than five pages) or in manuscript format (if they exceed five pages).
- *Why is the report being prepared?* **Informational reports** focus on facts; **analytical reports** include analysis, interpretation, conclusions, and recommendations.

Informational reports are usually organized around subtopics; analytical reports are generally organized around logical arguments and conclusions. Chapter 13 explains this difference in greater detail.

- *How receptive is the reader?* When the reader is likely to agree with the content of the report, the material is presented in direct order, starting with the main idea (key findings, conclusions, recommendations). If the reader may have reservations about the report, the material is presented in indirect order, starting with the details and leading up to the main idea.

As you can see, the origin, subject, timing, distribution, purpose, and probable reception of a report have quite an impact on its format, style, and organization.

How Electronic Technology Affects Business Reports

LEARNING OUTCOME 4
Weigh the advantages and disadvantages of electronic reports.

Reports aren't necessarily confined to paper in today's business environment. Virtually all of the report styles discussed in this chapter can be and are being adapted to computerized formats. Thousands of companies have set up electronic reporting procedures to communicate with employees, customers, and suppliers.

Electronic reports are becoming more popular.

Electronic reports fall into two basic categories: First are those that essentially replace paper reports. You can draft a report using your word processor, but rather than printing it and making copies, you can distribute the file electronically. Most e-mail systems now have the ability to attach files to support electronic-document distribution. The other category of electronic reports includes those that are unique to the electronic format. For example, an intranet site can offer text, video, and sound in a single integrated "report."

Report-writing software can pull information out of computerized databases and organize it in any format you want.

If you explore software for electronic reports, you'll discover a class of software known as *report writers* or *reporting tools*. Naturally, these tools don't magically write business reports for you. They are designed to extract and format data from computerized databases. For instance, you can use a personnel database to generate a report that ranks employees by salary or a customer database to generate mailing labels for all your customers. Once the report is generated, you can print it or distribute it electronically. Also, some report writers allow you to work interactively with the database, in effect creating a "live" report that responds to your queries and inputs.[2]

Electronic reports offer both advantages and disadvantages compared with their paper counterparts. Potential advantages include the following:

Electronic reports have distinct advantages.

- *Cost savings.* Assuming you have the necessary hardware and software in place, electronic reports can save a significant amount of money in terms of paper, printing or photocopying, and distribution.
- *Space savings.* A CD-ROM can hold the equivalent of hundreds of pages of text, so electronic reports can be stored in a much smaller space than paper reports. This can be a significant advantage for large businesses, businesses with heavy government reporting requirements, and businesses that must keep historical records for many years.
- *Faster distribution.* Electronic documents can reach their audiences in a few seconds, compared with the few hours or days it can take to send paper documents to other locations.
- *Multimedia communication.* You can integrate sound and video with electronic reports, bringing text to life.

- *Easier maintenance.* Documents on intranet and Internet Web sites are great examples of how much easier it is to correct and update electronic documents. If a single figure changes in a sales report after you've distributed it, your options with a paper report are to reprint and redistribute the entire thing, send out a corrected page, or send a memo to all the recipients asking them to pencil in the correction by hand. With an electronic report, you simply make the change and let everyone know via e-mail. When you offer your readers access to an electronic report on an intranet site, you have an added bonus: Because the only existing copy of the report is always current, you don't have to worry that people will hang on to obsolete or incorrect information.

For all their advantages, however, electronic reports are not a cure-all for business communication problems, nor are they without some risks and disadvantages:

Electronic reports have some disadvantages.

- *Hardware and software costs.* Naturally, you need a computer network to distribute electronic documents. If the system isn't already in place, its purchase, installation, and maintenance involve an extra expense.
- *System compatibility.* As discussed in Chapter 4, corporate intranets are helping business people get around the computer compatibility problem, but companies that lack intranets may find themselves with incompatible computer systems that inhibit the use of electronic documents.

BEHIND THE SCENES AT ACHIEVEGLOBAL

Consulting, Clarifying, Communicating

"Our company promises clients that we will take any strategy they have devised, clarify it, and bring it from strategy to results through their people," says Bill Stevens, a senior consulting partner at AchieveGlobal, an international consulting and training firm. Working for a business with a client base of more than 300 major organizations, employees of the company are continually planning or writing reports. Many are external, written for clients across Canada, and many are internal, directed toward colleagues, and report on such critical issues as profitability, revenue, growth, client retention, and capability development. Stevens explains, "Because AchieveGlobal's problem-solving approach is consultative and draws on a wide variety of solutions, there is a wide variety of both internal and external reports we produce." Examples are discussion, planning, implementation, follow-up, periodic, trip, progress, and project management, and recommendation reports as well as proposals.

Consultants consider reports essential to keep their clients up to date with projects and to communicate information and recommendations.

Reports are a significant part of Stevens's job, "either being worked on or completed frequently," he says. "A good example of a report I am currently working on involves an intervention with an executive team in a manufacturing organization. The initial stage of the project involved a series of interviews with each of the executive members. The purpose of the interviews was to assess the situation, to initiate leadership and communication development, and to make recommendations. To facilitate all of these things, I produced a report to serve as a discussion document."

Some reports require use of the indirect strategy, and others the direct strategy. One client didn't want recommendations, but only the detailed findings of the information he gathered through discussions with more than 250 people in the company, from executives and managers to employees on the shop floor, and through observing meeting behaviour. In this instance, the client wanted to do their own analysis and draw their own conclusions and recommendations. Stevens applied the indirect strategy by integrating his suggestions for changes in how the company operates and manages employees into various subsections of the report, rather than placing them at the beginning. In addition, in circumstances where clients "want to see the thought process and some or all of the considerations that went into the development of the recommendations," Stevens will use the

- *Training.* Beyond the ability to read, little extra training is required to read most paper business reports. However, reading electronic reports can require training in using Web browsers, accessing databases, or other skills.
- *Data security and integrity.* Because information in electronic reports is not fixed on paper, it's vulnerable to tampering and inadvertent corruption. Hackers may be able to penetrate a company's "secure" Web site where confidential information is transmitted and undermine the integrity of the organization's electronic communications. Even innocent computer errors can affect electronic reports. Sending word-processor files over the Internet is still a shaky proposition. Because the files are handled by various systems that don't always work in harmony, your carefully crafted document can arrive at its destination looking very different than the original.[3]

Many businesses see electronic documents as a way to cut costs while improving worker productivity and customer service, so you'll probably write and read many electronic reports on the job.

Planning Short Reports

LEARNING OUTCOME 5
Explain how short reports are developed.

When planning your report, you need to consider your audience, as well as your purpose and subject matter. These three elements influence the format and length of your report, as well as its basic structure.

indirect approach. On the other hand, for clients who want "clear and concise recommendations," Stevens will place his advice up front.

Stevens's reports are frequently read by both primary and secondary audiences—that is, not only by the person who will make the decision based on Stevens's findings and recommendations, but also by the entire executive team, who may need to understand the big picture; as well as by managers of departments where operational changes will be most felt or by managers in a firm's international locations where Stevens's information may be relevant. To accommodate the variety of readers, Stevens tries to include information that "provides perspective and context" and anticipates the impact of his findings, conclusions, and recommendations on all audiences.

Stevens's reports make use of such formatting devices as headings, bulleted points, and variations in font size to highlight information, making it easy for his readers to review specific details. He uses visual support, he explains, "when there is need for impact at a glance, summary of lots of detail, trend comparison, project progress, to compare one item with another (such as last year with this year), to show organizational structure."

For certain AchieveGlobal projects that he administers, Bill Stevens is not the sole report author. When collaborators are located in different cities, "technology helps a lot," he says. "The project leader distributes the draft report to team members by e-mail, and assigns each team member (sometimes including the client) a different colour of text. The colour legend is shared amongst team members, so that each individual's thoughts can be identified." After each person has made his or her colour-coded contribution to the master draft document, "it's a relatively easy matter to meet, discuss, gain consensus and convert the text to black—meaning it has been finalized."

For Canadian clients, sometimes the reports are translated into French, and sometimes written in French and translated into English. Depending on the level of translation, a bilingual employee will translate the document verbally or in written form. Fee-for-service writers are also used for translations. And editing and proofreading are essential stages in the report-writing process. As Stevens notes, these steps are "critical" because they "result in accuracy, credibility, and the elimination of distracters—people are trying to make decisions."[4]

APPLY YOUR KNOWLEDGE

1. If you were writing a report recommending a reduction in the number of employees in your client's firm because the jobs they were doing overlapped, would you use the direct or the indirect strategy? Why?
2. If you were writing the report described in question #1, and your primary audience was the vice-president of human resources, who might be your secondary readers? How would you adapt the report for these readers?

Going Online

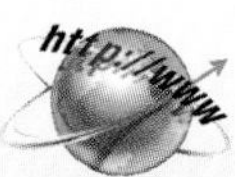

Spotlight on Business Reports

Gain an understanding of common types of business reports by visiting the Web site of the Management Assistance Program for Nonprofits. Click on "Free Management Library," then "Communications (Writing)," and, under "Basic Writing Skills," choose "Formatting: Recommended Headings for Business Reports and What Report Readers Want to Know." Here you will see a list of different reports, frequently used headings, and questions readers ask when evaluating reports. You can reach the page directly at **www.mapnp.org/library/writing/rechdngs.htm.**

Deciding on Format and Length

Decisions about format and length may be made for you by the person who requests the document. Such guidance is often the case with monitor/control reports, justification reports, proposals, progress reports, and compliance reports. Generally speaking, the more routine the report, the less flexibility you have in deciding format and length.

When you do have some leeway in length and format, your decisions are based on your readers' needs. As Frederick Smith can attest, your goal is to tell your audience what they need to know in a format that is easy for them to use. Whether you deliver your report on paper or electronically, when you select a format, you have four options:

You may present a report in one of four formats: preprinted form, letter, memo, or manuscript.

- *Preprinted form.* Basically for fill-in-the-blank reports. Most are relatively short (five or fewer pages) and deal with routine information, often mainly numerical. Use this format when it's requested by the person authorizing the report.
- *Letter.* Common for reports of five or fewer pages that are directed to outsiders. These reports include all the normal parts of a letter, but they may also have headings, footnotes, tables, and figures.
- *Memo.* Common for short (fewer than ten pages) informal reports distributed within an organization. Memos have headings at the top: *To, From, Date,* and *Subject.* In addition, like longer reports, they often have internal headings and sometimes have visual aids. Memos exceeding ten pages are sometimes referred to as memo reports to distinguish them from their shorter cousins. They also begin with the standard memo headings. The Checklist for Short Informal Reports at the end of this chapter provides guidelines for preparing memo reports and other short informal reports.
- *Manuscript.* Common for reports from a few pages to several hundred pages that require a formal approach. As their length increases, reports in manuscript format require more elements before the text of the report (prefatory parts) and after the text (supplementary parts). Chapter 14 explains these elements and includes additional instructions as well as a checklist for preparing formal reports.

Appendix A, "Format and Layout of Business Documents," contains more specific guidelines for physically preparing these four kinds of reports.

Length depends on
- ✧ Your subject
- ✧ Your purpose
- ✧ Your relationship with your audience

The length of your report obviously depends on your subject and purpose, but it's also affected by your relationship with your audience. If they are relative strangers, if they are skeptical or hostile, if the material is non-routine or controversial, you usually have to explain your points in greater detail. You can afford to be brief if you are on familiar terms with your readers, if they are likely to agree with you, and if the information is routine or uncomplicated. In general, short reports are more common in business than long ones, and you'll probably write many more five-page memos than 50-page formal reports.

Selecting the Information to Include

Should you cover all the material obtained during your research, or should you eliminate some of the data? When deciding on the content of your report, first put yourself in the audience's position. What do you think are your audience's major questions about the subject? By developing a **question-and-answer chain,** you can think ahead to the questions your readers may have and anticipate their sequence. Your objective is to answer all those questions in the order that makes the most sense.

Your audience usually has one question of greatest importance: "Why are we losing money?" or "What's the progress on this project?" No matter what the main question is, be sure to define it as precisely as you can before you begin formulating your answer. The main question is simply the reason you've been asked to write the report. Once you've defined it, you can sketch a general answer based on the information available. Your answer, like the question, should be broad.

Reports answer the audience's key questions.

Now you're ready to determine, on the basis of your answer to the main question, what additional questions your audience is likely to ask. A typical question-and-answer chain might look like the following:

Main question:	Why are we losing money?
General answer:	We're losing money because our production costs are higher than our prices.
Question 1:	Why are our production costs high?
Question 2:	Why are our prices low?

Your next step is to answer these questions, and your answers again raise additional questions. As you forge the chain of questions and answers, the points multiply and become increasingly specific (Figure 12.1). When you've identified and answered all of your audience's probable questions, you will have defined the content of your report or presentation. The process is similar to outlining.

The question-and-answer chain clarifies the main idea of the report (your answer to the main question) and establishes the flow of ideas from the general to the specific. Effective reports and presentations use a mix of broad concepts and specific details. When the mix is right, the message works: Members of the audience grasp both the general meaning of the ideas and the practical implications of those ideas. The general ideas sum up and give direction to the message, and the specific ideas clarify and illustrate their meaning. For every piece of information you are tempted to include, ask why the audience needs it and how it relates to the main question.

Pursue the chain of questions and answers from the general to the specific.

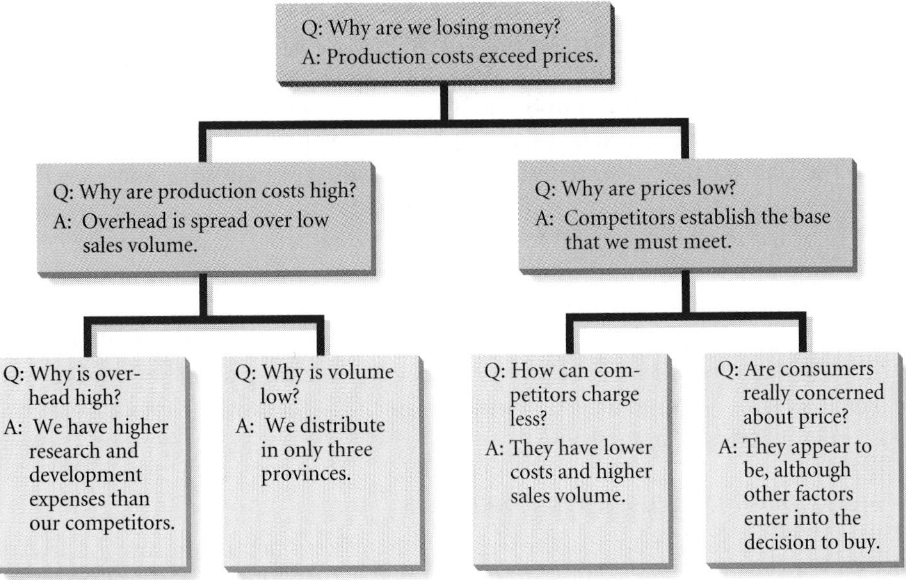

FIGURE 12.1
A Typical Question-and-Answer Chain

Choosing Direct or Indirect Order

The direct approach saves time and makes the report easy to understand by giving readers the main idea first.

As Chapter 6 explained, audience attitude is the basis for decisions about organization. When the audience is considered either receptive or open-minded, use the direct approach: Lead off with a summary of your key findings, conclusions, and recommendations. This up-front approach is by far the most popular and convenient order for business reports because it saves time and makes the rest of the report easy to follow. For those who have questions or want more information, later parts of the report provide complete findings and supporting details. In addition to being more convenient for readers, the direct approach also produces a more forceful report. You sound sure of yourself when you state your conclusions confidently at the outset.

The indirect approach helps overcome resistance by withholding the main idea until later in the report.

However, confidence may sometimes be misconstrued as arrogance. If you're a junior member of a status-conscious organization or if your audience is skeptical or hostile, you may want to use indirect order–introducing the complete findings and supporting details before the conclusions and recommendations, which come last. The indirect approach gives you a chance to prove your points and gradually overcome your audience's reservations. By deferring the conclusions and recommendations, you imply that you've weighed the evidence objectively without prejudging the facts. You also imply that you're subordinating your judgment to that of the audience, whose members are capable of drawing their own conclusions when they have access to all the facts.

Although the indirect approach has its advantages, some report readers will always be in a hurry to get to the answer, flipping to the recommendations immediately and defeating your purpose. For this reason, consider length when deciding on direct or indirect order. In general, the longer the message, the less effective an indirect approach is likely to be. Furthermore, an indirect argument is harder to follow than a direct argument. Because both the direct and indirect approaches have merit, business people often combine them. They reveal their conclusions and recommendations as they go along, rather than putting them either first or last.

Structuring Ideas

Topical organization is based on order of importance, sequence, chronology, location, spatial relationships, or categories. *Logical organization* is based on logical arguments that reflect the reasoning process behind the conclusions and recommendations.

What method of subdivision will make your material both clear and convincing? Should you use a topical organization, based on order of importance, sequence, chronology, location, spatial relationships, or categories? Should you use logical organization to arrange your ideas around logical arguments that reflect the reasoning behind the report's conclusions and recommendations? Regardless of whether you use the direct or the indirect approach, you must still deal with the question of how your ideas will be subdivided and developed. The key is first to decide whether the purpose of the report is to provide information or analysis. From there, you can choose an organizational plan that suits your topic and goals.

Informational and analytical reports differ in their purpose, organization, and focus.

Informational reports differ from analytical reports in their purpose and thus in their organization. Informational reports are intended mainly to educate readers, but analytical reports are designed to persuade readers to accept certain conclusions or recommendations. In informational reports the information alone is the focus of attention. In analytical reports the information plays a supporting role. The facts are a means to an end rather than an end in themselves. Typically, the end is either a decision or an action.

The purpose of informational reports is to explain, whereas analytical reports are meant to convince the audience that the conclusions and recommendations developed in the text are valid.

ORGANIZING INFORMATIONAL REPORTS

Informational reports are usually written to explain something in straightforward terms. Having hundreds of uses in business, informational reports include those for monitoring and controlling operations, statements of policies and procedures, most compliance reports, most personal activity reports, some justification reports, some reports documenting client work, and some proposals.

Make clarity your main objective in informational reports.

As with any business communication, in your informational reports your main concern is to be understood. As Frederick Smith knows, the facts and ideas must be presented logically and accurately so that readers will understand exactly what you mean and will be able to use the information in a practical way.

Before writing his reports, Bill Stevens, a senior consulting partner at AchieveGlobal, determines his purpose, analyzes his audiences, and organizes his information and ideas. Time spent thoroughly planning always results in a final product of value to its readers.

When structuring an informational report, you can let the nature of whatever you're describing serve as the point of departure. If you're describing a machine, each component can correspond to a part of your report. If you're describing an event, you can approach the discussion chronologically, and if you're explaining how to do something, you can describe the steps in the process.

Some informational reports, especially compliance reports and internal reports prepared on preprinted forms, are organized according to instructions supplied by the person requesting the information. In addition, many proposals conform to an outline specified in the request for a proposal issued by the client, which might include a statement of the problem, background, scope of work, restrictions, sources and methods, work schedule, qualifications of personnel, facilities, anticipated costs, and expected results.

Informational reports take many forms. The two examples that follow, a brief periodic report and a personal activity report on a seminar, will give you an idea of the typical organization and tone.

A Periodic Report A periodic report is a monitor/control report that describes what has happened in a department or division during a particular period. It is a recurring report, often prepared at regular intervals–monthly, weekly, or more frequently, depending on the situation. The purpose of a periodic report is to describe the status or progress of a project or some aspect of operations. A periodic report brings corporate managers up to date so they can keep informed and take corrective action, if necessary. Periodic reports are usually written in memo format and don't need much of an introduction; a subject line on the memo is adequate. They should follow the same general format and organization from period to period. Most are organized in this sequence:

Periodic reports are recurring monitor/control reports that keep managers informed about departments reporting to them.

Periodic reports expose any problems that exist.

- *Overview of routine responsibilities.* Briefly describes activities related to each of the writer's normal responsibilities. In some cases the overview focuses on statistical or financial results, and presents information in table format. In other cases, the overview focuses on operations, and is written in paragraph form.
- *Discussion of special projects.* Briefly describes any new or special projects that have been undertaken during the reporting period.
- *Plans for the coming period.* Gives a schedule of activities planned for the next reporting period.
- *Analysis of problems.* Discusses the possible causes of and solutions for any problems. Although often included in the overview of routine responsibilities or in the discussion of special projects, this analysis is sometimes set off in a separate section to call attention to areas that may require high-level intervention.

Most periodic reports are organized similarly:
✧ Overview
✧ Project discussion
✧ Coming plans
✧ Problem analysis

The important thing to remember when writing periodic reports is to be honest about problems as well as accomplishments. In fact, Frederick Smith will tell you that, at Federal Express, the bad news is probably more important than the good news because problems require action, whereas good news often doesn't.

The periodic report in Figure 12.2 was prepared by Roger Watson, real-estate director for a coffee retailer. According to Watson, "Real-estate scouting is a crucial activity for our company as we expand our operations. My manager needs to know that my department is making good decisions when we select new store locations."

The brief introduction orients the reader but doesn't waste time with unnecessary explanations.

Headings stand out to make report review easier for the reader.

The table organizes summary information in the most time-saving format.

Details of upcoming efforts help the reader maintain a timely overview of the progress.

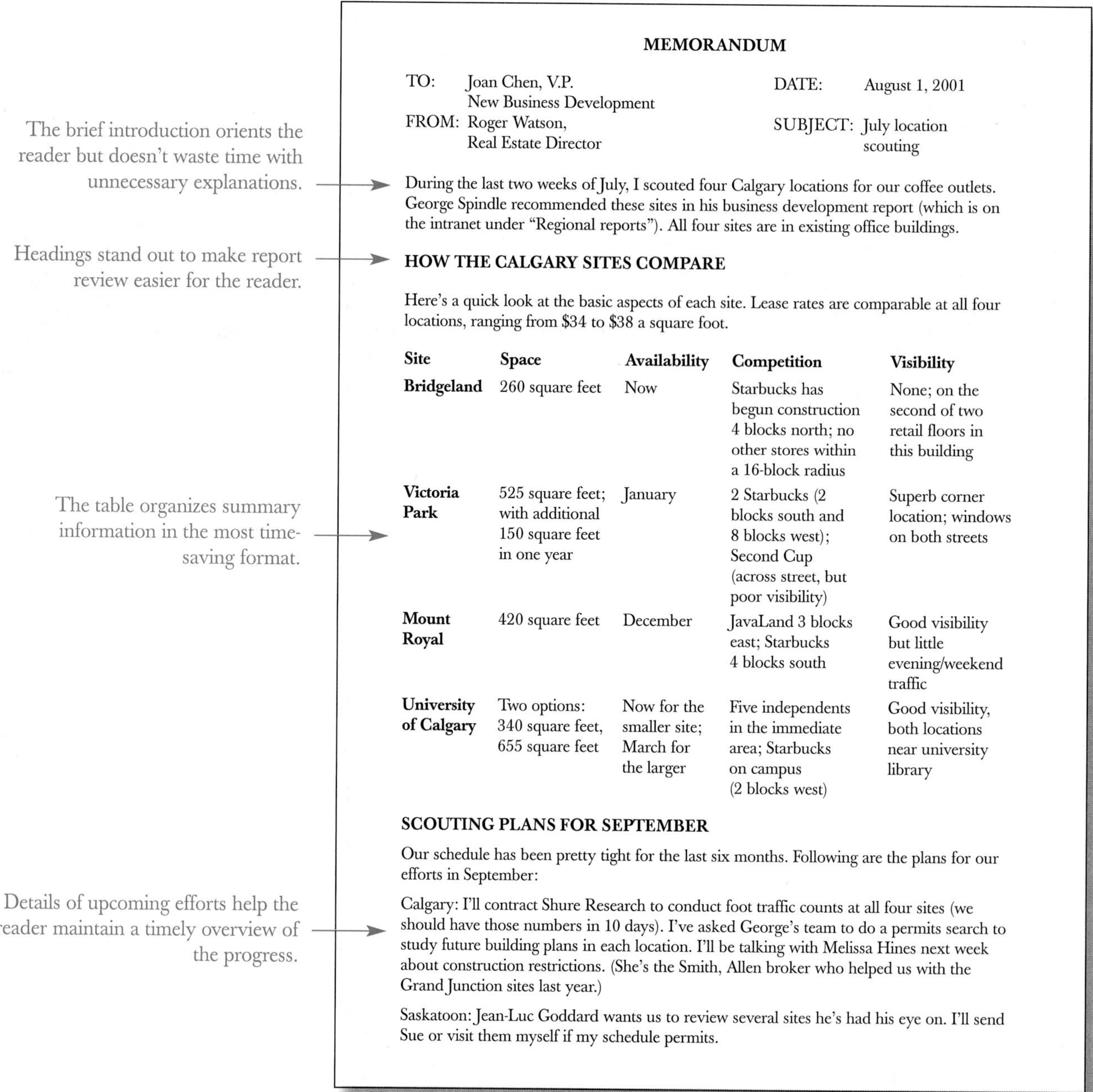

MEMORANDUM

TO: Joan Chen, V.P.
New Business Development

FROM: Roger Watson,
Real Estate Director

DATE: August 1, 2001

SUBJECT: July location scouting

During the last two weeks of July, I scouted four Calgary locations for our coffee outlets. George Spindle recommended these sites in his business development report (which is on the intranet under "Regional reports"). All four sites are in existing office buildings.

HOW THE CALGARY SITES COMPARE

Here's a quick look at the basic aspects of each site. Lease rates are comparable at all four locations, ranging from $34 to $38 a square foot.

Site	Space	Availability	Competition	Visibility
Bridgeland	260 square feet	Now	Starbucks has begun construction 4 blocks north; no other stores within a 16-block radius	None; on the second of two retail floors in this building
Victoria Park	525 square feet; with additional 150 square feet in one year	January	2 Starbucks (2 blocks south and 8 blocks west); Second Cup (across street, but poor visibility)	Superb corner location; windows on both streets
Mount Royal	420 square feet	December	JavaLand 3 blocks east; Starbucks 4 blocks south	Good visibility but little evening/weekend traffic
University of Calgary	Two options: 340 square feet, 655 square feet	Now for the smaller site; March for the larger	Five independents in the immediate area; Starbucks on campus (2 blocks west)	Good visibility, both locations near university library

SCOUTING PLANS FOR SEPTEMBER

Our schedule has been pretty tight for the last six months. Following are the plans for our efforts in September:

Calgary: I'll contract Shure Research to conduct foot traffic counts at all four sites (we should have those numbers in 10 days). I've asked George's team to do a permits search to study future building plans in each location. I'll be talking with Melissa Hines next week about construction restrictions. (She's the Smith, Allen broker who helped us with the Grand Junction sites last year.)

Saskatoon: Jean-Luc Goddard wants us to review several sites he's had his eye on. I'll send Sue or visit them myself if my schedule permits.

FIGURE 12.2

In-Depth Critique: Sample Periodic Report

Roger Watson doesn't want to burden his boss with a lot of details about every one of the company's more than 500 sites. His monthly reports are concise and presented in a summary format. "If Joan has questions about a specific location and needs more information," says Watson, "we usually just talk by phone after she's read my report."

Personal activity reports describe the facts and decisions that emerge during conventions, trips, and business meetings.

A Personal Activity Report A personal activity report is a form of monitor/control report that calls for a person's description of what occurred during a conference, convention, trip, or other activity. It's intended to inform management of any important information or decisions that emerged during the activity.

MEMORANDUM

TO:	Jeff Balou; all members of HR staff	DATE:	March 14, 2001
FROM:	Carrie Andrews	SUBJECT:	Recruiting and hiring seminar

As we all know, legal considerations frame the process of recruiting, screening, and hiring new employees. Because we don't have an in-house lawyer to advise us in our hiring decisions, it is critical for all of us to be aware of acceptable practice.

Last week I attended a Canadian Management Centre seminar on this subject. I got enough useful information to warrant updating our online personnel handbook and perhaps developing a training session for all interviewing teams. First, here's a quick look at the knowledge I gained.

AVOIDING LEGAL MISTAKES

- How to write recruiting ads that accurately portray job openings and that don't discriminate
- How to use an employment agency effectively and safely (without risk of legal entanglements)

SCREENING AND INTERVIEWING MORE EFFECTIVELY

- How to sort through résumés more efficiently (including looking for telltale signs of false information)
- How to avoid interview questions that are legally questionable
- When and how to check criminal records

MEASURING APPLICANTS

- Which types of preemployment tests have proven most effective
- Which drug-testing issues and recommendations affect us

As you can see, the seminar addressed a lot of important information. We cover the basic guidelines for much of this already, but a number of specific recommendations and legal concepts should be emphasized.

One eye-opening part of the seminar was learning about the mistakes other companies have made. Some companies have lost millions of dollars in employment-discrimination lawsuits. The risks are significant, and violating human rights during the hiring process can have considerable consequences for us.

It will take me two weeks to get the personnel handbook updated; as you know, we don't have any hiring plans for the foreseeable future. I'll keep the seminar handouts and my notes on my desk, in case you want to review them. After I've updated the handbook, we can get together and decide whether we need to train the interviewing team members and how we will approach doing this.

If you have any questions in the meantime, don't hesitate to e-mail me or drop by for a chat.

The introduction states Andrews's reason for attending the seminar.

The organization of this report around the three areas of knowledge gained by Andrews helps readers focus on what is important.

Bullets make the new knowledge stand out for easy reader reference.

Although reporting on personal activity, this report wastes no time on unimportant activities such as how many sessions were offered during the seminar or what was served for lunch. Rather, the report is full of the information needed by department members and the plans for how to disseminate it.

FIGURE 12.3

In-Depth Critique: Sample Personal Activity Report

Carrie Andrews attended a seminar on legal issues in employee recruiting and interviewing. Says Andrews, "I prepared this report for my boss, the company president, and the four people who work for me. We can't afford to send everyone in the department to seminars such as this, so it's important that I share the information I received with the people who couldn't attend."

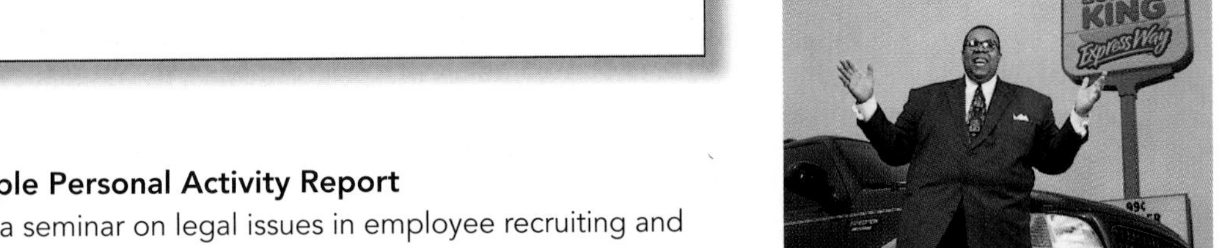

In order to stay profitable, hundreds of Burger King franchise owners rely on the kind of information a short report can convey: profit figures, market statistics, sales strategy recommendations, promotional plans, and so on. It's a quick way to gain a clear perspective—and make the right decisions.

Personal activity reports are ordinarily written in memo format. Because they're nonrecurring documents, they require more of an introduction than periodic reports. They're often organized chronologically, but some are organized around topics that reflect the audience's interests. Figure 12.3 is an example of a personal activity report organized by topic. This seminar attendance report was prepared by Carrie Andrews, the human resources manager of a small insurance firm.

ORGANIZING ANALYTICAL REPORTS

Analytical reports may be organized around conclusions and recommendations (direct approach) when the audience is receptive.

Analytical reports are usually written to respond to special circumstances. Most of the decision-oriented reports mentioned in this chapter are analytical, such as justification reports, research reports, and troubleshooting reports. So are many proposals and final reports to clients.

Analytical reports may be organized around logical arguments (indirect approach) when the audience is unreceptive.

Regardless of which type of analytical report you're writing, organize your ideas so that they will convince readers of the soundness of your thinking. Your choice of a specific approach is based on your estimate of the readers' probable reactions: direct if you think they are likely to agree with you, indirect if you think they will resist your message. If you use the direct approach, you can base the structure of the report on your conclusions and recommendations, using them as the main points of your outline. If you use an indirect approach, your organization can reflect the thinking process that will lead readers to your conclusions.

A Justification Report Justification reports are internal proposals used to persuade top management to approve an investment in a project. When your readers want to know what they ought to do as opposed to what they ought to conclude, the process you want your readers to follow forms the main subdivisions of your report. When organizing a report around recommendations, you usually take five steps:

1. Establish the need for action in the introduction, generally by briefly describing the problem or opportunity.
2. Introduce the benefit that can be achieved, without providing any details.
3. List the steps (recommendations) required to achieve the benefit, using action verbs for emphasis.
4. Explain each step more fully, giving details on procedures, costs, and benefits.
5. Summarize the recommendations.

The company's board of directors asked Alycia Jenn, the business development manager at a retail chain, to suggest whether the company should set up a retailing site on the World Wide Web, and, if so, how to implement the site. As Jenn noted, "Setting up shop on the Internet is a big decision for our company. We don't have the computer staff that our larger competitors have, and our business development team is stretched thin already. On the other hand, I know that more and more people are shopping online, and we don't want to be left out if this mode of retailing really takes off. After studying the issue for several weeks, I concluded that we should go ahead with a site, but we have to be careful about how we implement it." Her memo appears in Figure 12.4.

A BUSINESS PLAN PROPOSAL

A business plan explains overall goals and the ways they will be accomplished.

Focusing on conclusions or recommendations is the most forceful and efficient way to organize an analytical report, but it isn't the best solution for every situation. Sometimes you can achieve better results by encouraging readers to weigh all the facts before you present your conclusions or recommendations.

Business plans can be used as proposals to raise support and funding for an idea, a project, or a business.

A **business plan** documents an organization's overall goals and the operational methods it will use to reach those goals.[5] Small businesses, divisions of larger businesses, and non-profit organizations write business plans for internal use to guide operations and to provide benchmarks for measuring progress toward goals.[6] In addition, top managers and entrepreneurs frequently send their business plans to external audiences (such as bankers or consultants) when they need financing or are contracting for managerial support services.

MEMORANDUM

TO: Board of Directors, Executive Committee members
FROM: Alycia Jenn, Business Development Manager
DATE: July 6, 2001
SUBJECT: World Wide Web retailing site

In response to your request, my staff and I investigated the potential for establishing a retailing site on the World Wide Web. After analyzing the behaviour of our customers and major competitors and studying the overall development of electronic retailing, we have three recommendations:

1. Yes, we should establish an online presence within the next six months.
2. We should engage a firm that specializes in online retailing to design and develop the Web site.
3. We must take care to integrate online retailing with our store-based and mail-order operations.

WE SHOULD SET UP A WEB SITE

First, does a Web site make financial sense today? Studies suggest that our competitors are not currently generating significant revenue from their Web sites. Stallini's is the leader so far, but its sales haven't broken the $1 million mark. Moreover, at least half of our competitors' online sales are from current customers who would have purchased the same items in-store or by mail order. The cost of setting up a retailing site is around $120,000, so it isn't possible to justify a site based solely on current financial return.

Second, do we need to establish a presence now in order to remain competitive in the future? The online situation is too fluid and unpredictable to answer this question in a quantitative profit-and-loss way, but a qualitative view of strategy indicates that we should set up a site:

- As younger consumers (more comfortable with online shopping) reach their peak earning years (ages 35–54), they'll be more likely to buy online than today's peak spenders.
- The Web is erasing geographical shopping limits, presenting both a threat and an opportunity. Even though our customers can now shop Web sites anywhere in the world (so that we have thousands of competitors instead of a dozen), we can now target customers anywhere in the world.
- If the growth in online retailing continues, it will eventually become a viable market. Establishing a site now and working out any problems will prepare us for high-volume online business in the years ahead.

WE SHOULD ENGAGE A CONSULTANT TO IMPLEMENT THE SITE

Implementing a competitive retailing site can take anywhere from 1,000 to 2,500 hours of design and programming time. We have some of the expertise needed in-house, but the marketing and information systems departments have only 300 person-hours in the next six months. I recommend that we engage a Web-design consultant to help us with the design and to do all of the programming.

Jenn clarifies the purpose and origin of the report in the introduction.

For clarity, her recommendations are simple and to the point.

Her reasons for recommending that the firm establish a Web site are logically and clearly presented.

Her recommendations include not only establishing a Web site but also hiring a consultant to implement it and making sure to integrate it with existing systems.

FIGURE 12.4

In-Depth Critique: Sample Justification Report Focusing on Recommendations

In her justification report, Alycia Jenn uses her recommendations to organize her thoughts. Because the board of directors wouldn't be interested in a lot of technical detail, she focuses her discussion on the financial and marketing angle. She also maintains a formal and respectful tone for this audience.

Bruce Rogow was an engineering student when he was first struck by the idea of leading a team of students to design, build, and race a solar car at the World Solar Challenge race across the Australian outback. The race itself would be the least of Rogow's challenges: First he had to convince students and faculty of the project's benefits; then he had to keep them motivated (and working long, hard hours) while he tackled administrative and engineering roadblocks that even he couldn't predict.

Her close briefly summarizes her recommendations and the reasons behind them.

2

WE MUST INTEGRATE THE WEB INTO EXISTING OPERATIONS

The studies we reviewed showed that the most successful Web retailers are careful to integrate their online retailing with their store- and mail-based retailing. Companies that don't integrate carefully find themselves with higher costs, confused customers, and Web sites that don't generate much business. Before we begin designing our Web site, we should develop a plan for integrating the Web into our existing marketing, accounting, and production systems. The online site could affect every department in the company, so it's vital that everyone has a chance to review the plans before we proceed.

SUMMARY

1. Yes, establish a Web site now even though it doesn't make immediate financial sense, because we might lose business if we don't have a site in the near future.
2. Use the services of a Web designer, because we don't have enough person-hours available in-house.
3. Integrate the Web site with existing operations, particularly in marketing, accounting, and production.

FIGURE 12.4 (continued)

Ultimately, Rogow's solar car project succeeded, drawing involvement from various academic departments, dozens of student volunteers, several corporate benefactors, and many news organizations. Rogow challenged the science, engineering, and computer-science students on his team to design and test *Suntrakker* (as the car was named). But he also challenged business students to come up with a proposal that would help him raise the support *Suntrakker* needed.

"We needed to raise $145 000," Rogow recalls. "And since we had no faculty support in the beginning, we had to have something that would give us credibility. The business plan gave us much more than that."

Three students from an entrepreneurship class agreed to work with Rogow on a plan that eventually filled more than 70 pages. "The business plan mapped out every detail of our project, from start to finish, and made us look at things we had not considered. It also earned us respect from the faculty and was responsible for a $5000 donation from our local power company." Rogow now believes that the business plan made the difference between "thriving and just surviving" (Figure 12.5).

Liz Claiborne attributes the success of her clothing designs to the reports prepared by her marketing department: reports that analyze sales figures, define women's roles and issues, identify trends, and communicate recommendations that can be translated into fashions. When writing such analytical reports, it is important to use the facts in a convincing way.

A Troubleshooting Report Whenever a problem exists, someone must investigate it and propose a solution. A troubleshooting report is a decision-oriented document prepared for submission to top management. When you want your readers to concentrate on *why* your ideas make sense, your best bet is to let your logical arguments provide the structure for your report. The main points in your outline correspond to the reasons that underlie your conclusions and recommendations. You support each reason with the evidence you collected during your analysis.

Binh Phan, the national sales manager of a sporting goods company, was concerned about his company's ability to sell to its largest customers. His boss, the vice-president of marketing, shared these concerns and asked Phan to analyze the situation and recommend a solution. As Phan says, "We sell sporting goods to retail chains across the country. Large nationwide chains with superstores modelled after Toys'R' Us have been revolutionizing the industry, but we haven't had as much success with these big customers as we've had with smaller companies

THE EXECUTIVE SUMMARY

Purpose of the Plan

This document will acquaint the reader with three principal topics by

- Showing what the SUNTRAKKER project is
- Showing that the team-oriented, interdepartmental disciplines at our university possess the tenacity and know-how to build and race a solar-powered vehicle in the World Solar Challenge Race in Australia
- Defining and articulating how this business team expects to promote and generate the necessary support, funds, and materials from the student body, alumni, community, and local businesses to seize and execute this opportunity

Project Profile

The SUNTRAKKER Solar Car Project was conceived in July when a small group of engineering students, motivated by the successes of the General Motors Sunrayce, committed themselves to designing and building a superior solar-powered vehicle to compete in the World Solar Challenge.

From modest beginnings, the SUNTRAKKER project quickly evolved into a cross-disciplinary educational effort encompassing students from many programs. The project has provided student participants and volunteers with valuable real-life experiences, and brought them together in an effort that benefits not only the students and the university but also the environment.

Sponsors of this project are not only contributing to the success of the overall SUNTRAKKER project but will also enhance their goodwill, advertising, and name promotion by association with the project. In addition, the SUNTRAKKER offers a unique opportunity for companies that can donate parts and accessories to showcase their name and field test their products in this highly publicized international contest.

The Nature and Value of the Project

The explicit purpose of the project is to design, build, test, and race a world-class solar-powered car with the express purpose of spurring the technological development of energy-efficient vehicles. Although winning the World Solar Challenge is the explicit focus of the project, the implicit goal is to promote ongoing technological research in the field of alternative energy sources, with a view toward conserving the earth's precious nonrenewable natural resources and encouraging international cooperation.

Competitions such as the World Solar Challenge are catalysts for innovation; they provide focus and expand our perspectives beyond the present technology horizon in many different disciplines. The competition stimulates development of seemingly impractical vehicles, yet actually promotes interest and involvement in real-life educational and practical experiences culminating in tangible benefits to the global community. Futuristic and evolutionary projects such as the SUNTRAKKER provide a stimulus to researchers and forward-thinkers to strive toward the common goal of making alternative energy sources a viable reality.

The overall purpose of the business plan introduces readers to its main sections and focuses on the points that will convince your audience of the plan's feasibility.

A project profile provides the background that sponsors need to evaluate the project's worthiness. For a fundraising business plan, use the indirect approach to introduce your objectives, justification, and benefits. Include ample details supported by facts, figures, personnel qualifications, endorsements, and so forth.

Business plans may be prepared for external and internal readers. Not usually compared with competing plans (as are solicited proposals or bids), business plans must still motivate readers to invest or contribute. Many businesses periodically update their plans as their objectives change and as they seek funding from new sources.

FIGURE 12.5

In-Depth Critique: Bruce Rogow's Proposal (Business Plan Excerpt)

Bruce Rogow's business plan is a type of unsolicited proposal, with the benefits up front and the financial information at the close. Detailed and thorough, it includes sections describing the vehicle, the management team, and even "Critical Risks." Appendices include an organization chart, résumé, design schematics, letters of support, lists of volunteers and contributors, and a telemarketing script. Here is an excerpt from the executive summary (a mini-version of the report that gives busy executives a detailed overview).

that operate on only a local or a regional basis. With more and more of the industry in the hands of the large chains, we knew we had to fix the situation." The main idea of Phan's report is that the company should establish separate sales teams for its major accounts rather than continuing to service them through the

As the executive summary suggests, Bruce Rogow's business plan includes the résumés of participants to enhance the project's credibility and potential for success.

The confident tone of Rogow's executive summary reflects the tone of the business plan. The summary, like the plan, is composed of thoughtful, well-developed paragraphs. The business plan itself includes effective introductions and transitions, headings, and lists.

2

Form of Organization

The SUNTRAKKER project has been founded as a tax-exempt, non-profit student organization. The organization's primary purposes are to build the SUNTRAKKER and to enter it in the World Solar Challenge Race in 2001.

The SUNTRAKKER project is organized by function, with directors of marketing, design, production, logistics, public relations, and finance. Together, the departments constitute the management review committee in charge of all activities. Each department director reports to the project manager, Bruce Rogow. In turn, Mr. Rogow, who is responsible for coordinating the whole team effort, reports to a board of advisers. The advisory board, headed by Dr. William Guentzler, oversees the project and acts as a resource think thank to assist in critical problem solving. (See Appendix A for an organizational chart of the SUNTRAKKER project.)

Growth Trend of Market

Technology developed from the SUNTRAKKER project has direct applicability to the coming hybrid electric and solar-powered vehicle markets throughout the world. Because of massive pollution problems and rising population growth rates, transportation needs mandate that we find alternatives to the fossil-fuelled vehicles now in popular use.

In many regions of Canada, pollution has become the driving factor in the search for alternative vehicle power sources. The Canadian Vehicle Manufacturers' Association (CVMA) and the Association of International Automobile Manufacturers of Canada (AIAMC) are committed to equipping Canadian vehicles with emission control and monitoring equipment. The Canadian government gave $1.2 million dollars to the National Air Pollution Surveillance Network (NAPs), thus doubling funding for federal and provincial air pollution monitoring.

FIGURE 12.5
(continued)

company's four regional divisions. However, Phan knew that his plan would be controversial because it required a big change in the company's organization.

When Phan wrote the actual report, he used descriptive rather than informative headings to give his report an objective feel:

I. Introduction

II. Organizational Issues

III. Commission Issues

IV. Recommendation

V. Summary

By phrasing his headings in an objective manner, he reassured his readers and prevented them from reacting negatively to ideas that had not yet been fully explained. Figure 12.6 is a copy of Phan's report.

Organizing an analytical report around a list of reasons that collectively support your main conclusions or recommendations is a natural approach to take. Many problems are solved this way, and readers tend to accept the gradual accumulation of evidence, even though they may question one or two points. However, not every problem or reporting situation can be handled with this organizational plan. Some analytical reports are organized to highlight the pros and cons of a decision; others might be structured to compare two or more alternatives

MEMORANDUM

TO: Robert Mendoza, Vice-President of Marketing
FROM: Binh Phan, National Sales Manager
DATE: September 12, 2000
SUBJECT: Major accounts sales problems

INTRODUCTION

This report outlines the results of my investigation into the recent slowdown in sales to major accounts and the accompanying rise in sales- and service-related complaints from some of our largest customers.

As we discussed at last quarter's management retreat, major account sales dropped 12 percent over the last four quarters, whereas overall sales were up 7 percent. During the same time, we've all noticed an increase in both formal and informal complaints from larger customers regarding how confusing and complicated it has become to do business with us.

My investigation started with in-depth discussions with the four regional sales managers, first as a group and then individually. The tension I felt in the initial meeting eventually came to the surface during my meetings with each manager. Staff members in each region are convinced that other regions are booking orders they don't deserve, with one region doing all the legwork only to see another region get credited with the sale and, naturally, the commission and quota credit.

I followed up the sales manager discussions with informal talks and e-mail exchanges with several sales reps from each region. Virtually everyone who is involved with our major national accounts has a story to share. No one is happy with the situation, and I sense that some reps are walking away from major customers because the process is so frustrating.

ORGANIZATIONAL ISSUES

When we divided the national sales force into four geographical regions last year, the idea was to focus our sales efforts and clarify responsibilities for each prospective and current customer. The regional managers have gotten to know their market territories very well, and sales have increased beyond even our most optimistic projections.

Unfortunately, while solving one problem, we seem to have created another. In the past 12 to 18 months, several regional customers have grown to national status. In addition, a few national retailers have taken on (or expressed interest in) our products. As a result, a significant portion of both our current sales and our future opportunities lie with these large national accounts.

I uncovered more than a dozen cases in which sales reps from two or more regions found themselves competing with each other by pursuing the same customer from different locations.

Moreover, the complaints from our major accounts about overlapping or nonexistent account coverage are a direct result of the regional organization. In some cases,

Instead of summarizing his recommendations, Phan begins by discussing the report's purpose and scope, the background of the study, and his methods of research.

In the body, Phan presents the facts and his observations in an objective tone, without revealing his own point of view.

FIGURE 12.6

In-Depth Critique: Sample Troubleshooting Report

Binh Phan's troubleshooting report would definitely stir emotions, so he had to make sure the logic was solid. Moreover, he was careful that his introduction didn't reveal his position.

against a set of criteria. The best organizational approach in any given situation depends on the nature of the facts at your disposal. Essentially, you choose a structure that matches the reasoning process you used to solve the problem. The objective is to focus your reader's attention on the rationale for your conclusions and recommendations.

2

customers aren't sure which of our reps they're supposed to call with problems and orders. In others, no one has been in contact with them for several months.

An example should help illustrate the problem. CanSport, with retail outlets in the Maritimes and the west coast, was being pitched by reps from our West, Central, and East regions. Because we give our regional offices a lot of negotiating freedom, the three reps were offering the client different prices. But all of CanSport's buying decisions are made at their headquarters in Montreal, so all we did was confuse the customer.

The irony of this situation is that we're often giving our weakest selling and support efforts to the largest customers in the country.

COMMISSION ISSUES

The regional organization issues are compounded because of the way we assign commissions and quota credit. Salespeople in one region can invest a lot of time in pursuing a sale, only to have the customer place the order in another region. So a sales rep in the second region ends up with the commission on a sale that was partly or even entirely earned by someone in the first region.

Also, sales reps sometimes don't pursue leads in their regions if they think that a rep in another region will get the commission. For example, Athletic Express, with outlets in four provinces spread across all regions, finally got so frustrated with us that the company president called our headquarters. Athletic Express has been trying to place a large order for tennis and golf accessories, but none of our local reps seem interested in paying attention. I spoke with the rep responsible for Winnipeg, where the company is headquartered, and asked her why she wasn't working the account more actively. Her explanation was that last time she got involved with Athletic Express, the order was actually placed from their Vancouver regional office, and she didn't get any commission after more than two weeks of selling time.

RECOMMENDATION

Phan saves his recommendations for the fourth section, where he adds up the reasons.

Our sales organization should reflect the nature of our customer base. To accomplish that goal, we need a group of reps who are free to pursue accounts across regional borders–and who are compensated fairly for their work. The most sensible answer is to establish a national accounts group. Customers whose operations place them in more than one region would automatically be assigned to the national group.

Further, we need to modify our commission policy to reward people for team selling. I'll talk with the sales managers to work out the details, but in general, we'll need to split commissions whenever two or more reps help close a sale. This policy will also involve a "finder's fee" for a rep who pulls in leads at the regional level that are passed on to the national account team.

FIGURE 12.6 (continued)

LEARNING OUTCOME 6
Make reports readable.

Making Reports and Proposals Readable

Deciding on format, length, and basic organizational plan for your report comes first. Then, when you're ready to write your report, you must find the most effective way to communicate your message to your audience. Three more decisions affect the way your report will be received and understood by readers: It should have a proper degree of formality, a consistent time perspective, and appropriate structural clues.

3

SUMMARY

The regional sales organization is working at the regional and local levels but not at the national level. We should establish a national accounts group to handle sales that cross regional boundaries.

To make sure that the sales reps (at both the regional and national levels) are adequately motivated and fairly compensated, we need to devise a system of commission splitting and finders' fees. We'll then have one set of reps who are focused on the local and regional levels and another set who are pursuing national accounts. The two groups will have incentives to work together rather than against each other, as is now the case.

FIGURE 12.6
(continued)

Choosing the Proper Degree of Formality

The issue of formality is closely related to considerations of format, length, and organization. If you know your readers reasonably well and if your report is likely to meet with their approval, you can generally adopt a less formal tone. In other words, you can address readers personally, referring to yourself as *I* and to your readers as *you*. This personal approach is often used in brief memo or letter reports, although there are many exceptions.

Write informal reports in a personal style, using the pronouns *I* and *you*.

EFFECTIVE E-BUSINESS COMMUNICATION

Reporting in Many Languages

Global companies often prepare legally required financial reports and other business reports in different languages for different audiences. On the Web, however, you can allow readers to select their preferred language with a quick click. For example, Microsoft's annual report is prepared for investors and posted on the company's Web site in 11 languages (including French for Canadian readers and Portuguese for Brazilian readers). Readers simply click on the link for the language they want—and then read on.

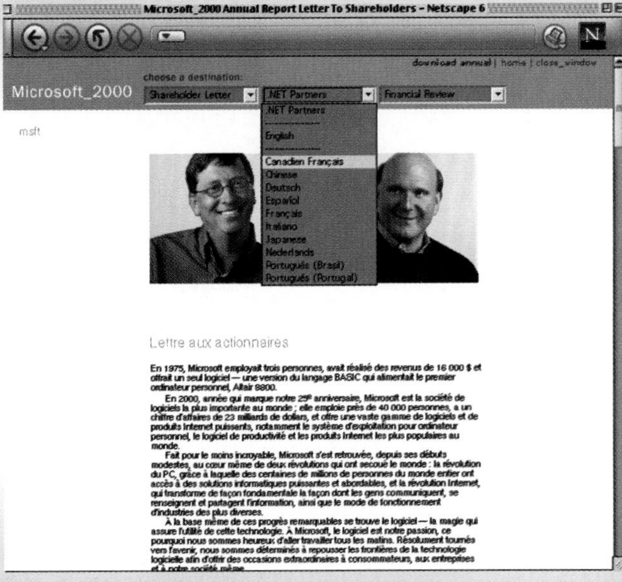

CAREER APPLICATIONS

1. When offering readers a choice of languages, must a company post translated versions of the graphics and every other element of the report?
2. What kinds of reports might companies post on their Web sites for access by audiences in multiple languages?

Being formal means putting your readers at a distance and establishing an objective, businesslike relationship.

Longer reports, especially those dealing with controversial or complex material, are traditionally handled in a more formal vein. You'll also tend to use a more formal approach when writing a report to be sent beyond your own work area to other parts of the organization, or to customers or suppliers. Communicating with people in other cultures often calls for more formality, for two reasons. First, the business environment outside Canada and the United States tends to be more formal in general, and that formality must be reflected in your communication style. Second, the things you do to make a document informal, such as using humour and idiomatic language, are the hardest things to transfer from culture to culture. Less formality in these cases increases the risk of offending people and of miscommunicating.

Intercultural communication often calls for more formal language.

You achieve a formal tone by using the impersonal style (as in Fig. 12.5), eliminating all references to *I* (including *we, us,* and *our*) and *you*. The style is borrowed from journalism, which stresses the reporter's objectivity. However, be careful that avoiding personal pronouns need not lead to overuse of such phrases as *there is* and *it is,* which are both dull and wordy. Also, avoiding personal pronouns makes it easy to slip into passive voice, which also tends to be dull and wordy.

When you write in a formal style, you impose a certain distance between you and your readers. You remain businesslike, unemotional, and objective. You use no jokes, no similes or metaphors, and very few colourful adjectives or adverbs. You eliminate your own subjective opinions and perceptions and retain only the objective facts.

You are not being objective if you
✧ Omit crucial evidence
✧ Use exaggerated language

The formal style does not guarantee objectivity of content, however. The fairness of a report is determined far more by the selection of facts than by the way they're phrased. If you omit crucial evidence, you're not being objective, even though you're using an impersonal style. In addition, you can easily destroy objectivity by exaggerating and using overblown language: "The catastrophic collapse in sales, precipitated by cutthroat pricing on the part of predatory and unscrupulous rivals, has jeopardized the very survival of the once-soaring hot-air balloon division." This sentence has no personal references, but its objectivity is highly questionable.

Despite such drawbacks, the impersonal style is a well-entrenched tradition. You can often find a tone appropriate for your readers in reports of a similar type in your company. If all the other reports on file are impersonal, you should probably adopt the same tone yourself, unless you're confident that your readers prefer a more personal style. Most organizations, for whatever reasons, expect an unobtrusive, impersonal writing style for business reports.

Establishing a Time Perspective

In what time frame will your report exist? Will you write in the past or present tense? The person who wrote this paragraph never decided:

Be consistent in the verb tense you use.

> Twenty-five percent of those interviewed *report* that they *are* dissatisfied with their present brand. The wealthiest participants *complained* most frequently, but all income categories *are* interested in trying a new brand. Only 5 percent of the interviewees *say* they *had* no interest in alternative products.

By flipping from tense to tense when describing the same research results, you only confuse your readers. Is the shift significant, they wonder, or are you just being sloppy? Such confusion can be eliminated by using tense consistently.

Follow a proper chronological sequence in your report.

Also be careful to observe the chronological sequence of events in your report. If you're describing the history or development of something, start at the beginning and cover each event in the order of its occurrence. If you're explaining the steps in a process, take each step in proper sequence.

Helping Readers Find Their Way

As you begin to write, remember that readers have no concept of how the various pieces of your report are related to one another. Because you have done the work and outlined the report, you have a sense of its wholeness and can see how each page fits into the overall structure, but readers see the report one page at a time. Your job is to give readers a preview or road map of the report's structure so that they can see how the parts of your argument are related. These directions are particularly important for people from other cultures and countries, whose language skills and business expectations may differ from yours–as Frederick Smith knows from his worldwide business dealings through Federal Express.

Your job is to guide readers through the structure of your report.

In a short report, readers are in little danger of getting lost. As the length of a report increases, however, so do readers' opportunities for becoming confused and losing track of relations among the ideas. If you want readers to understand and accept your message, help them avoid this confusion. Five tools are particularly useful for giving readers a sense of the overall structure of your document and for keeping them on track as they read along: the opening, headings and lists, smooth transitions, previews and reviews, and the ending.

THE OPENING

As the name suggests, the **opening** is the first section in any report. A good opening accomplishes at least three things:

In the opening tell readers what to expect, tell them why your subject is important, and orient them toward your organizational plan.

- Introduces the subject of the report
- Indicates why the subject is important
- Previews the main ideas and the order in which they will be covered

If you fail to provide readers with these clues to the structure of your report, they'll read aimlessly and miss important points, much like drivers trying to find their way through a strange city without a map.

If your audience is skeptical, the opening downplays the controversial aspects of your message while providing the necessary framework for understanding your report. Here's a good example of an indirect opening, taken from the introduction of a controversial memo on why a new line of luggage has failed to sell well. The writer's ultimate goal is to recommend a shift in marketing strategy.

> The performance of the Venturer line can be improved. In the two years since its introduction, this product line has achieved a sales volume lower than we expected, resulting in a drain on the company's overall earnings. The purpose of this report is to review the luggage-buying habits of consumers in all markets where the Venturer line is sold so that we can determine where to put our marketing emphasis.

The paragraph quickly introduces the subject (disappointing sales), tells why the problem is important (drain on earnings), and indicates the main points to be addressed in the body of the report (review of markets where the Venturer line is sold), without revealing what the conclusions and recommendations will be.

HEADINGS AND LISTS

A **heading** is a brief title at the start of a subdivision within a report that cues readers about the content of the section that follows. Headings are useful markers for clarifying the framework of a report. They visually indicate shifts from one idea to the next, and, when *subheadings* (lower-level headings) and headings are both used, they help readers see the relationship between subordinate and main ideas. In addition, busy readers can quickly understand the gist of a document simply by scanning the headings.

Use headings to give readers the gist of your report.

SHARPENING YOUR CAREER SKILLS

Writing Headings that Grab Your Reader

Headings help readers follow the main points of your report, but when carefully developed they also do much more. By capturing interest, they make readers want to read your entire report. By showing how your document is organized, they save readers time. By labelling the parts of your document, they help readers find the most important or most relevant parts. Moreover, headings help you organize your writing.

Each heading offers you an opportunity to make an important point. For example, instead of "Introduction," your opening section might be called "An Insight into the Need for Better Communication." This heading gets attention and sparks interest. The heading "Chart of Proposed Organization" gains impact when reworded as "Organizing for Results." So does "Cost Considerations" when retitled "A New Way to Cut Costs."

Headings fall into two categories. Descriptive (topical) headings, such as "Cost Considerations," identify a topic but do little more. However, they are fine in routine reports and in controversial reports, where they may defuse emotional reactions. Informative (talking) headings, such as "A New Way to Cut Costs," convey more information about the main idea of the report. They help readers think about your topic in a certain way. For more effective reports, concentrate on developing informative headings rather than descriptive ones. However, be aware that informative headings are more difficult to create.

Try to avoid vague headings. In a chronological history of your company, headings such as "The Dawning of a New Era" and "The Times They Are a-Changin'" may sound distinguished or cute, but readers will have no idea what period you are discussing. Preferable headings would be "The War Years: Bombardier's Military Vehicles" or "The 1990s See International Expansion."

Whatever headings you choose, try to keep them grammatically parallel. For example, this series of headings is parallel: "Cutting Costs," "Reducing Inventory," "Increasing Profits." This series of headings is not: "Cutting Costs," "Inventory Reduction," "How to Increase Profits."

CAREER APPLICATIONS

1. Think about newspaper headlines. What functions do they perform? How are they usually phrased? What can you learn from journalistic headlines that would apply to report writing?
2. For practice in writing headings, collect some brochures, newsletters, or similar items and rewrite the headings to convey more information about the theme or main idea.

Phrase all same-level headings within a section in parallel terms.

Headings within a given section that are of the same level of importance should be phrased in parallel form. In other words, if one heading begins with a verb, all same-level headings in that section should begin with verbs. If one is a noun phrase, all should be noun phrases. (A noun phrase is a phrase that functions as a noun; for example, "*Writing a report* involves research.") Putting comparable ideas in similar terms tells readers that the ideas are related. The only exception might be such descriptive headings as "Introduction" at the beginning of a report and "Conclusions" and "Recommendations" at the end. Many companies specify a format for headings. If yours does, use that format. Otherwise, try the scheme shown in Figure 12.7.

Use lists to set off important ideas and to show sequence.

A **list** is a series of words, names, or items arranged in a specific order. Setting off important ideas in a list provides an additional structural clue. Lists can show the sequence of ideas or visually heighten their impact. In addition, they facilitate the skimming process for busy readers. Like headings, list items should be phrased in parallel form. You might also consider multilevel lists, with subentries below each major item (much like an outline).[7]

When you're creating a list, you can separate items with numbers, letters, or bullets. Numbers are the best choice when you want to indicate sequence or priority, as in this example:

1. Find out how many employees would like on-site day-care facilities
2. Determine how much space the day-care centre would require
3. Estimate the cost of converting a conference room for the on-site facility

TITLE

The title is centred at the top of the page in all capital letters, usually boldfaced (or underlined if typewritten), often in a large font (type size), and often using a sans serif typeface. When the title runs to more than one line, the lines are usually double-spaced and arranged as an inverted pyramid (longer line on the top).

FIRST-LEVEL HEADING

A first-level heading indicates what the following section is about, perhaps by describing the subdivisions. All first-level headings are grammatically parallel, with the possible exception of such headings as "Introduction," "Conclusions," and "Recommendations." Some text appears between every two headings, regardless of their levels. Still boldfaced and sans serif, the font may be smaller than that used in the title but still larger than the typeface used in the text and still in all capital letters.

Second-Level Heading

Like first-level headings, second-level headings indicate what the following material is about. All second-level headings within a section are grammatically parallel. Still boldfaced and sans serif, the font may either remain the same or shrink to the size used in the text, and the style is now initial capitals with lower case. Never use only one second-level heading under a first-level heading. (The same is true for every other level of heading.)

Third-Level Heading

A third-level heading is worded to reflect the content of the material that follows. All third-level headings beneath a second-level heading should be grammatically parallel.

Fourth-Level Heading. Like all the other levels of heading, fourth-level headings reflect the subject that will be developed. All fourth-level headings within a subsection are parallel.

Fourth level headings are "run in"; that is, put on the same line as the following text. You can indicate further breakdowns in your ideas by using a list:

1. *The first item in a list.* You may indent the entire item in block format to set it off visually. Numbers are optional.
2. *The second item in a list.* All lists have at least two items. An introductory phrase or sentence may be italicized for emphasis, as shown here.

FIGURE 12.7
Heading Format for Reports

Howard Schultz, chairman and CEO of Starbucks Coffee Company and author of *Pour Your Heart Into It*, believes that "a company can provide long-term value for shareholders without sacrificing its core belief in treating its employees with respect and dignity." Every month Schultz carefully reviews reports that convey employee comments and criticisms along with the usual sales and profit analysis.

These three steps need to be taken in the order indicated, and the numbers make that clear. Letters and bullets help you indicate choices without implying order or hierarchy:

A. Convert an existing conference room

B. Build an add-on room

C. Lease space in an existing day-care centre

Bullets can add a decorative touch while helping readers distinguish the items in a list. Most word processors make it easy to add a variety of bullet styles, some more appropriate than others. The first list here is fine in this context; the second is frivolous:

➢ Cut everyone's salary by 10 percent
➢ Close the employee cafeteria
➢ Reduce travel expenses

☞ Cut everyone's salary by 10 percent
☞ Close the employee cafeteria
☞ Reduce travel expenses

When you use lists, make sure to introduce them clearly so that people know what they're about to read. If necessary, add further discussion after the lists (as this paragraph is doing). Moving your readers smoothly into and out of lists requires careful use of transitions–the subject of the next section.

SMOOTH TRANSITIONS

Use transitions consisting of a single word, a few words, or a whole paragraph to provide additional structural clues.

Such phrases as *to continue the analysis, on the other hand,* and *an additional concept* are another type of structural clue. These are examples of **transitions,** words or phrases that tie ideas together within a report and keep readers moving along the right track. Here is a list of transitions frequently used to move readers smoothly between sentences and paragraphs:

Additional detail:	moreover, furthermore, in addition, besides, first, second, third, finally
Causal relationship:	therefore, because, accordingly, thus, consequently, hence, as a result, so
Comparison:	similarly, here again, likewise, in comparison, still
Contrast:	yet, conversely, whereas, nevertheless, on the other hand, however, but, nonetheless
Conditional:	although, if
Illustration:	for example, in particular, in this case, for instance
Time sequence:	formerly, after, when, meanwhile, sometimes
Intensification:	indeed, in fact, in any event

Checklist for Short Informal Reports

A. Format

1. For brief external reports, use letter format, including a title or a subject line after the reader's address that clearly states the subject of the document.
2. For brief internal reports, use memo or manuscript format.
3. Present all short informal reports properly.
   a. Single-space the text.
   b. Double-space between paragraphs.
   c. Use headings where helpful, but try not to use more than three levels of headings.
   d. Call attention to significant information by setting it off visually with lists or indention.
   e. Include visual aids to emphasize and clarify the text.

B. Opening

1. For short, routine memos, use the subject line of the memo and the first sentence or two of the text as the introduction.
2. For all other short reports, cover these topics in the introduction: purpose, scope, background, restrictions (in conducting the study), sources of information and methods of research, and organization of the report.
3. If using direct order, place conclusions and recommendations in the opening.

C. Body (Findings and Supporting Details)

1. Use direct order for informational reports to receptive readers, developing ideas around subtopics (chronologically, geographically, categorically).
2. Use direct order for analytical reports to receptive readers, developing points around conclusions or recommendations.

Summary: in brief, in short, to sum up

Repetition: that is, in other words, as I mentioned earlier

Although transitional words and phrases are useful, they're not sufficient in themselves to overcome poor organization. Your goal is to put your ideas in a strong framework and then to use transitions to link them together even more strongly.

In longer reports transitions that link major sections or chapters are often complete paragraphs that serve as mini-introductions to the next section or as summaries of the ideas presented in the section just ending. Here's an example:

> Given the nature of this problem, the alternatives are limited. As the previous section indicates, we can stop making the product, improve it, or continue with the current model. Each of these alternatives has advantages and disadvantages. The following section discusses pros and cons of each of the three alternatives.

PREVIEWS AND REVIEWS

Previews tell readers where they're going.

You may have heard the old saying "Tell them what you're going to tell them, tell them, then tell them what you just told them." The more formal way of giving this advice is to tell you to use *preview sections* before important material in your report, and *review sections* after. Using a preview section to introduce a topic helps readers get ready for new information. Previews are particularly helpful when the information is complex or unexpected. You don't want the reader to get halfway into a section before figuring out what it is all about.

Reviews tell readers where they've been.

Review sections come after a body of material and summarize the information for your readers. Summaries that come at the end of chapters in some textbooks are review sections. Long reports and reports dealing with complex subjects can often benefit from multiple review sections, and not just a single review at the very end.

THE ENDING

Re-emphasize your main ideas in the ending.

Research shows that the **ending,** the final section of a report, leaves a strong and lasting impression. That's why it's important to use the ending to emphasize the main points of your message. In a report written in direct order, you may want to remind

3. Use indirect order for analytical reports to skeptical or hostile readers, developing points around logical arguments.

4. Use an appropriate writing style.

a. Use an informal style (*I* and *you*) for letter and memo reports, unless company custom calls for the impersonal third person.

b. Use an impersonal style for more formal short reports in manuscript format.

5. Maintain a consistent time frame by writing in either the present or the past tense, using other tenses only to indicate prior or future events.

6. Give each paragraph a topic sentence.

7. Link paragraphs by using transitional words and phrases.

8. Strive for readability by using short sentences, concrete words, and terminology that is appropriate for your readers.

9. Be accurate, thorough, and impartial in presenting the material.

10. Avoid including irrelevant and unnecessary details.

11. Include documentation for all material quoted or paraphrased from secondary sources, using a consistent format.

D. Ending

1. In informational reports summarize major findings at the end, if you wish.

2. Summarize points in the same order in which they appear in the text.

3. In analytical reports using indirect order, list conclusions and recommendations at the end.

4. Be certain that conclusions and recommendations follow logically from facts presented in the text.

5. Consider using a list format for emphasis.

6. Avoid introducing new material in the summary, conclusions, or recommendations.

readers of your key points or your conclusions and recommendations. If your report is written in indirect order, end with a summary of key points (except in short memos). In analytical reports, end with conclusions and recommendations as well as key points. Be sure to summarize the benefits to the reader in any report that suggests a change of course or some other action. In general, the ending ties up all the pieces and reminds readers how those pieces fit together. It provides a final opportunity to emphasize the wholeness of your message. Furthermore, it gives you one last chance to check that the report says what you really wanted to say.[8]

ON THE JOB
Solving a Communication Dilemma at Federal Express

Entrepreneur Frederick Smith was sure that his new transportation network would increase Federal Express's efficiency and decrease the cost of moving packages across the US and Canada. He wanted to fly packages from a central hub in Memphis, Tennessee, where they would be sorted and flown to their final destinations. To raise money for this venture, Smith used business reports, which have remained important through the years as he and his managers have built Federal Express into a global business with $18 billion in annual revenues.

For example, because of Federal Express's heavy orientation toward customer satisfaction, the company has a strong emphasis on training. Training costs money, and reports are used to justify training expenditures. One of those expenditures might be for computer-networking equipment to support the company's interactive training program. Of course, before managers buy equipment, these items are thoroughly and objectively investigated and analyzed. Then managers can read through special, non-recurring reports, study the justification for each major purchase, and weigh the pros and cons.

Reports are also important to the company's internal auditors, who are charged with studying how the company controls its finances, operations, and legal compliance. Internal auditors visit the departments they are assigned to examine, conduct their investigations, and then write reports to communicate their findings and any ideas for improvement. The analytical reports that Federal Express's auditors prepare contain recommendations as well as conclusions.

The human resources and internal audit departments are only two of the many Federal Express departments that prepare and receive reports. As Frederick Smith and his managers strive against competitors, work toward customer satisfaction, and keep the business running smoothly, business reports are sure to continue to play a key role at Federal Express.[9]

Your Mission: You have recently joined Federal Express as one of Frederick Smith's administrative assistants. Your job is to help him with a variety of special projects. During an average week, he might ask you to handle three or four assignments and then report back to him in writing. In each of the following situations, choose the best communication alternative from among those listed, and be prepared to explain why your choice is best.

1. To keep tabs on the industry, Smith has asked you to research two services offered by FedEx's top three competitors: the online pickup request (scheduling a pickup online rather than over the telephone) and package tracking (entering a tracking number on a Web site to see where a package is during transit). How should you introduce your report? Choose the best introduction from the four shown below.

a. Recognizing that Federal Express no longer has the overnight delivery business to itself, management has decided to examine the effect of online pickup-request and package-tracking services offered by other companies. Specifically, management wants to review two issues:

   1. What online pickup-request and package-tracking services are offered by the top three competitors?
   2. How can Federal Express use its own online services to compete more effectively?

   The following pages present the results of a two-week study of these questions.

b. Major changes are occurring in the overnight delivery business. Our online pickup-request and package-tracking services have attracted a great deal of customer use since we introduced them. Not surprisingly, however, we are not the only express shipping company offering such services.

   With more and more shippers and receivers conducting more and more business online, the demand for such services will only increase. Federal Express can capitalize on this market demand and compete more effectively if we (1) publicize our fast, easy online services more heavily and (2) introduce additional online services for time-pressured customers. These conclusions are examined in detail in the following pages.

c. I am happy to report that Federal Express is still ahead of all competitors. However, I have to point out that rivals are doing everything they can to keep up the pressure. The two-week study of competitors' online services that I recently conducted shows that UPS and others offer a variety of services similar to our own offerings.

Let me stress that customers have already tracked millions of packages and placed millions of pickup requests using these online services. Although this is obviously an important service, I want to emphasize that customers are going to continue expecting more and more of these online conveniences. Because of this trend, I want to present two recommendations that Federal Express might pursue.

d. Since Federal Express was founded nearly 35 years ago, the company has looked for ways to turn customer convenience into both a competitive advantage and a way to operate more efficiently (and therefore more profitably). In the past few years, the Internet has proven to be a very effective way to expand our customer-service options while decreasing the amount of time our customer-service representatives need to spend on the phone.

At the request of senior management, an examination of the online pickup-request and package-tracking services offered by competitors was conducted. The following pages present the findings of this study, which addressed the following questions:

1. What online pickup-request and package-tracking services do competitors offer?
2. How do Federal Express's services compare?
3. What challenges and opportunities do such services represent?

2. Smith has asked you to provide a brief overview of UPS, Airborne Express, and DHL Worldwide Express, three important Federal Express competitors. This overview will be handed out at a shareholder's meeting in Memphis. Because some shareholders may not be fully informed about the competition, Smith has asked you to write a brief informational memo on the subject. He wants you to cover the following points for each competitor: (1) annual sales, (2) number of employees, (3) names of top executives, and (4) main services. You have to write this immediately, so you'll just have to use whatever facts you can find. Which of the following versions is preferable?

a. The three companies in question, UPS, Airborne Express, and DHL Worldwide Express, are a mixed bag in terms of size. Their sales range from $27 billion (UPS) to $3 billion (Airborne Express) to $2 billion (DHL).

Similarly, the number of employees varies from competitor to competitor. Airborne is headed by CEO Robert Cline. Airborne employs about 24 000 people, DHL employs about 60 000, and UPS employs more than 358 000. James P. Kelly is the CEO of UPS. Patrick Foley was chairman of Hyatt Hotels and Braniff Airlines before joining DHL as CEO (the US segment of the company) in 1988. Victor Guinasso serves as CEO of DHL's international operations.

All three competitors offer domestic and international delivery. Although DHL offers delivery throughout the United States, it is better known for international delivery. In fact, DHL's market share outside the United States is larger than Federal Express's and UPS's combined. In contrast, only 2 percent of Airborne's deliveries are international. UPS went worldwide in 1985 and now serves more than 200 countries.

b. Federal Express's $18 billion in annual sales puts the company at about two-thirds of UPS sales, while DHL and Airborne Express both have sales less than 20 percent of FedEx. Federal Express's 145 000 employees puts it roughly halfway between UPS and the two smaller rivals.

Federal Express's founder, Frederick Smith, has been CEO since he began the company more than 20 years ago. James P. Kelly is CEO of UPS, Patrick Foley is CEO of DHL Airways, and Robert Cline is CEO of Airborne. All three competitors serve customers around the world as well as in Canada and the United States.

c. Here's the lowdown on the poor hapless souls that Federal Express will mow down in the next year:

- UPS is the top dog of delivery services. It has annual sales of $27 billion and employs something like 300 000 people. James P. Kelly is the top banana here. We know that UPS delivers around the world, but we don't know how many countries it serves or how many packages it sends around the globe every year.
- Airborne Express is teeny compared with UPS and with Federal Express. Its sales are puny–just a little over $3 billion or so–and only 24 000 people work for the company. A lot less than half of Airborne's deliveries go to international destinations. Robert Cline is the head honcho.
- DHL's Patrick Foley has the arduous task of being CEO and competing with Federal Express's vastly superior services. Like Airborne, DHL's annual sales of $2 billion are anemic when compared with UPS and Federal Express. But it does have 60 000 workers toiling away at domestic and international deliveries.

d. Here are the annual sales, number of employees, names of top executives, and international presence of three of our competitors:

- UPS is our largest competitor, with $27 billion in annual sales (compared with our own $18 billion in annual sales). UPS employs more than 350 000. The CEO is James P. Kelly. Since 1985, UPS has offered both domestic and international delivery service, but we don't have data on the number of global deliveries or the number of countries served.
- DHL has annual sales of $2 billion, and the number of employees is 60 000. CEO Patrick Foley was chairman of Hyatt Hotels and Braniff Airlines before joining DHL Airways (the domestic segment of the company) in 1988. Although DHL offers delivery throughout the United States, it is better known for international delivery, where it holds a 41 percent market share. The company handles more than 50 million international shipments every year.

- Airborne Express has annual sales of just over $3 billion, and the company employs 24 000 people. Robert Cline is Airborne's CEO. Like the other three competitors, Airborne offers both domestic and international delivery, but only 2 percent of its deliveries are to overseas destinations.

3. Smith wants to celebrate Federal Express's thirtieth anniversary by creating a special advertising insert on the company's history. He wants to distribute this insert inside the April issue of a national business magazine. The magazine's publisher is excited about the concept and has asked Smith to send her "something in writing." Smith asks you to draft the proposal, which should be no more than ten pages long. Which of the following outlines should you use?

a. Version One
   I. An overview of Federal Express's history
      A. How company was founded
      B. Overview of company services
      C. Overview of markets served
      D. Overview of transportation operations
   II. The Federal Express magazine insert
      A. Historic events to be included
      B. Employees to be interviewed
      C. Customers to be discussed
      D. Production schedule
   III. Pros and cons of Federal Express magazine insert
      A. Pros: Make money for magazine, draw new customers for Federal Express
      B. Cons: Costs, questionable audience interest

b. Version Two
   I. Introduction: Overview of the Federal Express special insert
      A. Purpose
      B. Content
      C. Timing
   II. Description of the insert
      A. Text
         1. Message from CEO
         2. History of Federal Express
         3. Interviews with employees
         4. Customer testimonials
      B. Advertising
         1. Inside front and back covers
         2. Colour spreads
         3. Congratulatory ads placed by customers
   III. Next steps
   IV. Summary

c. Version Three
   Who: Federal Express
   What: Special magazine insert
   When: Inserted in April issue
   Where: Coordinated by magazine's editors
   Why: To celebrate Federal Express's anniversary
   How: Overview of content, production responsibilities, and schedule

d. Version Four
   I. Introduction: The rationale for producing a magazine insert promoting Federal Express
      A. Insert would make money for magazine
      B. Insert would boost morale of Federal Express employees
      C. Insert would attract new customers
   II. Insert description
      A. Interview with founder Frederick Smith
      B. Interviews with employees
      C. Description of historic moments
      D. Interviews with customers
      E. Advertisements
   III. Production plan
      A. Project organization
      B. Timing and sequence of steps
      C. Federal Express's responsibilities
      D. Magazine's responsibilities
   IV. Detailed schedule
   V. Summary of benefits and responsibilities

4. Smith has asked you to think about ways of attracting new customers that need Federal Express's expertise in managing international parts and parcel distribution. You have talked with executives at Laura Ashley and National Semiconductor, two current customers, and discovered that they are most concerned about the time needed to process orders and deliver parts to stores or factories. Federal Express can cut the delivery time from as much as 21 days to as little as 4 days after ordering. You believe that an advertising campaign featuring testimonials from these two satisfied customers will give Federal Express a tremendous advantage over other competitors, who haven't yet developed a track record with large global companies. As a relatively junior person at Federal Express, you are a little apprehensive about suggesting your idea. You don't want to seem presumptuous, but on the other hand, you think your idea is good. You have decided to raise the issue with Smith. Which of the following approaches is preferable?

a. Instead of writing a report, arrange a meeting to discuss your ideas with Smith, the advertising manager, and an executive from the company's advertising agency. This allows you to address the issues and ideas first-hand in an informal setting.

b. You write the following short report:

   You recently asked me to give some thought to how Federal Express might attract new customers for its international parts distribution business. I decided to sound out two of our largest customers to get a feel for why they hired us to handle this operation. Interestingly, they didn't choose Federal Express because they wanted to reduce their shipping costs. Rather, they were interested in reducing the time needed to process and ship orders to stores and factories.

   Many companies are in the same situation as Laura Ashley and National Semiconductor. They're not just looking for the carrier with the lowest prices, they're looking for the carrier with the proven ability to process orders and get shipments to their destinations as quickly as possible. Instead of waiting as long as 21 days for shipments to reach their destination, these companies can promise delivery in 4 days.

Clearly, our track record with Laura Ashley and National Semiconductor is the key to capturing the attention of other global companies. After all, how many competitors can show they have the ability to cut as much as 17 days off the time needed to process and deliver an order? Of course, companies might be skeptical if we made this claim on our own, but they would be more likely to accept it if our customers told their own stories. That's why Federal Express should ask executives from Laura Ashley and National Semiconductor to offer testimonials in an advertising campaign.

c. You write the following short report:

In response to your request, I have investigated ways in which Federal Express might attract new customers for its international parts distribution business. In conducting this investigation, I have talked with executives at two of our largest customers, Laura Ashley and National Semiconductor, and discussed the situation with our advertising manager and our advertising agency. All agreed that companies are interested in more than merely saving money on international shipments.

Typically, a global company has to keep a lot of parts or materials on hand and be ready to ship these whenever a store or factory places an order. As soon as an order arrives, the company packages the parts and ships it out. The store or factory doesn't want to wait a long time because it, in turn, has to keep a lot of money tied up in parts to be sure it doesn't run out before the new shipment arrives. Thus, if the company can cut the time between ordering and delivery, it will save its stores or factories a lot of money and, at the same time, build a lot of customer loyalty.

As a result, shipping costs are less important than the need to process orders and get shipments to their destinations as quickly as possible. Instead of delivery in 21 days, these companies can promise deliveries in 4 days. If we can show global companies how to do this, we will attract many more customers.

d. You write the following short report:

This report was authorized by Frederick W. Smith on May 7. Its purpose is to analyze ways of attracting more customers to Federal Express's international parts distribution business. Laura Ashley and National Semiconductor are two large, global companies that use our international parts distribution service. Both companies are pleased with our ability to cut the time between ordering and parts delivery. Both are willing to give testimonials to that effect.

These testimonials will help attract new customers if they are used in newspaper, magazine, and television advertising. A company is more likely to believe a satisfied customer than someone who works for Federal Express. If the advertising department and the advertising agency start working on this idea today, it could be implemented within two months.

TAP Your Knowledge

Summary of Learning Outcomes

1. Define what is meant by a business report. Some reports are needed for internal communication; others for communicating with outsiders. Some are required as a permanent record; others to solve an immediate problem. In each instance, most business people think of reports as written, factual accounts that objectively communicate information about some aspect of a business.

2. Discuss six general purposes of reports. Reports are written to monitor and control operations (such as plans and personal activity reports), implement policies and procedures (such as guidelines and position papers), comply with regulatory requirements (such as reports for the Canadian Human Rights Commission and industry regulators), obtain new business or funding (such as sales proposals), document client work (such as progress reports), and guide decisions (such as research reports and justification reports). In each situation, you must determine the format, style, and order of the report, based on your purpose and audience.

3. Make decisions about report format, style, and organization based on six factors: who, what, when, where, why, and how. When preparing a report, ask yourself the following questions: (1) Who initiated the report? (2) What subject does the report cover? (3) When is the report prepared–is it a routine report, submitted on a recurring basis, or a special report, one that deals with a unique situation? (4) Where is the report being sent? (5) Why is the report being prepared? (6) How receptive is the reader? Your answers will guide you toward writing a report suited to your audience and purpose.

4. **Weigh the advantages and disadvantages of electronic reports.** Electronic reports offer many advantages: they save costs associated with paper, photocopying, distribution, and storage space (since mass storage devices hold the equivalent of thousands of pages). Electronic reports can be distributed quickly and are easy to correct or update. Furthermore, report writers can include sound and video with their electronic documents. On the other hand, there are risks linked to electronic reports. Without a computer system in place, start-up costs are significant. In addition, employees may need to be trained in using Web browsers and databases to access electronic reports. Finally, information in electronic reports is vulnerable to tampering, because it is not fixed on paper, and reports transmitted over the Internet may appear in a different format at the recipient's computer if the software isn't the same as the sender's.

5. **Explain how short reports are developed.** You will need to make several decision when developing short reports. What will be the format and length? You will need to decide if you should write a letter or memo report, or a manuscript report, for example. What information should you include? By developing a question-and-answer chain, you will be able to determine the questions your reader may ask and answer them in your report. Should you use the direct or indirect order? The direct approach gives readers the main idea first; the indirect approach helps overcome resistance by withholding the main idea until later in the report. How should you organize your ideas? You will need to review your material to decide on whether a topical organization or a logical organization would be best.

6. **Make reports readable.** The degree of formality, the time perspective, and structural clues all bear on the ability of your audience to easily understand your report. Whether you should relate to readers personally, using the pronouns "I" and "you," depends on how well you know them and if your report is likely to meet with their approval. A more formal tone puts your readers at a distance and uses the impersonal style, which stresses the report's objectivity. When using the impersonal style, it's important to avoid overusing such phrases as "it is" and "there are" and the passive voice, which can be dull and wordy. Furthermore, be consistent in the verb tense you use: inconsistent use can cause confusion. Finally, use structural devices to help your readers find their way. Write a clear opening that introduces the report's purpose and subject and previews the main ideas. Headings and lists will set off important ideas and show sequence. Previews will tell your readers where they are going, and reviews will tell them where they've been. Let your ending emphasize your key ideas for a final time.

Test Your Knowledge

Review Questions

1. Distinguish between voluntary reports and authorized reports.
2. What is an informational report? Give some examples and explain their features.
3. What is an analytical report? Give some examples and explain their features.
4. What are several key features of electronic reports?
5. Define a question-and-answer chain and give an example of one.
6. When should you consider using the direct order for a report? The indirect order?
7. Explain what a logical organization is for a report.
8. What is a troubleshooting report and why is it important?
9. Explain why transitions, previews, and reviews are important in report writing.
10. Briefly describe the informal and formal styles for report writing.

Apply Your Knowledge

Critical Thinking Questions

1. How do you explain the fact that so many kinds of documents qualify as reports? What makes them all reports? Please explain.
2. Have you ever written a report that led to a decision or action? Did your report achieve the desired results? Did you use direct or indirect order? Why? How did you subdivide the ideas, and why did you use that structure? How might you have applied some of the ideas presented in this chapter to make the report more effective? Briefly explain.
3. Could the increased speed of electronic reporting create any problems with the quality of the information people see or the decisions they make? Explain your answer.
4. What are the advantages and disadvantages of the direct and the indirect approaches? Briefly explain.
5. Why do you think some organizations prefer a formal tone for internal reports? What are the advantages and disadvantages of such a tone? Explain briefly.
6. How can a writer help readers understand the structure of a report? Please explain.

Practise Your Knowledge

Exercises

1. Team up with a classmate to research one of the following topics. Working together, plan an analytical report focusing on your conclusions. Write out the main idea, and draft an informative outline with first- and second-level headings.
   a. Trends in computer use among students at your school
   b. The impact on small businesses of recent increases in the minimum wage
   c. The impact of drug abuse in the workplace
2. Select one of the following topics and plan an analytical report focusing on your recommendations. Develop the main idea, and draft an informative outline with first- and second-level headings.
   a. How to reduce the amount of electricity consumed by your university or college
   b. How to prepare your home to withstand a severe weather problem, such as a strong tornado or a major snowstorm
   c. How to reduce the cost of car insurance
3. Team up with a classmate to practise writing informative openings. For the analytical report you outlined in either exercise 1 or exercise 2, draft an opening that tells what the report covers, explains why the subject is important, and previews the main ideas and the order in which ideas will be presented. Exchange your draft with your teammate and evaluate each other's opening section. Does each opening give sufficient clues to the structure of the report? How can these openings be improved?
4. Team up with a classmate to practise writing emphatic and informative endings. For the analytical report you outlined in exercise 1 or 2, draft an ending that includes conclusions, recommendations, and key points. Exchange with your teammate and compare each ending with the Checklist for Short Informal Reports. How well does each ending communicate the main points and the overall message? How can these endings be improved?
5. Attend the next meeting of your school's student government and take notes on what occurs. Then write a brief (two-page) personal activity report on the meeting, using the memo format. Think about what your audience, students in your business communication class, will want to know about the issues discussed and conclusions reached during the meeting. What key question should you answer in this report?
6. American Management Systems (AMS) has, for more than a quarter century, developed and implemented management plans and has placed management personnel in positions around the globe. The company's Canadian Web site, **www.amsinc.com/Canada/default.htm**, provides

perspective on the company's Canadian operations, as well as information about positions in management. Following suggestions in the Checklist for Short Informal Reports, prepare a brief internal report analyzing the clarity of presentation and the persuasive aspects of the AMS Web page.

Cases

1. My progress to date: Periodic report on your academic career As you know, navigating the bureaucratic process to get a degree or certificate is nearly as challenging as any course you could take.

Your Task: Prepare a periodic report detailing the steps you've taken toward completing your graduation or certification requirements. After examining the requirements listed in your school's catalogue, indicate a realistic schedule for completing those that remain. In addition to course requirements, include such steps as filing necessary papers and paying necessary fees. Use memo format for your report, and address it to anyone who is helping or encouraging you through school.

2. Gavel to gavel: Personal report of a meeting Meetings, conferences, and conventions abound in the academic world, and you may have attended at least one.

Your Task: Prepare a report on a meeting, convention, or conference that you have recently attended. Use memo format, and direct the report to other students in your field who were not able to attend.

3. The importance of a good breakfast: Justification report for longer business hours Imagine that you work for a restaurant that's near campus and that's open only for lunch and dinner. You think there is significant demand for a good place to eat breakfast, and you believe the restaurant could more than make up for the additional cost of opening at 6:00 A.M. instead of 11:30 A.M.

Your Task: Develop a budget for the expanded hours of operation, including personnel costs, management time, utilities, and changes to the food inventory. Next, write a report explaining your concept, describing the major budget items, and briefly predicting the benefits that this expansion will bring. (Feel free to make up any details you need, but keep it realistic.) Write your report in memo format to the owner or manager of the business.

4. Selling something special: Proposal to a business Pick a company or business that you know something about. Now think of a customized item or service that you believe the business needs. Examples might be a specially designed piece of equipment, a workshop for employees on improving their communication skills, a program for curtailing shoplifting, a catering service to a company's construction site, or a customized word-processing system, to name just a few possibilities.

Your Task: Write a proposal to the owners or managers of this business. Convince them that they need the product you're selling. Include a statement of the problem, purpose (benefits), scope (areas in which your product will help the business), methods and procedures, work plan and schedule, your qualifications, projected costs, and any other pertinent information. Use letter format.

5. Restaurant review: Report on a restaurant's food and operations Visit any restaurant, possibly your school's cafeteria. The workers and fellow customers will assume that you are an ordinary customer, but you are really a spy for the owner.

Your Task: After your visit write a short memo to the owner, explaining (a) what you did and what you observed, (b) any violations of policy that you observed, and (c) your recommendations for improvement. The first part of your report (what you did and what you observed) will be the longest. Include a description of the premises, inside and out. Tell how long the various steps of ordering and receiving your meal took. Describe the service and food thoroughly. You are interested in both the good and bad aspects of the establishment's decor, service, and food. For the second section (violations of policy), use some common sense. If all the servers but one have their hair covered, you may assume that policy requires hair to be covered; a dirty window or restroom obviously violates policy. The last section (recommendations for improvement) involves professional judgment. What management actions will improve the restaurant?

6. Pumping up gasoline sales: Report on suggested advertising approaches Gasoline advertising is heating up in Brazil, where Esso, Shell, Atlantic-Arco, Texaco, and Ipiranga compete with Petrobras, the state-owned monopoly. All are in a race to increase their share of Brazil's 5-billion-litre gasoline-products market. However, Brazilian drivers know that Petrobras actually produces and refines the gasoline that every one of its competitors sells. What differentiates one brand from another are the additives that the oil companies put into their individual formulations. Esso's advertising in Brazil is handled by the ad agency McCann-Erickson. Knowing that rivals put a variety of ingredients into their formulations, the agency recommends that Esso use a new advertising approach: Alert drivers to the differences among brands and warn them to look closely at the quality of the gasoline they use.

Your Task: As the McCann-Erickson manager assigned to the Esso account, draft a one-page memo to Esso's managers in which you justify your agency's recommendation. Use your contact's first name, Don, and your own first name in the memo heading. Explain why you believe Esso should adopt this new advertising approach, discuss the main benefit you see in using this approach, and summarize your position.[10]

7. **Preparing for the worst: Report on crisis management** When the anonymous call came in, Campbell Soup officials refused to take any chances. The caller claimed to have put poison in Campbell's tomato juice cans at a Maritime supermarket. The company quickly decided to yank the product from 30 area stores. Even though the call turned out to be a hoax, Campbell Soup believes it's best to be prepared for the worst. Moreover, an important part of any crisis-management plan is the way company officials tell the public about the situation.

Your Task: You're a public relations consultant with special expertise in crisis management. You've been asked to recommend how and when Campbell Soup should reveal any threats and the steps that have been taken in response. In addition, you want to suggest ways of reassuring consumers that Campbell Soup products are pure and completely safe. Draft the outline for an impersonal but informal analytical report to CEO Douglas R. Conant that includes your recommendations and the justifications for those recommendations. Be sure the headings you choose show what your report will cover, including the need for action, the benefits to be achieved, the list of recommendations (without details), and a summary.[11]

8. **Fishing for more revenue: Report for a non-profit organization** Imagine that Newfoundland's Burnt Cape Ecological Reserve has asked you to determine why revenues have been lower than expected and to suggest how to improve revenues. You've found two probable causes for the low revenue: (a) unusually bad weather during prime tourism periods and (b) shoddy, inexpensive merchandise in the gift shop.

Your Task: Draft a two-page troubleshooting report to present to the non-profit's trustees. Be sure to support your conclusions, and address the report to the trustees as a group. Make up whatever details you need about the merchandise and about ways to improve revenues. Bear in mind that the trustees originally approved the purchase of merchandise for the gift shop, so you'll want to use objective language to avoid offending them.

9. **On the books: Troubleshooting report on improving the campus bookstore** Imagine that you are a consultant hired to improve the profits of your campus bookstore.

Your Task: Visit the bookstore and look critically at its operations. Then draft a memo offering recommendations to the bookstore manager that would make the store more profitable, perhaps suggesting products it should carry, hours that it should remain open, or added services that it should make available to students. Be sure to support your recommendations.

Developing Your Internet Skills

Going Online: Spotlight on Business Reports, p. 308

Analyze the information presented on the "Formatting: Recommended Headings for Business Reports ..." page. Is the information presented useful for people who want to know how to write reports? Are the questions "What Report Readers Want to Know from Research/Activity Reports" helpful? Why? Why not? Would visitors to this Web page need more information about report writing? What additional information do you think they should have?

CHAPTER 13

Planning Long Reports

AFTER STUDYING THIS CHAPTER, YOU WILL BE ABLE TO

1. Develop a statement defining the problem to be solved and a statement defining the purpose of the report
2. Identify and outline the issues that have to be analyzed during your study
3. Prepare a work plan for conducting the investigation
4. Organize the research phase of the investigation, including the identification of secondary and primary sources of data
5. Draw sound conclusions and develop practical recommendations
6. Develop a final outline and visual aid plan for your report

ON THE JOB
Facing a Communication Dilemma at Harley-Davidson

Driven to Success, But Now What?

Success certainly is popular. Employees like it; business partners like it; investors, executives, and the local communities usually like it. Unfortunately, so do competitors.

The story of Harley-Davidson is a story of remarkable highs and equally remarkable lows. In the early 1970s, the company controlled 99.7 percent of the high-end US motorcycle market and saw no reason to panic when Japanese manufacturers began to push from low-cost bikes into the heavyweight segment. After all, if your customers love your product so much that they tattoo your logo on their chests, can't you count on their loyalty?

When Harley-Davidson saw its market share tumble to record lows, the CEO at the time, Richard F. Teerlink, realized that every facet of the operation needed careful analysis, which required equally careful reporting. Teerlink and all of Harley's managers received considerable amounts of information in the form of reports.

Unfortunately, Honda and the other Japanese manufacturers attacked Harley's two major weaknesses: cost and quality. Before long, Harley's market share had tumbled to 23 percent, and the company was staring at bankruptcy.

Harley responded in truly inspiring fashion, virtually reinventing itself in the late 1980s and early 1990s. In doing so, it also became a symbol of reinvigorated US business. In fact, business schools across Canada and the US now study the company's turnaround to learn more about contemporary product design and manufacturing. Market share climbed back into the 70-percent range, as Richard F. Teerlink, CEO at the time, and the rest of the Harley team capitalized on the one thing other manufacturers could never have—the Harley-Davidson mystique. A product that was once associated with biker gangs became a status symbol for successful professionals who wanted to feel like temporary outlaws.

Once again, though, Harley faces a challenge that will test its ingenuity and resourcefulness. Demand has outpaced production by such a degree that customers have had to wait as long as two years for a new Harley. Meanwhile, the Japanese makers, along with Germany's BMW, have studied Harley's reborn success and are hungry for a bigger piece of the pie. They're getting it, too, pushing Harley's market share in Canada and the US back below 50 percent by 1999.

Harley's current CEO, Jeffrey Bleustein, and his team realize that to stay in the fast lane, they need careful research and analysis of issues ranging from product design to inventory control to customer needs. If you were in charge of writing reports on these issues, how would you go about planning them? What steps would you take to define each problem, conduct the research, and analyze the data necessary for such reports?[1]

Five Steps in Planning Reports

Whether you're employed by Harley-Davidson or by another business, you usually have some work to do before you begin to write a report. Like other effective business communications, reports require careful planning. Even if you're preparing a strictly informational report that does nothing more than transmit facts, you must still gather those facts and arrange them in a convenient format. Before putting a single word on the page, follow the series of steps that form the foundation of any report:

1. Define the problem and the purpose.
2. Outline the issues for investigation.
3. Prepare a work plan.
4. Conduct research.
5. Analyze and interpret data, drawing conclusions and developing recommendations.

When planning most business reports, you define the problem and the purpose, outline the issues for investigation, prepare a work plan, conduct research, and then analyze and interpret data.

The relative importance of these five steps depends on the type of assignment. **Informational reports,** which contain facts alone, may require very little in the way of conclusions and recommendations. Monitor/control reports, statements of policies and procedures, interim progress reports, and many compliance reports are examples. On the other hand, **analytical reports** include conclusions and recommendations and require all five steps. Examples include decision-oriented reports, business plans, proposals, and final reports to clients.

Step 1: Defining the Problem and the Purpose

LEARNING OUTCOME 1
Develop a statement defining the problem to be solved and a statement defining the purpose of the report.

Narrow the focus of your investigation by defining your problem.

Your first step is to write a **problem statement,** a statement that defines the problem your report will cover. This problem may be negative or positive; it may deal with the problem of shrinking sales or the need for more child-care facilities. The problem is merely the matter you intend to deal with, whether you're gathering information, supporting a decision, or actually solving a problem. Be careful not to confuse a simple topic (campus parking) with a problem (the lack of enough campus parking). A clear problem statement helps you decide what information you'll need in order to complete your report. Also, be sure to consider the company's perspective and the individual perspectives of the people who will read your report.[2] If you're the only person who thinks this issue is a problem, the audience won't be very interested in your solution. You may have to spend some time convincing people that a problem exists.

Linda Moreno is a cost accounting analyst for Electrovision, a high-technology company. She was asked to find ways of reducing employee travel costs (her complete report appears in Chapter 14). Because she was supposed to suggest specific cost reductions, she phrased her problem statement carefully: "Electrovision needs to find ways to reduce travel costs while still enabling employees to work effectively." If her assignment had been restricted to simply reporting on spending patterns, her problem statement would have been phrased differently: "We need to understand how our travel budget is being spent." You can see from these two statements how much influence the problem statement has on your investigation. If Moreno's manager expected her to suggest cost reductions, but all she did was collect cost data, her report would have failed to meet expectations. Because she was assigned an analytical report rather than an informational report, Moreno had to go beyond mere data collection to draw conclusions and make recommendations. No matter what kind of report you're doing, however, defining the problem and the purpose requires asking questions to clarify the assignment.

You don't have to become an expert on every subject you undertake, but you must learn enough about the subject you are exploring to pose intelligent questions, just as detectives do when they investigate a case.

Asking the Right Questions

As in Moreno's case, the problem is often defined for you by the person who authorizes the report. When this is the case, talk over the objectives of the report before you begin your investigation–to ensure that you understand exactly what is required. Specifically, try to answer the following questions:

- What needs to be determined?
- Why is this issue important?
- Who is involved in the situation?
- Where is the trouble located?
- When did it start?
- How did the situation originate?

Not all these questions apply in every situation, but asking them helps you clarify the boundaries of your investigation. You can then draft a written statement of the problem being investigated, which will serve as a guide to whatever problem you're trying to solve or whatever question you're trying to answer in the report.[3]

Developing the Statement of Purpose

Prepare a written statement of your purpose, then review it with the person who authorized the study.

Once you've asked some preliminary questions and determined the problem, you're ready to write a clear **statement of purpose,** which defines the objective of the report. In contrast to the problem statement, which defines only what you're going to investigate, the statement of purpose defines what the report should accomplish.[4]

The most useful way to phrase your purpose is to begin with an infinitive phrase. If Linda Moreno had been given an informational assignment, she might have stated her purpose this way:

> PURPOSE: To summarize Electrovision's spending on travel and entertainment

However, her analytical report had to go beyond information:

> PURPOSE: To analyze Electrovision's travel costs and suggest practical ways to reduce these costs while still enabling employees to work effectively

Using an infinitive phrase (*to* plus a verb) encourages you to take control and decide where you're going before you begin. When you choose such a phrase—*to inform, to confirm, to analyze, to persuade, to recommend*—you pin down your general goal in preparing the report. At the same time, be sure to define the benefit (the information or recommended action) that your reader will gain from reading your report. The more specific your purpose, the more useful it will be as a guide to planning and writing the report.

Your audience's reaction dictates all the decisions you'll make about content, structure, outline, and so forth. So it's important to anticipate that reaction. Double-check your statement of purpose with the person who authorized the report. When the authorizer sees the purpose written down in black and white, she or he may decide to point the study in another direction.

Step 2: Outlining Issues for Investigation

LEARNING OUTCOME 2
Identify and outline the issues that have to be analyzed during your study.

Outline the issues you plan to study.

Once you've defined the problem and established the purpose of your report, you're ready to begin your investigation. To organize the research effort, you can break the problem into a series of logical, connected questions that try to identify causes and effects. This process is sometimes called **problem factoring.** You probably subconsciously approach most problems in this way. When your car's engine won't start, what do you do? You use the available evidence to organize your investigation, to start a search for cause-and-effect relationships. If the engine doesn't turn over at all, for instance, you might suspect a dead battery. In contrast, if the engine does turn over but won't fire, you can conclude that the battery is okay but perhaps you're out of gas. When you speculate on the cause of a problem, you're forming a **hypothesis,** a potential explanation that needs to be tested. By subdividing a problem and forming hypotheses based on available evidence, you can tackle even the most complex situations.

Linda Moreno used the factoring process to structure her investigation into cost reduction at Electrovision (Figure 13.1). "I began with a two-part question," says Moreno. "Why have our travel costs grown so dramatically, and how can we

FIGURE 13.1
Factoring the Travel-Cost Problem at Electrovision

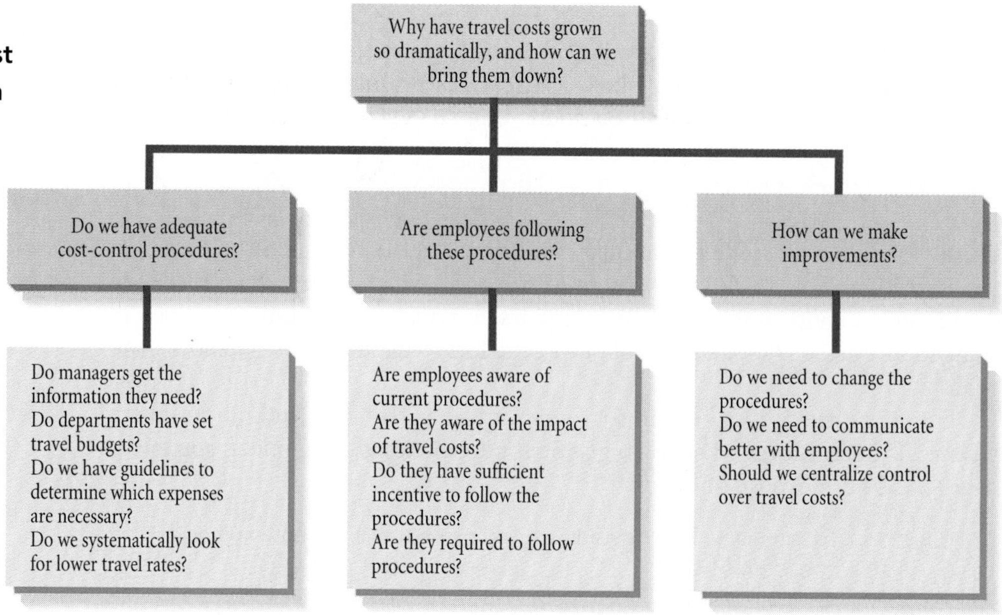

reduce them? Then I factored the first part into two sub-questions: Do we have adequate procedures for tracking and controlling costs? Are these procedures being followed?

"Looking into cost-control procedures, I speculated that the right kind of information was not reaching the executives who were responsible for these costs. From there, the questioning naturally led to the systems and procedures for collecting this information. If we didn't have the right procedures in place or if people weren't following procedures, the information wouldn't reach the people in charge."

The outline of issues for analysis is often different from the outline of the final report.

Once Moreno had determined what was wrong with Electrovision's cost-control system, she could address the second part of the main question: the problem of recommending improvements. The process of outlining the issues enabled Moreno and her colleagues to solve a problem methodically, just as outlining a report enables you to write in a systematic way. It's worth noting, however, that the way you outline an investigation may be different from the way you outline the resulting report. Solving the problem is one thing; selling the solution is another. During your investigation, you might analyze five possible causes of a problem and discover that only two are relevant. In your report, you might not even introduce the three unrelated possibilities that you investigated.

Developing a Logical Structure

Informational and analytical studies are factored differently.

Because any subject can be factored in many ways, your job is to choose the most logical method, the one that makes the most sense. Start by looking carefully at the purpose of your report. Informational assignments are structured differently from analytical ones.

Many assignments require both information and analysis, so it's up to you to discern the overall purpose of the report. Is your general goal to provide background information that someone else will use or interpret? Then an informational outline is appropriate overall, even though subsections of the study may require some analysis to discover and emphasize important facts. Is the purpose of your report to scrutinize the data and generate your own conclusions and recommendations? Then use an analytical outline overall, even though your opinions will obviously be based on facts. For problem solving you may use a variety of structural schemes, as long as you take care to avoid errors in logic.

INFORMATIONAL ASSIGNMENTS

Investigations that lead to factual reports, offering little analysis or interpretation of the data, are generally organized on the basis of subtopics dealing with specific subjects. These subtopics can be arranged in various ways:

Studies that emphasize discovering and reporting facts may be factored by subtopic.

- *According to importance.* If you're reviewing five product lines, you might organize your study in order of the sales for each product line, beginning with the line that produces the most revenue and proceeding to the one that produces the least revenue.
- *According to sequence.* If you're describing a process, proceed step by step–1, 2, 3, and so on. One instance is the process of organizing a conference. You would need to isolate each step and describe it sufficiently to inform and educate your readers.
- *According to chronology.* When investigating a chain of events, organize the study according to the time of its occurrence. For example, if you were reporting on the development of a product, you might organize your report by month, indicating the stages of the product's evolution in January, February, March, and so on. Another example is a report on the installation and testing of a large company's computer network; here, you might organize your account of this project's progress week by week.
- *According to geography.* If location is important, factor your study geographically. Here, a report investigating sites for a fast-food outlet in a particular city would report on the data collected for different neighbourhoods.
- *According to category.* If you're asked to review several distinct aspects of a subject, look at one category at a time, such as assembly, packaging, and shipping. If you're asked to compile data on a competitor's products, you would gather information on advertising, sales, market, and cost.

These methods of subdivision are commonly used when preparing monitor/control reports, policies and procedures, compliance reports, and interim progress reports.

ANALYTICAL ASSIGNMENTS

Analytical studies result in decision-oriented reports, final reports for clients, and some compliance reports. Such reports usually contain analyses, conclusions, and recommendations, and they're generally categorized by a problem-solving method. The two most common structural approaches for this method are (1) relative merit and (2) hypothesis.

Studies that focus on problem solving may be structured around hypotheses that the report writer plans to prove or disprove during the investigation.

When the problem is to evaluate how well various alternatives meet your criteria, the natural way to subdivide your analysis is to focus on the criteria. For example, if the problem is to decide where to build a new plant, you might factor the investigation along the following lines:

Where should we build a new plant?

I. Construction costs
   A. Location A
   B. Location B
   C. Location C

II. Labour availability
   A. Location A
   B. Location B
   C. Location C

III. Transportation facilities
   A. Location A
   B. Location B
   C. Location C

Another way of using relative merits is to identify the alternatives first and then analyze how well each one meets your criteria.

When the report's purpose is to discover causes, predict results, or suggest a solution to a problem, one natural way to proceed is to formulate hypothetical explanations. If your problem is to determine why your company is having trouble hiring secretaries, you could begin factoring the problem by speculating on the causes. Then you'd collect information to confirm or disprove each reason. Your outline of the major issues might look something like this:

Why are we having trouble hiring secretaries?

I. We don't pay them enough.
   A. What do we pay our secretaries?
   B. What do comparable companies pay their secretaries?
   C. How important is pay in influencing secretaries' job choices?

II. Our location is poor.
   A. Are we accessible by public transportation and major roads?
   B. Is the area physically attractive?
   C. Are housing costs affordable?
   D. Is crime a problem?

III. The supply of secretaries is diminishing.
   A. How many secretaries were available five years ago as opposed to now?
   B. What was the demand for secretaries five years ago as opposed to now?

In many cases, however, identifying and clarifying problems is only part of the challenge. You'll often be called on to suggest and implement solutions. Developing solid problem-solving skills will help not only your business reports but many other aspects of your career as well. You will be able to solve problems efficiently and effectively if you follow a clear problem-solving process.[5]

1. Define and limit the problem so that you know exactly what you're trying to solve–and what you're not trying to solve.
2. Analyze the problem and gather data about it.
3. Establish criteria for possible solutions.
4. Brainstorm possible solutions.
5. Choose the best possible solution, based on the criteria you set in step 3.
6. Implement the chosen solution.

You won't cover all six of these steps in every report you write, of course, but knowing how to solve problems will help you make better decisions and recommendations in your reports.

Preparing a Preliminary Outline

Organize your study by preparing a detailed preliminary outline.

As you go through the factoring process, you may want to use an outline format to represent your ideas. Of course, if a few notes are enough to guide you through a short, informal report in memo form, perhaps an outline isn't necessary. However, a preliminary outline gives you a convenient frame of reference for your formal investigation. Furthermore, a detailed outline can definitely be worthwhile under certain circumstances:

- When you're one of several people working on an assignment
- When your investigation will be extensive and will involve many sources and types of data
- When you know from experience that the person who requested the study will revise the assignment during the course of your investigation and you want to keep track of the changes

Two widely used systems of outlining, the alphanumeric system and the decimal system, are illustrated in Figure 13.2. Both are perfectly acceptable, but some companies favour one method over the other. Many outlining programs for personal computers give you a choice and then help you switch from outline format to report format as you write.

You usually write the headings at each level of your outline in the same grammatical form. In other words, if item I uses a verb, items II, III, and IV also use verbs. This parallel construction enables readers to see that the ideas are related, of similar importance, and on the same level of generality. It makes the outline a useful tool for establishing the table of contents and headings in your final report, and it is considered the correct format by most of the people who might review your outline.

Use the same grammatical form for each group of items in your outline.

When wording the outline, you must also choose between descriptive (topical) and informative (talking) headings. As Table 13.1 indicates, descriptive headings label the subject that will be discussed, whereas informative headings (in either question or summary form) suggest more about the meaning of the issues.

Although outlines with informative headings take a little longer to write, they're generally more useful in guiding your work, especially if written in terms of the questions you plan to answer during your investigation. In addition, they're easier for others to review. If other people are going to comment on your outline, they may not have a very clear idea of what you mean by the descriptive heading "Advertising." However, they will get the main idea if you use the informative heading "Cuts in ad budget may explain sales decline."

Informative outlines are generally more helpful than descriptive outlines.

FIGURE 13.2

Two Common Outline Formats

ALPHANUMERIC	DECIMAL
I. ______	1.0 ______
A. ______	1.1 ______
B. ______	1.2 ______
1. ______	1.2.1 ______
2. ______	1.2.2 ______
a. ______	1.2.2.1 ______
b. ______	1.2.2.2 ______
3. ______	1.2.3 ______
C. ______	1.3 ______
II. ______	2.0 ______
A. ______	2.1 ______
1. ______	2.1.1 ______
a. ______	2.1.1.1 ______
b. ______	2.1.1.2 ______
2. ______	2.1.2 ______
3. ______	2.1.3 ______
B. ______	2.2 ______

TABLE 13.1 Types of Outline Headings

Descriptive (Topical) Outline	Informative (Talking) Outline	
	Question Form	*Summary Form*
I. Industry Characteristics	I. What is the nature of the industry?	I. Flour milling is a mature industry.
A. Annual sales	A. What are the annual sales?	A. Market is large.
B. Profitability	B. Is the industry profitable?	B. Profit margins are narrow.
C. Growth rate	C. What is the pattern of growth?	C. Growth is modest.
1. Sales	1. Sales growth?	1. Sales growth averages less than 3 percent a year.
2. Profit	2. Profit growth?	2. Growth in profits is flat.

Remember that at this point you're only developing a preliminary outline to guide your investigation. Later on, when you've completed your research and are preparing a final outline or a table of contents for the report, you may want to switch from an outline of your questions to an outline that summarizes your findings.

Following the Rules of Division

Follow the rules of division to ensure that your study will be organized in a logical, systematic way.

Once you've prepared your outline, sit back for a minute and check it over. Ask yourself whether the structure is significant, consistent, exclusive, and complete:

- *Divide a topic into at least two parts.* A topic cannot be divided into only one part. For example, if you wanted to divide a topic such as "Alternatives for Improving Division Profits," you wouldn't look only at increasing sales. You would need at least one other subtopic, such as reducing production costs or decreasing employee absenteeism. If you were interested only in increasing sales, then that would be your topic, which you would probably divide into at least two subtopics.
- *Choose a significant, useful basis or guiding principle for the division.* You could subdivide production problems into two groups: problems that arise when the machines are turned off and problems that occur when the machines are turned on. However, this basis for breaking down the subject would not be of much use to anyone. A better choice might be dividing the subject into problems caused by human error versus problems caused by machine failure.
- *When subdividing a whole into its parts, restrict yourself to one category at a time.* If you switch from one category to another, you get a mixed classification, which can confuse your analysis. Say you're subdividing your study of the market for toothpaste according to sales of fluoride versus non-fluoride brands. You would upset the investigation by adding another category to your analysis (such as sales broken down by geographical region). If you are dealing with a long, complex subject, you'll no doubt have to use several categories of division before you complete your work, but the shift from one category to another must be made at a logical point, after you've completed your study of a particular issue. For example, after you've looked at sales of fluoride versus non-fluoride toothpaste, you might then want to look at toothpaste sales by geographical location or socioeconomic group.

WRONG	CORRECT
I. Toothpaste market by type of product	I. Toothpaste sales by type of product
A. Fluoride brands	A. Fluoride brands
B. Non-fluoride brands	B. Non-fluoride brands
C. Sales by geographical region	II. Toothpaste sales by region
	A. West
	B. Central
	C. East

- *Make certain that each group is separate and distinct.* As you divide a topic into groups, those groups must be mutually exclusive, or you'll end up talking about the same item twice, under two separate headings. Subdividing a population into males, females, and teenagers wouldn't make any sense because the categories overlap.
- *Be thorough when listing all the components of a whole.* It would be misleading to subdivide an engine into parts without mentioning the pistons. An important part of the whole would be missing, and the resulting picture of the engine would be wrong.

Most important, of course, is whether your outline follows a logical flow when compared with your investigation and its results. For instance, if you're searching for cause-and-effect relationships, you might want to start with the observed effects and work backward to the causes in a logical manner.

Step 3: Preparing the Work Plan

LEARNING OUTCOME 3
Prepare a work plan for conducting the investigation.

Once you've defined the problem and outlined the issues for analysis, you are ready to establish a work plan based on your preliminary outline. In business, most report writing situations involve a firm deadline with finite time and resources to get the job done. In other words, you not only have to produce quality reports, you have to do so quickly and efficiently. A carefully thought-out work plan is the best way to make sure you produce quality work on schedule.

Prepare a work plan that identifies the tasks you will perform.

If you are preparing this work plan for yourself, it can be relatively informal: a simple list of the steps you plan to take, an estimate of their sequence and timing, and a list of the sources of information you plan to use. If you're conducting a lengthy, formal study, however, you'll want to develop a detailed work plan that can guide the performance of many tasks over a span of time. Most proposals require a detailed work plan, which becomes the basis for a contract if the proposal is accepted. A formal work plan might include these elements (especially the first two):

- *Statement of the problem.* Include the problem statement so that anyone working with you is clear about the nature of the challenge you face. Including the problem statement can also help you stay focused on the core problem and avoid distractions that are likely to arise during your investigation and writing.
- *Statement of the purpose and scope of your investigation.* As you saw earlier in the chapter, your statement of purpose describes what you plan to accomplish with this report. The scope defines the boundaries of your work, explicitly stating which

issues you will cover and which issues you won't cover. If you've ever misunderstood a homework assignment and delivered something that didn't meet expectations, you know how frustrating misunderstandings about expectations can be for both the writer and the reader. Particularly with complex, lengthy investigations, make sure that the task is clearly defined before you start. If it's possible and appropriate, verify your purpose and scope with your intended audience before starting. As with homework, you usually won't have time to rework business reports if you discover at the last minute that you're on the wrong track.

- *Discussion of the sequence of tasks to be accomplished.* Indicate sources of information, required research, and any constraints (on time, money, personnel, or data). For simple reports, the list of necessary tasks will be short and probably rather obvious. Longer reports and complex investigations, however, require thorough planning. You may need to reserve time with customers or executives or schedule outside services such as telephone researchers.
- *Description of the end products that will result from the investigation.* In many cases, the output of your efforts will be the report itself. In other cases, though, you'll need to produce something above and beyond a report, such as a new marketing plan, some improvements to a business process, or even a tangible product. As with the rest of your work plan, make sure these expectations are clear up front, and make sure you've scheduled enough time and resources to complete the job.
- *Review of project assignments, schedules, and resource requirements.* Indicate who will be responsible for what, when tasks will be completed, and how much the investigation will cost. You may also want to include a brief section on coordinating the writing and production of the report if more than one person will be involved. Collaborative writing has some important advantages over writing a report by yourself, of course, but making sure everyone works together productively can also be a challenge. One way is to obtain firm commitments from participants at the outset.
- *Plans for following up after the report is delivered.* Follow-up can range from something as simple as making sure people received the information they needed to something as complex as conducting additional research to evaluate the results of proposals contained in the report. Even if follow-up isn't required or expected, doing some informal follow-up can help you find ways to improve your future reports. Following up is also a good way to communicate to your audience that you care about the effectiveness of your work and the impact you can have on the organization.

Some work plans also include a tentative outline of the report (Figure 13.3). With a plan in place you're ready to get to work, which usually means starting with research.

Step 4: Conducting the Research

LEARNING OUTCOME 4
Organize the research phase of the investigation, including the identification of secondary and primary sources of data.

The value of your report depends on the quality of the data you use. So when the time comes to gather facts and figures, your first concern is to get organized. If you're working alone on a project, getting organized may mean nothing more than setting up a file, checking out relevant books from the library, and compiling a list of articles from electronic databases. If you're part of a team, you will work out your assignments and coordinate activities. Your work plan will be a big help during this research effort.

STATEMENT OF THE PROBLEM

The rapid growth of our company over the past five years has reduced the sense of community among our staff. People no longer feel like part of an intimate organization where they matter as individuals.

Problem statement is clear enough for anyone to understand without background research.

PURPOSE AND SCOPE OF WORK

The purpose of this study is to determine whether a company newsletter would help rebuild employee identification with the organization. The study will evaluate the impact of newsletters in other companies and will attempt to identify features that might be desirable in our own newsletter. Such variables as length, frequency of distribution, types of articles, and graphic design will be considered. Costs will be estimated for several approaches. In addition, the study will analyze the personnel and the procedures required to produce a newsletter.

Statement of purpose is specific, delineating exactly what will be covered in the report.

SOURCES AND METHODS OF DATA COLLECTION

Sample newsletters will be collected from 50 companies similar to ours in size, growth rate, and types of employees. The editors will be asked to comment on the impact of their publications on employee morale. Our own employees will be surveyed to determine their interest in a newsletter and their preferences for specific features. Production procedures and costs will be analyzed through conversations with newsletter editors and printers.

Tasks to be accomplished are clearly laid out.

PRELIMINARY OUTLINE

I. Do newsletters affect morale?
   A. Do people read them?
   B. How do employees benefit?
   C. How does the company benefit?

II. What are the features of good newsletters?
   A. How long are they?
   B. What do they contain?
   C. How often are they published?
   D. How are they designed?

III. How should a newsletter be produced?
   A. Should it be written, edited, and printed internally?
   B. Should it be written internally and printed outside?
   C. Should it be totally produced outside?

IV. What would a newsletter cost?
   A. What would the personnel costs be?
   B. What would the materials costs be?
   C. What would outside services cost?

V. Should we publish a company newsletter?

VI. If so, what approach should we take?

Although no description of the end product is included here, a preliminary outline is presented for guidance.

WORK PLAN

Collect/analyze newsletters	09/01–09/14
Interview editors by phone	09/16–09/20
Survey employees	09/14–09/28
Develop sample	09/28–10/05
Develop cost estimates	10/07–10/10
Prepare report	10/10–10/24
Submit final report	10/25

This plan includes no plans for following up, but it clearly states the assignments and the schedules for completing them.

FIGURE 13.3

In-Depth Critique: Sample Work Plan for a Formal Study

This work plan was developed for a report on whether to launch a company newsletter.

Consult primary and secondary sources of information.

Work plans contain a list of the sources you'll consult. **Primary sources** of information provide, as the name implies, first-hand information that is collected for your report's specific purpose. In contrast, **secondary sources** of information have been previously collected for other purposes.[6] Most business reports call for a mix of both primary and secondary sources. However, you're likely to find that much of what you need to know has never been collected, so you'll have to conduct your own research. For example, you probably wouldn't locate much existing information on what a Harley-Davidson dealership should look like. Reliance on primary sources is one of the main differences between business reports and school reports. Even so, business report writers often begin by researching secondary sources.

Reviewing Secondary Sources

Conduct secondary research by locating information that has already been collected, usually in the form of books, periodicals, and reports.

Even though you may plan to rely heavily on primary sources, it's a good idea to begin your study with a thorough review of the information that has already been collected. By searching the literature, you avoid the embarrassment of failing to notice a key factor that's common knowledge. You also save yourself the trouble of studying something that has already been done. Once you gain a feel for the structure of the subject, you can decide what additional research will be required.

FINDING SOURCES

Depending on your subject, you may find useful information in general reference works, popular publications, or government documents. CD-ROM products offer a wide variety of research materials, from product databases to nationwide phone directories. You can also search online databases on the Internet or by using services such as Dialog (a gateway to more than 450 databases). As you learned in Chapter 4, the Internet offers a variety of search and retrieval tools to help you find articles, research reports, Web sites, and other sources of information (Figure 13.4).

In addition, each field of business has a handful of specialized references that are considered indispensable. You'll quickly come to know these sources once you've joined a particular industry. In addition, don't overlook internal sources. Often the most useful references are company reports, memos, and information stored in the company's databases. Also check company brochures, newsletters, and annual reports to shareholders.

If you're working for a large organization with a company library, you may have the help of a professional librarian to identify and obtain other useful materials for your investigation. If not, look for the nearest public library or university library, and ask the librarians there for help. Reference librarians are trained to know where to find just about everything, and many of them are pleased to help people pursue obscure information.

Going Online

Search Thousands of Full-Text Articles Instantly

The Electronic Library's easily searchable database contains more than 150 full-text newspapers; 900 full-text magazines; national and international newswires; 2000 literary works; over 18 000 photos, images, and maps; television and radio transcripts; and movie and software reviews. Use it free for a month. All materials can be downloaded and printed for your immediate use.

www.elibrary.com

CHOOSING AND USING SOURCES

When it comes to choosing your references, be selective. Avoid dated or biased material. If possible, check on who collected the data, the methods they used, their qualifications, and their professional reputations.[7] Common sense will help you judge the credibility of the sources you plan to use. Ask yourself the following questions about each piece of material:

- *Does the source have a reputation for honesty and reliability?* Naturally, you'll feel most comfortable using information from a source that has established a reputation for accuracy. But even a good reputation doesn't mean you can let your guard down completely; even the finest reporters and editors make mistakes.
- *Is the source potentially biased?* Some of the information you'll find in your research will have been produced and distributed by people or organizations with a particular point of view. Bias isn't necessarily bad; in fact, getting people to believe one thing and not another is the purpose of much of the world's communication efforts. If you gather some facts from the Beef Farmers of Alberta or the Canadian Association of Retired Persons, you have a fairly clear idea of what these organizations stand for and what biases their messages may have. However, organizations with neutral names, such as the Freedom Foundation of Canada, aren't as easy to categorize. Without knowing what these organizations stand for, you're at their mercy when it comes to interpreting the information they produce. Also, an organization's source of funding may influence its information output. Again, there is nothing inherently unethical about this type of reporting; you just need to be aware of it when you interpret the information.
- *Where did the source get its information?* Many secondary sources are themselves derived from other sources, making you even farther removed from the original information. If a newspaper article says that pollutants in a local river dropped by 50 percent in the last year, chances are the reporter who wrote the article didn't make those measurements directly. He or she got the number from someone else.
- *Can you verify the material independently?* A good way to uncover mistakes or biases is to search for the same information from another source. But be alert to the possibility that many versions come from a single source. Verifying material can be particularly important when the information goes beyond simple facts to include projections, interpretations, and estimates.
- *Will the source's claims stand up to thoughtful scrutiny?* Finally, step back and ask yourself whether the things you read or hear make sense. If a researcher claims that the market for a particular product will triple in the next five years, ask yourself what will have to happen for that prediction to come true. Will three times as many customers buy the product? Will existing customers buy three times as much as they currently buy? Why?

Ask questions about the reference works you use:
✧ Are they up to date?
✧ Are they objective?
✧ Who collected the data? How?
✧ What are the authors' qualifications and reputations?

You probably won't have time to conduct a thorough background check on all your sources, so focus your efforts on the most important or most suspicious pieces of information.

Stop when you reach the point at which additional effort provides little new information.

The amount of library research you do depends on the subject you're studying and the purpose of your investigation. Linda Moreno conducted fairly extensive research, both to analyze Electrovision's expense problems and to find potential solutions. Because travel costs are a concern to so many companies, business newspapers and magazines publish quite a few articles on the subject.

Regardless of the amount of research you do, retain complete and accurate notes on the sources of all the material you collect, using one of the systems explained in Appendix B, "Documentation of Report Sources." Documenting your sources through footnotes, endnotes, or some similar system lends credibility to your report. It also helps you avoid plagiarism.

FIGURE 13.4
Using Search Engines on the Internet

If you can think of a research topic, you can probably find information about it on the Internet. However, searching for that information can be frustrating if you don't know where or how to look. Search engines are Internet research tools that can help you identify and screen resources.

A **search engine** travels the Web, indexes documents it finds on Web sites, and places those documents in a database. When you enter key words or phrases to be searched, the engine scans its database and returns all documents or *hits* that contain a match. Effective searches often require linking key words together. **Boolean search operators,** such as *AND, WITH, NEAR, OR,* and *NOT,* can help you limit or expand your search. For example, if you searched for "Ford AND automobiles," you would receive documents that contain both words. Entering "Ford WITH automobiles" would retrieve documents in which the words appear beside each other. Entering "Ford NEAR automobiles" would return hits where the two words appear close to each other. Searching for "Ford OR automobiles," would return documents containing at least one, but not necessarily both words. And if you entered "Ford NOT automobiles" you would see all documents that refer to Ford but do not mention automobiles. The NOT operator can be especially effective for limiting unwanted hits. Most search engines recognize Boolean search operators, although some substitute symbols, such as plus and minus signs, to achieve the same results.

Each engine has qualities that distinguish it from the others. Some engines index all the pages they find. Others index only the most popular pages. Many will also search Usenet newsgroups instead of Web sites, depending on which one you specify when you enter your query. And each search engine updates its database on its own schedule. Scheduling differences create great variation in search results. It is always best, therefore, to try your search on several engines. Canada.com, Yahoo!, HotBot, Alta Vista, and Google are a few of the more popular search engines available. There are many others, however, some of which are designed for locating specific types of information.

Canada.com (**www.canada.com**) offers many useful options for searching the World Wide Web. You can direct your search to the entire Web or focus it on a geographical location, such as North America, Canada, or Southeast Asia, and can have the search engine look for specific media types, such as images, audio, or video. Drop-down menus make the word filters easy to use: you choose whether your search "must," "should," or "must not" contain the words, phrase, the person names, or links to the URL.

Yahoo! (**www.yahoo.com** and **www.yahoo.ca**) is actually called a **Web directory** because it files all of its documents in categories. It works best when you want to locate many similar sites under a particular subject or title. Yahoo! supports case-sensitive matching,

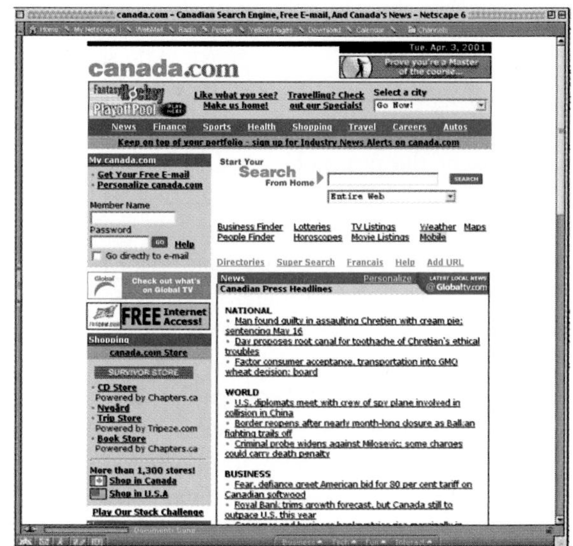

which can be very helpful when you are searching for documents containing proper names. For example, by entering "China," you are assured of receiving only documents that refer to the country, and not to porcelain dishes. The documents that Yahoo! returns are given priority when key words appear either in the title or multiple times in the text. Also, general categories are ranked higher than narrowly focused categories.

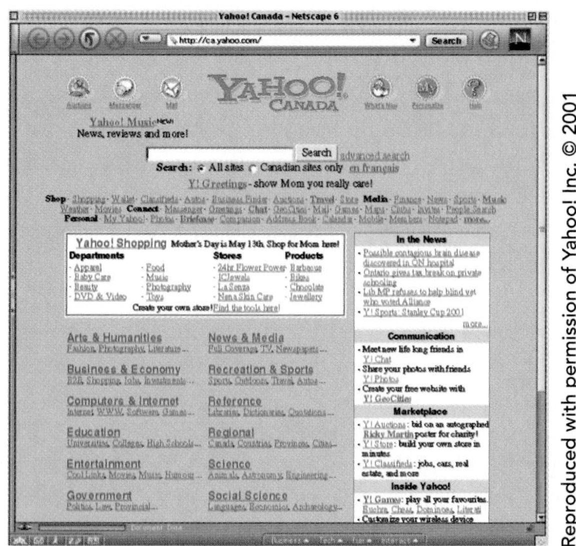

HotBot (**www.hotbot.com**) indexes more than 110 million sites and provides more updated sites than some search engines. Like Canada.com, HotBot both allows you to sort results by date or type of media and features drop-down menus where you can click on "and," "or," or "not" to simplify Boolean searches. Advanced search features include drop-down menus that let you specify not only a geographical region but also a particular domain for your search, such as .com, .net, .ca, .uk, .edu, and .org. HotBot is considered one of the top Internet search engines.

AltaVista (**www.altavista.com**) is commonly known as having the largest search engine database on the Web. It claims to contain well over 20 million pages. This distinction makes it the engine of choice when you want the most comprehensive results or when you are searching for obscure information. AltaVista allows you to limit your returns by date or by instructing the engine to prioritize documents that contain particular words. AltaVista also supports searches in 25 languages, including Japanese, Chinese, and Korean.

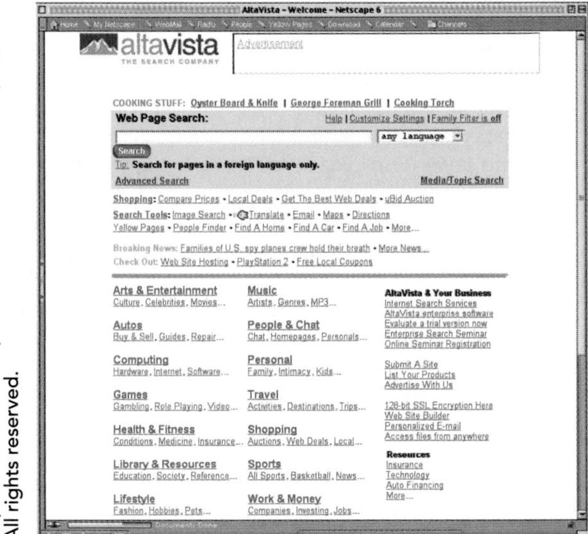

Google (**www.google.com**) is currently the largest search engine, indexing 1.25 billion Web pages. As a full-text index, it

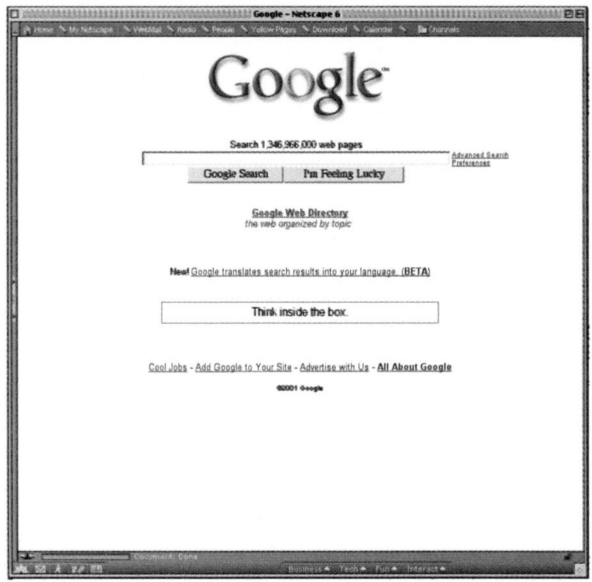

searches the entire HTML file. Advanced searching using Google allows you to limit your searches by including or excluding words or phrases. Google also supports searches in any language. With this engine, you can search by phrase by including the phrase in quotation marks.

You will also find metasearch tools useful, because they enable a search on several search engines at one time. The disadvantage of these metasearch tools is that they tend to be slow and you will obtain an extremely large number of hits. But if you need to do a broad search, they are handy. Metacrawler (**www.metacrawler.com**) is useful because it eliminates redundant URLs. AskJeeves (**www.askjeeves.com**) lets you search by asking questions in natural language, and returns a list of questions to help you narrow your search.

Regardless of which search engine you choose, your results will be best if you spend a few minutes becoming acquainted with it before initiating your search. Each engine has a "tips" or "help" page that explains which operators it uses, whether it recognizes misspellings, whether case-sensitivity is supported, how it ranks pages for relevancy, and whether it is capable of searching phrases. You should also become acquainted with each engine's advanced search capabilities, because they will usually bring the best hits. Getting to know each engine's strengths and weaknesses at the start of your search can save you a lot of time and frustration later on.

You can obtain more information about search engines by going to Search Engine Watch (**www.searchenginewatch.com**). This site discusses how search engines work and provides live links to dozens of different types of search engines, including news and specialty search engines. You'll also find search engine reviews and resources, as well as techniques for conducting advanced searches.

REPORT WRITER'S NOTEBOOK

Evaluating World Wide Web Resources

The World Wide Web has become the first stop for students, teachers, and researchers who need information for a report, essay, or study. Anyone who has gone online will agree that the Web offers the benefits of high speeds and enormous scope for people who want both convenience and wide access to a variety of information sources. A quick entry into an online search engine may harvest dozens, hundreds, or thousands of hits, confronting Web researchers with data ranging from essential to just plain worthless. If you are just starting to acquire research skills, or wish to refine them further, developing a critical sense of Web resources will help you become a better researcher.[8] Your reports could be more credible and beneficial to your audiences.

Broadly speaking, World Wide Web resources may be classified into the following areas:

- **Usenet:** Newsgroups are public discussions of specific topics. Usenet groups may be moderated by an individual who volunteers to monitor the relevance of the *articles*, as contributions are called, and ban those that don't meet the principles of the newsgroup's charter, which includes submission guidelines. Alternatively, some newsgroups may be unmoderated.
- **Commercial Web sites:** These are usually operated by small and large businesses, corporations, and online retailers. They often provide information about the company and advertise products and services. Sometimes they provide links to Web sites that share the same industry.
- **Organizational Web sites:** These are often operated by nonprofit, political, special interest, and advocacy groups. These sites typically provide information about the organization and endorse and promote the issues that concern them. You may find here links to organizations that share their concerns and activities.
- **Institutional Web sites:** Examples are sites operated by universities, hospitals, and other public institutions. Educational Web sites typically house the school's library catalogue and electronic databases.
- **Government Web sites:** Here you will find information about government services at the federal, provincial, and municipal levels as well as statistical information and research papers.
- **Individual Web sites:** These sites are created by people who frequently post personal information and may discuss topics of personal interest, such as hobbies, books and music, and political and social beliefs.

Analyzing the reliability of your Web information is not that much different from determining the trustworthiness of your secondary print sources, a topic already discussed in this chapter (see ***Choosing and Using Sources*** on p. 348). You must consider the source's reputation and potential bias. You must determine where your sources got their information, thereby providing yourself with a further check for reliability. You must also see if you can verify your source's information independently and if your source's claims meet the test of thoughtful scrutiny—in other words, do they make sense? With information you have accessed electronically, you should also ask yourself the following questions:

- **What is the URL (Universal Resource Locator)?** If the URL is a corporation or a political party, the information on the Web site may be particularly slanted. For example, if you are doing a study of the popularity of a certain snack food, the manufacturer's Web site will likely not include information you should know about competing products. And if the URL is a personal Web page, the information is more likely to be opinion than fact.
- **Who is the author? What are the author's qualifications?** An unsolicited book review downloaded from a major online bookseller, such as **Indigo.ca**, may be written by a fan of the author, or even a friend, who wants to promote the book by writing a favourable review. If you have obtained an article from a private or organizational Web site, look for a biography of the author and a list of her or his publications and affiliations. Check these carefully for clues to the author's attitudes and interests, which may betray a particular viewpoint. Sometimes the author is anonymous, often a clue that the information may not be reliable.
- **Who is the audience?** Noting the URL and investigating the Web site and its links will help you determine if the information is directed toward a particular group of people with common interests. If it is, the information you have obtained may be slanted. For example, information on Web sites established by environmental associations or associations that promote the interests of the tobacco industry should be analyzed carefully for signs of bias.
- **Is the information in its original format? If not, is the original source cited?** You must try to determine if the information is taken out of context, different from the original, or plagiarized. If the source isn't documented, it may not be trustworthy.
- **Has the information been filtered?** Filtering means that an author's article has undergone review by external readers. The author's peers, a publisher, or an editor has read it and probably asked the author for improvements in content and writing style. Look for an author's acknowledgements of reviewers and editors. Acknowledgements suggest that the work was submitted to this kind of quality control, which results in a more authoritative and reliable electronic document than one that wasn't.
- **How current is the Web site?** Web sites include a "last updated" feature that indicates the last time the site was revised. Stale-dated sites may contain out-of-date information. Be aware of the site's date, which can usually be found on the Web site's first page.

For information that is current and has undergone the peer-review process, your best bet is to search your school library's electronic journals or those located at your public library. Appendix B lists the electronic databases you will find most useful for your research.

Spending the time analyzing your Web sources will help you to become a credible and reliable researcher and writer. Your audiences will value your skills and respect you for your integrity.

Collecting Primary Data

When the information you need is not available from secondary sources, you collect and interpret the data yourself by doing primary research, going out into the real world to gather information through your own efforts. The four main ways of collecting primary data are examining documents, making observations, surveying people, and conducting experiments.

Conduct primary research by collecting information yourself.

DOCUMENTS

In business, a great deal of information is filed away for future reference. By scouring a company's files, you can often piece together an accurate, factual, historical record from the tidbits of evidence revealed in various letters, memos, and reports. Managers can gain valuable insight into current problems and situations by researching the company's previous positions on certain issues–seeking the origins of various policies.[9]

Documentary evidence and historical records are sources of primary data.

Business documents that qualify as primary data include sales reports prepared by field representatives, balance sheets and income statements, policy statements, correspondence with customers and suppliers, contracts, and log books. Many government and legal documents are also primary sources because they represent a decision made by the people who were present at some official proceeding.

A single document may be both a secondary source and a primary source. When citing summaries of financial and operations data from an annual report, you're using it as a secondary source. That same report, however, would be considered a primary source if you were analyzing its design features or comparing it with annual reports from other years or from other companies.

OBSERVATIONS

Informal observations are a rather common source of primary data in business. You simply use your five senses (especially your eyes and ears) to gather information. For instance, many reports are based on the writer's visiting a facility and observing operations. More objective information can be gathered through formal observations, which give observers a structure for noting what they see, thereby minimizing opportunities for interpretation.

Observation applies your five senses and your judgment to the investigation.

In general, observation is a useful technique when you're studying objects, physical activities, processes, the environment, or human behaviour. However, it can be expensive and time consuming, and the value of the observation depends on the reliability of the observer. Many people have a tendency to see what they want to see or to interpret events in light of their own experience. However, if the observer is trustworthy and has proper instructions, observation can provide valuable insights.[10]

Steve Jobs, co-founder of Apple Computer, sees an added dimension to researching what customers want: technology. He cautions that customers are unable to foresee what technology can do, so in addition to asking customers what they want, it's important to acquaint them with what's possible.

SURVEYS

Often the best way to obtain answers to your questions is to ask people with relevant experience and opinions. Such surveys include everything from conducting a single interview to distributing thousands of questionnaires.

When you need specialized information that hasn't been recorded anywhere, you may want to conduct a personal interview with an expert, which is the simplest form of survey. Many experts come from the ranks of your own organization: people from other departments who have specialized knowledge, your predecessor in the job, long-time employees who have seen it all. On occasion you may also want to talk with outsiders who have some special expertise.

Doing an interview may seem an easy way to get information, but it requires careful preparation. You don't want to waste anyone's time, and you want your efforts to be productive. Chapter 17 presents some helpful pointers on conducting effective interviews.

A formal survey is a way of finding out what a cross-section of people thinks about something.

Although they have the same purpose, interviews are quite different from formal, large-scale surveys in which a sample population answers a series of carefully tested questions. In Linda Moreno's work at Electrovision, she needed to know why people were travelling and whether there were suitable alternatives to frequent travel.

A formal survey requires a number of important decisions:

Two important research criteria are
- ✧ Reliability—when the same results would be obtained if the research were repeated
- ✧ Validity—when research measures what it is intended to measure

- ➤ Which type of survey–face-to-face interviews, phone calls, printed questionnaires, or computer-based surveys–will be most useful?
- ➤ How many individuals will you contact to get results that are **reliable** (that is, reproducible if the same study were repeated)? Who will those people be? What sample is an accurate reflection of the population?
- ➤ What specific questions will you ask to get a **valid** picture (a true reflection of the group's feelings on the subject)?[11]

Your answers to these questions have a profound effect on the results of your survey.

Having seen rival pre-election polls that come up with conflicting projections of who's going to win, you may wonder whether it makes sense to rely on survey results at all. The answer is it does, as long as you understand the nature of surveys. For one thing, surveys reveal only what people think about something at a specific time. For another, pollsters ask various people different questions in various ways, and not surprisingly get differing answers. Just because surveys produce differing results doesn't mean that surveys are a poor form of research. Conducting a reliable, valid survey is not easy. Generally speaking, it helps to have the advice of a specialist.

Developing an effective questionnaire requires care and skill.

One of the most crucial elements of a survey is the questionnaire. To develop one, begin by listing the points you're trying to determine. Then phrase these points as specific questions, choosing an appropriate type of question for each point (Figure 13.5 shows some variations). The following guidelines will help you produce valid results:

- ➤ *Provide clear instructions.* Respondents need to know exactly how to fill out the questionnaire.
- ➤ *Keep the questionnaire short and easy to answer.* People are most likely to respond if they can complete the questionnaire within 10 or 15 minutes. So ask only questions that are relevant to your research. In addition, don't ask questions that require too much work on the respondent's part. People aren't willing to dig up the answers to questions like "What was your monthly rate of water consumption in 2000?"
- ➤ *Formulate questions that provide easily tabulated or analyzed answers.* Numbers and facts are easier to deal with than opinions are. Nevertheless, you may be able to elicit countable opinions with multiple-choice questions or to group open-ended opinions into a limited number of categories.
- ➤ *Avoid questions that lead to a particular answer, because they bias your survey.* Harley-Davidson would gain little useful information by asking customers, "Do you prefer that our dealerships stay open on Sundays for your convenience?" The question obviously calls for a yes answer. A less biased question would be: "What day of the week are you most likely to visit one of our dealerships?"
- ➤ *Ask only one thing at a time.* A compound question like "Do you read books and magazines regularly?" doesn't allow for the respondent who reads one but not the other.
- ➤ *Avoid questions with vague or abstract words.* Instead of asking "Are you frequently troubled by colds?" ask, "How many colds did you have in the past 12 months?"
- ➤ *Include a few questions that rephrase earlier questions.* Such questions will help you cross-check the validity of respondents' answers.
- ➤ *Pretest the questionnaire.* Have a sample group identify questions that are subject to misinterpretation.[12]

Question Type	Example
OPEN-ENDED	How would you describe the flavour of this ice cream?
EITHER-OR	Do you think this ice cream is too rich? ________ Yes ________ No
MULTIPLE-CHOICE	Which description best fits the taste of this ice cream? (Choose only one.) a. Delicious b. Too fruity c. Too sweet d. Too intensely flavoured e. Bland f. Stale
SCALE	Please make an X on the scale to indicate how you perceive the texture of this ice cream. ◄──────────────► Too light Light Creamy Too creamy
CHECKLIST	Which flavours of ice cream have you had in the past 12 months? (Check all that apply.) _____ Vanilla _____ Chocolate _____ Strawberry _____ Chocolate chip _____ Coffee
RANKING	Rank these flavours in order of your preference, from 1 (most preferred) to 5 (least preferred): _____ Vanilla _____ Cherry _____ Maple nut _____ Chocolate ripple _____ Coconut
SHORT-ANSWER	In the past month, how many times did you buy ice cream in the supermarket? ____________ In the past month, how many times did you buy ice cream in ice cream shops? ____________

FIGURE 13.5
Types of Survey Questions

If you're mailing your questionnaire, rather than administering it in person, include a persuasive cover letter that explains why you're conducting the research. Try to convince readers that their response is important to you. If possible, offer to share the results with the respondent. Mention that you won't disclose information that can identify individual respondents. Include a preaddressed envelope with pre-paid postage so that the respondent won't have to find an envelope or postage to return the questionnaire to you. Remember, however, that even under the best of circumstances you may not get more than a 10 to 20 percent response.

Computer-based interviewing (CBI) can be an excellent way to gather and analyze data. Two big advantages of CBI are real-time customization (the computer can change the flow and content of the interview on the basis of each person's answers) and the ability to automatically sort and compile data during the interview. Computer-based interviewing can be conducted in several ways, including mailing survey disks or inviting people to respond at an Internet Web site.

TK Associates International is a Japanese consulting firm that helps international companies market to Japanese consumers and businesses. It has used its Web site to conduct a survey of more than 2000 Japanese computer users.[13] This application of CBI was particularly helpful because the company was researching Web-based marketing opportunities.

EXPERIMENTS

Experiments are far more common in technical fields than in general business. That's because an experiment requires extensive manipulation of the factors involved, which is often very expensive (and may even be unethical when people are one of the factors). Nevertheless, experiments do have their place. Say you want to find out whether a change in lighting levels increases the productivity of the pattern cutters in your dressmaking business. The most objective approach is to assign cutters randomly to two groups: one working under existing conditions and the other working under the new lighting.

The aim when conducting an experiment is to keep all variables the same except for the one you're testing.

When conducting an experiment, it's important to carefully control the factors (called variables) you're not testing. Thus, in the lighting experiment, for the results to be valid, the only difference between the two groups and their environments should be the lighting. Otherwise, differences in productivity could be attributed to such factors as age differences between the two groups or experience on the job. It's even possible that introducing any change in the pattern cutters' environment, whether it be lighting or something else entirely, is enough to increase their productivity.

Top Tips for Writing Reports that Mean Business

PROMOTING WORKPLACE ETHICS

Put nothing in writing that you're unwilling to say in public, and write nothing that may embarrass or jeopardize your employer. Does this mean you should cover up problems? Of course not. However, when you're dealing with sensitive information, be discreet. Present the information in such a way that it will help readers resolve a problem. Avoid personal gripes, criticisms, alibis, attempts to blame other people, sugar-coated data, and unsolicited opinions.

To be useful, the information must be accurate, complete, and honest. However, being honest is not always a simple matter. Each of us sees reality a little differently, and we describe what we see in our own way. To restrict the distortions introduced by differences in perception, follow these guidelines.

- **Describe facts or events in concrete terms.** Indicate quantities whenever you can. Say that "Sales have increased 17 percent," or that "Sales have increased from \$40 000 to \$43 000 in the past two months." Don't say, "Sales have skyrocketed."
- **Report all relevant facts.** Regardless of whether these facts support your theories or please your readers, they must be included. Omitting the details that undermine your position may be convenient, but it is misleading and inaccurate.
- **Put the facts in perspective.** Taken out of context, the most concrete facts are misleading. If you say "Stock values have doubled in three weeks," you offer an incomplete picture. Instead, say "Stock values have doubled in three weeks, rising from \$2 to \$4 per share."
- **Give plenty of evidence for your conclusions.** Statements such as "We have to reorganize the sales force or we'll lose market share" may or may not be true. Readers have no way of knowing unless you provide enough data to support your claim.
- **Present only verifiable conclusions.** Check facts, and use reliable sources. Don't draw conclusions too quickly (one sales rep may say that customers are unhappy, but that doesn't mean they all are). And don't assume that one event caused another—sales may have dipped right after you switched ad agencies, but that doesn't mean the new agency is at fault. The general state of the economy may be responsible.
- **Keep your personal biases in check.** Even if you feel strongly about your topic, keep those feelings from influencing your choice of words. Don't say, "Locating a plant in Kraymore is a terrible idea because the people there are mostly students who would rather play than work and who don't have the ability to operate our machines." Such language not only offends but also obscures the facts and provokes emotional responses.

CAREER APPLICATIONS

1. When would you use vague language instead of concrete detail? Would this action be unethical or merely one form of emphasizing the positive?
2. Recent budget cuts have endangered the day-care program at your local branch of a national company, and the effect on employees is grave. You're writing a report for headquarters about the impact on employees. Describe the situation in a single sentence that reveals nothing about your personal feelings but that clearly shows your position.

Step 5: Analyzing and Interpreting Data

After you've completed your research, you're ready to analyze your data and interpret the findings. The analytical process is essentially a search for relationships among the facts and bits of evidence you've compiled. By themselves, the data you've collected won't offer much meaning or insight. It's the *analysis* of these facts and the *interpretation of the findings* that give you the information you need in order to understand or solve a problem.

Looking at the data from various angles, you attempt to detect patterns that will enable you to answer the questions outlined in your work plan. Your mind begins to fit pieces together and to form tentative conclusions. As your analysis proceeds, you either verify or reject each conclusion. Your mind constantly filters, sorts, and combines ideas; so this is where your critical thinking skills will be put to the test.

Analyze your results by calculating statistics, drawing reasonable and logical conclusions, and, if appropriate, developing a set of recommendations.

Calculating Statistics

Much of the information you compile during the research phase will be in numerical form. If data have been collected carefully, this information is precise, measurable, and objective–and therefore credible. However, raw statistics are of little practical value. The numbers must be manipulated so that you and your readers can interpret their significance.

AVERAGES

One useful way of looking at data is to find the **average,** which is a number that represents a group of numbers. Consider the data presented in Figure 13.6, for example, showing the sales booked by a group of nine salespeople over one week. To analyze this information, you could calculate the average–but which average? Depending on how you planned to use the data, you could choose the mean, the median, or the mode.

The same set of data can be used to produce three kinds of averages: mean, median, and mode.

The most commonly used average is the **mean**, or the sum of all the items in the group divided by the number of items in the group. The mean is useful when you want to compare one item or individual with the group. In the example, the mean is $7000. If you were the sales manager, you might well be interested in knowing that Wimper's sales were average; that Wilson, Green, and Carrick had below-average sales; and that Keeble, Kim, O'Toole, Makryk, and Caruso's sales were above average. One problem with using the mean, however, is that it can give you a false picture if one of the numbers is extreme. Say that Caruso's sales for the week were $27 000. The mean would then be $9000, and eight of the nine salespeople would be performing "below average."

The **median** is the "middle of the road" average: It's found at the midpoint of a series.[14] Above and below the median are an equal number of items. In a numerical ranking like the one shown in Figure 13.6, the median is the number right in the middle of the list: $7500. The median is useful when one (or a few) of the numbers is extreme. For example, even if Caruso's sales were $27 000, the median would still be $7500.

The **mode** is the number that occurs more often than any other in your sample.[15] It's the best average for answering a question such as "What is the usual amount?" If you wanted to know what level of sales was most common, you would answer with the mode, which is $8500. Like the median, the mode is not affected by extreme values. It's much easier to find than the median, however, when you have a large number of items or individuals.

FIGURE 13.6

Three Types of Averages: Mean, Median, and Mode

Salesperson	*Sales*	
Wilson	$ 3 000	
Green	5 000	
Carrick	6 000	
Wimper	7 000	Mean
Keeble	7 500	Median
Kim	8 500	Mode
O'Toole	8 500	Mode
Makryk	8 500	Mode
Caruso	9 000	
Total	$63 000	

While you're analyzing averages, you should also consider the **range**, or the spread of a series of numbers. In the example, the fact that sales per person ranged from $3000 to $9000 may raise the question of why there is such a wide gap between Wilson's performance and Caruso's. A range tells you the context in which the averages were calculated and demonstrates what values are possible.

TRENDS

Trend analysis involves an examination of data over time so that patterns and relationships can be detected.

If you were overseeing the work of Wilson, Caruso, and the other salespeople, you might be tempted to make some important personnel decisions on the basis of the week's sales figures. You would be a lot smarter, however, to compare them with sales figures from other weeks, looking for a **trend,** a steady upward or downward movement in a pattern of events taking place over time. By examining the pattern over a number of weeks, you could begin to see which salespeople were consistently above average and which were consistently below. You could also see whether sales for the group as a whole were increasing, declining, or remaining steady and whether there were any seasonal fluctuations in the sales pattern.

This type of trend analysis is very common in business. By looking at data over a period of time, you can detect patterns and relationships that will help you answer important questions.

CORRELATIONS

Once you have identified a trend, look for the cause. Say that Caruso consistently produces the most sales. You would undoubtedly be curious about the secret of her success. Does she call on her customers more often? Is she a more persuasive person? Does she have larger accounts or a bigger sales territory? Is she simply more experienced than the others?

A correlation is a statistical relationship between two or more variables.

To answer these questions, you could look for a **correlation,** a statistical relationship between two or more variables. For example, if salespeople with the largest accounts consistently produced the highest sales, you might assume that these two factors were correlated, or related in a predictable way. You might conclude that Caruso's success was due, at least in part, to the average size of her accounts.

However, your conclusion might be wrong. Correlations are useful evidence, but they do not necessarily prove a cause-and-effect relationship. Caruso's success might well be the result of several other factors. To know for sure, you would have to collect more evidence.

Drawing Conclusions

LEARNING OUTCOME 5
Draw sound conclusions and develop practical recommendations.

Regardless of how much evidence you amass, at some point in every analysis you move beyond hard facts that can be objectively measured and verified. When you reach that point, you begin to formulate a **conclusion,** which is a logical interpretation of what the facts in your report mean. Reaching good conclusions based on the evidence at hand is one of the most important skills you can develop for your business career. A sound conclusion meets the following criteria:

Conclusions are interpretations about what the facts mean.

- *It fulfills the original statement of purpose.* After all, this is why you took on the project in the first place.
- *It is based strictly on the information included in the rest of the report.* In other words, the conclusion must consider all the information in the report and no information not included in the report. While drawing a conclusion, you cannot introduce any new information. (If it's important, it should be in the body of the report.) Nor can you ignore any information in your report that doesn't support your conclusion.

➤ *It is logical.* People sometimes toss the word *logical* into a conversation without thinking much about its true meaning. For the purposes of writing a business report, a logical conclusion is one that follows accepted patterns of reasoning.

Reasoning falls into two distinct categories. With **inductive reasoning,** you arrive at a general conclusion after analyzing many specific pieces of evidence. If every one of your stores experienced a sales decline during a recent blizzard (specific evidence), you could reasonably conclude that harsh weather can have a negative effect on sales (general conclusion).

Deductive reasoning, in contrast, works from general principles to specific conclusions. This includes the classic form of argumentation called a **syllogism**, in which you state a general principle (the major premise), then a specific case (the minor premise), and then draw a conclusion based on the relationship of the two premises. Say that you study employee productivity problems and discover that radios distract some employees from their work. If you were to conclude that radios are affecting productivity, you could construct a syllogism such as this:

MAJOR PREMISE:	Things that distract employees reduce productivity (general principle).
MINOR PREMISE:	Radios are distracting employees (specific case).
CONCLUSION:	Therefore, radios reduce productivity.

Ian Hamilton, a communications manager at steel producer Dofasco, writes the company's annual environmental report. His close attention to all facets of the report's creation—research, writing, gathering and producing the visual support—exemplifies the numerous tasks involved in writing any business report.

To support your conclusion, you have to be able to demonstrate that both premises are true. In addition, you need to consider cause-and-effect relationships. Maybe it's not radios themselves that are distracting people but the fact that employees argue constantly about which stations to listen to. The music may in fact help relieve stress or boredom, if only you could get people to agree.

Conclusions need to be logical, but this doesn't mean they automatically flow from the evidence. Most business decisions require assumptions and judgments; relatively few are based strictly on the facts. Your personal values or the organization's values may also influence your conclusions; just be sure that you are conscious of how these biases may be affecting your judgment. Nor can you expect members of a team to examine the evidence and all arrive at the same conclusion. One of the key reasons for bringing additional people into a decision is to gain the value of their unique perspectives and experiences.

Developing Recommendations

Recommendations are suggestions for action.

Drawing a conclusion is one thing; deciding what to do about it and then recommending action is another. Recommendations are inappropriate in a report when you're not expected to supply them, so be sure you know the difference between conclusions and recommendations. Recall that a conclusion is an opinion or interpretation of what the facts mean; a **recommendation** suggests what ought to be done about the facts. Here's an example of the difference:

CONCLUSION	RECOMMENDATION
I conclude that on the basis of its track record and current price, this company is an attractive buy.	I recommend that we write a letter to the president offering to buy the company at a 10 percent premium over the market value of its stock.

When you've been asked to take the final step and translate your conclusions into recommendations, be sure to make the relationship between them clear. Keep in

BEHIND THE SCENES AT DOFASCO

Planning Environmental Performance Reports

Ian Hamilton writes for Dofasco, one of Canada's largest steel manufacturers. A manager in the corporate communications department, among his many projects Hamilton prepares the company's Environmental and Energy Report, an annual document that describes the firm's environmental policies and management. The report's audiences include environmental organizations, government environmental officials at both the federal and provincial levels, members of Dofasco's local communities, employees, shareholders, financial analysts, the media, and other companies in the steel industry. Dofasco's Environmental and Energy Report, explains Hamilton, is "a forum in which we communicate our progress to all stakeholders, outline our priorities, and demonstrate our commitment."

Dofasco's environmental performance reports are the result of careful planning and research, and the collaboration of many employees.

The report, which numbered 16 pages in 1999, is written by one person, but requires the input of numerous employees. Accordingly, this complex document, an artful combination of text, graphics, and photographs, demands a finely tuned overall plan to see the document from conception to completion. So one individual has the project-management function, making him responsible for the budget, creating the critical paths that focus the report and drive it to publication, delegating work and responsibilities, and keeping the external suppliers, such as the printer and designer, in touch and on schedule. Hamilton explains that the project-management function is essential for meeting deadlines: "They are very rigid because of reporting requirements."

Determining the overall theme is a first step in the planning process, and is critical, says Hamilton, "as it sets the tone for the coming year." The theme is developed collaboratively by Dofasco's Director of Communications and Public Affairs, senior communications staff, outside designers, and consultants. The ultimate approval comes from senior management.

Much of the research is primary. Employees involved in the report process interview Environment and Energy staff who have responsibility for specific areas, such as air, water, waste, and energy. These staff are asked to contribute important "stories," Hamilton explains, such as "new projects, accomplishments and/or shortcomings, as well as context for the stories. At these meetings, images and photos are also discussed." To facilitate the process of collecting and

mind that your assumptions and personal values may enter into your recommendations, but to be credible they must be based on logical analysis and sound conclusions.

Good recommendations are
- ✧ Practical
- ✧ Acceptable to readers
- ✧ Explained in enough detail for readers to take action

When you develop recommendations of your own, consider whether your suggestions are practical and acceptable to your readers; they're the people who have to make the recommendations work. Be certain that you have adequately described the steps that come next. Don't leave your readers scratching their heads and saying, "This all sounds good, but what do I do on Monday morning?"

Preparing the Final Outline

LEARNING OUTCOME 6
Develop a final outline and visual aid plan for your report.

Once you've completed your research and analysis, you can prepare the final outline of the report. Sometimes you can use the preliminary outline that guided your research as a final blueprint for the report. More often, however, you have to rework it to take into account your purpose, your audience's probable reactions, and the things you learned during your study. As already mentioned, you generally organize *informational reports* around topics suggested by the information itself, such as steps in a process, divisions of a company, or results in various geographical areas. On the other hand, your organization of an *analytical report* depends on the audience response you expect: if receptive, organize around conclusions or recommendations; if skeptical or hostile, organize around problem-solving approaches.

The final outline of the report should be geared to your purpose and the audience's probable reaction.

passing of information to Hamilton and his colleagues, a single contact person in the Environment and Energy area is designated to "coordinate the interviews, tabulate data, and maintain a knowledge of the overall report content." Other primary research involves reading the annual and environmental reports other companies produce, both within and outside the steel industry. They are studied not only to establish a benchmark for Dofasco's report, but also, Hamilton comments, to "stimulate new ideas or reinforce the approaches we are taking."

Another step in creating the E & E Report is to develop the design concepts by bringing in the expertise of external designers and printers. Designers also help with the outline and pagination. Visual support is another essential part of the document, such as the graphics and charts, "which can communicate complex information in a couple of square inches," Hamilton remarks. These are prepared by the relevant department; for example, finance prepares the financial charts. Photography is also a necessary component; a single photograph can transmit a complicated concept, such as "growth," "confidence," or "direction." Photos also "put a human face on the company, and in showing, not telling, what we do," says Hamilton. Dofasco's staff photographers may search the company's photo library, which houses "thousands and thousands of images" to find the right ones, or take new photographs. Hamilton notes that "Dofasco photographers and the report designers are consulted and engaged in the report process from Day One."

As the annual Environmental and Energy Report moves toward completion, its overall format and appearance are determined. As Hamilton observes, "structural considerations are a part of every long report. Introductions, theme pages, visuals, highlight and summary sections, sidebars, and other features are used throughout to provide a lot of explanation in a confined space, as well as to maintain reader interest by being both visually engaging and possessing a logical flow."

Ian Hamilton notes that Dofasco "has a long history of communicating with external stakeholders. Our position is simply this: we will be honest, forthright, and open to dialogue with our stakeholders, whether they are industry peers or a group of concerned local citizens In our reports, we try to paint an accurate picture of where we are, how we're performing, and, importantly, where we're going."

APPLY YOUR KNOWLEDGE

1. One of the biggest worries of anyone doing long reports is that the report may not see the light of day. List the circumstances that might lead to a long report's being tabled before it can be read. If you're responsible for the preparation of a long report, what could you do to prevent the circumstances you've listed?
2. If you were an intern at Dofasco assigned to do research using World Wide Web sources, how would you plan your task? What search engines would you use? How would you refine your search?

The placement of conclusions and recommendations depends on the audience's probable response. Put them up front if you expect a positive reaction, toward the end if you anticipate resistance.

The final outline is phrased so that the points on the outline can serve as the headings that appear in the report. Bear in mind that the phrasing of the headings will affect the tone of the report. If you want a hard-hitting, direct tone, use informative phrasing. If you prefer an objective, indirect tone, use descriptive phrasing. Be sure to use parallel construction when wording the points on the outline.

Visual aid: Illustration in tabular, graphic, schematic, or pictorial form.

Once you have an outline in mind, you can begin to identify which points can be, and should be, illustrated with visual aids–tables, graphs, schematic drawings, or photographs. (See Chapter 14 for more details on visual aids.) Ask yourself whether there is some way to visually dramatize the key elements of your message. You might approach the problem as though you were writing a picture book or making a movie. Think of each main point in your outline as a separate scene. Your job is to think of a picture, chart, or graph, that will communicate that point to the audience.

Then take your analysis a step further. Undoubtedly, some of the supporting items on your outline involve the presentation of detailed facts and figures. This sort of information may be confusing and tedious when presented in paragraph form. Often the best approach is to display it in a table, which arrays the data in a convenient format. You might want to use flowcharts, drawings, or photographs to clarify physical relationships or procedures.

Use visual aids to simplify, clarify, and emphasize important information.

When planning the illustrations for your report or presentation, aim to achieve a reasonable balance between the verbal and the visual. The ideal blend depends on the nature of the subject. Some topics are more graphic than others and require more visual aids. But remember that illustrating every point dilutes the effectiveness of all your visual aids. In a written report, particularly, too many visuals can be a problem. If readers are told in every paragraph or two to consult a table or chart, they are likely to lose the thread of the argument you are trying to make. Furthermore, readers tend to assume that the amount of space allocated to a topic indicates its relative importance. If you use visual aids to illustrate a minor point, you may be sending a misleading message about its significance.

ON THE JOB
Solving a Communication Dilemma at Harley-Davidson

Harley-Davidson had regained its reputation for building dependable motorcycles, but higher demand had created two new problems for CEO Jeffrey Bleustein: how to increase production and boost sales without sacrificing quality and how to stay on top in a world where mammoth motorcycles have become status symbols. The crux of Harley's new problem was that many customers simply aren't willing to wait two years for a motorcycle. Bleustein refused to risk disappointing Harley customers by compromising quality for quantity. To keep Harley on track toward higher sales, he and his management team needed to collect and analyze mountains of information, much of it in the form of reports.

One key to Harley's stunning turnaround in the late 1980s and early 1990s was its revamped manufacturing process. After analyzing information on Honda's manufacturing processes, the Harley staff had installed a system of inventory management known as just-in-time (JIT). Similar systems have propelled some of the world's leading manufacturers to success. By lowering the number of parts and supplies held in waiting, JIT enabled Harley to funnel more money into research to improve product quality and to speed up the manufacturing process.

But more research and faster processes weren't the only changes wrought by JIT. It forced Harley to change everything—from its purchasing practices to the layout of its factories. Harley forged cooperative relationships with a select group of suppliers who could deliver high-quality parts on time. In turn, these relationships enabled the company to cut costs and increase quality. Because Harley now uses fewer suppliers, it can place larger orders that qualify for bulk discounts. Also, Harley's design and production teams can work more closely with a smaller number of suppliers to ensure the quality of parts and supplies.

By redesigning its production machinery and creating more-standardized parts for multiple bike models, Harley can now build individual models in smaller batches that allow product upgrades more frequently and that boost quality by limiting defects to fewer parts. Reports help Harley management stay informed about the details they need to keep this lean-and-mean manufacturing process running smoothly.

Thanks to the emphasis on quality rather than quantity, Harley's share of the US heavyweight motorcycle market is up to 64 percent, well ahead of second-place Honda. As it continues to expand its production capacity, Harley is eager to gain additional market share in Europe and Japan.

Bleustein's strategy is built on three related initiatives: double production levels to more than 200 000 bikes a year by 2003, improve customer satisfaction to keep brand loyalty high, and improve and expand the worldwide dealer network. To double its manufacturing capacity, Harley expanded its three factories in Wisconsin and Pennsylvania. Modifying large, complex factories requires numerous reports, ranging from site selection analyses and environmental impact statements to staffing and training plans.

Reports also play a key role in Harley's efforts to improve customer satisfaction. For example, performance reports can help managers track customer satisfaction and complaint resolution. Research reports help product planners gauge customer expectations and competitive strengths. For instance, knowing that European customers balk at the prices that Harley gets in other markets, the company retooled its European product offerings with an eye toward less expensive models.

Last, Bleustein and other Harley managers rely on reports to help them make decisions and monitor progress in the effort to improve the dealer network. Among the improvements planned in this area is an Internet-based system that provides fast two-way communication between individual dealers and Harley factory personnel.[16]

Your Mission: Harley management realizes that to stay on top, Harley can't afford to grow complacent and forget how intense the competition is today. Executives are particularly interested in continuing to improve customer service at Harley dealerships around the world. As a manager at Harley-Davidson's head office, you've been asked to plan a report that will outline ways to increase customer satisfaction by improving customer service. You'll need to conduct the necessary research, analyze the findings, and present your recommendations. From the following, choose the best responses, and be prepared to explain why your choices are best.

1. Which of the following represents the most appropriate statement of purpose for this study?

a. The purpose of this study is to identify any customer service problems in Harley-Davidson's worldwide dealer network.
b. This study answers the following question: "What improvements in customer service can our dealers make in order to increase overall customer satisfaction?"
c. This study identifies those dealers in the worldwide network who are most responsible for poor customer satisfaction.
d. This study identifies steps that dealers should take to change customer service practices.

2. You have tentatively identified the following factors for analysis:

I. To improve customer service, we need to hire more salespeople
   A. Compute competitors' employee-to-sales ratio
   B. Compute our employee-to-sales ratio
II. To improve customer service, we need to hire better salespeople
   A. Assess skill level of competitors' salespeople
   B. Assess skill level of our salespeople
III. To improve customer service, we need to retrain our salespeople
   A. Review competitors' training programs
   B. Review our training programs
IV. To improve customer service, we need to compensate and motivate our people differently
   A. Assess competitors' compensation levels and motivational techniques
   B. Assess our compensation levels and motivational techniques

Should you proceed with the investigation on the basis of this preliminary outline, or should you consider other approaches to factoring the problem?

a. Proceed with this outline.
b. Do not proceed. Factor the problem by asking customers how they perceive Harley's current customer service efforts. In addition, ask dealers what they think they should be doing differently.
c. Do not proceed. Factor the problem by considering what successful car dealers do in terms of customer service.
d. Do not proceed. Factor the problem by considering what the rest of the company, aside from the dealers, could be doing to improve customer service.

3. Which of the following work plans is the best option for guiding your study of ways to improve customer service?

a. Version One

Statement of Problem: As part of Harley-Davidson's continuing efforts to offer the most attractive heavyweight motorcycles in the world, Jeffrey Bleustein wants to improve customer service at the dealer level. The challenge here is to identify service improvements that are meaningful and valuable to the customer without being too expensive or time consuming.

Purpose and Scope of Work: The purpose of this study is to identify ways to increase customer satisfaction by improving customer service at our dealerships worldwide. A four-member study team, composed of the vice-president of marketing and three dealers, has been appointed to prepare a written service-improvement plan. To accomplish this objective, this study will survey customers to learn what changes they'd like to see in terms of customer service. The team will analyze these potential improvements in terms of cost and time requirements and then will design new service procedures that dealers can use to better satisfy customers.

Sources and Methods of Data Collection and Analysis: The study team will assess current dealer efforts by (1) querying dealership employees regarding their customer service, (2) observing employees in action dealing with customers, (3) surveying current Harley owners regarding their purchase experiences, and (4) surveying visitors to dealerships who decide not to purchase Harleys (by intercepting a sample of these people as they leave the dealerships). The team will also visit competitive dealerships to determine first-hand how they treat customers, and the team will mail questionnaires to a sample of registered motorcycle owners and classify the results by brand name. Once all these data have been collected, the team will analyze them to determine where buyers and potential buyers consider customer service to be lacking. Finally, the team will design procedures to meet their expectations.

<u>Schedule:</u>

Query dealer employees	Jan 10–Jan 20
Observe employees in action	Jan 21–Jan 30
Survey current Harley owners	Jan 15–Feb 15
Survey non-buyers at dealerships	Jan 20–Jan 30
Visit competitive dealerships	Jan 31–Feb 15
Conduct mail survey of registered owners	Jan 15–Feb 15
Analyze data	Feb 15–Mar 1
Draft new procedures	Mar 2–Mar 15
Prepare final report	Mar 16–Mar 25
Present to management/ dealer committee	Mar 28

b. Version Two

Statement of Problem: Harley's dealerships need to get on the ball in terms of customer service, and we need to tell them what to do in order to fix their customer-service shortcomings.

Purpose and Scope of Work: This report will address how we plan to solve the problem. We'll design new customer-service procedures and prepare a written report that dealers can learn from.

Sources and Methods of Data Collection: We plan to employ the usual methods of collecting data, including direct observation and surveys.

Schedule:

Collect data	Jan 10–Feb 15
Analyze data	Feb 15–Mar 1
Draft new procedures	Mar 2–Mar 15
Prepare final report	Mar 16–Mar 25
Present to management/ dealer committee	Mar 28

c. Version Three

Task 1–Query dealer employees: We will interview a sampling of dealership employees to find out what steps they take to ensure customer satisfaction. Dates: Jan 10–Jan 20

Task 2–Observe employees in action: We will observe a sampling of dealership employees as they work with potential buyers and current owners, in order to learn first-hand what steps employees typically take. Dates: Jan 21–Jan 30

Task 3–Survey current Harley owners: Using a sample of names from Harley's database of current owners, we'll ask owners how they felt about the purchase process when they bought their bikes and how they feel they've been treated since then. We'll also ask them to suggest steps we could take to improve service. Dates: Jan 15–Feb 15

Task 4–Survey non-buyers at dealerships: While we are observing dealership employees, we will also approach people who visit dealerships but leave without making a purchase. In the parking lot, we'll go through a quick survey, asking them what they think about Harley's customer service policies and practices and whether these had any bearing on their decisions not to buy a Harley. Dates: Jan 21–Jan 30

Task 5–Visit competitive dealerships: Under the guise of shoppers looking for new motorcycles, we will visit a selection of competitive dealerships to discover how they treat customers and whether they offer any special services that Harley doesn't. Dates: Jan 31–Feb 15

Task 6–Conduct mail survey of registered owners: Using vehicle registration files from several provinces, we will survey a sampling of motorcycle owners (of all brands). We will then sort the answers by brand of bike owned to see which dealers are offering which services. Dates: Jan 15–Feb 15

Task 7–Analyze data: Once we've collected all these data, we'll analyze them to identify (1) services that customers would like to see Harley dealers offer, (2) services offered by competitors that aren't offered by Harley dealers, and (3) services currently offered by Harley dealers that may not be all that important to customers. Dates: Feb 15–Mar 1

Task 8–Draft new procedures: From the data we've analyzed, we'll select new services that should be considered by Harley dealers. We'll also assess the time and money burdens that these services are likely to present, so that dealers can see whether each new service will yield a positive return on investment. Dates: Mar 2–Mar 15

Task 9–Prepare final report: This is essentially a documentation task, during which we'll describe our work, make our recommendations, and prepare a formal report. Dates: Mar 16–Mar 25

Task 10–Present to management/dealer committee: We'll summarize our findings and recommendations and will make the full report available to dealers at the quarterly meeting. Date: Mar 28

d. Version Four

Problem: To identify meaningful customer service improvements that can be implemented by Harley dealers.

Data Collection: Use direct observation and surveys to gather details about customer service at Harley dealers and at competing dealers. Have the study team survey current Harley owners, talk with people who visited Harley dealerships but did not buy, and send a questionnaire to registered motorcycle owners.

Schedule:

Step 1:	Data collection. Work will begin on January 10 and end on February 15.
Step 2:	Data analysis. Work will start on February 15 and end on March 1.
Step 3:	Drafting new procedures. Work will start on March 2 and end on March 15.
Step 4:	Preparation of the final report. Work will start on March 16 and end on March 25.
Step 5:	Presentation of the final report. The report will be presented to management and the dealer committee on March 28.

4. Assume that your survey results indicate that BMW motorcycle dealers rank highest in terms of customers' satisfaction with the treatment they received while buying motorcycles. Which of the following conclusions can you safely draw from this result?

a. Harley needs to improve its customer service.

b. BMW sells the most motorcycles in the regions of the country covered by the survey.

c. Because BMW is not one of the world's leading motorcycle manufacturers, customer service is not very important.

d. None of the above.

TAP Your Knowledge

Summary of Learning Outcomes

1. Develop a statement defining the problem to be solved and a statement defining the purpose of the report. You narrow the focus of your investigation when you define the problem. The problem is the matter you intend to deal with, whether you're gathering information, supporting a decision, or solving a problem. The statement of purpose defines the objective of the report, or what the report should accomplish.

2. Identify and outline the issues that have to be analyzed during your study. Identifying the issues your report will investigate is called *problem factoring*. Informational reports, studies that emphasize discovering and reporting facts, may be factored by subtopic. These subtopics may be arranged by importance, sequence, chronology, spatial orientation, geography, or category. Studies that focus on problem solving may be structured around hypotheses that you may prove or disprove during your investigation. *Hypotheses* are potential explanations that need to be tested. Outlining the issues will help you organize your study. When outlining, decide on an outline format and follow the rules of division to ensure that your study will be organized in a logical, systematic way.

3. Prepare a work plan for conducting the investigation. A work plan identifies the tasks you will perform and will help you not only produce quality reports, but also to do so efficiently. A formal work plan includes the following elements: (1) a statement of the problem; (2) a statement of the purpose and scope of your investigation; (3) discussion of the sequence of tasks to be accomplished; (4) description of the end products that will result from the investigation; (5) review of project assignments, schedules, and resource requirements; (6) plans for following up after the report is delivered.

4. Organize the research phase of the investigation, including the identification of secondary and primary sources of data. To work efficiently, create a work plan that reviews the problem, purpose, and sources and methods of data collection for your report. Conduct your secondary research by locating information that has already been collected; use electronic databases on CD-ROM and the Internet to expedite your search. Be sure your sources are up to date and objective. Conduct primary research by collecting information yourself. Documentary evidence and historical records are sources of primary data. Surveys such as face-to-face or telephone interviews and printed or computer-based questionnaires are methods for discovering what a cross-section of people think about something. Experiments are more common in technical fields than in business, but may be used in the workplace to gather primary evidence.

5. Draw sound conclusions and develop practical recommendations. A conclusion is a logical interpretation of what the facts mean. A sound conclusion meets the following criteria: (1) it fulfills the original statement of purpose; (2) it is based strictly on the information included in the rest of the report; (3) it is logical, following an accepted pattern of reasoning. A recommendation is a suggestion for action. When writing recommendations, be sure to base them on logical analysis and sound conclusions. Recommendations should be described in enough detail for the reader to take action.

6. Develop a final outline and visual aid plan for your report. The final outline of your report should be geared to your purpose and the audience's probable reaction. The final outline should be phrased so that the points can serve as the headings that appear in the report. After writing your outline, identify the points that should be illustrated with graphs, tables, diagrams, or photographs. Use visual support to simplify, clarify, and emphasize important information.

Test Your Knowledge

Review Questions

1. What questions should you ask to understand the problem you're trying to solve in your report?
2. Distinguish between a problem statement and a statement of purpose.
3. Define "hypothesis."
4. What are the differences in how informational assignments and analytical assignments are factored?
5. What are the rules of division in outlining? Why are they important?
6. Why is it important to have a work plan?
7. How do you determine the integrity of your sources?
8. What is a Boolean search?
9. What guidelines should you follow to produce valid survey results?
10. What is a trend? What is a correlation?

Apply Your Knowledge

Critical Thinking Questions

1. What are the advantages and disadvantages of knowing a lot about the problem you are researching? Explain.
2. Analyze any recent school or work assignment that required you to conduct research. Was the assignment informational, analytical, or a mix? How did you approach your investigation? Did you rely mostly on primary or on secondary sources? Now that you've studied this chapter, can you identify two ways to improve the research techniques you used during that assignment? Briefly explain.
3. Imagine you've detected a correlation in the trend data collected for an analytical report. What kind of research might help you determine whether a cause-and-effect relationship exists between the two variables? Why?
4. Put yourself in the position of a manager who is supervising an investigation but doing very little of the research personally. Why would a work plan be especially useful to the manager? To the researcher? Explain.
5. If you have a clear and detailed statement of purpose, why do you need a problem statement as well? Would it be a good idea to combine the two? Why or why not?
6. After an exhaustive study of an important problem, you have reached a conclusion that you know your company's management will reject. What do you do? Explain your answer.

Practise Your Knowledge

Exercises

1. Select any public company and find the following information:
   a. Names of the company's current officers
   b. List of the company's products or services
   c. Current issues in the company's industry
   d. Outlook for the company's industry as a whole
2. You're getting ready to launch a new lawn-care business offering mowing, fertilizing, weeding, and other services. The lawn surrounding a nearby shopping centre looks like it could use better care, so you target that business for your first sales proposal. To help prepare this proposal, write your answers to these questions:
   a. What problem statement and statement of purpose would be most appropriate? (Think about the reader's viewpoint.)
   b. What questions will you need answered before you can write a proposal to solve the reader's problem? Be as specific as possible.
   c. Will you conduct primary or secondary research? Why? What sources will you use?
   d. What conclusions and recommendations might be practical, acceptable to the reader, and specific enough for the shopping centre to take action? (Think about the purpose of the report.)
3. Now turn the situation around and assume that you're the shopping centre's facilities manager. You report to the general manager, who must approve any new contracts for lawn service. Before you contract for lawn care, you want to prepare a formal study of the current state of your lawn's health. The report will include conclusions and recommendations for your boss's consideration. Draft a work plan, including the problem statement, the statement of purpose and scope, a description of what will result from your investigation, the sources and methods of data collection, and a preliminary outline.
4. Assume that your university president has received many student complaints about campus parking problems. You are appointed to chair a student committee organized to investigate the problems and recommend solutions. The president turns over to you the file labelled "Parking: Complaints from Students," and you jot down the essence of the complaints as you inspect the contents. Your notes look like this:
   - Inadequate student spaces at critical hours
   - Poor night lighting near the computer centre
   - Inadequate attempts to keep resident neighbours from occupying spaces
   - Dim marking lines
   - Motorcycles taking up full spaces
   - Discourteous security officers

- Spaces (usually empty) reserved for university officials
- Relatively high parking fees
- Full fees charged to night students even though they use the lots only during low-demand periods
- Vandalism to cars and a sense of personal danger
- Inadequate total space
- Resident harassment of students parking on the street in front of neighbouring houses

Your first job is to organize for committee discussion four or five areas that include all (or most) of these specific complaints. Choose the main headings for your outline, and group these specific complaints under them.

5. As the new manager at The Gap clothing store, located in your local mall, you've been assigned to research and write a factual report about the day-to-day variations in store sales throughout a typical week. What's the most logical way to factor this problem and structure your informational report? Why? Indicate the subtopics you might use in your report.

6. You're getting ready to write a research paper on a topic of your choice. You decide to search for information using both the library databases and the Internet. Develop a search strategy.

a. What are some key words and phrases you might use?

b. Which Boolean operators would you use to narrow your search?

7. Deciding how to collect primary data is an important part of the research process. Which one or more of the five methods of data collection (examining documents, making observations, surveying people, conducting experiments, and performing interviews) would you use if you were researching these questions?

a. Has the litter problem on campus been reduced since the cafeteria began offering fewer take-out choices this year than in past years?

b. Has the school attracted more transfer students since it waived the formal application process and allowed students at other schools to send in transcripts with a one-page letter of application?

c. Have the number of traffic accidents at the school's main entrance been reduced since a traffic light was installed?

d. Has student satisfaction with the campus bookstore improved now that students can order their books over the Internet and pick them up at several campus locations?

8. After years of work, you've almost completed your first motion picture, the story of a group of unknown musicians finding work and making a reputation in a difficult world. Unfortunately, some of your friends leave the first complete screening saying that the 132-minute movie is simply too long. Others can't imagine any more editing cuts. You decide to test the movie on a regular audience, members of which will be asked to complete a questionnaire that may or may not lead to additional editing. You obtain permission from a local theatre manager to show your film at 4:30 and 8:30, after the regularly scheduled matinee and after the evening show. Design a questionnaire that can solicit valid answers.

9. Visit the Xerox Web site at **www.xerox.ca** and carefully review the products and services discussed on the site. Prepare a survey instrument that Xerox could use for customer feedback on these products. Remember to avoid questions that are leading, and pretest your questionnaire on family and friends before submitting it to your instructor.

10. Your company operates a Web site featuring children's games and puzzles. The vice-president of marketing needs to know more about the children who visit the site so she can plan new products. She has asked you to develop an online survey questionnaire to collect the data. What ethical issues do you see in this situation? What should you do?

11. Some students on your campus have complained about the high cost of textbooks. Team up with three other students to study the average cost of the textbooks purchased by students in this class. Start by designing a survey; then conduct the research, tabulate your results, and report the findings.

a. List the survey questions you'll ask and decide whether you'll interview the students or ask them to write down their own answers.

b. Pretest the questionnaire on several students to see whether the questions make sense.

c. Conduct the research.

d. Analyze the survey answers by determining the mean, median, and mode of the amounts spent on textbooks.

e. Write a one- or two-page summary of your findings, including an interpretation of the data you've gathered.

12. Your boss has asked you to analyze and report on your division's sales for the first nine months of this year. Using the following data from company invoices, calculate the mean for each quarter and all averages for the year to date. Then identify and discuss the quarterly sales trends.

January	$24 600	**June**	$26 800
February	25 900	**July**	29 900
March	23 000	**August**	30 500
April	21 200	**September**	26 600
May	24 600		

13. Because of the success of your pizza delivery service, you're considering whether to expand. You'll need at least one additional delivery van if you expand, but you know that buying a van will lead to other expenses, such as maintenance, insurance, and so on. Before you can make a decision, you want to factor the problem and develop an outline to guide your investigation. As you do so, include a list of at least six questions to research and answer.

14. You're the advertising manager at a regional ice cream company. Your boss, the director of marketing, has asked you to report on how the company should use advertising to support new-product introductions, using this statement of purpose:

Statement of purpose: To analyze various methods of advertising new products when they are introduced and to recommend the most effective and cost-efficient program

a. How should you factor this problem? Will you use descriptive or informative headings for your preliminary outline?

b. Develop an outline, following the rules of division.

c. Exchange outlines with a student in your class and evaluate each other's work. Comment on the organization, the logic, the consistency, and the completeness of the other student's outline. On the basis of the suggestions you receive, revise your own outline.

15. Now put yourself on the other side of the desk: You're the regional ice cream company's director of marketing. Your advertising manager has submitted a full report, and you're reviewing the conclusions. Identify and discuss the errors of logic underlying the following conclusions and recommendations in the report:

a. As soon as we started advertising the new Apricot Swirl on television, sales increased, so we need to advertise every new fruit-flavoured product on television.

b. Coupons really work, and if we don't use them to promote every new product we introduce, they will all fail.

c. Newspaper advertising didn't help Apricot Swirl, so let's not use it on any other new-product launch.

d. Peanut Swirl isn't as good a flavour as the other new products, so it shouldn't receive the same extensive advertising support.

Developing Your Internet Skills

Going Online: Search Thousands of Full-Text Articles Instantly, p. 348

You can test the search results of the Electronic Library without signing up even as a trial subscriber. Pick a topic you're required to research for a sample report and enter your key words or phrase. Choose the sources you want to search–newspapers and newswires, books, magazines, photo archives, and so forth. Now review the resulting list. (If you want to sign on as a trial subscriber, you will then be able to read the articles and view any photos. Otherwise, you should be able to make a comparative evaluation by reviewing the list.) How did your search results differ from results obtained from an ordinary search engine? Do you think this kind of information would be useful to you? How could you narrow or qualify your search to reap the kind of results that would be helpful?

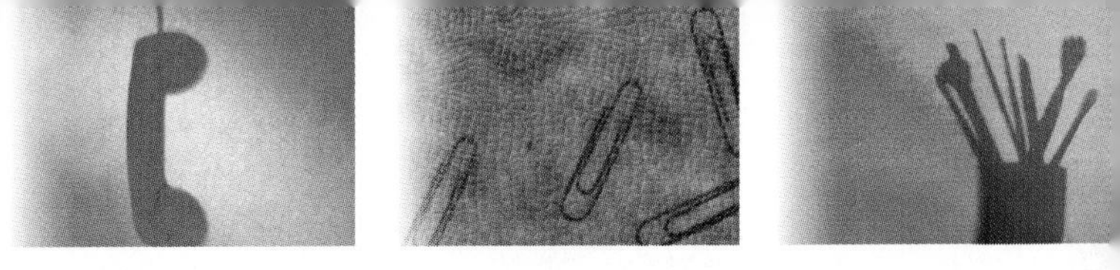

CHAPTER 14

Completing Formal Reports and Proposals

AFTER STUDYING THIS CHAPTER, YOU WILL BE ABLE TO

1. Describe how organizations produce formal reports and proposals
2. Explain all the prefatory parts of a formal report
3. Describe four important functions of a formal report's introduction, and identify the possible topics it might include
4. Explain how to incorporate visual support into your text
5. Discuss the four areas of specific information that must be covered in the body of a proposal

ON THE JOB
Facing a Communication Dilemma at Levi Strauss

Placing a High Value on Reports

Levi Strauss and Company is famous for taking both business ethics and business communication seriously. Former long-serving chairman and CEO Robert Haas, who is also the great-great-grandnephew of the firm's founder, Levi Strauss, defined Levi's goal as "responsible commercial success." In other words, he envisioned his company as being run according to principles such as teamwork, trust, ethical management, environment care, diversity, and individual respect.

Haas recognized the importance of communicating his vision throughout the company, to customers, and in the community. In fact, effective communication is one of the company's fundamental values, affecting everything from personal interactions to community relations.

Employees at Levi Strauss and Company know how important it is to produce reports that are easily understood, logical, attractive, persuasive, and thorough. So they include all the necessary components to accomplish these goals.

One way to communicate such a complex vision is through reports. So Haas made sure he knew everything he could about developing reports that were clear and well organized, and that contained all the elements necessary to promote easy understanding.

During his years as CEO, Haas created reports and relied on them to make decisions and to set company policy. If you were the current CEO at Levi Strauss, Philip Marineau, how would you approach the challenge of communicating complex ideas and issues? What steps would you take to make sure an audience gets what it needs from long reports? What features would you include to help readers find and understand the information in your reports? And how would you use reports in your own decision making?[1]

Report Production

LEARNING OUTCOME 1
Describe how organizations produce formal reports and proposals.

Experienced business communicators such as CEOs Robert Hass and Philip Marineau realize that planning a report or proposal, conducting the necessary research, developing visual aids, organizing the ideas, and drafting the text are demanding and time-consuming tasks. They also know that the process of writing a report or proposal doesn't end with these steps. After careful editing and rewriting, you still need to produce a polished final version.

How the final version is actually produced depends on the nature of your organization. Traditionally, company teams produced reports–secretaries and support personnel handled the typing, formatting, and routine tasks. For important, high-visibility reports, a graphics department would often help with charts, drawings, covers, and other visual elements.

In organizations that produce many reports and proposals, the preparation process often involves teamwork.

However, as personal computers have become commonplace in the business office, more and more employees are expected to handle most or even all of the formatting and production of their own reports. Many of the advances in computer hardware and software have been designed specifically to give all business people the ability to produce great-looking reports by themselves. The good news is that, with some practice, report writers can develop expertise with software suites such as Microsoft Office or Corel WordPerfect Office, and produce reports that may include graphics, tables, spreadsheet data, and even database records. With the advent of low-cost scanners and colour printers, it is easy to include photographs as well. Used effectively, colour helps improve both the reader's interest in your material and the effectiveness of your message.

Personal computers can automatically handle many of the mechanical aspects of report preparation.

The bad news is that continually improving computer tools increase your audience's expectations. People are impressed by packaging, so a handsomely bound report with full-colour graphics may influence many readers more than a plain, typewriter-style report containing exactly the same information. To make matters even more challenging, paper reports are starting to compete with various multimedia electronic reports, such as Web sites and CD-ROMs. Instead of producing a lengthy report full of tables and other information, you can now provide the information electronically and let readers pick and choose what they want to read.

No matter which tools you use, make sure you leave enough time for formatting and production. Murphy's law (which says that if something can go wrong, it will) applies to just about every aspect of using computers. Data communication problems, incompatible or corrupted disk files, printing problems, and other glitches can consume hours. You don't want computer trouble to sabotage all your thinking, planning, and writing, so make sure you can create and produce the report before the deadline.

Be sure to schedule enough time to turn out a document that looks professional.

Be sure to save your work frequently and to back it up to a floppy disk. Many report writers have gone through the agony of recreating lost work because they didn't follow this simple rule.

Once you've completed a major report and sent it off to your audience, you'll naturally expect a positive response, and quite often you'll get one–but not always. You may get halfhearted praise or no action on your conclusions and recommendations, or you may get some serious criticism. Try to learn from these experiences.

Ask for feedback, and learn from your mistakes.

Even worse, you may get no response at all. If you don't hear from your readers within a week or two, you might want to ask politely whether the report arrived. In hopes of stimulating a response, you might also offer to answer any questions or provide additional information.

Regardless of how the final product is produced, it will be up to you to make sure that all necessary components are included. Depending on the length and formality of your report, various prefatory and supplementary parts may be necessary. The more formal your report, the more components you'll include.

Components of a Formal Report

A formal report's manuscript format and impersonal tone convey an impression of professionalism. A formal report can be either short (fewer than ten pages) or long (ten pages or more). It can be informational or analytical, direct or indirect. It may be directed to readers inside or outside the organization. What sets a formal report apart from other reports is its polish.

A formal report conveys the impression that the subject is important.

The parts included in a report depend on the type of report you're writing, the requirements of your audience, the organization you're working for, and the length of your report. The components listed in Figure 14.1 fall into three categories, depending on where they are found in a report: prefatory parts, text of the report, and supplementary parts. For an illustration of how the various parts fit together, see Linda Moreno's Electrovision report in "In-Depth Critique: Analyzing a Formal Report," starting on page 390.

The three basic divisions of a formal report:

- Prefatory parts
- Text
- Supplementary parts

When a particular section is designed to stand apart, it generally starts on a new page, and the following material starts on a new page as well. Most prefatory parts (such as the table of contents, for example) should be placed on their own pages. Often, however, the parts in the text of the report need not stand alone. If your introduction is only a paragraph long, don't bother with a page break before moving into the body of your report. If the introduction runs longer than a page, however, a page break can signal the reader that a major shift is about to occur in the flow of the report.

FIGURE 14.1
Parts of a Formal Report

PREFATORY PARTS	TEXT OF THE REPORT	SUPPLEMENTARY PARTS
Cover	Introduction	Appendices
Title fly	Body	Bibliography
Title page	Summary	Index
Request for proposal	Conclusions	
Letter of transmittal	Recommendations	
Table of contents	Notes	
List of illustrations	Visual aids	
Synopsis or executive summary		

LEARNING OUTCOME 2
Explain all the prefatory parts of a formal report.

Prefatory Parts

Although the prefatory parts are placed before the text of the report, you may choose to write them after you've written the text. Many of these parts–such as the table of contents, list of illustrations, and executive summary–are easier to prepare after the text is complete because they directly reflect the contents. Other parts can be prepared at almost any time.

COVER

Many companies have standard covers for reports, made of heavy paper and imprinted with the company's name and logo. Report titles are either printed on these covers or attached with adhesive labels. If your company has no standard covers, you can usually find something suitable in a good stationery store. Make sure it can be labelled with the report title, the writer's name (optional), and the submission date (also optional).

Put a title on the cover that is informative but not too long.

Think carefully about the title you put on the cover. A business report is not a mystery novel, so give your readers all the information they need: the who, what, when, where, why, and how of the subject. At the same time, try to be reasonably concise. You don't want to intimidate your audience with a title that's too long, awkward, or unwieldy. One approach is to use a subtitle. You can reduce the length of your title by eliminating phrases such as *A report of, A study of,* and *A survey of.*

TITLE FLY AND TITLE PAGE

The **title fly** is a plain sheet of paper with only the title of the report on it. While the title fly may seem redundant, some situations require them because they enhance the formality of the report.

The title page usually includes four blocks of information.

The **title page** includes four blocks of information, as shown in Moreno's Electrovision report: (1) the title of the report; (2) the name, title, and address of the person, group, or organization that authorized the report (usually the intended audience); (3) the name, title, and address of the person, group, or organization that prepared the report; and (4) the date on which the report was submitted. On some title pages the second block of information is preceded by the words *Prepared for* or *Submitted to,* and the third block of information is preceded by *Prepared by* or *Submitted by.* In some cases the title page serves as the cover of the report, especially if the report is relatively short and intended solely for internal use.

LETTER OF AUTHORIZATION AND LETTER OF ACCEPTANCE

A letter of authorization usually follows the direct-request plan.

If you were authorized in writing to prepare the report, you may want to include in your report the letter or memo of authorization (and sometimes even the letter or memo of acceptance). The **letter of authorization** (or *memo of authorization*) is a document requesting that a report be prepared. It normally follows the direct-request plan described in Chapter 8, and it typically specifies the problem, scope, time and money restrictions, special instructions, and due date.

The **letter of acceptance** (or *memo of acceptance*) acknowledges the assignment to conduct the study and to prepare the report. Following the good-news plan, the acceptance confirms time and money restrictions and other pertinent details. This document is rarely included in reports.

A letter of authorization usually follows the direct-request plan.

LETTER OF TRANSMITTAL

The **letter of transmittal** (or *memo of transmittal*) conveys your report to your audience. The letter of transmittal says what you'd say if you were handing the report directly to the person who authorized it, so the style is less formal than the rest of the report. For example, the letter would use personal pronouns (*you, I, we*) and conversational language. Moreno's Electrovision report includes a one-page transmittal memo from Moreno to her boss (the person who requested the report).

Use a less formal style for the letter of transmittal than for the report itself.

In general, the transmittal letter appears right before the table of contents. However, if your report will be widely distributed, you may decide to include the letter of transmittal only in selected copies, in order to make certain comments to a specific audience. If your report discusses layoffs or other issues that affect people in the organization, you might want to discuss your recommendations privately in a letter of transmittal to top management. If your audience is likely to be skeptical of or even hostile to something in your report, the transmittal letter is a good opportunity to acknowledge their concerns and explain how the report addresses the issues they care about.

The letter of transmittal follows the routine and good-news plans described in Chapter 9. Begin with the main idea, officially conveying the report to the readers and summarizing its purpose. Such a letter typically begins with a statement like "Here is the report you asked me to prepare on ..." The rest includes information about the scope of the report, the methods used to complete the study, and the limitations that became apparent. In the middle section of the letter you may also highlight important points or sections of the report, make comments on side issues, give suggestions for follow-up studies, and offer any details that will help readers better understand and use the report. You may also wish to acknowledge help given by others. The concluding paragraph is a note of thanks for having been given the report assignment, an expression of willingness to discuss the report, and an offer to assist with future projects.

Use the good-news plan for a letter of transmittal.

If the report does not have a synopsis, the letter of transmittal may summarize the major findings, conclusions, and recommendations. This material would be placed after the opening of the letter.

The synopsis of short reports is often included in the letter of transmittal.

TABLE OF CONTENTS

The table of contents indicates in outline form the coverage, sequence, and relative importance of the information in the report. In fact, the headings used in the text of the report are the basis for the table of contents. Depending on the length and complexity of the report, your contents page may show only the top two or three levels of headings, sometimes only first-level headings. Of course, excluding some levels of headings may frustrate readers who want to know where to find every subject you cover. On the other hand, a simpler table of contents helps readers focus on the major points. No matter how many levels you include, make sure readers can easily distinguish between them (see the table of contents in the Electrovision report, p. 393).

The table of contents outlines the text and lists prefatory and supplementary parts.

Be sure the headings in the table of contents match up perfectly with the headings in the text.

The table of contents is prepared after the other parts of the report have been typed so that the beginning page numbers for each heading can be shown. The headings should be worded exactly as they are in the text of the report. Also listed on the contents page are the prefatory parts (only those that follow the contents page) and the supplementary parts. If you have fewer than four visual aids, you may wish to list them in the table of contents too; but if you have four or more visual aids, show them separately in a list of illustrations.

LIST OF ILLUSTRATIONS

For simplicity's sake, some reports refer to all visual aids as illustrations or exhibits. In other reports, as in Moreno's Electrovision report, tables are labelled separately from other types of visual aids, which are called figures. Regardless of the system used to label visual aids, the list of illustrations gives their titles and page numbers.

Put the list of illustrations on a separate page if it won't all fit on one page with the table of contents; start the list of figures and the list of tables on separate pages if they won't both fit on one page.

If you have enough space on a single page, include the list of illustrations directly beneath the table of contents. Otherwise, include the list on a separate page following the contents page. When tables and figures are numbered separately, they should also be listed separately. The two lists can appear on the same page if they fit; otherwise, start each list on a separate page.

SYNOPSIS OR EXECUTIVE SUMMARY

Provide an overview of the report in a synopsis or an executive summary.

A **synopsis** is a brief overview (one page or less) of a report's most important points, designed to give readers a quick preview of the contents. It's often included in long informational reports dealing with technical, professional, or academic subjects and can also be called an *abstract*. Because it's a concise representation of the whole report, it may be distributed separately to a wide audience; interested readers can then order a copy of the entire report.

Linking from Introduction to Topic Title

EFFECTIVE E-BUSINESS COMMUNICATION

A report's introduction gives readers just a brief overview of the main points covered. Readers who want more information must then flip back to the table of contents to locate the right page within the body. On the Web, however, your introduction can include links to bring readers directly to the report sections covering main points. For example, when the AT&T Foundation posted an executive summary of its philanthropic activities on the Web, it added links labelled "more" to encourage readers to click for more details on each activity.

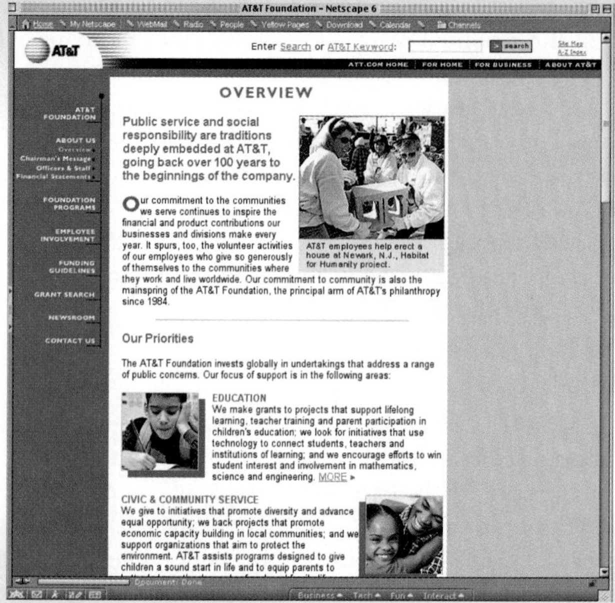

CAREER APPLICATIONS

1. Besides the table of contents, in what other prefatory parts of an online report would readers appreciate seeing links to more information?
2. How could you use links in the bibliography of an online report?

The phrasing of a synopsis can be either informative or descriptive, depending on whether the report is in direct or indirect order. In an informative synopsis, you present the main points of the report in the order in which they appear in the text. A descriptive synopsis, on the other hand, simply tells what the report is about, in only moderately greater detail than the table of contents; the actual findings of the report are omitted. Here are examples of statements from each type:

An informative synopsis summarizes the main ideas; a descriptive synopsis states what the report is about.

INFORMATIVE SYNOPSIS: Sales of super-premium ice cream make up 11 percent of the total ice cream market.

DESCRIPTIVE SYNOPSIS: This report contains information about super-premium ice cream and its share of the market.

The way you handle a synopsis reflects the approach you use in the text. If you're using an indirect approach in your report, you're better off with a descriptive synopsis. An informative synopsis, with its focus on conclusions and key points, may be too confrontational if you have a skeptical audience. You don't want to spoil the effect by providing a controversial beginning. No matter which type of synopsis you use, however, be sure to present an accurate picture of the report's contents.[2]

Use a descriptive synopsis for a skeptical or hostile audience, an informative synopsis for most other situations.

Many business report writers prefer to include an executive summary instead of a synopsis or an abstract. A synopsis is essentially a prose table of contents that outlines the main points of the report; an **executive summary** is a fully developed "mini" version of the report itself, intended for readers who lack the time or motivation to study the complete text. So an executive summary is more comprehensive than a synopsis, often as much as 10 percent as long as the report itself.

Put enough information in an executive summary so that an executive can make a decision without reading the entire report.

Unlike a synopsis, an executive summary may contain headings, well-developed transitions, and even visual aids. It is often organized in the same way as the report, using a direct or an indirect approach, depending on the audience's receptivity. However, executive summaries can also deviate from the sequence of material in the report.

After reading the summary, audience members know the essentials of the report and are in a position to make a decision. Later, when time permits, they may read certain parts of the report to obtain additional detail. See Linda Moreno's Electrovision report for an example of an executive summary.

Many reports require neither a synopsis nor an executive summary. Length is usually the determining factor. Most reports of fewer than 10 pages either omit such a preview or combine it with the letter of transmittal. However, if your report is over 30 pages long, you'll probably include either a synopsis or an executive summary as a convenience for readers. Which one you'll provide depends on the traditions of your organization.

Text of the Report

Apart from deciding on the fundamental issues of content and organization, you must also make decisions about the design and layout of the report. You can use a variety of techniques to present your material effectively. Many organizations have format guidelines that make your decisions easier, but the goal is always to focus readers' attention on major points and on the flow of ideas. Headings, typographical devices (such as capital letters, italics, and boldface type), white space, and so on are useful tools, as are visual aids. Also, as discussed in Chapter 12, use preview and review statements to frame sections of your text. This strategy keeps your audience informed and reinforces the substance of your message.

Aids to understanding the text of a report:

- ✧ Headings
- ✧ Typographical devices
- ✧ Visual aids
- ✧ Preview and review statements

LEARNING OUTCOME 3
Describe four important functions of a formal report's introduction, and identify the possible topics it might include.

An introduction has a number of functions and covers a wide variety of topics.

INTRODUCTION

The introduction of a report serves a number of important functions:

- Putting the report in a broader context by tying it to a problem or an assignment
- Telling readers the report's purpose
- Previewing the report's contents and organization
- Establishing the tone of the report and the writer's relationship with the audience

The length of the introduction depends on the length of the report. In a relatively brief report, the introduction may be only a paragraph or two and may not be labelled with a heading of any kind. On the other hand, the introduction to a major formal report may extend to several pages and can be identified as a separate section by the first-level heading "Introduction." (See Linda Moreno's Electrovision report.)

Here's a list of topics to consider covering in an introduction, depending on your material and your audience:

- *Authorization.* When, how, and by whom the report was authorized; who wrote it; and when it was submitted. This material is especially important when no letter of transmittal is included.
- *Problem/purpose.* The reason for the report's existence and what is to be accomplished as a result of the report's having been written.
- *Scope.* What is and what isn't going to be covered in the report. The scope indicates the report's size and complexity.
- *Background.* The historical conditions or factors that have led up to the report. This section enables readers to understand how the problem developed and what has been done about it so far.
- *Sources and methods.* The secondary sources of information used and the surveys, experiments, and observations carried out. This section tells readers what sources were used, how the sample was selected, how the questionnaire was constructed (a sample questionnaire and cover letter should be included in the appendix), what follow-up procedures were employed, and the like. It provides enough detail to give readers confidence in the work and to convince them that the sources and methods were satisfactory.
- *Definitions.* A brief introductory statement leading into a list of terms used in the report and their definitions. Naturally, if your audience is familiar with the terms you've used throughout the report, a list of definitions isn't necessary. Moreno's Electrovision report has no list of definitions because the topic doesn't involve any unfamiliar terminology. However, if you have any question about your readers' knowledge, be sure to include definitions of any terms that might lead to misinterpretation. In addition, if you've used familiar or general terms in a specific way, be sure to explain exactly what you mean. For example, the term *market* could be used in a number of different ways, from a physical location to a collection of potential customers. Note that terms may be defined in other places as well: in the body (when a term is first used), in explanatory footnotes, or in a glossary (an alphabetical listing of terms placed in the supplementary section).
- *Limitations.* Factors affecting the quality of the report, such as a budget too small to do all the work that should have been done, an inadequate amount of time to do all the necessary research, unreliability or unavailability of data, or other conditions beyond your control. This is the place to mention doubts about any aspect of the report. Although candour may lead readers to question the

Going Online

Design Effective Computer Graphics

Mambo is a jump station to more than 65 Web sites containing the latest information about the imaginative world of computer graphics. The site provides links to company, university, and government labs displaying colourful portfolios; Usenet groups; and software companies. It also includes frequently asked questions (FAQs), bibliographies, conferences, and utilities.
www.mambo.ucsc.edu/psl/cg.html

Only about thirty years ago, report writers commonly prepared their reports on manual or electric typewriters. What are the differences between using old-fashioned typewriters to prepare reports and using computers with word-processing software? Are there any advantages to typewriters? Any disadvantages to using computers? What are they?

results, it will also enable them to assess the results more accurately and help you maintain the integrity of your report. However, limitations are no excuse for conducting a poor study or writing a bad report.

➢ *Report organization.* The organization of the report (what topics are covered and in what order), along with a rationale for following this plan. This section is a road map that helps readers understand what's approaching at each turn of the report and why.

When grad student Jerry Yang partnered with David Filo to found Yahoo!, the popular Internet search engine, they wound up developing more than software. It took a business plan with convincing arguments for their "diversified media company," backed by solid facts and figures, to land their first $1 million financial stake.

Some of these items may be combined in the introduction; some may not be included at all. You can decide what to include by figuring out what kind of information will help your readers understand and accept the report. Also give some thought to how the introduction relates to the prefatory parts of the report. In longer reports you may have a letter of transmittal, a synopsis or an executive summary, and an introduction, all of which cover essentially the same ground.

To avoid redundancy, balance the various sections. If the letter of transmittal and synopsis are fairly detailed, for example, you might want the introduction to be relatively brief. However, remember that some people may barely glance at the prefatory parts, so be sure your introduction is detailed enough to provide an adequate preview of your report. If you feel that your introduction must repeat information that has already been covered in one of the prefatory parts, simply use different wording.

BODY

Restrict the body to those details necessary to prove your conclusions and recommendations.

The body of the report follows the introduction. It consists of the major sections (with various levels of headings) that present, analyze, and interpret the findings gathered as part of your investigation. These sections contain the "proof," the detailed information necessary to support your conclusions and recommendations. (See the body of Linda Moreno's Electrovision report.)

One of the decisions to make when writing the body of your report is how much detail to include. Your decision depends on the nature of your information, the purpose of your report, and the preferences of your audience. Some situations call for detailed coverage; others lend themselves to shorter treatment. In general, provide only enough detail in the body to support your conclusions and recommendations, and put additional details in tables, charts, and appendices.

You can also decide whether to put your conclusions in the body or in a separate section or both. If the conclusions seem to flow naturally from the evidence, you'll almost inevitably cover them in the body. However, if you want to give your conclusions added emphasis, you may include a separate section to summarize them. Having a separate section is particularly appropriate in longer reports; the reader may lose track of the conclusions if they're given only in the body.

SUMMARY, CONCLUSIONS, AND RECOMMENDATIONS

Summaries, conclusions, and recommendations serve different purposes.

The final section of the text of a report tells readers "what you told them." In a short report this final wrap-up may be only a paragraph or two. A long report generally has separate sections labelled "Summary," "Conclusions," and "Recommendations." Here's how the three differ:

➢ *Summary.* The key findings of your report, paraphrased from the body and stated or listed in the order in which they appear in the body.

➢ *Conclusions.* Your analysis of what the findings mean. These are the answers to the questions that led to the report.

- *Recommendations.* Opinions, based on reason and logic, about the course of action that should be taken. The author of the Electrovision report listed four specific steps the company should take to reduce travel costs.

If the report is organized in direct order, the summary, conclusions, and recommendations are presented before the body and are reviewed only briefly at the end. If the report is organized in indirect order, these three sections are presented for the first time at the end and are covered in detail. Many report writers combine the conclusions and recommendations under one heading because it seems like the natural thing to do. It is often difficult to present a conclusion without implying a recommendation. (See Moreno's Electrovision report.)

Whether you combine them or not, if you have several conclusions and recommendations, you may want to number and list them. An appropriate lead-in to such a list might be, "The findings of this study lead to the following conclusions." A statement that could be used for a list of recommendations might be, "Based on the conclusions of this study, the following recommendations are made." Present no new findings either in the conclusions or in the recommendations section.

In action-oriented reports, put all the recommendations in a separate section and spell out precisely what should happen next.

In reports that are intended to lead to action, the recommendations section is particularly important; it spells out exactly what should happen next. It brings all the action items together in one place and gives the details about who should do what, when, where, and how. Readers may agree with everything you say in

BEHIND THE SCENES OF ANNUAL REPORTS

Telling a Company's Story, Once a Year, Every Year

To some people, it's "nothing more than a storybook with pretty pictures." To others, it is, above all, a financial document. According to John Svicarovich, head of Merewords, a communications and project management firm, the annual report "is an organization's most prominent communication tool, and maybe its best platform for public accountability. It's the best principal format to assess the past year's performance, to tell stakeholders how their interests are being managed, and to outline important strategies and plans."

Large publicly held companies, such as Canada's banks and telecommunications firms, as well as smaller organizations like Gildan, a Montreal-based athletic wear manufacturer, are legally required to produce an annual report. Its primary purpose—and reason for being—is to tell shareholders about the firm's financial activities and results for the previous year. Alice Brink, a vice-president of Vollmer Public Relations, says, "For most companies, the audience that will read the report most closely, and have the greatest influence on the company's stock, is the professional investment community." This community includes stockbrokers, financial advisers, portfolio managers, and individual investors.

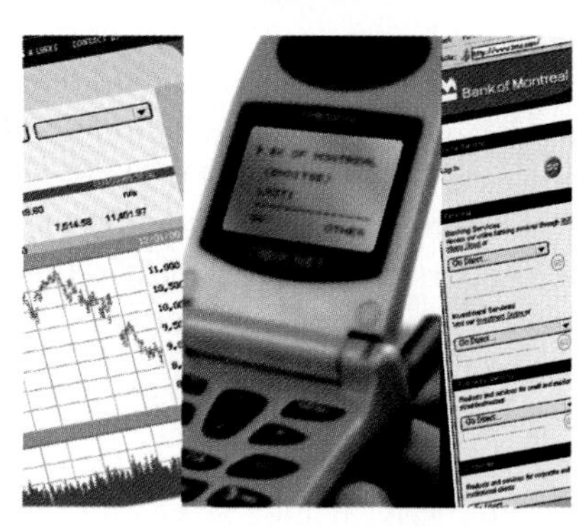

Annual reports are complex documents that describe the operations, financial performance, and culture of an organization.

But annual reports are not only financial documents; they have evolved into key communication tools that describe a firm's culture, employees, and social and environmental responsibilities as well as their operations and strategic direction. Not only do corporations produce them, but also nonprofit organizations, such as universities, hospitals, and social agencies. Nor is the audience confined to financial readers: the firm's employees, consumers, activist groups, government agencies, professional associations, students, educators, the media, and competitors all read annual reports to learn what the company does and where it is going.

As Brink notes, many corporations spend at least six months and more than $500 000 to produce a glossy, full-colour annual report. The report may be created internally, under the management of the director of corporate communications, in concert with the CEO and a designer. The process begins with preliminary planning and a timetable to track the stages of the report from beginning to distribution. Soon after, staff your report but still fail to take any action if you're vague about what should happen next. Your readers must understand what's expected of them and must have some appreciation of the difficulties that are likely to arise. So providing a schedule and specific task assignments is helpful because concrete plans have a way of commanding action.

SOURCE DOCUMENTATION

When writing the text of the report, you need to decide how to acknowledge your sources. You have an ethical and a legal obligation to give other people credit for their work. Acknowledging your sources also enhances the credibility of your report. By citing references in the text, you demonstrate that you have thoroughly researched the topic. Mentioning the names of well-known or important authorities on the subject also helps build credibility for your message.

On the other hand, you don't want to make your report read like an academic treatise, dragging along from citation to citation. The source references should be handled as conveniently and inconspicuously as possible. One approach, especially for internal reports, is simply to mention a source in the text:

> According to Lewis Morgan of Vision Consulting, the stress of dealing with rude customers accounts for the high turnover of telemarketers.

Linda J. Wachner is CEO of lingerie maker Warnaco and is often called on to make decisions based on reports. But if a report makes a recommendation and lacks the detail to support it, the recommendation is useless. Likewise, a recommendation buried in too much detail may be too difficult to uncover. Wachner advises balancing the amount of detail to complement the subject and its complexity.

involved in the project read previous annual reports, examine company documents, and interview key staff to develop the report's goals and themes. An initial design is developed, to be revised and fine-tuned over the weeks that follow. Meanwhile the text is being written, and photographs taken of company officers, directors, employees, locations, and products. A corporate communications, public-affairs specialist, or CEO prepares a draft of the letter to shareholders. This letter reviews the key events and financial results of the previous year, examines operational problems, and describes development for the next year. By about the fourth month of the production process, drafts of the narrative are sent to department heads for review, and by the fifth month, the design and layout is finalized and the text is confirmed. Finally, after the report is returned from the printer, staff proofread it and make final corrections.

Like many formal business reports, annual reports include standard components, some legally required: the table of contents, letter to shareholders, narrative section describing company operations, balance sheet and income statement, management discussion and analysis of the financials, and five-year statistical summary. Virtually all reports use headings and subheadings to segment information and make it easy to follow. Also included are photographs of company officers, employees, and products; as well as charts and tables to highlight and make accessible important quantitative information, such as details about sales and profits. As Karen Kahler Holliday, a marketing specialist, notes, "crisp writing and easy-to-understand graphics" are essential. Sid Cato, a recognized authority on annual reports and publisher of the *Newsletter on Annual Reports*, claims, "If the annual report isn't easy to follow, or the executives don't know how to relate the firm's story simply and clearly, then perhaps one's investment dollars should be placed elsewhere." And if the cover doesn't command the reader's attention by conveying the report's theme in a clear and attractive way, Cato advises to "heave the report into the nearest receptacle."

Canadian annual reports that make the grade are honoured with an Annual Report Award, sponsored by the Chartered Accountants of Canada and the *National Post* newspaper. The Bank of Montreal 1999 annual report received the "overall award of excellence." Praised as "an exceptional example of comprehensive coverage of a complex organization," the shareholders' letter was admired for being "up-front" and showing a "personal touch," being "logically organized and easy to follow," and using charts and graphs with captions that provided "more details and/or explanation." In the world of report writing, winning this award is equivalent to the film industry's Genie or Oscar.[3]

APPLY YOUR KNOWLEDGE

1. Sid Cato says readers should throw out an annual report if the cover doesn't immediately engage their interest. Why is an effective cover an important element of an annual report? Why do many experts believe it should express the report's theme?
2. Select one or two paper annual reports (rather than ones posted on the World Wide Web or prepared on a CD-ROM) and examine its use of headings, charts and tables, and general design. Is it easy or difficult to absorb the information? Why?

Give credit where credit is due.

However, you can supplement in-text references with additional information on where you obtained the data. Most university students are familiar with citation schemes suggested by the Modern Language Association (MLA) or the American Psychological Association (APA). The *Chicago Manual of Style* is a reference often used by typesetters and publishers. All of these encourage the use of *in-text citations,* in which you insert the author's last name and a year of publication or a page number directly in the text. An alternative is to use numbered footnotes (bottom of the page) or endnotes (end of the report). Linda Moreno's Electrovision report uses the author–page number system, whereas this textbook uses endnotes. For more information on citing sources, see Appendix B, "Documentation of Report Sources."

LEARNING OUTCOME 4
Explain how to incorporate visual support into your text.

VISUAL AIDS

Visual aids help communicators get through to an audience.

Reinforcing or explaining important ideas is the main reason business people include visual aids in their reports and proposals, but which comes first: visual aid or text? Say you've just completed the research for an important report or oral presentation. You're about to begin the composition phase. Your first impulse might be to start with the introduction and proceed page by page until you've completed the text or script. Almost as an afterthought you might throw in a few visual aids–tables, charts, graphs, schematic drawings, illustrations, photographs–to illustrate the words.

Beginning with your visual aids offers several advantages.

Although this approach makes some sense, many experienced business people prefer to begin with the visual aids, which has three advantages. First, if much of the fact-finding and analytical work is already in tabular or graphic form, you already have a visual point of departure. Sorting through and refining your visuals will help you decide exactly what you're going to say. Second, many important business projects involve both a written report and an oral presentation of results. Similar visual aids, modified for different media, can be used for both communication situations. By starting with the visual aids, you develop a graphic story line that serves two purposes. Finally, the text or script explains and refers to the tables, charts, and graphs; so you save time by having them ready before you start to compose, particularly if you plan to use more than four visuals. However, the illustrative material in a report or presentation should supplement the written or spoken word, not replace it, so restrict your use of visual aids to situations in which they do the most good. Table 14.1 helps you identify those situations.

In general, use visual aids only to supplement the story you are telling in words.

Refer to every visual aid by number.

Every visual aid you use should be clearly referred to by number in the text of your report. Some report writers refer to all visual aids as exhibits and number them consecutively throughout the report; many others number tables and figures separately (everything that isn't a table is regarded as a figure). In a very long report with numbered chapters (as in this book), visual aids may have a double number (separated by a period or a hyphen) representing the chapter number and the individual illustration number within that chapter.

Introduce each visual in your text before the visual appears.

Help your readers understand the significance of any visual aids by referring to them before they appear in the text. The reference helps readers understand why the table or chart is important. The following examples show how you can make this connection in the text:

> Figure 1 summarizes the financial history of the motorcycle division over the past five years, with sales broken into four categories.
>
> Total sales were steady over this period, but the mix of sales by category changed dramatically (see Figure 2).

TABLE 14.1 When to Use Visuals

Purpose	Application
To clarify	Support text descriptions of "graphic" topics: quantitative or numerical information; explanations of trends; descriptions of procedures, relationships, locations, or composition of an item.
To simplify	Break complicated descriptions into components that can be depicted with conceptual models, flowcharts, organization charts, or diagrams.
To emphasize	Call attention to particularly important points by illustrating them with line, bar, and pie charts.
To summarize	Review major points in the narrative by providing a chart or table that sums up the data.
To reinforce	Present information in visual and written form to increase readers' retention.
To attract	Make material seem more interesting by decorating the cover or title page and by breaking up the text with visual aids.
To impress	Build credibility by putting ideas in visual form to convey the impression of authenticity and precision.
To unify	Depict the relationships among points—for example, with a flowchart.

> The underlying reason for the remarkable growth in our sales of low-end fax machines is suggested by Table 4, which provides data on fax machine sales in Canada by region and model.

Ideally, it is best to place each visual aid right beside or right after the paragraph it illustrates so that readers can consult the explanation and the visual aid at the same time. Word-processing programs and desktop-publishing systems let you create layouts with artwork and text on the same page. These programs offer a number of creative options for including visual support.

Knowing what points you want to present visually and knowing exactly what format to use are separate things. The construction of visual aids requires a good deal of both imagination and attention to detail. Your main concern is always your audience. What format is most meaningful and convenient for them? When illustrating the text of any report, you face the problem of choosing the specific form that best suits your message. Moreover, good business ethics demands you choose a form of visual aid that will not mislead your audience.

Tables When you have to present detailed, specific information, choose a **table,** a systematic arrangement of data in columns and rows. Tables are ideal when the audience needs the facts–all the facts–and when the information would be either difficult or tedious to handle in the main text.

Use tables to help your audience understand detailed information.

Most tables contain the standard parts illustrated in Figure 14.2. A table is characterized by the grid that allows you to find the point at which two factors intersect. Every table includes vertical columns and horizontal rows, with useful headings along the top and side. Tables projected onto a screen during an oral presentation should be limited to three column heads and six row heads; tables presented on paper may include from one or two heads to a dozen or more. If the table has too many columns to fit comfortably between the margins of the page, turn the paper horizontally and insert it in the report with the top toward the binding.

FIGURE 14.2
Parts of a Table

TABLE 1 Title

Subhead	*Multicolumn Head* *Subhead*	*Multicolumn Head* *Subhead*	*Single Column Head*	*Single Column Head*
Line head	XXX	XXX	XX	XX
Line head				
Subhead	XX	XXX	XX	XX
Subhead	XX	XXX	XX	XX
Total	XXX	XXX	XX	XX

Source: (In the same format as a text footnote; see Appendix B).
*Footnote (to explain particular elements in the table; a superscript number or small letter may be used instead of an asterisk or other symbol).

Tabular information can be included in text without a formal title.

Although formal tables set apart from the text are necessary for complex information, you can present some data more simply within the text. You make the table, in essence, a part of the paragraph, typed in tabular format. These text tables are usually introduced with a sentence that leads directly into the tabulated information. Here's an example:

> Half the people surveyed are very concerned about artificial colouring in the prepackaged foods they eat. Women and older people are most concerned:

	Percentage Who Are Very Concerned	Percentage Who Are Slightly Concerned
Men	44	40
Women	53	39
Adults 18–49	49	40
Adults 50–65	55	32

> *Source:* "Artificial Colouring in Prepackaged Food," *Food Processing News,* January 1995, 113.

When preparing a numerical table, be sure to identify the units you're using: dollars, percentages, price per tonne, or whatever. All items in a column are expressed in the same unit. Although many tables are numerical, word tables can be just as useful. They are particularly appropriate for presenting survey findings or for comparing various items against a specific standard.

Use line charts to
✧ Indicate changes over time
✧ Plot the interaction of two variables

Line and Surface Charts A **line chart** illustrates trends over time or plots the relationship of two variables. In line charts that show trends, the vertical axis shows the amount, and the horizontal axis shows the time or the quantity being measured. Ordinarily, the two scales begin at zero and proceed in equal increments; however, the vertical axis can be broken to show that some of the increments have been left out. A broken axis is appropriate when the data are plotted far above zero, but be sure to clearly indicate the omission of data points.

A simple line chart may be arranged in many ways. One of the most common is to plot several lines on the same chart for comparative purposes, as shown in Figure 14.3. Try to use no more than three lines on any given chart, particularly if

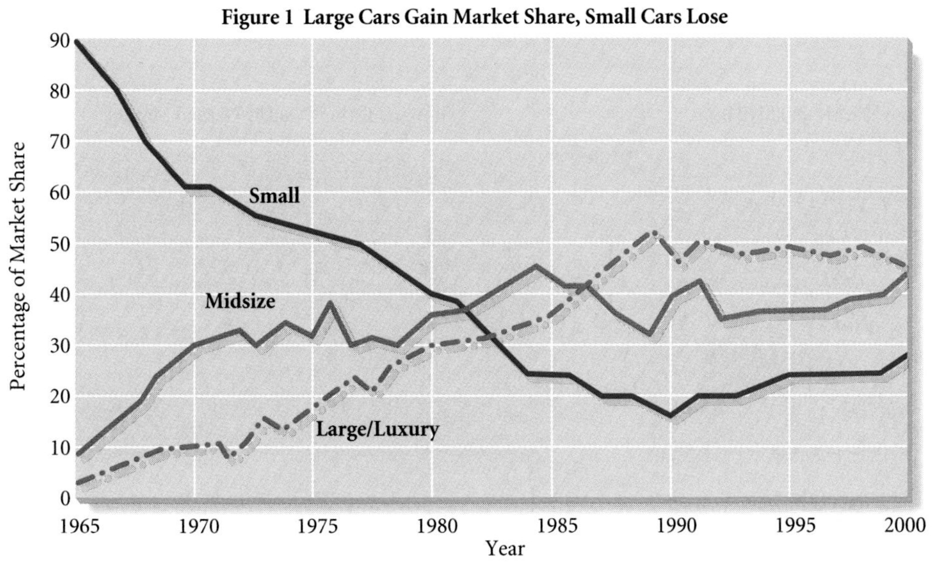

FIGURE 14.3
Line Chart Plotting Three Lines

the lines cross. Another variation of the simple line chart has a vertical axis with both positive and negative numbers. This arrangement is handy when you have to illustrate losses.

A **surface chart** is a form of line chart with a cumulative effect; the lower lines add up to the top line, which represents the total (Figure 14.4). This form of chart helps you illustrate changes in the composition of something over time. When preparing a surface chart, put the most important segment against the baseline, and restrict the number of strata to four or five.

A surface chart is a kind of line chart showing cumulative effect.

Bar Charts A **bar chart** is a chart in which amounts are visually portrayed by the height or length of bars. These bars may be rectangles, cylinders, or some other shape; the chart feature in word-processing software offers some variety. As Figure 14.5 illustrates, bar charts are particularly valuable when you want to

Bar charts, in which numbers are visually portrayed by rectangular bars, can take a variety of forms.

- Compare the size of several items at one time
- Show changes in one item over time
- Indicate the composition of several items over time
- Show the relative size of components of a whole

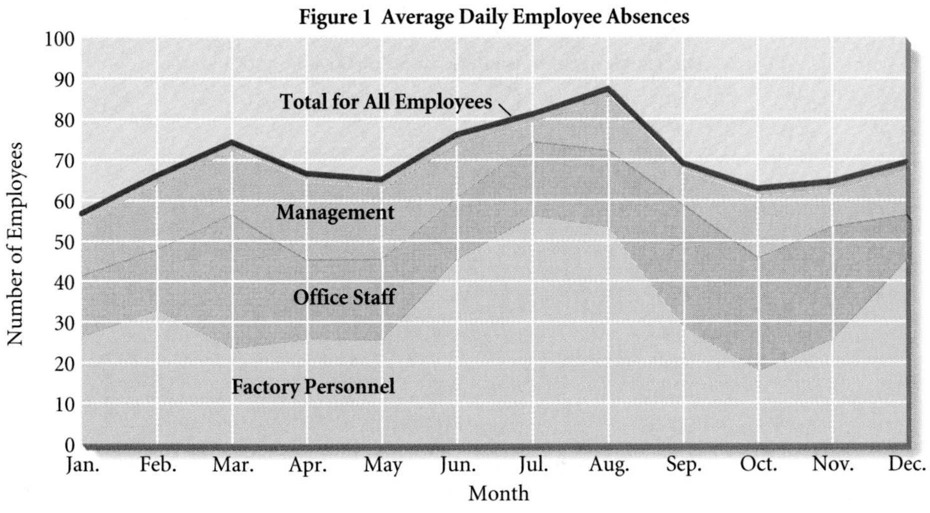

FIGURE 14.4
Surface Chart

FIGURE 14.5
The Versatile Bar Chart

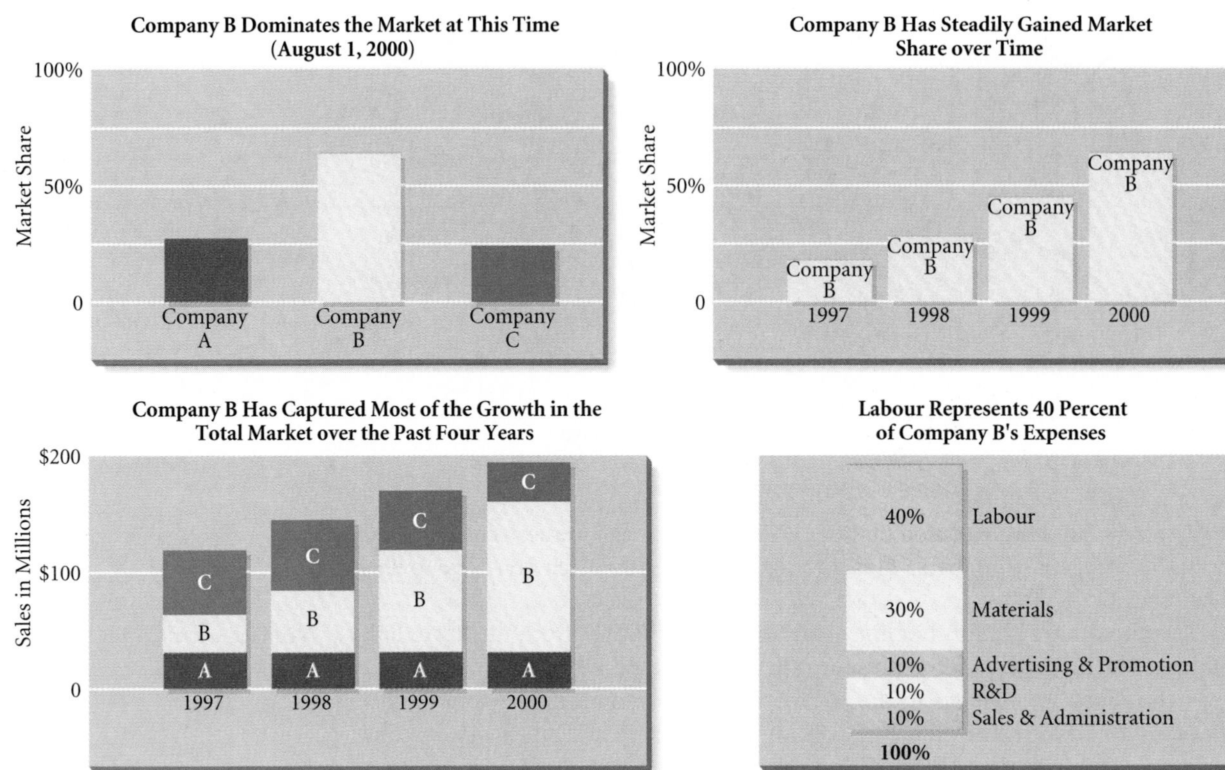

You can be creative with bar charts in many ways. You might align the bars either vertically or horizontally and double the bars for comparisons. You might even use bar charts to show both positive and negative quantities.

Pie Charts Another type of chart you see frequently in business reports is the **pie chart,** in which numbers are represented as sectors of a complete circle, or slices of a pie. As you can see from the pie chart in Figure 14.6, this type of chart helps you show exactly how each part is related to the whole. You can combine pie charts with tables to expand the usefulness of such visuals.

FIGURE 14.6
Pie Chart

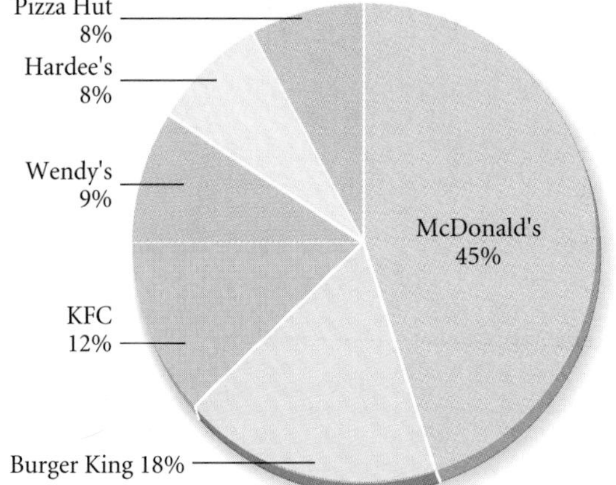

When composing pie charts, try to restrict the number of slices in the pie to a maximum of seven. Otherwise, the chart looks cluttered and is difficult to label. If necessary, lump the smallest pieces together in a "miscellaneous" category. Ideally, the largest or most important slice of the pie, the sector you want to emphasize, is placed at the twelve o'clock position; the rest are arranged clockwise either in order of size or in some other logical progression. You might want to shade the sector that is of the greatest interest to your readers or use colour to distinguish the various pieces. In any case, label all the sectors and indicate their value in either percentages or units of measure so that your readers will be able to judge the value of the wedges. The sectors must add up to 100 percent.

Use flowcharts to
- ✧ Show a series of steps from beginning to end
- ✧ Show relationships

Flowcharts and Organization Charts If you need to show physical or conceptual relationships rather than numerical ones, you might want to use a flowchart or an organization chart. A **flowchart** illustrates a sequence of events from start to finish. Flowcharts are indispensable for illustrating processes, procedures, and relationships. The various elements in the process you want to portray may be represented by pictorial symbols or geometric shapes, as shown in Figure 14.7.

Use organization charts to depict the interrelationships among the parts of an organization.

An **organization chart,** as the name implies, illustrates the positions, units, or functions of an organization and how they are related. An organization's normal communication channels are almost impossible to describe without the benefit of a chart like the one in Figure 14.8.

Use maps to
- ✧ Represent statistics by geographical area
- ✧ Show location relationships

Maps For certain applications, maps are ideal. One of the most common uses is to show concentrations of something by geographical area. In your own reports, you might use maps to show regional differences in such variables as your company's sales of a product. You might indicate proposed plant sites and their relationship to key markets.

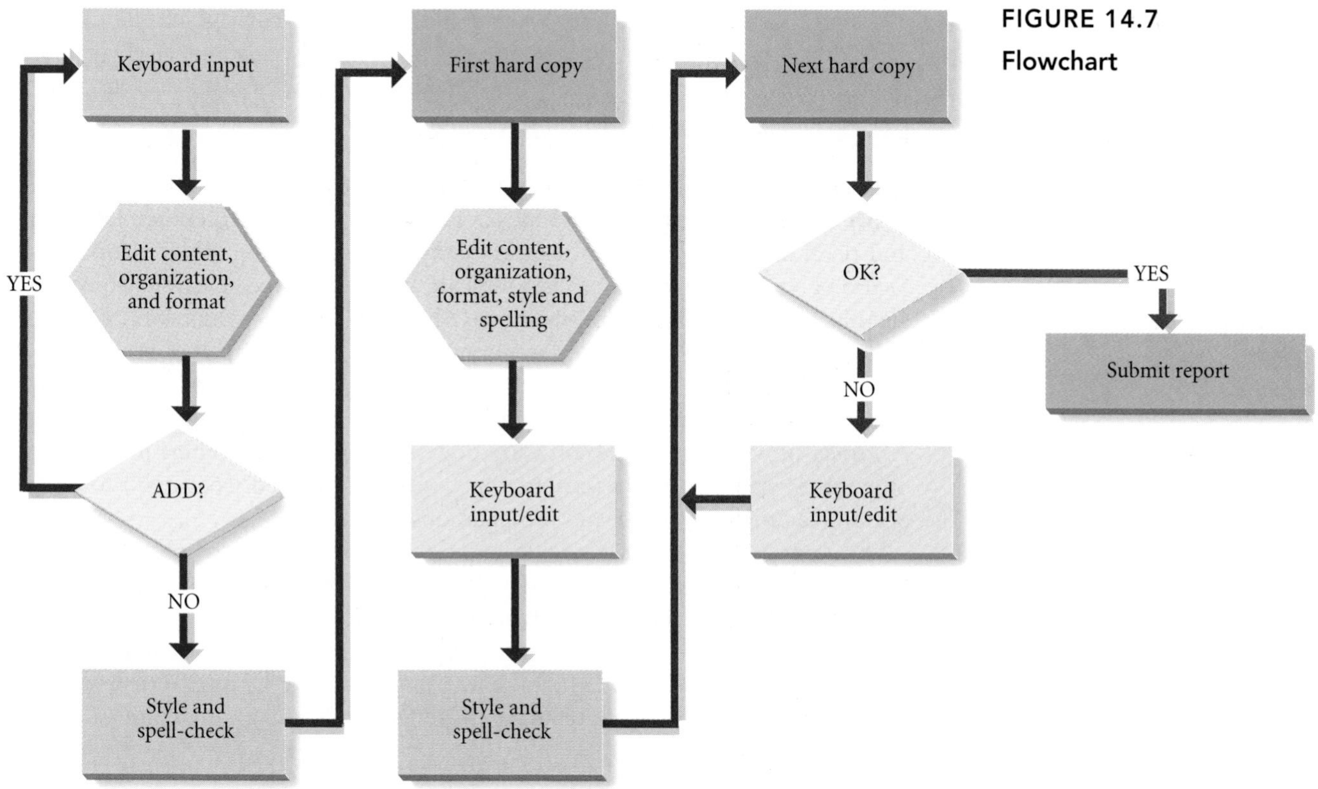

FIGURE 14.7
Flowchart

FIGURE 14.8
Organization Chart

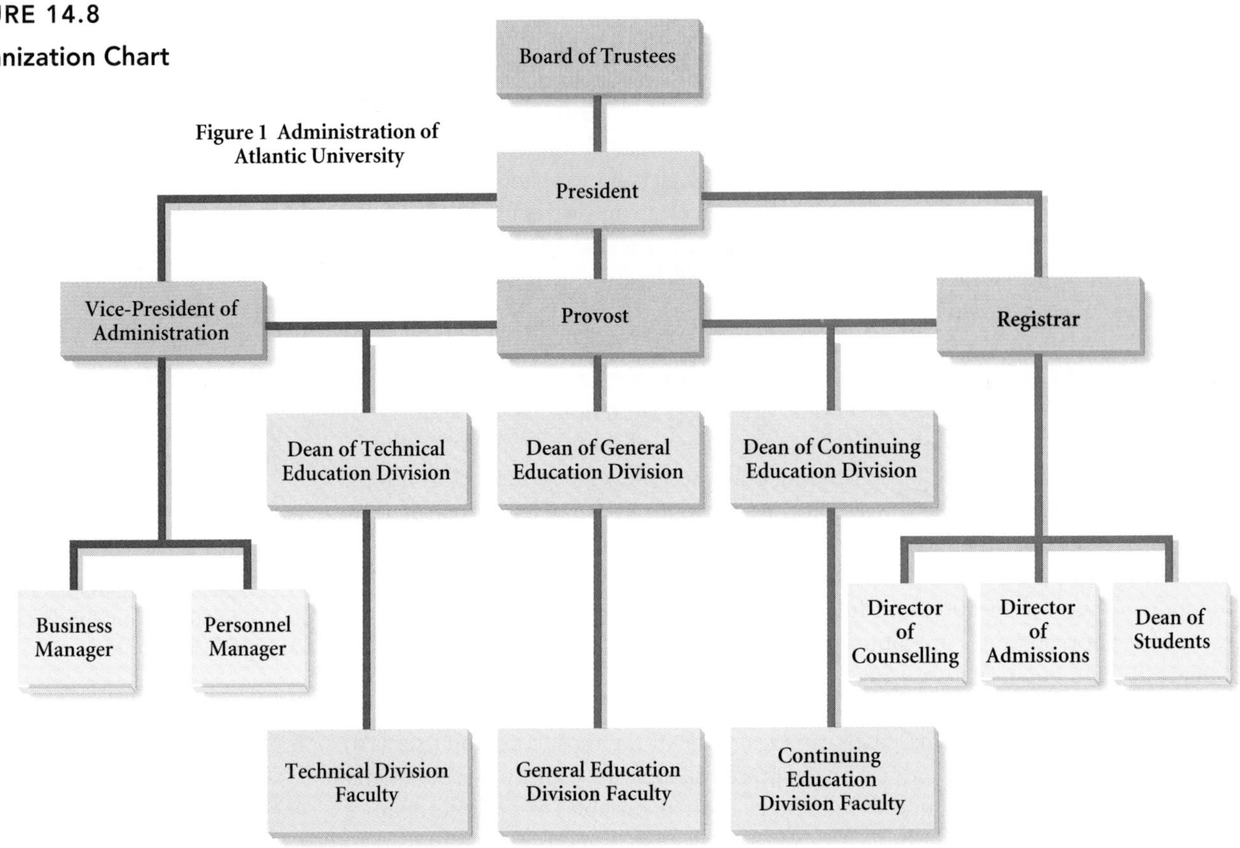

Figure 1 Administration of Atlantic University

Board of Trustees
President
Vice-President of Administration
Provost
Registrar
Dean of Technical Education Division
Dean of General Education Division
Dean of Continuing Education Division
Business Manager
Personnel Manager
Director of Counselling
Director of Admissions
Dean of Students
Technical Division Faculty
General Education Division Faculty
Continuing Education Division Faculty

Most office-supply stores carry blank maps of various regions of the world, including all or part of Canada. You can illustrate these maps to suit your needs, using dots, shading, colour, labels, numbers, and symbols. In addition, you can use specialized computer programs to select maps of various regions and insert just the portions you need into your business documents.

Use drawings and diagrams to show
✧ How something looks or works
✧ How something is made or used

Drawings, Diagrams, and Photographs Although less common than other visual aids, drawings, diagrams, and photographs are also used in business reports. Drawings and diagrams are most often used to show how something looks or operates. Figure 14.9 was prepared using Visio software and explains the benefits of converged communication networks over traditional networks. Diagrams can be much clearer than words alone when it comes to giving your audience an idea of how an item looks or how it can be used. In industries such as engineering and architecture, computer-aided design (CAD) systems produce detailed diagrams and drawings. A variety of widely available software programs for microcomputers provide files of symbols and pictures of various types that can be used (sparingly) to add a decorative touch to reports and presentations.

Use photographs
✧ For visual appeal
✧ To show exact appearance

Photographs have always been popular in certain types of business documents, such as annual reports, where their visual appeal is used to capture readers' interest. As the technology for reproducing photographs improves and becomes less expensive, even analytical business reports for internal use are beginning to include more photographs. Digital cameras now make it easy to drop photographic images directly into a report or presentation. Nothing can demonstrate the

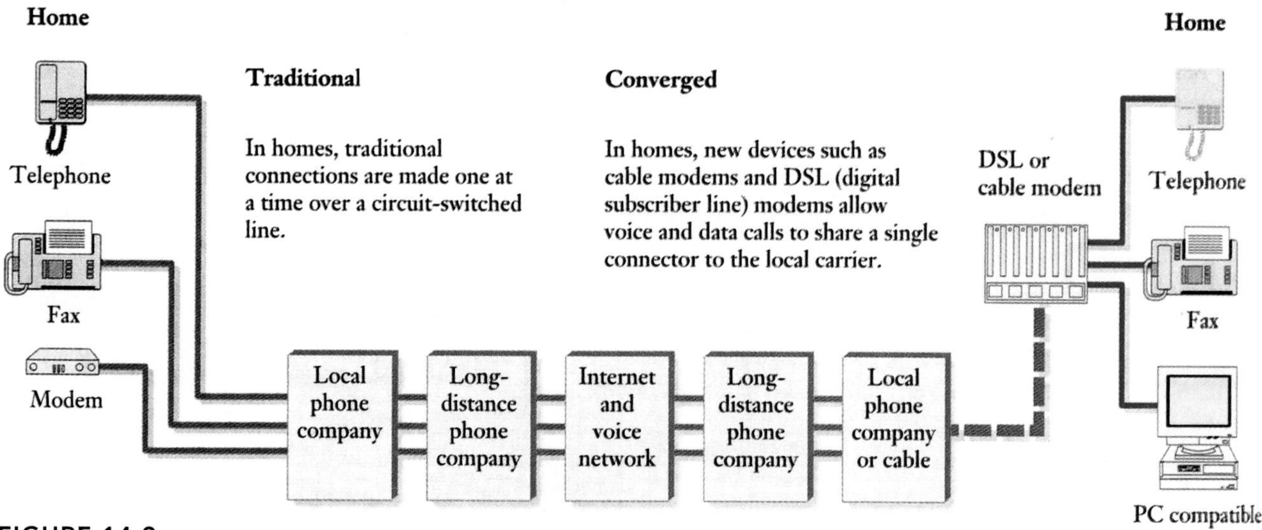

FIGURE 14.9
Diagram

exact appearance of a new facility, a piece of property or equipment, or a new product as well as a photograph. In some situations, however, a photograph shows too much detail. This is one of the reasons that repair manuals, for instance, frequently use drawings instead of photos. With a drawing, you can select how much detail to show and focus the reader's attention on particular parts or places.

Technology has created new opportunities and an important ethical concern for people who use photography in reports and other materials. Software such as Photoshop makes it easy for computer users to make dramatic changes to photos–without leaving a clue. Small changes to photos have been possible for a long time, of course (more than a few people have blemishes airbrushed out of their yearbook photos), but computers make drastic changes easy and undetectable. You can remove people from photographs, put Person A's head on Person B's body, and make products look more attractive than they really are. As with other technological tools, stop and ask yourself where the truth lies before you start editing photographs.[4]

Computer-graphics systems cut the time and cost involved in producing visual aids.

Supplementary Parts

Supplementary parts follow the text of the report and include appendices, the bibliography, and the index. They are more common in long reports than in short ones.

An **appendix** contains materials related to the report but not included in the text because they're too lengthy or bulky or because they lack direct relevance. Frequently included in appendices are sample questionnaires and cover letters, sample forms, computer printouts, and statistical formulas; a glossary of terms may be put in an appendix or may stand as a separate supplementary part. The best place to include visual aids is in the body of the text nearest the point of discussion. If any graphics are too large to fit on one page or are only indirectly relevant to your report, they may be put in an appendix. Some organizations specify that all visual aids be placed in an appendix.

Put into an appendix materials that are

✧ Bulky or lengthy

✧ Not directly relevant to the text

Each type of material deserves a separate appendix. Identify the appendixes by labelling them, for example, "Appendix A: Questionnaire," "Appendix B: Computer Printout of Raw Data," and the like. All appendices should be mentioned in the text and listed in the table of contents.

REPORT WRITER'S NOTEBOOK

Creating Colourful Visual Aids with Computers for Maximum Clarity and Impact

More and more people are learning to use graphics software to create striking and attractive visual aids. No matter which type of software you use, your design is likely to look more professional than a graphic drawn by hand. Once you've designed your visual, you can also use your computer and software to plan the colours.

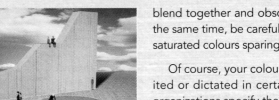

You know from your own experience that colour helps make a point more effectively than black and white. However, there's more to using colour than simply picking hues that appeal to you. To choose an effective colour scheme, ask yourself these questions:

- *What colours will best convey the effect I want?* As a general rule, bright, solid colours are more pleasing to the eye and easier to distinguish than pastel or patterned colours. Yellow, blue, and green are usually good choices, but the possibilities are numerous. Just keep in mind that too many colours may overwhelm the message. Use colour as an accent, bright colour for emphasis and darker or lighter colours for background information. Colour can also visually connect related points or set apart points that represent significant change.
- *Are these colours appropriate for my message, purpose, and audience?* Liking red is not a good reason for using it in all your graphic designs. It's too "hot" for some people and conveys the wrong message in some instances; for example, using red to show profits in an annual report might confuse readers because they're likely to associate your graphic with "red ink," or losses. Also remember that people in other cultures will make colour associations that differ from yours.
- *Is my audience familiar with these colours?* Unless your aim is to shake up your audience, avoid uncommon colours or unusual combinations. In general, conventional colours are best for conventional audiences. However, young or trendy audiences probably won't be jarred by unfamiliar colours.
- *Can I improve the effect by changing any of the colours?* When you have the opportunity to use more than one colour, choose them to contrast. Colours without contrast blend together and obscure the message. At the same time, be careful to use vivid or highly saturated colours sparingly.

Of course, your colour choices may be limited or dictated in certain situations. Some organizations specify the exact colour or combination to be used on company logos and other official symbols or illustrations. At other times you'll be free to decide on any combination of colours that works best for the visual aid you're preparing. That's when you'll find graphics software especially useful.

Depending on the capabilities of your software and your computer monitor, you can try out various colours and combinations and see the results immediately. Even the most basic program offers three colours. More sophisticated programs can give you thousands or even millions of colour and shading choices.

To start, select a background colour from the program's palette of available colours. Then choose a dominant colour to set the tone for the overall colour scheme. Continue adding colours as necessary, until you find the combination that works best. Because you can test many colours and combinations with a quick click of the mouse, you can come to a final decision more quickly (and with less effort) than if you had to do it without the software.

Once you've decided on colours, you can print out a hard copy or an acetate transparency using a colour printer or colour plotter. You can also create full-colour slides using a film recorder, or you can simply project the colourful image from your computer screen through an overhead projector to a large viewing screen.

APPLY YOUR KNOWLEDGE

1. Would you use green or red to shade a visual aid showing the geographic areas where your firm does business? Would you use green or red to shade the areas where your firm does not do business? Why?
2. How can you use colour in a line chart to help your audience differentiate between current and projected sales? Between expected and actual sales? Explain your answers.

PREFATORY PARTS	TEXT OF THE PROPOSAL	SUPPLEMENTARY PARTS
Cover	Introduction	Appendices
Title fly	Body	
Title page	Summary	
Request for proposal		
Letter of transmittal		
Table of contents		
List of illustrations		
Synopsis or executive summary		

FIGURE 14.10
Parts of a Formal Proposal

A **bibliography** is a list of sources consulted when preparing the report. Linda Moreno labelled her bibliography as "Sources" in her Electrovision report. You might also call this section "Works Cited" or "References." The construction of a bibliography is shown in Appendix B.

List your secondary sources in the bibliography.

An **index** is an alphabetical list of names, places, and subjects mentioned in the report and the pages on which they occur, as in the index for this book. An index is rarely included in unpublished reports.

Components of a Formal Proposal

Certain analytical reports are called **proposals**, including bids to perform work under a contract and pleas for financial support from outsiders. As Levi's Philip Marineau can tell you, such bids and pleas are nearly always formal. The goal is to impress the potential client or supporter with your professionalism, and that goal is best achieved through a structured and deliberate approach.

Formal proposals contain many of the same components as other formal reports (Figure 14.10). The difference lies mostly in the text, although a few of the prefatory parts are also different. With the exception of an occasional appendix, most proposals have few supplementary parts.

Formal proposals contain most of the same prefatory parts as other formal reports.

Prefatory Parts

The cover, title fly, title page, table of contents, and list of illustrations are handled the same as in other formal reports. However, other prefatory parts are quite different:

- *Copy of the RFP.* Instead of having a letter of authorization, a formal proposal may have a copy of the **request for proposal (RFP)**, which is a letter or memo soliciting a proposal or bid for a particular project. The RFP is issued by the client to whom the proposal is being submitted and outlines what the proposal should cover. If the RFP includes detailed specifications, it may be too long to bind into the proposal; in that case, you may want to include only the introductory portion of the RFP. Another option is to omit the RFP and simply refer to it in your letter of transmittal.

Use a copy of the request for proposal in place of the letter of authorization.

Use the good-news pattern for the letter of transmittal if the proposal is solicited; use the persuasive plan if the proposal is unsolicited.

- *Letter of transmittal.* The way you handle the letter of transmittal depends on whether the proposal is solicited or unsolicited. If the proposal is solicited, the transmittal letter follows the pattern for good-news messages, highlighting those aspects of your proposal that may give you a competitive advantage. If the proposal is unsolicited, the transmittal letter takes on added importance; in fact, it may be all the client reads. The letter must persuade the reader that you have something worthwhile to offer, something that justifies the time required to read the entire proposal. The transmittal letter for an unsolicited proposal follows the pattern for persuasive messages (see Chapter 11).

Most proposals do not require a synopsis or an executive summary.

- *Synopsis or executive summary.* Although you may include a synopsis or an executive summary for your reader's convenience if your proposal is quite long, these components are somewhat less useful in a formal proposal than they are in a formal report. If your proposal is unsolicited, your transmittal letter will already have caught the reader's interest, making a synopsis or an executive summary pointless. It may also be pointless if your proposal is solicited, because the reader is already committed to studying the text to find out how you propose to satisfy the terms of a contract. The introduction to a solicited proposal would provide an adequate preview of the contents.

REPORT WRITER'S NOTEBOOK

In-Depth Critique: Analyzing a Formal Report

The report presented in the following pages was prepared by Linda Moreno, manager of the cost-accounting department at Electrovision, a high-tech company. Electrovision's main product is optical-character-recognition equipment, which is used by postal services throughout the world for sorting mail. Moreno's job is to help analyze the company's costs. She has this to say about the background of this report:

"For the past three or four years, Electrovision has been on a roll. Our A-12 optical-character reader was a real breakthrough, and postal services grabbed up as many as we could make. Our sales and profits kept climbing, and morale was fantastic. Everybody seemed to think that the good times would last forever. Unfortunately, everybody was wrong. When one of our major clients announced they were postponing all new equipment purchases because of cuts in its budget, we woke up to the fact that we are essentially a one-product company. At that point management started scrambling around looking for ways to cut costs until we could diversify our business a bit.

"The vice-president of operations, Dennis McWilliams, asked me to help identify cost-cutting opportunities in the travel and entertainment area. On the basis of his personal observations, he felt that Electrovision was overly generous in its travel policies and that we might be able to save a significant amount by controlling these costs more carefully. My investigation confirmed his suspicion.

"I was reasonably confident that my report would be well received. I've worked with Dennis for several years and know what he likes: plenty of facts, clearly stated conclusions, and specific recommendations for what should be done next. I also knew that my report would be passed on to other Electrovision executives, so I wanted to create a good impression. I wanted the report to be accurate and thorough, visually appealing, readable, and appropriate in tone."

When writing the analytical report that follows, Moreno used an organization based on conclusions and recommendations, presented in direct order. The first two sections of the report correspond to Moreno's two main conclusions: that Electrovision's travel and entertainment costs are too high and that cuts are essential. The third section presents recommendations for achieving better control over travel and entertainment expenses. As you review the report, analyze both the mechanical aspects and the way Moreno presents her ideas. Be prepared to discuss the way the various components convey and reinforce the main message.

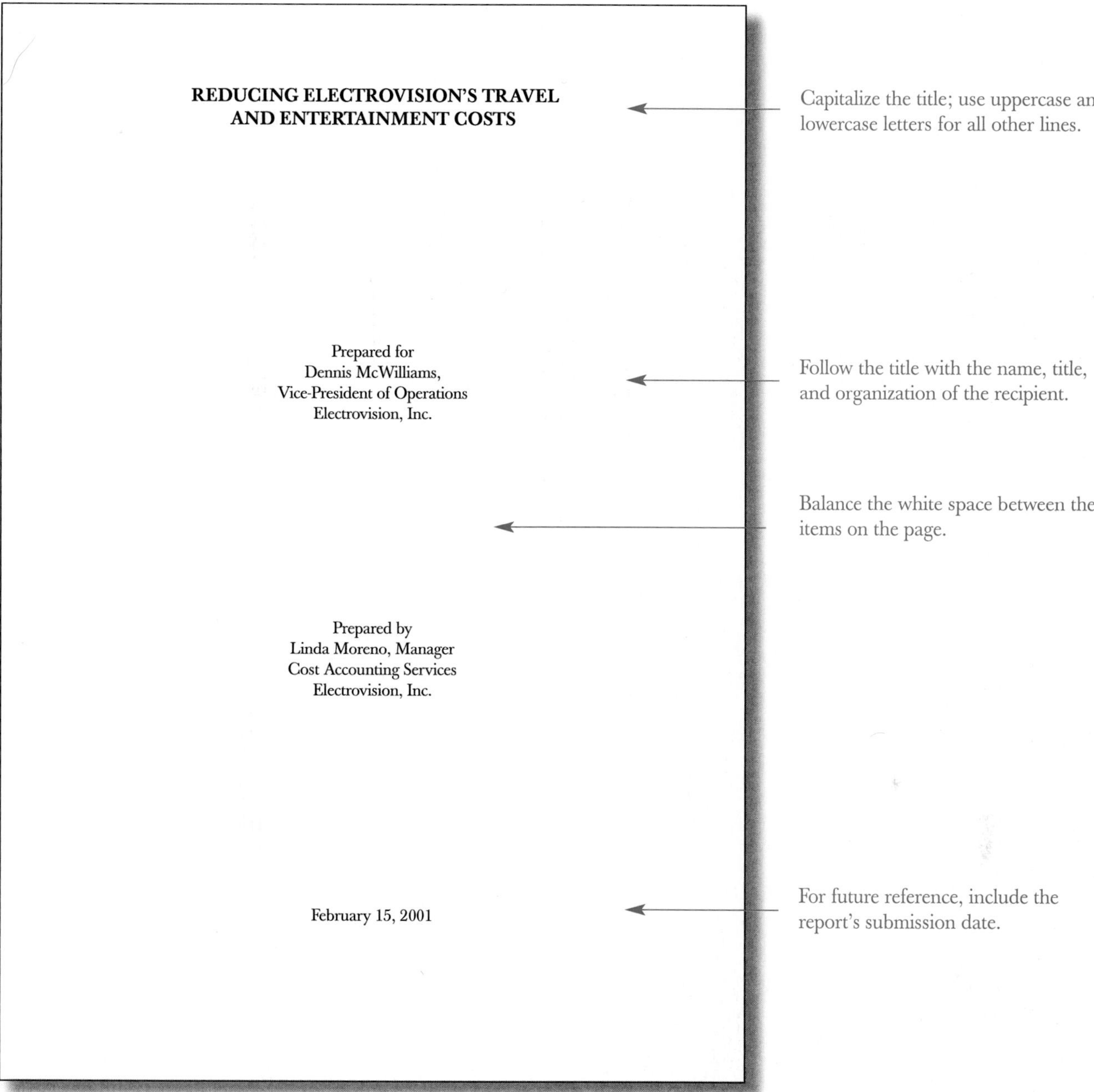
REDUCING ELECTROVISION'S TRAVEL AND ENTERTAINMENT COSTS

Prepared for
Dennis McWilliams,
Vice-President of Operations
Electrovision, Inc.

Prepared by
Linda Moreno, Manager
Cost Accounting Services
Electrovision, Inc.

February 15, 2001

Capitalize the title; use uppercase and lowercase letters for all other lines.
Follow the title with the name, title, and organization of the recipient.
Balance the white space between the items on the page.
For future reference, include the report's submission date.

The "how to" tone of Moreno's title is appropriate for an action-oriented report that emphasizes recommendations. A more neutral title, such as "An Analysis of Electrovision's Travel and Entertainment Costs," would be more suitable for an informational report.

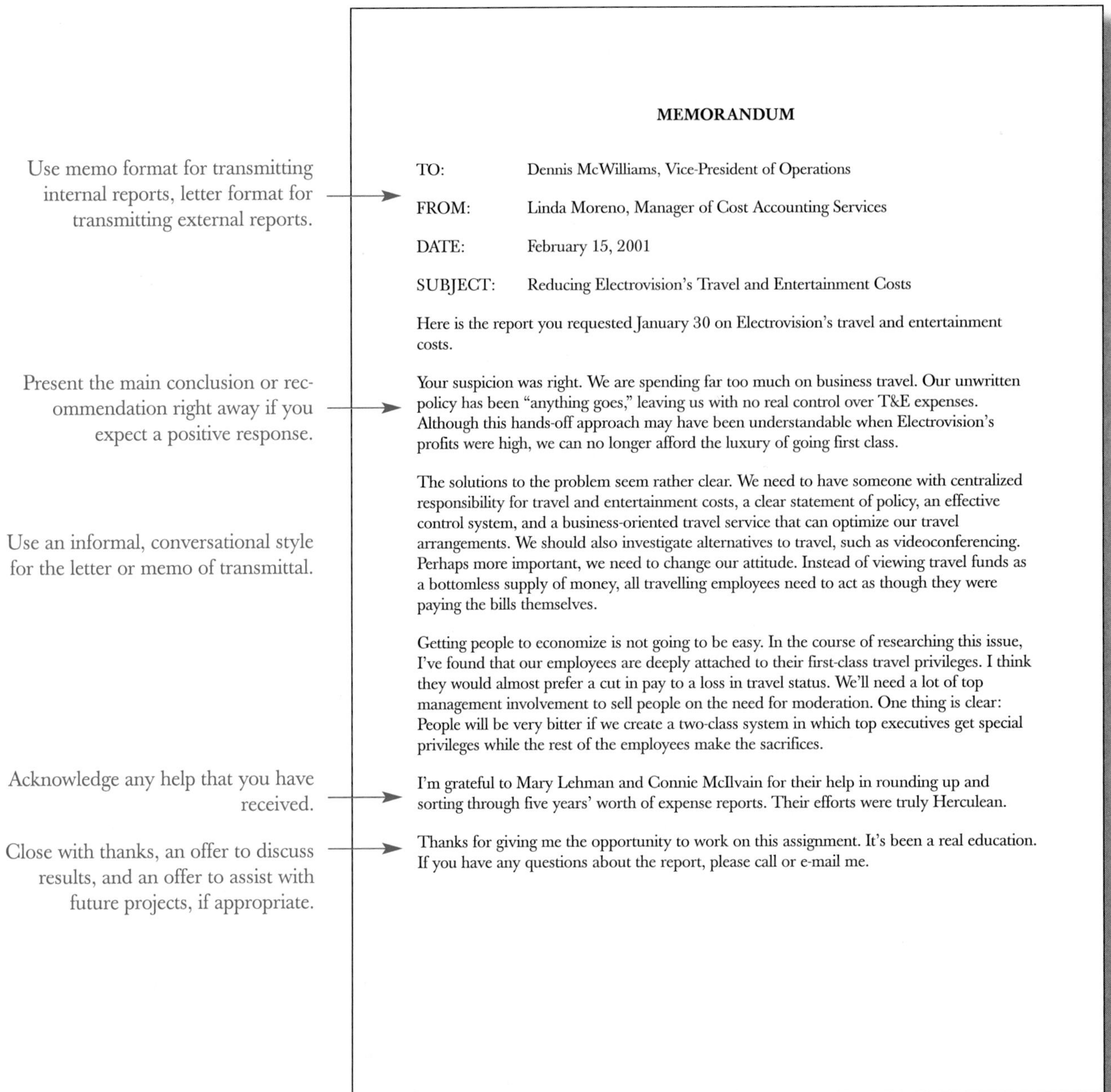

Use memo format for transmitting internal reports, letter format for transmitting external reports.

Present the main conclusion or recommendation right away if you expect a positive response.

Use an informal, conversational style for the letter or memo of transmittal.

Acknowledge any help that you have received.

Close with thanks, an offer to discuss results, and an offer to assist with future projects, if appropriate.

MEMORANDUM

TO: Dennis McWilliams, Vice-President of Operations

FROM: Linda Moreno, Manager of Cost Accounting Services

DATE: February 15, 2001

SUBJECT: Reducing Electrovision's Travel and Entertainment Costs

Here is the report you requested January 30 on Electrovision's travel and entertainment costs.

Your suspicion was right. We are spending far too much on business travel. Our unwritten policy has been "anything goes," leaving us with no real control over T&E expenses. Although this hands-off approach may have been understandable when Electrovision's profits were high, we can no longer afford the luxury of going first class.

The solutions to the problem seem rather clear. We need to have someone with centralized responsibility for travel and entertainment costs, a clear statement of policy, an effective control system, and a business-oriented travel service that can optimize our travel arrangements. We should also investigate alternatives to travel, such as videoconferencing. Perhaps more important, we need to change our attitude. Instead of viewing travel funds as a bottomless supply of money, all travelling employees need to act as though they were paying the bills themselves.

Getting people to economize is not going to be easy. In the course of researching this issue, I've found that our employees are deeply attached to their first-class travel privileges. I think they would almost prefer a cut in pay to a loss in travel status. We'll need a lot of top management involvement to sell people on the need for moderation. One thing is clear: People will be very bitter if we create a two-class system in which top executives get special privileges while the rest of the employees make the sacrifices.

I'm grateful to Mary Lehman and Connie McIlvain for their help in rounding up and sorting through five years' worth of expense reports. Their efforts were truly Herculean.

Thanks for giving me the opportunity to work on this assignment. It's been a real education. If you have any questions about the report, please call or e-mail me.

In this report Moreno decided to write a brief memo of transmittal and include a separate executive summary. Short reports (fewer than ten pages) often combine the synopsis or executive summary with the memo or letter of transmittal.

CONTENTS

Page

iii

Include no element that appears before the "Contents" page.

Word the headings exactly as they appear in the text.

Include only the page numbers where sections begin.

Moreno included only first- and second-level headings in her table of contents, even though the report contains third-level headings. She prefers a shorter table of contents that focuses attention on the main divisions of thought. She used informative titles, which are appropriate for a report to a receptive audience.

LIST OF ILLUSTRATIONS

Number the contents pages with lowercase Roman numerals centred at the bottom margin.

iv

Because figures and tables were numbered separately in the text, Moreno listed them separately here. If all had been labelled as exhibits, a single list of illustrations would have been appropriate.

EXECUTIVE SUMMARY

This report analyzes Electrovision's travel and entertainment (T&E) costs and presents recommendations for reducing those costs.

Travel and Entertainment Costs Are Too High

Travel and entertainment is a large and growing expense category for Electrovision. The company spends over $16 million per year on business travel, and these costs have been increasing by 12 percent annually. Company employees make roughly 1066 trips each year at an average cost per trip of $15 000. Airfares are the biggest expense, followed by hotels, meals, and rental cars.

The nature of Electrovision's business does require extensive travel, but the company's costs appear to be excessive. Every year Electrovision employees spend almost 50 percent more on T&E than the average business traveller. Although the location of the company's facilities may partly explain this discrepancy, the main reason for Electrovision's high costs is the firm's philosophy and managerial style. Electrovision's tradition and its hands-off style almost invite employees to go first class and pay relatively little attention to travel costs.

Cuts Are Essential

Although Electrovision has traditionally been casual about travel and entertainment expenses, management now recognizes the need to gain more control over this element of costs. The company is currently entering a period of declining profits, prompting management to look for every opportunity to reduce spending. At the same time, rising airfares and hotel rates are making travel and entertainment expenses more important to the bottom line.

Electrovision Can Save $6 Million per Year

Fortunately, Electrovision has a number of excellent opportunities for reducing its travel and entertainment costs. Savings of up to $6 million per year should be achievable, judging by the experience of other companies. Dallyce Macas, vice-president of national corporate consulting for the Rider Group, a corporate business travel management company, says that a sensible travel management program can save companies as much as 30 percent a year (Green, "Spelling Out the Rules" 56). Given that we purchase many more first-class tickets than the average company, we should be able to achieve even greater savings. The first priority should be to hire a director of travel and entertainment to assume overall responsibility for T&E spending. This individual should establish a written travel and entertainment policy and create a budget and a cost-control system. The director should also retain a nationwide travel agency to handle our reservations and should lead an investigation into electronic alternatives to travel.

v

Begin by stating the purpose of the report.

Present the points in the executive summary in the same order as they appear in the report; use subheadings that summarize the content of the main sections of the report without repeating those that appear in the text.

Type the synopsis or executive summary in the same manner as the text of the report. Use single spacing if the report is single spaced, and use the same format as used in the text for margins, paragraph indentions, and headings.

Moreno decided to include an executive summary because her report was aimed at a mixed audience. She knew that some readers would be interested in the details of her report and some would prefer to focus on the big picture. The executive summary was aimed at the big-picture group. Moreno wanted to give these readers enough information to make a decision without burdening them with the task of reading the entire report.

The frank tone of this executive summary is appropriate for a receptive audience. A more neutral approach would be better for hostile or skeptical readers.

At the same time, Electrovision should make employees aware of the need for moderation in travel and entertainment spending. People should be encouraged to forgo any unnecessary travel and to economize on airline tickets, hotels, meals, rental cars, and other expenses.

In addition to economizing on an individual basis, Electrovision should look for ways to reduce costs by negotiating preferential rates with travel providers. Once retained, a travel agency should be able to accomplish this.

Finally, we should look into alternatives to travel. Although we may have to invest money in videoconferencing systems or other equipment, we may be able to recover these costs through decreased travel expenses. I recommend that the new travel director undertake this investigation to make sure it is well integrated with the rest of the travel program.

These changes, although necessary, are likely to hurt morale, at least in the short term. Management will need to make a determined effort to explain the rationale for reduced spending. By exercising moderation in their own travel arrangements, Electrovision executives can set a good example and help other employees accept the changes. On the plus side, cutting back on travel with videoconferencing or other alternatives will reduce the travel burden on many employees and help them balance their business and personal lives much better.

Number the pages of the executive summary with lowercase roman numerals centred about 1 inch from the bottom of the page.

vi

This executive summary is written in an impersonal style, which adds to the formality of the report. Some writers prefer a more personal approach. Generally speaking, you should gear your choice of style to your relationship with the readers. Moreno chose the formal approach because several members of her audience were considerably higher up in the organization. She did not want to sound too familiar. In addition, she wanted the executive summary and the text to be compatible, and her company prefers the impersonal style for formal reports.

REDUCING ELECTROVISION'S TRAVEL AND ENTERTAINMENT COSTS

Centre the title of the report on the first page of the text, 2 inches from the top of the page.

INTRODUCTION

Electrovision has always encouraged a significant amount of business travel, believing that it is an effective way of operating. To compensate employees for the inconvenience and stress of frequent trips, management has authorized generous travel and entertainment (T&E) allowances. This philosophy has been good for morale, but the company has paid a price. Last year Electrovision spent $16 million on T&E–$7 million more than it spent on research and development.

Begin the introduction by establishing the need for action.

This year the cost of travel and entertainment will have a bigger impact on profits, owing to changes in airfares and hotel rates. The timing of these changes is unfortunate because the company anticipates that profits will be relatively weak for a variety of other reasons. In light of these profit pressures, Dennis McWilliams, Vice-President of Operations, has asked the accounting department to take a closer look at the T&E budget.

Purpose, Scope, and Limitations

The purpose of this report is to analyze the T&E budget, evaluate the impact of recent changes in airfares and hotel costs, and suggest ways to tighten management's control over T&E expenses. Although the report outlines a number of steps that could reduce Electrovision's expenses, the precise financial impact of these measures is difficult to project. The estimates presented in the report provide a "best guess" view of what Electrovision can expect to save. Until the company actually implements these steps, however, we won't know exactly how much the travel and entertainment budget can be reduced.

Sources and Methods

In preparing this report, the accounting department analyzed internal expense reports for the past five years to determine how much Electrovision spends on travel and entertainment. These figures were then compared with average statistics compiled by American Express's Survey of Canadian Business Management Travel. We also analyzed trends and suggestions published in a variety of business journal articles to see how other companies are coping with the high cost of business travel.

Mentioning sources and methods increases the credibility of a report and gives readers a complete picture of the study's background.

1

Use the Arabic numeral 1 for the first page of the report; centre the number about 1 inch from the bottom of the page.

In a brief introduction like this one, some writers would omit the subheadings within the introduction and rely on topic sentences and on transitional words and phrases to indicate that they are discussing such subjects as the purpose, scope, and limitations of the study. Moreno decided to use headings because they help readers scan the document. Also, to conserve space, Moreno used single spacing and 1-inch side margins.

Using Arabic numerals, number the second and succeeding pages of the text in the upper right-hand corner where the top and right-hand margins meet.

2

Report Organization

This report reviews the size and composition of Electrovision's travel and entertainment expenses, analyzes trends in travel costs, and recommends steps for reducing the T&E budget.

THE HIGH COST OF TRAVEL AND ENTERTAINMENT

Although many companies view travel and entertainment as an "incidental" cost of doing business, the dollars add up. At Electrovision the bill for airfares, hotels, rental cars, meals, and entertainment totalled $16 million last year. Our T&E budget has increased by 12 percent per year for the past five years. Compared to the average Canadian business traveller in our industry, Electrovision's expenditures are high, largely because of management's generous policy on travel benefits.

$16 Million per Year Spent on Travel and Entertainment

Electrovision's annual budget for travel and entertainment is only 8 percent of sales. Because this is a relatively small expense category compared with such things as salaries and commissions, it is tempting to dismiss T&E costs as insignificant. However, T&E is Electrovision's third-largest controllable expense, directly behind salaries and information systems.

Last year Electrovision personnel made about 1066 trips at an average cost per trip of $15 000. The typical trip involved a round-trip flight of 8000 km, meals and hotel accommodations for four or five days, and a rental car. Roughly 80 percent of the trips were made by 20 percent of the staff–top management and sales personnel travelled most, averaging 17 trips per year.

Place the visual aid as close as possible to the point it illustrates.

Figure 1 illustrates how the travel and entertainment budget is spent. The largest categories are airfares and lodging, which together account for $7 out of every $10 that employees

Placement of visual-aids titles should be consistent throughout a report. Options for placement include above, below, or beside the visual aid.

Give each visual aid a title that clearly indicates what it's about.

Figure 1
Airfares and Lodging Account for Over Two-Thirds of Electrovision's Travel and Entertainment Budget

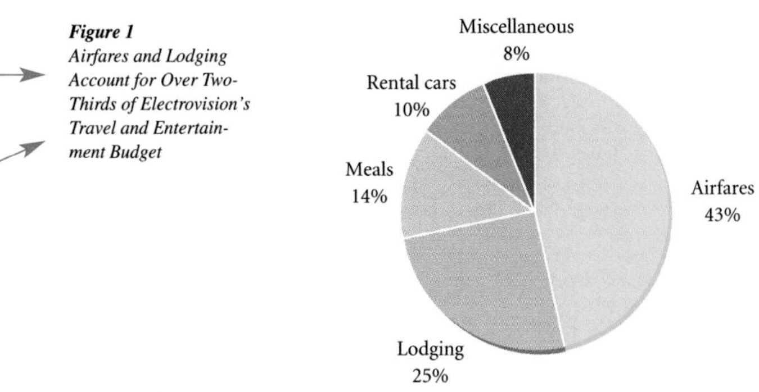

Moreno opened the first main section of the body with a topic sentence that introduces an important fact about the subject of the section. Then she oriented the reader to the three major points developed in the section.

3

spend on travel and entertainment. This spending breakdown has been relatively steady for the past five years and is consistent with the distribution of expenses experienced by other companies.

Although the composition of the T&E budget has been consistent, its size has not. As mentioned earlier, these expenditures have increased by about 12 percent per year for the past five years, roughly twice the rate of the company's growth in sales (see Figure 2). This rate of growth makes T&E Electrovision's fastest-growing expense item.

Introduce visual aids before they appear, and indicate what readers should notice about the data.

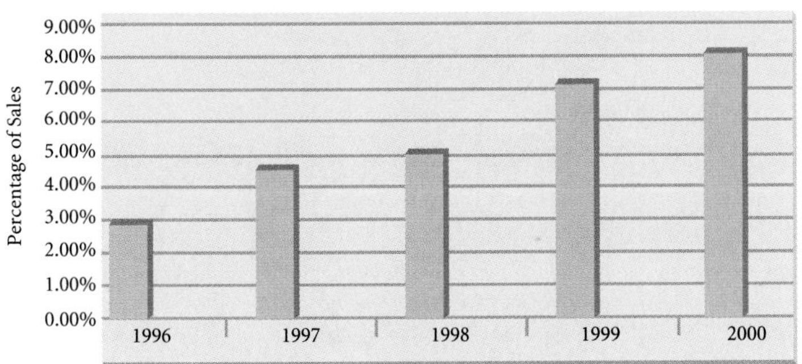

Figure 2
Travel and Entertainment Expenses Have Increased as a Percentage of Sales

Number the visual aids consecutively, and refer to them in the text by their numbers. If your report is a book-length document, you may number the visual aids by chapter: Figure 4-2, for example, would be the second figure in the fourth chapter.

Electrovision's Travel Expenses Exceed National Averages

Much of our travel budget is justified. Two major factors contribute to Electrovision's high travel and entertainment budget:

- With our headquarters in Kanata, Ontario and our major customers in the US, Central and South America, and Western Europe, we naturally spend a lot on international flights.
- A great deal of travel takes place between our headquarters here in Kanata and the manufacturing operations in Salt Lake City, UT, Seattle, WA, and Dublin, Ireland. Corporate managers and division personnel make frequent trips to coordinate these disparate operations.

However, even though a good portion of Electrovision's travel budget is justifiable, individuals spend considerably more on travel and entertainment than the average business traveller (see Figure 3).

Moreno originally drew the bar chart in Figure 2 as a line chart, showing both sales and T&E expenses in absolute dollars. However, the comparison was difficult to interpret because sales were so much greater than T&E expenses. Switching to a bar chart expressed in percentage terms made the main idea much easier to grasp. The chart in Figure 3 is very simple, but it creates an effective visual comparison. Moreno included just enough data to make her point.

4

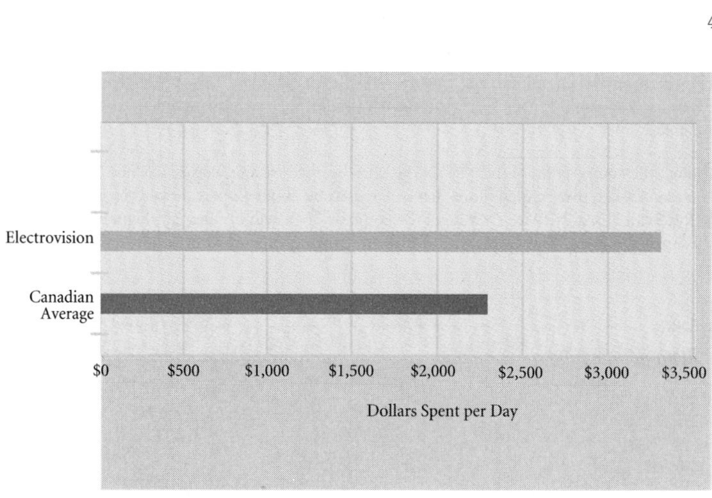

Figure 3
Electrovision People Spend Over Twice as Much as the Average Business Traveler
Source: American Express (Cuthbert C15) and company records

The 1997–98 American Express Survey of Canadian Business Travel Management indicates that Canadian companies spend approximately $9500.00 for each traveller, based on airfare, hotel rates, meals, and rental car rates (Cuthbert C15). If we adjust this amount by 5 percent each year for increases, the total amount Canadian companies spend is about $10 500.00. For a 4.5 day trip, the daily rate is about $2300 per day. In contrast, Electrovision's average daily expense over the past year has been about $3300, or about 43 percent higher than average. This figure is based on the average trip cost of $15 000 listed earlier and an average trip length of 4.5 days.

Leaving a bit more white space above a heading than below it helps readers associate that heading with the text it describes.

Spending Has Been Encouraged

Although a variety of factors may contribute to this differential, Electrovision's relatively high T&E costs are at least partially attributable to the company's philosophy and management style. Because many employees do not enjoy business travel, management has tried to make the trips more pleasant by authorizing first-class airfare, luxury hotel accommodations, and full-size rental cars. The sales staff is encouraged to entertain clients at top restaurants and to invite them to cultural and sporting events.

The cost of these privileges is easy to overlook, given the weakness of Electrovision's system for keeping track of T&E expenses:

Moreno was as careful about the appearance of her report as she was about its content.

5

- The monthly financial records provided to management do not contain a separate category for travel and entertainment; the information is buried under Cost of Goods Sold and under Selling, General, and Administrative Expenses.
- Each department head is given authority to approve any expense report, regardless of how large it may be.
- Receipts are not required for expenditures of less than $100.
- Individuals are allowed to make their own travel arrangements.
- No one is charged with the responsibility for controlling the company's total spending on travel and entertainment.

Bulleted lists make it easy for readers to identify and distinguish related points.

GROWING IMPACT ON THE BOTTOM LINE

During the past three years, the company's healthy profits have resulted in relatively little pressure to push for tighter controls over all aspects of the business. However, as we all know, the situation is changing. We're projecting flat to declining profits for the next two years, a situation that has prompted all of us to search for ways to cut costs. At the same time, rising airfares and hotel rates have increased the impact of T&E expenses on the company's financial results.

Lower Profits Underscore the Need for Change

The next two years promise to be difficult for Electrovision. After several years of steady increases in spending, many of our clients are tightening procurement policies for automated mail-handling equipment. As a consequence, the marketing department expects sales to drop by 15 percent. Although Electrovision is negotiating several promising R&D contracts with non-government clients, the marketing department does not foresee any major procurements for the next two to three years.

At the same time, Electrovision is facing cost increases on several fronts. As we've known for several months, the new production facility now under construction in Montreal is behind schedule and over budget. Labour contracts in Salt Lake City and Seattle expire within the next six months, and plant managers there anticipate that significant salary and benefits concessions may be necessary to avoid strikes. Moreover, marketing and advertising costs are expected to increase as we attempt to strengthen these activities to better cope with competitive pressures. Given the expected decline in revenues and increase in costs, the Executive Committee's prediction that profits will fall by 12 percent in the coming fiscal year does not seem overly pessimistic.

Informative headings focus readers' attention on the main points of the report. Thus they are most appropriate when the report is in direct order and is aimed at a receptive audience. Descriptive headings are more effective when a report is in indirect order and the readers are less receptive.

Airfares and Hotel Rates Are Rising

Business travellers have grown accustomed to frequent fare wars and discounting in the travel industry in recent years. Excess capacity and aggressive price competition, particularly in the airline business, made travel a relative bargain.

Because airfares represent Electrovision's biggest T&E expense, Moreno included a subsection that deals with the possible impact of trends in the airline industry. Airfares are rising, so it is especially important to gain more control over employees' air travel arrangements.

Documenting the facts adds weight to Moreno's argument.

Pointing out both the benefits and risks of taking action gives recommendations an objective flavour.

6

However, that situation has changed, as weaker competitors have been forced out and the remaining players have grown stronger and smarter. Airlines and hotels are better at managing inventory and keeping occupancy rates high, and high occupancy translates into higher prices because suppliers have less reason to compete on price. Last year saw some of the steepest rate hikes in years. All airfares between Canada and Europe have increased 5 percent to cover rising fuel prices, as well as an additional 5 percent for business class and 4 percent for first class. British Airways and Air Canada have both reduced their discount on business-class tickets (Fitzpatrick C1, C12; Lewis C1, C12). These trends are expected to continue.

Given the fact that air and hotel costs account for 70 percent of Electrovision's T&E budget, the trend toward higher prices in these two categories will have serious consequences on the company's expenses unless management takes action to control these costs.

METHODS FOR REDUCING TRAVEL AND ENTERTAINMENT COSTS

By implementing a number of reforms, management can expect to reduce Electrovision's T&E budget by as much as 30 percent or more. This estimate is based on the general assessment made by Dallyce Macas, vice-president of national corporate consulting for the Rider Group (Green, "Spelling Out the Rules" 56) and the fact that we have an opportunity to significantly reduce air travel costs by reducing or eliminating first-class travel. However, these measures are likely to be unpopular with employees. To gain acceptance for such changes, management will need to sell employees on the need for moderation in travel and entertainment allowances.

Four Ways to Trim Expenses

By researching what other companies are doing to curb travel and entertainment expenses, the accounting department has identified four prominent opportunities that should enable Electrovision to save about $6 million annually in travel-related costs.

Institute Tighter Spending Controls

A single individual should be appointed director of travel and entertainment to spearhead the effort to gain control of the T&E budget. According to American Express Canada, 48 percent of Canadian companies employ travel managers in an effort to keep costs in line ("Expanding Markets" 52–53). The director should be familiar with the travel industry and should be well versed in both accounting and information technology. The director should also report to the vice-president of operations. The director's first priorities should be to establish a written travel and entertainment policy and to implement a system for controlling travel and entertainment costs.

Moreno created a forceful tone by using action verbs in the third-level subheadings of this section. This approach is appropriate to the nature of the study and the attitude of the audience. However, in a status-conscious organization, the imperative verbs might sound a bit too presumptuous coming from a junior member of the staff.

Electrovision currently has no written policy on travel and entertainment, a step widely recommended by air travel experts (Green, "Business Travel" 9–12; Green, "Spelling Out the Rules" 56). Creating a policy would clarify management's position and serve as a vehicle for communicating the need for moderation. At a minimum, the policy should include the following provisions:

- All travel and entertainment should be strictly related to business and should be approved in advance.
- Except under special circumstances to be approved on a case-by-case basis, employees should travel by coach and stay in mid-range business hotels.
- The travel and entertainment policy should apply equally to employees at all levels in the organization. No special benefits should be allowed for top executives.

The bulleted-list format not only calls attention to important points but also adds visual interest. You can also use visual aids, headings, and direct quotations to break up large, solid blocks of print.

To implement the new policy, Electrovision will need to create a system for controlling travel and entertainment expenses. Each department should prepare an an-nual T&E budget as part of its operating plan. These budgets should be presented in detail so that management can evaluate how travel and entertainment dollars will be spent and recommend appropriate cuts.

When including recommendations in a report, specify the steps required to implement them.

To help management monitor performance relative to these budgets, the director of travel should prepare monthly financial statements showing actual travel and entertainment expenditures by department. The system for capturing this information should be computerized and should be capable of identifying individuals who consistently exceed approved spending levels. The recommended average should range between $4000 and $5000 per month for each professional employee, depending on the individual's role in the company. Because they make frequent trips, sales and top management personnel can be expected to have relatively high travel expenses.

The director of travel should also be responsible for retaining a business-oriented travel service that will schedule all employee business trips and look for the best travel deals, particularly in airfares. In addition to centralizing Electrovision's reservation and ticketing activities, the agency will negotiate reduced group rates with hotels and rental car agencies. By consolidating its travel planning in this way, Electrovision can increase its control over costs and achieve economies of scale. This is particularly important in light of the dizzying array of often wildly different airfares available between some cities (Rowe 30).

The director should also work with the agency to explore low-cost alternatives, such as buying tickets from airfare consolidators (the air travel equivalent of factory outlet malls). In addition, the director can help coordinate travel across the company to secure group discounts whenever possible (Barker 31; Miller B6).

Moreno decided to single space her report to save space; however, double spacing can make the text of a long report somewhat easier to read, and it provides more space for readers to write comments.

Reduce Unnecessary Travel and Entertainment

One of the easiest ways to reduce expenses is to reduce the amount of travelling and entertaining that occurs. An analysis of last year's expenditures suggests that as much as 30 percent of Electrovision's travel and entertainment is discretionary. The professional staff spent $2.8 million attending seminars and conferences last year. Although some of these gatherings are undoubtedly beneficial, the company could save money by sending fewer representatives to each function and by eliminating some of the less useful seminars.

Similarly, Electrovision could economize on trips between headquarters and divisions by reducing the frequency of such visits and by sending fewer people on each trip. Although there is often no substitute for face-to-face meetings, management could try to resolve more internal issues through telephone, electronic, and written communication.

Electrovision can also reduce spending by urging employees to economize. Instead of flying first class, employees can fly tourist class or take advantage of discount fares. Instead of taking clients to dinner, Electrovision personnel can hold breakfast meetings, which tend to be less costly. Rather than ordering a $50 bottle of wine, employees can select a less expensive bottle or dispense with alcohol entirely. People can book rooms at moderately priced hotels and drive smaller rental cars. In general, employees should be urged to spend the company's money as though it were their own.

Obtain Lowest Rates from Travel Providers

Apart from urging individual employees to economize, Electrovision can also save money by searching for the lowest available airfares, hotel rates, and rental car fees. Currently, few Electrovision employees have the time or specialized knowledge to seek out travel bargains. When they need to travel, they make the most convenient and most comfortable arrangements. However, if Electrovision contracts with a professional travel service, the company will have access to professionals who can more efficiently obtain the lower rates from travel providers.

Judging by the experience of other companies, Electrovision may be able to trim as much as 30 to 40 percent from the travel budget by looking for bargains in airfares and negotiating group rates with hotels and rental car companies. Electrovision should be able to achieve these economies by analyzing its travel patterns, identifying frequently visited locations, and selecting a few hotels that are willing to reduce rates in exchange for guaranteed business. At the same time, the company should be able to save up to 40 percent on rental car charges by negotiating a corporate rate.

Note how Moreno made the transition from one section to the next. The first sentence under the second heading on this page refers to the subject of the previous paragraph and signals a shift in thought.

9

The possibilities for economizing are promising, but it's worth noting that making the best arrangements is a complicated undertaking, requiring many trade-offs such as the following:

- The best fares might not always be the lowest. Indirect flights are often less expensive than direct flights, but they take longer and may end up costing more in lost work time.
- The cheapest tickets may have to be booked 30 days in advance, often impossible for us.
- Discount tickets may be non-refundable, which is a real drawback if the trip has to be cancelled at the last minute.

Pointing out possible difficulties demonstrates that you have considered all the angles and builds readers' confidence in your judgment.

Electrovision is currently ill-equipped to make these and other trade-offs. However, by employing a business-oriented travel service, the company will have access to computerized systems that can optimize its choices.

Replace Travel with Technological Alternatives

We might be able to replace a significant portion of our interdivisional travel with electronic meetings that utilize videoconferencing, real-time document sharing on PC screens, and other alternatives. Naturally, we don't want to reduce employee or team effectiveness, but many companies are using these tools to cut costs and reduce wear and tear on employees.

Rather than make specific recommendations in this report, I suggest that the new travel director conduct an in-depth study of the company's travel patterns as part of an overall cost-containment effort. A thorough analysis of why employees travel and what they accomplish will highlight any opportunities for replacing face-to-face meetings. Part of this study should include limited-scope tests of various communication systems as a way of measuring their impact on both workplace effectiveness and overall costs.

The Impact of Reforms

By implementing tighter controls, reducing unnecessary expenses, negotiating more favourable rates, and exploring "electronic travel," Electrovision should be able to reduce its travel and entertainment budget significantly. As Table 1 illustrates, the combined savings should be in the neighbourhood of $6 million, although the precise figures are somewhat difficult to project.

The informative title is consistent with other headings. This is appropriate for a report to a receptive audience. The complete sentence helps readers to see the point immediately.

Even though estimated savings may be difficult to project, including dollar figures helps management envision the impact of your suggestions.

10

TABLE 1

Electrovision Can Trim Travel and Entertainment Costs by an Estimated $6 Million per Year

Source of Savings	Amount Saved
Switching from first-class to coach airfare	$2 300 000
Negotiating preferred hotel rates	940 000
Negotiating preferred rental car rates	460 000
Systematically searching for lower airfares	375 000
Reducing interdivisional travel	675 000
Reducing seminar and conference attendance	1 250 000
TOTAL POTENTIAL SAVINGS	**$6 000 000**

To achieve the economies outlined in the table, Electrovision will incur expenses for hiring a director of travel and for implementing a T&E cost-control system. These costs are projected at $95 000 to $85 000 per year in salary and benefits for the new employee plus a one-time expense of $10 000 for the cost-control system. The cost of retaining a full-service travel agency is negligible because agencies normally receive a commission from travel providers rather than a fee from clients.

The measures required to achieve these savings are likely to be unpopular with employees. Electrovision personnel are accustomed to generous travel and entertainment allowances, and they are likely to resent having these privileges curtailed. To alleviate their disappointment

- Management should make a determined effort to explain why the changes are necessary.
- The director of corporate communication should be asked to develop a multifaceted campaign that will communicate the importance of curtailing travel and entertainment costs.
- Management should set a positive example by adhering strictly to the new policies.
- The limitations should apply equally to employees at all levels in the organization.

The table on this page puts Moreno's recommendations in perspective. Note how she called attention in the text to the most important sources of savings and also spelled out the costs required to achieve these results.

11

CONCLUSIONS AND RECOMMENDATIONS

Use a descriptive heading for the last section of the text. In informational reports, this section is generally called "Summary"; in analytical reports, it is called "Conclusions" or "Conclusions and Recommendations."

Electrovision is currently spending $16 million per year on travel and entertainment. Although much of this spending is justified, the company's costs appear to be high relative to competitors', mainly because Electrovision has been generous with its travel benefits.

Electrovision's liberal approach to travel and entertainment was understandable during years of high profitability; however, the company is facing the prospect of declining profits for the next several years. Management is therefore motivated to cut costs in all areas of the business. Reducing T&E spending is particularly important because the impact of these costs on the bottom line will increase as a result of fare increases in the airline industry.

Electrovision should be able to reduce travel and entertainment costs by as much as 40 percent by taking four important steps:

1. *Institute tighter spending controls.* Management should hire a director of travel and entertainment who will assume overall responsibility for T&E activities. Within the next six months, this director should develop a written travel policy, institute a T&E budget and a cost-control system, and retain a professional, business-oriented travel agency that will optimize arrangements with travel providers.

Emphasize the recommendations by presenting them in list format if possible.

2. *Reduce unnecessary travel and entertainment.* Electrovision should encourage employees to economize on travel and entertainment spending. Management can accomplish this by authorizing fewer trips and by urging employees to be more conservative in their spending.

3. *Obtain lowest rates from travel providers.* Electrovision should also focus on obtaining the best rates on airline tickets, hotel rooms, and rental cars. By channelling all arrangements through a professional travel agency, the company can optimize its choices and gain clout in negotiating preferred rates.

4. *Replace travel with technological alternatives.* With the number of computers already installed in our facilities, it seems likely that we could take advantage of desktop videoconferencing and other distance-meeting tools. This won't be quite as feasible with customer sites, since these systems require compatible equipment at both ends of a connection, but it is certainly a possibility for communication with Electrovision's own sites.

Do not introduce new facts in this section of the text.

Because these measures may be unpopular with employees, management should make a concerted effort to explain the importance of reducing travel costs. The director of corporate communication should be given responsibility for developing a plan to communicate the need for employee cooperation.

Because Moreno organized her report around conclusions and recommendations, readers have already been introduced to them. Thus she summarizes her conclusions in the first two paragraphs. A simple list is enough to remind readers of the four main recommendations. In a longer report she might have divided the section into subsections, labelled "Conclusions" and "Recommendations," to distinguish between the two. If the report had been organized around logical arguments, this would have been a reader's first exposure to the conclusions and recommendations, and Moreno would have needed to develop them more fully.

List references alphabetically by the author's last name or, when the author is unknown, by the title of the reference. See Appendix B for additional details on preparing reference lists.

12

WORKS CITED

Barker, Julie. "How to Rein in Group Travel Costs." *Successful Meetings* Feb. 1998: 31.

Cuthbert, Wendy. "Tighter Travel on the Company's Dime: Ticket to Rider [American Express Survey of Canadian Business Travel Management]." *Financial Post* (*National Post*) 24 May 1999: C15.

"Expanding Markets: Growth in Canadian Business Travel to be Filled by Mid-Sized Companies." *CMA Management,* 74, no. 5 (June 2000): 52-53.

Fitzpatrick, Peter. "Foreign Flights to Rise 10%: IATA Agreement. Prices Include 5% Fuel Charge, 3% to 5% General." *Financial Post* (*National Post*) 7 December 2000: C1, C12.

Green, Carolyn. "No Follow-Through After Travel: Survey [Rider Group]." *Financial Post* 18/20 October 1997: 57.

— "Spelling Out the Rules: Many Companies Have Travel Policies. But Monitoring Them is the Trick." *Financial Post* 18/20 October 1997: 56.

Lewis, Michael. "Air Fares Keep Rising with Fuel Prices: Tourist Ticket Up 20.5%." *Financial Post* (*National Post*) 25 September 2000: C1, C12.

Miller, Lisa. "Attention, Airline Ticket Shoppers." *Wall Street Journal* 7 July 1997: B6.

Phillips, Edward H. "Airlines Post Record Traffic." *Aviation Week & Space Technology* 8 Jan. 1998: 331.

Rowe, Irene Vlitos. "Global Solution for Cutting Travel Costs." *European* 12 Oct. 1997: 30.

Moreno's list of references follows the style recommended in the *MLA Style Manual*.

Text of the Proposal

The text of a proposal performs two essential functions: It persuades the client to award you a contract, and it spells out the terms of that contract. Your ideas should be practical; otherwise, you will be unable to fulfill your promises.

A proposal is both a selling tool and a contractual commitment.

If the proposal is unsolicited, you have some latitude in arranging the text. However, the organization of a solicited proposal is governed by the request for proposal. Most RFPs spell out precisely what you should cover, and in what order, so that all bids will be similar in form. This uniformity enables the client to evaluate the competing proposals in a systematic way. Many organizations assign particular sections of the proposals to appropriate expert members of an evaluation team. An engineer might review the technical portions of all the proposals submitted, and an accountant might review the cost estimates.

Follow the instructions presented in the RFP.

INTRODUCTION

The introduction orients readers to the rest of the proposal. It identifies your organization and your purpose and outlines the remainder of the text. If the proposal is solicited, the introduction should refer to the RFP; if not, it should mention any factors that led you to submit the bid. You might refer to previous conversations you've had with the client, or you might mention mutual acquaintances. Subheadings often include the following:

- *Background or statement of the problem.* Briefly reviews the client's situation, worded to establish the need for action. In business selling situations, the reader may not have the same perception of the problem as the writer has. With unsolicited proposals, potential clients and other readers may not even think they have a problem. You have to convince them a problem exists before you can convince them to accept your solution. You can do this by discussing the reader's current situation and explaining how the situation could be better–in a way that is meaningful to your reader.
- *Overview of approach.* Highlights your key selling points and their benefits, showing how your proposal will solve the client's problem. The heading for this section might also be "Preliminary Analysis" or some other wording that will identify this section as a summary of your solution to the problem.
- *Scope.* States the boundaries of the study, what you will and will not do.
- *Report organization.* Orients the reader to the remainder of the proposal and calls attention to the major divisions of thought.

As chairman of the board of Computer Associates International, Charles B. Wang must often make fast decisions on proposals. A clear purpose stated concisely saves time and promotes understanding, advises Wang, which allows your reader to make the right decision.

BODY

The core of the proposal is the body, which has the same purpose as the body of other reports. In a proposal, however, the body must cover some specific information:

LEARNING OUTCOME 5
Discuss the four areas of specific information that must be covered in the body of a proposal.

- *Proposed approach.* May also be titled "Technical Proposal," "Research Design," "Issues for Analysis," or "Work Statement." Regardless of the heading, this section is a description of what you have to offer: your concept, product, or service. If you're proposing to develop a new airplane, you might describe your preliminary design by using drawings or calculations to demonstrate the soundness of your solution. To convince the client that your proposal has merit, focus on the strengths of your product in relation to the client's needs. Point out any advantages that you have over your competitors. In this example, you might describe how your plane's unique wing design provides superior fuel economy, a particularly important feature specified in the client's request for proposal.

In the approach section, demonstrate the superiority of your ideas, products, or services.

Use the work plan to describe the tasks to be completed under the terms of the contract.

➤ *Work plan.* Describes how you will accomplish the work that must be done (necessary unless you're proposing to provide a standard, off-the-shelf item). For each phase of the work plan, describe the steps you'll take, their timing, the methods or resources you'll use, and the person or persons who will be responsible. Indicate any critical dates when portions of the work will be completed. If your proposal is accepted, the work plan will be considered firm. Any delay in the proposed schedule may jeopardize the contract or cost your organization a considerable amount of money. Therefore, don't promise to deliver more than you can realistically achieve within a given period.

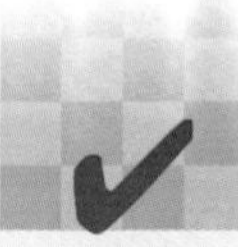

Checklist for Formal Reports and Proposals

A. Quality of the Research

1. Define the problem clearly.
2. State the purpose of the document.
3. Identify all relevant issues.
4. Accumulate evidence pertaining to each issue.
5. Check evidence for accuracy, currency, and reliability.
6. Justify your conclusions by the evidence.
   a. Do not omit or distort evidence in order to support your point of view.
   b. Identify and justify all assumptions.

B. Preparation of Reports and Proposals

1. Choose a format and length that are appropriate to your audience and the subject.
2. Prepare a sturdy, attractive cover.
   a. Label the cover clearly with the title of the document.
   b. Use a title that tells the audience exactly what the document is about.
3. Provide all necessary information on the title page.
   a. Include the full title of the document.
   b. Include the name, title, and affiliation of the recipient.
   c. Give the name, title, and affiliation of the author.
   d. Provide the date of submission.
   e. Balance the information in blocks on the page.
4. Include a copy of the letter of authorization or request for proposal, if appropriate.
5. Prepare a letter or memo of transmittal.
   a. Use memo format for internal documents.
   b. Use letter format for external documents.
   c. Include the transmittal letter in only some copies if it contains sensitive or personal information suitable for some but not all readers.
   d. Place the transmittal letter right before the table of contents.
   e. Use the good-news plan for solicited proposals and other reports; use the persuasive plan for unsolicited proposals.
   f. Word the letter to convey the document officially to the readers; refer to the authorization; and discuss the purpose, scope, background, sources and methods, and limitations.
   g. Mention any special points that warrant readers' attention.
   h. If you use direct order, summarize conclusions and recommendations (unless they are included in a synopsis).
   i. Acknowledge all who were especially helpful in preparing the document.
   j. Close with thanks, offer to be of further assistance, and suggest future projects, if appropriate.
6. Prepare the table of contents.
   a. Include all first-level headings (and all second-level headings or perhaps all second- and third-level headings).
   b. Give the page number of each heading.
   c. Word all headings exactly as they appear in the text.
   d. Include the synopsis (if there is one) and supplementary parts in the table of contents.
   e. Number the table of contents and all prefatory pages with lowercase Roman numerals centred at the bottom of the page.
7. Prepare a list of illustrations if you have four visual aids or more.
   a. Put the list in the same format as the table of contents.
   b. Identify visual aids either directly beneath the table of contents or on a separate page under the heading "List of Illustrations."
8. Develop a synopsis or an executive summary if the document is long and formal.
   a. Tailor the synopsis or executive summary to the document's length and tone.
   b. Condense the main points of the document, using either the informative approach or the descriptive approach, according to the guidelines in this chapter.

- *Statement of qualifications.* Describes your organization's experience, personnel, and facilities in relation to the client's needs. If you work for a large organization that frequently submits proposals, you can usually borrow much of this section intact from previous proposals. Be sure, however, to tailor any of this boilerplate material to suit the situation. The qualifications section can be an important selling point, and it deserves to be handled carefully.

In the qualifications section, demonstrate that you have the personnel, facilities, and experience to do a competent job.

- *Costs.* Typically has few words and many numbers but can make or break the proposal. If your price is out of line, the client will probably reject your bid. However,

The more detailed your cost proposal is, the more credibility your estimates will have.

c. Present the points in the synopsis in the same order as they appear in the document. Remember that an executive summary can deviate from the order of points made in the report.

9. Prepare the introduction to the text.

a. Leave a 2-inch margin at the top of the page, and centre the title of the document.

b. In a long document (ten pages or more), type the first-level heading "Introduction" three lines below the title.

c. In a short document (fewer than ten pages), begin typing three lines below the title of the report or proposal without the heading "Introduction."

d. Discuss the authorization (unless it's covered in the letter of transmittal), purpose, scope, background, sources and methods, definitions, limitations, and text organization.

10. Prepare the body of the document.

a. Carefully select the organizational plan (see Chapter 13).

b. Use either a personal or an impersonal tone consistently.

c. Use either a past or a present time perspective consistently.

d. Follow a consistent format in typing headings of different levels, using a company format guide, a sample proposal or report, or the format in this textbook as a model (see Appendix A).

e. Express comparable (same-level) headings in any given section in parallel grammatical form.

f. Group ideas into logical categories.

g. Tie sections together with transitional words, sentences, and paragraphs.

h. Give ideas of equal importance roughly equal space.

i. Avoid overly technical, pretentious, or vague language.

j. Develop each paragraph around a topic sentence.

k. Make sure all ideas in each paragraph are related.

l. Double space if longer than ten pages.

m. For documents bound on the left, number all pages with Arabic numerals in the upper right-hand corner (except for the first page, where the number is centred 1 inch from the bottom); for top-bound documents, number all pages with Arabic numerals centred 1 inch from the bottom.

11. Incorporate visual aids into the text.

a. Number visual aids consecutively throughout the text, numbering tables and figures (other visual aids) separately if that style is preferred.

b. Develop explicit titles for all visual aids except in-text tables.

c. Refer to each visual aid in the text, and emphasize the significance of the data.

d. Place visual aids as soon after their textual explanations as possible, or group them at the ends of chapters or at the end of the document for easy reference.

12. Conclude the text of reports and proposals with a summary and, if appropriate, conclusions and recommendations.

a. In a summary, recap the findings and explanations already presented.

b. Place conclusions and recommendations in their order of logic or importance, preferably in list format.

c. To induce action, explain in the recommendations section who should do what, when, where, and how.

d. If appropriate, point out the benefits of action, to leave readers with the motivation to follow recommendations.

13. Document all material quoted or paraphrased from secondary sources, using a consistent format (see Appendix B).

14. Include appendixes at the end of the document to provide useful and detailed information that is of interest to some but not all readers.

a. Give each appendix a title, such as "Questionnaire" or "Names and Addresses of Survey Participants."

b. If there is more than one appendix, number or letter them consecutively in the order they're referred to in the text.

c. Type appendices in a format consistent with the text of the report or proposal.

15. Include a bibliography if it seems that readers would benefit or the document would gain credibility.

a. Type the bibliography on a separate page headed "Bibliography" or "Sources."

b. Alphabetize bibliography entries.

c. Use a consistent format for the bibliography (see Appendix B).

before you deliver a low bid, remember that you'll have to live with the price you quote in the proposal. It's rarely worthwhile to win a contract if you're doomed to lose money on the job. Because it's often difficult to estimate costs on experimental projects, the client will be looking for evidence that your costs are realistic. Break down the costs in detail so that the client can see how you got your numbers: so much for labour, so much for materials, so much for overhead.

In a formal proposal it pays to be as thorough and accurate as possible. Carefully selected detail enhances your credibility. So does successful completion of any task you promise to perform.

SUMMARY

You may want to include a summary or conclusion section because it's your last opportunity to persuade the reader to accept your proposal. Summarize the merits of your approach, re-emphasize why you and your firm are the ones to do the work, and stress the benefits. Make this section relatively brief, assertive, and confident. To review the ideas and procedures presented in this chapter, consult the Checklist for Formal Reports and Proposals.

ON THE JOB
Solving a Communication Dilemma at Levi Strauss

Levi Strauss executives use reports to communicate to employees, customers, and the community. They are used to make decisions, to communicate special programs, and to recognize staff.

Former CEO Robert Haas believed that empowered employees lead to greater business success. That is, he concluded from one report that stock prices actually rise when people on the front lines are given greater authority to act and make decisions that are in the best interest of both the customer and the company.

A key report at Levi Strauss is based on Haas's vision of an ethically driven business. Called the Aspirations Statement, this report helps guide the decisions and actions of all 17 000 of Levi's employees. It clearly outlines the type of values and behaviours that the company expects from its employees. It covers issues ranging from trust to empowerment and even to good business-communication skills—all of which help the company become the organization that it aspires to be. By laying out these complex issues clearly and presenting them in a way that all employees can understand, Haas's report helps ensure that everyone is "reading off the same page." It helps lead the company forward.

Although most business reports are not accessible to the general public, anyone visiting Levi's corporate Web site, **www.levistrauss.com**, can see how much the company values the written word. The site makes a number of reports available to the public, including a complete history of the company and an overview of its corporate-giving program. All of these reports are clear and concise, and all have the components necessary for making the material easily understandable.[5]

Your Mission: As manager of internal communication, you are responsible for maintaining the communication channels up, down, and across the organization. One of your most important tasks is keeping Levi's 17 000 employees updated on the company's progress toward reaching the goals of the Aspirations Statement. Each year, you prepare a long report that is distributed both in printed form and online. Study the following questions, select the best answer in each case, and be prepared to support your choices.

1. From the boardroom to the warehouse, just about every employee in today's business world is overwhelmed with data and information. Because people have too much information to digest and too little time to read, the executive summary has become a particularly important part of corporate reports. Which of the following approaches would you take with the executive summary in your report this year?
   a. Use the executive summary to provide a quick score card for the company's performance in each of the areas addressed by the Aspirations Statement. Readers may be tempted to skip the detail contained in the body of the report, but at least they'll get the highlights in the executive summary.
   b. Use the executive summary to highlight changes in the report from previous years. You believe that the report is widely read within the company every year, so people will need guidance to understand how this new report differs in content and organization from the ones they've read in the past.

c. Do not use an executive summary at all. This report is made available to everyone in the company, not just a handful of executives, so an executive summary is not appropriate.

2. One of your responsibilities in preparing this report is to recommend specific steps the company can take to improve on any of the areas of concern that you've uncovered in your investigation. One of those areas involves one of the company's customer-service centres. Several customer-service reps complained to your staff that the centre's manager places so much emphasis on community service that the quality of the work is slipping. For example, employees who want to help out at AIDS-awareness rallies or environmental clean-up projects are allowed to do so on company time, as often as they want. This frequently leaves the centre short-handed, and employees who choose not to participate in these outside events are overloaded and increasingly resent both the volunteering program in general and particular employees who seem to be taking advantage of it. Remember, this report is distributed worldwide, so even though it's intended only for internal use, you must assume that people outside the company (including competitors and the news media) may gain access to it. How should you word your recommendation on this issue?

a. Another concern we uncovered at a customer service centre was a conflict between the company's desire to support the local community and the need to maintain a productive work environment. The specific problem involved too many employees taking too much volunteer time off work, leaving their co-workers overloaded. We've already discussed our concerns with the centre manager involved, who is working with the next level of management to resolve the situation in a way that better balances these sometimes-conflicting needs. However, it seems possible that similar situations might be developing at other locations. We recommend that all regional managers discuss the issue with their employees to see whether specific situations need to be resolved or whether the company's overall stance on volunteerism needs to be reviewed.

b. Our investigation raised some concerns about the management style of Sarah Blackstone, manager of the Montreal customer-service centre. Her commendable interest in supporting the local community through employee volunteerism is unfortunately in conflict with her responsibilities as a business manager. Too many employees are taking too much time off work to participate in community activities, leaving other employees behind to take up the slack. The result is both a decline in customer service and a growing resentment among the employees who stay in the office and have to work harder and longer to cover for their absent co-workers.

c. Our investigation raised some concerns about the management style of Sarah Blackstone, manager of the Montreal customer service centre. Her commendable interest in supporting the local community through employee volunteerism is unfortunately in conflict with her responsibilities as a business manager. Too many employees are taking too much time off work to participate in community activities, leaving other employees behind to take up the slack. The result is both a decline in customer service and a growing resentment among the employees who stay in the office and have to work harder and longer to cover for their absent co-workers. We strongly recommend that Ms. Blackstone retake the standard LS&Co management-training program to help realign her priorities with the company's business priorities.

3. Much of the information you've collected from your interviews around the world is difficult or impossible to represent numerically. However, you believe that readers would appreciate a brief summary of the interview results. For one of the issues you would like to summarize, you posed the following open-ended question to 153 employees and managers: "How would you describe our progress toward empowering front-line employees with the authority to make decisions and take actions that satisfy our customers quickly and completely?" The answers range from simple, one-sentence responses to long, involved answers complete with examples. All together, the responses fill 13 pages. What's the best way of summarizing your findings?

a. Pick a half dozen responses that in your opinion represent the range of responses. For example, you might include one that says "we've made no progress at all," one that says "I believe we've been very successful at our empowerment efforts," and four more that fall between these two extremes.

b. Create a five-step measurement scale that ranges from "little or no progress" to "completely successful." Together with a few experienced members of your staff, review each response and decide in which of the five categories it belongs. Then create a chart that shows how the 153 responses are distributed among the five categories. Explain how you developed the chart, and offer to provide a complete listing of the responses to any reader who requests one.

c. Because the information is not quantitative, it's impossible to summarize and boil down to a few facts and figures. It would therefore be inappropriate to summarize the information at all. Simply include all 13 pages of responses as an appendix in your report.

4. Assume that you chose answer (b) in question 3, and now you need to create the chart. Given the kind of information you're trying to communicate, which of the following chart types would be most effective? Explain your answer.

a. A line chart, with a point for each of five categories and a line connecting the five points.

b. A bar chart with five bars that indicate the number of responses in each category.

c. A pie chart with five slices that indicate the number of responses in each category.

TAP Your Knowledge

Summary of Learning Outcomes

1. Describe how organizations produce formal reports and proposals. As personal computers have become widespread in the workplace, employees are expected to handle most of the formatting and production requirement of their own reports and proposals. Software suites include word processing, graphics, spreadsheet, and database products that give employees the means to create professional-looking documents. The end result may be produced on paper or CD-ROM, or posted on a company intranet or on the World Wide Web.

2. Explain all the prefatory parts of a formal report. Depending on readers' preferences and familiarity, formal reports may include as many as nine of the ten possible prefatory parts: (1) The cover includes at least the report's title and perhaps the writer's name and submission date. (2) The title fly is a blank sheet of paper that adds a touch of formality. (3) The title page includes the report title; the name, title, and address of the person or group that authorized the report; the name, title, and address of the person or group that prepared the report; and the date of submission. (4) The letter (or memo) of authorization is the document requesting a report be written. (5) The letter (or memo) of *acceptance* acknowledges the assignment and is hardly ever included in reports. (6) The letter (or memo) of *transmittal* conveys the report to the audience and may appear in only selected copies of the report. (7) The table of contents lists report headings in outline form with page numbers. (8) The list of illustrations gives the titles and page numbers of visual aids. (9) A synopsis (or abstract) is a brief (one page or less) review of the report's most important points. (10) The executive summary is a fully developed "mini" version of the report that may contain headings and even visual aids. The executive summary would replace the synopsis, since both components would never be included in the same report.

3. Describe four important functions of a formal report's introduction and identify the possible topics it might include. Four important functions of introductions are (1) putting the report in a broader context by tying it to a problem or an assignment, (2) telling readers the report's purpose, (3) previewing the report's contents and organization, and (4) establishing the tone of the report and the writer's relationship with the audience. To accomplish these functions, an introduction might address topics such as authorization, scope, background, sources and methods, definitions, limitations, and organization.

4. Explain how to incorporate visual support into your text. Each visual aid you use should be referred to by number in the text of your report. Introduce each visual aid before it appears; the reference helps readers understand why the table or chart is important. Place each visual aid as close as possible to where it's mentioned first.

5. Discuss the four areas of specific information that must be covered in the body of a proposal. The body of a proposal must cover four specific areas of information. First, you must describe your proposed approach–your concept, product, or service. In this section, focus on how your approach satisfies reader needs and on any advantages you have over competitors. Second, describe your work plan–how you'll accomplish the task. Be clear about the steps you'll take, as well as when you'll take them and how. Clearly identify the person(s) responsible for the work and the completion dates for important portions of the work. Third, describe your qualifications to do the work. Include your organization's experience, personnel, and facilities, and make sure this material relates directly to the reader's particular situation. Fourth, describe the cost of the work. Break down all estimated costs so that readers can see how you arrived at your overall figure.

Test Your Knowledge

Review Questions

1. What are the elements of a report title?
2. What are the elements of a letter of transmittal?
3. What are the components of an executive summary?
4. Describe the elements of a report introduction.
5. What are the purposes of the summary, conclusion, and recommendation sections of a report?
6. How does a flowchart differ from an organization chart?

7. What tools can you use to help readers follow the structure and flow of information in a long report?
8. What ethical issue is raised by the use of technology to alter photographs in reports?
9. What information does a proposal introduction cover?
10. What are the important features of the approach section in a proposal?

Apply Your Knowledge

Critical Thinking Questions

1. What are the advantages and disadvantages of having managers and professional staff members (e.g., lawyers, accountants, engineers, and consultants) use such computer tools as page-layout programs, graphic-design software, and scanners? Explain your answer.
2. Would you include a letter of authorization with a periodic personal activity report? Would you include a letter of transmittal? Why or why not?
3. Under what circumstances would you include more than one index in a lengthy report? Explain your answer.
4. In what ways might visual aids help people overcome some of the barriers to communication discussed in Chapter 2? Please explain.
5. You're writing a report to the director of human resources on implementing participative management throughout your company. You want to emphasize that since the new approaches were implemented six months ago, absenteeism and turnovers have been sharply reduced in all but two departments. How do you visually present your data in the most favourable light? Explain.
6. If you were submitting a solicited proposal to build an indoor pool, would you include as references the names and addresses of other clients for whom you recently built similar pools? Would you include these references in an unsolicited proposal? Where in either proposal would you put these references? Why?

Practise Your Knowledge

Exercises

1. As the head of the career centre at a Canadian journalism school, you want to show students they have many options after graduation. Create a pie chart based on the following information, which shows career areas pursued by graduates of journalism schools during recent years. Summarize these findings (in two or three sentences) for publication in the student newspaper.

Media jobs	11 276
Newspapers/wire services	3 162
Broadcast/radio/TV	1 653
Public relations	2 407
Advertising	2 142
Magazines	286
Other media	1 626
Graduate study	1 346
Non-media jobs	5 324
Unemployed	2 454
Total graduates	20 400

2. The pet-food manufacturer you work for is interested in the results of a recent poll of Canadian pet-owning households. Look at the statistics that follow and decide on the most appropriate scale for this chart; then create a line chart of the trends in cat ownership. What conclusions do you draw from the trend you've charted? Draft a paragraph or two discussing the results of this poll and the potential consequences for the pet-food business. Support your conclusions by referring readers to your chart.

   In 1985, 210 000 Canadian households owned a cat. In 1990, 240 000 Canadian households owned a cat. In 1995 275 000 Canadian households owned a cat. In 2000, 310 000 Canadian households owned a cat.

3. Team up with a classmate to design graphics based on a comparison of the total tax burden of the Canadian taxpayer with that of people in other nations. One teammate should sketch a horizontal or vertical bar chart and the other should sketch pie charts from the estimates that follow. Then

exchange visual aids and analyze how well each conveys the situation of the Canadian taxpayer. Would the bar chart look best with vertical or horizontal bars? Why? What scale is best? How does using pie charts enhance or obscure the meaning or impact of the data? What suggestions can each student make for improving the other's visual aid?

Estimates show that Swedish taxpayers spend 51 percent of their incomes on taxes, British taxpayers spend 48 percent, French taxpayers spend 37 percent, Japanese taxpayers spend 28 percent, and US taxpayers spend 27 percent.

4. Last year's sales figures are in for the department store where you work (Table 14.2). Construct visual aids based on these figures that will help you explain seasonal sales variations among the departments to the store's general manager.
5. With a team of three or four other students, brainstorm and then sketch at least three ways to visually compare the populations of all 10 provinces and three territories. You can use any of the graphic ideas presented in this chapter, as well as any ideas or examples you find from other sources.
6. Because of your experience with creating and designing presentation materials, your company asks you to design its Web page. No one else in your company has the technical expertise to help you, so you begin by searching the Internet. You discover the Web sites at **www.pageresource.com** and **info.med.yale.edu/caim/manual/**. Explore the links to HTML Tutorials and JavaScript Tutorials on the *pageresource* site, and to Page Design and Web Graphics on the *info.med.yale.edu* site. Now try your hand at Web page design, and print a copy of your sample home page for submission.

TABLE 14.2 Store Sales in 2000 in Thousands

Month	Lingerie	Sporting Goods	Housewares
January	$39	$55	$83
February	37	50	81
March	37	51	78
April	25	55	77
May	26	60	79
June	30	65	85
July	30	65	79
August	27	60	77
September	27	51	77
October	27	53	78
November	31	60	82
December	40	65	85

Cases

Short Formal Reports

1. Keeping an eye on the kids: Report that summarizes survey data for an on-site day-care facility You're the human-resources manager at a 200-employee manufacturing firm. Employees at your company have expressed a strong desire for some kind of on-site child-care facility. You're in charge of investigating the situation and developing the company's response. You know that any facility will require a balance between what the company can afford to pay and what employees are willing to pay, relative to other day-care alternatives.

Table 14.3 indicates trends in on-site day care among local employers. Because you have to compete with other organizations for employees, offering comparable employee benefits such as on-site day care is an important business decision. Tables 14.4, 14.5, and 14.6 show the data collected in an internal employee survey.

Your Task: Write a report to your boss summarizing the survey results and suggesting the next step in the planning process.

TABLE 14.3 Day-Care Facilities Offered by Local Employers

	Percentage with On-Site Day-Care	
Organization Type	1995	2000
By Industry		
Retailing	6%	14%
Consumer services	8	11
Business services	11	25
Government and nonprofit	15	17
Manufacturing	27	30
By Size		
Up to 50 employees	2	2
51–100 employees	5	6
101–250 employees	12	14
251–500 employees	28	32
More than 500 employees	35	45

TABLE 14.4 Ages of Employee Dependants

Age Range	Number of Children
Under 1	14
2–3	32
4–5	25
6–7	22
8–9	13
10–11	28
Over 12	112

TABLE 14.5 Services and Features Desired in an On-Site Day-Care Facility

Service or Feature	Must Have	Nice to Have	Not Important
Nurse	3%	77%	0%
Arts and crafts	54	41	5
Outdoor play area	36	52	12
Educational activities	25	59	16
Organized games and contests	12	62	26
Sleeping arrangements	34	34	32
Evening hours (after 6 P.M.)	33	52	15
Early morning hours (before 8 A.M.)	7	48	45
Snacks	74	21	5
Lunch	88	12	0

TABLE 14.6 Amount Employees Are Willing to Pay

Per Child per Month	Percentage of Employees Willing to Pay
Less than $100	100%
$101–$200	95
$201–$300	89
$301–$400	64
$401–$500	50
$501–$600	28
More than $600	12

2. **Sailing past the sunsets: Report using statistical data to suggest a new advertising strategy** As manager of Distant Dreams, a travel agency in Halifax, Nova Scotia, you are interested in the information in Table 14.7. Dollar income seems to be shifting toward the 35–44 age group. Tables 14.8 and 14.9 are also broken down by age group. Your agency has traditionally concentrated its advertising on people nearing retirement–people who are closing out successful careers and now have the time and money to vacation abroad. Having examined the three sets of data, however, you realize that it's time for a major shift in emphasis.

Your Task: Write a report to Mary Henderson, who writes your advertisements, explaining why future ads should still be directed to people who want to explore far reaches

TABLE 14.7 Percentage of Total Canadian Household Income Earned by Various Age Groups

Age Group	1990	1995	2000
25–34	23%	24%	26%
35–44	22	25	28
45–54	22	21	19
55–64	19	17	15
Over 65	14	13	12

TABLE 14.8 Preferences in Travel Among Various Age Groups

	Age Group		
Travel Interests	18–34	35–54	55+
I am more interested in excitement and stimulation than rest and relaxation.	67%	42%	38%
I prefer to go where I haven't been before.	62	58	48
I like adventurous travel.	62	45	32
I love foreign and exotic things.	41	25	21
Vacation is a time for self-indulgence, regardless of the cost.	31	16	14
I don't see the need for a travel agent.	67	63	52

TABLE 14.9 Basic Desire for Travel Among Various Age Groups

Attitude Toward Travel	Age Group 18–34	35–54	55+
Travel is one of the most rewarding and enjoyable things one can do.	71%	69%	66%
I love the idea of travelling and do so at every opportunity.	66	59	48
I often feel the need to get away from everything.	56	55	33

of the world but to people in other age groups as well as those in their fifties and sixties. Justify your explanation by referring to the data you have examined.

3. Picking the better path: Report to help a client choose a career You are employed by Open Options, a career-counselling firm, and your main function is to help clients make career choices. Today a client with the same name as yours (a truly curious coincidence) came to your office and asked for help deciding between two careers, careers that you yourself had been interested in (an even greater coincidence!).

Your Task: Do some research on the two careers and then prepare a short report that your client can study. Your report should compare at least five major areas, such as salary, working conditions, and education required. Interview the client to understand her or his personal preferences regarding each of the five areas. For example, what is the minimum salary the client will accept? By comparing the client's preferences with the research material you collect, such as salary data, you will have a basis for concluding which of the two careers is better. The report should end with a career recommendation.

4. Selling overseas: Report on the prospects for marketing a product in another country Select (a) a product and (b) a country. The product might be a novelty item that you own (an inexpensive but accurate watch or clock, a desk organizer, or a coin bank). The country should be one that you are not now familiar with. Imagine that you are with the international sales department of the company that manufactures and sells the novelty item and that you are proposing to make it available in the country you have selected.

The first step is to learn as much as possible about the country where you plan to market the product. Check almanacs and encyclopedias for the most recent information, paying particular attention to descriptions of the social life of the inhabitants and their economic conditions. If your library carries resources such as *Yearbook of International Trade Statistics, Monthly Bulletin of Statistics,* or *Trade Statistics* (all put out by the United Nations), you may want to consult them. In addition, check the card catalogue and recent periodical indexes for sources of additional information; look for (among other matters) cultural traditions that would encourage or discourage use of the product. If you have online access, check both Web sites and any relevant databases you can find.

Your Task: Write a short report that describes the product you plan to market abroad, briefly describes the country you have selected, indicates the types of people in this country who would find the product attractive, explains how the product would be transported into the country (or possibly manufactured there if materials and labour are available), recommends a location for a regional sales centre, and suggests how the product should be sold. Your report is to be submitted to the chief operating officer of the company, whose name you can either make up or find in a corporate directory. The report should include your conclusions (how the product will do in this new environment) and your recommendations for marketing (steps the company should take immediately and those it should develop later).

5. The new way to advertise: Report summarizing Internet demographics The number of Internet users continues to grow rapidly in North America and around the world. For marketers, the Internet represents a veritable gold mine of potential customers. Unlike traditional print and broadcast media, an Internet site can be seen around the world at any time. The trick, however, is to get your target customers to take the time to visit your page.

As marketing strategist for a specialty foods mail-order company, you have been toying with the idea of going online for quite some time. Your company, Martha's Kitchen, has been selling its cakes, cheeses, fruit, and candy in printed catalogues for a little over a decade and has built up a loyal clientele. Most of your customers are affluent adults age 30 and over, and 75 percent of them are women. Of course, large portions of your sales come during the holidays.

As more and more customers ask about ordering on the Internet, you feel compelled to establish an Internet presence. Nevertheless, you have heard conflicting reports about whether companies actually make any money by selling over the Internet. Moreover, developing a top-notch Web site will likely cost a lot of money. How can you sort through the hype to find real answers?

Your Task: Write a short formal report to the director of marketing explaining whether Martha's Kitchen should develop an Internet presence. You will need some solid

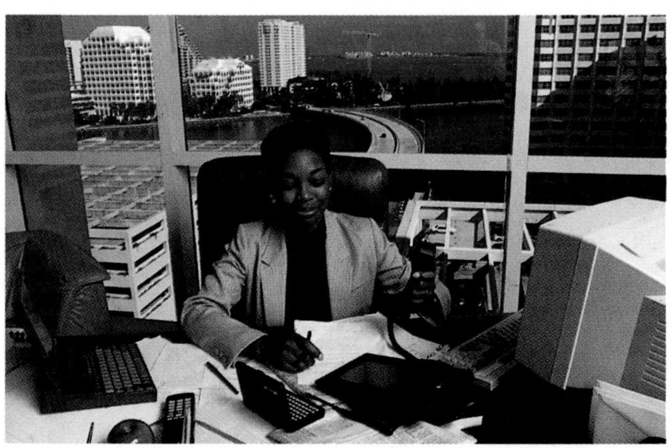

figures about the demographics of Internet users, their surfing habits, the types of products they purchase online, and growth trends in online commerce. The following are good resources to help you get started.

www.emarketer.com
www.cyberatlas.internet.com
www.ad-guide.com

(Hint: Type "Canada" in the search box.)

These sites also contain links to other sites with additional useful information. As background, you may also find it helpful to look at some competitors' sites, such as Harry and David **www.harryanddavid.com** and Norm Thompson **www.normthompson.com**.

On the basis of your findings, how do you think an Internet site will improve the company's bottom line? Use your imagination to fill in the details about the company.

Long Formal Report Requiring No Additional Research

6. Customer service crisis: Report summarizing and explaining customer service problems You are the operations manager for Continental Security Systems (CSS), a mail-order supplier of home-security systems and components. Your customers are do-it-yourself homeowners who buy a wide range of motion sensors, automatic telephone dialers, glass breakage detectors, video cameras, and other devices.

The company's aggressive pricing has yielded spectacular growth in the last year, and everyone is scrambling to keep up with the orders arriving every day. Unfortunately, customer service has often taken a back seat to filling those orders. Your boss, the company's founder and president, knows that service is slipping, and she wants you to solve the problem. You started with some internal and external surveys to assess the situation. Some of the most significant findings from the research are presented in Tables 14.10, 14.11, and 14.12.

Your Task: Prepare a report that explains the data you collected in your research. Keep the report factual and objective; everyone knows that growth has strained the company's resources, so you have no need to place blame. (For the purposes of this exercise, feel free to make up any additional facts you need about the company.)

TABLE 14.10 Customer Complaints over the Last 12 Months

Type of Complaint	Number of Occurrences	Percentage of Total
Delays in responding	67	30%
Product malfunction	56	25
Missing parts	45	20
No answer when calling for help	32	14
Rude treatment	18	8
Overcharge	5	2

Note: Percentages don't add to 100 because of rounding.

TABLE 14.12 Customer Perceptions And Opinions

Statement	Agree	Disagree
CSS offers a competitive level of customer service.	12%	88%
I recommended CSS to friends and colleagues.	4	96
I plan to continue buying from CSS.	15	85
I enjoy doing business with CSS.	9	91

TABLE 14.11 How Complaints Were Resolved

Resolution	Percentage
Employee receiving the phone call solved the problem	20%
Employee referred customer to manager	30
Customer eventually solved the problem by himself/herself	12
Unable to solve problem	23
Resolution unknown	15

Long Formal Reports Requiring Additional Research

7. Equipment purchase: Report on competitive product features Suppose that your office or home needs some new equipment. Choose one of the following, and figure out which brand and model would be the best buy.

a. Cellular phone
b. Calculator
c. Telephone answering machine
d. Home-security system
e. Photocopier
f. Personal computer
g. Word-processing software
h. Desktop scanner

Your Task: Write a long formal report describing the features of the available alternatives, listing the benefits and drawbacks of each, and making a clear recommendation. Be sure to include a discussion of the factors on which you've based your decision (including cost, reliability, and so on).

8. Group effort: Report on a large-scale topic The following topics may be too big for any one person, yet they need to be investigated:

a. A demographic profile (age, gender, socioeconomic status, residence, employment, educational background, and the like) of the students at your college or university
b. The best part-time employment opportunities in your community
c. The best of two or three health clubs or gyms in your community
d. Actions that can be taken in your community or province to combat alcohol (or other drug) abuse
e. Improvements that could be made in the food service at your college or university
f. Your college's or university's image in the community and ways to improve it
g. Your community's strengths and weaknesses in attracting new businesses

Your Task: Because these topics require considerable research, your instructor may wish to form groups to work on each. If your group writes a report on the first topic, summarize your findings at the end of the report. For all the other topics, reach conclusions and make recommendations in the report.

9. Secondary sources: Report based on library research Perhaps one of the following questions has been keeping you awake at night:

a. What's the best way for someone in your financial situation to invest a $5000 inheritance?
b. What can be done about parking problems on campus?
c. Of three careers that appeal to you, which best suits you?
d. How do other consumers regard a product that you use frequently?
e. Which of three cities that you might like to live in seems most attractive?
f. What's the surest and easiest route to becoming a millionaire?

Your Task: Answer one of these questions, using secondary sources for information. Be sure to document your sources in the correct form. Give conclusions and recommendations in your report.

10. Travel opportunities: Report comparing two destinations You are planning to take a two-week trip abroad sometime within the next year. Because there are a couple of destinations that appeal to you, you are going to have to do some research before you can make a decision.

Your Task: Prepare a lengthy comparative study of two countries that you would like to visit. Begin by making a list of important questions you will need to answer. Do you want a relaxing vacation or an educational experience? What types of services will you require? What will your transportation needs be? Where will you have the least difficulty with the language? Using resources in your library, the Internet, and perhaps travel agencies, analyze the suitability of these two destinations with respect to your own travel criteria. At the end of the report, recommend the better country to visit this year.

11. Doing business abroad: Report summarizing the social and business customs of a foreign country Your company would like to sell their products overseas. Before they begin negotiating on the international horizon, however, management must have a clear understanding of the social and business customs of the foreign countries where they intend to do business.

Your Task: Choose a non-English-speaking country, and write a long formal report summarizing the country's social and business customs. Review Chapter 3 and use that chapter's "Checklist for Doing Business Abroad" as a guide for the types of information you should include in your report.

Formal Proposals

12. Top Dog: Proposal to furnish puppies to Luv-A-Pet Stores You are the business manager of MukLuk Kennels of Whitehorse, Yukon, a breeder of Siberian huskies. Every year, you sell between 45 and 60 huskies to dog-sledding companies that run tours, and to men and women who participate in dog-sled races. Your average price for these mature huskies are about $250 each.

All your huskies are pedigreed animals with the Canadian Kennel Club and the American Kennel Club. In addition, they are sold with the required vaccinations and are guaranteed to be healthy.

Siberian huskies have become popular as personal pets in households across North America, and for several months you have been trying to win a long-term contract with Luv-A-Pet stores, a retail operation with stores in many Canadian cities. Finally, you've been invited to submit a proposal to provide 60 puppies a year to their outlets in western Canada. The specifications stipulate that you will ship approximately five dogs a month. The puppies should be eight to ten weeks old at the time of shipment and should have all the necessary shots and CKC papers. Luv-A-Pet stores is willing to pay $115 for each Siberian husky puppy.

Your Task: Using your imagination to supply the details, write a proposal describing your plans to provide the dogs.[6]

13. When is a program not a program? Proposal to produce a television infomercial. If you have cable television, you already know something about infomercials. As you flip through the channels, you can't help noticing these half-hour "programs" that extol the benefits of products ranging from baldness cures to exercise equipment to car wax. Many of the ads are in a talk-show format and feature celebrities talking with people who have used the product and want to share their success stories. Other infomercials focus primarily on product demonstrations.

This form of direct-response television has proliferated because the ads are relatively inexpensive to produce and because cable air time often comes cheap. Whereas producing a 30-second network commercial might cost $200 000, a marketer can get by with as little as $150 000 to produce a 30-minute infomercial. In addition, placing an infomercial can cost only hundreds or thousands of dollars instead of tens of thousands or hundreds of thousands.

You've recently joined the staff of American Telecast, one of the three major producers of infomercials, with annual revenues of $150 million. American Telecast's claims to fame include the highly successful Richard Simmons weight-loss-plan "long-form marketing program." Your boss has handed you a magazine ad for Audio-Forum, a company that sells audiocassettes that teach people how to speak foreign languages, how to play the piano or read music, how to improve their vocabulary or their speech, and even how to touch-type. "This looks like the kind of product we could really run with in an infomercial–especially the foreign language stuff," says your boss. She wants you to come up with an unsolicited proposal that will entice Audio-Forum into entering the infomercial game.

You look through the company's highly detailed ad, which you remember having seen in several magazines. The portion of the ad devoted to language-learning tapes says, "Learn to speak a foreign language fluently on your own and at your own pace" and goes on to give the course's credentials (developed for the Ministry of Foreign Affairs for diplomatic personnel who need to learn a language quickly), to describe what each course consists of, and to list the languages available. Both an order form and a toll-free number are provided. You remember reading somewhere that Audio-Forum has been quite successful with its magazine direct-marketing approach.

Your Task: Write a proposal to Audio-Forum, 413 Weldrick Road, Richmond Hill, Ontario, L4B 3M5, indicating American Telecast's desire to produce an infomercial for Audio-Forum's language-learning tapes. Use your imagination to fill in any additional details.[7]

Developing Your Internet Skills

Going Online: Design Effective Computer Graphics, p. 376

Find some information here that might help you visually enhance a business report. Write down a brief description of what you've found. What did you discover about computer graphics that you didn't know before? What resources did you find that might help future writing projects? Did you see anything visually arresting that gave you ideas for illustrating your own work? If so, what was it? Did you find anything that offended or confused you? Is so, what made it fail to impress you positively?

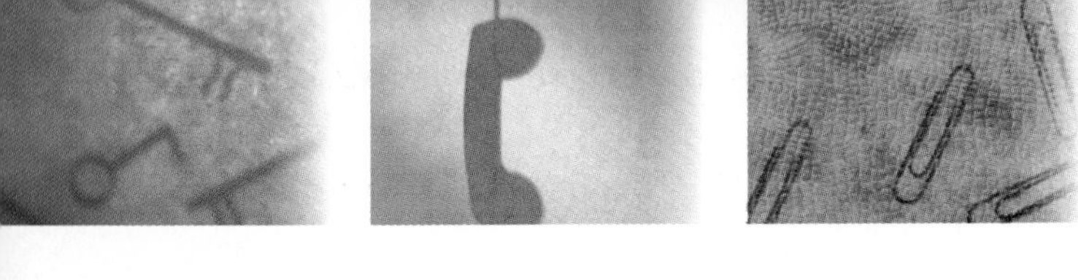

CHAPTER 15

Writing Résumés and Application Letters

AFTER STUDYING THIS CHAPTER, YOU WILL BE ABLE TO

1. Analyze your work skills and qualifications
2. Identify what type of job and employer you want
3. List your best prospects for employment
4. Develop a strategy for selling yourself to these prospects
5. Prepare an effective résumé
6. Define the purpose of application letters, and explain how to apply the AIDA organizational approach to them

ON THE JOB

Facing a Communication Dilemma at Pinkerton

Keeping a Private Eye on Hiring

When you screen more than a million job applicants a year, you're sure to gain an in-depth knowledge of employment messages. That's the kind of expertise that Pinkerton has developed. One of the many security and protection services Pinkerton performs around the world is screening job applicants for clients (as well as for its own operations), but the company takes great pride in matching the right person to the right job.

Like most companies today, Pinkerton is looking for applicants who are well educated, well trained, and well spoken. The process usually begins with a résumé and culminates with an interview.

In Canada, Pinkerton's clients include General Motors, which is paying $174 million over eight years to the agency for security services. In the US, the Academy of Motion Picture Arts and Sciences relies on Pinkerton to protect the rich and famous during the Academy Award presentations in Los Angeles. Uniformed security services make up the bulk of Pinkerton's business, but the company is working to become a one-stop shop for asset-protection services. These include electronic surveillance systems, undercover investigations, access control, insurance investigations, crisis management, ethics-monitoring programs, and a wide variety of related services.

Between 1994 and 1999, when he retired, CEO Denis Brown led Pinkerton through more than 35 acquisitions, a major global expansion, and the addition of new services to assure the company's future. His vision of a global security company was realized with Pinkerton's merger with Swedish firm Securitas AB, the largest security provider in Europe. This union has created the world's largest security business with annual revenues of $5.25 billion Canadian and 114 000 employees in more than 32 countries throughout the Western hemisphere, Europe, and Asia.

Brown's own background has been as diverse as Pinkerton's—his jobs have ranged from helping develop the Global Positioning System to turning around a troubled supercomputer maker. Throughout his career, Brown has reviewed plenty of job applications for all kinds of positions.

If you were Brown, what qualities would you look for in a job applicant? How would you want Pinkerton to evaluate the résumés and application letters it receives? What would you think constitutes a good résumé? A good application letter? What steps would you take to screen job candidates?[1]

Thinking About Your Career

LEARNING OUTCOME 1
Analyze your work skills and qualifications.

As Pinkerton's Denis Brown would tell you, getting the job that's right for you takes more than sending out a few letters or signing up with the university placement service. Planning and research are important if you want to find a company that suits you. So before you limit your employment search to a particular industry or job, analyze what you have to offer and what you hope to get from your work. Then you can identify employers who are likely to want you and vice versa.

What Do You Have to Offer?

What you have to offer:
✧ Functional skills
✧ Education and experience
✧ Personality traits

What are your marketable skills? First, jot down ten achievements you're proud of—learning to ski, taking a prizewinning photo, tutoring a child, editing the school paper. Analyze each achievement, and you'll begin to recognize a pattern of skills that are valuable to potential employers.

Second, look at your educational preparation, work experience, and extracurricular activities. What kinds of jobs have your knowledge and experience qualified you for? What have you learned from participating in volunteer work or class projects that could benefit you on the job? Have you held any offices, won any awards or scholarships, or mastered a second or third language?

Third, take stock of your personal characteristics to determine the type of job you'll do best. Are you aggressive, a born leader? Or would you rather follow? Are you outgoing, articulate, great with people? Or do you prefer working alone? Make a list of what you believe are your four or five most important traits. Ask a relative or friend to rate your traits as well. If you're having trouble figuring out your interests and capabilities, consult your university placement office or career guidance centre for advice.

What Do You Want to Do?

LEARNING OUTCOME 2
Identify what type of job and employer you want.

Knowing what you *can* do is one thing. Knowing what you *want* to do is another. Don't lose sight of your own values. Discover the things that will bring you satisfaction and happiness on the job.

Envision the ideal day at the office. What would you enjoy doing every day?

- *Decide what you'd like to do every day.* Talk to people in various occupations. You might contact relatives, local businesses, or former graduates (through your school's alumni relations office). Read about various occupations. Start with your university or college library or placement office, where they will have material on hand and will direct you to helpful sites on the World Wide Web, such as **www.workinfonet.ca**, an especially rich resource of career and employment information sponsored by Human Resources Development Canada. (You will find that Web sites such as this one will be more up to date than books, but don't ignore such works as Frank Feather's *Canada's Best Careers Guide*). Also consider how much independence you want on the job, how much variety you like, and whether you prefer to work with products, machines, people, ideas, numbers, or some combination of these. Do you like physical work, mental work, or a mix? Constant change or a predictable role?

How much do you want to earn, and how high do you hope to climb?

- *Establish some specific compensation targets.* What do you hope to earn in your first year on the job? What kind of pay increase do you expect each year? What's your ultimate earnings goal? Would you be comfortable with a job that paid on commission, or do you prefer a steady paycheque? What occupations offer the kind of money you're looking for? Are these occupations realistic for someone with your qualifications? Are you willing to settle for less money in order to do something you really love? Consider where you'd like to start, where you'd like to go from there, and the ultimate position you'd like to attain. How soon after joining the company would you like to receive your first promotion? Your next one? What additional training or preparation will you need to achieve them?

What type of industry and organization do you want to work for?

- *Consider the type of environment you prefer.* Think in broad terms about the size and type of operation that appeals to you, the location you prefer, the facilities you envision, and especially the corporate culture you'd be most comfortable with. Would you rather work for a small, entrepreneurial operation or a large company? A profit-making company or a non-profit organization? Are you attracted to service businesses or manufacturing operations? Do you want regular, predictable hours, or do you thrive on flexible, varied hours? Would you enjoy a seasonally varied job (say, in education, which may give you summers off, or in retailing, with its selling cycles)? Or would you prefer a steady pace year-round? Would you like to work in a city, a suburb, a small town, or an industrial area? Do you favour a particular part of the country? A country abroad? Do you like working indoors or outdoors? Is it important to you to work in an attractive place, or will simple, functional quarters suffice? Do you need a quiet office to work effectively, or can you concentrate in a noisy, open setting? Is access to public transportation or highways important? Perhaps the most important environmental factor is the corporate culture. Would you be happy in a well-defined hierarchy, where roles and reporting relationships are clear, or would you prefer a less structured situation? What qualities do you want in a boss? Are you looking for a paternalistic organization or one that fosters individualism? Do you like a competitive environment or one that rewards teamwork?

What type of corporate culture best suits you?

Where Do You Find Employment Information?

LEARNING OUTCOME 3
List your best prospects for employment.

Once you know what you have to offer and what you want, you can start finding an employer to match. If you haven't already committed yourself to any particular career field, first find out where the job opportunities are. Which industries are strong? Which parts of the country are booming, and which specific job categories offer the best prospects for the future?

Find out where the job opportunities are.

Whether your major is business, biology, or political science, start your search for information by keeping abreast of business and financial news. Subscribe to a major newspaper and scan the business pages every day. Watch TV programs that focus on business, such as *ROBTV* and *Wall Street Week*, and read the business articles in popular magazines such as *Maclean's* and *Time*. You might want to subscribe to a business magazine, such as *Canadian Business*, *Fortune*, or *Business Week*.

You can obtain information about the future for specific jobs in the *Dictionary of Occupational Titles*, *Occupational Outlook Handbook*, and through the World Wide Web. Two good Internet sources are Canada Prospects 2000 and Job Futures 2000–HRDC, both available through **www.workinfonet.ca**. For overviews of major industries, see the *Financial Post's Survey of Industrials*, *Globe and Mail Report on Business: Canada Company Handbook*, the annual Market Data and Directory issue of *Industrial Marketing*, and Standard & Poor's industry surveys.

Study professional and trade journals in the career fields that interest you. Also, talk to people in those fields; for names of the most prominent, consult *Standard & Poor's Register of Corporations, Directors and Executives* and the *Globe and Mail Report on Business: Canada Company Handbook*. You can find recent books about the fields you're considering by checking *Books in Print* at your library. It's often possible for students to network with executives in their field of interest by joining or participating in student business organizations, especially those with ties to organizations such as the American Marketing Association or the American Management Association, both of which have Canadian branches.

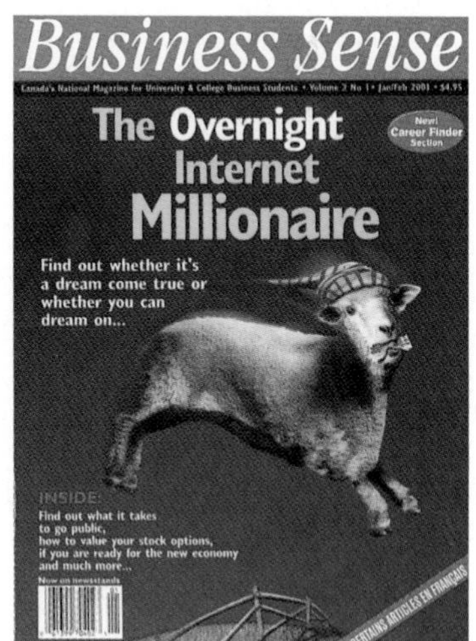

One of the best resources Canadians can consult for employment information is *Busienss $ense* magazine. Oriented toward university and college students, it includes information about résumés, interviewing, and career options. Read about *Business $ense* in Behind the Scenes in Chapter 6.

Once you've identified a promising industry and a career field, list specific organizations that appeal to you by consulting directories of employers, such as the *Canadian Student Employment Guide, The Career Directory*, and *Career: The Annual Guide to Business Opportunities*. (Other directories are listed in Chapter 16.) Write to the organizations on your list and ask for their most recent annual report and any descriptive brochures or newsletters they've published. If possible, visit some of the organizations on your list, contact their human resources departments, or talk with key employees.

You can find ads for specific job openings by looking in local and major newspapers. In addition, check the trade and professional journals in career fields that interest you; *Ulrich's International Periodicals Directory* (available at the library) lists these publications. So do electronic databases such as *Infotrac: General BusinessFile ASAP*, which is supplied by Information Access Company to many university libraries. Job listings can also be obtained from your university placement office and from government employment bureaus. A source of growing importance to your job search is the Internet, or more specifically the World Wide Web.

For helpful hints and useful Web addresses, you can turn to innumerable books, such as *What Colour Is Your Parachute?* by Richard Nelson Bolles (which is also available in an electronic edition on the Web). The World Wide Web offers information not only from employers seeking applicants but also from people seeking work. You can use the World Wide Web for a variety of job-seeking tasks:

- *Finding career counselling*. When analyzing your skills and work expectations, you can begin your self-assessment with the *Keirsey Temperament Sorter,* an online personality test at **www.advisorteam.com/user/kts.asp**. You'll find job-seeking pointers and counselling from online career centres. Some are run by universities and colleges that put a lot of effort into creating interesting and helpful sites. Others are commercial and can range from exceptional to unsatisfactory. So make sure the advice you get is both useful and sensible. You can also obtain online résumé assistance from sites such as Job Smart Résumé Guide, the Riley Guide, Career Mosaic's Résumé Writing Guide, and Intellimatch Power Résumé Builder.
- *Making contacts*. You can use the Web to locate and communicate with potential employers. Usenet newsgroups are dedicated to your field of interest, and members leave messages for one another on an electronic bulletin board. Listservs (or Internet mailing lists) are similar to Usenet newsgroups, except they mail each message to every member's e-mail address. Commercial systems such as Prodigy, America Online, and CompuServe have their own discussion groups (called Special Interest Groups, RoundTables, Clubs, or Bulletin Boards) that are also devoted to a particular interest, but they make a profit from the time users spend using their services. Once you locate a potential contact, you can communicate quickly and non-intrusively by using e-mail to request information or to let an employer know you're interested in working for that company.
- *Researching employers' companies*. By visiting a company's Web site, you can find out about its mission, products, annual reports, employee benefits, and job openings. You can locate company Web sites by knowing the URL (or Web address), by using links from other sites, or by using a search engine such as AltaVista.ca, Canada.com, or Hotbot.
- *Searching for job vacancies*. Online indexes list openings from multiple companies and include Career Mosaic, Careerclick.com, CanadaJobs.Com, Monster Board Canada, Recruiters Online Network, Workopolis, and many others. To locate any of these organizations, simply use a search engine such as AltaVista Canada or Canada.com. Of course, even the Web offers no central, unified marketplace, so plan on visiting hundreds of sites to learn what jobs are available. Also remember that only a small percentage of jobs are currently listed on the Web. Employers generally prefer to fill job vacancies through the "hidden job market," finding people without advertising, whether on the Internet or in newspapers (Figure 15.1).
- *Posting your résumé online*. You can post your résumé online either through an index service or on your own home page. To post your résumé on an index service, simply prepare the information to be input into the database and transmit it by mail, fax, modem, or e-mail. Then employers contact your index service, specifying all the key words to be found in qualifying résumés, and your index service sends the employer a list of names along with résumés or background profile sheets. By posting your résumé on your own home page, you can retain a nicer looking format, and you can even include links to papers you've written or recommendations you've received, and sound or video clips. Numerous campus placement offices have retooled to help you take advantage of Web opportunities. But keep in mind that many job openings are not listed on the Internet. The World Wide Web cannot replace other techniques for finding employment; it's just one more tool in your overall strategy.[2]

Employers find job candidates through
✧ Employee referrals
✧ On-campus interviews
✧ Unsolicited résumés
✧ Placement agencies
✧ Advertisements

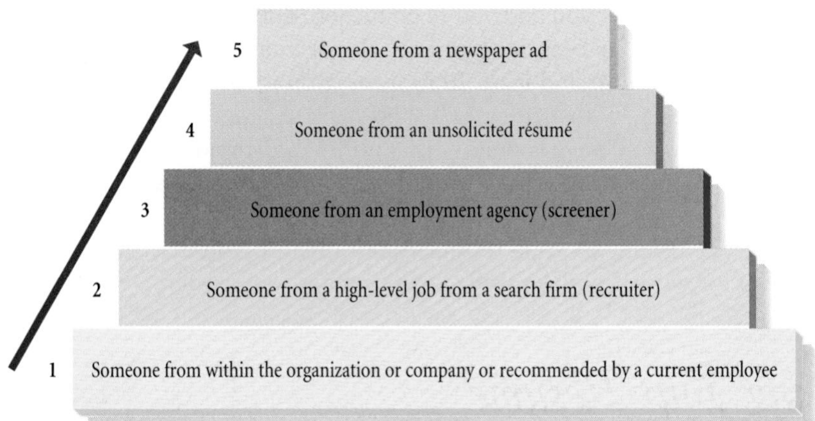

FIGURE 15.1

How Organizations Prefer to Find New Employees

Employers prefer filling positions from within their organization or from an employee's recommendation. Placing want ads is often viewed as a last resort. In contrast, typical job hunters begin pursuing work from the opposite direction (starting with want ads).

How Do You Build Toward a Career?

LEARNING OUTCOME 4
Develop a strategy for selling yourself to these prospects.

Employers are seeking people who are able and willing to adapt to diverse situations, who thrive in an ever-changing workplace, and who continue to learn throughout their careers. Companies want leaders who are versatile, and they are encouraging their managers to get varied job experience.[3] Employers want team players with strong work records, so try to gain skills you can market in various industries.

Consider keeping an employment portfolio. Get a three-ring binder and a package of plastic sleeves. Collect anything that shows your ability to perform, such as classroom or work evaluations, certificates, awards, and papers you've written. This employment portfolio accomplishes two things: it impresses employers that you're not just talking about what you've done but have tangible evidence of your professionalism. Also, it allows you to be relaxed because you can discuss your skills and accomplishments calmly and enthusiastically.

Your chances of getting a job are increased by career-building efforts:

- ✧ Developing an employment portfolio
- ✧ Gaining intercultural experience
- ✧ Participating in an internship program
- ✧ Networking with others in your field
- ✧ Taking interim jobs and classes
- ✧ Expanding your life experience
- ✧ Having at least a working knowledge of Canada's two official languages

Your chances of being hired are better if you've studied abroad and learned another language. At the least, employers expect graduates to have a sound understanding of international affairs. Companies are looking for employees with intercultural sensitivity and an ability to adapt in other cultures.[4]

Gain a competitive edge by participating in an internship program. Not only will an internship help you gain valuable experience and relevant contacts, but it will provide you with important references and items for your portfolio.[5]

Join networks of professional colleagues and friends who can help you stay abreast of where your occupation, industry, and company are going. As you search for a permanent job that fulfills your career goals, take interim job assignments and consider temporary work or freelance jobs. Employers will be more willing to find (or even create) a position for someone they've learned to respect–your temporary or freelance work gives them a chance to see what you can do.

Another way to gain experience is to start your own business. Many students do freelance secretarial or landscaping work, for example.

If you're unable to find actual job experience, work on polishing and updating your skills. While you're waiting for responses to your résumé or to hear about your last interview, take a computer course, or use the time to gain some other educational or life experience that would be difficult to get while working full time. Become familiar with the services offered by your campus career centre or placement office. They offer a variety of services, including individual placement counselling, credential services, job fairs, on-campus interviews, job listings, advice on computerized résumé-writing software, workshops in job-search techniques, résumé preparation, interview techniques, and more.[6]

Once an employer hires you and you're on the job, don't think you've reached the end of the process. The best thing you can do for your long-term career is to continue learning. Listen to and learn from those around you who have experience. Actively pursue new or better skills, and be ready and willing to take on new responsibilities. Employers appreciate applicants and employees who demonstrate a willingness and enthusiasm to learn, to listen, and to gain experience.

Of course, to get hired, you usually need an interview, and to get that interview, you usually need a résumé. A good résumé can distinguish you from all the other people looking for work. So make sure your résumé is well written.

Writing Your Résumé

LEARNING OUTCOME 5
Prepare an effective résumé.

A **résumé** is a structured, written summary of a person's education, employment background, and job qualifications. A résumé is a form of advertising, designed to help you get an interview. This interview may serve any number of purposes–to get a job, get a promotion, obtain membership in a professional organization, or become a member of a non-profit board. As in all forms of advertising, your objectives are to call attention to your best features and to downplay your disadvantages, without distorting or misrepresenting the facts.[7] You arrange these facts according to your purpose.

Your résumé is a structured, written summary of your educational and employment background, and it shows your qualifications for a job.

The purpose of the résumé is to get you an interview.

Executives like Pinkerton's Denis Brown believe a good résumé shows that a candidate (1) thinks in terms of results, (2) knows how to get things done, (3) is well rounded, (4) shows signs of progress, (5) has personal standards of excellence, (6) is flexible and willing to try new things, and (7) possesses strong communication skills. As you put your résumé together, think about how the format, style, content, and organization can help you convey these seven qualities.

Controlling the Format and Style

The key characteristics of a good résumé are

✧ Neatness
✧ Simplicity
✧ Accuracy
✧ Honesty

Quick! You have less than 45 seconds to make a good impression. That's the amount of time a typical recruiter devotes to each résumé before tossing it into either the "maybe" or the "reject" pile.[8] If your résumé doesn't *look* sharp, chances are nobody will read it carefully enough to judge your qualifications.

It's important to use a clean typeface on high-grade, letter-size bond paper (in white, off-white, light ivory, or other light earth tone). Be sure your application letter and envelope are on matching-coloured stationery. Leave ample margins all around, and be sure any corrections are unnoticeable. Avoid italic typefaces, which can be difficult to read. If you have reservations about the quality of your printer (dot-matrix printing is not suitable for any résumé) or typewriter, you might want to turn your résumé over to a professional service. To make duplicate copies, use offset printing or photocopying.

In terms of layout, your objective is to make the information easy to grasp.[9] Break up the text by using headings that call attention to various aspects of your background, such as your work experience and education. Underline or capitalize key points, or set them off in the left margin. Use indented lists to itemize your most important qualifications. Leave plenty of white space, even if doing so forces you to use two pages rather than one.

Pay attention to mechanics. Check the headings and itemized lists to make sure they're grammatically parallel. Be sure your grammar, spelling, and punctuation are correct. Because your résumé has only seconds to make an impression, the "you" attitude and audience focus are crucial. Keep your writing style simple and direct. Instead of whole sentences, use short, crisp phrases starting with action verbs. You might say, "Coached a Little League team to the regional playoffs" or "Supervised a fast-food restaurant with four employees."

As a rule of thumb, try to write a one-page résumé. If you have a great deal of experience and are applying for a higher-level position, you may wish to prepare a somewhat longer résumé. The important thing is to give yourself enough space to present a persuasive but accurate portrait of your skills and accomplishments.

Tailoring the Contents

Most potential employers expect to see certain items in any résumé. The bare essentials are name and address, academic credentials, and employment history. Otherwise, make sure your résumé emphasizes your strongest, most impressive qualifications. Think in terms of an image or a theme you'd like to project. Are you academically gifted? Are you a campus leader? A well-rounded person? A creative genius? A technical wizard? If you know what you have to sell, you can shape the elements of your résumé accordingly. Don't exaggerate, and don't alter the past or claim skills you don't have, but don't dwell on negatives, either. By focusing on your strengths, you can convey the desired impression without distorting the facts.

PROMOTING WORKPLACE ETHICS

Inflating Your Résumé: Is It Worth the Risk?

In an effort to put your best foot forward, you may be tempted to omit, enhance, or waltz around a few points that could raise questions about your résumé. Statistics on the prevalence of résumé inflation are difficult to gather, but most recruiters agree that distortion is common. The best guess is that up to 40 percent of all résumés either omit potentially damaging information or exaggerate the candidate's accomplishments. Some of the most frequent forms of deception include the following:

- ✧ **Claiming nonexistent educational credits.** Candidates may state (or imply) that they earned a degree when they never attended or did not complete the regular program.
- ✧ **Inflating grade-point averages.** Students feeling pressured to impress employers may claim a higher GPA than they actually achieved.
- ✧ **Stretching dates of employment to cover gaps.** Many candidates try to camouflage gaps in their work history by giving vague references to dates of employment.
- ✧ **Claiming to be self-employed.** Some candidates cover a period of unemployment by claiming to have operated an independent business during the time in question.
- ✧ **Leaving out any reference to jobs that might cause embarrassment.** To cover up a string of job losses, candidates may decide to drop a few positions, particularly if a reference check could prove embarrassing.
- ✧ **Exaggerating expertise or experience.** Candidates often inflate accomplishments by using verbs such as *supervised, managed, increased, improved,* and *created* to imply that the candidate was personally responsible for results actually achieved by a group effort.
- ✧ **Claiming to have worked for companies that are out of business.** Candidates who need to fill a gap in their work record sometimes say they worked for a firm that has gone out of business.

Think twice before trying one of these ploys yourself. Experienced recruiters are familiar with the games that candidates play to look better. Many employers have a policy of firing people who lied on their résumés.

If you misrepresent your background, your résumé may raise suspicions, and you will do yourself more harm than good. Sure, it's fine to stress your strongest, most impressive qualifications and to minimize your weaknesses. However, don't exaggerate, alter the past, or claim to have skills you don't have.

CAREER APPLICATIONS

1. You actually did quit your summer job as a door-to-door encyclopedia sales representative. Describe how you might handle that period on your résumé. Should you omit it? Can you mention it without revealing why you quit?
2. Consider one or two positions you've held (whether in a club, in a volunteer organization, or with a business). Write a realistic description of your responsibilities that doesn't inflate them but that presents them in a positive light.

NAME AND ADDRESS

The opening section shows at a glance
✧ Who you are
✧ How to reach you

The first thing an employer needs to know is who you are and where you can be reached: your name, address, and phone number (as well as your e-mail address or URL, if you have one). If you have an address and phone number at school and another at home, you may include both. At the same time, if you have a work phone and a home phone, list both and indicate which is which. Many résumé headings are nothing more than the name and address centred at the top of the page. You really have little need to include the word *Résumé,* but if you have a specific job in mind, you could use a heading that indicates that fact:

Qualifications of Craig R. Crisp for Insurance Sales Representative

Résumé of Mary Menendez, an Experienced Retail Fashion Buyer

Public Relations Background of Bradley R. (Brad) Howard

Susan Lee Selwyn's Qualifications for the Position of Teaching Assistant in the Waterloo School District

Profile of Michael de Vito for Entertainment Management

Whatever heading you use, make sure the reader can tell in an instant who you are and how to communicate with you.

CAREER OBJECTIVE OR SUMMARY OF QUALIFICATIONS

Stating your objective or summarizing your qualifications helps the recruiter categorize you.

Experts disagree about stating a career objective on your résumé. Some argue that your objective will be obvious from your qualifications. They also point out that such a statement is counterproductive (especially if you would like to be considered for a variety of openings) because it labels you as being interested in only one thing. Other experts point out that employers will undoubtedly try to categorize you anyway, so you might as well be sure they attach the right label. If you decide to state your objective, be as specific as possible about what you want to do:

Human Resources Management, requiring international experience

Advertising assistant, with print media emphasis

If you have two types of qualifications (such as a certificate in public administration and two years' experience in retail sales), prepare two separate résumés, each with a different objective. If your immediate objective differs from your ultimate one, combine the two in a single statement:

A marketing position with an opportunity for eventual managerial status

Proposal writer, with the ultimate goal of becoming a contracts administrator

As an alternative to stating your objective, you might want to summarize your qualifications in a brief statement that highlights your strongest points, particularly if you have had a good deal of varied experience. Use a short, simple phrase:

Summary of qualifications: Ten years of experience in commission selling

Hospital administrator responsible for 350-bed facility

EDUCATION

If you're still in school, education is probably your strongest selling point. So present your educational background in depth, choosing facts that support your theme. Give this section a heading, such as "Education," "Professional Training," or

"Academic Preparation." Then, starting with the school you most recently attended, list for each school the name and location, the term of your enrolment (in months and years), your major and minor fields of study, significant skills and abilities you've developed in your course work, and the degrees or certificates you've earned. Showcase your qualifications by listing courses that have directly equipped you for the job sought, and indicate any scholarships, awards, or academic honours you've received.

If education is your strongest selling point, discuss it thoroughly and highlight it visually.

The education section also includes off-campus training sponsored by business, industry, or government. Include any relevant seminars or workshops you've attended, as well as the certificates or other documents you've received. Mention high school or military training only if your achievements are pertinent to your career goals. Whether you list your grades depends on the job you want and the quality of your grades. If you choose to show grade-point averages for your total program or your major, be sure to mention if a 5-point scale is used instead of a 4-point scale.

Education is usually given less emphasis in a résumé after you've worked in your chosen field for a year or more. If work experience is your strongest qualification, save the section on education for later in the résumé and provide less detail.

WORK EXPERIENCE

Like the education section, the discussion of your work experience focuses on your overall theme. Tailor your description to highlight the relationship between your previous responsibilities and your target field. Call attention to the skills you've developed and the progression from jobs of lesser to greater responsibility.

The work experience section lists all the related jobs you've had:

- ✧ Name and location of employer
- ✧ What the organization does (if not clear from its name)
- ✧ Your functional title
- ✧ How long you worked there
- ✧ Your duties and responsibilities
- ✧ Your significant achievements or contributions

When describing your work experience, you'll usually list your jobs in chronological order, with the current or last one first. Include any part-time, summer, or intern positions even if the jobs have no relation to your present career objective. Employers will see that you have the ability to get and hold a job, which is an important qualification in itself. If you have worked your way through school, say so. Employers interpret this as a sign of character.

Each listing includes the name and location of the employer. Then, if the reader is unlikely to recognize the organization, briefly describe what it does. When you want to keep the name of your current employer confidential, identify the firm by industry only ("a large film-processing laboratory"), or use the name but request confidentiality in the application letter or in an underlined note ("Résumé submitted in confidence") at the top or bottom of the résumé. If an organization's name or location has since changed, state the current name or location and then "formerly ..."

Before or after each job listing, state your functional title, such as "clerk typist" or "salesperson." If you were a dishwasher, say so. Don't try to make your role seem more important by glamorizing your job title, functions, or achievements. You also state how long you worked on each job, from month/year to month/year. Use the phrase "to present" to denote current employment. If a job was part-time, say so.

Be honest about the positions you've held, the companies you've worked for, and your dates of employment. You'll be courting trouble if you list jobs you never held, claim to have worked for a firm when you didn't, or change dates to cover up a gap in employment. These days, more employers are checking candidates' backgrounds, so inaccuracies are likely to be exposed sooner or later.

Devote the most space to the jobs that relate to your target position. If you were personally responsible for something significant, be sure to mention it ("Devised a new collection system that accelerated payment of overdue receivables"). Facts about your accomplishments are the most important information you can give a prospective employer, so quantify your accomplishments whenever possible ("Designed a new ad that increased sales by 9 percent").

Quantify your accomplishments whenever possible.

RELEVANT SKILLS

Include miscellaneous facts that relate to your career objective:
- ✧ Command of other languages
- ✧ Computer expertise
- ✧ Date you can start working
- ✧ Availability of references

You may also want to include a section that describes other aspects of your background that pertain to your career objective. If you apply for a position with a multinational organization, you should mention your command of another language or your travel experience. Other skills you might mention include the ability to operate a computer, word processor, or other equipment. In fact, you might title a special section "Computer Skills" or "Language Skills" and place it near your "Education" or "Work Experience" section.

If your academic transcripts, samples of your work, or letters of recommendation might increase your chances of getting the job, insert a line at the end of your résumé offering to supply them on request. If your school placement office keeps these items on file for you, you can say "References and supporting documents available from ..."; be sure to include the exact address of the placement office. Many potential employers prefer that you list your references on the résumé. As a convenience for the prospective employer, you may also list the month and, if you know it, the day you will be available to start work.

ACTIVITIES AND ACHIEVEMENTS

Non-paid activities may provide evidence of work-related skills.

Your résumé also describes any volunteer activities that demonstrate your abilities. List projects that require leadership, organization, teamwork, and cooperation. Emphasize career-related activities such as "member of the Student Marketing Association." List skills you learned in these activities, and explain how these skills relate to the job you're applying for. Include speaking, writing, or tutoring experience; participation in athletics or creative projects; fund-raising or community service activities; and offices held in academic or professional organizations. (However, mention of political or religious organizations may be a red flag to someone with different views, so use your judgment.) Note any awards you've received. Again, quantify your achievements with numbers whenever possible. Instead of saying that you addressed various student groups, state how many and the approximate audience sizes. If your activities have been extensive, you may want to group them into divisions: "University Activities," "Community Service," "Professional Associations," "Seminars and Workshops," and "Speaking Activities." An alternative is to divide them into two categories: "Service Activities" and "Achievements, Awards, and Honours."

PERSONAL DATA

Provide only the personal data that will help you get the job.

To make your résumé distinctive, you might mention your hobbies, travel experiences, or personal characteristics, particularly if they suggest qualities related to your career goals. This section helps present you as a well-rounded person, and can be used to spark conversation during an interview.[10] For example, you and your interviewer may have a common interest in music or sports.

Choosing the Best Organizational Plan

Select an organizational pattern that focuses attention on your strengths.

Although you may want to include a little information in all categories, emphasize the information that has a bearing on your career objective and minimize or exclude any that is irrelevant or counterproductive. You do this by adopting an organizational plan–chronological, functional, or targeted–that focuses attention on your strongest points. The right choice depends on your background and goals.

THE CHRONOLOGICAL RÉSUMÉ

The most traditional type of résumé is the **chronological résumé,** in which a person's employment history is listed sequentially in reverse order, starting with the most recent experience. When you organize your résumé chronologically, the "Work Experience" section dominates the résumé and is placed in the most prominent slot, immediately after the name and address and the objective. You develop this section by listing your jobs in reverse order, beginning with the most recent position and working backward toward earlier jobs. Under each listing you describe your responsibilities and accomplishments, giving the most space to the most recent positions. If you are just graduating, you can vary the chronological plan by putting your educational qualifications before your experience, thereby focusing attention on your academic credentials.

Most recruiters prefer the chronological plan—a historical summary of your education and work experience.

The chronological approach is the most common way to organize a résumé, and many employers prefer it past and present. Robert Nesbit, a vice president with Korn/Ferry International, speaks for many recruiters: "Unless you have a really compelling reason, don't use any but the standard chronological format. Your résumé should not read like a treasure map, full of minute clues to the whereabouts of your jobs and experience. I want to be able to grasp quickly where a candidate has worked, how long, and in what capacities."[11]

The chronological approach is especially appropriate if you have a strong employment history and are aiming for a job that builds on your current career path. This is the case for Roberto Cortez, whose résumé appears in Figure 15.2.

THE FUNCTIONAL RÉSUMÉ

In a **functional résumé,** you organize your résumé around a list of skills and accomplishments, and then identify your employers and academic experience in subordinate sections. This pattern stresses individual areas of competence, and it's useful for people who are just entering the job market, people who want to redirect their careers, and people who have little continuous career-related experience. Figure 15.3 illustrates how a recent graduate used the functional approach to showcase her qualifications for a career in retail.

A functional résumé focuses attention on your areas of competence.

Posting Your Résumé Online

EFFECTIVE E-BUSINESS COMMUNICATION

Printing and mailing your résumé takes more time and effort offline than online. Instead of stuffing an envelope with each résumé, you can now post your résumé on the Web with a few keystrokes. At **workopolis.com**, click on "My workopolis" to post your résumé and to search for jobs. This site is used by employers and job seekers across Canada. It also provides tips and hints on composing your résumé. You can send it to an employer with a quick click—and leave it in the site's database for other employers to browse.

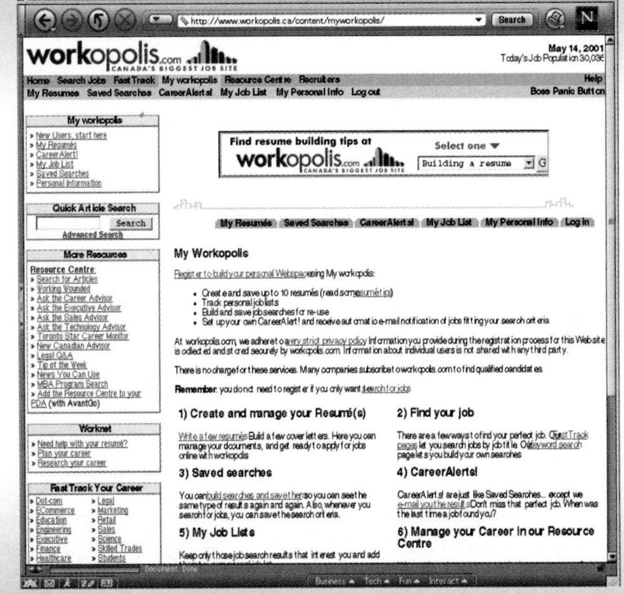

CAREER APPLICATIONS

1. What role do key words play in résumés that are posted online for employers to browse?
2. What style and formatting changes should you make before pasting your résumé into an online database?

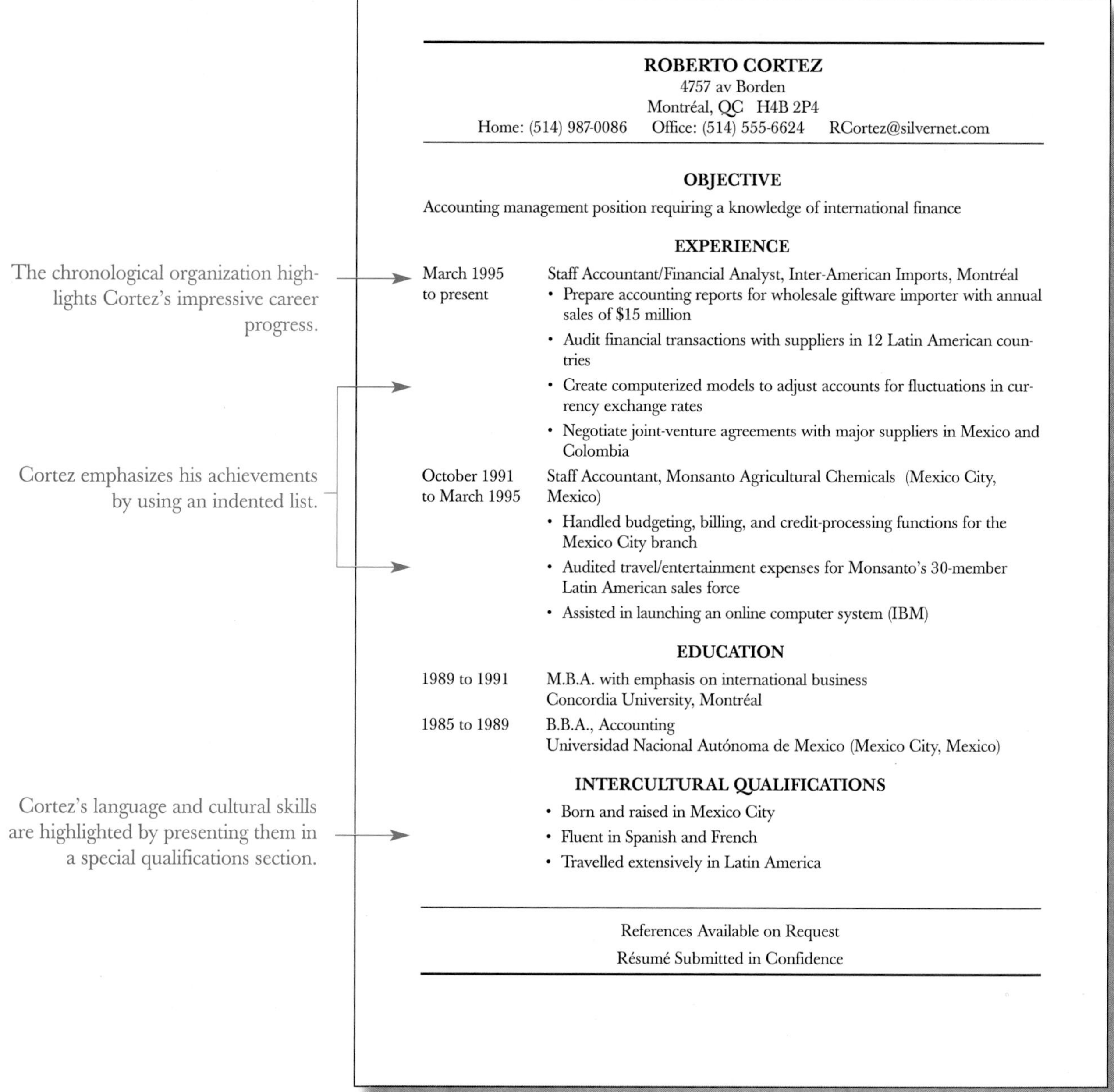

The chronological organization highlights Cortez's impressive career progress.
Cortez emphasizes his achievements by using an indented list.
Cortez's language and cultural skills are highlighted by presenting them in a special qualifications section.
ROBERTO CORTEZ
4757 av Borden
Montréal, QC H4B 2P4
Home: (514) 987-0086 Office: (514) 555-6624 RCortez@silvernet.com
OBJECTIVE
Accounting management position requiring a knowledge of international finance
EXPERIENCE
March 1995 to present
Staff Accountant/Financial Analyst, Inter-American Imports, Montréal
• Prepare accounting reports for wholesale giftware importer with annual sales of $15 million
• Audit financial transactions with suppliers in 12 Latin American countries
• Create computerized models to adjust accounts for fluctuations in currency exchange rates
• Negotiate joint-venture agreements with major suppliers in Mexico and Colombia
October 1991 to March 1995
Staff Accountant, Monsanto Agricultural Chemicals (Mexico City, Mexico)
• Handled budgeting, billing, and credit-processing functions for the Mexico City branch
• Audited travel/entertainment expenses for Monsanto's 30-member Latin American sales force
• Assisted in launching an online computer system (IBM)
EDUCATION
1989 to 1991
M.B.A. with emphasis on international business
Concordia University, Montréal
1985 to 1989
B.B.A., Accounting
Universidad Nacional Autónoma de Mexico (Mexico City, Mexico)
INTERCULTURAL QUALIFICATIONS
• Born and raised in Mexico City
• Fluent in Spanish and French
• Travelled extensively in Latin America
References Available on Request
Résumé Submitted in Confidence

FIGURE 15.2

In-Depth Critique: Chronological Résumé

Cortez calls attention to his achievements by setting them off in a bulleted list. Because they come first, his most recent achievements will get the most attention. The section titled "Intercultural Qualifications" emphasizes his international background and fluency in Spanish, which are important qualifications for his target position.

THE TARGETED RÉSUMÉ

A targeted résumé shows how you qualify for a specific job.

A **targeted résumé** is organized to focus attention on what you can do for a particular employer in a particular position. Immediately after stating your career objective, you list any related capabilities. This list is followed by a list of your achievements, which provide evidence of your capabilities. Schools and employers are listed in subordinate sections.

Glenda S. Johns

Home: 688 Crescent Rd.
Newmarket, ON L3Y 2C2
(905) 555-5971

School: 66 Bernick Drive
Barrie, ON L4M 2V6
(705)111-5254

OBJECTIVE

Retailing position that utilizes my experience

RELEVANT SKILLS

- Personal Selling/Retailing
  - Led housewares department in fewest mistakes while cashiering and balancing register receipts
  - Created end-cap and shelf displays for special housewares promotions
  - Sold the most benefit tickets during college fund-raising drive for local community centre
- Public Interaction
  - Commended by housewares manager for resolving customer complaints amicably
  - Performed in summer theatre productions in Newmarket
- Managing
  - Trained part-time housewares employees in cash register operation and customer service
  - Reworked housewares employee schedules as assistant manager
  - Organized summer activities for children 6–12 years old in Barrie–including reading programs, sports activities, and field trips

EDUCATION

- Certificate in Retail Management (3.81 GPA / 4.0 scale), Georgian College, Barrie, June 2000
- In addition to required retailing, buying, marketing, and merchandising courses, completed electives in visual merchandising, business information systems, principles of management, and business math

WORK EXPERIENCE

- Assistant manager, housewares, at The Bay store during off-campus work experience program, Barrie (winter 1999–spring 2000)
- Sales clerk, housewares, at The Bay store during off-campus work experience program, Barrie (winter 1998–spring 1999)
- Assistant director, Summer Recreation Program, Barrie (summer 1997)
- Actress, Resurgence Players, Newmarket (summer 1996)

REFERENCES AND SUPPORTING DOCUMENTS

Available from Placement Office, Georgian College, Barrie, ON L4M 3X9

Because she is a recent graduate, the applicant describes her skills first, based on details of her limited experience.

The use of action verbs and specific facts enhances this résumé's effectiveness.

The applicant's sketchy work history is described but not emphasized.

FIGURE 15.3

In-Depth Critique: Functional Résumé

Although Glenda Johns has not held any paid, full-time positions in retail sales, she has participated in work-experience programs, and she knows a good deal about the profession from doing research and talking with people in the industry. As a result, she was able to organize her résumé in a way that demonstrates her ability to handle such a position.

Targeted résumés are a good choice for people who have a clear idea of what they want to do and who can demonstrate their ability in the targeted area. This approach was effective for Erica Vorkamp, whose résumé appears in Figure 15.4.

Going Online

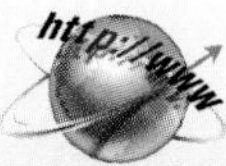

Link Your Way to a Better Résumé

Learn how to stand out in a crowded job market. Find a helpful list of dos and don'ts, some suggested résumé headings, a sample chronological résumé, a chart of action words to create an accomplishment-oriented impression, and a checklist for preparing scannable résumés.

www.bridgew.edu/depts/carplan/resume.htm

Erica Vorkamp
67 Garfield St., Moncton, NB E1C 3Z2
(506) 555-2153

Qualifications for Special Events Coordinator
for the City of Moncton

CAPABILITIES

- Plan and coordinate large-scale public events
- Develop community support for concerts, festivals, and entertainment
- Manage publicity for major events
- Coordinate activities of diverse community groups
- Establish and maintain financial controls for public events
- Negotiate contracts with performers, carpenters, electricians, and suppliers

The capabilities and achievements are all related to the specific job target, giving a very selective picture of the candidate's abilities.

ACHIEVEMENTS

- Arranged 2000's week-long Arts and Entertainment Festival for the Moncton Public Library, involving performances by 25 musicians, dancers, actors, magicians, and artists
- Supervised the 1999 PTA Halloween Carnival, an all-day festival with game booths, live bands, contests, and food service that raised $7600 for the PTA
- Organized the 1997 Atlantic convention for 300 members of the YWCA, which extended over a three-day period and required arrangements for hotels, meals, speakers, and special tours
- Served as chairperson for the 1996 Children's Home Society Fashion Show, a luncheon for 150 that raised $3,000 for orphans and abused children

EDUCATION

- B.A., Psychology, Mount Allison University (Sackville, NB), September 1979 to June 1984, First Class Honours

WORK HISTORY

- Bank of Nova Scotia, June 1984 to October 1986, personnel counsellor/campus recruiter; scheduled and conducted interviews with graduating M.B.A. students on 5 Atlantic campuses; managed orientation program for recruits hired for bank's management trainee staff
- Mount Allison University, November 1981 to June 1984, part-time research assistant; helped Professor Paul Harangozo conduct behavioural experiments using rats trained to go through mazes

This work history has little bearing on the candidate's job target, but she felt that recruiters would want to see evidence that she has held a paid position.

FIGURE 15.4

In-Depth Critique: Targeted Résumé

When Erica Vorkamp developed her résumé, she chose not to use a chronological pattern, which would focus attention on her lack of recent work experience. Instead, she used a targeted approach that emphasizes her ability to organize special events.

Adapting Your Résumé to an Electronic Format

An electronic résumé is helpful if your résumé will be scanned or if you post it on the Internet or submit it via e-mail.

Although it was once considered unacceptable to fax a résumé to a potential employer, many executives now say they would indeed accept a résumé by fax if they've given no other specific guidelines.[12] Moreover, if employers advertise job openings online and provide an e-mail address for responses, sending your résumé by e-mail and responding via the Internet is not only acceptable, it's preferable.

Roberto Cortez
4757 av Borden
Montréal, QC H4B 2P4

Home: (514) 987-0086 Office: (514) 555-6624

RCortez@silvernet.com

KEY WORDS

Financial executive, accounting management, international finance, financial analyst, accounting reports, financial audit, computerized accounting model, exchange rates, joint-venture agreements, budgets, billing, credit processing, online systems, M.B.A., fluent Spanish, fluent French

OBJECTIVE

Accounting management position requiring a knowledge of international finance

EXPERIENCE

Staff Accountant/Financial Analyst, Inter-American Imports (Montréal)
March 1995 to present

- o Prepare accounting reports for wholesale importer, annual sales of $15 million
- o Audit financial transactions with suppliers in 12 Latin American countries
- o Create computerized models to adjust for fluctuations in currency exchange rates
- o Negotiate joint-venture agreements with suppliers in Mexico and Colombia

Staff Accountant, Monsanto Agricultural Chemicals (Mexico City)
October 1991 to March 1995

- o Handled budgeting, billing, credit-processing functions for the Mexico City branch
- o Audited travel/entertainment expenses for Monsanto's 30-member Latin American sales force
- o Assisted in launching an online computer system (IBM)

EDUCATION

M.B.A. with emphasis on international business, Concordia University (Montréal) 1989 to 1991

B.B.A., Accounting, Universidad Nacional Autónoma de Mexico (Mexico City) 1985 to 1989

INTERCULTURAL QUALIFICATIONS

Born and raised in Mexico City
Fluent in Spanish and French
Travelled extensively in Latin America

References and formatted résumé available on request

Cortez has removed all boldfacing, rules, bullets, and two-column formatting.

Cortez uses a lowercase letter *o* in his indented lists.

If Cortez truly wanted to submit his résumé in confidence, he would not submit it to an online index or post it on a Web site, where his current employer might run across it; so, stating the need for confidentiality is no longer necessary.

The final note informs the reader of the availability not only of references but also of a fully formatted version of this electronic résumé.

FIGURE 15.5

In-Depth Critique: Electronic Résumé

If Roberto Cortez (see Figure 15.2) knows that the employers he's targeting will be scanning his résumé into a database, or if he wants to submit his résumé via e-mail or to post it on the Internet, he will change his formatting and add a key word list. The information he provides can remain essentially the same and appear in the same order.

Large companies have been storing résumés in centralized databases for some time. Now, when employers look for potential employees, more and more of them are searching online databases as well as their own in-house files.[13] Depending on where you wish to apply and how you wish to be perceived, you may want to consider the unique characteristics of electronic résumés—whether they are printed out and end up being scanned into a database, sent to employers by e-mail, or posted on the Internet. You can convert your traditional paper résumé into an electronic one in three steps (Figure 15.5):[14]

To make your résumé electronic
✧ Save it as an ASCII file
✧ Provide a list of key words
✧ Balance clear language with up-to-date jargon

1. *Save your résumé as a plain ASCII text file.* ASCII is a common text language that allows your résumé to be accessed by any word processor or easily read by any scanner. All word-processing programs allow you to save files as ASCII. However, this language does have its limitations. ASCII will not handle decorative or uncommon typefaces, underlining, italics, graphics, or shading. Stick to a popular Times New Roman or Helvetica typeface, and use blank spaces to align text (rather than tabs). To help your résumé appear more readable, you might sparingly use an asterisk or a lowercase letter *o* to indicate a bullet. Be sure to use a lot of white space to allow scanners and computers to recognize when one topic ends and another begins.
2. *Provide a list of keywords.* Emphasizing certain words will help potential employers select your résumé from the thousands they scan. Because employers set their databases to search for nouns (rather than the active verbs you've included in your traditional paper résumé), you can provide those key nouns in a separate list and place it right after your name and address. These keywords may or may not actually appear in your résumé, but they accomplish two things: They give potential employers a quick picture of you, and they show that you're sensitive to the requirements of today's electronic business world. When choosing your keywords, consider the following categories: job titles (staff accountant), job-related tasks (instead of "created a computerized accounting model" simply list "computerized accounting model"), skills or knowledge (Excel, fluent

BEHIND THE SCENES AT RECRUITSOFT

The Wired World of E-cruiting

"When you consider the fact that most companies spend an average of $6000 every time they hire someone," says Louis Tétu, "it quickly becomes clear that this turnover in the labour market represents an enormous expense." As CEO of Recruitsoft, a provider of electronic hiring systems, Tétu is showing companies how to use the power of the Internet to find new employees and help current ones pinpoint new jobs internally. The Quebec-born Tétu says, "Companies want a system that can automate the pre-screening process and enable them as recruiters to keep ongoing communication through the Web with prospective employees." Tétu says online systems can cut the time it takes to hire a new employee by half and costs by as much as 70 percent for each job posting. Bombardier Aerospace, for example, receives 30 000 résumés a year. Daniel Bouchard, a Bombardier human resources adviser, remarks that Recruitsoft's product allows the company "to shorten our recruitment time since we don't have to look at all the candidates." Using Bombardier's online pre-screening system, job applicants click on answers to questions designed to determine their qualifications for specific positions.

Electronic recruiting tools are gaining popularity among employers as a means to find qualified staff, but they are only one step in the recruitment process.

Recruitsoft's system, Recruitor WebTop, works by allowing recruiters to store candidate profiles in a database. Applicants need only apply for one opening; the software will automatically contact them by e-mail if another position that suits their qualifications comes open. As more and more people apply for jobs via a company's automated screening system, the database of potential employees grows. Consequently, recruiters become less dependent on such traditional recruiting media as newspapers and recruitment firms. The cost and time of finding new employees can be dramatically reduced.

Based in San Francisco, with offices in Boston and Quebec City, where the firm was founded, Recruitsoft works with their clients, such as Bank of Montreal, National Bank of Canada, Bombardier Inc., and many other North American companies,

French), degrees (M.B.A. or master of business administration), major (accounting major), certifications (C.G.A.), school (Memorial University), class ranking (top 20 percent), and interpersonal traits or skills (intercultural experience, organized, proven leader, willing to travel, written and oral communication skills).

3. *Balance common language with current jargon.* To maximize matches (or *hits*) between your résumé and an employer's search, use words that potential employers will understand. For example, don't call a keyboard an input device. Also, use abbreviations sparingly, except for common ones such as B.A. or M.B.A. At the same time, learn the important buzz words used in your field, and use them. Places to look for the most current trends include want ads in major newspapers such as *The Toronto Star* and the résumés in your field that are posted online. Be careful to check and recheck the spelling, capitalization, and punctuation of any jargon you include, and use only those words you see most often.

Make sure your name and address are the first lines on your résumé (with no text appearing above or alongside your name). Also, particular sections are sometimes omitted from electronic résumés–special interests and references, for example.[15] To find out what employers expect to see, check online résumés in your field. If most of them list a career objective, then perhaps you should too. If you're mailing your résumé, you may want to send both a well-designed traditional one and a scannable one.

Two other quick points. First, when sending your résumé to a public access area (such as a résumé database) or when posting it on your own home page, leave out social insurance numbers and other identification codes. You might also leave

to develop job descriptions and pre-selection questions to screen candidates. These questions seek data about education, work experience, professional abilities, and skill level. Their formats may be single- or multiple-choice questions, or open-text. The software invites candidates to copy and paste their résumés into the database or use Recruitsoft's "Résumé Builder." Essentially an online résumé template, "Résumé Builder" provides both drop-down menus where applicants can select answers about program of study, educational level, job function, start and end dates for past work. The template also includes areas for inputting descriptive information, such as duties and accomplishments in previous positions. Furthermore, the software allows employers to scan paper résumés into the database. Walk-in job applicants can complete an online questionnaire at an electronic kiosk.

According to Kevin Scott, Bank of Montreal's vice-president of strategic staffing, "The financial services industry in North America is in a period of rapid change as a result of the tremendous impact of technology." To ensure that the best person is hired for the job, the Bank of Montreal Web site uses Recruitsoft to streamline the selection process. Recruitsoft's "Candidate Profiler" lets applicants answer questions about desired job level, job type, shift, and work location preferences as well as salary preference.

But can online services ever replace traditional recruitment? Visitors to the Bank of Montreal Web site will see electronic options for job applicants, but they will also find a career library to help students and other job-seekers with traditional résumés, job application letters, and interviews. For example, the bank advises applicants to keep paper résumés to two pages, and to include extracurricular activities and community service, which often show leadership and organizational skills. As for interviews, Bank of Montreal tells applicants to listen carefully, link qualifications to the requirements of the job, and to "stop when you've said enough." Applicants may be asked to justify their area of study. They may also be invited to recount instances when they worked as a member of a team, tell why they are applying to a position at Bank of Montreal, and describe a time they adapted to significant change. According to Bruce Powell, an independent recruitment consultant, despite the benefits of technology in the recruitment process, there are many human subtleties "that can't be picked up by testing online."[16]

APPLY YOUR KNOWLEDGE

1. Bank of Montreal advises that job applicants who have personal Web sites should post their résumés on them. What are the benefits of posting your résumé on your Web site? The disadvantages?
2. Review the questions Bank of Montreal asks job applicants and construct answers to them that you would use in an actual job interview at the bank. Are your answers clear? Are they relevant? You might want to visit the Bank of Montreal's career Web site at **www.bmo.com/careers/body_studentcareer.html** for more questions that bank interviewers ask applicants.

out the names of references and previous employers. Simply say that references are available on request, and refer to "a large accounting firm" or "a wholesale giftware importer" rather than naming companies.

Second, avoid attaching fully designed résumés to e-mail messages. Your audience will have to spend extra effort to open your résumé, and there's a chance your résumé will be in a format your audience can't read.

Writing the Perfect Résumé

The perfect résumé responds to the reader's needs and preferences and avoids some common faults.

Regardless of whether your résumé is electronic or paper, and regardless of what organizational plan you follow, the key to writing the "perfect" résumé is to put yourself in the reader's position. Think about what the prospective employer needs, and then tailor your résumé accordingly.

People like Pinkerton's Denis Brown read thousands of résumés every year and complain about the following common résumé problems:

- *Too long.* The résumé is not concise, relevant, and to the point.
- *Too short or sketchy.* The résumé does not give enough information for a proper evaluation of the applicant.
- *Hard to read.* A lack of "white space" and of such devices as indentions and boldfacing makes the reader's job more difficult.
- *Wordy.* Descriptions are verbose, with numerous words used for what could be said more simply.
- *Too slick.* A résumé that appears to have been written by someone other than the applicant raises the question of whether the qualifications have been exaggerated.

Checklist for Résumés

A. Content and Style

1. Prepare the résumé before writing the application letter so you can summarize the facts the letter will be based on.
2. Present the strongest qualifications first.
3. Use short noun phrases and action verbs, not whole sentences.
4. Use facts, not opinions.
5. Avoid using too many personal pronouns.
6. Omit the date of preparation.
7. Omit mention of your desired salary, work schedule, or vacation schedule.

B. Contact Information

1. Use a title or your name and address as a heading.
2. List your name, address, area code, and telephone number–for both school or work and home, if appropriate.

C. Career Objective and Skills Summary (optional)

1. Be as specific as possible about what you want to do.
   a. State a broad and flexible goal to increase the scope of your job prospects.
   b. Prepare two different résumés if you can do two unrelated types of work.
2. Summarize your key qualifications.
3. State the month and, if you know it, the day on which you will be available to start work.

D. Education

1. List all relevant schooling and training since high school, with the most recent first.
   a. List the name and location of every postsecondary school you have attended, with the dates you entered and left and the degrees or certificates you obtained.
   b. Indicate your major (and minor) fields in university work.
   c. State the numerical base for your grade-point average, overall or in your major, if your average is impressive enough to list. Note the numerical scale (4.0 or 5.0).
2. List relevant required or elective courses in descending order of importance.
3. List any other related educational or training experiences, such as job-related seminars or workshops attended and certificates obtained. (Give dates.)

- *Amateurish.* The applicant appears to have little understanding of the business world or of the particular industry, as revealed by including the wrong information or presenting it awkwardly.
- *Poorly reproduced.* The print is faint and difficult to read.
- *Misspelled and ungrammatical throughout.* Recruiters conclude that candidates who make these kinds of mistakes don't have good verbal skills, which are important on the job.
- *Boastful.* The overconfident tone makes the reader wonder whether the applicant's self-evaluation is realistic.
- *Dishonest.* The applicant claims to have expertise or work experience that he or she does not possess.
- *Gimmicky.* The words, structure, decoration, or material used in the résumé depart so far from the usual as to make the résumé ineffective.

Guard against making these mistakes in your own résumé, and compare your final version with the suggestions in this chapter's Checklist for Résumés.

Also, update your résumé regularly. You'll need it whether you're applying for membership in a professional organization, working toward a promotion, or changing employers. People used to spend most of their career with one company, but today the average person beginning work in Canada will probably hold several jobs before retiring. So keeping your résumé updated is a good idea.

Whenever you submit your résumé, you accompany it with a cover or application letter. This document lets your reader know what you're sending, why you're sending it, and how your reader can benefit from reading it. Because your

E. Work Experience

1. List all relevant work experience, including paid employment, volunteer work, and internships.
2. List full-time and part-time jobs, with the most recent one first.
   a. State the month/year when you started and left each job.
   b. Provide the name and location of the firm that employed you.
   c. List your job title and briefly describe your responsibilities.
   d. Note on-the-job accomplishments, such as an award or a suggestion that saved the organization time or money.

F. Activities, Honours, and Achievements

1. List all relevant unpaid activities, including offices and leadership positions held; significant awards or scholarships not listed elsewhere; projects you have undertaken that show an ability to work with others; and writing or speaking activities, publications, and roles in academic or professional organizations.
2. In most circumstances, exclude mention of religious or political affiliations.

G. Other Relevant Facts

1. List other information, such as your keyboarding speed or your proficiency in languages other than English.
2. Mention your ability to operate any machines, equipment, or computer software used in the job.

H. Personal Data

1. Omit personal details that could be regarded negatively or be used to discriminate against you.
2. Omit or downplay references to age if it could suggest inexperience or approaching retirement.
3. List job-related interests and hobbies, especially those indicating stamina, strength, sociability, or other qualities that are desirable in the position you seek.

I. References

1. Offer to supply the names of references on request.
   a. Supply names of academic, employment, and professional associates–but no relatives (unless you worked for them in a family-owned or -operated business).
   b. Provide a name, a title, an address, and a telephone number (with area code) for each reference.
   c. List no name as a reference until you have that person's permission to do so.
2. Exclude your present employer if you do not want the firm to know you are seeking another position, or add "Résumé Submitted in Confidence" at the top or bottom of the résumé.

application letter is in your own style (rather than the choppy, shorthand style of your résumé), it gives you a chance to make a good personal impression.

Writing Application Messages

LEARNING OUTCOME 6
Define the purpose of application letters, and explain how to apply the AIDA organizational approach to them.

Follow the AIDA plan when writing your application letter: attention, interest, desire, action.

Like your résumé, your application letter is a form of advertising, so organize it like a sales letter. Use the AIDA plan; focus on the "you" attitude; and emphasize reader benefits (as discussed in Chapter 11). You need to stimulate your reader's interest before showing how you can satisfy the organization's needs. Make sure your style projects confidence–you can't hope to sell a potential employer on your merits unless you truly believe in them yourself and sound as though you do.

Of course, this approach isn't appropriate for job seekers in every culture. If you're applying for a job abroad or want to work with a subsidiary of an organization based in another country, you may need to adjust your tone. For instance, blatant self-promotion is considered bad form in some cultures. Other cultures stress group performance over individual contributions. And as for format, in some countries recruiters prefer handwritten letters to printed or typed ones. So research your company carefully before drafting your application letter.

For Canadian and US companies, let your letter reflect your personal style. Be yourself, but be businesslike too–avoid sounding cute. Don't use slang or a gimmicky layout. The only time to be unusually creative in content or format is when the job you're seeking requires imagination, such as a position in advertising. In most cases you'll use a printer or typewriter to produce your application letter.

Finally, showing that you know something about the organization can pay off. Imagine yourself in the recruiter's situation. How can you demonstrate that your background and talents will solve a particular problem or fill a need? By using a "you" attitude and showing you've done some homework, you'll capture the reader's attention and convey your desire to join the organization. The more you can learn about the organization, the better you'll be able to write about how your qualifications fit its needs.[17]

Also, during your research, find out the name, title, and department of the person you're writing to. Reaching and addressing the right person is the most effective way to gain attention. So be sure to avoid phrases such as "To Whom It May Concern" and "Dear Sir."

Writing the Opening Paragraph

You write a solicited application letter in response to an announced job opening.

You write an unsolicited application letter to an organization that has not announced a job opening.

A **solicited application letter** is one sent in response to an announced job opening. An **unsolicited letter,** also known as a *prospecting letter,* is one sent to an organization that has not announced an opening. When you send a solicited letter, you usually know in advance what qualifications the organization is seeking. However, you also have more competition because hundreds of other job seekers will have seen the listing and may be sending applications. In some respects, therefore, an unsolicited application letter stands a better chance of being read and of receiving individualized attention.

Whether your application letter is solicited or unsolicited, your qualifications are presented similarly. The main difference is in the opening paragraph. In a solicited letter, no special attention-getting effort is needed because you have been invited to apply. However, the unsolicited letter starts by capturing the reader's attention and interest.

Within a year of becoming president of Godfather's Pizza, Herman Cain returned the floundering chain to profitability. Now principal owner (following a leveraged buyout), Cain says his success springs from his love of the restaurant business. Simple ambition isn't enough to succeed in any business, he advises, so send résumés to companies whose business you have a real passion for.

GETTING ATTENTION

One way to spark attention in the opening paragraph is to show how your strongest work skills could benefit the organization. A 20-year-old secretary with one year of university education might begin like this:

> When you need a secretary in your export division who can take shorthand at 125 words a minute and transcribe notes at 70–in English, French, or Portuguese–call me.

Here's another attention-getter. It describes your understanding of the job's requirements and then introduces how well your qualifications fit the job, which you would develop in the body of the letter.

> Your annual report states that Petro-Canada runs training programs about workforce diversity for managers and employees. The challenges involved in running such programs can be significant, as I learned while teaching English as a second language last summer. My 12 students were enrolled in vocational training programs and came from different cultures.

Mentioning the name of a person known to and highly regarded by the reader is bound to capture some attention:

> When Janice McHugh of your franchise sales division spoke to our business communication class last week, she said you often need promising new marketing graduates at this time of year.

References to publicized company activities, achievements, changes, or new procedures can also be used to gain attention:

> Today's issue of the *Montreal Gazette* reports that you may need the expertise of computer programmers versed in robotics when your Joliette tire plant automates this spring.

Another type of attention-getting opening uses a question to demonstrate an understanding of the organization's needs:

> Can your fast-growing market research division use an interviewer with three years of field survey experience, a B.A. in public relations, and a real desire to succeed? If so, please consider me for the position.

A catch-phrase opening can also capture attention, especially if the job sought requires ingenuity and imagination:

> *Haut monde*–whether said in French, Italian, or Arabic–still means "high society." As an interior designer for your Vancouver showroom, not only could I serve and sell to your distinguished clientele, but I could do it in all these languages. I speak, read, and write them fluently.

Start a solicited application letter by mentioning how you found out about the open position.

In contrast, a solicited letter written in response to a job advertisement usually opens by identifying the publication in which the ad ran and then describes what the applicant has to offer:

> Your ad in the April issue of *Travel & Leisure* for a cruise-line social director caught my eye. My eight years of experience as a social director in the travel industry would allow me to serve your new Caribbean cruise division well.

Note that all these openings demonstrate the "you" attitude and many indicate how the applicant can serve the employer.

CLARIFYING YOUR REASON FOR WRITING

State in the opening paragraph that you are applying for a job.

The opening paragraph of your application letter also states your reason for writing: You are applying for a job, so the opening paragraph identifies the desired job or job area:

> Please consider my application for an entry-level position in technical writing.
>
> Your firm advertised a fleet sales position (on March 23, 2001, in the *Winnipeg Free Press*). With my 16 months of new-car sales experience, I believe I can be a benefit to your company.

Another way to state your reason for writing is to use a title at the opening of your letter:

> Subject: Application for accounts payable position

After this clear signal, your first paragraph can focus on getting attention and indicating how hiring you may benefit the organization.

Summarizing Your Key Selling Points

The middle section of an application letter

- ✧ Summarizes your relevant qualifications
- ✧ Emphasizes your accomplishments
- ✧ Suggests desirable personal qualities
- ✧ Justifies salary requirements
- ✧ Refers to your résumé

The middle section of your application letter presents your strongest selling points in terms of their potential benefit to the organization, thereby creating interest in you and a desire to interview you. If your selling points have already been mentioned in the opening, don't repeat them. Simply give supporting evidence. Otherwise, spell out your key qualifications, together with some convincing evidence of your ability to perform.

To avoid a cluttered application letter, mention only the qualifications that indicate you can do the job. Show how your studies and your work experience have prepared you for that job, or tell the reader about how you grew up in the business. Be careful not to repeat the facts presented in your résumé; instead, interpret those facts for the reader:

> Experience in customer relations and university courses in public relations have taught me how to handle the problem-solving tasks that arise in a leading retail clothing firm like yours. Such important tasks include identifying and resolving customer complaints, writing letters that build good customer relations, and above all, promoting the organization's positive image.

When writing a solicited letter responding to a help-wanted advertisement, discuss each requirement specified in the ad. If you are deficient in any of the requirements, stress other solid selling points to help strengthen your overall presentation.

Stating that you have all the necessary requirements for the job is rarely enough to convince the reader, so back up assertions of your ability by presenting evidence of it. Cite one or two of your key qualifications; then show how you have effectively put them to use.

> **INSTEAD OF THIS** I completed three university courses in business communication, earning an A in each course, and have worked for the past year at Imperial Construction.
>
> **WRITE THIS** Using the skills gained from three semesters of university training in business communication, I developed a collection system for Imperial Construction that reduced its 2000 bad-debt losses by 3.7 percent, or $9902, from those of 1999. The new system included collection letters that offered discount incentives for speedy payment rather than timeworn terminology.

This section of the letter also presents evidence of a few significant job-related qualities. The following paragraph demonstrates that the applicant is diligent and hard working:

> While attending university full time, I trained 3 hours a day with the varsity track team. In addition, I worked part-time during the school year and up to 60 hours a week each summer in order to be totally self-supporting while in college. I can offer your organization the same level of effort and perseverance.

Other relevant qualities worth noting include being able to learn quickly, to handle responsibility, and to get along with people.

Another matter to bring up in this section is your salary requirement–but only if the organization has asked you to state it. The best strategy, unless you know approximately what the job pays, is to suggest a salary range or to indicate that the salary is negotiable or open. You might also consult the Job Futures Web site of Human Resources Development Canada (**www.jobfutures.ca**), where you can search for salaries in specific occupations. If you do state a target salary, tie your request to the benefits you would provide the organization, much as you would handle price in a sales letter:

Oprah Winfrey has a humanistic approach to running her company, Harpo Productions. She's known to be demanding of her 135 employees, but she's also generous. Winfrey reminds applicants to get attention by emphasizing how they can help the employer. And don't be afraid to be yourself, she says.

> For the past two years, I have been helping a company similar to yours organize its database. I would therefore like to receive a salary in the same range (the mid-40s) for helping your company set up a more efficient customer database.

Toward the end of this section, refer the reader to your résumé. You may do so by citing a specific fact or general point covered in the résumé.

> You will find my people skills an asset. As you can see in the attached résumé, I've been working part-time with a local publisher since my second year, and during that time, I successfully resolved several client crises.

Writing the Closing Paragraph

Close by asking for an interview and making the interview easy to arrange.

The final paragraph of your application letter has two important functions: to ask the reader for a specific action and to make a reply easy. In almost all cases, the action you ask for is an interview. Don't demand it, however; try to sound natural and appreciative. Offer to come to the employer's office at a convenient time or, if the firm is some distance away, to meet with its nearest representative. Make the request easy to fulfill by stating your phone number and the best time to reach you. Refer again to your strongest selling point and, if desired, your date of availability:

> After you have reviewed my qualifications, could we discuss the possibility of putting my marketing skills to work for your company? Because I will be on spring break the week of March 8, I would like to arrange a time to talk then. You can reach me by calling (709) 235-6311 during the day or (709) 529-2873 any evening after 5:00.

An alternative approach is to ask for an interview and then offer to get in touch with the reader to arrange a time for it, rather than requesting a reply. Whichever approach you use, mail your application letter and résumé promptly, especially if they have been solicited.

Writing the Perfect Application Letter

The "perfect" application letter, like the "perfect" résumé, accomplishes one thing: It gets you an interview. It conforms to no particular model because it's a reflection

Glenda S. Johns

Home: 688 Crescent Rd., Newmarket, ON L3Y 2C2, (905) 555-5971
School: 66 Bernick Drive, Barrie, ON L4M 2V6, (705)111-5254

June 16, 2000

Ms. Patricia Downings, Store Manager
Zellers Inc.
Orillia Square Mall
Orillia, ON L3V 6H6

Dear Ms. Downings:

The applicant gains attention in the first paragraph.

You want retail clerks and managers who are accurate, enthusiastic, and experienced. You want someone who cares about customer service, who understands merchandising, and who can work with others to get the job done. When you're ready to hire a manager trainee or a clerk who is willing to work toward promotion, please consider me for the job.

The applicant points out personal qualities that aren't specifically stated in her résumé.

Working as clerk and then as assistant department manager in a large department store has taught me how challenging a career in retailing can be. Moreover, my certificate in retailing (including work in such courses as retailing, marketing, and business information systems) will provide your store with a well-rounded associate. Most important, I can offer Zellers' Orillia store more than my two years of study and field experience. You'll find that I'm interested in every facet of retailing, eager to take on responsibility, and willing to continue learning throughout my career. Please look over my résumé to see how my skills can benefit your store.

Knowledge of the company's policy toward promotions is sure to interest the reader.

Even though the last paragraph uses the word "I," the concern and the focus of the letter are clearly centred on the audience and convey a "you" attitude.

I understand that Zellers prefers to promote its managers from within the company, and I would be pleased to start out with an entry-level position until I gain the necessary experience. Do you have any associate positions opening up soon? Could we discuss my qualifications? I will phone you early next Wednesday to arrange a meeting at your convenience.

Sincerely,

Glenda Johns

Glenda Johns

Enclosure

FIGURE 15.6

In-Depth Critique: Sample Unsolicited Application Letter

In her unsolicited application letter, Glenda Johns manages to give a snapshot of her qualifications and skills without repeating what is said in her résumé (which appears in Figure 15.3).

of your special strengths. Nevertheless, an application letter contains some basic components. In Figure 15.6, an unsolicited letter for a retail position, the applicant gains attention by focusing on the needs of the employer. The letter in Figure 15.7, written in response to a help-wanted ad, highlights the applicant's chief qualifications. Compare your own letters with the items in this chapter's Checklist for Application Letters.

Kenneth Sawyer

2141 Michelle Cres., Kelowna, BC V1Z 2W2

February 2, 2001

Ms. Angela Singh
Director of Administration
Cummings and Welbane, Inc.
260 Harvey Ave., Suite 333
Kelowna, BC V1Y 7S5

Dear Ms. Singh:

In the January 31 issue of the *Daily Courier,* your ad mentioned "proven skills." I believe I have what you are looking for in an administrative assistant. In addition to experience in a variety of office settings, I am familiar with the computer software that you use in your office.

The opening states the reason for writing and links the writer's experience to stated qualifications.

I recently completed a three-course sequence at the University College of the Cariboo in Kamloops, on Microsoft Word and PowerPoint. I learned how to apply those programs to speed up letter- and report-writing tasks. A workshop on "Writing and Editing with the Unix Processor" gave me experience with other valuable applications such as composing and formatting sales letters, financial reports, and presentation slides.

By discussing how his specific skills apply to the job sought, the applicant shows that he understands the job's responsibilities.

These skills were invaluable to me as assistant to the director of UCC food-training (please refer to my résumé). I'm particularly proud of the order-confirmation system I designed, which has sharply reduced the problems of late shipments and depleted inventories.

Because "proven skills" are best explained in person, I would appreciate an interview with you. Please phone me any afternoon between 3 and 5 p.m. at (250) 555-6139 to let me know the day and time most convenient for you.

In closing, the writer asks for an interview and facilitates action.

Sincerely,

Kenneth Sawyer

Kenneth Sawyer

Enclosure: Résumé

FIGURE 15.7

In-Depth Critique: Sample Solicited Application Letter

Kenneth Sawyer grabs attention by focusing on a phrase the employer used in a want ad: "proven skills." Sawyer elaborates on his own proven skills throughout the letter, and he even uses the term in the closing paragraph.

Writing Other Types of Employment Messages

In your search for a job, you may prepare three other types of written messages: job-inquiry letters, application forms, and application follow-up letters.

Writing Job-Inquiry Letters

Use a job-inquiry letter to request an application form, which is a standardized data sheet that simplifies comparison of applicants' credentials.

Some organizations will not consider you for a position until you have filled out and submitted an **application form,** a standardized data sheet that simplifies comparison of applicants' qualifications. The inquiry letter is sent to request such a form. To increase your chances of getting the form, include enough information about yourself in the letter to show that you have at least some of the requirements for the position you are seeking:

> Please send me an application form for work as an interior designer in your home furnishings department. For my certificate in design, I took courses in retail merchandising and customer relations. I have also had part-time sales experience at Capwell's department store.

Instead of writing a letter of this kind, you may want to drop in at the office you're applying to. You probably won't get a chance to talk to anyone other than the receptionist or a human resources assistant, but you can pick up the form, get an impression of the organization, and demonstrate your initiative and energy.

Filling Out Application Forms

Your care in filling out application forms suggests to the employer that you will be thorough and careful in your work.

Some organizations require an application form instead of a résumé, and many require both an application form and a résumé. When filling out an application form, try to be thorough and accurate, because the organization will use this as a convenient one-page source for information about your qualifications. Be sure to have your résumé with you to remind you of important information. If you can't remember something and have no record of it, provide the closest estimate possible. If the form calls for information that you cannot provide because you have no background in it, such as military experience, write "Not applicable." When filling out applications on the premises, use a pen (unless specifically requested to use a pencil). If you're allowed to take the application form with you, use a typewriter to fill it out.

Checklist for Application Letters

A. Attention (Opening Paragraph)

1. Open the letter by capturing the reader's attention in a businesslike way.
   a. Summary opening. Present your strongest, most relevant qualifications, with an explanation of how they can benefit the organization.
   b. Name opening. Mention the name of a person who is well known to the reader and who has suggested that you apply for the job.
   c. Source opening. When responding to a job ad, identify the publication in which the ad appeared, and briefly describe how you meet each requirement stated in the ad.
   d. Question opening. Pose an attention-getting question that shows you understand an organization's problem, need, or goal and have a genuine desire to help solve or meet it.
   e. News opening. Cite a publicized organizational achievement, contemplated change, or new procedure or product; then link it to your desire to work for the organization.
   f. Personalized opening. Present one of your relevant interests, mention previous experience with the organization, or cite your present position or status as a means of leading into a discussion of why you want to work for the organization.
   g. Creative opening. Demonstrate your flair and imagination with colourful phrasing, especially if the job requires these qualities.
2. State that you are applying for a job, and identify the position or the type of work you seek.

B. Interest and Desire, or Evidence of Qualifications (Next Several Paragraphs)

1. Present your key qualifications for the job, highlighting what is on your résumé: job-related education and training; relevant work experience; and related activities, interests, and qualities.

Application forms rarely seem to provide the right amount of space or to ask the right kinds of questions to reflect one's skills and abilities accurately. Suppress your frustration, however, and show your cooperation by doing your best to fill out the form completely. If you get an interview, you'll have an opportunity to fill in the gaps. You might also ask the person who gives you the form if you may submit a résumé and an application letter as well.

Writing Application Follow-Ups

If your application letter and résumé fail to bring a response within a month or so, follow up with a second letter to keep your file active. This follow-up letter also gives you a chance to update your original application with any recent job-related information:

Use a follow-up letter to let the employer know you're still interested in the job.

> Since applying to you on May 3 for an executive secretary position, I have completed a course in office management at Coquitlam College. I received straight A's in the course. My keyboarding speed has also increased to 75 words per minute.
>
> Please keep my application in your active file, and let me know when you need a skilled Web site designer.

Even if you have received a letter acknowledging your application and saying that it will be kept on file, don't hesitate to send a follow-up letter three months later to show that you are still interested:

> Three months have elapsed since I applied to you for an underwriting position, but I want to let you know that I am still very interested in joining your company.
>
> I recently completed a four-week temporary work assignment at a large local insurance agency. I learned several new verification techniques and gained experience in using the online computer system. This experience could increase my value to your underwriting department.
>
> Please keep my application in your active file, and let me know when a position opens for a capable underwriter.

2. Adopt a mature and businesslike tone.
   a. Eliminate boasting and exaggeration.
   b. Back up your claims of ability by citing specific achievements in educational and work settings or in outside activities.
   c. Demonstrate a knowledge of the organization and a desire to join it by citing its operations or trends in the industry.
3. Link your education, experience, and personal qualities to the job requirements.
   a. Relate aspects of your training or work experience to those of the target position.
   b. Outline your educational preparation for the job.
   c. Provide proof that you learn quickly, are a hard worker, can handle responsibility, and get along well with others.
   d. Present ample evidence of the personal qualities and work attitudes that are desirable for job performance.
   e. If asked to state salary requirements, provide current salary or a desired salary range, and link it to the benefits of hiring you.
4. Refer the reader to the enclosed résumé.

C. Action (Closing Paragraph)

1. Request an interview at the reader's convenience.
2. Request a screening interview with the nearest regional representative if company headquarters is some distance away.
3. State your phone number (with area code) and the best time to reach you, to make the interview request easy to comply with, or mention a time when you will be calling to set up an interview.
4. Express appreciation for an opportunity to have an interview.
5. Repeat your strongest qualification, to help reinforce the claim that you have something to offer the organization.

Unless you inform them otherwise, the human resources office may assume that you've already found a job and are no longer interested in their organization. In addition, organizations' requirements change. Sending a letter like this demonstrates that you are sincerely interested in working for the organization, that you are persistent in pursuing your goals, and that you continue upgrading your skills to make yourself a better employee–it might just get you an interview.

ON THE JOB
Solving a Communication Dilemma at Pinkerton

Whether it's safeguarding movie stars or making sure a multinational corporation hires the right people, it's all in a day's work for Pinkerton. The security company founded by Allan Pinkerton in 1850 made its name with such exploits as tracking Butch Cassidy and the Sundance Kid. Thomas Wathen bought Pinkerton in 1987 and began expanding it into a worldwide network. Denis Brown took the reins in 1994 with the goal of continuing that growth while improving the company's profit margins.

With the company's services so dependent on the quality of people it hires, Pinkerton's management must screen job seekers and pick only those individuals who have the experience, attitude, and talent to perform well in whatever unique and demanding situation the company assigns them to. These security officers also need excellent communication skills to interact with the public and handle troubles that might range from petty theft to terrorism.

Pinkerton follows the same five-step approach to screening, evaluating, and selecting employees, regardless of whether it's filling internal openings or helping clients evaluate job candidates. In the first step, each candidate fills out a job application and sits through an initial interview with Pinkerton personnel. Only candidates whose qualifications meet Pinkerton's job requirements move to the second step. Next, prospective employees fill out questionnaires measuring attitudes toward honesty and willingness to follow company rules.

Again, only people who meet Pinkerton's standards advance. In the third step, candidates participate in a ten-minute interview session conducted over the telephone by a computerized voice system. They answer roughly 100 questions about job stability, career goals, work ethic, enthusiasm, and other aspects of their work history by pushing buttons on the telephone keypad—one button for yes, another for no, and a third for uncertain.

Just a few minutes after each candidate hangs up the phone, Pinkerton personnel can call the computer centre and get the results. This information helps the staff members pinpoint topics to be addressed in the fourth step of the process, an in-depth personal interview.

At least 30 percent of the applicants are weeded out by this point. In the fifth step, Pinkerton investigators check the backgrounds of those candidates who have completed the personal interview successfully. Once they have the results of the investigation, Pinkerton personnel are then able to decide which candidates to hire.[18]

Your Mission: As a member of Pinkerton's human resources department, you regularly review résumés that arrive uninvited. You're particularly on the lookout for recent university graduates who might be good candidates for management training positions in Pinkerton's comprehensive security operations for General Motors, which span Canada, the United States, and Mexico. General Motors accounts for roughly 10 percent of Pinkerton's annual revenue, so keeping this customer satisfied is extremely important. Give your manager your best advice regarding the following applicants, and be prepared to explain your recommendations.

1. You have received résumés from four people. On the basis of only the career objectives listed, which one of the candidates will you consider hiring as a management trainee?

   a. Career Objective: An entry-level management position in a large company
   b. Career Objective: To invest my management talent and business savvy and shepherd a business toward explosive growth
   c. Career Objective: A management position in which a degree in business administration and experience in managing personnel will be useful
   d. Career Objective: To learn all I can about personnel management in an exciting environment with a company whose reputation is outstanding

2. On the basis of only the education sections of another four résumés, which of the following candidates would you recommend?

   a. **EDUCATION**
   University of Calgary, Calgary, AB 1996–2000.
   Received B.A. degree with a major in Business Administration and a minor in Finance. Graduated with a 3.65 grade-point average. Played varsity football and basketball. Worked 15 hours per week in the library. Coordinated the local student chapter of the Treasury Management Association of Canada. Member of Alpha Phi Alpha social fraternity.
   b. **Education:** I attended Mohawk College in Hamilton for two years and then transferred to Ryerson University, Toronto

where I completed my studies. My program of study was urban planning, but I also took many business management courses, including employee motivation, leadership, history of management theory, and organizational behavior. I selected courses based on the professors' reputation for excellence, and I received mostly A's and B's. Unlike many students, I viewed the acquisition of knowledge–rather than career preparation–as my primary goal. I believe I have received a well-rounded education that has prepared me to approach management situations as problem-solving exercises.

c. **ACADEMIC PREPARATION**
St. Francis Xavier University, Antigonish, NS. Graduated with a B.A. degree in 1999. Majored in Physical Education. Minored in Business Administration. Graduated with a 2.85 average.

d. **Education: University of Regina, Regina, Saskatchewan**
Received B.A. and M.B.A. degrees. I majored in business as an undergraduate and concentrated in manufacturing management during my M.B.A. program. Received a special $2500 scholarship offered by Rotary International recognizing academic achievement in business courses. I also won the MEGA award in 1997. Dean's list.

3. Which of the following four candidates would you recommend, strictly on the basis of the experience sections?

a. **RELATED WORK EXPERIENCE**
McDonald's, The Pas, MB 1996–1997. Part-time cook. Worked 15 hours per week while attending high school. Prepared hamburgers, chicken bits, and french fries. Received employee-of-the-month award for outstanding work habits.
University Grill, Saskatoon, SK 1997–2000. Part-time cook. Worked 20 hours per week while attending university. Prepared hot and cold sandwiches. Helped manager purchase ingredients. Trained new kitchen workers. Prepared work schedules for kitchen staff.

b. **RELATED EXPERIENCE**
Although I have never held a full-time job, I have worked part-time and during summer vacations throughout my high school and university years. During my first two years in high school, I bagged groceries at the Safeway store three afternoons a week. The work was not terribly challenging, but I liked the customers and the other employees. During my third and fourth years, I worked at the YMCA as an after-school counsellor for elementary school children. The kids were really sweet, and I still get letters from some of them. During summer vacations while I was in university, I did construction work for a local home builder. The job paid well, and I also learned a lot about carpentry. The guys I worked with were a mixed bag who expanded my vocabulary and knowledge of the world. I also worked part-time in university in the student cafeteria, where I scooped food onto plates. This did not require much talent, but it taught me a lot about how people behave when standing in line. I also learned quite a bit about life from my boss, Sam "The Man" Benson, who has been managing the student cafeteria for 25 years.

c. **PREVIOUS WORK EXPERIENCE**
The Broadway Department Store, Moncton, NB. Summers, 1997–2000. Sales Consultant, Furniture Department. I interacted with a diverse group of customers, including suburban matrons, teenagers, career women, and professional couples. I endeavoured to satisfy their individual needs and make their shopping experience memorable, efficient, and enjoyable. Under the direction of the sales manager, I helped prepare employee schedules and fill out departmental reports. I also helped manage the inventory, worked the cash register, and handled a variety of special orders and customer complaints with courtesy and aplomb. During the 2000 annual storewide sale, I sold more merchandise than any other salesperson in the entire furniture department.

d. **EXPERIENCE RELATED TO MANAGEMENT**
Medicine Hat, AB. Civilian Member of Public Safety Committee, January–December 2000.

- Organized and promoted a lecture series on vacation safety and home security for the residents of Medicine Hat, recruited and trained 7 committee members to help plan and produce the lectures; persuaded local businesses to finance the program; designed, printed, and distributed flyers; wrote and distributed press releases; attracted an average of 120 people to each of three lectures
- Developed a questionnaire to determine local residents' home-security needs; directed the efforts of 10 volunteers working on the survey; prepared written report for city council and delivered oral summary of findings at town meeting; helped persuade city to fund new home-security program
- Initiated the Business Security Forum as an annual meeting at which local business leaders could meet to discuss safety and security issues; created promotional flyers for the first forum; convinced 19 business owners to fund a business security survey; arranged press coverage of the first forum

4. You've received the following résumé. What action will you take?

Maria Martin
911 Alfred Ave
Winnipeg MB R2X 0V1
(204) 555-0098

Career Objective: To build a management career in a growing Canadian company

Summary of Qualifications: As a student at the University of Manitoba in Winnipeg, carried out various assignments that have required skills related to a career in management. For example:

Planning Skills. As president of the university's foreign affairs forum, organized six lectures and workshops featuring 36 speakers from 16 foreign countries within a nine-month period. Identified and recruited the speakers, handled their travel arrangements, and scheduled the facilities.

Interpersonal Skills. As chairman of the parade committee for Homecoming Weekend, worked with the city of Winnipeg to obtain approval, permits, and traffic control for the parade. Also encouraged local organizations such as the Lion's Club, the Kiwanis Club, and the Boy Scouts to participate in the parade. Coordinated the efforts of the 5 fraternities and 6 sororities that entered floats in the parade. Recruited 4 marching bands from the surrounding area and coordinated their efforts with the university's marching band. Also arranged for local auto dealers to provide cars for the ten homecoming queen candidates.

Communication Skills. Wrote over 25 essays and term papers dealing with academic topics. Received an A on all but two of these papers. In final year, wrote a 20-page analysis of the paper products industry, interviewing the five top executives at the Abitibi paper company. Received an A on this paper.

a. Definitely recommend that Pinkerton take a look at this outstanding candidate.
b. Turn down the candidate. She doesn't give enough information about when she attended university, what she majored in, or where she has worked.
c. Call the candidate on the phone and ask for more information. If she sounds promising, send her an application form that requests more specific information about her academic background and employment history.
d. Consider the candidate's qualifications relative to those of other applicants. Recommend her if you do not have three or four other applicants with more directly relevant qualifications.

TAP Your Knowledge

Summary of Learning Outcomes

1. Analyze your work skills and qualifications. Analyzing what you have to offer an employer is the first step in your job search. To perform a thorough analysis, review your functional skills, education, work experience, extracurricular activities, and personal characteristics. A thorough self-analysis will help you understand the type of work you can do.

2. Identify what type of job and employer you want. To get the type of job you'd like to have, do some research. Talk to people in various occupations, perhaps relatives or friends. Ask yourself what you'd enjoy doing every day. Decide the amount of money you'd like to earn your first year on the job, and your ultimate earnings goal. Consider your ideal work environment–the size and type of operation, the location, the culture. This type of analysis will also help you target your preferred career.

3. List your best prospects for employment. Several methods will help you find your best prospects for employment. Look in such sources such as the *Financial Post's Survey of Industrials* and the *Canadian Student Employment Guide*. The Internet has useful sites, such as **www.workinfonet.ca**, to aid you in your job search. Making contacts, researching companies, searching for job vacancies online or in newspapers and trade magazines, and posting your résumé online will help you find employment.

4. Develop a strategy for selling yourself to these prospects. Sell yourself to your job prospects by keeping a portfolio of your best work and awards you've won. Gain intercultural experience through travel. Participate in internship programs, network with others in your field, take temporary jobs and courses to upgrade your skills, and demonstrate a willingness to learn, listen, and gain experience.

5. Prepare an effective résumé. The key characteristics of an effective résumé are neatness, simplicity, accuracy, and honesty. Use a clean typeface and high-grade paper and leave ample margins. Make your information easy to grasp by using headings that call attention to various aspects of your background, experience, and education and indented lists to highlight your qualifications. Keep your writing style simple and direct, and use crisp phrases that begin with action verbs. If education is your strongest selling point, discuss it thoroughly and highlight it visually. Your work experience section should list all the related jobs you have held, including employer's name and location, your title, length of service, duties, and achievements. Other sections are relevant skills, which may indicate computer expertise or command of other languages; and nonpaid activities, which reveal work-related skills.

6. Define the purpose of application letters, and explain how to apply the AIDA organizational approach to them. The purpose of an application letter is to convince readers to look at your résumé. This makes application letters a type of sales letter, so you'll want to use the AIDA organizational approach. Get attention in the opening paragraph by showing how your work skills could benefit the organization, by explaining how your qualifications fit the job, or by demonstrating an understanding of the organization's needs. Build interest and desire by showing how you can meet the job requirements, and be sure to refer your reader to your résumé near the end of this section. Finally, motivate action by making your request easy to fulfill and by including all necessary contact information.

Test Your Knowledge

Review Questions

1. What is the purpose of maintaining an employment portfolio?
2. What is a résumé, and why is it important to adopt a "you" attitude when preparing one?
3. In what ways can job-seekers use the Internet during their career and employment search?
4. How does a chronological résumé differ from a functional résumé, and when is each appropriate?
5. What elements are commonly included in a résumé?
6. What are some of the most common problems with résumés?
7. Why is it important to provide a key word summary in a scannable or electronic résumé?
8. What advantages do résumés sent by e-mail have over résumés sent by fax or by mail?
9. How does a solicited application letter differ from an unsolicited letter?
10. How does the AIDA approach apply to an application letter?

Apply Your Knowledge

Critical Thinking Questions

1. According to experts in the job-placement field, the average job seeker places too much importance on the résumé and not enough on other elements of the job search. Which elements do you think are most important? Explain.
2. How would you locate information about overseas employment opportunities in general? About job requirements at specific overseas companies? Briefly explain.
3. As an employer, what would you do to detect résumé inflation such as misrepresented job qualifications, salaries, and academic credentials? Please explain.
4. Stating your career objective might limit your opportunities by labelling you too narrowly. Not stating your career objective, however, might lead an employer to categorize you incorrectly. Which outcome is riskier? Do summaries of qualifications overcome such drawbacks? If so, how? Briefly explain.
5. When writing a solicited application letter and describing the skills requested in the employer's ad, how can you avoid using *I* too often? Explain and give examples.
6. How can you make your letter of application unique without being cute or gimmicky? Explain and give examples.

Practise Your Knowledge

Exercises

1. Working with another student, change the following statements to make them more effective for a traditional résumé by using active verbs.

   a. Have some experience with database design.
   b. Assigned to a project to analyze the cost accounting methods for a large manufacturer.
   c. I was part of a team that developed a new inventory control system.

d. Am responsible for preparing the quarterly department budget.
e. Was a manager of a department with seven employees working for me.
f. Was responsible for developing a spreadsheet to analyze monthly sales by department.
g. Put in place a new program for ordering supplies.

2. Using your team's answers to exercise 14.1, make the statements stronger by quantifying them (make up any numbers you need).
3. Assume that you achieved the results shown in exercise 14.1 not as an individual employee, but as part of a work team. Must you mention your team participation in your résumé? Explain your answer.
4. What work-related activities and situations do you prefer? Evaluate your preferences by deciding whether you strongly agree, agree, or disagree with each of the following statements. Use the results as a good start for guiding your job search.
    1. I want to work independently.
    2. I want variety in my work.
    3. I want to work with people.
    4. I want to work with products or machines.
    5. I want physical work.
    6. I want mental work.
    7. I want to work for a large organization.
    8. I want to work for a non-profit organization.
    9. I want to work for a small family business.
    10. I want to work for a service business.
    11. I want regular, predictable work hours.
    12. I want to work in a city location.
    13. I want to work in a small town or suburb.
    14. I want to work in another country.
    15. I want to work outdoors.
    16. I want to work in a structured environment.

Documents for Analysis

Read the following documents; then (1) analyze the strengths or weaknesses of each sentence and (2) revise each document so that it follows the guidelines presented in this chapter.

Document 15.A: Writing an Application Message

I'm writing to let you know about my availability for the brand manager job you advertised. As you can see from my enclosed résumé, my background is perfect for the position. Even though I don't have any real job experience, my grades have been outstanding considering that I went to a top-ranked business school.

I did many things during my undergraduate years to prepare me for this job:

- Earned a 3.4 out of a 4.0 with a 3.8 in my business courses
- Elected representative to the student governing association
- Selected to receive the Lamar Franklin Award
- Worked to earn a portion of my tuition

I am sending my résumé to all the top firms, but I like yours better than any of the rest. Your reputation is tops in the industry, and I want to be associated with a business that can pridefully say it's the best.

If you wish for me to come in for an interview, I can come on a Friday afternoon or anytime on weekends when I don't have classes. Again, thanks for considering me for your brand manager position.

Document 15.B: Writing an Application Message

I saw your ad for a finance major in our paper last week. I hope the position isn't already filled because I'd like to interview for it. I've enclosed my résumé, which includes the work I've done since graduation.

Your ad said you were looking for a motivated person who wouldn't mind travelling. That would be me! I've also done the type of work you mentioned: budgeting, forecasting, and working with information systems. I know quite a bit about computers.

I know you get many résumés and mine is probably not all that special, but there's one thing that sets me apart: I'm friendly and eager to work. My present position is with a Silicon Valley North company, which is in financial trouble. I'm afraid my whole division is going to be downsized, so I want to have something lined up in advance.

Could you send me some information about the financial stability of your company and its history of layoffs. I certainly wouldn't want to jump from the frying pan into the fire, so to speak. (Ha.) At any rate, thank you for considering my application and résumé. I hope you call me very soon.

Document 15.C: Writing Application Follow-Up Messages

Did you receive my résumé? I sent it to you at least two months ago and haven't heard anything. I know you keep résumés on file, but I just want to be sure that you keep me in mind. I heard you are hiring health-care managers and certainly would like to be considered for one of those positions.

Since I last wrote you, I've worked in a variety of positions that have helped prepare me for management. To wit, I've become lunch manager at the restaurant where I work, which involved a raise in pay. I now manage a wait-staff of 12 girls and take the lunch receipts to the bank every day.

Of course, I'd much rather be working at a real job, and that's why I'm writing again. Is there anything else you would like to know about me or my background? I would really like to know more about your company. Is there any literature you could send me? If so, I would really appreciate it.

I think one reason I haven't been hired yet is that I don't want to leave St. John's. So I hope when you think of me, it's for a position that wouldn't require moving. Thanks again for considering my application.

Cases

Thinking About Your Career

1. Taking stock and taking aim: Application package for the right job Think about yourself. What are some things that come easily to you? What do you enjoy doing? In what part of the country would you like to live? Do you like to work indoors? Outdoors? A combination of the two? How much do you like to travel? Would you like to spend considerable time on the road? Do you like to work closely with others or more independently? What conditions make a job unpleasant? Do you delegate responsibility easily, or do you like to take charge? Are you better with words or numbers? Better at speaking or writing? Do you like to be motivated by fixed deadlines? How important is job security to you? Do you want your supervisor to state clearly what is expected of you, or do you like the freedom to make many of your own decisions?

Your Task: After answering these questions, consult reference materials (from your university or college library or placement centre) and choose a location, a company, and a job that suits the profile you have just developed. With guidance from your instructor, decide whether to apply for a job you're qualified for now or one you'll be qualified for with additional education. Then, as directed by your instructor, write one or more of the following: (a) a job-inquiry letter, (b) a résumé, (c) a letter of application, or (d) a follow-up letter to your application letter.

2. Scanning the possibilities: Résumé for the Internet In your search for a position, you discover that **www.workopolis.com** is a Web site that lists hundreds of companies advertising on the Internet. Your chances of getting an interview with a leading company will be enhanced if you submit your résumé and cover letter electronically. On the Web, explore **www.adm.uwaterloo.ca/ infocecs/CRC/manual-home.html** and **www.careersite.com.**

Your Task: Prepare an electronic résumé that could be submitted to the site that best fits your qualifications, experience, and education. Print out the résumé for your instructor.

3. Online application: Electronic cover letter introducing a résumé *Motley Fool* is a Generation-X online financial magazine accessed via the World Wide Web. Their mission is to educate, enrich, and amuse individual investors around the world.

Your Task: Visit the *Motley Fool* Web site at **www.fool.com** and examine the news and the range of companies that interest the *Motley Fool.* Then, choose an area of the publication in which you could imagine having expertise that would contribute to their operation. Write an e-mail message that will serve as your cover letter, and attach your résumé as a file to be downloaded. Address your message to Brian Bauer, Managing Editor. Try to limit your message to one screen (about 23 lines). You'll need a creative "hook" and an assurance that you are the right person to help *Motley Fool.*

Writing a Résumé and an Application Letter

4. "Help wanted": Application for a job listed in the classified section Among the jobs listed in today's *Province* (200 Granville Street, Vancouver, BC V6C 3N3) are the following:

ACCOUNTANT/MANAGER
Supervisor needed for 3-person bookkeeping department. Degree in accounting plus collection experience helpful. L. Cichy, Reynolds Clothiers, 1818 2nd Ave W, Vancouver, BC V6J 1H9.

ACTIVIST–MAKE DEMOCRACY WORK
British Columbia's largest consumer-lobbying organization has permanent positions (full- or part-time) for energetic individuals with excellent communication skills who are interested in working for social change. Reply *The Province* Box 5432.

ATTENDANT
For video game room, 2359 Venable St, Vancouver BC V5L 2J5

CONVENIENCE FOOD STORE MANAGER
Vacancies for managers and trainees in Vancouver area. We are seeking energetic and knowledgeable individuals who will be responsible for profitable operation of convenience food stores and petroleum product sales. Applicants should possess retail sales or managerial training. Interested candidates mail résumés and salary requirements to Prestige Products, Inc., PO Box 23727, Airport Postal Outlet, Vancouver, BC V7B 1X9. Equal opportunity employer M/F.

Your Task: Send a résumé and an application letter to one of these potential employers.

Writing Other Types of Employment Messages

5. Crashing the last frontier: Letter of inquiry about jobs in the Yukon Your friend can't understand why you would want to move to the Yukon. So you explain: "What really decided it for me was that I've never seen the Northern Lights."

"But what about the bears? The 60-below winters? The permafrost?" asks your friend.

"No problem. Whitehorse doesn't get much colder than Saskatoon does. It is just windier and wetter. Anyhow, I want to live in the wilderness, by the famous Yukon River. Whitehorse has lots of small businesses, like a frontier town. I think I'd be able to buy a tract on the outskirts and build my own cabin there."

"Your plans seem a little hasty," your friend warns. "Maybe you should write for information before you just take off. How do you know you could get a job?"

Your Task: Take your friend's advice and write to the Chamber of Commerce, City of Whitehorse, 2121 2nd Avenue, Whitehorse, Yukon, Y1A 1C2. Ask what types of employment are available to someone with your education and experience, and ask who specifically is hiring year-round employees.

Developing Your Internet Skills

Going Online: Link Your Way to a Better Résumé, p. 435

Read over the section on using action words in your résumé, paying particular attention to the charts that give examples of "Action Statements with Accomplishment-Oriented Results" and "Positive Action Verbs." Then move on to read about something you may not have considered: the computer-scannable résumé. Now choose one or both of these tasks: (1) If you don't have a current résumé, look over the charts and examples and let them inspire you while you develop a new résumé that incorporates action verbs and accomplishment statements. (2) Turn your readable résumé into a computer-scannable résumé by following the guidelines on this site. Look over your new résumé(s) and think of ways to improve your presentation. Can you choose better words to describe your accomplishments? Can you eliminate any wordy job descriptions and then add more detail about your most important accomplishments? What words can you replace with action verbs? For the scannable résumé, have you missed any key words that could catch an employer's eye during a database search?

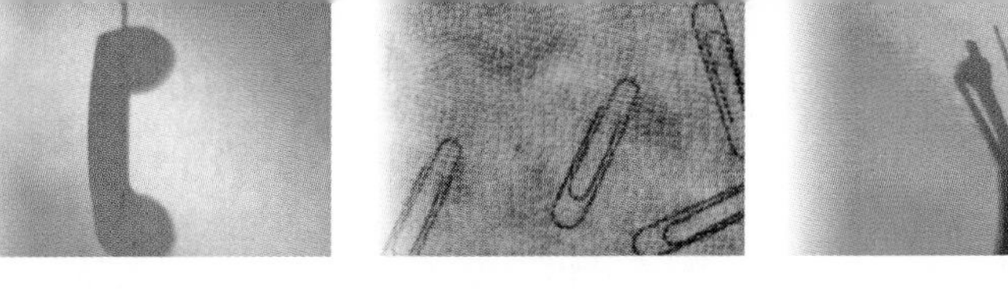

CHAPTER 16

Interviewing for Employment and Following Up

AFTER STUDYING THIS CHAPTER, YOU WILL BE ABLE TO

1. Describe the dual purpose of the job interview
2. Explain the steps in the interview process
3. Identify and adapt to various types of interviews
4. List the types of questions you are likely to encounter during a job interview
5. Discuss how to perform well during the three phases of a typical job interview
6. Write the six most common types of messages required to follow up after an interview

ON THE JOB
Facing a Communication Dilemma at Herman Miller, Inc.

How to Tell a Good Dancer Before the Waltz Begins

Looking for a company that cares about people? You might try Herman Miller, a highly successful establishment that manufactures office furniture in Zeeland, Michigan. Founded in 1923 by D. J. DePree, Herman Miller has gained an international presence over the years; Canadians have been furnishing their offices with stylish Herman Miller products since 1996. The firm is justifiably famous for its corporate culture. It may be the only company on the Fortune 500 list that actually has a *vice-president for people*. Participation is the name of the game in this organization. Employees at all levels are consulted about important decisions and reap the rewards if the business does well.

Herman Miller's recruiters look at a candidate's education and experience, but even more important is the candidate's personality. It's a challenge to find people who can operate in the company's participative environment without regarding the culture as permissive.

When Herman Miller's recruiters interview a job candidate, they look at the person's education and experience, of course, but they also look for something else: the ability to get along with others. If the candidate's personality is outstanding, the company may be willing to overlook a lack of relevant experience. A senior vice-president of research was once a high-school football coach. The senior vice-president of marketing and sales used to be the dean of agriculture at Michigan State. And the vice-president for people had been planning to become a prison warden but joined Herman Miller instead.

On the surface, these people didn't seem like good candidates for management jobs in the office furniture business, but Herman Miller looked beyond the superficial to see their true potential. The most important quality in a Herman Miller employee is the capacity for teamwork. "To be successful here," says one Herman Miller executive, "you have to know how to dance."

How do you know whether someone is a good dancer before you actually begin the waltz? That's the challenge facing Herman Miller's recruiters when they interview job candidates. The challenge facing candidates is how to prepare for a job interview. What would you do? What can you do during an interview? Is there anything you could do after the interview?[1]

Interviewing with Potential Employers

LEARNING OUTCOME 1
Describe the dual purpose of the job interview.

As Herman Miller's recruiters can tell you, the best way to prepare for a job interview is to think carefully about the job itself. With the right job, you stand to be happy in your work. Thus it pays to approach job interviews with a sound appreciation of their dual purpose. The organization's main objective is to find the best person available for the job; the applicant's main objective is to find the job best suited to his or her goals and capabilities.

An interview helps both the interviewer and the applicant achieve their goals.

By focusing on your audience, your potential employer, you will learn about the organization you want to work for and the people who will make the hiring decision. Planning and preparation are key elements for successful job interviews.

The Interview Process

An employment interview is a formal meeting in which employers and applicants ask questions and exchange information to learn more about each other.

Various types of organizations approach the recruiting process in various ways, so adjust your job search accordingly. In any case, once you get your foot in the door, you move to the next stage and prepare to meet with a recruiter during an **employment interview,** a formal meeting during which an employer and an applicant ask questions and exchange information to see whether the applicant and the organization are a good match. The purpose of an employment interview is two-fold: (1) to help the organization find the best person for the job, and (2) to help the applicant find the job best suited to his or her goals and capabilities. Applicants often face a series of interviews.

THE TYPICAL SEQUENCE OF INTERVIEWS

LEARNING OUTCOME 2
Explain the steps in the interview process.

Most employers conduct two or three interviews before deciding whether to offer a person a job. The first interview, sometimes held on campus, is the **preliminary screening interview,** which helps employers eliminate (screen out) unqualified applicants from the hiring process. Those candidates who best meet the organization's requirements are invited to visit company offices for further evaluation. Some organizations make a decision at that point, but many schedule a third interview to complete the evaluation process before extending a job offer.

Most organizations interview an applicant several times before extending a job offer.

Screening interviews are fairly structured, so applicants are often asked roughly the same questions. Many companies use standardized evaluation sheets to grade each applicant so that all candidates are measured against the same criteria. Your best approach to a screening interview is to follow the interviewer's lead. Keep your responses short and to the point. However, if an opportunity presents itself, emphasize the theme you used in developing your résumé. You want to give the interviewer a way to differentiate you from other candidates, and, at the same time, you want to demonstrate your strengths and qualifications.

The next round of interviews is designed to help the organization narrow the field a little further. Typically, if you're invited to visit a company, you will talk with several people: a member of the human resources department, one or two potential colleagues, and your potential supervisor. You might face a **panel interview,** meeting with several interviewers who ask you questions during a single session. Your best approach during this round of interviews is to show interest in the job, relate your skills and experience to the organization's needs, listen attentively, ask insightful questions, and display enthusiasm.

TYPES OF INTERVIEWS

LEARNING OUTCOME 3
Identify and adapt to various types of interviews.

Interviews take various forms, depending on what the recruiter is attempting to discover about the applicant. In the **directed interview,** generally used in screening, the employer controls the interview by preparing a series of questions to be asked in a set order. Working from a checklist, the interviewer asks you each question in order, staying within a specific time period. Your answers are noted. Although useful in gathering facts, the directed interview is generally regarded as too structured to measure an applicant's personal qualities.

Companies use a variety of interviewing techniques to evaluate various attributes.

In contrast, the **open-ended interview** is a less formal, unstructured interview with an open, relaxed format. By posing broad, open-ended questions, the interviewer encourages you to talk freely, perhaps even to divulge more than you should. This type of interview is good for bringing out an applicant's personality. Interviewers also ask behavioural or situational questions to determine how candidates would handle real-life work problems. Some companies interview several candidates simultaneously to see how they interact–whether they smile, support one another's comments, or try to score points at one another's expense.[2] Other companies ask candidates to participate in a series of simulated exercises, either individually or in a group. Trained observers evaluate their performance using predetermined criteria and then advise management on how well each person is likely to handle the challenges normally faced on the job.[3]

Perhaps the most unnerving type of interview is the **stress interview,** designed to see how well a candidate handles stressful situations (an important qualification for certain jobs). During a stress interview you might be asked pointed questions designed to irk or unsettle you. You might be subjected to long periods of silence, criticisms of your appearance, deliberate interruptions, and abrupt or even hostile reactions by the interviewer. Many corporate managers believe that stress interviews are inappropriate and unethical.[4]

Interviewing by video is an option that has worked for some job seekers. Manpower Canada uses a videoconferencing system to interview applicants at remote locations.[5] Some applicants use video "résumés" on CD-ROMs that can be played on office computers. These videos are more like interviews than résumés, and they require the same strategies as interviews. Such video interviews can save you time, showcase your strong personality, and facilitate long-distance job searches. But video interviews entail a risk: Your appearance may jog a negative memory or a dislike that the recruiter is unaware of, or you may encounter discrimination that you'll never know about.[6] Whatever types of interviews you face, even if you are successful you may still be asked to take one or more pre-employment tests before starting your new job.

PRE-EMPLOYMENT TESTING

Pre-employment tests attempt to provide objective, quantitative information about candidates' skills, attitudes, and habits.

Given the high cost of hiring unsuitable employees, more and more companies are turning to pre-employment testing to determine whether applicants have the necessary skills and psychological characteristics to handle a particular job. Even though many of the tests are related to specific job skills such as keyboarding ability, the real growth is occurring in tests designed to weed out dishonest candidates Many administer honesty tests, which ask applicants questions designed to bring out their attitudes toward stealing and work habits.

Some employers prefer not to go to the extra expense of administering such tests or feel that educated judgment works just as well. Some applicants question the validity of honesty tests or consider them an invasion of privacy. However, used in conjunction with other evidence, the tests attempt to provide an objective, quantitative measure of applicants' qualifications, which may work to the advantage of both employer and applicant.

What Employers Look For

Interviewers try to determine what you can do and what kind of person you are.

In general, employers are looking for two things: proof that a candidate can handle a specific job and evidence that the person will fit in with the organization. Employers are most concerned with attitude, communication skill, and work experience.[7] They also care about intelligence, enthusiasm, creativity, and motivation.

LEARNING OUTCOME 4
List the types of questions you are likely to encounter during a job interview.

QUALIFICATIONS FOR THE JOB

Every position requires specific qualifications. To become an auditor, for example, you must know accounting; to become a sales manager, you must have several years of sales experience. When you're invited to interview for a position, the interviewer may already have some idea of whether you have the right qualifications, based on a review of your résumé. During the interview, you'll be asked to describe your education and previous jobs in more depth so that the interviewer can determine how well your skills match the requirements. In many cases, the interviewer will be seeking someone with the flexibility to apply diverse skills in several areas.[8]

Suitability for the specific job is judged on the basis of
- ✧ Academic preparation
- ✧ Work experience
- ✧ Job-related personality traits

Another consideration is whether a candidate has the right personality traits for the job. A personal interview is vital because a résumé can't show whether a person is lively and outgoing, subdued and low key, able to take direction, or able to take charge. Each job requires a different mix of personality traits. The task of the interviewer is to find out whether a candidate will be effective in the job.

A GOOD FIT WITH THE ORGANIZATION

Interviewers try to determine more than whether the applicant has the right professional qualifications and personality for a particular job. They also try to decide whether the candidate will be compatible with the other people in the organization. Every interviewer approaches this issue a little differently. Features they may consider include:

Compatibility with the organization is judged on the basis of
✧ Appearance
✧ Age
✧ Personal background
✧ Attitudes and style

- *Physical appearance.* Includes clothing, grooming, posture, eye contact, handshake, facial expressions, and tone of voice.
- *Age.* If you feel that your youth could count against you, counteract its influence by emphasizing your experience, dependability, and mature attitudes.
- *Personal background.* To broaden your interests, hobbies, awareness of world events, and so forth, you can read widely, make an effort to meet new people, and participate in discussion groups, seminars, and workshops.
- *Attitudes and personal style.* Interviewers are likely to be impressed by openness, enthusiasm, interest, courtesy, sincerity, willingness to learn, and self-confidence.

What Applicants Need to Find Out

What things should you find out about the prospective job and employer? By doing a little advance research and asking the right questions during the interview, you can probably find answers to all the following questions and more:

Candidates are responsible for deciding whether the work and the organization are compatible with their goals and values.

- Are these my kind of people?
- Can I do this work?
- Will I enjoy the work?
- Is the job what I want?
- Does the job pay what I'm worth?
- What kind of person would I be working for?
- What sort of future can I expect with this organization?

In order to find out the answers to these questions, you'll need to keep your wits about you. The best way to do that is to be prepared for the interview.

How to Prepare for a Job Interview

It's perfectly normal to feel a little anxious before an interview. So much depends on it, and you don't know quite what to expect. But don't worry too much–preparation will help you perform well. Before the interview, do some basic research, think about questions, bolster your confidence, polish your interview style, and plan to look good. If you do these things, you'll be ready when you arrive.

DO SOME BASIC RESEARCH

Learning about the organization and the job is important because it enables you to review your résumé from the employer's point of view (Figure 16.1). Consider 360networks, for example. With a little research, you would discover that this Canadian company, a provider of optical cable, is moving aggressively into international markets.[9] Knowing this fact might help you pinpoint aspects of your background (such as language capabilities and communication skills) that would appeal to 360network's recruiters. The fastest way to learn about a company is by visiting its Web site.

Be prepared to relate your qualifications to the organization's needs.

WHERE TO LOOK	▪ *Annual report:* Summarizes year's operations; mentions products, significant events, names of key personnel ▪ *In-house magazine or newspaper:* Reveals information about company operations, events, personnel ▪ *Product brochures and publicity releases:* Provide insight into organization's operations and values (obtain from public relations office) ▪ *Stock research reports:* Help you assess stability and prospects for growth (obtain from local stockbroker) ▪ *Business and financial pages of local newspapers:* Contain news items about organizations, current performance figures ▪ *Periodicals indexes:* Contain descriptive listings of magazine and newspaper articles about organizations (obtain from library or online) ▪ *Better Business Bureau and Chamber of Commerce:* Distribute information about some local organizations ▪ *Former and current employees:* Have insight into job and work environment ▪ *School placement office:* Collects information on organizations that recruit and on job qualifications and salaries
WHAT TO FIND OUT	**About the Organization** ▪ *Full name:* What the organization is officially known as (for example, 3M is Minnesota Mining & Manufacturing Company) ▪ *Location:* Where the organization's headquarters, branch offices, and plants are ▪ *Age:* How long the organization has been in business ▪ *Products:* What goods and services the organization produces and sells ▪ *Industry position:* What the organization's current market share, financial position, and profit picture are ▪ *Earnings:* What the trends in the organization's stock prices and dividends are (if the firm is publicly held) ▪ *Growth:* What changes in earnings and holdings the organization has experienced in recent years and its prospects for expansion ▪ *Organization:* What subsidiaries, divisions, and departments make up the whole **About the Job** ▪ *Job title:* What you will be called ▪ *Job functions:* What the main tasks of the job are ▪ *Job qualifications:* What knowledge and skills the job requires ▪ *Career path:* What chances for ready advancement exist ▪ *Salary range:* What the organization typically offers and what pay is reasonable in this industry and geographic area ▪ *Travel opportunities:* How often, long, and far you'll be allowed (or required) to travel ▪ *Relocation opportunities:* Where you might be allowed (or required) to move and how often you might be moved

FIGURE 16.1
Finding Out About the Organization and the Job

THINK AHEAD ABOUT QUESTIONS

Practise answering interview questions.

Most job interviews are essentially question-and-answer sessions: You answer the interviewer's questions about your background, and you ask questions of your own to determine whether the job and the organization are right for you. By planning for your interviews, you can handle these exchanges intelligently.

Employers usually gear their interview questions to specific organizational needs, and many change their questions over time. In general, you can expect to be asked about your skills, achievements, and goals; your attitude toward work and school; your relationships with work supervisors, colleagues, and fellow students; and, occasionally, your hobbies and interests. For a look at the types of questions that are often asked, see Figure 16.2. Jot down a brief answer to each one. Then read the answers over until you feel comfortable with each one. You may want to tape record them and then listen to make sure they sound clear and convincing. Although practising your answers will help you feel prepared and confident, you don't want to memorize responses or sound over-rehearsed. Another suggestion is to give a list of interview questions to a friend or relative and have that person ask you various questions at random. Through practice you'll learn to articulate answers and to look at the person as you answer.

Questions About College

1. What courses in college or university did you like most? Why?
2. Do you think your extracurricular activities were worth the time you devoted to them? Why or why not?
3. When did you choose your area of study? Did you ever change your area of study? If so, why?
4. Do you feel you did the best scholastic work you are capable of?
5. Which of your college or university years was the toughest? Why?

Questions About Employers and Jobs

6. What jobs have you held? Why did you leave?
7. What percentage of your school expenses did you earn? How?
8. Why did you choose your particular field of work?
9. What are the disadvantages of your chosen field?
10. Have you served in the military? What rank did you achieve? What jobs did you perform?
11. What do you think about how this industry operates today?
12. Why do you think you would like this particular type of job?

Questions About Personal Attitudes and Preferences

13. Do you prefer to work in any specific geographical location? If so, why?
14. How much money do you hope to be earning in five years? In ten years?
15. What do you think determines a person's progress in a good organization?
16. What personal characteristics do you feel are necessary for success in your chosen field?
17. Tell me a story.
18. Do you like to travel?
19. Do you think grades should be considered by employers? Why or why not?

Questions About Work Habits

20. Do you prefer working with others or by yourself?
21. What type of boss do you prefer?
22. Have you ever had any difficulty getting along with colleagues or supervisors? With other students? With instructors?
23. Would you prefer to work in a large or a small organization? Why?
24. How do you feel about overtime work?
25. What have you done that shows initiative and willingness to work?

FIGURE 16.2
Twenty-Five Common Interview Questions

The questions you ask in an interview are just as important as the answers you provide. By asking intelligent questions, you can demonstrate your understanding of the organization and steer the discussion into those areas that allow you to present your qualifications to peak advantage. More important, you can get the information you need to evaluate the organization and the job. While recruiters like those at Herman Miller are trying to decide whether you are right for them, you must decide whether Herman Miller or any other company is right for you.

Types of questions to ask during an interview:

- ✧ Warm-up
- ✧ Open-ended
- ✧ Indirect

Before the interview, prepare a list of about a dozen questions, using a mix of formats to elicit various types of information. Start with a warm-up question to help break the ice. You might ask a Herman Miller recruiter, "What departments usually hire new graduates?" After that, you might build rapport by asking an open-ended question that draws out her opinion: for example, "How do you think the current economic environment will affect Herman Miller's ability to expand?" Indirect questions are another approach. You can get useful information and show that you've prepared for the interview with comments such as "I'd really like to know more about Herman Miller's plans for increasing product distribution" or "That recent *Canadian Business* article about the company was very interesting." Of course, any questions you ask should be put into your own words so that you don't sound like every other candidate. For a list of other good questions you might use as a starting point, see Figure 16.3.

Take your list of questions to the interview on a notepad or clipboard. If you need to, jot down the briefest notes during the meeting, and be sure to record them in more detail afterward. Having a list of questions should impress the inter-

FIGURE 16.3

Fifteen Questions to Ask the Interviewer

1. What are this job's major responsibilities?
2. What qualities do you want in the person who fills this position?
3. Do you want to know more about my related training?
4. What is the first problem that needs the attention of the person you hire?
5. What are the organization's major strengths? Weaknesses?
6. Who are your organization's major competitors, and what are their strengths and weaknesses?
7. What makes your organization different from others in the industry?
8. What are your organization's major markets?
9. Does the organization have any plans for new products? Acquisitions?
10. What can you tell me about the person I would report to?
11. How would you define your organization's managerial philosophy?
12. What additional training does your organization provide?
13. Do employees have an opportunity to continue their education with help from the organization?
14. Would relocation be required, now or in the future?
15. Why is this job now vacant?

viewer with your organization and thoroughness. It will also show that you're there to evaluate the organization and the job as well as to sell yourself.

BOLSTER YOUR CONFIDENCE

By overcoming your tendencies to feel self-conscious or nervous during an interview, you can build your confidence and make a good impression. The best way to counteract apprehension is to try to remove its source. You may be shy because you think you have some flaw that will prompt other people to reject you. Bear in mind, however, that you're much more conscious of your limitations than other people are. If some aspect of your appearance or background makes you uneasy, correct it or exercise positive traits to offset it, such as warmth, wit, intelligence, or charm. Instead of dwelling on your weaknesses, focus on your strengths so that you can emphasize them to an interviewer. Make a list of your good points and compare them with what you see as your shortcomings. Remember, too, that all the other candidates for the job are probably just as nervous as you are. In fact, even the interviewer may be nervous.

Going Online

Be Prepared for Challenging Interview Questions

The Royal Bank Web site provides typical questions asked at Royal Bank interviews, such as behavioural questions. Here you will also find information about résumé preparation and the job search.

www.royalbank.com/fastforward/interview.html

POLISH YOUR INTERVIEW STYLE

Confidence helps you walk into an interview, but the only way you'll walk out with a job is if you give the interviewer an impression of poise, good manners, and good judgment as well as self-confidence. One way to develop an adept style is to stage mock interviews with a friend. After each practice session, have your friend critique your performance, using the list of interview faults shown in Figure 16.4 to identify opportunities for improvement. You can even videotape these mock interviews and then evaluate them yourself. The taping process can be intimidating, but it helps you work out any problems before you begin actual job interviews.

As you stage your mock interviews, pay particular attention to your non-verbal behaviour. In Canada, you are more likely to be invited back for a second interview or offered a job if you maintain eye contact, smile frequently, sit in an attentive position, and use frequent hand gestures. These non-verbal signals convince the interviewer that you are alert, assertive, dependable, confident, responsible, and energetic.[10] Of course some companies based in Canada are owned and managed by people from other cultures. So during your basic research, find out about the company's cultural background and preferences.

FIGURE 16.4

Marks Against Applicants (in General Order of Importance)

1. Has a poor personal appearance
2. Is overbearing, overaggressive, conceited; has a superiority complex; seems to know it all
3. Is unable to express self clearly; has poor voice, diction, grammar
4. Lacks knowledge or experience
5. Is not prepared for interview
6. Has no real interest in job
7. Lacks planning for career; has no purpose or goals
8. Lacks enthusiasm; is passive and indifferent
9. Lacks confidence and poise; is nervous and ill at ease
10. Shows insufficient evidence of achievement
11. Has failed to participate in extracurricular activities
12. Overemphasizes money; is interested only in the best dollar offer
13. Has poor scholastic record; just got by
14. Is unwilling to start at the bottom; expects too much too soon
15. Makes excuses
16. Is evasive; hedges on unfavourable factors in record
17. Lacks tact
18. Lacks maturity
19. Lacks courtesy; is ill-mannered
20. Condemns past employers
21. Lacks social skills
22. Shows marked dislike for schoolwork
23. Lacks vitality
24. Fails to look interviewer in the eye
25. Has weak, limp, handshake

The way you speak is almost as important as what you say.

Like other forms of non-verbal behaviour, the sound of your voice can have a major impact on your success in a job interview.[11] You can work with a tape recorder to overcome voice problems. If you tend to speak too rapidly, practise speaking more slowly. If your voice sounds too loud or too soft, practise adjusting it. Work on eliminating speech mannerisms such as *you know, like,* and *um,* which might make you sound inarticulate. Speak in your natural tone, and try to vary the pitch, rate, and volume of your voice to express enthusiasm and energy. If you speak in a flat, emotionless tone, you convey the impression that you are passive or bored.

When non-verbal behaviour is less of a concern, you can use live chat rooms on the Internet to simulate interviews. For example, by using the chat rooms on America Online, CompuServe, or Yahoo!, you can create a private room and invite other Internet users to meet you there for a one-on-one mock interview.[12] You'll be able to practise answering questions, but you'll have no way of evaluating gestures, voice, or appearance over the Internet.

PLAN TO LOOK GOOD

To look like a winner
- ✧ Dress conservatively
- ✧ Be well groomed
- ✧ Smile when appropriate

When your parents nagged at you to stand up straight, comb your hair, and get rid of your gum, they were right. You can impress an interviewer just by how you look. The best policy is to dress conservatively. Wear the best-quality businesslike clothing you can, preferably in a dark, solid colour. Avoid flamboyant styles, colours, and prints.

Good grooming makes any style of clothing look better. Make sure your clothes are clean and unwrinkled, your shoes unscuffed and well shined, your hair neatly styled and combed, your fingernails clean, and your breath fresh. If possible, check your appearance in a mirror before entering the room for the interview. Don't spoil the effect by smoking just before the interview. Finally, remember that one of the best ways to look good is to smile at appropriate moments.

Be prepared for the interview:
- ✧ Take proof of your accomplishments
- ✧ Arrive on time
- ✧ Wait graciously

BE READY WHEN YOU ARRIVE

For the interview, plan to take a small notebook, a pen, a list of the questions you want to ask, two copies of your résumé protected in a folder, an outline of what you have learned about the organization, and any past correspondence about the position. You may also want to take a small calendar, a transcript of your university grades, a list of references, and your portfolio containing samples of your work, performance reviews, and certificates of achievement. Recruiters are impressed by such tangible evidence of your job-related accomplishments; visible proof of your abilities carries a lot of weight.[13]

Be sure you know when and where the interview will be held. The worst way to start any interview is to be late. Check the route you will take, even if it means phoning the interviewer's secretary to ask. Find out how much time it takes to get there; then plan to arrive early. Allow a little extra time just in case you run into a problem on the way.

Once you arrive, relax. You may have to wait a little while, so bring along something to read or occupy your time (the less frivolous or controversial, the better). If company literature is available, read it while you wait. In any case, be polite to the interviewer's assistant. If the opportunity presents itself, ask a few questions about the organization or express enthusiasm for the job. Refrain from smoking before the interview (nonsmokers can smell smoke on the clothing of interviewees), and avoid chewing gum in the waiting room. Anything you do or say while you wait may well get back to the interviewer, so make sure your best qualities show from the moment you enter the premises.

BEHIND THE SCENES AT IBM

Secrets to Winning an Interview

Jim Greenwood is an area manager in IBM's student recruiting program. His staff and IBM managers work year-round arranging career fairs, booking speaking engagements, and responding to inquiries—all to attract the best students for the company. Greenwood also coordinates recruiting activity at numerous campuses. Of the more than 8000 entry-level people hired by IBM in a recent year, 2800 were university graduates—75 percent of them from targeted campuses.

Whether at the IBM Information Day or any other career fair, be aware that the interview process begins when you step up to a company representative. "On that first day," says Greenwood, "the managers who want to recruit at a given school are there, so bring a résumé. Seek out managers in the skill group that is of interest to you. Talk with them about your background and interests. Our managers know their requirements, and if there's a match, they will sign you up to be interviewed the next day." That will be your second interview, the 30-minute job interview people mistakenly think of as the first interview.

IBM's Jim Greenwood encourages the members of his college and university recruiting staff to listen to the questions applicants ask. That way, they can judge how much applicants know about their field and the company.

"We do a total assessment," Greenwood says. At the site interview, managers explore technical background and breadth, interests, likes, and dislikes. "We're looking for people who can communicate. When you get into an environment, say a lab or a marketing department, you have to relate to people, sell your ideas, explain how things are to be done."

Greenwood listens for your level of interest. "If you did an internship at Hewlett-Packard, I might say, 'Tell me about your job.' Then I'll ask, 'What did you do? What did you like about it? What didn't you like? What kind of programming did you do? What languages? How proficient are you in those languages? Which do you like the best? Why? Do you like to program? Do you like to write code?'"

Greenwood also listens to the types of questions you ask. "They tell me how well informed you are, what you have done to prepare yourself for the interview, whether you researched

How to Be Interviewed

LEARNING OUTCOME 5
Discuss how to perform well during the three phases of a typical job interview.

The way to handle the actual interview depends on where you stand in the interview process. If you are being interviewed for the first time, your main objective is often to differentiate yourself from the many other candidates who are also being screened. Say you've signed up to talk with a recruiter on campus, who may talk with 10 or 15 applicants during the course of the day. Without resorting to gimmicks, you need to call attention to one key aspect of your background so that the recruiter can say, "Oh yes, I remember Jones–the one who sold used Toyotas in Oshawa." Just be sure the trait you accentuate is relevant to the job in question. In addition, you'll want to be prepared in case an employer such as Herman Miller expects you to demonstrate a particular skill (such as problem solving) during the screening interview.

Present a memorable "headline" during a screening interview.

If you have progressed to the initial selection interview, you should broaden your sales pitch. Instead of telegraphing the "headline," give the interviewer the whole story. Touch at least briefly on all your strengths, but explain three or four of your best qualifications in depth. At the same time, probe for information that will help you evaluate the position objectively. As important as it is to get an offer, it's also important to learn whether the job is right for you.

If you're asked back for a final visit, your chances of being offered a position are quite good. At this point, you'll talk to a person who has the authority to make the offer and negotiate terms. This individual may already have concluded that you have the right background for the job, so she or he will be concerned with sizing up your personality. In fact, both you and the employer need to find out whether

---

us, and whether you know about our products and our corporate culture. But don't try to bluff or tell us what you think we want to hear. Ask questions that matter and that make the right impression. Don't ask the interviewer, 'What do you do?' That shows a lack of preparation and interest. Instead ask about the future: 'What technology are you developing? Where's it going?' You should also raise legitimate concerns—the size of a company like IBM, for example. Ask, 'How are you structured? How do I get my ideas across? How do I interact with other departments?' "

Greenwood's goal is for you to leave the interview feeling positive about IBM and knowing when you will learn the outcome. He wants you to feel "that you were given a good, courteous interview." So, what about follow-up? "Don't write for the sake of writing," says Greenwood. "But if you want to stress special interests or reinforce skills, or if you feel you blew the interview and want to be reconsidered, write to the department manager."

Regarding that much-discussed situation of needing experience to get a job but needing a job to get experience, Greenwood offers this advice: "Getting experience is important, whether it's work-study, a cooperative education program, or work you did over the summers, maybe a pre-professional internship. Experience helps you focus your academic choices, prepares you for your job search, and lets you sift and sort out what you do and don't want. That shows in the interview—you have a sharper focus on your wants and needs." To come across well in an interview, you have to stress what experience you have and relate it to what you can do once you're employed.

APPLY YOUR KNOWLEDGE

1. You're scheduled for a job interview in your chosen profession. You anticipate that the interviewer will ask you to describe your job-related experience. Although you have no full-time experience, you've held positions in a pre-professional organization and have completed an internship in a job similar to the one for which you're applying. To prepare for your interview, write a description of your job-related experience, specifying what experience you have and relating it to what you can do for the employer once you get the job.
2. How would you handle this situation? A company—your first choice both as a career and as a place to work—has offered you a position, but the starting salary you've been offered is below your expectation and below what you've already been offered by another firm (your third choice as a career and as a workplace). Lay out a strategy that you think will get you both the position you most desire and the salary you expect.

Van Carlisle is CEO of FireKing International, maker of fireproof filing cabinets. As such, he tries to perform each task at the optimum level, and he likes working with people who do their homework and who are honest, energetic, and thorough. Carlisle advises applicants to show their own commitment to performance by being well prepared for interviews.

there is a good psychological fit. Be honest about your motivations and values. If the interview goes well, your objective should be to clinch the deal on the best possible terms.

Regardless of where you are in the interview process, every interview will proceed through three stages: the warm-up, the question-and-answer session, and the close.

THE WARM-UP

Of the three stages, the warm-up is most important, even though it may account for only a small fraction of the time you spend in the interview. Psychologists say that 50 percent of the interviewer's decision is made within the first 30 to 60 seconds, and another 25 percent is made within 15 minutes. If you get off to a bad start, it's extremely difficult to turn the interview around.[14]

Body language is important at this point. Because you won't have time to say much in the first minute or two, you must sell yourself non-verbally. Begin by using the interviewer's name if you're sure you can pronounce it correctly. If the interviewer extends a hand, respond with a firm but gentle handshake. Then wait until you are asked to be seated. Let the interviewer start the discussion, and listen for cues that tell you what she or he is interested in knowing about you as a potential employee.

THE QUESTION-AND-ANSWER STAGE

Questions and answers will consume the greatest part of the interview. During this phase, the interviewer will ask you about your qualifications and discuss many of the points mentioned in your résumé. You'll also be asked whether you have any questions of your own.

As questions are asked, tailor your answers to make a favourable impression. Don't limit yourself to yes or no answers. Be sure you pause to think before responding if you're asked a difficult question. Consider the direction of the discussion, and guide it where you wish with your responses.

Another way you can reach your goal is to ask the right questions. If you periodically ask a question or two from the list you've prepared, you'll not only learn something but demonstrate your interest as well. It's especially useful to probe for what the company is looking for in its new employees. Once you know that, you can show how you meet the firm's needs. Also try to zero in on any reservations the interviewer might have about you so that you can dispel them.

Paying attention to both verbal and non-verbal messages can help you turn the question-and-answer stage to your advantage.

Paying attention when the interviewer speaks can be as important as giving good answers or asking good questions. Listening should make up about half the time you spend in an interview. For tips on becoming a better listener, read Chapter 17. Be alert to non-verbal communication. The interviewer's facial expressions, eye movements, gestures, and posture may tell you the real meaning of what is being said. If the interviewer says one thing but sends a different message non-verbally, you may want to discount the verbal message. Be especially aware of how your comments are received. Does the interviewer nod in agreement or smile to show approval? If so, you're making progress. If not, you might want to introduce another topic or modify your approach.

Bear in mind that Canadian Human Rights legislation prohibits employers from discriminating against job candidates on the basis of race, national or ethnic origin, religion, age, sex (including pregnancy and childbirth), marital status, family status, mental or physical disability (including previous or present drug or alcohol dependence), pardoned conviction, or sexual orientation.[15] In the course of your interviews, however, you may be asked questions that are directly or indirectly related to

- Your religious affiliation or organizations and lodges you belong to
- Your marital status or former name
- The names or relationships of people you live with
- Your spouse, spouse's employment or salary, dependents, children, or child-care arrangements
- Your height, weight, gender, pregnancy, or any health conditions or disabilities that are not reasonably related to job performance
- Arrests or criminal convictions that are not related to job performance

How you respond depends on how badly you want the job, how you feel about revealing the information asked for, what you think the interviewer will do with the information, and whether you want to work for a company that asks such questions. If you don't want the job, you can tell the interviewer that you think a particular question is unethical and mention that you plan to contact the proper government agency. You can also simply refuse to answer.[16]

Think about how you might respond if you are asked to answer unlawful interview questions.

If you want the job (and you don't want to leave an unfavourable impression), you can choose a more tactful approach than simply refusing. You might (1) ask how the question is related to your qualifications for the job, (2) explain that the information is personal, (3) respond to what you think is the interviewer's real concern, or (4) answer both the question and the concern. Of course, if you answer an unethical question, you still run the risk that your answer may hurt your chances, so think carefully before answering.[17]

When a business can show that the safety of its employees or customers is at stake, it may be allowed to ask questions that would seem discriminatory in another context. Despite this exception, if you believe that an interviewer's questions are unreasonable, unrelated to the job, or designed to elicit information in an attempt to discriminate, you may complain to the Canadian or a provincial Human Rights Commission.

As senior vice-president of human resources at Levi Strauss and Company, Donna J. Goya believes that developing people is vital to successful business management. You want to be in a company that cares about people, says Goya. You can show that you care about people by expressing your thanks to the interviewer either by phone or in a letter.

THE CLOSE

Like the opening, the end of the interview is more important than its duration would indicate. In the last few minutes, you need to evaluate how well you've done and correct any misconceptions the interviewer might have.

You can generally tell when the interviewer is trying to conclude the session by watching for verbal and non-verbal cues. The interviewer may ask whether you have any more questions, sum up the discussion, change position, or indicate with a gesture that the interview is over. When you get the signal, respond promptly, but don't rush. Be sure to thank the interviewer for the opportunity and express an interest in the organization. If you can do so comfortably, try to pin down what will happen next, but don't press for an immediate decision.

If this is your second or third visit to the organization, the interview may culminate with an offer of employment. You have two options: accept it or request time to think it over. The best course is usually to wait. If no job offer is made, the interviewer may not have reached a decision yet, but you may tactfully ask when you can expect to know the decision.

Be realistic in your salary expectations and diplomatic in your negotiations.

If you do receive an offer during the interview, you'll naturally want to discuss salary. However, let the interviewer raise the subject. If asked your salary requirements, say that you would expect to receive the standard salary for the job in question. If you have additional qualifications, point them out: "With my 18 months of experience in the field, I would expect to start in the middle of the normal salary range."

If you don't like the offer, you might try to negotiate, provided you're in a good bargaining position and the organization has the flexibility to accommodate you. You'll be in a fairly strong position if your skills are in short supply and you have several other offers. It also helps if you're the favorite candidate and the organization is booming. However, many organizations are relatively rigid in their salary practices, particularly at the entry level.

INTERVIEW NOTES

Keep a written record of your job interviews.

If yours is a typical job search, you'll have many interviews before you accept a final offer. For that reason, keeping a notebook or binder of interview notes can be helpful. To refresh your memory of each conversation, jot down the names and titles of the people you met as soon as the interview ends. Next write down in capsule form the interviewer's answers to your questions. Then briefly evaluate your performance during the interview, listing what you handled well and what you didn't. Going over these notes can help you improve your performance in the future.[18] Whenever you need to review important tips, try consulting this chapter's Checklist for Interviews. In addition to improving your performance during interviews, interview notes will help you keep track of any follow-up messages you'll need to send.

Following Up After the Interview

LEARNING OUTCOME 6
Write the six most common types of messages required to follow up after an interview.

Touching base with the prospective employer after the interview, either by phone or in writing, shows that you really want the job and are determined to get it. It also brings your name to the interviewer's attention once again and reminds him or her that you're waiting to know the decision. As Herman Miller's recruiters will advise you, following up shows your continued interest in the job.

Checklist for Interviews

A. Preparation

1. Determine the requirements and general salary range of the job.
2. Research the organization's products, structure, financial standing, and prospects for growth.
3. Determine the interviewer's name, title, and status in the firm.
4. Prepare (but don't over-rehearse) answers for the questions you are likely to be asked about your qualifications and achievements, your feelings about work and school, your interests and hobbies.
5. Develop relevant questions to ask, such as what training the organization might offer to employees, what type of management system the firm has, whether its executives are promoted from within, and why the position is vacant.
6. Plan your appearance.
   a. Dress in a businesslike manner, regardless of the mode of dress preferred within the organization.
   b. Select conservative, good-quality clothing to wear to the interview.
   c. Check your clothing to make sure it's clean and wrinkle free.
   d. Choose traditional footwear, unscuffed and well shined.
   e. Wear a minimum of jewellery.
   f. Use fragrances sparingly, and avoid excessive makeup.
   g. Clean and manicure your fingernails.
   h. Check your appearance just before going into the interview, if possible.
7. In a briefcase or portfolio, take a pen and paper, a list of questions, copies of your résumé, and samples of your work (if appropriate).
8. Double-check the location and time of the interview.
   a. Map out the route beforehand, and estimate the time you'll need to get there.
   b. Plan your arrival for 10 to 15 minutes before the interview.
   c. Add 10 or 15 more minutes to cover problems that may arise en route.

B. Initial Stages of the Interview

1. Greet the interviewer by name, with a smile and direct eye contact.

The two most common forms of follow-up are the thank-you message and the inquiry. These are generally handled by letter, but a phone call is often just as effective, particularly if the employer seems to favour a casual, personal style. The other four types of follow-up messages–request for a time extension, letter of acceptance, letter declining a job offer, and letter of resignation–are sent only in certain cases. These messages are better in writing, because it's important to document any official actions relating to your employment. Regardless of which type of follow-up message you're sending, the principles outlined here will help you write it well.

Six types of follow-up messages:
- ✧ Thank-you message
- ✧ Inquiry
- ✧ Request for a time extension
- ✧ Letter of acceptance
- ✧ Letter declining a job offer
- ✧ Letter of resignation

Thank-You Letter

Express your thanks within two days after the interview, even if you feel you have little chance for the job. Acknowledge the interviewer's time and courtesy, and be sure to restate the specific job you're applying for. Convey the idea that you're still interested, and ask politely for a decision.

Keep your thank-you message brief (less than five minutes for a phone call or only one page for a letter), and organize it like a routine message. As do all good business messages, it demonstrates the "you" attitude, and it sounds positive without sounding overconfident. You don't want to sound doubtful about your chances of getting the job, but you don't want to sound arrogant or too sure of yourself either.

The following thank-you letter shows how to achieve all that in three brief paragraphs:

A note or phone call thanking the interviewer
- ✧ Is organized like a routine message
- ✧ Closes with a request for a decision or future consideration

> After talking with you yesterday, touring your sets, and watching the television commercials being filmed, I remain very enthusiastic about the possibility of joining your staff as a television/film production assistant. Thank you for taking so much time to show me around.

The opening reminds the interviewer of the reasons for meeting and graciously acknowledges the consideration shown to the applicant.

2. Offer a firm but not crushing handshake if the interviewer extends a hand.
3. Take a seat only after the interviewer invites you to be seated or has taken his or her own seat.
4. Sit with an erect posture, facing the interviewer.
5. Listen for cues about what the interviewer's questions are trying to reveal about you and your qualifications.
6. Assume a calm and poised attitude.
7. Avoid gum chewing and other displays of nervousness.

C. Body of the Interview

1. Display a genuine, not artificial, smile when appropriate.
2. Convey interest and enthusiasm.
3. Listen attentively so that you can give intelligent responses.
4. Take a few notes, and expand on key points later.
5. Sell the interviewer on hiring you.
   a. Relate your knowledge and skills to the position you are seeking.
   b. Stress your positive qualities and characteristics.
6. Answer questions wisely.
   a. Keep responses brief, clear, and to the point.
   b. Avoid exaggeration, and convey honesty and sincerity.
   c. Avoid slighting references to former employers.
7. Avoid alcoholic drinks if you are interviewed over lunch or dinner.

D. Salary Discussions

1. Put off a discussion of salary until late in the interview, if possible.
2. Let the interviewer initiate the discussion of salary.
3. If asked, state that you would like to receive the standard salary for the position. (Know the standard salary for the position in your region of the country.)

E. Closing Stages of the Interview

1. Watch for signs that the interview is about to end.
2. Tactfully ask when you will be advised of the decision on your application.
3. If you're offered the job, either accept or ask for time to consider the offer.
4. Thank the interviewer for meeting with you, with a warm smile and a handshake.

This paragraph indicates the writer's flexibility and commitment to the job if hired. It also reminds the recruiter of special qualifications.

During our meeting, I said that I would prefer not to relocate, but I've reconsidered the matter. I would be pleased to relocate wherever you need my skills in set decoration and prop design.

The letter closes on a confident and "you"-oriented note, ending with the request for a decision.

Now that you've explained the details of your operation, I feel quite strongly that I can make a contribution to the sorts of productions you're lining up. I would be an energetic employee and a positive addition to your crew. Please let me know your decision as soon as possible.

Even if the interviewer has said that you are unqualified for the job, a thank-you message like that shown in Figure 16.5 may keep the door open. A letter of this type will probably go into the file for future openings because it demonstrates courtesy and interest.

MICHAEL ESPINOSA
844 Newport Ave.
Thunder Bay, ON P7A 6K2

January 5, 2001

Ms. Gloria Reynolds, Editor
Northview Mirror
289 Balsam St.
Thunder Bay, ON P7A 5N6

Dear Ms. Reynolds:

The main idea is the expression of thanks for the interviewer's time and information.

Our conversation on Tuesday about your newspaper's opening for a food-feature writer was enlightening. Thank you for taking time to talk with me about it.

The writer specifically refers to points discussed in the interview. Enthusiasm and eagerness to improve skills are qualities that will impress the interviewer.

Your description of the profession makes me feel more certain than ever that I want to be a newspaper writer. Following your advice, I am going to enrol in an evening journalism course.

The letter closes on a confident and you-oriented note.

After I achieve the level of writing skills you suggested, I would deeply appreciate the chance to talk with you again.

Sincerely,

Michael Espinosa

Michael Espinosa

FIGURE 16.5

In-Depth Critique: Thank-You Note

After Michael Espinosa's interview with Gloria Reynolds, he sent the following thank-you message.

EFFECTIVE E-BUSINESS COMMUNICATION

The Fastest Thank You

Experts recommend sending a thank-you letter within two days after interviewing for a job. Even if you drop your letter in the mail one day after the interview, it may not arrive for a day or two. If your interviewer has an e-mail address, however, you can express your thanks immediately—with just a few keystrokes. Remember to include your e-mail address in the signature block at the close of the letter in case the interviewer wanted to contact you electronically. Michael Espinosa could have followed up after his recent job interview by sending his thank-you message by e-mail the same day.

CAREER APPLICATIONS

1. Why is there no inside address in this thank-you e-mail?
2. How else could a candidate make productive use of a thank-you e-mail?

TO: G_Reynolds@northviewmirror.net
SUBJECT: Thank you for today's interview

Dear Ms. Reynolds:

Our conversation this morning about your newspaper's opening for a food-feature writer was enlightening. Thank you for taking time to talk with me about it.

Your description of the profession makes me feel more certain than ever that I want to be a newspaper writer. Following your advice, I am going to enrol in an evening journalism course.

After I achieve the level of writing skills you suggested, I'd appreciate the chance to talk with you again.

Sincerely,

Michael Espinosa
844 Newport Avenue
Thunder Bay, ON P7A 6K2
(807) 555-6208
espinosam@sympatico.ca

Letter of Inquiry

If you're not advised of the interviewer's decision by the promised date or within two weeks, you might make an inquiry. An inquiry is particularly appropriate if you have received a job offer from a second firm and don't want to accept it before you have an answer from the first. The following inquiry letter follows the general plan for a direct request; the writer assumes that a simple oversight, and not outright rejection, is the reason for the delay.

An inquiry about a hiring decision follows the plan for a direct request.

> When we talked on April 7 about the fashion coordinator position in your York Avenue showroom, you said you would let me know your decision before May 1. I would still like the position very much, so I'm eager to know what conclusion you've reached.

The opening paragraph identifies the position and introduces the main idea.

> To complicate matters, another firm has now offered me a position and has asked that I reply within the next two weeks.

The reason for the request comes second. The writer tactfully avoids naming the other firm.

> Because your company seems to offer a greater challenge, I would appreciate knowing about your decision before Thursday, May 12. If you need more information before then, please let me know.

The courteous request for a specific action comes last, in the context of a clearly stated preference for this company.

Request for a Time Extension

If you receive a job offer while other interviews are still pending and you want more time to decide, write to the offering organization and ask for a time extension. Employers understand that candidates often interview with several companies. They want you to be sure you are making the right decision, and most of them are happy to accommodate you with a reasonable extension. Just be sure to preface your

A request for a time extension follows the plan for a direct request but pays extra attention to easing the reader's disappointment.

request with a friendly opening like the one shown in the following sample letter. Ask for more time, stressing your enthusiasm for the organization. Conclude by allowing for a quick decision if your request for additional time is denied. Ask for a prompt reply confirming the time extension if the organization grants it.

The letter begins with a strong statement of interest in the job.

> The customer relations position in your snack-foods division seems like an exciting challenge and a great opportunity. I'm very pleased that you offered it to me.

The writer stresses professional obligations, not her desire to learn what the other company may offer. Specific reasons for preferring the first job offer help reassure the reader of her sincerity.

> Because of another commitment, I would appreciate your giving me until August 29 to make a decision. Before our interview, I scheduled a follow-up interview with another company. I'm interested in your organization because of its impressive quality-control procedures and friendly, attractive work environment. But I do feel obligated to keep my appointment.

The expression of willingness to yield or compromise conveys continued interest in the position.

> If you need my decision immediately, I'll gladly let you know. However, if you can allow me the added time to fulfill the earlier commitment, I'd be grateful. Please let me know right away.

This type of letter is, in essence, a direct request. However, because the recipient may be disappointed, be sure to temper your request for an extension with statements indicating your continued interest.

Letter of Acceptance

A letter of acceptance follows the good-news plan.

When you receive a job offer that you want to accept, reply within five days. Begin by accepting the position and expressing thanks. Identify the job that you're accepting. In the next paragraph, cover any necessary details. Conclude by saying that you look forward to reporting for work.

The good-news statement at the beginning confirms the specific terms of the offer.

> I'm delighted to accept the graphic design position in your advertising department at the salary of $43 000.

Miscellaneous details are covered in the middle.

> Enclosed are the health insurance forms you asked me to complete and sign. I've already given notice to my current employer and will be able to start work on Monday, January 15.

The letter closes with another reference to the good news and a look toward the future.

> The prospect of joining your firm is very exciting. Thank you for giving me this opportunity for what I'm sure will be a challenging future.

As always, a good-news letter should convey your enthusiasm and eagerness to cooperate.

Written acceptance of a job offer is legally binding.

Be aware that a job offer and a written acceptance of that offer constitute a legally binding contract, for both you and the employer. So before you write an acceptance letter, be sure you want the job.

Letter Declining a Job Offer

A letter declining a job offer follows the bad-news plan.

After all your interviews, you may find that you need to write a letter declining a job offer. The best approach is to open warmly, state the reasons for refusing the offer, decline the offer explicitly, and close on a pleasant note, expressing gratitude. By taking the time to write a sincere, tactful letter like the one shown here, you leave the door open for future contact.

The opening paragraph is a buffer.

> One of the most interesting interviews I have ever had was the one last month at your Halifax shipping company. I'm flattered that you would offer me the computer-analyst position that we talked about.

During my job search, I applied to five highly rated firms like your own, each a leader in its field. Both your company and another offered me a position. Because my desire to work abroad can more readily be satisfied by the other company, I have accepted that job offer.

Tactfully phrased reasons for the applicant's unfavourable decision precede the bad news and leave the door open.

I deeply appreciate the hour you spent talking with me. Thank you again for your consideration and kindness.

A sincere and cordial ending lets the reader down gently.

The bad-news plan is ideally suited to this type of letter.

Letter of Resignation

If you get a job offer and are currently employed, you can maintain good relations with your employer by writing a letter of resignation to your immediate supervisor. Make the letter sound positive, regardless of how you feel. Say something favourable about the organization, the people you work with, or what you've learned on the job. Then state your intention to leave and give the date of your last day on the job. Be sure you give your current employer at least two weeks' notice.

A letter of resignation also follows the bad-news plan.

My sincere thanks to you and to all the other Emblem Corporation employees for helping me learn so much about serving the public these past 11 months. You have given me much help and encouragement.

An appreciative opening serves as a buffer.

You may recall that when you first interviewed me, my goal was to become a customer-relations supervisor. Because that opportunity has been offered to me by another organization, I am submitting my resignation. I regret leaving all of you, but I can't pass up this opportunity.

Reasons stated before the bad news itself and tactful phrasing help keep the relationship friendly, should the writer later want letters of recommendation.

I would like to terminate my work here two weeks from today but can arrange to work an additional week if you want me to train a replacement.

An extra paragraph discusses necessary details.

My sincere thanks and best wishes to all of you.

A cordial close tempers any disappointment.

This letter follows the bad-news plan. By sending one like it, you show that you are considerate and mature, and you also help ensure the good feeling that may help you get another job in the future. Compare your messages with the suggestions in this chapter's Checklist for Follow-Up Messages.

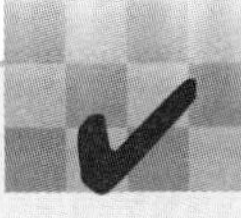

Checklist for Follow-Up Messages

A. Thank-You Messages

1. Thank the interviewer in writing within two days after the interview, and keep your letter to one page.
2. If you have no alternative, thank the interviewer by phone, keeping the message under five minutes.
3. In the opening, express thanks and identify the job and the time and place of the interview.
4. Use the middle section for supporting details.
   a. Express your enthusiasm about the organization and the job.
   b. Add any new facts that may help your chances.
   c. Try to undo any negative impressions you may have left during the interview.
5. Use an action ending.
   a. Offer to submit more data.
   b. Express confidence that your qualifications will meet the organization's requirements.
   c. Look forward to a favourable decision.
   d. Request an opportunity to prove that you can aid the organization's growth or success.

B. Inquiries

1. Phone or write an inquiry if you are not informed of the decision by the promised date, especially if another organization is awaiting your reply to a job offer.
2. Follow the plan for direct requests: main idea, necessary details, specific request.

C. Requests for a Time Extension

1. Send this type of letter if you receive a job offer while other interviews are pending and you want more time before making your decision.
2. Open with an expression of warmth.
3. In the middle section explain why you need more time and express your continuing interest in the organization.
4. Conclude by allowing for a quick decision if your request for more time is denied, or by asking the interviewer to confirm the time extension if it is granted.

D. Letters Accepting a Job Offer

1. Send this message within five days of receiving the offer. State clearly that you accept the offer with pleasure, and identify the job you're accepting.
2. Fill out the letter with vital details.
3. Conclude with a statement that you look forward to reporting for work.

E. Letters Declining a Job Offer

1. Open a letter of rejection warmly.
2. Fill out the letter with an explanation of why you are refusing the offer and an expression of appreciation.
3. End on a sincere, positive note.

F. Letters of Resignation

1. Send a letter of resignation to your current employer as soon as possible.
2. Begin with an appreciative buffer.
3. Fill out the middle section with your reasons for looking for another job and the actual statement that you are leaving.
4. Close cordially.

ON THE JOB
Solving a Communication Dilemma at Herman Miller, Inc.

Herman Miller's corporate culture reflects the philosophy of Max DePree, son of the firm's founder and, until recently, chairman of the board. DePree based his management style on his assumptions about human nature. In his view, the idea of motivating people is nonsense. "Employees bring their own motivation," he said. "What people need from work is to be liberated, to be involved, to be accountable, and to reach their potential."

DePree believed that good management consists of establishing an environment in which people can unleash their creativity. "My goal for Herman Miller is that when people both inside and outside the company look at all of us, they'll say, 'Those folks have a gift of the spirit.' " He wanted the organization, like its products, to be a work of art. To carry out his philosophy, DePree created an employee bill of rights, which includes "The right to be needed, the right to understand, the right to be involved, the right to affect one's own destiny, the right to be accountable, and the right to appeal."

The company's organizational structure, now in the hands of president and CEO Michael Volkema, reinforces DePree's philosophy. All employees are assigned to work teams. The team leader evaluates the workers every six months, and the workers evaluate the leader as well. Teams elect representatives to caucuses that meet periodically to discuss operations and problems. Through the team structure, employees have a say in decisions that affect them. They also have a vehicle for dealing with grievances. If a problem isn't resolved by the team supervisor, employees can go directly to the next executive level—all the way to Volkema, if needed.

But like all good things, Herman Miller's corporate culture has its downside. Teamwork takes time, and an egalitarian approach to decision making can be frustrating if you value efficiency. Although today's business environment requires decisive action, it takes a special kind of talent to draw the line between participation and permissiveness. Finding people who appreciate the distinction—and who can operate effectively in this climate—is a real challenge.

To identify people who have the right mix of attitudes, Herman Miller uses what it calls value-based interviewing. During an initial job interview, the staffing department probes the candidate's work style, likes, and dislikes by posing "what if" questions. By evaluating how the candidate would handle a variety of scenarios, the recruiter gets a good idea of how well the individual would fit into the company. If the fit seems good, the candidate is invited back for follow-up interviews with members of the department where she or he would be working. During these follow-up interviews, the candidate's functional expertise is evaluated along with her or his psychological makeup. By the end of the interview process, Herman Miller has a good idea of whether the candidate "knows how to dance."[19]

Your Mission: As a member of Herman Miller's staffing department, you are responsible for screening job candidates and arranging for candidates to interview with membbers of Herman Miller's professional staff. Your responsibilities include the development of interview questions and evaluation forms for use by company employees involved in the interview process. You also handle all routine correspondence with job candidates. In each of the following situations, choose the best alternative, and be prepared to explain why your choice is best.

1. Herman Miller has decided to establish a management training program for recent university and college graduates. The training program is designed to groom people for careers in finance, strategic planning, marketing, administration, and general management. To recruit people for the program, the firm will conduct on-campus interviews at several universities—something it has not generally done. You and the other Herman Miller interviewers will be talking with 30 or 40 applicants on campus. You will have 20 minutes for each interview. Your goal is to identify the candidates who will be invited to come to the office for evaluation interviews. You want the preliminary screening process to be as fair and objective as possible, so how will you approach the task?
   a. Meet with all the Herman Miller interviewers to discuss the characteristics that successful candidates will exhibit. Allow each interviewer to use his or her own approach to identify these characteristics in applicants. Encourage the interviewers to ask whatever questions seem most useful in light of the individual characteristics of each candidate.
   b. Develop a list of 10 to 15 questions that will be posed to all candidates. Instruct the Herman Miller interviewers to stick strictly to the list so that all applicants will respond to the same questions and be evaluated on the same basis.
   c. Develop a written evaluation form for measuring all candidates against criteria such as academic performance, relevant experience, capacity for teamwork, and communication skills. For each criterion, suggest four or five questions that interviewers might use to evaluate the candidate. Instruct the interviewers to cover all the criteria and to fill out the written evaluation form for each applicant immediately after the interview.
   d. Design a questionnaire for candidates to complete before their interviews. Then ask the interviewers to outline the ideal answers they would like to see a candidate offer for each item on this questionnaire. These ideal answers give you a standard against which to measure actual candidate answers.
2. During the on-campus screening interviews, you ask several candidates, "Why do you want to work for this organization?" Of the following responses, which would you rank the highest?
   a. "I'd like to work here because I'm interested in the office-furniture business. I've always been fascinated by industrial design and the interaction between people and their environment. In addition to studying business, I have taken courses in industrial design and industrial psychology. I also have some personal experience in building furniture. My grandfather is a cabinetmaker and an antique restorer, and I have been his apprentice since I was 12 years old. I've paid for university by working as a carpenter during summer vacations."
   b. "I'm an independent person with a lot of internal drive. I do my best work when I'm given a fairly free rein to use my creativity. From what I've read about your corporate culture, I think my working style would fit very well with your management philosophy. I'm also the sort of person who identifies very strongly with my job. For better or worse, I define myself through my affiliation with my employer. I get a great sense of pride from being part of a first-rate operation, and I think Herman Miller is first-rate. I've read about the design awards you've won and about your selection as one of America's most admired companies. The articles say that Herman Miller is a well-managed company. I think I would learn a lot working here, and I think my drive and creativity would be appreciated."
   c. "There are several reasons why I'd like to work for Herman Miller. For one thing, I'd like to stay in the area. Also, I have friends who work for Herman Miller, and they both say it's terrific. I've also heard good things about your compensation and benefits."
   d. "My ultimate goal is to start my own company, but first I need to learn more about managing a business. I read in *Fortune* that Herman Miller is one of America's most admired corporations. I think I could learn a lot by joining your management training program and observing your operations."
3. You are preparing questions for the professional staff to use when conducting follow-up interviews at Herman Miller's headquarters. You want a question that will reveal something about the candidates' probable loyalty to the organization. Which of the following questions is the best choice?
   a. If you knew you could be one of the world's most successful people in a single occupation, such as music, politics, medicine, or business, what occupation would you choose? If you knew you had only a 10 percent chance of being so successful, would you still choose the same occupation?
   b. We value loyalty among our employees. Tell me something about yourself that demonstrates your loyalty as a member of an organization.
   c. What would you do if you discovered that a co-worker routinely made personal, unauthorized long-distance phone calls from work?
   d. What other companies are you interviewing with?

4. In concluding an evaluation interview, you ask the candidate, "Do you have any questions?" Which of the following answers would you respond most favourably to?

a. "No. I can't think of anything. You've been very thorough in describing the job and the company. Thank you for taking the time to talk with me."

b. "Yes. I have an interview with one of your competitors, Steelcase, next week. How would you sum up the differences between your two firms?"

c. "Yes. If I were offered a position here, what would my chances be of getting promoted within the next 12 months?"

d. "Yes. Do you think Herman Miller will be a better or worse company 15 years from now?"

TAP Your Knowledge

Summary of Learning Outcomes

1. Describe the dual purpose of the job interview. An employment interview is a formal meeting during which an employer and an applicant ask questions and exchange information to see whether the two are a good match. The purpose of an employment interview is two-fold: (1) to help the organization find the best person for the job, and (2) to help the applicant find the job best suited to his or her goals and capabilities.

2. Explain the steps in the interview process. Most employers conduct two or three interviews when considering applicants for a position. The preliminary screening interview helps employers eliminate (or screen out) unqualified applicants from the hiring process. If you meet the organization's requirements, you may then be invited to a panel interview. Here you meet with several interviewers who ask you questions during a single session.

3. Identify and adapt to various types of interviews. The directed interview, the open-ended interview, and the stress interview are three common types job candidates may experience in the interview process. The directed interview, generally used in screening, is characterized by a series of questions asked in a set order. Used to gather facts, the directed interview is regarded as too structured to measure an applicant's personal qualities. The open-ended interview is a less formal, unstructured interview that poses broad, open-ended questions that encourages the candidate to talk freely. Interviewers ask behavioural or situational questions that determine how candidates would handle real-life work problems. The stress interview is designed to see how well a candidate handles stressful situations, an important qualification for certain kinds of work. During this type of interview you might be subjected to long periods of silence, criticisms, deliberate interruptions, and abrupt or hostile reactions by the interviewer.

4. List the types of questions you are likely to encounter during a job interview. Employers look for two things: proof that a candidate can handle a specific job and evidence that the person will fit in with the organization. During the interview, you will be asked to describe your education and previous jobs in depth so that the interviewer can determine how well your skills match the job requirements. They will also ask about your personal attitudes and preferences and about your work habits.

5. Discuss how to perform well during the three phases of a typical job interview. All employment interviews have three stages. The warm-up stage is the most important, because first impressions greatly influence an interviewer's decision. Be sure to pronounce the interviewer's name correctly, return a firm but gentle handshake, and wait until you are asked to be seated. The question-and-answer stage is the longest, during which you will answer and ask questions. Listening carefully and watching the interviewer's non-verbal clues help you determine how the interview is going. The close is also important, because you need to evaluate your performance to see whether the interviewer has any misconceptions that you must correct. Remember to thank the interviewer for the opportunity and express an interest in the organization.

6. Write the six most common types of messages required to follow up after an interview. The two most common types of follow-up messages are usually in letter form but can also be effective by phone or e-mail. You send the *thank-you* message within two days after your interview to show appreciation, express your continued interest in the job, and politely ask for a decision. You send an *inquiry* if you haven't received the interviewer's decision by the date promised or within two weeks of the interview–especially if you've received a job offer from another firm. The remaining four employment messages are best sent in letter form, to document any official action. You request a *time extension* if you receive a job offer while other interviews are pending and you want more time to complete those interviews before making a decision. You send a letter of *acceptance* within five days of receiving a job offer that you want to take. You send a letter *declining* a job offer when you want to refuse an offer tactfully and leave the door open for future contact. You send a letter of *resignation* when you receive a job offer that you want to accept while you are currently employed.

Test Your Knowledge

Review Questions

1. How does a structured interview differ from an open-ended interview and a situational interview?
2. What typically occurs during a stress interview?
3. Why do employers conduct pre-employment testing?
4. Why are the questions you ask during an interview as important as the answers you give to the interviewer's questions?
5. What are the three stages of every interview, and which is the most important?
6. How should you respond if an interviewer at a company where you want to work asks you a question that seems too personal or unethical?
7. What should you say in a thank-you message after an interview?
8. What is the purpose of sending a letter of inquiry after an interview?
9. What organization plan is appropriate for a letter of resignation, and why?

Apply Your Knowledge

Critical Thinking Questions

1. How can you distinguish yourself from other candidates in a screening interview and still keep your responses short and to the point? Explain.
2. What can you do to make a favorable impression when you discover that an open-ended interview has turned into a stress interview? Briefly explain your answer.
3. Should applicants ask about pre-employment testing during an interview? Explain your answer.
4. Why is it important to distinguish unethical or illegal interview questions from acceptable questions? Explain.
5. If you want to switch jobs because you can't work with your supervisor, how can you explain this reason to a prospective employer? Give an example.
6. If you think you've gotten off to a bad start during a preliminary screening, what can you do to try to save the interview? Explain your answer.

Practise Your Knowledge

Exercises

1. Divide the class into two groups. Half the class will be recruiters for a large chain of national department stores looking to fill manager trainee positions (there are 15 openings). The other half of the class will be candidates for the job. The company is specifically looking for candidates who demonstrate these three qualities: initiative, dependability, and willingness to assume responsibility.
   a. Have each recruiter select and interview an applicant for ten minutes.
   b. Have all the recruiters discuss how they assessed the applicant against each of the three desired qualities. In other words, what questions did they ask or what did they use as an indicator to determine whether the candidate possessed the quality?
   c. Have all the applicants discuss what they said to convince the recruiters that they possessed each of these qualities.
2. Select a large company (that you can easily find information on) where you might like to work. Use Internet sources to gather some preliminary research on the company.

   a. What did you learn about this organization that would help you during an interview there?
   b. What Internet sources did you use to obtain this information?
   c. Armed with this information, what aspects of your background do you think might appeal to this company's recruiters?
   d. If you choose to apply for a job with this company, what key words would you include on your résumé, and why?
3. Prepare written answers to ten of the questions listed in Figure 16.2, "Twenty-Five Common Interview Questions."
4. You have decided to accept a new position with a competitor of your company. Write a letter of resignation to your supervisor announcing your decision.
   a. Will you notify your employer that you are joining a competing firm? Please explain.
   b. Will you use the direct or the indirect approach? Please explain.
   c. Will you send your letter by e-mail, send it regular mail, or place it on your supervisor's desk?
5. Write a short memo to your instructor discussing what you feel are your greatest strengths and weaknesses from an employment perspective. Next, explain how you believe these strengths and weaknesses would be viewed by interviewers evaluating your qualifications.

Documents for Analysis

Read the following documents; then (1) analyze the strengths or weaknesses of each sentence and (2) revise each document so that it follows this chapter's guidelines.

Document 16.A: Thank-You Letter

Thank you for the really marvellous opportunity to meet you and your colleagues at Starret Engine Company. I really enjoyed touring your facilities and talking with all the people there. You have quite a crew! Some of the other companies I have visited have been so rigid and uptight that I can't imagine how I would fit in. It's a relief to run into a group of people who seem to enjoy their work as much as all of you do.

I know that you must be looking at many other candidates for this job, and I know that some of them will probably be more experienced than I am. But I do want to emphasize that my two years in the Navy involved a good deal of engineering work. I don't think I mentioned all my shipboard responsibilities during the interview.

Please give me a call within the next week to let me know your decision. You can usually find me in my residence room in the evening after dinner (phone: 250-555-9080).

Document 16.B: Letter of Inquiry

I have recently received a very attractive job offer from the Warrington Company. But before I let them know one way or another, I would like to consider any offer that your firm may extend. I was quite impressed with your company during my recent interview, and I am still very interested in a career there.

I don't mean to pressure you, but Warrington has asked for my decision within ten days. Could you let me know by Tuesday whether you plan to offer me a position? That would give me enough time to compare the two offers.

Document 16.C: Letter Declining a Job Offer

I'm writing to say that I must decline your job offer. Another company has made me a more generous offer, and I have decided to accept. However, if things don't work out for me there, I will let you know. I sincerely appreciate your interest in me.

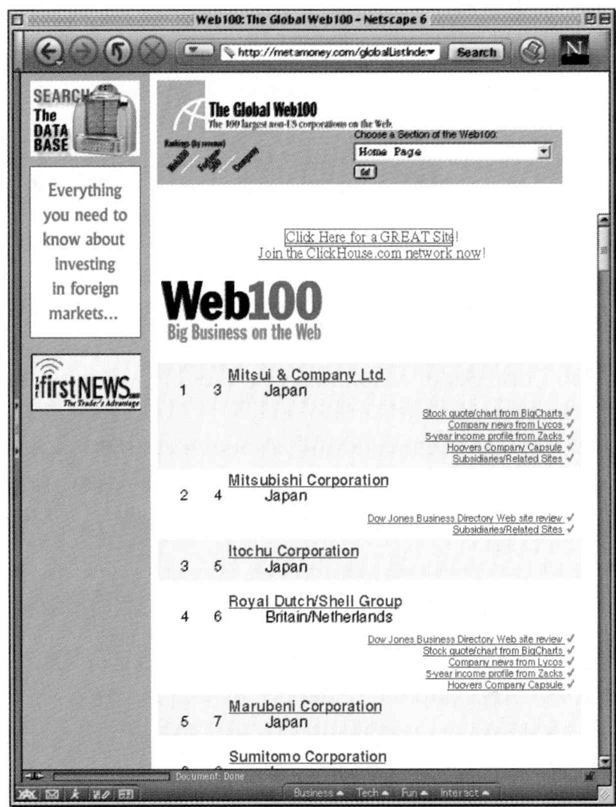

Cases

Interviewing With Potential Employers

1. Interviewers and interviewees: Classroom exercise in interviewing Interviewing is clearly an interactive process involving at least two people. So the best way to practise for interviews is to work with others.

Your Task: You and all other members of your class are to write letters of application for an entry-level or management-trainee position requiring a pleasant personality and intelligence but a minimum of specialized education or experience. Sign your letter with a fictitious name that conceals your identity. Next, polish (or prepare) a résumé that accurately identifies you and your educational and professional accomplishments.

Three members of the class, who volunteer as interviewers, divide equally among themselves all the anonymously written application letters. Then each interviewer selects a candidate who seems the most pleasant and convincing in his or her letter. At this time the selected candidates identify themselves and give the interviewers their résumés.

Each interviewer then interviews his or her chosen candidate in front of the class, seeking to understand how the items on the résumé qualify the candidate for the job. At the end of the interviews, the class may decide who gets the job and discuss why this candidate was successful. Then retrieve your letter, sign it with the right name, and submit it to the instructor for credit.

2. Internet interview: Exercise in interviewing Using the Global Web100 site at **metamoney.com/globalListIndex.html** locate the Web home page of a company you would like to work for. Then identify a position within the company you would like to apply for. Working with a partner, review each other's company home page.

Your Task: Interview your partner in person for her or his chosen position. Take notes during the interview. Now revisit your company's home page, and consider the information generated during your interview. Write a follow-up letter thanking your interviewer, and print it out along with your interview notes for submission to your instructor.

Following Up After the Interview

3. A slight error in timing: Letter asking for delay of an employment decision You botched up your timing and applied for your third-choice job before going after what you really wanted. What you want to do is work in retail marketing with Holt-Renfrew in Vancouver; what you have been offered is a similar job with Zellers in Regina.

You review your notes. Your Regina interview was three weeks ago with the human resources manager, R. P. Bronson, a congenial person who has just written to offer you the position. His address is PO Box 79801, Regina, SK S4N 0A0. Mr. Bronson notes that he can hold the position open for ten days. You have an interview scheduled with Holt-Renfrew next week, but it is unlikely that you will know the store's decision within this ten-day period.

Your Task: Write to R. P. Bronson, requesting a reasonable delay in your consideration of his job offer.

4. **Job hunt: Set of employment-related letters to a single company** Where would you like to work? Pick a real or an imagined company, and assume that a month ago you sent your résumé and application letter. Not long afterward, you were invited to come for an interview, which seemed to go very well.

Your Task: Use your imagination to write the following: (a) a thank-you letter for the interview, (b) a note of inquiry, (c) a request for more time to decide, (d) a letter of acceptance, and (e) a letter declining the job offer.

Developing Your Internet Skills

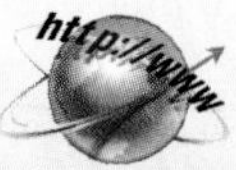

Going Online: Be Prepared for Challenging Interview Questions, p. 464

By now, you've probably read about and practised many different approaches to job interviews, including what you've learned from this chapter and the Royal Bank Web site. If you were going to write a "how-to" magazine article about job interviews and you didn't have space for everything, what interviewing advice would you include as the best and most important?

CHAPTER 17

Listening, Interviewing, and Conducting Meetings

AFTER STUDYING THIS CHAPTER, YOU WILL BE ABLE TO

1. Apply the composition process to your spoken comments
2. Summarize the skills involved in being an effective listener
3. Identify nine common types of business interview
4. Define four types of interview questions and clarify when to use each type
5. Describe how groups make decisions
6. Discuss the preparations and duties necessary for productive meetings

ON THE JOB
Facing a Communication Dilemma at Rockport

Convening an Unconventional Meeting

Calling a meeting isn't unusual; executives do it every day. Even so, few executives shut down entire companies to bring everyone to a meeting, but that's exactly what Rockport president John Thorbeck decided to do. Rockport is a footwear subsidiary of Reebok, and except for the handful of people left behind to answer telephones in the company's Marlboro, Massachusetts, headquarters, all 350 managers and employees were asked to gather in a huge room for a two-day meeting.

Many of Thorbeck's top managers questioned the need for halting the daily functions that had built Rockport's annual sales to $300 million. The chief financial officer complained: "A company as large as ours can't afford to lose two whole shipping days." He also doubted that the discussions would yield any concrete results. But Thorbeck believed this meeting was important enough to involve every employee at every level. His objective was nothing less than to increase the company's potential. "I felt that there was so much more we could do, given our profitability and resources," he said. "Our goals were far too modest."

If you were John Thorbeck, how would you use a two-day meeting to obtain input from your employees? What factors of oral communication would you use to get them talking? Would good listening skills be valuable? What would you do to be sure the meeting was productive?[1]

To be successful at Rockport, employees must be skilled in oral communication. Their skills are constantly put to the test, whether they're engaging in one-on-one interviews, dealing with customers, or participating in meetings.

Communicating Orally

Oral communication saves time and provides opportunities for feedback and social interaction.

Rockport's John Thorbeck knows that speaking and listening are the communication skills we use most. Given a choice, people would rather talk to each other than write to each other. Talking takes less time and needs no composing, keyboarding, rewriting, duplicating, or distributing.

More important, oral communication provides the opportunity for feedback. When people communicate orally, they can ask questions and test their understanding of the message; they can share ideas and work together to solve problems. They can also convey and absorb non-verbal information, which reveals far more than words alone can do. By communicating with facial expressions, eye contact, tone of voice, gestures, and postures, people can send subtle messages that add another dimension to spoken words. Oral communication satisfies our common need to be part of the human community and makes us feel good. Talking things over helps people in organizations build morale and establish a group identity.

Nonetheless, oral communication also has its dangers. Under most circumstances, oral communication occurs spontaneously. You have far less opportunity to revise your spoken words than to revise your written words. You can't cross out what you just said and start all over. Your dumbest comments will be etched in the other person's memory, regardless of how much you try to explain that you really meant something else entirely. Moreover, if you let your attention wander while someone else is speaking, you miss the point. You either have to muddle along without knowing what the other person said or admit you were daydreaming and ask the person to repeat the comment. One other problem is that oral communication is personal. People tend to confuse your message with you as an individual. They're likely to judge the content of what you say by your appearance and style of delivery.

Intercultural barriers can also be as much a problem in oral communication as in written communication. Naturally, it's best to know your audience, including any cultural differences you may have. Then communicate your message in the tone, manner, and situation your audience will feel most comfortable with. (Chapter 3 has more information on intercultural barriers.)

Whether you're using the telephone, engaging in a quick conversation with a colleague, participating in a formal interview, or attending a meeting, oral communication is the vehicle you use to get your message across. When talking to people, make it your goal to take advantage of positive features while minimizing the dangers. To achieve that goal, work on improving two key skills: speaking and listening.

Speaking

LEARNING OUTCOME 1
Apply the composition process to your spoken comments.

Because speaking is such an ingrained activity, we tend to do it without much thought, but that casual approach can be a problem in business. Be more aware of using speech as a tool for accomplishing your objectives in a business context. To do this, break the habit of talking spontaneously, without planning *what* you're going to say or *how* you're going to say it. Learn to manage the impression you create by consciously tailoring your remarks and delivery style to suit the situation. Become as aware of the consequences of what you say as you are of the consequences of what you write.

The spontaneous quality of oral communication limits your ability to edit your thoughts.

With a little effort, you can learn to apply the composition process to oral communication. Before you speak, think about your purpose, your main idea, and your audience. Organize your thoughts in a logical way, decide on a style that suits the occasion (for example, formal or informal, lecture or conversation), and edit your remarks mentally. Try to predict how the other person will react, and organize the message accordingly. Your audience may not react the way you expect, so have alternative approaches ready. As you speak, watch the other person, judging from verbal and nonverbal feedback whether your message is making the desired impression. If it isn't, revise and try again.

Learn to think before you speak.

Just as various writing assignments call for different writing styles, various situations call for different speaking styles. Your speaking style depends on the level of intimacy between you and the other person and on the nature of your conversation. When you're talking with a friend, you naturally speak more frankly than when you're talking with your boss or a stranger. When you're talking about a serious subject, you use a serious tone. As you think about which speaking style is appropriate, also think about the non-verbal message you want to convey. People derive less meaning from your words than they do from your facial expressions, vocal characteristics, and body language. The non-verbal message should reinforce your words. Perhaps the most important thing you can do to project yourself more effectively is to remember the "you" attitude, earning other people's attention and goodwill by focusing on them. For example, professionals like Rockport's John Thorbeck elicit opinions from others not only by asking them pointed questions but also by paying attention to their responses.

Adjust your speaking style to suit the situation.

Apply the "you" attitude to oral communication.

An important tool of oral communication, the telephone can extend your reach across town and around the world. However, if your telephone skills are lacking, you may waste valuable time and appear rude.[2] You can minimize your time on the phone while raising your phone productivity by delivering one-way information by fax or e-mail, jotting down an agenda before making a call, saving social chit-chat for the end of a call (in case your conversation is cut short), saving up all the short calls you need to make to one person during a given day, and making sure your assistant has a list of people whose calls you'll accept even if you're in a meeting.[3]

Much telephone communication now happens through voice mail rather than directly person to person. Organize your thoughts before you make the phone call so that your message will be concise and accurate. Be sure to take advantage of the system's review and editing features to make your message as effective as possible. And keep in mind that voice mail messages aren't necessarily private. Many systems make it easy to forward messages to other people, so be careful when recording sensitive or personal messages.

Listening

The ability to listen is a vital skill in business.

If you're typical, you spend over half your communication time listening.[4] Listening supports effective relationships within the organization, enhances the organization's delivery of products, alerts the organization to the innovation growing from both internal and external forces, and allows organizations to manage the growing diversity both in the workforce and in the customers they serve.[5] A person with good listening ability is likely to succeed; good listening enhances performance, leading to raises, promotions, status, and power.[6] However, no one is born with the ability to listen; the skill is learned and improved through practice.[7] Cultural barriers present a potential challenge with listening as well as with speaking. You might misinterpret what you hear if you fail to consider any cultural differences between you and the speaker. Even though most of us like to think of ourselves as being good listeners, the average person remembers only about half of what's said during a 10-minute conversation and forgets half of that within 48 hours.[8]

Most people need to improve their listening skills.

WHAT HAPPENS WHEN YOU LISTEN

Listening involves five steps: sensing, interpreting, evaluating, remembering, and responding.

Listening involves five related activities, which most often occur in sequence:[9]

- *Sensing* is physically hearing the message and taking note of it. This reception can be blocked by interfering noises, impaired hearing, or inattention. Tune out distractions by focusing on the message.
- *Interpreting* is decoding and absorbing what you hear. As you listen, you assign meaning to the words according to your own values, beliefs, ideas, expectations, roles, needs, and personal history. The speaker's frame of reference may be quite different from yours, so you may need to determine what the speaker really means. Pay attention to non-verbal cues–gestures, body language, facial expressions–but be careful not to assign meanings that aren't there. For example, speakers who nervously stumble over their words might be hiding something or might simply be nervous.
- *Evaluating* is forming an opinion about the message. Sorting through the speaker's remarks, separating fact from opinion, and evaluating the quality of the evidence require a good deal of effort, particularly if the subject is complex or emotionally charged. Avoid the temptations to dismiss ideas offered by people who are unattractive or abrasive and to embrace ideas offered by people who are charismatic speakers.
- *Remembering* is storing a message for future reference. As you listen, retain what you hear by taking notes or by making a mental outline of the speaker's key points.
- *Responding* is acknowledging the message by reacting to the speaker in some fashion. If you're communicating one on one or in a small group, the initial response generally takes the form of verbal feedback. If you're one of many

in an audience, your initial response may take the form of applause, laughter, or silence. Later on, you may act on what you have heard. Actively provide feedback to help the speaker refine the message.

Listening requires a mix of physical and mental activities and is subject to a mix of physical and mental barriers.

THE THREE TYPES OF LISTENING

The three forms of listening:

- ✧ Content listening enables you to understand and retain the message.
- ✧ Critical listening enables you to evaluate the information.
- ✧ Active listening is used to draw out the other person.

Various situations call for different listening skills. When you attend a briefing on the company's new medical insurance, you listen mainly for *content.* You want to know what the policy is. As the speaker describes the prescription drug plan, you begin to listen more *critically*, assessing the benefits of the new plan relative to your own needs. Later, as a friend talks to you about his medical problems, you listen *empathetically*, trying to understand his feelings.

These three types of listening differ not only in purpose but also in the amount of feedback or interaction that occurs. The goal of **content listening** is to understand and retain information imparted by a speaker. You may ask questions, but basically information flows from the speaker to you. Your job is to identify the key points of the message, so be sure to listen for clues to its structure: previews, transitions, summaries, and enumerated points. In your mind create an outline of the speaker's remarks; afterward silently review what you've learned. You may take notes, but you do this sparingly so that you can concentrate on the key points. It doesn't matter whether you agree or disagree, approve or disapprove–only that you understand.[10] When you listen to a regional sales manager's monthly report on how many of your products sold that month, you are listening for content.

The goal of **critical listening** is to evaluate the message at several levels. Is the argument logical? How strong is the evidence? Are the conclusions valid? What does the message imply for you or your organization? What are the speaker's intentions and motives? Did she leave out any important or relevant points?

Because it's hard to absorb information and evaluate it at the same time, reserve judgment until the speaker has finished. Critical listening generally involves interaction as you try to uncover the speaker's point of view. You are bound to evaluate the speaker's credibility as well. Non-verbal signals are often your best clue.[11] When the regional sales manager presents sales projections for the next few months, you listen critically, evaluating whether the estimates are valid and what the implications are for your manufacturing department.

The goal of **active,** or **empathic, listening** is to understand a speaker's feelings, needs, and wants so that you can appreciate their point of view, regardless of whether you share that perspective. By listening in an active or empathic way, you help the individual vent the emotions that prevent a dispassionate approach to the subject. Avoid the temptation to give advice. Try not to judge the person's feelings. Just let them talk.[12] You listen empathically when your regional sales manager tells you about the problems he had with his recreational vehicle while vacationing with his family.

All three types of listening can be useful in work-related situations, so it pays to learn how to apply them.

HOW TO BE A BETTER LISTENER

LEARNING OUTCOME 2
Summarize the skills involved in being an effective listener.

Regardless of whether the situation calls for content, critical, or active listening, you can improve your listening ability by becoming more aware of the habits that distinguish good listeners from bad (Table 17.1). In addition, use nonverbal skills to help you focus: maintain eye contact, react responsively with head nods or spoken signals, and pay attention to the speaker's body language. You might even test yourself from time to time. When someone else is talking, ask yourself whether

TABLE 17.1 Distinguishing Good Listeners from Bad Listeners

To Listen Effectively	The Bad Listener	The Good Listener
Find areas of interest	Tunes out dry subjects	Opportunizes; asks "What's in it for me?"
Judge content, not delivery	Tunes out the message if the delivery is poor	Judges content; skips over delivery errors
Hold your fire	Tends to enter into argument	Doesn't judge until comprehension is complete; interrupts only to clarify
Listen for ideas	Listens for facts	Listens for central themes
Be flexible	Takes extensive notes	Takes fewer notes
Work at listening	Shows no energy output; fakes attention	Works hard; exhibits active body state
Resist distractions	Is distracted easily	Fights or avoids distractions; tolerates bad habits; knows how to concentrate
Exercise your mind	Resists difficult expository material; seeks light, recreational material	Uses heavier material as exercise for the mind
Keep your mind open	Reacts to emotional words	Interprets emotional words; does not get hung up on them
Capitalize on the fact that thought is faster than speech	Tends to daydream with slow speakers	Challenges; anticipates; mentally summarizes; weighs the evidence; listens between the lines to tone of voice

Effective listening involves being receptive to both information and feelings.

you're actually listening to the speaker or mentally rehearsing how you'll respond. Above all, try to be open to the information that will lead to higher-quality decisions, and try to accept the feelings that will build understanding and mutual respect. If you do, you'll be well on the way to becoming a good listener–an important quality when conducting interviews on the job.

Conducting Interviews on the Job

An interview is any planned conversation with a specific purpose involving two or more people.

In addition to handling difficult interpersonal situations, planning what to say and developing good listening skills will also help you participate in on-the-job interviews. From the day you apply for your first job until the day you retire, you'll be involved in a wide variety of business **interviews**–planned conversations with a predetermined purpose that involve asking and answering questions. In a typical interview the action is controlled by the interviewer, the one who scheduled the session. This person poses a series of questions designed to elicit information from the interviewee. Interviews sometimes involve several interviewers or several interviewees, but more often only two people participate. The conversation bounces back and forth between them. Although the interviewer guides the conversation, the interviewee may also seek to accomplish a purpose, perhaps to obtain or provide information, to solve a problem, to create goodwill, or to persuade the other person to take action. If the participants establish rapport and stick to the subject at hand, both parties have a chance of achieving their objectives.

When both the interviewer and the interviewee achieve their purpose, the interview is a success.

Categorizing Interviews

LEARNING OUTCOME 3
Identify nine common types of business interview.

The interviewer establishes the style and structure of the session, depending on the purpose of the interview and the relationship between the parties, much as a writer varies the style and structure of a written message to suit the situation. Each situation calls for a slightly different approach, as you can imagine when you try to picture yourself conducting some of these common business interviews:

The various types of interviews call for different communication skills.

- *Job interviews.* The job candidate wants to learn about the position and the organization; the employer wants to learn about the applicant's abilities and experience. Both hope to make a good impression and to establish rapport. Initial job interviews are usually fairly formal and structured, but later interviews may be relatively spontaneous as the interviewer explores the candidate's responses.
- *Information interviews.* The interviewer seeks facts that bear on a decision or contribute to basic understanding. Information flows mainly in one direction: One person asks a list of questions that must be covered and listens to the answers supplied by the other person. This kind of interview is a valuable form of primary research. Of course, the person you interview must be credible and knowledgeable about the subject. It is also important to decide in advance what kind of information you want and how you will use it; this planning will save time and build goodwill.
- *Persuasive interviews.* One person tells another about a new idea, product, or service and explains why the other should act on the recommendations. Persuasive interviews are often associated with, but are certainly not limited to, selling. The persuader asks about the other person's needs and shows how the product or concept is able to meet those needs. Thus persuasive interviews require skill in drawing out and listening to others as well as the ability to impart information.
- *Exit interviews.* The interviewer tries to understand why the interviewee is leaving the organization or transferring to another department or division. A departing employee can often provide insight into whether the business is being handled efficiently or whether things could be improved. The interviewer tends to ask all the questions while the interviewee provides answers. Encouraging the employee to focus on events and processes rather than on personal gripes will elicit more useful information for the organization.

Marvin Ross is principal of Bridgeross Communications. An author of articles for medical and business journals, books on parenting and pet care, and other works, Ross gathers a portion of his information through one-on-one interviews. How do you think he plans his interview sessions?

- *Evaluation interviews.* A supervisor periodically gives employees feedback on their performance. Supervisor and employee discuss progress toward predetermined standards or goals and evaluate areas that require improvement. They may also discuss goals for the coming year, as well as the employee's longer-term aspirations and general concerns.
- *Counselling interviews.* A supervisor talks with an employee about personal problems that are interfering with work performance. The interviewer is concerned with the welfare of both the employee and the organization. The goal is to establish the facts, convey the company's concern, and steer the person toward a source of help. (Only a trained professional should offer advice on such problems as substance abuse, marital tension, or financial trouble.)
- *Conflict-resolution interviews.* Two competing people or groups of people (such as Smith versus Jones, day shift versus night shift, General Motors versus the Canadian Auto Workers) explore their problems and attitudes. The goal is to bring the two parties closer together, cause adjustments in perceptions and attitudes, and create a more productive climate.

- *Disciplinary interviews.* A supervisor tries to correct the behaviour of an employee who has ignored the organization's rules and regulations. The interviewer tries to get the employee to see the reason for the rules and to agree to comply. The interviewer also reviews the facts and explores the person's attitude. Because of the emotional reaction that is likely, neutral observations are more effective than critical comments.
- *Termination interviews.* A supervisor informs an employee of the reasons for the termination. The interviewer tries to avoid involving the company in legal action and tries to maintain as positive a relationship as possible with the interviewee. To accomplish these goals, the interviewer gives reasons that are specific, accurate, and verifiable.

Planning Interviews

Planning an interview is similar to planning any other form of communication. You begin by stating your purpose, analyzing the other person, and formulating your main idea. Then you decide on the length, style, and organization of the interview.

To accomplish their objectives, interviewees develop a communication strategy.

Even as an interviewee, you have some control over the conversation by anticipating the interviewer's questions and then planning your answers so that the points you want to make will be covered. You can also introduce questions and topics of your own. In addition, by your comments and non-verbal cues, you can affect the relationship between you and the interviewer. Think about your respective roles. What does this person expect from you? Is it to your advantage to confirm those expectations? Will you be more likely to accomplish your objective by being friendly and open or by conveying an impression of professional detachment? Should you allow the interviewer to dominate the exchange, or should you try to take control?

The interviewer assumes the main responsibility for planning the interview.

If you're the interviewer, responsibility for planning the session falls on you. On the simplest level, your job is to schedule the interview and see that it's held in a comfortable and convenient location. Good interviewers are good at collecting information, listening, and probing.[13] You will develop a set of interview questions and decide on their sequence. Having a plan will enable you to conduct the interview more efficiently, even if you find it advantageous to deviate from the plan during the interview. If your questions might require research or extensive thinking, or if you'd like to quote the interviewee in writing, consider providing a list of questions a day or two before the interview so that the person will have time to prepare more complete (and therefore more helpful) answers. You might also want to tape record the interview if the topic is complex or if you plan to quote or paraphrase the interviewee in a written document.

LEARNING OUTCOME 4
Define four types of interview questions and clarify when to use each type.

INTERVIEW QUESTIONS

The purpose of the interview and the nature of the participants determine the types of questions that are asked. When you plan the interview, bear in mind that you ask questions (1) to get information, (2) to motivate the interviewee to respond honestly and appropriately, and (3) to create a good working relationship with the other person. While you're drafting your questions, be aware of ethical implications. For example, asking someone to divulge personal information about a co-worker may be asking that person to make an unethical decision. Always be careful about issues of confidentiality, politics, and other sensitive issues.

To obtain both factual information and underlying feelings, you'll probably use various types of questions. **Open-ended questions** invite the interviewee to offer an opinion, not just a "yes," "no," or one-word answer: "What do you think your company wants most from its suppliers?" This kind of question is useful when you want to learn the reasons behind a decision rather than just the facts. You can learn some interesting and unexpected things from open-ended questions, but they diminish your control of the interview. The other person's idea of what's relevant may not coincide with yours, and you may waste some time getting the interview back on track. Use open-ended questions to warm up the interviewee and to look for information when you have plenty of time to conduct the conversation.

Four basic types of interview questions:

- ✧ Open-ended questions
- ✧ Direct open-ended questions
- ✧ Closed-ended questions
- ✧ Restatement questions

To suggest a response, use **direct open-ended questions.** For example, asking "What have you done about ..." assumes that something has been done and calls for an explanation. With direct open-ended questions you have somewhat more control over the interview, but you still give the other person some freedom in framing a response. This form is good to use when you want to get a specific conclusion or recommendation from someone: for example, "What would you do to improve customer satisfaction in the southern region?" Take care to avoid biasing the response with the way you word the question, however. Asking "What should Roger Vanque do to improve customer satisfaction in his region?" implies that Vanque is doing something wrong, which may not be the case.

Closed-ended questions require yes or no answers or call for short responses: "Did you make a reservation for the flight?" "Is your grade-point average 3.5 to 4.0, 3.0 to 3.5, 2.5 to 3.0, 2.0 to 2.5?" Questions like these produce specific information, save time, require little effort from the interviewee, and eliminate bias and prejudice in answers. The disadvantage is that they limit the respondent's initiative and may prevent important information from being revealed. They're better for gathering information than for prompting an exchange of feelings.

Questions that mirror a respondent's answer are called **restatement questions.** They invite the respondent to expand on an answer: "You said you dislike completing travel vouchers. Is that correct?" They also signal to the interviewee that you're paying attention. Restatements provide opportunities to clarify points and to correct misunderstandings. Use them to pursue a subject further or to encourage the other person to explain a statement. You can also use restatement questions to soothe upset customers or co-workers. The simple act of acknowledging the other person's complaint provides a wealth of gains in information, rapport, and mutual trust and respect.

Going Online

Meeting the High-Tech Way

Learn how to plan and run a videoconference. The site discusses meeting basics, equipment needs, visual aids, room arrangement, and interacting with colleagues at remote locations.

www.3m.com/meetingnetwork/readingroom/meetingguide_plan_video.html

www.3m.com/meetingnetwork/readingroom/meetingguide_run_video.html

INTERVIEW STRUCTURE

Good interviews have an opening, a body, and a close. The opening establishes rapport and orients the interviewee to the remainder of the session. You might begin by introducing yourself, asking a few polite questions, and then explaining the purpose and ground rules of the interview.

Use the opening to set the tone and orient the interviewee.

The questions in the body of the interview reflect the nature of your relationship with the interviewee. For an informational session, such as a market-research interview, you may want to structure the interview and prepare a detailed list of specific questions. This approach enables you to control the interview and use your time efficiently. It also facilitates repeating the interview with other participants. On the other hand, if the interview is designed to explore problems or to persuade the interviewee, you may prefer a less structured approach. You might simply prepare a checklist of general subjects and then let the interview evolve on the basis of the participant's responses.

In the body of the interview, use a mix of question types. One good technique is to use closed-ended questions to pin down specific facts that emerge during an open-ended response. You might follow up an open-ended response by asking, "How many people did you contact to get this information?" or "Can we get this product in stock before May 15?"

Use a mix of question types to give the body of the interview rhythm.

Use the close to sum up the interview and leave the interviewee with a cordial feeling.

"Today the drive is to go beyond competence to expertise," says Dr. Patricia Sachs, a senior research scientist at the Institute for Research on Learning. "But expertise takes place inside communities. Work communities—communities of practice—develop when people work together, when they coordinate their efforts, exchange information, and solve problems to get something done."

The close of the interview is when you summarize the outcome, preview what comes next, and underscore the rapport that has been established. To signal that the interview is coming to an end, you might lean back in your chair, smile, and use an open, palms-up gesture as you say, "Well, I guess that takes care of all my questions. Would you like to add anything?" If the interviewee has no comments, you might go on to say, "Thank you so much for your help. You've given me all the information I need to finish my report. I should have it completed within two weeks; I'll send you a copy." Then you might rise, shake hands, and approach the door. In parting, you could add a friendly comment to reaffirm your interest in the other person: "I hope you have a nice trip to Banff. I was there when I was a kid, and I've never forgotten the experience."

From a practical standpoint, you need to be certain that your interview outline is about the right length for the time you've scheduled. People can speak at the rate of about 125 to 150 words a minute. If you're using a mix of various types of questions, you can probably handle about 20 questions in half an hour—about the same amount of information in a 10- to 12-page single-spaced document. However, you may want to allow more or less time for each question and response, depending on the subject matter and the complexity of the questions. Bear in mind that open-ended questions take longer to answer than other types do.

When you've concluded the interview, take a few moments to write down your thoughts. If it was an information-gathering session, go over your notes. Fill in any blanks while the interview is fresh in your mind. In addition, you might write a short letter or memo that thanks the interviewee for cooperating, confirms understandings between you, and if appropriate, outlines the next steps. As a reminder of the tasks involved in interviews, see this chapter's Checklist for Interviews on the Job.

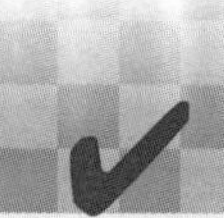

Checklist for Interviews on the Job

A. Preparation

1. Decide on the purpose and goals of the interview.
2. Outline your interview on the basis of your goals and the interview category.
   a. Set the level of formality.
   b. Choose a structured or an unstructured approach.
3. Determine the needs of your interviewee, and gather background information.
4. Formulate questions as clearly and concisely as possible, and plot their order.
5. Project the outcome of the interview, and develop a plan for accomplishing the goal.
6. Select a time and a site.
7. Inform the interviewee of the nature of the interview and the agenda to be covered.
8. Provide a list of questions in advance if the interviewee will need time to research and formulate quality answers.

B. Conduct

1. Be on time for the interview appointment.
2. Remind the interviewee of the purpose and format.
3. Clear the taking of notes or the use of a tape recorder with the interviewee.
4. Use ears and eyes to pick up verbal and non-verbal cues.
5. Follow the stated agenda, but be willing to explore relevant subtopics.
6. At the end of the interview, restate the interviewee's key ideas and review the actions, goals, and tasks each of you has agreed to.
7. Close the interview with a friendly comment to underscore the rapport that's been established.

C. Follow-Up

1. Write a thank-you memo or letter that provides the interviewee with a record of the meeting.
2. Provide the assistance that you agreed to during your meeting.
3. Monitor progress by keeping in touch with your interviewee.

Participating in Small Groups and Meetings

As in interviews, your speaking and listening skills are put to the test during meetings. Moreover, the skills you develop to handle difficult interpersonal situations and interviews are just as helpful when operating in small groups. By being a good listener, relying on a win-win strategy, and using the appropriate types of questions for each situation, you can contribute positively to any small group or meeting.

Don't try to cover more questions than you have time for.

As more and more corporations embrace the concept of **participative management** and involve employees in the company's decision making, the importance of teamwork has increased. Companies are looking for people who can interact successfully in small groups and make useful contributions during meetings. When Hewlett-Packard studied its most successful managers to identify the personality traits that contribute to their effectiveness, it found that all of them are good at team building. This finding prompted the company to emphasize team-building skills in its management-development program.[14]

Electronic Meetings: Work Together—Wherever You Are—to Get the Results You Want

USING THE POWER OF TECHNOLOGY

Imagine a meeting where everyone shares ideas, but no one knows who contributed them: a meeting in which people aren't talking, but typing. Computer-supported (or electronic) meetings have been popular with big corporations since IBM introduced the technology in the 1980s. Thanks to computer conferencing, the Internet, groupware, and a variety of new, affordable software packages, you can attend a virtual meeting in the morning and, in the afternoon, enter the electronic decision room to brainstorm ideas with colleagues.

Here's How It Works

Attending a *virtual meeting* means joining (by computer) an ongoing dialogue between two or more individuals communicating over telephone lines via computer modems. The exchange is similar to e-mail, but it's interactive (like chat rooms); that is, everyone sees everyone else's message as soon as it's sent. Participants may be separated by hundreds of kilometres, but they can exchange ideas as if they were in the same room.

Electronic meeting rooms go one step further with special electronic meeting systems (EMS), group decision support systems, and electronic voting systems. The simplest of these setups includes a large viewing screen, personal computers, and individual keypads (one for each participant). In general, the participants are all together, and the meeting is led by a trained facilitator who asks questions while participants type their responses.

With a simple keypad system, participants can view all responses, vote on an idea, and see the results immediately displayed on the large screen—whether as a graph, a simple number tally, or a complex breakdown of categories and voting trends. Discussion follows, along with subsequent votes on every aspect of the issues at hand. At the end of the meeting, the system provides a printed summary for everyone.

Are Electronic Meetings More Productive?

Electronic meetings are up to 55 percent faster than traditional meetings. Participants stay focused on the issues, and detailed statistical data helps guide decision-making. Plus, everyone speaks at the same time (typing responses simultaneously).

"It's the great equalizer," notes one communication expert. "Employees can share opinions anonymously—and honestly—without fear of displeasing superiors." Many employees are more candid in computer conferences than in traditional meetings or memos. Furthermore, because electronic meetings engender a true sense of shared decision-making, participants are more satisfied with the results.

Still, electronic meetings can't replace the synergy and spontaneity of face-to-face meetings. In fact, electronic-meeting keyboards are sometimes set aside for vigorous group discussion. After all, the purpose of electronic meetings isn't to dwell on the technology but to enhance the group process, gather information, elicit honest thoughts and ideas, and engage members in dialogue.

CAREER APPLICATIONS

1. What advantages do in-person, face-to-face meetings have over electronic meetings?
2. What potential risks face employees and companies that don't keep up with trends in electronic meeting technology?

Tom Chappell is the author of *The Soul of Business.* He believes a good portion of that soul comes from employees. "Flatten the hierarchy and create a circle of people who can offer diverse perspectives." A final decision often rests with one person of authority, "but that person always benefits from the dialogue," says Chappell.

At their best, meetings can be an extremely useful forum for making key decisions and coordinating the activities of people and departments. Theoretically, the interaction of the participants should lead to good decisions based on the combined intelligence of the group. Whether the meeting is held to solve a problem or to share information, the participants gain a sense of involvement and importance from their attendance. Because they share in the decision, they accept it and are committed to seeing it succeed.

At their worst, meetings are unproductive and frustrating. They waste everyone's time and they're expensive. More important, poor meetings may actually be counterproductive, because they may result in bad decisions. When people are pressured to conform, they abandon their sense of personal responsibility and agree to ill-founded plans.

Understanding Group Dynamics

A meeting's success depends not only on what the goal is but also on how the group approaches the task.

A meeting is called for some purpose, and this purpose gives form to the meeting. In addition, however, the interactions and processes that take place during a meeting, the **group dynamics,** affect the outcome. People are assembled to achieve a work-related task, but, at the same time, each person has a **hidden agenda,** private motives that affect the group's interaction. Sam might want to prove that he's more powerful than Sherry; Sherry might be trying to share the risk of making a decision; Don might be looking for a chance to postpone doing "real" work; and Rachel might be looking for approval from her peers. Each person's hidden agenda either contributes to or detracts from the group's ability to perform its task. Although it would be unethical for any group member to make decisions solely on the basis of their hidden agenda, a person's private motives cannot be left on a coat rack outside the conference room.

ROLE-PLAYING

Each member of a group plays a role that affects the outcome of the group's activities.

We all have many-faceted personalities: Sometimes we're carefree and fun-loving; sometimes we're serious and hard working. We assume various roles to suit various occasions, playing the part that's expected of us in a particular context. The roles are all consistent with our self-concept, but we vary the image we project depending on the demands of the situation and the cues we receive from other people.

The roles people play in meetings fall into three categories (Table 17.2). Members who assume **self-oriented roles** are motivated mainly to fulfill personal needs, and they tend to be less productive than the other two types. Far more likely to contribute to group goals are those who assume **group maintenance roles** to help members work well together and those who assume **task-facilitating roles** to help members solve the problem or make the decision.

To a great extent, the role we assume in a group depends on our status in that group: High-status people play dominant roles; low-status people play passive roles. Status depends on many variables, such as personal attractiveness, competence in a particular field, past successes, education, age, social background, and position in the organization. It also varies from group to group: You may have a high status in one group (say, a student council) and very low status in another (say, a Fortune 500 company).

Group members' personal motives may interfere with the group's efforts to accomplish its mission.

In most groups a certain amount of politics occurs as people try to establish their status. One or two people typically emerge as the leaders, but often an undercurrent of tension remains as members of the group vie for better positions in the pecking order. These power struggles often get in the way of the real work. One person might refuse to go along with a decision simply because it was suggested by a rival. Until roles and status have stabilized, the group may have trouble accomplishing its goals.

TABLE 17.2 Roles People Play in Groups

Self-Oriented Roles	Group Maintenance Roles	Task-Facilitating Roles
Controlling: dominating others by exhibiting superiority or authority **Withdrawing:** retiring from the group either by becoming silent or by refusing to deal with a particular aspect of the group's work **Attention seeking:** calling attention to oneself and demanding recognition from others **Diverting:** focusing group discussion on topics of interest to the individual rather than on topics relevant to the task	**Encouraging**: drawing out other members by showing verbal and nonverbal support, praise, or agreement **Harmonizing:** reconciling differences among group members through mediation or by using humour to relieve tension **Compromising:** offering to yield on a point in the interest of reaching a mutually acceptable decision	**Initiating:** getting the group started on a line of inquiry **Information giving or seeking:** offering (or seeking) information relevant to questions facing the group **Coordinating:** showing relationships among ideas, clarifying issues, summarizing what the group has done **Procedure setting:** suggesting decision-making procedures that will move the group toward a goal

GROUP NORMS

A group that meets regularly develops unwritten rules governing the behaviour of the members, and people are expected to conform to these norms. For example, there may be an unspoken agreement that it's okay to be 10 minutes late for meetings but not 15 minutes late. In the context of work, the most productive groups tend to develop norms that are conducive to business.

Some groups are more cohesive than others. When the group has a strong identity, the members all observe the norms religiously. They're upset by any deviation, and individuals feel a great deal of pressure to conform. This sense of group loyalty can be positive. Members generally have a strong commitment to one another, and they're highly motivated to see that the group succeeds. However, such group loyalty can also lead members into **groupthink,** the willingness of individual members to set aside their personal opinions and go along with everyone else, even if everyone else is wrong, simply because belonging to the group is important to them. Because decisions based on groupthink are more a result of group loyalty and conformity than of carefully considered opinion and fact finding, groupthink can lead to poor-quality decisions and ill-advised actions. Groupthink can even induce people to act against their own sense of ethics.

Because they feel pressured to conform, members of a group may agree to unwise decisions.

GROUP DECISION MAKING

LEARNING OUTCOME 5
Describe how groups make decisions.

Groups usually reach their decisions in a predictable pattern. The process can be viewed as passing through four phases. In the **orientation phase**, group members socialize, establish their roles, and agree on their reason for meeting. In the **conflict phase** members begin to discuss their positions on the problem. If group members have been carefully selected to represent a variety of viewpoints and expertise, disagreements are a natural part of this phase. The point is to air all the options and all the pros and cons fully. At the end of this phase, group members begin to settle on a single solution to the problem. In the **emergence phase** members reach a decision. Those who advocated different solutions put aside their objections, either because they're convinced that the majority solution is better or because they recognize that arguing is futile. Finally, in the **reinforcement phase** group feeling is rebuilt, and the solution is summarized. Members receive their assignments for carrying out the group's decision and make arrangements for following up on those assignments.[15]

Group decision making passes through four phases: orientation, conflict, emergence, reinforcement.

These four phases almost always occur, regardless of what type of decision is being considered. Group members naturally employ this decision process, even when they lack experience or training in group communication. However, just as a natural athlete can improve by practising, the group leader can make this natural decision process proceed more smoothly by preparing carefully.

Group decision-making software (also called electronic meeting systems) can save time and streamline the decision process. These systems can also make meetings more democratic by putting everyone on equal footing.

LEARNING OUTCOME 6
Discuss the preparations and duties necessary for productive meetings.

Arranging the Meeting

By being aware of how small groups of people interact, meeting leaders can take steps to ensure that their meetings are productive. The three most frequently reported problems with meetings are (1) getting off the subject, (2) not having an agenda, and (3) meeting for too long.[16] The key to productive meetings is careful planning of purpose, participants, agenda, and location. The trick is to bring the right people together in the right place for just enough time to accomplish your goals.

Before calling a meeting, ask yourself whether it is really needed.

- *Determining the purpose.* Rockport's John Thorbeck warns that the biggest mistake is having no specific goal. In general, the purpose of a meeting is either to get information or to make a decision, although many meetings comprise both purposes. An informational meeting is called so that the participants can share information and, possibly, coordinate actions. This type of meeting may involve individual briefings by each participant or a speech by the leader followed by questions from the attendees. Decision-making meetings are mainly concerned

BEHIND THE SCENES AT 3M

The Keys to Masterful Meetings

Virginia Johnson is the manager of 3M's Meeting Management Institute. Among American companies, 3M is known for its role in promoting the importance of effective meetings (as well as for producing such brand names as Scotch cellophane tape and Post-it notes). The company also produces graphics and presentation equipment, which suggests a natural connection between 3M's products and its emphasis on effective meetings. The company funds research, sponsors seminars, and publishes articles and books on the subject.

At 3M, meetings help participants share information, solve problems, make decisions, and train employees. As manager of 3M's Meeting Management Institute, Virginia Johnson believes that successful meetings depend on preparation.

"We define a meeting as three or more people gathering for an expected outcome," explains Johnson. Top executives spend 17 hours a week in such gatherings and another 6 hours preparing for them: a total of 38 percent of their typical 61-hour week. But why call meetings? Why not put what has to be said in writing and save everybody some time? Johnson says, "You can't accomplish some things without getting your people together—when you want to provide them direct access to an expert, for example, or show that avenues of communication in the company are open. Meetings here at 3M serve other needs too. They allow us to share information, build teams, brainstorm problems and solutions, reach decisions, and train people. Young companies, especially, and companies in trouble may find meetings indispensable."

To determine whether to hold a meeting, Johnson says she writes "one 25-word sentence stating what I expect people to know, do, and believe after attending. If I can't create that sentence, the need for a meeting isn't apparent." When a meeting is appropriate, she believes that preparation is what makes it successful. "I start by thinking in terms of the agenda. Once it's outlined, I create the visuals that will illustrate the points I want to make.

"Listening is an important skill. Traditionally you help yourself listen by taking notes. We've found that graphics also help people listen, enabling them to visualize and retain information. That's why I plan my graphics early." Johnson finishes by preparing notes containing her main ideas or key phrases. "I never write a speech," she explains. "Speeches are not meet-with persuasion, analysis, and problem solving. They often include a brainstorming session that is followed by a debate on the alternatives. These meetings tend to be somewhat less predictable than informational meetings.

- *Selecting the participants.* Try to invite only those whose presence is essential. The number of participants should reflect the purpose of the meeting. If the session is purely informational and one person will be doing most of the talking, you can include a relatively large group. However, if you're trying to solve a problem, develop a plan, or reach a decision, try to limit participation to between 6 and 12 people.[17] Of course, be sure to include those who can make an important contribution and those who are key decision makers.

Limit the number of participants, but include all key people.

- *Setting the agenda.* Although the nature of a meeting may sometimes prevent you from developing a fixed agenda, at least prepare a list of matters to be discussed (see Appendix A). Distribute the agenda to the participants several days before the meeting. The more participants know ahead of time about the purpose of the meeting, the better prepared they'll be to respond to the issues at hand.

Prepare a detailed agenda well in advance of the meeting.

- *Preparing the location.* Decide where you'll hold the meeting, and reserve the location. For work sessions, morning meetings are usually more productive than afternoon sessions. If you work for an organization with technological capabilities, you may want to use teleconferencing or videoconferencing for your meeting. Also, consider the seating arrangements. Are rows of chairs suitable, or do you need a conference table? Give some attention to such details as room temperature, lighting, ventilation, acoustics, and refreshments. These things may seem trivial, but they can make or break a meeting.

---

ings. My personal style is to be natural and extemporaneous. My agenda, visuals, and notes help me achieve that tone.

"For me, the toughest meeting to run is the creative session. Trying to bring out the child in adults, achieving fantasy and free thinking by breaking down management roles, is very demanding." A meeting to generate new ideas in sales training was Johnson's most recent challenge. "I used what I call a 'brain-writing' sheet. I asked the eight managers to write down three things about sales training they'd like to see added or changed. They handed their ideas in and took the sheet of another participant. They read that person's suggestions and wrote down three more. After a few rounds of this, they'd forgotten their jobs and titles and were busy scribbling. Each round triggered new ideas."

Johnson is more alert than most to the conduct of meetings, and, as a participant, she has the greatest trouble when there is little or no leadership from the meeting facilitator. "My mind wanders," she admits. "If a leader speaks more than 15 or 20 percent of the time, for example, he or she is not being effective. The role of the facilitator is to help other people get their opinions or questions out and responded to." To get the most out of her attendance, Johnson adopts a listening behaviour appropriate to the meeting. "If it's a formal meeting, I'll take notes to help me listen and for later recall. At creative sessions I may have to listen intently or shout out my responses. Either way, I want to be free of the technical aspects of meeting attendance." For Virginia Johnson and 3M, planning, conducting, or attending a well-run meeting rewards everyone involved. "If it produces that expected outcome, it's a job well done."

APPLY YOUR KNOWLEDGE

1. You followed Virginia Johnson's advice. For a meeting on the need to improve office telephone techniques, you created 30 visuals to guide you and eight managers through your agenda. On your way to the meeting, you lost the case with your visuals. What steps can you take to conduct a productive meeting anyway?
2. Determine the hourly cost of meetings. Create a grid of six vertical columns with these labels: Salary; (number of executives): 2, 4, 6, 8, and 10. Down the left side, under "Salary," label five lines with these annual salaries: $20 000, $40 000, $60 000, $80 000, and $100 000. Do the arithmetic and fill in the grid with how much a 1-hour meeting of each group would cost a company (assuming fifty 40-hour weeks to a year). For example, a 1-hour meeting of four executives earning $80 000 a year costs the company $160. Next, determine the cost of an all-morning (3-hour) meeting involving eight employees: one earning $20 000, three earning $40 000, one earning $60 000, two earning $80 000, and one earning $100 000.

EFFECTIVE E-BUSINESS COMMUNICATION

Calling a Meeting in Cyberspace

Working with team members in different locations is less of a challenge when you bridge the distance with WebEx or a similar Web-based service. Say you're going to call a cyberspace meeting. Following the WebEx prompts, you simply enter the meeting date and time, send e-mail announcements to attendees, and request features such as online polling. Then, at meeting time, participants log on to WebEx, click "Join Meeting," and enter a special code to attend your meeting.

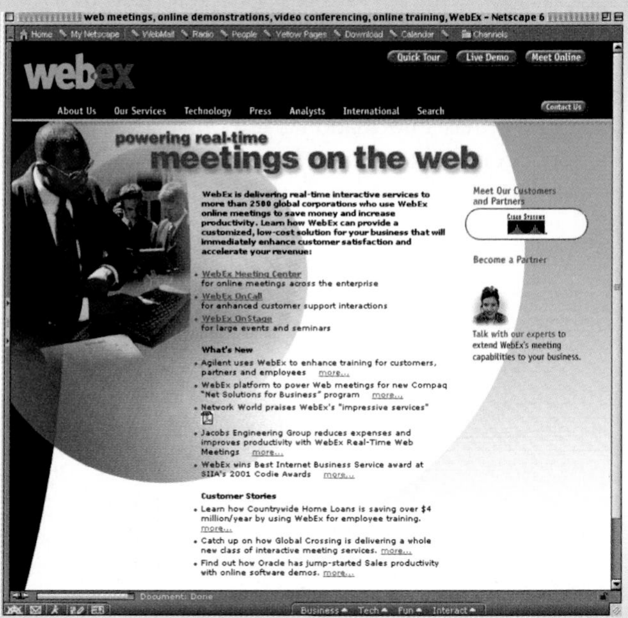

CAREER APPLICATIONS

1. What information should you include in your pre-meeting e-mail announcements to cyberspace meeting attendees?
2. Why would a company encourage teams to meet in cyberspace rather than travel to one central location for a meeting?

Contributing to a Productive Meeting

The meeting leader's duties:
- ✧ Pacing the meeting
- ✧ Appointing a note taker
- ✧ Following the agenda
- ✧ Stimulating participation and discussion
- ✧ Summarizing the debate
- ✧ Reviewing recommendations
- ✧ Circulating the minutes

Whether the meeting is conducted electronically or conventionally, its success depends largely on how effective the leader is. If the leader is prepared and has selected the participants carefully, the meeting will probably be productive. Moreover, according to Rockport's John Thorbeck, listening skills are especially important to meeting leaders. The leader's ability to listen well facilitates good meetings.

As meeting leader, you're responsible for keeping the ball rolling. Avoid being so domineering that you close off suggestions, but don't be so passive that you lose control of the group. If the discussion lags, call on people who haven't spoken. Pace the presentation and discussion so that you'll have time to complete the agenda. As time begins to run out, interrupt the discussion and summarize what has been accomplished. Another leadership task is either to arrange for someone to record the proceedings or to ask a participant to take notes during the meeting. (Appendix A includes an example of the format for minutes of meetings.)

As leader, you're expected to follow the agenda; participants have prepared for the meeting on the basis of the announced agenda. However, don't be rigid. Allow enough time for discussion, and give people a chance to raise related issues. If you cut off discussion too quickly or limit the subject too narrowly, no real consensus can emerge.

You can improve the productivity of a meeting by using **parliamentary procedure,** a time-tested method for planning and running effective meetings. Anyone belonging to an organization should understand the basic principles of parliamentary procedure. Used correctly, it can help groups in several important ways.[18]

- ➤ Transact business efficiently
- ➤ Protect individual rights
- ➤ Maintain order

- Preserve a spirit of harmony
- Help the organization accomplish its goals

The most common guide to parliamentary procedure is *Robert's Rules of Order,* available in various editions and revisions. Also available are less technical guides based on Robert's Rules. You can determine how strictly you want to adhere to parliamentary procedure. For small groups you may be quite flexible, but for larger groups you'll want to use a more formal approach.

As the meeting gets under way, you'll discover that some participants are too quiet and others are too talkative. To draw out the shy types, ask for their input on issues that particularly pertain to them. You might say something like, "Gino, you've done a lot of work in this area. What do you think?" For the overly talkative, simply say that time is limited and others need a chance to speak. The best meetings are those in which everyone participates, so don't let one or two people dominate your meeting while others doodle on their notepads. As you move through your agenda, stop at the end of each item, summarize what you understand to be the feelings of the group, and state the important points made during the discussion.

At the conclusion of the meeting, tie up the loose ends. Either summarize the general conclusion of the group or list the suggestions. Wrapping things up ensures that all participants agree on the outcome and gives people a chance to clear up any misunderstandings. Before the meeting breaks up, briefly review who has agreed to do what by what date.

As soon as possible after the meeting, the leader gives all participants a copy of the minutes or notes, showing recommended actions, schedules, and responsibilities. The minutes will remind everyone of what took place and will provide a reference for future actions.

Like leaders, participants have responsibilities during meetings. If you've been included in the group, try to contribute both to the subject of the meeting and to the smooth interaction of the participants. Use your listening skills and powers of observation to size up the interpersonal dynamics of the people; then adapt your behaviour to help the group achieve its goals. Speak up if you have something useful to say, but don't monopolize the discussion. To review the tasks that contribute to productive meetings, see this chapter's Checklist for Meetings.

Fernando Espinosa, CEO and founder of Andes Chemical, says that "You've got to work for a living; you might as well do it right." This *Hispanic Business* magazine's Entrepreneur of the Year says that "empowerment and employee involvement are the bonds that keep morale high and employees motivated."

Checklist for Meetings

A. Preparation

1. Determine the meeting's objectives.
2. Work out an agenda that will achieve your objectives.
3. Select participants.
4. Determine the location, and reserve a room.
5. Arrange for light refreshments, if appropriate.
6. Determine whether the lighting, ventilation, acoustics, and temperature of the room are adequate.
7. Determine seating needs: chairs only or tables and chairs.

B. Conduct

1. Begin and end the meeting on time.
2. Control the meeting by following the announced agenda.
3. Encourage full participation, and either confront or ignore those who seem to be working at cross-purposes with the group.
4. Sum up decisions, actions, and recommendations as you move through the agenda, and restate main points at the end.

C. Follow-Up

1. Distribute the meeting's notes or minutes on a timely basis.
2. Take the follow-up action agreed to.

ON THE JOB
Solving a Communication Dilemma at Rockport

Many executives shook their heads over John Thorbeck's idea of shutting down the entire Rockport operation so that everyone could attend a two-day meeting. They were even more baffled when they arrived at the cavernous distribution centre where the meeting was held. Instead of finding an agenda, a set of reading materials, or a keynote speaker, they were confronted by hundreds of chairs, loosely arranged in a circle. They also found large, empty sheets of paper; a pile of felt-tip markers; several rolls of masking tape; and 12 computers.

Nobody knew quite what to expect when Harrison Owen, a consultant hired by Thorbeck, stepped into the centre of the circle and began to talk. Rockport was holding an "open-space meeting," he explained, and what happened during the next two days was up to the participants. The rules were simple: Anyone who felt passionate about a business-related topic should step forward, announce the topic, write it on one of the sheets of paper, and tack it on the wall. The company's 350 managers and employees would then sign up to discuss the topics that interested them. The employee who initiated a particular idea would be responsible for leading the discussion in his or her group and for recording the minutes of that meeting.

Before leaving the circle, Owen outlined one more rule: "The Law of Two Feet." All discussions were voluntary, he said, so anyone who was bored, not learning anything, or not able to contribute information should simply walk out. Allowing people to leave any group at any time would serve as a safeguard against discussion leaders who acted pompous or self-important.

After Owen made his way out of the circle, the room was silent for a time. In the words of Keith Mathis, director of distribution, "I thought the meeting had ended right there. With so much of the top brass around, I fully expected that no one would write anything down. But one person rose tentatively, then another, and soon it was like ants going to sugar." One employee introduced the topic of compensation policy; another proposed a discussion of office politics; a third wanted to talk about reducing paperwork.

What had begun as a leaderless, agenda-less meeting soon turned into a series of smaller meetings, each with a real sense of purpose. More than 60 topics were tacked to the wall, and Rockport personnel eagerly signed up for the groups of their choice. The hottest topics drew 150 people, but even the smallest group had at least 5 participants. After each group met, its leader entered the results and recommendations into one of the 12 computers.

John Thorbeck knew that coming up with ideas was only the first step in releasing the company's potential. The next step was following through to see that the ideas were implemented. Rockport managers didn't have to worry about supervising this part of the process: The energized workforce got busy right after the meeting. All the recorded suggestions were assembled into a book, and many people who had led discussion groups went on to establish committees that put the recommended changes into practice.

Both large and small changes came about as a result of the meeting. Thanks to ideas contributed by people from sales, production, purchasing, and merchandising, the company found a way to cut its purchasing cycle and save $4 million. A security guard suggested a new line of shoes that is expected to bring in $20 million in annual sales. In addition, Rockport installed an e-mail system, hired a training specialist, and published an employee directory.

As effective as it was for Rockport, the open-space meeting isn't appropriate for every situation or every company. For example, an open-space meeting isn't a good way to implement a new word-processing system. It's also unlikely to yield results when top management wants to control the process and the outcome. But it can help when an organization wants to examine such open-ended questions as "What should we be doing?" and "How can we feel more involved and alive at work?"[19]

Your Mission: As John Thorbeck's executive assistant, you handle a wide range of assignments that put you in daily contact with managers and employees at all levels of the company. Oral communication skills are vitally important to your success in this key role. Choose the best alternative for handling the following situations, and be prepared to explain why your choice is best.

1. One of the employees who works at the distribution centre comes to you with the following complaint: "I told my supervisor that I could do my job better if he would arrange to adjust the lighting over my work area. It's so dark that I can hardly see what I'm doing. I know I could work faster if I could see without squinting and straining my eyes. Now you'd think that with everybody pushing to increase productivity, the supervisor would jump at the chance to boost my output, wouldn't you? But what does he do? He says, 'Hey, try bifocals.' It's a big joke to him. I don't think it's fair that people like me have to be held back by people like him, who are too lazy or too cheap to change the lighting." Which of the following remarks is the best way to begin your reply to the employee's complaint?

a. "It sounds as though you and your supervisor don't see eye to eye on this issue."
b. "I can see why you're provoked. I'd be annoyed too if somebody treated me that way."
c. "Maybe your supervisor has a good point. I think you should have your eyes checked and see if that might be the problem."
d. "I'd like to take a look at the situation. Let's go to your workstation right now so I can get a better idea of the lighting conditions there."

2. A benefits expert from the human resources department has asked you to attend a meeting and answer questions about using open-space meetings within departments that have fewer than 20 people. The benefits specialist launches the meeting by summarizing a variety of concerns about how small groups might react to open-space meetings. His comments last about 15 minutes. After responding to these points, you throw the meeting open to additional questions from the group. One employee stands up, crosses his arms in front of his chest, and says, "How do we know that management will allow us enough time to hold this kind of meeting when a department like ours sees the need to address important issues?" The question seems straightforward, but the employee's tone of voice strikes you as being belligerent. His posture is aggressive, and he has a sneer on his face. How would you interpret his question?
a. The employee is implying that management will not allow departmental employees to take time from their regular duties to hold open-space meetings when important issues should be addressed.
b. The employee is simply trying to learn about management's attitude toward future open-space meetings around the company.
c. The employee is implying that Rockport should encourage employees to take time from their regular duties to hold open-space meetings every week or two.
d. The employee wants to know whether future open-space meetings to address important issues will be long or short.

3. John Thorbeck has asked you to explain the electronic mail system to a new manager who will be running the company's accounting department. The manager is expected to exchange e-mail messages about accounting practices with people in other departments and other locations, so you want to be sure that he fully understands the system's details and will be able to use it. Which of the following versions would provide the best structure for this interview?
a. Version One
   1. Overview of e-mail and Rockport's reasons for adopting it
   2. Feature-by-feature description of the e-mail system
   3. Description of accounting department's use of e-mail
   4. Problems the manager might encounter in learning the e-mail system
   5. Questions the manager might have about the system
b. Version Two
   1. Do you have any experience with e-mail systems?
   2. What advantages and disadvantages do you see in using e-mail to communicate internally?
   3. If you were designing an e-mail system, what features would you include?
   4. What steps will you take to ensure that the e-mail system is used throughout your department?
   5. How will you deal with technical problems that might arise when you use the system?
c. Version Three
   1. The problem: Employees waste a lot of time waiting for memos to arrive in the interoffice mail.
   2. Background: Rockport implemented e-mail to eliminate paper memos.
   3. Objectives: To boost productivity and slash the time needed to send and receive messages.
   4. Alternatives: Various types of e-mail systems were evaluated (give a description and the pros and cons of each approach).
   5. Solution: Give key features of selected system.
   6. Next steps: Discuss manager's role in using e-mail in his department.
   7. Answer manager's questions.
d. Version Four
   1. Conclusions: Show how e-mail saves a lot of time and paper.
   2. Supporting details: Discuss specific time-saving features of the system, and mention how much paper is saved in a typical week, month, or year.
   3. External evidence: Introduce facts about how other companies have used e-mail systems to speed internal communication.
   4. Concerns: Bring out specific fears others have expressed about e-mail systems.

4. Some Rockport employees have been pushing the company to adopt a corporate statement of goals. In response, John Thorbeck has decided to call a companywide meeting to discuss goals. Which purpose should Thorbeck focus on during the meeting?
a. Purpose: To find out about competitors' goals and determine whether they are appropriate for Rockport
b. Purpose: To inform employees of his intention to evaluate all employees on the basis of their contributions to corporate goals
c. Purpose: To decide which employees should be asked to come to a meeting about corporate goals
d. Purpose: To reach agreement about Rockport's primary corporate goals

TAP Your Knowledge

Summary of Learning Outcomes

1. Apply the composition process to your spoken comments. Before you speak, think about your purpose, main idea, and audience. Organize your thoughts logically, decide on a style that suits the occasion, and edit your remarks mentally. Predict how your audience will react and arrange your message to suit your audience's attitudes, but have alternative approaches ready in case your audience does not respond as you expect them to.

2. Summarize the skills involved in being an effective listener. Effective listening involves being receptive to both information and feelings. You can become a better listener by finding areas of interest; judging content, not delivery; judging after comprehension is complete; listening for ideas, not facts; being flexible; resisting distractions; exercising your mind; and keeping your mind open. Effective listeners also use non-verbal skills to help them focus, such as maintaining eye contact, reacting responsively with head nods or spoken signals, and paying attention to the speaker's body language.

3. Identify nine common types of business interview. The nine common types of business interview are (1) job interviews, where the job candidate seeks information about the position and organization, and the employer seeks information about the applicant; (2) information interviews, where the interview seeks facts that bear on a decision or contribute to basic understanding; (3) persuasive interviews, which try to influence the listener to act on the speaker's recommendations; (4) exit interviews, which seek to understand why the interviewee is leaving an organization or transferring to another department or division; (5) evaluation interviews, conducted to determine an employee's performance; (6) counselling interviews, or discussions between an employee and a supervisor about personal problems that may be interfering with performance at work; (7) conflict-resolution interviews, used to explore and resolve problems and attitudes between competing groups of people; (8) disciplinary interviews, conducted to correct behaviour of employees who ignore the organization's rules and regulations; (9) termination interviews, where a supervisor informs an employee of the reasons for termination of employment.

4. Define four types of interview questions and clarify when to use each type. One type of interview question is the *open-ended* question, which invites the interviewee to offer an opinion, not just a yes-or-no answer. This kind of question is useful when the interviewer wants to learn the reasons behind a decision rather than just the facts. The *direct open-ended* question is phrased to suggest a response to the question. This type of question gives the interviewer more control over the interview, but still gives the respondent some freedom in phrasing a response; it is used when the interviewer wants to get a specific conclusion or recommendation from someone. The *closed-ended* question requires yes-or-no answers or calls for short responses. This type of question is used for gathering information rather than for prompting an exchange of feelings or ideas. *Restatement* questions mirror a respondent's answer. They provide opportunities to clarify points and to correct misunderstandings.

5. Describe how groups make decisions. Group decision making usually passes through four phases: orientation, conflict, emergence, and reinforcement. In the *orientation* phase, group members socialize, establish their roles, and agree on their reason for meeting. In the *conflict* phase, members begin to discuss their positions on the problem; at the end of this stage, group members begin to settle on a single solution to the problem. In the *emergence* phase, members reach a decision. Those who advocated different solutions put aside their objections, either because they're convinced that the majority solution is better or because they recognize that arguing is futile. Finally, in the *reinforcement* phase, group feeling is rebuilt and the solution is summarized, with members receiving their assignments for carrying out the group's decision.

6. Discuss the preparations and duties necessary for productive meetings. Prepare for meetings by deciding on your purpose, selecting participants who really need to be there, choosing a location and time that are conducive to your goals, and developing an agenda that is specific and thorough. Conduct productive meetings by pacing the discussion and encouraging everyone to participate. Before the end, summarize conclusions and review who has agreed to do what by what deadline. Follow up with minutes that show recommended actions, schedules, and responsibilities. As a participant in any meeting, do everything you can to contribute to the smooth interaction of attendees as well as to the subject.

Test Your Knowledge

Review Questions

1. What are the benefits of oral communication? What are its drawbacks?
2. Discuss the importance of the "you" attitude when communicating orally.
3. What happens when you listen?
4. Describe the three types of listening and discuss how to be a better listener.
5. Name at least five types of interviews and discuss their goals.
6. Why is it important to structure interviews?
7. What is meant by a hidden agenda?
8. What are the roles people play in meetings?
9. What is groupthink, and how can it affect an organization?
10. What is the purpose of parliamentary procedure?

Apply Your Knowledge

Critical Thinking Questions

1. Do you believe that you're best at sending written, oral, or non-verbal messages? Why does this form of communication appeal to you? When receiving messages, are you best at reading, listening, or interpreting non-verbal cues? Why do you think this is true?
2. Have you ever made a comment you later regretted? Describe the circumstances of your verbal blunder, and explain the consequences.
3. Canadians are considered consensus builders when negotiating with others and trying to come to an agreement. What are the strengths of being a consensus builder? Are there any drawbacks? Explain.
4. When was the last time you negotiated for something? Were you successful in achieving your aims? If you could repeat the experience, what would you do differently? Briefly explain.
5. Should meeting leaders always use a participatory style, or are there some circumstances when this might not be advisable? Explain your answer.
6. During your meeting with members of your project team, one member keeps raising objections to points of style in a rough draft of your group's report. At this rate, you'll be here for hours debating whether to use the word *criterion* or the word *parameter* on page 27. What should you do? Explain your answer.

Practise Your Knowledge

Exercises

1. Visit the 3M home page on the Internet at **www.3m.com**. To gain more information from 3M, write an e-mail message in which you ask two open-ended and two closed-ended questions about products and markets. Print out your e-mail message for submission.
2. Read through the following situations, and think about them from the viewpoint of both participants. For each participant, what is the general purpose of the interview? What sequence of conversation might best accomplish this purpose? What type of information should be sought or presented? Explain your answers.

   a. A high school debates coach has scheduled an appointment with the school principal in an attempt to obtain $250 to take her debate team to the provincial finals in Saint John, New Brunswick. The team is strong, and she feels that it has a good chance of winning some type of award. However, the school activities budget is limited.

b. A counsellor has scheduled an interview with a company employee who has a long, consistent record of excellent work. Recently, however, the employee has been coming to work late and often appears distracted on the job.

c. As part of the job-evaluation process and in an attempt to have her civil-service position upgraded, an employee has submitted a job description of her work. An evaluator from the civil-service administration has scheduled an interview at the job location to discuss the candidate's requested upgrading.

3. How good are your listening skills? Rate yourself on each of the following elements of good listening by answering always, frequently, occasionally, or never. Then examine your answers to identify where you are strongest and where you can improve, using the tips in this chapter. For the next 30 days, review your list and jot down any improvements you've noticed as a result of your effort.

a. I look for areas of interest when people speak.

b. I focus on content rather than delivery.

c. I wait to respond until I understand the content.

d. I listen for ideas and themes, not isolated facts.

e. I take notes only when needed.

f. I really concentrate on what speakers are saying.

g. I stay focused even when the ideas are complex.

h. I keep an open mind despite emotionally charged language.

4. With a classmate, attend a local community or campus meeting where you can observe group discussion as well as voting or another group action. Take notes individually during the meeting and then work together to answer the following questions.

a. What is your evaluation of this meeting? In your answer, consider (1) the leader's ability to clearly articulate the meeting's goals, (2) the leader's ability to engage members in a meaningful discussion, (3) the group's dynamics, and (4) the group's listening skills.

b. How did group members make decisions? Did they vote? Did they reach decisions by consensus? Did the naysayers get an opportunity to voice their objections?

c. How well did the individual participants listen? How could you tell?

d. Did any participants change their expressed views or their votes during the meeting? Why might that have happened?

e. Did you observe any of the communication barriers discussed in Chapter 1? Identify them.

f. Compare the notes you took during the meeting with those of your classmate. What differences do you notice? How do you account for these differences?

5. Two of your employees have personal differences that are beginning to interfere with their work. Suggest some ways that you might resolve the conflict. Put your suggestions and explanations into a memo to be submitted to your superior.

6. Describe a recent conflict you had with a team member at work or at school, and explain how you resolved it. Did you find a solution that was acceptable to both of you and to the team?

7. During team meetings, one member constantly calls for votes before all the members have voiced their views. As the leader, you asked this member privately about his behaviour. He replied that he was trying to move the team toward its goals, but you are concerned that he is really trying to take control. How can you deal with this situation without removing the member from the group?

8. Your company is opening a new office in Japan, and you are unfamiliar with Japanese culture and business practices. Suggest some ways you and your co-workers could learn more about the cultural differences that might affect work relationships. Briefly explain your suggestions.

Developing Your Internet Skills

http://www

Going Online: Meeting the High-Tech Way, *p. 491*

Read the articles and advice on the 3M meeting network Web site. Familiarize yourself with 3M's advice for planning and running videoconferences so that if you encounter a business associate who starts talking about this sort of technology, you'll be able to participate intelligently in the conversation. If you had such a system available to you right now, and if you knew there was another system available to business students at another university across the country, how could you use it to your benefit? What information could you share that you can't share through regular e-mail, file transfer, or Usenet or chat groups?

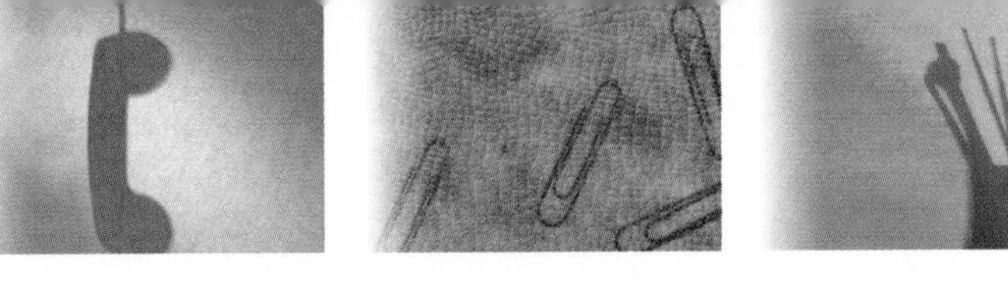

CHAPTER 18

Giving Speeches and Oral Presentations

AFTER STUDYING THIS CHAPTER, YOU WILL BE ABLE TO

1. Categorize speeches and presentations according to their purpose
2. Identify the audience characteristics that govern decisions about the style and content of speeches and presentations
3. Discuss four steps required in planning a speech or presentation
4. Develop an introduction, a body, and a close for a long formal presentation
5. Select, design, and use visual aids that are appropriate for various types of speeches and presentations
6. Explain techniques you can use to improve your public-speaking skills

ON THE JOB
Facing a Communication Dilemma at Lucent Technologies Canada

Speaking Her Mind, Persuading Her Listeners

Carol Stephenson gives speeches—lots of them. During her four-year tenure as CEO of the Stentor Resource Centre, an alliance of telephone service providers, she travelled across the country promoting the interests of Canada's phone companies. Now, as CEO of Lucent Technologies Canada, a manufacturer of next-generation communications software, hardware, and services, Stephenson continues to speak, to professional, civic, and social groups. Her topics are technology, communication, leadership, and the challenges facing women in business.

Stephenson started her career as an operator at Bell Canada. She had planned to enter social work, but changed her mind when she saw the opportunities offered by a large company. In 1973 she joined Bell as a management trainee, gradually working her way up through various management positions to the vice-presidential level. Along the way, she learned that her ability to listen to employees and to learn from them created a workplace culture that fostered initiative and respect, high morale and productivity.

Carol Stephenson is CEO of Lucent Technologies Canada. She credits her success to effective listening and open communication. She believes that these skills are essential to creating a productive and positive workplace.

Now, as Lucent Canada's CEO, she brings the same attitudes and abilities to her new job. She tells her audiences about the communications revolution and Lucent's place in it, and about the corporate culture that encourages open communication between employees and executives. Stephenson works hard to communicate Lucent's messages, both within the company and outside of it. If you were Carol Stephenson, whether you were addressing a large crowd or an audience of one, what would you need to know about preparing, developing, and delivering speeches? Can improving your speaking skills really lead to the success that Carol Stephenson has realized in her career?[1]

Speaking and Presenting in a Business Environment

As Carol Stephenson will tell you, giving speeches and oral presentations may be an integral part of your business career. Chances are you'll have an opportunity to deliver a number of speeches and presentations throughout your career. You may not speak before large audiences of employees or the media, but you'll certainly be expected to present ideas to your colleagues, make sales presentations to potential customers, or engage in other kinds of spoken communication. For most speeches and formal presentations, you'll follow three general steps:

1. Prepare to speak (by defining your purpose, analyzing your audience, and planning your speech's content, length, and style)
2. Develop your speech or presentation (including the introduction, body, close, question-and-answer period, and visual aids)
3. Deliver your speech or presentation

Preparing to Speak

Preparing speeches and oral presentations is much like preparing any other message: You define your purpose, analyze your audience, and plan how to present your points. However, because speeches and presentations are delivered orally under relatively public circumstances, they require a few special communication techniques. A speech is a one-shot event; your audience cannot leaf back through pages to review something you said earlier. For this reason, you must make sure audience members will hear what you say and remember it.

Define Your Purpose

LEARNING OUTCOME 1
Categorize speeches and presentations according to their purpose.

Speeches and presentations can be categorized according to their purpose, which helps you determine content, style, and audience participation. The four basic categories are to inform, to persuade, to motivate, and to entertain. Here are sample statements of purpose for business speeches:

The amount of audience interaction varies from presentation to presentation, depending on your purpose.

- To inform the accounting department of the new remote data-access policy
- To explain to the executive committee the financial ramifications of OmniGroup's takeover offer
- To persuade potential customers that our bank offers the best commercial banking services for their needs
- To motivate the sales force to close 10 percent more business this quarter

Many of your business speeches and presentations will be informative, and if you're involved in a marketing or sales position, you'll need to do persuasive presentations as well. Motivational speeches tend to be more specialized. Many companies bring in outside speakers who specialize in motivational speaking. Entertainment speeches are perhaps the rarest in the business world, and they are usually limited to after-dinner speeches and speeches at conventions or retreats. But no matter which kind of speech you plan to make, it will always start with understanding your audience.

Analyze Your Audience

LEARNING OUTCOME 2
Identify the audience characteristics that govern decisions about the style and content of speeches and presentations.

Once you have your purpose firmly in mind, you should think about another basic element of your speech or presentation–your audience. As Carol Stephenson would point out, analyzing your audience is an important step because you'll be gearing the style and content of your speech to your audience's needs and interests. When you're preparing to speak, be sure to review the discussion of audience analysis in Chapter 5. Of course, for even more insight into audience evaluation (including emotional and cultural issues) consult a good public-speaking textbook.

The nature of the audience affects your strategy for achieving your purpose.

If you're involved in selecting the audience, you'll certainly have information about their characteristics. However, you'll often be speaking to a group of people you know very little about. You'll have a much better chance of achieving your purpose if you investigate the audience's characteristics before you show up to speak. Ask your host or some other contact person for help with audience analysis, and supplement that information with some informed estimates of your own. The Checklist for Audience Analysis summarizes these points.

Gear the content, organization, and style of your message to the audience's size, background, and attitude.

Plan Your Speech or Presentation

LEARNING OUTCOME 3
Discuss four steps required in planning a speech or presentation.

Planning an oral message is similar to planning a written message. You establish the main idea, organize an outline, estimate the appropriate length, and decide on the most effective style.

The main idea points up how the audience can benefit from your message.

Mark Swartz is a career consultant, speaker, and author of *Get Wired, You're Hired*, a guide to using the Internet for job searches. He stresses that effective speakers take into account the needs of the audience, sticking to the agenda and the time limits, and maintaining a platform manner and speaking style that helps the audience understand and retain the message.

ESTABLISHING THE MAIN IDEA

What is the main idea, or theme, that you want to convey to the audience? Look for a one-sentence generalization that links your subject and purpose to the audience's frame of reference, much as an advertising slogan points out how a product can benefit consumers:

- Demand for low-calorie, high-quality frozen foods will increase because of basic social and economic trends.
- Reorganizing the data-processing department will lead to better service at a lower cost.
- We should build a new plant in Alberta to reduce operating costs and to capitalize on growing demand in the west.
- The new health plan reduces our costs by 12 percent while maintaining quality coverage.

Each of these statements puts a particular slant on the subject, one that is positive and directly related to the audience's interests. This sort of "you" attitude helps keep the audience's attention and convinces people that your points are relevant.

ORGANIZING AN OUTLINE

With a well-crafted main idea to guide you, you can begin to outline your speech or presentation. This outline will be affected by your subject, your purpose, and your audience, as well as by the time allotted for your presentation. If you have ten minutes or less to deliver your message, organize your thoughts much as you would for a letter or a brief memo. Use the direct approach if the subject involves routine information or good news; use the indirect approach if the subject involves bad news or persuasion. Plan your introduction to arouse interest and to give a preview of what's to come. For the body of the presentation, be prepared to explain the who, what, when, where, why, and how of your subject. In the final paragraph

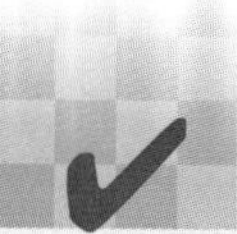

Checklist for Audience Analysis

A. Audience Size and Composition

1. Estimate how many people will attend.
2. Consider whether they have some political, religious, professional, or other affiliation in common.
3. Analyze the mix of men and women, age ranges, socioeconomic and ethnic groups, occupations, and geographical regions represented.

B. Probable Audience Reaction

1. Analyze why audience members are attending the speech or presentation.
2. Determine the audience's general attitude toward the topic.
   a. Decide whether the audience is very interested, moderately interested, or unconcerned.
   b. Find out how the audience has reacted to similar issues in the past.
   c. Determine which facets of the subject are most likely to appeal to the audience.
   d. Decide whether portions of your message will create problems for any members of the audience.
3. Analyze the mood that people will be in when you speak to them: tired from listening to other presentations like yours or fresh because your presentation comes early in the agenda; interested in hearing a unique presentation or restless from sitting too long in one position and needing a minute to stretch.
4. Figure out which sort of backup information will most impress the audience: technical data, statistical comparisons, cost figures, historical information, generalizations, demonstrations, samples, and so on.
5. Predict audience response.
   a. List ways that the audience will benefit from your message.

or two, review the points you've made, and close with a statement that will help your audience remember the subject of your speech (Figure 18.1).

Structure a short speech or presentation like a letter or a memo; organize long speeches and presentations like formal reports.

Long speeches and presentations are organized like reports (see Chapter 13 for specific suggestions). If the purpose is to entertain, motivate, or inform, use direct order and a structure imposed naturally by the subject (importance, sequence, chronology, spatial orientation, geography, category—as discussed in Chapter 13). If the purpose is to analyze, persuade, or collaborate, organize your material around conclusions and recommendations or around a logical argument. Use direct order if the audience is receptive and indirect if you expect resistance. Regardless of the length of your speech or presentation, bear in mind that simplicity of organization is especially useful in oral communication.

Use a clear, direct organization to accommodate your listeners' limitations.

A carefully prepared outline may be more than just the starting point for composing a speech or presentation. If you plan to deliver your presentation from notes rather than from a written text, your outline can also become your final script. The headings on this type of outline should be complete sentences or lengthy phrases rather than one- or two-word topic headings. Many speakers also include notes that indicate where visual aids will be used. You might want to write out the transitional sentences you'll use to connect main points. Experienced speakers often use a two-column format, which separates the "stage directions" from the content (Figure 18.2).

Use an outline as your script, but be prepared to deviate in response to audience feedback.

Presentation software can help you organize your speech. Packages such as PowerPoint and Freelance Graphics include special outline tools that simplify organizing and formatting your outline. Both provide a variety of ways to print notes and handouts. For example, PowerPoint allows you to view all your overhead transparencies and slides in thumbnails to help you choose the items you want to discuss and display.

Of course, you may have to adjust your organization in response to feedback from your audience, especially if your purpose is to collaborate. You can plan ahead by thinking of several organizational possibilities (based on "what if" assumptions about your audience's reactions). Then if someone says something that undercuts your planned approach, you can switch smoothly to another one.

b. Formulate an idea of the most desirable audience reaction and the best possible result (what you want the audience to believe or to do afterward).

c. Anticipate possible objections or questions.

d. Analyze the worst thing that might happen and how you might respond.

C. Level of Audience Understanding

1. Determine whether the audience already knows something about the subject.
   a. Analyze whether everybody has about the same amount of knowledge.
   b. Consider whether the audience is familiar with your vocabulary.
2. Estimate whether everybody is equally capable of understanding the message.
3. Decide what background information the audience will need to understand the subject.
4. Think about the mix of general concepts and specific details you will need to explain.
5. Consider whether the subject involves routine, recurring information or an unfamiliar topic.

D. Audience Relationship with the Speaker

1. Analyze how this audience usually reacts to speakers.
2. Determine whether the audience is likely to be friendly, open-minded, or hostile toward your purpose in making the speech or presentation.
3. Decide how the audience is likely to respond to you.
   a. Analyze what the audience expects from you.
   b. Think about your past interactions with the audience.
   c. Consider your relative status.
   d. Consider whether the audience has any biases that might work against you.
   e. Take into account the audience's probable attitude toward the organization you represent.
4. Decide which aspects of your background are most likely to build credibility.

This introduction will arouse interest and preview what is coming in the presentation.

Items II, III, and IV support the main idea (that an on-site fitness centre would be a good investment).

The conclusion will summarize all the evidence that makes the installation of the centre such a good business decision.

PHYSICAL FITNESS IS GOOD FOR BUSINESS

Purpose: To convince company officers to approve an on-site fitness centre.

I. Introduction

Mention the words *computer programmer,* and the picture that comes to mind is a person sitting in a cubicle and pounding away at a keyboard for 12 or more hours a day. This may be the stereotype, but it is outdated. Programmers and employees in general are more and more aware that physical activity makes them more healthy, happy and productive. Corporations have also learned the benefits of having healthy, fit employees.

II. The most obvious improvement is in lowered health costs. [slides]

A. People who are physically active generally are healthier and take fewer sick days.

B. Increased activity leads to better general health and fewer visits to the doctor, which means lower health insurance costs for the company and less absenteeism.

C. Better physical fitness results in a reduction in work-related injuries.

III. Improving employees' physical fitness increases company profitability.

A. Studies show that improved physical fitness increases employee productivity. [slide]

B. Physical activity also increases creativity.

IV. A survey of fourth-year university students showed fringe benefits to be the second most important factor (after salary) **in choosing a company.**

V. Conclusion: Installing an on-site fitness centre makes good business sense.

FIGURE 18.1

In-Depth Critique: Sample Outline for a Brief Speech

A human resources manager used this outline for a brief speech he delivered to persuade a group of executives to invest in an on-site fitness centre for employees.

ESTIMATING LENGTH

The average speaker can deliver about 125 to 150 words in a minute.

Time for speeches and presentations is often strictly regulated, so you'll need to tailor your material to the available time. You can use your outline to estimate how much time your speech or presentation will take. The average speaker can deliver about 125 to 150 words a minute (or roughly 7500 to 9000 words an hour), which corresponds to 20 to 25 double-spaced, typed pages of text an hour. The average paragraph is about 125 to 150 words in length, so most of us can speak at a rate of about one paragraph a minute.

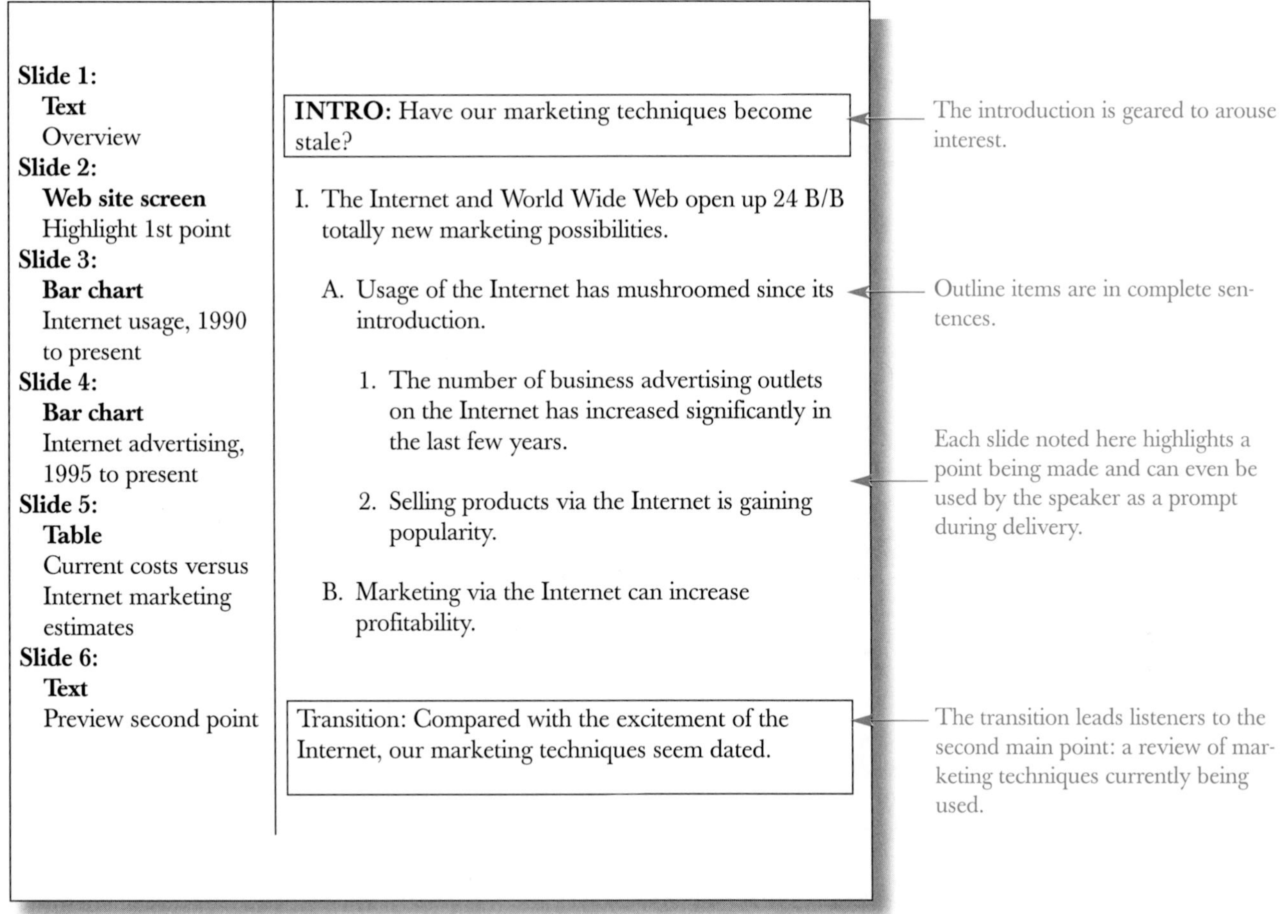
Slide 1:
Text
Overview
Slide 2:
Web site screen
Highlight 1st point
Slide 3:
Bar chart
Internet usage, 1990 to present
Slide 4:
Bar chart
Internet advertising, 1995 to present
Slide 5:
Table
Current costs versus Internet marketing estimates
Slide 6:
Text
Preview second point

INTRO: Have our marketing techniques become stale?

I. The Internet and World Wide Web open up 24 B/B totally new marketing possibilities.

A. Usage of the Internet has mushroomed since its introduction.

1. The number of business advertising outlets on the Internet has increased significantly in the last few years.

2. Selling products via the Internet is gaining popularity.

B. Marketing via the Internet can increase profitability.

Transition: Compared with the excitement of the Internet, our marketing techniques seem dated.

The introduction is geared to arouse interest.

Outline items are in complete sentences.

Each slide noted here highlights a point being made and can even be used by the speaker as a prompt during delivery.

The transition leads listeners to the second main point: a review of marketing techniques currently being used.

FIGURE 18.2

In-Depth Critique: Excerpt from Sample Outline with Delivery Notes

This excerpt is taken from a presentation that was made to persuade a company's marketing department to reassess its strategies.

Say you want to make three basic points. In a 10-minute speech, you could take about 2 minutes to explain each point, using roughly two paragraphs for each. If you devoted a minute each to the introduction and the conclusion, you would have 2 minutes left over to interact with the audience.

If you had an hour, however, you could spend the first 5 minutes introducing the presentation, establishing rapport with the audience, providing background information, and giving an overview of your topic. In the next 30 to 40 minutes, you could explain each of the three points, spending about 10 to 13 minutes on each point (the equivalent of five or six printed pages). Your conclusion might take another 3 to 5 minutes. The remaining 10 to 20 minutes would then be available for responding to questions and comments from the audience.

Be sure that your subject, purpose, and organization are compatible with the time available.

Which is better, the 10-minute speech or the hour-long presentation? If your speech doesn't have to fit into a specified time slot, the answer depends on your subject, your audience's attitude and knowledge, and the relationship you have with your audience. For a simple, easily accepted message, 10 minutes may be enough. On the other hand, if your subject is complex or your audience is skeptical, you'll probably need more time. Don't squeeze a complex presentation into a period that is too brief, and don't draw out a simple talk any longer than necessary.

DECIDING ON STYLE

Another important element in your planning is the style you choose. Will you present a formal speech in an impressive setting, with professionally produced visual aids? Or will you lead a casual, roll-up-your-sleeves working session? Choose your style to fit the occasion. The size of the audience, the subject, your purpose, your budget, and the time available for preparation all determine the style.

Use a casual style for small groups; use a formal style for large groups and important events.

In general, if you're speaking to a relatively small group, you can use a casual style that encourages audience participation. A small conference room, with the audience seated around a table, may be appropriate. Use simple visual aids. Invite the audience to interject comments. Deliver your remarks in a conversational tone, using notes to jog your memory if necessary.

On the other hand, if you're addressing a large audience and the event is an important one, you'll want to establish a more formal atmosphere. A formal style is well suited to announcements about mergers or acquisitions, new products, financial results, and other business milestones. During these formal presentations, the speakers generally stand behind a lectern on a stage or platform and use a microphone so that their remarks can be heard throughout the room. These speeches are often accompanied by multimedia presentations showcasing major products, technological breakthroughs, and other information that the speakers want audience members to remember.

Developing Your Speech or Presentation

LEARNING OUTCOME 4
Develop an introduction, a body, and a close for a long formal presentation.

Developing a major speech or presentation is much like writing a formal report, with one important difference: You need to adjust your technique to an oral communication channel. This channel presents both an opportunity and a challenge.

How formal speeches and presentations differ from formal reports:
- ✧ More interaction with the audience
- ✧ Use of non-verbal cues to express meaning
- ✧ Less control of content
- ✧ Greater need to help the audience stay on track

The *opportunity* lies in the interaction that is possible between you and the audience. When you speak before a group, you can receive information as well as transmit it. So you can adjust both the content and the delivery of your message as you go along, editing your speech or presentation to make it clearer and more compelling. Instead of simply expressing your ideas, you can draw out the audience's ideas and use them to reach a mutually acceptable conclusion.

To realize the benefits of oral communication, though, you need to plan carefully. The *challenge* of this channel is controlling what happens. As you develop each part of your speech or presentation, stop and think about how you plan to deliver the information. The more you plan to interact with your audience, the less control you'll have. Halfway through your presentation a comment from someone in the audience might force you to shift topics. If you can anticipate such shifts, you'll have a chance to prepare for them.

The Introduction

The introduction captures attention, inspires confidence, and previews the contents.

You'll have a lot to accomplish during the first few minutes of your speech or presentation, including arousing your audience's interest in your topic, establishing your credibility, and preparing the audience for what will follow. That's why preparing the introduction often requires a disproportionate amount of your attention.

AROUSING INTEREST

Connect the topic to the listeners' needs and interests.

Some subjects are naturally more interesting than others. If you will be discussing a matter of profound significance that will personally affect the members of your audience, chances are they'll listen regardless of how you begin. All you really have to do is announce your topic:

"Today I'd like to announce the reorganization of the company."

The best approach to dealing with an uninterested audience is to appeal to human nature. Encourage people to take the subject personally. Show them how they'll be affected as individuals. You might plan to begin your address to new clerical employees like this:

> If somebody offered to give you $200 000 in exchange for $5 per week, would you be interested? That's the amount you can expect to collect during your retirement years if you choose to contribute to the voluntary pension plan. During the next two weeks, you will have to decide whether you want to participate. Although for most of you retirement is many years away, this is an important financial decision. During the next 20 minutes, I hope to give you the information you need to make that decision intelligently.

Make sure your introduction matches the tone of your speech or presentation. If the occasion is supposed to be fun, you may begin with something light; but if you're talking business to a group of executives, don't waste their time with cute openings. Avoid jokes and personal anecdotes when you're discussing a serious problem. If you're giving a routine oral report, don't be overly dramatic. Most of all, be natural. Nothing turns off the average audience faster than a trite, staged beginning.

As founder of the consulting firm Success Strategies, Lynda R. Paulson addresses the "people needs" of companies of all sizes. A dynamic speaker, Paulson advises you to establish your credibility early on, including your listeners' acceptance of you and their respect for your opinion.

BUILDING CREDIBILITY

One of the chief drawbacks of overblown openings is that they damage the speaker's credibility, and building credibility is probably even more important than arousing interest. A speaker with high credibility is more persuasive than a speaker with low credibility.[2] So it's important to establish your credentials–and quickly; people will decide within a few minutes whether you're worth listening to.[3] You want

EFFECTIVE E-BUSINESS COMMUNICATION

Speeches That Live On and On

Ordinarily, a speech is a one-time event that helps you connect with a particular audience at a particular time and place. However, a Webcast speech, accessed through the company's Web site, can reach many thousands of people around the world. Companies such as Avon, Nike, and America Online use Webcast speeches to make live announcements of financial news, new products, and management changes, as shown on the Yahoo! Broadcast site. Webcast speeches are often available on the Web for later viewing, which increases the potential audience and keeps the message alive long after the speakers have left the podium.

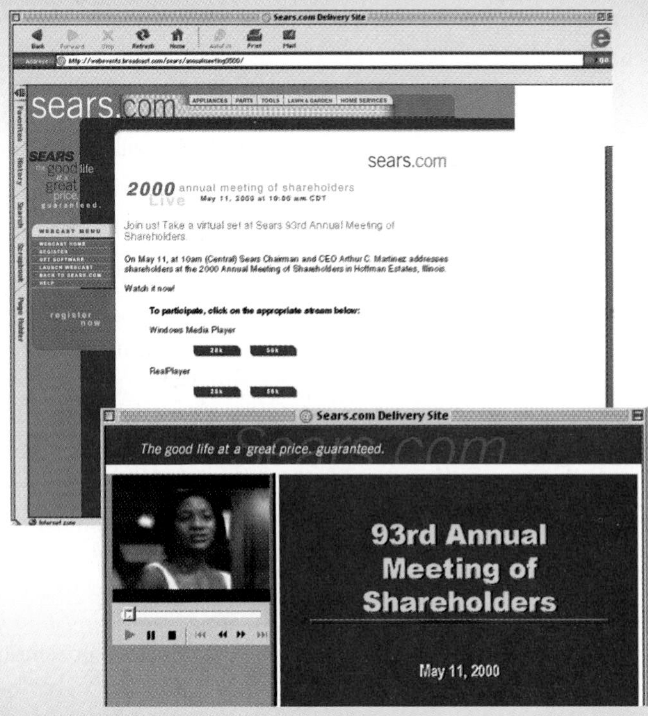

CAREER APPLICATIONS

1. What changes might you make to the text of your speech if you know it will be available on the Web for later viewing?
2. Would you use the same kind of visual aids for a Webcast speech and for a speech that will not be Webcast? Explain your answer.

A. Barry Rand is executive vice-president of operations for Xerox. Known as a persuasive and gifted speaker, Rand uses his talents to inspire employees and colleagues. "The more familiar you are with your subject, the better," says Rand. "Not only will you feel more comfortable during your speech, but your ease will come across as self-confidence."

the audience to like you as a person and to respect your opinion, and you have to plan for this while you're developing your speech.

Establishing credibility is relatively easy if you're speaking to a familiar, open-minded audience. The difficulty comes when you try to earn the confidence of strangers, especially those predisposed to be skeptical or antagonistic.

One way to handle the problem is to let someone else introduce you. That person can present your credentials so that you won't appear boastful, but make sure the person introducing you doesn't exaggerate your qualifications.

If you plan to introduce yourself, keep your comments simple. At the same time, don't be afraid to mention your accomplishments. Your listeners will be curious about your qualifications, so tell them briefly who you are and why you're there. Generally speaking, one or two aspects of your background are all you need to mention: your position in an organization, your profession, and the name of your company. You might plan to say something like this:

> I'm Jill Chen, a market research analyst with Information Resources Corporation. For the past five years, I've specialized in studying high-technology markets. Your director of engineering, John LaBarre, has asked me to brief you on recent trends in computer-aided design so that you'll have a better idea of how to direct your R&D efforts.

Without boasting, explain why you are qualified to speak on the subject.

This speaker would establish credibility by tying her credentials to the purpose of her presentation. By mentioning her company's name, her position, and the name of the audience's boss, she will let her listeners know immediately that she's qualified to tell them something they need to know. She connects her background to their concerns.

PREVIEWING THE PRESENTATION

Let the audience know what lies ahead.

Many effective speakers, like Carol Stephenson, strongly believe that you need to "tell them what you're going to tell them." Giving your audience a preview of what's ahead adds to your authority and, more importantly, helps people understand your message. In an oral presentation, the speaker provides the framework. Your introduction will summarize your main idea, identify the supporting points, and indicate the order in which you'll develop those points. Once you've established the framework, you can move into the body of the presentation, confident that the audience will understand how the individual facts and figures relate to your main idea.

The Body

Limit the body to three or four main points.

The bulk of your speech or presentation is devoted to a discussion of the three or four main points in your outline. Use the same organizational patterns you'd use in a letter, memo, or report, but keep things simple. Your goals are (1) to make sure the structure of your speech or presentation will be clear and (2) to make sure your speech will keep your audience's attention.

EMPHASIZING STRUCTURE

Help your audience follow your presentation
- ✧ By summarizing as you go along
- ✧ By emphasizing the transitions from one idea to the next

To show how ideas are related in an oral presentation, you rely more on words than you do in a written a report. For the small links between sentences and paragraphs, one or two transitional words are enough: *therefore, because, in addition, in contrast, moreover, for example, consequently, nevertheless, finally.* To link major sections of the speech or presentation, you need complete sentences or paragraphs, such as "Now that we've reviewed the problem, let's take a look at some solutions." Every time you shift topics, stress the connection between ideas. Summarize what's been said, and then preview what's to come.

The longer your presentation, the more important the transitions become. If you present many ideas, the audience will have trouble absorbing them and seeing the relationships among them. Listeners need clear transitions to guide them to the most important points. Furthermore, they need transitions to pick up any ideas they may have missed. If you plan to repeat key ideas in the transitions, you can compensate for lapses in the audience's attention. When you actually deliver your speech, you might also want to call attention to the transitions by using gestures, changing your tone of voice, or introducing a visual aid.

HOLDING THE AUDIENCE'S ATTENTION

To communicate your points effectively, you have to maintain the audience's attention. Here are a few tips for developing memorable speeches:

Make a special effort to capture wandering attention.

- *Relate your subject to the audience's needs.* People are interested in things that affect them personally. Plan to present every point in light of the audience's needs and values.
- *Use clear, vivid language.* People become bored quickly when they don't understand the speaker. If your presentation will involve abstract ideas, plan to show how those abstractions are connected with everyday life. Use familiar words, short sentences, and concrete examples.
- *Explain the relationship between your subject and familiar ideas.* Plan to show how your subject relates to ideas the audience already understands so that you give people a way to categorize and remember your points.[4]

You can also hold the audience's interest by introducing variety into your presentation. One useful technique is to pause occasionally for questions or comments from the audience. This technique helps you determine whether the audience understands key points before you launch into another section; it also gives the audience a chance to switch for a time from listening to participating. Visual aids will also help clarify points and stimulate interest.

The Close

The close of a speech or presentation is almost as important as the beginning because audience attention peaks at this point. Plan to devote about 10 percent of the total time to the ending. When developing your conclusion, begin by telling listeners that you're about to finish so that they'll make one final effort to listen intently. Don't be afraid to sound obvious. Consider saying something like "in conclusion" or "to sum it all up." You want people to know that this is the home stretch.

The close should leave a strong and lasting impression.

RESTATING THE MAIN POINTS

Once you've planned how to get everyone's attention, you'll repeat your main idea. Be sure to emphasize what you want the audience to do or think. Then state the key motivating factor. Reinforce your theme by repeating the three or four main supporting points. A few sentences are generally enough to refresh people's memories. Here's how one speaker ended a presentation on the company's executive compensation program:

Summarize the main idea, and restate the main points.

> We can all be proud of the way our company has grown. If we want to continue that growth, however, we will have to adjust our executive compensation program to reflect competitive practices. If we don't, our best people will look for opportunities elsewhere.
>
> In summary, our survey has shown that we need to do four things to improve executive compensation:

- Increase the overall level of compensation.
- Install a cash bonus program.
- Offer a variety of stock-based incentives.
- Improve our health insurance and pension benefits.

By making these improvements, we can help our company cross the threshold of growth into the major leagues.

The speaker repeats his recommendations and then concludes with a memorable statement that motivates the audience to take action.

DESCRIBING THE NEXT STEPS

Some speeches and presentations require the audience to reach a decision or agree to take specific action. In such cases the close provides a clear wrap-up. If the audience agrees on an issue covered in the presentation, plan to review the consensus in a sentence or two. If not, make the lack of consensus clear by saying something like "We seem to have some fundamental disagreement on this question." Then you'll be ready to suggest a method of resolving the differences.

Be certain that everyone agrees on the outcome and understands what should happen next.

If you expect any action to occur, you must explain who is responsible for doing what. One effective technique is to list the action items, with an estimated completion date and the name of the person responsible. Plan to present this list in a visual aid that can be seen by the entire audience, and ask each person on the list to agree to accomplish his or her assigned task by the target date. This public commitment to action is the best insurance that something will happen.

If the required action is likely to be difficult, make sure everyone understands the problems involved. You don't want people to leave the presentation thinking their tasks will be easy, only to discover later that the jobs are quite demanding. If that happens, they may become discouraged and fail to complete their assignments. You'll want everyone to have a realistic attitude and to be prepared to handle whatever arises. So when planning your presentation, use the close to alert people to potential difficulties.

ENDING ON A POSITIVE NOTE

Make sure that your final remarks are enthusiastic and memorable. Even if parts of your speech are downbeat, plan to close on a positive note. You might stress the benefits of action or express confidence in the listeners' ability to accomplish the work ahead. An alternative is to end with a question or a statement that will leave your audience thinking.

Be sure your close is natural as well as positive.

Remember that your final words round out the presentation. You'll want to leave the audience with a satisfied feeling, a feeling of completeness. The close is not the place to introduce new ideas or to alter the mood of the presentation. Although you want to close on a positive note, avoid using a staged finale. Keep it natural.

The Question-and-Answer Period

Along with the introduction, body, and close, include in your speech or presentation an opportunity for questions and answers. Otherwise, you might just as well write a report. If you aren't planning to interact with the audience, you're wasting the chief advantage of an oral format.

Encourage questions throughout your speech if you are addressing a small group, but ask a large audience to defer questions until later.

Specifics about handling questions from the audience are discussed in this chapter under the heading "Handling Questions." In general, the important things to consider when you're developing your speech are the nature and timing of audience interaction. Responding to questions and comments during the presentation can interrupt the flow of your argument and reduce your control of the situation. If you'll be addressing a large group, particularly a hostile or an unknown group, questions can be dangerous. Your best bet in this case is to ask people to hold their questions until after you have concluded your remarks. On the other hand, if you're working with a small group and need to draw out ideas, encourage comments from the audience throughout the presentation.

LEARNING OUTCOME 5
Select, design, and use visual aids that are appropriate for various types of speeches and presentations.

The Visual Aids

Visual aids create interest and clarify ideas. From a purely practical standpoint, visuals are a convenience for the speaker, who can use them as a tool for remembering the details of the message (no small feat in a lengthy presentation). Novice speakers also like visual aids because they draw audience attention away from the speaker. More important, visual aids dramatically increase the audience's ability to absorb and remember information.

Visual aids help both the speaker and the audience remember the important points.

DESIGNING AND PRESENTING VISUAL AIDS

Two types of visual aids are used to supplement speeches and presentations. **Text visuals** consist of words and help the audience follow the flow of ideas. Because text visuals are simplified outlines of your presentation, you can use them to summarize and preview the message and to signal major shifts in thought. On the other hand, **graphic visual aids** can illustrate the main points. They help the audience grasp numerical data and other information that would be hard to follow if presented only orally.

Two kinds of visual aids:
- ✧ Text visuals help listeners follow the flow of ideas.
- ✧ Graphic visuals present and emphasize important facts.

Simplicity is the key to effectiveness when designing both types of visual aids. Because people can't read and listen at the same time, the visual aids have to be simple enough for the audience to understand within a moment or two. As a rule, text visuals are most effective when they consist of no more than six lines, with a maximum of six words on each line. Produce them in large, clear type, using initial caps with lowercase lettering, and extra white space between lines of text. (All-capital letters are harder to read.) Make sure the type is large enough to be seen from any place in the room. Phrase list items in parallel grammatical form. Use telegraphic wording ("Compensation Soars," for example) without being cryptic ("Compensation"); including both a noun and a verb in each item is a good rule of thumb.

Visual aids are counterproductive if the audience can't clearly see or understand them within a few moments.

You can use any of the graphic visuals you might show in a formal report, including line, pie, and bar charts, as well as flowcharts, organization charts, diagrams, maps, drawings, and tables. However, graphic visuals used in oral presentations are usually *simplified* versions of those that appear in written documents. Eliminate anything that is not absolutely essential to the message. To help the audience focus immediately on the point of each graphic visual, use headings that state the message in one clear phrase or sentence: "Earnings have increased by 15 percent."

Children's book illustrator Chris K. Soentpiet (pronounced "soon-pete"), illustrator of *Peacebound Trains*, *The Last Dragon*, and other books, never dreamed he'd be travelling to schools to give inspirational talks, but now he enjoys it. He's learned to enliven speeches with anecdotes from his unique experiences as an adopted child, as a youthful success in a difficult career, and as one-half of a successful husband-wife business team.

When you present visual aids, you want people to have the chance to read what's there, but you also want them to listen to your explanation:

- ➤ Make sure that all members of the audience can see the visual aids.
- ➤ Allow the audience time to read a visual before you begin your explanation.
- ➤ Limit each visual to one idea.
- ➤ Illustrate only the main points, not the entire presentation.
- ➤ Avoid visual aids that conflict with your verbal message.
- ➤ Paraphrase the text of your visual aid; don't read it word for word.
- ➤ When you've finished discussing the point illustrated by the visual, remove it from the audience's view.[5]

The visual aids are there to supplement your words–not the other way around.

SELECTING THE RIGHT MEDIUM

Visual aids may be presented in a variety of media.

Visual aids for documents are usually limited to paper. For speeches and presentations, however, you can choose from a variety of media:

- *Handouts.* Even in an oral presentation, you may choose to distribute sheets of paper bearing an agenda, an outline of the program, an abstract, a written report, or supplementary material such as tables, charts, and graphs. Listeners can keep the handout to remind them of the subject and the main ideas of your presentation. In addition, they can refer to it while you're speaking. Handouts work especially well in informal situations in which the audience takes an active role; they often make their own notes on the handouts. However, handouts can be distracting because people are inclined to read the material rather than listen to you, so many speakers distribute handouts after the presentation.
- *Chalkboards and whiteboards.* When you're addressing a small group of people and want to draw out their ideas, use a board to list points as they are mentioned. Because visual aids using boards are produced on the spot, they provide flexibility. However, they're too informal for some situations.
- *Flip charts.* Large sheets of paper attached at the top like a tablet can be propped on an easel so that you can flip the pages as you speak. Each chart illustrates or clarifies a point. You might have a few lines from your outline on one, a graph or diagram on another, and so on. By using felt-tip markers of various colours, you can highlight ideas as you go along. Keep it simple–try to limit each flip-chart page to three or four graphed lines or to five or six points in list format.
- *Overheads.* One of the most common visual aids in business is the overhead transparency, which can be projected on a screen in full daylight. Because you don't have to dim the lights, you don't lose eye contact with your audience. Transparencies are easy to make using a typed original on regular paper, a copying machine, and a page-size sheet of plastic. Opaque projections are similar to transparencies but do not require as much preparation. You could use an opaque projector to show the audience a photograph or an excerpt from a report or manual.
- *Slides.* The content of slides may be text, graphics, or pictures. If you're trying to create a polished, professional atmosphere, you might find this approach worthwhile, particularly if you'll be addressing a crowd and don't mind speaking in a darkened room. However, remember that you may need someone to operate the projector and that you'll need to coordinate the slides with your speech. Take a few minutes before your speech to verify that the equipment works correctly.
- *Computers.* With special projection equipment, a personal computer can be turned into a large-screen "intelligent chalkboard" that allows you to create and modify your visual aids as the presentation unfolds. If you're discussing financial projections, you can type in a new number to show how a change in sales will affect profits. When the presentation is over, you can print out hard copies of the visual aids and distribute them to interested members of the audience. With this technology, you can prepare a multimedia presentation incorporating photos, sound, video, and animation.[6]
- *Other visual aids.* In technical or scientific presentations, a sample of a product or material allows the audience to experience your subject directly. Models built to scale are convenient representations of an object. Audiotapes are often used to supplement a slide show or to present a precisely worded and timed message. Filmstrips and movies can capture the audience's attention with colour and movement. Television and videotapes are good for showing demonstrations, interviews, and other events. In addition, filmstrips, movies, television, and videotapes can be used as stand-alone vehicles (independent of a speaker) to com-

Going Online

Speak Like a Pro

The Virtual Presentation Assistant offers leads to dozens of sites containing valuable help for business speakers and presenters. If you're stuck for a topic, need a good quote, want some speaking advice, need ideas and support for your ideas, want to link your topic to current events overseas, or just want to browse the latest tips or borrow some techniques from the experts, click on a few of the links provided here. Your thoughts will soon be filled with new material and renewed enthusiasm for your speaking project.

www.ukans.edu/cwis/units/coms2/vpa/vpa9.htm

municate with dispersed audiences at various times. For example, PepsiCo's CEO, Wayne Calloway, videotapes many of his important presentations and sends them to all the company's operating divisions to keep employees updated on the business.[7]

Table 18.1 summarizes some of the factors to consider when selecting a visual medium.

With all visual aids, the crucial factor is how you use them. Properly integrated into an oral presentation, they can save time, create interest, add variety, make an impression, and illustrate points that are difficult to explain in words alone.

Use visual aids to highlight your spoken words, not as a substitute for them.

Mastering the Art of Delivery

When you've planned all the parts of your presentation and have your visual aids in hand, you're ready to begin practising your delivery. Of the four main delivery methods, some are easier to handle than others:

- *Memorizing.* Unless you're a trained actor, avoid memorizing an entire speech, particularly a long one. You're likely to forget your lines. Furthermore, a memorized speech often sounds stiff and stilted. And in many business speaking situations, you'll need to address questions and comments from the audience during your speech, so you have to be flexible and sometimes adjust your speech as you go. On the other hand, memorizing a quotation, an opening paragraph, or a few concluding remarks can bolster your confidence and strengthen your delivery.

TABLE 18.1 Guidelines for Selecting Visuals

Visual	Optimal Audience Size	Degree of Formality	Design Complexity	Equipment and Room Requirements	Production Time	Cost
Handouts	Fewer than 110	Informal	Simple	Typed text and photocopying machine	Typing or drawing time; photocopying time	Inexpensive
Boards and flip charts	Fewer than 20	Informal	Simple	Chalkboard or whiteboard or easel and chart, with writing implements	Drawing time only	Inexpensive
Overheads	About 100	Formal or informal	Simple	Text, copy machine, plastic sheets, and projector screen	Drawing or typing time; photocopying time	Inexpensive—unless designed or typeset professionally
Slides	Several hundred	Formal	Anything that can be photographed	Slides, projector, and screen; dim lighting	Design and photographing time; at least 24 hours' production time	More expensive

- *Reading*. If you're delivering a technical or complex presentation, you may want to read it. Policy statements by government officials are sometimes read because the wording may be critical. If you choose to read your speech, practise enough so that you can still maintain eye contact with the audience. Triple-spaced copy, wide margins, and large type help too. You might even want to include stage cues for yourself, such as *pause, raise hands, lower voice*.

Speaking from notes is generally the best way to handle delivery.

- *Speaking from notes*. Making a presentation with the help of an outline, note cards, or visual aids is probably the most effective and easiest delivery mode. It gives you something to refer to and still allows for eye contact and interaction with the audience. If your listeners look puzzled, you can expand on a point or put it another way. (Note cards are generally preferable to sheets of paper; nervousness is more evident in shaking sheets of paper.)
- *Impromptu speaking*. You might give an impromptu, or unrehearsed, speech in two situations: when you've agreed to speak but have neglected to prepare your remarks or when you're called on to speak unexpectedly. Avoid speaking unprepared unless you've spoken countless times on the same topic or are an extremely good public speaker. When you're asked to speak off-the-cuff, take a moment or two to think through what you're going to say. Avoid the temptation to ramble.

Regardless of which delivery mode you use, be sure that you're thoroughly familiar with the subject. Knowing what you're talking about is the best way to build your self-confidence. It's also helpful to know how you'll approach preparing for successful speaking, delivering the speech, and handling questions.

BEHIND THE SCENES WITH LEANN ANDERSON

Improving Your Podium Power

When Leann Anderson prepares a speech, she doesn't worry about whether her audience is going to like her; instead she focuses on how she can offer useful information to her audience. As the owner of Anderson Business Resources, Anderson helps business people improve their business relationships by showing them how to enhance their image and become better public speakers. Anderson advises her clients to "know as much as possible about your audience." By understanding your audience, "you can create examples specifically for them, personalize your message, avoid sensitive topics, and appeal to the most important issues on their minds."

When Leann Anderson helps business people improve their public-speaking skills, she emphasizes learning as much as possible about the audience they will be addressing.

Anderson learns about her audience by being an active listener—something she believes is an essential skill for successful business people. Whether she is consulting with clients on how to project a favourable image or lecturing to university students on how to survive after they graduate, Anderson always focuses on giving something of value to her audience. She anticipates her audience's needs, carefully selects her topic, does extensive research, organizes her thoughts, and prepares her speeches meticulously. "Too many people wait until the last minute to work on their speeches, and once they've finished writing their rough drafts, they have no time left to edit and revise them."

Anderson advocates being a ruthless editor. "Most of us fall in love with our own words, and our presentations get too long and complicated. A good speech is built on an intriguing introduction, a substantive body, and a memorable conclusion. Eliminate anything that is not truly necessary to make your talk more interesting. Keep sentences simple, work from an outline if possible, and highlight key points. If you use generalized statements, be sure to follow them with specific examples and facts. Support your points with evidence, anec-

Getting Ready to Give Your Presentation

Before you speak
✧ Practise
✧ Prepare the location

In addition to knowing your material, you can build self-confidence by practising, especially if you haven't had much experience with public speaking. Even if you practise in front of a mirror, try to visualize the room filled with listeners. Put your talk on tape to check the sound of your voice and your timing, phrasing, and emphasis. If possible, rehearse on videotape to see yourself as your audience will. Go over your visual aids and coordinate them with the talk.

Whenever you can, check the location for your presentation in advance. Look at the seating arrangements, and make sure they're appropriate for your needs. If you want the audience to sit at tables, be sure tables are available. Check the room for outlets that may be needed for your projector or microphone. Locate the light switches and dimmers. If you need a flip-chart easel or a chalkboard, be sure it's on hand. Check for chalk, an eraser, extension cords, and any other small but crucial items you might need.

If you're addressing an audience that doesn't speak your language, consider using an interpreter. Of course, any time you make a speech or presentation to people from other cultures, you should take into account cultural differences in appearance, mannerisms, and other customs in addition to adapting the content of your speech. If you are working with an interpreter, the interpreter will be able to suggest appropriate changes for the audience or occasion. You will find useful suggestions in this chapter's box for Achieving Intercultural Communication.

dotes, and data to strengthen your message and reinforce your position as an expert."

However, being an expert is not enough. "Learn to be conversational. Cultivate the art of small talk—be an interesting person first; then be an expert in your field. When you talk to people, make them feel at ease with you—then they will be in a frame of mind to accept what you have to offer. When writing a speech, use *we* and *you* frequently to make your talk seem like more of a dialogue. Ask yourself, does that sound like something a person would say naturally—you have to sound conversational."

One way to increase your conversational ability is by reading magazines, books, journals, and newspapers. Anderson knows the value of being well-informed when preparing and delivering speeches, so she clips articles, collects meaningful quotes, jots down ideas, and collects words. "Words can distinguish you from others. By using visual words you catch people off guard, and they pay attention to what you have to say. ... For example, consider the words *seamless* and *embroidered*; both are visual words and have a greater impact than the words *smooth* and *included.* Economy of language is the real key to good communication—that means choosing the best way of saying something to get the desired result."

In fact, getting results is one of the many reasons Anderson's clients seek her advice. "If entrepreneurs knew how much they could improve the health of their businesses by becoming effective public speakers, more of them would jump on the bandwagon. ... When you are successful as a public speaker, most people will assume you are a successful business person too." So Anderson offers this advice: "Fine-tune your public-speaking skills. Be prepared and rehearse more than you think you need. The more you practise, the more confident and relaxed you will be." Anderson cautions speakers to "inject your personality into the speech. Have some fun with it. ... Stop concentrating on 'Will they like me?' and instead focus on 'What will they gain from hearing me?' "

APPLY YOUR KNOWLEDGE

1. Using the information in this chapter and the recommendations by Leann Anderson, discuss what it means to "fall in love with your own words," and why it is important not to do this.
2. List some of the things you should know about your audience before preparing a speech.

Delivering the Speech

LEARNING OUTCOME 6
Explain techniques you can use to improve your public-speaking skills.

When it's time to deliver the speech, you may feel a bit of stage fright. Many people do, even professional actors. A good way to overcome your fears is to rehearse until you're thoroughly familiar with your material.[8] Communication professionals have suggested other tips:

A little stage fright is normal.

- Prepare more material than necessary. Extra knowledge, combined with a genuine interest in the topic, will boost your confidence.
- Think positively about your audience, yourself, and what you have to say. See yourself as polished and professional, and your audience will too.
- Be realistic about stage fright. After all, even experienced speakers admit that they feel butterflies before they address an audience. A little nervous excitement can actually provide the extra lift that will make your presentation sparkle.
- Use the few minutes while you're arranging your materials, before you actually begin speaking, to tell yourself you're on and you're ready.
- Before you begin speaking, take a few deep breaths.
- Have your first sentence memorized and on the tip of your tongue.
- If your throat is dry, drink some water.
- If you feel that you're losing your audience during the speech, don't panic. Try to pull them back by involving them in the action.
- Use your visual aids to maintain and revive audience interest.
- Keep going. Things usually get better, and your audience will silently be wishing you success.

Perhaps the best way to overcome stage fright is to concentrate on your message and your audience, not on yourself. When you're busy thinking about your subject and observing the audience's response, you tend to forget your fears. Even so, as you deliver your presentation, try to be aware of the non-verbal signals you're transmitting. To a great degree, your effectiveness will depend on how you look and sound.

Don't rush the opening.

As you approach the speaker's lectern, breathe deeply, stand up straight, and walk slowly. Face the audience. Adjust the microphone. Count to three slowly; then survey the room. When you find a friendly face, make eye contact and smile. Count to three again; then begin your presentation.[9] Even if you feel nervous inside, this slow, controlled beginning will help you establish rapport.

Use eye contact, posture, gestures, and voice to convey an aura of mastery and to keep your audience's attention.

Once your speech is under way, be particularly careful to maintain eye contact with the audience. Pick out several people positioned around the room, and shift your gaze from one to another. Doing this will make you appear to be sincere, confident, and trustworthy; moreover, it will help you perceive the impression you're creating.

Your posture is also important in projecting the right image. Stand tall, with your weight on both feet and your shoulders back. Avoid gripping the lectern. In fact, you might step out from behind the lectern to help the audience feel more comfortable with you and to express your own comfort and confidence in what you're saying. Use your hands to emphasize your remarks with appropriate gestures. At the same time, vary your facial expressions to make the message more dynamic.

Finally, think about the sound of your voice. Studies indicate that people who speak with low voice tones at a slightly faster than average rate are perceived as being most credible.[10] Speak in a normal, conversational tone but with enough volume so that everyone in the audience can hear you. Try to sound poised and confident, varying your pitch and speaking rate to add emphasis. Don't ramble or use meaningless filler words such as *um, you know, okay,* and *like.* Speak clearly and crisply, articulating all the syllables, and sound enthusiastic about what you're saying.

ACHIEVING INTERCULTURAL COMMUNICATION

Five Tips for Making Presentations Around the World

In any successful presentation, getting your message across to an audience requires clear communication. But how can you communicate successfully with members of an international audience—especially if their fluency in your language ranges from expert to novice?

1. **Speak slowly and distinctly.** The most common complaint of international audiences is that English speakers talk too fast. If you speak too rapidly, your less-fluent listeners will be lost. Articulate every word carefully. Emphasize consonants for clarity, and make frequent pauses so that the audience will have time to absorb each key point.
2. **Repeat key words and phrases.** When audiences are less familiar with your language, they need to hear important information more than once. In addition, they may not be familiar with numerous synonyms, so refer to key points in the same way throughout your presentation. If you introduce the concept of *benefits*, for example, continue to use the same word. Don't refer to *advantages* later on.
3. **Aim for clarity.** Keep your message simple. Eliminate complex sentence structure, abbreviations, and acronyms. Avoid two-word verbs such as *look over* and *check out*. Such verbs are confusing because the definition of each separate word differs from the meaning of the two words combined. For clearer communication, use one specific term (substitute *review* for *look over*; *examine* for *check out*; *write* for *jot down*; *return* for *drop by*). Also, stay away from cultural idioms, such as "once in a blue moon," which may be unfamiliar to an international audience.
4. **Communicate with body language.** Establish a relationship with your audience through strong eye contact. And don't forget to smile! Smiles and other facial expressions are universally recognized. Moreover, multilingual audiences pay close attention to a speaker's body language to get clues about the meanings of unfamiliar words. For example, prepositions can often be confusing to multilingual listeners, so use gestures to illustrate the meaning of words such as *up*, *down*, or *under*.
5. **Support your oral message with visual aids.** For most audiences, visual messages support and clarify spoken words. Develop handouts, flip charts, or slides for your presentation, using simple words to describe your key points. To eliminate problems with rapid speech, unclear pronunciations, or strange accents, prepare captions both in English and in your audience's native language. Avoid confusion about quantities by presenting numbers in graphs or pie charts and by converting financial figures into local currency.

CAREER APPLICATIONS

1. As marketing director for an international corporation, you will be making a presentation to the company's marketing representatives in Germany. How will you communicate company goals and sales projections clearly?
2. Make a list of 10 two-word verbs. How does the meaning of each separate word differ from the definition of the combined words? Replace each two-word verb with a single, specific word that will be clearer to an international audience.

Handling Questions

Carol Stephenson believes that preparation is the key to handling questions effectively. Spend time before your speech thinking about the questions that might arise–including abrasive or difficult questions. Then be ready with answers. In fact, some experts recommend that you hold back some dramatic statistics as ammunition for the question-and-answer session.[11] Bear in mind, however, that circumstances may require some changes in the answers you've prepared.

Keep your answers short and to the point.

When someone poses a question, focus your attention on that individual. Pay attention to body language and facial expression to help determine what the person really means. Nod your head to acknowledge the question; then repeat it aloud to confirm your understanding and to ensure that the entire audience has heard it. If the question is vague or confusing, ask for clarification. Then give a simple, direct answer. Don't say more than you need to if you want to have enough time to cover all the questions. If giving an adequate answer would take too long, simply say, "I'm sorry, we don't have time to get into that issue right now, but if you'll see me after the presentation, I'll be happy to discuss it with you." If you don't know the answer, don't pretend that you do. Instead, say something like "I don't have those figures. I'll get them for you as soon as possible." Remember that you don't have to answer every question that is asked.

Don't let any member of the audience monopolize your attention or turn a question into a debate.

Don't allow one or two people to monopolize the question period. Try to give everyone a chance to participate; call on people from different parts of the room. If the same person keeps angling for attention, say something like "Several other people have questions; I'll get back to you if time permits." If audience members try to turn a question into an opportunity to mount their own soapboxes, it's up to you to maintain control. You might admit that you and the questioner have a difference of opinion and offer to get back to the questioner after you've done more research. Then call on someone else. Another approach is to respond with a brief answer, thus avoiding a lengthy debate or additional questions.[12] Finally, you might thank the person for the question and then remind the questioner that you were looking for specific questions. Don't indulge in put-downs, which may backfire and make the audience more sympathetic to the questioner.

When the time allotted for your presentation is up, call a halt to the question-and-answer session, even if more people want to talk. Prepare the audience for the end by saying: "Our time is almost up. Let's have one more question." After you've made your reply, summarize the main idea of the presentation and thank people for their attention. Conclude the way you opened: by looking around the room and making eye contact. Then gather your notes and leave the podium, shoulders straight, head up. The Checklist for Speeches and Oral Presentations is a reminder of the tasks involved in these types of oral communication.

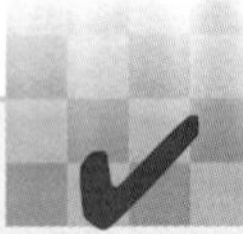

Checklist for Speeches and Oral Presentations

A. Development of the Speech or Presentation

1. Analyze the audience.
2. Begin with an attention-getter.
3. Preview the main points.
4. Limit the discussion to no more than three or four points.
5. Explain who, what, when, where, why, and how.
6. In longer presentations, include previews and summaries of major points as you go along.
7. Close by reviewing your main points and making a memorable statement.

B. Visual Aids

1. Use visual aids to show how things look, work, or are related to one another.
2. Use visual aids to highlight important information and to create interest.
3. Select appropriate visual aids.
   a. Use flip charts, boards, or transparencies for small, informal groups.
   b. Use slides or films for major occasions and large groups.
4. Limit each visual aid to three or four graphed lines or five or six points.
5. Use short phrases.
6. Use large, readable type.
7. Make sure equipment works.

C. Delivery

1. Establish eye contact.
2. Speak clearly and distinctly.
3. Do not go too fast.
4. Be sure everyone can hear.
5. Speak in your natural style.
6. Stand up straight.
7. Use gestures in a natural, appropriate way.
8. Encourage questions.
   a. Allow questions during the presentation if the group is small.
   b. Ask the audience to hold their questions until the end if the group is large or hostile.
9. Respond to questions without getting sidetracked.
10. Maintain control of your feelings despite criticism.

ON THE JOB
Solving a Communication Dilemma at Lucent Technologies Canada

In a speech called "The Female Style of Leadership," Carol Stephenson recalls the influences that gave her self-confidence and the values that would shape her management style. She says she was fortunate to "grow up with excellent female role models"—her grandmother, a co-owner and manager of a business college, and her mother, a nurse, who gave her "a determination to succeed." Stephenson also discovered that the "ferocious debates" around the family dinner table in her youth also shaped her management style. When the discussion "got too heated," she became the conciliator, showing her family where opposing opinions overlapped.

An early management job as a plant manager in a Bell Canada switching centre in downtown Toronto was an opportunity to put her values to work. The first female in this position, managing 60 male employees, Stephenson was told that she had accepted an "impossible job" and that she didn't have the technical skills to do it. But Stephenson has said that this job was one of the most successful and easiest she had ever assumed. The employees' main complaint was that they had been over-managed, and resented supervisors who tried to tell them what to do when they already knew how to do it. Stephenson's approach was to let them do the work without interference. She told them that she was there as a "resource person," to answer to their needs and requests, but would let them manage themselves as long as their performance levels stayed high. In the end, both Stephenson and her employees were satisfied.

A senior Bell executive, Owen McAleer, became her mentor. He encouraged Stephenson to communicate widely, within the company to employees and outside to customers, competitors, and the general public. As Stephenson's career progressed, she completed executive programs in Berkeley, California and at Harvard. During her twenty-year career at Bell Canada, from 1973 to 1993, her four-year tenure at Stentor Resource Centre, the now-disbanded alliance of nine Canadian telephone companies, from 1994 to 1998, her brief, six-month stay at BCE Media, and her current position as CEO of Lucent Technologies Canada, Stephenson has been applying her own management style of listening and conciliating between opposing groups. Through her speeches, she advises Canada's managers to "embrace communications, truth, and trust as their most precious skills." She says that a leader must "communicate a powerful vision and motivate others to buy into it." Lucent Technologies, a major manufacturer of telecommunications networks, software, and hardware, has 120 000 employees in more than 65 countries and territories around the world. Stephenson leads 350 employees across Canada from Lucent Canada's headquarters in Markham, Ontario.

Your Mission: As a member of Lucent Technologies Canada's corporate communications team, you help to write some of the speeches Carol Stephenson delivers to business and professional associations, civic and social groups, and employees. For the following assignments, choose the best solution and be prepared to explain your choice.[13]

1. Stephenson has agreed to give a 20-minute talk in Yorkton, Saskatchewan, to a group of approximately 35 business people who meet for lunch and networking on a monthly basis. The president of the group has suggested that Stephenson deal with the topic of e-commerce, conducting business over the Internet. Which of the following purposes do you think she should try to accomplish?
   a To inform the audience about the history of e-commerce in Canada.
   b. To inspire members of the audience to conduct business over the Internet if they haven't yet started doing so.
   c. To entertain the audience with stories about her previous experiences in the telecommunications industry.
   d. To analyze the impact of e-commerce on small, independently owned local businesses.
2. Stephenson has asked you to help plan a ten-minute speech that she can give to her Lucent employees in Markham, Ontario at the opening of the new Canadian headquarters. Management expects almost all the employees who work at that location to attend. Stephenson's speech is intended to celebrate the opening of the new, state-of-the-art building, where a "smart" cabling system handles all information traffic—voice, data, video. What general organizational scheme do you recommend for developing the theme of Stephenson's speech?
   a. *Chronological*: Highlights of Lucent Technologies' innovations over the years.
   b. *Geographical*: Descriptions of other "smart" buildings Lucent Technologies has constructed for its employees and operations.
   c. *Topical*: The contributions of Lucent Technologies' Canadian employees that have made Canada a world leader in telecommunications and have led to the construction of the new headquarters.
   d. *Comparison and contrast*: Lucent Technologies offices and the offices of competitors in the telecommunications industry.
3. You are helping Carol Stephenson write a speech on the *Communication Revolution*, which she will deliver to the Empire Club of Canada, an association of prominent business leaders. You are working on the introduction of the speech. Do you
   a. Begin with the first main point of the speech?
   b. Begin with background information about Carol Stephenson and then the first main point of the speech?
   c. Begin with some intriguing facts about modern electronic communications and then the first main point of speech?

d. Begin with information about Lucent Technologies and then the first main point of the speech?

4. In her role as CEO of Lucent Technologies Canada, Stephenson gives speeches about partnerships with telecommunications firms and acquisitions. You are helping her prepare a speech about a five-year, $400 million contract with Sprint Canada for network technology, equipment, and software. She is to deliver this speech to a group of about 25 financial advisers. How should you have her handle the quantitative financial details?
   a. You should prepare handouts that summarize the financial data in tabular and graphic form. As the audience arrives, a Lucent employee should give everyone a copy of the handout to refer to during the speech.
   b. Stephenson should write the information on a chalkboard while she delivers the speech.
   c. You should prepare simple overhead transparencies for Stephenson to use during the speech. As she concludes the speech, she should tell the audience that more detailed financial statements are available at the door for those who are interested.
   d. Given the size of the audience, you will prepare a software presentation, such as PowerPoint or Freelance, that summarizes the financial information in tabular and graphic forms. Stephenson is familiar with the technology used to display this kind of presentation.

TAP Your Knowledge

Summary of Learning Outcomes

1. Categorize speeches and presentations according to their purpose. Speeches and presentations are given to inform, persuade, motivate, or entertain. Many of your business presentations will be informative, educating your audience on a topic of concern or interest to them. Persuasive speeches try to sell a product or idea to an audience. Motivational speeches tend to be quite specialized, and companies may bring in outside speakers to deliver them. Entertainment speeches are usually limited to after-dinner speeches and speeches delivered at conventions or retreats.

2. Identify the audience characteristics that govern decisions about the style and content of speeches and presentations. Your audience's needs and interests will affect what you will say and how you will say it. To deliver an effective presentation, be sure to determine the size and composition of your audience, their probable reaction to your topic and purpose, their level of understanding, and whether they will be friendly, open-minded, or hostile toward your purpose in making the presentation.

3. Discuss four steps required in planning a speech or presentation. Apply the steps for planning written messages to your oral ones. First, establish the main idea, or what you want to convey to the audience. Construct a one-sentence generalization that highlights how the audience can benefit from your message. Second, prepare an outline, which may become your speaking notes or script. Third, estimate the length of your speech, because the delivery time will be strictly regulated. Tailor your delivery to the allotted time. Finally, decide on your speaking style: choose your style to fit the occasion. Mostly, you will choose a casual style for small groups, and a formal style for large groups and important events.

4. Develop an introduction, a body, and a close for a long formal presentation. As you develop each part of your speech, you must make sure that you accomplish specific tasks. In the introduction, you must arouse audience interest, build your credibility, and preview your presentation. In the body, you must connect your ideas and hold your audience's attention. In the close, you must restate your main points, describe the next steps, and end on a positive note. And in the question-and-answer period, you must plan how to control the situation and anticipate both questions and criticisms.

5. Select, design, and use visual aids that are appropriate for various types of speeches and presentations. Text visuals help listeners follow the flow of ideas; graphic visuals present and emphasize important facts. Simplicity is the key to effective visuals. Audiences need to be able to understand the visual in just a moment or two. So, text visuals should have no more than six lines of text, with not more than six words per line. Graphic visuals must be simplified versions of what would appear in a written report. The most effective visuals adhere to the following guidelines: limit each visual to one idea; illustrate your main points (not your entire presentation); and avoid visuals that conflict with your verbal message. Paraphrase the text of your visual, rather than read it word for word. Remove the visual aid from the audience's view when you've finished discussing the point it illustrates.

6. Explain techniques you can use to improve your public-speaking skills. Stage fright is common among speakers. To overcome this normal feeling, apply the following techniques: (1) Prepare more material than necessary; extra knowledge will increase your confidence. (2) Be realistic about stage fright, because all speakers experience it, and think positively about your audience. (3) Memorize your first sentence. (4) Take a few deep breaths to help yourself relax, and drink some water if your throat is dry. (5) Use visuals to maintain audience interest. (6) Keep going–your audience will be wishing you success.

Test Your Knowledge

Review Questions

1. What is the purpose of defining the main idea of a speech?
2. What is the relationship of your outline to your speech?
3. Why do you have to limit your scope when planning a presentation?
4. What do you want to achieve with the introduction part of your speech? With the close of your speech?
5. How can you hold your audience's attention when delivering a speech or presentation?
6. What types of visuals are commonly used in presentations?
7. How do you build credibility in your speech?
8. How does the delivery method of impromptu speaking differ from the delivery method of speaking from notes?
9. As a speaker, what non-verbal signals can you send to appear more confident?
10. What can speakers do to maintain control during the question-and-answer period of a presentation?

Apply Your Knowledge

Critical Thinking Questions

1. Would you rather (a) give a speech to an outside audience, (b) be interviewed for a news story, or (c) make a presentation to a departmental meeting? Why? How do the communication skills differ in each situation? Explain.
2. How might the audience's attitude affect the amount of audience interaction during or after a presentation? Explain your answer.
3. Have you ever attended a presentation or a speech in which the speaker's style seemed inappropriate? What effect did that style have on the audience? Briefly explain.
4. What similarities and differences would you expect to see in the introduction to a formal presentation and the introduction to a formal report? Explain.
5. What problems could result from using visual aids during your speech?
6. From the speaker's perspective, what are the advantages and disadvantages of responding to questions from the audience throughout a speech or presentation? From the listener's perspective, which approach would you prefer? Why?

Practise Your Knowledge

Exercises

1. For many years, Toastmasters has been dedicated to helping its members give speeches. Instruction, good speakers as models, and practice sessions aim to teach members to convey information in lively and informative ways. Visit the Toastmasters Web site at **www.toastmasters.org** and carefully review the linked pages about listening, speaking, voice, and body. Evaluate the information and outline a three-minute presentation to your class telling why Toastmasters and its Web site would or would not help you and your classmates write and deliver an effective speech.
2. Attend a speech at your school or in your area, or watch a speech on television. Categorize the speech as one that motivates or entertains, one that informs or analyzes, or one that persuades or urges collaboration. Then compare the speaker's delivery and use of visual aids with the Checklist for Speeches and Oral Presentations. Write a two-page report analyzing the speaker's performance and suggesting improvements.
3. Analyze the speech given by someone introducing the main speaker at an awards ceremony, a graduation, or some other special occasion. Does the speech fit the occasion and grab attention? Is it related to the audience's interests? How well does the speech motivate the audience to listen to the featured speaker? Does the speech provide the information necessary for the audience to understand, respect, and appreciate the speaker's background and viewpoint? Put yourself in the shoes of the person who made that introduction. Draft a brief (two-minute) speech that prepares the audience for the featured speaker.
4. Which media would you use for the visual aids that accompany each of the following speeches? Explain your answers.
   a. An informal ten-minute speech explaining the purpose of a new training program to 300 assembly-line employees
   b. An informal ten-minute speech explaining the purpose of a new training program to five vice-presidents
   c. A formal five-minute presentation explaining the purpose of a new training program to the company's 12-member board of directors
   d. A formal five-minute speech explaining the purpose of a new company training program to 35 members of the press
5. Select one of the following main ideas and outline a brief (three- to five-minute) persuasive speech to your business communication class.
   a. As a requirement for graduation, every university and college student should demonstrate proficiency in basic writing skills by passing a standardized national test.
   b. University students should be allowed access to their confidential academic records at least once a year and, if they choose, to submit a written statement disputing or correcting information in the files.
   c. Rather than ask all students to pay an activities fee to support campus sports, require only those students who participate to pay a special sports fee.
   d. The campus computer laboratory should remain open 24 hours a day throughout the week to give students the opportunity to complete their assignments at their own convenience.
   e. All university students should be required to complete a period of community service during their third or fourth year.
6. Observe and analyze the delivery of a speaker in a school, work, or other setting. What type of delivery did the speaker use? Was this delivery appropriate for the occasion? What nonverbal signals did the speaker use to emphasize key points? Were these signals effective? Which nonverbal signals would you suggest to further enhance the delivery of this speech–and why?
7. Think again about the speech you observed and analyzed in Exercise 6. How could the speaker have used nonverbal signals to unethically manipulate the audience's attitudes or actions?
8. You've been asked to give an informative ten-minute talk on vacation opportunities in your province. Draft your introduction, which should last no more than two minutes. Then pair off with a classmate and analyze each other's introductions. How well do these two introductions arouse the audience's interest, build credibility, and preview the presentation? Suggest how these introductions might be improved.

9. How good are you at planning, writing, and delivering speeches? Rate yourself on each of the following elements of the oral presentation process by answering always, frequently, occasionally, or never to the statements. Then examine your ratings to identify where you are strongest and where you can improve, using the tips in this chapter.

a. I start by defining my purpose.

b. I analyze my audience before writing a speech.

c. I match my speech length to the allotted time.

d. I begin my speeches with an attention-getting introduction.

e. I look for ways to build credibility as a speaker.

f. I cover only a few main points in the body of my speech.

g. I use transitions to help listeners follow my ideas.

h. I review main points and describe next steps in the close.

i. I choose visual aids appropriate for the audience and occasion.

j. I design simple visual aids to supplement my speech.

k. I practise my speech, with visuals, before the presentation.

l. I prepare in advance for questions and objections.

m. I conclude speeches by summarizing my main idea.

Developing Your Internet Skills

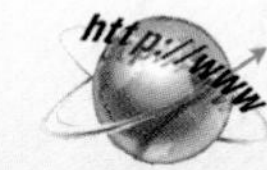

Going Online: Speak Like a Pro, p. 518

Take time to explore some linked sites from the Virtual Presentation Assistant Web site. Take a look at some of the advice offered by the experts found there. Look for material you can use in an upcoming classroom speaking project. Did your perusal of this site and its links cause you to make any changes in your speaking plans? What new ideas did you glean from this wealth of material? (If you didn't find anything to spark your interest, explain why.)

APPENDIX A

Format and Layout of Business Documents

An effective letter, memo, or report does more than store words on paper. It communicates with the right person, makes an impression, and tells the recipient who wrote it and when it was written. It may even carry responses back to the sender, if only to relate how and by whom it was received and processed.

Over the centuries certain conventions have developed for the format and layout of business documents. Of course, conventions vary from country to country, and, even within Canada, few hard-and-fast rules exist. Many organizations develop variations of standard styles to suit their own needs, adopting the style that's best for the types of messages they send and for the kinds of audiences that receive them. The conventions described here are more common than others. Whether you handle all your own communication on your computer or rely on someone else to handle it for you, knowing the proper form for your documents and knowing how to make them attractive to your readers are crucial.

First Impressions

A letter or other written document is often the first (sometimes the only) contact you have with an external audience. Memos and other documents used within an organization represent you to supervisors, colleagues, and employees. So it's important that your documents look neat and professional and that they're easy to read. Your audience's first impressions come from the paper you use, the way you customize it, and the general appearance of your document. These elements tell readers a lot about you and about your company's professionalism.

Paper

From your own experience, you know that a flimsy, see-through piece of paper gives a much less favourable impression than a richly textured piece. Paper quality is measured in two ways: The first measure of quality is weight, specifically the weight of four reams (each a 500-sheet package) of letter-size paper. The quality most commonly used by Canadian business organizations is 20-pound paper, but 16- and 24-pound versions are also used. The second measure of quality is the percentage of cotton in the paper. Cotton doesn't yellow over time the way wood pulp does, and it's both strong and soft. In general, paper with a 25 percent cotton content is an appropriate quality for letters and outside reports. For memos and other internal documents, lighter-weight paper and paper with a lower cotton content may be used. Also, airmail-weight paper may be more cost effective for international correspondence, but make sure it isn't too flimsy.[1]

In Canada the standard size of paper for business documents is 81/2 by 11 inches. Standard legal documents are 81/2 by 14 inches. Executives may have a box of correspondence note cards imprinted with their initials and a box of plain folded notes for condolences or for acknowledging formal invitations.

Stationery may vary in colour. Of course, white is standard for business purposes, although neutral colours such as gray and ivory are sometimes used. Memos are sometimes produced on pastel-coloured paper so that internal correspondence can be more easily distinguished from external. Memos are sometimes printed or typed on various colours of paper for routing to separate departments. Light-coloured papers are distinctive and often appropriate; bright or dark colours make reading difficult and may appear too frivolous.

Customization

For letters to outsiders, Canadian businesses commonly use letterhead stationery printed with the company's name and address, usually at the top of the page but sometimes along the left side or even at the bottom of the page. Other information may be included in the letterhead as well: the company's telephone number, fax number, cable address, Web site address, product lines, date of establishment, officers and directors, slogan, and logo. The idea is to give the recipient pertinent reference data and a good idea not only of what the company does but also of the company's image.[2] Nevertheless, the letterhead should be as simple as possible; too much information gives the page a cluttered look, cuts into the space needed for the letter, and may become outdated before all the letterhead has been used. If you do a lot of business abroad, be sure your letterhead is intelligible to foreigners, and make sure it includes the name of your country as well as your cable, telex, Web site and e-mail addresses, or fax information.

In Canada, company letterhead is always used for the first page of a letter. Successive pages are plain sheets of paper that match the letterhead in colour and quality, or some companies use a specially printed second-page letterhead bearing only the company's name. Other countries have other conventions. For example, Latin American companies use a cover page with their printed seal in the centre.

Many companies also design standardized forms for memos and for reports that are written frequently and always require the same sort of information (such as sales reports and expense reports). Electronic templates have become very common: employees complete them on computers and then print them out. Many businesses and institutions, however, still print frequently used forms in sets for use with carbon paper or in carbonless copy sets that produce multiple copies automatically with the original.[3]

Appearance

Most business documents are produced using a letter-quality (not a dot matrix) printer. Some short informal memos are handwritten, and it's appropriate to handwrite a note of condolence to a close business associate. Of course, the envelope is handwritten, printed, or typed to match the document. However, even a letter on the best-quality paper with the best-designed letterhead may look unprofessional if it's poorly produced.

Companies in Canada make sure that documents (especially external ones) are centred on the page, with margins of at least an inch all around. Using word-processing or desktop-publishing software, you can achieve this balanced appearance simply by defining the format parameters.

The most common line length is about 6 inches. Lines aren't usually full-justified because the resulting text can be hard to read, even with proportional spacing, and because the document generally looks too much like a form letter. Varying line length makes the document look more personal and interesting. If you're using a typewriter, the larger, pica type will give you 60 characters in a line; the smaller, elite type will give you 72 characters in a line. Sometimes a guide sheet, with the margins and the centre point marked in dark ink, is used as a backing. The number of lines between elements of the document (such as between the date line and inside address in a letter) can be adjusted to ensure that a short document fills the page vertically or that a longer document extends to at least three lines of body on the last page.

Another important aspect of a professional-looking document is the proper spacing after punctuation. For example, Canadian conventions include (1) leaving one space after commas and semicolons and (2) leaving two spaces after periods at the ends of sentences and after colons (unless your typeface is proportional, requiring only one space). Each letter in a person's initials is followed by a period and a single space. Abbreviations for organizations, such as YEA (Young Entrepreneur's Association), may or may not have periods, but they never have internal spaces. On computers and typewriters that have no special characters for dashes, use two hyphens with no space before, between, or after. Other details of this sort are provided in your company's style book or in most secretarial handbooks.

Finally, messy corrections are dreadfully obvious and unacceptable in business documents. Be sure that any letter, report, or memo requiring a lot of corrections is reprinted or retyped. Word-processing software and self-correcting typewriters can produce correction-free documents at the push of a button.

Letters

For a long time, letters have begun with some kind of phrase in greeting and have ended with some sort of polite expression before the writer's signature. In fact, books printed in the sixteenth century prescribed letter formats for writers to follow. Styles have changed some since then, but all business letters still have certain elements in common. Several of these elements appear in every letter; others appear only when desirable or appropriate. In addition, these letter parts are usually arranged in one of three basic formats.

Standard Letter Parts

All business letters typically include seven elements, in the following order: (1) heading, (2) date, (3) inside address, (4) salutation, (5) body, (6) complimentary close, and (7) signature block. The letter in Figure A.1 shows the placement of these standard letter parts.

HEADING

Letterhead (the usual heading) shows the organization's name, full address, and (almost always) telephone number. Executive letterhead also bears the name of an individual within the organization. Computers allow you to design your own letterhead (either one to use for all correspondence or a new one for each piece of

6412 Carleton Road
Lethbridge, AB T1H 9K4
June 22, 2001

Mr. Richard Lacroix
Director of Franchises
Snack Shoppes
9090 Portage Avenue
Winnipeg, MB R3C 1N1

Dear Mr. Lacroix:

Last Monday, my wife and I were on our way home from a long weekend, and we stopped at a Snack Shoppe for a quick sandwich. A sign on the cash register gave your address in the event customers were interested in operating a franchise of their own somewhere else. We talked about the idea all evening and into the night.

Although we had talked about changing jobs–I'm an administrative analyst for a utility company and my wife sells real estate–the thought of operating a franchised business had never occurred to us. We'd always thought in terms of starting a business from scratch. However, owning a Snack Shoppe is an intriguing idea.

We would appreciate your sending us full details on owning our own outlet. Please include the names and telephone numbers of other Snack Shoppe owners so that we can talk to them before we make any decision to proceed further. We're excited about hearing from you.

Cordially,

Peter Simond

Peter Simond

Heading
Date
Inside Address
Salutation
Body
Complimentary Closing
Typewritten Name

□ One blank space
· Variable space depending on length of letter

FIGURE A.1
In-Depth Critique: Standard Letter Parts
The writer of this business letter had no letterhead available, but correctly included a heading.

correspondence). If letterhead stationery is not available, the heading consists of a return address (but not a name) starting 13 lines from the top of the page, which leaves 2 inches between the return address and the top of the page.

DATE

If you're using letterhead, place the date at least one blank line beneath the lowest part of the letterhead. Without letterhead, place the date immediately below the return address. The standard method of writing the date in Canada uses the full name of the month (no abbreviations), followed by the day (in numerals, without *st, rd,* or *th*), a comma, and then the year: July 14, 1997 (7/14/97). Military and international standard places the year first, followed by the month and the day, using commas in the all-numeral form: 1997 July 14. To maintain the utmost clarity, always spell out the name of the month in dates for international correspondence.[4]

When communicating internationally, you may also experience some confusion over time. Some companies in Canada refer to morning (A.M.) and afternoon (P.M.), dividing a 24-hour day into 12-hour blocks so that they refer to four o'clock in the morning (4:00 A.M.) or four o'clock in the afternoon (4:00 P.M.). The military and European

TABLE A.1 Forms of Address

Person	In Address	In Salutation
	Personal Titles	
Man	Mr. [first & last name]	Dear Mr. [last name]:
Woman (marital status unknown)	Ms. [first & last name]	Dear Ms. [last name]:
Woman (single)	Ms. *or* Miss [first & last name]	Dear Ms. *or* Miss [last name]:
Woman (married)	Ms. *or* Mrs. [wife's first & last name] *or* Mrs. [husband's first & last name]	Dear Ms. *or* Mrs. [last name]:
Woman (widowed)	Ms *or* Mrs. [wife's first name & last name] *or* Mrs. [husband's first & last name]	Dear Ms. *or* Mrs. [last name]:
Woman (separated or divorced)	Ms. *or* Mrs. [first & last name]	Dear Ms. *or* Mrs. [last name]:
Two men (or more)	Mr. [first & last name] and Mr. [first & last name]	Dear Mr. [last name] and Mr. [last name]: *or* Messrs. [last name] and [last name]:
Two women (or more)	Ms. [first & last name] and Ms. [first & last name]	Dear Ms. [last name] and Ms. [last name]: *or* Mses. [last name] and [last name]:
	or	
	Mrs. [first & last name] and Mrs. [first & last name]	Dear Mrs. [last name] and Mrs. [last name]: *or* Dear Mesdames [last name] and [last name]: *or* Mesdames:
	or	
	Miss [first & last name] and Mrs. [first & last name]	Dear Miss [last name] and Mrs. [last name]:
One woman and one man	Ms. [first & last name] and Mr. [first & last name]	Dear Ms. [last name] and Mr. [last name]:
Couple (married)	Mr. and Mrs. [husband's first & last name]	Dear Mr. and Mrs. [last name]:
Couple (married with different last names)	[title] [first & last name of husband] [title] [first & last name of wife]	Dear [title] [husband's last name] and [title] [wife's last name]
Couple (married professionals with same title & same last name)	[title in plural form] [husband's first name] and [wife's first name] [last name]	Dear [title in plural form] [last name]:
Couple (married professionals with different titles & same last name)	[title] [first & last name of husband] [title] [first & last name of wife]	Dear [title] and [title] [last name]:

companies refer to one 24-hour period so that 0400 hours (4:00 A.M.) is always in the morning and 1600 hours (4:00 P.M.) is always in the afternoon.[5] Make sure your references to time are as clear as possible, and be sure you clearly understand your audience's time references.

INSIDE ADDRESS

The inside address identifies the recipient of the letter. For Canadian correspondence, begin the inside address one or more lines below the date, depending on how long the letter is. Precede the addressee's name with a courtesy title, such as *Dr., Mr.,* or *Ms.* The accepted courtesy title for women in business is Ms., although a woman known to prefer the title *Miss* or *Mrs.* is always accommodated. If you don't know whether a person is a man or a woman (and you have no way of finding out), do not use a courtesy title. For example, Terry Smith could be either a man or a woman. The first line of the inside address would be just Terry Smith, and the salutation would be Dear Terry Smith. The same is true if you know only a person's initials, as in S. J. Adams.

Spell out and capitalize titles that precede a person's name, such as *Professor* or *General* (see Table A.1 for the proper forms of address). The person's organizational

Person	In Address	In Salutation
	Professional Titles	
President of a college or university (doctor)	Dr. [first & last name], President	Dear Dr. [last name]:
Dean of a college or university	Dean [first & last name] *or* Dr., Mr., Mrs., or Miss [first & last name] Dean of [title]	Dear Dean [last name]: Dear Dr., Mr., Ms., Mrs., *or* Miss [last name]:
Professor	Professor [first & last name]	Dear Professor [last name]:
Physician	[first & last name], M.D.	Dear Dr. [last name]:
Lawyer	Mr., Ms., Mrs., *or* Miss [first & last name]	Dear Mr., Ms., Mrs., *or* Miss [last name]:
Service personnel	[full rank, first & last name, abbreviation of service designation] (add *Retired* if applicable)	Dear [rank] [last name]:
Company or corporation	[name of organization]	Ladies and Gentlemen *or* Gentlemen and Ladies
	Government Titles	
Prime Minister of Canada	The Right Honourable [name]	Dear Prime Minister
Federal Minister	The Honourable [name], PC, MP, Minister of ________	Dear Mr. or Ms. [name] *or* Dear Minister
Member of Parliament	Mr. or Mrs. [name], MP	Dear Mr. or Ms. [last name]
Judge	The Honourable [name]	Dear Mr. Justice [last name] Dear Madame Justice [last name]
Mayor	Mayor [name]	Dear Mr. or Ms. Mayor
Councillor	Councillor [name]	Dear Mr. or Ms. [name]

title, such as *Director,* may be included on this first line (if it is short) or on the line below; the name of a department may follow. In addresses and signature lines, don't forget to capitalize any professional title that follows a person's name:

Mr. Ray Johnson, Dean

Ms. Patricia T. Higgins, Assistant Vice-President

However, professional titles not appearing in an address or signature line are capitalized only when they directly precede the name.

President Kenneth Johanson will deliver the speech.

Maria Morales, president of ABC Enterprises, will deliver the speech.

The Honourable Ethel Blondin-Andrew, Member of Parliament for Western Arctic, Northwest Territories, will deliver the speech.

If the name of a specific person is unavailable, you may address the letter to the department or to a specific position within the department. Also, be sure to spell out company names in full, unless the company itself uses abbreviations in its official name.

Other address information includes the treatment of buildings, house numbers, and compass directions. Capitalize the names of buildings, and if you specify a location within a building (suite, room, and so on), capitalize it and use a comma to separate it from the building name.

Acme Building, Suite 1073

Use figures for all house or building numbers, except the number *one*.

One Trinity Lane
637 Adams Avenue, Apt. 7

Spell out compass directions that fall within a street address, but abbreviate compass directions that follow the street address:

1074 West Connover Street
783 Main Street, N.E., Apt. 27

Also remember that apartment, suite, and room numbers always appear in numerals (as in the examples already listed in this paragraph). The following example shows all the information that may be included in the inside address and its proper order for Canadian correspondence:

Ms. Linda Coolidge, Vice President
Dr. H. C. Armstrong
Research and Development
Commonwealth Mining Consortium
The Chelton Building, Suite 301
585 Second Street SW
Calgary, AB T2P 2P5

US addresses are similar:

Ms. Linda Rodriguez
Corporate Planning Department
Midwest Airlines
Kowalski Building, Suite 21-A
7279 Bristol Avenue
Toledo, OH 43617

When addressing correspondence for other countries, follow the format and information that appear in the company's letterhead. You want to be especially careful about the format of international correspondence because you want everything to be as clear as possible.[6] The order and layout of address information vary from country to country, so follow the conventions of the country of the recipient. When you're sending mail from Canada, however, be sure that the name of the destination country appears on the last line of the address in capital letters. Also, use the English version of the country name so that your mail is routed from Canada to the right country. Then, to be sure your mail is routed correctly within the destination country, use the foreign spelling of the city name (using the characters and diacritical marks that would be commonly used in the region). For example, the following address uses Köln, instead of Cologne:

H. R. Veith, Director	Addressee
Eisfieren Glaswerk	Company Name
Blaubachstraße 13	Street address
Postfach 10 80 07	Post office box
D-5000 Köln I	District, city
GERMANY	Country

Additional addresses might look similar to the following:

Mr. Toru Hasegawa
7-35 Kitashinagawa
6 Chome–141 Shinagawa-ku
Tokyo
JAPAN

Cairo
Cleopatra
165 El Corniche Road
Mrs. Ahmed Abbas Zaki
EGYPT

Crédit Lyonnais
c/o Claude Rubinowicz
19, Boulevard des Italiens
75002 Paris
FRANCE

Sr. Ari Matos Cardoso
Superintendent of Human Resources and Personnel
Av. República do Chile, 65
Centro-Rio de Janeiro, RJ
CEP 20035
BRAZIL

Be sure to get organizational titles right when addressing international correspondence. Job designations vary around the world. In England, for example, a managing director is often what a Canadian company would call its chief executive officer or president, and a British deputy is the equivalent of a vice president. In France, responsibilities are assigned to individuals without regard to title or organizational structure, and in China the title *project manager* has meaning, but the title *sales manager* may not. To make matters worse, business people in some countries sign correspondence without their names typed below. In Germany, for example, the belief is that employees represent the company, so it's inappropriate to emphasize personal names.[7]

SALUTATION

In the salutation of your letter, follow the first line of the inside address. That is, if the first line is a person's name, the salutation is *Dear Mr.* or *Ms. Name*. Base the formality of the salutation on your relationship with the addressee. If in conversation you would say "Mary," your letter's salutation should be *Dear Mary,* followed by a comma. In letters to people you don't know well enough to address personally, include the courtesy title and last name, followed by a colon. Presuming to write *Dear Lewis* instead of *Dear Professor Chang* demonstrates a disrespectful familiarity that a stranger will probably resent. If the first line is a position title such as Director of Personnel, then use *Dear Director;* if the addressee is unknown, use a polite description, such as *Dear Alumnus, Dear SPCA Supporter,* or *Dear Voter.* If the first line is plural (a department or company), then use *Ladies and Gentlemen* (look again at Table A.1). When you do not know whether you're writing to an individual or a group (for example, when writing a reference or a letter of recommendation), use *To whom it may concern.*

In Canada some letter writers use a salutopening on the salutation line. A salutopening omits *Dear* but includes the first few words of the opening paragraph along with the recipient's name. After this line, the sentence continues a double space below as part of the body of the letter, as in these examples:

Thank you, Mr. Brown,	Salutopening
for your prompt payment of your bill.	Body
Congratulations, Ms. Lake!	Salutopening
Your promotion is well deserved.	Body

Don't overlook an especially important point with personalized salutations: Whether they're informal or formal, make sure names are spelled right. A misspelled name is glaring evidence of carelessness, and it belies the personal interest you're trying to express.

BODY

The body of the letter is your message. Almost all letters are single-spaced, with double spacing (one blank line) before and after the salutation or salutopening, between paragraphs, and before the complimentary close. The body may include indented lists, entire paragraphs indented for emphasis, and even subheadings. If it does, all similar elements should be treated in the same way. Your department or company may select a format to use for all letters.

COMPLIMENTARY CLOSE

The complimentary close begins on the second line below the body of the letter. Alternatives for wording are available, but currently the trend seems to be toward using one-word closes, such as *Sincerely* and *Cordially.* In any case, the complimentary close reflects the relationship between you and the person you're writing to. Avoid cute closes, such as *Yours for bigger profits.* If your audience doesn't know you well, your sense of humour may be misunderstood.

SIGNATURE BLOCK

Leave three blank lines for a written signature below the complimentary close, and then include the sender's name (unless it appears in the letterhead). The person's title may appear on the same line as the name or on the line below:

> Cordially,
>
> Raymond Dunnigan
> Director of Personnel

Your letterhead indicates that you're representing your company. However, if your letter is on plain paper or runs to a second page, you may want to emphasize that you're speaking legally for the company. The accepted way of doing that is to place the company's name in capital letters a double space below the complimentary close and then include the sender's name and title four lines below that:

> Sincerely,
>
> WENTWORTH INDUSTRIES
>
> (Mrs.) Helen B. Yamaguchi
>
> President

If your name could be taken for either a man's or a woman's, a courtesy title indicating gender should be included, with or without parentheses. Also, women who prefer a particular courtesy title should include it:

Mrs. Nancy Winters
(Miss) Juana Flores
Ms. Pat Li

Additional Letter Parts

Letters vary greatly in subject matter and thus in the identifying information they need and the format they adopt. The following elements may be used in any combination, depending on the requirements of the particular letter, but generally in this order:

1. Addressee notation
2. Attention line
3. Subject line
4. Second-page heading
5. Company name
6. Reference initials
7. Enclosure notation
8. Copy notation
9. Mailing notation
10. Postscript

The letter in Figure A.2 shows how these additional parts should be arranged.

ADDRESSEE NOTATION

Letters that have a restricted readership or that must be handled in a special way should include such addressee notations as *Personal, Confidential,* or *Please Forward.* This sort of notation appears a double space above the inside address, in all capital letters.

ATTENTION LINE

Although an attention line is not commonly used today, you may find it useful if you know only the last name of the person you're writing to. An attention line can also be used to direct a letter to a position title or department. An attention line may take any of the following forms or variants of them: *Attention Dr. McHenry, Attention Director of Marketing,* or *Attention Marketing Department.* You may place the attention line on the first line and use the company name as the second line of the inside address. With either approach, the address on the envelope should always match the style of the inside address shown in Figure A.2, to conform to postal specifications.

SUBJECT LINE

The subject line lets the recipient know at a glance what the letter is about; it also indicates where to file the letter for future reference. It usually appears below the salutation—against the left margin, indented as the paragraphs in the body of the letter, or centred on the line. Sometimes the subject line is placed above the salutation or at the very top

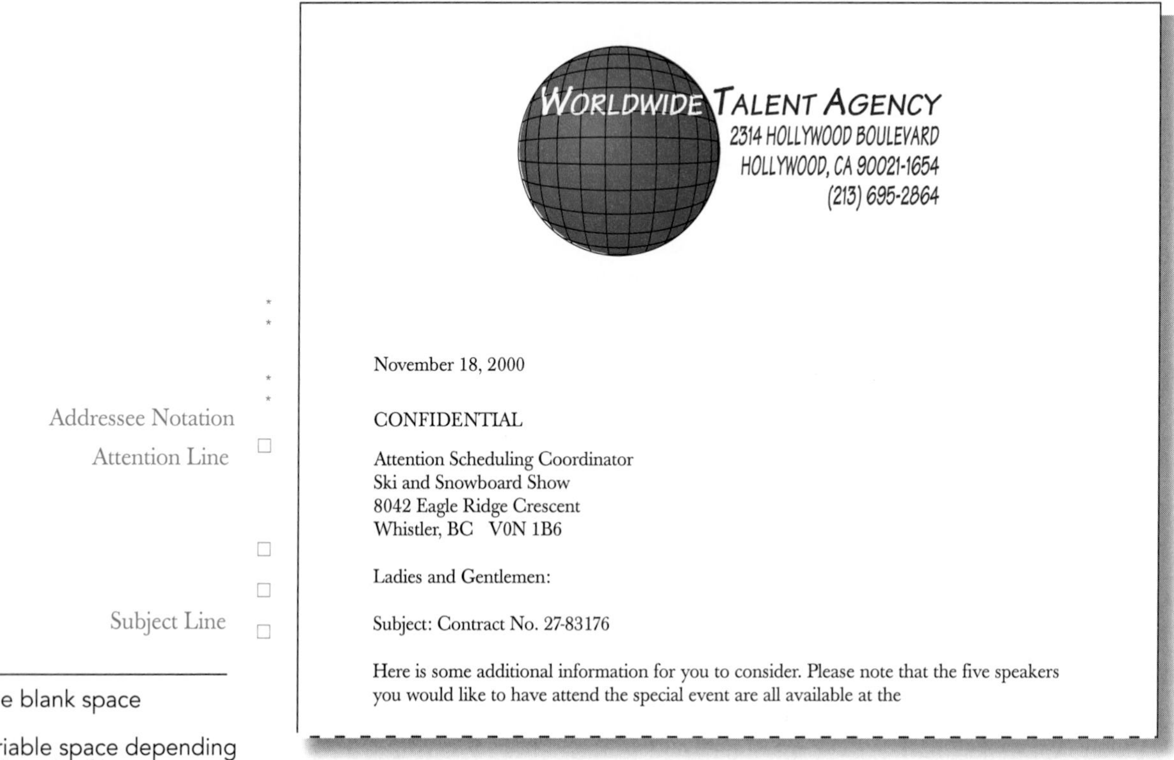

Addressee Notation
Attention Line
Subject Line
□ One blank space
* Variable space depending on length of letter
WORLDWIDE TALENT AGENCY
2314 HOLLYWOOD BOULEVARD
HOLLYWOOD, CA 90021-1654
(213) 695-2864
November 18, 2000
CONFIDENTIAL
Attention Scheduling Coordinator
Ski and Snowboard Show
8042 Eagle Ridge Crescent
Whistler, BC V0N 1B6
Ladies and Gentlemen:
Subject: Contract No. 27-83176
Here is some additional information for you to consider. Please note that the five speakers
you would like to have attend the special event are all available at the

FIGURE A.2

In-Depth Critique: Additional Letter Parts

This excerpt from a letter written by J. Elizabeth Spencer of the Worldwide Talent Agency includes many of the elements often appearing in business letters.

of the page. The subject line may take a variety of forms, including the following:

Subject: RainMaster Sprinklers
About your February 2, 2000, order
FALL 2000 SALES MEETING
Reference Order No. 27920

Sometimes the subject line (or the last line of a long subject "line") is underscored. Some writers omit the word *Subject* and put the other information all in capitals to distinguish it from the other letter parts. Organizations such as insurance and financial institutions, lawyers, and government offices may use the words *Re:* or *In re:* (meaning "concerning" or "in the matter of") rather than using the word *Subject.*

SECOND-PAGE HEADING

If the letter is long and an additional page is required, use a second-page heading. Some companies have second-page letterhead, with the company name and address on one line and in a smaller typeface than on the regular letterhead. In any case, the second-page heading bears the name that appears in the first line of the inside address (the person or organization receiving the letter), the page number, and the date of the letter; you can also include a reference number. All the following are acceptable:

Ms. Melissa Baker
May 10, 2000
Page 2

Ms. Melissa Baker, May 10, 2000, Page 2

Ms. Melissa Baker -2- May 10, 2000

Triple-space (leave two blank lines) between the second-page heading and the body. If a paragraph must be continued on a second page, make sure at least two lines of that paragraph appear on the first page and on the second page. Also, the closing lines of a business letter must never appear alone on a continued page. At least two lines of the body must precede the complimentary close or signature lines. And finally, don't hyphenate the last word on a page.

COMPANY NAME

If you include the company's name in the signature block, put it all in capitals letters a double space below the complimentary close. You usually include the company's name in the signature block only when the writer is serving as

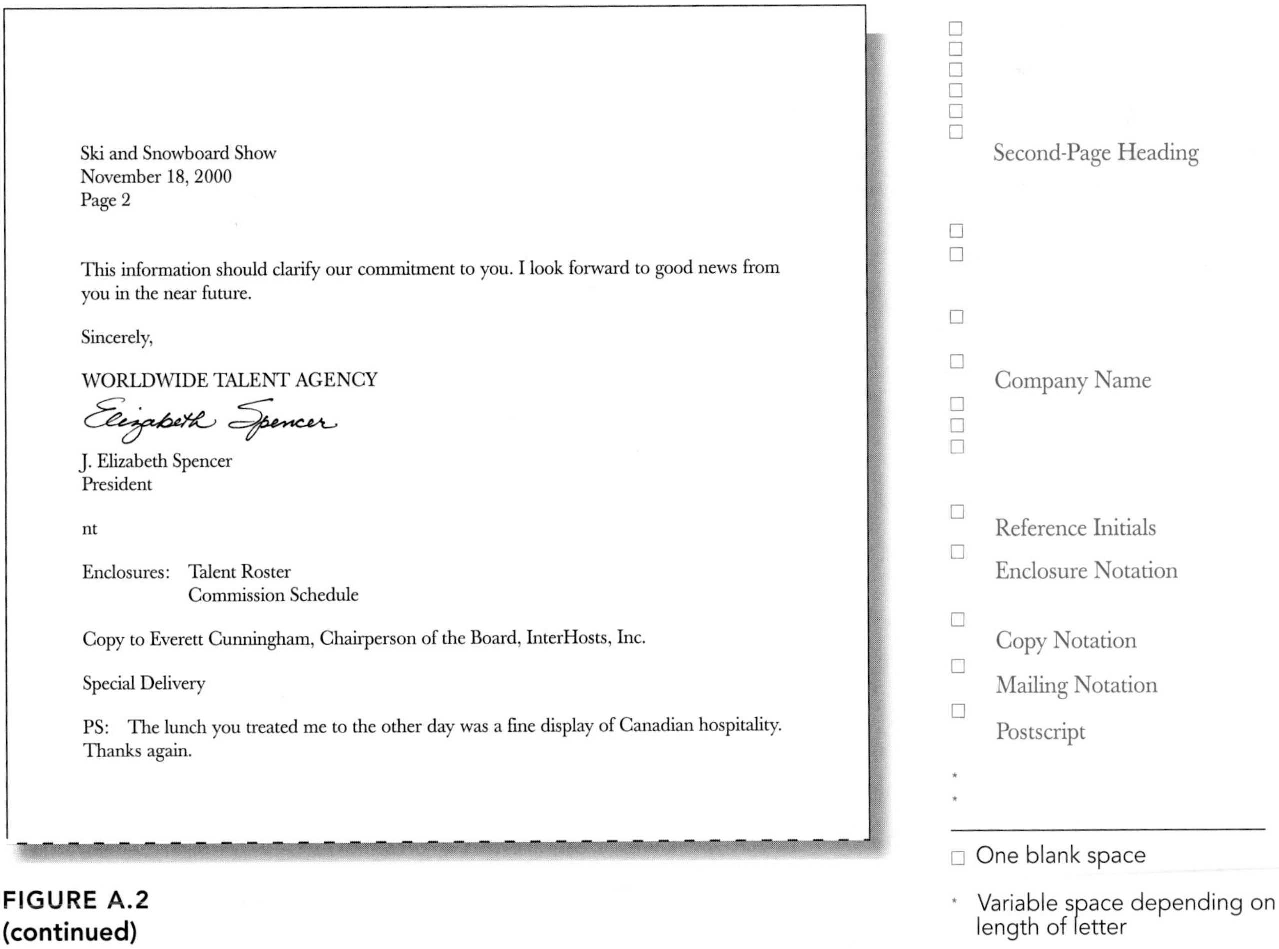

Ski and Snowboard Show
November 18, 2000
Page 2

This information should clarify our commitment to you. I look forward to good news from you in the near future.

Sincerely,

WORLDWIDE TALENT AGENCY

Elizabeth Spencer

J. Elizabeth Spencer
President

nt

Enclosures: Talent Roster
Commission Schedule

Copy to Everett Cunningham, Chairperson of the Board, InterHosts, Inc.

Special Delivery

PS: The lunch you treated me to the other day was a fine display of Canadian hospitality. Thanks again.

Second-Page Heading
Company Name
Reference Initials
Enclosure Notation
Copy Notation
Mailing Notation
Postscript

□ One blank space
* Variable space depending on length of letter

FIGURE A.2 (continued)

the company's official spokesperson or when letterhead has not been used.

REFERENCE INITIALS

Because it can happen in business that one person may dictate or write a letter and another person may produce it, reference initials are used to show who helped prepare the letter. Reference initials appear at the left margin, a double space below the last line of the signature block. When the writer's name has been included in the signature block, only the preparer's initials are necessary. If only the department name appears in the signature block, both sets of initials should appear, usually in one of the following forms:

RSR/sm

RSR:sm

RSR:SM

The first set of initials is the writer's; the second set is the preparer's.

Sometimes the writer and the signer of a letter are different people. In that case, at least the file copy of a letter should bear both their initials as well as those of the typist: JFS/RSR/sm (signer, writer, preparer). When business people keyboard their own letters, reference initials are not included, so such initials are becoming more and more rare.

ENCLOSURE NOTATION

Enclosure notations also appear at the bottom of a letter, one or two lines below the reference initials. Some common forms:

Enclosure

Enclosures (2)

Enclosures: Résumé Photograph

Attachment

COPY NOTATION

Copy notations may follow reference initials or enclosure notations. They indicate who's receiving a *courtesy copy* (cc). Some companies indicate copies made on a photocopier (*pc*), or they simply use *copy* (*c*). Recipients are listed in order of rank or (rank being equal) in alphabetical order. Among the forms used:

cc: David Wentworth

pc: Martha Littlefield

Copy to Hans Vogel

c: Joseph Martinez

In addition to the name of an individual, copy notations may include any combination of that person's courtesy title, position, department, company, and complete address, along with notations about any enclosures being sent with the copies.

On occasion, copies are sent to benefit readers other than the person who receives the original letter. In that case, place the notation *bc, bcc,* or *bpc* (for blind copy, blind courtesy copy, or blind photocopy) with the name, where the copy notation would normally appear–but only on the copy, not on the original.

MAILING NOTATION

You may place a mailing notation (such as *Priority Post* or *Registered Mail*) at the bottom of the letter, after reference initials or enclosure notations (whichever one is last) and before copy notations. Or you may place it at the top of the letter, either above the inside address on the left-hand side or just below the date on the right-hand side. For greater visibility, mailing notations may appear in capital letters.

POSTSCRIPT

Letters may also bear postscripts: afterthoughts to the letter, messages that require emphasis, or personal notes. The postscript is usually the last thing on any letter and may be preceded by *P.S., PS., PS:,* or nothing at all. A second afterthought would be designated *P.P.S.,* meaning "post postscript."

Postscripts usually indicate poor planning, so generally avoid them. However, they're commonly used in sales letters, not as an afterthought but as a punch line to remind the reader of a benefit for taking advantage of the offer.

Letter Formats

Although the basic letter parts have remained the same for centuries, ways of arranging them do change. Sometimes a company adopts a certain format as its policy; sometimes the individual letter writer or preparer is allowed to choose the format most appropriate for a given letter or to settle on a personal preference. In Canada, three major letter formats are commonly used:

- *Block format.* Each letter part begins at the left margin. The main advantage is quick and efficient preparation (Figure A.3).
- *Modified block format.* Same as block format, except the date, complimentary close, and signature block start near the centre of the page (Figure A.4). The modified block format does permit indentions as an option. This format mixes preparation speed with traditional placement of some letter parts. It also looks more balanced on the page than the block format does.

Beverly Hills Toys
3460 Rodeo Drive
Beverly Hills, California 90213
(310) 276-4839

September 5, 2000

Mr. Clifford Hanson,
General Manager
The Toy Trunk
3541 Fundy Drive
Saint John, NB E2M 5L4

Dear Mr. Hanson:

You should receive your shipment of Barbie dolls and accessories within two weeks, just in time for the holiday shopping season. The merchandise is being shipped by United Parcel Service. As the enclosed invoice indicates, the amount due is $352.32.

When preparing to ship your order, I noticed that this is your fifteenth year as a Mattel customer. During that period, you have sold over 3750 Barbie dolls! We sincerely appreciate the part you have played in marketing our toys to the public.

Your customers should be particularly excited about the new Barbie vacation outfits that you have ordered. Our winter advertising campaign will portray Barbie trekking through the jungle in her safari suit, climbing mountains in her down parka, and snorkeling off a coral reef in her diving gear.

Next month, you'll be receiving our spring catalogue. Notice the new series of action figures that will tie in with a TV cartoon featuring King Arthur and the Knights of the Round Table. As a special introductory incentive, you can receive a 15 percent discount on all items in this line until the end of January. Please send your order soon.

Sincerely,

Rhonda Rogers

Ms. Rhonda Rogers, ← either way
Customer Service Representative

/jhb — Typist initial same sender is the same, no need to type it, just put a / in front

Enclosure(s)

□ One blank space

* Variable space depending on length of letter

FIGURE A.3

In-Depth Critique: Block Letter Format

Rogers can be sure that her company's letterhead and the block format give her letter a crisp, businesslike appearance.

➤ *Simplified format.* Instead of using a salutation, this format often works the audience's name into the first line or two of the body and often includes a subject line in capital letters (Figure A.5). It also omits the complimentary close, so you sign your name after the body of the letter, followed by the printed (or typewritten) name (customarily in all capital letters). The advantages include convenience when you don't know your audience's name. However, some people object to this format because it seems mechanical and impersonal (a drawback that may be overcome with a warm writing style). In this format, the elimination of certain letter parts changes some of the spacing between lines.

These formats differ in the way paragraphs are indented, in the way letter parts are placed, and in some punctuation.

Fashion Sense

June 3, 2000

Ms. Clara Simpson, President
Young Volunteers Association
1295 Martindale Crescent
Brampton, ON L6X 3T1

Dear Ms. Simpson:

Thank you for inviting us to participate in the Young Volunteers Association Fashion Show. We will be delighted to provide some clothing samples for the May 15 event.

You indicated that you would like us to supply about 12 outfits from our designer collection, six in size 10 and six in size 12. We can certainly accommodate your request. To give your audience a representative overview of our merchandise, I suggest we provide the following: three tailored daytime dresses or pant suits, two dressy dresses, one formal ball gown, four casual weekend outfits, and two active sports outfits.

Please give me a call to schedule a "shopping" trip for you and your committee members. Together, I'm sure we can find exactly what you need to stage a well-rounded show. In the meantime, you might enjoy looking through the enclosed catalogue. It will introduce you to some of the options.

Sincerely,

Vera O'Donnell

(Mrs.) Vera O'Donnell
Special Events Manager

bcg

Enclosure

Fashion Sense, 1853 Queen Street, Brampton, ON L6X 3K8

□ One blank space

* Variable space depending on length of letter

FIGURE A.4

In-Depth Critique: Modified Block Letter Format

O'Donnell's choice of a modified block format appears no less crisp or businesslike than the previous figure, but indenting the date and the signature block can make the letter appear somewhat more balanced.

However, the elements are always separated by at least one blank line, and the printed (or typewritten) name is always separated from the line above by at least three blank lines to allow space for a signature. If paragraphs are indented, the indention is normally five spaces.

The most common formats for intercultural business letters are the block style and the modified block style. Use either the Canadian or the European format for dates. For the salutation, use *Dear (Title/Last name)*. Close the letter with *Sincerely* or *Cordially,* and sign it.

In addition to these three letter formats, letters may also be classified according to the style of punctuation they use. *Standard,* or *mixed, punctuation* uses a colon after the salutation (a comma if the letter is social or personal) and a comma

PERFORMANCE TOOLS INTERNATIONAL
9553 Tecumseh Road, Windsor, ON N8R 3Z9

May 5, 2000

Mr. Michael Ferraro
Pacific Coast Appliances
595 Briceland Street
Kingston, ON K7K 9L3

NEW PRODUCT INFORMATION

Thank you, Mr. Ferraro, for your recent inquiry about our product line. We appreciate your enthusiasm for our products, and we are confident that your customers will enjoy the improved performance of the new product line.

I have enclosed a package of information for your review, including product specifications, dealer prices, and an order form. The package also contains reprints of Performance Tools reviews and a comparison sheet showing how our products measure up against competing brands.

Please call with any questions you may have about shipping or payment arrangements.

Joanna Davis

JOANNA DAVIS
PRODUCT SPECIALIST

ek

Enclosures

□ One blank space

* Variable space depending on length of letter

FIGURE A.5

In-Depth Critique: Simplified Letter Format

Davis's use of the simplified format seems less personal than either the block or the modified block format.

after the complimentary close. *Open punctuation* uses no colon or comma after the salutation or the complimentary close. Although the most popular style in business communication is mixed punctuation, either style of punctuation may be used with block or modified block letter formats. Because the simplified letter format has no salutation or complimentary close, the style of punctuation is irrelevant.

Envelopes

The quality of the envelope is just as important for first impressions as the quality of the stationery. In fact, letterhead and envelopes should be of the same paper stock, have the same colour ink, and be imprinted with the same address and logo. Most envelopes used by Canadian businesses are No. 10 envelopes (91/2 inches long), which are sized to contain an 81/2-by-11-inch piece of paper folded in thirds. Some occasions call for a smaller, No. 63/4, envelope or for envelopes proportioned to fit special stationery. Figure A.6 shows the two most common sizes.

Addressing the Envelope

No matter what size the envelope, the address is always single-spaced and in block form–that is, with all lines aligned on the left. The address on the envelope is in the same style as the inside address and presents the same information. The order to follow is from the smallest division to the largest:

1. Name and title of recipient
2. Name of department or subgroup
3. Name of organization
4. Name of building
5. Street address and suite number, or post office box number
6. City, province, and postal code, or city, state, and zip code
7. Name of country (if the letter is being sent abroad)

Canada Post's optical scanning equipment can read both handwritten and typed addresses, and their addressing guidelines accommodate the requirements of French and English and the preferences of mailers. Businesses can use upper and lower case letters and accents when addressing envelopes and spell out and punctuate all addressing elements if they desire. However, Canada Post does encourage customers to follow specific formats because their mail will be handled more efficiently. For example, when a civic number suffix is present, there is no space when it is a letter (123A), and there is one space when it is a fraction (123 $\frac{1}{2}$). Canada Post prefers that common abbreviations be used for street types (such as ST and AVE), and directs that the only street types that may be translated are ST (RUE), AVE (AV), and BLVD (BOUL). A French street type is always placed before the street name, unless it is ordinal (1er, 2e) or cardinal (PREMIÈRE, DEUXIÈME). The street name is the official name recognized by each municipality and cannot be translated (for example, "Main" is not "Principale").

Canada Post also prefers that a province be written using the recognized two-letter symbol (see Table A.2) and requires that the postal code be in upper case and placed two spaces to the right of the province, with one space between the first three and the last three characters. Review the Canada Post Web site (**www.canadapost.ca/CPC2/addrm/addrguide/index.html**) for the numerous details governing address format.

Follow US Postal Service guidelines when addressing envelopes to customers in the United States. Like Canada Post, the US Postal Service prefers the two-character state

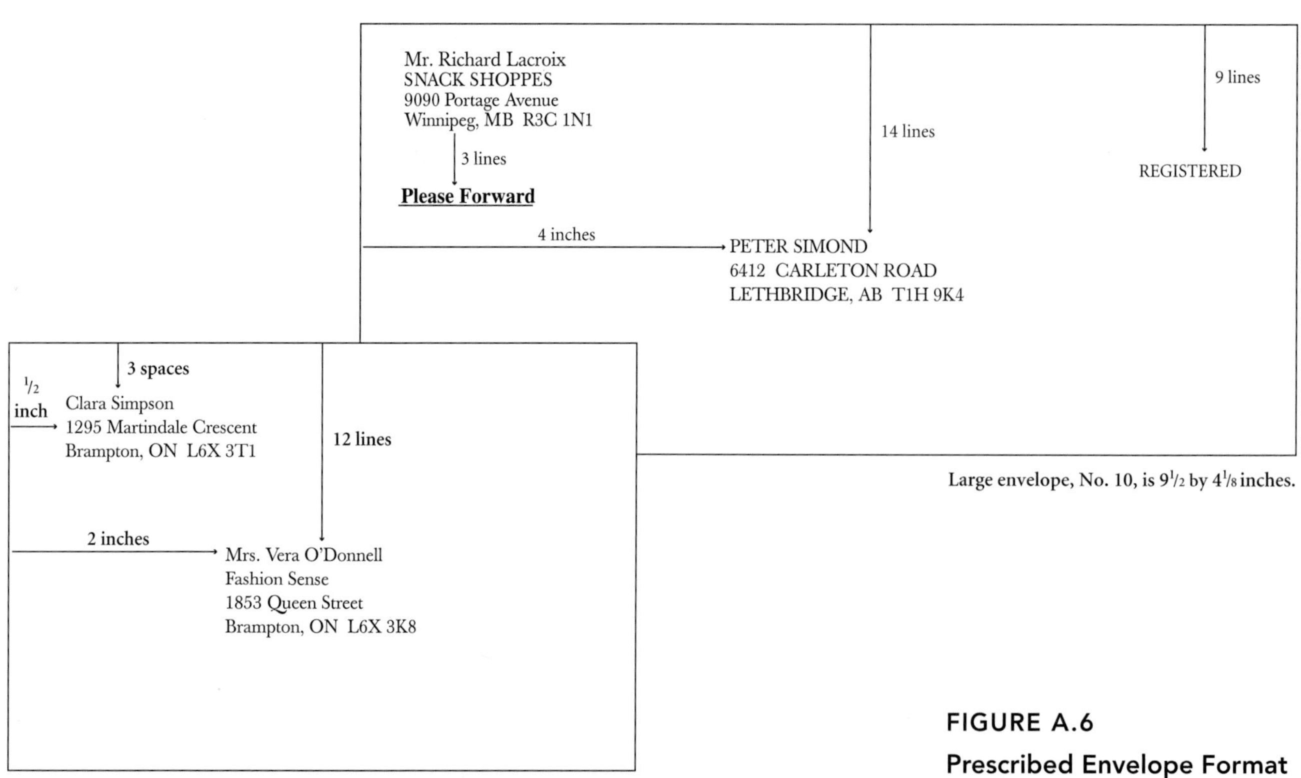

FIGURE A.6
Prescribed Envelope Format

TABLE A.2 Two-Letter Mailing Abbreviations For Canada and the United States

Province/State/ Territory	*Abbreviation*	*Province/State/ Territory*	*Abbreviation*	*Province/State/ Territory*	*Abbreviation*
Canada					
Alberta	AB	Northwest Territories	NT	Prince Edward Island	PE
British Columbia	BC	Nova Scotia	NS	Quebec	QC
Manitoba	MB	Nunavut	NU	Saskatchewan	SK
New Brunswick	NB	Ontario	ON	Yukon	YT
Newfoundland	NF				
United States					
Alabama	AL	Kentucky	KY	Ohio	OH
Alaska	AK	Louisiana	LA	Oklahoma	OK
Arizona	AZ	Maine	ME	Oregon	OR
Arkansas	AR	Maryland	MD	Pennsylvania	PA
American Samoa	AS	Massachusetts	MA	Puerto Rico	PR
California	CA	Michigan	MI	Rhode Island	RI
Canal Zone	CZ	Minnesota	MN	South Carolina	SC
Colorado	CO	Mississippi	MS	South Dakota	SD
Connecticut	CT	Missouri	MO	Tennessee	TN
Delaware	DE	Montana	MT	Trust Territories	TT
District of Columbia	DC	Nebraska	NE	Texas	TX
Florida	FL	Nevada	NV	Utah	UT
Georgia	GA	New Hampshire	NH	Vermont	VT
Guam	GU	New Jersey	NJ	Virginia	VA
Hawaii	HI	New Mexico	NM	Virgin Islands	VI
Idaho	ID	New York	NY	Washington	WA
Illinois	IL	North Carolina	NC	West Virginia	WV
Indiana	IN	North Dakota	NC	Wisconsin	WI
Iowa	IA	Northern Mariana Island	CM	Wyoming	WY
Kansas	KS				

abbreviation over the full state name (see Table A.2). The ZIP code must be separated from the state abbreviation by two spaces. The ZIP code may be five or nine digits. A hyphen separates the fifth and sixth digits. For example,

Mr. Damon Smith

1277 Morris Ave., Apt. 6-B

Bronx, New York 10451-4598

Folding to Fit

Trivial as it may seem, the way a letter is folded also contributes to the recipient's overall impression of your organization's professionalism. When sending a standard-size piece of paper in a No. 10 envelope, fold it in thirds, with the bottom folded up first and the top folded down over it (Figure A.7); the open end should be at the top of the envelope and facing out. Fit smaller stationery neatly into the appropriate envelope simply by folding it in half or in thirds. When sending a standard-size letterhead in a No. 63/4 envelope, fold it in half from top to bottom and then in thirds from side to side.

International Mail

When sending mail internationally, remember that postal service differs from country to country. It's usually a good

FIGURE A.7
Letter Folds for Standard-Size Letterhead

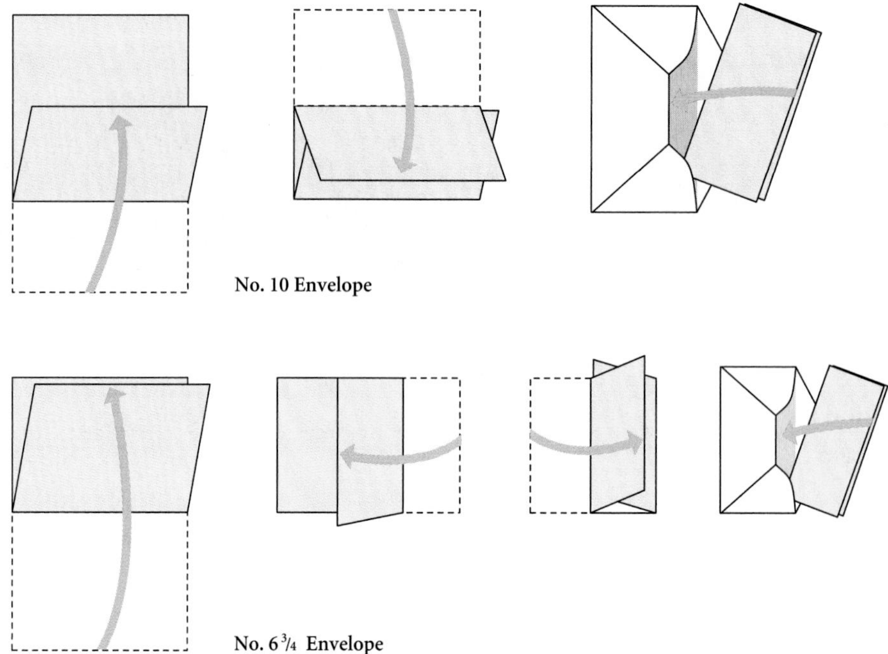

idea to send international correspondence by air mail and to ask that responses be sent that way as well. Also, remember to check the postage; rates for sending mail to most other countries aren't the same as the rates for sending mail within your own country.

Canada Post offers three methods for sending mail internationally:

- Purolator International, the most expensive service, offers next-day delivery to the US and 2 to 3 day delivery to 200 countries
- Air parcel, a medium-priced option, provides 6 to 10 day delivery to most international destinations
- Surface parcel, the economy service, offers 4 to 6 weeks delivery to most international destinations

When preparing documents for international destinations, follow Canada Post's instructions, available on their Web site, for size and weight limitations of letters and packages. In addition, observe customs requirements to avoid delays; you can access Revenue Canada Customs & Excise at **www.ccra-adrc.gc.ca/customs**.

Memos

Interoffice memos aren't distributed outside the organization, so they may not need the best-quality paper. However, they still convey important information, so clarity, careful arrangement, and neatness are important. As do those for letters, the guidelines for formatting memos help recipients understand at a glance what they've received and from whom.

Many organizations have memo forms printed, with labelled spaces for the recipient's name (or sometimes a checklist of all departments in an organization or all persons in a department), the sender's name, the date, and the subject (Figure A.8). If such forms don't exist, you can use plain paper or sometimes letterhead.

When using plain paper or letterhead, include a title such as *Memo* or *Interoffice Correspondence* (all in capitals) centred at the top of the page or aligned with the left margin. Also include the words *To, From, Date,* and *Subject*–followed by the appropriate information–at the top with a blank line between, as shown here:

MEMO

TO:

FROM:

DATE:

SUBJECT:

Sometimes the heading is organized like this:

MEMO

TO:	DATE:
FROM:	SUBJECT:

The subject may be presented with the letters *Re:*. You may want to include a file or reference number, introduced by the word *File*. Memo templates provided by many word processing programs offer a quick method for setting up your interoffice correspondence.

MEMO

TO: ____________

DEPT: ____________ FROM: ____________

DATE: ____________ TELEPHONE: ____________

SUBJECT: ____________ *For your* ☐ APPROVAL ☐ INFORMATION ☐ COMMENT

FIGURE A.8
Preprinted Memo Form

If you send a memo to a long list of people, include the notation *See distribution list* or *See below* in the *To* position at the top; then list the names at the end of the memo. Arranging such a list alphabetically is usually the most diplomatic course, although high-ranking officials may deserve more prominent placement. You can also address memos to groups of people–*All Sales Representatives, Production Group, Assistant Vice-Presidents.*

You don't need to use courtesy titles anywhere in a memo; first initials and last names are often sufficient. As a general rule, however, use a courtesy title if you would use one in face-to-face encounters with the person.

The subject line of a memo helps busy colleagues find out quickly what your memo is about. Although the subject "line" may overflow onto a second line, it's most helpful when it's short (but still informative).

Start the body of the memo on the second or third line below the heading. Like the body of a letter, it's usually single-spaced. Separate paragraphs with blank lines. Indenting them is optional. Handle lists, important passages, and subheadings as you do in letters. If the memo is very short, you may double-space it.

If the memo carries over to a second page, head the second page just as you head the second page of a letter.

Unlike a letter, a memo doesn't require a complimentary close or a signature, because your name is already prominent at the top. However, you may initial the memo–either beside the name appearing at the top of the memo or at the bottom of the memo–or you may even sign your name at the bottom, particularly if the memo deals with money or confidential matters. Treat all other elements–reference initials, enclosure notations, and copy notations–as you would in a letter.

Memos may be delivered by hand, by the post office (when the recipient doesn't work at the same location as the memo writer), or through inter-office mail. Inter-office mail may require the use of special reusable envelopes that have spaces for the recipient's name and department or room number; the name of the previous recipient is simply crossed out. If a regular envelope is used, the words *Interoffice Mail* appear where the stamp normally goes so that it won't accidentally be stamped and mailed with the rest of the office correspondence.

Informal, routine, or brief reports for distribution within a company are often presented in memo form (see Chapter 12). Don't include such report parts as a table of contents and appendixes, but write the body of the memo report just as carefully as you'd write a formal report.

E-Mail

Because e-mail messages can act both as memos (carrying information within your company) and as letters (carrying information outside your company and around the world), their format depends on your audience and purpose. You may choose to have your e-mail resemble a formal letter or a detailed report, or you may decide to keep things as simple as an inter-office memo. All e-mail messages include two major elements: the header and the body (Figure A.9).

Header

The e-mail header depends on the particular program you use. Some programs even allow you to choose between a shorter and a longer version. However, most headers contain similar information.

The *To:* line contains your audience's e-mail address. The most common e-mail addresses are Internet addresses, like the following:

- BellCustomizedEmail@bell.ca consumer information — Bell Canada
- editor_7@globeandmail.com financial news — Globe and Mail
- investor.relations@cantire.com investor relations division — Canadian Tire

HEADER (may vary from program to program)

Date: Includes the day, date, time, and time zone

To: Includes the recipient's address e-mail (perhaps addressee's proper name)

From: Includes your e-mail address (perhaps your proper name)

Subject (Re): Describes what your message concerns (an opportunity to gain interest)

Cc: Includes the address of anyone you want to receive a copy of the message

Bcc: Includes the address of anyone you want to receive a copy of the message but don't want listed as a receiver

Attachments: Includes the name of any files you have attached to your message

BODY (format depends on your audience and purpose)

Your own header (optional): Used only if this information isn't easily obtained from program's header

Greeting: Makes the message more personal

Message: Includes line space between paragraphs, and can include headings, lists, and other common devices used in letters and memos

Closing: Personalizes your message and resembles simple closings in letters

Signature: Can be simply your name typed or can be a signature file

Date: Tuesday, 25 April 2000, 9:34:27, PDT
To: bookco@artech.demon.co.uk
From: "Keith D. Wells" keithw@bluecrane.com
Subject: Please confirm shipping date

Re: Order # 1-SD-95466

Dated: 7 April 2000

Dear Jeffrey:

On 7 April 2000, we ordered the following books:

1 copy _Electronic Mail_
by Jacob Palme
(ISBN# 0-89006-802-X)

2 copies _Distance Learning Technology and Applications_
by Daniel Minoli
(ISBN# 0-89006-739-2)

Please confirm the date you shipped this order. My customers are eager to receive their copies and have been calling me almost daily.

You said in your last message that you would be shipping them by air parcel on 10 April, so I would have expected to receive them by now. Of course, I am used to ordering through your Boston office, so I may have misjudged the time it takes from London.

Anything you can tell me about when they were shipped will be most helpful.

Thank you,

Keith Wells, Proprietor

Blue Crane Books

Regina, Saskatchewan

FIGURE A.9
In-Depth Critique: A Typical E-Mail Message

On the Internet, everything on the left side of the @ symbol is the user name; everything on the right side is the domain name of the organization, or its service provider. This machine name usually ends with a country code (such as fr for France, dk for Denmark, hk for Hong Kong). Within Canada the country code, .ca, may be replaced with the type of organization that owns that particular name.

- .com business and commercial users
- .gov government and related groups
- .net network providers
- .org organizations and nonprofit groups

E-mail programs will allow you to send mail to an entire group of people all at once. First, you create a distribution list. Then you type the name of the list in the *To:* line instead of typing the addresses of every person in the group.

The *From:* line contains your e-mail address. The *Date:* line contains the day of the week, date (day, month, year), time, and time zone.

The *Subject:* line describes the content of the message and presents an opportunity for you to build interest in your message. The *cc:* line allows you to send copies of a message to more than one person at a time. It also allows everyone on the list to see who else received the same message. The *Bcc:* line lets you send copies to people without the other recipients knowing–a practice considered unethical by some.[8] The *Attachments:* line contains the name(s) of the file(s) you attach to your e-mail message. The file can be a word-processing document, a digital image, an audio or video message, a spreadsheet, or a software program.

Body

You might consider your message's header to be something like letterhead, because the rest of the space below the header is for the body of your message. In the *To:* and *From:* lines, some headers actually print out the names of the sender and the receiver in addition to the e-mail addresses.

Do include a greeting in your e-mail. As pointed out in Chapter 6, greetings personalize your message. Leave one line space above and below your greeting to set it off from the rest of your message. Again, depending on the level of formality you want, you may choose to end your greeting with a colon (most formal), a comma (conversational), or even two hyphens (informal).

Your message begins one blank line space below your greeting. Just as in memos and letters, skip one line space between paragraphs and include headings, numbered lists, bulleted lists, and embedded lists when appropriate. Limit your line lengths to a maximum of 80 characters by inserting a hard return at the end of each line. Many e-mail programs allow you to set the line length for an automatic word wrap; then, you do not need to insert hard returns at the ends of lines.

One blank line space below your message, include a simple closing, often just one word. A blank line space below that, include your signature. Whether you type your name or use a signature file, including your signature personalizes your message.

Time-Saving Messages

If there's a way to speed up the communication process, the organization stands to gain. Telephones and electronic mail systems are quick, as are mailgrams, telegrams, faxes, and the like. In addition, organizations have developed special formats to reduce the amount of time spent writing and typing short messages:

- *Fax cover sheets.* When faxing messages, you may use a fax cover sheet, which includes the recipient's name, company, fax number, and city; the sender's name, complete address, fax number, and telephone number; the number of pages being sent; a phone number to call if the faxed transmission isn't successful; and enough space for any brief message. The format for this information varies widely. When a document is self-explanatory, a cover sheet may be unnecessary, so be sure not to waste paper or transmission time.
- *Memo-letters.* Printed with a heading somewhat like a memo's, memo-letters provide a space for an inside address so that the message may be sent outside the company (see Figure A.10). When the memo is folded properly, the address shows through a window in the envelope, thereby eliminating the need to address the envelope separately. Memo-letters often include a space for a reply message so that the recipient doesn't have to print out or type a whole new letter in response; carbonless copy sets allow sender and recipient to keep on file a copy of the entire correspondence.
- *Short-note reply technique.* Popular in many organizations, this technique can be used even without a special form. The recipient of a memo (or sometimes a letter) simply handwrites a response on the original document, makes a copy for the files, and sends the annotated original back to the person who wrote it.
- *Letterhead postcards.* Ideal for short, impersonal messages, letterhead postcards are preprinted with a list of responses so that the "writer" merely checks the appropriate response(s) and slips the postcard into the mail. Organizations such as mail-order companies and government agencies use these time-saving devices to communicate frequently with individuals by mail.

The important thing to realize about these and all other message formats is that they've developed over time to meet the need for clear communication and to speed responses to the needs of customers, suppliers, and associates.

Reports

You can enhance your report's effectiveness by paying careful attention to its appearance and layout. Follow

MEMO

TO: Green Ridge Gifts
1786 Century Road
Nashua, NH 03060
USA

FROM: Whiteside Import/Export, Ltd.
1601 Ronson Drive
Toronto, Ontario M9W 3E3
CANADA

SUBJECT: Order for Royal Dorchester china completer sets

DATE: October 11, 2000

MESSAGE:

The six Wellington pattern completer sets that you ordered by telephone October 9 are on their way and should reach your shop by October 18.

The three Mayfield pattern completer sets are coming from the factory, however, and will not arrive here until October 26 or 27. That means you will get them around November 2 or 3.

Do you still want the Mayfield sets? Would you like us to bill you for the Wellington sets only so that you can pay for the Mayfield order separately? Please add your reply below, retain the yellow copy for your records, and send us the white and pink copies.

SIGNED: Barbara Hutchins

REPLY: PLEASE SEND THE MAYFIELD SETS AS SOON AS POSSIBLE. YOU MAY BILL FOR BOTH MAYFIELD AND WELLINGTON SETS.
DATE: OCT. 15, 2000

SIGNED: William L. Smith

□ One blank space

* Variable space depending on length of letter

FIGURE A.10

In-Depth Critique: Memo-Letter

Memo-letters such as this one are convenient for the writer, and, with the space for a reply message, they can be convenient for the recipient. However, they are much less formal than a business letter for outside correspondence.

whatever guidelines your organization prefers, but remember to be neat and consistent throughout. If it's up to you to decide formatting questions, the following conventions may help you decide how to handle margins, headings, spacing and indention, and page numbers.

Margins

All margins on a report page are at least 1 inch wide. Margins of 1 inch are customary for double-spaced pages, and margins of between 11/4 and 11/2 inches are customary for single-spaced pages. The top, left, and right margins are usually the same, but the bottom margins can be 11/2 times as deep as the others. Some special pages also have deeper top margins. You may set top margins as deep as 2 inches for pages that contain major titles, prefatory parts such as the table of contents or the executive summary, supplementary parts such as the reference notes or bibliography, and textual parts such as the first page of the text or the first page of each chapter.

If you're going to bind your report at the left or at the top, add half an inch to the margin on the bound edge (Figure A.11). Because of the space taken by the binding on left-bound reports, make the centre point of the page a quarter inch to the right of the centre of the paper. Be sure that centred headings are centred between the margins, not centred on the paper. Of course, computers can do this for you automatically. Other guidelines for formatting a report can be found in the sample in Chapter 14.

Headings

Headings of various levels provide visual clues to a report's organization. Figure 12.7, on page 325, illustrates one good system for showing these levels, but many variations exist. No matter which system you use, be sure to be consistent.

Spacing and Indentions

The spacing and indention of most elements of a report are relatively easy. If your report is double-spaced (perhaps to ease comprehension of technical material), indent all paragraphs five character spaces (or about 1/2 inch). In single-spaced reports, you can block the paragraphs (no indentions), leaving one blank line between them.

When using a typewriter, properly spacing the material on the title page is more complicated. For reports that will be bound on the left, start a quarter inch to the right of centre. From that point, backspace once for each two letters in the line so that the line will appear centred once the report is bound.

To correctly place lines of type on the title page, first count the number of lines in each block of copy, including blank lines. Subtract the total from 66 (the total number of lines on an 11-inch page) to get the number of unused lines. To allocate these unused lines equally among the spaces between the blocks of copy, divide the number of

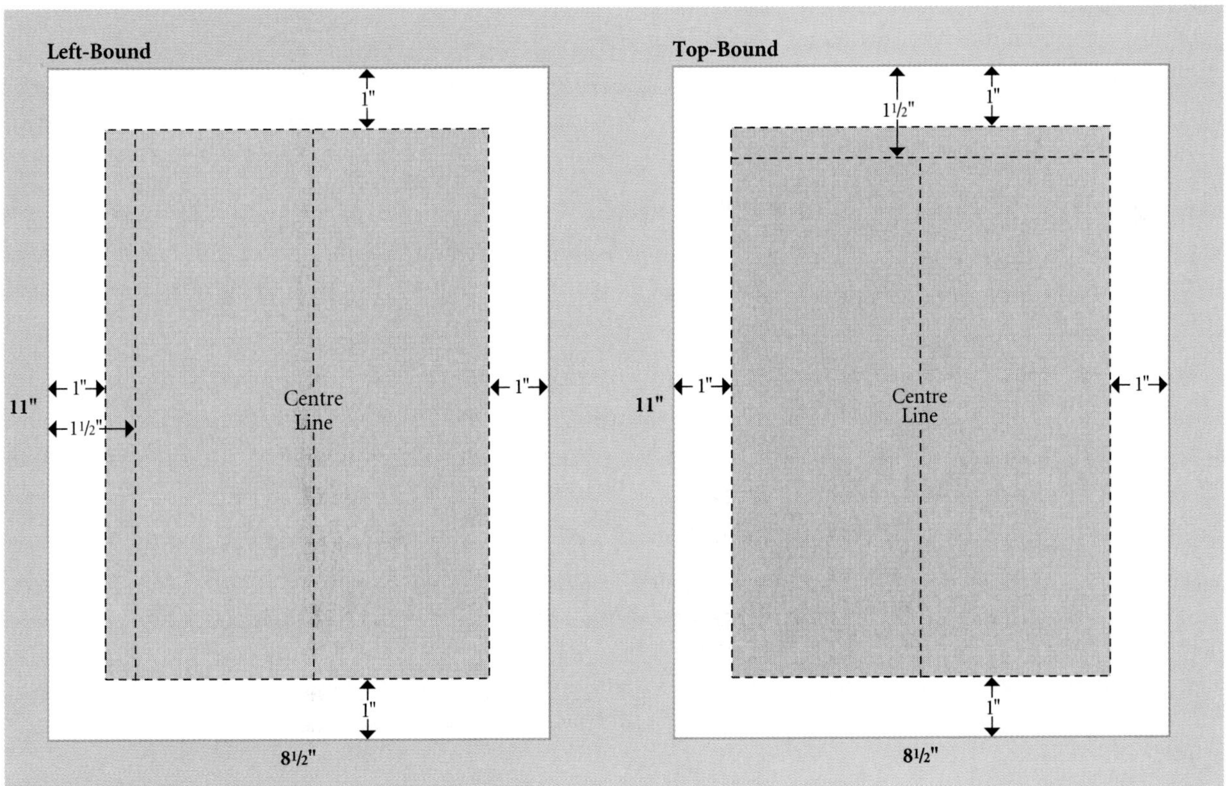

FIGURE A.11
Margins for Formal Reports

unused lines by the number of blank areas (always one more than the number of blocks of copy). The result is the number of blank lines to devote to each section. Of course, a computer with a good word-processing program will do these calculations for you at the click of a mouse. As the title page of the sample report in Chapter 14 shows, the title page should look well balanced.

Page Numbers

Remember that every page in the report is counted but that not all pages have numbers shown on them. The first page of the report, normally the title page, is not numbered. All other pages in the prefatory section are numbered with a lowercase roman numeral, beginning with ii and continuing with iii, iv, v, and so on. The unadorned (no dashes, no period) page number is centred at the bottom margin.

Number the first page of the text of the report with the unadorned arabic numeral 1, centred at the bottom margin (double- or triple-spaced below the text). In left-bound reports, number the following pages (including the supplementary parts) consecutively with unadorned arabic numerals (2, 3, and so on), placed at the top right-hand margin (double- or triple-spaced above the text). For top-bound reports and for special pages having 2-inch top margins, centre these page numbers at the bottom margin.

Meeting Documents

The success of any meeting depends on the preparation of the participants and on the follow-up measures they take to implement decisions or to seek information after the meeting. Meeting documents–agendas and minutes–aid this process by putting the meeting plan and results into permanent, written form. Although small informal meetings may not require a written agenda, any meeting involving a relatively large number of people or covering a lot of ground will run more smoothly if an agenda is distributed in advance. A written agenda helps participants prepare by telling them what will be discussed, and it helps keep them on track once the meeting begins. The typical agenda format (shown in Figure A.12) may seem stiff and formal, but it helps structure a meeting so that as little time as possible is wasted. It also provides opportunities for discussion, if that's what is called for.

The presentation, a special form of meeting that allows for relatively little group interaction, may also require an agenda or a detailed outline. Special visual aids such as flip charts help attendees grasp the message, and copies of the charts are often provided for future reference.

After a meeting the secretary who attended prepares a set of minutes for distribution to all attendees and to any other interested parties. The minutes are prepared in much the same format as a memo or letter, except for the heading, which takes this form:

MINUTES
PLANNING COMMITTEE MEETING
MONDAY, AUGUST 21, 2000

Present: [All invited attendees who were present are listed here, generally by rank, in alphabetical order, or in some combination.]

Absent: [All invited attendees who were not present are listed here, in similar order.]

The body of the minutes follows the heading, and it notes the times the meeting started and ended, all major decisions reached at the meeting, all assignments of tasks to meeting participants, and all subjects that were deferred to a later meeting. In addition, the minutes objectively summarize important discussions, noting the names of those who contributed major points. Outlines, subheadings, and lists help organize the minutes, and additional documentation (such as tables or charts submitted by meeting participants) are noted in the minutes and attached.

At the end of the minutes, the words *Submitted by* should be added, followed by a couple of blank lines for a signature and then the signer's printed (or typed) name and title (if appropriate). If the minutes have been written by one person and prepared by another, the preparer's initials should be added, as in the reference initials on a letter or memo.

An informal meeting may not require minutes. Attendees simply pencil their own notes onto their copies of the agenda. Follow-up is then their responsibility, although the meeting leader may need to remind them through a memo, phone call, or face-to-face talk.

AGENDA

PLANNING COMMITTEE MEETING

Tuesday, August 21, 2000
10:00 A.M.

Executive Conference Room

I. Call to Order

II. Roll Call

III. Approval of Agenda

IV. Approval of Minutes from Previous Meeting

V. Chairperson's Report

VI. Subcommittee Reports
   A. New Markets
   B. New Products
   C. Finance

VII. Unfinished Business

VIII. New Business
   A. Carson and Canfield Data
   B. Reassignments

IX. Announcements

X. Adjournment

FIGURE A.12
Agenda Format

APPENDIX B

Documentation of Report Sources

Documenting a report is too important a task to undertake haphazardly. By providing information about your sources, you improve your own credibility–as well as the credibility of the facts and opinions you present. By documenting your work, you give readers the means for checking your findings and pursuing the subject further. Also, documenting your report is the accepted way to give credit to the people from whose work you have drawn.

The specific style you use to document your report may vary from the styles recommended here. Experts recommend various forms, depending on your field or discipline. Moreover, your employer or client may use a form different from any the experts suggest. Don't let this discrepancy confuse you. If your employer specifies a form, use it; the standardized form is easier for colleagues to understand. However, if the choice of form is left to you, adopt a style like one of those described here. Just be consistent within any given report, using the same order, punctuation, and format from one reference citation or bibliography entry to the next. Of course, to document report sources, you have to find the information you need.

Finding Sources

Chapter 13 describes the difference between primary data and secondary data and tells how to gather both kinds of research. Primary research (such as conducting studies and surveys yourself) is documented within the text of your report through descriptions of your methods and findings. This appendix describes how to present the results of secondary research in your report. Secondary sources for business research can be obtained from libraries and computerized databases.

Libraries

The first step in getting information is to decide which library to visit or to phone with your query. The *American Library Directory* lists more than 3000 public, university, college and special libraries in Canada. In addition, many companies, nonprofit organizations, and professional associations have their own libraries, as do provincial legislatures. In many cases, the Internet can give you a good idea of what a library has to offer. Many libraries can be reached online for general information, access to the computerized catalogue, and even information about which books are out on loan and thus unavailable.

BASIC REFERENCES

Once you've decided which library to use, visit the reference section. A librarian with specialized knowledge of general sources of information can direct you to the appropriate dictionaries, encyclopedias, almanacs, atlases, biographical reference books, handbooks, manuals, directories of companies and associations, and perhaps even a collection of corporations' annual reports. In the absence of a knowledgeable reference librarian, consult *Reference Books: A Brief Guide* or *Business Information Sources,* or you can refer to Figure B.1, which lists the major reference books used by business researchers.

BOOKS AND ARTICLES

Both books and articles provide in-depth coverage of specific topics. Although articles are more timely than books, books have a broader focus. A combination of the two often provides the best background for your report.

Numerous books and articles are published every year, and libraries must be selective when choosing works to put on their shelves. So when you need specialized

- *Associations Canada:* directory of 20 000 Canadian and international associations.
- *Biography Index:* Cumulative index to biographical material in books and magazines.
- *Blue Book of Canadian Business:* Corporate and executive profiles.
- *Books in Print Plus–Canada:* Comprehensive list of published books indexed by subject, author, and title. See *Books in Print* for US books.
- *Canadian Almanac and Directory:* Statistical information about many events, people, and places. Indexes contain both subject headings and specific names.
- *Canadian Key Business Directory:* Comprehensive information about corporations.
- *Directory of Canadian Manufacturers (Dun & Bradstreet):* Provides basic information about manufacturers, including company officers, locations, products.
- *Directory of Canadian-Made Products:* Contains basic information about manufacturers, including company officers, locations, and products.
- *Dow Jones Interactive:* Includes full-text reports from 500 market research and investment firms; Dow Jones and Reuters newswires.
- *Encyclopedia of Consumer Brands:* Comprehensive list of brand names.
- *Financial Post Investment Reports:* Financial profiles.
- *Report on Business Magazine – The Top 1000 (Globe and Mail):* Comprehensive tables profiling leadership, products, and earnings of the top 1000 Canadian businesses. Appears annually.
- *Scott's Industrial Directories:* Organized by region; also includes a directory of exporters.
- *Standard and Poor's Registry of Corporations, Directors and Executives:* Lists officers, products, sales volume, and number of employees.
- *Who's Who in Canadian Business:* Profiles of key figures in the Canadian business scene.

FIGURE B.1
Major Reference Works

information, a public library may not be very useful. You'll have better luck finding books and articles on technical subjects at university and college libraries (assuming the school offers courses in those subjects) and in company libraries.

When you perform a search of a library's holdings, you will most likely use computerized catalogues. Computerized catalogues have, by and large, replaced traditional card catalogues, which contain vast numbers of index cards organized by subject, title, and author. A computerized catalogue is organized in the same way, but some systems offer more options for searching. For example, you may be able to perform a search by keywords in the title, subject, and author. Thus, if you enter only the author's last name–let's say it is "Lesley"–the catalogue will give you all works with the name "Lesley" in it, as the first, middle, or last name. A computerized catalogue may also support searches by call number. This kind of search can be useful because the summary list will display the titles with call numbers close to the call number you entered. In other words, you will be given the titles of books on the same subject.

You will find in some libraries microform or microfiche catalogues of their holdings. Like computerized catalogues, these take up far less room than traditional card catalogues, but are not as convenient to use as an electronic system.

ABSTRACTS

One way to find out a lot relatively quickly is to consult abstracts. Instead of just supplying a categorized list of article titles, as indexes do, abstracts summarize each article's contents as well. Many fields are served by abstracts that regularly review articles in the most useful periodicals. Figure B.2 lists the names of a few abstracts that may prove useful. Many are now provided online.

PERIODICAL DATABASES

You can now access newspaper, magazine, and journal articles electronically, either through a university or college library or public library. The companies that provide these electronic databases license them to the institution. Consequently, to use the database, you must either be a student of the university or college or a library customer with a valid library card. If you do not fit into either category, you will most likely have to pay for the service.

Canadian Research Index
Conference Paper Index
Dissertation Abstracts
EI Tech Index
ERIC–Educational Research Information Clearinghouse
Food Science and Technology Abstracts
Health and Safety Science Abstracts
ICONDA–International Construction Database
Pollution Abstracts
PsycInfo
Risk Abstracts
Social Services Abstracts
Sociological Abstracts (Sociofile)

FIGURE B.2
Selected Abstracts

When using periodical databases, you will find that many articles are provided in a full-text version, but not all. For those that aren't, you will find either a citation or brief abstract. Figure B.3 lists the indexes.

GOVERNMENT DOCUMENTS

When you want to know the exact provisions of a law, the background of a court decision, or the current population patterns and business trends, you can consult the government documents section of a library or online resources. This sort of research can be rather complicated, but a librarian will direct you to the information you need. All you have to know is the government body you're interested in (provincial legislature, Statistics Canada, Canada Customs and Revenue Agency) and some sort of identification for the specific information you need (such as the most recent census information or the tax cuts in the 2001 budget). If you have a date and the name of a publication containing the document, so much the better.

Using Source Information

Locating all this information is just the first step, of course. Once you have the necessary information, you'll want to use what you've found. You begin by recording information effectively. By taking down information that's complete and well organized, you'll capture the information you need and avoid backtracking to look up something you forgot. Moreover, to maintain your credibility and ethics, you'll want to keep current with the issues of copyright and fair use.

- *ABI/INFORM Global:* 1300 sources (350 from outside the US) indexed and abstracted. 600 available in full text.
- *Business & Industry:* 1000 trade and business publications covering over 180 countries. Includes leading trade magazines, newsletters, general business press, international dailies.
- *Canadian Business and Current Affairs (CBCA):* Canadian business, academic, and general interest magazines.
- *Canadian NewsDisc:* articles from Canadian newspapers and transcripts of national news broadcasts from CBC.
- *Canadian Periodicals Index (CPI.Q):* articles from general interest magazines and the *Globe and Mail.*
- *Computer Database:* articles from computer, business, and technology magazines.
- *Dow Jones Interactive:* includes more than 6000 global publications.
- *Expanded Academic ASAP:* articles from research and scholarly journals in all subjects.
- *General BusinessFile ASAP:* articles from business publications (mainly US) and international magazines.
- *Lexis/Nexis:* focuses on business, legal, and news resources. Includes journal and newspaper articles, broadcast transcripts, law reports, and company filings.
- *Repère:* Indexing and full-text articles from French-language magazines. The full-text is mainly Canadian; indexing is mainly international.

FIGURE B.3
Indexes of Articles in Newspapers, Magazines, and Journals
Major indexes are available online or on CD-ROM. Most of these indexes contain full-text articles.

Recording Information

The recording system that most students use (and many instructors recommend) is taking notes on 3-by-5-inch index cards, noting only one thought, quote, or other piece of information on each card. Try to summarize information in your own words, unless you think specific data or quotations may be useful. Using note cards has several advantages: Cards are easy to use, easy to carry around, and easy to sort and rearrange.

You're using these note cards to help you remember and retrieve useful information for your report, so be sure to record all bibliographical information carefully. Write the author's name, the title of the book or article, the publication information, and page numbers at the top of each card. (As an alternative, when you're collecting several pieces of information from each source, you might prepare a bibliography card for each one, number the cards, and then use these numbers to cross-reference your note cards.) It's helpful to note at the top of the card the general subject of the material (either in a simple phrase or with identifying numbers from your preliminary outline) so that you can sort your notes more easily when it comes time to write your report. Also indicate whether the information is a direct quote, a paraphrase of someone else's idea, or an idea of your own.[1] Figure B.4 shows a sample note card.

The card system works, without question. You won't go wrong with it. However computers can also help you capture and organize research information.[2] Here are three ways:

- *Organizing and outlining.* If you've used the outlining capability in a word processor, you already know how helpful it can be. You can quickly move headings and blocks of information–about as easily as you can shuffle a deck of index cards. And outliners have a major advantage over index cards in that they let you select the amount of information you want to see at any given time. Sometimes it's hard to see the big picture if you have 30 or 40 pieces of detailed information strewn across the table. Outliners let you collapse or expand your outline, showing as many levels as you want. This feature can be a great help when you're trying to organize the flow of your speech.
- *Searching.* Now where was that quote about water pollution? If you have more than a few dozen cards, which is easy to do, finding a specific piece of information can be time consuming. With the notes in your computer, you simply use the "find" function to locate the information. It's faster, and you have much less chance of missing whatever information you're looking for.
- *Linking.* This is not a feature found in the typical word processor, but software packages such as Info Select make it easy to weave "threads" through your research materials. For instance, for some research on water pollution, information-management software could highlight for you all the research notes that involve government regulation. If you had organized your notes by problems and solutions, in chronological order, or from general concepts to specific details, these bits of information about regulation would probably be spread throughout your outline. By reminding you of such links, the software helps you handle all the themes and subthemes of your report clearly and consistently.

You may find that using a combination of index cards (to capture information while you're reading it) and com-

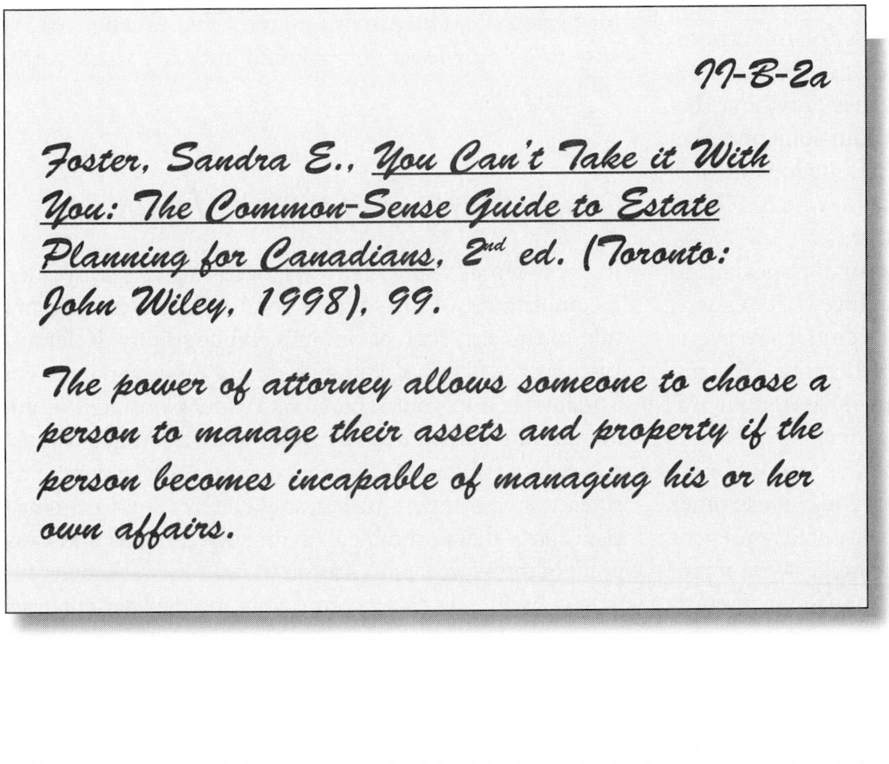

II-B-2a

Foster, Sandra E., <u>You Can't Take it With You: The Common-Sense Guide to Estate Planning for Canadians</u>, 2nd ed. (Toronto: John Wiley, 1998), 99.

The power of attorney allows someone to choose a person to manage their assets and property if the person becomes incapable of managing his or her own affairs.

FIGURE B.4
Sample Note Card

puter software (to manage the information once you've captured it) is the best solution. Whichever method you choose, be sure to record all the facts you need to responsibly credit your sources. Being thorough not only saves you time if you need to go back and check facts or quotes, but it is also your ethical responsibility.[3]

Understanding Copyright and Fair Use

You have an important reason for carefully documenting the sources you consult during secondary research: Although ideas belong to no one person, the way they're expressed provides the livelihood for many scholars, consultants, and writers. To protect the interests of these people, most countries have established copyright laws. If you transgress those laws, you or your company could be sued, not to mention embarrassed.

In addition to covering printed materials such as books and magazines, copyright law covers audiovisual materials, digital media, many forms of artistic expression, computer programs, maps, mailing lists, even answering machine messages. However, copyright law does not protect

- Titles, names, short phrases, and slogans
- Familiar symbols or designs
- Lists of ingredients or contents
- Ideas, procedures, methods, systems, processes, concepts, principles, discoveries, or devices (although it does cover their description, explanation, or illustration)

A work is considered copyrighted as soon as it's put into fixed form, even if it hasn't been registered.[4]

As discussed in Chapter 13, you can avoid plagiarism whenever you quote another person's work by telling where you found the statement. This documentation applies to books, articles, tables, charts, diagrams, song lyrics, scripted dialogue, letters, speeches–anything that you take verbatim (word for word) from someone else. Even if you paraphrase the material (putting in your own words), it's best to give credit to the person who has found an effective way of expressing an idea.

However, for general knowledge or for specialized knowledge that's generally known among your readers, you do not have to cite a source. For example, everyone knows that 1867 was the year of Confederation. You can say so on your own authority, even if you've read an article in which the author says the same thing.

Of course, merely crediting the source is not always enough. The fair use doctrine says that you can use other people's work only as long as you don't unfairly prevent them from benefiting as a result. For example, if you reproduce someone else's copyrighted questionnaire in a report you're writing (and identify the source thoroughly), you're preventing the author from selling a copy of that questionnaire to your readers.

In general, you do best to avoid relying to such a great extent on someone else's work. However, when you can't avoid it, contact the copyright holder (usually the author or publisher) for permission to reprint. You'll usually be asked to pay a fee.

Fair use is decided in the courts on a case-by-case basis. So you won't find any hard-and-fast rules about when to get permission. In general, however, you would probably request permission to use

- Any reproduction of a piece of artwork (including fully reproduced charts and tables) or excerpt from commercially produced audiovisual material
- Any dialogue from a play or line from a poem or song
- Any portion of consumable materials, such as workbooks
- Multiple copies of copyrighted works that you intend to distribute widely or repeatedly, especially for non-educational purposes

Under Canadian copyright law, a work is copyrighted until December 31 of the fiftieth year after the death of the creator of the work. Works that are jointly created are covered by copyright until December 31 of the fiftieth year after the death of the last creator.[5]

When deciding whether you may use someone else's work without permission, remember that the courts (if they get involved) will consider the length of your quotation in relation to the total length of the work from which it is taken, the type of work you are taking it from, your purpose, and the effect your action has on the original author's efforts to distribute the work. If you think you may be infringing on the author's rights, write for permission and provide a credit line. In any case, be sure to acknowledge the original author's work with a source note.

Preparing Reference Lists

In every report you write, you'll need to give your readers a complete list of the sources you used. You can assign a title to this list, such as Sources, Bibliography, Reference List, Works Cited (if you include only those sources you actually cited in your report), or Works Consulted (if you include uncited sources as well). Your reference list also serves as a reading list for readers who want to pursue the subject of your report further, so you may want to annotate each entry–that is, comment on the subject matter and viewpoint of the source, as well as on its usefulness. Annotations may be written in either complete or incomplete sentences:

Tammemagi, H.Y. *Writing Proposals: Writing to Get Results.* 2nd ed. Bellingham, WA: International Self-Counsel Press, 1999. Makes the process of writing proposals understandable for the inexperienced proposal writer. 105 pages.

Depending on the length of your report and the complexity and number of your sources, you may either place the entire bibliography at the end of the report (after the endnotes) or place relevant sections at the end of each chapter. Another way to make a long bibliography more manageable is to subdivide it into categories (a classified bibliography), either by type of reference (such as books, articles, and unpublished material) or by subject matter (such as government regulation, market forces, and so on).

Reference List Construction

When preparing the reference list, start each entry at the left margin, with the author's last name first. Entries are alphabetized and single-spaced (with a double space between entries). After the first line, these entries are usually indented (customarily five spaces or as few as two). See Figure B.5 and the Electrovision report that appears in Chapter 14.

Many schemes have been proposed for organizing the information in source notes, but all of them break the information into three main parts: (1) information about the author, (2) information about the work, and (3) information about the publication. The first part includes the author's name, last name first. The second part includes the title of the work, and such other identifying information as the edition and volume number. The third part includes the place of publication, the publisher, and the date of publication, followed by relevant page numbers. A few details about these elements are described in the sections that follow.

AUTHOR'S NAME

If the author of the work is only one person, spell out the name (last name first) and follow it with a period. For multiple authors, only the first author's name appears in reversed order. Two authors' names are separated with *and.* For three or more authors, separate the names with commas and insert *and* before the last author's name. For more than three authors, you usually list all the authors; however, it's also acceptable simply to insert *et al.* or *and others* after the first author's name, with no preceding comma.

TITLE OF THE WORK

Titles commonly appear uppercase and lowercase, which means that the first and last words start with a capital letter, as do all nouns, pronouns, verbs, adverbs, and adjectives. However, prepositions, conjunctions, and articles start with a lowercase letter; exceptions include prepositions that are an inseparable part of an expression (as in "Looking Up New Words") and often prepositions and conjunctions with more than four letters. For works that have a two-part title, use a colon to separate the two parts, and capitalize the letter that comes right after the colon.

How to Conduct Surveys: A Step-By-Step Guide

Titles of books, periodicals (journals and magazines published at regular intervals), and other major works are usually italicized on computer (or underlined on a typewriter). Sometimes they appear in all capitals (with no italics or underlining) to make the keyboarding task easier and to make the title stand out more. Titles of articles, pamphlets, chapters in books, and the like are most often placed in quotation marks.

PUBLICATION INFORMATION

Bibliographic entries referring to periodicals don't usually include the publisher's name and place of business, but entries for books, pamphlets, and other hard-to-find works do include such publication information. In a book entry, the first item of publication data is the city where the publisher is located. If the city is large and well known and if there are no other well-known cities by the same name, its name can appear alone. However, if necessary for proper identification, the province, state, or country should also be indicated. Abbreviations are used for states and provinces. A colon follows the name of the place.

The publisher's name comes after the colon, often in a shortened form. For example, Pearson Education Canada, Inc., can easily be identified when shortened to Pearson Education Canada. If you begin with shortened publishers' names, be sure to carry through with the same short forms throughout. Use a publisher's full name if it's not well known or if it might be confused with some other organization. The publisher's name is followed by a comma.

The publication date is the most recent year on the copyright notice. Ignore the dates of printing.

Manuals of Style

For more specific format guidelines about capitalization, punctuation, abbreviation, and order of the elements within these three main parts, follow the style established by your employer or consult a style manual. A wide variety of style manuals provide information on constructing reference lists (and on documentation in general):

Achtert, Walter S., and Joseph Gibaldi. *The MLA Style Manual.* New York: Modern Language Association, 1985. Basis for the note and bibliography style used in much academic writing and recommended in many university textbooks on writing term papers; provides a lot of examples in the humanities.

Reference List

Booth, Patricia. *Challenge and Change: Embracing the Team Concept*, The Conference Board of Canada, Report 123-94: Ottawa: The Conference Board of Canada, 1994.

Canadian Human Rights Commission. *The Canadian Human Rights Act Employer Guide.* Ottawa: Minister of Supply and Services Canada, 1981.

Cleese, John. *Meetings, Bloody Meetings.* London: Video Arts, 1993. [Videorecording].

Confederation Centre of the Arts. "The Charlottetown Festival May 31–October 14, 2000." [Brochure].

Davidson, Keith. "Function, Not Form, Drives Future Documents." *Canadian Printer*, 108, no. 1 (January 2000): 39–40.

Ennis, Pam. Interview by author. Toronto, Ontario. 16 September 1998.

Fink, Arlene and Jacqueline Kosecoff. *How to Conduct Surveys: A Step-By-Step Guide.* Thousand Oaks, CA: Sage Publications, 1998.

Foster, Sandra E. *You Can't Take it With You: The Common-Sense Guide to Estate Planning for Canadians*, 2nd ed. Toronto: John Wiley, 1998.

Goby, Valerie Priscilla and Justus Helen Lewis. "The Key Role of Listening in Business: A Study of the Singapore Insurance Industry." *Business Communication Quarterly*, 63, no. 2 (June 2000): 41–51.

"Hackers." *The 5th Estate.* CBC Television. 6 December 2000.

Kingston, Anne. "What's a Wife Worth?" *Saturday Night*, 12 May 2001, 22–30.

Landis, Dan and Rabi S. Bhagat, eds. *Handbook of Intercultural Training.* Thousand Oaks, CA: Sage, 1996.

"Mediation Better Way to Handle Conflicts: Companies Increasingly Looking for Alternatives to Legal Action." *Financial Post Daily*, 9(8), 15 February 1996, 18.

Meek, James T. Draft of remarks delivered to National Student Leaders' Orientation Conference, June 4, 1996. Print copy courtesy of Scotiabank.

Ravensbergen, Jan. "Software Firm Plays Hardball." *Montreal Gazette*, 2 December 1999, sec. C, 1.

Statistics Canada. *Place Name Lists: Quebec and Ontario.* Ottawa: Statistics Canada, 1993.

Steele, Peter A. "Implementation of Cyber Appliances Through Cable Television." Master's thesis, San Diego State University, 1996.

Sutherland, Robert J., Vice Chairman, Royal Bank of Canada, "The Benefits to Canadians of Building a Bank for the 21st Century." Delivered at the Annual Meeting of the Ontario Chamber of Commerce, May 3, 1998. http://www.royalbank.com/news/news/19980506_sp.html [accessed 7 September 1998].

Swartz, Mark. Personal e-mail, 11 June 1997.

Tammemagi, H.Y. *Writing Proposals: Writing to Get Results.* 2nd ed. Bellingham, WA: International Self-Counsel Press, 1999.

Telus. *2000 Annual Report.*

FIGURE B.5
Sample Reference List

American Psychological Association. *Publication Manual of the American Psychological Association.* 4th ed. Washington, D.C.: American Psychological Association, 1994. Details the author-date system, which is preferred in the social sciences and often in the natural sciences as well.

The Chicago Manual of Style. 14th ed. Chicago: University of Chicago Press, 1993. Known as the *Chicago Manual* and widely used in the publishing industry; detailed treatment of documentation in Chapters 15 and 16.

Gibaldi, Joseph. *MLA Handbook for Writers of Research Papers.* 5th ed. New York: Modern Language Association, 1999. One of the standard style manuals for footnote and bibliography form.

Gibaldi, Joseph. *MLA Style Manual and Guide to Scholarly Publishing.* 2d ed. New York: Modern Language Association, 1998. Full treatment of documentation and a discussion of scholarly publishing.

Harnack, Andrew, and Eugene Kleppinger. *Online! A Reference Guide to Using Internet Sources.* New York: St. Martin's Press, 1998. A comprehensive review of style for citing online references.

Turabian, Kate L. *A Manual for Writers of Term Papers, Theses, and Dissertations.* Revised and expanded by Bonnie Birtwhistle Honigsblum. 6th ed. Chicago: University of Chicago Press, 1995. Based on the *Chicago Manual*, but smaller and limited to matters of concern to report writers; many examples of documenting nonstandard references.

Reference List Entries

Because you're referring your reader to a work as a whole, bibliographic entries do not usually include page numbers (unless you're citing a chapter in a book or an article). To be sure you have all the information you need when it's time to construct a reference list, use the same format during your research that you'll be using in your report. Figure B.5 contains some sample bibliographic entries, based on guidelines recommended in the *Chicago Manual of Style*.

BOOKS

In their simplest form, references to books look like the Fink and Kosecoff entry in Figure B.5. Sometimes, however, you'll want to include additional information:

- For the edition of a book, place the information after the title (using abbreviations such as 1st, 2nd, 3rd, 4th, and so on–as in the Foster entry in Figure B.5).
- For more than one work by the same author, use three em dashes (or six hyphens) in place of the author's name. (However, repeat the name if one of the books is by a single author and another is by that author with others.)
- To cite a volume number, place *vol. 3* (or the correct number) after the title or edition number and before the publication data.
- To use the name of an editor instead of an author, simply place *ed.* after the editor's name (as in the Landis entry).

PERIODICALS

The typical periodical reference looks like the Davidson entry in Figure B.5. The article author's name (if there is one) is handled as a book author's is, but the title of the article appears in quotation marks. Like the title of a book, the title of the magazine or journal appears either in italics (underlined) or in all capital letters. The page numbers are always inclusive (that is, they show the page numbers for the entire article). Entries that have no author are listed alphabetically by title.

The rest of the periodical entry can be tricky, however. For popular and business magazines, you need include only the date and page number(s) after the title (as in the Kingston entry in Figure B.5). Be sure the date is inverted (2 May 2000)–unlike the dates you use in text. For scientific or academic journals, include the volume number and treat the page number(s) as shown in the Goby and Lewis entry in Figure B.5.

As a rule of thumb, use the more scholarly style if your report is weighted heavily toward serious research in professional journals; however, if popular and trade magazines dominate your references, you may stick with the simpler style that leaves out the volume number. Another option is to use both styles, depending on the type of periodical being referenced. Your guiding principle in choosing a style is to provide the information that your readers need to find your source easily.

NEWSPAPERS

When a newspaper article doesn't have an author, the citation begins with the name of the article (and the entry is alphabetized by the first word of that title). The name of the newspaper is treated like the title of a book or periodical. Many of the best-known newspapers–such as *The Globe and Mail, The National Post,* the *New York Times,* the *Wall Street Journal*–are not easily mistaken for other newspapers, but many smaller newspapers are less easily identified. If the name of the city (plus the province or state for obscure or small cities) doesn't appear in the title of these newspapers, put the place name in brackets after the title. Finally, a newspaper reference specifies the date of publication in the same way a magazine does, and it ends with a section name or number (if appropriate) and a page number (see the Ravensbergen entry in Figure B.5).

PUBLIC DOCUMENTS

Government documents and court cases are often useful in business reports, but bibliographic entries referring to them can be difficult to construct. As you struggle with a complex set of "authors" and publication data, remember that the goal is to provide just enough information to identify the work and to distinguish it from others. In Figure B.5, the entries for the Canadian Human Rights Commission and Statistics Canada are examples of how to format government documents.

UNPUBLISHED MATERIAL

Theses, dissertations, and company reports–which are usually prepared for a limited audience of insiders–are handled similarly. The title, like an article title, is in quotation marks, and "publication" data are included to help the reader find the work (see Figure B.5 entries for Meek and for Steele). This format can be used for any written source that doesn't fall into one of the other categories, such as a sales brochure or a presentation handout. Identify the author, title, and place and date of publication as completely as you can so that your readers have a way to refer to the source.

Formal letters, speeches, interviews, and other types of unpublished references are also identified as completely as possible to give readers some means of checking your sources. Begin with the name, title, and affiliation of the "author"; then describe the nature of the communication, the date and possibly the place, and if appropriate, the location of the files containing the document (as in Figure B.5 entry for Ennis). Casual letters, interviews, and telephone conversations are rarely included in bibliographies; however, in notes you can identify the communication as personal (see Figure B.5 entry for Swartz).

ELECTRONIC MEDIA

Television and radio programs, films, computer programs, Internet sources, electronic databases, and the like are also documented. It may be more difficult for a reader to refer to some of these media (especially television and radio programs), but you still want to acknowledge ideas and facts borrowed from someone else. Figure B.5 lists three electronic entries. The information provided in these entries is sufficient to give readers a clear idea of the works you consulted. For more details on the formatting of electronic sources, consult style manuals such as the *Chicago Manual of Style* and the *MLA Style Manual.*

Choosing a Method of In-Text Citation

Once you have constructed a complete and well-organized reference list, you can choose from several methods of documenting report sources in text. Three popular ways of handling citations are the author-date system, the key-number system, and the superscript system. Although the author-date system is preferred by many style manuals, the classic superscript system is still often used in scholarly works. The key-number system is least preferred by most authorities.

Author-Date System

When using the author-date system to make a reference citation in text, simply insert the author's last name and the year of the publication within parentheses. You can add a page number when necessary:

> Choosing someone to act on your behalf is a critical decision (Foster, 1998, 98).

An alternative is to weave the name of the author into the sentence:

> According to Foster (1998), choosing someone to act on your behalf ...

When no author is named, use a short form of the title of the work.

> ... mediators play a significant role ("Mediation Better Way")

If the "author" is an organization, then shorten the name of the organization.

When listing more than one work by the same author, rely on the year of publication to distinguish between them. A lowercase letter (*a, b,* and so on) after the year differentiates two works by the same author published in the same year.

The author-date system requires a reference list containing all your sources with all the pertinent publication information. The only variable is the placement of the year of publication; for the convenience of readers, the year of publication is placed just after the author's name:

> Foster, Sandra E. 1998. *You Can't Take it With You: The Common-Sense Guide to Estate Planning for Canadians,* 2nd ed. Toronto: John Wiley.
>
> Kingston, Anne. 2001. "What's a Wife Worth?" *Saturday Night,* 12 May, 22–30.

A modification of the author-date system uses author-page information. Like the author-date system, the author-page system lets you weave references into the text. However, instead of using the author's name with the year of publication, this system uses the author's name and a page reference:

> Choosing someone to act on your behalf is a critical decision (Foster, 98).

Parenthetical references can often be reduced to just the page number:

> In their article on listening and insurance industry employees in Singapore, Goby and Lewis note that students did not rank listening as the most important skill (44).
>
> Foster offers guidance for selecting the person to act on your behalf (102–103).

Key-Number System

To use the least preferred method of documenting sources, you number each reference-list entry in sequence, with an arabic numeral followed by a period. A key-number reference list is sometimes arranged in order of the appearance of each source in the text (rather than in alphabetical order).

In the text, references are documented with numbers. The first is the number assigned to the source, the second is the page number:

> the most important decision a person may make (11:99).

This reference cites page 99 of item 11 in the reference list. The goal of using the author-date, author-page, and key-number systems is to simplify the traditional method of documentation using superscripts.

Superscript System

Source information has been traditionally handled using superscripts, which are arabic numerals placed just above the line of type. Scholarly works in the humanities are still documented using this method. The superscript lets the reader know to look for source information either in a **footnote** (at the bottom of report pages) or in an **endnote** (at the end of each chapter or at the end of the report). Footnotes can be handier for readers, but some readers find them distracting. Endnotes are less intrusive, but readers may become annoyed with flipping to the end of the report to find them.

For the reader's convenience, you can use footnotes for **content notes** (which may supplement your main text with asides about a particular issue or event, provide a cross-reference to another section of your report, or direct the reader to a related source). Then you can use endnotes for **source notes** (which document direct quotations, paraphrased passages, and visual aids). Consider which type of note is most common in your report, and then choose whether to present them all as endnotes or all as footnotes. If all your sources are listed as endnotes, you may find that a bibliography is unnecessary. However, the larger and more formal the report, the greater the need for a separate reference list. Regardless of the method you choose for referencing textual information in your report, both content notes and source notes pertaining to visual aids are placed on the same page as the visual aid.

Superscripts usually come at the end of the sentence containing the referenced statement, but a superscript may be placed right after the referenced statement to avoid confusion:

> Rising interest rates put a damper on third-quarter profits in all industries,[1] and profits did not pick up again until the Bank of Canada loosened the money supply.[2]

The first superscript in this example comes after the comma. Superscripts follow all punctuation marks except the dash (which follows the superscript).

Superscripts are numbered consecutively throughout the report. (In very long reports, they may be numbered consecutively throughout each chapter instead, as in this textbook.) If a note is added or deleted, all the reference marks that follow must be changed to maintain an unbroken sequence. If you change the superscript, be sure to renumber the corresponding notes as well. (Of course, word-processing software contains a note feature that will automatically renumber for you.) Content notes appearing in visual aids are marked with asterisks and other symbols (or italicized lowercase letters if the visual aids contain many numbers).

SOURCE NOTE MECHANICS

Source notes generally follow the same order as bibliographic entries; however, commas are often substituted for periods, and the publication information appears in parentheses. A source note often refers to a specific page number. If it does, the closing parenthesis is followed by a comma, which in turn is followed by the page number(s):

> 13. H. Y. Tammemagi, *Writing Proposals: Writing to Get Results.* 2nd ed. (Bellingham, Wash.: International Self-Counsel Press, 1999), 34–40

Notes of all varieties are single-spaced and separated from one another by a double space. In footnotes to textual information, the identifying number is indented five spaces and followed by a period (as in the Tammemagi note just cited). However, endnotes begin at the left margin (see the "References" section at the end of this book). Notes referring to visual aids are handled differently too: A source note, preceded by the underlined (italicized) word *Source* and a colon, is placed at the bottom of the visual aid; content notes, if any, are listed below the source note. Figure 14.2 on page 382 shows the placement of these notes on visual aids.

When using footnotes, plan carefully to leave enough space for the footnote at the bottom of the page and still maintain the standard margin. Word-processing software handles the layout and numbering of notes for you, whether footnotes or endnotes. When using a typewriter, separate the footnotes from the text with a line (made using the underscore key) about 11/2 inches long (15 spaces in pica type, 20 in elite).

Quotations Quotations from secondary sources must always be followed by a reference mark. However, quotations may appear in one of two forms, depending on their length. A brief quotation (three lines or less) can be typed right into the main body of the text. Quotation marks at the beginning and end of the quotation separate the other person's words from your own.

Longer quotations must be set off as extracts. An extract begins on a new line, and both right and left margins are indented five to seven spaces. No quotation marks are needed. Although the main text may be single- or double-spaced, an extract is always single-spaced.

You'll often want to leave out some part of a quotation. Ellipsis points (or dots) are the three periodlike punctuation marks that show something is missing.

> Brant has demonstrated... a wanton disregard for the realities of the marketplace. His days at the helm are numbered.... Already several lower-level executives are jockeying for position.[3]

The second sentence in this example shows you how ellipsis points are handled between sentences: A period is followed by the three dots.

Repeated Notes When you cite the same reference more than once in the course of your report, you can save time and effort by using a full citation for the first source note and a shortened form for later references. The information in repeated source notes can be handled in two ways: in a formal, traditional style or in an informal style. The formal style uses Latin abbreviations to indicate certain information; the informal style uses shortened versions of the source information instead. Here are some repeated source notes using the formal style:

4. H. Y. Tammemagi, *Writing Proposals: Writing to Get Results.* 2nd ed. (Bellingham, WA: International Self-Counsel Press, 1999), 34–40.

5. Ibid., 42. [refers to page 42 in the Tammemagi book]

6. Dan Landis and Rabi S. Bhagat, eds., *Handbook of Intercultural Training.* Thousand Oaks, CA: Sage, 1996, 187.

7. Keith Davidson, "Function, Not Form, Drives Future Documents," *Canadian Printer*, 108, no. 1 (January 2000): 39.

8. Landis and Bhagat, op. cit., 64. [refers to a new page in the book cited in note 6]

9. Davidson, loc. cit. [refers to page 39 of the article cited in note 7]

Ibid. means "in the same place"–that is, the same reference mentioned in the immediately preceding entry but perhaps a different page (indicated by giving the page number). *Op. cit.* means "in the work cited"; because it's used when at least one other reference has come between it and the original citation, you must include the last name of the author. You must also use a new page number; otherwise, you would use *loc. cit.* ("in the place cited") and omit the page number.

The informal style, which is commonly used today, avoids Latin abbreviations by adopting a shortened form for the title of a reference that is repeated. In this style, the previous list of source notes would appear as follows:

4. H. Y. Tammemagi, *Writing Proposals: Writing to Get Results.* 2nd ed. (Bellingham, WA: International Self-Counsel Press, 1999), 34–40.

5. Tammemagi, *Writing Proposals*, 42.

6. Dan Landis and Rabi S. Bhagat, eds., *Handbook of Intercultural Training* (Thousand Oaks, CA: Sage, 1996), 187.

7. Keith Davidson, "Function, Not Form, Drives Future Documents," *Canadian Printer*, 108, no. 1 (January 2000): 39.

8. Landis and Bhagat, *Handbook of Intercultural Training,* 64.

9. Davidson, "Function, Not Form, Drives Future Documents," 64.

Only the author's last name, a short form of the title, and the page number are used in this style of repeated source note. If your report has a comprehensive alphabetical bibliography, you may opt to use the short form for all your source notes, not just for first citations.

Source Note Format

Source notes present the same information as bibliographic entries, in some cases with the addition of page numbers. Source note punctuation differs from bibliographic style, and parentheses are placed around the publication data. To emphasize the differences between source notes and bibliographic entries, the examples in Figure B.6 use the same sources as the references appearing in Figure B.5.

The exact information you provide for electronic references such as notes 27–30 depends on your subject and audience and on the context of the reference. For example, when you are citing a film, it may be appropriate to note the scriptwriter or director. When constructing source notes for electronic media, consult a good style manual and use good judgment about how much information is needed.

Books

10. Arlene Fink and Jacqueline Kosecoff, *How to Conduct Surveys: A Step-By-Step Guide* (Thousand Oaks, CA: Sage Publications, 1998), 14.

11. Sandra E. Foster, *You Can't Take it With You: The Common-Sense Guide to Estate Planning for Canadians*, 2nd ed. (Toronto: John Wiley, 1998), 99–102.

12. Dan Landis and Rabi S. Bhagat, eds., *Handbook of Intercultural Training* (Thousand Oaks, CA: Sage, 1996), 187–190.

13. H. Y. Tammemagi, *Writing Proposals: Writing to Get Results.* 2nd ed. (Bellingham, WA: International Self-Counsel Press, 1999), 34–40.

Periodicals and Newspapers

14. Keith Davidson, "Function, Not Form, Drives Future Documents," *Canadian Printer*, 108, no.1 (January 2000): 39–40.

15. Valerie Priscilla Goby and Justus Helen Lewis, "The Key Role of Listening in Business: A Study of the Singapore Insurance Industry," *Business Communication Quarterly*, 63, no. 2 (June 2000): 41–51.

16. Anne Kingston, "What's a Wife Worth?" *Saturday Night*, 12 May 2001, 22–30.

17. "Mediation Better Way to Handle Conflicts: Companies Increasingly Looking for Alternatives to Legal Action," *Financial Post Daily*, 9(8), 15 February 1996, p. 18.

18. Jan Ravensbergen, "Software Firm Plays Hardball." *Montreal Gazette*, 2 December 1999, sec. C, 1.

Public Documents

19. Patricia Booth, *Challenge and Change: Embracing the Team Concept*, The Conference Board of Canada, Report 123-94 (Ottawa: The Conference Board of Canada, 1994), 7.

20. Canadian Human Rights Commission, *The Canadian Human Rights Act Employer Guide.* (Ottawa: Minister of Supply and Services Canada, 1981).

21. Statistics Canada, *Place Name Lists: Quebec and Ontario.* (Ottawa: Statistics Canada, 1993).

Unpublished Materials

22. Confederation Centre of the Arts, "The Charlottetown Festival May 31–October 14, 2000" [brochure].

23. Pam Ennis, interview by author, Toronto, Ontario, 16 September 1998.

24. James T. Meek, draft of remarks delivered to National Student Leaders' Orientation Conference, June 4, 1996, 6. Print copy courtesy of Scotiabank.

25. Peter A. Steele, "Implementation of Cyber Appliances Through Cable Television." Master's thesis, San Diego State University, 1996.

26. Telus, *2000 Annual Report.*

Electronic Media

27. John Cleese, *Meetings, Bloody Meetings*, (London: Video Arts, 1993). [Videorecording]

28. "Hackers". *The 5th Estate.* CBC Television. 6 December 2000.

29. Robert J. Sutherland, Vice Chairman, Royal Bank of Canada, "The Benefits to Canadians of Building a Bank for the 21st Century," delivered at the Annual Meeting of the Ontario Chamber of Commerce, 3 May 1998. http://www.royalbank.com/news/news/19980506_sp.html [accessed 7 September 1998].

30. Mark Swartz, personal e-mail (11 June 1997).

FIGURE B.6
Sample Source Notes

HANDBOOK

Fundamentals of Grammar and Usage

Grammar is nothing more than the way words are combined into sentences, and usage is the way words are used by a network of people–in this case, the community of business people who use English. You'll find it easier to get along in this community if you know the accepted standards of grammar and usage. What follows is a review of the basics of grammar and usage, things you've probably learned but may have forgotten. Without a firm grasp of these basics, you risk not only being misunderstood but also damaging your company's image, losing money for your company, and possibly even losing your job.

1.0 Grammar

The sentence below looks innocent, but is it really?

> We sell tuxedos as well as rent.

You might sell rent, but it's highly unlikely. Whatever you're selling, some people will ignore your message because of a blunder like this. The following sentence has a similar problem:

> Vice President Eldon Neale told his chief engineer that he would no longer be with Avix, Inc., as of June 30.

Is Eldon or the engineer leaving? No matter which side the facts are on, the sentence can be read the other way. You may have a hard time convincing either person that your simple mistake was not a move in a game of office politics. Now look at this sentence:

> The year before we budgeted more for advertising sales were up.

Confused? Perhaps this is what you meant:

> The year before, we budgeted more for advertising. Sales were up.

Maybe you meant this:

> The year before we budgeted more for advertising, sales were up.

The meaning of language falls into bundles called sentences. A listener or reader can take only so much meaning before filing a sentence away and getting ready for the next one. So, as a writer, you have to know what a sentence is. You need to know where one ends and the next one begins.

If you want to know what a thing is, you have to find out what goes into it, what its ingredients are. Luckily, the basic ingredients of an English sentence are simple. They're called the parts of speech, and the content-bearing ones are nouns, pronouns, verbs, adjectives, and adverbs. They combine with a few functional parts of speech to convey meaning. Meaning is also transmitted by punctuation, mechanics, and vocabulary.

1.1 Nouns

A noun names a person, place, or thing. Anything you can see or detect with one of your other senses has a noun to name it. Some things you can't see or sense are also nouns–ions, for example, or space. So are things that exist as ideas, such as accuracy and height. (You can see that something is accurate or that a building is tall, but you can't see the idea of accuracy or the idea of height.) These names for ideas are known as abstract nouns. The simplest nouns are the names of things you can see or touch: car, building, cloud, brick.

1.1.1 PROPER NOUNS AND COMMON NOUNS

So far, all the examples of nouns have been common nouns, referring to general classes of things. The word *building* refers to a whole class of structures. Common nouns such as *building* are not capitalized.

If you want to talk about one particular building, however, you might refer to the Glazier Building. The name is capitalized, indicating that *Glazier Building* is a proper noun.

Here are three sets of common and proper nouns for comparison:

COMMON	PROPER
city	Kansas City
company	Blaisden Company
store	Books Galore

1.1.2 PLURAL NOUNS

Nouns can be either singular or plural. The usual way to make a plural noun is to add *s* to the singular form of the word:

SINGULAR	PLURAL
rock	rocks
picture	pictures
song	songs

Many nouns have other ways of forming the plural. Letters, numbers, and words used as words are sometimes made plural by adding an apostrophe and an *s*. Very often, '*s* is used with abbreviations that have periods, lowercase letters that stand alone, and capital letters that might be confused with words when made into plurals:

Spell out all *St.*'s and *Ave.*'s.

He divided the page with a row of *x*'s.

Sarah will register the *A*'s through the *I*'s at the convention.

In other cases, however, the apostrophe may be left out:

They'll review their *ABC*s.

The stock market climbed through most of the 1980s.

Circle all *the*s in the paragraph.

In these examples, the letters used as letters and words used as words *are italicized* (discussed later in the chapter).

Other nouns, such as those below, are so-called irregular nouns; they form the plural in some way other than simply adding *s:*

SINGULAR	PLURAL
tax	taxes
specialty	specialties
cargo	cargoes
shelf	shelves
child	children
woman	women
tooth	teeth
mouse	mice
parenthesis	parentheses
son-in-law	sons-in-law
editor-in-chief	editors-in-chief

Rather than memorize a lot of rules about forming plurals, use a dictionary. If the dictionary says nothing about the plural of a word, it's formed the usual way: by adding *s*. If the plural is formed in some irregular way, the dictionary shows the plural or has a note something like this: *ples.*

Exercise

Circle the nouns in the following sentences. Determine whether each is proper/common, singular/plural, and fill in the chart accordingly.

Basketball, one of the world's most popular sports, was invented by a Canadian. Dr. James Naismith was born in Ontario in 1861. While working at the YMCA Training School in Springfield, Massachusetts, Naismith was faced with the problem of finding a sport which his students could play indoors during the long winters. In 1891, the inaugural game of basketball was played with a soccer ball and two peach baskets serving as goals. Basketball was introduced at the Olympics in 1936.

	common	proper
singular		
plural		

1.1.3 POSSESSIVE NOUNS

A noun becomes possessive when it's used to show the ownership of something. Then you add *'s* to the word:

the man's car	the woman's apartment

However, ownership does not need to be legal:

the secretary's desk	the company's assets

Also, ownership may be nothing more than an automatic association:

a day's work	a job's prestige

An exception to the rule about adding *'s* to make a noun possessive occurs when the word is singular and already has two *s* sounds at the end. In cases like the following, an apostrophe is all that's needed:

crisis' dimensions	Mr. Moses' application

When the noun has only one *s* sound at the end, however, retain the *'s:*

Chris's book	Carolyn Nuss's office

With hyphenated nouns (compound nouns), add *'s* to the last word:

HYPHENATED NOUN	POSSESSIVE NOUN
mother-in-law	mother-in-law's
mayor-elect	mayor-elect's

To form the possessive of plural nouns, just begin by following the same rule as with singular nouns: add *'s*. However, if the plural noun already ends in an *s* (as most do), drop the one you've added, leaving only the apostrophe:

the clients'~~s~~ complaints	employees'~~s~~ benefits

Exercise

Form the possessive case of each word in parentheses.

1. Currently specializing in (ladies) lingerie, the company hopes to diversify into (children) clothing.
2. Her (father-in-law) opinion is that the assignment will be (child) play.
3. (Shakespeare) poetry is moving, but Tai-Cheung feels (Keats) is more melodic.
4. The (goddess) festival takes place at harvest time.
5. The (goddesses) festival brings the entire community together.
6. The (people) prayers were long and touching.
7. The (prayers) meaning was hard to discern.
8. The (drug) effect was instantaneous.
9. The (consultants) appraisal was discouraging.
10. (James) performance evaluation is impressive, but (Chris) shows several areas needing improvement.
11. The (women) movement has long roots.

12. (Clients) expectations have risen considerably.
13. The (duchess) complexion was perfect.
14. (Science) impact on our country is incalculable.
15. The (sciences) problem is a naïve faith in objectivity.
16. (North America) beauty is breathtaking.
17. (North Americans) manners leave much to be desired.
18. The (hurricanes) ravages were devastating.
19. The (Chans) daughter is charming.
20. (Manitobans) driving is more aggressive than (Newfoundlanders).
21. The (Winnipeg Blue Bombers) passing statistics are superior to the (Calgary Stampeders).
22. The (men) blood pressures were higher than the (women).
23. The twelve (jurors) decision differed from the (judge).
24. The (business) clientele is growing.
25. The (businesses) solution was to form a coalition. ■

1.2 Pronouns

A pronoun is a word that stands for a noun; it saves repeating the noun:

> *Drivers* have some choice of weeks for vacation, but *they* must notify this office of *their* preference by March 1.

The pronouns *they* and *their* stand in for the noun *drivers*. The noun that a pronoun stands for is called the antecedent of the pronoun; *drivers* is the antecedent of *they* and *their*.

When the antecedent is plural, the pronoun that stands in for it has to be plural; *they* and *their* are plural pronouns because *drivers* is plural. Likewise, when the antecedent is singular, the pronoun has to be singular:

> We thought the *contract* had been signed, but we soon learned that *it* had not been.

1.2.1 MULTIPLE ANTECEDENTS

Sometimes a pronoun has a double (or even a triple) antecedent:

> Kathryn Boettcher and Luis Gutierrez went beyond *their* sales quotas for January.

Kathryn Boettcher, if taken alone, is a singular antecedent. So is *Luis Gutierrez*. However, when together they are the antecedent of a pronoun, they're plural and the pronoun has to be plural. Thus the pronoun is *their* instead of *her* or *his*.

Exercise

Circle each pronoun in the following paragraph. If relevant, identify the pronoun's antecedent.

> When we think of millionaires, we often picture palatial homes, designer clothes, and exotic cars. In reality, experts say that most self-made millionaires cultivate a low-key existence. Rather than flaunting his or her wealth, the typical millionaire drives an old but reliable car, and lives in a modest house in a middle-class

neighbourhood. In fact, you may know a low-profile millionaire or two without even realizing it: statistics suggest that one out of every 85 Canadians has $1 million or more in financial assets.

1.2.2 UNCLEAR ANTECEDENTS

In some sentences the pronoun's antecedent is unclear:

> Sandy Wright sent Jane Brougham *her* production figures for the previous year. *She* thought they were too low.

To which person does the pronoun *her* refer? Someone who knew Sandy and Jane and knew their business relationship might be able to figure out the antecedent for *her*. Even with such an advantage, however, a reader might receive the wrong meaning. Also, it would be nearly impossible for any reader to know which name is the antecedent of *she*.

The best way to clarify an ambiguous pronoun is usually to rewrite the sentence, repeating nouns when needed for clarity:

> Sandy Wright sent her production figures for the previous year to Jane Brougham. *Jane* thought they were too low.

The noun needs to be repeated only when the antecedent is unclear.

Exercise

Rewrite the following sentences to eliminate unclear antecedents.

1. Mr. Ashat asked Mr. Lo to review his performance evaluation.
2. Because he felt Imola was more hard-working than Savita, he asked her to stay late.
3. Before I sold perfumes, I used to walk past the department-store displays, amazed at their variety.
4. We visit the Gaspé Peninsula every year, which I always enjoy.

1.2.3 GENDER-NEUTRAL PRONOUNS

The pronouns that stand for males are *he, his,* and *him*. The pronouns that stand for females are *she, hers,* and *her*. However, you'll often be faced with the problem of choosing a pronoun for a noun that refers to both females and males:

> Each manager must make up (his, her, his or her, its, their) own mind about stocking this item and about the quantity that (he, she, he or she, it, they) can sell.

This sentence calls for a pronoun that's neither masculine nor feminine. The issue of gender-neutral pronouns responds to efforts to treat females and males even-handedly. Here are some possible ways to deal with this issue:

> Each manager must make up *his* ...

(Not all managers are men.)

> Each manager must make up *her* ...

(Not all managers are women.)

> Each manager must make up *his or her* ...

(This solution is acceptable but becomes awkward when repeated more than once or twice in a document.)

> Each manager must make up *her* … Every manager will receive *his* … A manager may send *her* …

(A manager's gender does not alternate like a windshield wiper!)

> Each manager must make up *their* …

(The pronoun can't be plural when the antecedent is singular.)

> Each manager must make up *its* …

(*It* never refers to people.)
The best solution is to make the noun plural or to revise the passage altogether:

> Managers must make up *their* minds …
>
> Each manager must decide whether …

Be careful not to change the original meaning.

Exercise

If necessary, suggest gender-neutral alternatives to the following sentences.

1. At the end of the year, the top student will have his name in the local newspaper.
2. Each employee is asked to read her benefits package carefully.
3. Any client left off the list will have to submit his claim later.
4. Wireless technology is evolving so quickly that developers must continually update their skills.
5. Each salesperson has his own tried-and-true strategies. ■

1.2.4 CASE OF PRONOUNS

The case of a pronoun tells whether it's acting or acted upon:

> *She* sells an average of five packages each week.

In this sentence *she* is doing the selling. Because *she* is acting, *she* is said to be in the nominative case. Now consider what happens when the pronoun is acted upon:

> After six months Ms. Browning promoted *her*.

In this sentence the pronoun *her* is acted upon. The pronoun *her* is thus said to be in the objective case.

Contrast the nominative and objective pronouns in this list:

NOMINATIVE	OBJECTIVE
I	me
we	us
he	him
she	her
they	them
who	whom
whoever	whomever

Objective pronouns may be used as either the object of a verb (such as *promoted*) or the object of a preposition (such as *with*):

Rob worked with *them* until the order was filled.

In this example *them* is the object of the preposition *with* because Rob acted upon–worked with–them.

Here's a sample sentence with three pronouns, the first one nominative, the second the object of a verb, and the third the object of a preposition:

He paid *us* as soon as the cheque came from *them.*

He is nominative; *us* is objective because it's the object of the verb *paid; them* is objective because it's the object of the preposition *from.*

Every writer sometimes wonders whether to use *who* or *whom:*

(Who, Whom) will you hire?

Because this sentence is a question, it's difficult to see that *whom* is the object of the verb *hire.* You can figure out which pronoun to use if you rearrange the question and temporarily try *she* and *her* in place of *who* and *whom:* "Will you hire *she?*" or "Will you hire *her?*" *Her* and *whom* are both objective, so the correct choice is "*Whom* will you hire?" Here's a different example:

(Who, Whom) logged so much travel time?

Turning the question into a statement, you get:

He logged so much travel time.

Therefore, the correct statement is:

Who logged so much travel time?

Exercise

Select the correct pronoun in parentheses.

1. There is a rift between the office manager and _____ (*me, I*).
2. It's a private matter concerning only the CEO and _____ (*he, him*).
3. The strength of ____ (*we, us*) Canadians is an ability to recognize our weaknesses.
4. ___ (*We, Us*) Canadians possess an ability to recognize our weaknesses.
5. ___ (*Who, Whom*) is responsible for the fourth-quarter performance evaluations?
6. Since we had little sales experience, Jean-Claude and ____ (*I, me*) expected Ellen and ___ (*she, her*) to meet the quota first.
7. Wendy and _____ (*I, me*) summarized Gerald Schwartz's proposal for ____ (*they, them*).
8. If you do not understand the assignment, please see the project manager or ___ (*me, I*).
9. Java training will be given to ____________(*whoever, whomever*) requires it.
10. (*She, her*) _____ and Max disagree about _____ (*who, whom*) should initiate negotiations. ■

1.2.5 POSSESSIVE PRONOUNS

Possessive pronouns are like possessive nouns in the way they work: They show ownership or automatic association.

her job	their preferences
his account	its equipment

However, possessive pronouns are different from possessive nouns in the way they are written. That is, possessive pronouns never have an apostrophe.

POSSESSIVE NOUN	POSSESSIVE PRONOUN
the woman's estate	her estate
Roger Franklin's plans	his plans
the shareholders' feelings	their feelings
the vacuum cleaner's attachments	its attachments

The word *its* is the possessive of *it.* Like all other possessive pronouns, *its* doesn't have an apostrophe. Some people confuse *its* with *it's,* the contraction of *it is.* Contractions are discussed later.

Exercise

Fill in the blanks with the possessive "its" or the contraction "it's."

1. The Ontario Securities Commission has as _____ mandate to protect the integrity of the capital markets.
2. _____ paramount that the commission treat all of _____ constituents fairly.
3. Part of the OSC's responsibility is to communicate with a company in order to review _____ transactions and disclosures.
4. _____ important for participants in the capital markets to adhere strictly to securities law.
5. _____ the responsibility of each public company to ensure that ____ actions fall within the parameters of securities law.
6. The company's duty to _____ shareholders includes providing them with full and timely disclosure. ■

1.3 Verbs

A verb describes an action:

They all *quit* in disgust.

It may also describe a state of being:

Working conditions *were* substandard.

The English language is full of action verbs. Here are a few you'll often run across in the business world:

verify	perform	fulfill
hire	succeed	send
leave	improve	receive
accept	develop	pay

You could undoubtedly list many more.

The most common verb describing a state of being instead of an action is *to be* and all its forms:

I am, was, or will be; you are, were, or will be

Other verbs also describe a state of being:

It *seemed* a good plan at the time.

She *sounds* impressive at a meeting.

These verbs link what comes before them in the sentence with what comes after; no action is involved. (See Section 1.7.5 for a fuller discussion of linking verbs.)

1.3.1 VERB TENSES

English has three simple verb tenses: present, past, and future.

PRESENT: Our branches in Newfoundland *stock* other items.

PAST: When we *stocked* Purquil pens, we received a great many complaints.

FUTURE: Rotex Tire Stores *will stock* your line of tires when you begin a program of effective national advertising.

With most verbs (the regular ones), the past tense ends in *ed;* the future tense always has *will* or *shall* in front of it. But the present tense is more complex:

SINGULAR	PLURAL
I stock	we stock
you stock	you stock
he, she, it stocks	they stock

The basic form, *stock,* takes an additional *s* when *he, she,* or *it* precedes it.

In addition to the three simple tenses, there are three perfect tenses using forms of the helping verb *have.* The present perfect tense uses the past participle (regularly the past tense) of the main verb, *stocked,* and adds the present-tense *have* or *has* to the front of it:

(I, we, you, they) *have stocked.*

(He, she, it) *has stocked.*

The past perfect tense uses the past participle of the main verb, *stocked,* and adds the past-tense *had* to the front of it:

(I, you, he, she, it, we, they) *had stocked.*

The future perfect tense also uses the past participle of the main verb, *stocked,* but adds the future-tense *will have:*

(I, you, he, she, it, we, they) *will have stocked.*

Keep verbs in the same tense when the actions occur at the same time:

When the payroll checks *came* in, everyone *showed* up for work.

We *have found* that everyone *has pitched* in to help.

Of course, when the actions occur at different times, you may change tense accordingly:

> A shipment *came* last Wednesday, so when another one *comes* in today, please return it.
>
> The new employee *had been* ill at ease, but now she *has become* a full-fledged member of the team.

1.3.2 IRREGULAR VERBS

Many verbs don't follow in every detail the patterns already described. The most irregular of these verbs is *to be:*

TENSE	SINGULAR	PLURAL
Present:	I *am*	we *are*
	you *are*	you *are*
	he, she, it *is*	they *are*
Past:	I *was*	we *were*
	you *were*	you *were*
	he, she, it *was*	they *were*

The future tense of *to be* is formed in the same way that the future tense of a regular verb is formed.

The perfect tenses of *to be* are also formed as they would be for a regular verb, except that the past participle is a special form, *been,* instead of just the past tense:

> PRESENT PERFECT: you have been
>
> PAST PERFECT: you had been
>
> FUTURE PERFECT: you will have been

Here's a sampling of other irregular verbs:

PRESENT	PAST	PAST PARTICIPLE
begin	began	begun
shrink	shrank	shrunk
know	knew	known
rise	rose	risen
become	became	become
go	went	gone
do	did	done

Dictionaries list the various forms of other irregular verbs.

Exercise

Place the underlined verbs in the appropriate boxes in the table below.

> Ted Nolan's life has been a series of sharp ups and downs. A native Canadian, Nolan grew up on a reserve in a family of 12. Around him he saw lives ravaged by poverty, alcohol and violence. Hockey was his means of escape: hard work and dedication made him an NHL winger. However, an injury ended his playing

days when he was 28. Indomitable, he changed careers: if he had been a good hockey player, he was to be a great hockey coach. His superb work with the Buffalo Sabres led him to be named the NHL coach of the year at the age of 39. Strangely, though, he then lost his position, and many feel that racism has hampered his NHL coaching career.

Ted Nolan, however, is not to be daunted by adversity. Long a supporter of native youth, he has created Team Indigenous, a hockey club of Canadian aboriginal males. No one knows whether Nolan will ever return to the NHL, but it hardly matters anymore; a hero to his players, he instils hope, motivation and pride in aboriginal youth. At the end of his career, he will have made a difference not just on the ice, but also in the hearts and minds of the native peoples he has never forgotten. ■

simple past	simple present	simple future	past perfect	present perfect	future perfect

1.3.3 TRANSITIVE AND INTRANSITIVE VERBS

Many people are confused by three particular sets of verbs:

lie/lay sit/set rise/raise

Using these verbs correctly is much easier when you learn the difference between transitive and intransitive verbs.

Transitive verbs convey their action to an object; they "transfer" their action to an object. Intransitive verbs do not. Here are some sample uses of transitive and intransitive verbs:

INTRANSITIVE	TRANSITIVE
We should include in our new offices a place to *lie* down for a nap.	The workers will be here on Monday to *lay* new carpeting.
Even the way an interviewee *sits* is important.	That crate is full of stemware, so *set* it down carefully.
Salaries at Compu-Link, Inc., *rise* swiftly.	They *raise* their level of production every year.

The workers *lay* carpeting, you *set* down the crate, they *raise* production; each action is transferred to something. In the intransitive sentences, one *lies* down, an interviewee *sits,* and salaries *rise* without (at least grammatically) affecting anything else. Intransitive sentences are complete with only a subject and a verb; transitive sentences are not complete unless they also include an object, or something to transfer the action to.

Tenses are a confusing element of the *lie/lay* problem:

PRESENT	PAST	PAST PARTICIPLE
I *lie*	I l*ay*	I have *lain*
I *lay* (something down)	I *laid* (something down)	I have *laid* (something down)

The past tense of *lie* and the present tense of *lay* look and sound alike, even though they're different verbs.

Exercise

Select the correct verb in parentheses.

1. (*Lay, Lie*) your cards on the table: you're not pleased with the new intern's productivity.
2. He does tend to (*lie, lay*) around the office drinking coffee a little too much. Yesterday I had to (*lay, lie*) down company policy to him in no uncertain terms.
3. However, when I (*set, sit*) him a complex task, he often (*rises, raises*) to the challenge; he could be a first-class employee if he were to (*rise, raise*) his general level of productivity. ▫

1.3.4 VOICE OF VERBS

Verbs have two voices, active and passive:

ACTIVE: The buyer paid a large amount.

PASSIVE: A large amount was paid by the buyer.

The passive voice uses a form of the verb *to be.*

Also, the passive-voice sentence uses eight words, whereas the active-voice sentence uses only six words to say the same thing. The words *was* and *by* are unnecessary to convey the meaning of the sentence. In fact, extra words usually clog meaning. So be sure to opt for the active voice when you have a choice.

At times, however, you have no choice:

Several items *have been taken,* but so far we don't know who took them.

The passive voice becomes necessary when you don't know (or don't want to say) who performed the action; the active voice is bolder and more direct.

Exercise

Where possible, transform the following sentences from the passive voice to the active voice.

1. The invoice was faxed by the shipping department.
2. An explanatory letter will be sent to all customers.
3. The final cost of the Halifax project had been wildly underestimated by the consultants.
4. This task must be delegated by the vice-president of corporate affairs.
5. The national lacrosse team plays well under pressure. ▫

1.3.5 MOOD OF VERBS

You have three moods to choose from, depending on your intentions. Most of the time you use the indicative mood to make a statement or to ask a question:

> The secretary *mailed* a letter to each supplier.
>
> Did the secretary *mail* a letter to each supplier?

When you wish to command or request, use the imperative mood:

> Please mail a letter to each supplier.

Sometimes, especially in business, a courteous request is stated like a question; in that case, however, no question mark is required.

> Would you *mail* a letter to each supplier.

The subjunctive mood, most often used in formal writing or in presenting bad news, expresses a possibility or a recommendation. The subjunctive is usually signalled by a word such as *if* or *that.* In these examples, the subjunctive mood uses special verb forms:

> If the secretary *were to mail* a letter to each supplier, we might save some money.
>
> I suggested that the secretary *mail* a letter to each supplier.

Although the subjunctive mood is not used as often as it once was, it's still found in such expressions as *Come what may* and *If I were you.* In general, it is used to convey an idea that is contrary to fact: If iron *were* lighter than air.

Exercise

Identify the mood of each underlined verb.

1. In Spain let a handshake last five to seven strokes; pulling away too soon may be interpreted as rejection. In France, however, the preferred handshake is a single stroke.
2. Don't give a gift of liquor in Arab countries. If you were to give such a gift, offence would be taken.
3. In Pakistan don't be surprised when business people excuse themselves in the middle of a meeting to conduct prayers. Muslims pray five times a day.
4. Allow plenty of time to get to know the people you're dealing with in Africa; they are suspicious of people who are in a hurry. ■

1.4 Adjectives

An adjective modifies (tells something about) a noun or pronoun:

an *efficient* staff	a *heavy* price
brisk trade	*poor* you

Each of these phrases says more about the noun or pronoun than the noun or pronoun would say alone.

Adjectives always tell us something we wouldn't know without them. So you don't need to use adjectives when the noun alone, or a different noun, will give the meaning:

> a *company* employee

(An employee ordinarily works for a company.)

a *crate-type* container

(*Crate* gives the entire meaning.)

At times, adjectives pile up in a series:

It was a *long, hot,* and *active* workday.

Such strings of adjectives are acceptable as long as they all convey a different part of the phrase's meaning.

Verbs in the *ing* (present participle) form can be used as adjectives:

A *boring* job can sometimes turn into a *fascinating* career.

So can the past participle of verbs:

A freshly *painted* house is a *sold* house.

Adjectives modify nouns more often than they modify pronouns. When adjectives do modify pronouns, however, the sentence usually has a linking verb:

They were *attentive.*

He seems *interested.*

It looked *appropriate.*

You are *skilful.*

Most adjectives can take three forms: simple, comparative, and superlative. The simple form modifies a single noun or pronoun. Use the comparative form when comparing two items. When comparing three or more items, use the superlative form.

SIMPLE	COMPARATIVE	SUPERLATIVE
hard	harder	hardest
safe	safer	safest
dry	drier	driest

The comparative form adds *er* to the simple form, and the superlative form adds *est.* (The *y* at the end of a word changes to *i* before the *er* or *est* is added.)

A small number of adjectives are irregular, including these:

SIMPLE	COMPARATIVE	SUPERLATIVE
good	better	best
bad	worse	worst
little	less	least

When the simple form of an adjective is two or more syllables, you usually add *more* to form the comparative and *most* to form the superlative:

SIMPLE	COMPARATIVE	SUPERLATIVE
useful	more useful	most useful
exhausting	more exhausting	most exhausting
expensive	more expensive	most expensive

The most common exceptions are two-syllable adjectives that end in *y:*

SIMPLE	COMPARATIVE	SUPERLATIVE
happy	happier	happiest
costly	costlier	costliest

If you choose this option, change the *y* to *i,* and tack *er* or *est* onto the end.

1.5 Adverbs

An adverb modifies a verb, an adjective, or another adverb:

MODIFYING A VERB: Our marketing department works *efficiently.*

MODIFYING AN ADJECTIVE: She was not dependable, although she was *highly* intelligent.

MODIFYING ANOTHER ADVERB: His territory was *too* broadly diversified, so he moved *extremely* cautiously.

Most of the adverbs mentioned are adjectives turned into adverbs by adding *ly,* which is how many adverbs are formed:

ADJECTIVE	ADVERB
efficient	efficiently
high	highly
extreme	extremely
special	specially
official	officially
separate	separately

Some adverbs are made by dropping or changing the final letter of the adjective and then adding *ly:*

ADJECTIVE	ADVERB
due	duly
busy	busily

Other adverbs don't end in *ly* at all. Here are a few examples of this type:

often	fast	too
soon	very	so

Exercise

Identify each adverb and adjective in the following sentences. Note any examples of the comparative and superlative.

1. Given her high profile, Pamela Wallin is surprisingly accessible and engaging.
2. He duly noted that Mr. Wu felt that direct marketing, though initially costlier, would in the long run prove more efficient.
3. The best solution to declining morale is a policy which rewards the most innovative initiatives and the most effective trouble-shooting. ■

1.6 Other Parts of Speech

Nouns, pronouns, verbs, adjectives, and adverbs carry most of the meaning in a sentence. Four other parts of speech link them together in sentences: prepositions, conjunctions, articles, and interjections.

1.6.1 PREPOSITIONS

Prepositions are words like these:

of	to	for	with
at	by	from	about

They most often begin prepositional phrases, which function like adjectives and adverbs by telling more about a pronoun, noun, or verb:

of a type	*by* Friday
to the point	*with* characteristic flair

1.6.2 CONJUNCTIONS, ARTICLES, AND INTERJECTIONS

Conjunctions are words that usually join parts of a sentence. Here are a few:

and	but	because
yet	although	if

Using conjunctions is discussed in sections 1.7.3 and 1.7.4.

Only three articles exist in English: *the, a,* and *an.* These words are used, like adjectives, to specify which item you are talking about.

Interjections are words that express no solid information, only emotion:

Wow!	Well, well!
Oh no!	Good!

Such purely emotional language has its place in private life and advertising copy, but it only weakens the effect of most business writing.

Exercise

Identify the prepositions, conjunctions and articles in the following sentences.

1. He admires her skills, but told her in no uncertain terms that she must improve her ability to work with others.
2. Jatinder will have his associate chart profits to the end of the quarter.
3. The volatility of tech stocks is a concern, yet Binah feels that the company's risk-management strategies are adequate.
4. If she handles the situation with her usual tact, Vanita will successfully negotiate a compromise with the various parties. ■

Exercise

Place the underlined words in the appropriate boxes in the table below.

> The Canadian Ski Marathon began in 1967 when Olympic Nordic Ski Team member Don MacLeod decided to celebrate Canada's hundredth birthday by organizing a gruelling, 200-kilometre cross-country ski marathon. He chose as his starting point a shopping centre in suburban Montreal; since no one owned a gun, organizers signalled the start of the race by smashing an air-filled paper bag. The inaugural marathon presented unforeseen challenges: thanks to local pranksters who had removed trail markers, almost all the skiers got lost.
>
> Warm temperatures in the marathon's second year brought much riskier adventures. Many skiers broke through ice, and the Canadian army, ski patrol, police and marathon organizers had to rescue dozens of hypothermic skiers.

Astonishingly, there were no fatalities. One might think that such a disaster would signal the marathon's demise, but instead word spread about the event, and the following year drew more sponsors and skiers. This ultimate winter challenge is still going strong, and has never missed a year since its 1967 inception.

common noun	proper noun	pronoun	verb	adjective	adverb	preposition	conjunction	article

1.7 Sentences

Sentences are constructed with the major building blocks, the parts of speech.

Money talks.

This two-word sentence consists of a noun (*money*) and a verb (*talks*). When used in this way, the noun works as the first requirement for a sentence, the subject, and the verb works as the second requirement, the predicate. Now look at this sentence:

They merged.

The subject in this case is a pronoun (*they*), and the predicate is a verb (*merged*). This is a sentence because it has a subject and a predicate. Here is yet another kind of sentence:

The plans are ready.

This sentence has a more complicated subject, the noun *plans* and the article *the;* the complete predicate is a state-of-being verb (*are*) and an adjective (*ready*).

Without these two parts, the subject (who or what does something) and the predicate (the doing of it), no collection of words is a sentence.

Exercise

Rewrite the following paragraph to make it more effective, succinct, and stylistically pleasing. The paragraph is largely composed of simple sentences; you may find it useful to use some compound and complex sentences in your revisions.

Rick Mercer is one of the stars of a popular CBC show. This show is called *This Hour Has 22 Minutes.* This show is produced by Salter Street Films. This show is shot in Halifax. The other stars are Mary Walsh, Cathy Jones and Greg Thomey. Rick Mercer is one of Canada's most beloved comics. He does one of the show's funniest and most popular segments. This segment is called "Talking to Americans." Mercer did his first episode of "Talking to Americans" in 1998. One episode was particularly memorable. Mercer was in Iowa. Mercer spoke to several Americans. He spoke about Canada's 20-hour clock. He said for centuries Canada had operated on the 20-hour clock. He said that a Canadian hour was actually 75 American minutes. He said this system was confusing to American tourists visiting Canada. He said many tourists missed their buses, etc. He said Canada was finally switching to the 24-hour clock. He asked the Iowans' opinion. Most thought this was a sensible idea. They offered their congratulations to Canada for finally switching to American time. ■

1.7.1 COMMANDS

In commands, the subject (always *you*) is only understood, not stated:

(You) Move your desk to the better office.

(You) Please try to finish by six o'clock.

1.7.2 LONGER SENTENCES

More complicated sentences have more complicated subjects and predicates, but they still have a simple subject and a predicate verb. In the following examples, the simple subject is underlined once, the predicate verb twice:

Marex and Contron enjoy higher earnings each quarter.

(Marex [and] Contron did something; enjoy is what they did.)

My interview, coming minutes after my freeway accident, did not impress or move anyone.

(Interview is what did something. What did it do? It did [not] impress [or] move .)

In terms of usable space, a steel warehouse, with its extremely long span of roof unsupported by pillars, makes more sense.

(Warehouse is what makes.)

These three sentences demonstrate several things. First, in all three sentences the simple subject and predicate verb are the "bare bones" of the sentence, the parts that carry the core idea of the sentence. When trying to find the simple subject and predicate verb, disregard all prepositional phrases, modifiers, conjunctions, and articles.

Second, in the third sentence the verb is singular (*makes*) because the subject is singular (*warehouse*). Even though the plural noun *pillars* is closer to the verb, *warehouse* is the subject. So *warehouse* determines whether the verb is singular or plural. Subject and predicate must agree.

Third, the subject in the first sentence is compound (*Marex* [and] *Contron*). A compound subject, when connected by *and,* requires a plural verb (*enjoy*). Also in the second sentence, compound predicates are possible (*did* [not] *impress* [or] *move*).

Fourth, the second sentence incorporates a group of words—*coming minutes after my freeway accident*—containing a form of a verb (*coming*) and a noun (*accident*). Yet this group of words is not a complete sentence for two reasons:

- Accident is not the subject of coming. Not all nouns are subjects.
- A verb that ends in *ing* can never be the predicate of a sentence (unless preceded by a form of *to be,* as in *was coming*). Not all verbs are predicates.

Because they don't contain a subject and a predicate, the words *coming minutes after my freeway accident* (called a phrase) can't be written as a sentence. That is, the phrase can't stand alone; it can't begin with a capital letter and end with a period. So a phrase must always be just one part of a sentence.

Sometimes a sentence incorporates two or more groups of words that do contain a subject and a predicate; these word groups are called clauses.

> My interview, because it came minutes after my freeway accident, did not impress or move anyone.

The independent clause is the portion of the sentence that could stand alone without revision:

> My interview did not impress or move anyone.

The other part of the sentence could stand alone only by removing *because:*

> (because) It came minutes after my freeway accident.

This part of the sentence is known as a dependent clause; although it has a subject and a predicate (just as an independent clause does), it's linked to the main part of the sentence by a word (*because*) showing its dependence.

In summary, the two types of clauses–dependent and independent–both have a subject and a predicate. Dependent clauses, however, do not bear the main meaning of the sentence and are therefore linked to an independent clause. Nor can phrases stand alone, because they lack both a subject and a predicate. Only independent clauses can be written as sentences without revision.

1.7.3 SENTENCE FRAGMENTS

An incomplete sentence (a phrase or a dependent clause) that is written as though it were a complete sentence is called a fragment. Consider the following sentence fragments:

> Marilyn Sanders, having had pilferage problems in her store for the past year. Refuses to accept the results of our investigation.

This serious error can easily be corrected by putting the two fragments together:

> Marilyn Sanders, having had pilferage problems in her store for the past year, refuses to accept the results of our investigation.

Not all fragments can be corrected so easily. Here's more information on Sanders's pilferage problem.

> Employees a part of it. No authority or discipline.

Only the writer knows the intended meaning of these two phrases. Perhaps the employees are taking part in the pilferage. If so, the sentence should read:

> Some employees are part of the pilferage problem.

On the other hand, it's possible that some employees are helping with the investigation. Then the sentence would read:

> Some employees are taking part in our investigation.

It's just as likely, however, that the employees are not only taking part in the pilferage but are also being analyzed:

> Those employees who are part of the pilferage problem will accept no authority or discipline.

In fact, even more meanings could be read into these fragments. Because fragments can mean so many things, they mean nothing. No well-written memo, letter, or report ever demands the reader to be an imaginative genius.

One more type of fragment exists, the kind represented by a dependent clause. Note what *because* does to change what was once a unified sentence:

> Our stock of sprinklers is depleted.
>
> Because our stock of sprinklers is depleted.

Although the second version contains a subject and a predicate, adding *because* makes it a fragment. Words such as *because* form a special group of words called subordinating conjunctions. Here's a partial list:

since	though	whenever
although	if	unless
while	even if	after

When a word of this type begins a clause, the clause is dependent and cannot stand alone as a sentence. However, if a dependent clause is combined with an independent clause, it can convey a complete meaning. The independent clause may come before or after the dependent clause:

> We are unable to fill your order because our stock of sprinklers is depleted.
>
> Because our stock of sprinklers is depleted, we are unable to fill your order.

Another remedy for a fragment that is a dependent clause is to remove the subordinating conjunction. That solution leaves a simple but complete sentence:

> Our stock of sprinklers is depleted.

The actual details of a transaction will determine the best way to remedy a fragment problem.

The ban on fragments has one exception. Some advertising copy contains sentence fragments, written knowingly to convey a certain rhythm. However, advertising is the only area of business in which fragments are acceptable.

1.7.4 FUSED SENTENCES AND COMMA SPLICES

Just as there can be too little in a group of words to make it a sentence, there can also be too much:

> All our mail is run through a postage meter every afternoon someone picks it up.

This example contains two sentences, not one, but the two have been blended so that it's hard to tell where one ends and the next begins. Is the mail run through a meter every afternoon? If so, the sentences should read:

> All our mail is run through a postage meter every afternoon. Someone picks it up.

Perhaps the mail is run through a meter at some other time (morning, for example) and is picked up every afternoon:

> All our mail is run through a postage meter. Every afternoon someone picks it up.

The order of words is the same in all three cases; sentence division makes all the difference. Either of the last two cases is grammatically correct. The choice depends on the facts of the situation.

Sometimes these so-called fused sentences have a more obvious point of separation:

> Several large orders arrived within a few days of one another, too many came in for us to process by the end of the month.

Here the comma has been put between two independent clauses in an attempt to link them. When a lowly comma separates two complete sentences, the result is called a comma splice. A comma splice can be remedied in one of three ways:

- Replace the comma with a period and capitalize the next word: " ... one another. Too many ... "
- Replace the comma with a semicolon and do not capitalize the next word: " ... one another; too many ... " This remedy works only when the two sentences have closely related meanings.
- Change one of the sentences so that it becomes a phrase or a dependent clause. This remedy often produces the best writing, but it takes more work.

The third alternative can be carried out in several ways. One is to begin the blended sentence with a subordinating conjunction:

> Whenever several large orders arrived within a few days of one another, too many came in for us to process by the end of the month.

Another way is to remove part of the subject or the predicate verb from one of the independent clauses, thereby creating a phrase:

> Several large orders arrived within a few days of one another, too many for us to process by the end of the month.

Finally, you can change one of the predicate verbs to its *ing* form:

> Several large orders arrived within a few days of one another, too many coming in for us to process by the end of the month.

At other times a simple coordinating conjunction (such as *or, and,* or *but*) can separate fused sentences:

> You can fire them, *or* you can make better use of their abilities.
>
> Margaret drew up the designs, *and* Matt carried them out.
>
> We will have three strong months, *but* after that sales will taper off.

Be careful using coordinating conjunctions: Use them only to join simple sentences that express similar ideas.

Also, because they say relatively little about the relationship between the two clauses they join, avoid using coordinating conjunctions too often: *and* is merely an addition sign; *but* is just a turn signal; *or* only points to an alternative. Subordinating conjunctions such as *because* and *whenever* tell the reader a lot more.

Exercise

Rewrite the following paragraph to make it more effective, succinct, and stylistically pleasing. Make sure that each sentence is complete and correct.

> Evelyn Lau is one of Canada's exciting young writers, she was born in 1971, her hometown is Vancouver. She lived on the streets as a teen, she wrote about her harrowing experiences with prostitution and drugs in *Runaway: Diary of A Street Kid.* Having become a bestseller. Made into a T.V. movie. In the candid article "An Insatiable Emptiness" Evelyn writes about an aspect of her life little

> mentioned in *Runaway* her painful struggle with bulimia lasted many years. A moving piece of writing. She eventually came to a realization. The cause of her eating disorder not so much concern with her weight, but rather her troubled relationship with her parents. ■

1.7.5 SENTENCES WITH LINKING VERBS

Linking verbs were discussed briefly in the section on verbs (Section 1.3). Here you can see more fully the way they function in a sentence. The following is a model of any sentence with a linking verb:

> A (verb) B.

Although words such as *seems* and *feels* can also be linking verbs, let's assume that the verb is a form of *to be:*

> A *is* B.

In such a sentence, A and B are always nouns, pronouns, or adjectives. When one is a noun and the other is a pronoun, or when both are nouns, the sentence says that one is the same as the other:

> She is president.
>
> Rachel is president.

When one is an adjective, it modifies or describes the other:

> She is forceful.

Remember that when one is an adjective, it modifies the other as any adjective modifies a noun or pronoun, except that a linking verb stands between the adjective and the word it modifies.

Exercise

Circle the linking verbs in the following sentences.

> Tamara is president of the student council. She seems a good choice for the job, since she is a charming individual who can exert authority when necessary. ■

1.7.6 MISPLACED MODIFIERS

The position of a modifier in a sentence is important. The movement of *only* changes the meaning in the following sentences:

> *Only* we are obliged to supply those items specified in your contract.
>
> We are obliged *only* to supply those items specified in your contract.
>
> We are obliged to supply *only* those items specified in your contract.
>
> We are obliged to supply those items specified *only* in your contract.

In any particular set of circumstances, only one of these sentences would be accurate. The others would very likely cause problems. To prevent misunderstanding, place modifiers such as *only* as close as possible to the noun or verb they modify.

For similar reasons, whole phrases that are modifiers must be placed near the right noun or verb. Mistakes in placement create ludicrous meanings:

> Antia Information Systems has bought new computer chairs for the programmers *with more comfortable seats.*

The anatomy of programmers is not normally a concern of business writers. Obviously, the comfort of the chairs was the issue:

> Antia Information Systems has bought new computer chairs *with more comfortable seats* for the programmers.

Here is another example:

> I asked him to file all the letters in the cabinet *that had been answered.*

In this ridiculous sentence the cabinet has been answered, even though no cabinet in history is known to have asked a question. *That had been answered* is too far from *letters* and too close to *cabinet.* Here's an improvement:

> I asked him to file in the cabinet all the letters *that had been answered.*

In some cases, instead of moving the modifying phrase closer to the word it modifies, the best solution is to move the word closer to the modifying phrase.

Exercise

Correct any misplaced or dangling modifiers in the following sentences.

1. The pastries were served to the royals on fine crystal.
2. Frivolous, predictable and unrealistic, most females have lost patience with the typical women's magazine.
3. At the Juno and Genie Awards, several women are always snapped by photographers wearing daring evening gowns.
4. Professional and exacting, Peter Mansbridge is integral to the success of CBC's *The National.*
5. Waiting for the rescuers, a bat skimmed by my head. ■

2.0 Punctuation

On the highway, signs tell you when to slow down or stop, where to turn, when to merge. In similar fashion, punctuation helps readers negotiate your prose. The proper use of punctuation keeps readers from losing track of your meaning.

2.1 Periods

Use a period (1) to end any sentence that is not a question, (2) with certain abbreviations, and (3) between dollars and cents in an amount of money.

2.2 Question Marks

Use a question mark after any direct question that requests an answer:

> Are you planning to enclose a cheque, or shall we bill you?

Don't use a question mark with commands phrased as questions for the sake of politeness:

> Will you send us a cheque today.

2.3 Exclamation Points

Use exclamation points after highly emotional language. Because business writing almost never calls for emotional language, you will seldom use exclamation points.

2.4 Semicolons

Semicolons have three main uses. One is to separate two closely related independent clauses:

> The outline for the report is due within a week; the report itself is due at the end of the month.

A semicolon should also be used instead of a comma when the items in a series have commas within them:

> Our previous meetings were on November 11, 1997; February 20, 1999; and April 28, 2000.

Finally, a semicolon should be used to separate independent clauses when the second one begins with a word such as *however, therefore,* or *nevertheless* or a phrase such as *for example* or *in that case:*

> Our supplier has been out of part D712 for 10 weeks; however, we have found another source that can ship the part right away.

> His test scores were quite low; on the other hand, he has a lot of relevant experience.

Section 4.4 has more information on using transitional words and phrases.

2.5 Colons

Use a colon (1) after the salutation in a business letter, (2) at the end of a sentence or phrase introducing a list or (sometimes) a quotation, and (3) to separate two closely related independent clauses not joined by *and, but,* or *or.*

> Our study included the three most critical problems: insufficient capital, incompetent management, and inappropriate location.

In some introductory sentences, phrases such as *the following* or *that is* are implied by using a colon.

A colon should not be used when the list, quotation, or idea is a direct object or part of the introductory sentence:

> We are able to supply
>
> staples
>
> wood screws
>
> nails
>
> toggle bolts

> This shipment includes 9 videotapes, 12 CDs, and 14 cassette tapes.

2.6 Commas

Commas have many uses; the most common is to separate items in a series:

> He took the job, learned it well, worked hard, and succeeded.

> Put paper, pencils, and paper clips on the requisition list.

Company style often dictates omitting the final comma in a series. However, if you have a choice, use the final comma; it's often necessary to prevent misunderstanding.

A second place to use a comma is between independent clauses that are joined by a coordinating conjunction (*and, but,* or *or*) unless one or both are very short:

> She spoke to the sales staff, and he spoke to the production staff.
>
> I was advised to proceed and I did.

A third use for the comma is to separate a dependent clause at the beginning of a sentence from an independent clause:

> Because of our lead in the market, we may be able to risk introducing a new product.

However, a dependent clause at the end of a sentence is separated from the independent clause by a comma only when the dependent clause is unnecessary to the main meaning of the sentence:

> We may be able to introduce a new product, although it may involve some risk.

A fourth use for the comma is after an introductory phrase or word:

> Starting with this amount of capital, we can survive in the red for one year.
>
> Through more careful planning, we may be able to serve more people.
>
> Yes, you may proceed as originally planned.

However, with short introductory prepositional phrases and some one-syllable words (such as *hence* and *thus*), the comma is often omitted:

> Before January 1 we must complete the inventory.
>
> Thus we may not need to hire anyone.
>
> In short the move to Tulsa was a good idea.

Fifth, commas are used to surround nonrestrictive phrases or words (expressions that can be removed from the sentence without changing the meaning):

> The new owners, the Kowacks, are pleased with their purchase.

Sixth, commas are used between adjectives modifying the same noun (coordinate adjectives):

> She left Monday for a long, difficult recruiting trip.

To test the appropriateness of such a comma, try reversing the order of the adjectives: *a difficult, long recruiting trip*. If the order cannot be reversed, leave out the comma (*a good old friend* isn't the same as *an old good friend*). A comma is also not used when one of the adjectives is part of the noun. Compare these two phrases:

> a distinguished, well-known figure
>
> a distinguished public figure

The adjective-noun combination of *public* and *figure* has been used together so often that it has come to be considered a single thing: *public figure*. So no comma is required.

Seventh, commas should precede *Inc., Ltd.,* and the like:

> Cloverdell, Inc. Beamer, Ltd.

In a sentence, a comma also follows such abbreviations:

Belle Brown, Ph.D., is the new tenant.

Eighth, commas are used both before and after the year in sentences that include month, day, and year:

It will be sent by December 15, 2001, from our Moncton plant.

Some companies write dates in another form: 15 December 2001. No commas should be used in that case. Nor is a comma needed when only the month and year are present (December 2001).

Ninth, a comma may be used after an informal salutation in a letter to a personal friend. (In business letters, however, the salutation is followed by a colon.)

Tenth, a comma is used to separate a quotation from the rest of the sentence:

Your warranty reads, "These conditions remain in effect for one year from date of purchase."

However, the comma is left out when the quotation as a whole is built into the structure of the sentence:

He hurried off with an angry "Look where you're going."

Finally, a comma should be used whenever it's needed to avoid confusion or an unintended meaning. Compare the following:

Ever since they have planned new ventures more carefully.

Ever since, they have planned new ventures more carefully.

Exercise

Punctuate the following paragraph as necessary.

The most basic form of communication is **nonverbal communication** all the cues gestures vocal qualities spatial relationships and attitudes toward time that allow us to communicate without words Anthropologists theorize that long before human beings used words to talk things over our ancestors communicated with one another by using their bodies They gritted their teeth to show anger they smiled and touched one another to indicate affection Although we have come a long way since those primitive times we still use nonverbal cues to express superiority dependence dislike respect love and other feelings ■

2.7 Dashes

Use a dash to surround a comment that is a sudden turn in thought:

Membership in the IBSA–it's expensive but worth it–may be obtained by applying to our New York office.

A dash can also be used to emphasize a parenthetical word or phrase:

Third-quarter profits–in excess of $2 million–are up sharply.

Finally, use dashes to set off a phrase that contains commas:

All our offices–Toronto, Vancouver, and Regina–have sent representatives.

Don't confuse a dash with a hyphen. A dash separates and emphasizes words, phrases, and clauses more strongly than a comma or parentheses can; a hyphen ties two words so tightly that they almost become one word.

When typing a dash, type two hyphens with no space before, between, or after.

Exercise

Add dashes to the following sentences as appropriate.

1. I had hoped to visit Sabrina an old and dear friend if time permitted.
2. My favourite movies *The Terminator, The Matrix,* and *Crouching Tiger, Hidden Dragon* all have superb action sequences.
3. Inflation to no one's surprise appears to be rising again.

2.8 Hyphens

Hyphens are mainly used in three ways. The first is to separate the parts of compound words beginning with such prefixes as self-, ex-, quasi-, and all:

self-assured	quasi-official
ex-wife	all-important

However, hyphens are usually left out and the words closed up in words that have such prefixes as *pro*, *anti*, *non*, *un*, *inter*, and *extra:*

prolabour	nonunion
antifascist	interdepartmental

Exceptions occur when (1) the prefix occurs before a proper noun or (2) the vowel at the end of the prefix is the same as the first letter of the root word:

pro-Republican	anti-American
anti-inflammatory	extra-atmospheric

When in doubt, consult your dictionary.

Hyphens are also used in some compound adjectives, which are adjectives made up of two or more words. Specifically, you should use hyphens in compound adjectives that come before the noun:

an interest-bearing account	well-informed executives

However, you need not hyphenate when the adjective follows a linking verb:

This account is interest bearing.

Their executives are well informed.

You can shorten sentences that list similar hyphenated words by dropping the common part from all but the last word:

Check the costs of first-, second-, and third-class postage.

Finally, hyphens may be used to divide words at the end of a typed line. Such hyphenation is best avoided, but when you have to divide words at the end of a line, do so correctly (see Section 3.4). A dictionary will show how words are divided into syllables.

Exercise

Add hyphens to the following words as needed.

exhusband	quasiceremonial
thankyou letter	allconsuming
prolabour faction	previous boyfriend
intercontinental ▪	

2.9 Apostrophes

Use an apostrophe in the possessive form of a noun (but not in a pronoun):

> On *his* desk was a reply to *Bette Ainsley's* application for the *manager's* position.

Apostrophes are also used in place of the missing letter(s) of a contraction:

WHOLE WORDS	CONTRACTION
we will	we'll
do not	don't
they are	they're

Exercise

Add apostrophes to the following as necessary.

> Dont tell me that you cant help. I know perfectly well that youre tutoring Stephens child, so why shouldnt you spend some time with Bobbys as well? ▪

2.10 Quotation Marks

Use quotation marks to surround words that are repeated exactly as they were said or written:

> The collection letter ended by saying, "This is your third and final notice."

Remember: (1) When the quoted material is a complete sentence, the first word is capitalized. (2) The final comma or period goes inside the closing quotation marks.

Quotation marks are also used to set off the title of a newspaper story, magazine article, or book chapter:

> You should read "Legal Aspects of the Collection Letter" in *Today's Credit.*

The book title is shown here in italics. When typewritten, the title is underlined. The same treatment is proper for newspaper and magazine titles. (Appendix B explains documentation style in more detail.)

Quotation marks may also be used to indicate special treatment for words or phrases, such as terms that you're using in an unusual or ironic way:

> Our management "team" spends more time squabbling than working to solve company problems.

When using quotation marks, take care to put in both sets, the closing marks as well as the opening ones.

Although periods and commas go inside any quotation marks, colons and semicolons go outside them. A question mark goes inside the quotation marks only if the quotation is a question:

> All that day we wondered, "Is he with us?"

If the quotation is not a question but the entire sentence is, the question mark goes outside:

> What did she mean by "You will hear from me"?

2.11 Parentheses

Use parentheses to surround comments that are entirely incidental:

> Our figures do not match yours, although (if my calculations are correct) they are closer than we thought.

Parentheses are also used in legal documents to surround figures in arabic numerals that follow the same amount in words:

> Remittance will be One Thousand Two Hundred Dollars ($1,200).

Be careful to put punctuation (period, comma, and so on) outside the parentheses unless it is part of the statement in parentheses.

2.12 Ellipses

Use ellipsis points, or dots, to indicate that material has been left out of a direct quotation. Use them only in direct quotations and only at the point where material was left out. In the following example, the first sentence is quoted in the second:

> The Dow Jones Industrial Average, which skidded 38.17 points in the previous five sessions, gained 4.61 to end at 2213.84.
>
> According to the *The National Post,* "The Dow Jones Industrial Average … gained 4.61" on June 10.

The number of dots in ellipses is not optional; always use three. Occasionally, the points of ellipsis come at the end of a sentence, where they seem to grow a fourth dot. Don't be fooled: One of the dots is a period.

2.13 Underscores and Italics

Usually a line typed underneath a word or phrase either provides emphasis or indicates the title of a book, magazine, or newspaper. If possible, use italics instead of an underscore. Italics (or underlining) should also be used for defining terms and for discussing words as words:

> In this report *net sales* refers to after-tax sales dollars.
>
> The word *building* is a common noun and should not be capitalized.

Exercise

Make any necessary corrections to the following sentences.

1. Does he prefer the National Post or The Globe and Mail.
2. I asked him that same question, and he replied, "I don't have sufficient familiarity with the newer paper to be able to make a judgment.

3. My own opinion (for what it's worth) is that both national papers are kept on their toes by having such fierce competition.
4. According to one source I read, "Competition combats complacency [....] and fosters excellence in journalism, as in so many other fields".
5. Still, my friend John, who's taking journalism at a local college, feels that the country can only support one national newspaper. As few individuals buy two papers.
6. It is the case–and I know this from personal experience–that some readers buy the papers alternately.
7. My own father a long-time Globe reader, buys the weekend National Post because he enjoys reading Saturday Night, the magazine now included (at no extra charge).
8. My brother Stanley told me recently that he: "prefers to read the Sun, since the tone is more informal and engaging."
9. My brother Joseph–always an appreciator of the female form–likes the Sun for other reasons; though he claims to buy it only for the sports coverage. ■

3.0 Mechanics

The most obvious and least tolerable mistakes that a business writer makes are probably those related to grammar and punctuation. However, a number of small details, known as writing mechanics, demonstrate the writer's polish and reflect on the company's professionalism.

3.1 Capitals

You should, of course, capitalize words that begin sentences:

> *Before* hanging up, he said, "*We'll* meet here on Wednesday at noon."

A quotation that is a complete sentence should also begin with a capitalized word.

Capitalize the names of particular persons, places, and things (proper nouns):

> We sent *Ms. Larson* an application form, informing her that not all *applicants* are interviewed.
>
> Let's consider opening a branch in the *West*, perhaps at the *west* end of *Vancouver, British Columbia.*
>
> As office buildings go, the Kinney Building is a pleasant setting for TDG Office Equipment.

Ms. Larson's name is capitalized because she is a particular applicant, whereas the general term *applicant* is left uncapitalized. Likewise, *West* is capitalized when it refers to a particular place but not when it means a direction. In the same way, *office* and *building* are not capitalized when they are general terms (common nouns), but they are capitalized when they are part of the title of a particular office or building (proper nouns).

Titles within families, governments, or companies may also be capitalized:

> My *Uncle David* offered me a job, but I wouldn't be comfortable working for one of my *uncles*.
>
> We've never had a *president* quite like *President Sweeney*.

In addition, always capitalize the first word of the salutation and complimentary close of a letter:

Dear Mr. Andrews: *Yours* very truly,

Finally, capitalize the first word after a colon when it begins a complete sentence:

Follow this rule: *When* in doubt, leave it out.

Otherwise, the first word after a colon should not be capitalized (see Section 2.5).

Exercise

Add capital letters to the following as appropriate.

silicon valley's staggering success is due in large part to its ability to attract the best and brightest minds. canada is a rich source for such minds: an estimated 250 000 to 350 000 canadians reside in the valley, forming the bay area's largest invisible minority. at gatherings of these ex-pats, conversation frequently turns to hockey, tim hortons coffee, and canadian high-tech heroes like rob burgess and jeff skoll. ■

3.2 Abbreviations

Abbreviations are used heavily in tables, charts, lists, and forms. They're used sparingly in prose paragraphs, however. Here are some abbreviations often used in business writing:

ABBREVIATION	FULL TERM
b/l	bill of lading
ca.	circa (about)
dol., dols.	dollar, dollars
etc.	et cetera (and so on)
Inc.	Incorporated
L.f.	Ledger folio
Ltd.	Limited
mgr.	manager
NSF or N/S	not sufficient funds
P&L or P/L	profit and loss
reg.	regular
whsle.	wholesale

Because *etc.* contains a word meaning *and,* never write *and etc.*

Exercise

Write out the full term for each of the following common abbreviations.

1. ca.
2. etc.
3. Ltd.
4. mgr.
5. whsle. ■

3.3 Numbers

Numbers may correctly be handled many ways in business writing, so follow company style. In the absence of a set style, however, generally spell out all numbers from one to ten and use arabic numerals for the rest.

There are some exceptions to this general rule. First, never begin a sentence with a numeral:

> *Twenty* of us produced *641* units per week in the first *12* weeks of the year.

Second, use numerals for the numbers one through ten if they're in the same list as larger numbers:

> Our weekly quota rose from *9* to *15* to *27*.

Third, use numerals for percentages, time of day (except with *o'clock*), dates, and (in general) dollar amounts.

> Our division is responsible for *7* percent of total sales.
>
> The meeting is scheduled for *8:30* A.M. on August *2*.
>
> Add *$3* for postage and handling.

When writing dollar amounts, use a decimal point only if cents are included. In lists of two or more dollar amounts, use the decimal point either for all or for none:

> He sent two cheques, one for *$67.92* and one for *$90.00*.

Exercise

Correct the use of numbers in the following.

> 20 or so times a year, I like to get together with my friends for lunch at a new restaurant. Last week, we chose a Sri Lankan restaurant that proved surprisingly expensive. My meal cost $42.50; one of my friend's cost $80. We generally tip around fifteen to twenty %. ■

3.4 Word Division

In general, avoid dividing words at the ends of lines. When you must, follow these rules:

- Don't divide one-syllable words (such as *since, walked,* and *thought*); abbreviations (*mgr.*); contractions (*isn't*); or numbers expressed in numerals (*117 500*).
- Divide words between syllables, as specified in a dictionary or word-division manual.
- Make sure that at least three letters of the divided word are moved to the second line: *sin-cerely* instead of *sincere-ly.*
- Do not end a page or more than three consecutive lines with hyphens.
- Leave syllables consisting of a single vowel at the end of the first line (*impedi-ment* instead of *imped-iment*), except when the single vowel is part of a suffix such as *-able, -ible, -ical,* or *-ity* (*respons-ible* instead of *responsi-ble*).
- Divide between double letters (*tomor-row*), except when the root word ends in double letters (*call-ing* instead of *cal-ling*).
- Divide hyphenated words after the hyphen only: *anti-independence* instead of *anti-inde-pendence*.

Exercise

Correct any of the following words which are incorrectly divided.

jog-ged	fall-ing
fal-low	anti-quated
undoubted-ly	

4.0 Vocabulary

Using the right word in the right place is a crucial skill in business communication. However, many pitfalls await the unwary.

4.1 Frequently Confused Words

Because the following sets of words sound similar, be careful not to use one when you mean to use the other:

WORD	MEANING
accede exceed	to comply with to go beyond
accept except	to take to exclude
access excess	admittance too much
advice advise	suggestion to suggest
affect effect	to influence the result
allot a lot	to distribute much or many
all ready already	completely prepared completed earlier
born borne	given birth to carried
capital capitol	money; chief city a government building
cite sight site	to quote a view a location
complement compliment	complete amount; to go well with to flatter

WORD	MEANING
corespondent	party in a divorce suit
correspondent	letter writer
council	a panel of people
counsel	advice; a lawyer
defer	to put off until later
differ	to be different
device	a mechanism
devise	to plan
die	to stop living; a tool
dye	to colour
discreet	careful
discrete	separate
envelop	to surround
envelope	a covering for a letter
forth	forward
fourth	number four
holey	full of holes
holy	sacred
wholly	completely
human	of people
humane	kindly
incidence	frequency
incidents	events
instance	example
instants	moments
interstate	between states
intrastate	within a state
later	afterward
latter	the second of two
lead	a metal
led	guided
lean	to rest at an angle
lien	a claim
levee	embankment
levy	tax
loath	reluctant
loathe	to hate
loose	free; not tight
lose	to mislay

WORD	MEANING
miner minor	mineworker underage person
moral morale	virtuous; a lesson sense of well-being
ordinance ordnance	law weapons
overdo overdue	to do in excess past due
peace piece	lack of conflict a fragment
pedal peddle	a foot lever to sell
persecute prosecute	to torment to sue
personal personnel	private employees
precedence precedents	priority previous events
principal principle	sum of money; chief; main general rule
rap wrap	to knock to cover
residence residents	home inhabitants
right rite write	correct ceremony to form words on a surface
role roll	a part to play to tumble; a list
root rout route	part of a plant to defeat a traveller's way
shear sheer	to cut thin, steep
stationary stationery	immovable paper
than then	as compared with at that time
their there they're	belonging to them in that place they are

WORD	MEANING
to	a preposition
too	excessively; also
two	the number
waive	to set aside
wave	a swell of water; a gesture
weather	atmospheric conditions
whether	if

In the preceding list only enough of each word's meaning is given to help you distinguish between the words in each group. Several meanings are left out entirely. For more complete definitions, consult a dictionary.

Exercise

Select the appropriate word in parentheses.

1. In this (*instance, instants*), the (*effect, affect*) of the decision was immediate.
2. (*Discrete, Discreet*) employees (*accept, except*) the confidentiality requirements of (*there, their, they're*) firm.
3. As a matter of (*principle, principal*), the (*personal, personnel*) department is unwilling to (*wave, waive*) the educational requirement.
4. The president (*complimented, complemented*) the Montreal branch on the sound (*council, counsel*) it had offered concerning (*capital, capitol*) gains.
5. (*Allot, A lot*) of employees (*lose, loose*) sight of the importance of avoiding (*excess, access*) stress.
6. A (*wholly, holy, holey*) inappropriate mission statement would (*affect, effect*) company (*moral, morale*) more (*then, than*) individual productivity. ■

4.2 Frequently Misused Words

The following words tend to be misused for reasons other than their sound. Reference books (including the *Canadian Oxford English Dictionary*; *The Canadian Style: A Guide to Writing and Editing*, revised and expanded edition; and Fowler's *Modern English Usage*) can help you with similar questions of usage.

a lot: When the writer means "many," *a lot* is always two separate words, never one.

correspond with: Use this phrase when you are talking about exchanging letters. Use *correspond to* when you mean "similar to." Use either *correspond with* or *correspond to* when you mean "relate to."

disinterested: This word means "fair, unbiased, having no favourites, impartial." If you mean "bored" or "not interested," use *uninterested.*

etc.: This is the abbreviated form of a Latin phrase, *et cetera.* It means "and so on" or "and so forth." The current tendency among business writers is to use English rather than Latin.

imply/infer: Both refer to hints. Their great difference lies in who is acting. The writer *implies;* the reader *infers,* sees between the lines.

lay: This is a transitive verb. Never use it for the intransitive *lie.* (See Section 1.3.3.)

less: Use *less* for uncountable quantities (such as amounts of water, air, sugar, and oil). Use *fewer* for countable quantities (such as numbers of jars, saws, words, pages, and humans). The same distinction applies to *much* and *little* (uncountable) versus *many* and *few* (countable).

like: Use *like* only when the word that follows is just a noun or a pronoun. Use *as* or *as if* when a phrase or clause follows:

She looks *like* him.

She did just *as* he had expected.

It seems *as if* she had plenty of time.

many/much: See *less.*

regardless: The *less* ending is the negative part. No word needs two negative parts, so it is illiterate to add *ir* (a negative prefix) at the beginning.

to me/personally: Use these phrases only when personal reactions, apart from company policy, are being stated (not often the case in business writing).

try: Always follow with *to,* never *and.*

verbal: People in the business community who are careful with language frown on those who use *verbal* to mean "spoken" or "oral." Many others do say "verbal agreement." Strictly speaking, *verbal* means "of words" and therefore includes both spoken and written words. Be guided in this matter by company usage.

Exercise

Select the appropriate word in parentheses.

1. What was he (*implying, inferring*) when he said that he wished certain employees claimed (*fewer, less*) expenses?
2. I would (*imply, infer*) that he feels you are abusing your employee privileges.
3. Try (*and, to*) understand his point of view: just (*like, as*) you have to justify your expenses to him, he has to justify his to upper management.
4. In my (*disinterested, uninterested*) opinion, you do tend to use your business credit card somewhat too freely.
5. Since he receives (*a lot, alot*) of international inquiries, Atul corresponds (*with, to*) the Vancouver legal firm frequently. ■

4.3 Frequently Misspelled Words

All of us, even the world's best spellers, sometimes have to check a dictionary for the spelling of some words. People who have never memorized the spelling of commonly used words must look up so many that they grow exasperated and give up on spelling words correctly.

Don't expect perfection, and don't surrender. If you can memorize the spelling of just the words listed here, you'll need the dictionary far less often and you'll write with more confidence.

absence
absorption
accessible
accommodate
accumulate
achieve
advantageous
affiliated
aggressive
alignment
aluminum
ambience
analyze
apparent

appropriate
argument
asphalt
assistant
asterisk
auditor
bankruptcy
believable
brilliant
bulletin
calendar
campaign
category
ceiling
changeable
clientele
collateral
committee
comparative
competitor
concede
congratulations
connoisseur
consensus
convenient
convertible
corroborate
criticism
definitely
description
desirable
dilemma
disappear
disappoint
disbursement
discrepancy
dissatisfied
dissipate
eligible
embarrassing
endorsement
exaggerate
exceed
exhaust
existence
extraordinary
fallacy
familiar
flexible
fluctuation
forty
gesture
grievous
haphazard
harassment
holiday
illegible
immigrant
incidentally
indelible
independent
indispensable
insistent
intermediary
irresistible
jewellery
judgment
judicial
labelling
legitimate
leisure
litigation
maintenance
mathematics
mediocre
minimum
necessary
negligence

negotiable
newsstand
noticeable
occurrence
omission
parallel
pastime
peaceable
permanent
perseverance
persistent
personnel
persuade
possesses
precede
predictable
preferred
privilege
procedure
proceed
pronunciation
psychology
pursue
questionnaire
receive
recommend
repetition
rescind
rhythmical
ridiculous
saleable
secretary
seize
separate
sincerely
succeed
suddenness
superintendent
supersede
surprise
tangible
tariff
technique
tenant
truly
unanimous
until
vacillate
vacuum
vicious

Exercise

Correct the misspelled words in the following paragraphs.

1. I have recieved your most recent letter and the enclosed questionaire. Let me say that I admire your perserverence in trying to contact disatisfied customers. However, your agressive approach and your persistant attempts to minimize your own blame have exausted my patience; I will consider it harrassment if you try to contact me again.

   Yours truely, Dr. D. Chow

2. Many companies are conseding that the standard minimim fourty-hour work week is inconveniant for parents with young children. These companies now try to accomodate their employees' needs by offering a flexable scheduling option. Those familier with pyschology will not be surprised to learn that this arrangement often proves advantagous to the employers. Appreciative of the positive working ambiance, employees show their gratitude by producing brillient, independant work, and often become indispensible to the company.

3. Since our competiter is now offering lower prices on jewlery, it is desireable for us to find new ways of attracting clientel. Our company would risk bankrupcy if we were to undersell our competiter. However, we sinserely believe that we can offer priviliged customers a shopping experience that will exseed their expectations. We recomend that a commitee be struck to analize the situation and suggest an apropriate action plan.

4. The new assistent's handwriting is nearly illegeble. Moreover, standard operating prosedures remain a mystery to him, and he posesses an unerring instinct for mispelling even the simplest legal terms. You may think I exagerate, but many can coroborate what I say: it is apparant to all who work with him that the personel department made a greivous error in hiring him. The general concensus is that to avoid the company any further embarassment, we must ensure that he is removed from the department by the end of the calender year. ■

4.4 Transitional Words and Phrases

The following two sentences don't communicate as well as they might because they lack a transitional word or phrase:

> Production delays are inevitable. Our current lag time in filling orders is one month.

A semicolon between the two sentences would signal a close relationship between their meanings, but it wouldn't even hint at what that relationship is. Here are the sentences, now linked by means of a semicolon, with a space for a transitional word or phrase:

> Production delays are inevitable; _______ , our current lag time in filling orders is one month.

Now read the sentence with *nevertheless* in the blank space. Now try *therefore, incidentally, in fact,* and *at any rate* in the blank. Each substitution changes the meaning of the sentence.

Here are some transitional words (called conjunctive adverbs) that will help you write more clearly:

accordingly	furthermore	moreover
anyway	however	otherwise
besides	incidentally	still
consequently	likewise	therefore
finally	meanwhile	

The following transitional phrases are used in the same way:

as a result	in other words
at any rate	in the second place
for example	on the other hand
in fact	to the contrary

When one of these words or phrases joins two independent clauses, it should be preceded by a semicolon and followed by a comma, as shown here:

> The consultant recommended a complete reorganization; moreover, she suggested that we drop several products.

Exercise

Supply the appropriate transitional word or phrase. In some cases, more than one possibility exists.

1. John's interview was by far the best; __________, I will be recommending that we hire him.
2. Suzette will be leaving soon on maternity leave; _________, I would have offered her this plum assignment.
3. Francesco's skill set is outdated. ________________ , he lacks the familiarity with XML necessary to this project.
4. Mario has limited experience in sales; ________, he is such an engaging individual that I feel he will soon be meeting quotas.
5. Timothy has written the bar exam three times. ____________, success has crowned his efforts. ■

Answers to Exercises

1.1.1, 1.1.2 PROPER NOUNS, COMMON NOUNS, AND PLURAL NOUNS

Basketball, one of the world's most popular sports, was invented by a Canadian. Dr. James Naismith was born in Ontario in 1861. While working at the YMCA Training School in Springfield, Massachusetts, Naismith was faced with the problem of finding a sport which his students could play indoors during the long winters. In 1891, the inaugural game of basketball was played with a soccer ball and two peach baskets serving as goals. Basketball was introduced at the Olympics in 1936.

	common	**proper**
singular	basketball, world, problem, sport, game, soccer ball	Canadian Dr. James Naismith Ontario YMCA Training School
plural	sports students winters peach baskets	Olympics

1.1.3 POSSESSIVE NOUNS

1. ladies' lingerie, children's clothing.
2. father-in-law's opinion, child's play.
3. Shakespeare's poetry, Keats's
4. goddess's festival
5. goddesses' festival
6. people's prayers
7. prayers' meaning
8. drug's effect
9. consultants' appraisal
10. James's performance evaluation, Chris's
11. women's movement
12. Clients' expectations
13. duchess's complexion
14. Science's impact
15. sciences' problem
16. North America's beauty
17. North Americans' manners
18. hurricanes' ravages
19. The Chans' daughter
20. Manitobans', Newfoundlanders'
21. Blue Bombers' passing statistics, Stampeders'
22. men's blood pressures, women's
23. jurors' decision, judge's
24. business's clientele
25. businesses' solution

1.2, 1.2.1 PRONOUNS

When we think of millionaires, we often picture palatial homes, designer clothes, and exotic cars. In reality, experts say that most self-made millionaires cultivate a low-key existence. Rather than flaunting his or her wealth, the typical millionaire drives an old but reliable car, and lives in a modest house in a middle-class neighbourhood. In fact, you may know a low-profile millionaire or two without even realizing it: statistics suggest that one out of every 85 Canadians has $1 million or more in financial assets.

his - antecedent: the typical millionaire

her - antecedent: the typical millionaire

it - antecedent is the preceding clause

1.2.2 UNCLEAR ANTECEDENTS

The sentences may be rewritten in a variety of ways; two possibilities are given for each.

1. Mr. Ashat asked Mr. Lo to review the performance evaluation which Lo had received that morning.

   Mr. Ashat asked Mr. Lo to review the performance evaluation which Ashat had given him that morning.

2. Because he felt Imola was more hard-working than Savita, he asked the former to stay late.

   Because he felt Imola was more hard-working than Savita, he asked the latter to stay late.

3. Before I sold perfumes, I used to walk past the department-store displays, amazed at the variety of perfumes.

   Before I sold perfumes, I used to walk past the department-store displays, amazed at the displays' variety.

4. We visit the Gaspé Peninsula every year, a spot which I always enjoy.

   We visit the Gaspé Peninsula every year, a trip which I always enjoy.

1.2.3 GENDER-NEUTRAL PRONOUNS

There are multiple possibilities.

1. At the end of the year, the top student will have his or her name in the local newspaper.
2. All employees are asked to read their benefits packages carefully.
3. All clients left off the list will have to submit their claims later.
4. No change needed.
5. All salespersons have their own tried-and-true strategies.

1.2.4 CASE OF PRONOUNS

1. *me*
2. *him*
3. *us*
4. *We*
5. *Who*
6. *I, her*
7. *I, them*
8. *me*
9. *whoever*
10. *She, who*

Note regarding 9 and 10: The case of a subordinate clause embedded in a larger structure is tricky. You can settle uncertainty by mentally eliminating everything but the subordinate clause.

To take the example of 9: The subject of the subordinate clause *whoever requires it* belongs in the subjective case. Note that the object of "to" is the entire subordinate clause: *whoever requires it.*

1.2.5 POSSESSIVE PRONOUNS

1. its
2. It's, its
3. its
4. It's
5. It's, its
6. its

1.3.1 VERB TENSES

simple past	simple present	simple future	past perfect	present perfect	future perfect
saw	feel	will (ever) return	had been	has been	will have made
was	is			has hampered	
made	instils			has created	
ended					

1.3.3 TRANSITIVE AND INTRANSITIVE VERBS

1. Lay
2. lie, lay
3. set, rises, raise

1.3.4 VOICE OF VERBS

1. The shipping department faxed the invoice.
2. Not possible (no agent specified).
3. The consultants had wildly underestimated the final cost of the Halifax project.
4. The vice-president of corporate affairs must delegate this task.
5. Not possible (intransitive verb).

1.3.5 MOOD OF VERBS

1. <u>let</u> - imperative

   <u>is</u> - indicative

2. <u>Don't give</u> - imperative

   <u>were to give</u> - subjunctive

3. <u>pray</u> - indicative

4. <u>Allow</u> - imperative

   <u>are</u> - indicative

1.4., 1.5 ADJECTIVES AND ADVERBS

1. high - adjective; surprisingly - adverb; accessible, engaging - adjectives
2. duly - adverb; direct - adjective; initially - adverb; costlier - adjective (comparative); long - adjective; more efficient - adjective (comparative)
3. best - adjective (superlative); declining - adjective; most innovative - adjective (superlative); most effective - adjective (superlative)

1.6.1, 1.6.2 OTHER PARTS OF SPEECH

1. but - conjunction; in - preposition; that - conjunction; to - preposition; with - preposition
2. to - preposition; the - article; of - preposition; the - article
3. the - article; of - preposition; a - article; yet - conjunction; that - conjunction; the - article
4. if - conjunction; the - article; with - preposition; a - article; with - preposition; the - article

1.1–1.6 GENERAL REVIEW OF PARTS OF SPEECH

common noun	proper noun	pronoun	verb	adjective	adverb	preposition	conjunction	article
gun	Canadian Ski Marathon	He	signalled	inaugural	much	in	when	a
skiers	Don MacLeod	his	might think	unforeseen	astonishingly	by	since	an
fatalities	Montreal	its	spread	local		of	and	the
disaster			drew	warm		to	but	
demise				riskier		through		

1.7 SENTENCES

Multiple answers are possible. The following is one suggestion.

One of Canada's most beloved comics, Rick Mercer stars in CBC's *This Hour Has 22 Minutes* along with Mary Walsh, Cathy Jones and Greg Thomey. *This Hour* is produced in Halifax by Salter Street Films. In 1998, Mercer debuted one of the show's funniest and most popular segments, "Talking to Americans." In one particularly memorable episode, Mercer spoke to several Iowans about Canada's 20-hour clock, which he claimed had been in use for centuries. Mercer said that a Canadian hour was actually 75 American minutes, a fact which confused American tourists and often led to them missing buses and other modes of transportation. He asked the Iowans' opinion of Canada's recent decision to adopt the 24-hour clock. Many thought this was a sensible idea, and offered their congratulations to Canada for finally switching to American time.

1.7.3, 1.7.4 SENTENCE FRAGMENTS, FUSED SENTENCES AND COMMA SPLICES

Multiple answers are possible. The following is one suggestion.

One of Canada's exciting young writers, Evelyn Lau was born in Vancouver in 1971. Having lived on the streets as a teen, she wrote about her harrowing experiences with prostitution and drugs in *Runaway: Diary of A Street Kid.* This book became a bestseller and was made into a T.V. movie. In the moving and candid article "An Insatiable Emptiness," Evelyn writes about an aspect of her life little mentioned in *Runaway,* her long and painful struggle with bulimia. She eventually realized that her eating disorder was caused less by concern with her weight than by her troubled relationship with her parents.

1.7.5 SENTENCES WITH LINKING VERBS

is, seems, is

1.7.6 MISPLACED MODIFIERS

Various answers are possible.

1. Pastries on fine crystal were served to the royals.
2. Frivolous, predictable and unrealistic, the typical women's magazine annoys most females.
3. At the Juno and Genie Awards, several women wearing daring evening gowns are always snapped by photographers.
4. No correction needed.
5. As I waited for the rescuers, a bat skimmed by my head.

2.0 PUNCTUATION

The most basic form of communication is **nonverbal communication**: all the cues, gestures, vocal qualities, spatial relationships, and attitudes toward time that allow us to communicate without words. Anthropologists theorize that long before human beings used words to talk things over, our ancestors communicated with one another by using their bodies. They gritted their teeth to show anger; they smiled and touched one another to indicate affection. Although we have come a long way since those primitive times, we still use nonverbal cues to express superiority, dependence, dislike, respect, love, and other feelings.

2.7 DASHES

1. I had hoped to visit Sabrina–an old and dear friend–if time permitted.
2. My favourite movies–*The Terminator, The Matrix,* and *Crouching Tiger, Hidden Dragon*–all have superb action sequences.
3. Inflation–to no one's surprise–appears to be rising again.

2.8 HYPHENS

ex-husband

thank-you letter

correct

correct

quasi-ceremonial

all-consuming

correct

2.9 APOSTROPHES

Don't tell me that you can't help. I know perfectly well that you're tutoring Stephen's child, so why shouldn't you spend some time with Bobby's as well?

2.10–2.13 QUOTATION MARKS, PARENTHESES, ELLIPSES, UNDERSCORES AND ITALICS, GENERAL PUNCTUATION

1. Does he prefer *The National Post* or *The Globe and Mail*?
2. I asked him that same question, and he replied, "I don't have sufficient familiarity with the newer paper to be able to make a judgment."
3. No correction needed.
4. According to one source I read, "Competition combats complacency [...] and fosters excellence in journalism, as in so many other fields."
5. Still, my friend John, who's taking journalism at a local college, feels that the country can only support one national newspaper, as few individuals buy two papers.
6. No correction needed.
7. My own father, a long-time *Globe* reader, buys the weekend *National Post* because he enjoys reading *Saturday Night,* the magazine now included at no extra charge.
8. My brother Stanley told me recently that he prefers to read the *Sun,* since the tone is more informal and engaging.
9. My brother Joseph–always an appreciator of the female form–likes the *Sun* for other reasons, though he claims to buy it only for the sports coverage.

3.1 CAPITALS

Silicon Valley's staggering success is due in large part to its ability to attract the best and brightest minds. Canada is a rich source for such minds: an estimated 250 000 to 350 000 Canadians reside in the Valley, forming the Bay Area's largest invisible minority. At gatherings of these ex-pats, conversation frequently turns to hockey, Tim Hortons coffee, and Canadian high-tech heroes like Rob Burgess and Jeff Skoll.

3.2 ABBREVIATIONS

1. circa
2. et cetera
3. Limited
4. manager
5. wholesale

3.3 NUMBERS

Twenty or so times a year, I like to get together with my friends for lunch at a new restaurant. Last week, we chose a Sri Lankan restaurant that proved surprisingly expensive. My meal cost $42.50; one of my friend's cost $80.00. We generally tip around 15 to 20%.

3.4 WORD DIVISION

no division possible

correct

undoubt-edly

correct

correct

4.1 FREQUENTLY CONFUSED WORDS

1. instance, effect
2. Discreet, accept, their
3. principle, personnel, waive
4. complimented, counsel, capital
5. A lot, lose, excess
6. wholly, affect, morale, than

4.2 FREQUENTLY MISUSED WORDS

1. implying, fewer
2. infer
3. to, as
4. disinterested
5. a lot, with

4.3 FREQUENTLY MISSPELLED WORDS

1. received, questionnaire, perseverance, dissatisfied, aggressive, persistent, exhausted, harassment, truly
2. conceding, minimum, forty, inconvenient, accommodate, flexible, familiar, psychology, advantageous, ambience, brilliant, independent, indispensable
3. competitor, jewellery, desirable, clientele, bankruptcy, competitor, sincerely, privileged, exceed, recommend, committee, analyze, appropriate
4. assistant, illegible, procedures, possesses, misspelling, exaggerate, corroborate, apparent, personnel, grievous, consensus, embarrassment, calendar

4.4 TRANSITIONAL WORDS AND PHRASES

1. accordingly, consequently, therefore
2. otherwise
3. In other words
4. still, however, nevertheless, nonetheless
5. Finally

Proofreading Marks

Symbol	*Meaning*	*Symbol Used in Context*	*Corrected Copy*
═	Align horizontally	meaningful result	meaningful result
‖	Align vertically	1.‖Power cable 2.‖ Keyboard	1. Power cable 2. Keyboard
(uc)	Capitalize	(uc) Do not immerse.	DO NOT IMMERSE.
≡	Capitalize	Pepsico, Inc.	PepsiCo, Inc.
⁀‿	Close up	self- confidence	self-confidence
ℓ	Delete	harrassment ~~and abuse~~	harassment
(STET)....	Restore to original	none ~~of the~~ (STET)	none of the
^	Insert	tirquoise shirts (u; and white)	turquoise and white shirts
^,	Insert comma	a, b and c	a, b, and c
⊙	Insert period	Harrigan et al⊙	Harrigan et al.
/	Lowercase	TULSA, South of here	Tulsa, south of here
⊏	Move left	Attention:⊏ Security	Attention: Security
⊐	Move right	February 2, 1996 ⊐	February 2, 1996
⊔	Move down	Sincerely,	Sincerely,
⊓	Move up	THIRD-QUARTER SALES	THIRD-QUARTER SALES
⊐ ⊏	Centre	⊐Awards Banquet⊏	Awards Banquet
⌐L	Start new line	Marla Fenton, Manager, Distribution	Marla Fenton Manager, Distribution
⊂	Run lines together	Manager, Distribution	Manager, Distribution
¶	Start paragraph	¶The solution is easy to determine but difficult to implement in a competitive environment like the one we now face.	The solution is easy to determine but difficult to implement in a competitive environment like the one we now face.
#	Leave space	realestate testcase	real estate test case
◯	Spell out	(COD)	cash on delivery
(SP)	Spell out	(SP) Assn. of Biochem. Engrs.	Association of Biochemical Engineers
∿	Transpose	airy, light, casaul tone	light, airy, casual tone

Endnotes

Chapter 1

1. Adapted from Doug Glass, "Escaping the Rut Is Good Idea for Hallmark Artists, Writers; Creativity: Greeting Card Company Sends Its Employees on Retreats or to the Movies to Spark New Inspiration," Orange County Edition, *Los Angeles Times,* 6 June 1996, D-7; Gillian Flynn, "Sending a Quality of Life Message: Hallmark Cares," *Personnel Journal,* March 1996, 56; Karen Matthes, "Greetings from Hallmark," *HR Focus* 70 (August 1, 1993): 12.

2. Joseph N. Scudder and Patricia J. Guinan, "Communication Competencies as Discriminators of Superiors' Ratings of Employee Performance," *Journal of Business Communication* 26, no. 3 (Summer 1989): 217–29; Joseph F. Coates, "Today's Events Produce Tomorrow's Communication Issues," *IABC Communication World,* June–July 1991, 20–25.

3. J. Michael Sproule, *Communication Today* (Glenview, IL: Scott Foresman, 1981), 329; Ray Suutari, "Organizing for the New Economy: The Changing Role of Management," *CMA Management* 75, no. 2 (April 2001): 12–13.

4. Jaesub Lee and Fredric Jablan, "A Cross-Cultural Investigation of Exit, Voice, Loyalty and Neglect as Responses to Dissatisfying Job Conditions," *Journal of Business Communication* 23, no. 3 (1992): 203–28; Barron Wells and Nelda Spinks, "What Do You Mean People Communicate with Audiences?" *The Bulletin of the Association for Business Communication* 54, no. 3 (September 1991): 100–102.

5. Margot Gibb-Clark, "How to Keep Employees Informed," *The Globe and Mail,* 1 November 1996, B12.

6. Donald O. Wilson, "Diagonal Communication Links with Organizations," *Journal of Business Communication* 29, no. 2 (Spring 1992): 129–43.

7. Valorie A. McClelland and Richard E. Wilmot, "Communication: Improve Lateral Communication," *Personnel Journal,* August 1990, 32–38; Valorie A. McClelland and Dick Wilmot, "Lateral Communication: As Seen Through the Eyes of Employees," *IABC Communication World,* December 1990, 32–35.

8. Carol Hymowitz, "Spread the Word: Gossip Is Good," *Wall Street Journal,* 4 November 1988, B1; Donald B. Simmons, "The Nature of the Organizational Grapevine," *Supervisory Management,* November 1985, 40.

9. J. David Johnson, William A. Donohoe, Charles K. Atkin, and Sally Johnson, "Differences Between Formal and Informal Communication Channels," *Journal of Business Communication* 31, no. 2 (1994): 111–22; Patricia Karathanos and Anthony Auriemmo, "Care and Feeding of the Organizational Grapevine," *Industrial Management* 41, no. 26(5); Bob Smith, "Care and Feeding of the Office Grapevine," *Management Review* 85, no. 2 (February 1996): 6.

10. Maureen Weiss, "Manager's Tool Kit: Tapping the Grapevine," *Across the Board,* April 1992, 62–63.

11. "Walk More, Talk More," *Across the Board,* December 1992, 57; Jonathan H. Amsbary and Patricia J. Staples, "Improving Administrator/Nurse Communication: A Case Study of 'Management by Wandering Around,'" *Journal of Business Communication* 28, no. 2 (Spring 1991): 101–12; John Della Costa, "The Broken Promise of a Broken Paradigm: Rethinking Executive Leadership for an Age of Uncertainty," *Financial Post Magazine*, November 1998, 25–29.

12. Les Sillars, "Bureaucratic Serial Killers: Krever's Tainted Blood Inquiry Lays Bare in Meticulous Detail the Heavy Death from Political Correctness," *British Columbia Report,* 15 December 1997, 42–46.

13. Mike O'Brien (Executive Vice-President, Sunoco Group), "The Next Big Challenge: Moving from Downsizing to Growth," Speech delivered to the Ontario Club, Toronto, Ontario, 28 November 1996, http://www.suncor.com/about/speeches_961028.html (June 23, 1997).

14. John Huey, "Wal-Mart: Will It Take Over the World?" *Fortune,* 30 January 1989, 56; Patricia Sellers, "Getting Customers to Love You," *Fortune,* 13 March 1989, 39; Stephen Phillips and Amy Dunkin, "King Customer," *Business Week,* 12 March 1990, 91; Charles Leerhsen, "How Disney Does It," *Newsweek,* 3 April 1989, 52.

15. Phillip G. Clampitt and Cal W. Downs, "Employee Perceptions of the Relationship Between Communication and Productivity: A Field Study," *Journal of Business Communication* 30, no. 1 (1993): 5–28.

16. Douglas McGregor, *The Human Side of Enterprise* (New York: McGraw-Hill, 1960), 33–34, 47–48.

17. William G. Ouchi, *Theory Z: How American Business Can Meet the Japanese Challenge* (Reading, MA: Addison-Wesley, 1981), 17.

18. Shlomo Maital, "Zen and the Art of Total Quality," *Across the Board,* March 1992, 50–51; James C. Shaffer, "Seven Emerging Trends in Organizational Communication," *IABC Communication World,* February 1986, 18.

19. Former US Supreme Court Justice Potter Stewart, quoted in A. Thomas Young, "Ethics in Business: Business of Ethics," *Vital Speeches,* 15 September 1992, 725–30.

20. Bruce W. Speck, "Writing Professional Codes of Ethics to Introduce Ethics in Business Writing," *The Bulletin of the Association for Business Communication* 53, no. 3 (September 1990): 21–26; H. W. Love, "Communication, Accountability and Professional Discourse: The Interaction of Language Values and Ethical Values," *Journal of Business Ethics* 11 (1992): 883–92; Kathryn C. Rentz and Mary Beth Debs, "Language and Corporate Values: Teaching Ethics in Business Writing Courses," *Journal of Business Communication* 24, no. 3 (Summer 1987): 37–48.

21. Joseph L. Badaracco Jr., "Business Ethics: Four Spheres of Executive Responsibility," *California Management Review,* Spring 1992, 64–79; Kenneth Blanchard and Norman Vincent Peale, *The Power of Ethical Management* (Reprint, 1989; New York: Fawcett Crest, 1991), 7–17.

22. John D. Pettit, Bobby Vaught, and Kathy J. Pulley, "The Role of Communication in Organizations," *Journal of Business Communication* 27, no. 3 (Summer 1990): 233–49; Kenneth Labich, "The New Crisis in Business Ethics," *Fortune,* 20 April 1992, 167, 168, 172, 176; Kenneth R. Andrews, "Ethics in Practice," *Harvard Business Review,* September–October 1989, 99–104; Priscilla S. Rogers and John M. Swales, "We the People? An Analysis of the Dana Corporation Policies Document," *Journal of Business Communication* 27, no. 3 (Summer 1990): 293–313; Larry Reynolds, "The Ethics Audit," *Business Ethics,* July–August 1991, 120–22; Patrick E. Murphy, "Creating Ethical Corporate Structures," *Sloan Management Review* 30, no. 2 (Winter 1989): 81–87.

23. See Susan L. Fry, "How to Succeed in the New Europe," *Public Relations Journal,* January 1991, 17–21.

24. Laurel Hyatt, "Shedding Light on Canada's Ethnic Communities," *Broadcaster* 58, no. 3 (March 1999): 10.

25. Based on Zero Knowledge Systems Web site, http://www.zero-knowledge.com (25 May, 2000); Diane Francis, "Work is a Warm Puppy," *National Post,* 27 May 2000, W20; Hilary Davidson, "My Company is the Coolest," *Profit* 18, no. 7 (November 1999): 46–52; Jan Ravensbergen, "Software Firm Plays Hardbal," *Montreal Gazette,* 2 December 1999, C1.

26. Keith Davidson, "Function, Not Form, Drives Future Documents," *Canadian Printer* 108, no. 1 (January 2000): 39–40.

27. "Wireless Telecom" [advertising supplement], *Silicon Valley North* 3, no. 3 (May 1999): W1–W10.

28. Rick Tetzeli, "Surviving Information Overload, *Fortune,* July 1994, 60–65.

29. "Message Growth Spurt Speeds Pace of Work," *Computing Canada* 25, no. 41 (29 October 1999): 26.

30. "1995 Cost of a Business Letter," *Dartnell Study* (Chicago: The Dartnell Corporation, 1995).

31. Selwyn Feinstein, "Remedial Training," *Wall Street Journal*, 20 February 1990, A1.

32. Based on Glass, "Escaping the Rut"; Flynn, "Sending a Quality of Life Message"; Matthes, "Greetings from Hallmark."

33. Based on Keith Denton, "Improving Community Relations," *Small Business Reports,* August 1990, 33–34, 35–41.

34. Based on "When Rumours Disrupt Your Staff," *Working Women*, October 1992, 36.

Chapter 2

1. Adapted from Suncor Energy Inc. Web site, http://www.suncor.ca (16 May 2000).

2. David Givens, "You Animal? How to Win Friends and Influence Homosapiens," *The Toastmaster,* August 1986, 9; Judith A. Hall and Gregory B. Friedman, "Status, Gender, and Nonverbal Behavior: A Study of Structured Interactions Between Employees of a Company," *Personality & Social Psychology Bulletin* 25 (September 1999): 1082.

3. Mark L. Hickson III and Don W. Stacks, *Nonverbal Communication: Studies and Applications* (Dubuque, IA: Brown, 1985), 4.

4. Gerald H. Graham, Jeanne Unrue, and Paul Jennings, "The Impact of Nonverbal Communication in Organizations: A Survey of Perceptions," *Journal of Business Communication* 28, no. 1 (Winter 1991): 45–62.

5. David Lewis, *The Secret Language of Success* (New York: Carroll & Graf, 1989), 67, 170.

6. Nido Qubein, *Communicate Like a Pro* (New York: Berkley Books, 1986), 97.

7. Dale G. Leathers, *Successful Nonverbal Communication: Principles and Applications* (New York: Macmillan, 1986), 19.

8. Margaret Ann Baker, "Reciprocal Accommodation: A Model for Reducing Gender Bias in Managerial Communication," *Journal of Business Communication* 28, no. 2 (Spring 1991): 113–27; Graham, Unrue, and Jennings, "The Impact of Nonverbal Communication in Organizations," 45–62. Susan Burnette, "New Wave Women: For Women, the Road to the Top is Fraught with Twists, Turns and Potholes that Men Rarely Notice," *CMA Management* 73, no. 3 (April 1999): 14–17.

9. Graham, Unrue, and Jennings, "The Impact of Nonverbal Communication in Organizations," 45–62.

10. Stuart Berg Flexner, "From 'Gadzooks' to 'Nice,' the Language Keeps Changing," *U.S. News & World Report,* 18 February 1985, 59.

11. Erik Larson, "Forever Young," *Inc.,* July 1988, 56.

12. Phillip Morgan and H. Kent Baker, "Building a Professional Image: Improving Listening Behavior," *Supervisory Management,* November 1985, 35, 36.

13. Augusta M. Simon, "Effective Listening: Barriers to Listening in a Diverse Business Environment," *The Bulletin of the Association for Business Communication* 54, no. 3 (September 1991): 73–74.

14. Statistics Canada, *Literary Skills for the Knowledge Society* (Ottawa, ON: Ministry of Industry, 1997) quoted in "Literacy Facts," *ABC Canada,* http://www.abc-canada.org/literacy_ facts/index.asp#stats (22 June 2000).

15. Some material adapted from Courtland L. Bovée, John V. Thill, Marian Burk Wood, and George P. Dovel, *Management* (New York: McGraw-Hill, 1993), 537–38.

16. Much of the material contained in the entire section on communication barriers has been adapted from Bovée, Thill, Wood, and Dovel, *Management,* 549–57.

17. Adapted from C. Glenn Pearce, Ross Figgins, and Steve F. Golen, *Principles of Business Communication: Theory, Application, and Technology* (New York: Wiley, 1984), 520–38.

18. Linlin Ku, "Social and Nonsocial Uses of Electronic Messaging Systems in Organizations," *Journal of Business Communication* 33, no. 3 (July 1996): 297–325.

19. Boveé, Thill, Wood, and Dovel, *Management*, 555.

20. Based on information from the Enterprise Mediation Web site, http://www.enterprise-mediation.com (26 May 2000); "Mediation Better Way to Handle Conflicts: Companies Increasingly Looking for Alternatives to Legal Action," *Financial Post Daily* 9, no. 8 (15 February 1996): 18.

21. Based in information from the Suncor Web site, http://www.suncor.ca; "Automakers' Campaign Pushes for Cleaner Gasoline," *Plant* 58, no. 16 (8 November 1999): 2; Claudia Cattaneo, "Suncor Unveils new $750M Oilsands Project: Alberta Expansion Will Add 35,000 Barrels of Oil a Day," *Financial Post (National Post)* 2, no. 81 (28 January 2000): C1, C9.

Chapter 3

1. Based on information from the Malkam Cross-Cultural Training Web site, http://www.malkam.com (4 July 2000).

2. Bombardier, *Annual Report 2000*, 78.

3. Elizabeth Howard, "Going Global: What It Really Means to Communicators," *IABC Communication World*, April 1995, 12–15.

4. Paul Magnusson, "Free Trade? They Can Hardly Wait," *Business Week*, 14 September 1992, 24–25; Bill Javetski, "Continental Drift," *Business Week*, 5 October 1992, 34–36.

5. Laurel Hyatt, "Shedding Light on Canada's Ethnic Communities," *Broadcaster* 58, no. 3 (March 1999): 10.

6. Statistics Canada, "Immigrant Population by Place of Birth and Period of Immigration, 1996 Census, Canada," http://www.statcan.ca/english/Pgdb/People/Population/demo25b.htm (7 July 2000)

7. Gus Tyler, "Tokyo Signs the Paychecks," *New York Times Book Review*, 12 August 1990, 7.

8. Tzöl Zae Chung, "Culture: A Key to Management Communication Between the Asian-Pacific Area and Europe," *European Management Journal* 9, no. 4 (December 1991): 419–24.

9. Laraine Kaminsky, "Bridging the Culture Gap," *Exportwise*, July 2000. Quoted on Malkam Cross-Cultural Training Web site, http://www.malkam.com (4 July 2000).

10. Larry A. Samovar and Richard E. Porter, "Basic Principles of Intercultural Communication," in *Intercultural Communication: A Reader*, 6th ed., edited by Larry A. Samovar and Richard E. Porter (Belmont, CA: Wadsworth, 1991), 12.

11. Tim Jones, "Shrinking World Reshapes Auto Industry," *Chicago Tribune*, 10 May 1998, sec. 5, 1, 14.

12. Edmund L. Andrews and Laura M. Holson, "Significant Risks–The Largest Acquisition of a Company in U.S. by a Foreign Buyer," *New York Times*, 7 May 1998, A-1, C-4; Robyn Meredith, "Two Auto Makers With Long Histories Attempt a Trans-Atlantic Marriage," *New York Times*, 7 May 1998, C-4.

13. James Calvert Scott, "Using an International Business-Meal Function to Develop Sociocultural Skills," *Business Communication Quarterly* 58, no. 3 (1995): 55–57.

14. "What We're All About: What are the Ideals that Define Canadians?" *Canada and the World Backgrounder* 60, no.6 (April 1995): 38–39 (insert).

15. Sharon Oosthoek, "The Polite Canuck Gets an Attitude Adjustment; The stereotypical Canadian–always respectful of the powers-that-be–is a vanishing breed, observers say," *Edmonton Journal*, 17 August 1997, E3.

16. Paul Tellier (CEO, Canadian National Railways),"Leadership to Build Canada's Productivity," Speech delivered at the Summa Strategy Forum in Ottawa, Ontario, 16 March 1999, http://www.cn.ca (17 May 2000).

17. See Nancy J. Adler, "Women Managers in a Global Economy," *Training and Development* 48, no. 4 (April 1994): 30, and Charlene Marmur Solomon, "Global Operations Demand that HR Rethink Diversity," *Personnel Journal* 73, no. 7 (July 1994): 40.

18. "Pakistan: A Congenial Business Climate," *Nation's Business*, July 1986, 50.

19. Victor, *International Business Communication,* 234–39; Mohan R. Limaye and David A. Victor, "Cross Cultural Business Communication Research: State of the Art and Hypotheses for the 1990s," *Journal of Business Communication* 28, no. 3 (Summer 1991): 277–99.

20. Carley H. Dodd, *Dynamics of Intercultural Communication*, 3rd ed. (Dubuque, IA: Brown, 1991), 215.

21. Edward T. Hall, "Context and Meaning," in *Intercultural Communication*, Samovar and Porter, 46–55.

22. Dodd, *Dynamics of Intercultural Communication*, 69–70.

23. Porter and Samovar, "Basic Principles of Intercultural Communication," 5–22; David A. Victor, personal communication, 1993.

24. Jean A. Mausehund, Susan A. Timm, and Albert S. King, "Diversity Training: Effects of an Intervention Treatment on Nonverbal Awareness," *Business Communication Quarterly* 38, no. 1 (1995): 27–30. See also "Gestures Around the World," http://www.webofculture.com/worldsmart/gestures.html (12 July 2000).

25. Sharon Ruhly, *Intercultural Communication*, 2nd ed. MODCOM (Modules in Speech Communication) (Chicago: Science Research Associates, 1982), 14.

26. Karen P. H. Lane, "Greasing the Bureaucratic Wheel," *North American International Business*, August 1990, 35–37; Arthur Aronoff, "Complying with the Foreign Corrupt Practices Act," *Business America*, 11 February 1991, 10–11; Bill Shaw, "Foreign Corrupt Practices Act: A Legal and Moral Analysis," *Journal of Business Ethics* 7 (1988): 789–95. Claudia Cattaneo, "An Exporter of Ethics," *Financial Post (National Post)* 1, no. 93 (13 February 1999): D1, D6; Neville Nankivell, "New Legislation Forces Companies to Take Foreign Bribery Seriously: But Enforcing Anti-Corruption Law Will Be Tricky," *Financial Post (National Post)* 1 no. 91 (11 February 1999): C7; Mike Trickery, "Code of Ethics for Conduction Business Overseas Developed by Group of Canadian Firms," *Calgary Herald*, 5 September 1997 (Final Edition), D6.

27. Philip R. Harris and Robert T. Moran, *Managing Cultural Differences*, 3rd ed. (Houston: Gulf, 1991), 260.

28. David J. McIntyre, "When Your National Language Is Just *Another* Language," *IABC Communication World*, May 1991, 18–21.

29. Linda Beamer, "Teaching English Business Writing to Chinese-Speaking Business Students," *Bulletin of the Association for Business Communication* 57, no. 1 (1994): 12–18.

30. David A. Ricks, "International Business Blunders: An Update," *B&E Review*, January–March 1988, 12.

31. Based on information from the Terra Cognita Web site, http://www.terracognita.com (8 July 2000).

32. Mark Wilson, "Canadian Speaks to Asians," *The Province* (Vancouver), 20 October 1995 (Final Edition), A48.

33. Victor, *International Business Communication*, 36.

34. Doreen Mangan, "What's New in Language Translation: A Tool for Examining Foreign Patents and Research," *New York Times*, 19 November 1989, sec. 3, 15.

35. Victor, *International Business Communication*, 39; Harris and Moran, *Managing Cultural Differences*, 64.

36. Mona Casady and Lynn Wasson, "Written Communication Skills of International Business Persons," *The Bulletin of the Association for Business Communication* 57, no. 4 (1994): 36–40.

37. Geert Hofstede, *Cultures and Organizations* (London: McGraw-Hill, 1991), 211.

38. Richard W. Brislin, "Prejudice in Intercultural Communication," in *Intercultural Communication*, Samovar and Porter, 366–70.

39. Jensen J. Zhao and Calvin Parks, "Self-Assessment of Communication Behavior: An Experiential Learning Exercise for Intercultural Business Success," *Business Communication Quarterly* 58, no. 1 (1995): 20–26; Dodd, *Dynamics of Intercultural Communication*, 142–43, 297–99.

40. Susan A. Hellweg, Larry A. Samovar, and Lisa Skow, "Cultural Variations in Negotiation Styles," in *Intercultural Communication*, Samovar and Porter, 185–92.

41. Brian Dumaine, "P&G Rewrites the Marketing Rules," *Fortune*, 6 November 1989, 38.

42. Based on information from Malkam Cross-Cultural Training Web site.

43. Michael Copeland, specialist, international training, personal communication, 24 January 1990; Dumaine, "P&G Rewrites the Maketing Rules," 34–48; Procter & Gamble Company 1992 Annual Report, 24.

Chapter 4

1. Mike Stevens, systems technology specialist, Hewlett-Packard, Colorado Springs, Colorado, personal communication, April 1996; Hewlett-Packard Web site, http://www.hp.com (8 August 2000).

2. Eric J. Adams, "A Real Global Office," *World Trade*, October 1992, 97–98.

3. See http://www.taxpage.com and http://www.taxpage.com/taxlinks.htm.

4. Microsoft Corporation, *Encarta*, CD-ROM (Microsoft Corporation, 2000).

5. Inspiration demonstration, Disk (Inspiration Software, 1994).

6. Jack Nimersheim, "Grammar Checker Face-Off," *Home-Office Computing*, July 1992, 49–53.

7. Eric J. Adams, "The Fax of Global Business," *World Trade*, August–September 1991, 34–39.

8. Bill Eager, *Using the Internet* (Indianapolis: Que, 1994), 13.

9. Don Clark and Joan E. Rigdon, "Stripped Down PCs Will Be Talk of Comdex," *Wall Street Journal*, 10 November 1995, B1.

10. "All About E-Mail: Use E-Mail to Communicate with Anyone, Anywhere," *Microsoft Magazine*, April–May 1996, 14–26.

11. William Eager, Larry Donahue, David Forsyth, Kenneth Mitton, and Martin Waterhouse, *Net.search* (Indianapolis: Que, 1995), 226.

12. Sheri Rosen, "Who Says E-Mail Is Mundane?" *IABC Communication World*, September 1995, 42.

13. Jolie Solomon, "As Electronic Mail Loosens Inhibitions, Impetuous Senders Feel Anything Goes," *Wall Street Journal*, 10 December 1990, B1–B2.

14. Mike Snyder, "E-Mail Isn't as Private as You May Think," *USA Today*, 10 October 1995, 6D.

15. Karen Kaplan, "Your Voicemail Box May Have Ears," *Los Angeles Times*, 15 July 1996, D8; Virginia Galt, "Stop Snooping on Your Employees: Privacy Commissioner Says Confidential E-Mail is a Right," *The Globe and Mail*, 16 April 2001, B9.

16. Wayne Rash Jr., "Before You Press That Send Button, Keep in Mind That E-Mail Is Forever," *Communications Week*, 16 October 1995, 72.

17. Michael Mathiesen, *Marketing on the Internet* (Gulf Breeze, FL.: Maximum Press, 1995), 11–12.

18. Mathiesen, *Marketing on the Internet*, 12–14.

19. Amy Cortese, "Here Comes the Intranet," *BusinessWeek*, 26 February 1996 and *BusinessWeek Online*, 15 May 1996, http://www.businessweek.com/1996/09/b34641.htm.

20. "HP and Netscape Outline Strategic Alliance to Deliver Enterprise Intranet Solutions Across UNIX and NT System Platforms," press release, *Netscape*, Online, 14 May 1996.

21. "Internal Webs as Corporate Information Systems," White paper, *Netscape Communications*, Online, 25 April 1996.

22. Mike Bransby, "Voice Mail Makes a Difference," *Journal of Business Strategy*, January–February 1990, 7–10.

23. Harris Collingswood, "Voice Mail Hangups," *Business Week*, 17 February 1992, 46.

24. Andrew Kupfer, "Prime Time for Videoconferences," *Fortune*, 28 December 1992, 90–95; Charlotte Marmur Solomon, "Global Teams: The Ultimate Collaboration," *Personnel Journal* 74, no. 9 (September 1995): 6.

25. Michael Finley, "The New Meaning of Meetings," *IABC Communication World*, March 1991, 25–27.

26. Based on information from Chapters Web site, http://www.chapters.ca (6 June 2000); Chapters, Inc., *1999 Annual Report*; CCN Newswire, news release, 15 May 2000, http://www2.cdn-news.com/scripts/ccn-release.pl?2000/05/15/051512n.html?cp=chp (6 June 2000); Canadian NewsWire, "Chapters Expands Internet Presence," 23 April 1999, http://www.newswire.ca/releases/April1999/23/c5387.html (6 June 2000); Canadian NewsWire, "Chapters.ca and Chapters.Inc Bring 'Clicks and Mortar' Shopping to Canadians," September 1999, http://www.newswire.ca/releases/September 1999/09/c1584.html (6 June 2000); Stephanie Nolen, "Love Him, or Hate Him, He's Man of the Year," *The Globe and Mail*, 27 December 1999.

27. Chris Campbell, "Outerstreaming: The Fourth Communication Paradigm," *IABC Communication World*, December 1990, 18–22.

28. Based on Mike Stevens, personal communication, April 1996.

Chapter 5

1. Adapted from Mattel Barbie Web site, http://www.barbie.com (9 October 1997, 9 August 2000); *Mattel 1993 Annual Report*, 2–6; Cinda Chavich, "Tickled Pink; Herald Writer (and Barbie Fan) Cinda Chavich Attended Her First Collectors Convention Expecting a World of Wierdos: Instead She Found a Roomful of Dedicated Artists Working in Miniature," *Calgary Herald*, 19 September 1999, E1; Michelle Greene and Denise Gellene, "As a Tiny Plastic Star Turns 30, the Real Barbie and Ken Reflect on Life in the Shadow of the Dolls," *People,* 6 March 1989, 186–89; Denise Gellene, "Forever Young," *Los Angeles Times,* 29 January 1989, D1, D4; Ann Hornaday, "Top Guns: The Most Powerful Women in Corporate America," *Savvy,* May 1989, 57, 60; Jennifer Roethe, "Dolls and Dollars Go Together Like Ken and Barbie," *Cincinnati Business Courier,* 10 July 1989, 1.

2. Mary K. Kirtz and Diana C. Reep, "A Survey of the Frequency, Types, and Importance of Writing Tasks in Four Career Areas," *The Bulletin of the Association for Business Communication* 53, no. 4 (December 1990): 3–4.

3. Mary Cullinan and Ce Ce Iandoli, "What Activities Help to Improve Your Writing? Some Unsettling Student Responses," *The Bulletin of the Association for Business Communication* 54, no. 4 (December 1991): 8–10; Ruth Yontz, "Providing a Rationale for the Process Approach," *Journal of Business Communication* 24, no. 1 (Winter 1987): 17–19; Annette Shelby, "Note on Process," *Journal of Business Communication* 24, no. 1 (Winter 1987): 21.

4. Peter Bracher, "Process, Pedagogy, and Business Writing," *Journal of Business Communication* 24, no. 1 (Winter 1987): 43–50.

5. John J. Stallard, Sandra F. Price, and E. Ray Smith, "A Strategy for Teaching Critical-Thinking Skills in Business Communication," *The Bulletin of the Association for Business Communication* 55, no. 3 (September 1992): 20–22.

6. Rodney P. Rice and John T. Huguley Jr., "Describing Collaborative Forms: A Profile of the Team-Writing Process," *IEEE Transactions on Professional Communication* 37, no. 3 (1994), 163–70; Mary Beth Debs, "Recent Research on Collaborative Writing in Industry," *Technical Communication* (November 1991): 476–84.

7. William P. Galle Jr., Beverly H. Nelson, Donna W. Luse, and Maurice F. Villere, *Business Communication: A Technology-Based Approach* (Chicago: Irwin, 1996), 256.

8. Galle, Nelson, Luse, and Villere, *Business Communication,* 260.

9. Charles R. Stratton, "Collaborative Writing in the Workplace," *IEEE Transactions on Professional Communication* 32, no. 3 (1989): 178–82.

10. Debs, "Recent Research on Collaborative Writing in Industry," 476–84.

11. Sanford Kaye, "Writing Under Pressure," *Soundview Executive Book Summaries* 10, no. 12, part 2 (December 1988): 1–8.

12. Al Schlachtmeyer and Max Caldwell, "Communicating Creatively," *IABC Communication World,* June–July 1991, 28.

13. Morgan W. McCall Jr. and Robert L. Hannon, *Studies of Managerial Work: Results and Methods,* Technical Report no. 9 (Greensboro, NC: Center for Creative Leadership, 1978), 6–10.

14. Wendy MacNair, editor, Aboriginal Banking Newsletter, personal communication 28 August 2000, 29 August 2000, and 18 September 2000; Business Development Bank of Canada, *2000 Annual Report,* http://www.bdc.ca (18 September 2000); Business Development Bank of Canada, *Aboriginal Banking: The Key to Success* [pamphlet], August 1999; Business Development Bank of Canada, *Growth Capital for Aboriginal Business: Taking Entrepreneurs One Step Further* [pamphlet], September 1997.

15. Ernest Thompson, "Some Effects of Message Structure on Listener's Comprehension," *Speech Monographs* 34 (March 1967): 51–57.

16. Laurey Berk and Phillip G. Clampitt, "Finding the Right Path in the Communication Maze," *IABC Communication World,* October 1991, 28–32.

17. Schlachtmeyer and Caldwell, "Communicating Creatively," 26–29.

18. Adapted from Berk and Clampitt, "Finding the Right Path in the Communication Maze," 28–32.

19. Mohan R. Limaye and David A. Victor, "Cross-Cultural Business Communication Research: State of the Art and Hypotheses for the 1990s," *Journal of Business Communication* 28, no. 3 (Summer 1991): 277–99.

20. Berk and Clampitt, "Finding the Right Path in the Communication Maze," 28–32.

21. Berk and Clampitt, "Finding the Right Path in the Communication Maze," 28–32.

22. Based on Mattel Barbie Web site; *Mattel 1993 Annual Report*; Chavich, "Tickled Pink"; Green and Gellene, "As a Tiny Plastic Star Turns 30"; Gellene, "Forever Young"; Hornaday, "Top Guns"; Roethe, "Dolls and Dollars Go Together Like Ken and Barbie."

Chapter 6

1. Hoover's Online, "Club Mediterranee S.A.," http:/www.hoovers.com (22 January 1997); Elaine Underwood, "Club Med Continues to Broaden, Soften Image," *Brandweek*, 30 October 1995, 12; Jorge Sidron, "Club Med Finds Success Sticking to Key Formula: Fun, Relaxation," *Travel Weekly*, 25 November 1996, 100; Patrick Flanagan, "Don't Call 'Em Old, Call 'Em Customers," *Management Review*, October 1994, 18; Stewart Troy, "Storms, Terrorists–Why Is Club Med Smiling?" *Business Week*, 6 November 1995, 160C.

2. Carol S. Mull, "Orchestrate Your Ideas," *The Toastmaster*, February 1987, 19.

3. Susan Hall and Theresa Tiggeman, "Getting the Big Picture: Writing to Learn in a Finance Class," *Business Communication Quarterly* 58, no. 1 (1995): 12–15.

4. Based on the Pyramid Model developed by Barbara Minto of McKinsey & Company, management consultants.

5. Philip Subanks, "Messages, Models, and the Messy World of Memos," *The Bulletin of the Association for Business Communication* 57, no. 1 (1994): 33–34.

6. Anne Hoekstra, Editor-in-Chief, *Business $ense*, personal communication, 5 September 2000; Business $ense Web site, http://www.BusinessSense.com (24 August 2000); Ellen Roseman, "New Business Magazine Launched: Target Market is 120,000 Students," *Toronto Star*, 29 March 1999; Dawn Walton, "Magazine Targets Business Students," *Globe and Mail Report on Business: Enterprise*, 26 March 1999, B10; "What Do Employers Look for in Business Graduates?" *Canada NewsWire*, 10 January 2000.

7. See Iris I. Varner, "Internationalizing Business Communication Courses," *The Bulletin of the Association for Business Communication* 50, no. 4 (December 1987): 7–11.

8. Mary A. DeVries, *Internationally Yours* (New York: Houghton Mifflin, 1994), 61.

9. Elizabeth Blackburn and Kelly Belanger, "You-Attitude and Positive Emphasis: Testing Received Wisdom in Business Communication," *The Bulletin of the Association for Business Communication* 56, no. 2 (June 1993): 1–9.

10. Blackburn and Belanger, "You-Attitude and Positive Emphasis,"1–9.

11. DeVries, *Internationally Yours*, 61.

12. Annette N. Shelby and N. Lamar Reinsch Jr., "Positive Emphasis and You Attitude: An Empirical Study," *Journal of Business Communication* 32, no. 4 (1995): 303–22.

13. John S. Fielden, Jean D. Fielden, and Ronald E. Dulek, *The Business Writing Style Book* (Englewood Cliffs, NJ: Prentice Hall, 1984), 7.

14. Renee B. Horowitz and Marian G. Barchilon, "Stylistic Guidelines for E-Mail," *IEEE Transactions on Professional Communications* 37, no. 4 (December 1994): 207–12.

15. Jill H. Ellsworth and Matthew V. Ellsworth, *The Internet Business Book* (New York: Wiley, 1994), 91.

16. Lance Cohen, "How to Improve Your E-Mail Messages," http://galaxy.einet/galaxy/Business-and-Commerce/Management/Communications/How_to_Improve_Your_E_Mail.html.

17. David Angell and Brent D. Heslop, *The Elements of E-mail Style: Communicate Effectively via Electronic Mail* (Reading, MA: Addison-Wesley, 1994), 10.

18. Angell and Heslop, *The Elements of E-Mail Style*, 20.

19. Angell and Heslop, *The Elements of E-Mail Style*, 24.

20. Angell and Heslop, *The Elements of E-Mail Style*, 22.

21. Cohen, "How to Improve Your E-Mail Messages"; Angell and Heslop, *The Elements of E-Mail Style*, 20; Horowitz and Barchilon, "Stylistic Guidelines for E-Mail."

22. Angell and Heslop, *The Elements of E-Mail Style*, 18–19.

23. Angell and Heslop, *The Elements of E-Mail Style*, 21.

24. Angell and Heslop, *The Elements of E-Mail Style*, 20; Cohen, "How to Improve Your E-Mail Messages"; Ellsworth and Ellsworth, *The Internet Business Book*, 101.

25. Cohen, "How to Improve Your E-Mail Messages"; William Eager, *Using the Internet* (Indianapolis: Que, 1994), 99.

26. Angell and Heslop, *The Elements of E-Mail Style*, 30, 117; Ellsworth and Ellsworth, *The Internet Business Book*, 99; Eager, *Using the Internet*, 99; Cohen, "How to Improve Your E-Mail Messages"; William Eager, Larry Donahue, David Forsyth, Kenneth Mitton, and Martin Waterhouse, *Net.Search* (Indianapolis: Que, 1995), 225.

27. Based on Hoover's Online, "Club Mediterranee S.A."; Underwood, "Club Med Continues to Broaden, Soften Image"; Sidron, "Club Med Finds Success Sticking to Key Formula"; Flanagan, "Don't Call 'Em Old, Call 'Em Customers"; Troy, "Storms, Terrorists."

Chapter 7

1. Adapted from Brian Bremmer, "The Burger Wars Were Just a Warmup for McDonald's," *Business Week,* 8 May 1989, 67, 70; Richard Gibson and Robert Johnson, "Big Mac Plots Strategy to Regain Sizzle; Besides Pizza, It Ponders Music and Low Lights," *Wall Street Journal,* 29 September 1989, B1; Dyan Machan, "Great Hash Browns, But Watch Those Biscuits," *Forbes,* 19 September 1988, 192–96; Penny Moser, "The McDonald's Mystique," *Fortune,* 4 July 1988, 112–16; Thomas N. Cochran, "McDonald's Corporation," *Barron's,* 16 November 1987, 53–55; Lenore Skenazy, "McDonald's Colors Its World," *Advertising Age,* 9 February 1987, 37.

2. Iris I. Varner, "Internationalizing Business Communication Courses," *The Bulletin of the Association for Business Communication* 50, no. 4 (December 1987): 7–11.

3. Kevin T. Stevens, Kathleen C. Stevens, and William P. Stevens, "Measuring the Readability of Business Writing: The Cloze Procedure versus Readability Formulas," *Journal of Business Communication* 29, no. 4 (1992): 367–82; Alinda Drury, "Evaluating Readability," *IEEE Transactions of Professional Communication* PC-28 (December 1985): 11.

4. Portions of this section are adapted from Courtland L. Bovée, *Techniques of Writing Business Letters, Memos, and Reports* (Sherman Oaks, CA: Banner Books International, 1978), 13–90.

5. Randolph H. Hudson, Gertrude M. McGuire, and Bernard J. Selzler, *Business Writing: Concepts and Applications* (Los Angeles: Roxbury, 1983), 79–82.

6. Peter Crow, "Plain English: What Counts Besides Readability?" *Journal of Business Communication* 25, no. 1 (Winter 1988): 87–95.

7. Rose Knotts and Mary S. Thibodeaux, "Verbal Skills in Cross-Culture Managerial Communication," *European Business Review* 92, no. 2 (1992): 5–7.

8. Lisa Taylor, "Communicating About People with Disabilities: Does the Language We Use Make a Difference?" *The Bulletin of the Association for Business Communication* 53, no. 3 (September 1990): 65–67.

9. Charles E. Risch, "Critiquing Written Material," *Manage* 35, no. 4 (1983): 4–6.

10. Risch, "Critiquing Written Material."

11. Risch, "Critiquing Written Material."

12. Varner, "Internationalizing Business Communication Courses."

13. Drury, "Evaluating Readability," 12.

14. Portions of the following sections are adapted from Roger C. Parker, *Looking Good in Print,* 2nd ed. (Chapel Hill, NC: Ventana Press, 1990).

15. Laurie Murphy, Publicist, Confederation Centre of the Arts, interview with author, 27 September 2000; Confederation Centre of the Arts Web site, http://www.confederationcentre.com; *The Charlottetown Festival May 31-October 14, 2000* [brochure]; Curtis Barlow, Executive Director and CEO, Confederation Centre of the Arts, "The Charlottetown Festival" [promotional letter].

16. Raymond W. Beswick, "Designing Documents for Legibility," *The Bulletin of the Association for Business Communication* 50, no. 4 (December 1987): 34–35.

17. Beswick, "Designing Documents for Legibility."

18. "The Process Model of Document Design," *IEEE Transactions on Professional Communication* PC-24, no. 4 (December 1981): 176–78.

19. Based on Bremmer, "The Burger Wars Were Just a Warmup for McDonald's"; Gibson and Johnson, "Big Mac Plots Strategy to Regain Sizzle"; Machan, "Great Hash Browns"; Moser, "The McDonald's Mystique"; Cochran, "McDonald's Corporation"; Skenazy, "McDonald's Colors Its World."

Chapter 8

1. Based Indigo Books and Music Web site, http://www.indigo.ca (24 August 2000); Paul Brent, "High-stakes Holiday: The Chapters and Indigo Bookstore Chains are Spending Millions to Take their Main Street Rivalry into Electronic Commerce," *Financial Post,* 13 November 1999, D1; Mikala Folb, "Online Book Boom: Canadian Booksellers Aren't About to Equal Amazon.com's Revenues, but Sales of up to $50 million this Year ain't Shabby," *Marketing Magazine* 104, no. 3 (25 January 1999): 15–16; Geoff Kirbyson, "Bookseller has More than 200 Employees, Annual Revenues of $15 Million," *Winnipeg Free Press,* 15 September 2000, B5; John Lorinc, "The Indigo Way: Stylish and Savvy, Canada's #2 Chain Marches to Its Own Beat," *Quill & Quire* 66, no. 2 (February 2000): 22–23.

2. Based on Indigo Books and Music Web site, http://www.indigo.ca (24 August 2000, 8 December 2000); Brent, "High-Stakes Holiday"; Folb, "Online Book Boom"; Adrian Humphreys and Paul Waldie, "High-Flying Pair Know this Turf Well," *The Globe and Mail,* 29 November 2000, A3; Lorinc, "The Indigo Way"; Deborah Stokes, "Black and Blue and Read All Over Again: Minding Online Business," *Financial Post,* 8 September 1999, E1; Derek Weiler, "Indigo Launches Round Two of Expansion: New Stores, Internet Campaign Mark Chain's Renewed Growth as Competition with Chapters Intensifies," *Quill & Quire* 65, no. 9 (Spring 1999): 5–7.

3. Adapted from Kendall Hamilton, "Getting Up, Getting Air," *Newsweek,* 13 May 1996, 68.

4. Trinidad & Tobago advertisement, *Saveur,* March–April 1996, 79.

5. Adapted from Robirda's A Place for Canaries Web site, http://www. robirda.com (21 August 2000) and Herman Brothers Pet Products Web site, www.ddc.com/hermanbros (21 August 2000).

6. Based on "Ask an Expert", *Chatelaine.com,* http://www.chateleine.com/experts/askanexpert.html (11 December 2000).

7. Based on Canada's SchoolNet Web site, http://www.schoolnet.ca (11 December 2000).

8. Eben Shapiro, "Blockbuster Rescue Bid Stars Viacom Top Guns," *Wall Street Journal,* 7 May 1997, B1, B10.

9. Adapted from Michael M. Phillips, "Carving Out an Export Industry, and Hope, in Africa," *Wall Street Journal,* 18 July 1996, A8.

10. Adapted from Alexandra Peers, " Ruling Britannia, or a Little Portion of It," *Wall Street Journal,* 19 July 1996, B6.

11. Adapted from "Periscope: Beanie Mania," *Newsweek,* 3 June 1996, 8.

12. "Starters: Spearing the Best," *Bon Appétit,* March 1997, 20; Mary Alice Kellogg, "The Reel Dish," *Bon Appétit,* March 1997, 38.

Chapter 9

1. Adapted from Campbell Soup Web site, http://www.campbellsoup.com (13 October 1997, 12 December 2000); Hoover's Online, "Campbell Soup Company," http://www.hoovers.com (23 January 1997); *Campbell Soup 1993 Annual Report*; Joseph Weber, "Campbell: Now It's M-M-Global," *Business Week,* 15 March 1993, 52–54; Pete Engardio, "Hmm. Could Use a Little More Snake," *Business Week,* 15 March 1993, 53; Joseph Weber, "Campbell Is Bubbling, But for How Long?" *Business Week,* 17 June 1991, 56–57; Joseph Weber, "From Soup to Nuts and Back to Soup," *Business Week,* 5 November 1990, 114, 116; Alix Freedman and Frank Allen, "John Dorrance's Death Leaves

Campbell Soup with Cloudy Future," *Wall Street Journal,* 19 April 1989, A1, A14; Claudia H. Deutsch," Stirring Up Profits at Campbell," *New York Times,* 20 November 1988, sec. 3, 1, 22; Bill Saporito, "The Fly in Campbell's Soup," *Fortune,* 9 May 1988, 67–70.

2. Bob Angel, "CRM: The Upgrade," *Canadian Banker* 107, no. 3, 32-36; "CMA Member Internet Privacy Policy," Canadian Marketing Association Web site, http://www.the-cma.org/privacy/privacy.html (15 December 2000); "Data Privacy Issue Reaching Apex," *Canadian Underwriter* 66, no. 10 (October 1999): 75; Charles Mandel, "It's Not Just a Deal, It's a Relationship," *Canadian Business* 72, no. 2 (28 May 1999): 73–73; Scott McKinnon, "Truly, Madly, Deeply: How to Build a Meaningful Relationship with Your Customers," *Marketing Magazine* 104, no. 39 (18 October 1999): 23; John Saunders, "Canadian Manufacturers See Sales Rising Using CRM Strategies," *Computer Dealer News* 15, no. 37 (1 October 1999): 14; selected pages from Pivotal Corporation Web site, http://www.pivotal.com (12 December 2000).

3. Daniel P. Finkelman and Anthony R. Goland, "Customers Once Can Be Customers for Life," *Information Strategy: The Executive's Journal,* Summer 1990, 5–9.

4. Cathy Goodwin and Ivan Ross, "Consumer Evaluations of Responses to Complaints: What's Fair and Why," *Journal of Consumer Marketing* 7, no. 2 (Spring 1990): 39–46.

5. Stacey Ball, "Employers Should Exercise Care When Writing References for Former Employees," *Financial Post,* 1/3 June 1996, 21.

6. Claudia Mon Pere McIsaac, "Improving Student Summaries Through Sequencing," *The Bulletin of the Association for Business Communication,* September 1987, 17–20.

7. David A. Hayes, "Helping Students GRASP the Knack of Writing Summaries," *Journal of Reading,* November 1989, 96–101.

8. Adapted from Donna Larcen, "Authors Share the Words of Condolence," *Los Angeles Times,* 20 December 1991, E11.

9. Based on Campbell Soup Web site; Hoover's Online, "Campbell Soup Company"; *Campbell Soup 2000 Annual Report*; Weber, "Campbell"; Engardio, "Hmm"; Weber, "Campbell Is Bubbling, But for How Long"; Weber, "From Soup to Nuts and Back to Soup"; Freedman and Allen, "John Dorrance's Death Leave's Campbell Soup with Cloudy Future"; Deutsch, "Stirring Up Profits at Campbell"; Saporito, "The Fly in Campbell's Soup."

10. Adapted from Paul Dean, "Auto Makers Shift into New Gear," *Los Angeles Times,* 15 January 1997, E1, E6.

11. Adapted from Barbara Carton, "Farmers Begin Harvesting Satellite Data to Boost Yields," *Wall Street Journal,* 11 July 1996, B4.

12. Adapted from Campbell Soup Web site; Hoover's Online, "Campbell Soup Company"; *Campbell Soup 2000 Annual Report*; Weber, "Campbell"; Engardio, "Hmm"; Weber, "Campbell Is Bubbling, But for How Long"; Weber, "From Soup to Nuts and Back to Soup"; Freedman and Allen, "John Dorrance's Death Leaves Campbell Soup with Cloudy Future"; Deutsch, "Stirring Up Profits at Campbell"; Saporito, "The Fly in Campbell's Soup."

13. Adapted from "Entrepreneurs Across America," *Entrepreneur Magazine Online,* http://www.entrepreneurmag.com/entmag/50states5.hts#top (12 June 1997).

14. Adapted from Rodale's home page, http://www.rodalepress.com/ mssn2.html (17 July 1997); Kim Komando, "Computer Basics: The Perfect Garden Is a Mouse Click Away," *Los Angeles Times,* 31 March 1997, D5.

15. Adapted from "Group Accuses Nike of Vietnam Abuses," *Los Angeles Times,* 28 March 1997, D3; Greg Rushford, "Manager's Journal: Nike Lets Critics Kick It Around," *Wall Street Journal,* 12 May 1997; "Nike vs. Doonesbury," *People Online Daily,* http://pathfinder.com/@SX8oXwUA238MYHni/ people/daily/pages/peephole.html (6 June 1997).

16. Based on Ace Canada Web site, http://www.acecanada.ca (15 December 2000).

17. Based on ABC Canada Literacy Foundation Web site, http://www.abc-canada.org (18 December 2000).

Chapter 10

1. Based on Wal-mart Web site, http://www.walmartstores.com (19 December 2000).

2. James Calvert Scott and Diana J. Green, "British Perspectives on Organizing Bad-News Letters: Organizational Patterns Used by Major U.K. Companies," *The Bulletin of the Association for Business Communication* 55, no. 1 (March 1992): 17–19.

3. Iris I. Varner, "Internationalizing Business Communication Courses," *The Bulletin of the Association for Business Communication* 50, no. 4 (December 1987): 7–11.

4. Ram Subramanian, Robert G. Insley, and Rodney D. Blackwell, "Performance and Readability: A Comparison of Annual Reports of Profitable and Unprofitable Corporations," *Journal of Business Communication* 30, no. 2 (1993): 49–61.

5. "Are Service Charges a Rip-Off?" *Canadian Banker* 105, no. 5 (September/October 1998): 46; Richard Blackwell, "Royal's Ombudsman Calls for Openness on Transfers," *Financial Post Daily,* 16 December 1997, 8; Rod McQueen, "Bill Bailey is Low Key, Until a Client Needs His Help; Scotiabank's Ombudsman is Customer-Friendly," *Financial Post (National Post),* 11 October 1999, C3; Jill Vardy, "Martin Delivers Promised Help to the Little Guy: Ombudsman Created, Account Access Improved," *Financial Post (National Post),* 26 June 1999, D8; Canadian Banking Ombudsman Web site, http://www.bankingombudsman.com (19 December 2000); Bank of Montreal Web site, http://www.bmo.com (22 December 2000); Royal Bank Financial Group, "Office of the Ombudsman," http://www.royalbank.com/ombudsman (7 December 2000); Scotiabank, "Ombudsman Report," http://www.scotiabank.com/cda/content/0,1608,CID915_LIDen,00.html# (22 December 2000).

6. *Techniques for Communicators* (Chicago: Lawrence Ragan Communication, 1995), 18.

7. See "Case Notes," *Focus on Canadian Employment & Equality Rights* 5, no. 24 (December 1999): 188; Stacey Ball, "Employers Should Exercise Care When Writing References for Former Employees," *Financial Post,* 1/3 June 1996, 21; Howard Levitt, "If You Can't Say Something Good, Say Something Bad," *Financial Post (National Post),* 27 November 1998, C17; "Layoffs and Terminations Across Canada," *Employers Online,* http://employers.gc.ca (29 December 2000).

8. Gwendolyn N. Smith, Rebecca F. Nolan, and Yong Dai, "Job-Refusal Letters: Readers' Affective Responses to Direct and Indirect Organizational Plans," *Business Communication Quarterly* 59, no. 1 (1996): 67–73; Brice and Waung, "Applicant Rejection Letters."

9. Judi Brownell, "The Performance Appraisal Interviews: A Multipurpose Communication Assignment," *The Bulletin of the Association for Business Communication* 57, no. 2 (May 1994): 11–21; Tom Davis and Michael J. Landa, "A Contrary Look at Employee Performance Appraisal," *Canadian Manager* 24, no. 3 (Fall 1999): 18–19; Laura Fowlie, "Make Your Next Performance Review Count: Much of the Anxiety Surrounding the Dreaded Meeting Can Be Minimized With a Bit of Preparation," *Financial Post,* 11/13 April 1998, R14; Laura Ramsay, "Time to Examine the Exam: Mostly Everyone Dreads a Performance Appraisal, and for Good Reasons," *Financial Post (National Post),* 18 October 1999, C15.

10. Brownell, "The Performance Appraisal Interviews"; Fowlie, "Make Your Next Performance Review Count."

11. Judith A. Kolb, "Leader Behaviors Affecting Team Performance: Similarities and Differences Between Leader/Member Assessments," *Journal of Business Communication* 32, no. 3 (1995): 233–48.

12. Howard M. Bloom, "Performance Evaluations," *New England Business,* December 1991, 14; Levitt, "If You Can't Say Something Good, Say Something Bad."

13. Fowlie, "Make Your Next Performance Review Count"; Patricia A. McLagan, "Advice for Bad-News Bearers: How to Tell Employees They're Not Hacking It and Get Results," *Industry Week,* 15 February 1993, 42; Michael Lee Smith, "Give Feedback, Not Criticism," *Supervisory Management,* March 1993, 4; "A Checklist for Conducting Problem Performer Appraisals," *Supervisory Management,* December 1993, 7–9; Jane R. Goodson, Gail W. McGee, and Anson Seers, "Giving Appropriate Performance Feedback to Managers: An Empirical Test of Content and Outcomes," *Journal of Business Communication* 29, no. 4 (1992): 329–42.

14. Based on information from Wal-mart Web site, http://www.walmartstores.com (19 December 2000).

15. Adapted from Sewell Chan, "A Seattle Blend Is Praised as Rich, Smooth, and Better

Than Worms," *Wall Street Journal,* 16 July 1996, B1.

16. Adapted from Michael A. Champ and Michael W. Willinsky, "Farming the Oceans," *The World and I,* April 1994, 200–207.

17. Paschal Zachary, "Sun Microsystems Apologizes in Letter for Late Payments," *Wall Street Journal,* 11 October, B4.

18. Peter Fritsch, "It's Lighter Than Glass and Hurts Less When Thrown, But Can Plastic Stack Up?" *Wall Street Journal,* 24 July 1996, B1.

19. Adapted from Robert Johnson, "Your Little Monkey Is So Cuddly. Here, Let Me–OUCH!" *Wall Street Journal,* 2 December 1991, A1, A14.

20. Based on "Campbell Pulls School Program," *Marketing Magazine* 105, no. 9 (6 March 2000): 1; Danny Kucharsky, "Navigating Quebec's Promo Regulations," *Marketing Magazine* 105, no. 13 (3 April 2000): 20–21; Campbells Web site, http://www.campbellsoup.ca (17 December 2000).

21. Based on Reid Kanaley, "Resisting Computer Surveillance: Employees Assume They Have a Right to Privacy at Work. Well, That's Not the Case, as Many Firms Monitor E-mail and Net Use," *Financial Post (National Post),* 10 September 1999, C14; Timothy Pritchard, "Canada Strengthens Internet Privacy," *New York Times,* 23 December 2000, http://www.nytimes.com/2000/12/23/technology/23PRIV.html (3 January 2001); "Privacy of E-Mail and Internet Use in the Workplace," *Labour Notes,* 18 October 1999, http://204.187. 104.200/cbcaget.exe (1 January 2001).

Chapter 11

1. Based on Young Entrepreneurs' Association Web site, http://www.yea.ca (15 December 2000).

2. Jeanette W. Gilsdorf, "Write Me Your Best Case for . . . ," *The Bulletin of the Association for Business Communication* 54, no. 1 (March 1991): 7–12.

3. Gilsdorf, "Write Me Your Best Case for . . ."

4. Mary Cross, "Aristotle and Business Writing: Why We Need to Teach Persuasion," *The Bulletin of the Association for Business Communication* 54, no. 1 (March 1991): 3–6.

5. Abraham H. Maslow, *Motivation and Personality* (New York: Harper & Row, 1954), 12, 19.

6. Robert T. Moran, "Tips on Making Speeches to International Audiences," *International Management,* April 1980, 58–59.

7. Tamra B. Orr, "Persuasion Without Pressure," *The Toastmaster,* January 1994, 19–22; William Friend, "Winning Techniques of Great Persuaders," *Association Management,* February 1985, 82–86; Patricia Buhler, "How to Ask For–and Get–What You Want!" *Supervision,* February 1990, 11–13.

8. Based on e-mail interview with Dave Bedford, 27 December 2000.

9. Gilsdorf, "Write Me Your Best Case for . . ."

10. John D. Ramage and John C. Bean, *Writing Arguments: A Rhetoric with Readings,* 3rd ed. (Boston: Allyn and Bacon, 1995), 430–42.

11. Ramage and Bean, *Writing Arguments,* 102–17; Lauren M. Bernardi, "Law of Terminations," *Canadian Manager* 25, no. 3 (Fall 2000): 22-24.

12. James Suchan and Ron Dulek, "Toward a Better Understanding of Reader Analysis," *Journal of Business Communication* 25, no. 2 (1988): 29–45.

13. Jeanette W. Gilsdorf, "Executives' and Academics' Perceptions on the Need for Instruction in Written Persuasion," *Journal of Business Communication* 23 (Fall 1986): 67.

14. Robert L. Hemmings, "Think Before You Write," *Fund Raising Management,* February 1990, 23–24; Royal Bank Web site, http://www.royalbank.com/sponsorship/prog_02.html (1 May 2001).

15. Teri Lammers, "The Elements of Perfect Pitch," *Inc.,* March 1992, 53–55.

16. William North Jayme, quoted in Albert Haas Jr., "How to Sell Almost Anything by Direct Mail," *Across the Board,* November 1986, 50. See also Danna Yuhas, "Creating a Plan: A Creative Brief Allows Businesses to Both Develop and Evaluate Marketing Activities," *Computer Dealer News,* 3 September 1999, 30.

17. Hemmings, "Think Before You Write."

18. Hemmings, "Think Before You Write."

19. Conrad Squires, "How to Write a Strong Letter, Part Two: Choosing a Theme," *Fund Raising Management,* November 1991, 65–66.

20. Conrad Squires, "Getting the Compassion Out of the Box," *Fund Raising Management,* September 1992, 55, 60.

21. Squires, "How to Write a Strong Letter, Part Two."

22. Constance L. Clark, "25 Steps to Better Direct Mail Fundraising," *Nonprofit World,* July–August 1989, 11–13; Squires, "How to Write a Strong Letter, Part Two."

23. Squires, "How to Write a Strong Letter, Part Two."

24. Clark, "25 Steps to Better Direct Mail Fundraising."

25. Conrad Squires, "Why Some Letters Outpull Others," *Fund Raising Management,* January 1991, 67, 72.

26. Squires, "Why Some Letters Outpull Others"; Clark, "25 Steps to Better Direct Mail Fundraising"; Jerry Huntsinger, "My First 291/2 Years in Direct-Mail Fund Raising: What I've Learned," *Fund Raising Management,* January 1992, 40–43; Yuhas, "Creating a Plan: A Creative Brief Allows Businesses to Both Develop and Evaluate Marketing Activities."

27. Carolyn Green, "Cool, Calm, and Collecting: Effective Debt Collection is a Matter of Helping People Out of a Problem, Says this Specialist," *Canadian Banker* 104, no. 2 (March/April 1997): 10. "The Ideal Collection Letter," *Inc.,* February 1991, 59–61.

28. Based on Young Entrepreneurs' Association Web site.

29. Adapted from Jane Bryant Quinn, "A Primer on Downsizing," *Newsweek,* 13 May 1996, 50; Howard Levitt, "Employers Have a Custodial Obligation: Gamble With an Employee's Well-Being and They are Answerable," *Financial Post (National Post),* 19 July 1999, D10; Dean McMann, "The Roller-Coaster of Downsizing," *CMA Management* 73, no. 8 (October 1999): 42–46; Marshall Loeb, "What to Do If You Get Fired," *Fortune,* 15 January 1996, 43; and "Urohealth Sets Sights on Eighth Acquisition," *Los Angeles Times,* 5 May 1996, p. B1.

30. Adapted from Andrew Ferguson, "Supermarket of the Vanities," *Fortune,* 10 June 1996, 30, 32.

31. Adapted from Peter Coy, "Peddling Better Bike Designs," *Business Week,* 1 July 1996, 103.

32. Albert R. Karr, "Work Week: Wake Up and Read This," *Wall Street Journal,* 6 May 1997, A1.

33. Adapted from Cathy Werblin, "Korean Business Owners Want Signs to Mark Area," *Los Angeles Times,* 29 March 1997, B3.

34. Adapted from Steve Bass, "ISDN Not; The Agony, the Ecstasy, the Migraines," *Computer Currents,* 7 May 1996, 9.

35. Adapted from Goosehead Teen Entertainment Network Web site, http://www.goosehead.com (29 August 2000); Samantha Miller, "Home Work," *People Weekly,* 31 July 2000, 23.

36. Kevin M. Savetz, "Preventive Medicine for the Computer User," *Multimedia Online* 2, no. 2 (June 1996): 58–60.

37. Adapted from Marcia Joseph, Deodorant Stones of America (DSA), personal communication, 14 July 1994; DSA product literature.

38. Adapted from Karen E. Klein and Steve Scauzillo, "The Fuel Cell Future," *The World & I,* April 1994, 192–99; Ballard Power Systems Web site, http://www.ballard.com (1 May 2001), *1999 Ballard Power Systems Annual Report.*

37. Adapted from "Down These Aisles Is Matrimonial Bliss," *Los Angeles Times,* 22 March 1996, D3.

38. Adapted from Chris Pasles, "Long Beach Opera Cancels Rest of Season as Deal Nears," *Los Angeles Times,* 16 May 1996, F4, F9.

39. Adapted from Tom Morganthau and Seema Nayyar, "Those Scary College Costs," *Newsweek,* 29 April 1996, 52–56; Jane Bryant Quinn, "Save First, Then Borrow," *Newsweek,* 29 April 1996, 67–68. See also Alfred LeBlanc, "Getting Out of Student Straits," *Financial Post Magazine,* October 1998, 101–104.

40. Adapted from Edmund Sanders, "Subcontractors Still Waiting for Payoff from Giant Irvine Theater," *The Orange County Register,* 9 May 1996, 2.

Chapter 12

1. Adapted from Federal Express Web site, http://www.fedex.com (27 October 1997); UPS Web site, http://www.ups.com (27 October 1997, 19 January 2001); DHL Web site, http://www.dhl.com (27 October 1997, 19 January 2001); Airborne Express Web site, http://www.airborne.com (27 October 1997, 19 January 2001); Hoover's Online, http://www.hoovers.com (27 October 1997, 19 January 2001); "All Strung Up," *The Economist*, 17 April 1993, 70; Gary M. Stern, "Improving Verbal Communications," *Internal Auditor*, August 1993, 49–54; Gary Hoover, Alta Campbell, and Patrick J. Spain, *Hoover's Handbook of American Business 1994* (Austin, TX: Reference Press, 1993), 488–89; "Pass the Parcel," *The Economist*, 21 March 1992, 73–74; "Federal Express," *Personnel Journal*, January 1992, 52.

2. John Taschek, "New Report Writers Provide Improved Access to Data," *PC Week*, 6 February 1995, 81–85.

3. Stephan Manes, "E-Mail Troubles? You Have No Idea!" *PC World*, July 1996, 39.

4. Based on e-mail interview with Bill Stevens, 8 January 2001.

5. Dan Steinhoff and John F. Burgess, *Small Business Management Fundamentals*, 5th ed. (New York: McGraw-Hill, 1989), 37.

6. Joan F. Vesper and Karl H. Vesper, "Writing a Business Plan: The Total Term Assignment," *The Bulletin of the Association for Business Communication* 56, no. 2 (June 1993): 29–32.

7. Eleanor Rizzo, "Document Design Basics," *Technical Communication*, Fourth Quarter 1992, 645.

8. A. S. C. Ehrenberg, "Report Writing–Six Simple Rules for Better Business Documents," *Admap*, June 1992, 39–42.

9. Based on Federal Express Web site; UPS Web site; DHL Web site; Airborne Express Web site; Hoover's Online; "All Strung Up," *The Economist*; Stern, "Improving Verbal Communications"; Hoover, Campbell, and Spain, *Hoover's Handbook of American Business*; "Pass the Parcel," *The Economist*; "Federal Express," *Personnel Journal*.

10. Adapted from J. Roberto Whitaker-Penteado, "Oil Cos. Pump Up Advertising in Brazil," *Adweek*, 6 September 1993, 14.

11. Adapted from Nancy Jeffrey, "Preparing for the Worst: Firms Set Up Plans to Help Deal with Corporate Crises," *Wall Street Journal*, 7 December 1987, 23.

Chapter 13

1. Adapted from On Call Plus, Company News, *PRNewswire*, http://www.prnewswire.com/gh/cnoc/comp/106632.html (7 November 1997); *Harley-Davidson 1993 and 1999 Annual Reports*; Brian S. Moskal, "Born to Be Real," *Industry Week*, 2 August 1993, 14–18; Martha H. Peak, "Harley-Davidson: Going Whole Hog to Provide Stakeholder Satisfaction," *Management Review*, June 1993, 53–55; Gary Slutsker, "Hog Wild," *Forbes*, 24 May 1993, 45–46; Kevin Kelly and Karen Lowry Miller, "The Rumble Heard Round the World: Harleys," *Business Week*, 24 May 1993, 58, 60; James B. Shuman, "Easy Rider Rides Again," *Business Tokyo*, July 1991, 26–30; Holt Hackney, "Easy Rider," *Financial World*, 4 September 1990, 48–49; Roy L. Harmon and Leroy D. Peterson, "Reinventing the Factory," *Across the Board*, March 1990, 30–38; John Holusha," How Harley Outfoxed Japan with Exports," *New York Times*, 12 August 1990, F5; Peter C. Reid, "How Harley Beat Back the Japanese," *Fortune*, 25 September 1989, 155–64.

2. Bruce McComiskey, "Defining Institutional Problems: A Heuristic Procedure," *Business Communication Quarterly* 58, no. 4 (1995): 21–24.

3. Iris I. Varner, *Contemporary Business Report Writing*, 2nd ed. (Chicago: Dryden Press, 1991), 135.

4. F. Stanford Wayne and Jolene D. Scriven, "Problem and Purpose Statements: Are They Synonymous Terms in Writing Reports for Business?" *The Bulletin of the Association for Business Communication* 54, no. 1 (1991): 30–37.

5. Maridell Fryar and David A. Thomas, *Successful Problem Solving* (Lincolnwood, IL: NTC, 1989), 20.

6. David A. Aaker and George S. Day, *Marketing Research*, 2nd ed. (New York: Wiley, 1983), 79, 111.

7. Aaker and Day, *Marketing Research*, 88–89.

8. Four useful online sources of analyzing World Wide Web quality are Esther Grassian, *Thinking Critically about World Wide Web Resources*, http://www.library.ucla.edu/libraries/college/help/critical/index.htm (2 February 2001); Elizabeth E. Kirk, *Evaluating Information Found on the Internet*, http://milton.mse.jhu.edu:8001/research/education/net.html (2 February 2001); Hope N. Tillman, *Evaluating Quality on the Net*, http://www.hopetillman.com/findqual.html (2 February 2001); and *Why We Need to Evaluate What We Find on the Internet*, http://thorplus.lib.purdue.edu/~techman/eval.html (2 February 2001).

9. Lisa Gubernick, "Making History Pay," *Forbes*, 13 May 1991, 132.

10. Aaker and Day, *Marketing Research*, 124.

11. Paul L. Riedesel, "Understanding Validity Is Easy; Doing Right Research Is Hard," *Marketing News*, 12 September 1986, 24.

12. "How to Design and Conduct a Study," *Credit Union Magazine*, October 1983, 36–46. See also Arlene Fink and Jacqueline Kosecoff, *How to Conduct Surveys: A Step-By-Step Guide* (Thousand Oaks, CA: Sage Publications, 1998).

13. TK Associates International, Internet Web site, http://www.diyer.com (29 July 1996).

14. Charles L. Olson and Mario J. Picconi, *Statistics for Business Decision Making* (Glenview, IL: Scott, Foresman, 1983), 105.

15. Olson and Picconi, *Statistics for Business Decision Making*, 105.

16. Based on On Call Plus, Company News, *PRNewswire*; *Harley-Davidson 1993 Annual Report*; Moskal, "Born to Be Real"; Peak, "Harley-Davidson"; Slutsker, "Hog Wild"; Kelly and Miller, "The Rumble Heard Round the World"; Shuman, "Easy Rider Rides Again"; Hackney, "Easy Rider"; Harmon and Peterson, "Reinventing the Factory"; Holusha, "How Harley Outfoxed Japan with Exports"; Reid, "How Harley Beat Back the Japanese."

Chapter 14

1. "Responsible Commercial Success," "A Unique Company Culture at Levi Strauss & Co.," "Levi Strauss & Co. Global Sourcing & Operating Guidelines," "Levi Strauss & Co. General Information," Levi Strauss & Co. Web site, http://www.levistrauss.com (29 September 1997, 1 February 2000); Charlene Marmer Solomon, "Put Your Ethics to the Test," *Personnel Journal* 75, no. 1 (January 1996): 66–74; Russell Mitchell and Michael Oneal, "Managing by Values," *Business Week*, 1 August 1994, 46–52.

2. Oswald M. T. Ratteray, "Hit the Mark with Better Summaries," *Supervisory Management*, September 1989, 43–45.

3. Alice Brink, "Oh No! I Forgot to Evaluate the Annual Report!" *Communication World*, December 1998/January 1999, 24–27; Canadian Institute of Chartered Accountants, *Annual Reports Awards 2K*, Karen Kahler Holliday, "Annual Reports as Marketing Tools," *Bank Marketing*, August 1994, 22; H.R. Hutchins, "Annual Reports (...Who Reads Them?)," *Communication World*, October 1994, 18; Doug Newsome and Bob Carrell, *Public Relations Writing*, 5th ed. (Belmont, CA: Wadsworth, 1998); Doug Newsome, Judy VanSlyke Turk, and Dean Kruckeberg, *This is PR: The Realities of Public Relations*, 7th ed. (Belmont, CA: Wadsworth, 2000); Gerald D. Trites and Paul-Emile J. Roy, "Dispelling the Storybook Myth," *CA Magazine*, January 1992, 55; Sid Cato's Official Annual Report Web site, http://www.sidcato.com (7 February 2001).

4. Sheri Rosen, "What Is Truth?" *IABC Communication World*, March 1995, 40.

5. Based on "Responsible Commercial Success," "A Unique Company Culture at Levi Strauss & Company," "Levi Strauss & Co. Global Sourcing & Operating Guidelines," "Levi Strauss & Co. General Information," Levi Strauss & Co. Web site; Solomon, "Put Your Ethics to the Test"; Mitchell and Oneal, "Managing by Values."

6. Adapted from Nicholas E. Lefferts, "What's New in the Pet Business," *New York Times*, 3 August 1985, sec. 3, 15 ; Muktuk Kennels Web site, http://www.muktuk.com (14 February 2001); "Siberian Husky," *DogBiz.com*, http://www.dogbiz.com/dogs-grp3/siberian/siberian.htm (14 February 2001).

7. Adapted from David J. Jefferson and Thomas R. King, "'Infomercials' Fill Up Prime Time on Cable, Aim for Prime Time," *Wall Street Journal*, 22 October 1992, A1.

Chapter 15

1. Adapted from US Securities and Exchange Commission EDGAR database, http://www.sec.gov/Archives/edgar/data/78666/000089843 0-97-001002.txt (7 November 1997); Pinkerton Web site, http://www.pinkertons.com (7 November 1997); Seth Lubove, "High-Tech Cops," *Forbes,* 25 September 1995, 44–45; Hoover's Online, http://www.hoovers.com (23 January 1997); Bob Smith, "The Evolution of Pinkerton," *Management Review,* September 1993, 54–58; Smith, "Pinkerton Keeps Its Eye on Recruitment," *HR Focus,* 6 September 1993, 1, 6; "Oscar's News," *Security Management,* 14 June 1993, 14; *Pinkerton 1993 Annual Report.*

2. Adapted from Richard Nelson Bolles, *The 1997 What Color Is Your Parachute?* (Berkeley, CA.: Ten Speed Press, 1996), 129–66; Karen W. Arenson, "Placement Offices Leave Old Niches to Become Computerized Job Bazaars,"*New York Times,* 17 July 1996, B12; Lawrence J. Magid, "Job Hunters Cast Wide Net Online," *Los Angeles Times,* 26 February 1996, 20; Richard Van Doren, "On-Line Career Advice Speeds Search for Jobs," *Network World,* 4 March 1996, 54; Alex Markels, "Job Hunting Takes Off in Cyberspace," *Wall Street Journal,* 20 September 1996, B1, B2; Michael Chorost, "Jobs on the Web," *Hispanic,* October 1995, 50–53; Zane K. Quible, "Electronic Résumés: Their Time Is Coming," *Business Communication Quarterly* 58, no. 3 (1995): 5–9; Margaret Mannix, "The Home-Page Help Wanteds," *U.S. News & World Report,* 30 October 1995, 88, 90; Pam Dixon and Silvia Tiersten, *Be Your Own Headhunter Online* (New York: Random House, 1995), 53–69; Mark Swartz, *Get Wired, You're Hired,* 2nd ed. (Scarborough, ON.: Prentice Hall Canada, 1998), chaps. 4, 6, 9.

3. Amanda Bennett, "GE Redesigns Rungs of Career Ladder," *Wall Street Journal,* 15 March 1993, B1, B3.

4. Robin White Goode, "International and Foreign Language Skills Have an Edge," *Black Enterprise,* May 1995, 53.

5. Nancy M. Somerick, "Managing a Communication Internship Program," *The Bulletin of the Association for Business Communication* 56, no. 3 (1993): 10–20.

6. Cheryl L. Noll, "Collaborating with the Career Planning and Placement Center in the Job-Search Project," *Business Communication Quarterly* 58, no. 3 (1995): 53–55.

7. Pam Stanley-Weigand, "Organizing the Writing of Your Resume," *The Bulletin of the Association for Business Communication* 54, no. 3 (1991): 11–12.

8. Beverly Culwell-Block and Jean Anna Sellers, "Résumé Content and Format–Do the Authorities Agree?" *The Bulletin of the Association for Business Communication* 57, no. 4 (1994): 27–30.

9. Janice Tovey, "Using Visual Theory in the Creation of Resumes: A Bibliography," *The Bulletin of the Association for Business Communication* 54, no. 3 (1991): 97–99.

10. Myra Fournier, "Looking Good on Paper," *Managing Your Career,* Spring 1990, 34–35.

11. Adapted from Burdette E. Bostwick, *How to Find the Job You've Always Wanted* (New York: Wiley, 1982), 69–70.

12. Jennifer J. Laabs, "For Your Information," *Personnel Journal,* August 1993, 16.

13. Dixon and Tiersten, *Be Your Own Headhunter Online,* 75.

14. Bronwyn Fryer, "Job Hunting the Electronic Way," *Working Woman,* March 1995, 59–60, 78; Joyce Lane Kennedy and Thomas J. Morrow, *Electronic Resume Revolution,* 2nd ed. (New York: Wiley, 1995), 30–33; Mary Goodwin, Deborah Cohn, and Donna Spivey, *Netjobs: Use the Internet to Land Your Dream Job* (New York: Michael Wolff, 1996), 149–50; Zane K. Quible, "Electronic Résumés: Their Time Is Coming," *Business Communication Quarterly* 58, no. 3 (1995): 5–9; Alfred Glossbrenner and Emily Glossbrenner, *Finding a Job on the Internet* (New York: McGraw-Hill, 1995), 194–97; Dixon and Tiersten, *Be Your Own Headhunter Online,* 80–83; Swartz, *Get Wired, You're Hired,* chap. 4.

15. Quible, "Electronic Résumés"; Goodwin, Cohn, and Spivey, *Netjobs.*

16. Diane Lu-Hovasse, "Headhunters: Doomed By the Mouse?" *Financial Post,* 19 February 2001, E4; Tony Martell, "Résumé Volumes Push Firms to the Web," *ComputerWorld Canada,* 7 April 2000, 45; "Scoring Successes in the Wired World," *The Globe and Mail,* 15 November 2000; Sinclair Stewart, "Recruits du jour: Who Need Online Job Boards? Louis Tétu Founded Recruitsoft on the Hunch Companies Would Rather Do Their Own Online Recruiting," *Canadian Business* 73, no. 2 (7 February 2000), 78; Recruitsoft Web site, http://www.recruitsoft.com (20 February 2001); Bank of Montreal Web site, http://www.bmo.com (20 February 2001).

17. William J. Banis, "The Art of Writing Job-Search Letters," CPC Annual, *36th Edition 2* (1992): 42–50.

18. Based on US Securities and Exchange Commission EDGAR database; Pinkerton Web site; Lubove, "High-Tech Cops"; Hoover's Online; Smith, "The Evolution of Pinkerton"; Smith, "Pinkerton Keeps Its Eye on Recruitment"; "Oscar's News"; *Pinkerton 1993 Annual Report.*

Chapter 16

1. Adapted from On Call Plus Company News, *PRNewswire,* http://www.prnewswire.com/cgibin/liststory?406325^1 (9 November 1997); Herman Miller Web site, http://www.hermanmiller.com (9 November 1997); Hoover's Online, http://www.hoovers.com (23 January 1997); A. J. Vogl, "Risky Work," *Across the Board,* July–August 1993, 27–31; Kenneth Labich, "Hot Company, Warm Culture," *Fortune,* 27 February 1989, 74–78; George Melloan, "Herman Miller's Secrets of Corporate Creativity," *Wall Street Journal,* 3 May 1988, A31; Beverly Geber, "Herman Miller: Where Profits and Participation Meet," *Training,* November 1987, 62–66; Robert J. McClory, "The Creative Process at Herman Miller," *Across the Board,* May 1985, 8–22; Tom Peters and Nancy Austin, *A Passion for Excellence* (New York: Random House, 1985), 204–05.

2. Charlene Marmer Solomon, "How Does Disney Do It?" *Personnel Journal,* December 1989, 53.

3. Peter Rea, Julie Rea, and Charles Moonmaw, "Training: Use Assessment Centers in Skill Development," *Personnel Journal,* April 1990, 126–31.

4. Barron Wells and Nelda Spinks, "Interviewing: What Small Companies Say," *The Bulletin of the Association for Business Communication* 55, no. 2 (1992): 18–22; Clive Fletcher, "Ethics and the Job Interview," *Personnel Management,* March 1992, 36–39.

5. Greg Meckbach, "Your Next Job Interview Might be at Home," *Computing Canada* 23, no. 16 (August 5, 1997): 2.

6. Joyce Lain Kennedy and Thomas J. Morrow, *Electronic Resume Revolution* (New York: Wiley, 1995), 208–10.

7. "Read Between the Lines," *Inc.,* June 1995, 90.

8. Joel Russell, "Finding Solid Ground," *Hispanic Business,* February 1922, 42–44, 46.

9. See 360Networks Web site, http://www.360networks.com.

10. Robert Gifford, Cheuk Fan Ng, and Margaret Wilkinson, "Nonverbal Cues in the Employment Interview: Links Between Applicant Qualities and Interviewer Judgments," *Journal of Applied Psychology* 70, no. 4 (1985): 729.

11. Dale G. Leathers, *Successful Nonverbal Communication* (New York: Macmillan, 1986), 225.

12. Mary Goodwin, Deborah Cohn, and Donna Spivey, *Netjobs: Use the Internet to Land Your Dream Job* (New York: Michael Wolff, 1996), 170.

13. Shirley J. Shepherd, "How to Get That Job in 60 Minutes or Less," *Working Woman,* March 1986, 119.

14. Shepherd, "How to Get That Job in 60 Minutes or Less," 118.

15. Canadian Human Rights Commission, *The Canadian Human Rights Act: A Guide,* November 1998.

16. Gerald L. Wilson, "Preparing Students for Responding to Illegal Selection Interview Questions," *The Bulletin of the Association for Business Communication* 54, no. 2 (1991): 44–49.

17. Jeff Springston and Joann Keyton, "Interview Response Training," *The Bulletin of the Association for Business Communication* 54, no. 3 (1991): 28–30; Gerald L. Wilson, "An Analysis of Instructional Strategies for Responding to Illegal Selection Interview Questions," *The Bulletin of the Association for Business Communication* 54, no. 3 (1991): 31–35.

18. Harold H. Hellwig, "Job Interviewing: Process and Practice," *The Bulletin of the Association for Business Communication* 55, no. 2 (1992): 8–14.

19. Based on On Call Plus Company News, *PRNewswire*; Herman Miller Web site; Hoover's Online; Vogl, "Risky Work"; Labich, "Hot Company, Warm Culture"; Melloan, "Herman Miller's Secrets of Corporate Creativity"; Geber, "Herman Miller"; McClory, "The Creative Process at Herman Miller"; Peters and Austin, *A Passion for Excellence.*

Chapter 17

1. Adapted from Srikumar S. Rao, "Welcome to Open Space," *Training*, April 1994, 52–56; Claudia H. Deutsch, "Round-Table Meetings with No Agendas, No Tables," *New York Times*, 5 June 1994, sec. 3, 5; Charles D. Bader, "These Shoes Are Made for Walkin'," *Bobbin*, November 1991, 118–21.

2. Edward F. Walsh, "Telephone Tyranny," *Industry Week*, 1 April 1991, 24–26.

3. Madeline Bodin, "Making the Most of Your Telephone," *Nation's Business*, April 1992, 62.

4. Beverly Davenport Sypher, Robert N. Bastrom, and Joy Hart Seibert, "Listening, Communication Abilities, and Success at Work," *Journal of Business Communication* 26, no. 4 (Fall 1989): 293–301.

5. Augusta M. Simon, "Effective Listening: Barriers to Listening in a Diverse Business Environment," *The Bulletin of the Association for Business Communication* 54, no. 3 (September 1991): 73–74.

6. Sypher, Bastrom, and Seibert, "Listening, Communication Abilities, and Success at Work."

7. Thomas L. Means, "A Unit to Develop Listening Skill," *The Bulletin of the Association for Business Communication* 54, no. 3 (September 1991): 70–72.

8. Phillip Morgan and H. Kent Baker, "Building a Professional Image: Improving Listening Behavior," *Supervisory Management*, November 1985, 35–36.

9. Lyman K. Steil, Larry L. Barker, and Kittie W. Watson, *Effective Listening: Key to Your Success* (Reading, MA: Addison-Wesley, 1983), 21–22.

10. J. Michael Sproule, *Communication Today* (Glenview, IL: Scott, Foresman, 1981), 69.

11. Sproule, *Communication Today*, 69.

12. Sproule, *Communication Today*, 69.

13. Thomas L. Brown, "The Art of the Interview," *Industry Week*, 1 March 1993, 19.

14. Claudia H. Deutsch, "Teamwork or Tug of War?" *New York Times*, 26 August 1990, sec. 3, 27.

15. B. Aubrey Fisher, *Small Group Decision Making: Communication and the Group Process*, 2nd ed. (New York: McGraw-Hill, 1980), 145–49.

16. Ken Blanchard, "Meetings Can Be Effective," *Supervisory Management*, October 1992, 5.

17. William C. Waddell and Thomas A. Rosko, "Conducting an Effective Off-Site Meeting," *Management Review*, February 1993, 40–44.

18. Kathy E. Gill, "Board Primer: Parliamentary Procedure," *Association Management*, 1993, L-39.

19. Based on Rao, "Welcome to Open Space"; Deutsch, "Round-Table Meetings with No Agendas, No Table"; Bader, "These Shoes Are Made for Walkin'."

Chapter 18

1. Based on Lucent Web site, http://www.lucent.ca (3 March 2001); Len Scher, "Women at the Top," *Silicon Valley North* 4, no. 5 (July 2000): 23; Chris Talbot, "Lucent Canada's New CEO Can't Slow Down," *Silicon Valley North* 3, no. 5 (July 1999): 13.

2. Sherron B. Kenton, "Speaker Credibility in Persuasive Business Communication: A Model Which Explains Gender Differences," *Journal of Business Communication* 26, no. 2 (Spring 1989): 143–57.

3. Walter Kiechel III, "How to Give a Speech," *Fortune,* 8 June 1987, 180.

4. *Communication and Leadership Program* (Santa Ana, CA.: Toastmasters International, 1980), 44, 45.

5. *How to Prepare and Use Effective Visual Aids,* Info-Line series, Elizabeth Lean, managing ed. (Washington, DC: American Society for Training and Development, October 1984), 2.

6. Kathleen K. Weigner, "Visual Persuasion," *Forbes,* 16 September 1991, 176; Kathleen K. Weigner, " Showtime!" *Forbes,* 13 May 1991, 118.

7. Eric Arndt, "Nobody Does It Better," *IABC Communication World,* May 1988, 28.

8. Daniel Goleman, "For Victims of Stage Fright, Rehearsal Is the Therapy," *New York Times,* 12 June 1991, sec. B1; "Giving a Performance," *Royal Bank Letter* 76, no. 2 (March/April 1995), http://www.royalbank.com/english/news/letter/giving.html (16 June 1997).

9. Judy Linscott, "Getting On and Off the Podium," *Savvy,* October 1985, 44.

10. Iris R. Johnson, "Before You Approach the Podium," *MW,* January–February 1989, 7.

11. Sandra Moyer, "Braving No Woman's Land," *The Toastmaster,* August 1986, 13.

12. Teresa Brady, "Fielding Abrasive Questions During Presentations," *Supervisory Management,* February 1993, 6.

13. Based on Lucent Web site; Sher, "Women at the Top"; Talbot, "Lucent Canada's New CEO Can't Slow Down."

Appendix A

1. Mary A. DeVries, *Internationally Yours* (Boston: Houghton Mifflin, 1994), 9.

2. "When Image Counts, Letterhead Says It All," *The Advocate and Greenwich Time*, 10 January 1993, F4.

3. Mel Mandell, "Electronic Forms Are Cheap and Speedy," *D&B Reports,* July–August 1993, 44–45.

4. Linda Driskill, *Business & Managerial Communication: New Perspectives* (Orlando, FL: Harcourt Brace Jovanovich, 1992), 470.

5. Driskill, *Business & Managerial Communication*, 470.

6. DeVries, *Internationally Yours*, 8.

7. Lennie Copeland and Lewis Griggs, *Going International: How to Make Friends and Deal Effectively in the Global Marketplace*, 2nd ed. (New York: Random House, 1985), 24–27.

8. Bill Eager, *Using the Internet* (Indianapolis, IN: Que, 1994), 10.

9. Copeland and Griggs, *Going International*, 24–27.

Appendix B

1. Sherwyn Morreale and Courtland Bovée, *Excellence in Public Speaking* (Fort Worth, TX: Harcourt Brace, 1997), 173.

2. Morreale and Bovée, *Excellence in Public Speaking,* 174.

3. Morreale and Bovée, *Excellence in Public Speaking,* 174–175.

4. Dorothy Geisler, "How to Avoid Copyright Lawsuits," *IABC Communication World,* June 1984, 34–37.

Acknowledgements

Text, Figures, and Tables

5 (Figure 1.2): From David J. Rachman and Michael Mescon, *Business Today,* 5th edition, p. 27, 1987. McGraw Hill. **7** (Figure 1.4): From David J. Rachman and Michael Mescon, *Business Today,* 5th edition, p. 127, 1987. McGraw Hill. **9** (Figure 1.5): Letterhead courtesy of Swift Canoe & Kayak. **14** Copyright © Zero Knowledge Systems. Reproduced with permission. **28** (Figure 2.1): Reprinted by permission of publisher, from *Supervisory Management,* November 1985 © 1985. American Management Association, New York. http:wwww. amanet.org. All rights reserved. **47** (Figure 3.1): Courtesy of CHIN Radio. **78** (Figure 4.1): Courtesy of the Royal Ontario Museum. **81** (Figure 4.2): Courtesy of Yukon Brewing Company. **86** Copyright © Telus Corporation. Reproduced with permission. **100** Copyright © Canadian Broadcasting Corporation. Reproduced with permission. **107** (Figure 5.2): Courtesy of Cadbury Beverages Canada Inc. **150** (Figure 7.3): Adapted from Robert Gunning, *The Technique of Clear Writing* (New York: McGraw-Hill, rev. ed., 1973). Used with permission of copyright owners, Gunning-Mueller Clear Writing Institute, Inc. **167** (Figure 7.4): Courtesy of Lexmark Canada Inc. **188–189** (Behind the Scenes at Numa Financial Systems): Stephen Eckett, managing director of Numa Financial Systems, personal communication, July 1997. **243** Copyright © Land's End. Reproduced with permission. **267** Copyright © IBM. Reproduced with permission. **272** (Figure 11.1): Letterhead courtesy of Host Marriot. **321** Copyright © Microsoft Corporation. Reproduced with permission. **350–351** (Figure 13.4): Canada.com home page. Copyright © Canada.com. Reproduced with permission. Yahoo! Canada home page. Reproduced with permission of Yahoo! Inc. ©2001 Yahoo! and the Yahoo! Logo are trademarks of Yahoo! Inc. HotBot home page. Copyright Wired Digital, Inc. All rights reserved. AltaVista Canada home page. Reproduced with the permission of AltaVista Company. All rights reserved. Google home page. Copyright © Google Inc. **374** Copyright © AT&T. Reproduced with permission. **381** (Table 14.1): Adapted from Robert Lefferts, *Elements of Graphics,* pp. 18–35. Copyright 1981 by Robert Lefferts, Harper & Rowe. **382** (Unnumbered Table 14.1): *Food Processing News,* January 1995, 113. **384** (Figure 14.6): Nation's Restaurant News. **386** (Figure 14.8): From John M. Lannon, *Technical Writing,* 3rd edition. Copyright © 1985 by John M. Lannon. Reprinted by permission of Addison Wesley Educational Publishers, Inc. **387** (Figure 14.9): "How the Networks Deliver the Goods," Business Week, 6 April 1998, 91-92. **427** (Figure 15.1): Richard Nelson Bolles, *What Color Is Your Parachute,* Ten Speed Press 1997, p. 67. **433** Copyright © Workopolis.com, Canada's Biggest Job Site. **438** Copyright © 2001 Recruitsoft, Inc. **455** Copyright © Workopolis.com, Canada's Biggest Job Site. **488** (Table 17.1): Copyright Dr. Lyman K. Steil, President, Communication Development, Inc., St. Paul, MN. Prepared for Sperry Corporation, reprinted with permission of Dr. Steil & Unisys Corporation. **495** (Table 17.2): J. Michael Sproule, *Communication Today,* 1981. **496–497** (Behind the Scenes at 3M): Virginia Johnson, director of human relations, 3M, personal communication, June 1989. Used with permission. **499** Copyright © WebEx. Reproduced with permission. **513** Copyright © Sears. Reproduced with permission. **520–521** (Behind the Scenes with Leann Anderson): Adapted from Leann Anderson, personal interview, April 1997; Leann Anderson, "Speak Up," *Entrepreneur,* March 1997, pp. 94–95. **533** (Table A.1): Adapted from *How 7: A Handbook for Office Workers,* 7/e, by James L. Clark and Lyn R. Clark. Copyright © 1995. Used with permission of South-Western College Publishing, a division of International Thomson Publishing, Inc. Cincinatti, Ohio 45227. **541** (Figure A.3): Letterhead courtesy of Mattel Toys. **543** (Figure A.5): Letterhead courtesy of Black & Decker.

Photos

2 Churchill Klehr Photograpby. **12** Photo courtesy of Telus. **16** Courtesy of CN Media Relations. **24** Courtesy of Suncor Energy Inc. **27** Courtesy of Suncor Energy Inc. **31** CBC Photo Gallery. **34** Nawroki Stock Photo, Inc. **36** Courtesy of Habitat for Humanity. **46** Courtesy of Laraine Kaminsky. **50** William Coupon/Gamma-Liaison, Inc. **54** AP/World Wide Photos. **57** Patricia Diaz, B.B.A., President, Latin Access. **61** Courtesy of Seema Narula. **72** John Coletti/Stock Boston. **75** Peter Caton/Gerald Campbell Studios. **81** Courtesy of AOL Canada. **84** Courtesy of Marty Lippert. **94** John Coletti/Stock Boston. **96** Ballard Power Systems, Firoz Rasul, Chairman and CEO. **100** George Lange/Outline Press Syndicate, Inc. **101** Courtesy of Wendy MacNair. **102** *Transition* by Stewart Stranger **116** SUSNSTAR/Photo Researchers, Inc. **117** Courtesy of Marie Delorme. **121** Courtesy of Dofasco. **128** Courtesy of *Business $ense,* Canada's National Magazine for Business Students. **134** Christopher Pillitz/Matrix International. **136** Microsoft Corporation. **147** AP/World Wide Photos. **149** I. Uimonen/Sygma. **154** Courtesy of *Business $ense,* Canada's National Magazine for Business Students. **158** Laurie Murphy, Publicist, Confederation Centre of the Arts, Charlottetown, PEI. **168** Laurie Murphy, Publicist, Confederation Centre of the Arts, Charlottetown, PEI. **181** Courtesy of Indigo. **182** Essence Communications, Inc. **184** Kim Kullish/SABA Press Photos, Inc. **200** Gamma-Liaison, Inc. **203** D. Young Wolff/PhotoEdit. **204** AP/World Wide Photos. **207** McGraw-Hill Companies. **208** Darryl Estrine/Outline Press Syndicate, Inc. **210** Courtesy of Ann Cavoukian. **218** Courtesy of Suncor Energy Inc. **219** PhotoDisc Inc. **223** Steinway & Sons. **229** Cindy Lewis/Cindy Lewis Photography. **231** john Deere & Company. **232** Tom Mareschal/The Image Bank. **235** Ralf-Finn Hestoft/SABA Press Photos, Inc. **237** Dick Hemingway. **240** Kathleen Bellesiles. **259** Joel Grimes/Joel Grimes Photography. **261** Courtesy of Sherry Torchinsky. **265** Picture Perfect USA, Inc. **268** Photo by Peter Thompson/Permission granted by Jusith A. Walsh on behalf of Any Walsh. **270** PhotoDisc Inc. **274** Courtesy of the Rick Hansen Institute. **279** National Easter Society. **293** Ed Quinn/SABA Press Photos, Inc. **297** Deodorant Stones of America. **298** Keith Polakoff/Long Beach Opera. **302** George Disario/The Stock Market. **306** Real Life/Image Bank.

311 Courtesy of AchieveGlobal. **313** Urban City Foods. **316** Liz Claiborne, Special Markets. **325** Starbucks Coffee Company. **334** Churchill & Klehr Photography. **335** Susan Lapides/Lapides Photography. **337** Larter Creative. **338** Index Stock Imagery. **353** Kim Kullish/SABA Press Photos, Inc. **370** Najlah Feanny/SABA Press Photos, Inc. **376** PhotoDisc Inc. **377** Reglain Frederic/Gamma Liaison, Inc. **378** Courtesy of the Bank of Montreal. **379** Larry Ford Foto. **388** Picture Perfect USA, Inc. **390** SuperStock, Inc. **409** Computer Associates International, Inc. **419** Tom McCarthy/PhotoEdit. **421** © Dorling Kindersley. **423** Pinkerton Security and Investigation Services. **443** Godfathers Pizza. **445** Thomas Lau/Outline Press Syndicate Inc. **456** Jim Zuckerman/Westlight. **458** Courtesy of Herman Miller, Inc. **466** Monkmeyer Press. **468** FireKing International Inc. **469** Levi Strauss & Co. **484** RW Jones/Westlight. **489** Courtesty of Marvin Ross and Mike Grandmaison, photographer. **492** Institute for Research on Learning. **494** Tom's of Maine. **494** 3M Corporation. **499** Andes Chemical Corporation. **506** Courtesy of Carol Stephenson. **508** Courtesy of Mark Swartz. **513** Success Strategy, Inc. **514** Xerox Corporation. **517** Chris K. Soentpiet. **520** Shadowfax/Leann Anderson.

Index

D

E

F

G

M

P

X

Y

Z

"AS IS" LICENSE AGREEMENT AND LIMITED WARRANTY

READ THIS LICENSE CAREFULLY BEFORE OPENING THIS PACKAGE. BY OPENING THIS PACKAGE, YOU ARE AGREEING TO THE TERMS AND CONDITIONS OF THIS LICENSE. IF YOU DO NOT AGREE, DO NOT OPEN THE PACKAGE. PROMPTLY RETURN THE UNOPENED PACKAGE AND ALL ACCOMPANYING ITEMS TO THE PLACE YOU OBTAINED THEM. *THESE TERMS APPLY TO ALL LICENSED SOFTWARE ON THE DISK EXCEPT THAT THE TERMS FOR USE OF ANY SHAREWARE OR FREEWARE ON THE DISKETTES ARE AS SET FORTH IN THE ELECTRONIC LICENSE LOCATED ON THE DISK:*

1. **GRANT OF LICENSE and OWNERSHIP:** The enclosed computer programs <<and any data>> ("Software") are licensed, not sold, to you by Pearson EducationCanada Inc. ("We" or the "Company") in consideration of your adoption of the accompanying Company textbooks and/or other materials, and your agreement to these terms. You own only the disk(s) but we and/or our licensors own the Software itself. This license allows instructors and students enrolled in the course using the Company textbook that accompanies this Software (the "Course") to use and display the enclosed copy of the Software for academic use only, so long as you comply with the terms of this Agreement. You may make one copy for back up only. We reserve any rights not granted to you.

2. **USE RESTRICTIONS:** You may not sell or license copies of the Software or the Documentation to others. You may not transfer, distribute or make available the Software or the Documentation, except to instructors and students in your school who are users of the adopted Company textbook that accompanies this Software in connection with the course for which the textbook was adopted. You may not reverse engineer, disassemble, decompile, modify, adapt, translate or create derivative works based on the Software or the Documentation. You may be held legally responsible for any copying or copyright infringement which is caused by your failure to abide by the terms of these restrictions.

3. **TERMINATION:** This license is effective until terminated. This license will terminate automatically without notice from the Company if you fail to comply with any provisions or limitations of this license. Upon termination, you shall destroy the Documentation and all copies of the Software. All provisions of this Agreement as to limitation and disclaimer of warranties, limitation of liability, remedies or damages, and our ownership rights shall survive termination.

4. **DISCLAIMER OF WARRANTY: THE COMPANY AND ITS LICENSORS MAKE NO WARRANTIES ABOUT THE SOFTWARE, WHICH IS PROVIDED "AS-IS." IF THE DISK IS DEFECTIVE IN MATERIALS OR WORKMANSHIP, YOUR ONLY REMEDY IS TO RETURN IT TO THE COMPANY WITHIN 30 DAYS FOR REPLACEMENT UNLESS THE COMPANY DETERMINES IN GOOD FAITH THAT THE DISK HAS BEEN MISUSED OR IMPROPERLY INSTALLED, REPAIRED, ALTERED OR DAMAGED. THE COMPANY DISCLAIMS ALL WARRANTIES, EXPRESS OR IMPLIED, INCLUDING WITHOUT LIMITATION, THE IMPLIED WARRANTIES OF MERCHANTABILITY AND FITNESS FOR A PARTICULAR PURPOSE. THE COMPANY DOES NOT WARRANT, GUARANTEE OR MAKE ANY REPRESENTATION REGARDING THE ACCURACY, RELIABILITY, CURRENTNESS, USE, OR RESULTS OF USE, OF THE SOFTWARE.**

5. **LIMITATION OF REMEDIES AND DAMAGES: IN NO EVENT, SHALL THE COMPANY OR ITS EMPLOYEES, AGENTS, LICENSORS OR CONTRACTORS BE LIABLE FOR ANY INCIDENTAL, INDIRECT, SPECIAL OR CONSEQUENTIAL DAMAGES ARISING OUT OF OR IN CONNECTION WITH THIS LICENSE OR THE SOFTWARE, INCLUDING, WITHOUT LIMITATION, LOSS OF USE, LOSS OF DATA, LOSS OF INCOME OR PROFIT, OR OTHER LOSSES SUSTAINED AS A RESULT OF INJURY TO ANY PERSON, OR LOSS OF OR DAMAGE TO PROPERTY, OR CLAIMS OF THIRD PARTIES, EVEN IF THE COMPANY OR AN AUTHORIZED REPRESENTATIVE OF THE COMPANY HAS BEEN ADVISED OF THE POSSIBILITY OF SUCH DAMAGES.** SOME JURISDICTIONS DO NOT ALLOW THE LIMITATION OF DAMAGES IN CERTAIN CIRCUMSTANCES, SO THE ABOVE LIMITATIONS MAY NOT ALWAYS APPLY.

6. **GENERAL:** THIS AGREEMENT SHALL BE CONSTRUED AND INTERPRETED ACCORDING TO THE LAWS OF THE PROVINCE OF ONTARIO. This Agreement is the complete and exclusive statement of the agreement between you and the Company and supersedes all proposals, prior agreements, oral or written, and any other communications between you and the company or any of its representatives relating to the subject matter.

Should you have any questions concerning this agreement or if you wish to contact the Company for any reason, please contact in writing: Customer Service, Pearson EducationCanada, 26 Prince Andrew Place, Don Mills, Ontario, M3C 2T8.